A HISTORY OF INDIAN LOGIC

न्यायशास्त्रस्य इतिहासः ।

महामहोपाध्याय-विद्याभूषण-शास्त्रसुधाकर-सिद्धान्तमहोदधि-

त्रिपिटकवागीश्वर - एम,ए,- पि,एच,डि,-

एम,आर,ए,एस,- एफ,ए,एस्,बि,

इत्युपाधिधारिणा

श्रीसतीशचन्द्र आचार्य्येण सम्पादितः ।

Mahamahopadhyaya Dr. Satischandra Vidyabhushan.

A HISTORY OF
INDIAN LOGIC

Ancient, Mediaeval and
Modern Schools

Mahāmahopādhyāya
SATIS CHANDRA VIDYABHUSANA
M.A., PH.D., M.R.A.S., F.A.S.B.

MOTILAL BANARSIDASS PUBLISHERS
PRIVATE LIMITED • DELHI

Reprint: Delhi, 1971, 1978, 1988, 2002, 2006
First Indian Edition: Calcutta, 1920

ISBN: 81-208-0565-8

MOTILAL BANARSIDASS
41 U.A. Bungalow Road, Jawahar Nagar, Delhi 110 007
8 Mahalaxmi Chamber, 22 Bhulabhai Desai Road, Mumbai 400 026
236, 9th Main III Block, Jayanagar, Bangalore 560 011
203 Royapettah High Road, Mylapore, Chennai 600 004
Sanas Plaza, 1302 Baji Rao Road, Pune 411 002
8 Camac Street, Kolkata 700 017
Ashok Rajpath, Patna 800 004
Chowk, Varanasi 221 001

Printed in India
BY JAINENDRA PRAKASH JAIN AT SHRI JAINENDRA PRESS,
A-45 NARAINA, PHASE-I, NEW DELHI 110 028
AND PUBLISHED BY NARENDRA PRAKASH JAIN FOR
MOTILAL BANARSIDASS PUBLISHERS PRIVATE LIMITED,
BUNGALOW ROAD, DELHI 110 007

TO

THE HON'BLE SIR ASUTOSH MOOKHERJEE, Kt.,
C.S.I., M.A., D.L., D.Sc., Ph.D., F.R.A.S., F.R.S.E.,

Sarasvati, Sastra-Vachaspati, Sambuddhagama-Chakravarti, Offg. Chief Justice, High Court of Judicature, Fort William, Calcutta,

THE FOREMOST EDUCATIONIST OF HIS COUNTRY,
WHO HAS, FOR A NUMBER OF YEARS, SUCCESSFULLY
GUIDED THE POLICY OF HIGHER EDUCATION
IN BENGAL,
THIS BOOK IS DEDICATED
AS A TOKEN OF PROFOUND ESTEEM
BY
HIS HUMBLE ADMIRER,

THE AUTHOR.

प्रदीपः सर्व्वविद्यानामुपायः सर्व्वकर्म्मणाम् ।
आश्रयः सर्व्वधर्म्माणां शश्वदान्वीक्षिकी मता ॥

(KAUṬILYA.)

" Ānvīkṣikī (Logic) has ever been esteemed as the lamp of all sciences, the resource of all actions and the shelter of all virtues."

न्यायाम्बुधिर्दीधितिकारयुक्तिकल्लोलकोलाहलदुर्व्विगाहः ।
तस्यापि पातुं न पयः समर्थः किं नाम धीमत्प्रतिभाम्बुवाहः ॥

" Modern Logic is a veritable ocean whose water is saline and which is unapproachable owing to the tumults and uproars of the commentators. Is not then the water of that ocean capable of being drunk ? Why not ? Intelligent people, like clouds, can easily approach the ocean and drink its water pure and sweet."

PREFACE

It pleased His Excellency the Earl of Ronaldshay, G.C.I.E., the Governor of Bengal, to utter these memorable words while presiding at the Convocation of the Calcutta University in the year 1918 :—"That an Indian student should pass through a course of philosophy at an Indian University without ever hearing mention of, shall I say, Śaṅkara, the thinker who, perhaps, has carried idealism further than any other thinker of any other age or country, or of the subtleties of the Nyāya system which has been handed down through immemorial ages, and is to-day the pride and glory of the *tols* of Navadvīpa, does, indeed, appear to me to be a profound anomaly."

Words like these coming from one who is himself a keen and ardent student of Indian Philosophy and a scrupulous and sympathetic ruler, came upon me, who have the good fortune to belong to Navadvīpa, "with double sway" and supplied the inspiration which sustained me in this my humble attempt to present a history of Indian Logic or Nyāya Darśana before the English-knowing public.

It was my revered preceptors Mahāmāhopadhyaya Mohesh Chandra Nyāyaratna, C.I.E., Principal, Sanskrit College, Calcutta, and Mahāmahopadhyaya Jadunath Sārvabhauma of Navadvīpa, who (the first by his lecture on *Bhāṣāpuricheda* and *Siddhanta-muktāvalī*, and the second by his lectures on *Kusumāñjali* and *Ātma-tattva-viveka*) first awakened in me an interest in the study of Indian Logic. That was about the year 1892. Subsequently I read Modern Logic, viz. *Tattvacintāmaṇi* and *Śabda-śakti-prakāśikā* under Pandit Bāmācharan Nyāyāchārya and Raghunātha Śiromaṇi's *Dīdhiti* under Pandit Jībanāth Miśra, both of Benares College.

I searched out and studied most of the books and manuscripts on the subject of Hindu Logic to be found in the Sanskrit College Library and the Asiatic Society of Bengal and occasionally consulted works supplied by the Deccan College, Poona, and Benares Sanskrit College. I thus put myself in the way of acquiring some acquaintance with Indian Logic and from time to time published several books and articles on Nyāya.

With regard to Jaina Logic, I derived valuable help from my teacher, Śāstra-viśārada Jaināearya Vijayadharma Sūri, Pandit Indravijaya Upādhyāya and occasionally from Pandit Haragovind Seth Nyāyatīrtha. I gathered Jaina books from various Jaina Societies and Publishing Houses such as those at Benares,

Azimganj, Arrah, Bhavnagar, etc. I also used a large number of Jaina manuscripts, of the Asiatic Society of Bengal, Deccan College, Poona, etc., besides those in the possession of the aforesaid Venerable Vijayadharma Sūri.

As regards Buddhistic Logic, I could not get much help from Pali sources, because neither in the Buddhistic Scriptures introduced into Ceylon in 254 B.C. by Mahendra, son of Aśoka, nor in the Buddhistic books recorded in writing in 88 B.C. by Vatta-gāmini, is there any trace of a systematic culture of Nyāya. Even during my visit to Ceylon in 1909 (Appendix K), I did not come across in that island any evidence of Nyāya-study. On this subject I have derived materials to some extent from Chinese, but mostly from Tibetan sources. Professor Kimura occasionally helped me in dealing with Chinese materials. Concerning the Tibetan sources almost all the materials were derived from *Bstan-ḥgyur* some volumes whereof were lent to me by the India office through the courtesy of Dr. F. W. Thomas. Through the kindness of Lord Curzon, the then Viceroy of India, I was enabled to retain temporarily for my use some other volumes of *Bstan-ḥgyur* brought down from Gyantse during the Tibet Mission of 1904. To secure further materials bearing on the subject of Buddhistic Logic I visited Labrang and Pamyangchi monasteries in June 1907 and October 1908, respectively (Appendices I and J), and came across a world of facts for observation and comment. Since the opening of increased intercourse between India and Tibet consequent upon the Tashi Lama's visit to India in 1905 (of which an account is given in Appendix H), batches of Tibetan traders have been pouring into India and from them four copies of, *Bstan-ḥgyur* have been obtained since 1911, of which one is with me, one in the Asiatic Society, Calcutta, one (a fragmentary copy) in the Sāhitya-Parishad Library, and one in the Calcutta University Library.

In regard to the chapters on modern Logic I occasionally consulted some scholars among whom Mahāmahopādhyāya Pramatha Nath Tarkabhūṣaṇa, Mahāmahopādhyāya Gurucharan Tarka-darśana-tīrtha, Mahāmahopādhyāya Lakshman Śāstri, Mahāmahopādhyāya Vindhyeswari and Pandit Jāmini Nath Tarkavāgīśa may be gratefully mentioned.

My thanks are due to Hon'ble Mr. W. W. Hornell, Director of Public Instruction, Bengal, who very kindly looked through the first batch of manuscripts and made many suggestions which have stood me in great stead in preparing the volume. I am also grateful to Rev. A. Johnstone, M.A., Principal, C.M.S. College, for having revised manuscripts as well as the proofs of the portion dealing with ancient Logic. Mr. F. J. Monahan, I.C.S., Commissioner, Presidency Division, looked through a few galleys and when he left for England, the work of revision was very kindly undertaken by Dr. W. S. Urquhart, of the Scottish Churches College, to whom I offer my thanks. My special thanks are due to Dr. H. Stephen of the Calcutta University for the interest and thoroughness with which he examined all the proofs of the present volume.

The book however could not have seen the light nor assumed its present form were it not for help of various kinds received from that Macenas of letters—I mean the Hon'ble Justice Sir Asutosh Mukherji, Sarasvati, whose name is inseparably associated with every form of educational work in Bengal, who has spent the best years of his life in effecting various improvements in the status of the Calcutta University and who above anything else is the typical man of action—a great *Karmayogin*—unswerving in his aim and fixity of purpose, selfless in his devotion to work, pursuing it through life regardless of malediction or benediction, praise or blame.

CALCUTTA,
21st April, 1920.

SATIS CHANDRA VIDYABHUSANA.

The late Mahāmahopādhyāya Dr. Satis Chandra Vidyābhūṣana had seen this book through up to p. 384. After his rather sudden death the work of seeing the remainder of the book through the press, was entirely left to me. I am, therefore, entirely responsible for any defects to be found in those pages. I have been helped, however, very materially by Dr. W. S. Urquhart and by Pandit Pasupati Nath Sāstri, M.A., to both of whom I have to express my thanks. The Index has been prepared by my old pupil Prof. Surendranath Bhaṭṭācārya, M.A., of the Behar National College and for the Tibetan Index I have to thank Mr. Johan Van Manen, Librarian, Imperial Library, Calcutta.

I am well aware of my unfitness to undertake such a task requiring years of patient study. But I was tempted to do so, among other reasons, on account of the feeling of esteem and regard which I always entertained for my late friend, and I look upon this slight service to his memory as going a little way towards repaying the many kindnesses he had always shown to me ever since I first knew him.

CALCUTTA,
December, 1920.

I. J. S. TARAPOREWALA.

INTRODUCTION.

My object in this volume is to write the history of what is called *Nyāya*, one of the six schools into which orthodox philosophy in India is divided. The word 'logic,' although it is in common parlance held synonymous with Indian Nyāya, is not exactly identical with it. Logic covers some of the subjects of Nyāya as well as Vaiśeṣika and is not co-extensive with either.

Indian Logic has been differently defined in different ages but the definition generally accepted is the science which ascertains valid knowledge either by means of the six senses or by means of the five members of the syllogism; in other words, perception and inference are the subject-matter of Logic.

In my anxiety to assign a proper place to Jaina and Buddhistic Logic, which played no inconsiderable part in the development of the science of reasoning in India, I have made a departure from the time-honoured classification of Indian Logic into Ancient and Modern and have added an intermediate stage—thus dividing it into *three* periods. Ancient (650 B.C.—100 A.D.), Mediæval (up to 1200 A.D.) and Modern (from 900 A.D.). The standard texts for each of these periods were **Nyāya-Sutra** by Akṣapāda, **Pramāṇa-samuccaya** by Dignāga and **Tattva cintāmaṇi** by Gaṅgeśa Upādhyāya respectively. The wide popularity of these works is evidenced by the large numbers of commentaries that have been written upon them, as mentioned below:—

THE ANCIENT SCHOOL OF INDIAN LOGIC.

Text.

1. Nyāya-sūtra by Akṣapāda Gautama.

Commentaries.

2. Nyāya-bhāṣya by Vātsyāyana.
3. Nyāya-vārtika by Udyotakara.
4. Nyāya-vārtika-tātparya-ṭīkā by Vācaspati Miśra.
5. Nyāya-vārtika-tātparya-ṭikā-pariśuddhi by Udayanācārya.
6. Nyāya-nibandha-prakāśa by Vardhamāna.
7. Nyāyālaṅkara by Śrīkaṇṭha.
8. Nyāya-vṛtti by Abhayatilaka Upādhyāya.
9. Nyāya-sūtroddhāra by Vācaspati Miśra.
10. Nyāya-rahasya by Rāmabhadra.
11. Nyāya-siddhānta-mālā by Jayrāma.
12. Nyāya-sūtra-vṛtti by Viśvanātha Siddhāntapañcānana.
13. Nyāya-saṃkṣepa by Govinda Sannā.

The Mediæval School of Indian Logic.

Text.

1. Pramāṇa-samuccaya by Dignāga.

Commentaries.

2. Pramāṇa-samuccaya-vṛtti by Dignāga.
3. Pramāṇa-vārtika-kārikā by Dharmakīrti.
4. Pramāṇa-vārtika-vṛtti by Dharmakīrti.
5. Pramāṇa-vārtika-pañjikā by Devendrabodhi.
6. Pramāṇa-vārtika-pañjikā-ṭīkā by Śākyabodhi.
7. Pramāṇa-vārtika-vṛtti by Ravi Gupta.
8. Pramāṇa-samuccaya-ṭīkā (Viśālāmalavatī-nāmā) by Jinendrabodhi.
9. Pramāṇa-vārtikālaṅkāra by Prajñākara Gupta.
10. Pramāṇa-vārtikālaṅkāra-ṭīkā by Jina
11. Pramāṇa-vārtikālaṅkāra by Yamāri.
12. Pramāṇa-vārtika-ṭīkā by Śaṅkarānanda.

The Modern School of Indian Logic.

Text.

1. Tattva-cintāmaṇi by Gaṅgeśa.

Commentaries.

2. Tattva-cintāmaṇi-prakāśa by Vardhamana Upādhyāya.
3. Tattva-cintāmaṇi-āloka by Pakṣadhara Miśra.
4. Tattva-cintāmaṇi-prakāśa by Rucidatta.
5. Tattva-cintāmaṇi-mayūkha by Śaṅkara Miśra.
6. Anumāna-khaṇḍa-ṭīkā by Vācaspati Miśra.
7. Tattva-cintāmaṇi-prakāśa by Haridāsa Nyāyalāṅkāra.
8. Tattva-cintāmaṇi-dīdhiti by Raghunātha Siromaṇi.
9. Maṇī-vyākhyā by Kaṇāda Tarkavāgīśa.
10. Tattva-cintāmaṇi-rahasya by Mathurānātha.
11. Tatva-cintāmaṇi-dīdhiti prasāriṇī by Kṛṣṇadāsa Sārvabhauma.
12. Tattva-cintāmaṇi-mayūkha by Jagadīśa Tarkālaṅkāra.
13. Tattva-cintāmaṇi-ṭīkā by Bhavānanda Siddhāntavāgīśa.
14. Tattva-cintāmaṇi-ṭīkā by Harirāma Tarkavāgīśa.
15. Tattva-cintāmaṇi-gūḍhārtha-dīpikā by Raghudeva Nyāyālaṅkāra.
16. Tattva-cintāmaṇi-vyākhyā by Gadādhara Bhaṭṭācārya.

Sub-Commentaries.

17. Āloka-darpaṇa by Maheśa Thakkura.
18. Tattva-cintāmaṇi-āloka-pariśiṣṭa by Devanātha Thakura.
19. Tattva-cintāmaṇi-āloka-kaṇṭakoddhāra by Madhusūdana Thakkura.
20. Tattva-cintamaṇi-āloka-rahasya by Mathurānātha Tarkavāgīśa.

21. Dīdhiti-rahasya by Mathūranātha Tarkavāgīśa.
22. Tattva-cintāmaṇi-dīdhiti-prasāriṇī by Kṛṣṇadāsa Sārvabhauma.
23. Anumānāloka-prasāriṇī on Pakṣadhara by Kṛṣṇadāsa.
24. Sabdāloka-viveka by Guṇānanda Vidyāvāgīśa.
25. Dīdhiti-ṭīkā by Rāmabhadra Sārvabhauma.
26. Tattva-cintāmaṇi-dīdhiti-prakāśikā by JagadīśaTarkālaṅkāra.
27. Tattva-cintāmaṇi-dīdhiti-gūḍhārtha-vidyotana by Jayarāma Nyāyapañcānana.
28. Tattva-cintāmaṇi-dīdhiti-prakāśikā by Bhavānanda Siddhāntavāgīśa.
29. Tattva-cintāmaṇi-dīdhiti-parīkṣā by Rudra Nyāyavācaspati.
30. Dīdhiti-ṭīkā by Raghudeva Nyāyālaṅkāra.
31. Tattva-cintāmaṇi-dīdhiti-prakāśikā by Gadādhara.
32. Tattva-cintāmaṇi-dīdhiti-ṭīkā by Rāmarudra Tarkavāgīśa.

Glosses.

33. Tattva kālīśāṅkarī-patrikā by Kālīśaṅkara.
34. Tattva cāndri-patrikā by Candra Nārāyaṇa.
35. Tattva-raudri-patrikā by Rudra Nārāyaṇa, etc.

Of all the nations of the world the Hindus and the Greeks appear to have developed systems of logic to a large extent independently of each other. Hindu Logic in its rudimentary stage can be traced as early as the 6th century before Christ. Greek Logic assumed a definite form in the fourth century B.C. though its germs can be traced a little earlier in the controversies of the Sophists and Socrates. But so far as the five-limbed syllogism of Hindu Logic is concerned the Hindu logician may have been indebted some way or other to the Greeks. While the syllogism was definitely formulated as a logical doctrine by Aristotle in his Rhetoric, Prior Analytics and Posterior Analytics in the 4th century B.C., the Hindu logician shows but a vague conception of it as late as the 1st century B.C. It is not inconceivable that the knowledge of Aristotle's logic found its way through Alexandria, Syria and other countries into Taxila (*vide* Appendix A). This is rightly corroborated by the Hindu tradition that Nārada who visited Alexandria (Śvetadvīpa) and became an expert in the handling of the five limbed syllogism. So simple is syllogistic structure that it does not seem to require any theory of gradual development to explain its growth. And Aristotle might have conceived the idea of syllogistic form into which all reasoning could be put as a complete whole.

I am inclined, therefore, to think that the syllogism did not actually evolve in Indian Logic out of inference, and that the Hindu logician owed the idea of syllogism to the influence of Aristotle (*vide* Appendix B). To me it is one of the most important enquiries in the history of Indian Logic to ascertain at what stage the doctrine of inference, which was an indigenous growth, was happily amalgamated with the borrowed art of syllogism into a common structure of logical thought. The Buddhist work Kathāvatthu furnishes several logical terms, e.g. *upanayana*, *nigamana*, etc., of syllogistic reasoning. But we find not a single instance where these terms have been methodically combined so as to form a syllogism proper. An attempt has been made to discuss the point at issue in the Appendix B, and I leave it to the reader to take my views for what they are worth.

Ancient logic was called *Ānvīkṣikī*, or the science of debate, but with the introduction of syllogism or proper reasoning it came to be called Nyāya from the 1st century A.D. The Nyāya-Śāstra in its earliest age flourished in Mithilā with Gotama but it attained its high development in Prabhāsa with Akṣapāda. The mediaeval logic from the 4th century A.D. was called Pramāṇa Sāstra, inasmuch as it dealt with *pramāna*, the means of valid knowledge, i.e. perception and inference. Ujjaini in Malwa and Valabhi in Gujarat were the scenes of activity of the Jaina logicians of the Śvetāmbara sect. The Digambaras flourished principally in Pāṭaliputra and Drāviḍa (including Karṇātā) about the 8th century A.D. Buddhist logicians flourished in universities such as Kāñcīpura, Nālanda (*vide* Appendix C), Odantapurī, Śrīdhānya-kaṭaka, Kāśmīra and Vikramaśilā (*vide* Appendix E). In Bengal Buddhist Logic attained its highest development during the reigns of the kings of the Pāl dynasty (*vide* Appendix D). Modern Logic commenced from the 10th century A.D. and was, in its first stage, called *Prakaraṇa* or the Manual of Logic, but its real life began from the 13th century A.D., since when it has been called Tarka-Śāstra or the science of Dialectics. It flourished in the University of Mithilā (*vide* Appendix F) during 13th, 14th and 15th centuries, and afterwards that of Nadia (*vide* Appendix G) became its stronghold from the 16th century onwards.

CALCUTTA,
21st April, 1920.

SATIS CHANDRA VIDYABHUSAN

FOREWORD.

Mahāmahopādhyāya Dr. Satischandra Vidyabhushan came of a respectable Brahmana family of Faridpore. He was the third son of the well-known Pandit Pitambar Vidyāvāgīśa and was born on the 30th July, 1870, in the village of Khalkula in Faridpore. Satischandra was an infant four years old when he lost his father. The family was large and yet had no earning member; and the eldest son Biswamber Jyotiṣārṇava who was then only sixteen maintained the family under circumstances of great difficulty.

Satischandra first went to the village school at the early age of five and rapidly made his mark amongst his fellow students. He stood first in the Minor Vernacular Examination from his Division and secured a scholarship which enabled him to proceed to Navadvip and take admission into the Hindu School. He passed the Entrance Examination of the Calcutta University in 1888, and obtained a scholarship which helped him to come to Calcutta and take his admission into the City College. In due course he passed the F.A. Examination and then migrated to the Krishnagar College. He took his B.A. degree with Honours in Sanskrit in 1892, and in the following year passed the M.A. Examination in Sanskrit from the Calcutta Sanskrit College. Meanwhile he had distinguished himself at the Sanskrit Examination held by the Vidagdha Jananī Sabhā of Navadwip and had obtained the title of *Vidyābhūṣaṇa*. It may be mentioned here that while still an undergraduate student in the City College he had married in 1889 the youngest daughter of Babu Gaṇgadhar Acharyya, the first Principal of the Midnapore College.

In 1893, shortly after Satischandra had passed the M.A. Examination in Sanskrit, he settled at Krishnagar as Professor of Sanskrit in the local college. Here he had special opportunity to study Sanskrit Kāvya from Mahāmahopādhyāya Ajitnath Nyāyaratna and Sanskrit Nyāya from Mahāmahopādhyāya Jadunath Sārvabhauma, each the recognised authority on his special subject. Some years later his services were lent by the Government of Bengal to the Buddhist Text Society under whose auspices he edited a number of useful Pali Texts and published several original papers which attracted the attention of scholars in Europe and America. About this time he came into contact with Rai Saratchandra Das, Bahadur, C.I.E., the distinguished Tibetan Explorer at whose request his services were again lent by the Government for three years to assist in the preparation of a Tibetan-English Dictionary. He was in Darjeeling for this purpose from 1897-1900 and utilised the opportunity to acquire a thorough mastery over the Tibetan language with the help of the celebrated Lama Funchhog Wangdan of Lhasa, then resident at Darjeeling. In December, 1900, Satischandra came to Calcutta as a Professor in the Sanskrit College. At about this period he acquired a thorough knowledge of Pali from Sramanas of Ceylon and Burma. In November, 1901, he appeared a second time at the M.A. Examination of the Calcutta University and chose Pali as his special subject. The University authorities were placed in a difficulty to find a suitable examiner. Ultimately Mr. C. H. Tawney and Prof. E. B. Cowell who had for many years been connected with the University arranged with Professor T. W. Rhys Davids to conduct the examination. Satischandra achieved high distinction and his attainments were specially praised by the distinguished examiner. In March, 1902, he was transferred to the Presidency College as Professor of Sanskrit. In December, 1905, the Tashi Lama came to India in order to visit the places sacred to Buddhists. Satischandra was deputed by the Government to accompany him, to act as Interpreter and to explain to him the histories and customs at the old Buddhist holy places. The Tashi Lama was highly pleased and presented Satischandra with a *Khatag* (silken upper garment) in token of high regard. On the 1st January, 1906, the Governor-General bestowed upon him the coveted title of Mahāmahopādhyāya. In 1907, on my nomination, Lord Minto, then Chancellor of the Calcutta University appointed him an Ordinary Fellow. At the same time he became a Fellow of the Asiatic Society of Bengal and Joint Philological Secretary. In 1908, the University conferred on him the Degree of Doctor of Philosophy and awarded him the Griffith Prize for original research. About this time the question of Principalship of the Sanskrit College had come under the consideration of the Government of Bengal and the suggestion had been put forward that a European scholar should be appointed. The Lieutenant-Governor felt doubtful as to the advisability of such a step and discussed the matter with me as Vice-Chancellor of the University. I expressed my emphatic disapproval of the course proposed and expressed the opinion that Dr. Satischandra Vidyabhushan would be found admirably qualified for the Principalship if he were offered facilities for further training. This view prevailed and during 1909 and 1910 Satischandra was placed on deputation. In June 1909, he went to Ceylon and studied for six months with the venerable High Priest Sumangala, Principal of the Vidyodaya College at Colombo.

The first six months of the year 1910 he spent at Benares where, under the guidance of Dr. A. Venis, then Principal of the Queen's College, he studied under Subrahmanya Sastri, Bhagavatāchāryya, Sibakumar Sastri, Jibanath Jha and Bamacharan Nyāyāchāryya. After his return to Calcutta from Benares he studied for six months under the guidance of Dr. George Thibaut and acquired a good working knowledge of French and German. On the 1st December, 1910, he assumed charge of the Principalship of the Sanskrit College. In 1912 and 1916, he passed with great distinction the Preliminary and Final Examinations in Tibetan held by the Government, and carried off the sanctioned prizes on both occasions. He also acted as Lecturer on Pali and Tibetan in the University. His fame as a profound scholar of versatile attainments had rapidly spread and he was eagerly sought after in literary conferences. In 1913, he was the first President of the All India Digambar Jain Conference held at Benares. In 1914, he was President of the All India Svetambar Jain Conference held at Jodhpur and of the All India Sanskrit Conference held at Hardwar. In 1916, he was President of the Bengal Literary Conference held at Jessore, and of the District Literary Conference at Krishnagar. In 1919, he was a Vice-President of the First Oriental Conference held at Poona and President of the section on Pali and Buddhism. During all this period he worked strenuously as a scholar, and the value of his contributions to Sanskrit, Pali and Tibetan studies cannot be easily appraised by a single individual. In the University itself he was a leading figure, and from 1912, acted as a Member of the Syndicate. His services were invaluable in reorganising Sanskrit studies of the indigenous type and his work as Secretary to the Sanskrit Board and the Sanskrit Association founded by the Government will be gratefully remembered by Pandits of the present generation all over this Presidency. There can be little doubt that he overworked himself, and in 1919 the first signs of failing health were indicated by a mild stroke of paralysis. Friends and well-wishers implored him to spare himself, but he was deaf to their entreaties, for as he used to say, it is better to die than to remain invalid. Two other mild attacks followed and the recovery was slow and gradual. At last on the 25th April, 1920, he passed away as the result of a sudden attack of apoplexy.

The publication of the present volume has a melancholy interest for me. In 1901 I had come across a monograph on "Hindu Logic as preserved in China and Japan" by Sadajiro Sugiura who had offered it as a dissertation for the Degree of Doctor of Philosophy at the University of Pennsylvania. The work seemed to me of fascinating interest as opening up a new field of investigation full of untold possibilities. I suggested to Satischandra who at the time was engaged in the study of Tibetan that he should undertake to explore the materials available from Tibetan sources. The substance of his first researches in this direction was embodied in his thesis on "Mediaeval School of Indian Logic" which brought him the Degree of Doctor of Philosophy and the Griffith Prize. He was however not content with this preliminary survey and continued steadily to collect fresh materials. The present volume was the result. At his request I read through more than half of the work before it was finally printed off and this made me realise the true value of what he had accomplished. Professor Taraporewala has with loving care seen through the press all that had not been printed when Satischandra passed away

A list of his many and varied writings (complete as far as it has been possible to make it) has been compiled by several people and is herewith appended.

ASUTOSH MOOKERJEE.

A LIST OF THE WRITINGS OF THE LATE MAHĀMAHŌPĀDHYĀYA DR. SATISCHANDRA VIDYABHUSHAN.[1]

A. Works, original or edited.

1. Avadāna Kalpalatā: a Collection of Legendary Stories about the Bodhisattvas, by Kṣemendra, with its Tibetan version by Souton Lochava and Lakṣmīkara. Edited from a xylograph of Lhasa and Sanskrit MS. of Nepal by S. C. Das, H. M. Vidyabhushan and Mm. S. C. Vidyabhushan (Bib. Ind., Tib. Ser.—1888-1913).
2. Ātma-tattva-prakāś (A Bengali work on the Nyāya Philosophy)—1897.
3. Bhavabhūti and his Dramas (in Bengali)—1899.
4. Laṅkāvatāra-sūtra, Fabci. i-ii.—1900.
5. Kaccāyana s Pali Grammer (Edited in Devanāgari characters and translated into English)—1901.
6. Tibetan Primer, I. by Lama Wangdan.—Transcribed into Roman Characters. Revised and translated by MM. S. C. Vidyabhushan—1902.
7. Tibetan Primer, II— 1902.
8. Ratanautta (a Pali work).—Edited with an English translation—1902.
9. Notes on *Ratnāvali*, with English and Bengali Translations—1903.
10. Buddha-dev (in Bengali)—1904.
11. Grimm's Phonetic Law of the Indo-European Languages—1905.
12. Bauddha-stotra saṅgrahaḥ: a collection of Buddhist Hymns, Vol. I. (Bib. Ind., Tib. Ser.—1908).
13. Parīkṣāmukha-sūtram: a Digambara Jaina work on Logic (Nyāya) by Māṇikya Nandi (Bib. Ind., Sans. Ser.—1909).
14. History of the Mediaeval School of Indian Logic—1909.
15. Amarakośa: a Metrical Dictionary of the Sanskrit Language with the Tibetan Version (Bib. Ind., Tib. Ser—1911-12).
16. Amaraṭīkā Kāmadhenuḥ (Bib. Ind., Tib. Ser.—1912).
17. Maitrī or Maitrāyaṇīya Upaniṣad, edited by E. B. Cowell. Second edition revised by Mm. S. C. Vidyabhushan (Bib. Ind., Sans. Ser. 1913-1919, (*In progress.*)
18. The *Nyāya-sūtras* of Gotama, translated into English (Sacred Books of the Hindus, Vol. 8)—Allahabad, 1913.
19. Sāhitya-Pariṣat-Patrikā—Edited by Mm. S. C. Vidyabhushan from (1913-1916?)
20. Nyāyabindu: a Bilingual Index of Sanskrit and Tibetan words (Bib. Ind., Tib. Ser.—1917).
21. A Report on the Revival of Buddhism—1917.
22. A History of Indian Logic—1922.

B. Articles contributed to various English Journals.

(i) "*The Journal of the Royal Asiatic Society.*"

1. Mahāyāna and Hinayāna—1900.
2. Brahmanic References to the Buddhist Philosophy—1901.
3. Old Indian Alphabet—1904.
4. Laṅkāvatāra Sūtra—1905.
5. Uddyotakara—1914.
6. Influence of Aristotle on the Development of the Syllogism in Indian Logic—1918.

(ii) "*The Journal of the Asiatic Society of Bengal.*"

1. The Licchavi Race of Ancient India } (lxxi, 1.) Abstracts also printed in
2. Vrātyā and Saṅkara Theories of Caste } Proc. A.S.B., 1902.

---

[1] This list has been compiled from several sources and though extensive is by no means complete.

3. An Analysis of the *Laṅkāvatāra-Sūtra.*
4. Anuruddha Thera--a learned Pali author of Southern India in the 12th century A.D.
5. Diṅnāga and his *Pramāṇa-samuccaya*
6. Sarvajña-mitra: a Tāntrika Buddhist author of Kaśmira in the 8th cent. A.D.

(N.S., i.)

7. A Tibetan Almanac for 1906-07
8. The Gyantse Rock-Inscription of Chos-rgyal-ḥquis-pa, a Ruler under Śabyapa Hierarch in the 14th cent. A.D.
9. Romaka, or the City of Rome, as mentioned in the Ancient Pali and Sanskrit Works
10. *Hetu-cakra-hamaru*, or Diṅnāga's Wheel of Reason, recovered from Labrang in Sikkim

(N.S., ii.)

11. Indian Logic as preserved in Tibet—
12. ,, ,, ,, ,, —2
13. ,, ,, ,, ,, —3
14. Nyaya-praveśa

(N.S., iii.)

15. Saṁkhya Philosophy in the Land of the Lamas
16. Sanskrit works on Literature, Grammar, Rhetoric and Lexicography as preserved in Tibet
17. A Descriptive List of Works on the Mādhyamika Philosophy
18. Some rare Sanskrit works on Grammar, Lexicography and Prosody recovered from Tibet
19. Two Tibetan Charms obtained by Lt.-Col. Stuart H. Godfrey in Ladakh, one for chasing away Evil Spirits and the other for compelling Fortune

(N.S., iv.)

20. On the Date of a Copy of the *Svayambhū-purāṇa.* (N.S., v.)
21. Maharaja Kanika Lekha
22. Yaśovijaya Gaṇi (about 1608-1688, A.D.)

(N.S., vi.)

23. The Localisation of certain Hymns of the *Ṛgveda.* (N.S., x.)
24. *So-sor tha-pa.* or a Code of Buddhist Monastic Laws (edited and translated. (N.S., xi.)
25. The *Tattva-Cintāmaṇi.* a most advanced Work on Hindu Logic (Summarised in English.) (N.S., xiv.)

(ii. a) "*Proceedings of the Asiatic Society of Bengal.*"

1. The Śaraka Caste of India identified with the *Sériké* of Central Asia (1903.)
2. The Buddhist doctrine of "Middle Path" (1904).

[See also items 1 and 2 under heading ii, above.]

(ii. b) "*Memoirs of the Asiatic Society of Bengal.*"

1. On Certain Tibetan Scrolls and Images lately brought from Gyantse (i, 1.)
2. Sanskrit-Tibetan-English Vocabulary, being an edition of the *Mahāvyutpatti.* by Alexander Csoma de Körös. Edited by D. Ross and Mm. S C. Vidyabhushan (iv, 1-2.) [in progress.]
3. Srid-pa-ho: a Tibetan-Chinese Tortoise Chart of Divination. (v. 1.)

(iii) "*The Journal of the Buddhist Text Society of India.*"

1. Brahmanic References to the Maddhyamika School of Buddhist Philosophy. (iii. 2.)
2. The Madhyamika School of Buddhist Philosophy, together with a Short Sketch of the leading Indian Schools of Philosophy. (iii, 3.)
3. A Brief Survey of the Hindu Philosophical Doctrines of Salvation
4. The Madhyamika Aphorisms—2
5. How Buddhism became extinct in India
6. The Madhyamika Aphorisms—3 (the Examination of the Sense-Organs)
7. The Madhyamika Aphorisms—4 (the Examination of the *Skandhas.* the five Aggregates of Being or Existence)

(iv, 1.)

8. The Philosophy of *Prajnāpāramitā*; Absolute Knowledge. (iv, 3.)
9. The Philosopher Diṅnāga, a Contemporary of the Poet Kālidāsa } (iv, 4.)
10. The Mādhyamika Aphorisms—5 (the Examination of the Elements) } (iv, 4.)
11. The Mādhyamika Aphorisms—6 } (iv, 4.)
12. The Story of Haritika. (v, 1.)
13. The Mādhyamika Aphorisms—7 (the Examination of the *Saṁskāras*, Origination, Continuance and Extinction) (v, 3.)
14. History of the Mādhyamika Philosophy of Nāgārjuna. (v, 4.)
15. The Story of Mahākāśyapa } (vi, 1.)
16. Nirvāṇa } (vi, 1.)
17. The Influence of Buddhism on the Development of Nyāya Philosophy } (vi, 3.)
18. The Mādhyamika Aphorisms—8 } (vi, 3.)
19. The Buddhist Doctrine of the "Ego" or the "Soul" } (vi, 3.)
20. Synopsis of the Duties of a Buddhist according to Bodhicaryavrata } (vi, 4.)
21. The examination of "Fire and Fuel" } (vi, 4.)
22. *Pratītya-samutpada*, or the Buddhist Doctrine of Dependent Origination } (vii, 1.)
23. The Buddhist Version of the Nyāya Philosophy } (vii, 1.)

(iv) "*The Journal of the Mahabodhi Society.*"

1. The Law of Karma } (1899).
2. Life of Diṅnāga } (1899).
3. Buddhist Convocations } (1901).
4. Buddhism in India } (1901).
5. The History of Saṁkhya Philosophy } (1902).
6. Alexander Csoma de Körös } (1902).
7. Ratanasutta } (1902).
8. Prajñāpāramitā or Perfection of Wisdom } (1902).
9. Conversion of the People of Laṅkā by Buddha } (1902).
10. *Upasampada*, or Ordination ceremony of the Buddhist } (1902).
11. Influence of Buddhism on the Development of the Hindu Nyāya Philosophy } (1902).
12. The Northern and Southern Schools of Buddhism } (1902).
13. Nāgarjuna } (1902).

(v) "*The Dawn.*"

1. History of the Grammatical Literature of India } (1901).
2. The Ancient History of Magadha } (1901).
3. Dharmāraṇya, or Forest of Justice (1902).

(vi) "*The Bengalee.*"

1. The Influence of Bengali on the Nyāya Philosophy (1902).

(vii) "*The Indian Mirror.*"

1. An Apology for *Advaitavāda* or the Vedānta Philosophy I-III (1897).
2. History of the Pali Language (1900).
3. The University of Nālanda } (1901).
4. The University of Taxila } (1901).
5. The Ancient City of Taxila } (1901).
6. The Age of the Poet Māgha (1902).

(viii) "*The Open Court*" (*America*).

1. The Conversion of Rāvaṇa and of the People of Laṅkā by Buddha (1902).

C. Articles in Bengali contributed to Bengali Journals.[1]

(i) "The Rishi."

1. Fruits of Karma, a Tibetan Story (1899).

(ii) "The Panthā."

1. Jātaka Stories of the Pali Piṭakas (1901).

(iii) "The Baṅgadarśan."

1. The Pali Source of Æsop's Fables (1902).
2. The Foundation of the Building for the Baṅgīya Sāhitya Pariṣad (1903).

(iv) "The Kāyastha Samāchār

1. The Nyāya Philosophy of the Hindus (1902).

(v) "The Bāṇī."

1. Romaka (1905).
2. Departure from Laṅkā (1910).

(vi) "The Bhāratavarṣa."

1. Uddyotakara (1913).

(vii) "The Janmabhūmi.'

1. The Nyāya Doctrine of the Soul (1896).

(viii) "The Kalpa."

1. The Theory of the Soul according to Western Philosophers (1896).

(ix) "The Suhṛid"

1. The Study of Sanskrit in the University (1894).

(x) "The Sāhitya Pariṣad Patrikā."

1. Bhavabhūti (1899).
2. Life of Lord Buddha (1900).
3. The Mahāparinirvāṇa of Lord Buddha (1901).
4. Kāyastha Chākādās, Ṭaṅgadās and Bhuvanākar Śarma (1907).
5. Bauddha-nyāya (1915).

(xi) "The Sāhitya."

1. A Buddhist Picture from Tibet } (1905).
2. The Sixteen Mahāsthaviras of Tibet } (1905).
3. Vrātya and Saṅkara Theories of Caste (1906).

(xii) "The Sāhitya Saṁhita."

Anuruddhasthavira (1901).
2. Bauddha-darśana; a series of articles on the "Metaphysical Basket" of the Buddhist Scripture } (1902).
3. Nyāya-darśan } (1902).
4. Śaṁkhya-darśan } (1902).
5. Pratītya-samutpada, or the Chain of Causes } (1902).
6. Abhihammattha saṁgaha } (1902).

---

[1] The titles have been translated into English.

(*xiii*) "*The Navyabhārat.*"

1. The Existence, Immortality and Transmigration of the Soul } (1895).
2. The World. Pain and Emancipation }
3. The Hindu Theory of Rebirth (1896).
4. Panca-kandha (1897).
5. Notes on the Dhammapada (1899).
6. A brief History of the Pali Language (1900).
7. The *dharma-dīkṣā* of Rāvaṇa (1901)
8. History of Nyāya Philosophy } (1902).
9. Bauddha Dharma }

(*xiv*) "*The Bhārati.*"

1. Analysis of Śāntideva's Bodhicaryavrata (1899).
2. The Science of Language } (1901).
3. The Bengali Alphabet }
4. The Ancient History of Megadha }
5. The Letter *kṣa* }
6. The Relations of Grammar and Language }
7. The Missionaries of Ancient India }
8. Differences of Race and Differences of Language } (1902).
9. Aṅguttara Nikāya }
10. The Milk-drinking Swan of Sanskrit Poetry }
11. How Buddhism became extinct in India }
12. The Spirit of Self-help in Hindu Religion }
13. Nicchivi Jāti }
14. History of the Nyāya Philosophy }
15. Bauddha-dharma }
16. Prāti-mokṣa } (1903).
17. Ratnāvali }
18. The Grammar of Bengali } (1904).
19. Kumāra-jiva }
20. Amoghavajra } (1905).
21. Sarvajña-mitra }
22. Travels of the Tashī Lama in India (1906).
23. Travels in Sikkim } (1908).
24. The University of Vikramaśilā }
25. History of the Alphabet }
26. Buddha's Tooth in Ceylon (1910).
27. Natarāja Śiva in Ceylon (1911).

D. Presidential Addresses, etc.

1. The Birthplace of the great Poet Kālidasa and the place of his Death (Sāhitya Sammelan at Bhagalpur).
2. Nyāya-darśan.
3. Birthplace of Kālidasa (Sāhitya Sammelan at Calcutta).
4. Presidential Address (Sāhitya Sammelan at Jessore).
5. Presidential Address (Literary Section, Sāhitya Sammelan at Jessore.)

CONTENTS.

Page

Portrait of the late MM. Dr. Satischandra Vidyabhusana .. Frontispiece
Author's Preface ix
Introduction xiii
Foreword by Sir Asutosh Mukerjee xvii
A List of the writings of the late Mahāmahopādhyāya Dr. Satis Chandra Vidyabhushan xxi

PART I.

THE ANCIENT SCHOOL OF INDIAN LOGIC.

Section I.

Ānvīkṣikī—The Science of Inquiry (650 B.C.—100 A.D.).

Chapter I.

The Growth of Ānvīkṣikī into an Art of Debate.

1. The Early Literature of India 1
2. Problems of the Vedas 2
3. Development of the conception of soul 2
4. *Ātmavidyā*, the Science of soul 4
5. *Ānvīkṣikī*, which includes a Theory of Reasons 4
6. *Anvīkṣikī* bifurcates into Philosophy and Logic 5
7. *Ānvīkṣikī* in its Philosophical Aspect called Darśana .. 6
8. Various names for *Ānvīkṣikī* in its Logical Aspect .. 7

Chapter II.

The Teachers of Ānvīksikī (Philosophy and Logic).

9. Cārvāka, his Materialistic Doctrine 9
10. Kapila, his Doctrine of Matter and Soul 9
11. Dattātreya, his Parable of a Tree 10
12. Punarvasu Ātreya, his Dissertation on the Senses .. 11
13. Sulabhā, a Lady Ascetic, her Canons of Speech 12
14. Aṣṭāvakra, a Violent Debater, how he Defeated a Sophist 13
15. Aṣṭāvakra Solves Puzzles 16
16. Medhātithi Gautama, the Founder of *Anvīkṣikī* par excellence 17

Chapter III.

The Doctrines of Anvīkṣikī.

16. A Council of Debate (*Pariṣad*) 22
17. The Technical Terms used in the Council of Debate .. 23

Page

18. *Tantra Yukti*, the Terms of Scientific Argument .. 24
19. Medhātithi Gautama's Doctrines as reproduced in the *Carakasaṃhitā* 25
    i. *Kāryābhinirvṛtti*, the Aggregate of Resources for the Accomplishment of an Action 27
    ii. *Parīkṣā*, the Standard of Examination 28
    iii. *Sambhāṣā or vāda-vidhi*, the Method of Debate .. 28

Chapter IV.

Reception accorded to Anvīkṣikī.

20. *Ānvīkṣikī* condemned in certain circles 36
21. *Ānvīkṣikī* held in high esteem in some quarters 37

SECTION II.

NYĀYA-SASTRA—THE SCIENCE OF TRUE REASONING.

Chapter I.

The Growth of Nyāyaśāstra.

22. Origin of the name *Nyāya* 40
23. The Antiquity of *Nyāyaśāstra* 41
24. The Early Teachers of *Nyāyaśāstra* 42
25. Nārada, an Expert in *Nyāyaśāstra* 43
26. *Nyāya-sūtra*, the first systematic work on *Nyāyaśāstra* .. 46
27. Akṣapāda, the Author of the *Nyāya-sūtra* 47
28. Subjects of the *Nyāya-sūtra* 50
29. The Arrangement of Categories in the *Nyāya-sūtra* .. 52
30. The Process of Treatment of the Categories 53

Chapter II.

Contents of the Nyāya-sūtra.

31. The Categories: their Enunciation 54
32. The Categories: their Definition 54
    1. The means of Right knowledge (*pramāṇa*) 54
    2. The Objects of Right knowledge (*prameya*) 56
    3. Doubt (*saṃśaya*) 58
    4. Purpose (*prayojana*) 59
    5. Example (*dṛṣṭānta*) 59
    6. Tenet (*siddhānta*) 59
    7. Members of a Syllogism (*avayava*) 60
    8. Confutation (*tarka*) 61
    9. Ascertainment (*nirṇaya*) 62
    10. Discussion (*vāda*) 63

Page

11. Wrangling (*jalpa*) 63
12. Cavil (*vitaṇḍā*) 63
13. Fallacy (*hetvābhāsa*) 63
14. Quibble (*chala*) 65
15. Analogue (*jāti*) 65
16. A Point of Defeat (*nigrahasthāna*) 66

33. The Varieties of Analogue 67
1. Balancing the homogeneity 67
2. Balancing the heterogeneity 68
3. Balancing an excess 68
4. Balancing a deficit 69
5. Balancing the questionable 69
6. Balancing the unquestionable 70
7. Balancing the alternative 70
8. Balancing the question 71
9. Balancing the co-presence 71
10. Balancing the mutual absence 72
11. Balancing the infinite regression 73
12. Balancing the counter-example 73
13. Balancing the non-produced 74
14. Balancing the doubt 74
15. Balancing the point at issue or the controversial .. 75
16. Balancing the non-reason 75
17. Balancing the presumption 76
18. Balancing the non-difference 77
19. Balancing the demonstration 78
20. Balancing the perception 78
21. Balancing the non-perception 79
22 Balancing the non-eternal 79
23. Balancing the eternal 80
24. Balancing the effect 81
Application of the Analogues 81
Six-winged Disputation (*ṣaṭpakṣī kathā*) 82

34. Varieties of the points of the Defeat 84
1. Hurting the proposition 84
2. Shifting the proposition 85
3. Opposing the proposition 85
4. Renouncing the proposition 86
5. Shifting the reason 86
6. Shifting the topic 86
7. The meaningless 87
8. The unintelligible 87
9. The incoherent 87
10. The inopportune 87
11. Saying too little 88
12. Saying too much 88
13. Repetition 88
14. Silence 89

	Page
15. Ignorance ..	89
16. Non-ingenuity	89
17. Evasion ..	89
18. Admission of an opinion ..	89
19. Overlooking the censurable	89
20. Censuring the non-censurable	90
21. Deviating from a tenet ..	90
22. The fallacies of reason also furnish points of defeat or occasion for rebuke ..	90
35. Categories: their Examination (*parīkṣā*)	90
1. The Means of Right Knowledge (*pramāna*)	90
The means ..	90
Perception ..	92
Inference ..	93
Comparison ..	93
Verbal testimony	94
Other means ..	95
2. The objects of right knowledge (*prameya*)	97
The Soul ..	97
Body ..	99
Senses ..	99
Objects of sense	100
Intellect ..	101
Mind ..	101
Faults ..	101
Transmigration	101
Emancipation ..	102
3. Doubt (*saṁśaya*) ..	103
4. Discussion (*vāda*) ..	104
5. Wrangling and Cavil (*jalpa-vitaṇḍā*)	104
36. Topics Incidentally Examined	105
1. Parts and Whole (*avayava* and *avayavin*)	105
2. Atoms (*paramāṇu*) ..	105
3. The Three Times (*kāla*) ..	106
4. Words and their Meanings (*śabdārtha*) ..	106
5. The Veda ..	107
6. Sound (*śabda*)	109
7. Word (*pada*)	110
8. The eyes (*cakṣuḥ*) ..	111
9. Intellect (*buddhi*) ..	112
10. Memory (*smṛti*) ..	112
11. The fixed signification of numbers (*saṃkhyaikānta*) ..	114

Chapter III.

Commentaries on the Nyaya-sūtra.

36*a*. Nature of the Commentaries ..	115
37. Vātsyāyana, author of the *Nyāya-bhāṣya* ..	115

		Page
38.	Vātsyāyana criticises Nāgārjuna	117
39.	Vātsyāyana criticises other Doctrines of the Buddhists ..	120
40.	Vātsyāyana's Explanation of certain Doctrines	121
41.	Uddyotakara, Author of the *Nyāya-vārtika*	123
42.	Uddyotakara's Controversy with the Buddhists	125
43.	Uddyotakara criticises Vasubandhu and Nāgārjuna ..	127
44.	Uddyotakara criticises Dignāga	129
45.	Uddyotakara's Explanation of Perception	130
46.	Uddyotakara's Definition of Inference	130
47.	Uddyotakara's Theory of Verbal Knowledge	131
48.	Uddyotakara's Theory of Sufferings	132
49.	Vācaspati Miśra, Author of the *Nyāya-vārtika-tātparaya-ṭika*	133
50.	Vācaspati opposes Dignāga	135
51.	Vācaspati criticises Dharmakīrti	136
52.	Vacaspati's Explanation of Determinate and Indeterminate Perceptions, *savikalpaka* and *nirvikalpaka*	137
53.	Vācaspati's Theory of Right Knowledge and Wrong Knowledge (*pramā* and *apramā*)	138
53*a*.	Vācaspati's Theory of Condition (*upādhi*)	140
53*b*.	The Theory of Cause and Effect (*kārya-kāraṇa*) .. .	140
53*c*.	The Buddhist and Jaina Scriptures condemned	141
54.	Udayanācārya, Author of *Nyāya-vārtika-tātparya-ṭikā-pariśuddhi*	141
55.	Udayana combats the Buddhists	142
56.	Udayana opposes Kalyāṇa Rakṣita and Dharmottara ..	143
57.	Udayana's *Kusumāñjali*	143
58.	Udayana's *Ātma-tattva-viveka*	145
59.	Jayanta, Author of the *Nyāya-mañjarī*	146
60.	Jayanta's Explanation of Verbal Knowledge	147
61.	Jayanta criticises the Doctrines of Kalyāna Rakṣita and Dharmottara	149
62.	Jayanta's Review of several other Buddistic Doctrines ..	150
63.	Srīkaṇtha	151
64.	Abhayatilaka Upādhyāya	151
65.	Other commentators on the *Nyāya-sūtra*	151

Chapter IV.

The Nyāya recognized as a Branch of Orthodox Learning. 152

66.	A comparative Estimate of the *Anvīkṣikī* and the *Nyāya*	152
67.	The Nyāya included in Ṣaddarśana	152
68.	The Nyāya supports the Veda	153
69.	The Nyāya adapts itself to Śaivism	154
70.	The Popularity of Nyāya established	155

PART II.

THE MEDIAEVAL SCHOOL OF INDIAN LOGIC

CALLED *Pramāṇaśāstra*, THE SCIENCE OF RIGHT KNOWLEDGE.

SECTION I.

JAINA LOGIC.

Chapter I.

Topics of Logic mentioned in the Jaina Canons.

Page

1. The special Features of Mediaeval Logic.
Formation of the Mediaeval school.
2. Mahāvīra, the founder of Jainism 158
3. The Jaina sects, Śvetāmbara and Digambara 159
4. Indrabhūti Gautama, a Disciple of Mahāvīra 159
5. The canonical Scriptures of the Jainas 160
6. Logical Subjects in the Canons 161

Chapter II.

Early Jaina Writers on Logic.

Bhadrabāhu the Senior 164
Bhadrabāhu the Junior 164
7. Bhadrabāhu's Syllogism 165
8 Bhadrabāhu's Explanation of *Syādvāda* 167
9. Umāsvāti 168
10. Umāsvāti's Doctrine of *Pramāṇa* (Right Knowledge) .. 169
11. Umāsvāti's Explanation of *Naya* (the Mood of Statements) 170

Chapter III.

Jaina Writers on Systematic Logic.

12. The written Records of the Jainas 172
13. Systematic Jaina Logic 172
14. Siddhasena Divākara *alias* Kṣapaṇaka 173
15. Siddhasena's *Nyāyāvatāra* 174
Pramāṇa, Right knowledge 174
Naya, the Method of Descriptions 181
16. Jinabhadra Gaṇi Kṣamāśramaṇa 181
17. Siddhasena Gaṇi 182
18. Samantabhadra.. 182
19. Samantabhadra's *Āptamīmāṁsā* 184
20. Akalaṅkadeva 185
21. Vidyānanda 186
22. Māṇikya Nandi 188
23. Māṇikya Nandi's *Parīkṣāmukha-sūtra* 188
Valid Knowledge, *pramāṇa* 189
Syllogism, *vyāpti* 189

		Page
	Reason, *hetu*	190
	Example, *dṛṣṭānta*	191
	Inference, *anumāna*	192
	Verbal Testimony, *āgama*	192
	Scope of valid Knowledge, *viṣaya*	192
	Fallacy, *ābhāsa*	192
	References to Philosophers	193
24.	Prabhācandra	193
25.	Rabhasānanda	194
26.	Mallavādin	194
27.	Amṛtacandra Sūri	195
28.	Devasena Bhaṭṭāraka	195
29.	Pradyumna Sūri	196
30.	Abhayadeva Sūri	196
31.	Laghusamantabhadra	197
32.	Kalyāṇacandra	198
33.	Anantavīrya	198
34.	Deva Sūri	198
35.	Deva Sūri's *Pramāṇa-naya-tattvālokālaṅkāra*	200
	Fallacies of Naya	203
	The Soul, *ātmā*	204
	The Method of Debate	204
36.	Hemacandra Sūri	205
37.	Candraprabha Sūri	206
38.	Nemicandra Kavi	207
39.	Ānanda Sūri and Amaracandra Sūri, nicknamed Tiger-cub and Lion-cub	207
40.	Haribhadra Sūri	208
41.	Pārśvadeva Gaṇi	210
42.	Śrīcandra	210
43.	Devabhadra	211
44.	Candrasena Sūri	211
45.	Ratnaprabha Sūri	211
46.	Tilakācārya	212
47.	Malliṣena Sūri	212
48.	Rājaśekhara Sūri	213
49.	Jñānacandra	213
50.	Guṇaratna	214
51.	Śrutasāgara Gaṇi	215
52.	Dharma Bhūṣaṇa	215
52*a*.	Vinayavijaya	516
53.	Yaśovijaya Gaṇi	217
54.	Yaśovijaya's Works	218

Chapter IV.

Continuity of Jaina Logic.

55.	The conciliatory Character of Jaina Logic	221
56.	Royal Patronage and Persecution	222

Page

57. Support of the Jaina Community 223
58. Jaina Logic will not be extinct 224

SECTION II.

THE BUDDHIST LOGIC.

Chapter 1.

Topics of Logic mentioned in the old Buddhist Literature

59. Buddha Gautama 225
60. Origin of the Pāli Buddhist Literature .. 225
61. Logical Topics in the Pāli Literature 227
62. *Suttapiṭaka : Dīgha-nikāya : Brahmajāla Sutta* 227
63. *Suttapiṭaka : Majjhemanikāya Anumāna Sutta* 229
64. *Suttapiṭaka : Khuddaka Nikāya Udāna* 229
65. *Vinaya-piṭaka : Parivāra* 229
Four kinds of Cases for Settlement (*adhikarṇa*) .. 229
Seven Rules for the Settlement of Cases (*adhikaraṇa-samatha-dhamma*) 230
A Complaint (*codanā*) 231
A Complaint in Complainant and Respondent .. 231
A Judicial Council of Monks (*saṅgha*) 231
Members of a Council (*saṁgamāvacarabhikkhu*) .. 231
The Judge or Umpire (*anuvijjaka*) 231
66. *Vinaya piṭaka : pātimokkha* 232
67. *Abhidhamma-piṭaka : kathāvatthuppakaraṇa* .. 234
68. Methods of Disputation as illustrated in the *Kathāvatthu* .. 235
A Case presented by a Dispute in a regular Form (*anuloma*) 235
A Rejoinder by the Respondent (*paṭikamma*) 235
The Rejoinder causing Entanglement or Defeat on the Disputant (*niggaha*) 236
Application of the Reasoning of the Disputant to his own Case (*upanaya*) 236
Conclusion (*niggamana*) 237
A Case presented through a simple Comparison (*suddhikasaṁsandana*) 237
Definition of Terms (*lakkhaṇayutti kathā*) 238
Clearing the Meaning of Terms (*vacanaśodhana*) .. 238
A Case presented through an Analogy (*opamma saṁsandana*) 238
A Case presented through the four-fold Method (*catukkanayasaṁsandana*) 239
The Doctrine of Impermanence (*khaṇeka kathā*) 239
69. Milinda-pañha *alias* the Bhikṣu-Sūtra 240
70. Origin of the Mahāyāna 241
71. Origin of the Sanskrit Buddhist Literature 242
72. Logic mentioned in the Sanskrit Literature 242
73. The *Lalitavistara* 243
74. The *Laṅkāvatāra-sūtra* 243
75. Eighteen Sects of the Buddhists 246
76. Four Schools of Buddhist Philosophy 247

Chapter II.

Early Buddhist Writers on Logic.

		Page
77.	Rise of Buddhist Logic	251
78.	Ārya Nāgārjuna	251
79.	Nāgārjuna's *Mādhyamika-kārikā*	253
80.	Nāgārjuna's References to the Logical Doctrines of Akṣapāda	255
81.	Nāgārjuna's *Vigraha-vyāvartani-kārikā*	256
82.	Nāgārjuna's *Pramāṇa-vihetana* or *Pramāṇa vidhvaṁsana*	257
83.	*Upāya-kauśalya-hṛdaya-śāstra*	259
84.	Ārya Deva	261
85.	Maitreya	262
86.	Maitreya's *Abhisamayālaṅkāra-kārikā*	262
87.	Maitreya's Treatise on the Art of Debate	263
	1. The Subject of Debate	263
	2. The Place of Debate	263
	3. The Means of Debate	264
	4. The Qualifications of a Debater	264
	5. Points of Defeat (*nigrahasthāna*)	264
	6. Attending a Place of Debate	264
	7. Confidence of a Debater	264
88.	Ārya Asaṅga	265
89.	Vasubandhu	266
90.	Vasubandhu's *Tarka-śāstra*	267

Chapter III.

Systematic Buddhist Writers on Logic.

91.	The Commencement of Mediaeval Logic	270
92.	Ācārya Dignāga, the Father of Mediaeval Logic	270
93.	Life of Dignāga	272
94.	Dignāga's *Pramāṇa-samuccaya*	274
	Chapter I—Perception	276
	Chapter II—Inference for One's Self	280
	Chapter III—Inference for the Sake of Others	282
	Chapter IV—Reason and Example	286
	Chapter V—*Apoha*, Negation of the Opposite	287
	Chapter VI—Analogues or Far-fetched Analogy	288
95.	Dignāga's *Nyāya-praveśa*	289
	A Syllogism, *nyāyāvayava*	289
	The Minor Term	290
	The Middle Term and the Major Term	291
	Fourteen Fallacies	293
	The example	295
	Perception and Inference	298
96.	Dignāga's *Hetu-cakrahamaru*	299
97	*Pramāṇa-samuccaya-vṛtti*	299
98.	*Pramāṇa-śāstra-nyāya-praveśa*	300

Page

99. *Ālambana-parīkṣā* 300
100. *Ālambana-parīkṣā-vṛtti* 301
101. *Trikāla-parīkṣā* 301
102. Paramārtha 301
103. Śaṅkara Svāmin 302
104. Dharmapāla 302
105. Ācārya Śīlabhadra 303
106. Ācārya Dharmakīrti 303
107. *Pramāṇa-vārtika-kārikā* 306
108. *Pramāṇa-vārtikā-vṛtti* 308
109. *Pramāṇa-viniścaya* 308
110. *Nyāya-bindu* 309
Perception 310
Inference for One's Self 310
Inference for the Sake of Others 312
Dharmakīrti criticises Dignāga 315
111. *Hetu-bindu-vivaraṇa* 318
112. *Tarka-nyāya* or *Vāda-nyāya* 318
113. *Santānāntara-siddhi* 319
114. *Sambandha-parīkṣā* 319
115. *Sambandha-parīkṣā-vṛtti* 319
116. Devendrabodhi 319
117. Śākyabodhi 320
118. Vinīta Deva 320
119. Ravi Gupta 322
120. Jinendrabodhi 323
121. Santa Raksita 323
122. Kamalasīla 327
123. Kalyaṇa Rakṣita 328
124. Dharmottarācārya 329
125. Muktakumbha 331
126. Arcaṭa 331
127. Aśoka 332
128. Candragomin (Junior) 333
129. Prajñākara Gupta 336
130. Ācārya Jetāri 337
131. Jina 338
132. Ratna Kīrti 338
133. Ratna Vajra 339
134. Jina Mitra 340
135. Dānaśīla 340
136. Jñānaśrī Mitra 341
137. Jñānaśrī Bhadra 342
138. Ratnākara Śānti 342
139. Yamāri 343
140. Śaṅkarānanda 344
141. Subhākara Gupta 346
142. Mokṣakara Gupta 346

Chapter IV.

The Decline of Buddhist Logic.

		Page
143.	Contentious Spirit of Buddhist Logic	348
144.	Loss of Royal Patronage	349
145.	Advent of the Mahomedans	350
146.	The Brāhmaṇic Preachers	351
147.	Shelter in Foreign Countries	351
148.	Extinction of the Buddhists and their Doctrines in India..	353

PART III.

THE MODERN SCHOOL OF INDIAN LOGIC.

SECTION I.

Prakaraṇa—MANUAL OF LOGIC.

Chapter I.

The Nyāya-prakaraṇa reduces its categories to one.

1.	The Neo-Brāhmaṇic age	355
2.	Composition of the *Prakaraṇas*, Manual of Logic	355
3.	Four Classes of *Prakaraṇas*	356
4.	*Nyāya-prakaraṇa* developing the category of *pramāṇa* ..	357
5.	Bhāsarvajña	357
6.	Bhāsarvajña's *Nyāya-sāra*	358
	Nyāya-sāra follows no particular Work	358
7.	Contents of the *Nyāya-sāra*	359
	Perception, *pratyakṣa*	359
	Inference, *anumāna*	361
	Hetvābhāsa, Fallacy of Reason	362
	A. Unproved (*asiddha*)	362
	B. The Contradictory (*viruddha*)	363
	C. The Uncertain (*anaikāntika*)	365
	D. Non-tried or Non-conclusive (*anadhyavasita* or *anupasaṁhārī*)..	366
	E. Mistimed or Incompatible Reason (*kālātyayopadiṣṭa* or *bādhita*)	367
	F. Balancing the Controversy (*prakaraṇa-sama*) ..	367
	G. Non-erroneous Contradiction (*viruddhāvyabhicārī*) ..	368
	Example, *udāharaṇa*	368
	Verbal Testimony, *āgama*	370
	Emancipation, *mokṣa*	370
8.	Commentaries on the *Nyāya-sāra*	371

Chapter II.

Nyāya-prakaraṇas embodying Vaiśeṣika categories.

9.	The Nyāya incorporates the Vaiśeṣika	373
10.	Varadarāja	373

Page

11. *Tārkikarakṣā* 374
Valid knowledge, *pramāṇa* 375
Inference, *anumāna* 376
Syllogism, *avayana* 377
The Sign, *liṅga* 377
Debate, *kathā* 378
12 Commentaries on *Tārkikarakṣā* 380
13. Keśava Miśra 381
14. *Tarka-bhāṣā*, Technicality of Logic 381
Categories, *padārtha* 381
Instrument, *karaṇa* 382
Cause, *kāraṇa* 382
Perception, *pratyakṣa* 383
Inference, *anumāna* 383
Comparison, *upamānā* 384
Word, *śabda* 384
15 Commentaries on the *Tarka-bhāṣā* 384

Chapter III.

The Vaiśeṣika Prakaraṇa embodying the Nyāya category of Pramāṇa.

16. The Vaiśesika incorporates the Nyāya category 386
17. Vallabhācārya 386
18. *Nyāya-līlāvatī* 387
19. Commentaries on the *Nyāya-līlāvatī* 387
20. Annaṃ Bhaṭṭa 388
21. *Tarkasaṁgraha* 388
22. Commentaries on *Tarkasaṁgraha* 390
23. Viśvanātha Nyāyapañcānana.. 392
24. *Bhāṣā-pariccheda* 392
25. *Tarkāmṛta* 393
26. Laugākṣi Bhāskara 395
27. *Tarka-kaumudī* 395

Chapter IV.

Works treating of certain topics of the Nyāya and certain topics of the Vaiśeṣika.

28. The Nyāya and Vaiśeṣika promiscuously amalgamated .. 396
29. Śaśadhara 396
30. *Nyāya-siddhānta-dīpa* 396
31. Mādhavācārya 397
32. *Sarvadarśana-saṁgraha*, Aksapāda Darśana.. 398
Inference as a Means of Right knowledge 398
The Inference as a Means of Right Knowledge cannot be denied.. 400

Section II.

Tarka-Śāstra—the Science of Dialectics.

Chapter II.

Formation of the Tarka-śāstra.

Page

33. The Nyāya cannot be combined with Vaiśeṣika 402
34. Adoption of *Pramāṇa* alone 402
35. Adoption of the Vaiśeṣika Principles 402
36. Subtlety of Meanings aimed at 403
37. Fine Definition of Terms 403
38. The Use of Technical Terms 403

Chapter II.

Tattva-cintāmaṇi—the Earliest work on Tarka-śāstra.

39. Importance of *Tattva-cintāmani* 405
40. Gaṅgeśa, the Author of the *Tattva-cintāmani* 405
41. The Text of *Tattva-cintāmani*

Book I: Perception, *Prtayakṣa khaṇḍa* 407

Invocation of Blessings, *Maṅgala-vāda* 408

The Validity of Knowledge, *Prāmāṇya-vāda* 408

Invalid Knowledge, *Anyathā-khyāti* 409

Intercourse between Senses and their Objects—*Sannikarṣa*

Ordinary Perception (*laukika pratyakṣa*).. 411

Transcendent Perception (*alaukika pratyakṣa*) 412

Inference *Samanāya-vāda* 414

The Invalidity of Non-perception. *Anupalabdhi or prāmāṇya vāda* 414

Non-existence (or Negation). *Abhāva-vāda* 415

Causes of Perception, *Pratyakṣa-kāraṇa-vāda* 416

The Atomic Nature of the Mind, *Manoṇutva-vāda* 417

The Doctrine of Self-consciousness, *Anuvyavasāya-vāda* .. 418

Immediate Perception, *Nirvikalpa-vāda* 418

Mediate Perception, *Savikalpa-vāda* 419

Book II. : Inference, *Anumāna-khaṇḍa* 419

The Determination of Inferential Knowledge—*Anumiti-nirūpaṇa* 419

Inference distinct from Perception 420

Five Provisional Definitions of Invariable Concomitance, *Vyāpti-pañcakam* 421

Definition of Invariable Concomitance given by "Lion" and "Tiger", *Siṁha-vyāghrokta-vyāptilakṣaṇa* 423

Non-existence whose Counterpart is qualified by a Nature abiding in a different Locus, *Vyadhikaraṇa-dharmāvacchinnābhāvaḥ* 423

Other objectionable Definitions of Invariable Concomitance, *Pūrvapakṣaḥ* 424

Page

The conclusive Definition of Invariable Concomitance, *Siddhānta-lakṣaṇam* 424
Non-existence of the General Form, *Sāmānya bhāvaḥ* .. 425
Invariable Concomitance of Special Forms, *Viśeṣa-vyāpti* .. 426
The Means of apprehending Invariable Concomitance, *Vyapti-grahopāyaḥ* 426
Conclusion as to the Means of appending Invariable Concomitance, *Vyāpti-grahopāya-siddhānta* 428
Reasoning (or Confutation), *Tarka* 429
Comprehensiveness of Invariable Concomitance, *Vyāptyanugamaḥ* 429
Intercourse whose Character is General, *Sāmānya-lakṣaṇa* .. 429
Conclusion about the Intercourse whose Character is General, *Sāmānya-lakṣaṇa-siddhāntaḥ* 430
The Conditional Middle Term, *Upādhi-vādaḥ* 431
The State of Being the Locus or Minor Term, *Pakṣatā* .. 432
Consideration or Knowledge of Premises, *Parāmarśaḥ* .. 433
An Exclusively Affirmative Inference, *Kevalānvayyanumānam* 434
An Exclusively Negative Inference, *Kevalavyatirekyanumanam* 434
An Affirmative—negative Inference 435
Presumption, *Arthāpatti* 435
Inference for One's self, *Svārthānumāna* 435
Inference for the Sake of Others, *Parārthānumāna* 435
Syllogism, *Nyāyaḥ* 436
Parts of a Syllogism, *Avayavaḥ* 436
Fallacies, *Hetvābhāsaḥ* 438
Fallacies are serviceable as they point out Inefficiency .. 442
Inference of God, *Īśvarānumānam* 442
Book III : Comparison, *Upamāna*-khaṇḍa 443
Book IV : Verbal Testimony, *Śabda-khaṇḍa* 444
Definition of Verbal Testimony 444
Verbal Knowledge, *Śabda-bodhaḥ* 444
Speech as a Means of Valid-Knowledge 445
Expectancy, *Ākāṅkṣā-vādaḥ* 447
Consistency, *Yogyatā* 447
Contiguity, *Āsattiḥ* 447
Intention, *Tātparayam* 448
The Non-eternity of Sound 448
Injunction, *Vidhi-vādaḥ* 448
Merit and Demerit, *Apūrva-vādaḥ* 449
Potentiality, *Śakti-vādaḥ* 449
Implication, *Lakṣaṇā* 451
Compound Words, *Samāsa-vādaḥ* 453
Verbal Suffixes, *Ākhyāta-vādaḥ* 453
The Roots, *Dhātu-vādaḥ* 453
Prefixes, *Upasarga-vādaḥ* 453
Validity of the Four Means of Knowledge 453

Chapter III.

Commentaries on the Tattva-cintāmaṇi.

Page

42. The Popularity of *Tattva-cintāmaṇi* 454
43. The Mithilā School 454
44. Vardhamāna Upādhyāya 454
45. Pakṣadhara Miśra 455
46. Vāsudeva Miśra 456
47. Rucidatta Miśra 457
48. Bhagīratha or Megha Ṭhakkura 457
49 Maheśa Ṭhakaura 457
50. Śankara Miśra 458
51. Vācaspati Miśra (the Younger or Junior) 459
52. Misaru Miśra 460
53. Durgādatta Miśra 460
54. Devanātha Ṭhakkura 460
55. Madhusūdana Ṭhakkura 461
56. The Nadia School 461
57. Vāsudeva Sārvabhauma 461
58. Raghunātha Śiromaṇi 463
59. Haridāsa Nyāyālaṅkāra Bhaṭṭācārya 465
60. Jānakīnātha Śarma 466
61. Kaṇāda Tarkavāgīśa 466
62. Rāmakṛṣṇa Bhaṭṭācārya Chakravarti 466
63. Mathurānatha Tarkavagīśa 467
64. Kṛṣṇadāsa Srāvabhauma Bhaṭṭācārya 468
65. Guṇānanda Vidyāvāgīśa 468
66. Rāmabhadra Sārvabhauma 468
67. Jagadiśa Tarkālaṅkāra 469
68. *Śabda-śakti-prakāśikā* 470
69. Rudra Nyāyavācaspati 476
70. Jayarāma Nyayapañcānana 477
71. Gaurīkānta Sārvabhauma 478
72. Bhavānanda Siddhāntavāgīśa 479
73. Harirāma Tarkavāgīśa 479
74. Viśvanātha Siddhāntapañcānana 479
75. Rāmabhadra Siddhāntavāgīśa 480
76. Govinda Nyāyavāgīśa 480
77. Raghudeva Nyāyālaṅkāra 481
78. Gadādhara Bhāṭṭācharya 481
79. Nṛsinha Pañcānana 482
80. Ramadeva Cirañjīva 483
81. Rāmarudra Tarkavāgīśa 483
82. Srīkṛṣṇa Nyāyālaṅkāra 483
83. Jayarāma Tarkalaṅkāra 483
84. Rudrarāma 484
85. " Buno " Rāmanātha 484
86. Kṛṣṇakānta Vīdyāvāgīśa 484
87. Rājacūḍāmaṇimakhin 485

Page

88. Dharmarājādhvarin 485
89. Gopīnātha Mauni 485
90. Kṛṣṇa Bhaṭṭa Āḍe 486
91. Mahādeva Puntaṁkar 486
92. Raghunātha Śāstri (Parvata) 487

Chapter IV.

Present State of the Science of Dialectics.

93. Patronage of the Maharaja of Nadia 488
94. The Portuguese to be an Interest in Dialectics 488
95. British Government encourages Nyāya 490
96. Rise of Vernacular detrimental to Nyāya 492
97. The Universities on the Western Model 492

Appendices.

Appendix A. The University of Taxila 494
Appendix B. Influence of Aristotle on the Development of the Syllogism in Indian Logic 497
Appendix C. The University of Nālandā 514
Appendix D. A List of Kings of the Pāla Dynasty of Bengal and Behar 517
Appendix E. The Royal University of Vikramaśilā .. 519
Appendix F. University of Mithilā 521
Appendix G. The University of Nadia 523
Appendix H. The Tashi Lama's Visit to India 528
Appendix I. Reminiscences of a Visit to Labrang, Pamiyangchi and Padangi 530
Appendix J. Reminiscences of a Visit to Pamiyangchi .. 537
Appendix K. Journey to Ceylon 540

INDEXES.

Index of Subjects 542
Index of Books 579
Index of Authors 595
Index of Quotations 599
Index of Sanskrit Terms 611

Tibetan Indexes.

I. Logical Terms 634
II. Tibetan Quotations 638
III. Books 638
IV. Proper Names 644
V. Place Names 646
VI. Residuals 647
VII. Errata 647

A HISTORY

OF

INDIAN LOGIC.

PART I.

THE ANCIENT SCHOOL OF INDIAN LOGIC.

SECTION I.

Ānvīkṣikī—the Science of Inquiry (650 B.C.—100 A.D.).

CHAPTER I.

The growth of Ānvīkṣikī into an Art of Debate.

1. The Early Literature of India (circa 1500 B.C.—600 B.C.).

The Brāhmaṇas maintain that their religion is eternal (*sanātana*). It is based on scriptures which are said also to be eternal but revealed in different cycles of time to seers or sages called *Ṛṣis*. These scriptures are called the Vedas which comprise the Saṁhitās (Hymns) and the Brāhmaṇas (Rituals etc.).

The Vedas.

The Vedas are regarded even by modern scholars, who do not admit the perpetuity of their existence, to be the oldest records not only of India but of the whole Aryan world. The Saṁhitā of the Ṛgveda which is the oldest part of the Veda is said by them to have come down to us from about 1500 B.C., while the Brāhmaṇas such as the Aitareya, Kauśītakī, etc., are supposed to have belonged to a period between 900 B.C. and 600 B.C. The Āraṇyakas (Forest-treatises), which are theosophic in character, form the closing section of the Brāhmaṇas. The Upaniṣads which deal mainly with metaphysical questions are included in the Āraṇyakas and are as such older than 600 B.C.[1]

[1] Compare Macdonell's "History of Sanskrit Literature," p. 47; and my "Grimm's Phonetic Law of the Indo-European Languages."

2. Problems of the Vedas (circa 1500 B.C.—600 B.C.).

Prayer, Rituals and Knowledge.

From the standpoint of subject-matter the Vedas (composed between 1500 B.C. and 600 B.C.) may be divided into three sections (kāṇḍas), viz. *upāsanā* (Prayer), *karma* (Rituals) and *jñāna* (Knowledge). Under *upāsanā* come the Saṁhitās which embody expressions of wonder and awe at the Powers of Nature such as Light, Darkness, Wind, Water, Rain, etc. The Brāhmaṇas which treat mainly of the sacrificial rites come under the head *karma*. The *jñāna*-kāṇḍa as represented by the Āraṇyakas is concerned mainly with the nature of soul and its destiny.

3. Development of the Conception of Soul (900 B.C.—600 B.C.).

As already suggested, the Brāhmaṇas hold that the doctrine of the soul and its destiny propounded in the Āraṇyakas (Upaniṣads) has existed in India from the beginning of time. Their view, which seeks to place the Brāhmaṇic religion on a firm basis unshaken by the influences of time, does not however find favour with modern scholars according to whom all human civilizations, including even the civilizations of the Indian people, grew up by a process of evolution. The conception of the soul and its destiny, like every thing else, has undergone stages of development in the course of ages. These stages may be clearly seen if we examine the doctrine of the soul as given in the Saṁhitās, Brāhmaṇas and Upaniṣads.

Evolution in the Doctrine of Soul.

The Saṁhitās of the Ṛg-veda[1] and Atharva-veda[2] tell us that when a person dies his spirit (called *prāṇa*, breath, *asu*, breathing, or *manaḥ*, intelligence, characterised as *ajo bhāgo*, the unborn part), which leaves behind on earth all that is uncomfortable, is conveyed by the messenger of Yama (the Lord of Death) to the world of his forefathers where it obtains a delectable abode and enters upon a perfect life which will never cease.

Spirit in the Vedas.

The Śatapatha Brāhmaṇa[3] and other later vedic works, which mention the soul as *ātman* lay much stress on its good work called *dharma* (righteous-

Soul in the Śatapatha-Brāhmaṇa.

---

[1] Ṛg-veda Saṁhitā ix. 113, 9, 11; x. 14, 8-10; x. 15, 14; and x. 16, 2, 5.

[2] Atharva veda saṁhitā xviii. 2, 27. Vide also Muir's Sanskrit Texts, Vol. V, pp. 300-335.

[3] Śatapatha Brāhmaṇa vi. 2, 2, 27; x. 6, 3, 1; xi. 7, 2, 23. Vide Muir's Sanskrit Texts, Vol. V, pp. 300-335.

ness) which is described as the strength of strengths (*kṣatrasya kṣatram*).[1] According to them all persons are after death reborn into another world where they enjoy pleasures or suffer pains according to their good or evil deeds.

Soul in the Upaniṣads.

The upaniṣads offer a subtle treatment of the soul distinguishing carefully between *jñāna* (knowledge) and *karma* (work). According to the Chāndogya[2] and the Bṛhadāraṇyaka[3] a person who has acquired knowledge proceeds after death through the path of gods (*deva-yāna*) to the region of Brahma whence he does not return; while a person who has merely done useful work passing through the path of his forefathers (*pitṛ-yāna*) reaches the moon whence he, after the exhaustion of his merits, comes back to this world; and a person who has neither acquired knowledge nor has done any useful work traverses a third path—the path of transmigration (*saṁsāra*)—which leads him to continual births and deaths.

Soul in the Kaṭhopaniṣad.

The third path is more fully expounded in the Kaṭhopaniṣad[4] which gives a clear exposition of the nature of the soul called *ātman*. The soul is described as being distinct from the body. It is not born, it does not die, it sprang from nothing and nothing sprang from it. It is eternal and everlasting and is not killed though the body is killed. The wise man who knows the soul as bodiless within the body, as unchanging among changing things, as great and omnipresent, never grieves. The soul is comparable to a person who moves in a chariot, the body is the chariot, the intellect the charioteer, the mind the reins, the senses are the horses and the surrounding objects their spheres of operation. The soul is called the enjoyer when it is in union with the body, the mind and the senses. Fools run after outward pleasures and fall into the snare of death, but wise men cognizant of the imperishable nature of the soul never hanker after unstable things which give rise only to sufferings. As to the destiny of the soul after death, the Kaṭhopaniṣad says that some souls enter the womb to have bodies as organic beings, while others go into inorganic matter according to their work and knowledge. Such transmigration continues until all desires that dwell in the heart cease. Then the mortal becomes immortal and attains Brahman.

---

[1] तदेतत् क्षत्रस्य क्षत्रं यद्धर्मः । तस्माद् धर्मात् परं नास्ति (Bṛhadāraṇyaka 10-14).

[2] Chāndogyopaniṣad 4-15, 5, 16; 5-10-3; 5-10-8.

[3] Bṛhadāraṇyakopaniṣad 4-4-5; 6-2-15, and 16.

[4] Kaṭhopaniṣad 1-1-20; 1-2-18, 19; 1-2-22; 1-3-3, 4; 2-1-4; 2-5-6, 7; and 2-6-14, 15. *Vide* also Max Müller's translation of the Kaṭhopaniṣad in the S.B.E. series.

4. *Ātmavidyā*—THE SCIENCE OF SOUL (CIRCA 900 B.C.—600 B.C.).

The Upaniṣads (composed between 900 B.C. and 600 B.C.) which dealt with the soul and its destiny constituted a very important branch of study called *Ātma-vidyā*, the science of soul, *Adhyātma-vidyā*, the spiritual science or *Brahma-vidyā*, the Divine Science, which is the foundation of all other sciences. In the previous paragraph there has been given some idea of the nature of the soul—a concrete substance—as it was understood in the ages of the Upaniṣads as well as in those of the Saṁhitās and Brāhmaṇas. In the ages of the Upaniṣads there arose another idea—an abstract conception—regarding the soul which developed *pari passu* with the first idea. Thus in the Śatapatha Brāhmaṇa,[1] Bṛhadāraṇyakopaniṣad,[2] etc., we find that *ātmā*, which referred not only to the human soul but to the soul of other objects as well, signified the essence of an object as distinguished from its outward form, and as such was often designated as *Brahman* the pervading essence, that is, the essence which permeated the object in all its forms and changes. This second idea of the soul, which gave birth to the Vedānta system of philosophy, began to exercise considerable influence on the first idea which was supported in other systems of philosophy, and a compromise between the two ideas was effected when the soul belonging to our practical condition (*vyāvahārika daśā*) was stated to be of the first description while the soul belonging to our transcendental condition (*pāramārthika daśā*) was stated to be of the second description.

Two ideas regarding the Soul.

5. *Ānvīkṣikī*—WHICH INCLUDES A THEORY OF REASONS (CIRCA 650 B.C.—100 B.C.).

Ātma-vidyā was at a later stage called *Ānvīkṣikī*, the science of inquiry. Manu[3] uses Ānvīkṣikī as an equivalent for ātma-

---

[1] Śatapatha Brāhmaṇa 10-3-4 (Weber's edition).

[2] Bṛhadāraṇyakopaniṣad (3rd chapter, 7th Brāhmaṇa), Muṇḍakopaniṣad, i. 1, 1, Bhagavadgītā 10-32.

[3] त्रैविद्येभ्यस्त्रयीं विद्याद्
दण्डनीतिञ्च शाश्वतीम् ।
आन्वीक्षिकीं चात्मविद्यां
वार्त्तारम्भांश्च लोकतः ॥ (Manu Saṁhitā 7—43).

Kāmandaka too in his Nītisāra writes :—

आन्वीक्षिक्यात्मविज्ञानं धर्म्माधर्म्मौ त्रयीस्थितौ ।
अर्थानर्थौ च वार्त्तायां दण्डनीतौ नयानयौ ॥

vidyā, and his followers, the Mānavas,[1] describe it—evidently considering it synonymous with the Upaniṣad—as a branch of the Vedas. Ānvīkṣikī while comprising the entire function of Ātma-vidyā was in fact different from it, and consequently from the Upaniṣad too. Kauṭilya[2] (about 327 B.C.) recognized Ānvīkṣikī as a distinct branch of study over and above the three, *viz.* *Trayī* (the Vedas), *Vārttā* (Commerce) and *Daṇḍa-nīti* (Polity) enumerated in the school of Manu. The distinction between *Ātma-vidyā* and *Ānvīkṣikī* lay in this, that while the former embodied certain dogmatic assertions about the nature of the soul, the latter contained reasons supporting those assertions. Ānvīkṣikī dealt in fact with two subjects, *viz.* *ātmā*, soul, and *hetu*, theory of reasons. Vātsyāyana[3] observes that Ānvīkṣikī without the theory of reasons would have like the Upaniṣad been a mere *ātma-vidyā* or *adhyātma-vidyā*. It is the theory of reasons which distinguished it from the same. The Sāṁkhya, Yoga and Lokāyata, in so far as they treated of reasons affirming or denying the existence of soul, were included by Kauṭilya in the Ānvīkṣikī.[4] The formation of Ānvīkṣikī must have commenced in the period of the Upaniṣad in which some of its technical terms were forestalled, but it did not take any definite shapes until about 650 B.C. when it was recognized as a distinct branch of learning

The distinction between Ānvīkṣikī and Ātma-vidyā.

6. Ānvīkṣikī bifurcates into Philosophy and Logic (about 650 B.C.).

Ānvīkṣikī, as previously pointed out, treated of two subjects, viz. the soul and the theory of reasons. In so far as it was mainly concerned with the soul, Ānvīkṣikī was developed into Philosophy called *Darśana*[5]; and in so far as it dealt largely with the

The theory of soul and that of reasoning.

---

[1] त्रयी वार्ता दण्डनीतिश्चेति मानवाः । त्रयीविशेषो ह्यान्वीक्षकीति ।
(Arthaśāstra of Kauṭilya, 1—2, p. 6, Sham Śāstri's edition).

[2] आन्वीक्षकी त्रयी वार्ता दण्डनीतिश्चेति विद्याः ।
(Arthaśāstra of Kauṭilya, 1-2, p. 6).

[3] इमास्तु चतस्रो विद्याः पृथक् प्रस्थानाः प्राणभृतामनुग्रहायोपदिश्यन्ते यासां चतुर्थीयम् आन्वीक्षिकी न्यायविद्या । तस्याः पृथक् प्रस्थानाः संशयादयः पदार्थाः । तेषां पृथग्वचनमन्तरेण अध्यात्मविद्यामात्रमियं स्यात् यथोपनिषदः (Nyāyabhāṣya, 1-1-1).

[4] सांख्यं योगो लोकायतं चेत्यान्वीक्षकी (Arthaśāstra of Kauṭilya, 1-2, p. 6).

[5] In Sanskrit दर्शन, in Pāli दस्सन, in Prākṛta दंसण, and in Tibetan ལྟ་བ ।

theory of reasons it was developed into Logic called pre-eminently *the Ānvīkṣikī* or *Ānvīkṣikī par excellence.* This bifurcation of Ānvikṣikī into Philosophy and Logic commenced with the very formation of the science but specially about 550 B.C. when Medhātithi Gautama expounded the logical side of the Ānvīkṣikī. The Ānvīkṣikī continued however for many centuries to be used in the *general sense* of a science which embraced both the subjects of Philosophy and Logic.

7. Ānvīkṣikī in its philosophical aspect called *Darśana*.

An explanation of the term *darśana*.

As already observed, Ānvīkṣikī treating of the soul was called *Darśana* (philosophy). "Darśana" literally signifies *seeing*: it is in fact the science which enables us to see our soul. The Bṛhadāraṇyakopaniṣad [1] says that "the soul is verily to be seen," and the Yājñavalkya-saṁhitā [2] declares that "the highest virtue consists in seeing the soul through meditation." In the Muṇḍakopaniṣad [3] we find that "when the soul is *seen*, the knot of the heart is untied, all doubts are dispelled and all act-forces are exhausted." It was about the first century B.C. that the Ānvīkṣikī dealing with the soul was replaced by the word "Darśana." The Sāṁkhya, Yoga and Lokāyata which were incorporated in Ānvīkṣikī were designated as Darśana or branches of philosophy. The word Darśana in this special sense occurs in the Mahābhārata,[4] Bhāgavata Purāṇa,[5] Nyāya-bhāṣya,[6] Vedānta-bhāṣya,[7] etc.

---

[1] आत्मा वारे द्रष्टव्यः (Bṛhadāraṇyakopaniṣad, ii, 4–5).

[2] अयन्तु परमो धर्म्मो यद् योगेनात्मदर्शनम् (Yājñavalkya-saṁhitā, book i, verse 8).

[3] भिद्यते हृदयग्रन्थिः छिद्यन्ते सर्व्वसंशयाः
क्षीयन्ते चास्य कर्म्माणि तस्मिन् दृष्टे परावरे ॥ (Muṇḍakopaniṣad, ii, 2–8).

[4] तुल्यं शौचं तपोयुक्तं दया भूतेषु चानघ ।
व्रतानां धारणं तुल्यं दर्शनं न समं तयोः ॥ (Mahābhārata, Śāntiparva, 110–45).

[5] स्तूयमानो जनैरेभिः मायया नामरूपया ।
विमोहितात्मभिर्नाना दर्शनैर्न च दृश्यते ॥ (Bhāgavatapurāṇa, 8–14–10).

[6] यत् पुरुषधर्म्मो ज्ञानम् अन्तःकरणस्य इच्छा द्वेषप्रयत्नसुखदुःखानि धर्म्मा इति कस्यचिद् दर्शनं तत् प्रतिषिध्यते । (Nyāya-bhāṣya, 3–2–35).

[7] Śaṅkara-bhāṣya on the Vedānta sūtra 2–2–1

8. VARIOUS NAMES FOR ĀNVĪKṢIKĪ IN ITS LOGICAL ASPECT (FROM 650 B.C. ONWARDS).

As already observed, Ānvīkṣikī dealing with the theory of reasons was developed into Logic designated specially as *the Ānvīkṣikī*—or *Ānvīkṣikī par excellence.* We find the term Ānvīkṣikī [1] used in this *special sense* of Logic in the Manusaṁhitā,[2] Gautama-dharma-sūtra,[3] Rāmāyaṇa,[4] Mahābhārata,[5] etc. In about 327 B.C. Kauṭilya[6] characterised the Ānvīkṣikī (evidently Logic) as a highly useful science which furnished people with reasons for the estimation of their strength and weakness, kept their intellect unperturbed in prosperity and adversity, and infused into their intelligence, speech and action, subtlety and power.

The Ānvīkṣikī.

The Ānvīkṣikī, in virtue of the theory of reasons predominating it, was called *Hetu-śastra* or *Hetu-vidyā*,[7] the science of reasoning, as is evident from the Manusaṁhitā,[8] Mahābhārata,[9] etc.

Hetu-śāstra.

It was also called *Tarka-vidyā*,[10] the art of debate, or *Vāda-vidyā*, the art of discussion, inasmuch as it dealt with rules for carrying on disputations in learned assemblies called *pariṣad*.

Tarka-vidyā or Vāda-vidyā.

---

1 The *Ānvīkṣikī* is called in Tibetan རྩོད་པ rtsod-pa. (*Vide* the Amarakoṣa, Svargavarga, verse 155, edited in Sanskrit with Tibetan version by Satis Chandra Vidyabhusana, in the Bibliotheca Indica series, Calcutta).

2 Manusaṁhitā 7–43.

3 Gautama-dharma-sūtra, adhyāya 11.

4 Rāmāyaṇa, Ayodhyākāṇḍa, sarga 100, verse 36.

5 Mahābhārata, Śāntiparva, adhyāya, 180, verse 47.

6 धर्म्माधर्म्मौ त्रय्याम्। अर्थानर्थौ वार्त्तायाम्। नयानयौ दण्डनीत्याम्। बलाबले चैतासां हेतुभिरन्वीक्षमाणा लोकस्योपकरोति, व्यसनेऽभ्युदये च बुद्धिमवस्थापयति, प्रज्ञावाक्यक्रियावैशारद्यं च करोति—

प्रदीपः सर्व्वविद्यानामुपायः सर्व्वकर्म्मणाम्।
आश्रयः सर्व्वधर्म्माणां शश्वदान्वीक्षिकी मता॥

(Artha śāstra of Kauṭilya, p. 1–2, 7).

7 The Hetu-śāstra or Hetu-vidyā is called in Tibetan གཏན་ཚིགས་རིག་པ Gtan-tshigs-rig-pa (*vide* the Mahāvyutpatti, part I, p. 20, edited in Sanskrit, Tibetan and English by Dr. E. D. Ross and Satis Chandra Vidyabhusana in the Bibliothece Indica series, Calcutta. Also Bstan-hgyur, Mdo, Go, folios 223–377).

8 Manusaṁhitā, 2–11.

9 Mahābhārata, Ādiparva, adhyāya 1, verse 67. Śāntiparva, adhyāya 210, verse 22; Aśvamedhaparva, adhyāya 85, verse 27. Cf. J.R.A.S. 1891–92, pp. 1–39, and 412.

10 *Tarka-vidyā* is called in Tibetan རྟོག་གེ་རིག Rtog-ge-rig (*vide* Amarakoṣa, Svargavarga, verse 155, Satis Chandra Vidyabhusana's edition).

Nyāya-śāstra.

Tarka-vidyā or Vāda-vidyā is referred to in the Manusaṁhitā,[1] Mahābhārata,[2] Skandapurāṇa,[3] Gautama dharma-sūtra,[4] Ramāyāṇa,[5] Yājñavalkya saṁhitā,[6] etc. The Ānvīkṣikī was, as we shall see later, also called *Nyāya-śāstra,*[7] the science of true reasoning

---

1 Manusaṁhitā, 6–50; 8–269, 12–106, 111.

2 Mahābhārata, Śāntiparva, adhyāya 180, verse 47, and adhyāya 246, verse 18.

3 Skandapurāṇa, Kālikākhaṇḍa, adhyāya 17.

4 Gautama-dharma sūtra, adhyāya 11.

5 Rāmāyaṇa 1-13–23, 7–53–15.

6 Yājñavalkya-saṁhitā, 3–292; etc.

7 The *Nyāya* is called in Tibetan རིགས་པ Rigs-pa (*vide* the Mahāvyutpatti, part II, p. 133, edited in Sanskrit-Tibetan-English by Dr. E. D. Ross and Satis Chandra Vidyabhusana in the Bibliotheca Indica series, Calcutta; also—Bstan-hgyur, Mdo, Go, folios 223–377).

CHAPTER II.

The Teachers of Ānvīkṣikī (Philosophy and Logic).

9. CĀRVĀKA—HIS MATERIALISTIC DOCTRINE (CIRCA 650 B.C.).

The Vedic literature[1] refers to a class of men who did not believe in gods, and would not perform sacrifices. They were subsequently designated as the followers of Cārvāka, a pupil of Bṛhaspati. Cārvāka was perhaps not the name of any particular individual but represented the atheistic doctrine of olden times. In the Bṛhadāraṇyakopaniṣad[2] (before 600 B.C.) there is a reference to such doctrine according to which our soul (consciousness) is produced through the combination of four elements, viz. earth, water, fire and air, just as an intoxicating power is generated by the comixture of rice, molasses, etc.

The Lokāyata doctrine of soul.

The dissolution into those elements is our death, after which our consciousness disappears. In the Rāmāyaṇa[3] the same doctrine is elucidated by Jāvāla when he says that our parents are our progenitors, that there is no future life and that we should not believe in anything which cannot be proved through perception. This doctrine, which is referred to also in the Caraka-saṁhitā,[4] etc., and which attracted a very large number of adherents, is widely known as *Lokāyata* or that which prevails in the world.[5]

10. KAPILA—HIS DOCTRINE OF MATTER AND SOUL (ABOUT 650–575 B.C.).

The earliest orthodox writer on Ānvīkṣikī (Philosophy) as mentioned in the Śvetāśvatara[6] Upaniṣad was Kapila who is tradition-

---

1 *Vide* Ṛgveda, 10–38–3; 8–70–7: 8–71–8, etc.

2 अरेऽयमात्मा ऽनन्तरोऽबाह्यः कृत्स्नः प्रज्ञानघन एव
एतेभ्यो भूतेभ्यः समुत्थाय तान्येव अनुविनश्यति न प्रेत्य संज्ञाऽस्तीति ।
(Bṛhadāraṇyaka, 4–5–13).

3 स नास्ति परमित्येतत् कुरु बुद्धिं महामते ।
प्रत्यक्षं यत् तदातिष्ठ परोक्षं पृष्ठतः कुरु ॥
(Rāmāyana, Ayodhyākāṇḍa, sarga 108, verse 17).

4 Caraka-saṁhitā, Sūtra-sthāna, chap. XI.

5 For a history of the Lokāyata compare Prof. T. W. Rhys Davids' Introduction to the Kūṭadanta Sutta in "Dialogues of the Buddha, vol. II."

6 ऋषिं प्रसूतं कपिलं यस्तमग्रे ।
ज्ञानैर्बिभर्त्ति जायमानं च पश्येत् ॥ (Śvetāśvatara Upaniṣad, 5–2).

ally known to have been born at Puṣkara near Ajmere, but who according to the Padmapurāṇa dwelt in Indraprastha (Delhi). The doctrine propounded by him was orally transmitted to form at later times a system of philosophy called the *Sāṁkhya*. Kapila imparted his doctrine to Āsuri[1] who taught it to Pañcaśikha. The fact that Āsuri is mentioned in the Śatapatha Brāhmaṇa[2] as a teacher warrants us to suppose that he lived before 600 B.C. which is the latest date of composition of the Brāhmaṇas. Kapila as the fifth incarnation of Viṣṇu preceded Dattātreya. Seeing that Kapila preceded Buddha (circa 570–490 B.C.) we shall not be far wrong if we place the former at an age from 650 B.C. to 570 B.C. As the original work of Kapila has not come down to us we can say nothing about his doctrine beyond the fact that he treated of the soul under the name of *Puruṣa* and the primordial matter under the name of *Prakṛti*, both of which were, according to him, eternal.[3] The soul, which experiences pleasure and pain owing to its connection with matter, attains release when it realizes itself to be totally unconnected with the same.

The Sāṁkhya doctrine of soul, *puruṣa*.

11. DATTĀTREYA—HIS PARABLE OF A TREE (ABOUT 650 B.C.).

A sage named Dattātreya,[4] who as the sixth incarnation of Viṣṇu was junior to Kapila, is stated in the Bhāgavata purāṇa to have taught Ānvīkṣikī to Alarka, Prahlāda and others. The proper name of the sage was Datta while his family name was Ātreya. He lived on the Girnar hills in Kathiawar where a temple associated with his name still exists. It appears from the Mārkaṇḍeya purāṇa[5] that the Ānvīkṣikī-vidyā expounded by him consisted of

---

1 Sāṁkhya kārikā, verse 70.

2 Macdonell's History of Sanskrit Literature, p. 215.

3 अजामेकां लोहितशुक्लकृष्णां
बह्वीः प्रजाः सृजमानां सरूपाः ।
अजो ह्येको जुषमाणोऽनुशेते
जहात्येनां भुक्तभोगामजोऽन्यः ॥ (Śvetāśvatara, 4–5).

4 षष्ठमत्रेरपत्यत्वं वृतः प्राप्तोऽनसूयया ।
आन्वीक्षिकीमलर्काय प्रह्लादादिभ्य ऊचिवान् ॥
(Bhāgavata purāṇa, 1–3–12).

5 शृणु तात यथा योगो दत्तात्रेयेण धीमता ।
अलर्काय पुरा प्रोक्तः सम्यक् [illegible] विस्तरात् ॥
(Mārkaṇḍeya purāṇa, 16–12).

A sage named Ātreya is mentioned in the Kauśika sūtra of the Atharva-veda. *Vide* Weber's History of Sanskrit Literature, p. 153.

a mere disquisition on soul in accordance with the *yoga* philosophy. He preached the doctrines of transmigration and emancipation under the parable of a tree. To identify a gross object with "I" or to look upon it as "mine" is, according to him, the germ of selfishness which grows up into a large tree bearing the fruits of pleasure and pain. He in whom the tree of selfishness has not grown is freed from all bondage for ever. Things when looked upon in their true nature do not cause affliction but they become sources of great woes when we consider them as our own.

The yoga doctrine of soul.

From this summary we may conclude that Dattātreya expounded the philosophical side of Ānvīkṣikī and not its logical aspect.

12. PUNARVASU ĀTREYA: HIS DISSERTATION ON THE SENSES (CIRCA 550 B.C.).

In the Caraka-saṁhitā, the original author of which was Punarvasu Ātreya,[1] there is a dissertation on the senses (*indriya*)[2] which seems to belong to the Ānvīkṣikī system. The Caraka-saṁhitā, originally called the Āyurveda, is said to have been delivered by a sage named Punarvasu better known as Ātreya who resided at the side of the Himālayas. The sage was perhaps the same Ātreya[3] who is mentioned in the Tibetan books as a Professor of medicine under whom Jīvaka the physician of Buddha studied for several years at Taxila about 550 B.C. Ātreya was a countryman of Pāṇini as both of them flourished in the Punjab—one at Taxila (Takṣaśilā) and the other at Śalātura. Like the Aṣṭādhyāyī of Pāṇini, Ātreya's Āyurveda[4] was divided into eight books called "sthānas" or "places." The rule which Pāṇini lays down as to the use of the word Punarvasu in the singular number shows that Ātreya whose proper name was Punarvasu was a Vedic sage.

Professor Ātreya of Taxila.

It is not known whether the Caraka-saṁhitā, as it exists at present, contains any genuine teachings of Ātreya, but the most elementary doctrines of each book of the saṁhitā are by common consent ascribed to him. The eighth chapter of sūtra-sthāna

---

[1] Ātreya is called in Tibetan རྒྱུན་ཤེས་ཀྱི་བུ Rgyun-śes-kyi-bu (*vide* Mahāvyutpatti, p. 22, Bibliotheca Indica).

[2] अथात इन्द्रियोपक्रमणीयमध्यायं व्याख्यास्याम इति ह स्माह भगवान् आत्रेयः ।
(Caraka-saṁhitā, Sūtra-sthāna, adhyāya 8).

[3] Bkaḥ-ḥgyur, Dulva III. *Vide* Rockhill's Life of Buddha, p. 64. Cf. Pali Mahāvagga, Khandhakas I, VIII in which there occurs the name Aṭṭhaka.

[4] छन्दसि पुनर्वस्वोरेकवचनम् (Pāṇini's Aṣṭādhyāyī, 1-2-61).

of the work contains a dissertation on the senses a summary of which is given below:—

There are five organs of sense, viz. the eye, ear, nose, tongue and skin. The five elements of which these are made are fire, ether, earth, water and air. The five objects of sense are colour, sound, smell, taste and touch. The five kinds of sensuous knowledge are the visual, the auditory, the olfactory, the gustatory and the tactual. The mind, which is different from these senses, is one and as such cannot attend to them simultaneously. Hence we cannot perceive more than one thing at a time.

His doctrine of the senses.

Dissertations on the senses, like the one given above, contributed not a little to the development of the doctrine of soul which formed a part of the Ānvīkṣikī.

13. SULABHĀ—A LADY ASCETIC: HER CANONS OF SPEECH (ABOUT 550–500 B.C.).

In the Mahābhārata[1] there is mention of an old female ascetic named Sulabhā who delivered a discourse on what constituted the merits and defects of speech as belonging to the province of Ānvīkṣikī. Sulabhā, who was in all probability a fictitious person, represents the philosophical culture of the 6th century B.C. It is related that once she transforming herself by occult processes into a lady of blooming youth came to the court of Janaka the pious king of Mithilā, whose fame as a philosopher was established far and wide. After the rites of hospitality had been duly observed she was led to the royal presence. Janaka was not a little surprised to hear that her sole object in coming to his court was to ascertain, from a personal interview with him, wherein lay the secret of final release of the soul. Janaka pointed out the impudence of such a wish entertained by a lady whose ambition must be something gross and material, and who must have come to his court as a spy. He concluded by asking in a taunting tone what business a lady could have had with the doctrine of *Release*, seeing that her strength lay solely in her radiant youth and beauty. Though rebuked in such unpleasant, improper and ill-applied terms, Sulabhā was not in the least annoyed but maintained a tranquil and dignified attitude. In the course of her reply to the king she made the following observations, on the canons of a sound speech:—

Sulabhā's interview with king Janaka.

A speech properly so called should be subtle, discriminative and orderly. It should lead to a decision and indicate a purpose.

[1] Mahābhārata, Śāntiparva, adhyāya 320, verses 78–94.

A good speech is (1) fraught with sense, (2) unequivocal, (3) fair, (4) not pleonastic, (5) smooth, (6) determinative, (7) not bombastic, (8) agreeable, (9) truthful, (10) not harmful, (11) refined, (12) not too laconic, (13) not abstruse, (14) not unsystematic, (15) not far-fetched, (16) not superfluous, (17) not inopportune, and (18) not devoid of an object.

Characteristics of a sound speech.

A speech, if it is to be freed from the faults of judgment, should not be prompted by lust, wrath, fear, greediness, abjectness, crookedness, shamefulness, tenderness or conceit.

A speech is said to be lucid if there is agreement between it on one hand and the speaker and hearer on the other. A speech which, though clear to the speaker himself, is uttered without any regard for the hearer, produces no impression in the latter. That speech again, which does not convey the meaning of the speaker himself but is uttered solely out of regard for the hearer, is disingenuous and faulty. He alone is a speaker who employs words which, while expressing his own meaning, are also understood by his hearer.

14. Aṣṭāvakra—A Violent Debater: how he defeated a sophist (about 550–500 B.C.).

In the Mahābhārata[1] the sage Aṣṭāvakra ("crooked in eight parts"), who represents the culture of the 6th century B.C., is stated to have been a great logician. He was the son of Kahoḍa who was a disciple and son-in-law of Uddālaka, father of Śvetaketu. With the object of defeating a famous sophist named Vandin, otherwise known as the son of Suta or Varuṇa, Aṣṭāvakra while a mere boy came to attend a sacrificial ceremony at the palace of king Janaka in Mithilā. Being prevented at the gate Aṣṭāvakra addressed the king and said: "A road while there is no Brāhmaṇa on it belongs to the blind, the deaf, women, carriers of burden and the king respectively, but when a Brāhmaṇa is there it belongs to him alone." Hearing these words the king gave him permission to enter. The warder in offering an apology said, that Aṣṭāvakra was stopped because he was still a lad, and, under orders of Vandin lads were not permitted to enter the sacrificial ground. Aṣṭāvakra said: "If

Aṣṭāvakra's debate with Vandin.

this be the condition O warder, that the door is opened only to the old, I have a right to enter, I am old: I have observed sacred vows and am in possession of energy proceeding from the Vedic lore. A person is not old because his head is gray but the gods

[1] Mahābhārata, Vanaparva, Chaps. 132–134.

regard him as old who, though young in years, is possessed of knowledge." "Who is Vandin? Where is he now? Tell him to come here so that I may destroy him even as the sun destroys the stars."

Vandin was summoned to be present in the assembly of debate on the sacrificial ground. While he arrived there Aṣṭāvakra threatened him and exclaimed: "Do thou answer my questions and I shall answer thine!"

The doctrine of things fixed in number.

(1) Aṣṭāvakra asks: What things are signified by one?

Vandin replies: There is only one *fire* that blazes forth in various shapes, there is only one *sun* that illumines the whole world, there is only one lord of the gods named *Indra*, and the lord of the deceased forefathers is also one, named *Yama*.

(2) Vandin asks: What things are signified by two?

Aṣṭāvakra replies: There are two friends named *Indra* and *Agni* who move together, the two celestial sages are *Nārada* and *Parvata*, twins are the *Aśvinīkumāras*, two is the number of *wheels* of a car, and the *wife* and *husband* are likewise two that live together.

(3) Aṣṭāvakra asks: What things are signified by three?

Vandin replies: There are three classes of *beings* born in consequence of their acts, three are the *Vedas* which perform the Vājapeya sacrifice, at three times the *adhvaryu* priests commence sacrificial rites, three is the number of the *world*, and three also are the *divine lights*.

(4) Vandin asks: What things are signified by four?

Aṣṭāvakra replies: Four are the *stages* of a Brāhmaṇa's life, sacrifices are performed by four *orders*, there are four *cardinal points* as well as *colours*, and four is the number of the *legs* of a cow.

(5) Aṣṭāvakra asks: What things are signified by five?

Vandin replies: There are five *fires*, the metre *paṅkti* possesses five feet, the *sacrifices* are five and there are five *senses*, the *locks* of celestial nymphs are five, and five are the *rivers* of the Punjab.

(6) Vandin asks: What things are signified by six?

Aṣṭāvakra replies: Six *cows* are paid as a gratuity on the occasion of establishing the sacred fire, the *seasons* are six, six are the *senses*, six stars constitute the constellation *kṛttikā*, and six is the number of the *sādyaska* sacrifices.

(7) Aṣṭāvakra asks: What things are signified by seven?

Vandin replies: Seven is the number of *domesticated animals*, the *wild animals* are likewise seven, seven metres are used in completing a *sacrifice*, the *sages* are seven in number, seven forms of paying *homage* are extant in the world, and seven are the strings of a *lute*.

(8) Vandin asks: What things are signified by eight?

Aṣṭāvakra replies: Eight are the *hemp-threads* which carry a hundred weights, eight is the number of legs of the *stag* that preys upon a lion, eight *Vasu*-gods are among the celestials, and eight are the *angles of a stake* in a sacrificial rite.

(9) Aṣṭāvakra asks: What things are signified by nine?

Vandin replies: Nine is the number of *mantras* used in kindling fire for the manes, nine are the appointed functions in the process of *creation*, nine letters compose a foot of the metre *vṛhatī*, and nine is ever the number of *figures* in calculation.

(10) Vandin asks: What things are signified by ten?

Aṣṭāvakra replies: Ten is the number of *cardinal points*, ten times hundred make up a *thousand*, ten is the numher of *months* during which women bear, and ten are the *teachers* of true knowledge.

(11) Aṣṭāvakra asks: What things are signified by eleven?

Vandin replies: Eleven are the *modifications of senses*, the number of *yūpas* (stakes) is eleven, eleven are the *changes of the natural state*, and there are eleven *Rudras* among the gods in heaven.

(12) Vandin asks: What things are signified by twelve?

Aṣṭāvakra replies: Twelve months complete a *year*, a foot of the metre *jagatī* consists of twelve letters, there are twelve *minor sacrifices* and twelve is the number of the *Adityas*.

(13) Aṣṭāvakra asks: What things are signified by thirteen?

Vandin replies: The *thirteenth lunar day* is considered most auspicious, and thirteen *islands* exist on earth.

Having proceeded so far, Vandin stopped.

Aṣṭāvakra completed the reply thus:

Thirteen sacrifices are presided over by *Keśī*, and thirteen letters compose the *aticchandas* metre.

Shouts of victory for Aṣṭāvakra.

Seeing Aṣṭāvakra speaking and Vandin silent, the assembly broke into a loud uproar indicative of victory for one and defeat for the other. The Brāhmaṇas present there being pleased approached Aṣṭāvakra to pay him their homage. Aṣṭāvakra said: "This Vandin defeating the Brāhmaṇas in controversy used to cast them into water. Let him to-day meet with the same fate: seize him and drown him into water." Janaka remaining speechless, Aṣṭāvakra reproached him thus: "O King, has flattery robbed thee of thy sense so that pierced by my words, as elephants by the hooks, thou heedest them not!" Janaka replied: "Your words are excellent and superhuman. As you have defeated Vandin in debate, I place him at your disposal."[1]

15. Aṣṭāvakra Solves Puzzles.

At Mithilā King Janaka to test the ingenuity of Aṣṭāvakra[2] once made a statement as follows:—

"He alone is a learned man who knows the thing which is possessed of 360 spokes (i.e. days), 12 parts (i e. months) of 30 subdivisions (days) each, and 24 joints (i.e. new moons and full moons)."

Aṣṭāvakra who fully understood the significance of the statement replied as follows:—

Aṣṭāvakra's ingenuity elicits applause.

"May that ever-moving wheel (i.e. the sun) that has 24 joints (i e. new moons and full moons), six naves (i.e seasons), 12 peripheries (i.e. the signs of the zodiac or months) and 360 spokes (i.e. degrees or days) protect thee."

Janaka asked: "Who amongst the gods beget those two which go together like two mares yoked to a car and swoop like hawks?"

Aṣṭāvakra said: "May God, O King, forfend the presence of these two (i.e thunder and lightning) in thy house, yea even in the house of thy enemies. He (i.e. the cloud), whose charioteer is the wind, begets them."

Thereupon the king said: "What is it that does not close its eyes even while sleeping: what is it that does not move even when born; what is it that has no heart. and what does increase even in its own speed"?

Aṣṭāvakra said: "It is a fish that does not close its eye-lids while sleeping; it is an egg that does not move when produced; it is a stone that has no heart: and it is a river that increases in its own speed."

---

[1] The dialogue, which shows besides their ready wit, an acquaintance of the debaters with all branches of learning known at their time, is neither "enigmatical" nor "puerile," when we consider that in olden times the names of things stood for numbers, nay constituted the dictionary of numbers called *Aṅkūbhidhāna*. It bears to a certain extent an analogy to the novice's questions (*Kumāra pañha*) which appear from the Pāli canonical works to have been a necessary part of the training of a young Buddhist monk.

The doctrine involved in the dialogue was criticised by Akṣapāda in the Nyāya-sūtra (4-1-41) under the title of *Saṁkhyaikānta-vāda*, the doctrine of the fixity of things signified by numbers.

The dialogue is quite simple and natural, and I do not find in it an exposition of the doctrine of unity of the Supreme Being as supposed by Nīlakaṇṭha, a commentator on the Mahābhārata, who lived at Kūrpara to the west of the Godāvarī in Mahārāṣtra in the 16th century A.D.

[2] Mahābhārata, Vanaparva, chaps. 132-134.

The king amazed at Aṣṭāvakra's ingenuity remained silent for a while, and then applauded him thus: "O possessor of divine energy thou art no human being."

16. Medhātithi Gautama—the founder of Ānvīkṣikī *par excellence* (circa 550 B.C.).

While the teachers mentioned before dealt with some particular topics of Ānvīkṣikī, the credit of founding the Ānvīkṣikī in its special sense of a science is to be attributed to a sage named Gotama or Gautama. In the Padmapurāṇa,[1] Skandapurāṇa,[2] Gandharva tantra,[3] Kusumāñjali, Naiṣadha carita,[4] Nyāya-sūtra-vṛtti, etc., Gotama or Gautama is mentioned as the founder of the science of Ānvīkṣikī (Logic) or Anvīkṣikī *par excellence*. The people of Mithilā, too, ascribe the foundation of the science of Ānvīkṣikī or Logic to Gotama or Gautama and point out, as the place of his birth, a village named Gautama-sthāna[5] where a fair is held every year on the 9th day of the lunar month of Caitra (March-April). It is situated on the outskirts of Mithilā at a distance of 28 miles north-east of modern Darbhanga. There is a mud-hill of considerable height (supposed to be the hermitage of Gautama) at the base of which lies the celebrated Gautama-kuṇḍa ("Gautama's well"), the water whereof is like milk to the taste and feeds a perennial rivulet called on this account "Kṣīrodadhi" or "Khiroi" signifying literally the sea of milk.

The birth-place of Gautama.

Gautama lived with his wife Ahalyā who, for her flirtation with Indra, was, according to the Rāmāyaṇa,[6] cursed by her

---

1 कणादेन तु सम्प्रोक्तं शास्त्रं वैशेषिकं महत् ।
गोतमेन तथा न्यायं सांख्यं तु कपिलेन वै ।
(Padmapurāṇa, Uttarakhaṇḍa, chap. 263).

2 गोतमः स्वेन तर्केण खण्डयन् तत्र तत्र हि ।
(Skandapurāṇa, Kālikākhaṇḍa, chap. xvii).

3 गोतमप्रोक्तशास्त्रार्थनिरताः सर्व एव हि ।
शार्गालीं योनिमापन्नाः सन्दिग्धाः सर्वकर्मसु ॥
(Gandharva tantra quoted in Prāṇatoṣiṇī tantra).

4 मुक्तये यः शिलात्वाय शास्त्रमूचे सचेतसाम् ।
गोतमं तमवेक्ष्यैव यथा वित्थ तथैव सः ॥
(Naiṣadha carita, canto xvii).

5 The author of this book visited Gautama-sthāna in October 1913.

6 मिथिलोपवने तत्र आश्रमं दृश्य राघवः ।
पुराणं निर्जनं रम्यं पप्रच्छ मुनिपुङ्गवम् ॥ १ ॥

2

husband and transformed into a stone She remained in this stony state for some time until she was emancipated by Rāma-candra. Then she regained her human form and was admitted into heaven.

Gautama as described in the Rāmāyaṇa.

Ahalyā in her accursed state is at present represented by a slab of stone, which lies between a pair of trees in a village called Ahalyā-sthāna (Ahiria) two miles to the east of Gautama-sthāna already mentioned. In the vicinity of this slab there is a temple which commemorates the emancipation of Ahalyā by Rāma-candra

Gautama as mentioned in the Mahābhārata.

The Mahābhārata[1] which gives a different version of the story mentions a son of Ahalyā named Cirakārin who is said to have been ordered by his father to kill Ahalyā, but who, being of a reflective turn of mind, refrained from carrying out the order. Gautama, in consideration of the natural weakness of her sex, pardoned his wife and dwelt from that time forward in his hermitage without ever separating himself from her.

Medhātithi of Bhāsa.

In the Pratimā-nāṭaka[2] the poet Bhāsa, who is believed to have flourished during the Kuśāna period,[3] speaks of a sage named Medhātithi as the founder of the Nyāya-śāstra, a later appellation for the Ānvīkṣikī. In the Mahābhārata,[4] we find that Medhātithi and Gautama were the names of the same person, one being his proper name and the other his family name Therefore the full name of the founder of Ānvīkṣikī was Medhātithi Gautama

---

इदमाश्रमसंकाशं किंस्विद् मुनिवर्जितम् ।
श्रोतुमिच्छामि भगवन् कस्यायम्पूर्व्व आश्रमः ॥ १२ ॥
गौतमस्य नरश्रेष्ठ पूर्व्वमासीन्महात्मनः ।
आश्रमो दिव्यसंकाशः सुरैरपि सुपूजितः ॥ १३ ॥
स चात्र तप आतिष्ठदहल्यासहितः पुरा ।
वर्षं पूगान्यनेकानि राजपुत्र महायशः ॥ १४ ॥

(Rāmāyaṇa, Ādikāṇḍa, sarga 48).

[1] Mahābhārata, Śāntiparva, 272–9; and Aśvamedhaparva, 56–26.

[2] भोः काश्यपगोत्रोऽस्मि । साङ्गोपाङ्गं वेदमधीये, मानवीयं धर्मशास्त्रं, माहेश्वरं योगशास्त्रं, बार्हस्पत्यम् अर्थशास्त्रं, मेधातिथेर्न्यायशास्त्रं, प्राचेतसं श्राद्धकल्पं च ।

(Bhāsa's Pratimā-nāṭaka, Act V, p. 79, M.M. Gaṇapati Śāstri's edition).

[3] *Vide* A. M. Meerwarth's "The dramas of Bhāsa: a literary study" in J.A S.B., 1917.

[4] मेधातिथिर्महाप्राज्ञो गौतमस्तपसि स्थितः ।
विमृश्य तेन कालेन पत्न्याः संस्थाव्यतिक्रमम् ॥

(Mahābhārata, Śāntiparva, 265–45, Baṅgavāsi edition).

Family and tribe of Medhātithi Gautama.

Medhātithi Gautama seems to have belonged to the family and school of Naciketas Gautama[1] and to have sprung, like Buddha Gautama, from the Āṅgirasa[2] tribe. His remote ancestor was perhaps the sage Nodhā Gotama descended from that Gotama who is described in the Ṛgveda,[3] and the Śatapatha-Brāhmaṇa[4] of the White Yajurveda as having settled in a place the description of which tallies with that of Gautama-sthāna in Mithilā. The descendants of Gotama[5] were called Gotamāsaḥ, Gotama or Gautama.[6]

शान्तसङ्कल्पसुमना यथा स्याद्वीतमन्यु र्गौतमो माभिमृत्यो ।
त्वत्प्रसृष्टं माभिवदेत् प्रतीत एतत् त्रयाणां प्रथमं वरं वृणे ॥
यथोदकं शुद्धे शुद्धमासिक्तं तादृगेव भवति ।
एवं मुनेर्विजानत आत्मा भवति गौतम ॥
हन्त त इदं प्रवक्ष्यामि गुह्यं ब्रह्म सनातनम् ।
यथा च मरणं प्राप्य आत्मा भवति गौतम ॥

(Kaṭhopaniṣad, 1-1-10; 2-4-15; and 2-5-6).

[2] In the Pāli Mahāvagga Āṅgirasa (in Pāli Aṅgirasa) occurs as a name of Buddha Gautama who evidently belonged to the Āṅgirasa tribe:—

Aṅgīrasassa kāye anekavaṇṇā acciyo honti—

(Mahāvagga, paṭhamaṁ pāṭihāriyaṁ, I. 15.7, p. 25, Dr. Oldenberg's edition).

Aṅgīraso Sakyamuni sabbabhūtānukampako.

(Parivāra III. 5, edited by Dr. H. Oldenberg).

In the Mahābhārata and Brahmāṇḍa purāṇa, Gautama (husband of Ahalyā) and his son Cirakārin are described as having belonged to the Āṅgirasa tribe:—

अत्राप्युदाहरन्तीममितिहासं पुरातनम्
चिरकारेश्च यत्पूर्वं वृत्तमाङ्गिरसे कुले ॥
चिरकारी महाप्राज्ञो गौतमस्याभवत् सुतः ।
चिरेण सर्वकार्याणि विमृश्यार्थान् प्रपद्यते ॥

(Mahābhārata, Śāntiparva, chap. 265, verses 2–4; Calcutta, Baṅgavāsi edition).

वने त्वङ्गिरसः श्रेष्ठो गौतमो नाम योगवित् ।
तस्माद् भविष्यते पुत्रं गौतमं नाम सद्गमम् ॥

(Brahmāṇḍa purāṇa, anuṣaṅgapāda, chapter 23).

[3] Ṛgveda-saṁhitā, maṇḍala 1, sūkta 81, verse 3; sūkta 61, verses 14—16; sūkta 62, verse 6; sūkta 62, verse 13; sūkta 64, verse 1; sūkta 77, verse 5; sūkta 85, verse 11.

[4] Śatapatha Brāhmaṇa of the White Yajurveda, kāṇḍa 1, adhyāya 4, Mādhyandinīya recension. *Vide* also my article on "The Localization of certain hymns of the Ṛgveda" in J.A.S.B., February 1914.

[5] भृग्वत्र्यङ्गिरः कुत्सवसिष्ठगोतमेभ्यश्च । १९२ ॥

(Kātantra, Catuṣṭaya kārakaprakaraṇa).

[6] The story of Gautama as related above seems to be historical in so far as his family and native-place are concerned, but the legend of Ahalyā associated with the story is untrustworthy.

We thus find that Medhātithi, Gotama, Gautama and Medhātithi Gautama were the names for one and the same person, who founded the Ānvīkṣikī *par excellence*. His work on Ānvīkṣikī has not come down to us in its original form. We do not therefore know whether he treated of the soul and reasoning together in one volume, or dealt with them separately. His theory of reasoning has reached us in a crude form through the Caraka-saṁhita, and in a developed form through the Nyāya-sūtra, while we may gather some idea of his theory of soul through the same sources as well as through the Mahābhārata and the Pali Brahmajāla-sutta.

Medhātithi's work on Ānvīkṣikī.

Bhāsa[1] speaks of Medhātithi's "Nyāya-śāstra" The term *Nyāya* was prevalent in the day of Bhāsa, and by "Nyāya śāstra" he really meant its prototype the Ānvīkṣikī. In the Śāntiparva of the Mahābhārata,[2] there is mention of a Medhātithi who, along with certain other sages, revealed to the world the Upaniṣad-doctrine of emancipation. This Medhātithi seems to have been the same as our Medhātithi Gautama.

Gautama mentioned in the old Persian scripture.

Medhātithi Gautama is more often called simply Gautama. As previously noticed, Gautama was the name under which the founder of Ānvīkṣikī was best known in the Padmapurāna, Matsyapurāṇa, etc., and his art of debate is still designated as *Gautamī Vidyā* (Gotamide science). The fame of Gautama as a great master of the art of debate seems to have spread as far as Persia In one of the yashts[3] of the Khorda Avesta edited[4] during the reigns of the Sasanian Kings Ardashīr (A.D. 211–241) and Shapūr I (A.D. 242–272), we read[5] "how the Fravashis cause

---

[1] Bhāsa's Pratimā-nāṭaka, Act V, p. 79, M.M. Gaṇapati Śāstri's edition.

[2] चतुर्थश्चोपनिषदो धर्म्मः साधारणः स्मृत।
वानप्रस्थाद् गृहस्थाच्च ततोऽन्यः संप्रवर्त्तते॥
अस्मिन्नेव युगे तात विप्रैः सर्व्वार्थदर्शिभिः।
मेधातिथिर्बुधः। ... एवं धर्म्मं कृतवन्तः॥

(Mahābhārata, Śāntiparva, Mokṣadharma, adhyāya 243, verses 14–17).

[3] *Vide* the 13th yasht, para. 16.

[4] According to Arda-viraf-nāma, the Avesta written on cow-hides with golden ink, and given to the Persians by Zaratusht (Zoroaster), existed in its original form for 300 years until it was burnt by Iskander Rumi (Alexander the Great) who destroyed Persepolis about 325 B.C. The fragments that survived were put together by Zoroastrian priests under the name of Avesta, which was edited and proclaimed canonical during the reigns of Ardashīr and Shapūr of the Sasanian dynasty. It is suggested that it was in the Sasanian period that Indian traditions entered the scripture of the Persians. Cf. Dr. K. Geldner's "Persia" in the Encyclopaedia Britannica.

[5] *Vide* the 13th yasht, para. 16; and Early Religious Poetry of Persia, by J. H. Moulton, p. 141.

a man to be born who is a master in assemblies and skilled in sacred lore, so that he *comes away from debate* a victor over *Gaotema.*[1]"

Medhātithi Gautama's age.

In the Aṅguttara-nikāya[2] of the Pāli Sutta-piṭaka we meet with ten orders of non-Buddhist recluses of which "Gotamakā"[3] was one. This order referred most probably to the followers of Gotama or Gautama the founder of Ānvīkṣikī. The Brahmajāla-sutta[4] describes a sage designated as *takki* (argumentationist) and *vīmaṁsi* (casuist) who maintained that certain things were eternal and other things were non-eternal. If this sage was identical with the leader of the Gotamakā sect or the founder of the Ānvīkṣikī, it will be difficult to resist the conclusion that he was a senior contemporary of Buddha Śākyamuni. We may therefore fix the date of Medhātithi Gautama at about 550 B.C.

---

[1] "Gaotema," who is identified by Dr. Haug and J. H. Moulton, with the Buddha Gautama, is more probably the same as Medhātithi Gautama, the well-known founder of the art of debate and a descendant of Nodhā Gautama. "Yō Nāidyāoṅhō Gaotĕmahe paro-yāo parśtōitavāiti. (Yasht 13, para. 16).

[2] Aṅguttaranikāya, part III, chap. 65, pp 276-77, edited by Dr. Morris, Pāli Text Society.

[3] Prof. T. W. Rhys Davids in his Introduction to the Kassapa-siha-nāda sutta in the Dialogues of Buddha, pp. 220-21, observes: "the only alternative is that some Brāhmaṇa, belonging to the Gotama-gotta, is here referred to as having had a community of Bhikṣus named after him."

[4] The Brahmajāla sutta 1-32 included in the Dīgha Nikāya, p. 29, edited by Dr. T. W. Rhys Davids and J. E. Carpenter, London.

CHAPTER III.

The Doctrines of Ānvīkṣikī.

16. A Council of Debate (*Pariṣad*) (circa 900–500 B.C.).

The theory of reasons (*hetu*), which formed an important subject of Ānvīkṣikī, grew out of debates in councils of learned men. In the Chāndogya[1] and Bṛhadāraṇyaka[2] upaniṣads there are references to councils for the discussion of metaphysical subjects, e.g. the nature of the soul and the Supreme Being. The Praśnopaniṣad[3] reports the proceedings of a council, in which Sukeśā Bhāradvāja, Saivya Satyakāma Sauryāyaṇī Gārgya, Kauśalya Āśvalāyana, Bhārgava Vaidarbhi and Kabandhī Kātyāyana approach the sage Pippalāda and ask him a series of questions such as "how has this world been produced," "how is it sustained" and "how does the life-breath come into our body." Such a council was called *saṁsad*, *samiti*, *sabhā*, *pariṣad* or *parṣad*.

A Council of learned men.

In the socio-religious institutes of Manu,[4] Parāśara,[5] Yājñavalkya[6] and others, we find that the council consisted generally of four, ten or twenty-one Brāhmaṇs, who were learned in the Vedic and secular literatures and could give decisions in matters on which

---

1 श्वेतकेतुर्ह आरुणेयः पाञ्चालानां समितिमेयाय

(Chāndogyopaniṣad, 5-3-1).

2 श्वेतकेतुर्ह आरुणेयः पाञ्चालानां परिषदमाजगाम

(Bṛhadāraṇyaka, 6-2-1).

Max Müller's History of Ancient Sanskrit Literature, pp. 128–132.

3 Praśnopaniṣad, Praśna 1-6.

4 त्रैविद्यो हैतुकस्तर्की नैरुक्तो धर्म्मपाठकः ।
त्रयश्चाश्रमिणः पूर्व्वे परिषत् स्याद्दशावरा ॥

(Manu-saṁhitā, 12-110, 111).

5 अनाहिताग्नयो येऽन्ये वेदवेदाङ्गपारगाः ।
पञ्च त्रयो वा धर्म्मज्ञाः परिषत् सा प्रकीर्त्तिता ॥

(Parāśara-saṁhitā, 8-19).

6 चत्वारो वेदधर्म्मज्ञाः पर्षत् त्रैविद्यमेव वा ।
सा ब्रूते यं स धर्म्मः स्यादेको वाध्यात्मवित्तमः ॥

(Yājñavalkya-saṁhitā, 1-9).

people might ask their advice. The debates or dialogues, such as those described in the Praśnopaniṣad, the Chāndogyopaniṣad and the Bṛhadāraṇyaka, were in all probability the precursors of the theory of reasons (*hetu-vāda*) treated in the Ānvīkṣikī. The words, which had to be used in special senses to carry on debates in the councils, constituted the technical terms of the Ānvīkṣikī.

17. The Technical Terms used in the Councils of Debate (900–500 B.C.).

Some of the terms used in the Brāhmaṇas and Upaniṣads.

Some of the technical terms used in the councils of debate had grown up along with the Upaniṣads. For instance in the Taittirīya Āraṇyaka[1] we meet with four terms, viz. (1) *Smṛti* (scripture), (2) *pratyakṣa* (perception), (3) *aitihya* (tradition), and (4) *anumāna* (inference). These terms recur in the Rāmāyaṇa[2] with a little alteration as (1) *aitihya* (tradition), (2) *anumāna* (inference), and (3) *śāstra*, scripture. Three of these terms, are used in the Manu saṁhitā,[3] as (1) *pratyakṣa*, *anumāna* and *śāstra*.

Similarly in the Aitareya Brāhmaṇa, Kaṭhopaniṣad, etc., there occur such terms as *tarka*[4] (reasoning), *vāda*[5] (debate), *yukti*[6] (continuous argument), *jalpa*[7] (wrangling), *vitaṇḍā*[8] (cavil), *chala*[9] (quibble), *nirṇaya*[10] (ascertainment), *prayojana*[11] (purpose), *pramāṇa*[12] (proof), *prameya*[13] (the object of knowledge), etc.

---

1 स्मृतिः प्रत्यक्ष मैतिह्यम्। अनुमानश्चतुष्टयम्। एतैरादित्यमण्डलं। सर्व्वैरेव विधास्यते ॥
(Taittirīya âraṇyaka, 1-2).

2 ऐतिह्यमनुमानञ्च प्रत्यक्षमपि चागमम्।
यो हि सम्यक् परीक्षेत कृतस्याप्यनुवृत्तिना ॥ (Rāmāyaṇa, 5-87-23).

3 प्रत्यक्षञ्चानुमानञ्च शास्त्रञ्च विविधागमम्।
त्रयं सुविदितं कार्य्यं धर्म्मशुद्धिमभीप्सता ॥ (Manu-saṁhitā, 12-105).

4 *Tarka* occurs in Kaṭhopaniṣad, 2-9; Manusaṁhitā, 12-106; Mahābhārata, 2-453; and Bhāgavata purāṇa, 8-21-2.

5 *Vāda* occurs in Manu-saṁhitā, 6-59; Rāmāyaṇa, 1-13-23 and 7-53-15; and Yājñavalkya-saṁhitā, 3-292.

6 *Yukti* occurs in Aitareya Brāhmaṇa, 6-23; Rāmāyaṇa, 2-1-13; Bhāgavata purāṇa, 3-31-15; and Kāmandakīya-nītisāra, 1-49.

7 *Jalpa* occurs in Mahābhārata, 13-4322.

8 *Vitaṇḍā* occurs in Mahābhārata, 2-1310 and 7-3022; and Pāṇini, 4-4-102.

9 *Chala* occurs in Manu-saṁhitā, 8-49; and Rāmāyaṇa, 4-57-10.

10 *Nirṇaya* occurs in Mahābhārata, 13-7533, 7535.

11 *Prayojana* in Manu-saṁhitā, 7-100; Mahābhārata, 1-5805; and Yājñavalkya-saṁhitā, 3-133.

12 *Pramāṇa* occurs in Manu-saṁhitā, 2-13; Rāmāyaṇa, 2-37-21; and Mahābhārata, 13-5572; Kauṭilya 3-1.

13 *Prameya* occurs in Rāmāyaṇa, 1-52-13; Mahābhārata, 1-157 and 8-1449.

18. *Tantra-yukti*—THE TERMS OF SCIENTIFIC ARGUMENT (QUOTED BY KAUṬILYA ABOUT 327 B.C.).

In the last chapter of the Artha-śāstra (a work on polity), Kauṭilya gives a list of thirty-two technical terms called *Tantra-yukti* or "the forms of scientific argument" (*dvātriṁśadākārā-stantrayuktayaḥ*). This list appears also in the Caraka-saṁhitā [1] and the Suśruta-saṁhitā,[2] two authoritative works on medicine. It was evidently prepared neither by Kauṭilya nor by the authors of the two saṁhitās, but by a person or persons who wanted to establish debates on a scientific basis.

Tantra-yukti for the systematization of debates.

The terms included in the list are found to have been employed more widely in works on Nyāya Philosophy than in those on Polity or Medicine. Definitions of some of those terms have been actually quoted by Vātsyāyana [3] and other commentators on the Nyāya-sūtra. The *Tantra-yukti* which literally signifies "scientific argument" was compiled possibly in the 6th century B.C. to systematize debates in *Pariṣads* or learned councils. In the Suśruta-saṁhitā [4] it is distinctly stated that by means of Tantra-yukti

---

1 *Vide* Caraka saṁhitā, Siddhisthāna, chapter XII. The Tantra-yukti along with other matters was added to the Caraka-saṁhitā by the redactor Dṛḍhabala of Pañcanada (the Punjab). In the Caraka-saṁhitā the Tantra-yukti consists of 34 technical terms as enumerated in the following verses:—

चतुस्त्रिंशद् विविधाभिर्भूषितं तन्त्रयुक्तिभिः ।
तत्राधिकरणं योगो हेत्वर्थोऽर्थः पदस्य च ॥
प्रदेशोद्देशनिर्देशवाक्यशेषाः प्रयोजनम् ।
उपदेशातिदेशाख्यार्थापत्तिविनिर्णयाः ॥
प्रसङ्गैकान्तानैकान्ताः सापवर्गो विपर्ययः ।
पूर्वपक्षविधानानुमतव्याख्यानसंशयाः ।
अतीतानागतापेक्षा स्वसंज्ञा ह्यसमुच्चयाः ।
निदर्शनं निर्वचनं सन्नियोगो विकल्पनम् ॥
प्रत्युच्चारस्तथोद्धारः सम्भवस्तन्त्रयुक्तयः ।
तन्त्रे व्याससमासाभ्यां भवन्त्येतानि कृत्स्नशः ॥

2 *Vide* Suśruta-saṁhitā, Uttaratantra, chapter LXV. The Uttara-tantra is said to have been added to the Suśruta-saṁhitā by the redactor Nāgārjuna. The *Tantra-yukti* as embodied in the Suśruta-saṁhitā consists of 32 technical terms:—

द्वात्रिंशद् युक्तयो ज्ञेयास्तन्त्रसारगवेषणे ।
मया सम्यग्विनिश्चिताः शब्दन्यायार्थसंयुताः ॥

3 परमतमप्रतिषिद्धमनुमतमिति हि तन्त्रयुक्तिः
(Nyāya-bhāṣya of Vātsyāyana, 1-1-4).

4 असद्वादिप्रयुक्तानां वाक्यानां प्रतिषेधनम् ।
स्ववाक्यसिद्धिरपि च क्रियते तन्त्रयुक्तितः ॥
(Suśruta-saṁhitā, Uttaratantra, chapter LXV).

a debater can establish his own points and set aside those of his opponents who indulge in unfairness. In the department of Hetu-śāstra (Logic) there is indeed no work older than the Tantra-yukti which is a little manual on the systematization of arguments or debates.

The technical terms constituting the Tantra-yukti are the following :—

The thirty-two terms of Tantra-yukti.

(1) *Adhikaraṇa* (a subject), (2) *vidhāna* (arrangement), (3) *yoga* (union of words), (4) *padārtha* (category), (5) *hetvartha* (implication), (6) *uddeśa* (enunciation), (7) *nirdeśa* (declaration), (8) *upadeśa* (instruction), (9) *apadeśa* (specification), (10) *atideśa* (extended application), (11) *pradeśa* (determination from a statement to be made), (12) *upamāna* (analogy), (13) *arthāpatti* (presumption), (14) *saṁśaya* (doubt), (15) *prasaṅga* (a connected argument), (16) *viparyaya* (reversion), (17) *vākya-śeṣa* (context), (18) *anumata* (assent), (19) *vyākhyāna* (description), (20) *nirvacana* (etymological explanation), (21) *nidarśana* (example), (22) *apavarga* (exception), (23) *sva-saṁjñā* (a special term), (24) *pūrva-pakṣa* (question), 25) *uttara-pakṣa* (reply), (26) *ekānta* (certain), (27) *anāgatāvekṣaṇa* (anticipation), (28) *atikrāntāvekṣaṇa* (retrospection), (29) *niyoga* (injunction), (30) *vikalpa* (alternative), (31) *samuccaya* (aggregation), and (32) *ūhya* (ellipsis).

In the Caraka-saṁhitā the *Tantra-yukti*, which consists of thirty-four terms, includes the following :—

The list of Kauṭilya differs from that of the Caraka-saṁhitā.

(1) *Prayojana* (purpose), (2) *nirṇaya* (ascertainment), (3) *anekānta* (uncertain), (4) *pratyuccāra* (repetition), (5) *uddhāra* (citation), and (6) *sambhava* (probability).

19. Medhātithi Gautama's Doctrines as reproduced in the Caraka-saṁhitā (about 78 A.D.).

Who was Caraka ?

The Caraka-saṁhitā [1] gives a summary of the principal doctrines of Ānvīkṣikī possibly as propounded by Medhātithi Gautama. Caraka is a general name for the ancient *śākhās* (branches) of the Yajurveda as well as for the teacher of those śākhās. The word "Carakāḥ" signifies, according to Pāṇini,[2] the persons who study the Veda (i.e.

---

[1] As Ātreya communicated his Āyurveda-saṁhitā at first to Agniveśa, the Caraka-saṁhitā is also called the Agniveśa-tantra. Agniveśa is called in Tibetan མེ་བཞིན་འཇུག Me-bshin-hjug (*vide* Mahāvyutpatti, part I, p. 23, Bibliotheca Indica series).

[2] कठचरकाल्लुक् (Pāṇini's Aṣṭādhyāyī, 4-3-107).

Max Müller's History of Ancient Sanskrit Literature, 2nd edition, pp. 225, 350, 364, 369.

the śākhās of the Yajurveda) enounced by the teacher Caraka. Some say that the exact meaning of "Caraka," as applied to the Caraka-saṁhitā, is unknown. The expression "Caraka-saṁhitā" may, according to them, mean the Āyurveda-saṁhitā of the school of Carakāḥ or the Āyurveda-saṁhitā as redacted by a member of the Caraka[1] sect or by a physician named Caraka. According to the Nyāya mañjarī[2] Caraka was a physician, and the Chinese Tripiṭaka[3] describes him as a physician at the court of Kaniṣka, the Kuśāna king of Gāndhāra. Punarvasu Ātreya (about 550 B.C.) was the original author of the Caraka-saṁhitā called Āyurveda-saṁhitā, and the physician Caraka was perhaps the redactor of the Saṁhitā at the beginning of the Christian era.[4]

Medhātithi Gautama's doctrines reflected through the Caraka-saṁhitā.

The doctrines of Ānvīkṣikī did not evidently constitute a part of the original Āyurveda of Punarvasu Ātreya. These doctrines seem to have been incorporated into the Caraka-saṁhitā by the redactor Caraka in whose time they were widely known and studied. The doctrines (with the exception of those relating to *Kāryābhinirvṛtti*) seem to have been the productions of Medātithi Gautama who flourished in the 6th century B.C. Medhātithi Gautama's doctrines were embodied in the Caraka-saṁhitā[5] of Caraka as well as in the Nyāya-sūtra of Akṣapāda. But while Caraka accepted them in their crude forms, Akṣapāda pruned them thoroughly before they were assimilated in the Nyāya-sūtra.

The doctrines as we find them in the Caraka-saṁhitā are treated under three heads, viz.:—

(1) *Kāryābhinirvṛtti*, the aggregate of resources for the accomplishment of an action.
(2) *Parīkṣā*, the standard of examination, and
(3) *Sambhāṣā-vidhi*, or *vāda-vidhi*, the method of debate.

---

1 For an account of the wandering sect named Caraka see the Aṅguttara nikāya, part iii, p. 276; Ratnolkā dhāraṇī; Mahāvastu iii, 412, 7–10, etc. quoted by Prof. Rhys Davids in his "Indian sects or schools in the time of the Buddha," in the J.R.A.S. for 1898. See also Prof. C. Bendall's observations in the J.R.A.S. for 1901.

2 यथोच्यते अनादिरेवैषा चिकित्सकस्मृतिः व्याकरणादिस्मृतिवत् ।
संक्षेपविस्तरविवक्षयैव चरकादयः कर्त्तारः न तु ते सर्व्वदर्शिनः ॥

(Nyāya-mañjarī, chapter IV, p. 249, edited by Gaṅgādhar Śāstri, Vizianagram Sanskrit series).

3 Jolly, *Medicin* (Bühler's Grundriss, iii, 10), p. 11.

In the Journal Asiatique (1896), T. VIII, pp. 447–451, Mr. Sylvain Levi maintains on the authority of Chinese books that Caraka the author of the Caraka-saṁhitā lived in the court of Kaniṣka. The date of Kaniṣka has not yet been finally fixed, but I provisionally take it to be 78 A.D. *Vide* my "History of the Medieval School of Indian Logic," pp. 62–63. Kaniṣka's capital was at Puṣpapura (Peshwar) in Gāndhāra, but he held his Buddhist convocation at Jālandhara.

4 Professor L. Suali fixes the date of Caraka at about 100 A.D. (Filosofia Indiana, p. 28).

5 Caraka-saṁhitā, Vimāna-sthāna, adhyāya 8.

As regards *Kāryābhinirvṛtti*, it does not appear to have been a part of the Ānvīkṣikī of Medhātithi Gautama. Perhaps it was a part of the Vaiśeṣika philosophy in an early stage. *Parīkṣā* is redundant as the four terms coming under this head, viz.: *āptopadeśa*,

Which of the doctrines of the Caraka-saṁhitā emanated from Medhātithi Gautama?

pratyakṣa, *anumāna* and *yukti* reappear with a little modification in the names of *śabda*, *pratyakṣa*, *anumāna* and *aupamya* under the sub-head *vādamārga* of *sambhāṣā-vidhi*. It is uncertain as to whether the first four or the last four were included in the Ānvīkṣikī of Medhātithi Gautama. *Sambhāṣā-vidhi* or *vāda-vidhi* was undoubtedly the principal topic of Ānvīkṣikī-vidyā. Some of the terms coming under the sub-head *vāda-mārga* did not however form a part of the original *sambhāṣā vidhi*. For instance the terms *dravya*, *guṇa*, *karma*, *sāmānya*, *viśeṣa* and *samavāya* were borrowed from the Vaiśeṣika philosophy in its first stage and incorporated into the *vāda-mārga* by Caraka himself. There are other terms such as *pratijñā*, *sthāpanā*, *pratiṣṭhāpanā*, *hetu*, *upanaya*, *nigamana*, *uttara*, *dṛṣṭānta* and *siddhānta* which in their technical senses were perhaps unknown to Medhātithi Gautama and were introduced into the *vāda mārga* by Caraka while he compiled and redacted the Āyurveda saṁhitā in the first century A.D.

The terms coming under the three heads are explained in the Caraka-saṁhitā as follows :—

I. **Kāryābhinirvṛtti**—the aggregate of resources for the accomplishment of an action.

A person who is determined to accomplish an action successfully should examine the following resources :—

(1) *Kāraṇa* or *hetu*—the actor or agent who accomplishes an action.
(2) *Karaṇa*—the instrument which co-operates with the actor to accomplish the action.
(3) *Kārya-yoni*—the material cause which while undergoing modification is developed into the action.
(4) *Kārya*—the action for the accomplishment of which the actor moves.
(5) *Kārya-phala*—the effect for the attainment of which the action is undertaken.
(6) *Anubandha*—the adjunct, that is, that pleasurable or painful condition which resulting from the action attaches unavoidably to the actor.
(7) *Deśa*—the place of the action.
(8) *Kāla*—the time of the action.
(9) *Pravṛtti*—the activity or exertion put forth for achieving the action.
(10) *Upāya*—a favourable circumstance or that condition of the actor, instrument and the material cause in which they can well render facilities and aids to the action being accomplished.

II. Parīkṣā—THE STANDARD OF EXAMINATION.

Things, existent or non-existent, are tested by four standards, viz. (1) *āptopadeśa*, reliable assertion (2) *pratyakṣa*, perception, (3) *anumāna*, inference, and (4) *yukti*, continuous reasoning. These are collectively called *parīkṣā*[1] (examination), *hetu*[2] (reason), or *pramāṇa*[3] (means of valid knowledge).

Reliable assertion is the assertion of a person who is trustworthy, noble, wise and freed from evil propensities, whose perception runs unimpeded, and the truth of whose words is never called in question.

Perception is the knowledge which is produced through a union of the soul with the mind, senses and their objects.

Inference is preceded by perception and refers to three times, e.g. a fire is inferred from smoke, fruits are inferred from a seed, etc.

Continuous reasoning refers to the knowledge which beholds conditions resulting from the co-operation of many causes and abiding in three times. For instance, one's birth in the womb is due to a combination of the soul and the five primal essences of earth, water, fire, air and space; the soul alone is related to the next life; acts result from the union of an agent and certain means; acts that are done bear fruits, acts not done bear no fruits: there can be no sprout where there is no seed; good or bad fruits correspond to the good or bad acts that produce them; and one kind of seed cannot produce another kind of fruit.

III. Sambhāṣā OR vāda-vidhi[4]—THE METHOD OF DEBATE.

Utility of Debate (sambhāṣā-praśaṁsā).

If a person carries on debate with another person both being versed in the same science, it increases their knowledge and happiness. Besides, it produces dexterity, bestows eloquence and brightens reputation. If there was any misapprehension in a subject

---

[1] Caraka-saṁhitā, Sūtra-sthāna, 11th adhyāya :—

द्विविधमेव खलु सर्वं सच्चासच्च। तस्य चतुर्विधा परीक्षा। आप्तोपदेशः प्रत्यक्षमनुमानं युक्तिश्चेति।

[2] Caraka-saṁhitā, Vimāna-sthāna, adhyāya 8:—

हेतुर्नामोपलब्धिकारणं तत् प्रत्यक्षमनुमानमैतिह्यमौपम्यम्। हेतुभिर्यदुपलभ्यते तत् तत्त्वम्।

[3] Caraka saṁhitā, Sūtra-sthāna, 11th adhyāya :—

एवं प्रमाणैः चतुर्भिरुपदिष्टैः पुनर्भवे धर्मद्वारेष्ववधीयते

[4] Caraka-saṁhitā, Vimāna-sthāna, adhyāya 8.

already studied it removes that misapprehension, and if there was no misapprehension in the subject it produces zeal for its further study. It also makes debaters familiar with certain matters which were unknown to them. Moreover some precious mystic doctrines, which a preceptor imparted to his favourite pupil, come out in essence from the pupil who, owing to a temporary excitement and ambition for victory, is impelled to expound them in the course of the debate. Hence wise men applaud debate with fellow scholars

Two kinds of Debate (dvividhā sambhāṣā).

A debate with a fellow-scholar may be carried on either (1) peacefully (*sandhāya*) or (2) in a spirit of opposition (*vigṛhya*). The first is called a congenial debate (*anuloma sambhāṣā*), and the second a hostile debate (*vigṛhya sambhāṣā*). The congenial debate takes place when the respondent (or opponent) is possessed of erudition, wisdom, eloquence and readiness of reply, is not wrathful or malicious, is well versed in the art of persuasion, and is patient and sweet-speeched. In debating with such a person one should speak confidently, interrogate confidently and give answer in confidence. One should not be alarmed at suffering defeat from him nor should one rejoice in inflicting defeat on him It is improper to show obstinacy towards him, or to introduce before him matters which are irrelevant. While using persuasion with gentleness, one should keep in view the subject of debate. This kind of debate is called a peaceful or congenial debate.

A congenial debate.

Before entering upon a hostile debate with a person one should examine one's strength through a casual conversation with him and observation in any other way of his merits. Such an examination should settle the opportuneness or otherwise of entering upon the debate. The merits considered as good are erudition, wisdom, memory, ingenuity and eloquence. The demerits considered as bad are irritability, shallowness, shyness and inattentiveness.

A hostile debate.

Three classes of respondents (trividhaḥ paraḥ).

In consideration of the merits and demerits mentioned above the respondent (or opponent) may be of three kinds, viz. superior, inferior, and equal

A Council of Debate (pariṣad).

The assembly (*pariṣad*) in which a debate is to take place may be of two kinds, viz. (1) learned, i.e. an assembly of wise men, and (2) ignorant, i.e. an assembly of fools. Each of these may be subdivided as (*a*) friendly, (*b*) indifferent or impartial, and (*c*) hostile or committed to one side.

The Expedients of Debate (vādopāya).

How to vanquish a person of blazing fame.

It is not advisable to enter upon debate in a hostile assembly, no matter whether the assembly is learned or ignorant. In an ignorant assembly, friendly or indifferent, one may enter upon debate with a person who is of blazing fame, but who neither possesses erudition, wisdom and eloquence, nor is held in esteem by respectable people. In debating with such an opponent one may employ crooked and long-strung word-bolts. Now assuming a delightful countenance and now indulging in ridicule one should engage the assembly in such a way that the opponent does not find an opportunity of speaking. If the opponent utters an unusual word he should be immediately told that such a word is never used or that his original proposition has fallen to the ground. In the case of his attempting to offer challenge he should be stopped with the observation: "Go and study for a full year, sitting at the feet of your preceptor: this much that you have done to-day is enough." If in the meantime the shout of "vanquished, van quished" has even once been uttered, no further debate need be held with the opponent.

Respect for an old man.

Some say that this procedure may be adopted in debate even with a superior opponent, but experts do not approve of its adoption when the opponent happens to be an old man.

How to argue with an opponent of superior, inferior or equal merits.

In a friendly assembly one may enter upon debate with an opponent who is inferior or equal. In an indifferent (or impartial) assembly consisting of members that are endued with attentiveness, erudition, wisdom, memory and eloquence, one should speak with great care marking the merits and demerits of one's opponent. If the opponent appears to be superior, one should, without expressing one's inferiority, never engage in debate with him. If on the other hand the opponent happens to be inferior, one should at once defeat him An opponent, who is weak in the scriptures, should be defeated through citations of long passages from them. An opponent devoid of erudition should be defeated through the employment of unusual words and phrases. An opponent whose memory is not sharp should be defeated with crooked and long-strung word-bolts. An opponent devoid of ingenuity should be defeated through the use of same words bearing different meanings and different words bearing the same meaning. An opponent, who is devoid of eloquence, should be defeated through the jeering imitations of his half-uttered speeches. An opponent whose knowledge is shallow should be defeated by being put to shame on that account. An opponent of irritable temper should be defeated by being thrown into a state of nervous exhaustion. An opponent who is timid should be defeated through the excitement of his fear. An opponent who is inattentive should be defeated by being put under the restraint of a certain rule. Even in a hostile debate one should speak with propriety, an absence of which may provoke the opponent to say or do any thing.

How to influence a Council.

Influencing the assembly one should cause it to name that as the subject of debate with which one is perfectly familiar and which presents an insurmountable difficulty to one's opponent. When the assembly meets, one should observe silence after saying to one's opponent: "it is not now permissible for us to make any suggestions. Here is the assembly which will fix the subject and limits of debate agreeably to its wishes and sense of propriety." [1]

The Limits of Debate (vāda-maryādā).

The limits of debate consist of such directions, as: "This should be said, this should not be said, if this occurs defeat follows, etc." [2]

The Course of Debate (vāda-mārga).

The following are the categories [3] which should be studied for a thorough knowledge of the course of debate:—

(1) *Debate (vāda)*—a discourse between two parties agreeably to the scriptures and in a spirit of opposition on a subject such as "whether there is rebirth, or there is no rebirth." It is of two kinds, viz. (1) wrangling (*jalpa*) which is a debate for the purpose of defence or attack, and (2) cavil (*vitaṇḍā*) which is a perverse debate for the purpose of a mere attack.

(2) *Substance (dravya)*—that in which actions and qualities inhere and which can constitute a material cause, e.g. ether, air, fire, water, earth, soul, mind, and space.

(3) *Quality (guṇa)*—that which inheres in a substance and is inactive, e.g. colour, taste, odour, touch, sound, heavy and

---

[1] This trick, the knowledge of which is useful in guarding oneself against a cunning debater, should never be adopted in a fair debate.—S. C. Vidyabhusana.

[2] Udayanācārya (10th century A.D.) following the old laws of debate observes that an objection may be removed by debate, but on no account should it proceed beyond the limit of practical absurdity.

व्याघातावधिराशङ्का तर्कःशङ्कावधिर्मतः ॥ (Kusumāñjali, 3-7).

[3] The explanation of *substance*, *quality*, *action*, *generality*, *particularity* and *inherence* is given in the Caraka-saṁhitā, Sūtra-sthāna, adhyāya 1; and the explanation of the remaining terms in the Vimāna-sthāna, adhyāya 8. The terms (2-7) were evidently taken from the Vaiśeṣika philosophy and not from Ānvīkṣikī of Medhātithi Gautama.

light, cold and hot, intelligence, pleasure and pain, desire and aversion, dissimilarity, contrariety, union, separation, number, measure, etc.

(4) *Action* (*karma*)—that which is the cause of both union and separation, which inheres in a substance and represents the function which is to be performed, and which is not dependent on any other acton.

(5) *Generality* (*sāmānya*)—that which produces unity.

(6) *Particularity* (*viśeṣa*)—that which produces diversity.

(7) *Inherence* (*samavāya*)—a permanent relation between a substance and its qualities or actions in virtue of which they cannot exist separately.

(8) *Proposition* (*pratijñā*)—the statement of what is to be established e.g. the soul is eternal.

(9) *Demonstration* (*sthāpanā*)—the establishment of a proposition through the process of a reason, example, application and conclusion, e.g.

(i) The soul is eternal (*a proposition*).
(ii) Because it is a non-product (*reason*).
(iii) Just as ether which being a non-product is eternal (*example*).
(iv) The soul similar to ether is a non-product (*application*).
(v) Therefore the soul is eternal (*conclusion*).

(10) *Counter-demonstration* (*pratiṣthāpanā*)—the establishment of the counter-proposition, e.g.

(i) The soul is non-eternal (*a proposition*).
(ii) Because it is cognized by the senses (*reason*)
(iii) Just as a pot which being cognized by the senses is non-eternal (*example*).
(iv) The soul similar to a pot is cognized by the senses (*application*).
(v) Therefore the soul is non-eternal (*conclusion*).

(11) *Reason* (*hetu*)[1]—the source of knowledge such as perception (*pratyakṣa*), inference (*anumāna*), scripture (*aitihya*), and comparison (*aupamya*).

(12) *Application* (*upanaya*)—as shown above.

(13) *Conclusion* (*nigamana*)—as shown above.

(14) *Rejoinder* (*uttara*)—the proposition in a counter-demonstration.

(15) *Example* (*dṛṣṭānta*)—the thing about which an ordinary man and an expert entertain the same opinion, and which describes the subject, e.g. hot as "fire," stable as "earth," etc., or just as the "sun" is an illuminator so is the text of the Sāṁkhya.

---

[1] The word reason (*hetu*), which in the old Brāhmaṇic and Jaina works signified a source of knowledge, is not exactly identical with the reason (*hetu*) which constitutes the second member of a syllogism or demonstration. It seems that the doctrine of syllogism or demonstration was introduced into Hindu Logic at a comparatively late time, and the word *hetu* used in connection with this doctrine was allowed for some time to retain its old signification.

(16) *Tenet* or *conclusion* (*siddhānta*)—a truth which is established on examination by experts and on proof by reasons. It is of four kinds, viz. a truth accepted by all the schools, that accepted by a particular school, that accepted hypothetically, and that accepted by implication.

(17) *Word* (*śabda*)—a combination of letters. It is of four kinds, viz. that which refers to a matter which is seen, that which refers to a matter which is not seen, that which corresponds to what is real, and that which does not correspond to what is real.

(18) *Perception* (*pratyakṣa*)—that knowledge which a person acquires by himself through his mind conjoined with the five senses. Pleasure, pain, desire, aversion, and the like are objects of the mind while sound, etc., are objects of the five senses.

(19) *Inference* (*anumāna*)—a reasoning based on the knowledge of connected facts, e.g. fire is inferred from the power of digestion.

(20) *Comparison* (*aupamya*)—the knowledge of a thing acquired through its similarity to another thing.

(21) *Tradition* (*aitihya*)—consisting of reliable assertions, e.g. the Veda, etc.

(22) *Doubt* (*saṁśaya*)—uncertainty, e.g. is there, or is there not, untimely death ?

(23) *Purpose* (*prayojana*)—that for the accomplishment of which actions are undertaken, e.g. I shall live carefully "to avoid untimely death."

(24) *Uncertain* (*savyabhicāra*)—going astray, e.g. this medicine may be or may not be suited to this disease.

(25) *Inquiry* (*jijñāsā*)—examination.

(26) *Ascertainment* (*vyavasāya*)—determination, e.g. that disease is due to the disturbance of wind in the stomach, and this is its medicine.

(27) *Presumption* (*artha-prāpti*)—the knowledge of a thing implied by the declaration of another thing, e.g. when it is said that a person should not eat during the day, it is implied that he should eat during the night.

(28) *The originating cause* (*sambhava*)—that from which something springs out, e.g. the six ingredients (*dhātus*), constitute the originating cause of the foetus in the womb.

(29) *Censurable* (*anuyojya*)—a speech which is fraught with fault, e.g. a person makes a general statement while a particular one is required : instead of saying 'this disease is curable by medicine,' one should say 'this disease is curable by an emetic medicine or a purgative medicine.'

(30) *Non-censurable* (*ananuyojya*)—the reverse of the censurable.

(31) *Interrogation* (*anuyoga*)—an inquiry about a subject made by a person who studies it, e.g. when a person asserts that the soul is eternal, his fellow-scholar inquires "what is the reason ?" This inquiry is an interrogation.

(32) *Re-interrogation* (*pratyanuyoga*)—an inquiry about another inquiry, e.g. when one says that the soul is eternal because

it is non-produced, the re-interrogation will be "why it is non-produced?"

(33) *Defect of speech* (*vākya-doṣa*)—consisting of inadequacy, redundancy, meaninglessness, incoherence, contradiction, etc.

(*a*) "Inadequacy" or saying too little which occurs when there is an omission of the reason, example, application or conclusion.

(*b*) "Redundancy" or saying too much which consists of (i) "irrelevancy," e.g. a person talks of the polity of Vṛhaspati or Śukra while the subject of discourse is medicine, or (ii) "repetition," e.g. when a person repeats a word or its meaning several times, as *bhaiṣajya*, *sādhana*, *auṣadha*, etc., all of which signify medicine.

(*c*) "Meaninglessness"—consisting of a mere grouping of letters without any sense, e.g. k, kh, g, gh, ṅ, etc.

(*d*) "Incoherence"—a combination of words which do not convey a connected meaning, e.g. whey, wheel, race, thunder, morning, etc.

(*e*) "Contradiction"—consisting of opposition to the example, tenet or occasion, e.g. on the occasion of sacrifices, animals should be offered up. Any thing uttered inconsistently with the occasion is contradiction.

(34) *Excellence of speech* (*vākya-praśaṁsā*)—when a speech is freed from inadequacy, etc., is fraught with well-expressive words and is otherwise uncensurable, it is applauded as excellent, perfect or meritorious.

(35) *Quibble* (*chala*)—a speech consisting of mere words fraught with cunning, plausibility and diversion of sense. It is of two kinds, viz. (1) 'quibble in respect of a word,' e.g. a person uses the word 'navatantra' to signify a man who has studied nine scriptures, though he really intends to signify a man who has studied his scripture recently, or (2) 'quibble in respect of a generality,' e.g. the medicine which cures phthisis should also cure bronchitis, as both come under the genus 'disease.'

(36) *Non-reason or fallacy* (*ahetu*)—which is of three kinds, viz.:

(*a*) "Begging the question" ("prakaraṇa-sama") occurring when that which is to be proved is taken as the reason, e.g. the soul is eternal because it is distinct from the body: the body is non-eternal, and the soul being heterogeneous from the body must be eternal.

(*b*) "Assumption based on doubt" ("saṁśaya-sama") occurring when that which is a cause of doubt is regarded as dispelling the doubt, e.g. it is doubtful whether a person who has studied a portion of the science of medicine is a physician; this person has studied a portion of the science of medicine: hence he is a physician. This is another form of "begging the question."

(*c*) "Balancing the subject" ("varṇya-sama") occurring where the example is not different from the subject in respect of their questionable character, e.g. the intellect is non-eternal, because it is intangible, as a sound. Here the eternality of the intellect is as questionable as that of the sound.

(37) *Mistimed* (*atīta-kāla*)—a fallacy which arises when that which should be stated first is stated afterwards.

(38) *Attribution of censure* (*upālambha*)—imputation of defect to the reason adduced.

(39) *Avoidance of defect* (*parihāra*) which occurs when the defect is corrected or amended, e.g. when the soul resides in the body, the signs of life are noticeable; but when the soul leaves the body those signs are no longer noticed: hence the soul is distinct from the body.

(40) *Abandonment of a proposition* (*pratijñā-hāni*)—which occurs when a disputant, being attacked, abandons the proposition first advanced by him, e.g.

A person advances first a proposition, viz.
the soul is eternal;
and being attacked by an opponent, he abandons it saying,
the soul is not eternal.

(41) *Admission* (*abhyanujñā*)—the acceptance by a person of what is attributed to him by his opponent, whether agreeable or disagreeable, e.g.

A disputant says: "you are a thief."
His opponent replies: "you too are a thief."
The reply of the opponent is an admission.

(42) *Shifting the reason* (*hetvantara*)—which occurs when one instead of advancing the proper reason adduces a different one.

(43) *Shifting the topic* (*arthāntara*), e.g. A person cites the symptoms of gonorrhoea while he was to have cited those of fever.

(44) *A point of defeat* or *an occasion for rebuke* (*nigrahasthāna*)—which occurs when a disputant suffers defeat at the hands of his opponent. It consists in the disputant misapprehending, or being unable to apprehend, something repeated thrice in an assembly the members whereof have apprehended it. It may also occur when one censures that which is not censurable or abstains from censuring that which is censurable.

CHAPTER IV.

Reception accorded to Ānvīkṣikī.

(From 650 B.C. onwards).

20. Ānvīkṣikī condemned in certain Circles.

Ānvīkṣikī known as *Hetu-śāstra* or *Tarka-vidyā*, the general principles of which might be applied to test the validity or otherwise of the injunctions and prohibitions laid down in the Vedas and Dharma-sūtras, was not received with favour by a certain section of the Brāhmaṇas, who could never think of calling in question the authority of those injunctions and prohibitions. We are therefore not surprised to find Manu [1] enjoining excommunication upon those members of the twice-born castes who disregarded the Vedas and Dharma-sūtras relying upon the support of *Hetu-śāstra* or Logic. Similarly Vālmīki [2] in his Rāmāyaṇa discredits those persons of perverse intellect who indulge in the frivolities of *Ānvīkṣikī*, the science of Logic, regardless of the works on Sacred Law (Dharma-śāstra) which they should follow as their guide. Vyāsa [3] in the Mahābhārata, Śāntiparva, relates the dole-

Ānvīkṣikī opposed to the Vedas.

---

1 योऽवमन्येत ते मूले हेतुशास्त्राश्रयाद् द्विजः ।
स साधुभिर्बहिष्कार्य्यो नास्तिको वेदनिन्दकः ॥

(Manu-saṁhitā, adhyāya 2, verse 11).

2 धर्मशास्त्रेषु मुख्येषु विद्यमानेषु दुर्बुधाः ।
बुद्धिमान्वीक्षिकीं प्राप्य निरर्थं प्रवदन्ति ते ॥ 36–39 ॥

(Rāmāyaṇa, Ayodhyā kāṇḍa, sarga 100).

3 अहमासं पण्डितको हैतुको वेदनिन्दकः ।
आन्वीक्षिकीं तर्कविद्यामनुरक्तो निरर्थिकाम् ॥ 47 ॥
हेतुवादान् प्रवदिता वक्ता संसत्सु हेतुमत् ।
आक्रोष्टा चाभिवक्ता च ब्रह्मवाक्येषु च द्विजान् ॥ 48 ॥
नास्तिकः सर्व्वशङ्की च मूर्खः पण्डितमानिकः ।
तस्येयं फलनिर्वृत्तिः शृगालत्वं मम द्विज ॥ 49 ॥

(Mahābhārata, Śāntiparva, adhyāya 180).

In the Gandharva tantra we find :—

गौतम प्रोक्तशास्त्रार्थनिरताः सर्व्व एव हि ।
शार्गालीं योनिमापन्नाः सन्दिग्धाः सर्व्वकर्म्मसु ॥

(Quoted in Prāṇatoṣiṇī tantra).

ful story of a repentant Brāhmaṇa who, addicted to *Tarka-vidyā* (Logic), carried on debates divorced from all faith in the Vedas and was on that account turned into a jackal in his next birth as a penalty. In another passage of the Śāntiparva, Vyāsa[1] warns the followers of the Vedānta philosophy against communicating their doctrines to a *Tārkika* or Logician. Vyāsa[2] does not care even to review *Hetu-śāstra* in the Brahma-sūtra seeing that it has not been recognized by any worthy sage. Stories of infliction of penalties on those given to the study of *Tarka-vidya* are related in the Skandapurāna[3] and other works; and in the Naiṣadhacarita[4] we find Kali satirising the founder of *Ānvīkṣikī* as "Go-tama" the most bovine among sages.

21. Ānvīkṣikī held in high Esteem in some Quarters.

On the other hand Ānvīṣikī, while it attached due weight to the authority of the Vedas, was held in very high esteem. There were also people who could appreciate the value of reasoning for ascertaining truths. Thus the Gautama-dharma-sūtra[5] prescribes a course of training in *Ānvīkṣikī* (Logic) for the king, and acknowledges the utility of *Tarka* (reasoning) in the administra-

---

1 आत्मकामानिदं शास्त्रं वाच्यं पुत्रानुशासनम् ।

* * * * * * * *

न तर्कशास्त्रदग्धाय तथैव पिशुनाय च ॥ १८ ॥

(Mahābhārata Śāntiparva, adhyāya 246).

2 अपरिग्रहाच्चात्यन्तमनपेक्षा ॥ 17 ॥ (Vedānta-sūtra, 2-2).

3 गोतमः स्वेन तर्केण खण्डयन् तत्र तत्र हि ।

अतोऽथ मुनिभिस्तत्र शार्गाली योनिमाप्स्यति ।

पुनश्चानुगृहीतोऽसौ मुनिभिर्ध्वस्तकल्मषः ।

सर्वलोकोपकाराय तव शास्त्रं भविष्यति ॥

(Skandapurāṇa, Kālikākhaṇḍa, adhyāya 17).

4 मुक्तये यः शिलात्वाय शास्त्रमूचे महामुनिः ।

गोतमं तमवेतैव यथा वित्थ तथैव सः ॥ 75 ॥

(Naiṣadhacarita, canto xvii).

5 राजा सर्वस्येष्टे ब्राह्मणवर्जं, साधुकारी स्यात् साधुवादी, त्रय्याम् आन्वीक्षिक्यां चाभिविनीतः ।......न्यायाधिगमे तर्कोऽभ्युपायः । तेनाभ्यूह्य यथास्थानं गमयेत् । विप्रतिपत्तौ त्रैविद्यवृद्धेभ्यः प्रत्यवहृत्य निष्ठां गमयेत् ॥

(Gautama dharma-sūtra, adhyāya 11).

Ānvīkṣikī useful for ascertaining truths.

tion of justice, though in the case of conclusions proving incompatible, the ultimate decision is directed to be made by reference to persons versed in the Vedas. Manu[1] admits that *dharma* or duty should be ascertained by logical reasoning (*tarka*), but the reasoning should not, according to him, be opposed to the injunctions of the Vedas. He recommends Ānvīkṣikī (Logic) as a necessary study for a king[2] and a *Tarkī*[3] (logician) as an indispensable member of a legal assembly. Kauṭilya[4] in his Arthaśāstra characterises *Ānvīkṣikī* (Logic) as the lamp of all sciences, the resource of all actions and the permanent shelter of all virtues.

Yājñavalkya[5] counts *Nyāya* or Logic among the fourteen principal sciences while Vyāsa[6] admits that he was able to arrange and classify the Upaniṣads with the help of *Ānvīkṣikī* or Logic. In the Padmapurāṇa[7] *Nyāya* (Logic) is included among the fourteen principal branches of learning promulgated by God Viṣṇu, while in the Matsyapurāṇa,[8] Nyāya vidyā (the science of Logic) together

---

1 आर्षं धर्म्मोपदेशं च वेदशास्त्राविरोधिना ।
यस्तर्केणानुसन्धत्ते स धर्म्मं वेद नेतरः ॥
(Manu-saṁhitā, adhyāya 12, verse 106).

2 त्रैविद्येभ्यस्त्रयीं विद्याद् दण्डनीतिञ्च शाश्वतीम् ।
आन्वीक्षिकीञ्चात्मविद्यां वार्त्तारम्भांश्च लोकतः ॥
(Manu-saṁhitā, adhyāya 7, verse 43).

3 त्रैविद्यो हैतुकस्तर्की नैरुक्तो धर्म्मपाठकः ।
त्रयश्चाश्रमिणः पूर्व्वे परिषत् स्याद् दशावरा ॥
(Manu-saṁhita, adhyāya 12, verse 111).

4 प्रदीपः सर्व्वविद्यानामुपायः सर्व्वकर्म्मणाम् ।
आश्रयः सर्व्वधर्म्माणां शश्वदान्वीक्षिकी मता ॥
(Artha-śāstra of Kauṭilya, chap. II).

5 पुराणन्यायमीमांसा धर्म्मशास्त्राङ्गमिश्रिताः ।
वेदाः स्थानानि विद्यानां धर्म्मस्य च चतुर्दश ॥
(Yājñavalkya-saṁhitā, adhyāya 1, verse 3).

6 यथोपनिषदं तात परिशेषं तु पार्थिव ।
मथ्नामि मनसा तात दृष्ट्वा चान्वीक्षिकीं पराम् ॥
(Mahābhārata quoted by Viśvanātha in his Nyāya-vṛtti, 1-1-1).

7 अङ्गानि चतुरो वेदान् पुराणन्यायविस्तरान् ।
मीमांसां धर्म्मशास्त्रञ्च परिगृह्याथ साम्प्रतम् ॥
मत्स्यरूपेण च पुनः कल्पादावुदकार्णवे ।
(Padmapurāṇa. *vide* Muir's Sanskrit texts, Vol. III, p. 27).

8 अनन्तरञ्च वक्त्रेभ्यो वेदास्तस्य विनिःसृताः ।
मीमांसा न्यायविद्या च प्रमाणाष्टकसंयुता ॥ (Matsyapurāṇa, 3–2).

with the Vedas is said to have emanated from the mouth of Brahma himself. In fact so widespread was the study of *Nyāya* that the Mahābhārata is full of references to that science. In the Ādiparva[1] of the Mahābhārata, the *Nyāya* (Logic) is mentioned along with the Veda and Cikitsā (the science of medicine), and the hermitage of Kāśyapa[2] is described as being filled with sages who were versed in the *Nyāya-tattva* (categories of Logic), and who knew the true meaning of a demonstration, objection and conclusion. The Śāntiparva[3] refers to numerous tenets of *Nyāya* supported by reasoning and scripture, while in the Aśvamedhaparva[4] we find that the sacrificial ground of Yudhiṣṭhira was crowded by logicians (*Hetu-vādin*) who employed arguments and counter-arguments to vanquish one another. Similar other instances of the popularity of *Nyāya* (Logic) may be cited from the Mahābhārata and other works which were composed in their present forms about the beginning of the Christian era.

It seems that the unfavourable criticism to which Ānvīkṣikī (the science of Logic) had long been exposed, terminated practically in the first century A.D. when, under the name of *Nyāya-śāstra*, it accepted the authority of the Vedas and propounded the doctrine of syllogistic reasoning the validity of which was never challenged.

---

1 न्यायशिक्षा चिकित्सा च दानं पाशुपतं तथा ।
हेतुनैव समं जन्म दिव्यमानुषसंज्ञितम् ॥ 67 ॥
(Mahābhārata, Ādiparva, adhyāya 1).

2 न्यायतत्त्वात्मविज्ञानसम्पन्नैर्वेदपारगैः ॥ 42 ॥
स्थापनाक्षेपसिद्धान्तपरमार्थज्ञतां गतैः । 44 ॥
(Mahābhārata, Ādiparva, adhyāya 70).

3 न्यायतन्त्राण्यनेकानि तैस्तैरुक्तानि वादिभिः ।
हेत्वागमसदाचारैर्यदुक्तं तदुपास्यताम् ॥ 22 ॥
(Mahābhārata, Śāntiparva, adhyāya 21).

4 तस्मिन यज्ञे प्रवृत्ते तु वाग्मिनो हेतुवादिनः ।
हेतुवादान बहूनाहुः परस्पर-जिगीषवः ॥ 27 ॥
(Mahābhārata, Aśvamedhaparva, adhyāya 85).

SECTION II.

Nyāya-śāstra—the Science of True Reasoning.

(CIRCA 1 A.D.—1200 A.D.)

CHAPTER I.

The Growth of Nyāya-śāstra.

22. ORIGIN OF THE NAME NYĀYA.

The Ānvīkṣikī-vidyā designated as Nyāya-śāstra.

It has been previously observed that *Nyāya*[1] was one of the various names by which the *Ānvīkṣikī* was designated in its logical aspect. With the introduction of this word, the ancient school of Indian Logic entered upon the second stage of its development In the first stage Logic was generally designated as *Ānvīkṣikī*, *Hetu-śāstra* or *Tarka-vidyā*, but in the second stage it was, as we find in the Nyāya-bhāṣya, widely known as *Nyāya-śāstra*.

The popular meaning of *Nyāya*.

The word *nyāya* popularly signfies 'right' or 'justice.' The *Nyāya-śāstra* is therefore the science of right judgment or true reasoning. The Chinese *Caṅ-li*[2] and the Tibetan *Rigs-bstan-bcos*,[3] as equivalents of the Sanskrit *Nyāya-śāstra*, express exactly the same meaning.

The technical meaning of *Nyāya*.

Technically the word *nyāya* signifies a syllogism (or a speech of five parts), and the Ānvīkṣikī was called *Nyāya-śāstra*, when *nyāya* constituted its special topic. That the word *nyāya* actually signified a syllogism is evident from an observation quoted by Vātsyāyana[4] that "*nyāya* functions neither with regard to things

---

[1] Vātsyāyana observes :—

सेयमान्वीक्षिकी प्रमाणादिभिः पदार्थैर्विभज्यमाना...... (Nyāya bhāṣya, 1-1-1),

[2] Yuan Chwang (Hwen-thsang) translates *Nyāya* (*Caṇ-li*) by true reason (or reasoning)—*vide* Professor H. Ui's Vaiśeṣika Philosophy, p. 84.

[3] The *Nyāya-śāstra* is called in Tibetan རིགས་པའི་བསྟན་བཅོས Rigs-paḥi-bstan-bcos, the science of right judgment—*vide* Mahāvyutpatti, part ii, p. 133, edited by Dr. E. D. Ross and Dr. Satis Chandra Vidyabhusana in the Bibliotheca Indica series, Calcutta.

[4] तत्र नानुपलब्धे न निर्णीतेऽर्थे न्यायः प्रवर्तते किन्तर्हि संशयितेऽर्थे

(Nyāyabhāṣya 1-1-1 ; also Dr. Gaṅgā Nath Jhā's Translation of the Nyāya-sūtra in the Indian Thought, vol. IV, p. 174).

unknown nor with regard to things that are definitely known, but it functions only with regard to things that are doubtful." Vātsyāyana defines,[1] no doubt, *nyāya* as an examination of objects by evidences, but he takes evidences to signify a syllogism which consists of a 'proposition' based on verbal testimony, a 'reason' based on inference, an 'example' based on perception, an 'application' based on comparison, and a 'conclusion' based on all the previous four. Viśvanātha[2] explains *nyāya svarūpa* as the essential form of a syllogism which consists of its five parts, and Mādhavācārya[3] understands by the term *nyāya* an inference for the sake of others in which a syllogism is specially employed. In view of this technical meaning we may interpret *Nyāya-śāstra* as the science of syllogism or the science of inference for the sake of others, that is, the science of demonstration.

23. The Antiquity of Nyāya-Śāstra (from circa 1 A.D.).

Nyāya did not formerly signify Logic.

The term "Nyāya" in the sense of Logic does not appear to have been used in literature before the first century A.D. Pāṇini[4] (about 350 B.C.) did not know the word "Nyāya" in the sense of Logic, and even Patañjali[5] (about 150 B.C) does not seem to have been conversant with the word, which does not occur in his Bhāṣya on *ukthādi-gaṇa*. It does not find place, in this sense,[6] in the Artha-

---

1 प्रमाणैरर्थपरीक्षणं न्यायः (Nyāya-bhāṣya, 1-1-1).

2 *Vide* Viśvanātha's Nyāya sūtra-vṛtti, 1-1-25, 1-1-31, 1-138 and 1-1-40 in which *nyāya-svarūpa*, *nyāya-pūrvāṅga*, *nyāyottarāṅga* and *nyāyāśraya* are defined. The five parts of *nyāya* (syllogism) will be explained later.

3 Mādhavācārya's Sarvadarśana-saṁgraha, under the head Akṣapāda-darśana, p. 114, Calcutta edition.

4 Goldstucker in his Panini, p. 157, says that both Kātyāyana and Patañjali knew the Nyāya-sūtra. There is however no proof for the statement.

There is no doubt that Pāṇini derives the word *nyāya* (evidently in the sense of justice) from the root *nī* in his Aṣṭādhyāyī, 3-3-122 as follows :—अध्यायन्यायोद्याव संहाराश्च His Aṣṭādhyāyī, 4-2-60 क्रतुक्थादि सूत्रान्तात् ठक् does not, however, presuppose *nyāya* in the sense of "Logic."

5 Patañjali did not use the word *naiyāyika* (logician) as *nyāya* was not included in the *ukthādigaṇa* in his Bhāṣya. The Gaṇapāṭha, which includes it, is a later work. For *nyāyya vide* Aṣṭādhyāyī, 4-4-92.

6 *Nyāya* signifies just or justice, equitable or equity :

शास्त्रं विप्रतिपद्येत धर्मन्यायेन केनचित् ।
न्यायस्तत्र प्रमाणं स्यात् तत्र पाठो हि नश्यति ॥

(Artha śāstra, adhikaraṇa 3, chap. 1, p. 150)

śāstra [1] of Kauṭilya (about 327 B.C.). The term "Nyāya," which previously signified "right," "method," "analogy" or "maxim," is used in the sense of Logic for the first time in the Mahābhārata,[2] Viṣṇu purāṇa,[3] Matsya purāṇa,[4] Padma purāṇa,[5] Yājña-valkya-saṁhitā,[6] etc., in passages which are presumed to have been written after the beginning of the Christian era.

Nyāya used in the sense of Logic from about the 1st century A.D.

The Nyāya-śāstra was not so called before the subject of "Nyāya" (syllogism) was introduced into it. As the Caraka-saṁhitā,[7] so far as we know, contains for the first time an exposition of the doctrine of syllogism under the name of *sthāpanā* (demonstration), it is presumed that the word *Nyāya* as an equivalent for Logic came into use about the composition of that Saṁhitā, that is, about the opening of the Christian era The word became very popular about the second century A.D. when the Nyāya-sūtra was composed. Vātsyāyana (about 400 A.D.) uses the expression "*parama-nyāya*"[8] for the conclusion (*nigamana*) which combines in itself all the five parts of a syllogism. Dignāga (about 500 A.D.) explicitly mentions the five parts or members of a syllogism as *Nyāyāvayava.*[9]

24. The Early Teachers of Nyāya-śāstra (about 100 A.D.).

Nothing is definitely known about the early teachers of Nyāya-śāstra. In the Ādiparva of the Mahābhārata [10] we find that the hermitage of Kāśyapa was filled with sages who knew the true

---

1 संघमुख्यश्च संघेषु न्यायवृत्तिर्हितः प्रियः ।
दान्तो युक्तजनस्तिष्ठेत् सर्वचित्तानुवर्तकः ॥

(Artha-śāstra of Kauṭilya, adhikaraṇa 11, adhyāya 1, p. 379, Sham Śāstri's edition).

2 Mahābhārata, Ādiparva, adhyāya 1, verse 67: adhyāya 70, verses 42–44 and Śāntiparva, adhyāya 210, verse 22.

3 Viṣṇu purāṇa, third part, adhyāya 6.

4 Matsya purāṇa, 3–2.

5 Padma purāṇa, Uttarakhaṇḍa, chap. 263.

6 Yājñavalkya-saṁhitā, 1–3, etc.

7 Caraka-saṁhitā, Vimāna-sthāna, adhyāya 8.

8 सर्वेषामेकार्थसमवाये सामर्थ्यप्रदर्शनं निगमनमिति सोऽयं परमो न्यायः ।

(Nyāya bhāṣya, 1-1-1).

9 Nyāyāvayava called in Tibetan 'rigs-paḥi-yan-lag' occurs in the Pramāṇa-samuccaya, chap VI, as follows:—རིགས་པའི་ཡན་ལག་ལ་སོགས་པ་བཞིན །

(Tshad-ma-kun las-btus-pa, chap. vi. Bstan-ḥgyur, Mdo, Ce).

10 न्यायतत्त्वात्मविज्ञानसम्पन्नैर्वेदपारगैः ॥ 42 ॥
नानावाक्यसमाहार समवाय विशारदैः ।

meanings of demonstration, refutation and conclusion. As *sthāpanā*, *ākṣepa* and *siddhānta*, which are the Sanskrit equivalents for demonstration, refutation and conclusion, are the technical terms of Nyāya-śāstra as used in the Caraka-saṁhitā, it may be reasonably inferred that the sages who dealt with them in the hermitage of Kāśyapa were the early exponents of that śāstra. Kāśyapa [1] lived on the river Mālinī in the district of Saharanpur midway between Delhi and Hardwar.

25. Nārada—an Expert in Nyāya-śāstra (about 100 A.D.).

In the Sabhāparva of the Mahābhārata we find that a sage named Nārada [2] was an expert in Nyāya-śāstra.[3] He was skilful in distinguishing unity and plurality, conjunction and co-existence (inherence), genus and species, etc., capable of deciding questions through evidences (*pramāṇa*), and clever in ascertaining the validity and invalidity of a speech of five parts (*pañcāvayava-vākya*). The "speech of five parts" refers undoubtedly to a syllogism of five members, and it is interesting to note that Nārada,

Nārada's skill in syllogistic reasoning.

विशेषकार्यविद्भिश्च मोक्षधर्मपरायणैः ॥ 43 ॥
स्थापनाक्षेपसिद्धान्तपरमार्थज्ञतां गतैः ।
शब्दच्छन्दोनिरुक्तज्ञैः कालज्ञानविशारदैः ॥ 44 ॥
द्रव्यकर्मगुणज्ञैश्च कार्यकारणवेदिभिः ।

(Mahābhārata, Ādiparva, adhyāya 70).

1 मालिनीमभितो राजन् नदीं पुण्यां सुखोदकाम् ॥ २१ ॥
तस्यास्तीरे भगवतः काश्यपस्य महात्मनः ।
आश्रमप्रवरं रम्यं महर्षिगणसेवितम् ॥ २२ ॥

(Mahābhārata, Ādiparva, chap. 70).

2 Nārada is called in Tibetan མིས་སྦྱིན་གྱི་བུ་ Mis-sbyin-gyi-bu (*vide* Mahāvyutpatti, part I, p. 23, edited by Dr. E. D. Ross and Dr. Satis Chandra Vidyabhusana, in the Bibliotheca Indica series, Calcutta).

3 वेदोपनिषदां वेत्ता ऋषिः सुरगणार्चितः ।
इतिहासपुराणज्ञः पुराकल्पविशेषवित् ॥ 2 ॥
न्यायविद्धर्मतत्त्वज्ञः षडङ्गविदनुत्तमः ।
ऐक्यसंयोगनानात्वसमवायविशारदः ॥ 3 ॥
वक्ता प्रगल्भो मेधावी स्मृतिमान्नयवित् कविः ।
परापरविभागज्ञः प्रमाणकृतनिश्चयः ॥ 4 ॥
पञ्चावयवयुक्तस्य वाक्यस्य गुणदोषवित् ।
उत्तरोत्तरवक्ता च वदतोऽपि बृहस्पतेः ।
धर्मार्थकाममोक्षेषु यथावत् कृतनिश्चयः ॥

(Mahābhārata, Sabhāparva, adhyāya 5).

who, as we shall presently see, travelled in Śvetadvīpa (perhaps Alexandria), was one of the earliest experts in judging the merit and demerit of such a speech.

Nārada was perhaps a fictitious person of the 1st century A.D.

This Nārada represents the philosophical culture of the 1st century A.D. No work on Nyāya-śāstra written by him has come down to us. But Jayanta[1] in the Nyāya-mañjarī quotes a verse attributed to him which gives an exposition of a logical "point of defeat" (*nigraha-sthāna*) technically known as "the abandonment of a proposition (*pratijñā-hāni*)

Legends regarding Nārada.

The personality of Nārada is shrouded in mystery. He[2] is represented in the Mahābhārata and Purāṇas to have been himself very quarrelsome and clever in exciting quarrels among other people. Cursed by Brahmā he wandered over earth without staying at any fixed habitation. He was of an imposing figure with flowing braids of hair and a long grey beard—wearing a mendicant's garment, holding in one hand a staff of gold and in the other a beggar's bowl together with a lute of tortoise shell, and chanting always the name of Hari the Lord. He carried messages of gods to men and *vice versa*. Once he left heaven for a pleasant ramble on earth and repaired to the court of Sṛñjaya who ordered his daughter Sukumārī of unrivalled beauty to attend upon him. Nārada fell in love with her, and they were married; but owing to a curse he looked like a monkey to his bride He however worked off the curse by severe austerities, and Sukumārī could with difficulty be reconciled to him when he appeared, on the removal of the curse, in his resplendent beauty Nārada studied music for two years under two wives of Kṛṣṇa, Jāmbavatī and Satyabhāmā, but had to prolong his studies for another two years under the third wife of Kṛṣṇa named Rukminī to attain mastery over the notes of the musical scale.

He visited Śvetadvīpa[3] supposed to be identical with the

---

[1] यदाह नारदः—

सारवद् व्यवहाराणां प्रतिज्ञा समुदाहृता।
तद्धानौ हीयते वादी तरं स्तामुत्तरो भवेत्॥

(Nyāya-mañjarī, chap. XII, p. 640, Vizianagaram Sanskrit series).

[2] For legends about Nārada consult the Mahābhārata, Bhāgavata purāṇa, Brahmāṇḍa purāṇa, Viṣṇu purāṇa, Varāha purāṇa, Bhaviṣya purāṇa, Adbhuta Rāmāyaṇa, etc.

तस्माल्लोकेषु ते मूढ न भवेद् भ्रमतः पदम्। (Viṣṇu purāṇa, 1-15, ṭīkā).

[3] क्षीरोदधेरुत्तरतो हि द्वीपः। श्वेतः स नाम्ना प्रथितो विशालः।

(Mahābhārata, Śāntiparva, 335-8).

Śvetadvīpa may also be identified with Syria. *Cf.* "Comparative studies in Vaiṣṇavism and Christianity," by Dr. B. N. Seal, Calcutta.

country of which the capital was Alexandria where he became the guest of a merchant in a town called Dvaidal-nāyaka, and where he saw Viṣṇu (God) worshipped with fervour by devotees who attained their suitable end through His grace

In the Varāha purāṇa[1] Nārada is stated to have in a previous birth been a Brāhmaṇa, Sārasvata by name, in the city of Avantī, who offered oblations of water to his dead ancestors in the lake of Puṣkara at Ajmere.

Nārada's work on Smṛti.

There is extant a work on Smṛti[2] dated about the 4th century A.D., which is said to have been written by the sage Nārada. Other works such as the Nārada-pañca-rātra are also attributed to him.

The real Nārada.

The fiction about Nārada seems to have originated from one Nārada whose existence is unquestioned. This real Nārada is mentioned in the Sarvānukramikā of Kātyāyana as a descendant of Kaṇva[3] and a seer of certain mantras of the Ṛgveda. It appears from the Chāndogyopaniṣad[4] that he was versed in many sciences including *vāko-vākya*[5] (perhaps Logic). He was either the founder of a distinguished line, the succeeding members of which took up his renowned name, or the founder of a school of thought, the various followers of which were known to the world after him.

Was there a logician name Nārada?

Our Nārada, an expert in Nyāya-śāstra, was a descendant or follower of the real Nārada or was an altogether fictitious person requisitioned by the compilers of the Mahābhārata and Purāṇas who fathered upon him the sayings and doings of different ages and countries to make them authoritative.

---

1 Varāha purāṇa, adhyāya 2, verses 63-83, and adhyāya 3, verses 3-7, in the Bibliotheca Indica series).

2 The Nārada-smṛti seems to have been composed about the fourth century A.D. as it frequently mentions *dīnāra* (the Roman coin denarius) which was imported into India about the time of the Roman emperors. Compare नद्वादशसुवर्णस्तु दीनाराख्यः स एव च ॥

(Nārada-smṛti pariśiṣṭa 60, edited by Dr. J Jolly, Bibliotheca Indica series, Calcutta).

Vide also Dr. J. Jolly's Introduction to the Nārada-smṛti (Minor Law books), in the S.B.E. series, p. xviii.

Nārada-smṛti, the real author of which is unknown, represents the theories of Smṛti and Nyāya of the early centuries of Christ.

3 Sāyaṇa's commentary on the Ṛgveda, 8-3-13 and 9-104-6. Kaṇva was an ancestor of Kāśyapa already mentioned.

4 Chāndogyopaniṣad, prapāṭhaka 7, khaṇḍa 1, verse 2, and "The Upanishads" translated by F. Max Müller, S.B.E. series, p. 110.

5 *Vāko-vākya* may signify grammar, rhetoric or debate. Śaṅkara interprets it as Logic.

26. NYĀYA-SŪTRA—THE FIRST SYSTEMATIC WORK ON NYĀYA-ŚĀSTRA.

The Nyāya-sūtra reviews doctrines of various periods.

The first regular work on the Nyāya-śāstra is the Nyāya-sūtra or "aphorisms on true reasoning." It is divided into five books, each containing two chapters called *āhnikas* (diurnal portions). Perhaps the Nyāya-sūtra, as it exists at present, is not entirely the work of one person, but has been enlarged by interpolations from time to time. It contains references to the Sāṁkhya, Vaiśeṣika, Yoga, Mīmāṁsā, Vedānta and Buddhist systems of philosophy. There are in it passages which were quoted almost *verbatim* from the Laṅkāvatāra sūtra,[1] Mādhyamika sūtra,[2] and other Buddhist works which were composed about the third or fourth century A.D. It seems that these passages were interpolated by Vātsyāyana who is said to have written the first commentary called *Bhāṣya* on the Nyāya sūtra about 400 A.D. The Nyāya-sūtra contains in itself the principles both of Logic and Philosophy.

---

[1] बुद्ध्या विवेचनात्तु भावानां याथात्म्यानुपलब्धिः (Nyāya-sūtra, 4-2-26).
"There is no essence in things inasmuch as they are discerned by our intellect."

बुद्ध्या विविच्यमानानां स्वभावो नावधार्यते । (Laṅkāvatāra-sūtra, chap. II, x).
"We cannot ascertain the essence of things which are discerned by our intellect."

स्फटिकेऽप्यपरापरोत्पत्तेः क्षणिकत्वाद् व्यक्तीनामहेतुः (Nyāya-sūtra, 3-2-11).
"Even in the case of a crystal there is no cause for the production of one after another, because all individuals are momentary."

अनुत्पत्तिश्च धर्म्माणां क्षणिकार्थं वदाम्यहम् ॥ (Laṅkāvatāra-sūtra, chap. VI).
"By saying that a thing is momentary, I mean that it is not produced."

[2] न स्वभावसिद्धिरापेक्षिकत्वात् (Nyāya sūtra, 4-1-39).
"Things cannot be self-existent owing to their inter-relations."

नहि स्वभावो भावानां प्रत्ययादिषु विद्यते (Mādhyamika-sūtra, chap. I).
"There is no self-existence of things owing to their mutual relationship."

न सन् नासन् न सदसत् सतो वैधर्म्यात् (Nyāya-sūtra, 4-1-48).
"A thing is neither existent nor non-existent nor both, owing to the mutual incongruity of existence and non-existence."

न सन् नासन् न सदसन् धर्म्मो निर्वर्त्तते यदा (Mādhyamika sūtra, chap. VII).
"There cannot be production of a thing which is existent, non-existent or both."

मायागन्धर्वनगरमृगतृष्णिकावद् वा (Nyāya-sūtra, 4-2-32).
"The concept of things is like a trick of jugglery, the city of the celestial quire or a mirage."

27. Akṣapāda—the author of the Nyāya-sūtra (about 150 A.D.).

In the early commentaries on the Nyāya-sūtra the author of the Sūtra is distinctly named as Akṣapāda.[1] Vātsyāyana[2] in the Nyāya-bhāṣya (about 400 A.D.) says that the Nyāya philosophy manifested itself (in a regular form) before Akṣapāda the foremost of the eloquent; while Uddyotakara[3] in his Nyāya-vārtika (about 600 A.D.) affirms that it was Akṣapāda the most excellent of sages that spoke out the Nyāya-śāstra in a systematic way. In the Nyāya vārtika tātparya-ṭīkā[4] (81 A.D.) and the Nyāya-mañjarī,[5] Akṣapāda is stated to have been the promul-

Akṣapāda credited as the author of the Nyāya-sūtra.

यथा माया यथा स्वप्नो गन्धर्वनगरं यथा ।
तथोत्पादस्तथा स्थानम् तथा भङ्ग उदाहृतम् ॥

(Mādhyamika-sūtra, chap. VII).

"The origination, continuance and cessation of a thing are said to be like a trick of jugglery, a dream or the city of the celestial quire."

वर्त्तमानाभावः पततः पतित-पतितव्य कालोपपत्तेः (Nyāya-sūtra, 2-1-39).

"The present time is non-existent because the falling down of an object relates to the time during which the object fell down and to the time during which it will fall down."

गतं न गम्यते तावत् अगतं नैव गम्यते ।
गतागत विनिर्मुक्तं गम्यमानं न गम्यते ॥

(Mādhyamika-sūtra, chap. II).

"We are not passing a path which has already been passed, nor are we passing that which is yet to be passed; the existence of a path, which has neither been passed nor is yet to be passed, is beyond comprehension."

1 Akṣapāda is called in Tibetan རྐང་མིག་ཅན་ Rkaṅ-mig-can, "with eyes on his feet." (*Vide* Mahā-vyutpatti, part I, p. 22, edited in Sanskrit-Tibetan-English by Dr. Sir E. D. Ross and Dr. Satis Chandra Vidyabhusana, Bibliotheca Indica series. Calcutta.)

2 योऽक्षपादमृषिं न्यायः प्रत्यभाद्वदतां वरम् ।
तस्य वात्स्यायन इदं भाष्यजातमवर्त्तयत् ॥

(Nyāya-bhāṣya, colophon, Vizianagaram Sanskrit series).

3 यदक्षपादः प्रवरो मुनीनां शमाय शास्त्रं जगतो जगाद ।
कुतार्किकाज्ञाननिवृत्तिहेतोः करिष्यते तस्य मया निबन्धः ॥

(Nyāya-vārtika, opening lines).

4 अथ भगवता अक्षपादेन निःश्रेयसहेतौ शास्त्रे प्रणीते...

(Nyāya-vārtika-tātparya-ṭīkā, opening lines).

5 अक्षपादप्रणीतो हि विततो न्यायपादपः ।
सान्द्रामृतरसस्यन्दफलसन्दर्भनिर्भरः ॥

(Nyāya-mañjarī, chap. I).

gator of the Nyāya-śāstra, while Mādhavācārya in his Sarvadarśana-saṁgraha (about 1350 A D) designates the Nyāya philosophy as *Akṣapāda-darśana*, the philosophy of Akṣapāda.

Gautama too believed to be the author of the Nyāya-sūtra.

But in the Padma purāṇa,[1] Skanda purāṇa,[2] etc, the Nyāya-śāstra is stated to have been expounded by Gotama or Gautama. Viśvanātha[3] in his Nyāya-sūtra-vṛtti calls the Nyāya-sūtra as Gotama-sūtra, that is, the sūtra of Gotama. Now the question arises as to who. Gotama or Akṣapāda, was the real author of the Nyāya-sūtra. Anantayajvan[4] in his commentary on the Pitṛmedha sūtra supposes on grounds best known to himself that Gautama (Gotama) and Akṣapāda were the same person.

Is Akṣapāda the same person as Gautama?

The Nyāya-koṣa[5] mentions two legends to account for the name Akṣapāda as applied, according to it to Gautama. It is said that Gautama was so deeply absorbed in philosophical contemplation that one day during his w.\ks he fell unwittingly into a well, out of which he was rescued with great difficulty. God therefore mercifully provided him with a second pair of eyes in his feet, to protect the sage from further mishaps. This is a ridiculous story manufactured merely to explain the word "Akṣapāda" "as composed of, "Akṣa" (eye) and "Pāda" (feet).

Another legend which represents Vyāsa, a disciple of Gautama, lying prostrate before his master until the latter condescended to look upon him, not with his natural eyes, but with a new pair of eyes in his feet, may be dismissed with scant ceremony as the invention of a later generation of logicians, anxious to humiliate Vyāsa for the vilification of the Nyāya system in the Mahābhārata and Vedānta-sūtra.

---

[1] Padma purāṇa, Uttarakhaṇḍa, chap. 263, where the following verse occurs:—

कणादेन तु सम्प्रोक्तं शास्त्रं वैशेषिकं महत् ।
गौतमेन तथा न्यायं सांख्यं तु कपिलेन वै ॥

[2] गौतमः स्वेन तर्केण खण्डयन् तत्र तत्र हि ।
(Skanda purāṇa, Kālikā khaṇḍa, chap. XVII).

[3] एषा मुनिवर गोतम सूत्रवृत्तिः श्रीविश्वनाथ कृतिना सुगमाल्पवर्णा ।
श्रीकृष्णचन्द्र चरणाम्बुज चञ्चरीक श्री मच्छिरोमणिवचः प्रचयैरकारि ॥
(Nyā-sūtra-vṛtti, concluding verse).

[4] To the Gṛhya-sūtras of the Sāma-veda probably belong also Gautama's Pitṛmedha-sūtra (cf. Burnell, p. 57: the commentator Anantayajvan identifies the author with Akṣapāda, the author of the Nyāya-sūtra), and Gautama-dharma-sūtra.—Weber's History of Indian Literature, p. 85.

[5] Nyāya-koṣa (2nd edition, by M.M. Bhīmācārya Jhalakīkara, Bombay).

Akṣapāda different from Gautama.

In fact Gotama or Gautama, the founder of Ānvīkṣikī, was quite different from Akṣapāda. While one lived in Mithilā, the other flourished at Prabhāsa in Kathiawar. The Brahmāṇḍa purāṇa[1] describes Akṣapāda and Kaṇāda as the sons of a Brāhmaṇa named Soma-śarmā who was Śiva incarnate, and well known for his practice of austerities at the shrine of Prabhāsa[2] during the time of Jātūkarṇya Vyāsa.

Gautama and Akṣapāda were both authors of the Nyāya-sūtra.

It is by no means easy to determine who was the real author of the Nyāya-sūtra. Gautama and Akṣapāda seem both to have contributed to the production of the work. The Nyāya-sūtra treats mainly of five subjects, viz. (1) *pramāṇa*, the means of right knowledge, (2) *prameya*, the object of right knowledge, (3) *vāda*, a debate or discussion, (4) *avayava*, the members of a syllogism, and (5) *anyamataparīkṣā*, an examination of contemporaneous philosophical doctrines. The second and the third subjects, and possibly also the first subject in its crude form, ample references to which are met with in the old Brāhmaṇic, Buddhistic, and Jaina books, were in all probability first handled by Gautama whose *Ānvīkṣikī-vidyā* was constituted by them. The

---

1

सप्तविंशतिमे प्राप्ते परिवर्त्ते क्रमागते ।
जातुकर्ण्यो यदा व्यासो भविष्यति तपोधनः ॥
तदाप्यहं संभविष्यामि सोमशर्म्मा द्विजोत्तमः ।
प्रभासतीर्थमासाद्य योगात्मा लोकविश्रुतः ॥
तत्रापि मम ते पुत्रा भविष्यन्ति तपोधनाः ।
अक्षपादः कणादश्च उलूको वत्स एव च ॥

(Brahmāṇḍa purāṇa published under the name of Vāyu purāṇa by A.S.B., adhyāya 23).

2 Prabhāsa washed on its western side by the river Sarasvatī, and reputed as the residence of Kṛṣṇa, is mentioned in the Śrīmad Bhāgavata thus:—

न वस्तव्यमिहास्माभिर्जिजीविषुरार्यकाः ।
प्रभासं सुमहत्पुण्यं यास्यामोऽद्यैव माचिरम् ॥

(Bhāgavata, Skandha II, adhyāya 6).

स्त्रियो बालाश्च वृद्धाश्च शंखोद्धारं व्रजन्त्वितः ।
वयं प्रभासं यास्यामो यत्र प्रत्यक् सरस्वती ॥

(Bhāgavata, Skandha II, adhyāya 30).

Prabhāsa was situated beyond the rock of Girnar in Kathiawar, where we come across all the edicts of Aśoka as well as an inscription of Rudradāman supposed to be the first inscription in Sanskrit about 150 A.D. which mentions Candra Gupta and Aśoka by names. There are also some inscriptions in Gupta characters, and there is no doubt that Prabhāsa situated on the Sarasvatī acquired celebrity in very old times.

Cf. Archaeological Survey of Western India, Vol. II, p. 128.

Poet Bhavabhūti of Vidarbha introduces himself as the son of Jātukarṇī (*vide* Uttararāma-carita).

fourth and fifth subjects, and possibly also the first subject in its systematic form, were introduced by Akṣapāda into the *Ānvīkṣikī-vidyā* which in its final form was styled the Nyāya-sūtra. Akṣapāda was therefore the real author of the Nyāya sūtra which derived a considerable part of its materials from the *Ānvīkṣikī-vidyā* of Gautama. Just as Caraka was the redactor of the Agniveśa-tantra or the Āyurveda of Ātreya,. Akṣapāda was the redactor of the *Ānvīkṣikī* of Gautama. Hence *Nyāya* is called *Gautamī-vidyā* as well as *Akṣapāda-darśana*.

We know nothing of Jātūkarṇya Vyāsa except that the name Jātūkarṇya widely prevailed in Vidarbha (Berar), and that the word Vyāsa usually signified a compiler. It seems that after king Kaniṣka had held the fourth Buddhist Council at Jālandhara in the first century A.D to collect the teachings of Buddha, the Brāhmaṇic sages too in the following centuries met togther in groups to compile the Purāṇas and other śāstras. Jātūkarṇya was probably one of the compilers at Vidarbha, and Akṣapāda, the compiler of the Nyāya-sūtra, was one of his contemporaries.

Age of Akṣapāda.

The Nyāya-sūtra, which was criticised by Nāgārjuna, referred perhaps to the Caraka-saṁhitā under the name of Āyurveda.[1] Akṣapāda seems therefore to have flourished before Nāgārjuna (circa 250-320 A.D.) who employs many logical terms presumably from the Nyāya-sūtra, and after Caraka whose Saṁhitā compiled about 78 A.D. embodies logical doctrines of a cruder form than those of the Nyāya-sūtra The date of Akṣapāda[2] may therefore be approximately fixed at about 150 A.D.

28. Subjects of the Nyāya-sūtra.

The principal subjects treated in the Nyāya-sūtra may be grouped under the following heads:—

(1) *Pramāṇa*—the means of knowledge, which comprises *pratyakṣa* (perception), *anumāna* (inference), *upamāna* (comparison), and *śabda* (verbal testimony). Of these, *śabda* (verbal testimony) as defined in the Nyāya-sūtra combines in itself the

---

1 मन्त्रायुर्वेद प्रामाण्यवच्च तत्प्रामाण्यमाप्तप्रामाण्यात् ।

(Nyāya-sūtra, 2-1-69, p. 42, Sacred Books of the Hindus series, Allahabad).

2 The Japanese scholar Professor H. Ui observes:—The date of Nyāya sūtra seems to be between Nāgārjuna (the second-third century) and Vasubandhu (the fourth century). (The Vaiśeṣika Philosophy, p. 16).

The Italian scholar Professor L. Suali places the date between 300 A.D. and 350 A.D. (Filosofia Indiana, p. 14).

Dr. H. Jacobi places the date between 200 A.D. and 450 A.D. on the ground that the Nāya-sūtra attacks Śūnyavāda, but does not allude to Vijñāna-vāda.

(Journal of the American Oriental Society, vol. xxxi, 1911, p. 29).

meanings of *āptopadeśa* (reliable assertion), *śabda* (word), and *aitihya* (tradition), as explained in the Caraka-saṁhitā. *Aupamya* or *upamāna* (comparison) included in the Tantra-yukti and mentioned in the Jaina works is accepted here as a means of knowledge (*pramāṇa*). The term "pramāṇa" in the sense given here was not widely used even in the days of Caraka (about 78 A.D.) inasmuch as he employed three terms, viz. *parīkṣā*, *hetu*, and *pramāṇa*, to signify the means of knowledge.

(2) *Prameya*—the object of knowledge, which comprises the soul, body, senses, objects of sense, intellect, mind, activity, fault, transmigration, fruit, pain, and release. It corresponds to Ātmavāda of the Ānvīkṣikī. Though the word "prameya" in the sense of an object of knowledge occurs in the Caraka-saṁhitā, it does not there refer specially to the twelve objects enumerated in the Nyāya-sūtra. The word, as already shown, is mentioned in the sense of an object of knowledge, also in the Rāmāyaṇa, Mahābhārata, and Manu-saṁhitā.

(3) *Vāda*—a discussion. In the Caraka-saṁhitā *vāda* as a substitute for *kathā* (discourse) includes *jalpa* (wrangling) and *vitaṇḍā* (cavil). The categories of the Nyāya-sūtra beginning with *saṁśaya* (doubt) are subsidiaries to *vāda* in the carrying on of which they are to be employed. The subject of *vāda* as treated in the Nyāya-sūtra represents the *sambhāṣā-vidhi* (the method of debate) as explained in the Caraka-saṁhitā. *Jāti* (analogue), *hetvābhāsa* (fallacy) and *nigrahasthāna* (the point of defeat) are included in the subject of *vāda*. "Jāti" is the same as "uttara" (rejoinder) and "hetvābhāsa" (fallacy) is the same as "ahetu" (non-reason) mentioned in the Caraka-saṁhitā. The grounds covered by the two sets of terms are however not exactly identical. The term "jāti" in the sense of "analogue" or "futile rejoinder" does not occur in any work anterior to the Nyāya-sūtra, but when it was introduced it incorporated in it "ahetu" as explained in the Caraka-saṁhitā. The term "nigraha" in the sense of "defeat" was extensively used in the Pāli literature, and "nigraha-sthāna" (the point of defeat or occasion for rebuke) was a technical term in the Caraka-saṁhitā. The doctrine of "nigraha-sthāna" attained a high development in the Nyāya-sūtra.

(4) *Avayava*—consists of five parts or members of a syllogism. It covers the same ground as *sthāpanā* (demonstration) explained in the Caraka-saṁhitā. Some of the five parts seem to have been known by name to the old Brāhmaṇic writers as well as to the authors of the Jaina sthānāṅga sūtra and Pāli Kathāvatthuppakaraṇa, but not in their technical senses nor as members of a syllogism. We do not find the five parts combined together in the form of a syllogism before the composition of the Nyāya-sūtra and the Caraka-saṁhitā.

(5) *Anya-mata-parīkṣā*—the examination of the doctrines of other

systems of philosophy. There is in the Nyāya-sūtra an examination of various philosophical doctrines, e.g. in Book III, chap. II there is a criticism of the Sāṁkhya doctrine of intellect (*buddhi*) and the Saugata doctrine of momentariness (*kṣaṇika-vāda*); in Book IV. chap. 1 there is a review of the (Buddhist) doctrine of voidness (*Śūnyatā*) and the Vedānta doctrine of the transformation of Brahma (*Brahma-pariṇāma-vāda*). etc.

29. The Arrangement of Categories in the Nyāya-sūtra.

The Nyāya-sūtra treats of sixteen categories which comprise all the topics of *vāda-mārga* (the course of debate) as enumerated in the Caraka-saṁhitā. While there is apparently no order among the topics of the Caraka-saṁhitā, there exists evidently a regular arrangement among the categories of the Nyāya-sūtra The categories are, according to the commentaries[1] on the Nyāya-sūtra, supposed to represent stages in the course of a debate between a disputant and his respondent. The first of the categories is (1) *pramāṇa*, which signifies the means of knowledge, and the second is (2) *prameya*, which refers to the objects of knowledge. These two categories, which constitute the basis of a debate, supply the thesis or case which a disputant is to prove. The third category, (3) *saṁśaya* (doubt), having roused a conflicting judgment about the case, the disputant in pursuance of his (4) *prayojana* (purpose) cites a parallel case called (5) *dṛṣṭānta* (a familiar instance) which is not open to such a doubt. The case is then shown to rest on (6) *siddhāntas* (tenets) which are accepted by both the parties. That the case is valid is further shown by an analysis of it into five parts called (7) *avayava* (members). Having carried on (8) *tarka* (confutation) against all contrary suppositions the disputant affirms his case with (9) *nirṇaya* (certainty). If his respondent, not being satisfied with this process of demonstration, advances an antithesis, he will have to enter upon (10) *vāda* (discussion) which will necessarily assume the form of (11) *jalpa* (a wrangling) and (12) *vitaṇḍā* (a cavil). Failing to establish his antithesis, he will employ (13) *hetvābhāsa* (fallacious reasons), (14) *chala* (quibbles), and (15) *jāti* (analogues), the exposure of which will bring about his (16) *nigrahasthāna* (defeat).

The categories represent the stages of a debate.

---

[1] Vātsyāyana in his Nyāya-bhāṣya and Viśva-nātha in his Nyāya-sūtra-vṛtti, while explaining the sixteen categories, justify the gradual order of their succession. Dr. Ballantyne in his translation of the Nyāya-sūtra, and Dr. Robert Adamson in his "History of Logic" (pp. 165-166), point out that the categories represent stages in dialectic or in the process of clearing up knowledge by discussion.

30. The Process of Treatment of the Categories.

Enunciation, definition and examination.

As pointed out by Vâtsyâyana,[1] the Nyâya-sûtra treats of its categories through the processes of enunciation (*uddeśā*), definition (*lakṣaṇa*), and examination (*parīkṣā*). *Enunciation* is the mere mention of the categories by name; *definition* consists in setting forth that character of a category which differentiates it from other categories; and *examination* is the settlement, by reasoning, of the question whether the definition of a certain category is really applicable to it. Book I of the Nyāya-sūtra deals with the enunciation and definition of the sixteen categories, while the remaining four books are concerned with a critical examination of the categories.

---

[1] Vâtsyâyana observes:—

त्रिविधा चास्य शास्त्रस्य प्रवृत्तिः । उद्देशो लक्षणं परीक्षा चेति ।

(Nyāya-bhāṣya, 1-1-2).

CHAPTER II.

Contents of the Nyāya-sūtra.[1]

31. The Categories: their Enunciation.

As the Nyāya-sūtra is the foremost work on Nyāya-śāstra, a full summary of its doctrines is given here. Akṣapāda says that supreme felicity, *summum bonum* (*niḥśreyasa*), is attained by the true knowledge of the sixteen categories treated in his Nyāya-sūtra. The categories[2] are enumerated as follows:—

(1) The means of right knowledge (*pramāṇa*), (2) the object of right knowledge (*prameya*), (3) doubt (*saṁśaya*), (4) purpose (*prayojana*), (5) example (*dṛṣṭānta*), (6) tenet (*siddhānta*), (7) members (*avayava*), (8) confutation (*tarka*), (9) ascertainment (*nirṇaya*), (10) discussion (*vāda*), (11) wrangling (*jalpa*), (12) cavil (*vitaṇḍā*), (13) fallacy (*hetvābhāsa*), (14) quibble (*chala*), (15) analogue (*jāti*), and (16) the point of defeat (*nigrahasthāna*).

32. The Categories: their Definition.

Definitions of the sixteen categories are given below:—

(1) The Means of Right Knowledge (*pramāṇa*).

Perception (*pratyakṣa*), inference (*anumāna*), comparison (*upamāna*), and word or verbal testimony (*śabda*), are the means of right knowledge.

---

[1] *Vide* "The Nyāya-sūtras of Gotama" translated by Dr. Satis Chandra Vidyabhusana in the "Sacred Books of the Hindus" series, Allahabad; also Dr. Ballantyne's translation of the Nyāya-sūtras, first four books, Benares.

[2] In Tibetan the sixteen categories, *ṣoḍaśa padārthāḥ* (ཚིག་གི་དོན་བཅུ་དྲུག tshig-gi-don bcu-drug), are designated respectively as follows:—

(1) ཚད་མ tshaḍ-ma (source of right cognition), (2) གཞལ་བྱ gshal-bya (object of right cognition), (3) ཐེ་ཚོམ་ the-tshom (doubt), (4) དགོས་པ dgoṣ-pa (motive), (5) དཔེ ḍpe (example), (6) ཆ་ཤས་ cha-śaṣ (member of a syllogism), (7) གྲུབ་པའི་མཐའ grub-pah̲i-ṃthah̲ (established tenet), (8) རྟོག་གེ ṛtog-ge (corroborating a proposition by showing that its denial is impossible, *reductio ad absurdum*), (9) གཏན་ལ་དབབ་པ gtan-la-ḍwab-pa (demonstration or ascertainment), (10) རྩོད་པ ṛtsoḍ-pa (discussion), (11) བརྗོད་པ bṛjoḍ-pa (wrangling), (12) སུན་འབྱིན་དུ་རྒོལ་བ་ sun-h̲byin-du-ṛgol-wa (cavil or reducing a proposition *ad absurdum* without caring to establish one's own view), (13) རྒྱུ་ལྟར་སྣང་བ ṛgyu-ḻtar-ṣnaṅ-wa (fallacious middle term), (14) ཚིག་དོར tshig-dor (quibble), (15) ལྟག་ཆོད ltag-choḍ (evasive answer), and (16) ཆད་པའི་གནས chaḍ-pah̲i-gnaṣ (a reason why one may be declared unfit to continue the controversy).—*Vide* Mahāvyutpatti, part II, p. 133, Bibliotheca Indica series; also Bṣtan-h̲gyur, M̲do, Go, folios 233–377.

Perception[1] is the knowledge which arises from the intercourse of a sense with its object, being determinate, unnameable, and non-erratic.

Sense—includes the mind. The knowledge of the soul, pleasure, pain, etc., is produced by their intercourse with the mind which, according to the Bhāṣya 1-1-4 of Vātsyāyana, is a sense-organ.

Determinate—this epithet distinguishes perception from indeterminate (doubtful) knowledge; as for instance, a man looking from a distance cannot ascertain whether there is smoke or dust. His knowledge, which is of a doubtful character, is not perception.

Unnameable—signifies that the knowledge of a thing derived through perception has no connection with the name which the thing bears. It arises in fact without the aid of language.

Some say that there is no perception entirely free from verbal representation. All things have names: there is nothing devoid of a name. Whenever a thing is perceived it is perceived as bearing a name. The thing being inseparably connected with its name, the perception of the thing involves that of the name also. Hence there is no perception which is not invariably accompanied by a name.

Akṣapāda does not accept the above view on the ground, as explained in the Bhāṣya 1-1-4 of Vātsyāyana, that we can perceive a thing although we may not know its name, and when we know the name we perceive the thing as entirely distinct from it. Thus our perception of a thing is totally independent of its name. It is, however, admitted that the name is useful in communicating our perception to our fellow-men. They cannot comprehend our perception unless we give a name to it. It is therefore concluded that the name of a thing is not necessarily present and operative at the time when the thing is perceived.

Non-erratic—In summer the sun's rays coming in contact with earthly heat (vapour) quiver and appear to the eyes of men as water. The knowledge of water derived in this way is not perception. To eliminate such cases the epithet non-erratic has been used.

[The Sanskrit Sūtra defining perception may also be translated as follows:—

Perception is knowledge which arises from the contact of a sense with its object, and which is non-erratic, being either indeterminate ("nirvikalpaka" as "this is something") or determinate ("savikalpaka" as "this is a Brāhmaṇa")].

---

[1] In Tibetan the definition is stated as follows:—

དབང་པོ་དང་དོན་འཕྲད་པ་ལས་བྱུང་བའི་ཤེས་པ་མངོན་སུམ་གཏན་དུ་མེད་པ་འཁྲུལ་པ་མེད་པ་རྟོག་པའི་བདག་ཉིད། Dwaṅ-po-daṅ-don-ḥphrad-pa-las-byuṅ-wahi-śes-pa-mṅon-sum-gtan-du-med-pa-ḥphrul-pa-med-pa-rtog-pahi-bdag-ñid. It has been translated by Alexander Csoma de Koros as follows: Perception is cognition [which is] produced through contact between an organ of sense and its object, [which is] not contained in the word, not discrepant from its object, and the essence of which is certainty. Mahāvyutpatti, part II, p. 134, Bibliotheca Indica series, Calcutta; also Bstan-ḥgyur Mdo, Go, folios 233–377.

Inference is knowledge which is preceded by perception, and is of three kinds, viz. 'â priori,' 'â posteriori,' and 'commonly seen.'

Â priori (*pūrvavat*) is the knowledge of effect derived from the perception of its cause, e.g. one seeing clouds infers that there will be rain.

Â posteriori (*śeṣavat*) is the knowledge of cause derived from the perception of its effect, e.g. one seeing a river swollen infers that there was rain.

'*Commonly seen*' (*sāmānyato dṛṣta*) is the knowledge of one thing derived from the perception of another thing with which it is commonly seen or seen together, e.g. seeing a beast possessing horns, one infers that it possesses also a tail, or one infers the presence of water from the presence of cranes.

[Vātsyāyana, the first commentator on the Nyāya-sūtra, takes the last to be "not commonly seen" (*sāmānyato 'dṛṣta*), which he interprets as the knowledge of a thing which is *not* commonly seen, e.g. observing affection, aversion and other qualities one infers that there is a substance called soul].

Comparison is the knowledge of a thing through its similarity to another thing previously well known.

A man hearing from a forester that a *bos gavaeus* is like a cow resorts to a forest where he sees an animal like a cow. Having recollected what he heard he institutes a comparison, by which he arrives at the conviction that the animal which he sees is *bos gavaeus*. This is knowledge derived through comparison.

Word or verbal testimony is the instructive assertion of a reliable person.

'A reliable person' is one (*a ṛṣi, ārya or mleccha*) who as an expert in a certain matter is willing to communicate his experiences of it. Suppose a young man coming to the side of a river cannot ascertain whether the river is fordable or not, and immediately an old experienced man of the locality, who has no enmity against him, comes and tells him that the river is easily fordable: the assertion of the old man is to be accepted as a means of right knowledge called *word* or verbal testimony.

Word is of two kinds, *viz* (1) that which refers to matter which is seen, e.g. a physician's assertion that physical strength is gained by taking butter; and (2) that which refers to matter which is not seen, e.g. a religious teacher's assertion that one conquers heaven by performing horse-sacrifices.

Rumour (*aitihya*), presumption (*arthāpatti*), probability (*sambhava*), and non-existence (*abhāva*), are not separate means of right knowledge as they are included in the four stated above.

(2) The Objects of Right Knowledge (*prameya*).

The soul (*ātmā*), body (*śarīra*), senses (*indriya*), objects of sense (*artha*), intellect (*buddhi*), mind (*manaḥ*), activity (*pravṛtti*), fault (*doṣa*), transmigration (*pretyabhāva*), fruit (*phala*), pain (*duḥkha*), and emancipation (*apavarga*), are the (principal) objects of right knowledge.

Desire, aversion, volition, pleasure, pain and cognition are the marks of the **soul**.

These are the qualities of the substance called soul.

Desire is a sign which proves the existence of "soul." A soul, having experienced pleasure in a certain thing, *desires* again to acquire it through recognition of the same. Aversion is another sign, inasmuch as the soul feels aversion against a thing from which it suffered pain. Similarly volition, etc., are also signs of the soul. The existence of soul is thus, according to the Nyāya-bhāṣya and Nyāya-vārtika, 1-1-10, proved on the basis of recognition involved in our desire, aversion, etc. The soul is an eternal entity which is from time to time connected with a body suitable to its desert (merit and demerit). The connection of the soul with a body is its birth while their mutual separation is its death. Transmigration, which consists in a series of births and deaths, is the source of all our sufferings When our desert is completely exhausted, our soul, freed from transmigration, attains emancipation or release (*mokṣa*).

The **body** is the site of gestures, senses and sentiments.

Body is the site of *gestures* inasmuch as it strives to reach what is desirable and to avoid what is hateful. It is also the site of *senses* for the latter act well or ill, according as the former is in good or bad order *Sentiments* which comprise pleasure and pain are also located in the body which experiences them.

The nose, tongue, eye, skin and ear are the **senses**, which are produced from elements.

Earth, water, light, air, and ether—these are the elements. The *nose* is of the same nature as earth, the *tongue* as water, the *eye* as light, the *skin* as air, and *ear* as ether

Smell (odour), taste (savour), colour, touch and sound which are qualities of the earth, etc., are **objects of the senses**.

Smell which is the prominent quality of earth is the object of the nose, *taste* the prominent quality of water is the object of the tongue, *colour* the prominent quality of light is the object of the eye, *touch* the prominent quality of air is the object of the skin, and *sound* the quality of ether is the object of the ear.

Intellect is the same as apprehension or knowledge.

The mark of the **mind** is that there do not arise in the soul more acts of knowledge than one at a time.

It is impossible to perceive two things simultaneously. Perception does not arise merely from the contact of a sense-organ with its object, but it requires also a conjunction of the mind. Now, the mind, which is an atomic substance, cannot be conjoined with more than one sense-organ at a time, hence there cannot occur more acts of perception than one at a time.

Activity is that which makes the voice, mind and body begin their action.

There are three kinds of action, *viz. bodily*, *vocal*, and *mental*, each of which may be subdivided as good or bad.

Bodily actions which are *bad* are :—(1) killing, (2) stealing, and (3) committing adultery.

Bodily actions which are *good* are :—(1) giving, (2) protecting, (3) and serving.

Vocal actions which are *bad* are :—(1) telling a lie, (2) using harsh language, (3) slandering, and (4) indulging in frivolous talk.

Vocal actions which are *good* are :—speaking the truth, (2) speaking what is useful, (3) speaking what is pleasant, and (4) reading sacred books.

Mental actions which are *bad* are :—(1) malice, (2) covetousness, and (3) scepticism.

Mental actions which are *good* are :—(1) compassion, (2) generosity, and (3) devotion.

Faults are those which cause activity.

They are affection (attachment), aversion, and stupidity.

Transmigration means rebirths.

As already explained, it is a series of births and deaths. *Birth* is the connection of a soul with a body which includes the sense-organs, mind, intellect, and sentiments. Death is the soul's separation from them.

Fruit is the thing produced by activity and faults.

It is the enjoyment of *pleasure* or suffering of *pain*. All activity and faults end in producing pleasure which is acceptable and pain which is fit only to be avoided.

Pain is that which causes uneasiness.

It is affliction which every one desires to avoid. The Sanskrit Sūtra defining "pain" may also be translated as follows: *Pain* is the mark of hindrance to the soul.

Emancipation or release is the absolute deliverance from pain.

A soul, which is no longer subject to transmigration, is freed from all pains. Transmigration, which consists in the soul's leaving one body and taking another, is the cause of its experiencing pleasure and pain. The soul attains emancipation as soon as there is an end of the body, and consequently of pleasure and pain.

(3) Doubt (*saṁśaya*).

Doubt, which is a conflicting judgment about the precise character of an object, arises from the recognition of properties common to many objects, or of properties not common to any of the objects, from conflicting testimony, and from irregularity of perception and non-perception.

(1) *Recognition of common properties*—e.g. seeing in the twilight a tall object we cannot decide whether it is a man or a post, for the property of tallness belongs to both.

(2) *Recognition of properties not common*—e.g. hearing a sound, one questions whether it is eternal or not, for the property of soundness abides neither in man, beast, etc., that are non-eternal, nor in atoms which are eternal.

(3) *Conflicting testimony*—e.g. merely by study one cannot decide whether the soul exists, for one system of philosophy affirms that it does, while another system states that it does not.

(4) *Irregularity of perception*—e.g. we perceive water in the tank where it really exists, but water appears also to exist in a mirage where it really does not exist.

A question arises, whether water is perceived only when it actually exists or even when it does not exist.

(5) *Irregularity of non-perception*—e.g. we neither perceive water in the radish where it really exists, nor on dry land where it does not exist.

A question arises, whether water is not perceived only when it does not exist, or also when it does exist.

(4) Purpose (*prayojana*).

Purpose is that with an eye to which one proceeds to act.

It refers to the thing which one endeavours to attain or avoid. A man collects fuel for the purpose of cooking his food.

(5) Example (*dṛṣṭānta*).

An example is the thing about which an ordinary man and an expert entertain the same opinion.

With regard to the general proposition "wherever there is smoke there is fire," the example is a kitchen in which fire and smoke abide together, to the satisfaction of an ordinary man as well as an acute investigator.

(6) Tenet (*siddhānta*).

A **tenet** is a dogma resting on the authority of a certain school, hypothesis, or implication.

The tenet is of four kinds owing to the distinction between a dogma of all the schools' (*sarva-tantra*), 'a dogma peculiar to some school' (*prati-tantra*), 'a hypothetical dogma' (*adhikaraṇa*), and 'an implied dogma' (*abhyupagama*).

A dogma of all the schools is a tenet which is not opposed by any school and is claimed by at least one school.

The existence of five elements or five objects of sense is a tenet which is accepted by all the schools.

A dogma peculiar to some school is a tenet which is accepted by similar schools, but rejected by opposite schools.

"A thing cannot come into existence out of nothing"—this is a peculiar dogma of the Sāṁkhyas.

A hypothetical dogma is a tenet which if accepted leads to the acceptance of another tenet.

"There is a soul apart from the senses, because it can recognize one and the same object by seeing and touching." If you accept this tenet you must also have accepted the following :—(1) That the senses are more than one, (2) that each of the senses has its particular object, (3) that the soul derives its knowledge through the channels of the senses, (4) that a substance which is distinct from its qualities is the abode of them, etc.

An implied dogma is a tenet which is not explicitly declared as such, but which follows from the examination of particulars concerning it, e.g. the discussion whether sound is eternal or non-eternal presupposes that it is a substance.

(7) Members of a Syllogism (*avayava*).

The **members** (of a syllogism) are signalised by a proposition (***pratijñā***), a reason (***hetu***), an explanatory example (***udāharaṇa***), an application of the example (***upanaya***), and a statement of the conclusion (***nigamana***).

A *proposition* is the statement of what is to be proved. e.g. the hill is fiery.

A *reason* is the means for proving what is to be proved through the homogeneous or heterogeneous (affirmative or negative) character of the example, e.g.

because it (the hill) is smoky.

Here "smoke" is the reason.

A ***homogeneous*** (or ***affirmative***) ***example*** is a familiar instance which is known to possess the property to be proved, and which implies that this property is invariably contained in the reason given. e.g.

whatever is smoky is fiery, as a kitchen.

Here "kitchen" is a familiar instance which possesses fire. and implies that fire invariably goes with smoke which is the reason given.

N.B.—*An affirmative example* may, according to the Nyāya-bhāṣya, 1-1-36, be defined as a familiar instance, which being similar to the minor term (subject) possesses the property of that term as copresent with the reason.

A *heterogeneous* (or *negative*) *example* is a familiar instance which is devoid of the property to be proved, and which implies that the absence of this property is incompatible with the reason given, e.g.

whatever is not fiery is not smoky, as a lake.

Here the lake is a familiar instance which is known to be devoid of fire, and implies that absence of fieriness is incompatible with the smoke, which is the reason.

Application is the winding up, with reference to the example, of what is to be proved as being so or not so.

Application is of two kinds: (1) *affirmative*, and (2) *negative*. The affirmative application, which is expressed by the word "so," occurs when the example is of an affirmative character. The negative application, which is expressed by the phrase "not so," occurs when the example is of a negative character.

Affirmative application—"So" is this hill (smoky).
Negative application—This hill is "not so" (not smoky).

Conclusion is the re-statement of the proposition after the reason has been mentioned.

It is the confirmation of the proposition after the reason and the example have been mentioned

Conclusion—Therefore the hill is fiery.

The five members may be fully set forth as follows:—

(i) *Proposition*—This hill is fiery.
(ii) *Reason*—Because it is smoky.
(iii) *Example*—Whatever is smoky is fiery, as a kitchen (*homogeneous* or *affirmative*).
(iv) *Application*—"So" is this hill (smoky)—(*affirmative*).
(v) *Conclusion*—Therefore this hill is fiery.

(8) Confutation (*tarka*).

Confutation,[1] which is carried on for ascertaining the real character of a thing of which the character is not known, is reasoning which reveals the character by showing the absurdity of all contrary characters.

Is the soul eternal or non-eternal? Here the real character of the soul, viz. whether it is eternal or non-eternal, is not known. In ascertaining the character we reason as follows: If the soul were non-eternal it would be impossible for it to enjoy the fruits of its own actions, to undergo transmigration, and to attain final emancipation. But such a conclusion is absurd: such possibilities are known to belong to the soul: therefore, we must admit that the soul is eternal.

---

[1] *Tarka* may be rendered also as 'argumentation,' 'reasoning,' 'hypothetical reasoning,' 'reductio ad absurdum,' etc.

(9) Ascertainment (*nirṇaya*).

Ascertainment is the determination of a question through the removal of doubt, by hearing two opposite sides.

A person wavers and doubts if certain statements advanced to him are supported by one of two parties, but opposed by the other party. His doubt is not removed until by the application of reason he can vindicate one of the parties. The process by which the vindication is effected is called ascertainment. Ascertainment is not, however, in all cases preceded by doubt, for instance, in the case of perception things are ascertained directly. So also we ascertain things directly by the authority of scriptures. But in the case of investigation (inference), doubt must precede ascertainment.

(10) Discussion (*vāda*).

Discussion is the adoption, by two parties, of two opposite theses which are each analysed in the form of five members, and are supported or condemned by any of the means of right knowledge, and by confutation, without deviation from the established tenets.

A *dialogue*, disputation or controversy (*kathā*) is the adoption of a side or thesis by a disputant, and its opposite one by his opponent. It is of three kinds, viz. *discussion* (*vāda*) which aims at ascertaining the truth, *wrangling* (*jalpa*) which aims at gaining victory, and *cavil* (*vitaṇḍā*) which aims at finding mere faults. A *discutient* is one who engages himself in a disputation as a means of seeking the truth.

An instance of discussion is given below :—

Discutient—There is soul.

Opponent—There is no soul.

Discutient—Soul is existent (proposition).

Because it is an abode of consciousness (reason).

Whatever is not existent is not an abode of consciousness, as a hare's horn (negative example).

Soul is not so, that is, soul is an abode of consciousness (negative application).

Therefore soul is existent (conclusion)

Opponent—Soul is non-existent (proposition).

Because it is not perceptible by any of our senses (reason).

Whatever is not perceptible by any of our senses is non-existent, as a hare's horn (positive example).

Soul is so (is not perceptible any of our senses) (positive application).

Therefore soul is non-existent (conclusion).

Discutient—The scripture which is a means of right knowledge declares the existence of soul.

Opponent—The scripture (of certain sects) denies the existence of soul.

Discutient—If there were no soul, it would not be possible to apprehend one and the same object through sight and touch.

Opponent—If there were soul, there would be no change of cognitions.

Discutient—The doctrine of soul harmonises well with the various tenets which we hold, viz. that there are eternal things, that everybody enjoys pleasure or suffers pain according to his own actions, etc. Therefore there is soul.

(11) Wrangling (*jalpa*).

Wrangling, which aims at gaining victory, is the defence or attack of a proposition in the manner aforesaid by quibbles, analogues, and other processes which deserve rebuke.

A *wrangler* is one who, engaged in a disputation, aims only at victory, being indifferent whether the arguments which he employs, support his own contention or that of his opponent provided that he can make out a pretext for bragging that he has taken an active part in the disputation.

(12) Cavil (*vitaṇḍā*).

Cavil is a kind of wrangling which consists in mere attacks on the opposite side.

A *caviller* does not endeavour to establish any thing, but confines himself to mere carping at the arguments of his opponent.

(13) Fallacy (*hetvābhāsa*).

Fallacies of reason are the erratic (*savyabhicāra*), the contradictory (*viruddha*), the controversial (*prakaraṇa-sama*), the counter-questioned (*sādhyasama*), and the mistimed (*kālātīta*).

The *erratic* is the reason which leads to more conclusions than one.

An instance of the *erratic* reason is given below:—

Proposition—Sound is eternal.
Erratic reason—Because it is intangible.
Example—Whatever is intangible is eternal as atoms.
Application—So is sound (intangible).
Conclusion—Therefore sound is eternal.

Again:

Proposition—Sound is non-eternal.
Erratic reason—Because it is intangible.
Example—Whatever is intangible is non-eternal, as cognition.
Application—So is sound (intangible).
Conclusion—Therefore sound is non-eternal.

Here from the reason (intangible) there have been drawn two opposite conclusions, viz. that sound is eternal, and that sound is non-eternal. The reason (or middle term) is erratic when it is not pervaded by the major term, that is, when there is no connection between the major term and middle term, as pervader and pervaded. 'Intangible' is pervaded neither by 'eternal' nor by 'non-eternal.'

The *Contradictory* is the reason which opposes what is to be established.

Proposition—A pot is produced.

Contradictory reason—Because it is eternal.

Here the reason is contradictory because that which is eternal is never produced.

The *controversial* or *balancing the point at issue* is a reason which is adduced to arrive at a definite conclusion while it is really one which can give rise to mere suspense as to the point.

Proposition—Sound is non-eternal.

Reason—Because it is not possessed of the attribute of eternality.

The reason that "sound is not possessed of the attribute of eternality" does not throw any new light, but keeps the parties in suspense as before.

The *counter-questioned* or *balancing the question* is a reason which not being different from what is to be proved stands in need of proof for itself.

Proposition—Shadow is a substance.

Reason—Because it possesses motion.

That which possesses quality and motion is a substance. To say that shadow possesses motion is the same as to say that it is a substance. Hence the reason stands as much in need of proof as the proposition itself. This is a counter-questioned reason or a reason which balances the question.

The *mistimed* is the reason which is adduced when the time is past in which it might hold good.

Proposition—Sound is durable.

Mistimed reason—Because it is manifested by union, as a colour.

The colour of a jar is manifested when the jar comes into union with a lamp, but the colour existed before the union took place, and will continue to exist after the union has ceased. Similarly, the sound of a drum is manifested when the drum comes into union with a rod, and the sound must, after the analogy of the colour, be presumed to have existed before the union took place, and to continue to exist after the union has ceased. Hence sound is durable. The reason adduced here is *mistimed*, because the manifestation of sound does not take place at the time when the drum comes into union with the rod, but it takes place at a subsequent moment when the union has ceased. In the case of colour, however, the manifestation takes place just at the time when the jar comes into union with the lamp. As the time of their manifestation is different, the analogy between colour and sound is not complete, therefore, the reason is mistimed.

[Some interpret the aphorism as follows: The *mistimed* is a reason which is adduced in a wrong order among the five members, for instance, if the reason is stated before the proposition. But this interpretation, according to Vātsyāyana, is wrong

for a word bears its legitimate connection with another word (in a Sanskrit sentence) even if they are placed at a distance from each other, and, on the other hand, even the closest proximity is of no use if the words are disconnected in their sense. Moreover the placing of members in a worng order is noticed in the Nyāya-sūtra as a *nigraha-sthāna* called *aprāpta-kāla* (inopportune)].

(14) Quibble (*chala*).

Quibble is the opposition offered to a proposition by the assumption of an alternative meaning.

It is of three kinds, viz. quibble in respect of a term (*vāk-chala*), quibble in respect of a genus (*sāmānya-chala*), and quibble in respect of a metaphor (*upacāra-chala*).

Quibble in respect of a term consists in wilfully taking the term in a sense other than that intended by the speaker who happened to use it ambiguously.

A speaker says: "this boy is *nava-kambala* (possessed of a new blanket).

A quibbler replies: "this boy is not certainly *nava-kambala* (possessed of nine blankets) for he has only one blanket.

Here the word *nava*, which is ambiguous, was used by the speaker in the sense of "new," but has been wilfully taken by the quibbler in the sense of "nine."

Quibble in respect of a genus consists in asserting the impossibility of a thing which is really possible, on the ground that it belongs to a certain genus which is very wide.

A speaker says: "this Brāhmaṇa is possessed of learning and conduct."

An objector replies: "it is impossible, for how can this person be inferred to be possessed of learning and conduct from his being merely a Brāhmaṇa? There are little boys who are Brāhmaṇas, yet not possessed of learning and conduct.''

Here the objector is a quibbler, for he knew well that possession of learning and conduct was not meant to be an attribute of the whole class of Brāhmaṇas, but it was ascribed to "this" particular Brāhmaṇa who lived long enough in the world to render it possible for him to pursue studies and acquire good morals.

Quibble in respect of a metaphor consists in denying the proper meaning of a word, by taking it literally while it was used metaphorically, and *viceversa*.

A speaker says: "the scaffolds cry out."

An objector replies: "it is impossible for scaffolds to cry out, for they are inanimate objects."

Here the objector is a quibbler, for he knew well that the word "scaffolds" was used to signify those standing on the scaffolds.

(15) Analogue (*jāti*).

Analogue, also called an analogous rejoinder or far-fetched analogy, consists in offering opposition founded on mere similarity or dissimilarity.

A disputant says: "the soul is inactive because it is all-pervading as ether."

His opponent replies: "if the soul is inactive because it bears similarity to ether as being all-pervading, why is it not active because it bears similarity to a pot as being a seat of union"?

The reason of the opponent is futile, because it bears only a far-fetched analogy to that of the disputant.[1]

or again:

Disputant—Sound is non-eternal, because, unlike ether, it is a product.

Opponent—If sound is non-eternal because, as a product, it is dissimilar to ether; why is it not eternal because, as an object of auditory perception, it is dissimilar to a pot?

The reason employed by the opponent is futile because the analogy which it bears to that of the disputant is far-fetched.[2]

(16) A Point of Defeat (*nigrahasthāna*).

A point of defeat, also called a clincher, an occasion for rebuke or a place of humiliation, arises when one misunderstands or does not understand at all.

If a person begins to argue in a way which betrays his utter ignorance, or wilfully misunderstands and yet persists in showing that he understands well, it is of no avail to employ counter-arguments. He is quite unfit to be argued with, and there is nothing left for his opponent, but to turn him out or quit his company, rebuking him as a block-head or a knave.

An instance of the point of defeat:—

Whatever is not quality is substance;
because there is nothing except colour, etc. (quality).

A person who argues in the above way is to be rebuked as a fool, for his reason (which admits only quality) opposes his proposition (which admits both quality and substance).

Another instance:

Disputant—Fire is not hot.

Opponent—But the evidence of touch disproves such a statement.

---

[1] The opposition is futile, because it overlooks the universal connection between the middle term and the major term which is existent in the arguments of the disputant, but wanting in the arguments of the opponent. Whatever is all-pervading is inactive, but whatever is a seat of union is not necessarily active.

[2] The opposition is futile because it overlooks the disconnection between the middle term and the absence of the major term. There is an utter disconnection between "a product" and "not non-eternal," but there is no such disconnection between "an object of auditory perception" and "not eternal."

Disputant, in order to gain the confidence of the assembled people, says—"O learned audience, listen, I do not say that fire is not hot," etc.

It is only meet that the opponent should quit the company of a man who argues in this way.

33. The Varieties of Analogue.

The analogues are as follows: (1) Balancing the homogeneity (*sādharmya-sama*), (2) balancing the heterogeneity (*vaidharmya-sama*), (3) balancing an excess (*utkarṣa-sama*), (4) balancing a deficit (*apakarṣa sama*), (5) balancing the questionable (*varṇya-sama*), (6) balancing the unquestionable (*avarṇya sama*), (7) balancing the alternative (*vikalpa sama*), (8) balancing the question (*sādhya-sama*), (9) balancing the co-presence (*prāpti-sama*), (10) balancing the mutual absence (*aprāpti-sama*), (11) balancing the infinite regression (*prasaṅga-sama*), (12) balancing the counter-example (*pratidṛṣṭānta-sama*), (13) balancing the non-produced (*anutpatti-sama*), (14) balancing the doubt (*saṁśaya-sama*), (15) balancing the point at issue (*prakaraṇa-sama*), (16) balancing the non-reason (*ahetu-sama*), (17) balancing the presumption (*arthāpatti-sama*), (18) balancing the non-difference (*aviśeṣa-sama*), (19) balancing the demonstration (*upapatti-sama*), (20) balancing the perception (*upalabdhi-sama*), (21) balancing the non-perception (*anupalabdhi-sama*), (22) balancing the non-eternal (*anitya-sama*), (23) balancing the eternal (*nitya-sama*) and (24) balancing the effect (*kārya-sama*).

(1) Balancing the homogeneity.—If, against an argument based on a homogeneous example, one offers an opposition merely based on the same kind of example, the opposition, futile as it is, will be called "balancing the homogeneity."

A certain person, to prove the non-eternality of sound, argues as follows:—

Sound is non-eternal,
because it is a product,
like a pot.

A certain other person offers the following futile opposition :—

Sound is eternal,
because it is incorporeal,
like the ether.

The argument, viz. sound is non-eternal, is based on the homogeneity of sound with the non-eternal pot, on the ground of both being products. The opposition, viz. sound is eternal, is said to be based on the homogeneity of sound with the eternal sky, on the alleged ground of both being incorporeal. This sort of opposition, futile as it is, is called "balancing the homogeneity," which aims at showing an equality of the arguments of two sides only in respect of the homogeneity of examples employed by them.[1]

(2) **Balancing the heterogeneity.** – If against an argument based on a heterogeneous example one offers an opposition based merely on the same kind of example, the opposition, futile as it is, will be called "balancing the heterogeneity."

A certain person, to prove the non-eternality of sound, argues as follows:—

Sound is non-eternal,
because it is a product,
whatever is eternal is not a product, as the ether.

A certain other person offers a futile opposition thus:—

Sound is eternal,
because it is incorporeal,
whatever is not eternal is not incorporeal, as a pot.

The argument, viz. sound is non-eternal, is based on the heterogeneity of sound from the eternal ether. The opposition, viz. sound is eternal, is said to be based on the heterogeneity of sound from the not-incorporeal pot. This sort of opposition, futile as it is, is called "balancing the heterogeneity," which aims at showing an equality of the arguments of two sides merely in respect of the heterogeneity of examples employed by them.[2]

(3) **Balancing an excess.**—If against an argument based on a certain character of the example, one offers an opposition based on an additional character thereof, the opposition, futile as it is, will be called "balancing an excess."

A certain person, to prove the non-eternality of sound, argues as follows:—

Sound is non-eternal,
because it is a product,
like a pot.

A certain other person offers a futile opposition thus:—

Sound is non-eternal (and must be corporeal),
because it is a product,
like a pot (which is non-eternal as well as corporeal).

---

[1] The opposition is futile because it is based on a mere homogeneous example. In the argument—"sound is non-eternal, because it is a product, like a pot"—the homogeneous example "pot" exhibits a universal connection between productivity and non-eternality, all products being non-eternal, but in the opposition "sound is eternal, because it is incorporeal like the sky" the homogeneous example "sky" does not exhibit a universal connection between incorporeality and eternality, because there are things, such as intelligence or knowledge, which are incorporeal but not eternal.

[2] In the opposition "sound is eternal, because it is incorporeal, whatever is not eternal is not incorporeal, as a pot," the heterogeneous example "pot" does not exhibit a universal disconnection between incorporeality and absence of eternality, because there are things, such as intelligence or knowledge, which are incorporeal but not eternal. Hence the opposition is futile.

The opponent alleges that if sound is non-eternal like a pot, it must also be corporeal like it: if it is not corporeal, let it be also not non-eternal. This sort of futile opposition is called "balancing an excess," which aims at showing an equality of the arguments of two sides in respect of an additional character (possessed by the example and attributed to the subject).

It is based on the false supposition of a complete equality of the subject and the example. Though there is no denial of an equality of the subject and the example in certain characters, there is indeed a great difference between them in other characters. Thus the equality supposed to exist between the pot and sound in respect of corporeality, is not warranted by the reason (viz. being a product) because there are things, such as intelligence or knowledge, which are products but not corporeal.

(4) **Balancing a deficit.**—If against an argument based on a certain character of the example, one offers an opposition based on another character wanting in it, the opposition, futile as it is, will be called "balancing a deficit."

A certain person, to prove the non-eternality of sound, argues as follows :—

Sound is non-eternal,
because it is a product,
like a pot.

A certain other person offers the following futile opposition :—

Sound is non-eternal (and cannot be audible),
because it is a product,
like a pot (which is non-eternal and not audible).

The opponent alleges that if sound is non-eternal like a pot, it cannot be audible, for a pot is not audible; and if sound is still held to be audible, let it be also not non-eternal. This sort of futile opposition is called "balancing a deficit," which aims at showing an equality of the arguments of two sides in respect of a certain character wanting in the example (and supposed consequently to be wanting also in the subject).

The equality alleged to exist between "sound" and "pot" is not warranted by the reason (viz. being a product).

(5) **Balancing the questionable**—If one opposes an argument by maintaining that the character of an example is as questionable as that of the subject, the opposition, futile as it is, will be called "balancing the questionable."

A certain person, to prove the non-eternality of sound, argues as follows :—

Sound is non-eternal,
because it is a product,
like a pot.

A certain other person offers a futile opposition thus:—

A pot is non-eternal,
because it is a product,
like sound.

The opponent alleges that if the non-eternality of sound is called in question, why is not that of the pot too called in question, as the pot and sound are both products? His object is to set aside the argument on the ground of its example being of a questionable character. This sort of futile opposition is called "balancing the questionable," which aims at showing an equality of the arguments of two sides in respect of the questionable character of the subject as well as of the example. It puts an end to all kinds of inference by ignoring the difference between the subject and the example altogether.

(6) **Balancing the unquestionable.**—If one opposes an argument by alleging that the character of the subject is as unquestionable as that of the example, the opposition, futile as it is, will be called "balancing the unquestionable."

A certain person, to prove the non-eternality of sound, argues as follows:—

Sound is non-eternal,
because it is a product,
like a pot.

A certain other person offers a futile opposition thus:—

A pot is non-eternal,
because it is a product,
like sound.

The opponent alleges that, if the non-eternality of a pot is to be unquestionable, why is not that of sound too held to be so, as the pot and sound are both products? This sort of futile opposition is called "balancing the unquestionable," which aims at showing the equality of the arguments of two sides in respect of the unquestionable character of the example as well as of the subject.

It ignores totally the difference between the subject and the example, and thus puts an end to all kinds of inference.

(7) **Balancing the alternative.**—If one opposes an argument by attributing alternative character to the subject and the example, the opposition, futile as it is, will be called "balancing the alternative."

A certain person, to prove the non-eternality of sound, argues as follows:—

Sound is non-eternal,
because it is a product,
like a pot.

A certain other person offers a futile opposition thus:—

Sound is eternal and formless,
because it is a product,
like a pot (which is non-eternal and has forms).

The opponent alleges that the pot and sound are both products, yet one has form and the other is formless: why on the same principle is not one (the pot) non-eternal and the other (sound) eternal? This sort of futile opposition is called "balancing the alternative," which aims at showing an equality of the arguments of two sides in respect of the alternative characters attributed to the subject and the example.

It introduces an equality between the pot and sound in respect of a character (viz. being eternal) which is not warranted by the reason (viz. being a product).

(8) **Balancing the question.**—If one opposes an argument by alleging that the example requires proof as much as the subject does, the opposition, futile as it is, will be called "balancing the question."

A certain person, to prove the non-eternality of sound, argues as follows:—

Sound is non-eternal,
because it is a product,
like a pot.

A certain other person offers a futile opposition thus:—

A pot is non-eternal,
because it is a product,
like sound.

The opponent alleges that, the pot and sound being both products, one requires proof for its non-eternality as much as the other does. Sound is to be proved non-eternal by the example of a pot, and the pot is to be proved non-eternal by the example of sound. This leads to a reciprocity of the pot (example) and sound (subject), resulting in no definite conclusion as to the eternality or noneternality of sound. This sort of opposition is called "balancing the question," which attempts to bring an argument to a standstill by alleging the reciprocity of the subject and the example.

It is based on the false supposition that the example stands exactly on the same footing as the subject. The example does not in fact stand in need of proof as to its characters, a "pot" being known to all as a product and non-eternal. Hence the opposition is futile.

(9) **Balancing the co-presence.**—If against an argument based on the co-presence of the reason and the predicate, one offers an opposition based on the same kind of co-presence, the opposition, futile as it is, will, on account of the reason being non-distinguished from the predicate, be called "balancing the co-presence."

A certain person, to prove that there is fire in the hill, argues as follows:—

The hill has fire,
because it has smoke
like a kitchen.

A certain other person offers a futile opposition thus :—

The hill has smoke,
because it has fire,
like a kitchen.

The arguer has taken the smoke to be the reason, and the fire to be the predicate. The opponent raises a question as to whether the smoke is present at the same site which is occupied by the fire or is absent from that site. If the smoke is present with fire at the same site, there remains, according to the opponent, no criterion to distinguish the reason from the predicate. The smoke is, in his opinion, as much a reason for the fire as the fire for the smoke. This sort of futile opposition is called "balancing the co-presence," which aims at stopping an argument on the alleged ground of the co-presence of the reason and the predicate.

Seeing that a potter cannot produce a pot without getting clay within his reach, it is affirmed that a thing is accomplished sometimes by the cause being present at its site. "Balancing the co-presence," which attaches an undue importance to the proximity of sites, is therefore a totally futile opposition.

(10) **Balancing the mutual absence.**—If against an argument based on the mutual absence of the reason and the predicate, one offers an opposition based on the same kind of mutual absence, the opposition, futile as it is, will, on account of the reason being non-conducive to the predicate, be called "balancing the mutual absence."

A certain person, to prove that there is fire in the hill, argues as follows :—

The hill has fire,
because it has smoke,
like a kitchen.

A certain other person offers a futile opposition thus :—

The hill has smoke,
because it has fire,
like a kitchen.

The opponent asks: "Is the smoke to be regarded as the reason because it is absent from the site of the fire?" "Such a supposition is indeed absurd." The reason cannot establish the predicate without being connected with it, just as a lamp cannot exhibit a thing which is not within its reach. If a reason unconnected with the predicate could establish the latter, then the fire could be as much the reason for the smoke as the smoke for the fire.

This sort of futile opposition is called "balancing the mutual absence" which aims at bringing an argument to a close on the alleged ground of the mutual absence of the reason and the predicate.

Seeing that an exorcist can destroy persons by administering spells from a distance, it is affirmed that a thing is accomplished sometimes by the cause being absent from its site. "Balancing the mutual absence," which attaches too much importance to remoteness of sites, is therefore a totally futile opposition.

(11) **Balancing the infinite regression.**—If one opposes an argument on the ground of the example not having been established by a series of reasons, the opposition, futile as it is, will be called "balancing the infinite regression"

A certain person, to prove the non-eternality of sound, argues as follows:—

> Sound is non-eternal,
> because it is a product,
> like a pot.

A certain other person offers a futile opposition thus:—

If sound is proved to be non-eternal by the example of a pot, how is the pot again to be proved as non-eternal? The reason which proves the non-eternality of the pot is itself to be established by further reasons. This gives rise to an infinite regression which injures the proposition "sound is non-eternal" not less than the proposition "sound is eternal." This sort of opposition is called "balancing the infinite regression," which aims at stopping an argument by introducing an infinite regression which is said to beset the example.

Now, an example is a thing the characters of which are well known to an ordinary man as well as to an expert. It does not require a series of reasons to reveal its character.

Hence the opposition called "balancing the infinite regression" is not founded on a sound basis.

(12) **Balancing the counter-example.**—If one opposes an argument on the ground of the existence of a mere counter example, the opposition, futile as it is, will be called "balancing the counter-example."

A certain person, to prove the non-eternality of sound, argues as follows:—

> Proposition—Sound is non-eternal.
> Reason—because it is a product.
> Example—like a pot.

A certain other person offers a futile opposition thus:—

> Proposition—Sound is eternal,
> Example—like the ether.

The opponent alleges that if sound is held to be non-eternal by the example of a pot, why it should not be held to be eternal by the example of the ether? If the example of the ether is set aside, let the example of the pot too be set aside. This sort of futile opposition is called "balancing the counter-example," which aims at setting aside an argument by the introduction of a mere counter-example.

A mere counter-example without a reason attending it cannot be conducive to any conclusion. We can rely on an example attended by reason, but not on a counter-example unattended by reason. Hence the opposition which is founded on a mere counter-example is to be rejected as futile.

(13) Balancing the non-produced.—If one opposes an argument on the ground of the property connoted by the reason being absent from the thing denoted by the subject while it is not yet produced, the opposition, futile as it is, will be called "balancing the non-produced."

A certain person, to prove that sound is non-eternal, argues as follows :—

Sound is non eternal,
because it is an effect of effort,
like a pot.

A certain other person offers a futile opposition thus :—

Sound is eternal,
because it is a non-effect-of-effort,
like the sky.

The opponent alleges that the property connoted by the reason, viz. being an effect of effort, is not predicable of the subject, viz. sound (while it is not yet produced). Consequently sound is not non-eternal, it must then be eternal. There is, according to the opponent, an apparent agreement between the two sides as to the sound being eternal on account of its being a non-effect-of-effort. This sort of opposition is called "balancing the non-produced," which pretends to show an equality of the arguments of two sides assuming the thing denoted by the subject to be as yet non-produced.

It is futile because the subject can become such only when it is produced, and that there is, then, no obstacle to the property of the reason being predicated of it. The opposition, viz. "sound (while non-produced) is eternal, because it is not then an effect of effort," carries no weight with it, since we do not take the sound to be the subject before it is produced. Sound, while it is produced, is certainly an effect of effort, and as such is non-eternal.

(14) Balancing the doubt.—If one opposes an argument on the ground of a doubt arising from the homogeneity of the eternal and the non-eternal, consequent on the example and its general notion being equally objects of perception, the opposition, futile as it is, will be called "balancing the doubt."

A certain person, to prove the non-eternality of sound, argues as follows :—

Sound is non-eternal,
because it is a product,
like a pot.

A certain other person offers a futile opposition thus :—

Sound is non-eternal (or eternal),
because it is an object of perception,
like a pot (or potness).

The opponent alleges that sound is homogeneous with a pot as well as potness inasmuch as both are objects of perception; but the pot being non-eternal and potness (the general notion of all pots) being eternal, there arises a doubt as to whether the sound is non-eternal or eternal. This sort of opposition is called "balancing the doubt," which aims at discarding an argument in consequence of a doubt arising from the homogeneity of the eternal and the non-eternal.

It is futile because sound cannot be said to be eternal on the mere ground of its homogeneity with potness, but it must be pronounced to be non-eternal on the ground of its heterogeneity from the same in respect of being a product. Though on the score of homogeneity we may entertain doubt as to whether sound is eternal or non-eternal, we can, however, on the score of heterogeneity pronounce it undoubtedly to be non-eternal. In this case we must bear in mind that we cannot ascertain the true nature of a thing unless we weigh it in respect of its homogeneity with, as well as heterogeneity from, other things. If even then there remains any doubt as to its true nature, that doubt will never end.

(15) **Balancing the point at issue, or the controversial.**—It is an opposition which is supposed to be conducted on the ground of homogeneity with (or heterogeneity from) both sides.

A certain person, to prove the non-eternality of sound, argues as follows:—

Sound is non-eternal,
because it is a product
like a pot.

A certain other person offers a futile opposition thus:—

Sound is eternal,
because it is audible,
like soundness.

The opponent alleges that the proposition, viz. sound is non-eternal, cannot be proved because the reason, viz. audibility which is homogeneous with both sound (which is non-eternal) and soundness (which is eternal), serves only to give rise to suspense for the removal of which it was employed. This sort of opposition is called "balancing the point at issue" which hurts an argument by giving rise to suspense which was to be removed.

It is futile and cannot set aside the main argument because it leads to a point which happens to support one side quite as strongly as it is opposed by the other side.

(16) **Balancing the non-reason.**—It is an opposition which is supposed to be based on the reason being shown to be impossible at all the three times.

A certain person, to prove the non-eternality of sound, argues as follows:—

Sound is non-eternal,
because it is a product,
like a pot.

Here "being a product" is the reason for "being non-eternal," which is the predicate.

(*a*) The reason does not precede the predicate, because the former is called a reason only when it establishes the latter. It is impossible for the reason to be called such before the establishment of the predicate.

(*b*) The reason does not succeed the predicate because a reason would be useless if the predicate could be established without it.

(*c*) The reason and the predicate cannot exist simultaneously. for they will then be reciprocally connected like the right and left horns of a cow. A reason which is dependent on the predicate cannot establish the latter. This sort of opposition is called "balancing the non-reason," which aims at setting aside an argument by showing that the reason is impossible at all the three times.

There is in fact no impossibility for the reason to operate. The knowledge of the knowable and the establishment of that which is to be established, take place from reason, which must precede that which is to be known and established. If the reason is held to be impossible, why then is not the opposition itself, which depends on reason, held to be so ? . In the event of the opposition being impossible, the original argument will hold good.

(17) **Balancing the presumption.**—If one advances an opposition on the basis of a presumption, the opposition, futile as it is, will be called "balancing the presumption."

A certain person, to prove the non-eternality of sound, argues as follows :—

Sound is non-eternal
because it is a product,
like a pot.

A certain other person offers a futile opposition thus :—

Sound is presumed to be eternal,
because it is incorporeal,
like the ether.

The opponent alleges that if sound is non-eternal on account of its homogeneity with non-eternal things (e.g. in respect of its being a product), it may be concluded by presumption that sound is eternal on account of its homogeneity with eternal things (e.g. in respect of its being incorporeal). This sort of opposition is called "balancing the presumption." which aims at stopping an argument by setting presumption as a balance against it.

The opposition is futile because if things unsaid could come by presumption, there would arise a possibility of the opposition itself being hurt on account of the presumption being erratic and conducive to an unexpected conclusion.

Sound is eternal,
because it is incorporeal,
like the ether.

If by presumption we could draw a conclusion unwarranted by the reason, we could from the opposition cited above draw the following conclusion :—

> Sound is presumed to be non-eternal,
> because it is a product,
> like a pot.

This would hurt the opposition itself. In fact the presumption as adduced by the opponent is erratic. If one says that "sound is non-eternal because of its homogeneity with non-eternal things," the presumption that naturally follows is that "sound is eternal because of its homogeneity with eternal things," and *vice versa*. There is no rule that presumption should be made in one case and not in the case opposed to it; and in the event of two mutually opposed presumptions no definite conclusion would follow. Hence the opposition called "balancing the presumption" is untenable.

(18) **Balancing the non-difference.**—If the subject and example are treated as non-different in respect of the possession of a certain property on account of their possessing in common the property connoted by the reason, it follows as a conclusion that all things are mutually non-different in respect of the possession of every property inasmuch as they are all existent: this sort of opposition is called "balancing the non-difference."

A certain person, to prove the non-eternality of sound, argues as follows :—

> Sound is non-eternal,
> because it is a product,
> like a pot.

A certain other person offers a futile opposition thus: If the pot and sound are treated as non-different in respect of non-eternality in consequence of their both being products, it follows as a conclusion that all things are mutually non-different in respect of the possession of every property, inasmuch as all of them are existent. Therefore, there being no difference between the eternal and the non-eternal, sound may be treated as eternal. This sort of opposition is called "balancing the non-difference," which aims at hurting an argument by assuming all things to be mutually non-different.

It is futile because the property possessed in common by the subject and the example, happens in certain instances to abide in the reason, while in other instances, it does not abide in the same.

> Sound is non-eternal,
> because it is a product,
> like a pot.

Here the pot and sound possessing in common the property of being a product, are treated as non-different in respect of the possession of non-eternality. On the same principle if all things are treated as non-different in consequence of their being existent, we should like to know in what respect they are non-different. If they are treated as non-different in respect of non-eternality, then the argument would stand thus :—

All things are non-eternal,
because they are existent,
like (?).

In this argument "all things" being the subject, there is nothing left which may serve as an example. A part of the subject cannot be cited as the example because the example must be a well-established thing, while the subject is a thing which is yet to be established. The argument, for the want of an example, leads to no conclusion. In fact all things are not non-eternal since some at least are eternal. In other words, non-eternality abides in some existent things and does not abide in other existent things. Hence all things are not mutually non-different, and the opposition called "balancing the non-difference" is unreasonable.

(19) **Balancing the demonstration.**—If an opposition is offered by showing that both the demonstrations are justified by reasons, the opposition will be called "balancing the demonstration."

A certain person demonstrates the non-eternality of sound as follows :—

Sound is non-eternal,
because it is a product,
like a pot.

A certain other person offers an opposition by the alleged demonstration of the eternality of sound as follows :—

Sound is eternal,
because it is incorporeal,
like the ether.

The reason in the first demonstration supports the non-eternality of sound, while that in the second demonstration supports the eternality of sound, yet both the demonstrations are alleged to be right. The opponent advanced the second apparent demonstration as a balance against the first to create a dead-lock. This sort of opposition is called "balancing the demonstration."

It is futile because there is an admission of the first demonstration. The opponent having asserted that both the demonstrations are justified by reasons, has admitted the reasonableness of the first demonstration which supports the non-eternality of sound. If to avoid the incompatibility that exists between the two demonstrations, he now denies the reason which supports non-eternality, we would ask why does he not deny the other reason which supports the eternality of sound, for he can avoid incompatibility by denying either of the reasons. Hence the opposition called "balancing the demonstration" is not well founded.

(20) **Balancing the perception.**—If an opposition is offered on the ground that we perceive the character of the subject even

without the intervention of the reason, the opposition, futile as it is, will be called "balancing the perception."

A certain person, to prove the non-eternality of sound, argues as follows:—

Sound is non-eternal,
because it is a product,
like a pot.

A certain other person offers a futile opposition thus:—

Sound can be ascertained to be non-eternal even without the reason that it is a product, for we *perceive* that sound is produced by the branches of trees broken by wind. This sort of opposition is called "balancing the perception," which aims at demolishing an argument by setting up an act of perception as a balance against it.

The opposition is futile, because the character of the subject can be ascertained by other means as well. The argument, viz. "sound is non-eternal, because it is a product, like a pot," implies that sound is proved to be non-eternal through the reason that it is a product. It does not deny other means, such as perception, etc., which also may prove sound to be non-eternal. Hence the opposition called "balancing the perception" does not set aside the main argument.

(21) **Balancing the non-perception.**—If against an argument proving the non-existence of a thing by the non-perception thereof one offers an opposition aiming at proving the contrary by the non-perception of the non-perception, the opposition, futile as it is, will be called "balancing the non-perception."

If the non-perception of a thing proves its non-existence, the non-perception of the non-perception must, in the opinion of the opponent, prove the existence of the thing. This sort of opposition is called "balancing the non-perception," which aims at counteracting an argument by setting up non-perception as a balance against it.

The opposition of this kind is not valid because non-perception is merely the negation of perception. Perception refers to that which is existent, while non-perception to that which is non-existent. The non-perception of non-perception which signifies a mere negation of non-perception cannot be interpreted as referring to an existent thing. Hence opposition called "balancing the non-perception" is not well founded.

There is, moreover, an internal perception of the existence as well as of the non-existence of the various kinds of knowledge. There are internal perceptions of such forms as "I am sure," "I am not sure," "I have doubt," "I have no doubt," etc., which prove that we can perceive the non-existence of knowledge as well as the existence thereof. Hence the non-perception itself is perceptible, and as there is no non-perception of non-perception, the opposition called "balancing the non-perception" falls to the ground.

(22) **Balancing the non-eternal.**— If one finding that things which are homogeneous possess equal characters, opposes an argu-

ment by attributing non-eternality to all things, the opposition, futile as it is, will be called "balancing the non-eternality."

A certain person, to prove the non-eternality of sound, argues as follows:—

Sound is non-eternal,
because it is a product,
like a pot.

A certain other person offers a futile opposition thus: If sound is non-eternal on account of its being homogeneous with a pot which is non-eternal, it will follow as a consequence that all things are non-eternal because they are in some one or other respect homogeneous with the pot—a consequence which will render all inferences impossible for want of heterogeneous examples. This sort of opposition is called "balancing the non-eternal" which seeks to counteract an argument on the alleged ground that all things are non-eternal.

It is futile because nothing can be established from a mere homogeneity. We cannot ascertain the character of a thing from its mere homogeneity with another thing: in doing so we must consider the logical connection between the reason and the predicate. Sound, for instance, is non-eternal not merely because it is homogeneous with a non-eternal pot but because there is a connection between "being a product" and "being non-eternal." Hence it will be unreasonable to conclude that all things are non-eternal simply because they are homogeneous with a non-eternal pot in one or another respect. Similarly a mere homogeneity of all things with the eternal ether in one or another respect, does not prove all things to be eternal. The opposition called "balancing the non-eternal" is therefore not founded on a sound basis.

(23) **Balancing the eternal.**—If one opposes an argument by attributing eternality to all non-eternal things on the ground of these being eternally non-eternal, the opposition, futile as it is, will be called "balancing the eternal."

A certain person, to prove the non-eternality of sound, argues as follows:—

Sound is non-eternal,
because it is a product,
like a pot.

A certain other person offers a futile opposition thus:—

You say that sound is non-eternal. Does this non-eternality exist in sound always or only sometimes? If the non-eternality exists *always*, the sound must also be always existent, or in other words, sound is eternal. If the non-eternality exists only *sometimes*, then too the sound must in the absence of non-eternality be pronounced to be eternal. This sort of opposition is called "balancing the eternal," which pretends to counteract an argument by setting up eternality as a balance against it.

The opposition is baseless because the thing opposed is always non-eternal on account of the eternality of the non-eternal. By speaking of eternality of the non-eternal you have admitted sound to be *always* non-eternal, and cannot now deny its non-eternality. The eternal and non-eternal are incompatible with each other: by admitting that sound is non-eternal you are precluded from asserting that it is also eternal. Hence "balancing the eternal" is not a sound opposition.

(24) **Balancing the effect.**—If one opposes an argument by showing the diversity of the effects of effort, the opposition, futile as it is, will be called "balancing the effect."

A certain person, to prove the non-eternality of sound, argues as follows :—

> Sound is non-eternal,
> because it is an effect of effort.

A certain other person offers a futile opposition thus :—

The effect of effort is found to be of two kinds, viz. (1) the production of something which was previously non-existent, e.g. a pot, and (2) the revelation of something already existent, e.g. water in a well. Is sound an effect of the first kind or of the second kind? If sound is an effect of the first kind it will be non-eternal, but if it is of the second kind it will be eternal. Owing to this diversity of the effects of effort, it is not possible to conclude that sound is non-eternal. This sort of opposition is called "balancing the effect."

It is futile because in the case of sound effort does not give rise to the second kind of effect. We cannot say that sound is revealed by our effort because we are unable to prove that it existed already. That sound did not exist previously is proved by our non-perception of the same at the time. You cannot say that our non-perception was caused by a veil because no veil covered sound. Hence sound is an effect which is not revealed but produced.

If an argument is to be set aside owing to an ambiguous meaning of the word "effect," why is not the opposition too set aside on the same ground? The reason in the argument is as erratic as that in the opposition. Just as there is no special ground to suppose that the "effect" in the argument signified "a thing produced and not revealed," so also there is no special ground to suppose that the word in the opposition signified "a thing revealed and not produced." Hence the opposition called "balancing the effect" is self-destructive.

Application of the Analogues.

In showing the futility of analogues we may test them in the light of the following principles :—

(i) If a special meaning is to be attached to a word in the opposition, the *same meaning* will have to be attached to the word in the original argument, e g the word "effect" should be used in one and the same sense by a disputant and his opponent.

(ii) Defect attaches to the *opposition of the opposition* just as it attaches to the opposition itself.

A certain person, to prove the non-eternality of sound, argues as follows:—

Sound is non-eternal,
because it is an effect of effort.
[Here "effect" signifies "a thing produced"].

A certain other person, seeing that the effect is of diverse kinds, offers an opposition thus:—

Sound is eternal,
because it is an effect of effort.
[Here "effect" signifies "a thing revealed"].

The arguer replies that sound cannot be concluded to be eternal because the reason "effect" is erratic (which may mean "a thing produced"). The opponent rises again to say that sound cannot also be concluded to be non-eternal because the reason "effect" is erratic (which may mean "a thing revealed"). So the defect which is pointed out in the case of the opposition, may also be pointed out in the case of the opposition of the opposition.

(iii) If one admits the defect of his opposition in consequence of his statement that an equal defect attaches to the opposition of the opposition, it will be called "*admission of an opinion*" (*matānujñā*).

A certain person lays down a proposition which is opposed by a certain other person. The first person, viz. the disputant, charges the opposition made by the second person, viz. the opponent, with a defect, e.g. that the reason is erratic. The opponent instead of rescuing his opposition from the defect with which it has been charged by the disputant, goes on charging the disputant's opposition of the opposition with the same defect. The counter-charge which the opponent brings in this way is interpreted by the disputant to be an admission of the defect pointed out by him. The disputant's reply consisting of this kind of interpretation is called "admission of an opinion."

(iv) "Admission of an opinion" also occurs when the disputant, instead of employing reasons to rescue his side from the defect with which it has been charged, proceeds to admit the defect in consequence of his statement that the *same defect* belongs to his opponent's side as well.

By overlooking the four principles stated here a person may entangle himself in a six-winged disputation.

Six-winged Disputation (*ṣaṭpakṣī kathā*).

The first wing. A certain disputant, to prove the non-eternality of sound, says:—

Sound is non-eternal,
because it is an effect of effort.

[The disputant evidently took the word "effect" in the sense of "a thing produced," but he did not make his meaning clear].

The second wing. An opponent, seeing that the word "effect" is ambiguous, offers an opposition thus:—

Sound is eternal,
because it is an effect of effort.

Here the opponent evidently took the word "effect" in the sense of "a thing revealed."

The third wing.

The disputant, seeing that the reason "effect" is erratic, charges the opposition with a defect thus:—

Sound is *not* eternal,
because it is an effect of effort.

He means that sound cannot be inferred to be eternal from its being an effect, because "effect," which is the reason here, admits of two different meanings, viz. (1) a thing [that did not previously exist but is now] produced, and (2) a thing [that already existed and is now] revealed. The reason being erratic the conclusion is uncertain.

The fourth wing.

The opponent finding that the reason "effect," which is erratic, proves neither the eternality nor the non-eternality of sound, brings a counter-charge against the disputant thus:—

Sound is also *not* non-eternal,
because it is an effect of effort.

He alleges that the defect (viz. the erraticity of the reason) with which his opposition (viz. sound is eternal) is charged, also attaches to the opposition of the opposition made by the disputant (viz. sound is *not* eternal, that is, is non-eternal).

The fifth wing.

The disputant finding that the counter-charge brought against him amounts to his opponent's admission of self-defect says:—

The opponent by saying that "sound is also not non-eternal" has (by the force of the word "also") admitted that it is also not eternal. In other words the counter-charge has proved the charge, that is, it has indicated that the opponent admits the disputant's opinion.

The sixth wing.

The opponent finding that the disputant instead of rescuing his argument from the counter-charge has taken shelter under his opponent's admission of the charge says:—

The disputant by saying that "sound is also not eternal" has (by the force of the word "also") admitted that it is also not non-eternal. In other words, if the counter-charge proves the charge, the reply to the counter-charge proves the counter-charge itself.

The first, third and fifth wings belong to the disputant while the second, fourth and sixth to the opponent. The sixth wing is a repetition of the fourth while the fifth wing is a repetition of the third. The sixth wing is also a repetition of the meaning of the fifth wing. The third and fourth wings involve the defect of "admission of an opinion." All the wings except the first three are unessential.

The disputation would have come to a fair close at the third wing if the disputant or the opponent had pointed out that the word "effect" had a special meaning, viz. "a thing produced" or "a thing revealed," or if they had agreed that the word "effect" being ambiguous no conclusion could be drawn. Instead of stopping at the proper limit they have obstinately carried on their disputation which is found after all to be totally futile.[1]

34. Varieties of the Points of Defeat.

The points of defeat, also called clinchers, occasions for rebuke or places of humiliation, are the following:—

(1) Hurting the proposition (*pratijñā-hāni*), (2) shifting the proposition (*pratijñāntara*), (3) opposing the proposition (*pratijñā-virodha*), (4) renouncing the proposition (*pratijñā-sannyāsa*), (5) shifting the reason (*hetvantara*), (6) shifting the topic (*arthāntara*), (7) the meaningless (*nirarthaka*), (8) the unintelligible (*avijñātārtha*), (9) the incoherent (*apārthaka*), (10) the inopportune (*aprāpta-kāla*), (11) saying too little (*nyūna*), (12) saying too much (*adhika*), (13) repetition (*punarukta*), (14) silence (*ananubhāsaṇa*), (15) ignorance (*ajñāna*), (16) non-ingenuity (*apratibhā*), (17) evasion (*vikṣepa*), (18) admission of an opinion (*matānujñā*), (19) overlooking the censurable (*paryanuyojyopekṣaṇa*), (20) censuring the non-censurable (*niranuyojyānuyoga*), (21) deviating from a tenet (*apasiddhānta*), and (22) the semblance of a reason (*hetvābhāsa*).

"A point of defeat," which is the same as "a clincher," "an occasion for rebuke," "a place of humiliation" or "a point of disgrace." arises generally from a misemployment of the proposition or any other part of an argument and may implicate any disputant whether he is a discutieut, wrangler or caviller.

(1) **Hurting the proposition** occurs when one admits in one's own example the character of a counter-example.

A disputant argues as follows:—

> Sound is non-eternal,
> because it is cognisable by sense,
> whatever is cognisable by sense is non-eternal as a pot,
> sound is so (cognisable by sense),
> therefore sound is non-eternal.

---

[1] *Vide* Nyāya-sūtra, 5-1-43.

Jayanta observes:—

षट्पक्ष्यामुभयोरशक्तिः ।
वाच्यमुत्तरमतो निरवद्यं जातिवादिनमपि प्रति तज्ज्ञैः ।
कल्पनोत्तरगिरा न तु कार्या पक्षषट्क परिकल्पनगोष्ठी ।

(Nyāya-mañjarī, chap. 12, p. 637, Vizianagaram Sanskrit series).

An opponent counter-argues thus :—

A genus (e.g. potness or pot-type), which is cognisable by sense, is found to be eternal: why cannot then the sound which is also cognisable by sense be eternal ?

The disputant being thus opposed says :—

Whatever is cognisable by sense is eternal as a pot,
sound is cognisable by sense,
therefore sound is eternal.

By thus admitting in his example (the pot) the character (the eternality) of a counter-example (the genus or type), that is, by admitting that a pot is eternal, he hurts his own proposition (viz. sound is non-eternal). A person who hurts his proposition in this way deserves nothing but rebuke.

(2) **Shifting the proposition** arises when a proposition being opposed one defends it, by importing a new character to his example and counter-example.

A certain person argues as follows :—

Sound is non-eternal,
because it is cognisable by sense,
like a pot.

A certain other person offers an opposition thus :—

Sound is eternal,
because it is cognisable by sense,
like a genus (or type).

The first person in order to defend himself says that a genus (or type) and a pot are both cognisable by sense, yet one in all-pervasive and the other is not so: hence the sound which is likened to a pot is non-all-pervasive.

The defence thus made involves a change of proposition. The proposition originally laid down was :—

Sound is non-eternal.

The proposition now defended is :—

Sound is non-all-pervasive.

A person who shifts his proposition in this way is to be rebuked inasmuch as he does not rely upon his original reason and example.

(3) **Opposing the proposition** occurs when the proposition and its reason are opposed to each other.

Substance is distinct from quality,
because it is perceived to be non-distinct from colour, etc.

In this argument it is to be observed that if substance is distinct from quality, it must also be distinct from colour, etc., which constitute the quality. The reason, viz. substance is non-distinct from colour, etc., is opposed to the proposition, viz. substance is distinct from quality. A person who thus employs a reason. which opposes his proposition. is to be rebuked as a fool.

(4) **Renouncing the proposition.**—If one disclaims a proposition when it is opposed, it will be called "renouncing the proposition."

A certain person argues as follows:—

Sound is non-eternal,
because it is cognisable by sense.

A certain other person offers an opposition thus: Just as a genus (or type) is cognisable by sense and is not yet non-eternal, so sound is cognisable by sense and is not yet non-eternal.

The first person, as a defence against the opposition, disclaims his proposition thus:—

Who says that sound is non-eternal?

This sort of denial of one's own proposition is called "renouncing the proposition" which rightly furnishes an occasion for rebuke.

(5) **Shifting the reason** occurs when the reason of a general character being opposed, one attaches a special character to it.

A certain person, to prove the non-eternality of sound, argues as follows:—

Sound is non-eternal,
because it is cognisable by sense.

A certain other person says that sound cannot be proved to be non-eternal through the mere reason of its being cognisable by sense, just as a genus (or type) such as potness (or pot-type) is cognisable by sense and is not yet non-eternal

The first person defends himself by saying that the reason, viz. being cognisable by sense, is to be understood as signifying that which comes under a genus (or type) and is as such cognisable by sense. Sound comes under the genus (or type) "soundness" and is at the same time cognisable by sense; but a genus or type such as pot-ness or pot-type does not come under another genus or type such as pot-ness-ness or pot-type-type though it is cognisable by sense. Such a defence, which consists in shifting one's reason, rightly furnishes an occasion for rebuke.

(6) **Shifting the topic** is an argument which setting aside the real topic introduces one which is irrelevant.

A certain person, to prove the eternality of sound, argues as follows:—

Sound is eternal (proposition),
because it is intangible (reason).

Being opposed by a certain other person he attempts, in the absence of any other resource, to defend his position as follows:—

Hetu which is the Sanskrit equivalent for "reason" is a word derived from the root "hi" with the suffix "tu." A word, as a part of a speech, may be a noun, a verb, or an indeclinable. A noun is defined as, etc., etc. The defence made in this way furnishes an instance of defeat through non-relevancy. The person who makes it deserves rebuke.

(7) **The meaningless** is an argument which is based on a nonsensical combination of letters in a series.

A certain person, to prove the eternality of sound, argues as follows:—

Sound is eternal,
because k, c, ṭ, t and p are j, v, g. ḍ and d.
like jh, bh, gh, ḍh and dh.

As the letters k, c, ṭ, etc., convey no meaning, the person who employs them in his argument deserves rebuke.

(8) **The unintelligible** is an argument, which although repeated three times, is understood neither by the audience nor by the opponent.

A certain person being opposed by another person and finding no means of self-defence, attempts to hide his inability in disputation by using words of double *entendre* or words not in ordinary use or words very quickly uttered which as such are understood neither by his opponent nor by the audience although they are repeated three times. This sort of defence is called "the unintelligible" which rightly furnishes an occasion for rebuke.

(9) **The incoherent** is an argument which conveys no connected meaning on account of the words being strung together without any syntactical order.

A certain person being opposed by another person and finding no other means of self-defences argues as follows:—

Ten pomegranates, six cakes, a bowl, goat's skin and a lump of sweets.

This sort of argument, which consists of a series of unconnected words, is called "the incoherent," which rightly presents an occasion for rebuke.

(10) **The inopportune** is an argument, the parts of which are mentioned without any order of precedence.

A certain person, to prove that the hill has fire, argues as follows:—

The hill has fire (proposition),
whatever has smoke has fire, as a kitchen (example),
because it has smoke (reason),
the hill has fire (conclusion),
the hill has smoke (application).

This sort of argument is called "the inopportune," which rightly presents an occasion for rebuke. Since the meaning of an argument is affected by the order in which its parts are arranged, the person who overlooks the order cannot establish his conclusion and is therefore rebuked.

(11) **Saying too little.**—If an argument lacks even one of its parts, it is called "saying too little."

The following is an argument which contains all its five parts :—

(1) The hill has fire (proposition).
(2) Because it has smoke (reason).
(3) All that has smoke has fire, as a kitchen (example).
(4) The hill has smoke (application).
(5) Therefore the hill has fire (conclusion).

As all the five parts or members are essential, a person who omits even one of them should be scolded as "saying too little."

(12) **Saying too much** is an argument which consists of more than one reason or example.

A certain person, to prove that the hill has fire, argues as follows :—

The hill has fire (proposition).
Because it has smoke (reason).
And because it has light (reason).
Like a kitchen (example).
And like a furnace (example).

In this argument the second reason and the second example are redundant.

A person, who having promised to argue in the proper way (according to the established usage), employs more than one reason or example is to be rebuked as "saying too much."

(13) **Repetition** is an argument in which (except in the case of reinculcation) the word or the meaning is said over again.

Repetition of the word—Sound is non-eternal,
Sound is non-eternal.

Repetition of the meaning—Sound is non-eternal, echo is perishable, what is heard is impermanent, etc.

There is a difference between "repetition" and "re-inculcation" inasmuch as the latter serves some useful purpose

In re-inculcation a special meaning is deduced from the word reinculcated, e.g.

The hill has fire (proposition).
Because it has smoke (reason).
All that has smoke has fire, as a kitchen (example).
The hill has smoke (application).
Therefore the hill has fire (conclusion).

In this argument the "conclusion" is a re-inculcation of the "proposition" serving a special purpose (viz. in showing the fifth member of the syllogism).

Repetition consists also in mentioning a thing by name although the thing has been indicated through presumption, e.g.

"A thing which is not non-eternal does not possess the character of a product"—this is a mere repetition of the following:—

"A thing possessing the character of a product is non-eternal."

(14) **Silence** is an occasion for rebuke which arises when the opponent makes no reply to a proposition although it has been repeated three times by the disputant within the knowledge of the audience.

How can a disputant carry on his argument if his opponent maintains an attitude of stolid silence? The opponent who takes up such an attitude is to be rebuked.

(15) **Ignorance** is the non-understanding of a proposition.

Ignorance is betrayed by the opponent who does not understand a proposition although it has been repeated three times within the knowledge of the audience. How can an opponent refute a proposition the meaning of which he cannot understand. He is to be rebuked for his ignorance.

(16) **Non-ingenuity** consists in one's inability to hit upon a reply.

A certain person lays down a proposition. If his opponent understands it and yet cannot hit upon a reply, he is to be scolded as wanting in ingenuity.

(17) **Evasion** arises if one stops an argument in the pretext of going away to attend another business.

A certain person having commenced a disputation in which he finds it impossible to establish his side, stops its further progress by saying that he has to go away on a very urgent business. He who stops the disputation in this way courts defeat and humiliation through evasion.

(18) **The admission of an opinion** consists in charging the opposite side with a defect by admitting that the same defect exists on one's own side

A certain person addressing another person says: "You are a thief."

This person, instead of removing the charge brought against him, throws the same charge on the opposite side whereby he admits that the charge against himself is true. This sort of counter-charge or reply is an instance of the "admission of an opinion" which brings disgrace on the person who makes it.

(19) **Overlooking the censurable** consists in not rebuking a person who deserves rebuke.

It is not at all unfair to censure a person who argues in a way which furnishes an occasion for censure. Seeing that the person himself does not confess his shortcoming, it is the duty of the audience to pass a vote of censure on him. If the audience failed to do their duty they would earn rebuke for themselves on account of their "overlooking the censurable."

(20) **Censuring the non-censurable** consists in rebuking a person who does not deserve rebuke.

A person brings discredit on himself if he rebukes a person who does not deserve rebuke.

(21) **Deviating from a tenet.**—A person who after accepting a tenet departs from it in the course of his disputation, is guilty of "deviating from a tenet."

A certain person promises to carry on his argument in consonance with the Sāṁkhya philosophy which lays down that (1) what is existent never becomes non-existent, and (2) what is non-existent never comes into existence, etc. A certain other person opposes him by saying that all human activity would be impossible if the thing now non-existent could not come into existence in the course of time, and that no activity would cease if what is existent now could continue for ever. If the first person being thus opposed admits that existence springs from non-existence and non-existence from existence, then he will rightly deserve rebuke for his deviation from the accepted tenet.

(22) **The fallacies of reason** also furnish points of defeat or occasions for rebuke.

Fallacies are mere semblances of reason. A person who employs them in a disputation certainly deserves rebuke.

There are infinite points of defeat or occasions for rebuke, of which only twenty-two have been enumerated here.

35. Categories: their Examination (*parīkṣā*).

A critical examination should be made of each case where there is room for doubt. In case of well-known facts admitted by all, examination is unnecessary. A critical examination of some of the categories is given below:—

(1) The Means of Right Knowledge (*pramāṇa*).

The means.

The means of right knowledge are said to be invalid.

Some[1] say that perception and other so-called *means of right knowledge* are invalid as they are impossible at all the three times. Perception is impossible at the present, past and future times inasmuch as it can neither be prior to, nor posterior to, nor simultaneous with, the objects of sense. If perception occurred anteriorly it could not have arisen from the contact

[1] The sūtras from 2-1-8 to 2-1-19 of the Nyāya-sūtra contain a critical examination of *pramāṇa* (the means of right knowledge).

of a sense with its object. With reference to the perception of colour, for instance, it is asked whether the colour preceded perception or the perception preceded colour. If one says that perception occurred anteriorly or preceded the colour, one must give up one's definition of perception. viz. that perception arises from the contact of a sense with its object. If perception is supposed to occur posteriorly, it cannot be maintained that objects of sense are established by perception. Colour, for instance, is an object which is said to be established by visual perception. But this conclusion will have to be abandoned if perception is supposed to occur posteriorly to the object. If perception were simultaneous with its object, there would not be any order of succession in our cognitions as there is no such order in their corresponding objects. Various objects of sense can exist at one time, e.g. colour and smell exist in a flower at the same time. If we hold that perception is simultaneous with its object, we must admit that the colour and the smell can be perceived at the same time, that is, our perception of colour must be admitted to be simultaneous with our perception of smell. This is absurd because two acts of perception, nay, two cognitions cannot take place at the same time. As there is an order of succession in our cognitions, perception cannot be simultaneous with its object. Perception and other so-called means of right knowledge are therefore not only invalid but also impossible. Moreover, if an object of knowledge is to be established by a means of knowledge, this latter needs also to be established by another means of knowledge. Just as a balance is an instrument when it weighs a thing, but is an object when it is itself weighed in another balance, so a means of knowledge is an instrument when it establishes an object, but is an object when it is itself to be established. Finally if a means of knowledge does not require another means of knowledge for its establishment, let an object of knowledge be also established without any means of knowledge.

Validity of the means of right knowledge established.

In reply it is stated that if perception and other means of right knowledge are impossible, then the denial of them is also impossible, for owing to absence of the matter to be denied the denial itself will be inoperative. If there is no means of knowledge to establish any thing, how is the denial itself to be established? If on the other hand the denial is held to be based on a certain means of knowledge, we are thereby to acknowledge the validity of that means. When we deny a thing on the ground of its not being perceived, we acknowledge by implication that perception is a means of right knowledge. Similarly inference, etc., are also means of knowledge. There is no fixed rule that the means of knowledge should precede the objects of knowledge or should succeed them or be simultaneous with them. They resemble sometimes a drum which precedes its sound, sometimes an illumination which succeeds the sun, and another time a smoke which is synchronous with the fire. The means of knowledge are self-established like the illumination of a lamp. Just as a lamp illumines itself and other objects, so the means of knowledge establish themselves and the objects of knowledge. Though a lamp which illumines other objects is itself illumined by our eye, we cannot deny a general notion of illuminator as distinguished from that of the objects illuminated. Similarly we must admit a general notion of the means of knowledge as distinguished from that of the objects of knowledge. The means of knowledge are therefore neither invalid nor impossible.

Perception.

The definition of perception is said to be defective.

Some say that the definition of perception as given before is defective, as it does not notice the conjunction of soul with mind and of mind with sense, which are also causes of perception. From the contact of a sense with its object no knowledge arises unless, it is said, there is also conjunction of soul with mind. A sense coming in contact with its object produces knowledge in our soul only if the sense is conjoined with the mind. Hence the conjunction of soul with mind should be mentioned as a necessary element in the definition of perception. Moreover the contact of a sense with its object is sometimes not found to be the cause of perception, e.g. a person listening to a song does not see colour though it comes in contact with his eye.

The definition of perception defended.

In reply it is stated that if the conjunction of soul with mind is to be mentioned as a necessary element in the definition of perception, then direction ("dik"), space ("deśa"), time ("kāla") and ether ("ākāśa") should also be enumerated among the causes of perception. But such an enumeration is held on all hands to be undesirable. The soul, we point out, has not been excluded from our definition of perception inasmuch as knowledge is a mark of the soul. Perception has been described as knowledge, and knowledge implies the soul which is its abode. Consequently in speaking of knowledge the soul has, by implication, been mentioned as a condition in the production of perception. The mind too has not been omitted from our definition inasmuch as we have spoken of the non-simultaneity of acts of knowledge. Perception has been defined as knowledge. An essential character of knowledge is that more than one act of knowing cannot take place at a time. This characteristic is due to the mind, an atomic substance, which is conjoined with the sense, when knowledge is produced. Hence in speaking of knowledge we have by implication mentioned the mind as a condition of perception. The contact of a sense with its object is mentioned as the special cause of perception. There are many kinds of knowledge, such as perception, recollection, etc. Conjunction of soul with mind is a cause which operates in the production of all kinds of knowledge, while the contact of a sense with its object is the cause which operates only in perception. In our definition of perception we have mentioned only the special cause, and have omitted the common causes which precede not only perception, but also other kinds of knowledge. By saying that perception is knowledge which arises from the contact of a sense with its object, we have distinguished five special kinds of knowledge, viz. (1) the visual perception also called eye-knowledge or colour-knowledge, (2) the auditory perception also called ear-knowledge or sound-knowledge, (3) the olfactory perception also called nose-knowledge or smell-knowledge. (4) the gustatory perception also called tongue-knowledge or taste-knowledge, and (5) the tactual perception also called skin-knowledge or touch-knowledge. It is admitted that a person while listening to a song may not see colour though the latter comes in contact with his eye. Yet the instance does not prove that the contact of a sense with its object, is not the cause of perception, for it is to be understood that his intent listening prevents him from seeing the colour. In other words, the auditory perception supersedes the visual perception, because the song is more attractive than the colour.

Is Perception a mere inference?

Perception, some say, is inference because it apprehends a thing by grasping only a part of the same. We are said to perceive a tree while we really perceive only a part of it. This knowledge of the tree, as a whole, derived from the knowledge of a part of it, is said to be a mere inference.

In reply it is stated that perception is not inference for even the objectors admit that at least a part of the tree is actually perceived. Hence perception as a means of knowledge is not altogether denied, on the contrary it is accepted as different from inference.

Inference

Is inference a means of right knowledge?

Inference, some say, is not a means of right knowledge, as it errs in certain cases. For instance, if we see a river swollen we infer that there has been rain, if we see ants carrying off their eggs, we infer that there will be rain, and if we hear a peacock scream, we infer that clouds are gathering. These inferences are said to be not necessarily correct, for a river may be swollen because of its being embanked, the ants may carry off their eggs because their nests have been damaged, and the supposed screaming of a peacock may be nothing but the voice of a man.

Inference, we reply, is really a means of right knowledge, as the errors alleged to be involved in it may be explained away. The swelling of a river caused by rain is different from that which results from the embankment of a part of it; the former is attended by a great rapidity of currents, an abundance of foam, a mass of fruits, leaves, wood, etc. The manner in which ants carry off their eggs just before rain is quite different from the manner in which they do so when their nests are damaged. The ants run away quickly in a steady line when rain is imminent, but fear makes them fly in disorder when their nests are damaged. The screaming of a peacock which suggests gathering clouds is quite different from a man's imitation of it, for the latter is not natural. If in such cases any wrong inference is drawn, the fault is in the person, not in the process.

Comparison.

Is comparison a means of right knowledge?

Comparison, some say, is not a means of right knowledge, as the knowledge of a thing cannot be established through its similarity to another thing, no matter whether the similarity is complete, considerable or partial. On the ground of complete similarity we never say "a cow is like a cow"; on the ground of considerable similarity we do not say "a buffalo is like a cow"; and on the ground of partial similarity we do not say "a mustard seed is like Mount Meru." Hence comparison is regarded by some as not a means of right knowledge, for it has no precise standard.

This objection does not, we maintain, carry any weight, for comparison is established through similarity in a high degree. The similarity in a high degree exists between such well-known objects as a cow and a *bos gavaeus*, etc.

Is comparison a mere perception?

Some hold that comparison is not a separate means of knowledge, for when one notices the likeness of a cow in a strange animal, one really performs an act of perception. In reply it is urged that we cannot deny comparison as a separate means of knowledge, for how otherwise does the name *bos gavaeus* convey the general notion of the animal called *bos gavaeus*? That the name *bos gavaeus* signifies one and all members of the *bos gavaeus* class is not a result of perception, but the consequence of a distinct knowledge called comparison.

Is comparison a mere inference?

Comparison, some say, is not different from inference, for both seek to establish the unperceived by means of the perceived. We recognize a *bos gavaeus* at first sight through its special similarity to a cow which we have often perceived. This knowledge of a previously unperceived object derived through its similarity to a perceived object is said to be nothing but inference.

In reply we maintain that it is not in a bos gavaeus *unperceived* that we find the real matter of comparison. The matter of comparison is similarity, e.g. between a cow and a *bos gavaeus*. The bos gavaeus in which we notice the similarity is first perceived, that is, on perceiving a bos gavaeus we notice its similarity to a cow. Hence comparison supplies us with knowledge of a *perceived* thing through its similarity to another thing also *perceived*. This characteristic distinguishes it from inference which furnishes us with knowledge of an *unperceived* thing through that of a thing *perceived*. Comparison is not identical with inference because the former is established through the compendious expression "so." "As is a cow, *so* is a *bos gavaeus*—": this is an instance of comparison. This use of 'so' makes it clear that comparison is a distinct means of right knowledge.

Verbal testimony.

Is "word" or verbal testimony a mere inference?

Verbal testimony, some say, is inference because the object indicated by it is not perceived but inferred. Inference gives us the knowledge of an unperceived object through that of an object which is perceived. Verbal testimony too enables us to acquire the knowledge of an unperceived object through that of a word which is perceived (heard). In inference as well as in verbal testimony we pass to an unperceived object through an object which is perceived. Just as in inference there is a certain connection between a sign (e.g. smoke), and the thing signified by it (e.g. fire), so in verbal testimony there is connection between a word and the object signified by it. Verbal testimony does not therefore differ from inference.

In reply we say that there is a great difference between inference and verbal testimony. The knowledge gained by verbal testimony is correct, not simply because it comes through the medium of words, but because it comes through words spoken by a reliable person. There are, it is said, paradise, nymphs, *uttarakurus*, seven islands, ocean, human settlements, etc. We accept them as realities not simply because they are known through words, but because they are spoken of by persons who are reliable. Hence verbal testimony is not inference. The two agree in conveying knowledge of an object through its sign, but the sign in one is different from the sign in the other. In the case of verbal testimony the special point is to decide whether the sign (word) comes from a reliable person. Moreover the connection between a word and the object signified by it is conventional and not a natural one We acknowledge that a word indicates a certain object, but we deny that the object is naturally or necessarily connected with the word. Hearing, for instance, the word "cow," we think of the animal signified by it, nevertheless the word and the animal are not connected with each other by nature or necessity. In the case of inference, however, the connection between a sign (e.g. smoke), and the thing signified (e.g. fire), is natural and necessary. The connection involved in inference is not, therefore, of the same kind as that involved in verbal testimony. In the case of verbal testimony there is no perception of the connection. The connection between a sign and the thing signified, which is the basis of inference, is obvious to perception. For instance, the inference that "the hill is fiery because it is smoky" is based on a certain connection between smoke and fire, which is actually perceived in a kitchen or elsewhere. The connection between a word and the object signified by it, which is the basis of verbal testimony, is not obvious to perception. The word *uttarakuru*, for instance, signifies the country of that name, but the connection between the word and the country is not perceived, as the latter lies beyond our observation. Hence verbal testimony is not inference.

Are there any other means of right knowledge?

Some say that the means of right knowledge are more than four because there are such other means of right knowledge as *rumour* ("aitihya"), *presumption* ("arthāpatti"), probability ("sambhava") and *non-existence* ("abhāva").

In reply we say that the means of right knowledge are really four, inasmuch as *rumour* is included in verbal testimony, and *presumption*, *probability* and *non-existence* are included in inference.

Other means.

Rumour.

Rumour is an assertion which has come from one to another without any indication of the source from which it first originated, e.g. on this tree there live goblins

It is not a separate means of knowledge, but partakes of the general characteristics of verbal testimony and is a special kind of it.

Presumption.

Presumption is the deduction of one thing from the declaration of another thing, e.g. from the declaration that 'unless there is cloud there is no rain,' we deduce that 'if there is rain there must have been cloud.'

Some say that presumption is not valid as it leads to uncertainty. "If there is no cloud there will be no rain"—from this we are said to presume that if there is a cloud there will be rain. But it often happens that a cloud is not followed by rain. So presumption does, according to the objectors, lead to uncertainty. In reply we say, that if there is uncertainty it is due to the objectors supposing that to be a presumption which is not really so. "If there is no cloud there will be no rain." From this we are entitled to presume that if there is rain there must have been cloud. But if one pretends to presume that "if there is a cloud there will be rain," one's so-called presumption will be an invalid one.

Presumption is thus found to be the knowledge of a thing derived through the consideration of it from the opposite standpoint. It does not differ from inference since both pass from a perceived thing to an unperceived one through a certain connection.

Probability.

Probability consists in cognising the existence of a thing from that of another thing in which it is included, e.g. knowledge of the measure of an *ādhaka* from that of a *droṇa* of which it is a fourth part.

Probability is inference because it is the cognizance of a part from that of a whole with which it is inseparably connected.

Non-existence or negation.

Of two opposite things, the *non-existence* of one establishes the existence of the other, e.g. the non-existence of rain indicates the existence of an obstruction [1] of the cloud which was to have brought it down.

Some say that non-existence is not a means of right knowledge, as there is no object which is known by it. Though a mark may distinguish the object which is marked, the non-existence (absence) of the mark cannot, it is said, distinguish the object which is not marked. A blue pot is distinguished by the blueness which is its mark. But how can we distinguish an unmarked object by the non-existence (absence) of the mark which it does not possess?

In reply we say that non-existence serves to mark out an object unmarked by the mark which characterises other objects. Suppose a person wants to bring a pot which is not blue. The absence of blueness is a mark which will enable him to mark out the particular pot he wants to bring, and to exclude the other pots which are blue. Thus an object may be known through the non-existence (absence) of its mark. If you say that the non-existence (absence) of a mark is impossible where there was no mark at all, it is, we reply, not so, because the non-existence (absence) is possible in reference to a mark elsewhere. We can, says an objector, talk of a mark being non-existent (absent) if it was previously existent (present). A pot is said to be not blue only in reference to its having been blue previously. In reply

[1] When there is an obstruction of cloud by wind, drops of water cannot fall in spite of their weight.

we say that it is not so. "Not blue" is no doubt possible only in reference to "blue." but that blueness may exist elsewhere. For instance, we can talk of this pot being not blue in contrast to that pot which is blue. Moreover, we perceive non-existence as a mark antecedent to the production of a thing. When we say that there will be a jar, we perceive the mark of non-existence of the jar in the halves (parts) which are destined to compose it.

Non-existence or negation is not however a separate means of knowledge It is included in inference. It infers one thing from the absence of another thing through the mutual connection of the two things, as follows: If a particular thing existed, it would have been seen; it is not seen: therefore it does not exist.

In the Nyāya-sūtra. 2-2-12, non-existence or negation (*abhāva*) is divided into two kinds[1] viz. (1) *prāgabhāva*, prior non-existence, that is, the non-existence of a thing before it is brought into existence, and (2) *pradhvaṁsābhāva*. posterior non-existence or destruction, that is, the disappearance of a thing after it has come into existence.

(2) The Objects of Right Knowledge (*prameya*).

The Soul.

The soul is different from the senses.

A sense is not *soul* because we can apprehend an object through both sight and touch. "Previously I saw the jar and now I touch it": such recognition will be impossible if "I" is not different from the eye which cannot touch and from the skin which cannot see. In other words, the "I" or soul is distinct from the senses.

Some say that the soul is not different from the senses. as there is a fixed relation between a sense and its object. Colour, for instance, is an exclusive object of the eye, sound of the ear, smell of the nose, and so on. It is the eye that apprehends colour. and there is no necessity for assuming a soul distinct from the eye for the purpose of explaining the apprehension of colour. In reply we say that the soul is certainly distinct from the senses. There is, no doubt, a fixed relation between a sense and its object, and in virtue of such relation the sense cannot apprehend more than one object; but the "I" can apprehend many objects, that is, the "I" can see colour, hear sound, and so on. Hence the "I" or soul, which confers unity on the various kinds of apprehension, is different from the senses each of which can apprehend only one object.

---

[1] In the Nyāya-vārtika-tātparya-ṭīkā, 2-2-9, negation (*abhāva*) is divided into (1) negation of identity (*tādātmyābhāva*), and (2) negation of correlation (*saṁsargābhāva*): and the latter is subdivided into (*a*) prior negation (*prāgabhāva*), (*b*) posterior negation (*pradhvaṁsābhāva*), and (*c*) absolute negation (*atyantābhāva*).

In the Nyāya vārtika, 1-1-1, existence and non-existence are both spoken of as things, and in the Nyāya-bhāṣya, 1-1-1, the non-existence of a thing is said to be perceived by the same means as the existence of it, e.g. the non-existence of colour is perceived by the eye.

The body is not soul.

If the body were soul there should be release from sins as soon as the body was destroyed But in reality a person is not freed from sins although his body is destroyed, inasmuch as the sins pursue him in his subsequent lives. Hence the body is not soul.

The soul is different from the mind.

Some say that the soul is not different from the mind inasmuch as the arguments which are adduced to establish the soul are applicable to the mind as well. I can see an object by my eye and touch it by my skin. The agent which sees the object and touches it, is, no doubt, different from both the eye and the skin. Let however the agent, says an objector, be identified with the mind. Since an agent requires an instrument to accomplish a thing, it is, we reply, a mere verbal trick to apply the name "mind" to that which is really the "soul." To explain the acts of seeing, touching, etc., you admit an agent distinct from the senses which are called its instruments. The sense or instrument by which the act of thinking is performed is called the "mind." The agent sees by the eye, hears by the ear, smells by the nose, tastes by the tongue, touches by the skin and thinks by the "mind." Hence we must admit the agent (soul) over and above the instrument (mind). If you call the agent "mind," you will have to invent another name to designate the instrument. This verbal trick will not, after all, affect our position. Moreover, the mind cannot be the agent as it is atomic in nature. An atomic agent cannot perform such diverse acts as seeing, hearing, knowing, feeling, etc.

The soul is the seat of knowledge (cognitions).

Knowledge is not a natural quality of the body because it does not, in some cases, continue quite as long as the body does. Knowledge belongs neither to a sense nor to its object because it continues even on their destruction. If knowledge had been a quality of the sense, it could not continue after the sense had been destroyed. But knowledge in the form of memory is found actually to abide even after the sense has perished. Hence the sense is not the abode of knowledge. Similarly knowledge does not abide in an object of sense, and does not belong to the mind.

As two or more things cannot be known (perceived) simultaneously, it is to be concluded that the mind, which is an instrument of our knowledge, is an atom in dimension. If we supposed this mind to be the abode of knowledge we could not call it an instrument in the acquisition of the same, and knowledge as a quality of an atom would in that case be imperceptible Knowledge must therefore be admitted, by the principle of exclusion, to be a quality of the soul. The soul is all-pervading, but it cannot perceive many things simultaneously, on account of the absence of contact of the mind with many sense-organs at a time. Though many objects can come in proximity with their corresponding senses simultaneously, the mind, which is an atom, can come in conjunction with only one sense at a time. Hence two or more things are not perceived simultaneously although the soul which perceives them is all-pervading.

Immortality of the soul.

The soul is immortal inasmuch as we find in a child joy, fear and grief which arise from the memory of things previously experienced. A new-born child manifests marks of joy, fear and grief. This is inexplicable unless we suppose that the child perceiving certain things in this life remembers the corresponding things of its past life. The things which used to excite joy, fear and grief in past life continue to do so in this life. The memory of the past proves the pre-existence of the soul. Moreover, if we do not admit our soul to be eternal, we shall be confronted by many absurdities such as "loss of merited action" (*kṛta-hāni*), and "gain of unmerited action" (*akṛtābhyāgama*). A man who has committed a certain sin may not suffer its consequences in this life, and unless there is a soul continuing to his next life he will not suffer them at all. This is a "loss of merited action." Again, we often find a man suffering the consequences of action which he never did in this life. This would be a "gain of unmerited action," unless we believe that his soul did the action in his previous life.

Body.

Our body is made of earth.

Our body is earthy because it possesses the special qualities of earth. In other worlds there are beings whose bodies are watery, fiery, airy or ethereal. Though our body is composed of all the five elements we call it earthy owing to the preponderance of earth in it.

The senses are material.

The senses are material substances inasmuch as they invariably receive obstruction. Nothing can offer obstruction to a non-material all-pervading substance. The senses receive obstruction from wall, etc., and are therefore material substances.

Senses.

The senses are five.

Some[1] say that the senses are not many as all of them are dependent on touch (skin). The eye, ear, nose and tongue are said to be mere modifications of touch (skin) which pervades them, that is, there is only one sense, viz. touch (skin), all others being merely its forms.

It is, we reply, not so because the objects of other senses are not perceived by touch (skin). If there had been only one sense, viz. touch (skin), then it could have seen colour, heard sound, and so on. But a blind man possessing the sense of touch cannot see colour. Hence it is concluded that senses are many. Moreover, had there been only one sense, viz. touch, it would have in conjunction with the mind produced the functions of seeing, hearing, smelling, tasting, etc., simultaneously. But we cannot perform different functions at once. This proves that the senses are many. The mind, which is an atomic substance, being unable to come in contact with many senses at a time cannot produce many functions simultaneously. Further, touch can perceive only those

[1] Compare—All the senses are only modifications of touch.—Democritus.

objects which are near (contiguous), but it cannot perceive objects which are far off. We can, however, perceive colour and sound from a great distance. This is certainly not the function of touch, but of some other sense which can reach distant objects.

In fact, the senses are five. There are five objects, viz. colour, sound, smell (odour), taste (savour), and touch which are cognised respectively by the eye, ear, nose, tongue and skin. There are therefore five senses corresponding to the five objects. The senses must be admitted to be five also on the following grounds :—(*a*) The characters of knowledge—there are five senses corresponding to the five characters of knowledge, viz. visual, auditory, olfactory gustatory and tactual. (*b*) The sites—the senses are five on account of the various sites they occupy. The visual sense rests on the eye-ball, the auditory sense on the ear-hole, the olfactory sense on the nose, the gustatory sense on the tongue, while the tactual sense occupies the whole body. (*c*) The processes—there are five senses involving five different processes, e.g. the visual sense apprehends a colour by approaching it through the (ocular) ray, while the tactual sense apprehends an object which is in association with the body, and so on. (*d*) The forms—the senses are of different forms, e.g. the eye partakes of the nature of a blue ball, and the ear is not different from ether, etc. (*e*) The materials—the senses are made up of different materials : the eye is fiery, the ear is ethereal, the nose is earthy, the tongue is watery, and the skin (touch) is airy.

Objects of Sense.

The objects of sense: their distribution.

The earth possesses four qualities, viz. odour (smell), savour (taste), colour, and tangibility. In water there are three qualities, viz. savour, colour, and tangibility. Colour and tangibility are known to be the qualities of fire while tangibility and sound belong respectively to air and ether. Some say that the earth does not possess four qualities, but possesses only one quality, viz. odour (smell), which is apprehended by the nose; that water does not possess three qualities but only one quality, viz. savour (taste), which is apprehended by the tongue; and that the other elements too do, each of them, possess only one quality. In reply, we say, that the earth really possesses four qualities, water three, fire two, air one, and ether one. Had the earth possessed only odour (smell) and the water only savour (taste), then it would have been impossible for us to see the earthy and watery things. We are competent to see only those things which possess colour, and if the earth and water had not possessed colour, how could we have seen them ? Since we can see the earthy and the watery, it follows that they possess colour. If you say that the earth and water are visible, because they are mixed with the fiery things which possess colour, why then the air and ether too are not visible ? There is no rule that it is only the earth and water that can be mixed with fiery things, but that the air and ether cannot be so mixed. Proceeding in this way we find that the earth, etc., do not each possess only one quality.

Intellect.

Intellect (*buddhi*) is not permanent.

Some maintain that the intellect is permanent, because it possesses the capacity of recognizing objects. A thing which was known before is known again now—this sort of knowledge is called recognition. It is possible only if the intellect which knew an object in the past continues also at the present, that is, if the intellect is persistent or permanent. Recognition would have been impossible if the intellect had been transitory. Hence the intellect which recognizes objects is said to be permanent. In reply we say that the intellect does not recognize objects, but it is the soul that does so. Knowledge cannot be attributed to an unconscious instrument the intellect, but it must be admitted to be a quality of a conscious agent the soul. Hence the intellect is not permanent.

Mind.

The mind is one.

The mind being one, there are no simultaneous cognitions. If there had been more minds than one, they could have come in contact with many senses at a time so that many cognitions could have been produced simultaneously. As many cognitions are never produced at once, the mind must be admitted to be one.

The mind is an atom.

If the mind had been possessed of magnitude, it could have come in contact with many senses at a time so that many cognitions could have taken place simultaneously. Since this has been found to be impossible, the mind is an atom.

Faults.

The faults: their subdivision.

The faults are divided into three groups, viz. affection, aversion, and stupidity. Affection includes lust, avarice, avidity and covetousness. Aversion includes anger, envy, malignity, hatred and implacability. Stupidity includes misapprehension, suspicion, arrogance and carelessness. Of the three, stupidity is the worst because it is only a stupid person who may be influenced by affection and aversion.

Transmigration.

Transmigration belonging to the soul.

Transmigration belongs to the soul and not to the body. The series of births and deaths implied by transmigration, is possible only if the soul is eternal. If the soul were destructible, it would be victim to two unexpected chances, viz. destruction of actions done by it (*kṛta-hāni*), and suffering from actions not done by it (*akṛtābhyāgama*).

God is the giver of fruits.

Seeing that man does not often reap fruits proportionate to his acts, some maintain that the acts are entirely subservient to God (Īsvara) [1] who alone can provide them with fruits. This view is opposed

---

[1] It may be noted that in the Nyāya-sūtra there is only a casual mention of God.

by others who say that if God were the only source of fruits, man could attain them even without any acts. Reconciling the two views we conclude that man performs acts which are endowed with fruits by God. The acts do not produce any fruits by themselves: they become fruitful only through the grace of God.

Time of production of the fruits.

The fruit is not produced immediately, because it is capable of being enjoyed after a lapse of time. The fruit, e.g. of maintaining the sacred fire, is the attainment of heaven, which is not possible until the time of death when the soul departs from our body. Just as a tree, whose roots are now nourished with water, will produce fruits in future, so the sacred fire which is maintained now will enable the maintainer to attain heaven after death.

Birth is pain.

Birth is nothing but pain, because it consists of our connection with the body, the senses and the intellect, which bring us various distresses. The body is the abode in which pain resides, the senses are the instruments by which pain is experienced, and the intellect is the agent which produces in us the feeling of pain. Our birth—as connected with the body, the senses and the intellect—is necessarily a source of pain. We do not altogether deny pleasure which often arises amidst pains. Some persons, thinking that pleasure is the *summum bonum*, are addicted to the world which causes them various distresses through birth, infirmity, disease, death, connection with the undesirable, separation from the desirable, etc. It is therefore clear that one who pursues pleasure, does in reality pursue pain, or in other words, pleasure is a synonym for pain.

Emancipation.

Attainment of emancipation.

Some say that there is no opportunity for us to attain emancipation because of the continual pressure of our debts,[1] troubles and activities. As soon as we are born we incur, according to them, three debts which we must go on clearing off until the time of our decay and death; and troubles are our constant companions while activities pursue us throughout our life. There is then no opportunity for us to attain emancipation. In reply we say that there is no lack of opportunity for our emancipation, because the sacrifices to be performed for clearing off our debts may be trusted to our soul. A person, while old, should refrain from all searches after sons, wealth and retinue. He should retire from the world when he has trusted to his soul the sacrifices which he used to perform to clear off his debts. By so doing he will imagine that his soul is the sacrificial fire in which his physical actions are offered as oblations. Freed from all debts, he will live on alms and find an ample opportunity for effecting his own emancipation. As there is no distress in a person who enjoys a sound

---

[1] The three debts are: (1) Debt to sages (*ṛṣi-ṛṇa*)—which can be cleared off only by undergoing a course of student life. (2) Debt to gods (*deva-ṛṇa*)—from which we can be freed only by performing sacrifices. (3) Debt to our progenitors (*pitṛ-ṛṇa*)—which cannot be cleared off except by begetting children.

sleep, so there is no pressure of troubles and activities in one who has attained emancipation. Emancipation is the condition of supreme felicity marked by perfect tranquillity and not tainted by any defilement. A person, by the true knowledge of the sixteen categories, is able to remove his misapprehensions. When this is done, his faults, viz. affection, aversion and stupidity, disappear. He is then no longer subject to any activity and is consequently freed from transmigration and pains. This is the way in which his emancipation is effected and supreme felicity secured.

(3) Doubt (*saṁśaya*).

Doubt is said to be impossible.

1. Some say that doubt cannot arise from the recognition of common and uncommon properties, whether conjointly or separately. It is said that doubt about an object is never produced, if *both* the common and uncommon properties of the object are recognized. For instance, if we see in the twilight a tall object which moves, we do not doubt whether it is a man or a post. We at once decide that it is a man, for though tallness is a property possessed in common by man and post, locomotion is a property which distinguishes a man from a post. Likewise doubt about an object is said never to be produced if *only* the common or the uncommon properties are recognized. For instance, if we see a tall object in the twilight we have no reason to doubt whether it is a man or a post. Tallness is certainly a property possessed in common by man and post, but the tallness of a man is not identical with that of a post: it merely resembles it. Now the knowledge of similarity between the tallness of a man and that of a post presupposes a knowledge of the man and the post. of which the two kinds of tallness are attributes If there is already a knowledge of the man and the post, there cannot be any doubt about them, for knowledge is the vanquisher of doubt. 2. It is further said that doubt cannot arise either from conflicting testimonies or from the irregularity of perception and non-perception. In the case of conflicting testimonies there is, according to them. a strong conviction on each side. Suppose a disputant says: there is soul. His opponent replies: there is no soul. The disputant and his opponent are quite sure that their respective statements are correct. Hence there is no doubt, but on the contrary there is conviction. in the minds of both. 3. Doubt. they say. does not arise from the irregularity of perception and non-perception, because in the irregularity itself there is regularity. An irregularity may be designated as such with reference to something else, but with reference to itself it is a settled fact. If the irregularity is settled in itself. it is regular and cannot cause doubt. On the other hand. if the irregularity is not settled in itself. it is devoid of its own character and cannot cause doubt. 4. Likewise there is. they say, the chance of an endless doubt owing to the continuity of its cause. Recognition of properties common to many objects is. for instance. a cause of doubt. The common properties continue to exist and hence there will. they say. be no cessation of doubt.

Doubt is not impossible.

1. In reply we say that doubt does arise from the recognition of common and uncommon properties conjointly. The recognition of properties common to many objects is certainly a cause of doubt, if there is no reference to the precise characters of the objects. There is indeed a common (non-distinctive) knowledge about a man and a post suggested by the tall object, but there is no precise (distinctive) knowledge about them. Precise knowledge (that is, knowledge of the precise character which distinguishes a man from a post) being absent, doubt must arise. Similar arguments will apply to doubt arising from the recognition of uncommon properties alone. 2. In the case of conflicting testimonies there is certainly a ground for doubt. When a disputant and his opponent make conflicting statements, one is led to believe that both statements are worth consideration, but is unable to penetrate into the precise characters of the statements. Hence though the disputant and his opponent are both confident of their respective contentions, the umpire and the audience are thrown into doubt by their conflicting statements. 3. It has been said that doubt cannot arise from the irregularity of perception and non-perception as the irregularity is settled in itself. This objection is untenable, as the irregularity cannot be concealed by mere verbal tricks. The irregularity though settled in itself does not lose its irregular character until the objects to which it is related are removed. 4. It has been urged that there is the possibility of an endless doubt inasmuch as its cause is continuous. In reply we say that though materials of doubt, such as common properties, etc., continue to exist, we do not always recognize them. Unless there is recognition of the common properties, etc., there cannot be doubt.

(4) Discussion (*vāda*).

With whom to hold discussion?

One should hold discussions with unenvious[1] persons, such as disciples, preceptors, fellow-students and seekers of tho *summum bonum*. In case of a necessity for the search of truth, discussion may be held even without an opposing side. A person desirous of knowledge may submit his views for examination by simply expressing his curiosity for truth without an attempt to establish the views.

(5) Wrangling and Cavil (*jalpa-vitaṇḍā*).

Use of wrangling and cavil.

Wranglings and cavils may be employed to keep up our zeal for truth, just as fences of thorny boughs are used to safeguard the growth of seeds. Certain talkative people propound philosophies which are mutually opposed, while others violate all sense of rectitude out of a bias for their own side. Seeing that these people have not attained true knowledge, and are not freed from faults, we may, in our disputation against them, employ wranglings and cavils which do not in themselves produce any profit or deserve any encomium.

[1] The epithet "unenvious" excludes those who do not seek truth but desire victory.

36. Topics Incidentally Examined.

(1) Parts and Whole (*avayava* and *avayavin*).

Some say that *parts* alone are realities and that there is no *whole* behind them. A tree, for instance, is yellow in some parts and green in other parts. If the tree were one whole, then the contradictory qualities of yellowness and greenness could not have belonged to it simultaneously. Hence the parts alone must, according to them, be regarded as real.

The parts alone are said to be real.

In reply Akṣapāda says that nothing would be perceptible if the *whole* were denied. Suppose that the parts alone are real. Then since a part is not of a fixed dimension, it may itself be divided into parts, these latter again into further parts and so on, until we reach the atoms which are the ultimate parts. Now the atoms which possess no bulk are not perceptible. Consequently the thing which is said to consist merely of parts is also not perceptible. We must therefore admit a whole beyond its parts. Moreover, if there were no whole, we could not have held or pulled an entire thing by holding or pulling a part of it. We say 'one jar,' 'one man,' etc. This use of 'one' would vanish if there were no whole. If any one were to say that just as a single soldier or a single tree may not be seen from a distance, but an army consisting of numerous soldiers or a forest consisting of numerous trees is seen, so a single atom may not be perceptible, but a jar consisting of numerous atoms will be perceptible, and these atoms being called 'one jar,' the use of 'one' will not vanish. The analogy, we reply, does not hold good because the soldiers and trees possess bulk and so are perceptible, whereas the atoms do not possess bulk and are individually not perceptible. It is absurd to conclude that because soldiers and trees are perceptible in the mass, atoms too are perceptible in the mass; to avoid this conclusion we must admit the existence of a whole beyond the parts.

There is certainly a whole beyond its parts.

(2) Atoms (*paramāṇu*).

In the Nyāya-sūtra 4-2-16, it is stated that there can never come a time when there will be an utter annihilation of things. Even at the dissolution of the world (*pralaya*), things will continue to exist in the form of atoms. An atom is that which is not divisible into parts: it is a whole without parts. The view that an atom cannot be devoid of parts because it is pervaded by ether (ākāśa) in its inner and outer sides, is not tenable because the terms "innerside" and "outerside" are not applicable to an eternal atom which is altogether different from an ordinary thing a constituent of which encloses, or is enclosed by, another constituent of it. It is no doubt admitted that the ether is all-pervading, but it neither obstructs anything nor is repelled by anything, so that the question of inner side or outer side does not arise at all. Those who argue that an atom must possess parts because it can come in conjunction with another atom only in some of its parts, should bear in mind that their argument gives rise to a *regressus ad infinitum* which is not proper. If an atom is held to be divisible into parts. those parts again must be supposed to be divisible into further parts. This would lead to the fallacy of an infinite regression which should be avoided. A thing although repeatedly divided and subdivided does not lose itself. There remains a particle called *atom* which does not perish even at the dissolution of the world.

[According to commentators two atoms make a *dvyaṇuka* (dyad or binary compound) and three dvyaṇukas make a *tryasareṇu* (triad or a tertiary compound). All things which we perceive are composed of *tryasareṇus*.]

(3) The Three Times (*kāla*).

Some deny the present time.

There is, some[1] say, no *present* time, because when a thing falls we can know only the time through which it has fallen, and the time through which it will fall. When a fruit, for instance, falls from a tree we recognize only the past time taken up by the fruit in traversing a certain distance, and the future time which will be taken up by the fruit in traversing the remaining distance. There is no intervening distance which the fruit can traverse at the so-called present time. Hence they say there is no present time.

The present time established.

In reply we say that there is the present time, as the past and future times are related to it. The past is that which precedes the present, and the future is that which succeeds it. Hence if there is no present time, there cannot be any past or future time. If the past is defined as that which is not the future and the future is defined as that which is not the past, the definition would involve a fallacy of mutual dependency. Hence we must admit the present time to which the past and future are related.

The present time is indicated by the very existence of things. If the present time is denied, there cannot be any perception which can arise only in connection with a thing which is present in time; and in the absence of perception all kinds of knowledge would be impossible. Hence the present time is established by the principle of *reductio ad absurdum*. The present time is indicated by what continues, the past by what has been finished, and the future by what has not yet begun.

(4) Words and their Meanings (*śabdārtha*).

Is the connection between a word and its meaning natural?

Some say that there is a fixed connection between words and their meanings. A particular word bears a particular meaning, e.g. the word 'cow' denotes the animal of that name, but it does not denote a horse, a jar or any other thing. There is therefore a fixed connection between a word and its meaning.

---

[1] The sūtras from 2-1-39 to 2-1-43 which contain a critical examination of the present time (*vartamāna*) seem to have been interpolated into the Nyāya-sūtra by Vātsyāyana inasmuch as the objections raised therein emanated most probably from Nāgārjuna (*q.v.*).

In reply we say that it is through convention that the meaning of a word is understood. The connection between a word and its meaning is conventional and not natural. The connection is fixed by man and is not inseparable. Moreover there is no universal uniformity of connection between a word and its meaning. The *ṛṣis*, *āryas* and *mlecchas* use the same word in different senses, e.g. the word "yava" is used by the āryas to denote a long-awned grain, but by the mlecchas to denote a panic-seed. So the connection between a word and its meaning is not everywhere uniform.

The connection is conventional.

(5) The Veda.[1]

Some say that the Veda is unreliable, as it involves the faults of untruth, contradiction and tautology. For instance, the Veda affirms that a son is produced when a sacrifice for the sake of a son (*putreṣṭi*) is performed. It often happens that a son is not produced though the sacrifice has been performed. Besides, there are many contradictory injunctions in the Veda, e.g. it declares "let the oblation be offered after sun-rise," "let the oblation be offered before sun-rise," etc., and at the same time "the oblation offered after sun-rise, is eaten up by the brown dog," "the oblation offered before sun-rise, is eaten up by the motley-coloured dog," etc. There is also tautology such as "let the first hymn be recited thrice," "let the last hymn be recited thrice," etc.

Is the Veda unreliable?

In reply we say that the so-called untruth in the Veda comes from some defect in the act, operator or materials of sacrifice. Defect in the act consists in sacrificing not according to rules, defect in the operator (officiating priest) consists in his not being a learned man, and the defect in the materials consists in the fuel being wet, butter being not fresh, remuneration to the officiating priest being small, etc. A son is sure to be produced as a result of performing the sacrifice if these defects are avoided. There is therefore no untruth in the Veda. Neither is there any contradiction. Let a person offer the oblation before sun-rise or after sun-rise, if he has agreed upon doing it at either of the times. Two alternative courses being open to him, he can perform the sacrifice before sun-rise or after sun-rise according to his agreement or desire. The deprecatory texts, that the oblations are eaten up by dogs, indicate that the time agreed upon should not be altered. The Veda cannot be charged with the fault of contradiction if it enjoins such alternative courses. There may be re-inculcation in the Veda, but there is no tautology in it. Tautology means a useless repetition, which never occurs in the Veda. If there is any repetition there, it is either for completing a certain number of syllables, or for explaining a matter briefly expressed, etc. "Let the first hymn be recited thrice," "let the last hymn be recited thrice"—such instances embody a useful repetition.

The Veda involves no faults.

---

[1] It is interesting to note how the Nyāya-śāstra defends the Veda from the attacks made against it perhaps by the followers of Ānvīkṣikī.

The principle of classification of the Vedic speech.

The two main divisions of the Veda are: (1) hymn (*saṁhitā*), and (2) ritual (*Brāhmaṇa*). The ritual portion admits of three sub-divisions, viz. the injunctive (*vidhi*), descriptive (*arthavāda*), and re-inculcative (*anuvāda*).

An injunction (*vidhi*), which may be either mandatory or permissive, is that which exhorts us to adopt a certain course of action [as the means of attaining good], e.g. "let him, who desires paradise, perform the fire-sacrifice." This is a mandatory injunction.

Description (*arthavāda*) is of four kinds, viz. valedictory, deprecatory, illustrative, and narrative. The valedictory (*stuti*) is a speech which persuades us to adopt a certain course of action, by extolling its consequences, e.g. "By the Sarvajit sacrifice gods conquered all; there is nothing so efficacious as the Sarvajit sacrifice, it enables us to obtain everything and to vanquish every one, etc." Here there is no direct command on us, but the Sarvajit sacrifice is extolled in such a way that we are persuaded to perform it. The deprecatory (*nindā*) is a speech which persuades us to adopt a certain course of action, by acquainting us with the undesirable consequences of neglecting it, e.g. "one who performs any other sacrifice neglecting the Jyotiṣṭoma falls into a pit and decays there." Here one is persuaded to perform the Jyotiṣṭoma sacrifice the neglect of which brings about evil consequences. The illustrative (*parakṛti*) is the mentioning of a course of action, the obstruction of which by some particular person led to bad consequences, e.g. on presenting oblation one is to take the fat first and the sprinkled butter afterwards, but alas! the Caraka priests first took the sprinkled butter which was, as it were, the life of fire, etc. Here the foolish course of action adopted by the Caraka priests should serve as a warning to other priests who ought to avoid the course. The narrative (*purākalpa*) is the mentioning of some thing as commendable on account of its antiquity, e.g. "By this the Brāhmaṇas recited the Sāma hymn, etc."

Re-inculcation (*anuvāda*) is the repetition of that which has been enjoined by an injunction. Re-inculcation may consist of the repetition of an injunction or the repetition of that which has been enjoined. The first is called verbal re-inculcation and the second objective re-inculcation. "Non-eternal, not eternal" this is a verbal repetition. "Non-eternal, possessing the character of extinction"—this is an objective repetition.

The reliability of the Veda established.

The Vedas are reliable like the spells or mantras and the medical science, because of the reliability of their authors. Spells counteract poison, etc., and the medical science prescribes correct remedies. The authority which belongs to them is derived from their authors, the sages, who were reliable persons. The sages themselves were reliable because (1) they had an intuitive perception of truths, (2) they had great kindness for living beings, and (3) they had the desire of communicating their knowledge of the truths. The authors (lit. the seers and speakers) of the Vedas were also the authors of the spells and the medical science. Hence like the spells and medical science, the Vedas must be accepted as authoritative.

(6) Sound (*śabda*).

There are conflicting opinions about the nature of sound. Some say that sound is a quality of ether and that it is all-pervading, eternal and capable of being manifested. Others say that sound like smell, etc., is a quality of the substance in which it abides, and is capable of being manifested. Sound is said by others to be a quality of ether and to be subject to production and destruction like knowledge. Others again say that sound arises from the concussion of elements, requires no abode, and is subject to production and destruction.

The nature of sound.

Sound, according to the Nyāya-sūtra 2-1-14, is non-eternal because (1) it has a beginning, i.e. arises from the concussion of two hard substances, e.g. an axe and a tree, etc.; (2) is cognised by one of our senses (the ear); and (3) is spoken of as possessing the properties of an artificial object, e.g. is described as grave, acute, etc.

Sound is non-eternal.

Some say that the so-called beginning of a sound is merely a manifestation of it, that is, sound does not really begin, but is merely manifested by the concussion of two hard substances. In reply it is said that the concussion does not manifest but produce sound. You cannot suppose the concussion to be the manifester and sound the manifested, unless you can prove that the concussion and sound are simultaneous. But the proof is impossible as a sound is heard at a great distance, even after the concussion of the substances has ceased. So sound is not manifested by the concussion. It is however legitimate to suppose that sound is produced by the concussion, and that one sound produces another sound, and so on until the last sound is heard at a great distance.

Sound having a beginning is non-eternal.

Some say that it is not true that whatever has a beginning is non-eternal. Look! the non-existence (destruction) of a jar, which began when the jar was broken, is eternal (indestructible). In reply it is said that, that which is really eternal belongs to three times. But the non-existence (destruction) of a jar does not belong to three times as it was impossible before the jar was broken. Hence the non-existence (destruction) of a jar, which has a beginning, is not really eternal.

Whatever is cognised by our senses is non-eternal: this is also said to be an unsound argument. When, for instance, we perceive a jar, we perceive also its genus (i.e. jar-ness) which is eternal. In reply we say that not all things cognised by our senses are non-eternal, but only those that belong to a certain genus.[1] A jar, for instance, is non-eternal because we perceive it as

Sound being cognised by our senses is non-eternal.

[1] The aphorism (Nyāya-sūtra 2-1-17) may also be interpreted as follows:—Sound is non-eternal because it is inferred to advance in a series. We do not say that whatever is cognised by our sense is non-eternal: our intention is to say that

belonging to the genus jar-ness. But jar-ness which is cognised by our sense is not non-eternal, because it does not belong to a further genus named jarness-ness. Similarly sound is non-eternal, because it is cognised by our sense as belonging to the genus called sound-ness.

Artificial properties attributed to sound.

It is said that the attribution of the properties of an artificial object to sound does not make it non-eternal. It is often alleged that we attribute to eternal things the properties of an artificial object. e.g. we speak of the extension of ether as we speak of the extension of a blanket. In reply we say that when we speak of the extension of ether, we really mean that the extension belongs to an artificial thing which has for its substratum the ether. Hence we do not in reality attribute to eternal things the properties of artificial objects. Sound is in fact non-eternal, because neither do we perceive it before utterance, nor do we notice any veil which covers it. If sound were eternal it would be perceived before utterance. You cannot say that sound really existed before utterance, but was covered by some veil, for we do not notice any such veil.

Traditionary teaching.

Some say that sound should be regarded as eternal because there is traditionary teaching. A teacher delivers, in the form of a lecture, certain sounds which are found to be repeated by his pupil after a long interval. This repetition, according to them, would be impossible if the sounds were perishable. In reply it is pointed out that the sounds, which have not been audible after their delivery by the teacher, are reproduced or imitated by his pupil. On the ground of the inaudibility, reproducibility and imitability, the sounds must be pronounced to be non-eternal.

The substratum of sound.

Sound has not for its substratum any of the tangible substances, viz. earth, water, fire, and air. Its substratum is ether which pervades all space. Hence sound is produced even in a vacuum which is devoid of smell, taste, colour, and touch—the qualities of tangible substances. The reason why the sound produced in a vacuum does not reach our ears, is that there is no air to carry it. The fact of having an intangible substance for its substratum, is no bar to the sound being non-eternal. Sound, though its substratum is the intangible ether, is produced by the contact of two hard substances. One sound produces another sound, and so on until the last sound ceases owing to some obstacle. Sound is therefore non-eternal.

(7) Word (*pada*).

The letters ended with an affix[1] form a word (*pada*) which is of two kinds, viz. a noun, and a verb. In assimilating an affix the letters may be transformed. The transformation takes place by substitution

---

things cognised by our sense as advancing in a series are non-eternal. Sound is cognised in that manner (i.e. sound advances like a wave), and hence sound is non-eternal.

[1] The indeclinables (*avyaya*) which drop their affixes are also words (Pāṇini 2-4-82).

(*ādeśa*), and not by modification (*vikāra*), e.g. in *bho + ti* (*bhū + ti = bhavati*), *o* vacates a place which is occupied by its substitute *av*.

What is expressed by a word—a genus, an individual or a form?

What does a word signify? A word presents to us an *individual*, a *form* and a *genus* (type). The word 'cow' reminds us of an individual (a four-footed animal), its form (limbs) and its genus or type (cowhood or cow-type). Now, it is asked what is the real signification of a word—an individual, a form or a genus (type)? Some say that the word denotes an individual, because it is only in respect of individuals that we can make any statement, e.g. "that cow is going"—here "that" can be used only in reference to an individual cow. Others say that the word denotes form by which an entity is recognised, e.g. we use such expressions as 'this is a cow,' and 'this is a horse.' only with reference to the forms of the cow and the horse. Others hold that the word must denote genus (type), for if we did not take genus into consideration the word cow might denote any individual of any kind.

In reply we say that the word signifies all the three, though prominence is given to one of them. For the purpose of distinction the individual is prominent. In order to convey a general notion, pre-eminence is given to the genus (type). In practical concerns much importance is attached to the form. As a fact the word ordinarily presents to us the form, denotes the individual, and connotes the genus (type).

Individual.

An *individual* (*vyakti*) is that which has a definite form and is the abode of particular qualities. An individual is any substance which is cognised by the senses as a limited abode of colour, taste, smell, touch, weight, solidity, tremulousness, velocity or elasticity.

Form.

The *form* (*ākṛti*) is that which is called the token of the genus. The genus, cowhood for instance, is recognized by a certain collocation of the dewlap which is a form. We cannot recognize the genus of a formless substance.

Genus.

A *genus* or type (*jāti*) is that whose nature is to produce the same conception. Cowhood is a genus (or type) which underlies all cows. Seeing a cow somewhere we acquire a general notion of cows (i.e. derive knowledge of cowhood). This general notion enables us on all subsequent occasions to recognize individual cows.

(8) The eyes (*cakṣuḥ*).

Are the eyes two?

Some say that the eyes are not two: the conceit of duality arises from the single organ of vision being divided by the bone of the nose. In reply we say that the eyes are really two, because the destruction of one does not cause the destruction of the other.

Is the eye a material substance?

The eye is said by some to be a material substance inasmuch as its function is limited by its contact. A thing is seen when it has contact with the eye, but it is not seen when the eye is not connected. In other words, the eye, like any other material substance, exercises its function only in virtue of its contact with things. Others say that if the eye had been a material substance, it could have apprehended only those things which coincided with itself in bulk. But we find it can apprehend things of greater and smaller bulk. So it is contended that the eye is a non-material substance.

In reply we say that though the eye does not coincide with things which are greater or smaller in bulk, yet the rays issuing from the eye reach the things to their entire extent. Hence in spite of the eye being a material substance, there is no impossibility for it to apprehend the great and the small

(9) Intellect (*buddhi*).

Is knowledge a function of the permanent intellect?

Some philosophers[1] [the sāṁkhyas] maintain that the intellect is permanent as it is capable of recognizing objects. A thing which was known before, is known now as the identical thing. This sort of identifying knowledge is called recognition, which is possible only if the intellect which existed in the past continues also at the present time, that is, if the intellect is permanent. Knowledge which is a function of the intellect is not different from the latter.

Akṣapāda opposes them by saying that the intellect, which is an unconscious instrument, cannot recognize objects, recognition being really a function of a conscious agent, the soul. If knowledge were not different from the permanent intellect, then various sorts of knowledge could have as permanent entities existed simultaneously, and there would have been no cessation of knowledge or recognition. Finding the absurdity of such contingencies, we cannot admit the intellect to be a permanent entity and knowledge a function of it.

(10) Memory (*smṛti*).[2]

Memory.

Memory (*smṛti*) belongs to the soul which possesses knowledge of the past, present and future. Memory is awakened by such causes as attention, context, exercise, signs, marks, likeness, possession, relation of protector and

---

[1] *Vide* Nyāya-sūtra, 3-2-1.

[2] Compare—The king said: 'In how many ways, Nāgasena, does memory spring up?'

'In sixteen ways, O king. That is to say; by personal experience, as when the Venerable Ānanda, or the devoted woman Khajjuttarā, or any others who had that power, called to mind their previous births—or by outward aid as when others continue to remind one who is by nature forgetful—or by the impression made by the greatness of some occasion, as kings remember their coronation day, or as we remember the day of our conversion—by the impression made by joy, as when one remembers that which gave him pleasure—or by the impression made by sorrow, as when one remembers that which pained him - or from similarity of appearance, as on seeing one like them we call to mind the mother or father or sister or brother, or on seeing a camel or an ox or an ass we call to mind others like them—or by difference of appearance as when we remember that such and such a colour, sound, smell, taste or touch belong to such and such a thing—or by the knowledge of speech, as when one who is by nature forgetful is reminded by others and then himself remembers—or by a sign, as when we recognize a draught bullock by a brand mark or some other sign—or from effort to recollect, as when one by nature

protegé. immediate subsequency, separation, similar employment, opposition. excess, receipt, intervention. pleasure and pain, desire and aversion, fear. entreaty. action. affection. and merit and demerit.

Attention—enables us to fix our mind on an object by restraining it from wandering away to any other object.

Context—is the connection of subjects such as proof (*pramāṇa*), that which is to be proved (*prameya*), etc.

Exercise—is the constant repetition which confirms an impression.

Sign—may be (1) connected, (2) inseparable (intimate), (3) correlated, or (4) opposite. e g. smoke is a sign of fire with which it is connected; a horn is a sign of a cow from which it is inseparable; an arm is a sign of a leg with which it is correlated; and the non-existent is a sign of the existent by the relation of opposition.

Mark—a mark on the body of a horse awakens the memory of the stable in which it was kept.

Likeness—as the image of Devadatta drawn on a board reminds us of the real person.

Possession—such as a property awakens the memory of the owner and *vice versa*.

Protector and Protégé—such as a king and his attendants.

Immediate subsequency—as sprinkling the rice and pounding it in a wooden mortar.

Separation—as of husband and wife.

Similar employment—as of a fellow-disciple.

Opposition—as between a snake and ichneumon.

Excess—awakening the memory of that which exceeded.

Receipt—reminding us of one from whom some thing has been or will be received.

Intervention—such as a sheath reminding us of the sword.

Pleasure and pain—reminding us of that which caused them.

Desire and aversion—reminding us of one whom we liked or hated.

Fear—reminding us of that which caused it, e.g. death.

Entreaty—reminding us of that which was wanted or prayed for.

---

forgetful is made to recollect by being urged again and again: "try and think of it"—or by calculation, as when one knows by the training he has received in writing, that such and such a letter ought to follow after such and such a one—or by arithmetic, as when accountants do set sums by their knowledge of figures—or by learning by heart, as the repeaters of the scriptures by their skill in learning by heart recollect so much—or by meditation, as when a Bhikkhu calls to mind his temporal states in days gone by—by reference to a book, as when kings calling to mind a previous regulation, say: "Bring the book here." and remind themselves out of that—or by a pledge, as when, at the sight of goods deposited, a man recollects (the circumstances under which they were pledged)—or by association, as when one remembers a thing because one has seen it, or a sound because one has heard it, or an odour because one has smelt it, or a touch because one has felt it, or a concept because one has perceived it."

'Very good, Nāgasena!'

(The questions of King Milinda—Book III, chapter 7, pp. 122-123, translated by T. W. Rhys Davids, S.B.E. Series).

Action—such as a chariot reminding us of the charioteer.
Affection—as recollecting a son or wife.
Merit and *demerit*—through which there is recollection of the causes of joy and sorrow experienced in a previous life.

(11) The fixed signification of numbers[1] (*saṁkhyaikānta*).

Saṁkhyaikānta-vāda, the doctrine of the fixed signification of numbers.

Some say that there is only *one* thing, viz. Brahma. Others say that things are *two*, viz. the eternal and non-eternal. Some find the things to be *three*, viz. the knower, the knowable and knowledge; while others treat of *four* things, viz. the agent of knowledge, means of knowledge, object of knowledge and act of knowledge. In this way philosophers indulge themselves in a *fixed number* of things. Akṣapāda opposes them by saying that the fixity of number cannot be established. In establishing the fixed number, there must be a reason. Now is the reason included in the number or excluded from it, or identical with it? If the reason is included in the number, it is as unfixed as the number itself. If the reason is excluded from the number, the fixity of number must be abandoned. If the number and the reason are identical, there will remain no means to establish the fixity of number.

---

[1] This doctrine, which occurs in the Nyāya-sūtra, 4-1-41, throws some light on the dialogue between Aṣṭāvakra and Vandin related in the Mahābhārata, Vana-parva, chaps. 132–134 (*vide* ante). It bears an analogy to the novice's question (Kumāra-pañha) which runs as follows:—

1. एकं नाम किं?	1. सब्बे सत्ता आहारट्ठितिका।
What is one?	Food is a thing on which all animals subsist.
2. द्वे नाम किं?	2. नामञ्च रूपञ्च।
What are two?	Name and form.
3. तीणि नाम किं?	3. तिस्सो वेदना।
What are three?	Three kinds of feeling.
4. चत्तारि नाम किं?	4. चत्तारि अरियसच्चानि।
What are four?	The four noble truths.
5. पञ्च नाम किं?	5. पञ्चुपादानक्खन्धा।
What are five?	The five constituent aggregates, etc., etc.

(Khuddakapāṭha of the Pāli sutta Piṭaka).

CHAPTER III.

Commentaries on the Nyāya-sūtra.

36*a*. Nature of the Commentaries.

Commentaries are store-houses of information.

In the previous chapter there has been given a summary of Nyāya-sūtra, the fundamental work on Nyāya Philosophy of the second century A.D. The Nyāya-sūtra was not followed, for several hundred years, by any other original treatises on Nyāya from the pen of the Brāhmaṇic writers. But these writers brought out numerous commentaries which served not only to elucidate and develop the Nyāya-sūtra, but to review critically, in the light of the sūtra, the various theories of contemporaneous philosophies. The commentaries are therefore store-houses of valuable information on Philosophy and Logic. It is not possible to give here a complete analysis of the commentaries, but a passing reference to some of their leading topics will be made in the following pages.

37. Vātsyāyana, author of the Nyāya-bhāṣya (about 400 A.D.).

Previous Commentaries.

The earliest commentary extant on the Nyāya-sūtra is the **Nyāya-bhāṣya** by Vātsyāyana [1] or Pakṣila Svāmī.[2] In it there are references to previous logicians designated as *eke* (some), *kecit* (certain), or *anye* (others), who were perhaps authors of commentaries [3] which have not come down to us. The Nyāya-bhāṣya

---

[1] The name Vātsyāyana occurs in the colophon of Uddyotakara's Nyāya-vārtika thus :—

यदक्षपादप्रतिमो भाष्यं वात्स्यायनो जगौ ।
अकारि महतस्तस्य भारद्वाजेन वार्त्तिकम् ॥

(Nyāya-vārtika, Book V, Chap. II, last line).

[2] Vācaspati Miśra mentions the name Pakṣila Svāmin thus :—

अथ भगवता अक्षपादेन निःश्रेयसहेतौ शास्त्रे प्रणीते व्युत्पादिते च भगवता पक्षिलस्वामिना किमपरमवशिष्यते यदर्थं वार्त्तिकारम्भ इति

(Nyāyavārtika-tātparyaṭīkā, opening lines).

[3] Vātsyāyana in his Nyāya-bhāṣya, 1-2-9, criticises, in connection with his definition of *kālātita*, the opinion of a previous commentator by saying—

अवयव विपर्य्यास वचनं न सूत्रार्थः ।

was separated from the Nyāya-sūtra by at least two centuries, as we find in it explanations of certain terms which became almost unintelligible at the time.[1]

Vātsyāyana preceded Dignāga and Vasubandhu.

Vātsyāyana must have flourished before Dignāga (q.v.), as the latter criticises him in connection with his explanation of the mind (*manas*) as a sense-organ,[2] and possibly also before Vasubandhu whose theory of syllogism, so antagonistic to that of Akṣapāda, has not been controverted, nay even referred to, by Vātsyāyana in his Nyāya-bhāṣya.

Vātsyāyana followed Nāgārjuna and the Laṅkāvatāra.

The Nyāya-sūtra, as already observed, contains certain aphorisms which refer to the doctrines expounded in such well-known Buddhist works as the Mādhyamika-sūtra, Laṅkāvatāra-sūtra, etc. These aphorisms do not constitute an essential part of the Nyāya-sūtra, and were evidently interpolated into it before or during the time of Vātsyāyana[3] who wrote *Bhāṣya*, commentary, on it. Vātsyāyana must therefore have flourished after the composition of the Buddhist works, the doctrines of which were interpolated into the Nyāya-sūtra.

Age of Vātsyāyana.

Hence the earliest limit of his age is A.D. 300, when the Mādhyamika-sūtra and Laṅkāvatāra-sūtra are supposed to have been composed. As Dignāga lived about 500 A.D. and Vasubandhu about 480 A.D., Vātsyāyana who preceded them could not have lived after the latter date. Taking the mean between the earliest and the latest dates we may approximately fix the date of Vātsyāyana[4] at about 400 A.D.

Vātsyāyana, in extolling the *Nyāya-śāstra* (called the *Ānvīkṣiki*), quotes a verse from the *Artha-śāstra*[5] of Kauṭilya (about

---

[1] Dr. H. Jacobi observes:—When commenting on Nyāya-sūtra, 1-1-5, Vātsyāyana gives two different explanations of the terms *pūrvavat*, *śeṣavat*, and *sāmānyato dṛṣṭam*, the names of the three subdivisions of inference, showing thereby that the meaning of these important terms had become doubtful at his time. (The dates of the philosophical sūtras, p. 6, Journal of the American Oriental Society for 1911).

[2] *Vide* Nyāya-bhāṣya, 1-1-4; and Pramāṇa-samuccaya, chapter I.

[3] Dr. Hermann Jacobi observes:—The text of the sūtras as we have them is at best that which the oldest scholiast chose to comment upon, and it cannot be safely traced further back—J.A.O.S., for 1911, the dates of philosophical sūtras, pp. 2-3.

[4] *Vide* my "Vātsyāyana, author of the Nyāya-bhāṣya" in the Indian Antiquary for April 1915.

[5] सेयमान्वीक्षिकी प्रमाणादिपदार्थैर्विभज्यमाना
"प्रदीपः सर्व्वविद्यानामुपायः सर्व्वकर्म्मणाम्।
आश्रयः सर्व्वधर्म्माणां विद्योद्देशे प्रकीर्त्तिता"
(Nyāya-bhāṣya, 1-1-1, and Artha-śāstra, chap. II).

327 B.C.), and in giving an example of "the incoherent" (*apārthaka*) extracts a sentence from the Mahābhāṣya[1] of Patañjali (150 B.C.).

Birthplace of Vātsyāyana.

Vātsyāyana, also designated as Drāmila[2] (same as Drāviḍa), was in all probability a native of Drāviḍa (the Deccan), of which the capital was Kāñcīpura, modern Conjeeveram. The title "Svāmin"[3] appended to "Pakṣila" in the name "Pakṣila Svāmin" also points to the same country as his birthplace. We may add that Kāñcī was a famous centre not only of Brāhmanic learning, but also of Buddhistic culture, and it was here that Dignāga (500 A.D.) and Dharmapāla (600 A.D.) and other Buddhist logicians lived and flourished. It may be of some interest to note that Vātsyāyana[4] makes a reference to the boiling of rice which is a staple food of the people of Drāviḍa. This Vātsyāyana who lived about 400 A.D., when Candra Gupta II, called Vikramāditya, was king of Magadha, should not be confounded with the sage or sages of that name, who compiled the Artha-śāstra and the Kāma-sūtra.

38. Vātsyāyana criticises Nāgārjuna.

The Mādhyamika doctrine of inter-relation, *apekṣā* or *pratyaya* criticised.

The sūtras 4-1-39 and 4-1-40 which seem to have been, as previously observed, interpolated into the Nyāya-sūtra[5] deal with the Buddhist doctrine of inter-relation (*apekṣā* or *pratyaya*) evidently taken from the Mādhyamika-sūtra[6] (Chapters I and XV) of Nāgārjuna who flourished about

---

[1] दश दाडिमानि षडपूपाः
कुण्डमजाजिनं पललपिण्डः ।
(Nyāya-bhāṣya, 5-1-10, and Mahābhāṣya, 1-1-3).

[2] Jaina Hemacandra supposes Drāmila to be another name for Vātsyāyana:—

वात्स्यायनो मल्लनागः कौटिल्यश्चणकात्मजो
द्रामिलः पक्षिलस्वामी विष्णुगुप्तोऽङ्गुलश्च सः ॥
(Abhidhāna-cintāmaṇi).

Vātsyāyana would not have been called Drāmila, had he been a native of Vatsa, the capital of which was Kauśāmbī near Allahabad.

[3] Svāmin is a common surname in Madras. In Pāli books, however, we read of a sage named Vacchagotta or Vātsyāyana living in Ayodhyā.

[4] Nyāya-bhāṣya, 2-1-40, edited by Jaya Narayan Tarkapañcānana, Bibliotheca Indica series.

[5] The Nyāya-sūtra of Gotama, translated by Satis Chandra Vidyabhusana, S.B.H. Series, Allahabad.

[6] रूपादिव्यतिरेकेण यथा कुम्भो न विद्यते ।
वाय्वादिव्यतिरेकेण तथा रूपं न विद्यते ॥
(Mādhyamika-sūtra, Chapter I, verse 3, p. 19, B.T.S. edition, Calcutta).

250–300 A.D. In the Bhāṣya on the sūtras, Vâtsyāyana summarises the doctrine as follows :—

Some say that things are not self-existent as they exist merely in relation to one another A thing is called short only in relation to another thing which is long, and *vice versa*. The long and short are inter-related, but not self-existent.

In the same Bhāṣya Vātsyāyana controverts the doctrine on the ground that it is self-destructive. If the long and short are not self-existent, it will be impossible to establish a relation between them, and in the absence of all relations the doctrine of inter-relation will fall to the ground.

The Mādhyamika doctrine of *śūnyatā*, voidness, criticised.

The sūtras 4-2-31, 4-2-32 and 4-2-33, of the Nyāya-sūtra,[1] seem also to have been interpolations. In the Bhāṣya on those sūtras, Vātsyāyana criticises the doctrine, evidently taken from the Mādhyamika-sūtra,[2] according to which our means and objects of knowledge are as unreal as things appearing in a dream or exhibited in jugglery or as the city of the celestial choirs or as a mirage.[3]

न संभवः स्वभावस्य युक्तः प्रत्ययहेतुभिः ।
स्वभावः कृतको नाम भविष्यति पुनः कथम् ॥
(Mādhyamika-sūtra, Chap. XV, p. 93, B.T.S. edition, Calcutta).

न स्वभावसिद्धिरापेक्षिकत्वात् । (Nyāya-sūtra, 4-1-39).

व्याहतत्वादयुक्तम्
(Nyāya-sūtra, 4-1-40, S.B.H. series, Allahabad).

1 स्वप्नविषयाभिमानवदयं प्रमाणप्रमेयाभिमानः ॥ 4-2-31
मायागन्धर्वनगरमृगतृष्णिकावद्वा ॥ 4-2-32

(Nyāya-sūtra translated into English by Satis Chanda Vidyabhusana, S.B.H. Series, Allahabad).

2 यथा माया यथा स्वप्नो गन्धर्वनगरं यथा ।
तथोत्पादस्तथा स्थानं तथा भङ्ग उदाहृतम् ॥
(Mādhyamika-sūtra, chapter VII).

यथैव गन्धर्वपुरं मरीचिका यथैव मायासुपिनं यथैव ।
स्वभावशून्या तु निमित्तभावना तथोपमान् जानथ सर्वधर्मान् ॥
(Quoted in the Mādhyamika-vṛtti, p. 57, B.T. Society's edition, Calcutta).

3 As explained in the Buddhist works (such as the Mādhyamika-sūtra, Laṅkāvatāra sūtra, Dvyardha-śatikā, etc.). The doctrine of inter-relation *pratyaya* or *apekṣā*) leads to that of voidness (*śūnyatā*). Compare—

यः प्रतीत्यसमुत्पादः शून्यतां तां प्रचक्षते ।.....
यश्च स्वभावेनानुत्पादो भावानां सा शून्यता ।
यः प्रत्ययैर्जायति स ह्यजातो
न तस्य उत्पादः स्वभावतोऽस्ति ।

Nāgārjuna's logical theory of examples, *udāharaṇa*, criticised.

Nāgārjuna in his Upāyakauśalya-sūtra, chapter I, says that a thesis can be established through a reason and an example (*udāharaṇa*), which may be either affirmative or negative. A syllogism, according to him, consists of three members and not of five, the last two members, viz. application (*upanaya*) and conclusion (*nigamana*) being superfluous and not better than "analogous rejoinders" (*jātyuttara*).

Vātsyāyana[1] in his Nyāya-bhāṣya, 1-1-39, answers these objections as follows:—

The application (*upanaya*) and conclusion (*nigamana*) are essential parts of a syllogism inasmuch as they serve on the strength of the general principle involved in the example, to confirm the reason and reassert decisively the proposition which, when first advanced, was of a doubtful character. After an invariable relation

---

यः प्रत्ययाधीनः स शून्य उक्तो
यः शून्यतां जानाति सोऽप्रमत्तः ॥ इति ॥

तथाचार्य्यलङ्कावतारे — स्वभावानुत्पत्तिं सन्धाय महामते सर्व्वधर्म्माः शून्या इति मया देशिता इति ॥ आर्य्यसमाधिराजे शून्याः सर्व्वधर्म्माः निःस्वभाव योगेन । इति ॥

(Mādhyamika vṛtti, Chap. XXIV, pp. 184–185, Calcutta Buddhist Text Society's edition).

एवं शून्यमुपादानमुपादाता च सर्व्वशः ।
प्रज्ञप्यते च शून्येन कथं शून्यस्तथागतः ॥

(Mādhyamika vṛtti, Chap. XXII, p. 160, Calcutta Buddhist Text Society's edition).

The doctrine of voidness (*śūnya-vāda*) flourished between 200 A.D. and 500 A.D. Compare Dr. L. Suali's Filosofia Indiana, p. 8.

1 Vātsyāyana observes:—

उपनयनिगमनान्तरेण साध्येऽनुपसंहृतः साधको धर्म्मो नार्थं साधयेत् । निगमनाभावे चानभिव्यक्तसम्बन्धानां प्रतिज्ञादीनामेकार्थेन प्रवर्त्तनं तथेति प्रतिपादनं करोति । ... न चैतस्यां हेतूदाहरणपरिशुद्धौ सत्यां साधर्म्यवैधर्म्याभ्यां प्रत्यवस्थानस्य विकल्पात् जातिनिग्रहस्थानबहुत्वं न प्रक्रमते, अव्यवस्थाप्य खलु साध्यसाधनभावम् उदाहरणे जातिवादी प्रत्यवतिष्ठते व्यवस्थिते तु खलु धर्म्मयोः साध्यसाधनभावे दृष्टान्तस्थे गृह्यमाणे साधनभूतस्य धर्म्मस्य हेतुत्वेनोपादानं न साधर्म्यमात्रस्य न वैधर्म्यमात्रस्य वेति

(Nyāya-bhāṣya, 1-1-39, pp. 34–35, published under the name of Nyāya-darśana, Bibliotheca Indica series, Calcutta).

Uddyotakara too in his Nyāya-vārtika, 1-1-39, cites the opinion of a certain sage who held that the application (*upanaya*) and conclusion (*nigamana*) were not separate members of a syllogism, as they served no purpose different from that of the reason and the proposition:—

उपनयनिगमने नावयवान्तरे अर्थाविशेषात् ।

(Nyāya-vārtika, 1-1-39, p. 140, edited by M.M. Vindhyeśvarī Prasāda, in the Bibliotheca Indica series).

The sage referred to was very probably Nāgārjuna. It is however to be noted that neither Vātsyāyana nor Uddyotakara mentions Nāgārjuna by name.

between the reason (middle term) and the predicate (major term) has been proved in the example, there is no occasion for an opponent to say that the application (*upanaya*) is a mere analogous rejoinder because it is based not on a mere similarity or dissimilarity indicated by its particle "so" or "not so," but on the general principle established by the example.

39. VĀTSYĀYANA CRITICISES OTHER DOCTRINES OF THE BUDDHISTS.

Vijñāna-vāda—idealism

The Yogācāra doctrine of *vijñāna*, knowledge, criticised.

The sūtras 4-2-26 and 4-2-27, which seem to have been interpolated into the Nyāya-sūtra,[1] deal with the Buddhist doctrine of the reality of knowledge (*vijñāna*) alone, evidently taken from the Laṅkāvatāra-sūtra,[2] chapters II and X. In the Nyāya-bhāṣya, 4-2-26, Vātsyāyana[3] summarises the Buddhist doctrine as follows:—

Some say that things do not possess a reality independent of our thoughts just as a web does not possess a reality indepen-

---

[1] Vātsyāyana seems here to have referred to the Laṅkāvatāra-sūtra.

बुद्ध्या विवेचनात्तु भावानां याथात्म्यानुपलब्धिस्तन्त्वपकर्षणे पटसद्भावानुपलब्धिवत् तदनुपलब्धिः ॥

Nyāya-bhāṣya, 4-2-26 translated by Satis Chandra Vidyabhusana, S.B.H. Series, Allahabad).

[2]

बुद्ध्या विविच्यमानानां स्वभावो नावधार्यते ।
यस्मादनभिलाप्यास्ते निःस्वभावाश्च देशिताः ॥

(Laṅkāvatāra-sūtra, chap. II, p. 50, and chapter XI, p. 115, of the Asiatic Society of Bengal).

བློ་ཡིས་རྣམ་པར་གཞིགས་ན་ཡང་།
གང་ཕྱིར་རང་བཞིན་མི་རིག་སྟེ།
དེ་ཕྱིར་དེ་དག་བརྗོད་དུ་མེད།
ངོ་བོ་ཉིད་ཀྱང་མེད་པར་བསྟན།།

(Bkaḥ-gyur, Mdo, ca, folio 150, also 253).

[3] The Nyāya-sūtras, 4-2-26 and 4-2-27, may be interpreted in such a way that they refer to the Mādhyamika philosophy rather than to the Yogācāra. In fact Dr. H. Jacobi J.A.O.S. for 1911, p. 29, maintains that the Yogācāra or *Vijñāna-vāda* did not commence until the 5th century A.D. when Asaṅga lived. But we should not forget that Maitreyanātha was a great expounder of *Vijñāna vāda* about 400 A.D., and that there is an exposition of it in the Laṅkāvatāra-sūtra about 300 A.D. I therefore conclude that though Akṣapāda (150 A.D.) was not conversant with the Yogācāra or *Vijñāna-vāda*, Vātsyāyana (about 400 A.D.) knew the doctrine and criticised it in his Nyāya-bhāṣya, 4-2-26, 4-2-27 and 3-2-11. Dr. Sher-batski on the authority of Vācaspati and Vātsyāyana observes that the Nyāya-sūtra, 4-2-26, is directed against the school of the Vijñāna-vādins (J.A.O.S. for 1911, p. 5).

dent of its threads. Hence it is our thoughts alone, they say, that are real, the external things are all unreal.

Vātsyāyana controverts this Buddhist doctrine by saying that it is self-destructive, because if things are capable of being separated from our thoughts they cannot be unreal and on the other hand if things are unreal they are incapable of being separated from our thoughts The holder of the doctrine commits, according to Vātsyāyana, a contradiction by saying that things are unreal, and at the same time by going on to separate them from our thoughts.

Kṣaṇika-vāda—the Theory of Impermanence.

The doctrine of momentariness, *kṣaṇika-vāda*, criticised.

The sūtra 3-2-11, which refers to the doctrine of momentariness (*kṣaṇikatva*) as explained in the Laṅkāvatāra-sūtra, etc., was evidently interpolated by Vātsyāyana into the Nyāya-sūtra.[1] In his *Bhāṣya*—commentary—on the sūtra, Vātsyāyana cites the opinion of *kṣaṇik-vādins* according to whom all entities are momentary, as they exist for a moment only. We feel the momentariness of entities on seeing their growth and decay which imply production and destruction.

Vātsyāyana in his Nyāya-bhāṣya, 3-2-12, 3-2-13, controverts the doctrine of momentariness by saying that there is no absolute certainty for an entity to be replaced by another entity after the lapse of a moment, and that there is a connecting link between the origination of an entity and its cessation.[2]

40. Vātsyāyana's Explanation of Certain Doctrines.

A Syllogism of Ten Members.

Vātsyāyana in his Nyāya-bhāṣya, 1-1-32, alludes to certain logicians according to whom a syllogism consisted of ten members as follows:—

Five ordinary members

1. Proposition (*pratijñā*).—This hill is fiery.
2. Reason (*hetu*).—Because it is smoky.
3. Example (*udāharaṇa*).—Whatever is smoky is fiery, as a kitchen.

---

[1] स्फटिकेऽप्यपरापरोत्पत्तेः क्षणिकत्वाद् व्यक्तीनामहेतुः । 3-2-11.
नियमहेत्वभावाद् यथादर्शनमभ्यनुज्ञा । 3-2-12.
नोत्पत्तिविनाशकारणोपलब्धेः । 3-2-13.
(Nyāya-sūtra, pp. 86–87, edited and translated by Satis Chandra Vidyabhusana. S.B.H. Series, Allahabad).

[2] *Vide* the Laṅkāvatāra-sūtra, chap. VI, called Kṣaṇika-parivarta, p. 99, Bengal Asiatic Society's MSS.
Cf. All is in a state of flux—Heraclitus.

4. Application (*upanaya*).—So is this hill (smoky).
5. Conclusion (*nigamana*).—Therefore this hill is fiery.

Five additional members.

1. (*a*) Inquiry as to the proposition (*jijñāsā*).—Is this hill fiery in all its parts, or in a particular part?
2. (*a*) Questioning the reason (*saṁśaya*).—That which you call smoke may be nothing but vapour.
3. (*a*) Capacity of the example to warrant the conclusion (*śakya-prāpti*).—Is it true that smoke is always a concomitant of fire? In a kitchen there are of course both smoke and fire, but in a red-hot iron ball there is no smoke.
4. (*a*) Purpose for drawing the conclusion (*prayojana*).—Purpose consists in the determination of the true conditions of the hill, in order to ascertain whether it is such that one can approach it, or such that one should avoid it, or such that one should maintain an attitude of indifference towards it.
5. (*a*) Dispelling all questions (*saṁśaya-vyudāsa*).—It is beyond all questions that the hill is smoky, and that smoke is an invariable concomitant of fire.

The five additional members serve no doubt to make our cognition clear, but they do not *prove* any thing. Hence they cannot, according to Vātsyāyana, be regarded as essential members or parts of a syllogism.[1]

God—Īśvara.

Akṣapāda in his Nyāya-sūtra, 4-1-16, casually mentions Īśvara (God) whose nature is described by Vātsyāyana in the Nyāya-bhāṣya 4-1-21, as follows:—

God is a soul specially endowed with qualities. He is freed from misapprehension, carelessness, etc., and is rich with merit, knowledge and concentration. He possesses eight supernatural powers which are the consequences of his merit and concentration. His merit, which conforms to his will, produces merit in each person, and sets the earth and other elements in motion. God is, as it were, the father of all beings. Who can demonstrate the existence of Him who transcends the evidences of perception, inference and scripture?

Emancipation—mokṣa.

In the Nyāya bhāṣya, 1-1-22, there is mention of certain philosophers who maintained that in emancipation there was manifesta-

[1] Here Vātsyāyana refers perhaps to the Jaina syllogism of ten members as illustrated in the Daśavaikālika-niryukti of Bhadrabāhu who, I suppose, was a contemporary of Chandra Gupta II, called Vikramāditya, about 375 A.D. The Jain logician, Anantavīrya, in his commentary on the Nyāyāvatāra, verse 13, says that the best form of syllogism consists of ten parts, the mediocre of five parts and the worst of two parts only.

tion of eternal pleasure of the soul. They based their view on the ground that human activity being always directed towards the attainment of pleasure, it was natural that the end of such activity was the enjoyment of eternal pleasure. They also relied on the scripture-texts (*upaniṣads*) which, according to them, declared that absolute pleasure belonged to the soul that attained emancipation.

Vātsyāyana in the Nyāya-bhāṣya, 1-1-22, opposed the above-mentioned philosophers by saying that emancipation or release (*mokṣa*), which was a condition of immortality freed from fear and change, was attended with a total cessation of pain, but there was no cause for production in the emancipated soul of any pleasure which was eternal. He further said that human activity was directed towards the removal of pain and not to the attainment of pleasure, which was invariably mixed up with pain and which could merely bring about bondage of an intricate form. As regards the scripture-texts these, according to Vātsyāyana, spoke, no doubt, of the essence of soul as being pleasure, but pleasure signified nothing but perfect freedom from pain. Hence emancipation or release was not, according to him, eternal pleasure but an absolute deliverance from pain.

41. Uddyotakara, author of the Nyāya-vārtika (about 635 A.D.).

The latest date assigned to Uddyotakara.

Uddyotakara was the author of a sub-commentary on the Nyāya-sūtra called the Nyāya-vārtika.[1] The Vāsavadattā,[2] an immortal work of the poet Subandhu, mentions Uddyotakara as a rescuer of the Nyāya, while the Vāsavadattā itself is mentioned in the Harṣacarita[3] by Bāṇa as a classical work which humbled the pride of all previous poets. The Harṣacarita[4] describes Bāṇa as a poet who lived at the court of King Śrī Harṣa or Harṣavardhana, and the manner in which the poet introduces himself into the work leaves no room for doubt that he was very young while his patron the king was mature in age and

---

[1] यदक्षपादप्रतिमो भाष्यं वात्स्यायनो जगौ ।
अकारि महतस्तस्य भारद्वाजेन वार्त्तिकम् ॥
(Nyāya-vārtika, closing lines).

[2] न्यायस्थितिमिवोद्द्योतकरस्वरूपां बौद्धसंगतिमिवालङ्कारभूषिताम्..वासवदत्तां ददर्श
(Vāsavadattā, p. 235, Hall's edition).

[3] कवीनामगलद्दर्पो नूनं वासवदत्तया ।
शक्त्येव पाण्डुपुत्राणां गतया कर्णगोचरम् ॥
(Harṣa-carita, ucchvāsa 1).

[4] (Harṣa-carita, ucchvāsa II, p. 58, Iśvara candra Vidyāsāgara's edition).

experience. King Harṣa reigned in Thāneśvara during the whole of the period (A.D. 629–644) that the Chinese pilgrim Hiuen-thsang travelled through India. This leads us to conclude that Bāṇa flourished about A.D. 635, which is the latest date that can be assigned to Uddyotakara.

The date of Uddyotakara.

In the Nyāya-vārtika Uddyotakara mentions a Buddhist treatise on Logic called the Vādavidhi[1] which seems to be only another name for the Vādanyāya by Dharmakīrti. On the other hand Dharmakīrti in his Nyāya-bindu[2] mentions a śāstra which evidently refers to the Nyāya-vārtika, and a śāstra-kāra who seems to be the same as Uddyotakara. Hence we conclude that Dharmakīrti[3] and Uddyotakara were contemporaries who flourished about A.D. 635.

Various names of Uddyotakara.

The name Bhāradvāja,[4] as applied to Uddyotakara, is derived from the family to which he belonged, while he is called Pāśupatācārya[5] on account of his having been a preceptor of the Pāśupata Śaiva sect.

Residence of Uddyotakara.

Nothing is definitely known as to the place where Uddyotakara was born. The only place mentioned by him is Śrughna[6] which is situated on the Western Jumna canal, 40 miles north of Thāneśvara.[7] It seems to me that Uddyotakara, while writing

---

[1] यदपि वादविधौ साध्याभिधानं प्रतिज्ञेति प्रतिज्ञालक्षणमुक्तम् ।

(Nyāya-vārtika, 1-33, pp. 121, A.S.B.).

དམ་བཅས་པ་ཡང་བསྒྲུབ་བྱ་བརྗོད་པའི་ཕྱིར་རོ །

(Vādanyāya of Dhamakīrti in Bstan-ḥgyur, Mdo, Ce. fol. 399).

It is reported that Vasubandhu too wrote a treatise called Vādavidhi, which is no longer extant.

[2] स्वयमिति वादिना यदा साधनमाह । एतेन यदपि क्वचिच्छास्त्रे स्थितः साधनमाह । तच्छास्त्रकारेण तस्मिन् धर्मिणि...

(Nyāya-bindu, chap. III, pp. 110–11, Peterson's edition).

[3] For the date of Dharmakīrti see my "Uddyotakara, a contemporary of Dharmakīrti" in the Journal of the Royal Asiatic Society of Great Britain and Ireland, for July 1914.

[4], [5] इति श्री परमर्षिभारद्वाजपाशुपताचार्य्य श्रीमदुद्द्योतकरकृतौ न्यायवार्त्तिके पञ्चमोऽध्यायः ।

(Nyāya-vārtika, colophon).

[6] एष पन्थाः स्रुघ्नं गच्छति

(Nyāya-vārtika 1-33, p. 113, M.M. Vindhyeśvarī Prasāda Dvivedin's edition).

[7] It was very probably this route by which Hiuen-thsang reached Śrughna on April 1, A.D. 635. (*Vide* Beal's Buddhist Records, pp. 186-90) Cunningham observes: "The importance of the position [of Śrughna] is shown by the fact that

the Nyāya-vārtika, resided at Thāneśvara which was connected with Śrughna by a high road. It is not unlikely that he received some time in his career patronage at the court of Thāneśvara.

42. Uddyotakara's Controversy with the Buddhists.

His aim was to refute the Buddhist doctrines.

The main object which prompted Uddyotakara to write his sub-commentary was to oppose Dignāga, Nāgārjuna, and other Buddhist logicians that preceded him. This is evident from the opening lines of the Nyāya-vārtika in which he says: "Akṣapāda the foremost of sages propounded a śāstra (body of doctrines) for the peace of the world; and I shall write an expository treatise on it to remove the veil of error cast by quibblers." [1]

Dignāga is throughout designated as *Bhadanta* [2] (a venerable Buddhist monk) whose definition of perception (*pratyakṣa*) is criticised in the Nyāya-vārtika (1-1-4), and whose denial of the evidences of comparison (*upamāna*) and verbal testimony (*śabda*) is reviewed in the same work (1-1-6, 7).

Do Buddhists deny the Soul?

The Buddhistic denial of the soul criticised.

In the Nyāya-vārtika, 3-1-1,[3] Uddyotakara points out a certain inconsistency among the doctrines maintained by Bhadanta. Uddyotakara observes: "If you (Buddhists) say that

---

it stands on the high road leading from the Gangetic Doab, *via* Mirat, Saharanpur, and Ambala, to the Upper Panjab and commands the passage of the Jumna By this route Mahmud of Ghazni returned from his expedition to Kanoj, by this route Timur returned from his plundering campaign at Haridwar, and by this route Baber advanced to the conquest of Delhi."

(Ancient Geography of India, p. 347).

1 यदक्षपादः प्रवरो मुनीनां
शमाय शास्त्रं जगतो जगाद ।
कुतार्किकाज्ञाननिवृत्तिहेतुः
करिष्यते तस्य मया निबन्धः ॥

(Nyāya-vārtika, opening lines).

2 अपरो प्रमाणाभिमता भदन्तस्य यथा गवयशब्दस्य प्रतिपत्तेः संज्ञासंज्ञिसम्बन्धं प्रतिपद्यते इति सूत्रार्थः

(Nyāya-vārtika, 1-1-6, p. 61, A.S.B.).

3 न चात्मानमनभ्युपगच्छता तथागत दर्शनम् अर्थवत्तायां व्यवस्थापयितुं शक्यम्, न चेदं वचनं नास्ति सर्वाभिसमयसूत्रेऽभिधानात् । तस्मान्नास्ति आत्मेति ब्रुवाणः सिद्धान्तं बाधत इति ।

(Nyāya-vārtika, 3-1-1, pp. 341-42).

there is no soul, you make an assertion contrary to your own doctrine. Your doctrine is that "I" is identical neither with *rūpa* (form) nor with *vedanā* (feeling), *saṁjñā* (sensation) *saṁksāra* (impression) and *vijñāna* (knowledge). Your scripture declares: 'O monk, I am not *rūpa* nor am I *vedanā*; I am not *saṁjñā*. *saṁskāra* is not myself; and neither am I *vijñāna*).' The "I" which is not identical with the five *skandhas* (aggregates of being) is in fact the soul. One who does not admit the soul can make no sense out of the philosophy of Tathāgata. The text quoted above about the existence of the soul cannot be denied) as it actually occurs in the Sarvābhisamaya-sūtra.' It is therefore clear that if Bhadanta says, 'there is no *ātman*,' he hurts his own system."

"A further text speaking of the soul is as follows:—'I shall teach you, O Bhikṣus, the burden and the burden-bearer: the five *skandhas* are the burden, and the *pudgala* is the burden-bearer.' He who says, 'there is no *ātman*,' is a heretic."[2]

---

[1] तथा भारं वो भिक्षवो देशयिष्यामि भारहारं च भारः पञ्चस्कन्धा भारहारश्च पुद्गल इति। यश्चात्मा नास्तीति स मिथ्यादृष्टिको भवतीति सूत्रम्;

भारं वो भिक्खवे देसिस्सामि। भारहारं च। कतमो भिक्खवे भारो। पञ्चुपादानक्खन्धा तिस्स वचनीयम्। कतमो च भिक्खवे भारहारो। पुग्गलो तिस्स वचनीयं।

(Nyāya-vārtika, 3-1-1, p. 342, quoted from Saṁyutta nikāya part III, chap. III, p. 25, Pali Text Society's edition).

[2] The following correspondence, on the Buddhistic denial of the soul, quoted from the Journal of the Royal Asiatic Society of Great Britain and Ireland for 1901, pp. 307-308, and p. 573, will be read with interest:—

"*Buddhist sūtras quoted by Brāhmaṇa authors.*

Dear Mr. Rhys Davids,—Several months ago I invited my friend Professor Satis Chandra Vidyabhusana, the joint editor of the Buddhist Text Society's Journal—whose essays are eulogised in the last Bulletin of M. Barth [of Paris]—to collect the numerous references to Buddhist sayings or tenets, scattered in the treatises of Uddyotakara, Udayana, Vācaspati Miśra, etc. I heard from the Paṇḍita that, just at the same time, he had been urged by yourself to devote himself to that work. A few weeks ago, he sent me copious materials: their publication will, no doubt, prove itself a contribution of some importance to our knowledge of the great schools of the Mahāyāna Philosophy, and of the polemical relations between these schools and the orthodox adherents of the Darśanas.

We shall first publish, in the *Muséon*, our observations and references to the Bauddha chapter of the Sarva-darśana-saṁgraha, without any claim to philological or historical accuracy and exhaustion of the subject—of course! We intend to show only the practicability and usefulness of such inquiries, if trained scholars would but care for it. Nevertheless, two discoveries of Professor S. C. Vidyabhusana deserve actual notice in a more *conspicuous* journal.

The first is the following:—The Śālistamba-sūtra quoted by Candrakīrti in chap. xxvi of the Madhyamakavṛtti, by Śāntideva in the Śikṣāsamuccaya, also by Prajñākaramati in the Bodhicaryāvatāratīkā as giving a complete *exposé* of the **Pratītya-samutpāda,** is quoted (without any mention of its name) with remark-

43. Uddyotakara criticises Vasubandhu and Nāgārjuna.

The Buddhist theory of example, *dṛṣṭānta*, criticised.

In his Vārtika on the Nyāya-sūtra, 1-1-37, Uddyotakara refers to a Buddhist philosopher (identified with Vasubandhu) who remarked that the three parts of a syllogism as defined by Akṣapāda were not so ingenious as they

---

able fidelity by the celebrated author of the Bhāmatī, *ad* Brahma-sūtra ii, 2, 19. Fragments of the same sūtra are to be found in the Sarvadarśana. . . . . .

. . . .

The second also is curious :—The sūtra of "the burden and the burden-bearer," as well known from the Abhidharmakośa, the Bodhicaryāvatāraṭīkā, and the Tibetan authorities, was one of the most decisive authorities referred to by the "Pudgalavādins." This very sūtra is cited by Uddyotakara against its Buddhist opponents: —" therefore, if [a Buddhist] says, '[there] is no *ātman*,' he hurts [his own] system. It has been said: 'I shall teach you, Bhikṣus, the burden and the burden-bearer: the five *skandhas* are the burden, and the *pudgala* is the burden-bearer.' 'Who says [there] is no *ātman* is heretic.' Such is the sūtra."

Are these last words authentic ?... This seems very hard; but you know, dear Mr. Rhys Davids, that I cannot help thinking that the *pudgalavāda* is more in harmony with the *duḥkha satya* and the law of *karman* than the *nairātmyavāda*, etc.....

Ghent, Louis De La Vallée Poussin.
January 7, 1901.

The Sūtra of the Burden-bearer.

Wurzburg,

April 22, 1901.

Dear Professor Rhys Davids,—It will probably not have escaped your notice that the "sūtra of the Burden and the Burden-bearer," which Professor de la Vallee Poussin, in his letter in your last issue (p. 308), refers to as quoted by the Pudgalavādins as an authority on their side, is actually to be found in our Pali Piṭaka, at vol. iii, p. 25, of the Saṁyutta Nikāya.

The manner in which this ancient sutta was appealed to by the opponents of the Bauddhas as being against the Bauddhas' doctrine of the *non-ātman* is very instructive.

Far from being entitled, on the ground of this sutta, to consider the *pudgalavāda* as a genuine portion of the ancient doctrine, it is just the other way. For we have in it a proof that *puggala* in the sense of a soul (*attā*) was unknown to the author of the sutta. He uses the word quite clearly as referring simply to the five *skandhas*, and indeed states so in so many words. To him *bhāra* and *hāra*, Burden and Bearer, form one inseparable unity, and the laying down of the Burden, that is of the skandhas, is synonymous and simultaneous with the laying down of the Bearer (Bhāranikkhepana = hāranikkhepana).

Uddyotakara, in his use of the sutta, is guilty of what we call, in logic, a *sub reptio*.

Yours sincerely,

E. Hardy.

[From the point of view of absolute truth the soul is unreal, but from the empirical standpoint it is real. The illusory relation between the fivefold aggregate and the soul as a burden and its bearer will continue until their absorption into Śūnyatā or nirvāṇa.]

appeared.[1] Vācaspati Miśra in his Vārtika-tātparya-ṭikā[2] on the Nyāya-sūtra, 1-1-37, quotes the same remark which he explains by saying that "here Subandhu [evidently the same as Vasubandhu] observes that the three parts of a syllogism beginning with 'proposition' as defined by Akṣapāda are badly confounded." Uddyotakara does not examine the remark, but satirically says that the person from whom it emanated was a mighty logician!!! In this connection there is however an examination of the definition, given by a Buddhist logician, of an example (*dṛṣṭānta*)[3] in which, according to him, the reason (middle term) and the predicate (major term) co-abide, e.g. in a syllogism, viz. sound is non-eternal, because it is a product, like a pot—the non-eternality and producibility co-abide in a pot. Uddyotakara asks: how can a Buddhist, a holder of the doctrine of momentariness, maintain that non-eternality (which refers to posterior non-existence) and producibility (which refers to prior non-existence) co-exist in a pot (which possesses a mere momentary existence)?

Nāgārjuna criticised.

On similar grounds Uddyotakara attacks the Buddhist logician Nāgārjuna[4], who in his Pramāṇa-vihetana or Pramāṇa-vidhvaṁsana (q.v.) defines an example as the place in which is decisively shown the relation between the reason (middle term) and its invariable companion the predicate (major term). It is impossible for a Buddhist to show the correlation of the reason (e.g. the fact that it is a product) and the predicate (e.g. non-eternality), since the two cannot, according to him, co-exist.

---

[1] तदेतस्मिन्नवयवत्रये एवं लक्षणेनोपपादिते तेषां त्रयो दुर्विभावा इति । अनेन वाक्येन महानैयायिकत्वमात्मनः ख्यापितं भवति ।

(Nyāya-vārtika, 1-1-37, p. 139, Bibliotheca Indica series).

[2] अत्र सुबन्धुना प्रतिज्ञादयस्त्रयोऽवयवा दुर्विहिता अक्षपादलक्षणेनेत्युक्तं तद्दूषयति ।

(Nyāya-vārtika-tātparya-ṭīkā, 1-1-37, p. 203, Vizianagaram Sanskrit series).

[3] तथा सिद्धो दृष्टान्त इत्यन्ये ।

(Nyāya-vārtika, 1-1-37, p. 139, Bibliotheca Indica series).

[4] In the Pramāṇa-vihetana (*vidhvaṁsana*), an example (*dṛṣṭānta*, in Tibetan: dpe) is defined by Nāgārjuna thus:—

དཔེ་ཞེས་པ་ནི་གཏན་ཚིགས་ཀྱི་ཕྱོགས་ཁྱབ་པ་དང་འབྲེལ་བ་གཏན་ལ་དབབ་པའི་གཞིར་འདོད་ལ །

(Bstan-hgyur, Mdo, ha, folio 417).

Uddyotakara opposes the above definition as follows :—

एतेन तयोः सम्बन्धि निदर्शनं दृष्टान्त इति प्रत्युक्तम् ।

(Nyāya-vārtika, 1-1-37, pp. 139-140, edited by M. M. Vindhyeśvarī Prasād in the Bibliotheca Indica series, Calcutta).

44. Uddyotakara criticises Dignāga.

The theory of perception, *pratykṣa*, controverted.

Uddyotakara in his Nyāya-vārtika[1] mentions a Buddhist logician Bhadanta (same as Dignāga)[2] who defines perception (*pratyakṣa*) as a knowledge which is free from reflection (*kalpanā*),[3] that is, which is not connected with a name or genus. Perception is in fact a pure sense-knowledge which is not expressed by a name or specified by a genus, which is specific in itself and cognised by itself.

This definition of perception is declared by Uddyotakara to be absurd. If a certain knowledge were not expressible by a name, how could it be called perception? The word perception would be meaningless if the knowledge corresponding to it were not capable of being expressed by a name. In the same way if perception referred to a specific individual (*svarūpa*) and not to a genus, it could not, according to Uddyotakara, be grasped in our mind and expreseed to our fellowmen, since our cognition of an object invariably assumes a generic form.

---

[1] अपरे तु मन्यन्ते प्रत्यक्षं कल्पनापोढमिति । अथ केयं कल्पना नाम जातियोजनेति । यत् किल न नाम्नाभिधीयते न च जात्यादिभिर्व्यपदिश्यते विषयस्वरूपानुविधायि परिच्छेदकमात्मसंवेद्यं तत् प्रत्यक्षमिति ।...... ......अथास्य वाक्यस्य कोऽर्थो यदि प्रत्यक्षं व्याख्यातः कथं प्रत्यक्षं कल्पनापोढमिति यानेन वाक्येनाभिधीयते न चाभिधेयमिति कोऽन्यो भदन्तादस्मादर्हति ।

(Nyāya-vārtika, 1-1-4, pp. 44–45, Bibliotheca Indica series).

[2] Vācaspati Miśra in his gloss on the above observes:—

संप्रति दिङ्नागस्य लक्षणमुपन्यस्यति अपरे इति

(Nyāya-vārtika-tātparya-ṭīkā, 1-1-4, p. 102, Vizianagaram Sanskrit series).

[3] Vācaspati and Jayanta observe that *kalpanā*, reflection, is the connection of an object with its adjuncts enumerated below:—

(1) Name (*nāma*), e.g. dittha, etc.
(2) Genus (jāti), e.g. cow, etc.
(3) Quality (*guṇa*), e.g. dark, etc.
(4) Action (*kriyā*), e.g. walking, etc.
(5) An adventitious entity (*dravya*), e.g. a load (on the back), etc.

A knowledge unconnected with any of these adjuncts is perception. For instance, our perception of an individual cow consists of a specific knowledge into which the name, genus, etc., of the individual cow do not enter.

Cf. पञ्च चैताः कल्पना भवन्ति जातिकल्पना गुणकल्पना क्रियाकल्पना नामकल्पना द्रव्यकल्पना चेति ।

(Jayanta's Nyāya-mañjarī, chapter II, p. 93, edited by Gaṅgādhar Sastri, Vizianagaram, Sanskrit series; compare also Vācaspati Miśra's Nyāya-vārtika-tātparya-ṭīkā, 1-1-4, p. 102, edited by Gaṅgādhar Sāstri, Vizianagaram Sanskrit series).

The word *kalpanā* seems to have been used in a different sense by Dignāga (q.v.). The idea of genus (*jāti*), quality (*guṇa*), action (*kriyā*), and name (*nāma*) was derived from the Mahābhāṣya of Patañjali.

45. Uddyotakara's Explanation of Perception.

Perception (*pratyakṣa*), as defined by Akṣapāda, is knowledge which is produced by the intercourse of a sense with its object.

The *intercourse* (*sannikarṣa*), which is of six kinds, is explained in the Nyāya-vārtika (1-1-4) of Uddyotakara as follows:—

(1) Conjunction (*saṁyoga*)—e.g. a jar is perceived through its conjunction with our eye.

(2) Conjoined-inherence (*saṁyukta-samavāya*)—e.g. in perceiving the colour of a jar there is conjunction of our eye with the jar in which colour inheres.

(3) Conjoined-inherent inherence (*saṁyukta-samaveta-samavāya*)—e.g. in perceiving the generic nature of the colour (colourness) there is conjunction of our eye with the jar in which inheres colour wherein again colourness is inherent.

(4) Inherence (*samavāya*)—e.g. we perceive sound which inheres in our ear-cavity.

(5) Inherent-inherence (*samaveta-samavāya*)—e.g. we perceive soundness (the generic nature of sound) which inheres in sound which in its turn is inherent in our ear-cavity.

(6) Qualification or particularity (*viśeṣaṇatā*)—e.g. we perceive the non-existence of a thing through the particularisation of the spot which the thing could occupy on earth.

46. Uddyotakara's Definition of Inference.

Uddyotakara in his Nyāya-vartika, 1-1-5, defines inference [1] (*anumāna*) as that knowledge which is preceded by perception of the reason (middle term) and remembrance of its invariable concomitance with the predicate (major term). For an instance, I perceive that this hill has smoke which I remember to be invariably concomitant with fire, and hence I infer that this hill has fire. The form of inference is as follows:—

(1) Whatever is smoky is fiery.
(2) This hill is smoky.
(3) Therefore this hill is fiery.

Inference is divided by Uddyotakara as (1) exclusively—affirmative (*anvayī*), (2) exclusively—negative (*vyatirekī*), and (3) affirmative-negative (*anvaya-vyatirekī*). Exclusively—affirmative is the inference in which the middle term abides in the major term as well as in things homogeneous with it, there being nothing which is heterogeneous from the major term, e.g. this is nameable, because it is

---

[1] स्मृत्यनुगृहीतो लिङ्गपरामर्शोऽनुमानम् ।

(Nyāya-vārtika, 1-1-5, p. 47, M.M. Vindheśvarī Prasada's edition).

Inference is *liṅga-parāmarśa* (a syllogism from sign) as aided by remembrance.

knowable. Exclusively-negative is the inference in which the middle term abides in the minor term alone, there being nothing else in which that term is known to be present, e.g the earth is different from other elements, because it possesses smell. Affirmative—negative is the inference in which the middle term, while abiding in things homogeneous with the major term, does not abide in any thing heterogeneous from the same, e.g. sound is non-eternal, because it is cognised by our senses.

47. Uddyotakara's Theory of Verbal Knowledge.

The signification of letters.

If a word is a mere combination of letters, how do we cogn'se a thing on hearing the word?

How does a word signify a thing?

The *Nyāya* theory of Uddyotakara.

Uddyotakara in his Vârtika on the Nyāya-sūtra, 2-2-55, says we become cognisant of a thing on hearing the last letter of its corresponding word as aided by the recollection of the preceding letters, i.e. when we hear the last letter, there is a collective recollection of all the previous letters. For instance, the word "cow" cannot present to us any thing until we have heard its last letter, viz. *w*, as aided by our recollection of the preceding letters, viz. *c* and *o*. The letters *c*, *o* and *w* by a conventional association produce in us the cognition of the thing called cow. This is the way in which things are signified by letters or rather words composed of letters, in accordance with the Nyāya philosophy followed by Uddyotakara.

Sphoṭa-vāda—the doctrine of phonetic explosion.

A rival theory.

Sphoṭa the outburst of a conglomerate sound.

Uddyotakara in his Nyâya-vārtika, 2-2-55, alludes, however, to certain sages who held that things could not be signified by letters. These sages, as pointed out by Vācaspati Miśra in his Nyāya-vārtika tātparya-ṭikā, 2-2-55, were supporters of *sphoṭa-vāda*, the theory of phonetic explosion. According to them, a thing is not signified by letters -no matter whether the letters are taken in their separate or collective form. No single letter of a word can produce cognition of a thing corresponding to the word. Neither *c* nor *o* nor *w* as separated from one another can produce in us the cognition of a thing called cow. The letters in their collective form too cannot produce the cognition, because each letter, as soon as it is pronounced, perishes and does not continue long to form a whole word. *C*, *o* and *w* not being able to exist simultaneously cannot produce the cognition of a cow.

We cannot also, they say, derive the cognition of a thing from a word on hearing its last letter as aided by the recollection of the preceding letters, because the recollection of letters can bring about only the *letters*, but not the *things* corresponding to them. Yet nobody can deny that on hearing the word "cow" we become cognisant of the thing called "cow." Hence there must be something over and above the letters which produces the cognition of the thing. This something is a conglomerate sound which bursts out after each letter has been uttered. It is distinct from the letters but revealed by them. This outburst of a conglomerate sound, that is, of a word as a whole, is called *sphoṭa*, which literally signifies an explosion of sounds. When we utter the first letter of a word there is revelation of the *sphoṭa*, which becomes more and more explicit along with the utterance of the following letters, until at last we become cognisant of the thing signified by the word.

Apoha—negation of the opposite.

Does a word denote *apoha*, exclusion?

In the Nyāya-vārtika, 2-2-65, Uddyotakara mentions the Buddhists who hold that what forms the denotation of a word is really *apoha*,[1] exclusion of the opposites. A word bears, according to them, a denotation of exclusion; that is, it denotes exclusion of what is denoted by other words. Thus the denotation of a cow is the exclusion of the denotation of a non-cow, that is, a cow is that which is not a non-cow. This theory is controverted by Uddyotakara on the ground (1) that we cannot conceive of a negative denotation, that is, the denotation of exclusion, unless we have previously conceived of a denotation of a positive character, e.g. a man can form no idea of a non-cow until he has formed the idea of a cow from which the former idea is to be excluded, and if he has already conceived of the denotation of a cow, there is no necessity for a further denotation of exclusion; (2) though in the case of two opposite (contradictory) words the denotation of one word may exclude that of the other, the exclusion will not be possible in the case of such a word as "all" which has nothing to exclude.

48. Uddyotakara's Theory of Sufferings.

Channels of sufferings.

Uddyotakara in his Nyāya-vārtika, 1-1-1, says that pain or suffering (*duḥkha*) is of twenty-one kinds, viz. (1) the body, (2-7) the six senses (the

---

[1] For a full criticism of the Vaiyākaraṇa doctrine of *apoha* consult the Nyāya-mañjarī, chapter VI. Cf. also Nyāya-vārtika, 2-2-65, Bibliotheca Indica, Mīmāṁsā-vārtika, and Vaiyākaraṇa-bhūṣaṇa-sāra of Kauṇḍa Bhaṭṭa.

eye, ear, nose, tongue, skin and mind), (8–13) the six objects of sense (colour, sound, odour, flavour touch and desire, etc.), (14–19) the six cognitions (visual, auditory, olfactory, gustatory, tactual and mental), (20) pleasure, and (21) pain. Of these the body is regarded as "pain" because it is the abode of all painful experiences; the senses, objects and cognitions are called "pains," because they constitute the channels through which pain reaches us; pleasure is designated as pain because it is always accompanied by the latter; and pain is by its very nature painful.

49. VĀCASPATI MIŚRA, AUTHOR OF THE NYĀYA-VĀRTIKA-TĀTPARYA-ṬĪKĀ (ABOUT 841 A.D.).

Vācaspati supports the Brāhmanic interpretations.

Dharmakīrti and several other Buddhist logicians[1] having compiled treatises subversive of the interpretations of Vātsyāyana and Uddyotakara, a Brāhmaṇa logician of great erudition named Vācaspati Miśra wrote, in support of the Brāhmaṇa commentators, an elaborate gloss on the Nyāya-vārtika called the **Nyāya-vārtika-tātparya-ṭīkā**.[2]

Vācaspati's place and time.

Vācaspati, who is reputed to be a native of Mithilā (modern Darbhanga in North Behar), must have flourished in the ninth century A.D., as he compiled his **Nyāya-sūci-nibandha**[3] in the year 898, which evidently refers to the *saṁvat* era and corresponds to 841 A.D. He preceded the Buddhist logician Ratnakīrti[4] (about 1000 A.D.) who quotes him.

---

[1] यद्यपि भाष्यकृता कृतव्युत्पादनमेतत् तथापि दिङ्नागप्रभृतिभिरर्वाचीनैः कुहेतुसन्तमस-समुत्थापनेनाच्छादितं शास्त्रं न तत्त्वनिर्णयाय पर्याप्तम् ।

(Nyāya-vārtika-ṭātparya-ṭīkā, opening lines, edited by M.M. Gaṅgadhar Sastri in the Vizianagaram Sanskrit series).

[2] In order to prevent interpolations into the Nyāya-sūtra, Vācaspati compiled an Index of the sūtras of the work called Nyāya-sūci-nibandha.

[3] न्यायसूचीनिबन्धोऽसावकारि सुधियां मुदे ।
श्रीवाचस्पतिमिश्रेण वस्वङ्कवसुवत्सरे ।

(Nyāya-sūci-nibandha, colophon).

The year 898, if it refers to the saṁvat era, corresponds to 841 A.D., but if it refers to the śaka era, corresponds to 976 A.D.

[4] Apoha-siddhi, p. 7; Kṣaṇabhaṅga-siddhi, p. 58 (included in Six Buddhist Nyāya Tracts, edited by H. P. Shāstri).

Trilocana, preceptor of Vācaspati.

Vācaspati Miśra, whose patron was king Nṛga,[1] received instruction in philosophy from a teacher named Trilocana.[2] Vācaspati plainly admits that his explanation of *pratyakṣa* (perception), in so far as it refers to its division into *savikalpaka* (the determinate), and *nirvikalpaka* (the indeterminate), is derived neither from the commentary of Vātsyāyana nor from the subcommentary of Uddyotakara, but reflects directly the teaching of his preceptor Trilocana. This Trilocana, evidently a writer on Vaiśeṣika philosophy, must have flourished before 1000 A.D. when his doctrines of generality[3] (*samavāya*) and causality[4] (*kārya, sahakārikāraṇa*), etc., were criticised by the Buddhist logician Ratnakīrti the famous author of Apoha-siddhi and Kṣaṇabhaṅga-siddhi. Rājaśekhara (about 917 A.D.) mentions Trilocana[5] to whom is ascribed a poem called Pārtha-vijaya.

Vācaspati's other works.

Vācaspati Miśra's Nyāya-kaṇikā,[6] a work on logic, is not now available. He is said to have written commentaries on the works of all the schools of philosophy. His commentary on the Vedānta-bhāṣya called Bhāmatī-ṭīkā and that on the Sāṁkhya-kārikā called Sāṁkhya-

---

1 नरेश्वरा यच्चरितानुकारम् इच्छन्ति कर्त्तुं न च पारयन्ति ।
तस्मिन महीपे महनीयकीर्त्तौ श्रीमन्नृगेऽकारि मया निबन्धः ॥

(Bhāmatī, last line).

अस्माभिः
2 त्रिलोचन गुरून्नीतमार्गानुगमनोन्मुखैः ।
यथामानं यथावस्तु व्याख्यातमिदमीदृशम् ॥

(Nyāya-vārtika-tātparya-ṭīkā, 1-1-4, p. 87, M.M. Gangadhar Sastri's edition).

3 यत्तु त्रिलोचनः । सकल गोत्वादीनां सामान्यविशेषाणां स्वाश्रये समवायः सामान्यम् .....

(Ratnakīrti's Apoha-siddhi, p. 13, included in the "Six Buddhist Nyāya Tracts," edited by M.M. Hara Prasad Shastri in the Bibliotheca Indica series, Calcutta).

4 त्रिलोचनस्त्वाशयं संक्षिप्तार्थः । कार्य्यमेव हि सहकारिणमपेक्षते । न कार्य्योत्पत्ति हेतुः ।

(Ratnakīrti's Kṣaṇabhaṅga-siddhi, p. 58, included in the "Six Buddhist Nyāya Tracts").

5 The following stanza, which is said to belong to the Sūkti-muktāvali of Rājaśekhara, refers to Trilocana:—

कर्तुं त्रिलोचनादन्यः कः पार्थं विजयं क्षमः ।
तदर्थः शक्यते द्रष्टुं लोचनद्वयिभिः कथम् ॥

Who else but Trilocana is able to compose a Pārtha-vijaya? How can its purport be perceived by the two-eyed? [It took a three-eyed *Trilocana* to compose the poem, how can a two-eyed mortal understand it?]

(Sanskrit Poems of Mayūra, Introduction, p. 53, Columbia University series, edited by Dr. G. P. Quackenbos).

6 Mentioned in the Nyāya-vārtika-tātparaya-ṭīkā, p. 395, Vizianagram Sanskrit series.

tattva-kaumudī occupy a most important place in the philosophical literature of India. Being equally at home in all the systems of philosophy and yet following no one of them as his own, Vācaspati was designated as *Sarva-tantra-svatantra*, "master of all systems but reliant on no one of them in particular."

Reference to the four Buddhist schools.

In the Nyāya-vārtika-tātparya-ṭikā Vācaspati mentions four schools of Buddhist philosophy,[1] viz. the Mādhyamika, Vijñāna-vāda, Sautrāntika and the Vaibhāṣika including the doctrine of the Vātsīputrīya sect; and repeatedly criticises Dignāga and Dharmakīrti.[2]

50. Vācaspati opposes Dignāga.

The analogue (*jāti*) called "balancing the effect," *kārya-sama*, criticised.

Vācaspati Miśra, in his Nyāya-vārtika-tātparya-ṭikā, criticises the definition of the analogue called "balancing the effect," *kārya-sama*, as given by the Buddhist logician Dignāga, about 500 A.D.[3] "Balancing the effect"[4] is defined by Dignāga as an opposition which one offers by showing that the effect referring to the subject is different from the one referring to the example.

For instance, a disputant argues as follows:—

Sound is non-eternal,
because it is an effect of exertion,
like a pot.

His respondent opposes this argument by saying that no conclusion can be drawn from it, because a sound is not an effect of exertion of the same kind as a pot, the former being caused by a vibration of winds, but the latter by a lump of clay. This sort of futile opposition is, according to Dignāga, signified by the analogue called "balancing the effect."

Vācaspati[5] controverts Dignāga by saying, that the latter's

---

1 Nyāya-vārtika-tātparya-ṭikā, 1-1-23; 1-2-1; 3-1-1; 4-1-33; 4-2-35, etc.

2 Nyāya-vārtika-tātparya-ṭikā, 1-1-1; 1-1-4; 1-1-5; 1-1-6; 1-1-8; 5-2-5, etc.

3 Vācaspati Miśra's Nyāya-vārtika-tātparya-ṭikā, 5-1-37, pp. 488-489, Vizianagaram Sanskrit series, where Dignāga is called Bhadanta.

4 Dignāga defines *kārya-sama* (balancing the effect) as follows:—

कार्य्यत्वान्यत्वलेशेन यत् साध्यासिद्धिदर्शनम् ।
तत् कार्य्यसमम् ॥

(Pramāṇa-samuccaya, chap. VI, quoted by Vācaspati).

5 The Tibetan version runs as follows:—

འབྲས་ཉིད་གཞན་གྱི་ཆ་ཡིས་ནི།
བསྒྲུབ་བྱ་མ་གྲུབ་པར་མཐོང་གང་།
དེ་ནི་འབྲས་མཚུངས་ས་འདི་ཡང་ནི།།

(Pramāṇa-samuccaya, chap. VI, Tshad-ma-kun-las-btus-pa, chap. VI, B̲stan-h̲gyur, M̲do, Ce, folio 13).

definition of "balancing the effect" is untenable, inasmuch as an effect of exertion, in so far as it signifies "coming into a state of existence from that of non-existence," is exactly the same in the case of a sound as in that of a pot. Moreover, if Dignāga's definition were accepted, then the Buddhistic denial of a Maker of the universe would be futile.

Those who believe in God argue as follows :—

The universe has a Maker,
because it is a product,
like a pot.

If Dignāga were to oppose this argument by saying that the universe is not a product of the same kind as a pot, his opposition, continues Vācaspati, would constitute an analogous rejoinder called "balancing the effect." In fact Vācaspati prefers the definition of "balancing the effect" as given by Akṣapāda[1] (q.v.) according to whom an effect of exertion, even when it refers to the subject alone, may be of diverse kinds.

51. Vācaspati criticises Dharmakīrti.

The point of defeat, *nigrahasthāna*.

In the Nyāya-vārtika-tātparya-ṭīkā Vācaspati says that according to the Buddhist logician Kīrti (Dharmakīrti about 635 A.D.) there are only two kinds[2] of the point of defeat (*nigrahasthāna*), which occur respectively (1) when one adduces a reason which is not a proper one (*asādhanāṅga-vacana*), and (2) when one alleges defect in that where there is really no defect (*adoṣodbhāvana*). It is not, continues Kīrti, proper to say that there are twenty-two varieties of the point of defeat inasmuch as all these are included in the two main kinds just mentioned.

Vācaspati controverts the above criticism by saying that sage Akṣapāda too laid down two kinds of the point of defeat which occur respectively (1) when one misunderstands an argument (*Vipratipatti*) or (2) does not understand it at all (*apratipatti*). While in respect of the division of the point of defeat into two

---

Kīrti or Dharmakīrti gives a similar definition :—

साध्येनानुगमात् कार्य्यसामान्येनापि साधने ।
सम्बन्धिभेदाद् भेदोक्तिदोषः कार्य्यसमो मतः ॥

(Quoted by Vācaspati in the Nyāya-vārtika-tātparya-ṭīkā, 5-1-37).

[1] Nyāya-sūtra, 5-1-37.

[2] Vācaspati says :—According to Dharmkīrti there are twenty-two varieties of *nigrahasthāna* which come under two main heads.

आह :—

असाधनाङ्गवचनमदोषोद्भावनं द्वयोः ।
निग्रहस्थानमन्यत्तु न युक्तमिति–नाम् प्रति आह ॥

(Nyāya-vārtika-tātparya-ṭīkā, 5-2-1, p. 492, Vizianagaram Sanskrit series).

kinds, the view of Dharmakīrti does not differ from that of Akṣapāda, the two kinds as laid down by the latter are clearer than those laid down by the former. For instance, non-ingenuity (*apratibhāna*), which consists in one's inability to hit upon a reply, is recognized as a point of defeat, but it is included rather in the two kinds of the point of defeat laid down by Akṣapāda than in those laid down by Kīrti.[1] A person defeated on the score of non-ingenuity may remain speechless or may talk irrelevantly This speechlessness (*tūṣṇīmbhāva*) and irrelevant talk (*pralapita*) are not new points of defeat, although they are recognized as such by Kīrti

Kīrti further observed that "renouncing the proposition" (*pratijñā-saṁnyāsa*) as a point of defeat, is identical with a fallacy of reason (*hetvābhāṣa*), because it involves a reason which is uncertain. Vācaspati opposes him by saying that the uncertainty of reason being pointed out after the proposition has been renounced, the point of defeat must in this case be designated as "renouncing the proposition."[2]

Considering their special characters even Dharmakīrti[3] admits that there are twenty-two varieties of the point of defeat.

52. Vācaspati's Explanation of Determinate and Indeterminate Perceptions, *Savikalpaka* and *Nirvikalpaka*.

Savikalpaka and *Nirvikalpaka* defined.

Vâcaspati[4] following his preceptor Trilocana[5] divides perception into two kinds, viz. determinate or mediate (*savikalpaka*) and indeterminate or immediate (*nirvikalpaka*). The determinate

---

1 Jayanta similarly observes :—

यच्च कीर्त्तिराह द्वाविंशतिधा निग्रहस्थानानि विभज्यन्ते .. . .

(Nyāya-mañjarī, āhnika 12, p. 639, Vizianagaram Sanskrit series).

2 Vācaspati says :—

तस्माद् यदुक्तं कीर्त्तिना किमिदानीं हेत्वाभासादुत्तरप्रतिज्ञासंन्यासापेक्षया तस्य प्रति-वादिनो हेत्वाभास एव वाच्यं निग्रहस्थानमिति तदपास्तम् ।

(Nyāya-vārtika-tātparya-ṭīkā, 5–2–5, p. 499, Vizianagaram Sanskrit series).

3 Jayanta says :—

एतेषां धर्म्मकीर्त्तेरपि च न विमतिर्निग्रहस्थानतायाम् ।

(Nyāya-mañjarī, p. 659, Vizianagaram Sanskrit series).

4 Vācaspati writes :—

व्यवसायात्मकपदं साक्षात् सविकल्पकस्य वाचकं, तथापि व्यवसायो विनिश्चयो विकल्प इत्यनर्थान्तरम् । स एव चात्मा रूपं यस्य तत् सविकल्पकं प्रत्यक्षम् । तदेतदतिस्फुटत्वात् निर्व्वक्तव्ये एव इति भाष्यवार्त्तिककाराभ्याम् न व्याख्यातम् ।

(Nyāya-vārtika-tātparya-ṭīka, p. 87).

5 अवाभि त्रिलोचनगुरूनीतमार्गानुगमनोन्मुखैः ।
यथामानं यथावस्तु व्याख्यातमिदमीदृशम् ॥

(Nyāya-vārtika-tātparya-ṭīkā, p. 87).

is knowledge which admits of specification: it is the knowledge of an object as particularised by its genus, etc., e g. this is a *man* (an individual coming under the genus 'man'). The indeterminate perception on the contrary is that knowledge which admits of no specification: it is the knowledge of an object derived through its first intercourse with one of our senses, e.g. this is *something*.

Niruktakāras criticised.

Vācaspati further observes that the doctrine of determinate and indeterminate perceptions is very easy to comprehend, and has not on that account been explained by Vātsyāyana in his Bhāṣya or Uddyotakara in his Vārtika. The Niruktakāras[1] who flourished before Vācaspati used the term *nirvikalpaka*, but they explained it as the knowledge of an object in which its general (*sāmānya*) and particular (*viśeṣa*) features were combined. Vācaspati controverts the view of the Niruktakāras by saying that if, in the *nirvikalpaka* stage, an object were to combine in itself its general and particular attributes, how could, in the *savikalpaka* stage, the two, viz. the general and the particular, be separated so that one might be predicated of the other in the form, "this (particular) is man (general)."

53. Vācaspati's Theory of Right Knowledge and Wrong Knowledge (*Pramā* and *Apramā*).

Right knowledge (*Pramā* or *tattva-jñāna*) defined in the Nyāya-vārtika, 1-1-2, is the knowledge of a thing as it is, while wrong knowledge or error (*apramā*, *bhrama* or *mithyā jñāna*) is the knowledge of a thing as it is not.

There are conflicting theories as to the exact nature of the wrong knowledge. Vācaspati Miśra in his Nyāya-vārtika-tātparya-ṭīkā, 1-1-2, mentions five different theories which may be summarised as follows:—

(1) *Ātma-khyāti* (manifestation of the self)—is a wrong knowledge in which our cognition, which exists in our mind alone, manifests itself as a thing existing outside of us. The Yogācāra Buddhists, who follow this theory, say that our cognition (or knowledge) alone is real, and its manifestation as external objects is a wrong knowledge.

---

[1] यथाहुर्निरुक्तकाराः । निर्विकल्पकबोधेन द्व्यात्मकस्यापि वस्तुनो ग्रहणम् । तथा—

ततः परं पुनर्वस्तु धर्मैर्जात्यादिभिर्यया ।
बुद्ध्यावसीयते सापि प्रत्यक्षत्वेन संमता ॥

(Nyāya-vārtika-tātparya-ṭīkā, p. 89, Vizianagaram Sanskrit series).

Vātsyāyana and Uddyotakara did not treat of the doctrine of *nirvikalpaka* and *savikalpaka pratyakṣa*. The *Niruktakāras* who treated them cannot be identified. Kumārila Bhaṭṭa, author of the Mīmāṁsā-vārtika (about 630 A.D.), was perhaps the earliest writer who dealt with the doctrine.

(2) *Asat-khyāti* (manifestation of the unreal)—is a wrong knowledge in which a thing, which is non-existent or unreal, manifests itself as existent or real, e.g. when a piece of shell is mistaken for a piece of silver. The piece of silver. being non-existent or unreal, its manifestation is a wrong knowledge. The Mādhyamika Buddhists, who hold this theory. say that all are void and the manifestation to us of our internal states and the external objects is a wrong knowledge.

(3) *Anirvacanīya-khyāti* (manifestation of the undefinable)—is a wrong knowledge in which a thing manifests itself in such a way that we cannot define it either as existent or as non-existent, e.g. when a piece of shell is mistaken for a piece of silver. our knowledge is neither that of a piece of silver (which is not present) nor that of a piece of non-silver (there being an apparent presence of a piece of silver), but that of a thing the nature of which we cannot define. The Advaita-vedāntins. who hold this theory, say that if we regard the external things as real, it will be a wrong knowledge, inasmuch as the things are undefinable, that is. neither do they possess a real existence nor are they devoid of an empirical or apparent existence.

(4) *A-khyāti* (non-manifestation)—is knowledge in which the difference of one thing (subject) from another thing (predicate) is not manifested on account of certain defects of our senses, etc., and owing to this non-manifestation we say that the one (subject) is identical with the other (predicate), e.g. when a piece of shell is supposed by us to be a piece of silver. in the form "this is silver," there are *perception* of "this" (shell) and *recollection* of "silver" together with a non-manifestation of their difference caused by the defects of our senses, etc. This theory is upheld by the Prābhākaras.

(5) *Anyathā-khyāti* (a converse manifestation)—is a wrong knowledge in which one thing is mistaken for another thing on the perception of those properties of the first thing which are possessed in common by the second thing, and a thing possessed of these common properties is particularised not as the first thing (whose special properties are not, owing to certain defects of our senses, etc., cognised by us), but as the second thing which presents itself to our recollection at the time, e.g. when a piece of shell is mistaken for a piece of silver in the form "this is silver," the properties common to both (shell and silver), are supposed, by the person who commits the mistake, to abide not in "this" (shell), but in "silver" which he remembers at the time. This theory is propounded by the Naiyāyikas.

In a wrong knowledge when a person mistakes one thing (e.g. a shell) for any other thing (e.g. a piece of silver), there is an actual perception, through imagination (*jñāna-lakṣaṇa*), of that "other thing," because if he had not perceived it at all, he would not have exerted himself to pick it up. In fact when our mistake is discovered we remember that we actually perceived the thing. Hence the only rational theory, according to Vācaspati Miśra, is that of *anyathākhyāti* which satisfactorily explains the origination of wrong knowledge.

53a. Vācaspati's theory of *Condition* (*upādhi*).

Vācaspati Miśra, in his Nyāya-vārtika-tātparya-ṭīkā, 1-1-1, says that an inference is based on the invariable concomitance (*vyāpti*) of its middle term with the major term. Now, what is the nature of this invariable concomitance? The Buddhists say that the middle term is in invariable concomitance with the major term, if the former stand to the latter in causal relation (*kārya kāraṇa*) or the relation of identity (*svabhāva*).

Seeing that the Buddhistic definition is too narrow and too wide, Vācaspati sets it aside by saying that the invariable concomitance is that relation of the middle term with the major term which is freed from all conditions (*upādhi*). A condition is illustrated in the following inference:—

The hill is full of smoke,
because it is full of fire.

This is a wrong inference, because smoke always accompanies fire, but fire does not always accompany smoke.

The inference will, however, be right if we attach a condition to its middle term in the following way:—

The hill is full of smoke,
because it is full of fire (fed by wet fuel).

Here 'wet fuel' is a condition (*upādhi*), which is attached to the middle term 'fire.' A fire by itself may not always accompany smoke, but when it is fed by wet fuel it is always attended by the same.

This kind of condition should not qualify the middle term, which must be perfectly free from all conditions. If an inference is to be right, a disputant must remove from it all conditions which are suspected (*śaṅkita*) by himself or with which he is charged (*samāropita*) by his opponent.

53b. The Theory of Cause and Effect (*kārya-kāraṇa*).

In the Nyāya-kaṇikā as also in the Nyāya-vārtika-tātparya-ṭīkā, 3-2-17, Vācaspati Miśra criticises, on one hand, those who hold that an effect (*kārya*) springs up from nothing (*asataḥ sajjāyate*) and, on the other hand, the sāṁkhyas who hold that an effect pre-exists in its cause (*sataḥ sajjāyate*). He expounds the doctrine of the Naiāyikas that an effect does not pre-exist in its cause, but that from a cause something originates which did not exist before such origination.

53c. The Buddhist and Jaina Scriptures condemned.

Vācaspati Miśra in his Nyāya-vārtika-tātparya-ṭīkā, 2–2–68, says that the author of the Brāhmaṇic scripture is God, while that of the Buddhist and Jaina scriptures is Buddha and Ṛṣabhadeva. While our God is omniscient and all-powerful, Buddha and Ṛṣabhadeva are not so. How can we then place any confidence in the latter? While the Brāhmaṇic scripture legislates for men divided into four classes and passing through four stages of life, the scriptures of the Buddhists and Jainas do not concern themselves much with the regulation of practical life. At the dissolution of the world the Buddhist and Jaina scriptures will disappear, while the tradition of the Brāhmaṇic scriptures will be kept up by God.

---

54. Udayanācārya, Author of the Nyāya-vārtika-tātparya-ṭīkā-pariśuddhi (984 A.D.).

Vācaspati Miśra was criticised by a host of Buddhist logicians, and it was to vindicate him against their attacks that Udayanācārya or Udayakara, a Brahmaṇa logician of Mithilā, wrote a sub-gloss on Vācaspati's work called the **Nyāya-vārtika tātparya-ṭīkā-pariśuddhi.**[1] He wrote several other works such as the Kusumāñjalī, Ātma-tattva-viveka,[2] Kiraṇāvalī and Nyāya-pariśiṣṭa (also called Bodha siddhi or Bodha-śuddhi).

Udayana's works.

[1] The Nyāya-vārtika-tātparya-ṭīkā-pariśuddhi embodies elaborate notes on the Nyāya-vārtika-tātparya-ṭīkā of Vācaspati Miśra whose words Udayana proposes to elucidate by the grace of the Goddess of Speech, thus:—

मातः सरस्वति पुनः पुनरेष नत्वा
बद्धाञ्जलिः किमपि विज्ञपयाम्यवेहि ।
वाक्चेतसोर्मम तथा भव सावधाना
वाचस्पतेर्वचसि न स्खलतो यथैते ॥

(Nyāya-vārtika-tātparya-ṭīkā-pariśuddhi, 1-1-1, edited by M.M. Vindhyesvari Prasad Dvivedin and M.M. Lakshman Śāstri, in the Bibliotheca Indica series.

[2] बकुलर परतन्त्र प्रान्तर ध्वान्तभीत स्तिमित पथिकरत्या सार्थवाहेन यस्मात् ।
इदमुदय करेण न्याय सौधा समाप्ता मतिभनिनवभूष मतिर्न गर्त्ता गुणैः ॥

(Ātma-tattva-viveka, last lines).

His place and time.

Udayana, better known as Ācārya, was the author of another work called Lakṣaṇāvalī,[1] in the introduction to which he says that he composed the book in the Śaka year 906 corresponding to A.D. 984. He was born in Maṅ-roṇi, a village 20 miles north of Darbhanga in Mithilā on the east bank of the river Kamalā.

55. Udayana combats the Buddhists.

Udayana's victory over the Buddhists causes his death.

It is said of Udayana that he frequently defeated the Buddhists[2] in religious discussions, but the latter did not admit his victory over them. One day, there was a very hot contest between him and the Buddhists on the question of the existence of God. Not being able to make them believe in God by arguments, Udayana ascended the top of a hill, taking a Brāhmaṇa and a Śramaṇa (Buddhist) with him. He hurled both of them down from the top of the hill. When falling down on the ground, the Brāhmaṇa cried aloud 'there is God,' while the Śramaṇa exclaimed 'there is no God.' It so happened that the Śramaṇa died of the fall, while the Brāhmaṇa came to the ground unhurt. This fact was considered as a convincing proof of the existence of God.

Udayana gained victory but was blamed as a murderer. Becoming penitent, he proceeded to the temple of Jagannātha at Purī. After he had lived there for three days and three nights, he was told in a dream that Jagannātha would not appear before him until he was cleansed of his sin, by performing the penitentiary rites of *tuṣānala* at Benares. Accordingly he went to that city, where he put an end to his life by *tuṣānala*, i.e. by burning himself in a slow fire. It is said that Udayana was not pleased with the decision of Jagannātha, as that deity did not show any mercy towards him in consideration of the services he had rendered to maintain his glorious existence. Udayana, while dying, thus addressed Jagannātha:—

"Proud of thy prowess thou despisest me—upon whom thy existence depended when the Buddhists reigned supreme!"[3]

---

1 तर्काम्बराङ्क प्रमितेष्वतीतेषु शकान्ततः ।
वर्षेषूदयनश्चक्रे सुबोधां लक्षणावलीम् ॥
(Lakṣaṇāvalī, colophon).

2 *Vide* my article on "Buddhism in India" in the Journal, Buddhist Text Society, part I, 1896.

3 ऐश्वर्यमद मत्तः सन् मामवमन्यसे ।
पुनर्बौद्धे समायाते मदधीना तव स्थितिः ॥

56. Udayana opposes Kalyāṇa Rakṣita and Dharmottara.

The doctrine of *apoha*, *kṣaṇa-bhaṅga*, etc., criticised.

Kalyāṇa Rakṣita (about 829 A.D) and Dharmottarācārya (about 847 A D), two Buddhist logicians whose accounts will be given hereafter, were opposed by Udayanācārya. The arguments advanced by Kalyāṇa Rakṣita in his Īśvara-bhaṅga-kārikā to refute the existence of God were controverted by Udayana in his Kusumāñjali. In the Ātma-tattva-viveka Udayana criticised the theories of *apoha* (the knowledge of a thing by the exclusion of its opposites), *kṣaṇa-bhaṅga* (the momentary existence), *śrutyaprāmāṇya* (denial of the authority of the Veda), etc., propounded by Kalyāṇa Rakṣita in his Anyāpoha-vicārakārikā, śruti-parīkṣā, etc., and by Dharmottara in his Apoha-nāma-prakaraṇa and Kṣaṇa-bhaṅga-siddhi.

57. Udayana's Kusumāñjali.

God—*Iśvara*.

The Kusumāñjali (literally "a handful of flowers"), which is divided into five chapters called clusters, treats of the supreme soul (*Paramātmā*) or God (*Īśvara*) whose worship enables us, according to Udayana, to attain paradise and emancipation. "Although all men worship Him alike under various names, there is," says he, "no harm in carrying on a logical investigation about Him which may also be called His worship."

Proof of the existence of God, *Iśvara*.

In the course of the investigation, Udayana says that there is an unseen cause called desert (*adṛṣṭa*)[1] which determines our happiness and misery. When we perform a good or bad action, the merit or demerit that ensues therefrom resides in our soul under the name of *adṛṣṭa* or desert. Associated with a suitable time, place and object, it produces in us pleasure or pain. Since a non-intelligent cause cannot produce its effect without the superintendence of an intelligent spirit, it is to be admitted that there is a Supreme Agent called the All-powerful God who bestows on us pleasure and pain as the effects of our desert.

---

[1] That there is an unseen cause called *adṛṣṭa* (desert) is proved on the following grounds:—

(*a*) An effect proceeds from a cause. If there had been no interdependence of a cause and its effect, the latter would have been found everywhere and always. But an effect is only occasional and hence it is dependent on a cause. Our happiness and misery are dependent on a cause called *adṛṣṭa*.

(*b*) A cause again is only an effect in relation to its preceding cause, which is linked with another cause and so on. The world having no beginning, the succession of cause and effect is eternal like a continued series of seed and plant. The desert on which our happiness and misery depend cannot also be traced to its first beginning.

Some people deny God, relying merely on the efficacy of sacrifices, etc., enjoined by the Veda. Udayana asks them: whence does the Veda derive its authority? The Veda is certainly not eternal, as everything in the world is subject to creation and destruction. Non-eternal as it is, it cannot be a source of right knowledge unless we suppose its author to be an infallible person. That person is God. Those who deny God, do thereby overthrow the authority of the Veda.

Some say that there is no God, as we do not perceive Him. Udayana silences them by stating that the non-perception of an object can prove its non-existence only if the object is one which is ordinarily perceptible. God is not ordinarily perceptible, and hence our non-perception of Him does not prove His non-existence.

It has been contended that God is no authority to us, inasmuch as He does not possess right knowledge. A right knowledge, nay, knowledge of any kind, concerns itself with an object unknown before. God's knowledge, which is not limited by time and space, cannot come under this description because it never refers to an object previously unknown. Udayana meets the contention by saying that the description of right knowledge cited above is incorrect. A right knowledge should, in his opinion, be defined as an independent apprehension which corresponds to its object in the external world. God is the source of such knowledge and is therefore the supreme authority to us.

There are many proofs to establish the existence of God. The earth being a product like a pot must have a maker. The maker must be an intelligent being possessing a will to bring atoms together and to support them. That intelligent being is God. It is He who introduced the traditional arts such as carpentry, weaving, etc., which have come down to us from time immemorial.

(c) The effects which are diverse in character imply a diversity of causes. As our happiness and misery are diverse in character, we cannot say that God or nature alone is their cause. They must be due to the diversity of our deserts.

(d) It is a universal practice to perform good actions and avoid bad actions as the means of gaining happiness and avoiding misery. The actions themselves disappear, but they leave behind them certain traces which operate in bringing about happiness and misery. The trace of a good action is called merit while that of a bad action is called demerit and the two together are called desert (*adṛṣṭa*). The desert resides in (the soul of) the person who performs an action and not in the thing from which he derives happiness or misery.

The above reasons are summarised thus:—

सापेक्षत्वादनादित्वाद् वैचित्र्याद् विश्ववृत्तितः ।
प्रत्यात्मनियमाद् भुक्तेरस्ति हेतुरलौकिकः ॥

(Kusumāñjali, stavaka I).

God having made this world causes it to collapse, and having destroyed it remakes it as a magic-show. His will manifests itself unhindered in all actions.

Perceiving suitable materials (atoms) for creation, and conceiving a desire for the same, He made this wonderful universe which is supported by His will.

Udayana offers prayer to God, at the concluding part of his Kusumāñjali, as follows:—

"Iron-souled are they in whose hearts Thou canst find no place, though repeatedly washed by the inundations of ethics and sacred texts; still in time, O Merciful One, Thou in Thy goodness wilt save those people too, because even in going to controvert Thy existence they have earnestly meditated on Thee."[1] "As for us, O Thou Essential Beauty, though our minds have been long plunged in Thee, the ocean of joy, yet are they verily restless still and unsatisfied: therefore, Oh Lord, haste to display thy mercy, that, our minds being fixed only on Thee, we may no more be subject to the afflictions of death.[2]"

58. Udayana's Ātma-tattva-viveka.

An analysis of the Ātma-tattva-viveka.

The **Ātma-tattva-viveka** (lit. a discussion about the true nature of the soul) is otherwise called **Bauddhādhikāra** (a discourse concerned with the Buddhists) or **Bauddha-dhikkāra** (Fie to the Buddhists). It[3] proposes to refute four Buddhistic theories in order to establish a permanent soul. The four theories are: (1) *kṣaṇa-bhaṅga*—that every thing is momentary; (2) *vāhyārtha-bhaṅga*—that things possess no external reality; (3) *guṇa-guṇi-bheda-bhaṅga*—that a substance is not distinct from its qualities;

---

1 इत्येवं श्रुतिनीतिसंप्लवजलैर्भूयोऽभिराक्षालिते
येषां नास्पदमादधासि हृदये ते शैलसाराशयाः ।
किन्तु प्रस्तुतविप्रतीपविधयोऽप्युच्चैर्भवच्चिन्तकाः
काले कारुणिक त्वयैव कृपया ते तारणीया नराः ॥

(Kusumāñjali, stavaka 5, edited and translated by E. B. Cowell and M. C. Nyāyaratna, Calcutta).

2 अस्माकन्तु निसर्गसुन्दर चिराच्चेतो निमग्नं त्वयि
अद्धानन्दनिधौ तथापि तरलं नाद्यापि सन्तृप्यते ।
तन्नाथ त्वरितं विधेहि करुणां येन त्वदेकाग्रतां
याते चेतसि नाप्नुयाम शतशो याम्याः पुनर्यातनाः ॥

(The Kusumāñjali, stavaka 5, edited and translated by E. B. Cowell and M. C. Nyāyaratna, Calcutta).

3 The Ātma-tattva-viveka, edited by Jaya Nārāyaṇa Tarkapañcānana, pp. 1, 9, 10, 24, 30, 31, 32, 34, 38, 39, 45, 46, 47, 53, 69, 89, 92, 93, etc.

and (4) *anupalambha*—that the world is void The book is divided into five sections of which the first four are concerned with the refutation of these theories, while the fifth concerns itself with the establishment of a permanent soul.

The Buddhists say that whatever is existent is momentary. A seed, for an instance, cannot continue up to the time when a plant springs out of it. The consequent cannot in fact come into being until the antecedent has ceased to exist. By the principle of *apoha* differentiation, we cognise an object as different from other objects, e.g. a cow is cognised as that which is not a not-cow. Some of the Buddhists (e.g. the *yogācāras or vijñāna vādins*) maintain that there are no external objects corresponding to our cognitions and that the cognitions alone are real. *Ālaya-vijñāna*, the abiding-cognition (or the abode of cognitions) called "ego" is the continuous flow of momentary cognitions called *pravṛtti-vijñāna.* Certain Buddhists go so far as to say that there is no substance distinct from its qualities, and that the world is void. A substance could not be defined if it existed apart from its qualities; and the substance and qualities are both to be denied if they are supposed to be identical. In fact a substance exists in relation to its qualities and the latter exist in relation to the former. It is this net of relations or conditions which constitutes the veil (*samvṛti*), called the world, of which the essence is voidness.

Udayana's contention.

These theories are set aside by Udayana who maintains that there is a permanent soul (*ātmā*) whose emancipation consists in getting rid of sufferings for ever. As to whether the soul is a principle of self-illumination and essence of bliss, the interrogator may consult the Upaniṣads or appeal to his own heart. The Naiyāyikas are satisfied if the soul is completely freed from the sufferings which are of twenty-one kinds.

Udayana says that the injunctions such as "do not kill" are respected by the followers of the Vedic as well as the Buddhistic religions. 'Shaving the head,' 'making magic circles,' etc., are the special practices of the Buddhists. The Buddhist scripture is disregarded in so far as it opposes the Vedas, controverts the doctrines of our great men and persuades people to build *caityas*, wear tattered robes, etc., in antagonism to our religion.

59. Jayanta, Author of the Nyāya-mañjarī (about the 10th century A.D.).

Life of Jayanta.

Another Brāhmaṇa logician who fought hard against the Buddhists was Jayanta, author of the Nyāya-mañjarī, an independent commentary on the Nyāya-sūtra. Jayanta, invincible in debate and well known as *Vṛttikāra*, was the son of Paṇḍita Candra.[1] If we suppose him to be identical with his namesake the great-grandson of Śakti Svāmin,[2] minister of King Muktāpīḍa, he must have flourished in Kāśmīra in the 10th century A.D.

Date of Jayanta.

He could not have lived earlier than the 9th and later than the 11th century A.D. as he quotes Vācaspati Miśra[3] (841 A.D.) and Māgha[4] (about 905 A.D.) in the Nyāya-mañjarī, and is himself quoted in the Ratnā-vatārikā[5] by Ratnaprabha (1181 A.D.), and in the Syādvāda-ratnākara[6] by Deva Sūri (1086–1169 A.D.).

60. Jayanta's Explanation of Verbal Knowledge.

Words and their meanings.

Abhihitānvaya-vāda and *Anvitābhidhāna-vāda.*

In explaining verbal knowledge Jayanta reviews two theories[7] called respectively the *Connection of the Expressed* (*abhihitānvaya-vāda*) and the *Expression of the Connected* (*anvitābhidhāna-vāda*). The Bhāṭṭa Mīmāṁsakas, who uphold the first theory, main-

---

1
वादेष्वाप्तजयो जयन्त इति यः ख्यातः सतामग्रणीः
अन्वर्थो नववृत्तिकार इति यं शंसन्ति नाम्ना बुधाः ।
सूनुर्व्याप्तदिगन्तरस्य यशसा चन्द्रस्य चन्द्रत्विषा
चक्रे चन्द्रकलावचूड चरणध्यायी स धन्यां कृतिम् ॥

(Nyāya-mañjarī, chapter XII, colophon, p. 659, Vizianagaram Sanskrit series).

2 The lineage of Jayanta is described in the opening verses of the Kādambarī-kathāsāra which was composed by his son Abhinanda.

3 यदपि उच्यते—नानिष्पन्नस्य सम्बन्धो निष्पत्तौ पुनरिष्यते—इति तदपि परिहृतमाचार्य्यैः जातं च संबद्धं चेत्येकः काल इति वदद्भिः ॥

(Nyāya-mañjarī, p. 312, edited by M.M. Gangadhar Śāstrī, in the Vizianagaram Sanskrit Series).

4 Nyāya-mañjarī, p. 84. Māgha is said to be a cousin of Siddharṣi, author of Upamiti-bhava-prapañcā Kathā.

5 तथा च जयन्तः -

स्वरूपादुद्भवत् कार्य्यं सहकार्य्युपबृंहितात् । न हि कल्पयितुं शक्यं शक्तिं..............

(Ratnāvatārikā, chap. IV).

6
यदत्र शक्तिं संसिद्धौ मन्यत्युदयन द्विपः ।
जयन्त हन्त का तत्र गणना त्वयि कीटके ॥

(Syādvāda-ratnākara, chap. II).

In 1348 A.D. Rājaśekhara Sūri quotes Jayanta as follows :—

जयन्ताचार्य्यैरचितो न्यायतर्कोऽतिदुस्तरः ।

(Maladhāri Rājaśekhara Sūri's Saḍdarśana-samuccaya, verse 100, chapter on Śaiva darśana).

7 Nyāya-mañjarī, chapter VI, pp. 402-403, Vizianagaram Sanskrit series.

tain that verbal knowledge depends upon the connection which is automatically perceived among the meanings expressed by words individually in a sentence; that is, the words of a sentence after conveying their respective meanings disappear, and then the meanings themselves produce in us a knowledge of their mutual connection which is called verbal knowledge. The Prābhākara Mīmāṁsakas, who uphold the second theory, say that it is only in a sentence that words can express to us any meanings, and produce in us the knowledge of a mutual connection among those meanings called verbal knowledge.

The Nyāya doctrine of *tātparya*, intention.

Jayanta dismisses the second theory on the ground that it presupposes a word to bear various meanings in connection with various words in a sentence. It is indeed absurd to suppose that a word bears no definite meaning. He also does not completely accept the first theory inasmuch as words alone do not produce verbal knowledge, as is evident from the fact that a sentence composed of disorderly and ungrammatical words does not express a systematic meaning. As an amendment of the first theory we must assume that a sentence, if it is to convey a consistent meaning, must have, underlying it, a power called intention (*tātparya*) over and above its component words.

Jayanta opposes sphoṭa-vāda.

Sphoṭa-vāda—the theory of phonetic explosion.

Jayanta examines *sphoṭa*,[1] the theory of phonetic explosion, which he pronounces to be untenable. The grammarians (*Vaiyākaraṇa*), who propound the theory, define *sphoṭa* (explosion) as the essence of sound revealed by a letter, word or sentence. The sound-essence, which is revealed by a letter, is called *varṇa-sphoṭa*, a letter-explosion; that revealed by a word is called *pada-sphoṭa*, a word-explosion; and that revealed by a sentence is called *vākya-sphoṭa*, a sentence-explosion. As there is a constant relation between a sound and the thing signified by it, the sound-essence of a letter, word or sentence, as soon as we hear it, reminds us of a thing corresponding to the same.

Suppose a person utters the word *cow* composed of the letters *c*, *o* and *w*. As soon as we hear *c*, there is revealed to us the sound-essence *cow* in an indistinct form; and then as we go on hearing *o*, the same sound-essence is revealed though still in an indistinct form, until we hear the last letter *w* which reveals to us the sound-essence in a distinct form. This revelation of sound-

---

[1] Nyāya-mañjarī, āhnika 6. Cf. Bhartṛhari's Vākyapadīya, kāṇḍa 1; Vaiyākaraṇa-bhūṣaṇa-sāra and Śabda-kaustubha, and Max Muller's Six Systems of Indian Philosophy, p. 402.

essence of the entire word in a distinct form is called *sphoṭa* or phonetic explosion,

A single letter, unless it is a complete word, cannot signify any thing. While some, the advocates of *pada-sphoṭa*, say that a sound-essence, significant of a thing, can be revealed only by a word (*pada*), others, the advocates of *vākya-sphoṭa*, hold that it is a sentence (*vākya*) alone that can reveal a significant sound-essence. According to the latter, a sentence is the beginning of speech, the words are mere parts of a sentence and the letters are parts of words.

Now, what is the nature of a sound-essence (*sphoṭa*)? A sound-essence is eternal and self-existent, bearing a permanent relation to the thing signified by it. It is *revealed* by a letter, word or sentence, but is not *produced* by any of them. Had there been no sound-essence, nothing would have been signified by letters, words or sentences. When we hear the word *cow*, the letters *c*, *o* and *w* may successively perish, but the sound-essence *cow*, which is eternal, persists to signify the thing called *cow*.

Jayanta's criticism of *sphoṭa-vāda*.

Jayanta, as a Naiyāyika, opposes the above theory by saying that it is a most cumbrous one. In the case of the word "cow," *c* and *o*, after being heard, no doubt pass away, but they leave on our soul (which is eternal) impressions which coupled with our audition of *w*, produce in us knowledge of the thing called *cow*. If in this way the letters themselves (as constituents of words) are sufficient to signify things, what is the necessity for admitting an additional entity called *sphoṭa*, sound-essence, which can neither be perceived nor inferred? Moreover, it is asked: Is the thing signified by a *sphoṭa* manifest by nature or does it require a cause for its manifestation? If it is manifest by nature, why do we not perceive it in all times and everywhere? If, on the other hand, it requires a cause for its manifestation, what is that cause? Jayanta says that the cause is not other than letters which constitute words. It is therefore superfluous to assume a sphoṭa over and above letters.

61. Jayanta criticises the Doctrines of Kalyāṇa Rakṣita (about 829 A.D.) and Dharmottara (847 A.D.).

Apoha, Kṣaṇa-bhaṅga, Īśvara-bhaṅga, etc.

Jayanta in his Nyāya-mañjarī (chapters V, VII, IV and III) severely criticises the doctrines of *apoha* (the knowledge of a thing by the exclusion of its opposites), *kṣaṇa-bhaṅga* (the momentary existence), *śrutyaprāmāṇya* (denial of the authority of the Veda),

Īśvara-bhaṅga (the non-existence of God), etc., propounded by Kalyāṇa Rakṣita, (q.v.) in his Anyāpoha-vicāra-kārikā, Īśvara-bhaṅga-kārikā, and Śruti-parīkṣā, and by Dharmottara (q.v.) in his Apoha-nāma-prakaraṇa, Kṣaṇa-bhaṅga-siddhi, etc.

62. Jayanta's Review of several other Buddistic Doctrines.

The Mādhyamika, Yogācāra, Sautrāntika and Vaibhāṣika, etc.

In the Nyāya-mañjarī, chapters I–III, Jayanta criticises the definition of *pratyakṣa* (perception) as given by Dharmakīrti who is designated as a *Bhikṣu*, *Saugata*, *Bauddha* or *Śākya*. He tries also to refute the Buddhist theories that there are only two means of right knowledge (perception and inference) and that pleasure, pain, etc., are mere species of our cognitions from which they are not distinct. It is perhaps the disputation with Dignāga that is referred to by the expression *Bhadanta-kalaha* in chapter III. The Buddhistic objections against the soul as a separate substance are mentioned and criticised in chapters VII and IX. In chapter IX there is also a criticism of the doctrine of those Buddhists who hold that the external world is unreal. In chapter XII the Vaibhāṣikas are mentioned as holding that the external objects are both real and perceptible. In the same chapter we find that the Sautrāntikas maintain that the external objects are undoubtedly real, but they are not perceptible, as we can know them only through inference. The Yogācāras are referred to as saying that the so-called external objects are mere forms of our cognition which alone is real. The Mādhyamikas are said to hold that the world is void as our cognition is transparent and formless.

In chapter XII Jayanta observes that even Dharmakīrti maintained that Points of Defeat (*nigrahasthāna*) were of 22 kinds. In the same chapter as an instance of the incoherent (*apārthaka*), Jayanta cities the metaphysical views of the Vaibhāṣika, Sautrāntika, Yogācāra and Mādhyamika.

Jayanta carried on such a vehement crusade against the Buddhists that in the Nyāya-mañjarī he actually reproached them as follows :—

Reproach of the Buddhists.

"You, Bauddhas, hold that there is no soul, yet you construct *caityas* (towers) to enjoy pleasure in paradise after death; you say that everything is momentary, yet you build monasteries with the hope that they will last for centuries; and you say that the world is void, yet you teach that wealth should be given to spiritual guides. What a strange character the Bauddhas possess, they are verily a monument of conceit."[1]

63. ŚRĪKAṆṬHA (BEFORE 1409 A.D.).

About 1409 A.D. Guṇaratna, a Jaina philosopher, in his Saḍdarśana-samuccaya-vṛtti mentions a Brāhmaṇa logician named Śrīkaṇṭha[2] who wrote a commentary on the Nyāya-sūtra called **Nyāyālaṅkāra.**

64. ABHAYATILAKOPĀDHYĀYA (BEFORE 1409 A.D.).

In the Saḍdarśana-samuccaya-vṛtti the Jaina philosopher Guṇaratna mentions a Brāhmaṇa logician named Abhayatilakopādhyāya[3] who wrote a commentary on the Nyāya-sūtra called **Nyāya-vṛtti.**

65. OTHER COMMENTATORS ON THE NYĀYA-SŪTRA.

These are the principal Brāhmaṇa commentators on the Nyāya-sūtra. Subsequently there arose a number of commentators such as **Vardhamāna**, author of the Nyāya-nibandha-prakāśa, **Vācaspati Miśra** the junior, author of Nyāya-tattvāloka, **Visvanātha**, author of Nyāya-vṛtti, etc., whose names are not mentioned here as they belong to the modern school of Nyāya in respect of their style and method of interpretation.

---

1 नास्त्यात्मा फलभोगमात्रमथ च स्वर्गाय चैत्यार्चनं
संस्काराः क्षणिका युगस्थितिभृतश्चैते विहाराः कृताः ।
सर्वं शून्यमिदं वसूनि गुरवे देहीति चादिश्यते
बौद्धानां चरितं किमन्यदियती दम्भस्य भूमिः परा ॥

(Nyāya-mañjarī, 7th āhnika, p. 467, Gaṅgādhara Śāstri's edition).

2, 3 Guṇaratna observes :—

एषां तर्कग्रन्था न्यायसूत्र-भाष्य-वार्त्तिक-तात्पर्य्यटीका-तात्पर्य्य परिशुद्धि न्यायालङ्कार-वृत्तयः । क्रमेण अक्षपाद-वात्स्यायन-उद्योतकर-वाचस्पतिमिश्र-श्रीउदयन-श्री कण्ठ-अभयतिलकोपाध्याय विरचिताः ५४०० ।

(Ṣaḍdarśana-samuccaya-vṛtti called Nyāya (Tarka)-rahasya-dīpikā, chap. II, p. 94, edited by Dr. L. Suali, in the Bibliotheca Indica).

CHAPTER IV.

The Nyāya recognized as a Branch of Orthodox Learning.

66. A Comparative Estimate of the Ānvīkṣikī and the Nyāya.

The means for gaining recognition.

The Indian Logic at its first stage called *Ānvīkṣikī* was often looked upon with positive disfavour and subjected to adverse criticisms, as its deductions were held apparently to be sophistical and heterodox. But at the second stage when it was named *Nyāya*, it gradually got a steady foothold and an increasing number of followers, nay it succeeded, as we read in the writings of Yājña-valkya [1] and others, in gaining recognition as a branch of orthodox learning. On account of its intrinsic worth it became the most prominent of the six systems of philosphy called *Ṣaḍdarśana.* Attempting to prove the infallibility of the *Veda* and adapting itself to the *Śaiva* cult the Nyāya got access into the orthodox community from which it received an unequivocal approbation.

67. The Nyāya included in *Ṣaḍdarśana.*

The Jaina writers include Nyāya in Ṣaḍdarśana.

After the term *darśana* (philosophy) had come into use at the beginning of the Christian era, widely divergent systems of thought were designated by this common appellation. We learn that at a later period six systems of philosophy were specially called Ṣaḍdarśana. Opinions differ as to which six of the numerous systems constitute *Ṣaḍdarsana,* but it is generally agreed that the Nyāya system is included therein. According to the Jaina philosopher Haribhadra Sūri,[2] author of Ṣaḍdarśana-samuccaya (about 1168 A D.), the six systems were the Buddhist, the *Nyāya,* the Sāṁkhya (including yoga), the Jaina, the Vaiśeṣika and the Jaiminīya (comprising the Mīmāṁsā and the Vedānta). Jinadatta Sūri [3] (about 1220 A.D.) reviews the same six

---

[1] The Yājñavalkya-saṁhitā, 1-3.

[2] बौद्धं नैयायिकं सांख्यं जैनं वैशेषिकं तथा ।
जैमिनीयं च षड् विधानि दर्शनानाममून्यहो ॥
(Ṣaḍdarśana-samuccaya, verse 3, Dr. Suali's edition).

[3] About the date of Jinadatta Sūri, Sir R. G. Bhandarkar in his Report of Sanskrit Manuscripts for 1883–84, p. 156, observes: "Jinadatta therefore lived in the first half of the 13th century of the Christian era." Klatt in his Onomasticon, no. 44, maintains on the authority of Sukṛta-saṁkīrtana and Prabandha-

systems in his Viveka-vilāsa under the head of *Ṣaḍdarśana vicāra*. Another Jaina writer named Maladhāri Śrī Rājaśekhara Sūri[1] (1348 A.D.) enumerates the same six systems in a different order, viz. the Jaina, the Sāṁkhya (including the Yoga), the Jaiminīya (comprising the Mīmāṁsā and the Vedānta), the Yauga or Śaiva (which is the same as *Nyāya*), the Vaiśeṣika and the Saugata or Buddhist.

The Brāmanic writers recognize Nyāya as a constituent of *Ṣaḍdarśana*.

The Brāhmaṇic writer Nārāyaṇa,[2] in his commentary called Prakāśa on the Naiṣadhacarita, speaks of *Ṣaḍdarśana* in which he evidently includes the *Nyāya*. In the Hayaśīrṣa-pañcarātra,[3] a Brāhmaṇic work supposed to have been introduced into Bengal by Rājā Vallāla Sena (about 1158–1170 A.D.) as well as in the Gurugītā of the Viśvasāra-tantra, the six systems comprising *Ṣaḍdarśana* are specified as the philosophies of Gotama (*Nyāya*), Kaṇāda (Vaiśeṣika), Kapila (Sāṁkhya), Patañjali (Yoga), Vyāsa (Vedānta) and Jaimini (Mīmāṁsā). By the term *ṣaḍdarśana* the Brāhmaṇic writers understand at present these six systems to the exclusion of the Jaina and the Buddhist which are considered by them as lying outside the pale of it.

68. THE NYĀYA SUPPORTS THE VEDA.

Authority of the Veda established.

In the Nyāya-mañjarī[4] Jayanta observes that the authority of the Veda was to a large extent established through the aid of the science of reasoning called the Nyāya. The reasoning

cintāmaṇi that Jinadatta Sūri was present at the pilgrimage of Vastupāla in *saṁvat* 1277 or 1220 A.D.

1 जैनं सांख्यं जैमिनीयं योगं वैशेषिकं तथा ।
सौगतं दर्शनान्येवं नास्तिकं तु न दर्शनम् ॥

(Maladhāri Rājaśekhara Sūri's Ṣaḍdarśana-samuccaya, p. 1, Yaśovijaya-granthamālā, Benares).

2 सार्द्धं प्रयच्छति न पक्षचतुष्टये तां
तल्लाभशंसिनि न पञ्चमकोटिमात्रे ।
श्रद्धां दधे निषधराड् विमतौ मतानाम्
अद्वैततत्त्व इव सत्यतरेऽपि लोकः ॥ (Naiṣadhacarita, 13–36).

In the commentary on this verse Nārāyaṇa says:—

मतानां सांख्यादि षड् दर्शनानां मध्ये .....परमार्थतो विद्यमानेऽपि अद्वैततत्त्वे तत्त्वे......
युक्त्याद्युक्तविचार ग्रन्थो जनो यथा श्रद्धां न धत्ते ।

3 गौतमस्य कणादस्य कपिलस्य पतञ्जलेः ।
व्यासस्य जैमिनेश्चापि दर्शनानि षडेव हि ॥

(Hayaśīrṣa-pañcarātra, a work which is quoted by Raghunandana in his Devapratiṣṭhā-tattva). This verse is quoted in the Gurugītā of the Viśva-sāra-tantra.

4 The Nyāya-mañjarī, pp. 4–5, edited by Gaṅgādhara Śāstri, Vizianagaram Sanskrit series.

required for the establishment of such authority has been dealt with in the Nyāya more fully than in any other system of philosophy. The Mīmāṁsā treats of the Vedic injunctions and prohibitions, but it does not examine their worth through the employment of reasoning. The Nyāya[1] alone demonstrates that the Veda is authoritative, because it was delivered by sages who were trustworthy persons. It is true that the Buddhists and Jainas too wrote treatises on reasoning, but these being opposed to the Veda cannot properly be included in the Nyāya, one of the fourteen branches of orthodox learning. In fact it is the work of Akṣapāda that should really be called Nyāya the supporter of Veda. The Nyāya-sūtra actually defends the Veda from the attacks of those who find in it untruth, contradiction and tautology, and declares the sacred text to be infallible like a spell or the medical science.

69. THE NYĀYA ADAPTS ITSELF TO ŚAIVISM.

The Naiyāyikas are Śaivas.

In the Ṣaḍdarśana-samuccaya of Haribhadra Sūri[2] (1168 A.D.) as well as in that of Maladhāri Rājaśekhara Sūri[3] (1348 A.D.), the followers of the Nyāya philosophy have been called the Śaivas while those of the Vaiśeṣika system have been called the *Pāśupatas*. In the Vivekavilāsa, Jinadatta Sūri includes both Naiyāyikas and Vaiśeṣikas in the Śaiva sect. According to the Devīpurāṇa[4] the Nyāya-śāstra was promulgated by the gracious Śiva himself.

---

[1] The Nyāya-sūtras, 2-1-58 and 2-1-69, translated by Satischandra Vidyabhusana, S.B.H. series, Allahabad.

[2] The Naiyāyikas were also called Yaugas.

अथादौ नैयायिकानां यौगापराभिधानानां लिङ्गादिव्यक्तिरुच्यते । ......सदा शिवभक्तत्वात् शैवा इत्युच्यन्ते । वैशेषिकास्तु पाशुपता इति । तेन नैयायिकशासनं शैवमाख्यायते । वैशेषिकदर्शनं च पाशुपतमिति ।......

अक्षपादमते देवः सृष्टिसंहारकृच्छिवः ।
विभुर्नित्यैकसर्वज्ञो नित्यबुद्धिसमाश्रयः ॥

(Ṣaḍdarśana-samuccaya of Haribhadra Sūri, edited by Dr. Suali, pp. 49–52).

[3] Ṣaḍdarśana-samuccaya of Maladhāri Rājaśekhara Sūri, pp. 8–11, published in the Yaśovijaya-granthamālā series, Benares.

[4]
शम्भोः कृपामनुप्राप्य यदोचामकरोन्मुनिः ।
तेन चान्वीक्षिकीसंज्ञां विद्यां प्रावर्त्तयत् क्षितौ ॥
आदेशेन शिवस्यैव स शिष्यान् दशभिर्दिनैः ।
पाठयामास तां विद्यां नाखिलामसत नाशिनीम् ॥

(Devīpurāṇa, Śumbha-niśumbha-mathana-pāda, chapter XVI, MSS. in the collection of Paṇḍita Pañcānana Tarkaratna of Bhāṭpārā).

Characteristics of the Naiyāyikas.

The Naiyāyikas are called Śaivas because they look upon, as their tutelary deity, Śiva who is the creator and destroyer of the universe. As described by Maladhāri Rājaśekhara Sūri the Naiyāyikas, identified with Śaivas, walked nude, wore matted hair, besmeared their bodies with ash and subsisted on roots and fruits. They always meditated upon Śiva and worshipped his eighteen figures, muttering the formula *oṁ namaḥ Śivāya*, "hail! obeisance to Śiva."

Naiyāyikas salute Śiva.

Akṣapāda, author of the Nyāya-sūtra, was a son of Soma-Śarmā[1] who was Śiva incarnate. Vātsyāyana begins his Nyāya-bhāṣya with obeisance to the *Pramāṇas* (Means of Knowledge), but in the body of the book he describes God[2] (*Īśvara*) in a style applicable only to Maheśvara (Śiva).

Whatever might have been the faiths of Akṣapāda and Vātsyāyana, there is no doubt that all the Brāhmanic Naiyāyikas from Uddyotakara downwards were Śaivas. Uddyotakara, as is evident from the colophon of his Nyāya-vārtika, was a leader of the Pāśupata Śaiva sect. The Nyāya-vārtika-tātparya-ṭīkā of Vācaspati Miśra opens with salutation to Pinākin (Śiva) while the Nyāya works of Udayana[3] contain abundant proofs that their author was a Śaiva by faith. Bhāsarvajña, author of the Nyāya-sāra,[4] and Gaṅgeśa Upādhyāya, author of the Tattvacintāmaṇi, begin their works with salutation to Śambhu or Śiva "the Supreme Lord and the Seer of all truths."

70. The Popularity of Nyāya established.

Three causes make Nyāya popular.

From the above it is clear that three distinct causes contributed to the popularity and predominance of Nyāya as a school of philosophy. The first was the intrinsic worth of the system which was acknowledged as most useful in carrying on processes

---

[1] Brahmāṇḍapurāṇa published under the name of Vāyupurāṇa by the Asiatic Society of Bengal, adhyāya 23, verses 200 seq.

[2] Nyāya-bhāṣya, 4-1-16, 22.

[3] Kusumāñjali, chapter I, opening line; chapter II, last verse; chapter IV, last verse; etc.

[4] प्रणम्य शम्भुं जगतः पतिम्परं
समस्ततत्त्वार्थविदं स्वभावतः ।
शिष्यप्रबोधाय मयाभिधास्यते
प्रमाणतद्भेद तदन्यलक्षणम् ॥

(Nyāya-sāra, p. 1, edited by Satis Chandra Vidyabhusana in the Bibliotheca Indica series, Calcutta).

of reasoning and which obtained for the system the foremost rank among the schools of philosophy called *Ṣaḍdarsana*. In the second place we notice that having supported the authority of the Veda the Nyāya was readily recognized as an approved branch of learning, and the charge of heterodoxy levelled against it at its early stage was proved to be baseless. Thirdly, the fact that Nyāya adopted the Śaiva cult gave it a positive stamp of orthodoxy and gained for it an unquestionable recognition.

PART II.

THE MEDIÆVAL SCHOOL OF INDIAN LOGIC

CALLED

PRAMĀṆA-ŚĀSTRA—THE SCIENCE OF RIGHT KNOWLEDGE.

(400 A.D.—1200 A.D.).

SECTION I.

The Jaina Logic (400 A.D.—1700 A.D.).

CHAPTER I.

Topics of Logic mentioned in the Jaina Canons

1. The Special Features of Mediæval Logic (from circa 599 B.C. onwards).

Termination of the Ancient School.

In Part I a short account has been given of the Ancient School of Indian Logic which deals, as we have seen, with the doctrine of the soul and its salvation, as well as with the rules of debate and true reasoning. The Ancient School, which reached the height of its development at the hands of Akṣapāda about 150 A.D., extended over a period of one thousand years, beginning with Gautama about 550 B.C. and ending with Vātsyāyana about 400 A.D. It must not however be supposed that the Ancient School became extinct at 400 A.D. A host of commentators such as Uddyotakara, Vācaspati Miśra and Udayanācārya, who flourished subsequently, kept the stream of that Logic flowing. But the thousand years from 550 B.C. to 400 A.D. represent what may be termed the period of organic growth of the Ancient School.

Formation of the Mediæval School.

Part II will represent a system of logic called the Mediæval School, the foremost exponents of which were the Jainas and the Buddhists—two powerful sects that were founded by Mahāvīra and Buddha about 600 B.C. At the time of the founders, and in subsequent times, the Jaina and Buddhist writers occasionally handled the principles of pure logic in expounding the dogmas of their own religion and metaphysics. Some of the writers even brought out regular treatises on logic, but those were either fragments or résumés of the Ancient Logic. By about 450 A.D. the Buddhist logician Dignāga and the Jaina logician Siddhasena Divākara, by differentiating the principles of logic from those of religion and metaphysics, laid the true foundation of what is termed the Mediæval School of Indian Logic. This school covered a period of nearly eight hundred years from 400 A.D. to 1200 A.D. In matter and method the Mediæval School conducted by the Jainas and Buddhists differs markedly from the Ancient School which was essentially Brāhmaṇic. The Ancient Logic dealt with sixteen categories such as *pramāṇa*, *prameya*, etc., comprising such heterogeneous elements as doctrine of salvation and nature of the soul, etc. The Mediæval Logic, on the contrary, concerns itself with one category, viz. *pramāṇa*, which touches upon other categories only in so far as these are necessary for its proper elaboration. The doctrine of *pramāṇa* is treated in such a way that it may be equally applied to the religious systems of the Brāhmaṇas, Jainas and Buddhists. Inference, a kind of *pramāṇa*, which was briefly noticed in the Ancient Logic, receives a full treatment in the Mediæval School. Numerous technical terms are coined and great subtleties are introduced into the definition of terms, the theory of syllogism, etc. *Prameya*, the object of knowledge, is rejected on the ground that it is useless in works on logic to treat of the soul, birth, death, etc., which are comprised under this category. The Mediæval Logic thus formed is called in Sanskrit *Pramāṇa-śāstra*, the science of right knowledge.

The works on Mediæval Logic written by the Jainas constitute the Jaina Logic, while those written by the Buddhists constitute the Buddhist Logic. Seeing that Mahāvīra, the founder of Jainism, preceded Buddha, the founder of Buddhism, I shall first treat of the Jaina Logic.

2. Mahāvīra—the founder of Jainism. (599–527 B.C.).

The Jainas maintain that their religion is coeval with time. According to their traditions there appeared at various periods in the world's history sages whom they call *Jinas*, conquerors of their passions, or *Tīrthaṅkaras*, builders of a landing place in the sea of existence. These sages preached the religion of the Jainas. The Jainas hold that in every cycle of time (*utsarpiṇī* or *avasarpiṇī kāla*[1]) 24 sages are born. The first sage of the last series was

[1] Period of evolution or involution.

Ādinātha or Ṛṣabhadeva, the 24th was Mahāvīra or Vardhamāna, who was born at Kṣatriya-kuṇḍagrāma in 599 B.C. and attained *nirvāṇa* at Pāvā in 527 B.C.[1] The scriptures which the Jainas obey are founded on the teachings of Mahāvīra. No one disputes this, and scholars generally regard Mahāvīra as the founder of Jainism, and hold that the theory of the existence of *Jinas* previous to him, except Pārśvanātha the 23rd Tīrthaṅkara, was a subsequent invention.

3. The Jaina sects—Śvetāmbara and Digambara (First century A.D.).

The Jainas are divided into two sects, the *Śvetāmbaras*, those who are clothed in white, and the *Digambaras*, those who are sky-clad or naked. The *Śvetāmbaras* claim to be more ancient than the *Digambaras*, whose existence as a separate sect is said to date from A.D. 82,[2] i.e. 609 years after the attainment of *nirvāṇa* by Mahāvīra.

4. Indrabhūti Gautama—a disciple of Mahāvīra (607 B.C.—515 B.C.).

The teachings of Mahāvīra as represented in the scriptures are said to have been collected[3] by a disciple of his, called Indrabhūti. This disciple is often known as Gautama or Gotama. He

---

1 पणछस्सय वस पणमास जुदं गमिय वीरणिवुइदो सगराजो। (Trilokasāra of the Digambara sect). "Mahāvīra attained *nirvāṇa* 605 years 5 months before the Śaka King (78 A.D.) came to the throne," that is, in 527 B.C As he lived 72 years he must have been born in 599 B.C.

According to Vicāraśreṇī of Merutuṅga, Tīrthakalpa of Jinaprabha Sūri, Vicāra-sāra-prakaraṇa, Tapāgaccha-paṭṭāvalī, etc., of the Śvetāmbara sect—Mahāvīra attained *nirvāṇa* 470 years before Vikrama Saṁvat or in B.C. 527.

Dr. Jacobi of Bonn, in his letter dated the 21st October, 1907, kindly writes to me as follows:—

"There is however another tradition which makes this event [viz. the *nirvāṇa* of Mahāvīra] come off 60 years later, in 467 B.C. (see Pariśiṣṭa Parvan, Introduction, p. 4 f.; also Kalpasūtra, Introduction, p. 8). The latter date cannot be far wrong because Mahāvīra died some years before the Buddha whose death is now placed between 470–480 B.C."

2 The Śvetāmbaras say:—छव्वास सयाइं नवुत्तराइं तइया सिद्धिंगयस्स वीरस्स तो बोडियाण दिट्ठी रहवीरपुरे समुप्पन्ना। "The Digambara doctrine was preached in Rathavīrapura 609 years after the attainment of *nirvāṇa* by Mahāvīra" (Āvaśyaka niryukti—52). But the Digambaras deny this and say that the Śvetāmbaras rose in Vikrama 136 or 79 A.D. Cf. Bhadrabāhucarita IV. 55:

मृते विक्रमभूपाले षट्त्रिंशदधिके शते ।
गतेऽब्दानामभूल्लोके मतं श्वेताम्बराभिधम् ॥

3 षष्ठ सप्तर्षिसम्पन्नं श्रुतार्थं जिनभाषितम् ।
द्वादशाङ्गश्रुतं सम्यं सोपाङ्गं गौतमो व्यधात् ॥

(Jaina Harivaṃśa Purāṇa).

was [1] a *Kevalin* [2] and the first of the Gaṇa-dharas [3] or leaders of the assembly. His father's name was Brāhmaṇa Vasubhūti, and his mother's name was Brāhmaṇī Pṛthvī. He was born in the village of Gorbara [4] in Magadha and died at Guṇava in Rājagṛha (Rajgir) at the age of ninety-two, 12 years after the attainment of *nirvāṇa* by Mahāvīra.[5] Assuming that Mahāvīra attained *nirvāṇa* in 527 B.C., Indrabhūti's birth must be assigned to 607 B.C. and his death to 515 B.C.

5. The Canonical Scriptures of the Jainas.

Aṅga and Upāṅga.

Those scriptures of the Jainas which are generally regarded as canonical are divided into 45 *siddhāntas* or *āgamas*, classified as 11 Aṅgas, 12 Upāṅgas, etc. "For the benefit of children, women, the old, and the illiterate,"[6] these were composed in the Ardha-Māgadhi or Prākṛta language. On the same principle the scriptures of the Buddhistic canon were originally written in Māgadhī or Pāli. It is maintained

---

[1] Indrabhūti Gautama and Sudharma Svāmi were the joint compilers of the Jaina scriptures. But Indrabhūti became a *Kevalin* or attained *kevalajñāna* (absolute knowledge) on the day on which Mahāvīra attained *nirvāṇa*. He did not therefore occupy the chair of his teacher Mahāvīra, but relinquished it to his spiritual brother Sudharma Svāmi. Cf. इन्द्रभूति प्रभृतीनां त्रिपदीं व्याहरत् प्रभुः ॥ (Hemacandra's Mahāvīracarita, chap. v. MSS. lent by Muni Dharmavijaya and Indravijaya).

[2] Possessor of absolute knowledge. For a further reference to this title see R. G. Bhandarkar's Report, 1883-84, p. 122.

[3]
यत्प्रज्ञाप्रसरेऽतिमाथिनि तथा प्रालेयशैलोन्नते
जैनो गौरवरश्मिपद्यपि यथा सद्यः पदैः कोटिशः ।
चक्रोपाङ्गसमुद्दया समभवच्छैलोक्यसंचारिणी
वन्द्योऽसौ गणभृद्गणप्रथमगुरुर्मामिन्द्रभूतिः सताम् ॥ ४ ॥

(Siddhajayantī-caritra-ṭīkā, noticed in Peterson's 3rd Report, App. 1, p. 38).

[4]
श्रीमन्तं मगधेषु गोर्वर इति ग्रामोऽभिरामः श्रिया
तत्रोत्पन्नमसन्नचित्तमनिशं श्रीवीरसेवाविधौ ।
ज्योतिःसंश्रयगौतमान्वयवियत्प्रद्योतनद्योमणिं
तापोत्तीर्णसुवर्णवर्णवपुषं भक्त्येन्द्रभूतिं स्तुवे ॥

(Gotamastotra by Jinaprabha Sūri, extracted in Kāvyamālā, 7th Gucchaka, p. 110).

[5] For particulars about Indrabhūti Gautama, *vide* Dr. J. Klatt's Paṭṭāvalī of the Kharataragaccha in the Indian Antiquary, Vol. XI, Sept. 1882, p. 246; and Weber's Die Handschriften Verzeichnisse der Königlichen Bibliothek zu Berlin, pp. 983 and 1030, in which are noticed Sarvarājagaṇi's Vṛtti on Gaṇadhara-sārdha-śatakam of Jinadattasūri, and Śrī-paṭṭāvalī-vācanā of the Kharataragaccha.

[6] Haribhadra-sūri, in his Daśa-vaikālika-vṛtti (Chap. III), observes:—

बालस्त्रीवृद्धमूर्खाणां नृणां चारित्रकाङ्क्षिणाम् ।
अनुग्रहार्थं तत्त्वज्ञैः सिद्धान्तः प्राकृतः कृतः ॥

that originally the Aṅgas were 12 in number. The 12th Aṅga, which was called Dṛṣṭivāda or the presentation of views, was written in Sanskrit.[1]

The Dṛṣṭivāda.

The **Dṛṣṭivāda** is not extant. It consisted apparently of five parts, in the first of which logic is said to have been dealt with. The Dṛṣṭivāda is reputed to have existed in its entirety at the time of Sthūlabhadra[2] who, according to the Tapāgachapaṭṭāvalī, died in the year in which the 9th Nanda was killed by Candra Gupta (i.e. about 327 B.C.). By 474 A.D. the Dṛṣṭivāda had disappeared altogether. Nothing is known as to the way in which logic was treated in the Dṛṣṭivāda.[3]

6. Logical subjects in the Canons.

Pramāṇa and Naya.

The subject-matter of logic is touched upon in several of the 45 Prākṛta scriptures of the Jainas. In the **Bhagavatī-sūtra,**[4] **Sthānāṅga-sūtra**, etc. which are Aṅgas, and in the **Prajñāpanā-sūtra** which is an Upāṅga, there is a description of *Naya*, or the method of comprehending things from particular standpoints. In the **Sthānāṅga-sūtra, Bhagavatī-sūtra**, etc.,[5] there is a complete classification of valid knowledge called *pramāṇa*, *pamāṇa*, *jñāna*, *nāna* or *hetu*.

---

[1] Vardhamāna-sūri, in his Ācāra-dinakara, quotes the following passage from Āgama :—

सुत्तूण दिट्ठिवायं कालिय उक्कालियंग सिद्धंतं ।
थीबालवायणत्थं पाइय सुइयं जिनवरेहिं ॥

[2] *Vide* Cūrṇika of Nandī Sūtra, page 478, published by Dhanapat Singh, Calcutta, and Peterson's 4th Report on Sanskrit MSS., p. cxxxvi.

[3] For a full history of the Dṛṣṭivāda (called in Prākṛta Ditthivāo) see Weber's Sacred Literature of the Jainas, translated by Weir Smyth in the Indian Antiquary, Vol. XX, May 1891, pp. 170–182.

[4] In the Bhagavatī-sūtra and Prajñāpanā-sūtra, *Naya* is divided into seven kinds, viz. *naigama*, *saṅgraha*, *vyavahāra*, *ṛju-sūtra*, *śabda*, *samabhirūḍha* and *evaṁbhūta*. For an explanation of these terms see Umāsvāti, who instead of dividing *Naya* into seven kinds, first divides it into five kinds, and then subdivides one of the five, viz. *śabda*, into three kinds.

[5] In the Sthānāṅga-sūtra, knowledge (*jñāna*) is divided into (1) *Pratyakṣa* (direct knowledge) and (2) *Parokṣa* (indirect knowledge). *Pratyakṣa* again is subdivided as *Kevala jñāna* (entire knowledge) and *Akevala jñāna* (defective knowledge). The *Akevala jñāna* is subdivided as *avadhi* and *manaḥ-paryāya*. The *Parokṣa jñāna* is subdivided as *abhinibodha* (*mati*) and *śruta*. *Vide* the Sthānāṅga-sūtra, pp. 45–48, and the Nandī-sūtra, pp. 120–134: both published by Dhanapat Singh and printed in Calcutta. See also what is said in the account of Umāsvāti *seq.* पमाणे चउव्विहे पण्णत्ते, दुविहे णाणे पण्णत्ते, तं जहा पच्चक्खे चेव परोक्खे चेव।

(Sthānāṅga-sūtra, chap. 6, p. 45).

Hetu.

The word "Hetu" is found in the Prākṛtra scriptures, but its use in these works makes it clear that it had not at this period acquired a very definite significance. In the Sthānāṅga-sūtra[1] it is used not only in the sense of reason, but also as a synonym for valid knowledge (*Pramāṇa*) and inference (*Anumāna*). *Hetu* as identical with valid knowledge (*Pramāṇa*) is stated to be of four kinds, viz.:—

(1) knowledge derived from perception (*Pratyakṣa*);
(2) knowledge derived from inference (*Anumāna*);
(3) knowledge derived through comparison (*Upamāna*); and
(4) knowledge derived from verbal testimony or reliable authority (*Āgama*).

When *Hetu* is used in the sense of inference (*Anumāna*), it is classified according to the following types:—

(1) This *is*, because that *is*: There is a fire, because there is smoke.
(2) This *is not*, because that *is*: It is not cold, because there is a fire.
( ) This *is*, because that *is not*: It is cold here, because there is no fire.
(4) This *is not*, because that *is not*: There is no *śiṁśapā* tree here, because there are no trees at all.

Several terms of debate.

In the Sūtrakṛtāṅga[2] there is mention of *vitarka* (in Prākṛta: *viyakka*) in the sense of speculation, *tarka* (in Prākṛta: *takka*) in the sense of reasoning or debate, *pakṣa* (in Prākṛta: *pakkha*) in the sense of a party, and *chala* in the sense of quibble.

1

अथवा हेऊ चउव्विहे पन्नत्ते तं जहा
पच्चक्खे अनुमाणे उवमे आगमे ।
अथवा हेऊ चउव्विहे पन्नत्ते तं जहा
अत्थि तं अत्थि सा हेऊ अत्थि तं ।
अ त्थि सो हेऊ अत्थि त अत्थि सो
हेऊ अत्थि त अत्थि सो हेऊ ॥

(Bhagavatī-sūtra, p. 336; and Sthānāṅga-sūtra, pp. 309-310, published by Dhanapat Singh and printed in Calcutta).

2

सच्चिासभावं न गिरा गहीए. बे मुम्मुई चोर अपापवाई ।
इमं दुपक्खं इममेगपक्खं आइंसु छलायतणं च एगं ॥ ५ ॥
एवमेगे वियक्काहि. नो अन्न पज्जुवासिया
अप्पणा य वियक्काहिं, अयमंजू हि दुम्मई ॥ २१ ॥
एवं तक्काहि साहिंता, धम्माधम्मे अकोविया ।
दुक्खं ते नाइतुट्टंति, सउणी पंजरं जहा ॥ २० ॥

(Sūtrakṛtāṅga, p. 62, published by Dhanapat Singh, Calcutta).

Various kinds of example.

In the Sthānāṅga-sūtra[1] an example, called in Prākṛta *ṇāa* (in Sanskrit *jñāta*), is divided into four kinds, viz. (1) *āharaṇa*, a complete example which bears similarity to the thing exemplified in all respects, (2) *āharaṇa-taddesa*, a limited example which bears similarity to the thing exemplified only in respect of a part, (3) *āharaṇa-taddoṣa*, a defective example, and (4) *upanyāsopanaya*, an anecdote used as an example.

Expedients in a debate (*vivāda*).

In the Sthānāṅga-sūtra[2] the following are enumerated as expedients in a hostile debate or debate *a l'outrance*. (1) *Asakkaittā*, taking some time in making oneself ready, (2) *ussakkaittā*, gaining enthusiasm after the enjoyment of leisure, (3) *aṇulomaittā*, propitiating the authorities or making them favourable, (4) *pratilomaittā*, making the authorities hostile (against one's respondent), (5) *bhaittā*, serving the authorities, (6) *bheyaittā*, creating divisions.

In the Sthānāṅga-sūtra[3] the following are enumerated as the defects (*doṣa*) of a debate :—

The defects of a debate.

(1) *Tajjāta-doṣa*, the defect arising from a disputant being agitated in mind, (2) *matibhaṅga-doṣa*, the defect arising from the failure of his memory, (3) *praśāstṛ-doṣa*, the defect arising from the authorities, e.g. the president or the members, showing partiality, (4) *pariharaṇa-doṣa*, avoidance of the charges brought by a disputant, (5) *lakṣaṇa-doṣa*, the defect of definition [which may be too wide, too narrow or altogether incomprehensible], (6) *kāraṇa-doṣa*, the defect of arguing, (7) *hetu-doṣa*, committing fallacies, (8) *saṁkramaṇa-doṣa*, diversion to other subjects, (9) *nigraha-doṣa*, the defect of understanding, and (10) *vastu-doṣa*, the defect of the subject (of debate).

---

[1] चउव्विहे णाए पन्नत्ते, तं जहा, आहरणे, आहरणतद्देसे, आहरणतद्दोसे, उवन्नासोवणए।

(Sthānāṅga-sūtra, p. 300, published by Dhanapat Singh, Calcutta).

[2] छव्विहे विवादे पन्नत्ते, तं जहा, उसक्कइत्ता, अणुलोमइत्ता, पडिलोमइत्ता, भइत्ता, भेयइत्ता।

(Sthānāṅga-sūtra, p. 421, published by Dhanapat Singh, Calcutta).

[3] दसविहे दोसे पन्नत्ते, तं जहा, तज्जायदोसे, मइभंगदोसे, पसत्थारदोसे परिहरणदोसे, सलक्खण-कारण हेउदोसे, संकामणं, निग्गह वत्थुदोसे।

(Sthānāṅga-sūtra, p. 560, published by Dhanapat Singh, Calcutta).

CHAPTER II.

Early Jaina writers on Logic.

BHADRABĀHU THE SENIOR (CIRCA 433–357 B.C.).

BHADRABĀHU THE JUNIOR (CIRCA 375 A.D. OR 450–520 A.D.).

Though we come across some technical terms of Ancient Logic in the canonical scriptures of the Jainas, yet we have no proof that the Jainas undertook at that stage to write any regular work on logic. The early Jaina writers who discussed definite problems of logic, were Bhadrabāhu and Umāsvāti. An elaborate discussion of certain principles of logic is found in a Prākṛta commentary on the Daśa-vaikālika sūtra, called Daśavaikālika-niryukti. This commentary was the work of one Bhadrabāhu [1] of the Prācīna Gotra. For 45 years this sage lived the ordinary life of the world; 17 years he passed in the performance of religious vows (*Vratas*); and for 14 years he was acknowledged by the Jainas to be the foremost man of his age (*Yuga-pradhāna*).[2] He was a *Śrutakevalin*,[3] that is, one versed in the 14 *Pūrvas* of the Dṛṣṭivāda.

The above-mentioned incidents are generally accepted as facts in the life of the author of the commentary. There is, however, some doubt as to the time in which he lived.[4] According to the records [5] of the *Śvetāmbaras* he was born in 433 B.C. and died in 357 B.C. The *Digambaras* maintain there were two Bhadrabāhus; that the first (Bhadrabāhu the senior) lived to 162 years from the

---

[1] For particulars *vide* Dr. J. Klatt's Kharataragaccha-paṭṭāvalī in the Indian Antiquary, Vol. XI, Sept. 1882, p. 247; Weber II, p. 999; Peterson's 4th Report on Sanskrit MSS., p. lxxxiv; and Dr. H. Jacobi's edition of the Kalpasūtra, Introduction, pp. 11–15. Bhadrabāhu (senior) seems to have lived between 380 B.C. and 314 B.C., if he was really a contemporary of King Candra Gupta (Maurya), but about 375 A.D. if he lived at the time of Candra Gupta II, called Vikramāditya, of the Gupta dynasty.

[2] In the Vicāra-ratna-saṁgraha by Jayasoma-sūri noticed by Peterson in his 3rd Report on Sanskrit MSS., pp. 307–308, Bhadrabāhu is included among the Yuga-pravaras or Yuga-pradhānas.

[3] For further particulars about this title see R. G. Bhandarkar's Report, 1883–84, p. 122.

[4] In Weber II, p. 999, in which the Gurvāvalī-sūtra of Mahopādhyāya Dharmasāgaragaṇi is noticed, we read of Sambhūtivijaya and Bhadrabāhu "Ubhau-pi ṣaṣṭhapaṭṭadharau."

[5] अथस्थिमः पूर्व्वभृतां द्वितीयः
श्रीभद्रबाहुश्च (७) गुरुः श्रियाय ।
कल्प पञ्चमादिद्वरस्तवं यो
ररच सङ्घ धरणाचिंतान्धिः ॥ ११ ॥

nirvāṇa of Mahāvīra, that is, up to 365 B.C., and that the second [1] (Bhadrabāhu the junior) to 515 years from the *nirvāṇa* of Mahāvira, that is, up to 12 B.C. They do not state definitely which of these Bhadrabāhus was the author of the Daśavaikālika-niryukti, but they hold the view that the second was the author of several of the existing Jaina works. The *Śvetāmabara* records do not contain any mention of the second Bhadrabāhu, but in the Ṛṣimaṇḍala-prakaraṇa-vṛtti [2] and Kalpa-sūtra-subodhikā-vṛtti,[3] two commentaries of the *Śvetāmbaras*, and in the Caturviṁśati prabandha, it is stated that Bhadrabāhu lived in the south in Pratiṣṭhāna and was a brother of Varāhamihira. Now Varāhamihira is popularly believed to have lived in the first century B.C. It is possible therefore, even according to the *Śvetāmbaras*, that the Daśavaikālika-niryukti was the work of a commentator who, if we rely on popular belief, lived about the time of the opening of the Christian era. As a fact Bhadrabāhu could not have lived much earlier than 500 A.D. if he was a brother of Varāhamihira.

From the confusing traditions preserved by the Jainas, it may be concluded that Bhadrabāhu lived in the reign of Candra Gupta II, called Vikramāditya, about 375 A.D.

Whatever was his date, the author of the Daśavaikālika-niryukti wrote commentaries (niryuktis) on the following Jaina scriptures:—Āvaśyaka-sūtra, Uttarādhyayana-sūtra, Ācārāṅga-sūtra, Sūtra-kṛtāṅga-sūtra, Daśāśruta-skandha-sūtra, Kalpa-sūtra, Vyavahāra-sūtra, Sūrya-prajñapti-sūtra, and Ṛṣibhāṣita-sūtra.

7. Bhadrabāhu's Syllogism.

Bhadrabāhu did not set himself to analyse knowledge with the object of evolving a system of logic. His object was to illus-

---

निर्यूढ सिद्धान्तपयोधिपार
स्वर् यय वीरात् सनंदवर्षे १७० ।
तयोर्विनेयः कृतविश्वभद्रः
श्रीस्थूलभद्रस्य ददातु भद्रं ॥ १४ ॥

(Gurvāvali by Munisundara-sūri published in the Jaina Yaśovijaya-granthamālā of Benares, p. 4).

1 *Vide* the Sarasvatī-gaccha-paṭṭāvalī in the Indian Antiquary, October 1891, and March 1892.

2 *Vide* Dr. R. G. Bhandarkar's Reports on Sanskrit MSS. during 1883–84, p. 138. Bhadrabāhu must have lived as late as the 6th century A.D., if he was really a brother of that Varāhamihira who was one of the nine Gems at the court of Vikramāditya. Munis Dharmavijaya and Indravijaya maintain that Bhadrabāhu's brother was not the same Varāhamihira that adorned the court of Vikramāditya.

3 प्रतिष्ठानपुरे वराहमिहिर भद्रबाहु द्विजौ प्रव्रजितौ । भद्रबाहोराचार्य्यं पददाने ततः सन् वराहो द्विजवेषमादाय वाराहीं संहितां कृत्वा निमित्तैर्जीवति ।

(Kalpa-sūtra-subodhikāvṛtti printed in Bombay).

trate the truth of certain principles of the Jaina religion. To do this, he, in his Daśavaikālika-niryukti,[1] elaborated a syllogism consisting of ten parts (*daśāvayava-vākya*), and then demonstrated how the religious principles of Jainism satisfied the conditions of this syllogism.

The following is an example:—

The Syllogism of ten parts.

(1) The proposition (*Pratijñā*),—"to refrain from taking life is the greatest of virtues."

(2) The limitation of the proposition (*Pratijñā-vibhakti*)—"to refrain from taking life is the greatest of virtues, according to the Jaina Tīrthaṅkaras."

(3) The reason (*Hetu*),—"to refrain from taking life is the greatest of virtues, because those who so refrain are loved by the gods and to do them honour is an act of merit for men."

(4) The limitation of the reason (*Hetu-vibhakti*),—"none but those who refrain from taking life are allowed to reside in the highest place of virtue."

(5) The counter-proposition (*Vipakṣa*),—"but those who despise the Jaina Tīrthaṅkaras and take life are said to be loved by the gods, and men regard doing them honour as an act of merit. Again, those who take life in sacrifices are said to be residing in the highest place of virtue. Men, for instance, salute their fathers-in-law as an act of virtue, even though the latter despise the Jaina Tīrthaṅkaras and habitually take life. Moreover, those who perform animal sacrifies are said to be beloved of the gods."

(6) The opposition to the counter-proposition (*Vipakṣapratiṣedha*),—"those who take life as forbidden by the Jaina Tīrthaṅkaras do not deserve honour, and they are certainly not loved by

---

[1] ते उ पइन्न विभत्ती हेउ-विभत्ती विवक्खपडिसेहो ।
दिट्ठंतो आसंका तप्पडिसेहो निगमणं च ॥ १४२ ॥

(Daśavaikālika-niryukti, p. 74, published under the patronage of Dhanapat Singh by the Nirṇaya Sāgara Press, Bombay; and Dr. E. Leumann's edition of Daśavaikālika-niryukti, p. 649).

The Jainas characterise a syllogism of ten parts as the best (*uttama*), a syllogism of five parts as the mediocre (*madhyama*), and a syllogism of two parts as the worst (*jaghanya*). Candra Prabha Sūri (1102 A.D.) observes:—

अवयवापेक्षया जघन्य मध्यमोत्कृष्टास्तिस्रः कथा भवन्ति इति। तत्र हेतुप्रतिपादनमात्रं जघन्या। पञ्चावयवनिवेदनं मध्यमा, संपूर्णं दशावयवकथनमुत्कृष्टा।

(Nyāyāvatāra-vivṛti on verse 20 of Nyāyāvatāra, p. 8, edited by Satis Chandra Vidyabhusana, Calcutta). Similarly Ratnaprabha Sūri (1181 A.D.) says:—

पक्षादिप्रयवच पञ्चपाख्याः। तत उत्कृष्टं दशावयवं परार्थानुमानम् इत्युक्तं भवति। मध्यमं तु नवावयवादारभ्य यावत् द्व्यवयवम्। जघन्यं पुनः साधनमात्रोपन्यास स्वरूपम्। प्रतिपाद्यानां मन्दव्युत्पन्नातिव्युत्पन्नत्वात्।

(Syād-vāda-ratnā-karā-vatārikā, p. 20, Chap. III, edited by Hara Govind Das and Bechar Das in the Yaśovijaya Series, Benares).

the gods. It is as likely that fire will be cold as that they will be loved by the gods or to do them honour will be regarded by men as an act of merit Buddha, Kapila and others, though really not fit to be worshipped, were honoured for their miraculous sayings, but the Jaina *Tīrthaṅkaras* are honoured because they speak absolute truth."

(7) An instance or example (*Dṛṣṭānta*),—"the *Arhats* and *Sādhus* do not even cook food, lest in so doing they should take life. They depend on householders for their meals."

(8) Questioning the validity of the instance or example (*Āśaṅkā*),—"the food which the householders cook is as much for the *Arhats* and *Sādhus* as for themselves. If, therefore, any insects are destroyed in the fire, the *Arhats* and *Sādhus* must share in the householders' sin. Thus the instance cited is not convincing."

(9) The meeting of the question (*Āśaṅkā-pratiṣedha*),—"the *Arhats* and *Sādhus* go to householders for their food without giving notice and not at fixed hours. How, therefore, can it be said that the householders cooked food for the *Arhats* and *Sādhus*? Thus the sin, if any, is not shared by the *Arhats* and *Sādhus*."

(10) Conclusion (*Nigamana*),—"to refrain from taking life is therefore the best of virtues, for those who so refrain are loved by the gods, and to do them honour is an act of merit for men."

8. Bhadrabāhu's Explanation of *Syādvāda*.

Syādvāda.

Bhadrabāhu in his Sūtra-kṛtāṅga-niryukti[1] mentions another principle of the Jaina Logic called *Syādvāda* (*Syat* "may be" and *Vāda* "assertion," or the assertion of possibilities) or *Saptabhaṅgī-naya* (the sevenfold paralogism).

The *Syādvāda*[2] is set forth as follows:—(1) May be, it is, (2) may be, it is not, (3) may be, it is and it is not, (4) may be, it

---

1 असियसयं किरियाणं
अकिरियाणं च होइ चुलसीति ।
अन्नाणिय सत्तट्ठी
वेणइयाणं च बत्तीसा ॥ २१ ॥

(Śūtra-kṛtāṅga-niryukti, skandha 1, adhyāya 12, p. 448, edited by Bhim Singh Manak and printed in the Nirṇaya Sāgara Press, Bombay).

Cf. Sthānāṅga-sūtra, p. 316, published by Dhanapat Singh, Benares edition.

2 Cf. Sarvadarśana-saṁgraha, translated by Cowell and Gough, p. 55. For full particulars about Syādvāda or Saptabhaṅgī-naya *vide* Saptabhaṅgī-taraṅgiṇī by Vimala Dāsa printed in Bombay.

is indescribable, (5) may be, it is and yet is indescribable, (6) may be, it is not and it is also indescribable, (7) may be, it is and it is not and it is also indescribable.

9. Umāsvāti (1–85 A.D.).

The Tattvārthādhigama sūtra.

Jaina philosophy recognises seven categories, viz. (1) the soul (*Jīva*), (2) the soul-less (*Ajīva*), (3) action (*Āsrava*), (4) bondage (*Bandha*), (5) restraint (*Saṁvara*), (6) destruction of the consequences of action (*Nirjarā*), and (7) release or salvation (*Mokṣa*). According to the **Tattvārthādhigama-sūtra**[1] which with a *Bhāṣya* or commentary was composed by one Umāsvāti, these categories can be comprehended only by *Pramāṇa*, the means of valid knowledge and by *Naya*, the method of comprehending things from particular standpoints.

Umāsvāti's life.

Umāsvāti is better known as Vācaka-śramaṇa: he was also called Nāgaravācaka, this title being probably a reference to his Śākhā (spiritual genealogy). The Hindu philosopher Mādhavācārya calls him Umāsvāti-vācakācārya.[2] He lived for 84 years, 8 months, and 6 days and ascended heaven in Saṁvat 142, i.e. in 85 A.D. In the Tattvārthādhigama-sūtra Umāsvāti gives the following account[3] of himself:—He was born in a village called Nyagrodhikā, but he wrote the Tattvārthādhigama-sūtra in Pāṭliputra or Kusumapura (modern Patna). He belonged to the Kaubhīṣaṇin-gotra. His father was Svāti and he was consequently sometimes called Svāti-

---

[1] There are commentaries on the **Tattvārthādhigama-sūtra** by **Pūjyapāda Svāmin** called **Sarvārtha-siddhi**, by **Akalaṅkadeva** called **Tattvārtha-vartikālaṅkāra**, etc., which will be mentioned later.

[2] *Vide* Sarvadarśana-saṁgraha, chapter on Jaina darśana.

[3]

न्यग्रोधिकाप्रसूतेन विहरता पुरवरे कुसुमनाम्नि ।
कौभीषणिना स्वातितनयेन वात्सीसुतेनार्घ्यम् ॥ ३ ॥
अर्हद्वचनं सम्यग्गुरुक्रमेणागतं समुपधार्य्य ।
दुःखार्तं च दुरागमविहतमतिं लोकमवलोक्य ॥ ४ ॥
इदमुच्चैर्नागरवाचकेन सत्त्वानुकम्पया दृब्धम् ।
तत्त्वार्थाधिगमाख्यं स्पष्टमुमास्वातिना शास्त्रम् ॥ ५ ॥

(Tattvārthādhigama-sūtra, chap. X, p. 233, edited by Mody Keshavlal Premchand in the Bibliotheca Indica series, Calcutta).

A similar account is found in the commentary on the Tattvārthādhigama-sūtra by Siddhasenagaṇi. This account is mentioned by Peterson in his 4th Report on Sanskrit Manuscripts, p. xvi.

For further particulars about Umāsvāti see Peterson's 4th Report on Sanskrit Manuscripts, p. xvi, where he observes that in the Digambara Paṭṭāvalī published by Dr. Hoernle in the Indian Antiquary, XX, p. 341, Umāsvāmin (probably the

tanaya. He was also known as Vātsī-suta, because his mother was Umā of the Vatsagotra. In the Tīrthakalpa of Jinaprabha-sūri, it is stated that Umāsvāti was the author of 500 Sanskrit prakaraṇas (treatises). He is said to have belonged to the *Śvetāmbara* sect, though it is probable that the distinction between that sect and the *Digambaras* had not in his time come into existence.

10. Umāsvāti's Doctrine of *Pramāṇa* (Right Knowledge).

Parokṣa, indirect knowledge, and *Pratyakṣa*, direct knowledge.

In the Tattvārthādhigama-sūtra *Pramāṇa* fluctuates between the meanings of valid knowledge and the means of valid knowledge. In its former sense *Pramāṇa*, according to this Sūtra, is of two kinds: (1) *Parokṣa*, indirect knowledge, which is acquired by the soul through external agencies such as the organs of sense, and (2) *Pratyakṣa*, direct knowledge, which is acquired by the soul without the intervention of external agencies. *Parokṣa*, indirect knowledge, includes *mati*[1] and *śruta*, for these are acquired by the soul through the medium of the senses and the mind. Knowledge which is attained by *Yoga* (concentration) in its three stages of *avadhi*, *manaḥparyāya* and *kevala* —is a species of *Pratyakṣa*, direct knowledge, because it is acquired by the soul not through the medium of the senses.

Umāsvāti contends[2] that inference (*Anumāna*), comparison

---

same as Umāsvāti) is included as the sixth Digambara Sūri of the Sarasvatī-gaccha, between Kundakunda and Lohācārya II. According to Dr. Hoernle (*vide* "Two Paṭṭāvalīs of the Sarasvatīgaccha" by Dr. Hoernle in the Indian Antiquary, Vol. XX, October 1891, p. 351) the date of Umāsvāmin's accession is 44 A.D., and he lived for 84 years, 8 months and 6 days. Dr. Hoernle adds, the Kāṣṭhāsaṁgha arose in the time of Umāsvāmin.

Umāsvāti's Tattvārthādhigama-sūtra with his *bhāṣya*, together with Pūjā-prakaraṇa, Jambudvīpa-samāsa and Praśamarati, has been published by the Asiatic Society of Bengal, Calcutta, in one volume, which ends thus:—

इति: सिताम्बराचार्यस्य महाकवेरुमास्वातिवाचकस्य कृति ॥

(Jambudvīpa-samāsa, p. 38, published as Appendix C to the Tattvārthādhigama-sūtra in the Bibliotheca Indica series).

The Tattvārthādhigama-sūtra has been translated into English by Mr. J. L. Jaini of Indore.

[1] *Mati* is knowledge of existing things acquired through the senses and the mind.

Śruta is knowledge of things (past, present and future) acquired through reasoning and study.

Avadhi is knowledge of things beyond the range of our perception.

Manaḥparyāya is knowledge derived from reading the thoughts of others.

Kevala is unobstructed, unconditional and absolute knowledge.

[2] In the *bhāṣya* on aphorism 12, of Chapter 1 of the Tattvārthādhigama-sūtra, Umāsvāti observes:—

अनुमानोपमानागमार्थापत्तिसम्भवाभावानपि च प्रमाणानीति केचिन्मन्यन्ते तत्कथमेतदिति अत्रोच्यते । सर्वाण्येतानि मतिश्रुतयोरन्तर्भूतानि इन्द्रियार्थसन्निकर्षनिमित्तत्वात् ॥

(Tattvārthādhigama-sūtra, p. 15).

(*Upamāna*), verbal testimony or reliable authority (*Āgama*), presumption (*Arthāpatti*), probability (*Sambhava*), and non-existence (*Abhāva*), are not separate sources of valid knowledge: he includes them under *Parokṣa* (indirect knowledge). According to his theory the majority of them are the result of the contact of the senses with the objects which they apprehend; and some of them are not sources of valid knowledge at all.

It is interesting to note that according to Umāsvāti and the earlier Jaina philosophers all sense-perceptions (visual perception, auditory perception, etc.) are indirect apprehensions, inasmuch as the soul acquires them not of itself but through the medium of the senses. The words *Parokṣa* and *Pratyakṣa* are thus used by these authors in senses quite opposite to those which they bear in Brâhmaṇic logic and in the later Jaina Logic.[1]

11. UMĀSVĀTI'S EXPLANATION OF *Naya* (THE MOOD OF STATEMENTS).

Naya, the method of descriptions or mood of statements.

In the Tattvârthâdhigama-sûtra, *Naya*[2] is described as the method by which things are comprehended from particular standpoints. It is of five kinds:—(1) *Naigama*, the non-distinguished or non-analytical, (2) *Saṁgraha*, the collective, (3) *Vyavahāra*, the practical, (4) *Ṛju-sūtra*, the straight or immediate, (5) *Śabda*, the verbal or nominal.

Naigama.

Naigama, the non-analytical, is the method by which an object is regarded as possessing both general and specific properties, no distinction being made between them. For instance, when you use the word "bamboo," you are indicating a number of properties some of which are peculiar to the bamboo, while others are possessed by it in common with other trees. You do not distinguish between these two classes of properties.

In his *bhāṣya* on 1—6 of the Tattvārthādhigama-sūtra, Umāsvāti observes:—

चतुर्विधमित्यके । (Tattvārthādhigama-sūtra, p. 9).

In his *bhāṣya* on 1—35 he mentions the four Pramāṇas thus:—

यथा वा प्रत्यक्षानुमानोपमानाप्तवचनैः प्रमाणैरेकोऽर्थः प्रमीयते स्वविषयनियमात् न च ता विप्रतिपत्तयो भवन्ति तद्वन्नयवादा इति ॥ (Tattvārthādhigama-sūtra, p. 35).

These four kinds of *Pramāṇa* seem to refer to those in the Nyāya-Sūtra of the Hindu logician Akṣapāda. But the same four kinds are also referred to as subdivisions of *Hetu* in the Sthānāṅga Sūtra of the Jainas, p. 309, published by Dhanapat Singh and printed in Calcutta.

[1] Here *Parokṣa* stands for *sāṁvyavahārika pratyakṣa* while *Pratyakṣa* for *pāramārthika pratyakṣa* (*vide* Pramāṇa-naya-tattvālokālaṅkāra, chapter II).

[2] नैगमसंग्रहव्यवहारर्जुसूत्रशब्दा नयाः ॥ १-३४ ॥

(Tattvārthādhigama-sūtra, p. 32).

Saṁgraha.

Saṁgraha, the collective, is the method which takes into consideration generic properties only, ignoring particular properties.

Vayavahāra.

Vyavahāra, the practical, is the method which takes into consideration the particular only. The general without the particular is a nonentity. If you ask a person to bring you a plant, he must bring you a particular plant, he can not bring plant in general.

Ṛju-sūtra.

Ṛjū-sutra, the straight or immediate, is the method which considers a thing as it exists at the moment, without any reference to its past or its future. It is vain to ponder over a thing as it was in the past or as it will be in the future. All practical purposes are served by considering the thing itself as it exists at the present moment. For instance, a man who in a previous birth was my son is now born as a prince, but he is of no practical use to me now. The method of *Ṛju-sūtra* recognises the entity itself (*bhāva*), but does not consider its name (*nāma*) or image (*sthāpanā*), or the causes which constituted it (*dravya*). The fact that a cowherd is called *Indra* does not make him lord of the heavens. An image of a king can not perform the functions of the king. The causes, which exist in me now and will necessitate my being born hereafter with a different body, can not enable me to enjoy that body now.

Śabda.

Śabda,[1] the verbal, is the method of correct nomenclature. It is of three kinds, viz. *Sāmprata*, the suitable, *Samabhirūḍha*, the subtle, and *Evaṁbhūta*, the such-like. In Sanskrit a jar is called *ghaṭa*, *kumbha* or *kalasa*, and these are synonymous terms. *Sāmprata* consists in using a word in its conventional sense, even if that sense is not justified by its derivation. For example the word "*Śatru*," according to its derivation, means "destroyer," but its conventional meaning is "enemy." *Samabhirūḍha* consists in making nice distinctions between synonyms, selecting in each case the word which on etymological grounds is the most appropriate. *Evaṁbhūta* consists in applying to things such names only as their actual condition justifies. Thus a man should not be called *Śakra* (strong), unless he actually possesses the *Śakti* (strength) which the name implies.

---

[1] Umāsvāti in his *bhāṣya* on 1–35 observes :—

यथार्थाभिधानं शब्दः नामादिषु प्रसिद्धपूर्वाच्छब्दादर्थे प्रत्ययः साम्प्रतः सत्सु अर्थेषु असंक्रमः समभिरूढः । व्यञ्जनार्थयोरेवम्भूत इति ॥

(Tattvārthādhigama-sūtra, p. 32).

CHAPTER III.

Jaina writers on Systematic Logic.

12. THE WRITTEN RECORDS OF THE JAINAS (COMMENCING FROM 453 A.D.).

Historical period.

The teachings of Mahāvīra as contained in the Jaina *Āgamas* are said to have been handed down by memory for several centuries until in Vīra Saṁvat 980 or A.D. 453, they were codified in writing by Devardhi Gaṇi,[1] otherwise known as Kṣamāśramaṇa, at a council held at Valabhi (near Bhavanagara in Guzerat). According to this theory the authentic history of the Jaina literature commences from 453 A.D., and all that preceded that period is to be regarded as merely traditional.

13. SYSTEMATIC JAINA LOGIC.

During the era of tradition there existed no systematic Jaina treatise on Logic, its principles being included in the works on metaphysics and religion. With the commencement of the historical period in 453 A.D. there grew up, among the Jainas of both the Śvetāmbara and Digambara sects, a band of scholars who devoted themselves to the study of logic with great interest and enthusiasm. They wrote treatises on logic the rules of which clashed neither with the religious dogmas of the Brāhmaṇas nor with those of the Buddhists and Jainas. These treatises, along with the similar works of the Buddhists, contributed to the formation of the Mediæval School of Indian Logic.

---

[1] *Vide* Dr. Klatt's Paṭṭāvalī of the Kharataragaccha in the Indian Antiquary, Sept. 1882, Vol. XI, p. 247; and Dr. Jacobi's Kalpasutra, Introduction, p. 15. See also Vinaya Vijaya Gaṇi's commentary on the Kalpasūtra which quotes the following text:—

वलहिपुरंमि नयरे ।
देवड्ढि पमुह सयलसंघेहिं ।
पुव्वे आगम लिहिउ ।
नवसय असौ आउ वीराउ ॥ १ ॥

(Sukhabodhikā-ṭīkā to Kalpasūtra, p 433, printed in Kathiwar by Hira Lal Haṁsarāja).

In Devardhi Gaṇi's redaction of the Kalpasūtra (*vide* Dr. Jacobi's edition of the Kalpasūtra, p. 67) we read:—

Samaṇassa bhagavao Mahāvīrassa jāva savva-dukkha-ppahīṇassa navavāsasayāiṁ vikkaṁtaiṁ dasamassa ya vāsa-sayassa, ayaṁ asī ime saṁvacchare kāle gacchai iti (148).

14. SIDDHASENA DIVĀKARA *alias* KṢAPAṆAKA (ABOUT 480—550 A.D.).

The first Jaina writer on systematic logic was Siddhasena Divākara. It was he who for the first time laid the foundation of a science called Logic among the Jainas by compiling a treatise called **Nyāyāvatāra** [1] in thirty-two short stanzas.

Siddhasena Divākara is also famous as the author of the **Sammatitarka-sūtra** which is a work in Prākṛta on general philosophy containing an elaborate discussion on the principles of logic. This author, who belonged to the Śvetāmbara sect, has been mentioned by Pradyumna Sūri (*q.v.*) in his Vicāra-sāra-prakaraṇa [2] and by Jina Sena Sūri in the Ādipurāṇa dated 783 A.D.

Siddhasena's date.

Siddhasena, who was a pupil of Vṛddha-vādisūri, received the name of Kumuda-candra [3] at the time of ordination. He is said to have split, by the efficacy of his prayers, the Liṅga, the Brāhmaṇical symbol of Rudra, in the temple of Mahākāla at Ujjayinī, and to have called forth an image of Pārśvanātha by reciting his Kalyāṇa-mandira-stava. He is believed by Jainas to have converted Vikramāditya to Jainism 470 years after the *nirvāṇa* of Mahāvīra, that is, in 57 B.C.[4]

But Vikramāditya of Ujjainī does not seem to be so old, as he has been identified by scholars with Yaśodharma Deva, king of Malwa, who, on the authority of Alberuni, defeated the Huns at Korur in 533 A.D. This view of scholars agrees well with the statement of the Chinese pilgrim Hwen-thsang, who visited India in 629 A.D. and says that a very powerful king, presumably Vikramāditya, reigned at Ujjainī 60 years before his arrival there.[5] Moreover, Varāhamihira, who was one of the nine Gems at the court of Vikramāditya, is known to have lived between 505 A.D.

---

[1] *Vide* No. 741 in the list of MSS. purchased for the Bombay Government as noticed by Peterson in his 5th Report, p. 289. A manuscript of the Nyāyāvatāra with Vivṛti was procured for me from Bhavanagara, Bombay, by Muni Dharmavijaya and his pupil Śrī Indravijaya. The Nyāyā-vatāra with commentary and translation edited by Satis Chandra Vidyabhusana is available in Calcutta and Arrah.

[2] पंचेव य वरिसमए सिद्धसेणदिवायरो य जयपयडो ।
छसय वीसहिए सहुयुक पव्वराकिवपह ॥ २९ ॥
(Vicāra sāra-prakaraṇa, noticed by Peterson in his 3rd Report, p. 272).

[3] Cf. Prabhāvakacaritra VIII, V. 57.

[4] For other particulars about Siddhasena Divākara see Dr. Klatt's Paṭṭāvalī of the Kharataragaccha in the Indian Antiquary, Vol. XI, Sept. 1882, p. 247. *Vide* also Dr. R. G. Bhandarkar's report on Sanskrit MSS., during 1883-84, pp. 118, 140. Also the Prabandha-cintāmaṇi translated by Mr. Tawney in the Bibliotheca Indica series of Calcutta, pp. 10-14.

[5] *Vide* Beal's Buddhist Records, Vol. II, p. 261.

and 587 A.D.[1] It is therefore very probable that Vikramāditya and his contemporary Siddhasena Divākara lived at Ujjainī about 530 A.D. I am inclined to believe that Siddhasena was no other than *Kṣapaṇaka*[2] (a Jaina sage) who is traditionally known to the Hindus to have been one of the nine Gems that adorned the court of Vikramāditya.

Siddhasena Divākara seems to have been a senior contemporary of Jinabhadra Gaṇi Kṣamāśramaṇa (484–588 A.D.) who criticises Dvātriṁśat-dvātriṁśikā of which the Nyāyāvatāra is a part.

15. Siddhasena's Nyāyāvatāra.

The **Nyāyāvatāra** written in Sanskrit verse gives an exposition of the doctrine of *Pramāṇa* (sources of valid knowledge) and *Naya* (the method of comprehending things from particular standpoints).

Pramāṇa—Right Knowledge.

Perception.

Pramāṇa is right knowledge which illumines itself as well as other things without any obstruction. It is of two kinds: (1) direct valid knowledge or perception (*Pratyakṣa*) and (2) indirect valid knowledge (*Parokṣa*). Direct valid knowledge (*Pratyakṣa*) is two-fold: (1) practical (*Vyāvahārika*) which is the knowledge acquired by the soul

---

[1] Varāhamihira chose Śaka 427 or A.D. 505 as the initial year of his astronomical calculation, showing thereby that he lived about that time:

सप्ताश्वि वेदसंख्यं शककालमपास्य चैत्रशुक्लादौ ।
अर्धास्तमिते भानौ यवनपुरे सौम्य दिवसाद्ये ॥ ८ ॥

(Pañcasiddhāntikā, chap. 1, edited by Dr. G. Thibaut and Sudhākara Dvivedi).

Vide also Dr. Thibaut's Introduction to the Pañcasiddhāntikā, p. xxx.

[2] The nine Gems are:—

धन्वन्तरिः क्षपणकोऽमरसिंहः शङ्कु
वेतालभट्ट घटखर्पर कालिदासाः ।
ख्यातो वराहमिहिरो नृपतेः सभायां
रत्नानि वै वररुचिर्नव विक्रमस्य ॥

(Jyotirvidābharaṇa).

In the Pañcatantra and other Brahmanic Sanskrit works as well as in the Avadānakalpalatā and other Buddhist Sanskrit works the Jaina ascetics are nicknamed as Kṣapaṇaka:

भगवद्भाषितं तत्तु सुभद्रेण निवेदितम् ।
श्रुत्वा क्षपणकः क्षिप्रमभूद् द्वेषविषाकुलः ॥ ९ ॥
तस्य सर्वज्ञतां वेत्ति सुभद्रो यदि मद्गिरा ।
तदेष क्षपणश्रद्धां त्यक्ष्यतीति श्रमणादरात् ॥ ११ ॥

(Avadānakalpalatā, Jyotiṣkāvadāna).

through the five senses (the eye, ear, nose, tongue and touch) and the mind (*Manas*), and (2) transcendental (*Pāramārthika*) which is the infinite knowledge that comes from the perfect enlightenment of the soul: it is called *Kevala* or absolute knowledge.

Verbal Testimony.

Indirect valid knowledge (*Parokṣa*) is also of two kinds: (1) inference (*Anumāna*) and (2) verbal testimony (*Śabda*). Verbal testimony is the knowledge derived from the words of reliable persons including knowledge from scripture. Suppose a young man coming to the side of a river cannot ascertain whether the river is fordable or not, and immediately an old experienced man of the locality, who has no enmity against him, comes and tells him that the river is easily fordable: the word of the old man is to be accepted as a source of valid knowledge called personal testimony or *Laukika Śābda.* Scripture is also a source of valid knowledge for it lays down injunctions on matters which baffle perception and inference: for instance, it teaches that misery is the consequence of vice. Knowledge derived from this source is called scriptural testimony or *Śāstraja Śābda. Scripture* is defined as that which was first cognised or composed by a competent person, which is not such as to be passed over by others, which is not incompatible with the truths derived from perception, which imparts true instruction and which is profitable to all men and is preventive of the evil path.[1]

Inference.

Inference (*Anumāna*) is the correct knowledge of the major term (*Sādhya*) derived through the middle term (*Hetu*, reason, or *Liṅga*, sign) which is inseparably connected with it. It is of two kinds: (1) inference for one's own self (*Svārthānumāna*) and (2) inference for the sake of others (*Parārthānumāna*).

The first kind is the inference deduced in one's own mind after having made repeated observations. A man by repeated observations in the kitchen and elsewhere forms the conclusion in his mind that fire is always an antecedent of smoke. Afterwards, he is not certain whether a hill which he sees has fire on it or not. But, noticing smoke, he at once brings to mind the inseparable connection between fire and smoke, and concludes that there must be fire on the hill. This is the inference for one's own self.

If the inference is communicated to others through words, it

---

[1] आप्तोपज्ञमनुल्लङ्घ्यमदृष्टेष्टविरोधकम् ।
तत्त्वोपदेशकृत् सार्वं शास्त्रं कापथघट्टनम् ॥

(Verse 9, Nyāyāvatāra).

is called an inference for the sake of others. A type of this kind of inference is as follows:—

(1) The *hill* (minor term or *Pakṣa*) is full of *fire* (major term or *Sādhya*);
(2) because it is full of *smoke* (middle term or *Hetu*);
(3) whatever is full of smoke is full of fire, as, e.g. a *kitchen* (example or *Dṛṣṭānta*);
(4) so is this hill full of smoke (application or *Upanaya*):
(5) therefore this hill is full of fire (conclusion or *Nigamana*).

Terms of a syllogism.

In a proposition the subject is the minor term (*Pakṣa*) and the predicate the major term (*Sādhya*). The minor term is that with which the connection of the major term is to be shown. In the proposition "the hill is full of fire," the *hill* is the minor term and *fire* major term. The middle term (*Hetu*) is defined as that which cannot occur otherwise than in connection with the major term. Thus in the proposition: "the hill is full of fire because it is full of smoke," *smoke* is the middle term which cannot arise from any other thing than fire which is the major term. The example (*Dṛṣṭānta*) is a familiar case which assures the connection between the major term and the middle term. It is of two kinds. (1) homogeneous or affirmative (*Sādharmya*), such as "the hill is full of fire because it is full of smoke, as a *kitchen*," and (2) heterogeneous or negative (*Vaidharmya*) which assures the connection between the middle term and major term by contrariety, that is, by showing that the absence of the major term is attended by the absence of the middle term, such as "where there is no fire there is no smoke, as in a *lake*."

In an inference for the sake of others the minor term (*Pakṣa*) must be explicitly set forth, otherwise the reasoning might be misunderstood by the opponent, e.g. This hill has fire because it has smoke.

This instance, if the minor term is omitted, will assume the following form:—

Having fire, | Because having smoke.

Here the opponent might not at once recollect any instance in which fire and smoke exist in union, and might mistake a lake for such an instance. In such a case the whole reasoning will be misunderstood.

If that of which the major term or predicate is affirmed, is opposed by evidence, public opinion, one's own statement, etc., we have that which is known as the fallacy of the minor term (*Pakṣābhāsa*) of which there are many varieties.

Fallacies of the minor term.

The semblance or fallacy of the minor term (*Pakṣābhāsa*) arises when one attributes to it as a proved fact that which is yet to be proved, or which is incapable of being proved, or when it is opposed to perception and inference, or inconsistent with public opinion or incongruous with one's own statement, thus :—

(1) "The jar is corporeal (*paudgalika*)"—this is a conclusion which is yet to be proved to the opponent.

(2) "Every thing is momentary"—this is a Saugata conclusion which, according to the Jainas, is incapable of being proved.

(3) "The general particular (*sāmānya viśeṣa*) things are without parts, are distinct from each other and are like themselves alone"—this is opposed to perception.

(4) "There is no omniscient being"—this is, according to the Jainas, opposed to inference.

(5) "The sister is to be taken as wife"—this is inconsistent with public opinion.

(6) "All things are non-existent"—this is incongruous with one's own statement.

Inseparable connection.

Inseparable connection or invariable concomitance (*Vyāpti*) is the constant accompaniment of the middle term by the major term. In the inference: "this hill is full of fire, because it is full of smoke," the connection between fire and smoke, that is, the constant presence of fire with smoke, is called *Vyāpti* or Inseparable Connection. It is of two kinds: (1) Intrinsic, and (2) Extrinsic.

Antar-vyāpti.

Intrinsic inseparable connection (*Antar-vyāpti*) occurs when the minor term (*pakṣa*), itself as the common abode of the middle term (*hetu*) and the major term (*sādhya*), shows the inseparable connection between them, thus :—

(1) This hill (minor term) is full of *fire* (major term) :

(2) because it is full of *smoke* (middle term).

Here the inseparable connection between fire and smoke is shown by the hill (minor term) in which both of them abide.

Bahir-vyāpti.

Extrinsic inseparable connection (*Bahir-vyāpti*) occurs when an example (*dṛṣṭānta*) from the outside is introduced as the common abode of the middle term (*hetu*) and the major term (*sādhya*) to assure the inseparable connection between them, thus :—

(1) This hill is full of *fire* (major term) ;

(2) because it is full of *smoke* (middle term) ;

(3) as a *kitchen* (example).

Here the reference to the kitchen is no essential part of the inference, but is introduced from without as a common instance of a place in which fire and smoke exist together, and so it reaffirms the inseparable connection between them.

Some logicians hold that that which is to be proved, that is, the major term (*sādhya*), can be established by intrinsic inseparable connection (*Antar-vyāpti*) only: hence the extrinsic inseparable connection (*Bahir vyāpti*) is superfluous.

Fallacies of the middle term.

The semblance of reason or fallacy of the middle term (*Hetvābhāsa*) arises from doubt, misconception or non-conception about it (the middle term). It is of three kinds:—

(1) The unproved (*Asiddha*): This is fragrant, because it is a sky-lotus.

Here the reason (middle term), viz. the sky-lotus, is unreal.

(2) The contradictory (*Viruddha*): "This is fiery, because it is a body of water."

Here the reason alleged is opposed to what is to be established.

(3) The uncertain (*Anaikāntika*): "Sound is eternal, because it is always audible."

Here the reason or middle term is uncertain, because audibleness may or may not be a proof of eternity.

Fallacies of homogeneous of example.

The fallacy of example (*Dṛṣṭāntābhāsa*) may arise in the homogeneous or heterogeneous form, from a defect in the middle term (*hetu*) or major term (*sādhya*) or both, or from doubt about them.

Fallacies of the homogeneous example (*Sādharmya-dṛṣṭāntābhāsa*) are as follows:—

(1) Inference is *invalid* (major term), because it is a *source of knowledge* (middle term), like *perception* (homogeneous example).

Here the example involves a defect in the major term (*sādhya*), for perception is not invalid.

(2) Perception is *invalid* (major term), because it is a *source of valid knowledge* (middle term), like a *dream* (homogeneous example).

Here the example involves a defect in the middle term (*hetu*), for the dream is not a source of valid knowledge.

(3) The omniscient being is not *existent* (major term), because he is not *apprehended by the senses* (middle term), like a *jar* (homogeneous example).

Here the example involves a defect in both the major and middle terms (*sādhya* and *hetu*), for the jar is both existent and apprehended by the senses.

(4) This person is *devoid of passions* (major term), because he is *mortal* (middle term), like the *man in the street* (homogeneous example).

Here the example involves doubt as to the validity of the major term, for it is doubtful whether the man in the street is devoid of passions.

(5) This person is *mortal* (major term), because he is *full of passions* (middle term), like the *man in the street* (homogeneous example).

Here the example involves doubt as to the validity of the middle term, for it is doubtful whether the man in the street is devoid of passions.

(6) This person is *non-omniscient* (major term), because he is *full of passions* (middle term), like the *man in the street* (homogeneous example).

Here the example involves doubt as to the validity of both the major and middle terms, for it is doubtful whether the man in the street is full of passions and non-omniscient.

It is stated in the Nyāyāvatāra-vivṛti that some unnecessarily lay down three other kinds of fallacy of the homogeneous example (*Sādharmyadṛṣṭāntābhāsa*), viz. :—

(1) Unconnected (*Ananvyaya*), such as: This person is *full of passions* (major term), because he is a *speaker* (middle term), like a *certain man in Magadha* (example).

Here though a certain man in Magadha is both a speaker and full of passions, yet there is no inseparable connection between "being a speaker" and "being full of passions."

(2) Of connection unshown (*Apradarśitānvaya*), such as :—

Sound is *non-eternal* (major term), because it is *produced* (middle term), as a jar (example).

Here though there is an inseparable connection between "produced" and "non-eternal," yet it has not been shown in the proper form as :—

"Whatever is produced is non-eternal, as a jar."

(3) Of inverted connection (*Viparītānvaya*), such as :—

Sound is non-eternal (major term), because it is *produced* (middle term).

Here if the inseparable connection (*vyāpti*) is shown thus—

"Whatever is non-eternal is produced as a jar," instead of—

"Whatever is produced is non-eternal as a jar," the example would involve the fallacy of inverted connection.

Fallacies of heterogeneous example.

Fallacies of the heterogeneous example (*Vaidharmyadṛṣṭāntābhāsa*) are of six kinds, thus :—

(1) Inference is *invalid* (major term), because it is a *source of knowledge* (middle term): whatever is not invalid is not a source of knowledge, as a *dream* (heterogeneous example).

Here the example involves in the heterogeneous form a defect in the major term (*sādhya*), for the dream is really invalid though it has been cited as not invalid.

(2) Perception is *non-reflective* or *nirvikalpaka* (major term), because it is a *source of knowledge* (middle term): whatever is reflective or *savikalpaka*, is not a source of knowledge, as *inference* (heterogeneous example).

Here the example involves in the heterogeneous form a

defect in the middle term (*sādhana*), for inference is really a source of knowledge though it has been cited as not such.

(3) Sound is eternal and *non-eternal* (major term), because it is an *existence* (middle term): whatever is not eternal and non-eternal is not an existence, as a jar (heterogeneous example).

Here the example involves in the heterogeneous form a defect in both the major and middle terms (*sādhya* and *sādhana*), for the jar is both "eternal and non-eternal" and "an existence."

(4) Kapila is not *omniscient* (major term), because he is not a *propounder of the four noble truths* (middle term): whoever is omniscient is propounder of the four noble truths, as *Buddha* (the heterogeneous example).

Here the example involves in the heterogeneous form a doubt as to the validity of the major term (*sādhya*), for it is doubtful whether Buddha was omniscient.

(5) This person is *untrustworthy* (major term), because he is *full of passions* (middle term): whoever is trustworthy is not full of passions, as *Buddha* (heterogeneous example).

Here the example involves doubt as to the validity of the middle term (*hetu*), for it is doubtful whether Buddha is not full of passions.

(6) Kapila is not devoid of *passions* (major term), because he did *not give his own flesh to the hungry* (middle term): whoever is devoid of passions gives his own flesh to the hungry, as *Buddha* (heterogeneous example).

Here the example involves doubt as to the validity of both the major and middle terms (*sādhya* and *sādhana*), for it is doubtful whether Buddha was devoid of passions and gave his own flesh to the hungry.

It is stated in the Nyāyāvatāra-vivṛti that some unnecessarily lay down three other kinds of fallacy of the heterogeneous example (*Vaidharmyadṛṣṭāntābhāsa*), *viz.*—

(1) Unseparated (*Avyatireki*): This person is not *devoid of passions* (major term), because he is a *speaker* (middle term): whoever is devoid of passions is not a speaker, as a *piece of stone* (heterogeneous example).

Here, though a piece of stone is both "devoid of passions" and "not a speaker," yet there is no invariable separation (*vyatireka vyāpti*) between "devoid of passions" and "a speaker."

(2) Of separation unshown (*Apradarśitavyatireka*):

Sound is *non-eternal* (major term), because it is *produced* (middle term); as ether (example).

Here, though there is an invariable separation between "*produced*" and "eternal," yet it has not been shown in the proper form, such as: "Whatever is non-non-eternal is not produced, e.g. ether."

(3) Of contrary separation (*Viparīta-vyatireka*):

Sound is *non-eternal* (major term), because it is produced (middle term): whatever is not produced is non-non-eternal, e.g. ether (example).

Here the example has been put in a contrary way, for the proper form should have been: Whatever is non-non-eternal is not produced, e.g. ether."

Refutation.

Refutation (*Dūṣaṇa*) is the pointing out of defects or fallacies in the statements of the opponent in any of the forms enumerated above. The semblance of a refutation (*Dūṣaṇābhāsa*) is the contrivance to allege defects where there are no defects at all.

Consequence of *pramāṇa.*

The immediate effect of *Pramāṇa* (valid knowledge) is the removal of ignorance. The consequence of the transcendental perception (*Pāramārthika Pratyakṣa Pramāṇa*) is bliss and equanimity consisting in salvation (*Mokṣa* or final emancipation), while that of the other kinds of *Pramāṇa* (direct and indirect knowledge) is the facility which they afford us to choose the desirable and reject the undesirable things.

Naya—the method of descriptions.

Naya or the method of comprehending things from particular standpoints.

Naya is the method of comprehending things from particular standpoints. Thus we may conceive rose either as a flower possessing the attributes common to all flowers or as a thing possessing attributes which are peculiar to the rose as distinguished from other flowers. The *Naya* is of seven kinds: *naigama, saṁgraha, vyavahāra, ṛjusūtra, śabda, samabhirūḍha,* and *evaṁbhūta.*

Syādvāda.

Knowledge which determines the full meaning of an object through the employment, in the scriptural method, of one-sided *nayas,* is called *Syādvāda-śruta.* It is the perfect knowledge of things taken from all possible standpoints. Thus a thing may be, may not be, both may or may not be, etc., according as we take it from one or other standpoint.

The soul (*Jīva*) is the knower, the illuminator of self and non-self, doer and enjoyer. It undergoes changes of condition and is self-conscious, being different from the earth, water, etc.

This system of *Pramāṇa* and *Naya,* with which all of us are familiar and which serves to perform all practical functions, cannot be traced to its beginning or followed to its end.

16. JINABHADRA GAṆI KṢAMĀŚRAMAṆA (484—588 A.D.).

Jinabhadra Gaṇi, author of a commentary on the Āvaśyaka-niryukti called **Viśeṣāvaśyaka Bhāṣya**, was born in Saṁvat 541 or 484 A.D. He was well known as Kṣamāśramaṇa, and continued to be pontiff from 528 A.D. to 588 A.D.[1]

---

[1] Peterson's Fourth Report, p. xxxix.

17. SIDDHASENA GAṆI (600 A.D.).

Siddhasena Gaṇi, who belonged to the Śvetāmbara sect, was the author of a commentary on Umāsvāti's Tattvārthādhigama-sūtra called **Tattvārthaṭīkā**,[1] in which the logical principles of *Pramāṇa* (the sources of knowledge), and *Naya* (the method of comprehending things from particular standpoints), have been fully discussed. He was a pupil of Bhāsvāmin[2] who was a spiritual successor of Siṁhasūri, himself a disciple of Dinna Gaṇi. Siddhasena Gaṇi[3] is generally believed to have been a contemporary of Devardhigaṇi Kṣamāśramaṇa, who flourished 980 years after Mahāvīra, or about 453 A.D. But as he has in his Tattvārthaṭīkā quoted Siddhasena Divākara and was posterior to Siṁhagiri or Siṁhasūri, a contemporary of Vikramāditya, I am inclined to suppose that he lived after 533 A.D. or about 600 A.D.

18. SAMANTABHADRA (600 A.D.).

Samantabhadra, who belonged to the Digambara sect of Southern India, was famous as the author of a well-known commentary on Umāsvāti's Tattvārthādhigama-sūtra called **Gandhahasti-mahābhāṣya**. The introductory part of this commentary is called **Devāgamastotra**[4] or **Āptamīmāṁsā**, and is replete with discussions of logical principles besides a review of the contemporary schools of philosophy including the Advaita Vāda.[5] The Āptamī-

---

[1] A palm-leaf manuscript of the Tattvārthaṭīkā in the temple of Śāntinātha, Cambay, has been noticed by Peterson in his 3rd Report, pp. 83–86.

[2] तस्मादृरजोऽपथयः सख्यागमशेमुषीकपङ्काप्तः ।
तस्यार्थभास्वटीकामिमां व्यधात् सिद्धसेनगणिः ॥ ७

(Tattvārthaṭīkā, noticed in Peterson's 3rd Report, p. 85).

[3] Siṁhasūri is identified by Peterson with Siṁhagiri who was a contemporary of Vikramāditya.

(Peterson's 4th Report, pp. cxxxi and cxxviii).

Muni Dharmavijaya and his pupil Indra-vijaya tell me that Siddhasena Gaṇi was a contemporary of Devardhigaṇi Kṣamāśramaṇa, who flourished 980 years after the *nirvāṇa* of Mahāvīra. *Vide* also Uvāsagadasāo edited by A. F. R. Hoernle, Appendix III, page 50.

[4] In the Pāṇḍavapurāṇa Samantabhadra is extolled as the author of the Devāgamastotra :—

समन्तभद्रो भद्रार्थो भातु भारतभूषणः
देवागमेन येनात्र व्यक्तो देवागमः कृतः ॥

(Pāṇḍavapurāṇa, noticed in Peterson's 4th Report, p. 157).

[5] अद्वैतैकान्तपक्षेऽपि दृष्टो भेदो विरुध्यते ।
कारकाणां क्रियायाश्च नैकं स्वस्मात् प्रजायते ॥ २४ ॥

(Āptamīmāṁsā, verse 24).

māṁsā has been cited by the Hindu philosopher Vācaspati Miśra [1] in explaining Śaṅkarācārya's criticism of the Syādvāda doctrine in the Vedānta-sūtra.

His age.

Samantabhadra, who was styled a Kavi and whose works were commented on by Vidyānanda [2] and Prabhācandra, was also the author of the Yuktyanuśāsana, the Ratnakaraṇḍaka (also called Upāsakādhyayana), the Svayambhū-stotra, and the Caturviṁśati-jina-stuti. He is mentioned by Jina Sena in the Ādipurāṇa composed about 838 A.D., and is referred to by the Hindu philosopher Kumārila.[3] Kumārila, a contemporary of the Buddhist logician Dharmakīrti, is generally held to have lived in the 7th century A.D. Samantabhadra is supposed to have flourished about 600 A.D.

---

[1] Vācaspati Miśra in his Bhāmatī-ṭīkā on Śaṅkara's exposition of the Vedānta Sūtra, 2-2-33, quotes the following verse:—

स्याद्वादः सर्वथैकान्तत्यागात् किंवृत्तचिद्विधः ।

सप्तभङ्गनयापेक्षो हेयादेयविशेषकृत् ॥

(Bhāmatī, Bibliotheca Indica, p. 458).

The same verse occurs in the Āptamīmāṁsā as follows:—

स्याद्वादः सर्वथैकान्तत्यागात् किंवृत्तचिद्विधः ।

सप्तभङ्गनयापेक्षो हेयादेयविशेषकः ॥ १०४ ॥

(MSS. of the Āptamīmāṁsā, verse 104, borrowed from Mr. Jain Vaidya of Jaipur).

[2] Vidyānanda at the closing part of his commentary on the Āptamīmāṁsā (called Āpta-mīmāṁsālaṅkṛti-ṭīkā aṣṭasāhasrī) refers to Samantabhadra thus:—

येनाशेषकुनीतिवृत्तिसरितः प्रेक्षावतां शोषिताः

यद्वाचोऽप्यकलङ्कनीतिरुचिरास्तत्त्वार्थसार्थद्युतः ।

स श्रीस्वामिसमन्तभद्रयतिभृद् भूयाद् विभुर्भानुमान्

विद्यानन्दघनप्रदोऽनघधियां स्याद्वादमार्गाग्रणीः ॥

(Folio 218, Āptamīmāṁsālaṅkṛti-ṭīkā, Govt. Collection, in the Asiatic Society of Bengal, No. 1525).

Prabhācandra in his commentary on the Ratnakaraṇḍaka (or Upāsakādhyayana) observes:—

येनाज्ञानतमो विनाश्य निखिलं भव्यात्मचेतोगतं

सम्यग्ज्ञानमहांशुभिः प्रकटितः सागारमार्गोऽखिलः ।

स श्रीरत्नकरण्डकामलरविः संसृत्सरिच्छोषको

जीयादेष समन्तभद्रमुनिपः श्रीमत्प्रभेन्दुर्जिनः ॥

(Upāsakādhyayana with the commentary of Prabhācandra noticed in Peterson's 4th Report, pp. 137–38)

[3] *Vide* Dr. R. G. Bhandarkar's Report on Sanskrit MSS. during 1883–84, p. 118, and J.B.B.R.A.S., for 1892, p. 227.

19. Samantabhadra's Āptamīmāṁsā.

Syād-vāda.

The Āptamīmāṁsā consists of 115 stanzas in Sanskrit, divided into ten chapters called *Paricchedas*, in the course of which a full exposition of the seven parts of the *Syād-vāda* or *Sapta bhaṅgī-naya* has been given. The first and second parts of the doctrine, viz. *Syād-asti* ("may be, it is"), and *Syād-nāsti* ("may be, it is not"), have led to a most interesting discussion of the relation between *asti*, that is, *bhāva* or existence, and *nāsti*, that is, *abhāva* or non-existence.

Non-existence.

Non-existence (*Abhāva*) is divided into four kinds: (1) antecedent non-existence (*prāgabhāva*), e.g. a lump of clay becomes non-existent as soon as a jar is made out of it, so the jar is an antecedent non-existence with reference to the lump of clay; (2) subsequent non-existence (*pradhvaṁsābhāva*), e.g. the lump of clay is a subsequent non-existence with reference to the jar; (3) mutual non-existence (*anyonyābhāva* or *anyāpoha*), e.g. a jar and a post are mutually non-existent with reference to each other; and (4) absolute non-existence (*samavāyābhāva* or *atyantābhāva*), e.g. the inanimate is not a living object.

It is observed [1] that, on the supposition of mere existence to the entire exclusion of non-existence, things become all-pervading, beginningless, endless, indistinguishable and inconceivable. For instance, if the antecedent non-existence is denied, action and substance become beginningless, while on the denial of the subsequent non-existence, they become endless, and in the absence of

---

1
भावैकान्ते पदार्थानामभावानामपह्नवात् ।
सर्वात्मकमनाद्यन्तमस्वरूपमभावकम् ॥ ९ ॥
कार्य्यद्रव्यमनादि स्यात् प्रागभावस्य निह्नवे ।
प्रध्वंसस्य च धर्म्मस्य प्रच्यवेऽनन्ततां व्रजेत् ॥ १० ॥
सर्वात्मकं तदेकं स्यादन्यापोहव्यतिक्रमे ।
अन्यत्र समवायेन व्यपदिश्येत सर्वथा ॥ ११ ॥
अभावैकान्तपक्षेऽपि भावापह्नववादिनाम् ।
बोधवाक्यप्रमाणं न केन साधनदूषणम् ॥ १२ ॥
विरोधान्नोभयैकात्म्यं स्याद्वादन्यायविद्विषाम् ।
अवाच्यतैकान्तेऽप्युक्तिर्नावाच्यमिति युज्यते ॥ १३ ॥
कथंचित्ते सदेवेष्टं कथंचिदसदेव तत् ।
तथोभयमवाच्यं च उपयोगान्न सर्वथा ॥ १४ ॥

(Āptamīmāṁsā, MSS., verses 9–14, lent to me by Mr. Jain Vaidya of Jaipur).

mutual non-existence, they become one and all-pervading, while on absolute non-existence being denied, they are to be supposed as existing always and everywhere.

In the same way on the supposition of mere non-existence to the entire exclusion of existence, it becomes impossible to establish or reject anything (since it is non-existent). If on the other hand existence and non-existence, which are incompatible with each other, are simultaneously ascribed to a thing, it becomes indescribable. Therefore the truth is as follows:—

Sevenfold paralogism.

(1) A thing *is* existent—from a certain point of view.
(2) It *is non*-existent—from another point of view.
(3) It is *both* existent and non-existent *in turn*—from a third point of view.
(4) It is *indescribable* (that is, both existent and non-existent simultaneously)—from a fourth point of view.
(5) It *is* existent and *indescribable*—from a fifth point of view.
(6) It *is non*-existent and *indescribable*—from a sixth point of view.
(7) It *is both* existent and *non*-existent and *indescribable*—from a seventh point of view.

20. Akalaṅkadeva (about 750 A.D.).

His works.

Akalaṅka, otherwise known as Akalaṅkadeva or Akalaṅkacandra, was a famous logician who belonged to the Digambara sect of Southern India. He was designated as a *Kavi*[1] (poet)—a title of special honour given to writers of repute. He wrote a commentary on Samantabhadra's Āptamīmāṁsā called **Aṣṭa-śatī**[2] which is a most precious work on the Jaina philosophy, dealing mainly with logic. Māṇikyanandi's Parīkṣāmukha-sūtra (q.v.) was based on another work on logic, called **Nyāya-viniścaya**, written by Akalaṅka, to whom the following works are also attributed: **Tattvārtha-vārtika-vyākhyānālaṅkāra**, Laghīyastraya, Akalaṅka-stotra, Svarūpa-sambodhana and Prāyaścitta. Laghusamantabhadra[3] in his Aṣṭa-sāhasrī-viṣama-pada-tātparya-ṭīkā calls Akalaṅka as *Sakala-tārkika-cakra-cūḍā-maṇi* or "the crest gem of the circle of all logicians."

---

[1] For an explanation of the term "Kavi" *vide* R. G. Bhandarkar's Report on Sanskrit MSS. during 1883-84, page 122.

[2] A manuscript of the Aṣṭa-śatī was kindly supplied to me by Mr. Jain Vaidya of Jaipur early in 1907.

[3] *Vide* Aṣṭasāhasrī-viṣamapada-tātparya-ṭīkā by Laghusamanta-bhadra, noticed by Peterson in his 5th Report, p. 217.

In the Pāṇḍavapurāṇa[1] reference is made to a legend according to which Akalaṅka was embarrassed in a controversy with a Buddhist antagonist. Finding that the antagonist was effectively prompted by Māyādevī concealed in a jar, Akalaṅka is said to have put an end to that prompting or inspiration by kicking the jar over with his foot.

His age.

Akalaṅka, though mentioned along with Dharmakīrti[2] as a logician, flourished at a considerably later time. He is held to have been a contemporary of Rāṣṭrakūṭa king Śubhatuṅga[3] or Kṛṣṇarāja I. As Kṛṣṇarāja's son, Govind II, lived in Śaka 705[4] or 783 A.D., Kṛṣṇa-rāja I, and consequently his contemporary Akalaṅka, must have flourished about 750 A.D.

21. VIDYĀNANDA (ABOUT 800 A.D.).

His works.

Vidyānanda, mentioned by the Hindu philosopher Mādhavācārya,[5] was a Digambara logician of Pāṭalīputra. He was the author of the **Āptamīmāṁsālaṅkṛti**, otherwise called **Aṣṭasāhasrī**, an exhaustive subcommentary on the Āptamīmāṁsā, containing an elaborate exposition of various logical principles. Vidyānanda, in the opening and the closing lines of his Aṣṭasāhasrī,[6] makes an indirect reference

---

[1] अकलङ्कोऽकलङ्कः स कलौ कलयतु श्रुतम् ।
पादेन ताडिता येन मायादेवी घटस्थिता ॥

(Pāṇḍavapurāṇa, noticed by Peterson in his 4th Report, p. 157).

[2] वाचकमुख्यविरचितानि सकलशास्त्रचूडामणिभूतानि तत्त्वार्थसूत्राणीति यद्येवमकलङ्क-धर्मकीर्त्यादिवत् प्रकरणमेव किं नारभ्यते किमनया सूत्रकारत्वाहोपुरुषिकया ।

(Pramāṇa-mīmāṁsā, by Hemacandra, noticed by Peterson in his 5th Report, p. 148).

[3] *Vide* K. B. Pathak's article on "Bhartṛhari and Kumārila" in the Journal of the Bombay Branch of the Royal Asiatic Society, Vol. XVIII, 1892.

It is reported that Akalaṅka and Niṣkalaṅka were two sons of Śubhatuṅga whose capital was Mānyakheta. Śubhatuṅga is another name of Kṛṣṇarāja the Rāṣṭrakūṭa king who reigned in the Deccan between 753–775 A.D. Akalaṅka forsook his father's palace and became an ascetic. (*Vide* Peterson's Report II, p. 79).

[4] *Vide* R. G Bhandarkar's "Early History of the Deccan," 2nd edition, p. 78.

[5] *Vide* the chapter on the Jaina system in the Sarvadarśana-saṁgraha translated by Cowell and Gough, p. 56.

[6] The opening lines of the Aṣṭasāhasrī are:—

श्रीवर्धमानमभिवन्द्य समन्तभद्रमुद्भूतबोधमहिमानमनिन्द्यवाचम् ।
शास्त्रावताररचितस्तुतिगोचराप्तमीमांसितं कृतिरलंक्रियते मयास्य ॥ १ ॥

The closing lines of the Aṣṭasāhasrī are:—

श्रीमदकलङ्कशशधरकुलविद्यानन्दसम्भवा भूयात् ।
गुणमीमांसालंकृतिरष्टसहस्री सतामृद्ध्यै ॥

to Samantabhadra and Akalaṅka respectively, while in chapter X of the work he distinctly says that he followed the Aṣṭa-śatī of Akalaṅka in explaining the Āptamīmāṁsā. Another logical treatise called Pramāṇa-parīkṣā is attributed to him. He was also the author of the Tattvārtha, śloka-vārtika and Āpta-parīkṣā.

His age.

He has, in his Aṣṭasāhasrī, criticised the doctrines of the Sāṁkhya, Yoga, Vaiśeṣika, Advaita, Mīmāṁsaka and Saugata, Tāthāgata or Bauddha philosophy; and has mentioned Dignāga, Uddyotakara, Dharmakīrti,[1] Prajñākara,[2] Bhartṛhari,[3] Śabarasvāmi, Prabhākara, Sureśvara[4] and Kumārila. Vidyānanda was otherwise named Pātra Kesari or Pātra Kesari Svāmi, who has been praised by Jina

---

The lines in Chapter X referred to run thus :—

श्रीमदकलङ्कविवृतां समन्तभद्रोक्तिमत्र संक्षेपात् ।
परमागमार्थविषयामष्टसहस्रीं प्रकाशयति ॥

(Aṣṭasāhasrī, MSS., Asiatic Society of Bengal).

[1] यदुक्तं धर्मकीर्तिना :—

अतद्रूप परावृत्त वस्तुमात्र प्रवेदनात् ।
सामान्यविषयम्प्रोक्तं लिङ्गभेदाप्रतिष्ठितेः ।

(Quoted in Aṣṭasāhasrī, chap. I).

अर्थोपयोगेऽपि पुनः स्मार्त्तं शब्दानुयोजनम् :
अक्षधीर्यद्यपेक्षेत सोऽर्थो व्यवहितो भवेत् ।

(Quoted in Aṣṭasāhasrī, chap. I).

[2] प्रज्ञाकरस्येदं वच :—

क्रमप्रतीतेरेवं स्यात् प्रथमस्यावमा मतिः ।
तस्यामर्थात् पुनः पश्चाद् यतः कर्ता प्रतीयते ॥

(Quoted in Aṣṭasāhasrī, chap. I).

This extract may be an interpolation, or else this Prajñākara must be different from the Buddhist logician Prajñākara Gupta to be mentioned hereafter.

[3] न सोऽस्ति प्रत्ययो लोके यः शब्दानुगमादृते ।
अनुविद्धमिवाभाति सर्वं शब्दे प्रतिष्ठितम् ॥

(This verse of Vākyapadīya by Bhartṛhari is quoted in the Aṣṭasāhasrī, *vide* J B.B.R.A.S. for 1892, p. 221).

[4] यदुक्तं सुरेश्वरेण वार्त्तिके :—

आत्मापि सदिदं ब्रह्म मोहात् पारोक्ष्य दूषितम् ।
ब्रह्मापि स तथैवात्मा स द्वितीय तयेष्यते ॥..............

इति कश्चित् सोऽपि न प्रेक्षावान्

(Aṣṭasāhasrī).

Cf. Preface to Tattvārtha-ślokavārtika, edited by Manohar Lal, Bombay.

Sena in the Ādi Purāṇa[1] composed about Śaka 760[2] or A.D. 838. He is believed to have lived early in the 9th century A.D.[3] at Pāṭalīputra.[4]

22. MĀṆIKYA NANDI (ABOUT 800 A.D.).

His age.

Māṇikya Nandi was a Digambara author, whose **Parīkṣā-mukha-śāstra**[5] or **Parīkṣā-mukha-sūtra** is a standard work on Jaina logic. As his work is based on that of Akalaṅka,[6] he must have lived after 750 A.D. The earliest commentary on the Parīkṣāmukha-śāstra is the Prameya-kamala-mārtaṇḍa of Prabhācandra. Vidyānanda, Māṇikya Nandi and Prabhācandra have been pronounced to be contemporaries.[7] So Maṇikya Nandi seems to have lived about 800 A.D.

23. MĀṆIKYA NANDI'S PARĪKṢĀMUKHA-SŪTRA.

Subjects.

The Parīkṣāmukha-sūtra is divided into six chapters thus: (1) the characteristic of valid knowledge (*Pramāṇa-svarūpa*); (2) direct apprehension or perception (*Pratyakṣa*); (3) indirect apprehension (*Parokṣa*); (4) the object of valid knowledge (*Viṣaya*); (5) the result of valid knowledge (*Phala*); and (6) the semblances or fallacies (*Ābhāsa*).

---

1 भट्टाकलंक श्रीपाल पात्रकेसरिणां गुणाः ।
विदुषां हृदयारूढा हारायन्तेऽतिनिर्मलाः ॥ ५३ ॥

(Ādipurāṇa, quoted by Mr. K. B. Pathak, J.B.B.R.A.S., for 1892, p. 222).

Mr. Pathak has quoted Samyaktvaprakāśa to show that Vidyānanda and Pātrakesari were identical:—

तथा श्लोकवार्त्तिके विद्यानन्द्यपरनाम पात्रकेसरिस्वामिना यदुक्तं तच्च लिख्यते तत्त्वार्थश्रद्धानं सम्यग्दर्शनम् । (J.B.B.R.A.S., for 1892, pp. 222, 223).

2-3 *Vide* K. B. Pathak's article on Bhartṛhari and Kumārila in J.B.B.R.A.S., for 1892, pp. 227, 229.

4 *Vide* Brahmanemidatta's Kathākoṣa, life of Pātrakesari *alias* Vidyānanda.

5 A manuscript of the Parīkṣā-mukha-śāstra was kindly lent to me by Mr. Jain Vaidya of Jaipur (Rajputana), and subsequently another manuscript of the work was procured from the Deccan College, Poona. I have published the work in the Bibliotheca Indica series of Calcutta.

6 Peterson in his 4th Report, p. 155, notices Parikṣāmukhaṁ saṭīkam. The Ṭīkā is the Prameya-ratna-mālā or Parīkṣāmukhapañjikā of Anantavīrya, which opens thus:—

अकलङ्कवचोऽम्भोधेरुद्दध्रे येन धीमता ।
न्यायविद्यामृतं तस्मै नमो माणिक्यनन्दिने ॥ १ ॥

7 *Vide* K. B. Pathak's article on Bhartṛharī and Kumārila in J.B.B.R.A.S., for 1892, pp. 219, 220, 221. Mr. Pathak says that Māṇikya Nandi has mentioned Vidyānanda, but in the text of the Parīkṣā-mukha-śāstra itself I have not come across any such mention.

Valid knowledge—*Pramāṇa.*

Right knowledge.

Pramāṇa, valid knowledge, is defined by Māṇikya Nandi as the knowledge which ascertains the nature of what was uncertain to one's self. It generally arises in the form : "I know the jar by myself," which consists of a subject, an object, an act, and an instrument. Just as a lamp illumines itself as well as the surrounding objects, so the *Pramāṇa* exhibits the knower as well as the thing known.

Kinds of right knowledge.

Pramāṇa is of two kinds: (1) direct knowledge (*Pratyakṣa*) which arises through the senses, etc., and (2) indirect knowledge (*Parokṣa*) consisting of recollection (*Smṛti*), recognition (*Pratyabhijñāna*), argumentation (*Tarka* or *Ūha*), inference (*Anumāna*), and the scripture (*Āgama*). Recollection is a knowledge of the form "that" which arises through the awaking of impressions, thus: "that Devadatta." Recognition is a knowledge which arises from perception through recollection in the forms, "this is that," "this is like that," "this is different from that," "this is the counterpart of that," etc., thus: "this is that Devadatta," "the *bos gavaeus* is like the cow," "the buffalo is different from the cow," "this is far from that," "this is a tree," etc. Argumentation is a knowledge of the connection between the middle term and the major term based on the presence or absence of the latter, in the form, "if this is, that is, if this is not, that is not," thus smoke arises only if there is fire, but it cannot arise if there is no fire. Inference[1] is the knowledge of the major term arising through the middle term : there is fire here, because there is smoke.

Syllogism—*Vyāpti.*

Terms of a Syllogism.

Pervasion[2] or inseparable connection (*Vyāpti or Avinābhāva*) is the universal attendance of the middle term by the major term in simultaneity or succession : thus fire and smoke may abide simultaneously or the latter may follow the former.

If the middle term and the major term exist simultaneously, the former is called *vyāpya*, pervaded or contained, and the latter *vyāpaka*, pervader or container.

But if the middle term follows the major term, the former is called effect (*kārya*), and the latter cause (*kāraṇa* or *hetu*), thus fire is the cause of smoke. Ordinarily, however, the major term is called *sādhya* or that which is to be proved, and the

---

[1] साधनात् साध्यविज्ञानमनुमानम् ॥ ९ ॥ (Parikṣa-mukha-sūtra).

[2] सहक्रमभावनियमोऽविनाभावः ॥ ११ ॥ (Parikṣā-mukha-sūtra).

middle term is called *sādhana* or that by which it is to be proved. Sometimes the major term is also called *dharma* or predicate, and the middle term *liṅga*, mark or sign.

The minor term is called *Pakṣa*, the place or locus in which the major term abides, or *Dharmin*, the subject, thus: "this place is fiery"; "sound is mutable": here "this place" and "sound" are the minor terms. No philosophers, who divide the middle term (reason) into three phases, should dispense with the minor term in an inference.

The middle term (*Hetu*) is defined as that which is inseparably connected with the major term, or in other words, which cannot come into existence unless the major term exists. For instance, smoke could not come into existence unless the fire existed.

Reason—*hetu*.

Different phases of the middle term.

The middle term or reason (*Hetu*) is divided as (1) perceptible (*upalabdhi*), and (2) imperceptible (*anupalabdhi*). Each of these again may occur in the form of an affirmation (*vidhi*) or negation (*pratiṣedha*).

The *perceptible* reason in the *affirmative* form admits of six subdivisions according as it is :—

(i) the pervaded (*vyāpya*)—sound is mutable, because it is factitious;

(ii) an effect (*kārya*)—this man has got intellect, because there are (intellectual) functions in him;

(iii) a cause (*kāraṇa*)—there is a shadow here, because there is an umbrella;

(iv) prior (*pūrva*)—the Rohiṇī stars will rise, for the Kṛttikās have risen;

(v) posterior (*uttara*)—the Bharaṇī stars certainly rose for the Kṛttikās have risen;

(vi) simultaneous (*sahacara*)—the man had a mother, for he had a father; or this mango has a particular colour, because it has a particular flavour.

The *perceptible* reason in the *negative* form admits of six subdivisions as follows :—

(i) the pervaded (*vyāpya*)—there is no cold sensation, because of heat;

(ii) an effect (*kārya*)—there is no cold sensation because of smoke;

(iii) a cause (*kāraṇa*)—there is no happiness in this man, because of the shaft in his heart;

(iv) prior (*pūrva*)—the Rohiṇī stars will not rise shortly, for the Revatī [only] has risen.

(v) posterior (*uttara*)—the Bharaṇī did not rise a moment ago, for the Puṣyā has risen.

(vi) simultaneous (*sahacara*)—there is no doubt of the existence of the other side of this wall, for this side of it is perceived.

The *imperceptible* reason in the *negative* form admits of seven subdivisions as follows :—

(i) identity (*svabhāva*)—there is no jar here, because it is imperceptible ;

(ii) the pervaded (*vyāpya*)—there is no Śiṁśapā here, because there is no tree at all ;

(iii) an effect (*kārya*)—there is no smouldering fire here, because there is no smoke ;

(iv) a cause (*kāraṇa*)—there is no smoke here, because there is no fire ;

(v) prior (*pūrva*)—Rohiṇī stars will not rise in a moment, for the Kṛttikās are not perceptible ;

(vi) posterior (*uttara*)—the Bharaṇī did not rise a moment ago, for the Kṛttikās are not perceptible ;

(vii) simultaneous (*sahacara*)—in this even balance there is no bending upwards, because it is not perceptible.

The *imperceptible* reason in the affirmative form may appear in the following ways :—

(i) as an effect (*kārya*)—in this man there is some disease, because there is no healthy movement in him ;

(ii) as a cause (*kāraṇa*)—this man is sorrowful, because he has no union with his beloved ones ;

(iii) as an identity (*svabhāva*)—there is uncertainty here, because certainty is not discernible.

Example—*dṛṣṭānta*.

Example is superfluous.

The middle term and the major term are the parts of an inference, but the example (*udāharaṇa*) is not. Nevertheless for the sake of explaining matters to men of small intellect, the example (*udāharaṇa* or *dṛṣṭānta*), nay, even the application (*upanaya*) and the conclusion (*nigamana*), are admitted as parts of an inference. The example is of two kinds: (1) the affirmative or homogeneous (*anvayi* or *sādharmya*) which shows the middle term as covered by the major term, such as: wherever there is smoke, there is fire, as in a *kitchen*; and (2) the negative or heterogeneous (*vyatireki* or *vaidharmya*) by which the absence of the middle term is indicated by the absence of the major term, e.g. wherever there is no fire, there is no smoke, as in a *lake*.

Inference—*anumāna.*

Two kinds of Inference.

Inference is of two kinds, viz. (1) inference for one's own self (*svārthānumāna*), and (2) inference for the sake of others (*parārthānumāna*). An instance of the latter kind of inference is given below :—

(1) Sound (minor term) is mutable (major term)—proposition ;
(2) because it is factitious (reason or middle term) ;
(3) whatever is factitious is mutable, as a jar (affirmative or homogeneous example) ;
(4) sound is factitious (application) ;
(5) therefore sound is mutable (conclusion).

Or,

(3) whatever is not mutable is not factitious, as the milk of a barren woman's breast (negative or heterogeneous example) ;
(4) but sound is factitious (application) ;
(5) therefore sound is mutable (conclusion).

Verbal Testimony—*āgama.*

Verbal Testimony

Testimony (*Āgama*) is a knowledge of objects derived from the words of reliable persons or scriptures in virtue of their natural fitness or suggestiveness—e.g. the north pole exists.

Scope of Valid Knowledge—*Viṣaya.*

Objects of valid knowledge.

Objects of valid knowledge are either general (*sāmānya*) or particular (*viśeṣa*). The general is of two kinds : (1) homogeneous (*tiryak*), including many individuals of like nature, as the "cow" is a general notion which signifies many individual cows as Śabalā, Khamba, Mumbha, etc. ; and (2) heterogeneous (*ūrddhvatā*), including many individuals of dissimilar nature, as, "gold" is a general notion comprising a bracelet, necklace, ear-ring, etc. The particular is also of two kinds : (1) relating to things (*vyatireka*), e.g. cow, buffalo, elephant, dog, are four particular things distinguished from one another ; and (2) relating to action such as pleasure, pain, etc., experienced by the soul.

Result of valid knowledge.

The result or consequence of valid knowledge is the cessation of ignorance, enabling one to choose the desirable and reject the undesirable.

Fallacy—*ābhāsa.*

Various kinds of Fallacies.

Fallacy or semblance consists of the knowledge of that which is different from the real thing. It is of many kinds, such as the fallacy—

(1) of perception (*pratyakṣābhāsa*). e.g.—to mistake a post for a man ;

(2) of recollection (*smaraṇābhāsa*)—in trying to recollect Jinadatta to say: "O, that Devadatta";
(3) of recognition (*pratyabhijñānābhāsa*)—on seeing a greyhound to say: "this is a tiger";
(4) of argumentation (*tarkābhāsa*)—"whoever is his son must be black";
(5) of the minor term (*pakṣābhāsa*)—"sound is impermanent": This is a fallacy of the minor term according to the Mīmāṁsakas, for they do not attribute impermanency to sound; or fire is not hot, because it is a substance as water;
(6) of the middle term or reason (*hetvābhāsa*)—sound is eternal, because it is factitious;
(7) of example (*dṛṣṭāntābhāsa*)—sound is eternal, because it is corporeal, like a jar;
(8) of verbal testimony (*āgamābhāsa*)—"there is a heap of sweetmeats on the side of the river, run you boys"; "there are a hundred elephants on his finger"; "the Jainas are allowed to eat in the night" [as a fact they are not so allowed by their scripture].

References to Philosophers.

References to contemporaneous systems of philosophy.

Māṇikya Nandi in the Parīkṣā-mukha-sūtra (chapter vi, aph. 56–57) has mentioned the Laukāyatika, Saugata, Sāṁkhya, Yoga, Prābhākara, Jaiminīya, etc. In the 3rd chapter of the work he observes—"no philosopher, who admits three kinds of reason or middle term (*hetu*), can dispense with the minor term (*pakṣa*)."[1]

He concludes his work by describing it as a mirror through which a man can see what is to be accepted and what rejected.[2]

24. Prabhā Candra (about 825 A.D.).

Prabhā Candra, styled a *Kavi*, a member of the Digambara sect, was the author of the famous logical treatise called **Prameya-kamala mārtaṇḍa** (the sun of the lotus of knowledge), the earli-

1 साध्याविनाभावित्वेन निश्चितो हेतुः ॥ १० ॥
को वा त्रिधा हेतुमुक्त्वा समर्थयमानो न पक्षयति ॥ २१ ॥
(Parīkṣā-mukha-sūtra, MSS. lent to me by Mr. Jain Vaidya of Jaipur).

2 परीक्षामुखमादर्शं हेयोपादेयतत्त्वयोः ।
संविदे मादृशो बालः परीक्षादक्षवद् व्यधाम् ॥
(Parīkṣā-mukha-sūtra, chap. VI, MSS. lent to me by Mr. Jain Vaidya of Jaipur). Parīkṣā-mukha-sūtra of Māṇikya Nandi with the commentary of Anantavīrya has been edited by Satis Chandra Vidyabhusana and published in the Bibliotheca Indica Series of Calcutta.

est commentary on the Parīkṣā-mukha-sūtra of Māṇikya Nandi. He was also the author of the Nyāya-kumuda-candrodaya (or briefly Candrodaya), a commentary on the Laghīyastraya of Akalaṅka He has in his Prameya-kamala-mārtaṇḍa mentioned Bhagavān Upavarṣa, Śabarasvāmi, Bhartṛhari, Bāṇa,[1] Kumārila,[2] Prabhākara, Dignāga, Uddyotakara, Dharmakīrti, Vidyānanda and others. He himself has been mentioned by Jina Sena in the Ādi-purāṇa[3] composed about Śaka 760 or A.D. 838. Prabhā Candra, as a contemporary of Māṇikya Nandi and Vidyānanda, is believed to have lived in the first half of the 9th century A.D.

25. Rabhasa Nandi
(circa 850 A.D.).

Rabhasa Nandi, probably a Digambara, wrote a work called **Sambandhoddyota**, which seems to be a commentary on the Sambandha-parīkṣā of the Buddhist logician Dharmakīrti. The work must have been composed after 635 A.D. when Dharmakīrti lived, and before 1444 A.D., which is the date of the copy of the work acquired for the Bombay Government.[4]

26. Mallavādin
(about 827 A.D.).

He belonged to the Śvetāmbara sect and was the famous author of a commentary on the Buddhist logical treatise Nyāya-

---

[1] Prabhā Candra has quoted the following verse from Bāṇa's Kādambarī :—

रजोजुषे जन्मनि सत्त्ववृत्तये
स्थितौ प्रजानां प्रलये तमःस्पृशे ।
अजाय सर्गस्थिति-नाश-हेतवे
त्रयीमयाय त्रिगुणात्मने नमः ॥

(Prameya-kamala-mārtaṇḍa, Deccan College, MSS., p. 21*a*, quoted by Mr. K. B. Pathak in J.B.B.R.A.S., for 1892, p. 221).

[2] Prabhā Candra refers to Kumārila, otherwise called Bhaṭṭa, thus :—

तथा चार्थापत्तिरपि प्रमाणान्तरं तल्लक्षणं चार्थापत्तिरपि दृष्टः श्रुतो वा अर्थोऽन्यथा नोपपद्यते इत्यदृष्टार्थकल्पना, कुमारिलोऽपि एतदेव भाष्यकारवचो व्याचष्टे ।

(Prameya-kamala-mārtaṇḍa, quoted by Mr. K. B. Pathak in the J.B.B.R.A.S., for 1892, p. 227).

[3] In the Ādipurāṇa Prabhā Candra is thus mentioned :—

चन्द्रांशुशुभ्रयशसं प्रभाचन्द्रं कविं स्तुवे ।
कृत्वा चन्द्रोदयं येन शश्वदाह्लादितं जगत् ॥ ४७ ॥

(Quoted by Mr. K. B. Pathak in J.B.B.RA.S., for 1892, p. 222).

On p. 227 of the same journal, the date of the Ādipurāṇa is fixed at Śaka 760 or 838 A.D.

[4] Peterson's Third Report, p. 407.

binduṭīkā called **Dharmottara-ṭippanaka**. According to a Jaina legend,[1] Malla was the son of King Śilāditya's sister. He was called *vādin* or logician, because, having vanquished the Buddhists in a dispute, he re-established the Jaina faith and brought to its former glory the great figure of Ādinātha on Mount Śatruñjaya (in Kathiwar).

A palm-leaf manuscript[2] of the Dharmottara-ṭippanaka is preserved at Anhilwad Patan and is said to be dated Saṁvat 1321 or 1174 A.D. According to the Prabhāvakacaritra[3], Mallavādin was also the author of a work called the Padmacaritra and lived in Vīra Saṁvat 884 or 357 A.D. But this is impossible, as Dharmottara (q.v.), on whose Nyāyabinduṭīkā Mallavādin wrote Ṭippanaka, lived about 837 A.D. On the other hand Mallavādin is mentioned[4] by Hem Candra Sūri, who lived during 1088—1172 A.D. It seems therefore probable that the year 884 in which Mallavādin lived does not refer to Vīra Saṁvat, but to Vikrama or Saka Saṁvat. On this supposition Mallavādin lived in 827 A.D. or 962 A.D.

27. Amṛta Candra Sūri (905 A.D.).

Amṛta Candra Sūri,[5] who belonged to the Digambara sect, was the author of **Tattvārtha-sāra**, **Ātmakhyāti**,[6] etc., and lived in Saṁvat 962 or 905 A.D.

28. Devasena Bhaṭṭāraka (899—950 A.D.).

Devasena,[7] a pupil of Rāmasena, was the author of **Naya-cakra**, etc. He was born in Saṁvat 951 or 894 A D., and wrote his **Daṁsaṇa-sāra** (Darśana-sāra) in Saṁvat 990 or 933 A.D.

---

1 Peterson 4, pp. 3-4, in which is mentioned the legend from the Prabandha-cintāmaṇi (Rāmacandra's edition, Bombay, p. 273).

2 इति धर्म्मोत्तरटिप्पनके श्रीमल्लवाद्याचार्य्यकृते तृतीयः परिच्छेदः समाप्तः मङ्गलं महाश्रीः ॥ संवत् १२३१ वर्षे भाद्रपद शुदि १२ रवौ (Peterson's Report V, p. 3).

संवत् १२३१ वर्षे भाद्रपद शुदि १२ रवौ अद्येह अंबावल्लिग्राम वास्तव्य श्रेष्ठिमहणसुत पाल्हणेन धर्म्मार्थं धर्म्मोत्तर-टिप्पनकं लिखापितम् ॥ (Noticed in Peterson 5, App. p. 3).

3 *Vide* Klatt, Vienna Oriental Journal, Vol IV, p. 67

4 अनु मल्लवादिनं तार्किकाः ।
तस्मादन्ये हीना इत्यर्थः ॥
(Siddha Hema Śabdānuśāsana-bṛhat-ṭīkā, 2-2-39)

5 Peterson's fourth Report, p. ix.

6 Ātmakhyāti, which is a commentary on the Samaya-prābhṛta of Kunda-kundācārya, has been edited by Paṇḍita Gajādhar Lal Nyāyaśāstri.

7 Peterson's Fourth Report, p. lvi.

29. PRADYUMNA SŪRI (ABOUT 980 A.D.).

He[1] belonged to the Rājagaccha of the Śvetāmbara sect. In Māṇikyacandra's Pārśvanātha-caritra,[2] his prowess in logical discussions is referred to in the following terms :—

"There was born the preceptor Pradyumna Sūri—the first healer of disease of the world—who entirely removed all corruptions from the body of men (or detected all defects in disputation committed by men) and who, using sharp logical expressions, made his irrelevant opponents to sweat and thereby to be cured of the fever of pride."

In the same work reference is made to his victory over the Digambaras of Veṅkapaṭṭa in the presence of the king of that province. He delighted the kings of various countries by no fewer than eighty-four triumphs in discussion. He was eleventh in ascent from Māṇikyacandra Sūri, who wrote his Pārśvanātha-caritra in Saṁvat 1276 or 1219 A.D. Pradyumna must have flourished about 980 A.D., for he was the preceptor of Abhayadeva Sūri (q.v.) who lived a little before 1039 A.D.

30. ABHAYADEVA SŪRI (ABOUT 1000 A.D.).

Abhayadeva Sūri belonged to the Śvetāmbara sect[3], and was the pupil and successor of Prdyumna Sūri of the Rājagaccha. He was an eminent logician and author of Vādamahārṇava, a treat-

---

[1] For further particulars about Pradyumna Sūri, see Peterson's /4th Report, p. lxxix.

[2]
पुंसां विग्रहजं विकारमखिलं निर्मूलमुन्मूलयं-
स्तथाद्यः समभूद् भवामयभिषक् प्रद्युम्नसूरिर्गुरुः ।
येन स्वेदयता प्रयुज्य तरलां तर्कोज्ज्वलां भारतीं
वादीन्द्राः प्रविलापिनो द्रुततरं दर्पज्वरं त्याजिताः ॥ ४ ॥
दिगम्बरसमाक्रान्तवेङ्कपट्टं समाददे ।
यः प्रत्यक्षं नरेन्द्रस्य जगतस्तस्य यः पुनः ॥ ५ ॥
गौरागतानिधौ राजगच्छभूर्गुणवारिधिः ।
सूरिः प्रद्युम्नसूर्याख्यः पूर्वं यः पूर्वजोऽभवत् ॥ १८ ॥
सपादलक्षगोपालत्रिभुवनगिर्यादिदेशभूपालान् ।
यश्चतुरधिकाशीत्या वादजयैरंजयामास ॥ १८ ॥
श्रीअभयदेवसूरिस्तच्छिष्यस्तर्कभूरभूत् ।
भग्नासनाखिलतुमुलाङ्घ्रीर्यदास्यमशिश्रियत् ॥ १९ ॥
(Pārśvanātha-caritra as noticed by Peterson in his 3rd Report, pp. 57-164.)

[3]
तर्कग्रन्थविचारदुर्गमवनीसञ्चारपञ्चानन-
स्तत्पट्टेऽभयदेवसूरिरजनि श्वेताम्बरग्रामणीः ।

ise on logic called the Ocean of Discussions, and of a commentary on the Sammati-tarka-sūtra called **Tattvārtha-bodha-vidhāyinī.**[1] "He is described as a lion that roamed at ease in the wild forest of books on logic. That the rivers of various conflicting opinions might not sweep away the path of the good, Abhayadeva[2] wrote his Vāda-mahārṇava." He was succeeded by Jineśvara Sūri, a contemporary of King Muñja.[3] He was the ninth predecessor of Siddhasena Sūri, who wrote Pravacana-sāroddhāra-vṛtti in Saṁvat 1242 or 1185 A.D. It was probably this Abhayadeva Sūri, who was "world-renowned" and a teacher of Śānti Sūri[4] who died in Saṁvat 1096 or 1039 A.D.

31. LAGHUSAMANTABHADRA (ABOUT 1000 A.D.).

He[5] wrote a commentary on the Aṣṭasāhasrī of Vidyānanda called the **Aṣṭasāhasrī-viṣamapada-tātparya-ṭīkā**[6] and seems to have belonged to the Digambara sect and lived about 1000 A.D.

सद्वाक्यश्रुतिलालसा मधुकरी कोशावलामश्लिष्टी
हित्वा विद्वरपङ्कजं श्रितवती ब्राह्मी यदीयाननम् ॥ ६ ॥
दृक्-निम्नगाः सत्पथभेदमेता
ध्रुवं करिष्यन्ति जडैः समेताः ।
इतीव रोधाय चकार तार्था
ग्रन्थं नवं वादमहार्णवं यः ॥ ७ ॥
विद्रुमवत्समौलिमण्डनमणिः प्रेक्षत्तपोऽस्तर्षि-
र्लिर्यन्योऽपि जिनेश्वरः समजनि श्रीमांस्ततः सद्गुरुः ।
यः श्रूर्जन्नृपपुङ्गवस्य सौविध्याोः पुरः प्रशिसान् ।
वादे वादिवरान् विजित्य विजयश्रीसंपदं च व्यधात् ॥ ८ ॥

(Pārśvanātha-caritra by Māṇikyacandra, noticed by Peterson in his Third Report, pp. 158–59).

1 See R. Mitra's Catalogue, X, pp. 39–40.

2 For particulars about Abhayadeva Sūri, see Peterson's Fourth Report, p. iii.

3 Weber's Die Handschriften-verzeichnisse, etc., p. 851, vv. 1, 2, and p. 121, vv. 4–5. Jineśvara Sūri was probably a spiritual brother of Dhaneśvara Sūri.

4 यस्याभ्युदयरागमे गुणनिधिः श्रीसर्वदेवाभिधः
सूरीशोऽभयदेव सूरिरचितमख्यातप्रमाणोऽपि च ।
तस्येयं सुगुरुद्वयादधिगत (?) दक्षात्मविद्यागुरु (?)
प्रत्याख्याय चिरं भुवि प्रचरतु श्रीशान्तिसूरेः कृतिः ॥

(Uttarādhyayana-bṛhadvṛtti by Śāntyācārya, noticed by Dr. R. G. Bhandarkar in his Report on Sanskrit MSS. for 1883–84, p. 44).

See also Weber's Die Handschriften-verzeichnisse der Königlichen Bibliothek zu Berlin, p. 827.

5 *Vide* Peterson's Sixth Report, p. xxiii.

6 The Aṣṭasāhasrī-viṣama-pada-tātparya-ṭīkā has been noticed in Peterson's Fifth Report, pp. 216–219, where we read :—

देवं स्वामिनममलं विद्यानन्दं प्रणम्य निजभक्त्या ।
विवृणोम्यष्टसहस्रीविषमपदं लघुसमन्तभद्रोऽहम् ॥

32. Kalyāṇa candra (about 1000 A.D.).

Kalyāṇacandra was the author of **Pramāṇa-vārtika-ṭikā** which is a commentary on the Pramāṇa-vārtika (probably of Dharmakīrti who lived about 635 A.D.). It must have existed before 1350 A.D. when Jñānacandra mentioned it in his Ratnākarāvatārikā-ṭippana.[1]

33. Ananta-vīrya (about 1039 A.D.).

Ananta-vīrya was the Digambara author of a commentary on the Parikṣāmukha of Māṇikya Nandi called **Parīkṣā-mukha-pañjikā** or **Prameya-ratnamālā**, as also a commentary on Akalaṅka's Nyāya-viniścaya called the **Nyāya-viniścaya-vṛtti**. He wrote the former for Śanti-ṣena at the request of Hirapa, son of Vijaya and Nāṇambā.[2] Now Śāntī-ṣena, supposed to be identical with Śānti Sūri, died in Saṁvat 1096 or A.D. 1039. His contemporary Ananta-vīrya must, therefore, have flourished about that time.[3] Ananta-vīrya must have lived before the 14th century, for he is mentioned by Mādhavācārya in the chapter on Jaina darśana in the Sarvadarśana-saṁgraha.

34. Deva Sūri (1086—1169 A.D.).

His Life.

Deva Sūri, called Vādipravara or the foremost of disputants, belonged to the Śvetāmbara sect and was a pupil of Municandra Sūri. He was the author of the well-known treatise on logic called **Pramāṇa-naya-tattvālokālaṅkāra** on which he himself wrote an elaborate commentary named **Syādvādaratnākara**.[4] He totally vanquished the Digambara Kumudacandrācārya in a dispute over the

---

1 तेनान्यापोहविषयाः प्रोक्ताः सामान्यगोचराः ।

यच्च व्याख्या तेनाचार्य्ये दिङ्नागेन... ..प्रोक्ताः । एतदर्थश्च विस्तारार्थिना प्रमाणवार्त्तिके कल्याणचन्द्र टीकातोऽवधेयः ॥

(Ratnākarāvatārikā-ṭippana, p. 7, Yaśovijaya granthamālā series, Benares).

2 वैजेयप्रियपुत्रस्य हीरपस्योपरोधतः ।

शान्तिषेणार्थमारब्धा परीक्षामुखपञ्जिका ॥ १ ॥

(Parīkṣā-mukhaṁ saṭīkam, noticed in Peterson's Fourth Report, p. 155).

3 *Vide* the Indian Antiquary, Vol. XI, p. 253; and Dr. R. G. Bhandarkar's Report on Sanskrit MSS. during 1883–84, p. 129.

4 स्याद्वादरत्नाकर इत्यस्ति ग्रन्थो महत्तमः ।

वादिवृन्दारकश्रीमद्देवसूरिविनिर्मितः ॥ ४ ॥

Maladhāri Rājśekhara Sūri's Pañjikā on Syādvāda-ratnākarāvatārikā.

salvation of women [at the court of Jaya-siṁha-deva at Anahilla-purapattana in N. Guzerat] and thereby practically stopped the entrance of the Digambaras into that town. The dispute[1] took place in Saṁvat 1181 or 1124 A.D.

Ratnaprabha Sūri, a pupil of Deva Sūri, in his Upadeśamālā-ṭīkā,[2] composed in Saṁvat 1238 or A.D. 1181, writes :—

"Lord Śrī Deva Sūri, who was the crest-gem of the pupils of the esteemed Municandra Sūri and succeeded him in his paṭṭa (sacred chair), conquered the Digambaras in the council-room of King Jaya-siṁha Deva and raised a pillar of victory by maintaining the nirvāṇa or salvation of women [that is, holding that even women were capable of attaining nirvāṇa]."

---

1 चन्द्राष्टशिववर्षेऽत्र वैशाखे पूर्णिमादिने ।
आकृतौ वादिशालायां तौ वादिप्रतिवादिनौ ॥

(Prabhāvakacar., XXI, v. 95, quoted by Dr. Klatt in his article on "Historical Records of the Jains" in the Indian Antiquary, Vol. XI, Sept. 1882, p. 254).

2 Ratnaprabha Sūri observes :—

शिष्यः श्रीमुनिचन्द्रसूरिसुगुरोर्मौलावचूडामणिः
पट्टे तस्य निवेशितस्तदनु च श्रीदेवसूरिप्रभुः ।
आस्थाने जयसिंहदेवनृपतेर्येनाजितदिग्वाससां
श्रीनिर्वाणसमर्थनेन विजयस्तम्भः समुत्तम्भितः ॥
तत्पट्टप्रभवो भवभय गुणग्रामाभिरामोदयाः
श्रीभद्रेश्वरसूरयः सुविधियत्नाजनप्रीतये ।
श्रीरत्नप्रभसूरिभिः शुभकृते श्रीदेवसूरिप्रभोः
शिष्यैः सेयमकारि सन्मदकृते वृत्तिर्विशेषार्थिनाम् ॥

(Upadeśamālāṭikā, noticed by Peterson in his Third Report, p. 167).

Munisundara Sūri, in his Gurvāvalī composed in Sāṁvat 1466, gives a similar account :—

येनार्हतचतुरशीति सुवादिलीला-
लब्धोज्ज्वलस्थिरमामदकेलिशाली ।
वादाहवे कुमुदचन्द्रदिगम्बरेन्द्रः
श्रीसिद्धभूमिपतिसंसदि पत्तनेऽस्मिन् ॥ ७४ ॥
स्याद्वादरत्नाकरतर्कवेधा
मुदे स केषां नहि देवसूरिः ।
यतश्चतुर्विंशतिसूरिशाखं
यस्येव नाम्ना विदितं बभूव ॥ ७५ ॥
वेदमुनीशमितेऽब्दे
देवगुरुर्जन्मदनुत्तरोऽभ्युदितः ।
श्रीमुनिचन्द्रगुरोरिति
शिष्या नव वोऽभवन् विदिताः ॥ ७६ ॥

(Gurvāvalī published in the Jaina Yaśovijaya-granthamālā of Benares, pp. 18–19).

In Saṁvat 1204 or 1147 A.D. Deva Sūri founded a caitya, raised a *bimba* at Phalavardhigrāma, and established an image of Neminātha at Arāsana.[1] He was born in Saṁvat 1143 or 1086 A.D., attained the rank of Sūri in 1174 Saṁvat or 1117 A.D., and ascended to heaven in Saṁvat 1226 or 1169 A.D.[2]

35. Deva Sūri's Pramāṇa-naya-tattvālokālaṅkāra

Pramāṇa—right knowledge.

Subjects of the Pramāṇa-naya-tattvālokālaṅkāra.

The **Pramāṇa-naya-tattvālokālaṅkāra**[3] consists of eight chapters (*paricchedas*), viz.—(1) Determination of the nature of valid knowledge (*pramāṇa-svarūpa-nirṇaya*); (2) determination of the nature of perception (*pratyakṣa-svarūpa-nirṇaya*); (3) determination of the nature of recollection, recognition, argumentation and inference (*smaraṇa-pratyabhijñāna-tarkānumāna-svarūpa-nirṇaya*); (4) determination of the nature of valid knowledge derived from verbal testimony or scripture (*āgamākhya-pramāṇa-svarūpa-nirṇaya*); (5) determination of the nature of objects of knowledge (*viṣaya-svarūpa-nirṇaya*); (6) determination of the consequences and fallacies of knowledge (*phala-pramāṇa-svarūpādyābhāsa-nirṇaya*); (7) determination of the nature of one-sided knowledge (*nayātma-svarūpa-nirṇaya*); and (8) determination of the right procedure of a disputant and his opponent (*vādi-prativādi-nyāya-nirṇaya*).

As this work is written on the same plan as Māṇikya Nandi's Parīkṣāmukha-sūtra or Akalaṅka's Nyāya-viniścaya as well as Siddhasena Divākara's Nyāyāvatāra, I shall pass over the common points, mentioning only its special features.

Nature of right or valid knowledge.

Pramāṇa or valid knowledge is defined here as the knowledge which ascertains the nature of itself as well as other things. The intercourse between the sense-organs and the objects of

---

1 *Vide* Peterson's Fourth Report, p. lv.; also Klatt, Ind. Ant. XI, p. 254.

2
शिखिवेदशिवे जन्म दीक्षा युग्मशरेश्वरे ।
वेदाश्वशंकरे वर्षे सूरित्वमभवत् प्रभोः ।
रसयुग्मरवौ वर्षे श्रावणे मासि संगते ।
कृष्णपक्षस्य सप्तम्यामपराह्णे गुरोर्दिने ॥
मर्त्यलोकस्थितं लोकं प्रतिबोध्य पुरन्दर-
बोधका इव ते जग्मुर्दिवं श्रीदेवसूरयः ॥

(Prabhāvakacar., XXI, vv. 287 seq., quoted by Dr. Klatt in his article on "Historical Records of the Jains" in the Indian Antiquary, Sept. 1982, Vol. XI, p. 254). According to some authorities Deva Sūri was born in Saṁvat 1134 or 1077 A.D.

3 The Pramāṇa-naya-tattvālokālaṅkāra has been printed and published in Benares in the Jaina Yaśovijaya series.

sense is not *pramāṇa* (valid knowledge), for though it can ascertain the nature of objects outside itself, it cannot ascertain its own nature, since it has no consciousness. *Pramāṇa* must certainly be *knowledge*, for it is capable of choosing what is desirable and rejecting what is undesirable. It must also be definite in character, for it is opposed to superimposition (*samāropa*). Superimposition is of three kinds: (1) inversion (*viparyaya*)—such as looking upon a pearl-oyster as a piece of silver; (2) doubt (*saṁśaya*)—such as: is this a post or a man? and (3) uncertainty (*anadhyavasāya*) consisting in a mere cogitation in the mind as to what the thing might be.

Direct knowledge. Perception.

Pramāṇa (valid knowledge) is of two kinds: (1) direct (*pratyakṣa*, perception) and (2) indirect (*parokṣa*, outside the senses). The direct knowledge or perception is of two kinds: practical (*sāṁvyavahārika*) and transcendental (*pāramārthika*). The practical direct knowledge again is subdivided as that which arises through the sense-organs (*indriya-nibandhana*) and that which does not arise through the sense-organs (*anindriya-nibandhana*) but through the mind (*manas*). Each of these passes through four stages,[1] viz.: (1) *avagraha*, distinguishing the type whether it be, e.g., horse or man, but not discerning the characteristics; (2) *īhā*, inquiring, e.g., whence came the man and from what country came the horse; (3) *avāya*, arriving at a correct identification of the above; and (4) *dhāraṇā*, recollecting the thing particularised and keeping it in mind.

The transcendental direct knowledge (*pāramārthika*) is that which comes exclusively from the illumination of the soul and is profitable to emancipation. It is two-fold: (1) *vikala* (defective) including *avadhi-jñāna* (limited knowledge), i.e. knowledge of special objects which, near or remote, are not differentiated, and *manaḥ-paryāya*, i.e. definite knowledge of another's thoughts and the laying bare of the secrets of the heart; and (2) *sakala*, i.e. perfect, which is the unobstructed intuition of the entire aspects of a thing. One who possesses that perfect transcendental knowledge is called an *arhat*, i.e. one freed from all faults or obstructions.

Indirect knowledge.

Indirect knowledge (*parokṣa*) is of five kinds: viz., (1) recollection (*smaraṇa*); (2) recognition (*pratyabhijñāna*); (3) argumentation (*tarka*); (4) inference (*anumāna*); (5) verbal testimony or the knowledge derived from the words of a reliable person or scripture (*āgama*).

---

[1] The explanation of *avagraha*, etc., as given here is taken from Col. Jarrett's translation of the Ain-i-Akbari, published by the Asiatic Society of Bengal, vol. III, p. 100, as the portion related to *pramāna* in the Jaina chapter of Ain-i-Akbari very closely resembles that in the *Pramāṇa-naya-tattvālokalaṅkāra*. Dr. R. G. Bhandarkara's explanation of these terms given on p. 93, footnote, of his Report on Sanskrit MSS., for 1883-84. is, however, different.

Inference.

Inference is of two kinds: (1) *svārtha*, for one's own self, and (2) *parārtha*, for the sake of others. *Hetu* (reason or the middle term) is defined as that which cannot happen except in connection with the major term. The definition that the *hetu* (middle term) is that which possesses three characteristics, is to be rejected as involving fallacies.[1] Those who maintain the threefold characteristic or division of the *hetu* (reason or middle term), cannot but admit the necessity of using the minor term (*pakṣa*) in an inference.[2]

According to some, as the connection or absence of connection between the middle and the major terms can be shown by internal inseparable connection (*antar-vyāpti*), the example forming the external inseparable connection (*bahirvyāpti*) is useless.[3] For instance:—

> The hill (minor term) is fiery (major term), because it is smoky (middle term), as a kitchen (example).

Uselessness of the example.

Here the hill is an integral part of the inference, and in it may be found the necessary connection between fire and smoke. Why then should we burden our inference with an example from without? The kitchen certainly shows the same connection; fire and smoke are found together there: but it is not an essential part of the inference, and so for the purpose in hand the connection which it proves may be described as the external inseparable connection. We must look to logical neatness, and the economy of mental labour, since the mind is liable to be confused when the unessential is brought across its track.

The application (*upanaya*) and conclusion (*nigamana*) as

---

1 निश्चितान्यथानुपपत्त्येकलक्षणो हेतुः न तु त्रिलक्षणकादिः ।
तस्य हेत्वाभासस्यापि सम्भवात् ॥ ११ ॥

(Pramāṇa-naya-tattvālokālaṅkāra, Chap. III).

This is an attack on Dharmakīrti and other Buddhist logicians who define the three characteristics of *hetu* as follows:—

त्रैरूप्यं पुनर्लिङ्गस्य अनुमेये सत्त्वमेव ।
सपक्ष एव सत्त्वम् । असपक्षे चासत्त्वमेव निश्चितम्

(Nyāyabindu, Chapter II).

2 त्रिविधं साधनमभिधायैव तत्समर्थनं विदधानः कः खलु न पक्षप्रयोगम् अङ्गीकुरुते ॥ २२ ॥

(Pramāṇa-naya-tattvālokālaṅkāra, Chap. III).

3 अन्तर्व्याप्त्या हेतोः साध्यप्रत्यायने शक्तावशक्तौ च बहिर्व्याप्तेरुद्भावनं व्यर्थम् ॥ ३५ ॥

(Pramāṇa-naya-tattvālokālaṅkāra, Chap. III).

parts of the syllogism are also useless, but these together with the example are to be employed to convince men of small intellect.[1]

Parts of a syllogism.

Avayava or parts of an inference or syllogism are therefore stated to be the following :—

(1) *Pakṣa-prayoga* (use of the minor term, otherwise called proposition, *pratijñā*)—the hill is fiery.
(2) *Hetu-prayoga* (use of the middle term)—because it is smoky.
(3) *Dṛṣṭānta* (example)—whatever is fiery is smoky, as a kitchen.
(4) *Upanaya* (application)—this hill is smoky.
(5) *Nigamana* (conclusion)—therefore this hill is fiery.

Non-existence.

Non-existence (*abhāva* or *anupalabdhi*) is subdivided as (1) antecedent (*prāgabhāva*); (2) subsequent (*pradhvaṁsābhāva*); (3) mutual (*itaretarābhāva*); and (4) absolute (*atyantābhāva*). Various kinds of *ābhāsa* or fallacy are also enumerated. Under verbal testimony (i.e. *āgama*) as also under the method of one-sided interpretation (*naya*), there is given an elaborate exposition of the *Saptabhaṅgī-naya* (sevenfold paralogism). The mediate and immediate results of valid knowledge (*pramāṇa*) have been clearly laid down.

The results of knowledge and the practical use made of them are stated to be not illusory (*saṁvṛti*), but real (*pāramārthika*).

Fallacies of *Naya*.

Under *naya* (the method of comprehending a thing from particular points of view), the fallacies of it (*nayābhāsa*) are enumerated thus :—

Fallacies of Naya.

(1) *Naigamābhāsa* (the fallacy of the *naigama*)—e.g. in estimating a soul we make a distinction between its "existence" (generic property) and its "consciousness" (specific property).

(2) *Saṁgrahābhāsa* (the fallacy of the collective)—occurs when we call a thing real if it possesses the generic property alone, altogether losing sight of its specific properties, as when we say a bamboo is real so far as it is a tree, but it has no specific properties.

(3) *Vyavahārābhāsa* (the fallacy of the practical)—e.g., the Cārvāka philosophy which makes a wrong distinction of substance, quality, etc.

(4) *Ṛjusūtrābhāsa* (the fallacy of the straight or immediate)—as the Tathāgata philosophy which altogether denies the reality of things.

---

[1] मन्दमतींस्तु व्युत्पादयितुं दृष्टान्तोपनयनिगमनान्यपि प्रयोज्यानि ॥ १८ ॥
(Pramāṇa-naya-tattvālokālaṅkāra, Chap. III).

(5) *Śabdābhāsa* (the verbal fallacy)—occurs when we recognize the distinction of times into past, present and future, but go on attaching one and the same meaning to a word in all the three cases, e.g. if we now use the word "kratu" (sacrifice) in the sense of "strength" which it signified a thousand years ago.

(6) *Samabhirūḍhābhāsa* (the fallacy of the subtle)—occurs when we interpret synonymous words such as Indra, Śakra, Purandara, etc., signifying altogether different things.

(7) *Evambhūtābhāsa* (the fallacy of the such-like)—occurs when a thing is discarded simply because it does not, at the moment, possess the properties implied by the name, e.g. Rāma is not a man (a thinking animal), because he is not at present thinking.

The Soul—*ātmā.*

The soul (*ātmā*) which is the doer and enjoyer, and an embodiment of consciousness, is of the same size as its body. In every person there is a separate soul which, having got rid of the bondage of its *karma* (act-fruits), attains emancipation.

The Method of Debate.

The last chapter expounds the method of debate. Discussion (*Vāda*) consists in assertion and counter-assertion for the establishment of a certain proposition by rejecting its opposite. The disputant or the person who opens the discussion may be eager either to gain a victory or to ascertain a truth. The truth may be sought either for one's own self as a disciple seeks it, or for others as a teacher seeks it. The same remarks apply to the opponent or respondent. There are four constituents of a council of discussion, viz. (1) the disputant (*vādī*); (2) the opponent (*prativādī*); (3) the members (*sabhya*); and (4) the president (*sabhāpati*). The duty of the disputant and his opponent consists in establishing his own side and opposing the other side by means of proof. The members must be acceptable to both the parties in respect of the skill in grasping their dogmas; they must have a good memory, be very learned, and possess genius, patience and impartiality. Their duties consist in stating the assertions and replies of the disputant and his opponent with reference to the particular subject of discussion, in estimating the merits and demerits of their arguments and counter-arguments, in occasionally interrupting them for setting forth some established conclusions, and in, as far as possible, declaring the result of the discussion. The President must be endowed with wisdom, authority, forbearance and impartiality. His duty consists in judging the speeches of the

Rules of Debate.

parties and the members, as also in preventing quarrels, etc., among them. In the event of the parties being desirous of victory alone, they may continue the discussion with vigour as long as the members wish ; but if they are eager to ascertain the truth alone, they may continue the discussion so long as the truth is not ascertained and so long as they retain their vigour.

36. Hemacandra Sūri.
(1088—1172 A.D.).

Hemacandra Sūri[1] (surnamed *Kalikāla-sarvajña*), born at Dhandhuka in Ahmedabad, was a pupil of Devacandra of the Vajraśākhā. He was a contemporary of King Jaya Siṁha and is said to have been the preceptor of Mahārāja Kumāra Pāla of Guzerat about Saṁvat 1199-1229. He was the author of a large number of works such as Kāvyānuśāsana vṛtti, Chandonuśāsanavṛtti, Abhidhāna-cintāmaṇi or Nāmamālā, Anekārthasaṁgraha, Dvāśraya-mahā-kāvya, Triṣaṣṭiśalākāpuruṣa-caritra (a part of which is called Mahāvīracaritra and the appendix called Pariśiṣṭaparva), Yogaśāstra, Nighaṇṭuśeṣa, etc.

He was also the author of a most important work on logic called **Pramāṇa-mīmāṁsā**,[2] on which he himself wrote a commentary. This work, which is divided into five chapters, is written in the *Sūtra* or aphoristic style, and not in the form of a *prakaraṇa* (expository treatise).

He was a spiritual brother of Pradyumna Sūri,[3] was born in Saṁvat 1145 or 1088 A.D., took the vow (*vrata*) in 1150 Saṁvat or 1093 A.D., attained the rank of Sūri in 1166 Saṁvat

---

[1] For details about Hemacandra, see Bühler's "Ueber das Lebens des Jaina Monches Hemacandra"; Peterson's Fourth Report, p. cxli, and p. 82; and also Peterson's lecture on the story of Hema Candra published in the *Bombay Gazette*, August 29, 1895.

[2] A manuscript of the **Pramāṇa-mīmāṁsā** with a commentary by the author himself has been noticed by Peterson in his Fifth Report on Sanskrit MSS., pp. 147–148. In explaining why the Pramāṇa-mīmāṁsā was written in the form of aphorisms, Hemacandra in the first chapter of the commentary says:—

वाचकमुख्यविरचितानि सकलशास्त्रचूडामणिभूतानि तत्त्वार्थसूत्राणीति यद्येवमकलङ्क-धर्मकीर्त्त्यादिवत् प्रकरणमेव किं नारभ्यते किमनया सूत्रकारत्वाहोपुरुषिकया मैवं वोचः । भिन्नरुचिर्ह्ययं जनस्ततो नास्य स्वेच्छाप्रतिबन्धो लौकिकराजकीयं वा शासनमस्तीति यत्किञ्चिदेतत् तत्र वर्णसमूहात्मकैः पञ्चभिरध्यायैः शास्त्रमेतदरचयदाचार्यः । तस्य च प्रेक्षावत् प्रवृत्त्यङ्गमभिधातुमिदमादिसूत्रम् । अथ प्रमाणमीमांसा अथ इत्यस्य अधिकारार्थत्वात् ।

(Quoted in Peterson's Fifth Report, p. 148).

[3] श्रीमांश्चन्द्रकुलेऽभवद्गुणनिधिः प्रद्युम्नसूरिप्रभु-
र्बन्धुर्यस्य स शिष्यहेमविषये श्रीहेमसूरिर्विधिः ॥

(Candrasena's commentary on Utpādasiddhiprakaraṇa, a manuscript of which is noticed in Peterson's Third Report, p. 209).

or 1109 A.D., and ascended to heaven (died) in 1229 Saṁvat or 1172 A.D.[1]

37. Candraprabha Sūri (1102 A.D).

Candraprabha Sūri (born in Guzerat), who founded the Pūrṇimāgaccha[2] in Saṁvat 1159 or 1102 A.D., was a pupil of Jayasiṁha Sūri and preceptor of Dharmaghoṣa. He[3] was the author of Darśanaśuddhi, otherwise called Samyaktva-prakaraṇa, of Prameya-ratnakoṣa and possibly also of Nyāyāvatāra-vivṛti.[4] He was a great logician, and in debate appeared as a lion before the opponents who resembled elephants.[5]

The Nyāyāvatāra-vivṛti is an excellent commentary on the Nyāyāvatāra of Siddhasena Divākara. In it mention is made of the Buddhist logicians Dharmottara, Arcaṭa[6] and others, and

---

1 शरवेदेश्वरे वर्षे कार्त्तिके पूर्णिमादिने ।
जन्माभवत् प्रभोर्व्योमबाणशंभौ व्रतं तथा ॥
रसषट्केश्वरे सूरिप्रतिष्ठा समजायत ।
नन्दद्वयरवौ वर्षेऽवसानमभवत् प्रभोः ॥

(Prabhāvakacar., XXII, v. 851 seq., quoted by Klatt in Ind. Ant., Vol. XI, Sept. 1882, p. 254).

2 For the origin of the Pūrṇimāgaccha see Dr. R. G. Bhandarkar's Report, 1883–84, p. 147.

3 For Candraprabha Sūri see also Peterson's Fourth Report, p. xxvii.

4 The manuscript of Nyāyāvatāra-vivṛti, which I consulted, was obtained from Bhavanagar, Bombay, through Munis Dharmavijaya and Indravijaya. In the Nyāyā-vatāra-vivṛti itself there is no mention of Candraprabha Sūri. Elsewhere I have seen it stated that it was the work of that author. The authorship must, however, for the present, remain an open question. In the colophon of the Nyāyāvatāra-vivṛti it is stated that it was the work of Siddhasena Divākara-vyākhyānaka or simply Siddha-vyākhyānaka which was evidently a surname. Munis Dharmavijaya and Indravijaya relying on the line व्याख्यातृचूडामणिसिद्धनामा (quoted from Ratnaprabha Sūri's Upadeśamālā-viśeṣa-vṛtti in Peterson's Third Report, p. 168) are inclined to identify Siddha-vyākhyānaka with Siddharṣi who lived in Saṁvat 962 or 905 A.D. (as is evident from Peterson's Fourth Report, p. cxxix). There is another commentary on the Nyāyāvatāra by Haribhadra Sūri. For Darśana-śuddhi, *vide* Peterson 3, App. p. 91; and for the Nyāyāvatāra-vivṛti *vide* Peterson 3, p. xvi. The Prameya-ratna-koṣa, known to Guṇaratna, has been published in Bhavanagara under the editorship of Dr. L. Suali of Italy. In one of its opening verses Candraprabha Sūri is thus mentioned:—

प्रमेयरत्नकोशोऽयं क्रियते कृतिवल्लभः ।
हितार्थं धीदरिद्राणां श्रीचन्द्रप्रभसूरिभिः ॥ २ ॥

5 तीर्थे वीरविभोः सुधर्मगणभृत्सन्तानलक्ष्मीव्रति
वारिधोज्ज्वलचन्द्रगच्छजलधिप्रीणासमोतद्युतिः ।
साहित्यागमतर्कलक्षणमहाविद्यापगासागरः
श्रीचन्द्रप्रभसूरिरद्भुतमतिर्वादीभसिंहोऽभवत् ॥ १ ॥

(Daśavaikālikaṭīkā by Tilakācārya, noticed in Peterson's Fifth Report, p. 65).

6 प्रमाणेत्यादि अनेन च तादात्म्यतदुत्पत्तिलक्षणसंबन्ध विकलतया ध्वनेर्बहिरर्थं प्रति प्रामाण्ययोगाद् अभिधेयादिसूचनद्वारोत्पन्नार्थसंशयमुखेन श्रोतारः श्रवणं प्रति प्रोत्साह्यन्ते इति धर्मोत्तरो मन्यते ... ... अर्चटस्तु आह न श्रावकोत्साहकमेतत् प्रामाण्याभावात् तेषां चाप्रमाणात्प्रवृत्तेः । (Nyāyāvatāra-vivṛti, on verse 1).

there is also a criticism of the views of Saugata, Naiyāyika, Mīmāṁsaka, Vaiśeṣika, Sāṁkhya, Cārvāka, Bauddha, Śauddhodani, Kaṇabhakṣa Akṣapāda, Brahama-vādī, etc.

38. Nemicandra Kavi (about 1150 A.D.).

Nemicandra, born in Guzerat, who combated the views of the Hindu philosopher Kaṇāda, was a great teacher of logic.[1] He was a pupil of Vairasvāmi and preceptor of Sāgarendu (Sāgaracandra) Muni (alive in Saṁvat 1200 or 1143 A.D.), as mentioned by Māṇikyacandra, Sāgarendu Muni's pupil, in his Pārśvanātha-caritra written in Saṁvat 1276 or 1219 A.D. As Māṇikyacandra flourished about 1219 A.D., his preceptor's preceptor Nemicandra[2] must have lived about 1150 A.D. Nemicandra was styled a *Kavi*[3]

39. Ānanda Sūri and Amaracandra Sūri, nicknamed Tiger-cub and Lion-cub (1093—1135 A.D.).

These two, born in Guzerat, were great logicians who, even in their boyhood, overcame their elephant-like opponents in dispute, and were nicknamed respectively *Vyāghra-śiśuka* (Tigercub) and *Siṁha-śiśuka* (Lion-cub).[4] They[5] were the twin pupils and suc-

---

1 षट्तर्कीकमलाविलासवसतिस्तस्वतपोऽदर्पति
स्तत्पट्टोदयचन्द्रमाः समजनि श्रीनेमिचन्द्रप्रभुः ।
निःसामान्यगुणैर्भुवि प्रसमरैः प्रालेयशैलोज्ज्वलैः
यस्याग्रे कणभोजिनो मुनिपतेर्व्यर्थं मतं सर्वतः ॥ १६ ॥

(Pārśvanātha caritra, noticed in Peterson 3, p. 160).
The same verse is quoted almost verbatim in the Kāvya-prakāśa-saṁketa by Māṇikyacandra Sūri, noticed in Person 3, p. 321.

2 For Nemicandra, see also Peterson 4, p. lxxi.

3 See Dr. R. G. Bhandarkar's Report, 1883-84, p. 122.

4 Udayaprabha Sūri, who was the successor of Haribhadra Sūri through Vijayasena Sūri, in his Dharmābhyudaya-mahākāvya, noticed by Peterson in his Third Report, pp. 16-19, writes:—

आनन्दसूरिरिति [तस्य बभूव] शिष्यः
पूर्वोऽपरः प्रशमधरोऽमरचन्द्रसूरिः ।
धर्मद्विपस्य दशनाविव पापपक्ष-
क्षोदक्षमौ जगति यौ विशदौ विभातः ॥ ३ ॥
अस्तावधवाङ्मयपयोनिधिमन्दराद्रि-
मुद्राजुषोः किमनयोः स्तुमहे महिम्नः
बाल्येऽपि निर्दलितवादिगजौ जगाद
यौ व्याघ्रसिंहशिशुकाविति सिद्धराजः ॥ ४ ॥

5 For further particulars of Ānanda Sūri and Amaracandra Sūri see Peterson 4, p. vii.

cessors of Mahendra Sūri in the Nāgendragaccha, and were succeeded by Haribhadra Sūri. As Siddharāja, from whom they received their nicknames, ascended the throne in Saṁvat 1150 or 1093 A.D., they must have flourished at the beginning of the 12th century A.D. It is probably these two logicians who are referred to by the Hindu logician Gaṅgeśa Upādhyāya in his Tattva-cintāmaṇi under *Siṁha vyāghrī-lakṣaṇa* of Vyāpti.

40. Haribhadra Sūri (About 1120 A.D.).

We find mention of at least two Śvetāmbara Jaina authors bearing the name Haribhadra Sūri. One died [1] in Saṁvat 535 or 478 A.D., while the other was a pupil of Ānanda Sūri and Amaracandra Sūri of the Nāgendragaccha who lived about 1093–1135 A.D.[2] The second Haribhadra Sūri, who was called "Kalikāla-Gautama"[3], must therefore have flourished about 1120 A.D. He must have been an eminent logician if we suppose him to be the author [4] of the **Ṣaḍdarśana-samuccaya**, the **Daśavaikālika-niryukti-ṭīkā**, the **Nyāya-praveśaka-sūtra** and the **Nyāyāvatāra-vṛtti**. There are strong grounds for supposing that the Ṣaḍdarśana-samuccaya was not the work of the first Haribhadra Sūri, as it refers in the

---

[1] पंचसए पणतीए विक्कमकालाओ झत्ति अत्थमिओ ।
हरिभद्दसूरिसूरो निव्वुओ दिसउ सिवसुक्खं ॥ १०० ॥

(Gacchotpatti-prakīrṇaka quoted in the Gāthāsāhāsrī noticed in Peterson 3, p. 284).

[2] Klatt refers to Bühler's Sukṛtasaṁkīrtana, pp. 24–25; see Peterson 4, pp. cxxxix, cxl.

[3] सिद्धान्तोपनिषन्निषण्णहृदयो श्रीजम्भभिन्मन्त्रयोः
पट्टे श्रीहरिभद्रसूरिरभवच्चारित्रिणामग्रणीः ।
यान्त्वा ग्रन्थसनाश्रयैरतिचिराद्धर्मभ्रष्टजनः
सम्भृष्टः कलिकालगौतम इति ख्यातिर्विवेने गुणैः ॥ ५ ॥

(Dharmābhyudaya-mahākāvya by Udayaprabha Sūri noticed in Peterson 3, Appendix I, p. 18).

[4] In the concluding lines of the Daśavaikālika-niryukti-ṭīkā, it is stated that the author of that work was one Haribhadra Sūri who was a *dharmaputra* of *Yākinī*. A similar description of Haribhadra, the author of Ṣaḍdarśana-samuccaya, is found in the opening sentences of Guṇaratna's commentary on that work (dated about 1407 A.D.). The Caturviṁśati-prabandha by Rājaśekhara Sūri, composed in Saṁvat 1405 or 1348 A.D., makes a like reference to Haribhadra, the author of Nyāyāvatāra-vṛtti. Now the *dharmaputra* of *Yākinī* is generally held to be a surname of the first Haribhadra Sūri whose disciples were Haṁsa and Paramahaṁsa, as is evident from Prabhācandra Sūri's Prabhāvaka-caritra dated about 1277 A.D.

In the Gacchotpatti-prakaraṇa, Gāthā-sāhasrī, Vicāra-sāra-prakaraṇa, Vicārāmṛta-saṁgraha, Tapāgacchapaṭṭāvalī, Kharataragaccha-paṭṭāvalī, etc., Haribhadra Sūri I. is stated to have flourished in Saṁvat 535 or 478 A.D.

Now the Nyāyāvatāra which is alleged to have been commented on by Haribhadra Sūri I. was itself composed about 533 A.D. (that is, after 478 A.D.), and Dharmakīrti, whose logical doctrines have been referred to in the Ṣaḍdarśana-samuccaya, lived about 650 A.D. These facts prove that Haribhadra, the author of Nyāyāvatāra-vṛtti and Ṣaḍdarśana-samuccaya, lived after 650 A.D.

chapter on the Bauddhadarśana to the views of such authors as Dignāga, Dharmakīrti,[1] and others who flourished long after the 5th century A.D. The six systems (Ṣaḍdarśana) treated by him are (1) Bauddha, (2) Naiyāyika, (3) Sāṁkhya, (4) Jaina, (5) Vaiśeṣika, and (6) Jaiminīya.

In the Anekānta-jaya-patākā-ṭīkā[2] attributed to Haribhadra Sūri, there are passages quoted from the works of Dinna or Dignāga, Dharma Pāla, Dharmakīrti, Bhartṛhari, Siddhasena Divākara, Samanta Bhadra, Mallavādin and Śubha Gupta. As the last mentioned two writers lived respectively in the 9th century and the 11th century A.D., we shall not be far wrong if we place Hari Bhadra early in 12th century A.D.

Haribhadra Sūri is often described[3] as having protected the

---

Dr. Jacobi in his letter, dated the 21st October 1907, writes to me that "Haribhadra uses the word *viraha* in the Samaraiccakahā, which is alluded to by Siddharṣi who wrote in 905 A.D."

Regarding the dates of the Ṣaddarśana-samuccaya, etc., he observes :—These are "unanimously ascribed to the first Haribhadra," "whose date, I believe, with Prof. Leumann, to have been wrongly referred to the Saṁvat era instead of the Valabhi or *Gupta era*, which commenced in 319 A.D."

According to Dr. Jacobi, therefore, the Ṣaḍdarśana-samuccaya, etc., were written by the first Haribhadra Sūri, who died in 535 Gupta Saṁvat or 854 A.D.

Dr. Jacobi's theory removes many of our difficulties, yet it is far from being conclusive, as the Jaina authors very seldom used the Gupta era. Moreover, it is inexplicable why Vācaspati Miśra and Udayanācārya did not refer to such an excellent compendium of Indian philosophy as the Ṣaḍdarśana-samuccaya if it existed as early as the 9th or 10th century A.D. I am therefore inclined to believe that Haribhadra Sūri II was the author of the Ṣaḍdarśana-samuccaya, Nyāyāvatāra-vṛtti, etc., while the Samaraiccakahā and other treatises might be the works of the first Haribhadra Sūri.

But I must confess that the modern Jaina Paṇḍitas such as Munis Dharmavijaya and Indravijaya firmly believe that the author of all these works was the first Haribhadra Sūri who, according to them, flourished in 535 Vikrama Saṁvat, or 478 A.D.

1 प्रत्यक्षं कल्पनापोढमभ्रान्तं तत्र बुध्यताम् ।
त्रिरूपाल्लिङ्गतो लिङ्गिज्ञानं त्वनुमानसंज्ञितम् ॥

(Ṣaḍdarśana samuccaya, chapter on Bauddha-darśana. p. 38, edited by Dr. Suali).

This verse refers without doubt to the definition of *Pratyakṣa* and *Anumāna* given by Dharmakīrti who lived about 650 A.D.

2 Anekānta-jaya-patākā-ṭikā, chap. III, p. 116, 117; p. 150; pp. 35, 76, 79, 116, 120, 159, 170, 175, 192, 192; pp. 134, 127; p. 3; p. 131; pp. 19, 38.

उक्तञ्च वादिमुख्येन मल्लवादिना सन्मतौ ।

(Anekānta-jaya-patākā, pp. 19, 38).

यथोक्तं वार्त्तिकानुसारिणा शुभगुप्तेन ॥

(Anekānta-jaya-patākā, p. 117).

3 Klatt in his "Paṭṭāvalī of the Kharataragaccha" in the Ind. Ant., Vol. XI, Sept. 1882, p. 247; also Peterson 3, p 35. Also:

स्तौमि श्रीहरिभद्रं तं येनार्हद्बीजमव्ययम् ।
चतुर्दशप्रकरणशत्यागोप्यत मातृवत् ॥ १९ ॥

Amarasvāmicarita by Muniratna Sūri noticed in Peterson 3, p. 91

word of the Arhats like a mother by his 1,400 works. He is said to have used the word *viraha* (separation or sorrow) as his mark in the last verse of each of his works He was by birth a Brāhmaṇa and was chaplain to king Jitāri whose capital was Chittore near the Citrakūṭa hill.[1] He was instructed in the Jaina doctrine by Jinabhaṭa. Two of his pupils, named Haṁsa and Paramahaṁsa, are said to have left him as missionaries of the Jaina faith, and to have been slain in the Bhoṭa country (Tibet) by the fanatical Buddhists whom they sougnt to convert. The sorrow caused by the death of these two pupils is said to have been symbolised in the word *viraha.*

It is generally supposed that Haribhadra Sūri, whose pupils were killed in Tibet, was the first author of that name. But there will be no inconsistency if we suppose him to be the second Haribhadra Sūri, for the religious intercourse between India and Tibet was more frequent in the 12th century A.D. than in the 5th century, when Tibet had scarcely emerged into the ken of history.

41. PĀRŚVADEVA GAṆI (1133 A.D.).

Pārśvadeva was the author of a commentary on Nyāyapraveśa, called **Nyāyapraveśapañjikā.**[2] He assisted Āmradeva Sūri in Saṁvat 1190 or 1133 A.D. in writing his commentary on the Ākhyāna-maṇi-koṣa of Nemicandra.[3]

42. ŚRICANDRA (ABOUT 1137—1165 A.D.).

Candra or rather Śrī Candra,[4] a disciple of Hema Candra Sūri of the Harṣapurīya gaccha, wrote about 1137 A.D. a work on Logic called the **Nyāya-praveśa-ṭippana,** a super-commentary on the Nyāya-praveśa-vṛtti of Haribhadra Sūri. His Pradeśa-vyākhyā-ṭippanaka[5] on the Āvaśyaka Sūtra appeared in Saṁvat 1222 or 1165 A.D.

---

[1] *Vide* Introduction to Ṣaḍdarśana-samuccaya published in the Chowkhamba series, Benares; and Peterson's Third Report, p. 35.

[2] दुर्वारमारवारि कुम्भतटप्रभेदकण्ठीरवं जिनपतिं वरदं प्रणम्य ।
न्यायप्रवेशकमिति प्रथिते सुशास्त्रे प्रारभ्यते मनुधियापि हि पञ्जिकेयम् ॥
(Quoted in Peterson's First Report, p. 81).

[3] Peterson's Fourth Part, p. lxxvii.

[4] *Vide* "Jainistic Notices" by Professor N. D. Mironow published as a Bulletin of the Imperial Academy of Sciences, St. Petersbourg, 1911.

[5] *Vide* Peterson's Fourth Report, pp. xxvii-xxviii.

43. Devabhadra
(about 1150 A.D.).

Devabhadra,[1] a disciple of both Hemacandra Sūri and Śrī Candra,[2] was the author of a logical treatise entitled the **Nyāyāvatāra-ṭippana**, a super-commentary on the Nyāyāvatāra-vivṛti. In this work there are quotations from Vindhyavāsin, Dharmakīrti, Dharmottara, Jñānaśrī Mitra[3] and others. He lived about 1150 A.D.

44. Candrasena Sūri
(about 1150 A.D.).

Candrasena, who seems to have been a pupil of Pradyumna Sūri, wrote, with the assistance of Nemicandra, a work called **Utpāda-siddhi-prakaraṇa** with a commentary on the same in Sanskrit in Saṁvat 1207 or 1150 A.D.[4]

45. Ratnaprabha Sūri
(1181 A.D.).

Ratnaprabha Sūri, who belonged to the Śvetāmbara sect, was a logician of repute, being the author of a light commentary (*laghu-ṭīkā*) on the Pramāṇa-naya-tattvālokālaṅkāra called **Syādvāda-ratnākarāvatārikā**,[5] in which are quoted the views of the Buddhist logicians Arcaṭa (q.v.) and Dharmottara (q.v.).

---

1 *Vide* "Devabhadra and his Nyāyāvatāra-ṭippana" in the Jainistic Notices by Professor N. D. Mironow published as a Bulletin of the Imperial Academy of Sciences, St. Petersbourg, 1911.
Vide also Peterson's Fourth Report, p. liv.

2 श्रीमदेवेऽभ्यस्ततां तर्के रतिं तत्रैव वाञ्छता ।
तस्य शिष्य लवेनेदं चक्रे किमपि टिप्पनम् ॥
(Praśasti of Pāṇḍava-caritra).

3 Devabhadra, in his Nyāyāvatāra-ṭippana, quotes Jñāna-śrī Mitra thus:—
ननु चार्थक्रियासामर्थ्यमेव सत्त्वं नान्यत् । तथा च ज्ञानश्रीः—— यदि नाम प्रतिदर्शनं सत्त्वभेदस्तथापीहार्थक्रियासामर्थ्यमेव सत्त्वमभिप्रेतमिति ।

4 द्वादशवर्षशतेषु श्रीविक्रमतो गतेषु मुनिभिः ।
चैत्रे सम्पन्नमिदं साहाय्यं चात्र मे नेमेः ॥
(Colophon of Saṭīka Utpāda-siddhiprakaraṇa quoted in Peterson's Third Report, p. 209).

5 प्रमाणे च प्रमेये च बालानां बुद्धिसिद्धये ।
किञ्चिद् वचनचातुर्य्यचापलायेयमादधे ॥
प्रमेयरत्नकोटीभिः पूर्णो रत्नाकरो महान् ।
तत्रावतारमात्रेण त्वेतस्याः कृतार्थता ॥
(Syādvāda-ratnākarāvatārikā, Muni Dharmavijaya's MSS., p. 99). A part of the Syādvāda-ratnākarāvatārikā has been printed and published in the Benares Jaina Yaśovijaya series.

While in Broach at the Aśvāvabodhatīrtha in Saṁvat 1238 or 1181 A.D., he wrote another work called Upadeśamālāvṛtti [1] to please Bhadreśvara Sūri and in payment of the debt he owed to Vijayasena Sūri, the brother of Bhadreśvara. There he gives his spiritual descent in the Vṛhadgaccha as follows: (1) Municandra Sūri; (2) Deva Sūri; (3) Bhadreśvara Sūri; and (4) Ratnaprabha Sūri.[2]

46. TILAKĀCĀRYA (ABOUT 1180—1240 A.D.).

Tilaka Ācārya, who belonged to the Candragaccha of the Śvetāmbara sect, was a spiritual descendant of Candraprabha Sūri through Dharmaghoṣa, Cakreśvara and Śivaprabha. He was author of several works such as the Āvaśyaka-laghu-vṛtti written in 1239 A.D., and, the Pratyeka-buddha-caritra in 1204 A.D.[3]

47. MALLIṢEṆA SŪRI (1292 A.D.).

Malliṣeṇa belonged to the Nagendra Gaccha of the Śvetāmbara sect, and was the author of the Syādvādamañjarī, a commentary on Hemacandra's Vītarāga-stuti or Dvātriṁśikā. The Syādvāda-mañjarī contains an exposition of the *Pramāṇa*, *Saptabhaṅgī-naya*, etc., and criticises Akṣapāda's theories of *Pramāṇa*, *Chala*, *Jāti*, *Nigrahasthāna*, etc. The doctrines of the Sāṁkhya, Aulūkya, Jaiminīya, Bhaṭṭapāda, Vedānta, Yogācāra, Mādhyamika, Cārvāka, etc., have also been his favourite subjects of attack. At the close of his work Malliṣeṇa describes himself as a pupil of Udayaprabha Sūri and as having composed the work in Śaka 1214 or A.D. 1292.[4]

---

[1] श्रीरत्नप्रभसूरिभिः शुभकृते श्रीदेवसूरिप्रभोः ।
शिष्यैः सेयमकारि षण्मदकृते वृत्तिर्विशेषार्थिनाम् ॥
विक्रमाद्वसुलोकार्के (१२३८) वर्षे माघे समर्थिता ।
एकादशसहस्राणि सार्द्धं पञ्चशतं तथा ॥

(Upadeśamālā-vṛtti, noticed in Peterson 5, p. 124).

[2] For other particulars of Ratnaprabha Sūri, *vide* Peterson 4, p. cii. Compare also Weber II, p. 922, note 7.

[3] *Vide* Peterson's Fourth Report, p. xlviii, and Fifth Report xxvi.

[4] श्रीमल्लिषेणसूरिभिरकारि तत्पदगगनदिनमणिभिः ।
वृत्तिरियं मनुरविमितशकाब्दे दीपमहसि शनौ ॥ १ ॥

(Syādvādamañjarī, p. 220, printed in the Benares Chowkhamba Sanskrit Series, and edited by Dāmodara Lal Gosvāmi).

48. Rājaśekhara Sūri (1348 A.D.).

Rājaśekhara Sūri, or Maladhāri Śrī Rājaśekhara Sūri, belonged to the Śvetāmbara sect and was the author of the **Ratnāvatārikā-pañjikā**,[1] a sub-commentary on the Pramāṇa-naya-tattvālokālaṅkāra, as also of two other works called Syādvāda-kalikā and Caturviṁśatiprabandha.[2] He is also the author of a Pañjikā (commentary) on the Nyāya-kandalī of the Hindu philosopher Śrī-dhara. He studied the Nyāya-kandalī under the guidance of Jinaprabha,[3] and completed his Caturviṁśatiprabandha in Saṁvat 1405 or 1348 A.D.[4]

49. Jñāna Candra (1350 A.D.).

He belonged to the Śvetāmbara sect and was the author of a gloss on the Ratnākarāvatārikā called the **Ratnākarāvatārikā-ṭippana**, which discusses many abstruse points of logic and criticises the views of Dignāga[5] and others. He composed this work[6] under orders from his preceptor Rājaśekhara Sūri, who flourished in 1348 A.D. Jñāna Candra's date may approximately be fixed at about 1350 A.D.

---

1 A part of the Ratnākarāvatārikā-pañjikā has been printed and published in the Benares Jaina Yaśovijaya series.

2 This work has been published by Hira Lal Haṁsarāja at Jāmanagara in Kathiawar.

3 श्रीमज्जिनप्रभविभोरधिगत्य न्यायकन्दलीं किञ्चित् ।
तस्यां विवृतिलवमहं करवै स्वपरोपकाराय ॥

(Nyāyakandalī of Śrīdhara with the Pañjikā of Rājaśekhara noticed in Peterson 3, p. 273; cf. also Peterson 3, pp. 28–29).

4 *Vide* Weber II, p. 1207.

शरगगनमनुमिताब्दे ज्येष्ठामूलीयधवलसप्तम्याम् ।
निष्पन्नमिदं शास्त्रं श्रोतृध्येत्रोः सुखं तन्यात् ॥

(Colophon of Caturviṁśatiprabandha).

5 तेनान्यापोहविषयाः प्रोक्ताः सामान्यगोचराः ।
शब्दाश्च बुद्धयश्चैव वस्तुन्येषामसम्भवात् ॥
यच्च व्याख्या तेनाचार्यदिङ्नागेन
अन्यापोहविषयाः ... प्रोक्ताः ॥

Jñānacandra's Ratnākarāvatārikā-ṭippana, chap. I, p. 7, published in Yaśovijaya-granthamālā of Benares.

6 रत्नाकरावतारिका वरटिप्पनं तत्
ज्ञानेन्दुरल्पतरधीः स्वमतिः प्रबद्धौ ।
तच्छिष्यको रचितवान् मलधारिपूज्य-
श्रीराजशेखरगुरोश्च निदेशमाप्य ॥

Quoted from the MSS. of Ratnākarāvatārikā-ṭippanaka, lent to me by Muni Dharmavijaya. A part of this work has been printed and published in the Benares Jaina Yaśovijaya series.

50. GUṆARATNA (1409 A.D.).

Guṇaratna belonged to the Tapāgaccha of the Śvetāmbara sect, and was the distinguished author of a commentary on the Ṣaḍdarśana-samuccaya[1] called **Ṣaḍdarśana-samuccaya-vṛtti** or **Tarka-rahasya-dīpikā** in which the Nyāya (logic) along with other systems has been lucidly explained. He also wrote the Kriyā-ratna-samuccaya.

He is mentioned by Ratna-śekhara Sūri in the Śrāddha-pratikramaṇa-sūtra-vṛtti composed in Saṁvat 1496 or A.D. 1439.[2] In that work Guṇaratna is mentioned as a pupil of Devasundara, who attained the exalted position of Sūri at Anahillapattana in Saṁvat 1420 or A.D. 1363.[3] Guṇaratna must, therefore, have lived between A.D. 1363 and A.D. 1439. Devasundara Sūri, teacher of Guṇaratna, was a contemporary of Muni-sundara Sūri, the famous author of the Gurvāvalī[4] composed in Saṁvat 1466 or A.D. 1409. Guṇaratna himself says that his Kriyāratna-samuccaya[5] was composed in Saṁvat 1466 or A.D. 1409.

Guṇaratna, in his elaborate commentary (*Vṛtti*) on the Ṣaḍdarśana-samuccaya, has mentioned Śauddhodani, Dharmottarā-

---

[1] Ṣaḍdarśana-samuccaya with Vṛtti, edited by Dr. Suali, and published by the Asiatic Society of Bengal. There is another commentary on Ṣaḍdarśana-samuccaya called Laghuvṛtti by Maṇibhadra. It has been published in the Chowkhamba series.

[2] The Śrāddha-prati-kramaṇa-sūtra-vṛtti, by Ratnaśekhara Sūri, has been noticed in Peterson 3, pp. 226–227, whence the following lines are quoted:—

विख्याततपेत्याख्या जगति जगच्चन्द्रसूरयोऽभूवन् ।
श्रीदेवसुन्दरगुरूत्तमाश्च तदनुक्रमाद्विदिताः ॥ १ ॥
पञ्च च तेषां शिष्यास्तेष्वाद्या ज्ञानसागरा गुरवः ।
कुलमण्डना द्वितीयाः श्रीगुणरत्नास्तृतीयाश्च ॥ २ ॥
षड्दर्शनवृत्तिक्रियारत्नसमुच्चयविचारनिचयसृजः ।
एषां श्रीसुगुरूणां प्रसादतोऽब्दे षडङ्कविश्वमिते ।
श्रीरत्नशेखरगणिर्वृत्तिमिमामकृत कृतिसुहिताम् ॥ ३ ॥

[3] *Vide* Dr. Klatt on the Paṭṭāvalī of the Kharataragaccha in the Ind. Ant., Vol. XI, September 1882, pp. 255–256; cf. also Weber II, p. 884 and Dr. R. G. Bhandarkar's Report, 1883–84, p. 157.

[4] रसरसमनुमितवर्षे १४६६ मुनिसुन्दरसूरिणा कृता पूर्वम् ।
मध्यचैरवधार्या गुर्वावलीयं जयश्रीदा ॥ ९१ ॥
(Gurvāvalī, Jaina-Yaśovijaya granthamālā series, p. 109).

[5] काले षड्रसपूर्वे १४६६ वत्सरमिते श्रीविक्रमार्काद्गते
गुर्वादेशवशाद्विमृश्य च सदा स्वान्योपकारं परम् ।
ग्रन्थं श्रीगुणरत्नसूरिरतनोत् प्रज्ञाविहीनोऽप्यमुं
निर्हेतूपकृतिप्रधानजननैः शोध्यस्त्वयं धीधनैः ॥ ९१ ॥
(Kriyāratna-samuccaya. Jaina Yaśovijaya granthamālā series, p. 309).

cārya, Arcaṭa, Dharmakīrti, Prajñākara, Kamalaśīla, Dignāga, and other Buddhist authors, as well as Tarkabhāṣā, Hetubindu, Arcaṭa-tarkaṭīkā, Pramāṇa-vārtika, Tattvasaṁgraha, Nyāyabindu, Nyāyapraveśaka, and other Buddhist works on logic, etc., in the chapter on the Bauddha system. Mention has also been made, in the chapter on the Nyāya, of such Hindu logicians as Akṣapāda, Vātsyāyana, Uddyotakara, Vācaspati, Udayana, Srīkaṇṭha, Abhayatilakopādhyāya, Jayanta, and of such works as Nyāya-sūtra, Nyāyabhāṣya, Nyāyavārtika, Tātparyaṭīkā, Tātparyapariśuddhi, Nyāyālaṅkāra, Nyāyālaṅkāravṛtti, etc. The Nyāya-sāra of Bhā-sarvajña and the eighteen commentaries on it such as Nyāyabhūṣaṇa, Nyāyakalikā, Nyāyakusumāñjali, etc., have also been mentioned.

51. Śrutasāgara Gaṇi (about 1493 A.D.).

Śrutasāgara Gaṇi, author of **Tattvārthadīpikā**, was a pupil of Vidyānandin of the Sarasvatī Gaccha of the Digambaras. Nemidatta, who wrote in Saṁvat 1585 or 1528 A.D., describes himself as devoted to the service of Śrutasāgara whose literary activity must be referred to about Saṁvat 1550 or 1493 A.D.[1]

52. Dharma-bhūṣaṇa (about 1600 A.D.).

Dharmabhūṣaṇa, a disciple of Vardhamāna Bhaṭṭāraka, was a Digambara who wrote the **Nyāya-dīpikā** about 300 years ago. He has been mentioned in the Tarkabhāṣā by Yaśovijaya Gaṇi.

The Nyāya-dīpikā begins with a salutation to Arhat Vardhamāna. It is divided into three chapters (*Prakāśa*), viz. (1) general characteristics of valid knowledge, *pramāṇa-sāmānya-lakṣaṇa*; (2) perception, *pratyakṣa*; and (3) indirect knowledge, *parokṣa*, including recollection, *smṛti*, recognition, *pratyabhijñāna*, argumentation, *tarka*, inference, *anumāna*, tradition, *āgama*, and the method of comprehending things from particular standpoints, *naya*.

The technical terms of logic have been defined and minutely examined, and the views of other logicians, specially of the Buddhists, have been severely criticised. There are references to Sugata, Saugata, Bauddha, Tāthāgata, Mīmāṁsaka, Yauga, Naiyāyika, Bhāṭṭa, Prābhākara, Dignāga, Samanta Bhadra, Akalaṅka Deva, Śālikā Nātha, Jainendra, Syādvāda-vidyāpati, Māṇikya Nandi Bhaṭṭāraka, Kumāra Nandi Bhaṭṭāraka, Udayana and others. The following works are also mentioned:—Prameya kamala-mārtaṇḍa, Rājavārtika, Ślokavārtika, Ślokavārtika-bhāṣya,

1. Peterson's Fourth Report, p. cxxiii.

Tattvārtha-sūtra, Tattvārtha-bhāṣya, Tattvārtha-śloka-vārtika, Āptamīmāṁsā vivaraṇa, Nyāyaviniścaya, Pramāṇa-nirṇaya, Pramāṇa-parīkṣā, Parīkṣāmukha, Nyāyabindu, etc.

52a. VINAYAVIJAYA (1613 A D.—1681 A.D.).

Vinayavijaya was born in a Vaiśya family in Guzerat in Saṁvat 1670 or A.D. 1613. His spiritual teacher Kīrtivijaya [1] was a disciple of Hīravijaya, the well-known sūri of Akbara's time. Vinayavijaya, after prosecuting his studies in Jaina scriptures under Kīrtivijaya, proceeded to Benares to study the grammar and philosophy of the Brāhmaṇas. Yaśovijaya, another Jaina ascetic, whose account will be given shortly, joined him in his journey to that famous seat of Brāhmaṇic learning. After undergoing a course of training for twelve years in Benares, Vinayavijaya travelled over various parts of India until he came to Junāgaḍh in Kathiawaḍ on his pilgrimage to the Girnar hills in 1651 A.D. He visited Surat, Marwaḍ, etc., and died at Rander in Guzerat in 1681 A.D. Of the numerous works written by him the undermentioned treatise on Jaina Nyāya deserves a special notice :—

Naya-karṇikā—"an ear-ring of *Naya*, the method of descriptions," which was composed at Diva near Junāgaḍh in Kathiawaḍ in 1651 A.D. for the satisfaction of *Guru* Vijayasiṁha Sūri.[2] *Naya* aims at describing things from all possible standpoints. There are altogether seven standpoints, viz. *naigama*, *saṁgraha*, *vyavahāra*, *ṛjusūtra*, *śabda*, *samabhirūḍha* and *evaṁbhūta*, explanations of which have already been given. The first four of the standpoints come under a group called *dravyāsti-kāya*, noumenal or that which refers to a substance, and the last three under a group called *paryāyāsti kāya*, phenomenal or that which refers to an attribute. The treatise ends with the observation [3] that

---

1 *Vide* the concluding verses of the chapters of Vinayavijaya's Lokaprakāśa.

2 इत्थं मयार्थकणवः कुतुकैर्विमैर्दु-
मौंशोषितः सविनयं विनयाभिधेन ।
श्रीदीपबन्दरवरे विजयादिदेव
सूरीशितुर्विजयसिंहगुरोश्च तुष्ट्यै ॥ २२ ॥

(Naya-karṇikā).

3 सर्वे नया अपि विरोधभृतो मिथस्ते
संभूय साधुसमयं भगवन् भजन्ते ।
भूपा इव प्रतिभटा भुवि सार्वभौम-
पादाम्बुजं प्रधनयुक्ति पराजिता द्राक् ॥ २१ ॥

(Naya-karṇikā).

though the standpoints are mutually conflicting, they serve collectively to establish the dogmas of the Jaina scripture.[1]

53. Yaśovijaya Gaṇi (1608—1688 A.D.).

Yaśovijaya's life.

Yaśovijaya Gaṇi, a member of the Śvetāmbara sect, was a distinguished logician who flourished at Dabhoi in the Baroda State (Guzerat), approximately between 1608 A.D. and 1688 A.D. He was a spiritual descendant of Hīravijaya Sūri, the well-known Jaina High-priest of the time of the Moghul Emperor Akbar.[2] In about 1626 A.D. he came to Benares,[3] where he studied Nyāya-śāstra in the disguise of a Brāhmaṇa ascetic. By about 1638 A.D. he confessed that he was a Jaina and was asked at once to leave the Sanskrit academies of the Brāhmaṇas. On account of his vast erudition in Logic and Metaphysics he obtained the titles of Upādhyāya, Nyāya-viśārada and Nyāyācārya. He died at Dabhoi in 1688 A.D.[4]

1 *Vide* Introduction to Naya-karṇikā edited by Mohan Lal Desai, pp. 3-4:— The doctrine of *Naya* is often illustrated by the parable of an elephant and blind men. Several blind men desirous of knowing what an elephant was like, touched separate parts of its body and went home with the knowledge they derived in this way. Sitting down to compare notes, they discovered that there was no agreement among them as to the form of the animal. The man who had only touched its leg described it as a huge column, another man who had touched only the ear described it as a winnowing fan, and so forth. They quarrelled among one another until a person who was not blind came before them. He took great pains to explain that their knowledge was only partial, and as such caused confusion. He said that all the different aspects of a thing must be examined in order to gain the complete knowledge of the thing. "A partial knowledge," continues he, "leads to conflict while a complete knowledge establishes harmony."

2

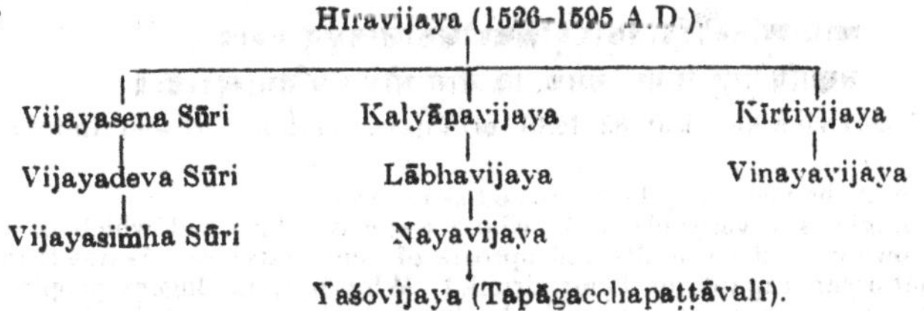

3 रचिया काशीमठे लेवयो मे भवो ।
न्यायदर्शन विपुलभाव पाया ॥ (Mandharastuti).

4 पूर्वं न्यायविशारदत्वबिरुदं काश्यां प्रदत्तं बुधैः
न्यायाचार्यपदं ततः कृतशतग्रन्थस्य यस्यार्पितम् ।
शिष्यप्रार्थनया नयादिविजयप्राज्ञोत्तमानां शिशुः
तत्त्वं किञ्चिदिदं यशोविजय इत्याख्याभृदाख्यातवान् ॥
(Tarkabhāṣā).

His review of other writers.

Yaśovijaya wrote more than one hundred works (in Sanskrit and Guzerati) in which he has preserved a detailed criticism on the Logic of Mithilā and Nadia as taught in the Benares academies of the 17th century A.D. He must have been a man of extraordinary talent, or else he would not have ventured to attack Śiromaṇi, the greatest exponent of Modern Logic in Nadia. He satirises this Brāhmaṇa logician by saying [1] "woe to Bengal where there is Śiromaṇi blind of one eye!"

Conscious of his own erudition he observes in another place: "The ocean of Logic is hard to approach owing to the uproar of waves of the Dīdhiti—Commentary (of Śiromaṇi); yet, is not the water of that ocean capable of being drunk by our cloud-like genius?" [2]

54. Yaśovijaya's Works.

Yaśovijaya was the author of several rare works on Logic such as **Nyāya-pradīpa**, **Tarkabhāṣā**, **Nyāya-rahasya**, **Nyāyāmṛta-taraṅgiṇī** and **Nyāya-khaṇḍa-khādya**. He also wrote a commentary on the Digambara work Aṣṭasāhasrī called **Aṣṭasāhasrī-vṛtti**.[3]

The **Tarkabhāṣā**, which begins with a salutation to Jina,[4] consists of three chapters, viz. (1) Valid knowledge, *pramāṇa*; (2) Knowledge from particular standpoints, *naya*; and (3) Imposition, *niḥkṣepa*. There is also an occasional discussion on *vyāpti-graha*, induction or the process of ascertaining a universal connection between the middle term and the major term.

---

1 अभाग्यं गौडदेशस्य यत्र काणः शिरोमणिः ।

(Nyāyakhaṇḍakhādya, leaf 43, MSS. in possession of Vijayadharma or Dharmavijaya Sūri).

2 न्यायाम्बुधिर्दीधितिकार[illegible]कल्लोलकोलाहलदुर्विगाहः ।
तथापि पातुं न पयः समर्थः किं नाम धीमत् प्रतिभाम्बुवाहः ॥

(Aṣṭasāhasrī vivaraṇa, leaf 82, MSS. of Vijaya-dharma Sūri and Indravijaya Sūri).

The idea of the verse may be expressed as follows:—

Indian Logic is a veritable ocean whose water is saline and which is unapproachable owing to the tumults and uproars of commentators. Is not then the water of that ocean capable of being drunk? Why not, intelligent people, like clouds, can easily approach the ocean and drink its water pure and sweet!

3 For other particulars about Yaśovijaya, see Peterson 6, p. xiv. For his works see the Jaināgama List published in Bombay.

To perpetuate the memory of Yaśovijaya there has been established at Benares a college called Jaina Yaśovijaya-pāṭhaśālā, under the auspices of which the sacred works of the Jainas are being published in a series called Jaina Yaśovijaya-granthamālā.

4 ऐन्द्रवृन्दनतं नत्वा जिनं तत्त्वार्थदेशिनम् ।
प्रमाणनयनिःक्षेपैस्तर्कभाषां तनोम्यहम् ॥

(Tarkabhāṣā. Chapter I).

The **Nyāyāloka** begins with a salutation to Mahāvīra[1] as Paramātman (the supreme spirit) and ends with an entreaty[2] that its author may be freed from lust and hatred, which are the causes of all sufferings. The work discusses the nature of soul (*ātman*), emancipation (*mukti*), inference (*anumāna*), testimony (*āgama*), direct knowledge (*pratyakṣa jñāna*), indirect knowledge (*parokṣa jñāna*), validity of external things[3] (*vāhyārtha-siddhi*), inherence (*samavāya*), negation (*abhāva*), ether (*ākāśa*), substance (*dravya*), etc.

The undermentioned philosophers, philosophical treatises and systems are quoted:—

Naiyāyika, Ucchṛṅkhala Naiyāyika, Sāṁkhya, Cārvāka, Tautātita, Vedāntin, Nyāya, Yauktika, Bauddha, Aupaniṣada, Digambara, Syādvāda-rahasya, Syādvāda-ratnākara, Sammati ṭīkā, Jñānārṇava, Bhāṣyakāra, Jinabhadra Gaṇi Kṣamā-śramaṇa, Bṛhaspati, Dharmakīrti, Ācārya, Cintāmaṇikṛt, Maṇikṛt, Miśra, Vardhamāna, and Pakṣadhara Miśra.

The **Nyāya khaṇḍa khādya**[4] is otherwise called Mahāvīra stavana. It consists of 108 verses composed in eulogy of Mahāvīra and at the same time embodying solutions of the deepest problems of Logic.[5] There is an elaborate commentary in prose by the author himself, elucidating many intricate points in the precise style of modern logicians. The work opens with a salutation to Mahāvīra who is called Śambhu and ends with a brief account of the author himself. The topics treated in the work are:—Soul (*atman*), emancipation (*mukti*), momentariness (*kṣaṇikatva*), origination (*utpatti*), destruction (*dhvaṁsa*), syādvāda, class and individual (*jāti* and *vyakti*), space and time (*deśa* and *kāla*), middle

---

1 प्रणम्य परमात्मानं जगदानन्ददायिनम् ।
न्यायालोकं वितनुते धीमान् न्यायविशारदः ॥
(Nyāyāloka).

2 कृत्वा न्यायालोकं प्रवचनरागाद् यदर्जितं पुण्यम् ।
तेन मम दुःखहेतू रागद्वेषौ विलीयेताम् ।
(Nyāyāloka).

3 यदुक्तं गौतमप्रधानेन,—
चित्तमेव हि संसारो रागादिक्लेशवासितम् ।
तदेव तैर्विनिर्मुक्तं भवान्त इति कथ्यते ॥
(Nyāyāloka, leaf 13, printed at Ahmedabad).

4 The Nyāyakhaṇḍa-khādya has been printed in Bombay.

5 [illegible] ।
सूक्तैर्विकाशिकुसुमैस्तव वीर शम्भोरम्भोजयोश्चरणयोर्वितनोमि पूजाम् ।
(Nyāyakhaṇḍa-khādya).

term and major term (*vyāpya-vyāpaka*), knowledge and external world (*vijñānavāda-vāhyārthavāda*), etc. The undermentioned philosophers, philosophical treatises and systems are referred to :—

Sāṁkhya, Kaṇabhakṣa, Akṣapāda, Naiyāyika, Bauddha, Mādhyamika, Prabhākara, Mīmāṁsaka, Bhāṣya, Vārtika, Ṭīkā, Samantabhadra, Gandhahasti, Sammati, Miśra, Bhaṭṭa, Śrīdhara, Udayana, Nārāyaṇa,[1] Nārāyaṇācārya, Śiromaṇi,[2] Dīdhiti-kāra, Vardhamāna, and Guṇānanda.[3]

The Aṣṭasāhasrī-vivaraṇa,[4] which is a gloss on the Aṣṭasāhasrī of Vidyānanda, opens with an obeisance to Indrabhūti Gautama. The work makes reference to the undermentioned philosophers, philosophical treatises and systems :—Vācaspati, Naiyāyika, Maṇḍana Miśra, Prajñākara, Bhaṭṭa, Prābhākara, Hemacandra, Vācakacakravartī (Umāsvāti), Vaidānti-paśu, Kusumāñjali, Gurumata, Murāribhaṭṭa, Murāri Miśra, Gautamīya, Udayanācārya, Bhaṭṭācārya Jarannaiyāyika, Raghudeva Bhaṭṭācārya,[5] Bhūṣaṇasāra,[6] etc.

---

1 सत्येनैव क्षणभङ्गो वक्तव्य इत्ययमभिप्राय इति नारायणाचार्य्यः ।

(Nyāyakhaṇḍa-khādya, leaf 3. Bombay).

2 जातेर्हि दृष्टिनियमो नहि नः स्वभावाद्
जातिं विना न च ततो व्यवहारसिद्धिः ।
उत्प्रेक्षितं ननु शिरोमणि काणदृष्टेः
तद्वाक्य बोधरचितस्य न किञ्चिदेव ॥

(Nyāyakhaṇḍa-khādya, leaf 42, Bombay).

3 यच्चेयं यति नवये भावभूतव्यूहकालाप्रतिसिद्धावपि प्रागभावस्य कालतया व्यवहारधारणाय चेत्यपि प्रयोजनवदिति गुणानन्देनोक्तं तदसत् ॥

(Nyāyakhaṇḍa-khādya, leaf 2. Bombay).

4 ऐन्द्रमहः प्रणिधाय न्यायविशारदयतिर्यशोविजयः ।
विषमामष्टसहस्रीमष्टसहस्र्या विवेचयति ॥

(Āṣṭasāhasrī-vivaraṇa, MSS. belonging to Vijayadharma Sūri and Indravijaya Sūri).

5 Raghudeva is referred to in leaves 4, 22 of Aṣṭasāhasrī.

6 The Bhūṣaṇasāra (Vyākaraṇa) is referred to in leaves 34, 35, etc.

CHAPTER IV.

Continuity of Jaina Logic.[1]

55. THE CONCILIATORY CHARACTER OF JAINA LOGIC.

No conflict with the Brāhmaṇas.

In the previous pages there has been given an indication of the services rendered by the Jainas and the Buddhists in the formation of the Mediæval School of Indian Logic. Since the Brāhmaṇas did not in respect of their social practices differ so markedly from the Jainas as they did from the Buddhists, their attack on the Jaina Logic was not so violent as that on the Buddhist Logic. In fact the logical theories of the Jainas are in many instances akin to those of the Brāhmaṇas. The terms *pratyakṣa* (perception), *anumāna* (inference), *upamāna* (comparison), *āgama* (verbal testimony), *āharaṇa* or *udāharaṇa* (example), *chala* (quibble), etc., of the Sthānāṅga-sūtra and the Sūtra-kṛtāṅga of the Jainas are in their meanings similar to, if not altogether identical with, the corresponding terms of the Caraka saṁhitā and the Nyāya-sūtra of the Brāhmaṇas. There was in the Logic of the Brāhmaṇas a casual review of the syllogism of ten members as propounded in certain works of the Jainas, but there was no protracted quarrel on that account between the two parties. The Jaina logicians quoted Brāhmaṇic authors[2] generally in an academic spirit. The special Jaina doctrines of *Naya* (method) and *sapta-bhaṅgī* (sevenfold paralogism), though occasionally criticised, did not receive any rude blows from the Brāhmaṇas.

No bitter rivalry with the Buddhists.

The Jainas, in so far as they wrote regular treatises on Logic, did not differ much from the Buddhists in respect of their subject and style. The Nyāyāvatāra, by the Śvetāmbara Jaina logician Siddhasena Divākara (500 A.D.), traverses almost the same ground as the Nyāya praveśa of the Buddhist logician Dignāga (450–530 A.D.). Rabhasa Nandi, a Digambara Jaina logician, wrote a commentary called Sambandhoddyota on the Sambandha parīkṣā of the Buddhist logician Dharmakīrti (635

---

[1] See Satis Chandra Vidyabhusana's "Mediæval School of Indian Logic," his edition of "Nyāya-sāra" with the Nyāya-tātparya-dīpikā of Jaya-siṁha Sūri; V.A. Smith's "Early History of India" and "Akbar"; Epigraphia Indica Vol. II; and "Jaina Inscriptions" compiled by Puran Chand Nahar.

[2] Akṣapāda was attacked by Siddhasena Divākara in his Sammatitarka, and by Haribhadra Sūri in his Śāstravārtāsamuccaya and Anekānta-jayapatākā. Uddyotakara (Vārtikakāra) was attacked by Abhayadeva Sūri of Rājagaccha.

A.D.). The Pramāṇa-vārtika-ṭīkā of Jaina Kalyāṇa-candra is likewise a commentary on the Pramāṇa-vārtika of the Buddhist Dharmakīrti (635 A.D.). Dharmottara-ṭippanaka is the title of a Jaina commentary by Mallavādin (about 962 A.D.) on the Buddhist work Nyāya-bindu-ṭīkā of Dharmottara (847 A.D.). If the Buddhist author Śānta Rakṣita (749 A.D.) instituted in his Tattvasaṁgraha an inquiry into the Jaina doctrine of soul, the Jaina author Haribhadra Sūri (1129 A.D.) gave in his Ṣaḍdarśana-samuccaya a complete summary of the Buddhist philosophy. In fact there was no bitter rivalry between the Jainas and the Buddhists.

56. Royal Patronage and Persecution.

Patronage.

From time to time Jainism enjoyed patronage as well as suffered persecution at the hands of the rulers. King Candra Gupta,[1] who carried on controversies in the spirit of scholars, was a great supporter of the Jaina religion which spread widely in Northern India and was introduced into Mysore by Bhadrabāhu. Samprati, a grandson of Emperor Aśoka, accepted the Jaina faith which was welcomed throughout the Deccan about 215 B.C. The Śvetāmbara Jaina logician Siddhasena Divākara (Kṣapaṇaka) was patronised at the court of Vikramāditya in Ujjainī about 500 A.D. The Chinese pilgrim Hwen-thsang, who visited the Pallava, Coḷa and Pāṇḍya kingdoms in 640 A.D., found that Jainism was the prevailing religion in Drāviḍa, old Trichinopoly and Malakūṭa, and that it was popular in Mathurā, Vaiśālī, Eastern Bengal and Southern Mārāṭhā country. The Digambara Jaina logician Akalaṅka Deva enjoyed favour at the court of the Rāṣṭrakūṭa King Kṛṣṇarāja I or Subhatuṅga about 750 A.D. Hema Candra Sūri, surnamed Kalikāla-sarvajña, was the preceptor of Mahārāja Kumāra Pāla of Guzerat about 1142–1172 A.D.

Persecution.

In the latter half of the seventh century A.D. there occurred, however, a terrible persecution of Jainism in Southern India. King Kūna, Sundara or Nedumāran Pāṇḍya, who had been brought up as a Jaina, became a pupil of Saint Tirujñāna Sambandar and accepted the Śaiva faith. Displaying the zeal of a convert he persecuted with savage cruelty his late co-religionists of whom no fewer than eight thousand were put to death. Mahendra Varman of the Pallava dynasty, whose rule extended to Trichinopoly, was

[1] If we suppose this Candra Gupta to be identical with Candra Gupta Maurya, the date of introduction of Jainism into Mysore must be about 309 B.C. On the contrary if he is the same as Candra Gupta II, Mysore could not have welcomed Jainism before 375 A.D. The date of Bhadrabāhu will have to be determined accordingly.

originally a Jaina. Through the influence of a Tamil saint he accepted Śaivism, and destroyed the large Jaina monastery of Pāṭaliputtriam in South Arcot at about 610 A.D. In the Cālukya Kingdom of Vātāpi, where Jainism flourished to a certain extent during 550–750 A.D., Buddhism was supplanted by Śaivism and Vaiṣṇavism. King Amoghavarṣa of the Rāṣṭrakūṭa line, whose capital was at Mānyakheṭa (in the Nizam's Dominions) devoted the last part of his life to ascetic practices and patronised the Digambara Jaina faith during 815–877 A.D. Jainism made a rapid progress in his kingdom up to the 10th century A D. Ajaya Deva, a Śaiva King of Guzerat (about 1174–76 A.D) mercilessly persecuted the Jainas and put their leader to death.

No hostility from the Mahomedans.

In spite of such persecutions the Jaina religion went on flourishing in the Hindu period up till 1200 A.D. During the Mahomedan rule which followed, Jainism remained unperturbed. The Pathan King, Firoz Shah Tughlak (1351–1388 A.D.), was kind towards the Jainas, and the Moghal Emperors showed them great favours. Three eminent Jaina teachers—Hīravijaya Sūri, Vijayasena Sūri and Bhānucandra Upādhyāya—were received with high honours at the court of Akbar who is said to have been a convert to Jainism and to have prohibited the killing of animals on certain days.

57. Support of the Jaina Community.

Rights and privileges of the laity.

Though in all periods the Jainas enjoyed a fair share of royal patronage, the main source of their stay and strength lay in the community of Jaina laymen. The founder of Jainism left the church not entirely at the mercy of the monks (*sādhu*) and nuns (*sādhvī*), but placed it also in the hands of the laymen (*śrāvaka*) and laywomen (*śrāvikā*) called respectively the male and female devotees. In all religious and social ceremonies the lay people exercise control in the full measure. It is at their choice and with their permission that the head of the church called *Ācārya* can be appointed. The management of temples and places of pilgrimage is entrusted entirely to the lay people, who select the residence of monks and nuns.

Aid to literary men.

It is on account of the mutual help of the monks and lay people that the Jaina church has continued undisturbed. The lay people, who belong mainly to the Vaiśya (merchant) community command the wealth of India. They have uniformly supported Jaina authors, and so long as they continue, the Jaina logicians will never have to recede from literary pursuits for want of funds.

58. Jaina Logic will not be extinct.

We have seen that the Jaina monks were very seldom militant against the Brāhmaṇas or Buddhists. They also avoided, as far as practicable, incurring the displeasure of their rulers, and framed their ecclesiastical rules in liberal spirit to ensure the sympathy of the laity. Under such circumstances it is not at all strange that Jainism has not died and there is no fear that the Jaina Logic will ever be extinct.

SECTION II.

The Buddhist Logic.

(CIRCA 570 B.C.—1200 A.D.).

CHAPTER I.

Topics of Logic mentioned in the old Buddhist Literature.

59. BUDDHA GAUTAMA (570 B.C.—490 B.C.).

The Buddhists maintain that their religion is eternal. It was taught at different cycles by sages called Buddhas (the Enlightened Ones) or Tathāgatas (those who have realized the truth). In the present cycle, called *Mahā-bhadra-kalpa* (the very blessed cycle), four Buddhas are said to have already appeared, *viz.* Krakucchanda, Kanaka Muni, Kāśyapa and Gautama, while the fifth, *viz.* Maitreya, is yet to be born.[1]

Of the past Buddhas the last, *viz.* Buddha Gautama, otherwise called Śākya Muni, was born at Kapilavastu (modern Nigliva in the Nepal Terai) about 570 B.C., and attained *nirvāṇa* at Kuśīnagara (modern Kuśinārā or Kasia near Gorakhpur) about 490 B.C.[2] He passed almost his whole life in Magadha (modern Behar). He is regarded by modern scholars as the real founder of Buddhism, while his predecessors are considered as purely mythical.

60. ORIGIN OF THE PĀLI BUDDHIST LITERATURE (490 B.C.—76 B.C.).

Buddha Gautama is said to have delivered his teachings in the Māgadhī or Pāli language. On his death these teachings were rehearsed by the Buddhist monks in three councils[3] held at Rāja-

---

1 *Vide* Hardy's Manual of Buddhism, second edition, pp. 88—91.

2 The exact date of Buddha is unknown. According to the Mahāvaṁsa, Buddha was born in 623 B.C. and attained nirvāṇa in 543 B.C. The date of Buddha's nirvāṇa is placed by European scholars between 470—480 B.C. Cf. Dr. Fleet's article on "The Date of Buddha's Death" in the Journal of the Royal Asiatic Society of Great Britain and Ireland, January 1904. We shall not be far wrong if we place Buddha's birth in 570 B.C. and his nirvāṇa in 490 B.C. There is a positive statement in chapter V of the Mahāvaṁsa that Aśoka was installed on the throne of Magadha 218 years after the nirvāṇa of Buddha. As Aśoka's installation took place about 272 B.C., the date of Buddha's nirvāṇa could approximately be placed in 490 B.C. Buddha, who lived 80 years, seems, therefore, to have been born about 570 B.C.

3 For an account of the first and second councils, *vide* Vinaya Piṭaka, Culla

gṛha, Vaiśālī and Pāṭalīputra under the patronage of kings Ajātaśatru, Kālāśoka and Aśoka about the year 490 B.C., 390 B.C. and 255 B.C.[1] respectively. The texts of the teachings as discussed and settled in these councils form the sacred scripture of the Buddhists. This scripture is called in Pāli *Tipiṭaka* or *Piṭakattaya* and in Sanskrit *Tripiṭaka* or *Piṭakatraya*, which signifies 'Three Baskets.' It consists of the Sermon Basket (Sutta Piṭaka), Discipline Basket (Vinaya Piṭaka), and the Metaphysical Basket (Abhidhamma Piṭaka), each of which embodies a large number of distinct works.

The monks assembled in the First Council, that is, in the Council of Kāśyapa, in 490 B.C., were called (1) Theras, and the scripture canonised by them was the basis of Theravāda. Subsequently ten thousand monks of Vaiśālī having violated certain rules of Theravāda were, by the decision of the Second Council in 390 B.C, expelled from the community of the Theras. These excluded priests were called (2) Mahāsāṅghikas, who were the first heretical sect of the Buddhists. They made certain additions and alterations in the Theravāda. Afterwards, within two hundred years from the *nirvāṇa* of Buddha, 14 other heretical sects[2] arose, *viz.* (3) Gokulika, (4) Ekabbohārika, (5) Paññatti (6) Bāhulika, (7) Cetiya, (8) Sabbatthi, (9) Dhammaguttika, (10) Kassapīya, (11) Saṅkantika, (12) Sutta, (13) Himavata, (14) Rājagirīya, (15) Siddhatthika, (16) Pubbaselīya, (17) Aparaselīya, and (18) Vajiriya.

Just at the close of the Third Council about 255 B.C., the teachings of Buddha as canonised by the Theras in the form of the *Tipiṭaka*, were carried[3] by Mahinda, son of Emperor Aśoka, to the island of Ceylon where they were perpetuated by priests in oral tradition They are said to have been committed to writing[4], for the first time in Ceylon, in the reign of Vaṭṭagāmaṇi during 104—76 B.C. Besides the *Tipiṭaka* there were numerous other works written in Pāli which have immensely added to the bulk of the Pāli literature.

Vagga. 11th and 12th Khandhakas, translated by Rhys Davids and Oldenberg, S.B.E. series, vol. XX, pp. 370, 386. For an account of the third council as also of the first and second, *vide* Wijesiṁha's translation of the Mahāvaṁsa, chapter V, pp. 25-29, as also chapters III and IV.

1 The first council was held in the year of Buddha's nirvāṇa, while the second council took place 100 years later. Aśoka ascended the throne in 272 B.C. (*vide* Vincent A. Smith's Aśoka, p. 63), and it was in the 17th year of his reign, that is, in 255 B.C., that the third council took place (*vide* Wijesiṁha's Mahāvaṁsa, p. 29).

2 For a discussion about the variant names and subdivisions of these sects, *vide* Wijesiṁha's Mahāvaṁsa, part I, chapter V, p. 15; and Dr. Rhys Davids' "Schools of Buddhist Belief" in the Journal of the Royal Asiatic Society of Great Britain and Ireland, 1892, pp. 1—37.

3 *Vide* the Mahāvaṁsa, chapter XII.

4 *Vide* the Mahāvaṁsa, chapter XXXIII. Cf. also Dr. Alwis's Lecture on the Pali Language in the Journal of the Pali Text Society, London, 1883, p. 42.

61. LOGICAL TOPICS IN THE PĀLI LITERATURE.

In the *Tipiṭaka*—nay in the whole Pāli literature[1]—there is not a single treatise on Logic. *Paṭicca-samuppāda* (the Chain of Interdependent Causes or the Wheel of Life), which represents the central teaching of Buddha, throws some light on the doctrines of self (or soul) and sufferings, but none on logic or processes of reasoning. The only topic bearing upon Logic which has been touched on in the Pāli works, is the division of knowledge into six kinds. In the Tipiṭaka[2] knowledge (*Viññāṇa*[3]) has been classified as (1) ocular (*cakkhu-viññāṇaṁ*), (2) auditory (*sota viññāṇaṁ*), (3) olfactory (*ghāna-viññāṇaṁ*), (4) gustatory (*jivhā-viññāṇaṁ*), (5) tactual (*kāya-viññāṇaṁ*), and (6) mental (*mano-viññāṇaṁ*). But this classification has not been carried far enough to lay the foundation of a Logic that deserves the name of science.

In the Tipiṭaka there are, however, occasional references to logical topics and to a class of men who were called *Takki* (in Sanskrit: *Tarkin*) or *Takkika* (in Sanskrit: *Tārkika*)—that is, those versed in reasoning. It is not known whether these men were Buddhists, Jainas or Brāhmaṇas, perhaps they were recruited from all communities. They were not logicians in the proper sense of the term, but they appear to me to have been sophists who indulged in quibble and casuistry.

62. Suttapiṭaka: Dīgha-nikāya: Brahmajāla sutta (490 B.C.).

Casuists and sophists.

In the Brahma-jāla-sutta,[4] which forms a part of the Dīgha Nikāya of the Sutta Piṭaka and was rehearsed in the First Buddhist Council about 490 B.C., there is mention of certain Śramaṇas and Brāhmaṇas who were *takki* (argumentationists) and *vīmaṁsi* (casuists) and indulged in *takka* (argumentations) and *vīmaṁsa* (casuistry). These Śramaṇas and Brāhmaṇas from the standpoints of their philo-

---

[1] Consult Mrs. Rhys Davids' article on Logic (Buddhist) in Dr. James Hastings' Encyclopaedia of Religion and Ethics.

[2] For an explanation of Paṭicca-samuppāda or *Pratītya-samutpāda*, the doctrine of mutual dependence, see Satis Chandra Vidyabhusana's article on the subject in the Journal of the Buddhist Text Society, Vol. VII, part I. For the division of knowledge, *vide* the Aṅguttara Nikāya III, 61. 8, edited by Dr. Morris in the Pāli Text Society series of London. *Vide* also the Dhammasaṅgaṇi, and compare Pariccheda IV of the Abhidhammatthasaṅgaha which, though not included in the Tipiṭaka, sums up the topics of the Abhidhamma Piṭaka.

[3] *Viññāṇa* is translated as knowledge or consciousness, such as *cakkhuviññāṇa* signifies ocular knowledge or eye-consciousness.

[4] The Brahmajāla-sutta, chaps. I—III, included in Dialogues of the Buddha, translated by Prof. T. W. Rhys Davids, London. The Brahmajāla-sutta, bhāṇavāraṁ 1—3, included in the Dīgha Nikāya, edited by T. W. Rhys Davids and J. E. Carpenter, London.

sophical views were divided into various classes such as the eternalists (*sassata-vādā*), eternalist-non-eternalists (*ekacca-sassatikā ekacca-asassatikā*), and the annihilationists (*uccheda-vādā*).

With regard to the eternalists who were perhaps the followers of (the Sāṁkhya philosophy of) Kapila, Buddha says :—

Eternalists.

There are, brethren, some recluses and Brāhmaṇas who are eternalists, and who, on four grounds, proclaim that both the soul and the world are eternal. . . . . They are addicted to logic and reasoning [argumentation and casuistry], and give utterance to the following conclusion of their own, beaten out by their argumentations and based on their sophistry : "eternal is the soul; and the world, giving birth to nothing new, is steadfast as a mountain-peak, as a pillar firmly fixed; and these living creatures, though they transmigrate and pass away, fall from one state of existence and spring up in another, yet they are for ever and ever."

With regard to the eternalist-non-eternalists who were perhaps the followers (of the Ānvīkṣikī) of Medhātithi-Gautama, Buddha says :—

Eternalists-non-eternalists.

There are, brethren, some recluses and Brāhmaṇas who are eternalists with regard to some things, and in regard to others non-eternalists; who on four grounds maintain that the soul and the world are partly eternal and partly not. . . . . They are addicted to logic and reasoning [argumentation and casuistry], and give utterance to the following conclusion of their own, beaten out by their argumentations and based on their sophistry : "This which is called eye and ear and nose and tongue and body is a self which is impermanent, unstable, not eternal, subject to change. But this which is called heart, or mind, or consciousness, is a self which is permanent, steadfast, eternal, and knows no change, and will remain for ever and ever."

With regard to the annihilationists who were perhaps the followers of the Lokāyata philosophy, Buddha observes :—

Annihilationists.

There are, brethren, recluses and Brāhmaṇas who are annihilationists, who in seven ways maintain the cutting off, the destruction, the annihilation of a living being . . . . In the first place, brethren, they put forth the following opinion, the following view : "Since, sir, this soul has form, is built up of the four elements, and is the offspring of father and mother, it is cut off, destroyed on the dissolution of the body; and does not continue after death; and then, sir, the soul is completely annihilated."

There are other classes of Śramaṇas and Brāhmaṇas such as

a class of fortuitous-originists (*adhicca-samuppannika*) of whom Buddha speaks as follows :—

"In this case, brethren, some recluse or Brāhmaṇa is addicted to *logic* [sophism] and *reasoning* [casuistry]." He gives utterance to the following conclusion of his own, beaten out by his *argumentations* and based on his *sophistry*: "The soul and the world arose without a cause."

63. **Suttapiṭaka : Majjhimanikāya : Anumāna sutta**
(490 B.C.).

"Anumāna sutta," which presupposes the use of the word *anumāna* in the sense of "inference" or rather "guess," is the title of a chapter of the **Majjhima Nikāya**, while the word *vāda* in the sense of discussion occurs in the Upālivāda-sutta of the same Nikāya of the Suttapiṭaka.[1]

64. **Suttapiṭaka : Khuddaka Nikāya : Udāna**
(490 B.C.).

In the **Udāna**, which is included in the Khuddaka Nikāya of the Sutta Piṭaka and is supposed to have been rehearsed in the three Buddhist Councils during 490 B.C.—255 B.C., we read :—

"As long as the perfect Buddhas do not appear, the *Takkikas* [sophists] are not corrected nor are the Sāvakas: owing to their evil views they are not released from misery."[2]

This passage leaves no doubt that the *Takkikas* were sophists.

65. **Vinaya-piṭaka : Parivāra**
(490 B.C.).

The logical procedure of a Judicial Council of Monks.

Four kinds of cases for settlement (*adhikaraṇa*).

In the **Parivāra**,[3] a work of the Vinaya-piṭaka, there is mention of four kinds of *adhikaraṇa*, cases for settlement, *viz.*: (1) *vivādādhikaraṇa*, a case pertaining to differences of opinion, (2) *anuvādādhikaraṇa*, a case in which one party accuses another party of the violation of a rule of good conduct; (3) *āpattādhikaraṇa*, a case in

---

[1] *Vide* Majjhima Nikāya, vol. I, 15th sutta, and vol. II, 5th sutta.

[2] The original of this passage runs as follows :—
Yāva sammā sambuddhā loke n'uppajjanti, na *takkikā* sujjhanti na c'āpi sāvakā, dudditthī na dukkhā pamuccare'ti.
—Udānaṁ, vi, 10, edited by Paul Steinthal in the Pāli Text Society series, London.

[3] The Parivāra, chapters IX—XIII, included in the Vinaya-piṭakaṁ, vol. V, edited by Dr. H. Oldenberg. *Vide* also the Pātimokkha of the Vinaya-piṭakaṁ.

which a monk has actually transgressed an established rule of good conduct; and (4) *kiccādhikaraṇa*, a case relating to the formal procedure of an ecclesiastical act.

Seven rules for the settlement of cases (*adhikaraṇa-samathā dhammā*).

There are laid down seven rules for the settlement of cases (*adhikaraṇa-samathā dhammā*), *viz* :—

(1) *Sammukhā vinaya*, settlement in presence, which applies to a case that must be conducted in the presence of a council of monks (*saṅgha*), the complainant and the respondent, in accordance with the sacred procedure appropriate for it.

(2) *Sati vinaya*, settlement from recollection, which applies to a case in which an Arhat (passionless person) is implicated. Such a case, which is evidently false, may be settled simply by asking the Arhat to recollect his past misdeeds, if any. An Arhat, being totally devoid of passions, is not at all liable to the transgression of any rule. Still to try him through *sati-vinaya*, is to settle the present charge and to grant him immunity from all further charges.

(3) *Amūḷha-vinaya*, settlement for the insane, which applies to a case in which a person while committing a crime was in an abnormal state of mind, and was therefore not liable to any charge for the committal of the crime. If at the time of his trial he denies all knowledge about the crime, he will be exempted from the charge once for all.

(4) *Paṭiññāya kāretabbaṁ*, settlement by an undertaking, applies to a case in which the person implicated admits his guilt and promises to refrain from committing it in the future.

(5) *Yebhuyyasikā*, settlement by a majority, applies to a case which is settled by the majority of votes of the members.

(6) *Tassa pāpiyyasikā*, settlement with the prospect of further inquiry, applies to a case in which, the respondent having neither admitted nor denied a charge, the council of monks (*saṅgha*), with a view to awakening him to a sense of responsibility, declares that he will be expelled from the council any day that the charge is proved true, but will be welcomed into the council when the charge is proved false.

(7) *Tiṇa vatthāraka*, covering over with grass, applies to a case in which a complainant and his respondent go on bringing charges and counter-charges against each other. The council of monks (*saṅgha*), finding no easy way to settle the case. hush it up without listening to either of the parties.

Of the four cases enumerated above the first may be settled by rules 1 and 5, the second by rules 1, 2, 3 and 6, the third by rules 1, 4 and 7, and the fourth by rule 1 alone.

A complaint (*codanā*).

A complaint, complainant and respondent.

A *complaint* (*codanā*) is intended for humiliating a person by reminding him of the nature of his criminal action. The complaint may be well founded or unfounded. It may arise from any thing seen, heard or apprehended.

The *complainant* or *plaintiff* (*codaka*) must institute his complaint at the proper time, in its true detail, in gentle and relevant terms and in good spirit.

The *respondent, accused* or *defendant* (*cuditaka*) must speak the truth and must not show temper.

A judicial council of monks (*saṅgha*).

A *council of monks* (*saṅgha*) engaged in trying a case, must receive the arguments of the complainant and the respondent who are the parties of the case. Deliberation (*matikamma*) must be shared in by each member of the council.

Members of a council (*saṁgāmāvacara bhikkhu*).

The monks who constitute the members of a judicial council (called in Pāli *saṁgāmāvacara bhikkhu*) must approach the council with meekness of spirit. They must know how to take their respective seats. They must refrain from irrelevant and useless talk. They may speak on good law, or they may solicit their brother-monks to speak on it, or they may remain absolutely silent.

The members must ascertain the nature of the case under trial, the nature of the breach of morality, the section of the moral code applicable to the case and the nature of the personnel of the council and the parties. They must not be biassed. They should, when necessary, employ persuasion and exhortation towards the respondent and should at times express their satisfaction at his conduct.

They must not, on account of their own superiority in knowledge or seniority in age, hold anybody in contempt.

The judge or umpire (*anuvijjaka*).

The judge (*anuvijjaka*), elected by the council to act as such, must not talk rashly or in haste. He must refrain from talking of a subject which is in itself unprofitable, and which may rouse dispute or ill-feeling. He must hear attentively what the parties have to say. Having the welfare of all at heart, he must not hastily accept the version of one party as true. The complainant will say that the respondent "is guilty," *āpanno*, while the respondent himself will plead "not guily," *anāpanno*. Instead of discarding the statement of either of the parties, the judge must see that each party is consistent with his first statement.

The judge must satisfy himself that the complainant understands the nature of the complaint he makes. As regards the respondent the judge must not put to him questions which may refer to his preceptor, teacher, brother-priest, resident pupil, caste, name, family, tradition, clan or native place. The reason is that thereby the judge may be biassed towards or prejudiced against the respondent, and his judgment may be influenced by affection, hatred, fear or delusion.

The judge must have respect for the whole council and not for a particular individual, for justice and not for private interest, for what is really good and not for what is agreeable to a particular company in which he is interested. He must investigate the case in season and not out of season, as it is and not as it is not, gently and not rudely, with good will and with his limbs and sense-organs duly restrained.

He must control the complainant and the respondent, must take note of what they say, and must not add any thing that they do not say. He must make the languid cheerful, the timid hopeful, and the angry cool He must not act from affection, hatred, fear or delusion. A judge who behaves himself in this way is a true follower of Buddha and is justly loved by all people.

66. Vinaya-piṭaka: Pātimokkha (490 B.C.).

As an instance of the method in which monks combined in a council (*saṅgha*) used to perform an ecclesiastical act (*kiccādhikaraṇa*), I explain the several stages and requisites of the Buddhist sabbath called *uposatha*[1] in accordance with the Pātimokkhupadesa[1] of the Vinaya-piṭaka.

An ecclesiastical act.

Uposatha (*Sabbath*).

1. *Pubba-karaṇa*, preparation, which refers to the following requisites:—

(*a*) *Sammajjanī*, brooming or cleansing the ground, on which monks are to assemble.

(*b*) *Padīpa*, lighting a lamp, if the uposatha is celebrated in the night

[1] *Vide* the Pāli Pātimokkha of the Vinaya-piṭaka, and also the translation of the Vinaya texts by T. W. Rhys Davids and H. Oldenberg. Compare also the Tibetan version of the Pātimokkha called So-sor-thar-pa edited with the Tibetan text and an English translation by Dr. Satis Chandra Vidyabhusana in J.A.S.B., nos. 3 and 4, 1915. *Pubba-karaṇa* and *pubba-kicca* are explained fully in the Kaṅkhā-vitaraṇī and Samantapāsādikā of Buddhaghoṣa.

(c) *Udaka*, water, for drinking or washing one's face and leg.
(d) *Āsana*, seat, on which monks are to sit.

2. *Pubba-kicca*, the preliminary acts, which refer to the following :—

(a) *Chanda*, vote by proxy. If a monk cannot, owing to any unavoidable cause, attend a council, he may authorize a brother-monk to exercise his vote. The formula of authorization runs thus :-

chandaṁ dammi, I give authority;
chandaṁ me hara, do ye receive my authority;
chandaṁ me ārocehi, do ye convey my authority to the council

(b) *Pārisuddhi*, purity. A monk who cannot attend a council of sabbath, must inform it of his purity through a brother-monk.

(c) *Utukkhāna*, naming the season. In a year there are three seasons, *viz* the winter, summer and rain, in each of which there are celebrated eight *uposathas* (sabbaths). The third and seventh *uposathas* of every season are held on the 14th day of the moon while the remaining six are held on the 15th day of the moon. *Uposathas* are of three kinds, *viz.* those held on the 14th day of the moon, those held on the 15th day of the moon, and those held on any day, by the common consent of a council of monks, to establish amity between two contending parties.

(d) *Bhikkhu-gaṇanā*, counting the number of monks present in a council A council may consist of four, five, ten, twenty or more monks.

(e) *Ovāda*, arrangement for the instruction to be imparted to a council of nuns by a monk deputed for the purpose.

3. *Pattakallaṁ*, in season. When the *pubba-karaṇa* and *pubba-kicca* are over, the council should see whether it was the right time when every thing was in order and there was nothing objectionable.

4. *Pātimokkhuddesa*, recitation of the code of monastic laws.

The introductory part of the Pātimokkha, called *nidāna*, is cited below :—

O brethren, listen to me, I pray. To-day is the 14th (or 15th) day of the lunar month for the celebration of sabbath by the council of monks. If it is convenient to the council, let us celebrate sabbath and recite the (rules of) Pātimokkha.

Have the preliminary acts been performed ? O brethren, do ye now express your purity. I shall recite the Pātimokkha.

We shall all listen to it calmly and bear the same in mind.

Whosoever among you has committed any fault, let him confess it. If there is no fault, say nothing whatsoever. If nothing is said I am to understand that the brethren are perfectly pure. As a monk gives an answer if a question is put to him individually, so each monk is to give an answer when I repeat my question three times in a council of monks like this. Whatsoever monk, in such a council, thus interrogated three times, does not confess a fault of which there is recollection, is guilty of uttering a deliberate lie. The uttering of a deliberate lie has, O brethren, been declared by Lord Buddha to be a sin called obstacle. Therefore a monk, who has committed a fault and desires to be cleansed therefrom, should confess it if he remembers the same. Having made confession he will reside in happiness. But if he does not confess or declare his fault, he will not be happy.

O brethren, I have recited the Introduction to the Pātimokkha. I now ask you whether you are perfectly pure. I ask you a second time and a third time. The brethren are perfectly pure; therefore they say nothing; so do I understand.

Then are recited the four rules of defeat, thirteen rules of suspension from monkhood, two rules regarding undetermined matters, thirty rules regarding sins which involve forfeiture, ninety-two rules regarding sins which require expiation, four rules regarding matters which must be confessed, one hundred and twelve rules which must be learnt (committed to memory), and seven rules for the settlement of cases. If any monk makes any confession, it is noted and considered.

5. After the Pātimokkha in its entirety has been recited, the monks should leave the sabbath hall with a feeling of universal love.

67. Abhidhamma-piṭaka: Kathāvatthuppakaraṇa (ABOUT 255 B.C.).

The **Kathāvatthuppakaraṇa**, a work of the Abhidhamma-piṭaka, composed by Moggaliputta Tissa at the Third Buddhist Council during the reign of Aśoka about 255 B.C.,[1] mentions *anuyoga* (inquiry), *āharaṇa* (illustration), *paṭiññā* (in Sanskrit: *pratijñā*, proposition), *upanaya* (in Sanskrit, too: *upanaya*, appplication of reason), *niggaha* (in Sanskrit: *nigraha*, humiliation or defeat), etc.,[2] which are the technical terms of Logic. Though Moggaliputta Tissa has not made any reference to a specific work on Logic, his mention of some of its technical terms warrants us to suppose that that science in some shape existed in India in his time, about 255 B.C.

---

[1] Aśoka ascended the throne of Magadha in 272 B.C. (*vide* Vincent A. Smith's Aśoka, p. 63). In the seventeenth year of his reign the Third Buddhist Council took place (Wijesiṁha's Mahāvaṁsa, p. 29).

[2] *Niggaha-catukkaṁ* is the name of a section of the first chapter of the Kathāvatthuppakaraṇa. *Upanaya-catukkaṁ* is the name of another section of that work. A passage, in which the terms *paṭiññā* and *niggaha* occur, is quoted below:—

No ca mayaṁ tayā tattha hetāya paṭiññāya hevaṁ paṭijānantā hevaṁ niggahetabbo (Kathāvatthuppakaraṇa, Siamese edition, p. 3, kindly lent to me by Anagārika H. Dharmapāla).

In the commentary on the above passage even *chala* (quibble), which is another technical term of Logic, has been used.

Evaṁ tena, chalena niggahe āropite idāni tass'eva paṭiññāya dhammena samena attavāde jayaṁ dassetuṁ anulomanaye pucchā sakavādissa attano nissāya paṭiññām paravādissa laddhiya okāsaṁ adatvā. . . .

68. Methods of Disputation as illustrated in the Kathāvatthu.

As a specimen of the method of reasoning carried on during the time of Aśoka, the following controversy (*kathā*) between a Theravādin (a Buddhist disputant who did not admit the existence of the soul, *puggala*, as a genuine reality) and a Puggalavādin (a heretic respondent who asserted that there was a genuine reality called soul, *puggala*) is quoted from the Kathāvatthu[1]:—

A case presented by a disputant in a regular form (*anuloma*).

Theravādin: Is the soul (*puggala*) known in the sense of a genuinely real thing?

Puggalavādin: Yes.

Theravādin: Is the soul known in the same way as a genuinely real thing?

Puggalavādin: No, that cannot be said.

Theravādin: Acknowledge your defeat.

(i) If the soul is known in the sense of a genuinely real thing, then, good sir, you should also say that the soul is known in the same way as any other genuinely real thing is known.

(ii) That which you say here is wrong, *viz.* (*a*) the soul is known in the sense of a genuinely real thing, but not (*b*) known in the same way as any other genuinely real thing is known.

(iii) If the statement (*b*) is not admitted, then indeed the statement (*a*) cannot be admitted either.

(iv) In admitting the statement (*a*) but in denying the statement (*b*), you are wrong.

A rejoinder by the respondent (*paṭikamma*).

Puggalavādin: Is the soul not known in the sense of a genuinely real thing?

Theravādin: No, it is not known.

Puggalavādin: Is it unknown in the same way as a genuinely real thing is known?

Theravādin: No, that cannot be said.

Puggalavādin: Acknowledge the rejoinder.

(Kathāvatthuppakaraṇa-aṭṭhakathā, published by the Pali Text Society of London, p. 13).

[1] Kathāvatthu, vol. I, pp. 1–69, edited by A. C. Taylor and published by the Pāli Text Society, London.

Compare the English translation called "Points of Controversy," by Mr. Shwe Zan Aung and Mrs. Rhys Davids, published by the Pāli Text Society, London, pp. 1–70.

(i) If the soul is not known in the sense of a genuinely real thing, then, good sir, you should also say that the soul is unknown in the same way as a genuinely real thing is known.

(ii) That which you say here is wrong, *viz.* (*a*) the soul is not known in the sense of a genuinely real thing, but not (*b*) unknown in the same way as a genuinely real thing is known.

(iii) If the statement (*b*) is denied, then the statement (*a*) cannot be admitted either.

(iv) In admitting the statement (*a*) but in denying the statement (*b*), you are wrong.

The rejoinder causing entanglement or defeat on the disputant (*niggaha*).

Puggalavādin: If in your opinion we should say that the soul is not known in the sense of a genuinely real thing but not unknown in the same way as a genuinely real thing is known, then, you have, by your own proposition, assented to the truth of our statement and have acknowledged defeat.

(i) Your statement—that the soul is not known in the sense of a genuinely real thing, but not unknown in the same way as a genuinely real thing is known—is wrong.

(ii) You should not say that the statement (*a*) is to be admitted, but the statement (*b*) is not to be admitted.

(iii) If the statement (*b*) is not admitted, then the statement (*a*) cannot be admitted either.

(iv) In admitting the statement (*a*) but in denying the statement (*b*), you are wrong.

Application of the reasoning of the disputant to his own case (*upanaya*)

Puggalavādin: If the defeat we have inflicted on you is considered unfair, do ye apply your reasoning to your own case.

We said: "(*a*) the soul is known in the sense of a genuinely real thing, but (*b*) unknown in the same way as a genuinely real thing is known."

You observed: "if the statement (*b*) is not admitted, then the statement (*a*) cannot be admitted either."

Now, you say: "(*a*) the soul is not known in the sense of a genuinely real thing, but not (*b*) unknown in the same way as a genuinely real thing is known."

Following you we observe: "if you do not admit the statement (*b*), you cannot admit the statement (*a*) either."

Conclusion (*niggamana*).

Puggalavādin : As for ourselves we do not deserve any defeat.

The following assumptions which you made are wrong :—

(i) If the soul is known in the sense of a genuinely real thing, it must also be known in the same way as a genuinely real thing is known.

(ii) It is wrong to couple the statement (*a*), *viz.* the soul is known in the sense of a genuinely real thing, with the statement (*b*), *viz.* the soul is not known in the same way as a genuinely real thing is known.

(iii) If the statement (*b*) is denied, then the statement (*a*) must also be denied.

(iv) If the statement (*a*) is admitted, then the statement (*b*) must also be admitted.

The defeat you propose to inflict on us is unfair. But our rejoinder is fair and demonstration well done.

The above is an instance of First Defeat (*pathamo niggaho*). The argument is suitably repeated in the Second Defeat (adverse controversy, *paccaṁka-niggaho*) in which the respondent is a Theravādin. In the Third, Fourth or Fifth Defeat the question runs respectively as follows: " Is the soul known *everywhere*, *always* or *in everything* in the sense of a genuinely real thing ? " " In the Sixth, Seventh and Eighth Defeats *not known* is substituted for *known* in the question.

A case presented through a simple comparison (*suddhika saṁsandana*).

Theravādin : Is the soul known in the sense of a genuinely real thing, and is matter also known in the same sense ?

Puggalavādin : Yes.

Theravādin : Is matter one thing and the soul another ?

Puggalavādin : No, that cannot be said.

Theravādin : Acknowledge defeat.

If the soul and matter be each known in the sense of a genuinely real thing, then, good sir, you should have admitted that they are distinct things. You are wrong to admit the former proposition and not the latter. If the latter cannot be admitted, neither should the former be admitted. To say that the soul and matter are both known in the sense of genuinely real things but that they are not mutually distinct things, is wrong.

If the soul is known in the sense of a genuinely real thing, then, good sir, you should also have admitted one of the four alternatives. Your position is untenable. If you cannot admit any of the four alternatives, then indeed, good sir, you should not assent to the proposition that the soul is known in the sense of a genuinely real thing.

Definition of terms (*lakkhaṇāyutti-kathā*).

Theravādin : Is the soul known in the sense of a genuinely real thing ?

Puggalavādin : Yes.

Theravādin : Is the soul related or absolute, compounded or uncompounded, eternal or temporal, is possessed of form or without form ?

Puggalavādin : No, these cannot be said.

Theravādin : Acknowledge defeat.

Clearing the meaning of terms (*vacana-sodhana*).

The extension of the subject in relation to its predicate is clearly set forth in the following controversy :—

Theravādin : Is the soul (subject) known, and is that which is known (predicate) the soul ?

Puggalavādin : The soul is known, but of that which is known a portion is soul and the remaining portion is not soul.

Theravādin : Do you say this with respect to the subject also, *viz.* of the soul, a portion is known and the remaining portion is not known.

Puggalavādin : No, that cannot be said, etc.

A case presented through an analogy (*opamma-saṁsandana*).

Theravādin : Matter (*rūpa*) is, you have admitted, known as a genuinely real thing. Feeling (*vedanā*) too is known as such. Now, is matter one thing and feeling another ?

Puggalavādin : Yes.

Theravādin : Is the soul known also in the sense of a genuinely real thing, as matter is known ?

Puggalavādin : Yes.

Theravādin : Then, is matter one thing, the soul another thing ?

Puggalavādin : No, that cannot be admitted.

Theravādin : Acknowledge defeat.

If matter and feeling are both known as genuinely real things and yet are two different things, then by analogy, if the soul and matter are both known as genuinely real things, they, good sir, can equally be two different things. Your position in admitting the first pair of propositions but not the second pair, is wrong. If you cannot admit the second pair, neither should you have admitted the first pair. Your position is wrong.

A case presented through the four-fold method (*catukka-naya-saṁsandana*).

Theravādin : Is the soul known in the sense of a genuinely real thing ?

Puggalavādin : Yes.

Theravādin : (i) Is matter the soul ? or (ii) Is the soul in matter ? or (iii) Is the soul apart from matter ? or (iv) Is matter in the soul ?

Puggalavādin : No, that cannot be said.

Theravādin : Acknowledge defeat.

The doctrine of impermanence (*khaṇika-kathā*).

The doctrine of momentariness (*khaṇika-kathā*)[1] in its crude form is discussed in the following dialogue :—

Theravādin : Do all things exist in our consciousness for a moment only ?

Pubbaseliyas : Yes.

Theravādin : Do you mean that it is in our consciousness that there exist the earth, ocean, Sumeru, water, fire, wind, grass, twigs and trees ?

Pubbaseliyas : No.

Theravādin : Do you mean that our sense-organs have grown along with our sense-cognitions ?

Pubbaseliyas : No.

Theravādin : Do you mean that the sense organs are coincident in time with our sense-cognitions ?

Pubbaseliyas : Yes.

Theravādin : Do you accept the authority of the scripture which declares that there will be no cognition, if the sense-organs are conjoined with their objects but not with the mind, or with the mind but not with the objects, and that there will be cognition only when the sense-organs, their objects and the mind—all these three—are conjoined ?

Pubbaseliyas : Yes.

Theravādin : Therefore you can not say that the sense-organs are coincident in time with our sense-cognitions.

Pubbaseliyas : Should we say that things do not exist in our mind for a moment only ?

Theravādin : Yes.

---

1 Kathāvatthu, Khaṇika-kathā XXII—8, pp. 620—621, edited by A. C. Taylor in the Pāli Text Society. Compare also the translation called "Points of Controversy" by S. Z. Aung and Mrs. Rhys Davids. Also Majjhima Nikāya, i, 190.

Pubbaseliyas: Are all things eternal, stable, permanent and immutable ?

Theravādin: No.

Pubbaseliyas: Therefore all things exist in our mind for a moment only.

69. Milinda-pañha *alias* THE Bhikṣu-sūtra (ABOUT 100 A.D.).

The only Pāli work in which an explicit reference to Logic called *Nīti* (or *Nyāya*) occurs is the Milinda-pañha otherwise known as the Bhikṣu-sūtra, which was composed about 100 A.D.[1] It was translated into Chinese under the Eastern Tsin dynasty A.D. 317—420.[2] In the Chinese collection of the Indian books it is designated as the Nāgasena-Bhikṣu-sūtra. This work contains questions of Milinda (the Greek King Menander of Bactria) and replies of Bhikṣu Nāga Sena on various abstruse matters. In it Milinda, who was versed in Logic (*Nīti* or *Nyāya*), is thus described :—

Hetuvidyā or Nyāya.

"Many were the arts and sciences he knew—holy tradition and secular law; the Sāṁkhya, Yoga, *Nyāya* and Vaiśeṣika systems of philosophy; arithmetic; music; medicine; the four Vedas, the Purāṇas, and the Itihāsas; astronomy, magic; *causation* and spells; the art of war; poetry; conveyancing—in a word, the whole nineteen.

As a disputant he was hard to equal, harder still to overcome; the acknowledged superior of all the founders of the various schools of thought. And as in wisdom so in strength of body, swiftness, and valour, there was found none equal to Milinda in all India. He was rich, too, mighty in wealth and prosperity, and the number of his armed hosts knew no end...... The king, who was fond of wordy disputation, and eager for discussion with *casuists*, *sophists*, and gentry of that sort, looked at the sun (to ascertain the time). and then said to his ministers."[3]

The following dialogue between Milinda and Nāga Sena is quoted to show what was thought to be the proper mode of carrying on debate in the days of those notable persons[4] :—

A scholarly debate.

The King said: 'Reverend Sir, will you discuss with me again ?'

'If your Majesty will discuss as a scholar (Paṇḍita), well; but if you will discuss as a king, no.'

'How is it then that scholars discuss ?'

---

1 For discussions about date *vide* Rhys Davids' Introduction to "the Questions of King Milinda" in the S.B.E. series, vol. xxxv. Menander seems to have belonged to the family of Enkratides and to have invaded India about 155 B.C.

2 *Vide* Bunyiu Nanjio's Catalogue of the Chinese Tripitaka, No. 1358.

3 Taken from Rhys Davids' translation of the Milinda-pañha called "the Questions of King Milinda" in S.B.E. series, vol. xxxv, pp. 6–7.

Nyāya is taken as an equivalent for the original *Nīti*, *causation* for *Hetu*, *casuists* for *Lokāyata* and *sophists* for *Vitaṇḍa*.

Nīti means "polity," but placed between Yoga and Vaiśeṣika it may signify *Nyāya*. Causation, *hetu*, very probably stands for *Hetu-vidyā*, *Nyāya* or Logic.

4 *Vide* Rhys Davids' Questions of King Milinda in the S.B.E. series, vol. xxxv, p. 46.

'When scholars talk a matter over with one another, then is there a winding up, an unravelling; one or other is convicted of error, and he then acknowledges his mistake, distinctions are drawn, and contradistinctions; and yet thereby they are not angered. Thus do scholars, O King, discuss.'

'And how do kings discuss?'

'When a king, Your Majesty, discusses a matter, and he advances a point, if any one differ from him on that point, he is apt to fine him, saying: "Inflict such and such a punishment upon that fellow!" Thus, Your Majesty, do kings discuss.'

'Very well. It is as a scholar, not as a king, that I will discuss. Let Your Reverence talk unrestrainedly, as you would with a brother, or a novice, or a lay disciple, or even with a servant. Be not afraid!'

70. Origin of the Mahāyāna (about 78 A.D.).

At the opening of the Christian era the north-western part of India was invaded by the Kuśānas, Turuṣkas or Scythians. Kaniṣka,[1] who was one of their chiefs, conquered Kāśmīra, Palhava and Delhi, and is said to have founded the era called *Śakābda* in 78 A.D. He accepted the Buddhist faith and established a new system of Buddhism called *Mahāyāna*,[2] the Great Vehicle. The old system of Buddhism as promulgated in the Pāli Tipiṭaka was henceforth nicknamed *Hīnayāna*, the Little Vehicle. The *Mahāyāna* gradually spread to Nepal, Tibet, Mongolia, China, Japan, Corea, etc., while the *Hīnayāna* continued in Ceylon and thence spread to Burmah, Siam, etc. In India both the systems prevailed.

---

[1] Hwen-thsang, in the 7th century A.D., records a prophecy of Buddha that 400 years after his nirvāṇa, Kaniṣka would be born: *vide* Beal's Buddhist Records of the Western World, vol. I, p. 99. The same prophecy is mentioned by Fa-hian about 399 A.D., showing thereby that Kaniṣka was regarded as historical even at that time. According to Tibetan books such as the Sum-paḫi-chos-byun, Kaniṣka flourished in 33 B.C., that is, 400 years after the nirvāṇa of Buddha which is said to have taken place in 433 B.C. Dr. J. F. Fleet holds that Kaniṣka founded the Vikrama era in 58 B.C. (*vide* Traditional Date of Kaniṣka in the Journal of the Royal Asiatic Society of Great Britain and Ireland, October 1906). Dr. R. G. Bhandarkar places Kaniṣka at the last quarter of the 3rd century A.D., as appears from "A peep into the early history of India" in the Journal of the Bombay Branch of the Royal Asiatic Society for 1897—98, p. 396. Vincent A. Smith places Kaniṣka in 125 A.D., while Sylvain Lévi assigns him an earlier date of 50 A.D. (*vide* J.R.A.S., January 1905, pp. 52—53). But Mr. Beal, Mr. Lassen, Professor Kern and others adopt the view that the Śaka era dates from Kaniṣka in 78 A.D. In the Bstan-ḫgyur, Mdo, Gi, there is *Mahārāja-Kanika-lekha*, which is a letter addressed by Maticitra (Aśvaghoṣa) to King Kaniṣka, an account of which has been published by Dr. Satis Chandra Vidyabhusana in the Journal of the Asiatic Society of Bengal, no. 9, for 1910. It seems that Kaniṣka, who was a contemporary of Aśvaghoṣa and Nāgārjuna, was different from the king of that name under whose patronage the fourth Buddhist Council was held. Indeed Kaniṣka was often taken as a general name for the Kuśāna kings.

[2] *Vide* Takakusu's I-tsing, p. xxv; also Satis Chandra Vidyabhusana's "Mahāyāna and Hīnayāna" in the Journal of the Royal Asiatic Society of Great Britain and Ireland, January 1900.

71. ORIGIN OF THE SANSKRIT BUDDHIST LITERATURE (ABOUT 78 A.D)

Under the patronage of Kaniṣka, a council [1] was held at Jālandhara under the superintendence of Pārśva (or Pūrṇaka) and Vasu-Mitra. It consisted of 500 monks who composed in Sanskrit three works explanatory of the Pāli *Tipiṭaka*, viz. Ṣūtra Upadeśa of the Sutta Piṭaka, Vinaya Vibhāṣā of the Vinaya Piṭaka, and Abhidharma Vibhāṣā of the Abhidhamma Piṭaka. These three, works written in Sanskrit, were the earliest canonical books of the Mahāyāna School.

It must not, however, be supposed that there had been no Buddhist books written in Sanskrit before Kaniṣka held his council. As a fact Kaniṣka thought it expedient to introduce Sanskrit as the medium of Buddhistic communication, because there already existed many valuable Buddhist books in that language. For instance, the Abhidharma-vibhāṣā, or rather the Abhidharma mahāvibhāṣā-śāstra, which was compiled at the council of Kaniṣka, was a mere commentary on Kātyāyanī-putra's Abhidharma-jñāna-prasthāna-śāstra.[2] This last is a Sanskrit work explanatory of the Pāli Abhidhamma Piṭaka. It was composed 300 years after the nirvāṇa of Buddha or 100 years before the time of Kaniṣka. Though Kaniṣka was not thus the first founder of the Sanskrit Buddhist literature, it cannot but be acknowledged that it was he, who for the first time proclaimed Sanskrit as the language of the Buddhist Canon. Since his time there have been composed innumerable Buddhist works in Sanskrit of which nine called the *Nava Dharmas* [3] are specially worshipped by the Mahāyāna Buddhists.

72. LOGIC MENTIONED IN THE SANSKRIT BUDDHIST LITERATURE.

None [4] of the works composed during or before the time of Kaniṣka has come down to us in its Sanskrit original, and I have

---

[1] An account of this council is given by Rai Sarat Chandra Das, C.I.E., in an article named "Some Historical facts connected with the rise and progress of Mahāyāna School of Buddhism, translated from the Sumpaḥi-chos-byuṅ" in the Journal of the Buddhist Text Society of Calcutta, vol. I, part III, p. 18. *Vide* also Watters' "On Yuan Chwang,' vol. I, p. 27 ; and also Monier Williams' Buddhism, pp. 68–69.

[2] *Vide* Bunyiu Nanjio's Catalogue of the Chinese Tripiṭaka, nos. 1263, 1273 and 1275. Regarding the authorship of Abhidharma-mahāvibhāṣā, or simply Mahāvibhāṣā, *vide* Takakusu in the Journal of the Royal Asiatic Society of Great Britain and Ireland, January 1905, p. 159.

[3] The *Nava Dharmas* or Nine Sacred Works are :—

(1) Aṣṭa-sāhasrikā Prajñāpāramitā, (2) Gaṇḍa-vyūha, (3) Daśa-bhūmīśvara, (4) Samādhi-rāja, (5) Laṅkāvatāra, (6) Saddharma-puṇḍarīka, (7) Tathāgata-guhyaka, (8) Lalitavistara, and (9) Suvarṇa-prabhāsa.

Vide Hodgson's Illustrations of the Literature and Religion of the Buddists, p. 19.

[4] Dr. Rhys Davids in his Buddhist India, p. 316, observes that the three works composed at the Council of Kaniṣka are extant in European libraries.

had no opportunity of examining the Chinese or Tibetan version of the same. I cannot, therefore, say whether there is any mention of Logic in those works. But we have before us a very large collection of Sanskrit Buddhist works composed after the time of Kaniṣka. Many of these works, such as some of the *Nava Dharmas*, contain references to Logic, and several works are even replete with logical discussions.

73. The **Lalitavistara** (before 250 A.D.).

The **Lalitavistara**, which is one of the *Nava Dharmas*, was translated into Chinese in 221—263 A.D.[1] The Sanskrit original of it must have been prepared in India before that time. In this work Logic, under the name of *Hetu-vidyā*,[2] is mentioned along with the Sāṁkhya, Yoga, Vaiśeṣika, etc., in all of which the Bodhisattva (Buddha Gautama) is said to have acquired distinction.

74. The **Laṅkāvatāra sūtra** (about 300 A.D.).

The **Laṅkāvatāra sūtra**[3] is a very sacred work, as it is one of the *Nava Dharmas*. The exact date of it is unknown, beyond the fact that it was translated into Chinese in 443 A.D.[4] The approximate date seems to be 300 A.D., for, it mentions four heretical schools, refuted later by Ārya Deva.[5] The four schools, as mentioned in the Chinese Tripiṭaka, are (1) the Sāṁkhyas who believe

---

[1] The Lalitavistara was translated into Chinese four times. The first and third translations were lost by 730 A.D. The first was prepared under the Han dynasty A.D. 221—263, the second under the Western Tsin dynasty A.D. 265—316, the third under the earlier Sun dynasty A.D. 420—479, and the fourth under the Thāṅ dynasty A.D. 683. *Vide* Bunyiu Nanjio's Catalogue of the Chinese Tripiṭaka, nos. 159 and 160.

[2] निर्घण्टे निगमे पुराणे इतिहासे वेदे व्याकरणे निरुक्ते शिक्षायां छन्दसि यज्ञकल्पे ज्योतिषि सांख्ये योगे क्रियाकल्पे वैशेषिके वैशिके अर्थविद्यायां बार्हस्पत्ये आश्चर्ये आसुरे मृगपक्षिरुते हेतुविद्यायां जतुयन्त्रे ...... सर्वत्र बोधिसत्त्व एव विशिष्यते स्म ॥

Lalitavistara, edited by Dr. Rajendra Lal Mitra in the Bibliotheca Indica series, Calcutta, Chapter XII, p. 179.

[3] The Sanskrit original of this work has been published by the Buddhist Text Society of Calcutta under the editorship of Rai Sarat Chandra Daṣ and Dr. Satis Chandra Vidyabhusana. The work also exists in Chinese and Tibetan. Hwenthsang mentions the **Laṅkāvatāra**; *vide* Beal's Buddhist Records of the Western World, Book XI, p. 251. *Vide* an account of the **Laṅkāvatāra sūtra** by Satis Chandra Vidyabhushana in the Journal of the Royal Asiatic Society of Great Britain and Ireland, 1906.

[4] *Vide* Bunyiu Nanjio's Catalogue of the Chinese Tripiṭaka, nos. 175, 176 and 177.

[5] Bunyiu Nanjio's Catalogue of the Chinese Tripiṭaka, nos. 1259, 1260 and Appendix I, no. 4.

in oneness,[1] (2) the Vaiśeṣikas who believe in difference, (3) the Nirgrantha-putras who believe in both, and (4) the Jñātiputras who believe in neither.[2]

Reference to Logic and Logicians.

The Laṅkāvatāra speaks in a prophetic style of the *Naiyāyikas* (logicians) and *Tārkikas* (dialecticians). Thus in Chapter II of the work Mahāmati asks Buddha :—

"Say how in time to come *Naiyāyikas* will flourish ?"[3]
"How is *tarka* (reasoning) corrected, and how is it carried on ?"[4]
"What is the nature of the doctrine that draws conclusion from a reason and an example ?"[5]

In Chapter X of the work we read :—

"Whatever is produced is destructible : this is the conclusion of the *Tārkikas*."[6]

---

[1] Here the word Sāṁkhya stands for the Upaniṣad or Vedānta. The Sāṁkhya as mentioned in the Mahābhārata really teaches the doctrine of oneness. Even Vijñāna Bhikṣu, the author of Sāṁkhya-bhāṣya, admits that the Sāṁkhya philosophy is not opposed to the doctrine of oneness. Cf

एकमेवाद्वितीयं तत्त्वम् इति श्रुतिस्मृतिप्रवादश्च सर्व्वात्मनां पुरुषे विभागेन अविभक्तिमद्भेदेनैत्यविरोधः । (Sāṁkhya-bhāṣya, Chap. 1, Sūtra 61).

[2] *Vide* Bunyiu Nanjio, no. 1259. Cf. Laṅkāvatāra-sūtra, A.S.B. MSS., leaf 135 :—

साङ्ख्या वैशेषिका नग्ना विप्राः पाशुपतास्तथा ।
असत्सद्दृष्टिपतिता विविक्तार्थविवर्जिताः ॥

[3] The Sanskrit original runs as follows :—

नैयायिकाः कथं ब्रूहि भविष्यन्ति अनागताः ।

(Laṅkavatāra sūtra, Asiatic Society of Bengal's MSS. Chap. II, leaf 11).
The Tibetan version runs thus :—

རྟོ་བ་རྣམས་ཀྱང་ཇི་ལྟ་བུར །
མ་འོངས་དུས་ན་འབྱུང་བ་གསུངས ॥

(Bkaḫ-ḫgyur. Mdo, vol. V, Asiatic Society of Bengal's xylograph).

[4] कथं हि शुध्यते तर्कः कथं तर्कः प्रवर्त्तते ।
(Laṅkāvatāra sūtra, Chap. II, leaf 11, A.S.B. MSS.).

ཇི་ལྟར་རྟོག་གེ་ཅི་ཡི་སྐད་དུ་འབྱུང་ །

(Bkaḫ-ḫgyur, Mdo, vol. V).

[5] दृष्टान्तहेतुभिर्युक्तः सिद्धान्तो हैमना कथम् ?
Laṅkāvatāra sūtra, p. 36, Buddhist Text Society's edition).

[6] कृतकस्य विनाशः स्यात् तार्किकाणामयं नयः ॥
(Laṅkāvatāra sūtra, Chap. X, leaf 143, A.S.B, MSS.).

བྱས་ན་རྣམ་པར་འཇིག་པར་འགྱུར །
འདི་ནི་རྟོག་གེ་ཅན་གྱི་ཚུལ ॥ (Bkaḫ-ḫgyur, Mdo, vol. V).

Idealism (*vijñāna-vāda*).

In Chapter II, the doctrine of idealism[1] (*vijñāna-vāda*) is explained. According to this doctrine our knowledge alone is real and the so-called external objects are mere manifestations of it. Knowledge (*vijñāna*) is stated to be of two kinds, *viz.* (1) the potential knowledge (*khyāti-vijñāna*) which remaining in us from time immemorial as a mass of potentialities, reminiscences, tendencies or impressions tends to produce the so-called external objects; and (2) the objectified knowledge (*vastu-prativikalpa vijñāna*) or knowledge which is manifested as external objects through the act-force (*karma*) inherent in our aforesaid potentialities, reminiscences, tendencies or impressions.

These two kinds of knowledge combined constitute what is called *pravṛtti-vijñāna*, presentative knowledge which produces the external world drawing us towards it. The seat of *pravṛtti-vijñāna* is called *ālaya-vijñāna*, the basic knowledge. While the latter is compared to an ocean, the former is compared to high winds which agitate it.

This basic knowledge, *ālaya-vijñāna*, is otherwise called an ego (*aham*). As we pass on our *pravṛtti-vijñāna* changes but our ego persists. By means of concentration (*yoga*) we can understand the true nature of the ego. It alone is perfect (*pariniṣpanna*). Non-ego or the external world is false (*parikalpita*) and conditional (*paratantra*). When emancipated, our *pravṛtti-vijñāna* totally disappears, but the ego or *ālaya-vijñāna* continues.[2] The

---

[1] Vijñāna-vāda is called in Tibetan ṛnam-par-śes-paḥi-lta-wa, རྣམ་པར་ཤེས་པའི་ལྟ་བ. It is designated in Sanskrit as *yogācāra-darśana* corresponding to Tibetan ṛnal-ḥbyor-paḥi-lta-wa, རྣལ་འབྱོར་པའི་ལྟ་བ། *Pravṛtti-vijñāna* is called in Tibetan: len-paḥi-ṛnam-par-śes, ལེན་པའི་རྣམ་པར་ཤེས, signifying knowledge as received. *Ālayavijñāna* is called in Tibetan: kun-gshi-ṛnam par-śes-pa, ཀུན་གཞི་རྣམ་པར་ཤེས་པ, signifying knowledge which constitutes the basis or foundation of all. *Pariniṣpanna* is called in Tibetan: yoṅs-grub, ཡོངས་གྲུབ, complete in itself; *paratantra*: gshan-dwaṅ, གཞན་དབང་, dependent on others; and *parikalpita*: kun-bṛtags, ཀུན་བརྟགས, fanciful or erroneous.

[2] It is perhaps not quite accurate to say that when emancipated the ego or *ālaya* of the vijñāna-vādins becomes identical with the void or *śūnyatā* of the Mādhyamikas, because while the former look upon *ālaya* as perfect (*pariniṣpanna*), the latter do not consider *Śūngatā* to be so.

The *ālaya* of the vijñāna-vādins corresponds to *ahaṁkāra* (and *puruṣa*) of the Sāṁkhya philosophy. In emancipation *ahaṁkāra*, according to the Sāṁkhyas, disappears, but *ālaya* according to the vijñāna-vādins persists. The sāṁkhyas do however assume an additional principle called *puruṣa* (soul) which continues to exist. This contrast with the Sāṁkhya doctrine is noted in the following passage of the Laṅkāvatāra sūtra:—

आलयविज्ञाने पुनर्निबध्यमाने निर्विशिष्टः तीर्थकरोच्छेदवादेन अयं वादः स्यात् । ... कारणं पुनः महामते प्रधानपुरुषेश्वरकालाणुप्रवादः ॥

(Laṅkāvatāra sūtra, Chap. II, p. 45, edited by Sarat Chandra Das and Satis Chandra Vidyabhusana).

ego, unruffled by the external world and freed from all potentialities, reminiscences, tendencies or impressions, attains its pristine purity. This is its emancipation or final rest.

In chapter VI of the Laṅkāvatāra-sūtra entitled *kṣaṇika-parivarta* (a chapter on momentariness), there is a clear explanation of the theory that everything is momentary. In a passage of the sūtra the author observes as follows [1]:—

The doctrine of momentariness.

"A momentary thing is that which is inactive, distinct in itself, and not liable to cessation By calling things momentary, I mean that they are not produced. I do not, O fools, say that they are destroyed after being produced."

75. Eighteen Sects of the Buddhists.

We have previously found that within 200 years after the *nirvāṇa* of Buddha there arose in India 17 heretical sects besides the orthodox priesthood called the Theras. In course of time some of these sects disappeared while new ones grew up, the result being that at the time of Kaniṣka, about 78 A.D., the Buddhists had already been divided into 18 sects [2] grouped into four classes as follows:—

I. Ārya Sarvāstivāda
- (1) Mūla Sarvāstivāda
- (2) Kāśyapīya
- (3) Mahīśāsaka
- (4) Dharma-guptīya
- (5) Bahuśrutīya
- (6) Tāmraśāṭīya
- (7) Vibhajyavādin

II. Ārya Sammitīya
- (8) Kurukullaka
- (9) Āvantika
- (10) Vātsīputrīya

} Belonging to the *Vaibhāṣika* School of Philosophy.

---

1 निर्व्यापारं क्षणिकं विविक्तं क्षयवर्जितम् ।
अनुत्पत्तिञ्च धर्माणां क्षणिकार्थं वदाम्यहम् ।
उत्पत्त्यनन्तरं भङ्गं न वै देशेमि बालिशाः ॥
(Laṅkāvatāra sūtra, Chap. VI, p. 99, Bengal Asiatic Society's MSS.).

2 *Vide* the Journal of the Buddhist Text Society of Calcutta, vol. I, part III, p. 18; Takakusu's I-tsing, pp. xxiii, xxiv and xxv; Rhys Davids' article in the Journal of the Royal Asiatic Society of Great Britain and Ireland, 1891, p. 411, and 1892, pp. 1—37; Rockhill's Buddha, p. 181 f; Tārānātha's Geschichte des Buddhismus von Schiefner, pp. 270—274; and Wijesiṁha's Mahāvaṁsa, part I, Chapter V, p. 15.

III. Ārya Mahāsāṁghika
(11) Pūrva-śaila
(12) Apara-śaila
(13) Haimavata
(14) Lokottaravādin
(15) Prajñaptivādin
IV. Ārya Sthavira
(16) Mahāvihāra
(17) Jetavanīya, and
(18) Abhayagirivāsin.

} Belonging to the *Sautrāntika* School of Philosophy.

All the sects mentioned above belonged to the *Hīnayāna*, though later on they joined the *Mahāyāna* too.

76. Four Schools of the Buddhist Philosophy.

The philosophical views of the sects mentioned above were gradually formulated into two schools, *viz.* the (1) *Vaibhāṣika* and (2) *Sautrāntika*. The Mahāyāna sect of the Buddhists founded by Kaniṣka established two other schools of philosophy, *viz.* the (3) *Mādhyamika* and *Yogācāra*. So there were altogether four schools of philosophy, two of the *Hīnayāna* and two of the *Mahāyāna*.[1]

Vaibhāṣika.

Vaibhāṣika was a later appellation of the philosophy of the Sarvāstivāda (Pali: Sabbatthivāda) sect[2] who, as their name implies, admitted the reality of the world—internal and external. In fact the Vaibhāṣika said that our cognition and its corresponding external object were both real. The fundamental philosophical work of this sect is Kātyāyanī-putra's Abhidharma-jñāna-prasthāna-śāstra,[3] or simply Jñāna-prasthāna-śāstra, composed 300 years after the *nirvāṇa* of Buddha The next work of this sect is the Abhidharma-mahā-vibhāṣā-śāstra,[4] or simply Vibhāṣā, compiled at the council of Kaniṣka about 78 A.D. It was from this *Vibhāṣā* that the name *Vaibhāṣika*[5] was derived. *Vibhāṣā* means "commentary," and the

---

1 *Vide* Beal's Buddhist Records of the Western World, vol. I, pp. 121, 139 n; and Takakusu's I-tsing, p. xxii.

2 *Vide* Takakusu's I-tsing, p. xxi. The Ārya Sammitīyas, at any rate their subclass called the Vātsiputrīyas, were followers of the Vaibhāṣika philosophy. The Hindu philosopher Vācaspati Miśra in his Nyāya vārtika-tātparyaṭīkā 3-1-1 quotes the opinions of the Vaibhāṣikas who were called Vātsīputras.

3 This work exists in Chinese and Tibetan: *vide* Bunyiu Nanjio's Catalogue of the Chinese Tripiṭaka, nos. 1273, 1275.

4 This work, too, exists in Chinese and Tibetan: *vide* Bunyiu Nanjio's Catalogue of the Chinese Tripiṭaka, nos. 1263, 1264.

5 Compare the explanation of *Vaibhāṣika* given by the Hindu philosopher Mādhavācārya in his Sarvadarśana-saṁgraha, chapter on Bauddha-darśana, translated by Cowell and Gough, second edition, p. 24. *Vide* also Satis Chandra Vidyabhusana's "Mādhyamika School" in the Journal of the Buddhist Text Society of Calcutta for 1895, part II, p. 4.

Vaibhāṣika philosophy seems to have been so called because it was based on the commentaries rather than on the original texts of the teachings of Buddha. Saṅghabhadra's Nyāyānusāra-śāstra,[1] otherwise called Koṣa-kāraka-śāstra, composed about 489 A.D.,[2] is a most learned work of the *Vaibhāṣika* philosophy.

Sautrāntika.

Sautrāntikas admit cognition and therefrom infer the existence of the external objects. The name *Sautrāntika*[3] was derived from *Sūtrānta*, called in Pāli *Suttanta*, meaning "original text." The *Sautrāntika* philosophy seems to have been so called, because it was based on the original text of the teachings of Buddha rather than on the commentaries thereon. The text, on which the *Sautrāntika* philosophy was based, belonged to the sect of Ārya Sthaviras, called in Pāli Theras, who held the First Council in 490 B.C., and possibly also to the sect of the Mahāsāṁghikas[4] who were the first dissenters in 390 B.C. The philosophical principles of this school are said to have been formulated in Kāśmīra[5] during the reign of Kaniṣka about 78 A.D. by a sage named Dharmottara or Uttara-dharma.[6] But the Chinese pilgrim Hwen-thsang who visited India early in the 7th century A.D., states that the renowned teacher Kumāralabdha[7] of Takṣaśilā (Taxila in the Punjab) was the founder of the *Sautrāntika* school and wrote several very valuable treatises on it. He is supposed to have lived about 300 A.D., as he was a contemporary of Nāgārjuna (q.v.), Ārya Deva (q.v.), and Aśvaghoṣa. There was another very famous teacher named Śrīlabdha[8] who wrote *Vibhāṣā-śāstra* (or commentary on a work) of the *Sautrāntika* school. Hwen thsang saw in Ayodhyā the ruins of a Saṅghārāma where Śrīlabdha resided.

---

1 This work exists in Chinese and Tibetan; *vide* Bunyiu Nanjio's Catalogue of the Chinese Tripitaka, no. 1265.

2 *Vide* Bunyiu Nanjio's Catalogue of the Chinese Tripitaka, Appendix II, no. 95. For Saṅgha-bhadra, *vide* also Hwen-thsang's Travel in Beal's Buddhist Records of the Western World, vol. I, pp. 193—194.

3 Compare the explanation of the term *Sautrāntika* given by the Hindu philosopher Mādhavācārya in the Sarvadarśana-saṁgraha, chapter on Bauddha-darśana, translated by Cowell and Gough, second edition, p. 26. *Vide* also Satis Chandra Vidyabhusana's "Mādhyamika School" in the Journal of the Buddhist Text Society of Calcutta for 1895, part II, p. 4.

Vide Rhys Davids' Buddhist India, p. 168, and Beal's Fahian and Sungyun, p. 143.

4 *Vide* Watters' "On Yuan Chwang," vol. II, p. 161.

5 *Vide* the Journal of the Buddhist Text Society of Calcutta, vol. I, part III, pp. 18, 19; and Tārānātha's Geschichte des Buddhismus von Schiefner, p. 59

6 For the Dhammuttariya or Dharmottara sect, *vide* Wassilief's Buddhism, p. 233; and Mahāvaṁsa, part I, chapter V, p. 15, Wijesiṁha's foot note.

7 *Vide* Beal's Buddhist Records of the Western World, vol. II, p. 302; and Tārānātha's Geschichte des Buddhismus von Schiefner, p. 78, where Kumāra-lābha stands for Kumāra-labdha.

8 *Vide* Beal's Buddhist Records of the Western World, vol. I, pp. 225, 226; and Tārānātha's Geschichte des Buddhismus von Schiefner, p. 67.

Yogācāras maintained that the external objects were unreal but the reality of our cognition could not be denied. The word[1] *yogācāra* (called in Tibetan : rnal-ḫbyor-waḫi lta-wa) is compounded of *yoga* meaning 'meditation' and *ācārā* meaning 'practice.' The *yogācāra* or the contemplative system was so called, because it emphasised the practice of meditation as the means of attaining *bhūmis*[2] or the seventeen stages of Buddhistic Perfection. The chief dogma established in it is *ālaya-vijñāna*,[3] the basis of conscious states, which is the same as our 'ego' or 'soul.' It is not known who was the founder of the *yogācāra* school, but in the Tibetan and Chinese books[4] the Laṅkāvatāra sūtra, Mahāsamaya sūtra,[5] Bodhisattva-caryā-nirdesa and Saptadaśa-bhūmi-śāstra-yogācārya have been named as the prominent old works of the system. Maitreyanātha and Ārya Asaṅga were the early teachers of it. The *yogācāra* school seems to have originated about 300 A.D. when the Laṅkāvatāra sūtra etc. were composed.

Yogācāra.

Mādhyamikas held that our cognition and its corresponding external object were neither absolutely real nor totally unreal. The name *Mādhyamika*[6] (called in Tibetan : Dwu-ma) was derived from *madhyama*, the

Mādhyamika.

---

[1] The yogācāra philosophy is generally known in China, Tibet and Nepal as *yogācārya*. For an account of this system, *vide* Watters' "On Yuan Chwang," vol. 1, p. 356; Dr. Schlagintweit's Buddhism, chap. V. Compare explanation of the word *yogācāra* given by the Hindu philosopher Mādhavācārya in the Sarvadarśana-saṁgraha, chapter on Buddha-darśana, translated by Cowell and Gough, second edition, p. 24. *Vide* also Satis Chandra Vidyabhusana's "the Mādhyamika School" in the Journal of the Buddhist Text Society of Calcutta, 1895, part II, p. 4.

[2] *Vide* Dharmasaṁgraha LXIV and LXV, edited by Max Müller and Wenzel.

[3] For an explanation of *ālaya vijñāna*, see Satis Chandra Vidyabhusana's note on p. 2 of the Laṅkāvatāra sūtra, Calcutta Buddhist Text Society's edition, and also see p. 45 of the same work.

[4] *Vide* section Mdo of the Bstan-ḫgyur; Lama Tāranātha's Geschichte des Buddhismus von Schiefner, p. 111 f; Bunyiu Nanjio's Catalogue of the Chinese Tripitaka, Appendix I, no. 1; Beal's Buddhist Records of the Western World, vol. I, p. 226, vol. II, pp. 220, 275; and Watters' "On Yuan Chwang," vol. I, p. 371.

[5] *Vide* Schlagintweit's Buddhism, chap. V.

[6] Compare—

यतो भावाभावान्तद्वयरहितत्वात् सर्वस्वभावानुत्पत्तिलक्षणा शून्यता मध्यमा प्रतिपन्मध्यमो मार्ग इत्युच्यते ।

(Mādhyamikā vṛtti, chap. XXIV, p 185, Calcutta Buddhist Text Society's edition).

Compare the explanation of the term *Mādhyamika* given by the Hindu philosopher Mādhavacārya, in the Sarvadarśana-saṁgraha, chapter on Bauddha-darśana, translated by Cowell and Gough, second edition, p. 24; and also Dr. Satis Chandra Vidyabhusana's History of the Mādhyamika philosophy of Nāgārjuna in the Journal of the Buddhist Text Society of Calcutta, 1897, part IV, pp. 7—20.

Vide Dr. Satis Chandra Vidyabhusana's "Descriptive list of works on the Mādhyamika Philosophy, no. I" in the Journal of the Asiatic Society of Bengal, no. 7, 1908.

middle. The *Mādhyamika* philosophy was so called because it avoided two extremes, i.e. advocated neither the theory of absolute reality, nor that of total unreality, of the world, but chose a *middle path*, inculcating that the world had only a conditional existence. The school is said to have been founded by Ārya Nāgārjuna about 250—320 A.D. In fact the doctrines of the school are contained in older works such as the Prajñāpāramitā. The Mādhyamika-kārikā by Nāgārjuna, Mūla-madhyama-vṛtti by Buddha Pālita, Hastabala by Ārya Deva, Madhyama-hṛdaya-kārikā by Bhavya, Madhyama-pratītya-samutpāda by Kṛṣṇa, Mādhyamika-vṛtti by Candra Kīrti and Mādhyamikāvatāra-ṭīkā by Jayānanta—are the principal works of the Mādhyamika School. Mūla-madhyamaka-vṛtti-akutobhaya, a work of Nāgārjuna, was translated into Tibetan, under orders of the great king D̲pal-lha-tsan-po, by the Indian sage Jñāna-garbha and the Tibetan official interpreter K̲luh̲i-r̲gyal-m̲tshan. The translation closes by mentioning eight expounders of the Mādhyamika philosophy, viz. Ārya Nāgārjuna, Sthavira Buddha Pālita, Candra Kīrti, Dev Śarmā, Guṇa-śrī, Guṇa-mati, Sthira-mati and Bhavya (or Bhāva-viveka).

CHAPTER II.

Early Buddhist Writers on Logic.

77. RISE OF THE BUDDHIST LOGIC.

With the growth of the four philosophical schools just mentioned, the study of Logic spread far and wide in the Buddhist community. The adherents of each of the schools considered it advantageous to employ logical arguments in defending their own dogmas and attacking those of their opponents. This is clear from the writings of Nāgārjuna and Ārya Deva of the Mādhyamika School, and Maitreya, Asaṅga and Vasubandhu of the yogācāra. The arguments employed in the course of the defence and attack of the schools served to popularise the Ancient Logic of Akṣapāda, and to produce a band of logicians among the Buddhists.

78. ĀRYA NĀGĀRJUNA (ABOUT 250—320 A.D.).

Nāgārjuna or rather Ārya Nāgārjuna, the founder of the Mādhyamika School, was a great logician. He was born at Vidarbha (modern Berar) in Mahākośala,[1] during the reign of King Sadvāha or Sātavāhana[2] [of the Andhra dynasty],[3] and passed many of his days in meditation in a cave-dwelling of the Śrī-parvata,[4] that bordered on the river Kṛṣṇā. He was a pupil of Śaraha and is said to have converted a powerful king, named Bhoja Deva,[5] to Buddhism.

---

[1] *Vide* Hwon-thsang's Travel in Beal's Buddhist Records of the Western World, vol. II, Book VIII, p. 97, and Book X, p. 210; Watters' "On Yuan Chwang," vol. II, pp. 201—202; and Wassiljew quoted by Schiefner in the Geschichte de Buddhismus, p. 301.

[2] Sadvāha is the same as Sātavāhana, which is a general name of the kings of the Andhra dynasty.—*Vide* Dr. R. G. Bhandarkar's Early History of the Dekkan, second edition, pp. 25—37.

Nāgārjuna wrote an instructive letter to Sātavāhana, whose private name in Chinese was Sh'-yen-töh-cia. This letter is called Ārya Nāgārjuna Bodhisattva Suhṛllekha. It was translated into Chinese in 434 A.D. An English translation of this letter has appeared in the Journal of the Pali Text Society of London, 1883. pp 71—75. The Tibetan version of *Suhṛllekha*, called Ḇśes-pahi-ṣpriṅ-yig (sent by Nāgārjuna to his friend Udayibhadra), is contained in the Ḇstan-ḫgyur, M̱do, gi.

[3] The Andhra kings ruled the northern portion of the Madras Presidency and the whole of Kaliṅga, and overthrew the Kaṇva dynasty in northern India about 31 B.C. They remained powerful up to 436 A.D. They were Buddhists, and it was by them that the magnificent marble stūpa at Amarāvatī was erected.—*Vide* Sewell's Lists of Antiquities in Madras, vol. II, pp. 141—146.

[4] For an account of Śrī-parvata or Śrī-śaila see Hwen-thsang's Life, Introduction, p. xi, by Beal; Tārānātha's Geschichte des Buddhismus von Schiefner, p. 84; Wilson's Mālatī-Mādhava, act I; and Satis Chandra Vidyabhusana's Notes on Ratnāvalī, pp. 27—29.

[5] *Vide* Tārānātha's Geschichte des Buddhismus von Schiefner, pp. 66, 69—73.

Nāgārjuna is said to have lived four hundred years [1] after the *nirvāṇa* of Buddha, that is, in 33 B.C. But he does not appear to me to have had so early a date, as he was one of the early patrons or founders of the university of Nālandā, [2] which had not, perhaps, come into existence in the 1st century B.C., and was insignificant [3] even in 399 A.D., when the Chinese pilgrim Fa-hian came to visit India. Nāgārjuna called in Tibetan "Klu-sgrub" is stated by Lama Tārānātha to have been a contemporary of King Nemi Candra, who is supposed to have reigned about 300 A.D. [4] The latest date that can be assigned to Nāgārjuna is 401 A D., [5] when [6] his biography was translated into Chinese by Kumārajīva.

---

[1] It is prophesied in the Mañju-śrī-mūla-tantra (called in Tibetan Hjam-dpal-rtsa-rgyud) that:—

དེ་བཞིན་གཤེགས་པ་མྱ་འདས་ནས།
ལོ་ནི་བཞི་བརྒྱ་ལོན་པ་ན།
དགེ་སློང་ཀླུ་ཞེས་དེ་འབོད་འབྱུང་།
བསྟན་པ་ལ་ནི་དད་ཅིང་ཕན།།

(Quoted in the Introduction to Śes-rab-sdoṅ-bu published in Calcutta).

"Four hundred years after Buddha's departure from the world there will appear a Bhikṣu, named Nāgārjuna, who will do good to the believers in the doctrine."

It should be noted that according to some books of Tibet, Buddha was born in 514 B.C., lived 81 years and attained *nirvāṇa* in 433 B.C. Nāgārjuna, who was born 400 years after the *nirvāṇa*, must, at this calculation, be placed in 33 B.C.

[2] *Vide* Tārānātha's Geschichte des Buddhismus von Schiefner, pp. 66, 69—73.

[3] Fahian describes Nālandā as a mere village Nā-lo: *vide* Beal's Travels of Fa-hian and Sung-yun, p. 111.

[4] According to Lama Tārānātha, Nāgārjuna was a contemporary of King Nemi Candra, whose genealogy is thus traced:—

Akṣa Candra | Jaya Candra | Nemi Candra	Ruled in Aparāntaka.
Phaṇi Candra | Bhaṁśa Candra | Śāla Candra | Candra Gupta	Ruled in Magadha.

The six kings, beginning with Akṣa Candra to Śāla Candra, are stated to have been weak and insignificant, while Candra Gupta, the seventh king, is described as having been very powerful. This Candra Gupta, who "did not take refuge in Buddha," may be the same who founded the Gupta era in 19 A.D. The reigns of his predecessors were very short. Nemi Candra may be assigned to about 300 A.D.—Cf. Tārānātha's Geschichte des Buddhismus von Schiefner, pp. 80—83

[5] *Vide* Bunyiu Nanjio's Catalogue of the Chinese Tripiṭaka, Appendix I, No. 3.

[6] For an account of some of the works on the Tantra by Nāgārjuna, *vide* Satis Chandra Vidyabhusana's Introduction to the Sragdharā-stotra in the "Bibliotheca Indica" series. For the latest researches, in the medical works, of Nāgārjuna, see Dr. Palmyr Cordier's "Introduction A L'Etude des Traites Medicaux Sanscritas"

79. NĀGĀRJUNA'S **Mādhyamika-kārikā.**
(ABOUT 300 A D).

The middle path doctrine—Madhyama-mārga.

The **Mādhyamika-kārikā** [1] is the first regular work on the Mādhyamika philosophy.

The doctrine, which permeates this work, is that of the middle path [2] which is to be comprehended from four aspects, viz. (1) in contradistinction to onesidedness, (2) as the abnegation of one-sidedness, (3) as unity in plurality, and (4) in the sense of absolute truth.

As we cannot conceive of being (existence) independently of non-being (non-existence), it will be taking an onesided view if we are to say that the world *exists* or that it *does not exist*. The middle path furnishes a contrast to this onesidedness by avoiding the two extremes of being and non-being. This is the first aspect of the middle path.

Four aspects of the middle path.

Denying the two extremes the middle path reveals itself through a complete harmony between them, that is, it transcends the extremes of being and non-being which are unified. This is the second aspect of the middle path.

The middle path, which unifies all particulars, does not lie beyond them. The particulars attain their characters of particularity only through our conception of the unity among them.

---

printed in Hanoi, 1903; and for his hymns such as **धर्म्मधातुस्तव, निरुपमस्तव** etc., *vide* Ḇsạn-ḫgyur, Ḇstod-pa, vol. *Ka.*

For an account of other works, *vide* the article "Indian Logic as preserved in Tibet, No. 3," by Satis Chandra Vidyabhusana, in the Journal of the Asiatic Society of Bengal, new series, vol. III, No. 7, 1907. For the philosophical works of Nāgārjuna, see Bunyiu Nanjio's Catalogue of the Chinese Tripiṭaka, Appendix I, no. 3.

The Nyāya-dvāra-tarka-śāstra or Hetu-vidyā nyāya dvāra śāstra, as noticed in Bunyiu Nanjio's Catalogue of the Chinese Tripiṭaka, Nos. 1223, 1224, is not a work of Nāgārjuna but of Dignāga.

1 The Mādhyamika-kārika with the Vṛtti of Candra Kīrti has been published by the Buddhist Text Society of Calcutta. It has also appeared in the St. Petersburg Buddhist Text Series under the editorship of Professor Louis de La Vallee Poussin. Dr. Satis Chandra Vidyabhusana's translation of the Kārikās with notes appeared in several numbers of the Journal of the Buddhist Text Society of Calcutta, 1895-1900.

2 **अतो भावाभावान्तद्वयरहितत्वात् सर्व्वस्वभावानुत्पत्तिलक्षणा**
शून्यता मध्यमा प्रतिपद् मध्यमोमार्ग इत्युच्यते ॥

(Mādhyamikā vṛtti, chap. XXIV, p. 185, Buddhist Text Society's edition, Calcutta).

For an Indian account of the Mādhyamika philosophy or the middle path doctrine, see Satis Chandra Vidyabhusana's articles on the subject published in the Journal of the Buddhist Text Society, 1895-1900. For the Chinese account, see Dr. T. Suzuki's article named "the Mādhyamika School in China" published in the Journal of the Buddhist Text Society, part IV, 1898.

Had there been no unifying principle, the particulars would have ceased to be such. This is the third aspect of the middle path.

By "middle path" it is not to be understood that there is something between the two extremes of being and non-being. In fact, we must avoid not only the two extremes, but also the middle.[1] The middle path, which discards all limitations, expresses the human conception of the absolute truth. This is the fourth aspect of the middle path.

The absolute (*śūnyatā* or *void*)[2] is demonstrated through the assumption of two truths—the conditional (*sanvṛti*) and the transcendental (*paramārtha*).[3] Judged by the transcendental truth no object comes into being or dissolves into non-being. It is from the point of view of the conditional truth alone that we can speak of the existence or non-existence of an object. As a fact no object has a nature or self-existence: objects come into existence in virtue of certain relations or conditions. Taking a substance and its qualities we find that the latter exist in relation to the former, and the former exists in relation to the latter. So a whole exists in relation to its parts, and the latter exist in relation to the former. Proceeding in this way we find that the world is an aggregate of relations or conditions in virtue of which it revolves like a water-wheel. These conditions being causes of confusion, the whole world is no better than an illusion.

The conditional and the transcendental truth.

Origination and cessation, persistence and discontinuance, unity and plurality, coming and going—these are the eight fundamental conceptions of relation or condition.[4] These conceptions, which are in es-

---

1 आर्य्यसमाधिराजे चोक्तं भगवता —
अस्तीति नास्तीति उभेऽपि अन्ताः ।
शुद्धीति अशुद्धीति इमेऽपि अन्ताः ॥
तस्मादुभे अन्ते विवर्जयित्वा ।
मध्येऽपि स्थानं न करोति पण्डितः ॥

(Quoted in Mādhyamikā Vṛtti, Chap. V, p. 41, Buddhist Text Society's edition, Calcutta).

2 Śūnya-vāda is called in Tibetan: stoṅ-pa-ñid, སྟོང་པ་ཉིད ། Saṁvṛti satya is called in Tibetan: Kun-rdsob-bden-pa, ཀུན་རྫོབ་བདེན་པ ། Paramārtha satya is called: don-dam-paḥi-bden-pa, དོན་དམ་པའི་བདེན་པ །

Vide Satis Chandra Vidyabhusana's article on the "absolute" in Dr. Hastings' Dictionary of Religion, J and T. Clark, Edinburgh.

3 द्वे सत्ये समुपाश्रित्य बुद्धानां धर्मदेशना ।
लोकसंवृतिसत्यञ्च सत्यञ्च परमार्थतः ॥

(Mādhyamikāvṛtti, chap. XXIV, p. 180, Buddhist Text Society's edition, Calcutta).

4 अनिरोधमनुत्पाद मनुच्छेदमशाश्वतम्
अनेकार्थमनानार्थं मनागममनिर्गमम् ।

sence unreal, give rise to our prejudices and wrong judgments. There nestles in them the principle of unrest and misery, and as people cling to them, their life is an everlasting prey to the pendulous feeling of exultation and mortification.

Where there is conditionality, there is no truth. Truth and conditionality are incompatible. Therefore, to attain truth, conditionality must be completely cast aside. When our mind is purified from the smirch of conditionality, there will come out the serene moon-light of "suchness" (*tathatā*) or transcendental truth (*paramārtha*), otherwise known as the void or absolute (*śūnyatā*).

The absolute: Śūnyatā and Nirvāṇa.

It may be asked as to whether there is actually a thing called 'suchness," "transcendental truth," or "the absolute." The answer will be that the thing which lies beyond conditionality, cannot be expressed in terms of "is" and "is not" or "being" and "non-being." It avoids the two extremes of "being" and "non-being," nay, it unifies both by underlying each of them. This so-called thing (*śūnyatā*) is called *Nirvāṇa*,[1] which is an unconditional condition in which all contradictions are reconciled. Attempts have been made to express this condition by the term "Infinite," "Eternal," "Profound," "Unconditioned," "Absolute" or "Blissful," but in reality no language can give adequate expression to it.[2]

80. Nāgārjuna's references to the Logical Doctrines of Akṣapāda.

Technicalities of Logic.

In the Mādhyamika-kārikā Nāgārjuna has occasionally referred to certain technical terms of Ancient Logic, such as *punarukta* (repetition) in

---

यः प्रतीत्य समुत्पादं प्रपञ्चोपशमं शिवं
देशयामास सम्बुद्धस्तं वन्दे वदतां वरम् ॥

(Mādhyamika-sūtra, chap. 1).

1 न चाभावोऽपि निर्वाणं
कुत एवास्य भावना ।
भावाभाव परामर्श-
क्षयो निर्व्वाण मुच्यते ॥

(Ratnāvalī quoted in Mādhyamikā vṛtti, p. 194).

2 अनक्षरस्य धर्मस्य श्रुतिः का देशना च का ।
श्रूयते तच्च यथापि समारोपादनक्षरम् ॥

(Mādhyamikāvṛtti, chap. V).

chapter II, *siddha-sādhana* [1] (demonstration of what has already been established) in chapter III, and *sādhya-sama* (*petitio principii*) as well as *parīhāra* (avoidance) in chapter IV.

Criticism of the Nyāya doctrine of *Pramāṇa*.

There is also a criticism of Akṣapāda's doctrine of *Pramāṇa* (evidence). Akṣapāda says that just as a lamp illumines itself and other objects, so does a *pramāṇa* establish itself as well as other objects. Nāgārjuna opposes him by saying that a lamp cannot illumine itself as there is no darkness in it. If a lamp could remove darkness even without coming in contact with it, why could it not, standing here, remove the darkness of the entire universe? [2]

81. Nāgārjuna's Vigraha-vyāvartanīkārikā (about 300 A.D).

The Tibetan and Chinese versions.

Vigraha-vyāvartanīkārikā is a work on the Mādhyamika philosophy which eventually criticises the Nyāya-theory of *pramāṇa*, the evidence or means of knowledge, as laid down by Akṣapāda. The work, the Sanskrit original of which is lost, is called in Tibetan Rtsod-pa-bzlog-pahi tshig-lehur-byas-pa, signifying memorial verses on quelling disputes. It consists of folios 26—29 of the Bstan-hgyur Mdo, tsa. The original Sanskrit text, which had been composed by Ārya Nāgārjuna, was translated into Tibetan by the Indian sage Jñāna-garbha and the Tibetan interpreter Ka-wa-dpal-brtsegs. Subsequently the translation was recast by the Kāśmīrian Paṇḍita Jayānanta and the interpreter Khu mdo-sde-dpal.

---

[1] The following verse refers to the fallacy of *sādhya-sama*:—

विग्रहे यः परीहारं कृते शून्यतया वदेत् ।
सर्वं तस्यापरिहृतं समं साध्येन जायते ॥

(Mādhyamika-kārikā, chapter IV).

[2] Akṣapāda says:—

न प्रदीपप्रकाशवत् तत्सिद्धेः

(Nyāya sūtra, 2-1-19).

Nāgārjuna says:—

प्रदीपः स्वपरात्मनोः सम्प्रकाशयिता यथा ।
प्रदीपे नान्धकारोऽस्ति यत्र चासौ प्रतिष्ठितः ॥
अप्राप्यैव प्रदीपेन यदि वा निहतं तमः ।
इहस्थः सर्वलोकस्थं स तमो निहनिष्यति ॥

(Mādhyamika Kārikā, chap. VII, p. 47, Calcutta Buddhist Text Society's edition).

Bunyiu Nanjio's Catalogue of the Chinese Tripiṭaka, no. 1251.

Bstan-hgyur, Mdo, tsa, folios 27—28.

Cf. Prof. H. Ui's Vaiśeṣika Philosophy, pp. 84—85.

The Chinese version of the Vigraha-vyāvartanī kārikā is noticed by Bunyiu Nanjio under the name of **Vivāda-śamana-śāstra.** It was translated into Chinese by the sage Vimokṣa-prajña and others in 541 A.D.

In the Vigraha-vyāvartanī kārikā (as reproduced in Tibetan) Nāgārjuna criticises the validity of *pramāṇa*, the evidence or means of knowledge, as follows:—

If you establish objects through a *pramāṇa*, the *pramāṇa* itself must be established through another *pramāṇa* and that again by a fresh *pramāṇa*, until you commit the fallacy of *regressus ad infinitum*. If, on the other hand, you attempt to establish objects without a *pramāṇa*, your tenet (viz. that objects are established through *pramāṇa*) falls to the ground.

The validity of Akṣapāda's *pramāṇa* criticised.

A *Pramāṇa* is not self-established. Had it been so, there would have been a complete cessation of gloom or ignorance. The view that a *pramāṇa* establishes itself as well as other objects, is untenable. A fire, which is cited as an illustration, can illumine other objects by removing darkness which besets them, but it cannot illumine itself inasmuch as a fire never co-abides with darkness.

A *pramāṇa* cannot be so called, if it is totally independent of *prameya* (objects). If, on the other hand a *pramāṇa* is dependent on *prameya* (objects), how can it, having no self-existence, establish the latter? etc., etc.

82. NĀGĀRJUNA'S **Pramāṇa-vihetana** OR **Pramāṇa-vidhvaṁsana** (ABOUT 300 A.D.).

To Nāgārjuna is attributed the composition of a logical treatise called **Pramāṇa-vihetana** or **Pramāṇa-vidhvaṁsana**, which literally signifies "the quelling of *pramāṇa*," and which was in fact a review of the definition of the sixteen categories as given by Akṣapāda. The Sanskrit original of this work is not available. There is however extant the Tibetan version of a commentary on the work called **Pramāṇa-vihetana-ṭeppitaka-vṛtti** or **Pramāṇa-vidhvaṁsana-saṁbhāṣita-vṛtti** dated probably about 650 A.D. It extends over folios 415—418 of the Bstan-ḥgyur, Mdo, ha. In Tibetan the commentary is called Tshad-ma-rnam-par-ḥjoms-pa mdor-bśad-paḥi-ḥgrel, which literally signifies "a magic-stick commentary on Pramāṇa-vihetana, or Pramāṇa-vidhvaṁsana." [1]

[1] Called by P. Cordier in his Tibetan Catalogue as Pramāṇa-vidhvaṁsana-ṭepptaka-vṛtti.

This work does not perhaps represent the views of Nāgārjuna but refers to those of the commentator.

The commentator, whose name is not mentioned, pays obeisance to Mañju-śrī-kumāra-bhūta and introduces his work as follows:—

To please the learned people, I give an exposition of the vihetana or vidhvaṁsana [*i.e.* Pramāṇa-vihetana or Pramāṇa-vidhvaṁsana].[1]

Then he observes that the instructions on Nyāya delivered by Nāgārjuna are put together to constitute the present work.

A legend about Nāgārjuna.

He further observes that Nāgārjuna, who bore special marks of greatness, proceeded once for the dissemination of culture to the region of the Nāgas. They exhibited their magical powers which could not overcome him. Beholding his superhuman greatness Upendra, king of the Nāgas, offered him his daughter, while the other Nāgas worshipped him in a befitting manner. They took orders and coming to the region of men practised the austerities of monks.

The commentator reproduced Nāgārjuna's definition of the categories which are stated in Tibetan as follows:—

Categories defined in the work.

(1) Tshad-ma (*pramāṇa*), (2) gshal-bya (*prameya*), (3) the-tshom (*saṁśaya*), (4) dgos-pa (*prayojana*), (5) dpe (*dṛṣṭānta*), (6) grub-pahi-mthah (*siddhānta*), (7) cha-śas (*avayava*), (8) rtog-ge (*tarka*), (9) gtan-la-phab-pa (*nirṇaya*), (10) smra-wahi-mthah (*vāda*), (11) rtsod-pahi-mthah (*jalpa*), (12) rnam-par-rtsod-pahi-mthah (*vitaṇḍā*), (13) gtan-tshigs-ltar-snaṅ-wa (*hetvābhāsa*), (14) tshig-dor (*chala*), (15) ltag-gcod (*jāti*), and (16) tshar-gcod-pa (*nigraha sthāna*).

A syllogism (cha-śas, *avayava*) is shown to consist of three members, *viz.* a proposition, a reason, and an example. It may be put in the affirmative or negative way.[2]

The reasons[3] (gtan-tshigs, *hetu*) may appear in one of the following relations, *viz.* (1) an effect (hbras-bu, *kārya*), (2) an identity (rnam-bshin, *svabhāva*), and (3) non-perception (mi-dmigs, *anupalabdhi*).

An example[4] (dpe, dṛṣṭānta) is defined as the place in which

---

1 མཁས་པ་དགའ་བ་བསྐྱེད་པའི་ཕྱིར། །
རྣམ་པར་འཇོམས་པའི་དོན་བཤད་བྱ། །

(Bstan-hgyur, Mdo, ha, folio 415).

2 ཆོས་ཅན་གྱི་ཆུས་པ་དང་གཏན་ཚིགས་དང་དཔེ་དང་བསྒྲུབ་བྱ་རང་ཉིད་ཀྱིས་ལྡན་པ་དང་། རྗེས་སུ་འགྲོ་བ་དང་། ལྡོག་པ་ངེས་པར་འགྱུར་བའི་ཚུལ་པའོ། །

(Bstan-hgyur, Mdo, ha, folio 417).

3 It is doubtful whether this was the original doctrine of Nāgārjuna. It might be a later development known to the author of the vṛtti.

4 དཔེ་ཞེས་པ་ནི་གཏན་ཚིགས་ཀྱི་གྲོགས་ཁྱབ་པ་དང་འབྲེལ་པ་གཏན་ལ་དབབ་པའི་གཞིར་འདོད་ལ། །

(Bstan-hgyur, Mdo, ha, folio 417).

is decisively shown the connection between the reason (middle term) and its universal companion the predicate (major term).

83. Upāya-kauśalya-hṛdaya-śāstra. (ABOUT 300 A.D.).

The **Upāya-kauśalya-hṛdaya-śāstra**,[1] the Essence of Skill in the Accomplishment of Action, is stated to be a work on the art of debate by Bodhisattva Nāgārjuna. In Chinese this work is called Fāṅ-pien-sin-lun. It was translated into Chinese by Ci-cia-ye and Thān-yāo in A.D. 472.

Seeing that the Vaiśeṣika and other systems were obscure in their terminology, Nāgārjuna, it is reported, undertook to write this book to give a clear exposition of the art of debate. The book is divided into four chapters styled respectively as (I) an elucidation of debate [*vāda-viśadīkaraṇa*], (II) an explanation of the points of defeat [*nigraha-sthāna*], (III) an explanation of the truths [*tattva-vyākhyāna*], and (IV) the analogue or far-fetched analogy [*jāti*].

(I) The first chapter consists of eight sections which treat respectively of (1) an example (*udāharaṇa*), (2) a tenet, truth or conclusion (*siddhānta*), (3) the excellence of speech (*vākya praśaṁsā*), (4) the defect of speech (*vākya-doṣa*), (5) the knowledge of inference (*anumāna* or *hetu-jñāna*), (6) the appropriate or opportune speech (*samayocita-vākya*), (7) the fallacy (*hetvābhāsa*), and (8) the adoption of a fallacious reason (*duṣṭa-vākyānusaraṇa*).

(1) The *example* is necessary to clear the reasons of a disputant and his respondent. It is of two kinds: (1) the affirmative or homogeneous example (*anvayi udāharaṇa*), and (2) the negative or heterogeneous example (*vyatireki udāharaṇa*).

(2) The *tenet, truth* or *conclusion* is of four kinds, *viz.* (1) that accepted by all the schools (*sarvatantra siddhānta*), (2) that accepted by a particular school (*pratitantra siddhānta*), (3) that accepted hypothetically (*adhikaraṇa siddhānta*), and (4) that which is implied or accepted on assumption (*abhyupagama siddhānta*).

The means, by which the tenets, truths or conculsions are established, are called *pramāṇas* (the sources of valid knowledge) which are of four kinds, *viz.* perception (*pratyakṣa*), inference (*anumāna*), comparison (*upamāna*), and scripture (*āgama*).

This definition is criticised by Uddyotakara in his Vārtika on Nyāya-sūtra, 1-1-37.

[1] Some suspect that the work was not composed by Nāgārjuna whose name, though mentioned by some Chinese editors, does not appear in the Chinese version. In the absence of any introduction to the Chinese version we cannot deny altogether the authorship of Nāgārjuna. *Vide* Bunyiu Nanjio's Catalogue of the Chinese Tripiṭaka, no. 1257.

(3) A *speech is said to be excellent* if its words are neither inadequate nor redundant, and its reason and example well expressed.

(4) A *speech is said to be defective* if its words are inadequate, or redundant, or if it employs the same word to convey different meanings or different words to convey the same meaning.

(5) The *inference* is of three kinds, *viz.* (1) *â priori* (*pūrvavat*), (2) *ā posteriori* (*śeṣavat*), and (3) *commonly, seen* (*sāmānyato dṛṣta*). The respective examples are: on seeing a cloud one infers that there will be rain; on seeing a swollen river one infers that there was rain; and on seeing a man move from one place to another, one infers that the sun, who rises in the east and sets in the west, must have moved.

(6) The *appropriate or opportune speech* consists in its being pertinent to the subject and occasion, *e.g.* in the discussion as to whether there will be rain to-morrow, one may appropriately speak of the condition of the sky of the previous day.

(7) The *fallacies* signify reasons which are derived from an imperfect perception, inference, or comparison, or which deviate from the scripture. There are various kinds of fallacies designated respectively as follows:—

(*a*) The *quibble in respect of a term* (*vāk-chala*), *e.g.* a man pretends to use the term *nava-kambala* in the sense of nine blankets while he really means a new blanket.

(*b*) The *erratic* reason or *undistributed middle term* (*savyabhicāra*), *e.g.* to say that all external things are non-eternal is to employ an erratic reason, because the sky is an external thing which is eternal.

(*c*) *Balancing the doubt* or *false assumption* (*saṁśaya-sama*), *e.g.* there is doubt as to a certain tall object being a post or a man, and yet if we proceed to act on the assumption that it is a man, we commit the fallacy of false assumption.

(*d*) The *mistimed* (*kālātīta*), *e.g.* we attempt to prove the eternity of the Veda on the ground that sound is eternal, when no proof has been given for the eternity of sound.

(*e*) *Balancing the point in dispute* or *begging the question* (*prakaraṇasama*), *e.g.* the soul is eternal, because it is distinct from the body [It is a matter of dispute if a thing which is distinct from the body is eternal or not].

(*f*) *Balancing the predicate* (*sādhya-sama*), *e.g.* the sky is eternal, because it is intangible.

(*g*) *Showing absurdity* (*vyāghāta-pradarśana*), *e.g.* the five objects are non-eternal, because they are apprehended by the senses: the four elements being also so apprehended are non-eternal. If you say so it will follow that a tortoise possesses hair and salt possesses smell, because they are apprehended by the mind: this is absurd.

(*h*) The *contradictory* (*viruddha*)—either in respect of the example or in respect of the conclusion.

(8) The *adoption of a fallacious reason*—If in the course of one's argument one commits fallacies, one will be thrown into difficulties and disgrace.

(II) "The points of defeat" are the following :—

(1) The unintelligible (*avijñātārtha*), (2) non-ingenuity (*apratibhā*), (3) silence (*ananubhāṣaṇa*), (4) saying too little (*nyūna*), (5) saying too much (*adhika*), (6) the meaningless (*nirarthaka*), (7) the inopportune (*aprāptakāla*), (8) the incoherent (*apārthaka*), (9) hurting the proposition (*pratijñā-hāni*).

(III) "An explanation of the truths" deals mainly with the admission of an opinion (*matānujñā*).

(IV) The "analogue" or far-fetched analogy is of various kinds as follows :—

(1) Balancing an excess (*utkarṣa-samā*), (2) balancing a deficit (*apakarṣa-samā*), (3) balancing the unquestionable (*avarṇya-samā*), (4) balancing the non-reason (*ahetu-samā*), (5) balancing the co-presence (*prāpti-samā*), (6) balancing the mutual absence (*aprāpti-samā*), (7) balancing the doubt (*saṁśaya-samā*), and (8) balancing the counter-example (*pratidṛṣṭānta-samā*).

84. Ārya Deva (about 320 A.D.).

Deva,[1] or rather Ārya Deva, was the next writer on the *Mādhyamika* philosophy. He is otherwise known as Karṇaripa, Kāṇa Deva, Nīla-netra and Piṅgala-netra. He was born in Southern India and was an eminent disciple of Nāgārjuna. According to Hwen-thsang,[2] he visited the countries of Mahākośala, Srughna, Prayāga, Coḷa and Vaiśālī, in all of which he won great renown by defeating the Tīrthikas and preaching the true doctrines of Buddha. According to Lama Tārānātha,[3] Deva resided for a long time in Nālandā, where he was a Paṇḍita. He flourished during the reign of Candra Gupta, whose date is supposed to be about 320 A.D.[4] The latest date that can be assigned to Deva is 401 A.D.,[5] when his biography was translated into Chinese by Kumārajīva. He wrote numerous works on the *Mādhyamika* philosophy, such as the **Śataka śāstra, Bhrama-prama-**

---

[1] *Vide* Bunyiu Nanjio's Catalogue of the Chinese Tripiṭaka, Appendix I, No. 4; and Watters' "On Yuan Chwang," vol. I, p. 321, vol. II, pp. 225—226.

[2] *Vide* Beal's Buddhist Records of the Western World, vol. I, Book IV, pp. 186—190, Book V, p. 231; vol. II, Book X, pp. 210, 227, Book XII, p. 302, Book VIII, pp. 98—102.

[3] *Vide* Lama Tārānātha's Geschichte des Buddhismus von Schiefner, pp. 83—86 and 93.

[4] *Vide* Nāgārjuna. Cf. Dr. Jacobi's "Dates of philosophical sūtras," J.A.O.S. for 1911, p. 2.

[5] *Vide* Bunyiu Nanjio's Catalogue of the Chinese Tripiṭaka, Appendix I, No. 4.

thana-yukti-hetu-siddhi,[1] etc., all of which bear evidences of his knowledge of Logic.

85. MAITREYA (ABOUT 400 A.D.).

His life and age.

Maitreya,[2] or rather Maitreya-nātha, who was an eminent teacher of the Yogācāra School, was called in Chinese 'Mirok' and in Tibetan 'Byams-pahi-mgon-pa.' He was the author of several works such as the Bodhisattva-caryā-nirdeśa which was translated into Chinese during 414—421 A.D., the Saptadaśa-bhūmi-śāstra-yogācārya which was translated into Chinese in 646—647 A.D., and the Abhisamayālaṅkāra-kārikā which was translated into Tibetan during 1059—1109 A.D. Maitreya, who lived 900 years after the *nirvāṇa* of Buddha, that is, about 400 A.D.,[3] is reported by Hwen-thsang to have communicated the materials of three Buddhist treatises to Ārya Asaṅga while the latter was residing in a monastery in Ayodhyā.[4]

86. MAITREYA'S Abhisamayālaṅkāra-kārikā.[5]

Doctrines of Momentariness and Voidness.

Maitreya strongly supported the doctrines of momentariness (*kṣaṇika-vāda*) and voidness (*śūnya-vāda*). This is evident from the Abhisamayālaṅkāra kārikā in which he says that when we attain perfect wisdom our thought neither precedes nor follows it, just as a lamp which removes darkness neither precedes nor follows the same. Profound indeed are the eight characters of objects.[6] Profound is the origination of an object, and so are its

---

[1] *Vide* Satis Chandra Vidyabhusana's "Indian Logic as preserved in Tibet No. 3" in the Journal of the Asiatic Society of Bengal, new series, vol. III, No. 7, 1907.

[2] *Vide* Bunyiu Nanjio's Catalogue of the Chinese Tripiṭaka, Appendix I, no. 1; Dr. P. Cordier's Tibetan Catalogue, p. 273.

[3] *Vide* "Hindu Logic as preserved in China and Japan," by Dr. Sugiura, p. 30.

[4] *Vide* Watters' "On Yuan Chwang," Vol. I, pp. 355—56. The three treatises are:—

Saptadaśa-bhūmi-śāstra-yogācārya, Sūtrālaṅkāra-ṭikā, and Madhyāntavibhāga-śāstra.

[5] The Abhisamayālaṅkāra-kārikā, a Sanskrit text of which is available in the library of the Asiatic Society of Bengal, was translated into Tibetan by Paṇḍita Amara Gomin and the interpreter Blo-ldan-śes-rab during 1059—1109 A.D. It extends over folios 1—14 of the Bstan-hgyur, Mdo, ka. The author of the work is named in Sanskrit as Maitreyanātha and in Tibetan as Byams-pahi-mgon-pa.

[6] पूर्व्वेण बोधिचित्तस्य नमसा पश्चिमेन वा ।
दीपदृष्टान्तयोगेन गम्भीरा धर्म्मताष्टधा ॥
उत्पादे च निरोधे च तथतायां गभीरता ।

cessation and suchness. The knowable, knowledge, action, means and expedients are all profound. Inasmuch as the objects partake of the character of a dream, there is no reality underlying our existence and its emancipation

Taking one's stand on the dreamy character of objects, one while practising charity, etc., realizes that these are void. One perceives in a moment that a dream and a seer of the dream are not connected but are non-dual in their essence.[1]

The knowledge of objects and their connection and separation, is momentary.[2]

87. Maitreya's treatise on the Art of Debate.

In the 15th volume of Maitreya's Ṣaptadaśa-bhūmi-śāstra-yogācārya[3] there is a treatise on the art of debate. It consists of seven chapters styled respectively as follows :—

1. *The subject of debate.*

Subjects of the treatise.

In beginning a debate on a subject, we must first see that the subject is a useful one. A useless subject should be abandoned.

2. *The place of debate.*

Debate should not be entered upon in any and every place. It should be carried on in the presence of scholars, in the palace of a king or the office of a minister or in a council (*pariṣad*).

ज्ञेयज्ञाने च चर्य्यायां सद्वयोपाय गोचरे ।
स्वप्नोपमत्वाद् धर्म्माणामभवशान्त्योरकल्पना ॥

(Abhisamayālaṅkāra-kārikā, Chap. IV, p. 22, MSS. of the Asiatic Society of Bengal).

1 स्वप्नोपमेषु धर्म्मेषु स्थित्वा दानादिचर्य्यया ।
अलक्षणत्वं धर्म्माणां क्षणेनैकेन बिध्यति ॥
स्वप्नं तद्दर्शनञ्चैव द्वययोगेन नेक्षते ।
धर्म्माणामद्वयतत्त्वं क्षणेनैकेन पश्यति ॥

(Abhisamayālaṅkāra-kārikā, Chap. VII, p. 28, MSS. of the Asiatic Society of Bengal).

2 धर्मज्ञानान्वयज्ञान क्षान्तिज्ञान क्षणात्मकः ।

(Abhisamayālaṅkāra-kārikā, Chap. III, p. 14, MSS. of the Asiatic Society of Bengal).

3 It is perhaps this work which is called *yoga* by Dr. Sugiura ; *vide* its Chinese version Yuka Ron, Book XV.

3. *The means of debate.*

The thesis (*sādhya* or that which is to be established) is of two kinds, *viz.* (1) that concerning one's self (*ātma-sambandha*), and (2) that concerning others (*para-sambandha*). The proof (or that which helps in establishing the thesis) may be of eight kinds as follows:—

(1) A proposition, tenet or conclusion (*siddhānta*), (2) reason (*hetu*), (3) example (*udāharaṇa*), (4) the affirmative example (*sādharmya*), (5) the negative example (*vaidharmya*), (6) perception (*pratyakṣa*), (7) inference (*anumāna*), and (8) scripture (*āgama*).

4. *The qualifications of a debater.*

(*a*) The debaters must be versed in each other's scriptures.

(*b*) They must not, under any circumstances, use sordid or disrespectful language. In addressing each other they should employ words of dignity.

(*c*) They must remain fearless.

(*d*) They must speak continuously without any break, and must be intelligible to the entire audience.

(*e*) They must speak in harmony—sometimes slowly and sometimes aloud—to please the audience.

5. *Points of defeat* (*nigrahasthāna*).

(*a*) If a debater at first opposes an assertion and afterwards speaks in agreement with it, he is defeated.

(*b*) If a debater being unable to defend the subject which he has been discussing introduces another subject, he is defeated.

(*c*) If a debater talks irrelevantly (*atīta-vākya*), he is defeated.

6. *Attending a place of debate.*

(*a*) A person, in proceeding to a place of debate, should consider whether the debate will be of any benefit to him.

(*b*) He should, before proceeding there, consider whether the debate will exercise any good influence on the debater, the opponent, the umpire, and the audience.

(*c*) He should consider whether the debater and his opponent are persons worthy of carrying on debate through the process of a proposition (*siddhānta*), a reason (*hetu*), an example (*udāharaṇa*), etc.

7. *Confidence of a Debater.*

The debater should appear to the audience in such a way that he is, as it were, sure to gain victory. He should be understood by them to be one who knows the scripture of both the parties, who is self-possessed and full of enthusiasm, and who can speak without a break.

It is evident from the titles of the chapters just mentioned that Maitreya mainly discussed the practical questions of Logic. But occasionally there was mixed with the discussions some Pure Logic also. A thesis [*pratijñā*], according to Maitreya, is to be supported by a reason [*hetu*] and two examples [*dṛṣṭānta*]. Validity of the reason and of the examples requires that they be based either (1) on fact or perception [*pratyakṣa*], (2) on inference [*anumāna*], or (3) on holy saying [*āgama*]. Analogy or Comparison [*upamāna*] is omitted. The form of his reasoning is illustrated as follows:—

(1) Sound is non-eternal,
(2) Because it is a product,
(3) Like a pot, but not like ether [*ākāśa*],
(4) A product like a pot is non-eternal,
(5) Whereas, an eternal thing like ether is not a product.[1]

88. Ārya Asaṅga (about 405—470 A.D.).

His life.

Asaṅga,[2] called in Chinese Mucak and in Tibetan Thogs-med, was born in Gāndhāra (modern Peshwar). He was at first an adherent of the Mahīśāsaka[3] sect and followed the *Vaibhāṣika* philosophy of the *Hīnayāna*. Later on he became a disciple of Maitreya and adopted the *Yogācāra* philosophy of the *Mahāyāna*. He is said to have lived for some years as a paṇḍiṭa in Nālandā[4] He lived about 450 A.D.[5] The latest date that can be assigned to him is 531 A.D.,[6] when one of his works, called the Mahāyāna-samparigraha-śāstra, was translated into Chinese. Hwen-thsang in the 7th century A.D. saw the ruins of *Saṅghārāmas* in Kauśāmbī and Ayodhyā, where Asaṅga resided for some years.[7] He wrote 12 works, most of which still exist in Chinese and Tibetan versions.[8]

His logical views.

A short summary of the Logic of Asaṅga is found in the 11th volume of **Prakaraṇārya vācā śāstra**[9] and 7th and 16th volumes of **Mahāyānābhidharma-saṁyukta-saṅgīti-śāstra**. The first work called in Chinese

---

1 *Vide* "Hindu Logic as preserved in China and Japan," p. 30.
2 *Vide* Hwen-thsang's Travel in Beal's Buddhist Records of the Western World, Vol. I, pp 98, 227 and 236.
3 *Vide* Watters' "On Yuan Chwang," Vol I, p. 357.
4 *Vide* Tāranātha's Geschichte des Buddhismus von Schiefner, p. 122.
5 Asaṅga is approximately placed at 450 A.D. as he was the eldest brother of Vasubandhu (q.v.) who lived about 480 A.D.
6 *Vide* Bunyiu Nanjio's Catalogue of the Chinese Tripiṭaka, Appendix I, No. 5.
7 *See* Beal's Buddhist Records, Vol I, pp. 98, 227, 236.
8 *Vide* Bunyiu Nanjio's Catalogue of the Chinese Tripiṭaka, Appendix I, No. 5.
9 Bunyiu Nanjio's Catalogue of the Chinese Tripiṭaka, Nos. 1177, 1178.

Hhien-yāṅ-shaṅ-ciāo-lun (signifying 'a śāstra on expounding the holy teaching') was composed by Bodhisattva Asaṅga. It was translated into Chinese by Hwen-thsang (Yuan chwang) of the Thāṅ dynasty in A.D. 645—646. The second work called in Chinese Tā-shaṅ ö-phi-tā-mo-tsā-tsi-lun was compiled by Bodhisattva Sthitamati. It was translated into Chinese by Hwen-thsang of the Thāṅ dynasty in A.D. 646.

In logical views Asaṅga follows Maitreya except in respect of the theory of proof (*sādhaka* or that which helps in establishing a thesis). A proof is subdivided by Asaṅga as follows: (1) A proposition (*pratijñā*), (2) a reason (*hetu*), (3) an example (*udāharaṇa*), (4) an application (*upanaya*), (5) a conclusion (*nigamana*), (6) perception (*pratyakṣa*), (7) comparison (*upamāna*), and (8) scripture (*āgama*).

The first five subdivisions constitute what is called an inference (*anumāna*).

Asaṅga's form of reasoning, which is somewhat different from Maitreya's, is given below:—

(1) Sound is non-eternal,
(2) Because it is a product,
(3) Like a pot (but not like ether);
(4) Because a pot is a product it is non-eternal; so is sound, as it is a product:
(5) Therefore we know sound is non-eternal.

89. Vasubandhu (about 410—490 A.D.).

His life.

Vasubandhu,[1] called in Chinese Seish and in Tibetan D̲wyig-gñen, was born in Gāndhāra (modern Peshwar), where a tablet to his memory was seen by Hwen-thsang in the 7th century A.D. His father's name was Kauśika. He began his career as a *Vaibhāṣika* philosopher of the Sarvāstivāda sect, but was later converted by his eldest brother Asaṅga to the *Yogācāra* school of the *Mahāyāna*. He passed many years of his life in Śākala, Kauśāmbī and Ayodhyā, in the last of which places he died at the age of eighty years. He was a friend of Manoratha, a master of the Vaibhāṣika Śāstra, who flourished in the middle of the thousand years after the *nirvāṇa* of Buddha, that is before 500 A.D. He was a contemporary of another *Vaibhāṣika* teacher, named Saṅghabhadra, who lived about 489 A.D.[2]

---

[1] *Vide* Hwen-thsang's Travel in Beal's Buddhist Records of the Western World, Vol. I, pp. 98, 105, 172, 193, 225, 236; and Watters' "On Yuan Chwang," Vol. I, p. 210.

[2] Saṅgabhadra translated Vibhāṣā-vinaya into Chinese in 489 A.D. *Vide* Bunyiu Nanjio's Catalogue of the Chinese Tripiṭaka, Appendix II, No. 95.

Vāmana,[1] who lived at the end of the 8th and beginning of the 9th century A.D., quotes a verse alluding to Vasubandhu as a counsellor (possibly of Kumāra Gupta during 413—455 A.D.). A biography[2] of Vasubandhu was translated from Sanskrit into Chinese during 557—569 A.D Paramārtha,[3] the translator of the biography (499—569 A.D.), tells us that Vasubandhu, who was patronised by Vikramāditya (possibly Skanda Gupta), died at the age of eighty years during the reign of Bālāditya Narasiṁha Gupta (485—490 A.D.). He was therefore a contemporary of Kumāra Gupta, Skanda Gupta, Pura Gupta and Bālāditya (from about 410 A.D. to about 490 A.D.).

His works.

Vasubandhu was the author of a large number of very valuable works,[4] some of which are available in Sanskrit and the rest in Chinese and Tibetan translations.

In the 7th century A.D. while Hwen-thsang was travelling in India, he saw three works on the art of debate attributed to Vasubandhu.[5] The Sanskrit originals of these works as well as their Chinese versions are now lost. The works were styled in Chinese as (1) **Ronki** (*Vāda-vidhi*—the method of debate), (2) **Ronshiki** (*Vāda-mārga*—the course of debate), and (3) **Ronshin** (*Vāda-kauśala*—the expedients of debate).

90. Vasubandhu's Tarka-Śāstra.

Besides these three works, there was a treatise on Logic called

---

Mr. Takakusu, in a very learned article called "Paramārtha's Life of Vasubandhu and the date of Vasubandhu" published in the Journal of the Royal Asiatic Society of Great Britain and Ireland, January 1905, says that Saṅghabhada, contemporary of Vasubandhu, was the translator of the Samantapāsādikā of Buddhaghoṣa into Chinese in 488 A.D

1 साभिप्रायत्वं यथा,——

सोऽयं संप्रति चन्द्रगुप्ततनयश्चन्द्रप्रकाशो युवा ।
जातो भूपतिराश्रयः कृतधियां दिष्ट्या कृतार्थश्रमः ॥

आश्रयः कृतधियामित्यस्य च सुबन्धुसाचिव्योपक्षेपपरत्वात् साभिप्रायत्वम् ।

(Kāvyālaṅkāra-sūtra-vṛtti, 3-2-2, p. 85, Benares Sanskrit series).

2 *Vide* Bunyiu Nanjio's Catalogue of the Chinese Tripiṭaka, No. 1463 and Appendix I, No. 6. The statement that there was an older translation of the life of Vasubandhu by Kumārajīva A.D. 401—409, but that it was lost in 730 A.D., cannot be accepted without further testimony. Takakusu says that "some catalogues mention by mistake that such a work was then in existence": *vide* Journal of the Royal Asiatic Society of Great Britain and Ireland, January 1905, p. 39.

3 *Vide* Takakusu in J.R.A.S. 1905, pp. 33—53; Prof. K. B. Pathak in Indian Antiquary, pp. 170—171, for June 1911; V. A Smith's Early History of India, pp. 293 and 327 (3rd edition); and Dr. Hoernle's correspondence in the Indian Antiquary for September 1911, p. 264.

4 *Vide* Bunyiu Nanjio's Catalogue of the Chinese Tripiṭaka, Appendix I, No. 6.

5 *Vide* Dr. Sugiura's "Hindu Logic as preserved in China and Japan," p. 32.

Tarka-śāstra[1] composed by Vasubandhu. There exists a Chinese version of this work called Zu-shih-lun. The Chinese version was prepared by Paramārtha of the Chan dynasty in A.D. 550. The Tarka-śāstra consists of three chapters dealing respectively with (1) the five parts of a syllogism (*pañcāvayava*), (2) the analogous rejoinder (*jāti*), and (3) the points of defeat (*nigraha-sthāna*).

An analysis of the Tarka-śāstra.

In chapter I, Vasubandhu treats of a proposition (*pratijñā*), a reason (*hetu*), an example (*udāharaṇa*), an application (*upanaya*), and a conclusion (*nigamana*), which constitute the five parts of a syllogism.

Though according to the Tarka-śāstra a syllogism consisted of five parts, in the Ronki, quoted by Kwei-ke, Vasubandhu maintained that a thesis could be proved by two parts only, *viz.* a proposition and a reason, and that, therefore, the necessary terms in a syllogistic inference were only three, *viz.* the minor term (*pakṣa*), the major term (*sādhya*), and the middle term (*hetu*).[2]

In chapter II, there is an account of the Analogous Rejoinder (*jāti*) which is subdivided under three heads as follows:—

A. A rejoinder on the basis of reversion (*viparyaya-khaṇḍana*) which consists of (1) balancing the homogeneity (*sādharmya-samā*), (2) balancing the heterogeneity (*vaidharmya-samā*), (3) balancing the thesis (*sādhya-samā*), (4) balancing the unquestionable (*avarṇya-samā*), (5) balancing the mutual absence (*aprāpti-samā*), (6) balancing the non-reason (*ahetu-samā*), (7) balancing the demonstration (*upapatti-samā*), (8) balancing the doubt (*saṁśaya-samā*), (9) balancing the non-difference (*aviśeṣa-samā*), and (10) balancing the effect (*kārya-samā*).

B. A rejoinder on the ground of meaninglessness (*nirartha-khaṇḍana*) which consists of (11) balancing the point in dispute (*prakaraṇa-samā*), (12) balancing the counter-example (*pratidṛṣṭānta-samā*), and (13) balancing the infinite regression (*prasaṅga-samā*).

C. A contrary rejoinder (*viparīta-khaṇḍana*), which consists of (14) balancing the non-produced (*anutpatti-samā*), (15) balanc-

---

[1] Bunyiu Nanjio's Catalogue of the Chinese Tripiṭaka, No. 1252.

[2] The Jaina logician Siddhasena Divākara probably refers to Vasubandhu, when he says that according to some logicians *antarvyāpti* (internal inseparable connection) consisting of *pakṣa* or minor term, *sādhya* or major term and *hetu* or middle term, is quite enough in establishing a thesis, and that *dṛṣṭanta* or example is altogether useless. Siddhasena Divākara writes:—

अन्तर्व्याप्त्यैव साध्यस्य सिद्धेर्बहिरुदाहृतिः ।
व्यर्था स्यात्तदसद्भावेऽप्येवं न्यायविदो विदुः ॥ २० ॥

(Nyāyāvatāra of Siddha-sena Divākara, edited by Dr. Satis Chandra Vidyabhusana and published by the Indian Research Society of Calcutta).

ing the eternal (*nitya-samā*), and (16) balancing the presumption (*arthāpatti-samā*).

Chapter III deals with twenty-two kinds of points of defeat (*nigraha-sthāna*) enumerated below:—

(1) Hurting the proposition (*pratijñā-hāni*), (2) shifting the proposition (*pratijñāntara*), (3) opposing the proposition (*pratijñā-virodha*), (4) renouncing the proposition (*pratijñā-saṁnyāsa*), (5) shifting the reason (*hetvantara*), (6) shifting the topic (*arthāntara*), (7) the meaningless (*nirarthaka*), (8) the unintelligible (*avijñātārtha*), (9) the incoherent (*apārthaka*), (10) the inopportune (*aprāpta-kāla*), (11) saying too little (*nyūnatā*), (12) saying too much (*adhika*), (13) repetition (*punarukta*), (14) silence (*ananubhāṣaṇa*), (15) ignorance (*ajñāna*), (16) non-ingenuity (*apratibhā*), (17) evasion (*vikṣepa*), (18) admission of an opinion (*matānujñā*), (19) overlooking the censurable (*paryanuyojyopekṣaṇa*), (20) censuring the non-censurable (*niranuyojyānuyoga*), (21) deviating from a tenet (*apasiddhānta*), and (22) the semblance of a reason or fallacy (*hetvābhāsa*).

It is to be regretted that neither the Ronki nor its Sanskrit original is available. Vasubandhu seems, however, to have used two forms of syllogism, *viz.* a syllogism of five parts at the time of a debate and a syllogism of two parts on an ordinary occasion. The two forms are exhibited below:—

A syllogism of five parts.

(1) Sound is non-eternal.
(2) Because it is a product.
(3) Products are non-eternal like a pot, which is a product and is non-eternal,
(4) Sound is an instance of a product.
(5) Therefore sound is non-eternal.

A syllogism of two parts.

(1) Sound is non-eternal.
(2) Because it is a product.

CHAPTER III.

Systematic Buddhist Writers on Logic.

91. THE COMMENCEMENT OF MEDIÆVAL LOGIC (450—1200 A.D.).

In the previous chapter we have seen that from the origin of Buddhism in the 6th century B.C. to its expansion into four philosophical schools in the 4th century A.D., there were no systematic Buddhist works on Logic, but only a few stray references to that science in the works on philosophy and religion. Nāgārjuna, about 300 A.D., wrote a tract on Logic which was a mere review of the common topics of the Ancient School of Brāhmaṇic Logic. During 400—500 A.D., Maitreya, Asaṅga and Vasubandhu handled Logic, but their treatment of it was merely incidental, being mixed up with the problems of the *Yogācāra* and *Vaibhāṣika* schools of philosophy. Vasubandhu's three works [1] on Pure Logic mentioned by Hwen-thsang are now lost and consequently their merits cannot be judged. With 450 A.D. began a period when Logic was completely differentiated from general philosophy, and a large number of Buddhist writers gave their undivided attention to that branch of learning. The works brought out by these writers, along with those brought out by the Jainas, constitute the Mediæval School of Indian Logic. Dignāga is the earliest known writer of this school.

92. ĀCĀRYA DIGNĀGA—FATHER OF MEDIÆVAL LOGIC (CIRCA 450—520 A.D.).

A portrait of Dignāga.

Dignāga is justly regarded as the Father of Mediæval Logic. Both in matter and in manner his works marked a distinct departure from those of his predecessors. The keenness of his insight and the soundness of his critical acumen combined to stamp him with an individuality all his own. No praise seems too high for him. Indeed he may fittingly be styled as the first and last of Indian logicians. His likeness recovered from Tibet is reproduced below.

Recovered from the land of snow.

The likeness of Dignāga reproduced here is taken from the Tibetan Bstan hgyur (Mdo, Ce, folio 1) which was put in its present form by the celebrated Lama Bu-ston, who passed the last days of his life at the monastery of Sha-lu, twelve miles south-east of Tashi-lhun-po. Bu-ston, who lived at the close of the thirteenth

---

[1] *Vide* Book II, Chapter I, under the head "Vasubandhu."

century A.D., must have copied the likeness from some earlier specimen, which was taken to Tibet during her intercourse with India between 600 A.D. and 1200 A.D.

A peculiarity of this likeness is its cap. In the early Buddhist Church monks were not allowed to wear any head-dress (*vide* the Pātimokkha rules of the Vinaya Piṭaka). With the introduction of Mahāyāna in the first century A.D. by Kaniṣka, a great change was effected in the dress of monks, and caps of various shapes were invented. The hat worn here is called Panchen-shwa-ḍmar[1] or "Paṇḍita's red cap," with a pointed peak and long lappets. The lappets of the cap were lengthened in proportion to the rank of the wearer.

It is not known when the "Paṇḍita's cap" was first introduced. It is said to have been taken to Tibet in 749 A.D. by Śānta Rakṣita. "Paṇḍita" was a degree which was conferred by the Vikramaśilā University on its successful candidates. It is not known what title the University of Nālandā conferred on its distinguished

བསྟན་འགྱུར་མདོ་ཅེ་གཅིག།

སློབ་དཔོན་ཕྱོགས་གླང་ལ་ནམོ །།

[1] *Vide* Waddell's Lamaism, pp. 194–196.

students. Perhaps in that University, too, the title "Paṇḍita" was recognized and "Paṇḍita's cap" was possibly a distinctive badge of the scholars of that famous University where Dignāga distinguished himself in philosophical controversies.

The woollen *shawl* in the figure is indicative of the fact that after Buddhism had spread into cold climes, monks like Brāhmaṇic sages were allowed to put on suitable warm clothes. There is also in the palms of the image a thunderbolt called in Sanskrit *Vajra* and in Tibetan *Rdorje*, which is a remover of all evils. The halo round the head of the image indicates that Dignāga was a saint.

93. Life of Dignāga.

Dignāga, or rather Ācārya Dignāga, is called in Tibetan Phyogs-glaṅ. He[1] was born in a Brāhmaṇa family in Siṁhavaktra near Kāñcī, modern Conjeeveram in the Madras Presidency. By Nāgadatta, a Paṇḍita of the Vātsīputrīya sect, he was admitted to the religious system of that sect and attained erudition in the *Tripiṭaka* of the *Hīnayāna*. Afterwards he became a disciple of Ācārya Vasubandhu with whom he studied all the Piṭakas of the *Mahāyāna* and *Hīnayāna*. He miraculously saw the face of Mañjuśrī, the Buddhist god of learning, from whom he received inspiration in the Law (Dharma). A few years later he was invited to Nālandā where he defeated Brāhmaṇa Sudurjaya and other Tīrtha dialecticians and won them to the doctrine of Buddha. Since he had refuted chiefly the Tīrtha controversialists he was called a "Fighting Bull" or a "Bull in discussion" (Sanskrit: *Tarka-puṅgava*, and Tibetan: Rtsod-pahi-khyu-mchog). He travelled through Orissa and Mahārāṣṭra to the south, meeting the Tīrtha controversialists in discussions. In Mahārāṣṭra he is said to have resided frequently in the Ācāra's Monastery.[2] In Orissa he converted Bhadra Pālita, Treasury-minister of the King of the country, to Buddhism. He was a man of vast learning and wisdom, and practised during his life-time twelve tested virtues. He lived a considerable part of his life in Andhra (Telingana) in the Madras Presidency. He is said to have died in a solitary wood in Orissa.

Dignāga must have lived before 557—569 A.D.[3] when two of

---

[1] *Vide* Lama Tāranātha's Geschichte des Buddhismus von Schiefner, pp. 130—135. Lama Tāranātha also relates that Dignāga frequently resided in Orissa in a cavern of a mountain called Bhoraśilā where he used to give himself up to contemplation. He was specially versed in incantation formulas. It is stated that the stem of a myrobalan tree called Muṣṭiharītakī in the garden of Bhadra Pālita in Orissa entirely withered, but it revived in seven days after Dignāga had uttered an incantation for its restoration. For a fuller account of Dignāga *vide* Satis Chandra Vidyabhusana's "Dignāga and his Pramāṇa-samuccaya" in the Journal of the Asiatic Society of Bengal, Vol. I, No. 9, 1905.

[2] *Vide* Watters' On Yuan Chwang, Vol. II, p. 122.

[3] *Vide* Bynyiu Nanjio's Catalogue of the Chinese Tripitaka, App. 1, No. 10, where Dignāga is called Jina. The Chinese name of Dignāga has been wrongly rendered as Jina by Japanese writers as well as by the Rev. Mr. Beal.

his works were translated into Chinese. The early limit of his date is 480 A.D. when his teacher Vasubandhu lived. Dignāga flourished possibly about 500 A.D. when the Buddhist kings of the Pallava [1] dynasty ruled the eastern coast of Southern India.

We have already seen that Dignāga travelled in Nālandā, Orissa, Mahārāṣṭra and Dakṣiṇa (Madras), entering everywhere into disputes with controversialists. He attacked his opponents as frequently as he was attacked by them. His whole life was passed in giving blows and receiving counter-blows. Even his death did not terminate the great intellectual war in which he had been engaged: though he could no longer offer any violence, his opponents continued to fall upon him with force. Mark the volleys on his dead body coming from no mean warriors! Kālidāsa,[2] the prince of poets, warns his poem to avoid the "rugged hand" (*sthūla-hasta*) of Dignāga. Uddyotakara,[3] the eminent logician, calls Dignāga "a quibbler" (*Kutārkika*). Vācaspati Miśra[4] describes him as "an erring one" (*bhrānta*) and speaks of his "blunders" (*bhrānti*). Mallinātha[5] compares him with a "rock" (*adri-kalpa*). Kumārila Bhaṭṭa and Pārtha-sārathi Miśra[6] turn their arrows against him. The Vedāntins and Jainas[7] were not in-

---

1 On the downfall of the Andhras in 436 A.D., the Pallavas rose to power. They were in their turn driven out of their northern possessions, the kingdom of Veṅgi, by Kubja Viṣṇuvardhana of the Eastern Chalukya dynasty During 552—589 A.D., Kāñcī, the capital of the Pallava kings, was captured by Vikramāditya I. of the Western Chalukya dynasty. *Vide* Sewell's Lists of Antiquities, Madras, Vol. II, pp. 141, 146, 148, 149 and 211, 212.

2 *Vide* Meghadūta, Pūrva-megha, verse 14.

3
यदक्षपादः प्रवरो मुनीनां
शमाय शास्त्रं जगतो जगाद।
कुतार्किकाज्ञाननिवृत्तिहेतुः
करिष्यते तस्य मया निबन्धः॥

Uddyotakara's Nyāya-vārtika, Introductory stanza, p 1, in the Bibliotheca Indica series. Compare also Nyāya-vārtika, 1-1-4, pp. 43—44; 1-1-5, p. 52; 1-1-6, pp. 60—61; 1-1-7, p. 63, etc.

4 *Vide* Vācaspati Miśra's Nyāya-vārtika-tātparya-ṭīkā, edited by Gangadhara Sastri, 1-1-1, pp. 1, 31; 1-1-4, pp. 76—77, 97—98, 102; 1-1-5, p. 102; 1-1-6, p 135, etc.

5 Mallinātha's commentary on verse 14 of the Meghadūta, Pūrva-megha.

6 *Vide* Pārtha sārathi's gloss on verses 59—60, Anumānaparicchedа of Kumārila Bhaṭṭa's vārtika on the 5th Sūtra of Jaimini.

7 *Vide* the works of Prabhācandra and Vidyānanda referred to in the J.B.B. R.A.S., Vol. XVIII, p. 229. The Digambara Jaina logician Dharma-bhūṣaṇa, in controverting the Vaiśeṣika doctrine of *Sāmānya*, generality, quotes in support of his own conclusion the following verse of Dignāga:—

न याति न च तत्रास्ते न पश्चादस्ति नांशवत्।
जहाति पूर्वं नाधारमहो व्यसनसन्ततिः॥
इति दिग्नागभिक्षुविरचितदूषणमणिप्रकरणात्

(Quoted in Dharmabhūṣaṇa's Nyāya-dīpikā, Chapter III).

active in their hostility. Even Dharmakīrti,[1] a Buddhist sage, attempted to oppose him. Dignāga must have been a very strongly built man, both physically and mentally, otherwise he could hardly have lived for a single day under assaults from so many sides. Those of his works which still exist enable us to measure, to some extent, his strength and his weakness.

94. Dignāga's Pramāṇa-samuccaya.[2]

The Pramāṇa-samuccaya is one of the grandest literary monuments of Dignāga. It is said to have been composed while he was residing on a solitary hill near Veṅgi in Andhra[3] (modern Telingāna) in the Madras Presidency. Seeing that the Śāstras on Dialectics written earlier by him remained scattered about, he resolved to collect them. Accordingly, putting together fragments from particular works, he engaged himself in compiling in verse a compendium called the Pramāṇa-samuccaya. While he was writing the opening lines, the earth trembled and all the places were filled with light and a great tumult was audible. A Brāhmaṇa named Īśvarakṛṣṇa[4] surprised at this wonder came to

Dignāga and Īśvara-kṛṣṇa.

The same verse has been quoted in a little altered form by the Hindu philosopher Mādhavācārya as follows :—

न याति न च तत्रासीदस्ति पश्चान्न चांशवत् ।
जहाति पूर्वं नाधारमहो व्यसनसन्ततिः ॥

(Sarvadarśana saṁgraha, chapter on Bauddhadarśana).

[1] *Vide* the head "Dharmakīrti" which follows.

[2] For an account of the composition of the Pramāṇa-samuccaya *vide* Lama Tārānātha's Geschichte des Buddhismus von Schiefner, pp. 13, 133; and the Tibetan Dpag-bsam-ljon-bzaṅ edited by Rai Sarat Chandra Das, Bahadur, C.I.E., pp. 62, 75, 100 and LXVII.

[3] *Vide* Hwen-thsang's Travel in Beal's Buddhist Records of the Western World, Vol. II, pp. 218, 219 and 220, where the Chinese term for Dignāga is wrongly rendered as Jina. Hwen-thsang gives the following account of the composition of the Pramāṇa-samuccaya :—"When Dignāga began to compose a useful compendium [presumably the Pramāṇa-samuccaya] for overcoming the difficulties of the Hetuvidyā-śāstra, the mountains and valleys shook and reverberated; the vapour and clouds changed their appearance, and the spirit of the mountain appeared before him, asking him to spread abroad the śāstra (Hetuvidyā). Then the Bodhisattva (Dignāga) caused a bright light to shine and illumine the dark places. Surprised at this wonder, the king of the country (Andhra) came near him and asked whether he was entering into *nirvāṇa*. When the king spoke of the infinite bliss of *nirvāṇa* Dignāga resolved to enter into it. Mañjuśrī, the god of learning, knowing his purpose was moved with pity. He came to Dignāga and said: "Alas! how have you given up your great purpose, and only fixed your mind on your own personal profit, with narrow aims, giving up the purpose of saving all." Saying this he directed him to explain the Yogācāryabhūmi-śāstra and Hetuvidyā-śāstra. Dignāga receiving these directions, respectfully assented and saluted the saint. Then he devoted himself to profound study and explained the Hetuvidyā-śāstra and the Yoga discipline.

[4] Īśvarakṛṣṇa here referred to was very probably the author of the Sāṁkhya kārikā.

Ācārya Dignāga, and finding that he had gone out to collect alms, wiped out the words he had written. Dignāga came and rewrote the words and Īśvara-kṛṣṇa wiped them out again. Dignāga wrote them a third time and added: "Let no one wipe these out even in joke or sport, for none should wipe out what are of great importance: if the sense of the words is not right, and one wishes to dispute on that account, let him appear before me in person." When after Dignāga had gone out to collect alms, the Brāhmaṇa again came to wipe out the writings, he saw what was added and paused. The Ācārya returning from his rounds for a meal met the Brāhmaṇa: they began a controversy, either staking his own doctrine. When he had vanquished the Tīrtha (Brāhmaṇa) several times and challenged him to accept the Buddhist doctrine, the Tīrtha scattered ashes, pronouncing incantations over them, and burnt all the goods of the Ācārya that happened to lie before him; and while the Ācārya was kept back by fire, the Tīrtha ran away. Thereupon Dignāga reflected that, since he could not work the salvation of this single individual, he would not be able to work that of others. So thinking he was on the point of giving up his purpose of compiling the Pramāṇa-samuccaya when the Bodhisattva Ārya Mañjuśrī miraculously appeared before him in person and said:—

"Son, refrain, refrain: the intellect is infected by arguing with mean persons. Please know that when you have demonstrated it, this Śāstra cannot be injured by the host of Tīrthas. I undertake to be your spiritual tutor till you have attained the stage of perfection. In later times this śāstra will become the sole eye of all the śāstras."[1]

So saying Mañjuśrī disappeared, and Dignāga resumed his work and completed Pramāṇa-samuccaya.

The Tibetan version of Pramāṇa-samuccaya.

The Pramāṇa-samuccaya[2] is a Sanskrit work written in *anuṣṭubh* metre. The Sanskrit original of it is lost, but a Tibetan translation still exists. The translation was prepared by an Indian sage named Hema (or Kanaka) Varma (in Tibetan: Gser-gyi-go-cha) and a Tibetan interpreter named Dad-pahi-śes-rab in the monastery of Śes-pahi-dge-gnas. It occupies folios 1—13 of the Bstan-hgyur,

1 བུ་མ་བྱེད་མ་བྱེད་སྐྱེ་བོ་དམན་དང་འཐུད་ལས་བློ་གྲོས་ངན་སྐྱེ་སྟེ། ཁྱོད་ཀྱི་བསྟན་ནས་འཆོས་འདི་ལ་མུ་སྟེགས་ཚོགས་ཀྱིས་གནོད་མི་ནུས་པར་ཤེས། ཁྱོད་ཀྱིས་ས་མ་ཐོབ་ཀྱི་བར་དུ་དགེ་བའི་བཤེས་སུ་ང་འགྱུར་གྱི། ཕྱི་མའི་དུས་སུ་བསྟན་བཅོས་ཀུན་གྱི་མིག་གཅིག་ཏུ་ནི་འདི་འགྱུར་རོ།།

Dpag-bsam-ljon-bzaṅ, edited by Rai Sarat Chandra Das, Bahadur, C.I.E., p. 101.

2 Probably the same as "The Śāstra on the grouped inferences," *vide* Takakusu's I-tsing, p. 167.

section Mdo, volume Ce.[1] In Tibetan it is called Tshad-mahi-Mdo-kun-las-btus-pa (=Pramāṇa-sūtra-samuccaya) or briefly Tshad-ma-kun-las-btus-pa (=Pramāṇa-samuccaya) signifying a compilation of aphorisms on Pramāṇa, valid knowledge. It begins thus:— "Bowing down before Sugata—the teacher and protector—who is *Pramāṇa* incarnate, and benefactor of the world, I, for the sake of expounding Pramāṇa (valid knowledge), put together here various scattered matters, compiled from my own works."[2] In the closing lines it is stated that "Dignāga, the subduer of controversialists in all regions and the possessor of elephantine strength, compiled this from his own works."[3]

It is divided into six chapters which are named respectively: (1) Perception (Sanskrit: *Pratyakṣa*, Tibetan: Mṅon-sum); (2) Inference for one's own self (Sanskrit: *Svārthānumāna*, Tibetan: Raṅ-don-gyi-rje-dpag); (3) Inference for the sake of others (Sanskrit: *Parārthānumāna*, Tibetan: Gshan-gyi-don-gyi-rje-dpag); (4) Reason and example (Sanskrit: *Hetu-dṛṣṭānta*, Tibetan: Gtan-tshigs-daṅ-dpe); (5) Negation of the opposite (Sanskrit: *Apoha*, Tibetan: Tshan-sel-wa); and (6) Analogue (Sanskrit: *Jāti*, in Tibetan: ltag-gcod.

Chapter I—Perception.

In opposition to Akṣapāda who propounded four *pramāṇas* (means of valid knowledge), Dignāga[4] states in Chapter I of the Pramāṇa-samuccaya

Pramāṇa.

---

[1] The volume Ce of the Bstan-hgyur, section Mdo, was put at my disposal by the India Office, London, through Mr. Thomas.

[2] ཚད་མར་གྱུར་པ་འགྲོ་ལ་ཕན་པར་བཞེད། །
སྟོན་པ་བདེ་གཤེགས་སྐྱོབ་ལ་ཕྱག་འཚལ་ནས། །
ཚད་མ་བསྒྲུབ་ཕྱིར་རང་གི་གཞུང་ཀུན་ལས། །
བཏུས་ཏེ་སྣ་ཚོགས་འཐོར་རྣམས་འདིར་གཅིག་བྱ། ། ||

(Bstan-hgyur, Mdo, Ce, folio 1).

[3] ཕྱོགས་རྣམས་ཀུན་གྱི་ཕས་ཀྱི་རྒོལ་བ་རྣམས། །
འཇོམས་པར་བྱེད་ལ་གླང་པོའི་སྟོབས་ལྡན་པ། ||
ཕྱོགས་ཀྱི་གླང་པོའི་གཞུང་ཀུན་ལས་བཏུས་པ། ||

(Bstan-hgyur, Mdo, Ce, folio 13).

[4] མངོན་སུམ་དང་ནི་རྗེས་སུ་དཔག་
ཚད་མ་དག་ནི་མཚན་ཉིད་གཉིས། །
གཞལ་བྱ་དེ་ལ་རབ་སྦྱོར་ཕྱིར
ཚད་མ་གཞན་ནི་ཡོད་མ་ཡིན། ||

(Tshad-ma-kun-las-btus-pa, Chapter I).

that *pramāṇas* are only two, viz. perception (*pratyakṣa*) and inference (*anumāna*). All objects being known through them, there is no other *pramāṇa*.

Dignāga's description of Perception.

Dignāga does not give any formal definition of Perception, which is well known as the knowledge of objects derived through the channel of the senses. But he describes Perception as that which, being freed from preconception, is unconnected with name, genus, etc.[1] Suppose a man in twilight mistakes a rope for a snake: his knowledge of the snake is a preconception and is not, according to Dignāga, an act of Perception. Dignāga contends that Perception is not connected with the name, as we can perceive a thing without knowing its name. It is also unconnected with genus, so that the perception of a thing consists of the knowledge of its individual characteristics alone. Suppose I see a cow. This cow, which I see, is a peculiar one. Its infinite peculiarities can only be realised by me who have seen it. If I proceed to indicate this cow to other persons by saying that I saw a cow which is named Dittha or which is red, etc., I can only convey to those persons the idea of a cow of a certain class, that is, a cow possessing the common characteristics of a class of cows, but can never express to them the individual cow which I saw. Hence it follows that (a result of) Perception cannot be properly expressed by name, genus, etc. But very different is the case with inference. Knowledge derived through inference is general, and can be well expressed by name, genus, etc., whereas that derived through Perception is particular, and is incapable of being properly communicated to others by name, genus, etc.

The Sanskrit original may be restored as follows:—

प्रत्यक्षमनुमानञ्च प्रमाणे हि द्विलक्षणम् ।
प्रमेयं तत्र सिद्धं हि न प्रमाणान्तरं भवेत् ॥

(Pramāṇa-samuccaya, Chapter I).

[1] In Chapter I of the Pramāṇa-samuccaya, Dignāga describes Perception as follows:—

མངོན་སུམ་རྟོག་པ་དང་བྲལ་བ །
མིང་དང་རིགས་སོགས་མི་འབྲེལ་པའོ ||

The Sanskrit equivalents for those two lines are as follows:—

प्रत्यक्षं कल्पनापोढं
नामजात्याद्यसंयुतम् ॥

(Pramāṇa-samuccaya, Chapter I).

The first of these lines has actually been quoted, and Dignāga's whole theory of Perception severely criticised, by the Hindu logician Uddyotakara in his Nyāya-vārtika, 1-1-4.

Perceptions as defined in other schools.

Dignāga reviews the doctrines of perception of the Yogins[1] (or Yogācāras called in Tibetan R̲nal-h̲byor-pa) and the Sāṁkhyas (called in Tibetan Grańs̲-can-pa) or Kāpilas[2] (called in Tibetan Ser-s̲kya-wa).

Dignāga criticises the definition of perception as given by Akṣapāda and Vātsyāyana.

Akṣapāda, whom Dignāga designates as Naiyāyika (in Tibetan: rigs̲-pa-can), defines *perception*[3] as knowledge which arises from the intercourse of sense-organs with their objects, being determinate, unnameable and non-erratic. Vātsyāyana in his *Bhāṣya*, commentary,[4] admits that this definition enumerates only the special factors of perception. The soul (*ātman*), etc., which co-operate in producing not only perception but also inference, etc., are general factors and as such not mentioned in the definition. As to the objection that the definition fails to enumerate even the special factor of perception, *viz*. the mind (*manas*) which through its intercourse with the soul, pleasure, etc., brings about their perception, Vātsyāyana observes that the mind is included in the sense-organs, it has been designated a sense-organ in the Vaiśeṣika philosophy, and the designation has been tacitly

---

1 རང་རིག་རྟོག་པ་མེད་པ་ཡིན། །
རྣལ་འབྱོར་རྣམས་ཀྱི་བླ་མས་བསྟན། །

(Pramāṇa-samuccaya, Chapter I).

2 གང་ཚེ་དོན་དང་དབང་པོ་ཡིད། །
སྐྱེས་བུ་སྦྱོར་བ་འདུ་བྱེད་ལྟར། །
བློ་སྐྱེ་བ་ཡི་ཚོགས་པ་ལ། །
མངོན་སུམ་བརྗོད་པ་དེ་ཞི་ལྟར། །

(Pramāṇa-samuccaya, Chapter I).

3 The definition of the Naiyāyika is quoted by Dignāga as follows :—

རིགས་པ་ཅན་རྣམས་ནི ——

དབང་པོ་དང་དོན་ཕྲད་པ་ལས་སྐྱེས་པའི་ཤེས་པ་ཐ་སྙད་དུ་བྱ་བ་མ་ཡིན་པ་འཁྲུལ་པ་མེད་པ་ཞེན་པའི་བདག་ཉིད་ཅན་ནི་མངོན་སུམ་མོ་ཞེས་ཟེར་རོ། །

(Pramāṇa-samuccaya, Chapter I).

4 The Sanskrit original runs as follows :—

इन्द्रियार्थसन्निकर्षोत्पन्नं ज्ञानमव्यपदेश्यमव्यभिचारि व्यवसायात्मकं प्रत्यक्षम् ।

(Nyāya-sūtra, 1-1-4).

नचैतन्मन्तव्यम् आत्ममनःसन्निकर्षजमेवानवधारणज्ञानमिति । ..... आत्मादिषु सुखादिषु च प्रत्यक्षलक्षणं वक्तव्यम् । अनिन्द्रियार्थसन्निकर्षजं हि तदिति इन्द्रियस्य वै सतो मनस इन्द्रियेभ्यः पृथगुपदेशो धर्मभेदात् । .... मनसश्चेन्द्रियभावान्न वाच्यं लक्षणान्तरमिति । तन्त्रान्तरसमाचाराच्चैतत् प्रत्येतव्यमिति परमतमप्रतिषिद्धमनुमतमिति हि तन्त्रयुक्तिः ।

(Nyāya-bhāṣya, 1-1-4)

accepted in the Nyāya philosophy according to the scientfic axiom, *viz.* " if I do not oppose a theory of my opponent, it is to be understood that I accept it."

Dignāga laughs at Vātsyāyana by saying that the Naiyāyika (Akṣapāda) takes pride in borrowing his definition of perception (*pratyakṣa*) from the Sūtra of the Vaiśeṣikas,[1] *viz.* that perception is knowledge which arises from the intercourse of the soul with the mind, the mind with a sense-organ, and the sense-organ with its object. The Naiyāyika is however careful not to connect his perception with generality (*sāmānya*), particularity (*viśeṣa*), substance (*dravya*), quality (*guṇa*) and action (*karma*) on which, as pointed out by Dignāga, the Vaiśeṣika's intercourse is dependent. Oh! what a strange consistency.

---

[1] Dignāga quotes the Vaiśeṣika definition as follows :—

བྱེ་བྲག་པ་རྣམས་ཀྱི་མདོ་ལས ——

བདག་དང་དབང་པོ་དང་ཡིད་དང་ །

དོན་དུ་ཕྲད་པ་ལས་གང་གྲུབ་པ་དེ་གཞན་ཡིན་ནོ་ཞེས་ཟེར་རོ ||

(Pramāṇa-samuccaya, Chapter I).

The Sanskrit original should stand thus :—

आत्मेन्द्रियमनोऽर्थसन्निकर्षाद् यन्निष्पद्यते तदन्यत् ।

But it is actually found in the Vaiśeṣika-sūtra as follows :—

आत्मेन्द्रियार्थसन्निकर्षाद् यन्निष्पद्यते तदन्यत् ।

(Vaiśeṣika-sūtra, 3-1-18, p. 121, Sacred Books of the Hindus, Allahabad).

In another place of the Vaiśeṣika-sūtra in connection with the perception of pleasure, etc., the definition of perception, which includes the mind, is stated as follows :—

आत्मेन्द्रियमनोऽर्थसन्निकर्षात् सुखदुःखे ।

(Vaiśeṣika-sūtra, 5-2-15, p. 181, Sacred Books of the Hindus, Allahabad).

In the Bhāṣya of Praśastapāda, the mind (मनस्) is explicitly mentioned as a sense-organ :—

यथापि इन्द्रियाणि घ्राणरसनचक्षुस्त्वक्श्रोत्रमनांसि षट् ।

(Praśastapāda Bhāṣya, p. 186, Vizianagram Sanskrit Series).

Dignāga quotes the explanatory portion of the Vaiśeṣika definition as follows :—

སྤྱི་དང་ཁྱད་པར་ལ་བལྟོས་པ་དང་ །

རྫས་དང་ཡོན་ཏན་དང་ལས་ལ་བལྟོས་པ་ནི་

མངོན་སུམ་མོ་ཞེས་སྦྱོར་བར་མི་བྱ་སྟེ ||

(Pramāṇa-samuccaya, Chapter I).

The Sanskrit original of this portion should stand thus :—

सामान्यविशेषापेक्षं द्रव्यगुणकर्मापेक्षं च प्रत्यक्षमिति न योजितम् ।

Compare Praśasta-pāda who gives a definition of perception (*pratyakṣa*) which is similar to the one criticised by Dignāga :—

सामान्यविशेषद्रव्यगुणकर्मविशेषणापेक्षाद् आत्ममनःसन्निकर्षात् प्रत्यक्षमुत्पद्यते ।

(Praśastapāda Bhāṣya, p. 186, Vizianagaram Sanskrit Series).

As to the mind it is not, says Dignāga, a sense-organ, and pleasure (*sukha*), etc., are not objects of knowledge. The view, that the Naiyāyika, not having opposed the mind as a sense-organ, tacitly accepts it as such, is untenable. If non-opposition was a proof of assent, it was useless for the Naiyāyika to have mentioned the other sense-organs.[1]

Chapter II—Inference for one's self.

Inference (called in Sanskrit *anumāna* and in Tibetan ṟjes-ḏpag) is of two kinds, *viz.* inference for one's self and inference for the sake of others.

Definition.

An inference for one's self[2] (*svārthānumāna*, raṅ-don-gyi-ṟjes-ḏpag) is defined as the knowledge of a thing derived through its mark or sign of three characters.

Three characters of the middle term.

The mark or sign (reason or middle term) should possess one of the following three characters:—

(1) *Effect* (*kārya*, ẖbras-bu)—the mark may be an effect of the thing to be inferred (predicate or major term); *e.g.* smoke of fire.

(2) *Identity* (*svabhāva*, raṅ-ḇshin)—the mark may be in essence identical with the thing to be inferred; *e.g. a simśapā* identical with a tree.

---

[1] Dignāga observes:—

བདེ་སོགས་གཞལ་བྱ་མིན་པའམ་
དབང་པོ་གཞན་ཡོད་ཡིད་དབང་པོ། །
བཀག་པ་མེད་ཕྱིར་ཚོབ་ཅེ་ན
དབང་པོ་གཞན་གྱི་སྒྲ་དོན་མེད། །

(Pramāṇa-samuccaya, Chapter I).

The original Sanskrit text of the verse is quoted by Vācaspati Miśra thus:—

न सुखादि प्रमेयं वा मनो वास्तीन्द्रियान्तरम् ।
अनिषेधादुपात्तं चेद् अन्येन्द्रियरुतं वृथा ॥

(Nyāya-vārtika-tātparya-ṭīkā, 1-1-4).

What Dignāga meant to say is:—

The Nyāya-sūtra distinctly mentions the eye, ear, nose, tongue and touch as sense-organs, but says nothing as to whether the mind (*manas*) is a sense-organ or not. The presumption from this silence is that the mind is not a sense-organ according to the Nyāya-sūtra.

But Vātsyāyana, the famous Hindu commentator on the Nyāya-sūtra, interprets the silence in a quite different way, concluding therefrom that the mind (*manas*) is a sense-organ according to the Nyāya-sūtra.

Dignāga contends "if silence was a proof of assent why did the Nyāya-sūtra not remain silent regarding the other five sense-organs too?"

[2] རྗེས་དཔག་རྣམ་གཉིས་རང་དོན་ནི། །
ཚུལ་གསུམ་རྟགས་ལས་དོན་མཐོང་བའོ། །

(Pramāṇa-samuccaya, chapter II).

(3) *Non-perception* (*anupalabdhi*, mi-ḏmigs-pa)—non-perception of the mark may be due to the non-existence of the thing to be inferred; *e.g* non-preception of a pot is a mark of non-existence thereof.

Inference.

Dignâga mentions the views of some logicians who from smoke, which is the middle term, infer *fire*, the major term, which is inseparably connected with it, and also of others, who from smoke infer the *connection* between fire (the major term) and the hill (the minor term). He argues against the first mentioned logicians saying that if they infer *fire* from smoke they gain no new knowledge from this inference, for it is already known that smoke is inseparably connected with fire. His argument against the other logicians is that they are not able to infer the *connection*, for connection implies two things, whereas here only one thing, *viz.* the hill, is visible, but the other, *viz.* fire, is not visible What then do we really infer from smoke? Dignāga says it is not fire nor the connection between it and the hill, but it is the *fiery* hill that is inferred.[1]

---

[1] Dignāga writes :—

རྟགས་ནི་འཁྲུལ་པ་མེད་པའི་ཕྱིར། །
ཁ་ཅིག་ཆོས་གཞན་དཔོག་བྱས་ཟེར། །
ཆོས་དང་ཆོས་ཅན་གྲུབ་པའི་ཕྱིར། །
ཁ་ཅིག་འབྲེལ་བ་འདོད་པ་ཡིན། །
ཆོས་ལ་རྟགས་ནི་གྲུབ་ཅེ་ན། །
གཞན་ངེས་ཅི་ཞིག་དཔག་བར་བྱེད། །
ཅི་སྟེ་ཆོས་ཅན་ལ་དེ་ཉིད། །
ཅི་ཕྱིར་རྗེས་སུ་དཔོག་མི་བྱེད། །
འབྲེལ་པ་ལ་ཡང་གཉིས་པོ་མེད། །
དེ་ལྡན་ལ་ནི་རྟག་པ་ཐོས། །
བརྗོད་མིན་དོན་གྱིས་གཟུང་པར་འགྱུར། །
འདི་ལ་རྟགས་དང་འབྲེལ་མ་ཡིན། །
རྟགས་ཀྱི་མི་འཁྲུལ་པ་ཡང་ན། །
ཆོས་དང་གཞན་དུ་བསྟན་པར་བྱ། །
དེ་ལ་གྲུབ་ན་ཆོས་ཅན་ནི། །
དེ་དང་ལྡན་པར་རྟོགས་པར་འགྱུར། ། ||

(Pramāṇa-samuccaya, chapter II).

The Sanskrit originals of these lines are as follows :—

केचिद्धर्मान्तरं मेयं लिङ्गस्याव्यभिचारतः।
संबन्धं केचिदिच्छन्ति सिद्धत्वाद्धर्मधर्मिणोः॥
लिङ्गं धर्मे प्रसिद्धं चेत् किमन्यत् तेन मीयते।
अथ धर्मिणि तस्यैव किमर्थं नानुमेयता॥

Chapter III—Inference for the sake of others.

Definition.

An inference for the sake of others[1] (called in Sanskrit *parārthānumāna* and in Tibetan gshan-gyi-don-gyi-rjes-dpag) takes place when a person demonstrates to others the conclusion drawn by him through an inference for one's self.

Predicate.

The predicate[2] or major term (called in Sanskrit *anumeya* or *sādhya* and in Tibetan dpag-bya or bsgrub bya) is the object which is desired by one's self to be predicable of (attributed to) the subject (or minor term) and which is not opposed to perception, inference or verbal testimony; *e.g.* the hill is *fiery*.

संबन्धेऽपि द्वयं नास्ति षष्ठी श्रूयते तद्वति ।
अवाच्योऽनुगृहीतत्वान्न चासौ लिङ्गसंगतः ॥
लिङ्गस्याव्यभिचारस्तु धर्म्मेणान्यत्र दृश्यते ।
तत्र प्रसिद्धं तद्युक्तं धर्म्मिणं गमयिष्यति ॥

(Pramāṇa-samuccaya, chapter II).

The Hindu logician Vācaspati Miśra has quoted and criticised these lines in the Nyāya-vārtika-tātparya-ṭikā, 1-1-5.

[1] Dignāga observes :—

གཞན་གྱི་དོན་གྱི་རྗེས་དཔག་ནི །
རང་གིས་མཐོང་དོན་གསལ་བྱེད་ཡིན །།

(Pramāṇa-samuccaya, chapter III).

The Sanskrit original of this verse runs thus :—

परार्थानुमानन्तु स्वदृष्टार्थप्रकाशनम् ।

(Quoted in Ślokavārtika-ṭīkā, p. 252).

Praśastapāda defines parārthānumāna thus :—

पञ्चावयवेन वाक्येन स्वनिश्चितार्थप्रतिपादनं परार्थानुमानम् ।

(Praśastapāda Bhāṣya, p. 231, edited by M.M. Vindhyeśvari Prasad Dvivedin, Vizianagaram Sanskrit Series).

[2] Dignāga observes :—

རང་གི་ངོ་བོ་ཁོ་ན་བསྟན་
བདག་འདོད་རང་གི་ཆོས་ཅན་ལ །
མངོན་སུམ་དོན་དང་རྗེས་དཔག་དང་
ཡིད་ཆེས་གྲགས་པས་མ་བསལ་བའོ །།

(Pramāṇa-samuccaya, chapter III).

The Sanskrit original should run thus :—

स्वरूपेणैव निर्देश्यः
स्वयमिष्टः स्वधर्म्मिणि ।
प्रत्यक्षार्थानुमानेन
चाप्तवाचाऽनिराकृतः ॥

(Pramāṇa-samuccaya, chapter III).

The law of extension.—The law of extension of the middle term (called in Sanskrit *pakṣa-dharma*[1] and in Tibetan phyogs-chos), which refers to the local area of a reason or middle term in relation to its minor and major terms, is stated as follows:—

(1) The reason or middle term must cover the subject or minor term (*pakṣa*).
(2) The reason or middle term must be present in the homologue (*sapakṣa*) of the predicate or major term.
(3) The reason or middle term must be absent from the heterologue (*vipakṣa*) of the predicate or major term.

Nine Reasons.—It is possible to conceive of nine reasons or middle terms[2] which are present in or absent from the homologues or heterologues wholly or partly. The reasons or middle terms, which are wholly or partly present in the homologues but wholly absent from the heterologues, are valid, their opposites are contradictory and the others are uncertain.[3]

A table of nine reasons, in reference to their homologues and heterologues, is given below:—

---

[1] ཕྱོགས་ཆོས་མཐུན་ཕྱོགས་ཡོད་མེད་དང་
རྣམ་གཉིས་རེ་རེ་དག་ལ་ཡང་ །
རྣམ་གསུམ་མི་མཐུན་ཕྱོགས་ལའང་
ཡོད་མེད་རྣམ་པ་གཉིས་ཕྱིར་རོ ॥

(Pramāṇa-samuccaya, chapter III).

The Sanskrit originals of these lines are quoted by Vācaspati Miśra as follows:—

सपक्षे सन्नसन् द्वेधा
पक्षधर्मः पुनस्त्रिधा ।
प्रत्येकमसपक्षे च
सदसद् द्विविधत्वतः ॥

(Pramāṇa-samuccaya, chapter III, quoted in Nyāyavārtika-tātparya-ṭīkā on Nyāya-sūtra, 1-1-35, p. 198, Vizianagaram Sanskrit series).

[2] In the commentaries on Nyāya-sūtra, 1-1-35, Uddyotakara and Vācaspati Miśra both severely criticize Dignāga's theory of Nine Reasons. Dignāga too reviews the definitions of a proposition (*pratijñā*) as given by Akṣapāda and the Mīmāṁsaka.

[3] དེར་གང་མཐུན་ཕྱོགས་ལ་ཡོད་དང་
རྣམ་གཉིས་དེ་མེད་ལ་མེད་པ །
དེ་རྟགས་དེ་ལས་བཟློག་པ་ནི
འགལ་བ་གཞན་ནི་མ་ངེས་ཉིད ॥

(Pramāṇa-samuccaya, chapter III).

The Sanskrit originals quoted by Vācaspati run thus:—

तत्र यः सन् सजातीये
द्वेधा चासन् तदत्यये ।

Nine reasons.

No.	Homologue of the major term (*sapakṣa*).	Heterologue of the major term (*vipakṣa*).	Nature of the reason.
1	The reason is wholly present (*sat*) in the homologue.	The reason is wholly present (*sat*) in the heterologue.	The reason is uncertain.
2	The reason is wholly present (*sat*) in the homologue.	The reason is wholly absent (*asat*) from the heterologue.	The reason is **valid.**
3	The reason is wholly present (*sat*) in the homologue.	The reason is partly present (*sadasat*) in the heterologue.	The reason is uncertain.
4	The reason is wholly absent (*asat*) from the homologue.	The reason is wholly present (*sat*) in the heterologue.	The reason is contradictory.
5	The reason is wholly absent (*asat*) from the homologue.	The reason is wholly absent (*asat*) from the heterologue.	The reason is uncertain.
6	The reason is wholly absent (*asat*) from the homologue.	The reason is partly present (*sadasat*) in the heterologue.	The reason is contradictory.
7	The reason is partly present (*sadasat*) in the homologue.	The reason is wholly present (*sat*) in the heterologue.	The reason is uncertain.
8	The reason is partly present (*sadasat*) in the homologue.	The reason is wholly absent (*asat*) from the heterologue.	The reason is **valid.**
9	The reason is partly present (*sadasat*) in the homologue.	The reason is partly present (*sadasat*) in the heterologue.	The reason is uncertain.

Illustration of the nine reasons.—The nine reasons [1] are illustrated by Dignāga in his Hetucakra (Wheel of Reasons) in which he assumes the following as reasons (or middle terms) and major terms respectively :—

Reasons or middle terms (*hetu* [1])—(1) knowable (*prameya*), (2) a product (*kṛtaka*), (3) non-eternal (*anitya*), (4) produced

---

स हेतु र्विपरीतोऽस्माद्
विरुद्धोऽन्यस्त्वनिश्चितः ॥

(Pramāṇa-samuccaya, chapter III, quoted in Nyāyavārtika-tātparya-ṭīkā on 1-1-35, p. 198, Vizianagaram Sanskrit Series).

[1] The Sanskrit originals are quoted by Vācaspati Miśra from Pramāṇa-samuccaya, chapter III, as follows :—

(*kṛta*), (5) audible (*śrāvaṇa*), (6) a product of effort (*yatnaja*), (7) non-eternal (*anitya*), (8) a product of effort (*yatnaja*), and (9) tangible (*sparśaja*).

Predicates or major terms (*sādhya*[1])—(1) eternal (*nitya*), (2) non-eternal (*anitya*), (3) a product of effort (*yatnaja*), (4) eternal (*nitya*), (5) non-eternal (*anitya*), (6) eternal (*nitya*), (7) a non-product of effort (*ayatnaja*), (8) non-eternal (*anitya*), and (9) eternal (*nitya*).

Application of the Law of Extension.—Applying the Law of Extension to the Table of Nine Reasons or the Wheel of Reasons we find that the second and the eighth reasons are valid, and the remaining seven are invalid inasmuch as these are either contradictory or uncertain. Take the case illustrating the first reason in the Wheel of Law. It stands thus:—

> Sound is eternal,
> Because it is knowable,
> Like ether and like a pot.

Here "knowability," the reason, is wholly present in "sound" which is the subject and in "ether" which is a homlogue of "eternal" the predicate. But being wholly present also in "a pot" which is a heterologue of the "eternal," knowability becomes an uncertain reason. Take the case illustrating the eighth reason which stands thus:—

> This sound is non-eternal,
> Because it is a product of effort,
> Like a pot, unlike lightning and ether.

Here "a product of effort" abides in "this sound" which is the subject, and in "a pot" which is a homologue of "non-eternal" the predicate, but does not abide in "lightning" which is also a

---

प्रमेय कृतकानित्यकृत श्रावण यत्नजाः ।
अनित्य यत्नजस्पर्शा नित्यत्वादिषु ते नव ॥

(Nyāyavārtika-tātparya-ṭīkā on 1-1-35, p. 198, Vizianagram Sanskrit series).

The Tibetan version runs thus:—

གཞལ་བྱ་བྱས་མི་རྟག་དང་
བྱས་དང་མཉན་བྱུང་རྩོལ་ལས་བྱུང་ །
མི་རྟག་རྩོལ་བྱུང་རེག་བྱ་མིན་
རྟག་སོགས་རྣམས་ལ་དེ་དགུར ། །

(Pramāṇa-samuccaya, chap. III).

The Sanskrit originals are quoted by Vācaspati Miśra from Pramāṇa-samuccaya, chapter III, thus:—

1 नित्यानित्यप्रयत्नोत्थमध्यम त्रिक साधनाः ।
अयत्नानित्यनित्याश्च प्रमेयत्वादि साधनाः ॥

(Nyāyavārtika-tātparya-ṭīkā on 1-1-35).

homologue and in "ether" which is a heterologue of the predicate. Here the reason is partly present in the homologue and wholly absent from the heterologue and as such is valid.

Chapter IV—Reason and Example.

Affirmative and negative reasons.

From a certain point of view, the reason or middle term (called in Sanskrit *hetu* and in Tibetan gtan-tshigs) is of two kinds,[1] *viz.* affirmative (*anvayi*) and negative (*vyatireki*). The affirmative reason signifies that the thing signified by it is invariably accompanied by the thing signified by the predicate or major term, *e.g.* the hill is fiery, because it is smoky (where *smoke* is an affirmative reason). The function of the negative reason is stated thus: wherever there is absence of the thing signified by the major term, there is also absence of the thing signified by the reason or middle term, *e.g.* the hill is not smoky, because it is not fiery.

A person who desires to produce in others, as in his own self, a definite conclusion, should state (in words) the subject, the predicate and the reason as also their mutual connection, in reference to the Law of Extension.[2]

Examples, *dṛṣṭānta.*

In pointing out the connection of the reason with the major term he should state examples[3] (called in Sanskrit *dṛṣṭānta* and in Tibetan dpe) which are of two kinds, *viz.* affirmative or homogeneous (*anvayi* or

---

1 གཏན་ཚིགས་བསྒྲུབ་བྱའི་རྗེས་འགྲོ་བ།
བསྒྲུབ་བྱ་མེད་ལ་མེད་པ་ཉིས།།

(Pramāṇa-samuccaya, chapter IV).

2 རང་ལ་ངེས་བཞིན་གཞན་དག་ལ་
ངེས་པ་བསྐྱེད་པར་འདོད་པ་ཡིས།
ཕྱོགས་ཆོས་ཉིད་དང་འབྲེལ་བ་དང་
བསྒྲུབ་བྱ་བརྗོད་བྱ་གཞན་དག་སྔང་།།

(Pramāṇa-samuccaya, chapter IV).

A similar idea is expressed in the Nyāyāvatāra of the Jaina logician Siddhasena Divākara :—

स्वनिश्चयवदन्येषां निश्चयोत्पादनं बुधैः
परार्थं मानमाख्यातं वाक्यं तदुपचारतः ॥ १० ॥

(Nyāyāvatāra, edited by Satis Chandra Vidyabhusana, Buddhist Text Society. Calcutta).

3 དེ་ཕྱིར་དཔེ་ནི་གཉིས་ཡིན་ནོ།
... ...
རྗེས་འགྲོ་བཟློག་པ་གཉིས་དག་སྟེ།།

(Pramāṇa-samuccaya, chapter IV).

sādharmya) and negative or heterogeneous (*vyatireki* or *vaidharmya*). An illustration of the examples is given below :—

> The hill is fiery,
> Because it is smoky,
> That which is smoky is fiery, as a kitchen (affirmative example),
> But that which is not fiery is not smoky, as a lake (negative example).

The two examples are in fact identical as they both point out the connection of the reason with the predicate or major term.

Chapter V—Apoha—negation of the opposite.

Apoha.

According to the doctrine of *Apoha*[1] (called in Tibetan gshan-sel-wa), an entity is defined as being the negation of its opposite, *e.g.* a cow is that which is not a not-cow. There is, in this connection, a review of the mutual relations of substance (*dravya*, rdsas), quality (*guṇa*, yon-tan), action (*karma*, las), particularity (*viśeṣa*, bye-brag, or, khyad), generality (*sāmānya*, spyi), and inherence (*samavāya*, hdu-wa).

Comparison, *upamāna.*

According to Dignāga, Comparison[2] (*upamāna*, ñer-hjal) is useless as it is not a separate source of knowledge. He says that when we recognise a thing through perception of a similar thing, we really perform an act of Perception. Hence Comparison or Recognition of Similarity is not a separate source of knowledge, but is included in Perception.

Credible word, *śabda.*

Credible Word[3] or Verbal Testimony (*śābda*, yid-ches-tshig, sgra-las-byuṅ-wa, or, ṅag-don) is also rejected as not being a separate source of

---

1 ཐུམ་ཐོགས་བརྟན་དུ་རང་དོན་ལ། །
གཞན་སེལ་བས་ནི་རྗོད་པར་བྱེད། །
(Pramāṇa-samuccaya, chapter V).

2 ཉེར་འཇལ་བརྙན་དུ་དོན་མེད་ཡིན། །
(Pramāṇa-samuccaya, chapter IV).

Vide a very interesting discussion on it in the Nyāyavārtika, 1-1-6, where the Brāhmaṇa Logician Uddyotakara defends the Nyāya-sūtra and the Nyāya-bhāṣya from the attacks of Dignāga.

3 སྒྲ་ལས་བྱུང་བ་རྗེས་དཔག་ལས། །
ཚད་མ་གཞན་མིན་དེ་ལྟར་ནི། །
(Pramāṇa-samuccaya, chapter V).

Compare—

यथानुमानमेवेदं बौद्धैर्वैशेषिकैः स्थितम् ॥
(Ślokavārtika, śabda pariccheda, verse 15).

knowledge. Dignāga asks: "What is the significance of a Credible Word? Does it mean that the person who spoke the word is credible, or that the fact he averred is credible?" "If the person," continues he, "is credible, it is a mere inference. On the other hand if the fact is credible, it is a case of Perception." Hence Dignāga concludes that Credible Word or Verbal Testimony is not a separate source of knowledge, but is included in Perception and Inference.[1]

Law governing the middle term.

The mark (middle term)[2] is present where the thing to be inferred (major term) or its homologue is present, but absent where the thing or its homologue is non-existent, *e.g.* smoke is present only where there is fire or any thing homogeneous with it, but absent where there is no fire nor any thing homogeneous with the same.

Chapter VI—Analogues or Far-fetched analogy.

In this chapter there is an explanation of the **Analogue**[3] or **Far-fetched Analogy** (called in Sanskrit *jāti* and in Tibetan ltag-gcod) which is of various kinds[3]; such as (1) *prāptisamā* (phrad-mtshuns), (2) *aprāptisamā* (ma-phrad-mtshuns), (3) *varṇyasamā*

शब्दानुमानयोरैक्यं धूमादग्न्यनुमानवत् । २९ ॥
अन्वयव्यतिरेकाभ्यामेकं प्रत्यक्षदर्शनात् ।
सम्बन्धपूर्वकत्वाच्च प्रतिपत्तिरितो यतः ॥ २९ ॥
प्रत्यक्षाद्यप्रमाणत्वात्तद्दृष्टार्थबोधनात् ।
सामान्यविषयत्वाच्च त्रैकाल्यविषयाश्रयात् ॥ ३० ॥

(Ślokavārtika, śabda pariccheda).

1 ཡིད་ཆེས་ཚིག་ནི་མི་བསླུ་བ །
སྤྱི་ལས་རྗེས་སུ་དཔག་པའི་ཉིད །།

(Pramāṇa-samuccaya, chapter II).

The Sanskrit original is quoted by Vācaspati Miśra thus:—

आप्तवाक्याविसंवादसामान्यादनुमानता ॥

(Nyāyavārtika-tātparya-ṭīkā on Nyāya-sūtra, 1-1-7).

Vide Uddyotakara's rejoinder in the Nyāyavārtika, 1-1-7.

2 རྗེས་དཔག་བྱ་དང་དེ་མཚུངས་ལ །
ཡོད་དང་མེད་ལ་མེད་པའོ །།

(Pramāṇa-samuccaya, chapter II).

The Sanskrit originals of these lines, which have been quoted and criticised by Uddyotakara, run as follows:—

अनुमेयेऽथ तत्तुल्ये । सद्भावो नास्तिताऽसति ॥

(Nyāyavārtika, 1-1-5, p. 58, Bibliotheca Indica, Calcutta).

3 For an explanation of these terms *vide* the Nyāya-sūtra.

(brjod-mtshuṅs), (4) *avarṇya-samā* (ma-brjod-mtshuṅs), (5) *anutpatti-samā* (ma-skyes-mtshuṅs), (6) *kārya samā* (ḥbras-mtshuṅs), (7) *sādharmya-samā* (chos-mthun-mtshuṅs), (8) *vaidharmya-samā* (chos-mi mthun-mtshuṅs), (9) *vikalpa-samā* (rnam-rtog-mtshuṅs), (10) *upalabdhisamā* (dmigs-pa-mtshuṅs), (11) *saṁśaya-samā* (the-tshom-mtshuṅs), (12) *arthāpatti samā* (don-rtogs-mtshuṅs), (13) *sādhyasamā* (bsgrub-bya mtshuṅs) and (14) *prasaṅga-samā* (thal-wa-mtshuṅs) Some other kinds of *analogue* are said to be enumerated in the Tīrthika works.

95. Dignāga's **Nyāya-praveśa.**

The **Nyāya-praveśa**[1], or rather "Nyāya-praveśo-nāma pramāṇa-prakaraṇa," is another excellent work on Logic by Dignāga. The Sanskrit original is lost. There exists a Tibetan translation of it which extends over folios 183—188 of the Bstan-ḥgyur, section Mdo, volume Ce. The translation was prepared by the great Kāśmīrian Paṇḍita Sarvajña-śrī Rakṣita and the Śākya monk Grags-pa rgyal-mtshan-dpal-bzaṅ, in the great Sā-skya monastery of Western Tibet. The work in Tibetan is called Tshad-ma-rigs-par-ḥjug-paḥi-sgo signifying the "Door of Entrance to Logic." It opens thus:—

"Demonstration and refutation together with their fallacies are useful in arguing with others; and Perception and Inference together with their fallacies are useful for self-understanding: seeing these I compile this Śāstra."[2]

A Syllogism—Nyāyāvayava.

Parts of a Syllogism.[3] Some of the subjects discussed in the work are noticed below:—

---

[1] I consulted the Nyāya-praveśa in the volume Ce of the Tibetan Bstan-ḥgyur which was placed at my disposal by the India Office, London. I have also brought a copy of the Nyāya-praveśa from the monastery of Labrang in Sikkim which I visited in May 1907. This is probably the same as "Nyāya-dvāra-tarka-śāstra": *Vide* Takakusu's I-tsing, p. 186, and Bunyiu Nanjio's Catalogue of the Chinese Tripitaka, Nos. 1223 and 1224. Cf. Dr. Sugiura's "Hindu Logic as preserved in China and Japan," pp. 36, 60, where Śaṅkara Svāmin's Nyāya-prāveśa-tarka-śāstra is noticed.

[2] སྒྲུབ་པ་དང་ནི་སུན་འབྱིན་ཉིད།
ལྟར་སྣང་བཅས་པ་གཞན་རྟོགས་ཕྱིར།
མངོན་སུམ་དང་ནི་རྗེས་སུ་དཔག།
ལྟར་སྣང་བཅས་པ་བདག་རིག་ཕྱིར།
ཅེས་པ་བསྟན་བཅོས་བསྡུས་པའོ།།

(Nyāya-praveśa).

[3] In Tibetan: Rigs-paḥi-yan-lag (རིགས་པའི་ཡན་ལག) and in Sanskrit: Nyāyāvayava (न्यायावयव) ।

19

Reasoning, according to the Nyāya-praveśa, is carried on by means of a minor term, a major term, a middle term and two examples. The minor term is also called the subject (in Sanskrit: *pakṣa* or *dharmin*, and in Tibetan phyogs or chos-can). The major term is otherwise called the predicate (in Sanskrit: *sādhya* or *dharma*, in Tibetan: bsgrub-par-bya or chos). The middle term is also called the reason or mark (in Sanskrit: *hetu*, *liṅga* or *sādhana*, in Tibetan: gtan-tshigs or bsgrub-par-byed). The example (called in Sanskrit: *dṛṣṭānta*, in Tibetan: dpe-brjod) is of two kinds, *viz.* (1) homogeneous (in Sanskrit: *sādharmya*, in Tibetan: chos-mthun-pa) and (2) heterogeneous (in Sanskrit: *vaidharmya*, in Tibetan: chos-mi-mthun-pa).

Form of a Syllogism.

The form of reasoning is as follows:—

(1) This hill is fiery,
(2) Because it has smoke,
(3) All that has smoke is fiery like a kitchen, and whatever is not fiery has no smoke, like a lake.

Here 'hill' is the minor term, 'fiery' the major term, 'smoke' the middle term, 'kitchen' a homogeneous example, and 'lake' a heterogeneous example.

The Minor Term.

Thesis.

A minor term and a major term linked together constitute a proposition, *e.g.*

The *hill* (minor term) is *fiery* (major term).

A proposition which is offered for proof is a Thesis.

There are certain types of thesis which cannot stand the test of proof and are therefore fallacious.

The Fallacies of Thesis.[1]

The following theses are fallacious:—

(1) A thesis incompatible with perception, such as: "sound is inaudible."

(2) A thesis incompatible with inference, such as: "A pot is eternal."

(Really "A pot is non-eternal, because it is a product.")

(3) A thesis incompatible with the public opinion, such as: "Man's head is pure, because it is the limb of an animate being." (Or, "money is an abominable thing." I or some men like me may say "money is an abominable thing," but the world does not say so).

---

[1] In Tibetan: phyogs-ltar-snaṅ (ཕྱོགས་ལྟར་སྣང་); and in Sanskrit: pakṣābhāsa (पक्षाभास)।

(4) A thesis incompatible with one's own belief or doctrine, such as: A Vaiśeṣika philosopher saying "sound is eternal."

(5) A thesis incompatible with one's own statement, such as: "My mother is barren."

(6) A thesis with an unfamiliar minor term, such as: The Buddhist speaking to the Sāṁkhya, "Sound is perishable." (Sound is a subject well known to the Mīmāṁsaka, but not to the Sāṁkhya).

(7) A thesis with an unfamiliar major term, such as: The Sāṁkhya speaking to the Buddhist, "The soul is animate."

(8) A thesis with both the terms unfamiliar, such as: The Vaiśeṣika speaking to the Buddhist, "The soul has feelings as pleasurable, etc."

(The Buddhist deals neither with the soul nor with its feelings).

(9) A thesis universally accepted, such as: "Fire is warm." (This thesis cannot be offered for proof, as it is accepted by all).

The Middle Term and the Major Term.

Three Characteristics of the Middle Term.[1]

The Middle Term (*hetu*) must possess three characteristics, *viz.*:—

(1) The whole of the minor term (*pakṣa*) must be connected with the middle term, *e.g.*

Sound is non-eternal,
Because it is a product,
Like a pot, but unlike ether.

In this reasoning, "product" which is the middle term includes the whole of "sound" which is the minor term.

(2) All things denoted by the middle term must be homogeneous with things denoted by the major term, *e.g.*

All things produced are non-eternal, as a pot.

(3) None of the things heterogeneous from the major term must be a thing denoted by the middle term, *e.g.*

No non-non-eternal (that is, no eternal) thing is a product, as ether.

If we suppose the minor term or subject to be 'S,' the middle term or reason to be 'R,' and the major term or predicate to be 'P,' then the above-mentioned three characteristics of the middle term may be symbolically set forth as follows:—

(1) All S is R.
(2) All R is P.
(3) No R is non-P.

---

[1] Called in Tibetan: Gtan-tshigs-ni-tshul-gsum (གཏན་ཚིགས་ནི་ཚུལ་གསུམ) and in Sanskrit: Liṅgasya trairūpyam (लिङ्गस्य त्रैरूप्यम्)।

Now, the negative aspect of the middle term, *viz.* no R is non-P, only confirms the truth conveyed by one of the positive aspects, *viz.* all R is P. Hence we may put aside the negative aspect, and exhibit the positive aspects as follows :—

(1) All S is R.
(2) All R is P.

Again, in the above instance 'R' and 'P' may be taken in their whole extent or partially. So the two positive aspects mentioned above may be fully exhibited as follows :—

(1) (*a*) All S is all R.
(*b*) All S is some R.

(2) (*a*) All R is all P.
(*b*) All R is some P.

Combining aspect (1) and aspect (2) together, we find that a syllogism may be of any one of the following forms :—

(1) All S is all P (conclusion) :
Because All S is all R,
All R is all P.

(2) All S is some P (conclusion) :
Because All S is all R,
All R is some P.

(3) All S is some P (conclusion) :
Because All S is some R,
All R is all P.

(4) All S is some P (conclusion) :
Because All S is some R,
All R is some P.

Hence we find that Dignāga admits only two conclusions, *viz.*

All S is all P, and
All S is some P.

Relative extension of the Middle Term and the Major Term.

The second and third of the characteristics mentioned above indicate the relative extension of the middle term and major term. They show that the middle term is universally, invariably, or inseparably connected with the major term. This universal, invariable, or inseparable connection between them is called in Sanskrit *Vyâpti* and in Tibetan *Khyab* which was, as far as I find, first discovered by Dignāga.

Supposing that the middle term or reason is R, and the major term or predicate is P, the connection between the two terms may be symbolically set forth as follows :—

(1) All R is all P, and
(2) All R is some P.

Fourteen Fallacies.

Fallacies of the Middle Term.[1]

Owing to the violation of one or more of the three characteristics, there occur Fallacies of the Middle Term which may be of fourteen kinds as follows:—

A. The *unproved* (Sanskrit: *Asiddha*, Tibetan: Ma-grub) which occurs:

(1) When the lack of truth of the middle term is recognized by both the parties, *e.g.*

Sound is non-eternal,
Because it is *visible*.

(Neither of the parties admits that sound is visible).

(2) When the lack of truth of the middle term is recognized by one party only, *e.g.*

Sound is evolved,
Because it is a *product*.

(The Mīmāṁsakas do not admit that sound is a product).

(3) When the truth of the middle term is questioned, *e.g.*

The hill is fiery,
Because there is *vapour*.

(Vapour may or may not be an effect of fire, and may or may not be connected with it otherwise).

(4) When it is questioned whether the middle term is predicable of the minor term, *e.g.*

Ether is a substance,
Because it has qualities.

(It is questioned whether ether has qualities).

B. The *uncertain* (Sanskrit: *Aniścita*, Tibetan: Ma-ṅes-pa) which occurs:

(5) When the middle term is too general, abiding equally in the major term as well as in the opposite of it, *e.g.*

Sound is eternal,
Because it is *knowable*.

(The 'knowable' is too general, because it abides in the eternal as well as the non-eternal. This is a fallacy of being too general, called in Sanskrit: *Sādhāraṇa*, and in Tibetan: Thun-moṅ).

(6) When the middle term is not general enough, abiding neither in the major term nor in its opposite, *e.g.*

Sound is eternal,
Because it is audible.

[1] In Tibetan: Gtan-tshigs-ltar-snaṅ (གཏན་ཚིགས་ལྟར་སྣང་) and in Sanskrit: Hetvābhāsa (हेत्वाभास)।

(This is a fallacy of being not general enough, called in Sanskrit: *Asādhāraṇa*, and in Tibetan: Thun-moṅ-ma-yin).

(7) When the middle term abides in some of the things homogeneous with, and in all things heterogeneous from, the major term, *e.g.*

Sound is not a product of effort,
Because it is *non-eternal.*

(The non-eternal abides in some of the things which are not products of effort, such as lightning, and abides in all things which are not non-products of effort).

(8) When the middle term abides in some of the things heterogeneous from, and in all things homogeneous with, the major term, *e.g.*

Sound is a product of effort,
Because it is non-eternal.

(The non-eternal abides in some of the things which are not products of effort, as lightning, and abides in all things which are products of effort).

(9) When the middle term abides in some of the things homogeneous with, and in some heterogeneous from, the major term, *e.g.*

Sound is eternal,
Because it is incorporeal.

(Some incorporeal things are eternal as ether, but others are not as intelligence).

(10) When there is a non-erroneous contradiction, that is, when a thesis and its contradictory are both supported by what appear to be valid reasons, *e.g.*

The Vaiśeṣika speaking to the Mīmāṁsaka:

"Sound is non-eternal,
Because it is a product."

The Mīmāṁsaka speaking to the Vaiśeṣika:

"Sound is eternal,
Because it is always audible."

(Both of the reasonings are correct, but as they lead to contradictory conclusions they are classed as *uncertain*).

C. The *contradictory* (Sanskrit: *Viruddha*, Tibetan: Ḫgal-wa) which occurs:

(11) When the middle term is contradictory to the major term, *e.g.*

Sound is eternal,
Because it is a product.

(Product is inconsistent with eternal).

(12) When the middle term is contradictory to the implied major term, *e.g.*

The eyes, etc., are serviceable to some being,
Because they are made of particles,
Like a bed, seat, etc.[1]

(Here the major term "serviceable to some being" is ambiguous, for, the apparent meaning of 'some being' is 'the body,' but the implied meaning of it is 'the soul.' Though things 'made of particles' are serviceable to the body, they are not, according to the Sāṁkhya, serviceable to the soul which is attributeless. Hence there is contradiction between the middle term and the implied major term).

(13) When the middle term is inconsistent with the minor term, *e.g.*

Sāmānya (generality) is neither a substance, nor a quality, nor an action;

Because it depends upon one substance and possesses quality and action.

Like generality-particularity—(*Sāmānya* or generality does not depend upon one substance, etc).

(14) When the middle term is inconsistent with the implied minor term, *e.g.*

Objects are stimuli of action;
Because they are apprehended by the senses.

("Objects" is ambiguous, meaning (1) things and (2) purposes. The middle term is inconsistent with the minor term in the second meaning).

The Example.

Dignāga's theory of examples. Examples converted to universal propositions.

An example before the time of Dignāga served as a mere familiar case which was cited to help the understanding of the listener, *e.g.*

The hill is fiery,
Because it has smoke,
Like a kitchen (example)

Dignāga converted an example into a universal proposition, that is, a proposition[2] expressive of the universal, invariable or

---

[1] This example may lead us to presume that the author of Nyāya-praveśa knew Īśvara Kṛṣṇa's Sāṁkhya-kārikā which is the oldest of the works on Sāṁkhya philosophy that have come down to us.

[2] The universal proposition, that is, the proposition expressive of the universal relation between the middle term and the major term, serves as the major premise in a syllogism of the celebrated Greek logician Aristotle. It was long unknown in India. Dignāga's discovery of the universal proposition marks a new era in the

inseparable connection between the middle term and the major term, which stand to each other in the causal relation or in the relation of inherence, *e.g.*

The hill is fiery,
Because it has smoke,
All that has smoke is fiery as a kitchen (homogeneous example).

The above example is homogeneous. A heterogeneous example is thus given :—

Whatever is not fiery has no smoke as a lake.

Examples have already been stated to be of two kinds, *viz.* (1) Homogeneous and (2) Heterogeneous. Each of these kinds becomes fallacious under certain circumstances. Fallacies of the homogeneous example are the following :—

Fallacies of the homogeneous example.[1]

(1) An example not homogeneous with the middle term, *e.g.*

Sound is eternal,
Because it is incorporeal,
That which is incorporeal is eternal as the atoms.

(The atoms cannot serve as an example, because they are not incorporeal. This is called a fallacy of the Excluded Middle Term).

(2) An example not homogeneous with the major term, *e.g.*

Sound is eternal,
Because it is incorporeal,
That which is incorporeal is eternal as intelligence.

(Intelligence cannot serve as an example, because it is not eternal. This is called a fallacy of the Excluded Major Term).

(3) An example homogeneous with neither the middle term nor the major term, *e.g.*

Sound is eternal,
Because it is incorporeal,
That which is incorporeal is eternal, as a pot.

(The pot cannot serve as an example, because it is neither incorporeal nor eternal. This is called a fallacy of the Excluded Middle and Major Terms).

(4) A homogeneous example showing a lack of universal connection between the middle term and the major term, *e.g.*

This person is passionate,
Because he is a speaker,

---

history of Indian Logic, and shows a great development of the principle of induction.

[1] Called in Tibetan: Chos-mthun-dpe-ltar-snaṅ-wa (ཆོས་མཐུན་དཔེ་ལྟར་སྣང་བ) and in Sanskrit: Sādharmya-dṛṣṭāntābhāsa (साधर्म्यदृष्टान्ताभास)।

> Whoever is a speaker is passionate, as a certain man in Magadha.

(Though a certain man in Magadha may be both a speaker and passionate, there is nevertheless no universal connection between being a speaker and being passionate. This is a fallacy of Absence of Connection, called in Sanskrit: *Ananvaya*, in Tibetan: Ṟjeṣ-su-ẖgro-wa-meḏ).

(5) A homogeneous example showing an inverse connection between the middle term and the major term, *e.g.*

> Sound is non-eternal,
> Because it is a product of effort,
> Whatever is non-eternal is a product of effort, as a pot.

(The pot cannot serve as an example, because though it is both non-eternal and a product of effort, the connection between the major term and the middle term has been inverted, *i.e.* all products of effort are non-eternal: but all non-eternals are not products of effort. This is a fallacy of Inverse Connection called in Sanskrit: *Viparītānvaya*, in Tibetan: Ṟjeṣ-su-ẖgro-wa-phyin-ci-log-pa).

Fallacies of the heterogeneous example.[1]

Fallacies of the heterogeneous example are the following:—

(6) An example not heterogeneous from the opposite of the middle term, *e.g.*

> Sound is eternal,
> Because it is incorporeal,
> Whatever is non-eternal is not incorporeal, as intelligence.

(Intelligence is non-eternal, yet incorporeal. This is a fallacy of Included Middle Term in a heterogeneous example).

(7) An example not heterogeneous from the opposite of the major term, *e.g.*

> Sound is eternal,
> Because it is incorporeal.
> Whatever is non-eternal is not incorporeal, as atoms.

(The atoms are not incorporeal, yet they are eternal. This is a fallacy of included Major Term in a heterogeneous example).

(8) An example heterogeneous from neither the opposite of the middle term nor the opposite of the major term, *e.g.*

> Sound is eternal,
> Because it is incorporeal,
> Whatever is non-eternal is not incorporeal, as a pot.

---

[1] Called in Tibetan: Choṣ-mi-ṃthun-ḏpe-ltar-snaṅ-wa (ཆོས་མི་མཐུན་དཔེ་ལྟར་སྣང་བ) and in Sanskrit: Vaidharmya-dṛṣṭāntābhāsa वैधर्म्यदृष्टान्ताभास)।

(A pot is neither eternal nor incorporeal. This is called a fallacy of Included Middle and Major Terms in a heterogeneous example).

(9) A heterogeneous example showing an absence of disconnection between the middle term and the major term, *e.g.*

This person is passionate,
Because he is a speaker,
Whoever is non-passionate is not a speaker, as a piece of stone.

(This is called a fallacy of Absence of Disconnection of a heterogeneous example).

(10) A heterogeneous example showing an absence of inverse disconnection between the middle term and the major term, *e.g.*

Sound is non-eternal,
Because it is a product,
Whatever is non-product is not non-eternal, as ether.

The example should be inverted as:

Whatever is non-non-eternal, *i.e.* eternal, is not a product, as ether. This is called a fallacy of Inverted Negation of a heterogeneous example.

All the three kinds of fallacies—of the Thesis, Middle Term and Example—are fallacies of reasoning. Refutation (called in Sanskrit: *Dūṣaṇa*, and in Tibetan: Sun-ḫbyin) consists in finding out in the reasoning of the opponent any one of the fallacies aforementioned. Fallacy of Refutation (called in Sanskrit: Dūṣaṇābhāsa, and in Tibetan: Sun-ḫbyin-ḻtar-ṉnaṅ-wa) consists in alleging a fallacy where there is no fallacy at all.

Perception and Inference.

Perception and Inference.

Perception and their Fallacies.

Perception and Inference are the two kinds of valid knowledge for one's own self. Perception (called in Sanskrit: *Pratyaksa*, and in Tibetan: M̱ṅon-sum) is knowledge derived through the senses. It is free from illusory experiences and is not connected with name, genus, etc. Inference (called in Sanskrit: *Anumāna*, and in Tibetan: Ṟjeṉ-su-ḏpag) is the knowledge of objects derived through a mark (Tibetan: Ṟtagṉ) or middle term which has three characteristics. There are Fallacies of Perception as well as of Inference (called respectively Pratyakṣābhāsa and Anumānābhāsa in Sanskrit, and M̱ṅon-sum-ḻtar-naṅ and Ṟjeṉ-ḏpag-ḻtar-ṉnaṅ in Tibetan).

96. DIGNĀGA's Hetu-cakra-hamaru.

(*Logic of Nine Reasons*).

The **Hetu-cakra-hamaru** [1] is another small treatise on Logic by Dignāga. The Sanskrit original is lost, but a Tibetan translation is preserved in the Ḇstan-ẖgyur, section M̱do, folios 193-194. The Tibetan translation was prepared by the sage Bodhisattva of Za-hor and the Bhikṣu Dharmāśoka. The work in Tibetan is called G̱tan-ṯshigs̱-kyi-ẖkhor-lo-g̱tan-la-ḏwab-pa signifying "the Wheel of Reasons put in order." [2] It begins thus :—

"Bowing down to the Omniscient One (Buddha), who has destroyed the net of errors, I explain the system of three characteristics of the Reason (or Middle Term)." [3]

In this work Dignāga has analysed all nine possible relations between the middle and the major terms and has found that there are among them two relations which conform to the three characteristics of the middle term already laid down, and the remaining seven relations are at variance with those characteristics. Accordingly he has concluded that only two relations are valid as will be evident from the annexed diagram.

97. Pramāṇa-samuccaya-vṛtti.

The **Pramāṇa-samuccaya-vṛtti** is a commentary on the Pramāṇa-samuccaya by Dignāga himself. The Sanskrit original of this work is lost, but there exists a Tibetan translation which extends over folios 13—96 of the Ḇstan-ẖgyur, section M̱do, volume Ce. The Tibetan translation was prepared, at the command of king Rigs̱-ḻdan-ṟgyal-po, by the famous Indian sage Vasudhara Rakṣita, who was as it were the crest-gem of logicians, and the Tibetan interpreter Sha-ma-ḏge-ḇsñen-siṅ ṟgyal. In Tibetan it is called Tshaḏ-ma-kun-las̱-ḇtus̱-paẖi-ẖgrel-wa. It is divided into six chapters corresponding to those of the Pramāṇa-samuccaya itself. At

---

[1] I brought a copy of the Tibetan version of the Hetu-cakra-hamaru from the monastery of Labrang in Sikkim which I visited in June 1907. This work is probably the same as the Hetu-dvāra-śāstra : *vide* Takakusu's I-tsing, p. 187

[2] The *Hetu-cakra* is also called in Sanskrit *Pakṣadharma-cakra* and in Tibetan Phyogs̱-chos̱-ḏguẖi-ẖkhor-lo.

[3] འཁྲུལ་པའི་དྲ་བ་འཇོམས་མཛད་པའི། །
ཐམས་ཅད་མཁྱེན་ལ་ཕྱག་འཚལ་ནས། །
གཏན་ཚིགས་ཚུལ་གསུམ་ཁོ་བོ་ཡི། །
གཏན་ལ་དབབ་པ་བཤད་པར་བྱ། ། ||

(Hetu--chakra-hamaru).

the end of the work it is stated that "led on by the command of Mañjunātha (the god of learning), Dignāga the great dialectician of sharp intellect, wrote this śāstra which is as deep as the ocean."

There is another translation of the **Pramāṇa-samuccaya-vṛtti** in Tibetan extending over folios 96—183 of the Bstan-ḥgyur, section Mdo, volume Ce. It was prepared by the Indian sage Hema or Kanaka Varma (called in Tibetan Gser-gyi-go-cha) and the Tibetan interpreter Dad-pa-śes-rab in the monastery of Śi-waḥi-dge gnas.

98. Pramāṇa-śāstra Nyāya-praveśa.

Pramāṇa-śāstra Nyāya-praveśa [1] is another work by Dignāga. It was translated into Chinese by the Chinese interpreter Tha-sam-tsan. The Chinese version [2] was translated into Tibetan by the Chinese scholar Dge-śes-siṅ-gyaṅ and the Tibetan monk ston-gshon in the sa-skya monastery of Western Tibet. The very venerable Chinese monk Dharmaratna (called in Tibetan Chos-kyi-rin-chen), who edited the Tibetan version, compared it thoroughly with the Chinese version. The Sanskrit original of the work appears to be lost but the Tibetan version still exists. It consists of folios 188—193 of the Bstan-ḥgyur, section Mdo, volume Ce. In Tibetan the work is called Tshad-maḥi-bstan-bcos-rig-pa-la-ḥjug-pa signifying "An Entrance to the Science of Logic." The Chinese title of the work is Gyen-miṅ-gshiḥi-ciṅ-liḥi-lun.

99. Ālambaṇa-parīkṣā.

The **Ālambaṇa-parīkṣā** [3] is another work by Dignāga. The Sanskrit original of this work appears to be lost, but there exists a Tibetan translation which consists of one folio only (folio 180)

---

[1] At the kind suggestion of Prof. H. Ui (*vide* his Vaiśeṣika Philosophy, p. 68), I have re-examined the *Pramāṇa-Nyāya-praveśa* (fully entitled as Nyāya-praveśo-nāma-pramāṇa-prakaraṇa) and Pramāṇa-śāstra-Nyāya-praveśa (fully called Pramāṇa-śāstra-Nyāya-praveśo-nāma), and find that they are identical in their contents. One was translated into Tibetan direct from Sanskrit and the other through the Chinese language. The original Sanskrit work, of which these two are translations was perhaps called simply *Nyāya-praveśa*. The Bstan-ḥgyur ascribes this work to Dignāga who dealt in it with fourteen fallacies besides other subjects. The *Hetu-cakra*, which treats of nine reasons, is a part of it. The Nyāya-praveśa and the Hetu-cakra combined together constitute Dignāga's "Logic of nine reasons and fourteen fallacies."

[2] The Nyāya-praveśa corresponds to Nos. 1223 and 1224 of Bunyiu Nanjio's Catalogue of the Chinese Tripitaka. No. 1223 represents I-tsing's translation of the Nyāya-praveśa brought out in 711 A.D., while No. 1224 is Hwen-thsang's translation finished in 648 A.D.

[3] I have consulted the Tibetan xylograph of this work as contained in the India Office, London. This is probably the same as "Ālambaṇa-pratyaya-dhyāna-śāstra": *vide* Bunyiu Nanjio's Catalogue of the Chinese Tripiṭaka, No. 1173, and Takakusu's I-tsing, p. 188.

of the Bstan-hgyur, section Mdo, volume Ce. The work in Tibetan is called Dmigs-pa-brtag-pa signifying "An Examination of the Objects of Thought." It begins with an invocation to Buddha and all Bodhisattvas.

100. Ālambana-parīkṣā-vṛtti.

The Ālambana-parīkṣā-vṛtti [1] is a commentary on the Ālambana-parīkṣā by Dignāga himself. The Sanskrit original of this work appears to be lost, but there exists a Tibetan version which is embodied in the Bstan-hgyur, section Mdo, volume Ce, folios 180—182. The work in Tibetan is called Dmigs-pa-brtag-pahis-hgrel.

101. Trikāla-parīkṣā.

The Trikāla-parīkṣā [2] is a work by Dignāga. The Sanskrit original of this work appears to be lost, but there exists a Tibetan version in the Bstan-hgyur, section Mdo, volume Ce, folios 182—183. This version was prepared by the great Paṇḍita Śāntakara Gupta and the interpreter-monk Tshul-hkhrims-rgyal-mtshan. The work in Tibetan is called Dus-bsum-brtag-pa signifying "An Examination of Three Times."

102. Paramārtha (498 A.D.—569 A.D.).

Paramārtha,[3] born in 498 A.D., was a Buddhist ascetic (*Śramaṇa*) at Ujjainī in Western India. He was placed by Jīvita Gupta I or Kumāra Gupta, as an interpreter at the disposal of a Chinese mission sent to Magadha by the Liang Emperor Wu-ti in 539 A.D. Paramārtha taking a large number of Sanskrit manuscripts went to China with the mission which spent several years in India. He reached Canton in 546 A.D. and was presented to the Emperor in 548 A.D. He arrived in 546 A.D. at Nankin where he translated numerous works into Chinese. His death took place in China in 569 A.D.

In 550 A.D. he translated Vasubandhu's Tarka-śāstra into Chinese. He is said to have translated the Nyāya-sūtra too. It

---

[1] I have consulted the xylograph of this work as contained in the India Office, London.

[2] I have consulted the Tibetan xylograph of this work as contained in the India Office, London. This work is probably the same that is called by Takakusu "The Śāstra on the Meditation of the Three Worlds": *vide* Takakusu's I-sing, p. 187. The "worlds" evidently stand for "times."

[3] *Vide* Bunyiu Nanjio's Catalogue of the Chinese Tripiṭaka, Appendix II, Nos. 104, 105. Cf. V. A. Smith's Early History of India, p. 313, third edition, *Vide* Bunyiu Nanjio's Catalogue of the Chinese Tripiṭaka No. 1252.

is further reported that he wrote a work called **Nyāya-bhāṣya** [1] or an explanation of the Nyāya-sūtra in five volumes.

103. Śaṅkara Svāmin (about 550 A.D.).

Śaṅkara Svāmin,[2] as it appears from Chinese records, was a pupil of Dignāga. He seems to have been a native of Southern India. Logic is said to have been handed down by Dignāga through Śaṅkara Svāmin and ten other masters to Śīlabhadra, who was the head of the Nālandā University, and the favourite teacher of the Chinese pilgrim, Hwen-thsang, in 635 A.D. According to the Chinese Tripiṭaka Śaṅkara Svāmin was the author of a work called **Hetuvidyā Nyāya-praveśa-śāstra, or Nyāya-praveśa Tarka-śāstra,**[3] which was translated into Chinese by Hwen-thsang in 647 A.D. This work seems to be different[4] from the "Nyāya-praveśa" or more fully the "Nyāya-praveśo-nāma-pramāṇa-prakaraṇa" which, as we have seen, is ascribed by the Tibetans to Dignāga.

104. Dharmapāla. (about 600—635 A.D.).

Dharmapāla,[5] a logician, was a native of Kāñcīpura in Drāviḍa (modern Conjeeveram in Madras). He was the eldest son of a great minister of the country. From his childhood he exhibited much cleverness, and as he was a young man the king and queen of the country condescended to entertain him at a feast. In the evening of that day his heart was oppressed with sorrow and, assuming the robes of a Buddhist recluse, he left home and applied himself with unflagging earnestness to learning. He was admitted into the University at Nālandā in which he acquired great distinction. Subsequently he became the head

---

1 Professor H. Ui observes:—
He (Paramārtha) also translated......the Caṅ-shwo (or lun-) tao-li-lun (one vol.); and he wrote a commentary (5 vols.) on the last, called the Explanation of the Caṅ-lun. All have been lost.......Caṅ-shwo (or lun) tao-li-lun......may have been the translation of *Nyāya*......that the commentary consisted of five volumes suggests the five adhyāyas of Nyāya-sūtra. (Vaiśeṣika Philosophy, p. 84).

2 *Vide* Dr. Sugiura's Hindu Logic as preserved in China and Japan, pp. 36, 37.

3 *Vide* Bunyiu Nanjio's Catalogue of the Chinese Tripiṭaka, No. 1216, and Appendix I, No. 13.

4 The Tibetans do not know Śaṅkara Svāmin at all. The Chinese pilgrim I-tsing, who visited India during 671—695, speaks of Dignāga and Dharmkīrti, but does not mention Śaṅkara Svāmin. Even Hwen-thsang in his Travel does not mention him. Śaṅkara Śvāmin's Nyāva-praveśa Tarka-śāstra seems to correspond to No. 1216 of Bunyiu Nanjio's Catalogue, Is the original Sanskrit text of 1216 different from that of 1224?

5 *Vide* Beal's Buddhist Records of the Western World, vol. 1, p. 237; vol. 11, pp. 110—223, 229 and 230. *Vide* also Takakusu's I-tsing, p. lvii, and Bunyiu Nanjio's Catalogue of the Chinese Tripiṭaka, Appendix I, No. 16.

of the University. He must have retired from Nālandā before 635 A.D., when Hwen-thsang visited it, and found that Śīlabhadra had succeeded him in the headship of the University. Dharmapāla conjointly with Bhartṛhari composed a Beḍā-vṛtti on Pāṇini's grammar.

He was a follower of the Yogācāra philosophy, and was the author of several works such as (1) Ālambaṇa-pratyaya-dhyāna-śāstra-vyākhyā; (2) Vidyāmātra-siddhi-śāstra-vyākhyā; and (3) Śata-śāstra-vaipulya-vyākhyā which was translated into Chinese in 650 A.D. Hwen-thsang, who visited India in 629 A.D., found in Kauśāmbī the ruins of a monastery where Dharmapāla had refuted the arguments of the heretics.

105. Ācārya Śīlabhadra (635 A.D.).

Śīlabhadra[1] belonged to the family of the king of Samataṭa (Bengal), and was of the Brāhmaṇa caste. He was a pupil of Dharmapāla at the Nālandā University of which subsequently he became the head. The Chinese pilgrim, Hwen-thsang, was his pupil[2] in 635 A.D. Śīlabhadra was a great logician and master of śāstras.

106. Ācarya Dharmakīrti (about 635—650 A.D.).

Darmakīrti's life.

The excellent Dharmakīrti,[3] called in Tibetan Chos-grags, according to the accounts of all earlier sages, was born in the south in the kingdom of Cūḍāmaṇi.[4] Since, however, there is now no country of that name, and since on the other hand all the orthodox and heterodox alike name Trimalaya as the birth-place of Dharmakīrti, it is to be accepted that in olden times Trimalaya was called the kingdom of Cūḍāmaṇi. His father was a Tīrtha of the Brāhmaṇa caste, Parivrājaka Korunanda by name. Endowed from childhood up with a very keen intellect he attained to great skill in the fine arts, in the Vedas and Vedāṅgas, in the art of healing, in grammar, and in all the theories of the Tīrthas. When only sixteen or eighteen years old, he was already deeply versed in

---

1 *Vide* Beal's Buddhist Records of the Western World, vol. II, p. 110; and Takakusu's I-tsing, p. 181.

2 *Vide* Takakusu's I-tsing, p. xlv.

3 *Vide* Lama Tārānātha's Geschichte des Buddhismus vou Schiefner, pp. 175—185.

4 Cūḍāmaṇi is probably the same as Coḍa or Chola country in the Eastern Deccan. As a fact Dharmakīrti was born in the Deccan. *Vide* Pramāṇa-vārtika-kārikā.

the philosophy of the Tīrthas. Occasionally he attended lectures of the Buddhists, and realised that the teachings of Buddha were without faults. There grew up in him a strong inclination towards Buddhism. He donned the dress of a Buddhist Upāsaka (devotee). When the Brāhmaṇas inquired the reason of this he praised the excellence of Buddhism for which he was out-casted. Thereupon he came to Madhyadeśa[1] (Magadha), was received into the Saṅgha (priesthood) by Ācārya Dharmapāla, attained to great learning in the three Piṭakas, and knew in all 500 sūtras and dhāraṇīs by heart.

Dharmakīrti and Kumārila.

Dharmakīrti, desiring to become acquainted with the secret doctrine of the Tīrtha system, donned a slave-attire and went southward. On inquiring who was versed in the Tīrtha system, he was informed that the Brāhmaṇa Kumārila was an incomparable master of the same. The assertion that Kumārila was an uncle of Dharmakīrti is unsupported by Indian authority. Kumārila had received a large fortune from his king, owned many rice fields, five hundred male slaves and five hundred female slaves and many hundred men. When Dharmakīrti, after entering their service, performed the work of fifty slaves indoors and outdoors, Kumārila and his wife were satisfied. They allowed him to hear the secret doctrines. Obtaining knowledge of the secret teaching from Kumārila, he left his house. With the wages which he received from Kumārila for his special services he gave a great feast to the Brāhmaṇas in the night of his departure.

Thereupon he challenged the followers of the system of Kaṇāda named Kaṇāda Gupta and other followers of the Tīrtha system and entered upon debates with them. The debates lasted for three months, during which he withstood all his opponents and converted many of them to Buddhism. Upon this Kumārila was enraged and appeared with 500 Brāhmaṇas for debate. He proposed the condition that whoever was defeated should be killed. Dharmakīrti, who did not desire the death of Kumārila, induced the latter to enter upon the condition that whoever was defeated should accept the doctrine of the winner. Putting

---

[1] In Tibetan literature Madhya-deśa signifies Magadha (Behar). But Manu defines Madhya-deśa as the country lying between the Himālayas on the north, the Vindhya mountains on the south, Prayāga in the east, and the river Sarasvatī on the west:

हिमवद्विन्ध्ययोर्मध्यं यत् प्राग् विनशनादपि ।
प्रत्यगेव प्रयागाच्च मध्यदेशः प्रकीर्तितः ॥

(Manusaṁhitā 2 : 21).

In this connection *vide* a very learned article named "Note on the Middle Country of Ancient India" by Rhys Davids in the Journal of the Royal Asiatic Society, January 1904.

Dharma (doctrine) up as the prize they began the debate, and finally Dharmakīrti was victorious. Kumārila and his 500 followers became followers of Buddha.[1]

Dharmakīrti's triumph.

Dharmakīrti further withstood the Nirgranthas (Jainas), Rāhuvratin and others, who lived within the range of the Vindhya mountains.[2] Returning to Dravali (Drāviḍa) he challenged by criers those who were ready for debate. The majority of the Tīrthas fled; and some actually confessed that they were not equal to the fight. He re-established all the religious schools that had fallen into decay in that country, and lived in the loneliness of the forest given up to meditation.

Dharmakīrti towards the end of his life erected a vihāra in the land of Kaliṅga, and after having converted many people to the Law (*Dharma*) passed away. Those of his pupils, who by their lives had become like Brahma, carried him to the cemetery for cremation. Then there fell a heavy rain of flowers, and for seven days the whole country was filled with fragrance and music.

This Ācārya (Dharmakīrti) and the Tibetan king Sroṅ-tsan-gam-po are said to have been contemporaries, which statement might be accepted as authoritative.

Dharmakīrti's age.

From this account it is evident that Dharmakīrti was a pupil of Dharmapāla. As the latter lived in 635 A.D., Dharmakīrti must also have lived about that time. This date agrees well with the statement that Dharmakīrti was a contemporary of the Tibetan king Sroṅ-

---

1 This tradition, which is recorded in the Chos-byuṅ of Tāranātha, is repeated in the Ḏpag-bsam-ljon-bzaṅ, as follows :—

དེའི་ཚེ་གཞོན་ནུ་རོལ་པས་ཐོས་ནས་ཁྲོས་ཏེ་འཁོར་ལྔ་བརྒྱ་བཅས་ཁོང་ནས་བརྩོམས་ཚེ་ཕོ་བོའི་ཐུན་མོང

མིན་པའི་དམ་བཅས་ལྔ་བརྒྱ་པོ་སྲུན་ཕྱུང་སྟེ་ནང་པར་གནུགས །

(Ḏpag-bsam-ljon-bzaṅ, edited by Sarat Chandra Das, p. 106).

The extract may be translated thus :—Upon this Kumārila was enraged and appeared with 500 attendants for debate. Being defeated he and his attendants became, in pursuance of his extraordinary pledge, followers of Buddha.

2 While sojourning in the Vindhya mountains Dharmakīrti was invited by a neighbouring king who, as a token of honour, had the following inscription recorded on his gate :—

གལ་ཏེ་ཆོས་ཀྱི་གྲགས་པ་ཡི།
སྨྲ་བའི་ཉི་མ་ནུབ་པ་ན།
ཆོས་རྣམས་གཉིད་ལོག་ཡང་ན་ཤི།
ཆོས་མ་ཡིན་རྣམས་ད་གཏོད་ལོངས།།

(Ḏpag-bsam-ljon-bzaṅ, p. 106).

If Dharmakīrti, the sun among disputants, sets and his doctrines sleep or die, the false doctrines of the Tīrthikas will then rise.

tsan-gam-po who lived during 627—698 A.D.[1] It seems that in 635 A.D., Dharmakīrti was very young as Hwen-thsang does not mention him. On the other hand I-tsing, who travelled over India during 671—695 A.D., declares eloquently how "Dharmakīrti made further improvement in Logic"[2] after Dignāga. The Brāhmanic logician Uddyotakara[3] is attacked by Dharmakīrti. The Mīmāṁsaka Sureśvarācārya,[4] author of the Bṛhadāraṇyaka-vārtika, and the Digambara Jaina Vidyānanda, author of the Aṣṭa-sāhasrikā,[5] have on the contrary criticised the definition of perception (*Pratyakṣa*) as given by Dharmakīrti, who is sometimes designated by the shorter name Kīrti. Vācaspati Miśra[6] too quotes Dharmakīrti to criticise him.

107. Pramāṇa-vārtika-kārikā.

Dharmakīrti is the author of numerous works on Logic. The Pramāṇa-vārtika-kārikā is one of them. A verse[7] of this work was quoted by the Hindu philosopher Mādhavācārya in the 14th

---

[1] *Vide* Wassilief, p. 54; and Csoma de Koros's Tibetan Grammar, p. 183.

[2] Takakusu's I-tsing, p. lviii.

[3] *Vide* K. B. Pathak's "Bhartṛhari and Kumārila," *Journal of the Bombay Branch of the Royal Asiatic Society*, 1892, vol. xviii, p. 229.

[4] Cf. निश्चेय ह्यविनाभावादिति धर्म्मकीर्त्तिना ।
प्रत्यक्षादि प्रतिज्ञेयं चीयेताशो न संशयः ॥
(Sureśvara's Bṛhadāraṇyaka-vārtika, chap. vi.)

[5] Vide *Journal of the Bombay Branch of the Royal Asiatic Society*, vol. xix, 1895—97, p. 56.

[6] Cf. यथाह धर्म्मकीर्त्तिः:—
तस्मान्नार्थे न च ज्ञाने स्थूलाभासस्तदात्मनः ।
एकत्र प्रतिषिद्धत्वाद्बहुष्वपि न सम्भवः ॥
(Vācaspati's Bhāmatī on Vedānta-sūtra, 2-2-28).

[7] The verse runs thus:—
भेदश्च भ्रान्तिविज्ञानैः दृश्येतेन्दाविवाद्वये ॥
(Pramāṇa-vārtika-kārikā quoted in Mādhavācārya's Sarvadarśanasaṁgraha, chapter on Bauddha darśana).

The Tibetan version of the verse runs as follows:—
རྣམ་ཤེས་འཁྲུལ་པས་ཟླ་བ་གཉིས ||
མེད་པར་ཐ་དད་མཐོང་བ་བཞིན ||
(Pramāṇa-vārtika-kārikā embodied in the Bstan-ḫgyur, Mdo, Ce, folio 230. *Vide* Louis de la Vallee Poussin's Le Bouddhisme d'après les sources brahmaniques, p. 34).

century A.D. The following story [1] is told regarding the composition of this work :—

Composition of the work.

It is said that Dharmakīrti studied many dialectic śāstras, but his spirit was not satisfied. Once at the house of one Īśvara Sena,[2] a pupil of Dignāga, he heard the Pramāṇa-samuccaya Having heard it for the first time, he at once became as proficient as Īśvara Sena who had minutely studied the work. When he heard it the second time, he became like Dignāga, the author of the work, and when he heard it the third time, he recognized several errors in the work. When he mentioned them to Īśvara Sena, the latter so far from being displeased, told him that he was at liberty to condemn all the mistakes of the work and to prepare a critical commentary on it. With the permission thus received he composed a metrical commentary on the Pramāṇa-samuccaya called the Pramāṇa-vārtika-kārikā.

Subjects of the work.

The Sanskrit original of the Pramāṇa-vārtika appears to be lost, but there exists a Tibetan translation [3] of it in the B̲stan-h̲gyur, section M̲do, volume Ce, folios 194—258. This translation was prepared by the Indian sage Subhūti-śrī-śānti and the Tibetan interpreter D̲ge-wah̲i-b̲lo-gros̲. The work in Tibetan is called Tshad̲-ma-r̲nam-h̲grel-gyi-tshig signifying "Memorial Verses explanatory of *Pramāṇa* or Sources of Knowledge." The work is divided into four chapters as follows :—(1) Inference for one's own self (in Tibetan : Raṅ-gi-don-rjes̲-su-d̲pag-pa, in Sanskrit : *Svārthānumāna*) ; (2) Establishment of *Pramāṇa* (in Tibetan : Tsad̲-ma-grub-pa, in Sanskrit : *Pramāṇa-siddhi*) ; (3) Perception (in Tibetan : Mṅon-sum, in Sanskrit : *Pratyakṣa*) ; and (4) Words for the sake of others (in Tibetan : G̲shan-gyi-don-gyi-tshig, in Sanskrit : *Parārtha-vākya*). The colophon [4] of the work runs as follows :—" Here is finished

---

[1] *Vide* Tāranātha's Geschichte des Buddhismus von Schiefner, p. 176.

[2] It seems that Īśvara Sena, in whose house Dharmakīrti heard the Pramāṇa-samuccaya, was not a direct pupil of Dignāga, for, while Dignāga lived about 500 A.D., Dharmakīrti lived about 635 A.D.

[3] I have consulted the copy of this work embodied in the B̲stan-h̲gyur of the India Office, London.

[4] ཚད་མ་རྣམས་འགྲེལ་ཚིག་ལེའུར་བྱས་པ།
ཡུལ་ལྷོ་ཕྱོགས་ཀྱི་རྒྱུད་དུ་བྱུང་བ།
གཞུང་ལུགས་ངན་པ་ཐམས་ཅད་ཚོས་ཤིན་ཏུ་འཁྲུལ་པར་འཇུག་པ།
སྙན་པའི་གྲགས་པས་སའི་སྟེང་མ་ལུས་པ་ཁྱབ་པ།
འགྲན་ཟླ་མེད་པའི་མཁས་པ་ཆེན་པོ་དཔལ་ཆོས་ཀྱི་གྲགས་པས་མཛད་པ་རྫོགས་སོ།།

(Pramāṇa-vārtika-kārikā in B̲stan-h̲gyur, M̲do, Ce, leaf 258).

Vide Dr. Satis Chandra Vidyabhusana's Introduction to " Bilingual Index of Nyāyabindu" published in the Bibliotheca Indica series of Calcutta.

the Pramāṇa-vartika-kārikā of Śrī Dharmakīrti who was born in a family of the Deccan, who exposed largely the errors of all the vicious texts (of the Tīrthikas), whose fame filled the entire earth, and who as a great sage had no rival"

108. Pramāṇa-vārtika-vṛtti.

There was a sub-commentary on the Pramāṇa-vārtika-kārikā called **Pramāṇa vārtika-vṛtti** by Dharmakīrti himself. The Sanskrit original of this work is lost. There exists, however, a Tibetan translation[1] of it in the Ḇstan-ẖgyur, M̱do, Ce, folios 420–535. In Tibetan the work is named Tshaḏ-ma-ṟnam ẖgrel-gyi-ẖgrel-wa. In the concluding lines of the work Dharmakīrti is described as "a great teacher and dialectician, whose fame filled all quarters of the earth and who was, as it were, a lion, pressing down the head of elephant-like debaters."[2]

109. Pramāṇa viniścaya.

Pramāṇa-viniścaya, quoted[3] by Mādhavācārya, is another work on Logic by Dharmakīrti. The Sanskrit original of this

---

[1] I have consulted the Tibetan xylograph of this work embodied in the Ḇstan-ẖgyur of the India Office, London.

[2] རིགས་པ་ཆེན་པོ་སའི་སྟེང་མ་ལུས་པ་ན་ སྨྲ་བའི་གླང་པོ་ཆེའི་སྤྱི་བོ་གནོན་པར་མཛད་པའི་སེང་གེ་ཕྱོགས་མ་ལུས་པར་སྙན་པར་གྲགས་པ་ཅན་དཔལ་སློབ་དཔོན་ཆོས་གྲགས་སྨྲས་པ །

(Pramāṇa-vārtika-vṛtti opening lines).

[3] The following verses of Pramāṇa-viniścaya were quoted in the Sarvadarśana-saṁgraha, chapter on Bauddha darśana, by the Hindu philosopher Mādhavācārya in the 14th century A.D. :—

नान्योऽनुभाव्यो बुद्ध्यास्ति तस्या नानुभवोऽपरः ।
ग्राह्यग्राहकवैधुर्यात् स्वयं सैव प्रकाशते ॥ (क)
सहोपलम्भनियमाद् अभेदो नीलतद्धियोः ॥ (ख)
अविभागोऽपि बुद्ध्यात्मा विपर्यासितदर्शनैः ।
ग्राह्यग्राहकसंवित्तिभेदवानिव लक्ष्यते ॥ (ग)

(Pramāṇa-viniścaya, chap. I).

Prof. Louis de la Vallee Poussin in his "Le Bouddhisme d'après les sources brahmaniques," pp. 32 and 34, identifies the above verses with their Tibetan versions as follows :—

བློ་ཡིས་ཉམས་མྱོང་བ་གཞན་ཡོད་མེད ||
དེ་ཡི་མྱོང་བ་གཞན་ཡོད་མིན ||
གཟུང་དང་འཛིན་པ་མེད་པའི་ཕྱིར ||
དེ་ཉི་དེ་ལྟར་རང་ཉིད་བསལ || (ཀ)
ལྷན་ཅིག་དམིགས་པ་ངེས་པའི་ཕྱིར ||
སྔོ་དང་དེ་བློ་གཞན་མ་ཡིན || (ཁ)

work appears to be lost, but there exists a Tibetan translation[1] of it in the B̲s̲tan-h̲gyur, M̲do, Ce, folios 259—347. The translation was prepared by the Kāśmīrian Paṇḍita Parahita Bhadra and the Tibetan interpreter B̲lo-l̲dan-śes̲-rab in the matchless city of Kāśmīra. The work in Tibetan is called Tshad̲-ma r̲nan-par-ṅes̲-pa signifying "Determination of Pramāṇa or Sources of Knowledge." The work is divided into three chapters as follows :—(1) System of Perception (in Tibetan : Mṅon-sum-g̲tan-la-dwab-pa, in Sanskrit : *Pratyakṣa-vyavasthā*) ; (2) Inference for one's own self (in Tibetan : Raṅ-gi-don-gyi-r̲jes̲-su-d̲pag-pa, in Sanskrit : *Svārthānumāna*) ; and (3) Inference for the sake of others (in Tibetan : G̲shan-gyi-don-gyi-r̲jes̲-su-d̲pag-pa, in Sanskrit : *Parārthānumāna*). In the concluding lines Dharmakīrti is described as a great sage of unrivalled fame born in Southern India.

110. Nyāya-bindu.

AN ANALYSIS OF THE NYĀYA-BINDU.

Subjects.

Nyāya-bindu is another excellent work on Logic by Dharmakīrti. The Sanskrit original of this work was discovered among the palm-leaf manuscripts preserved in the Jaina temple of Śāntinātha, Cambay, and has been published in the Bibliotheca Indica series of Calcutta by Professor Peterson. There exists a Tibetan translation[2] of the work in the B̲s̲tan-h̲gyur, M̲do, Ce, folios 347—355. The work in Tibetan is called Rigs̲-pah̲i-thigs̲-pa signifying "A Drop of Logic." It is divided into three chapters as follows : (1) Perception (in Tibetan : M̲ṅon-sum, in Sanskrit : *Pratyakṣa*) ; (2) Inference for one's own self (in Tibetan : B̲dag-gi-don gyi-r̲jes̲-su-d̲pag-pa, in Sanskrit : *Svārthānumāna*) ; and (3) Inference for the sake of others (in Tibetan : G̲shan-gyi-don-r̲jes̲-su-d̲pag-pa, in Sans-

---

སྨྲ་བདག་ཉམ་པར་དབྱར་མེད་ཀྱང་ ||
མཐོང་བ་ཕྱིན་ཅི་ལོག་ཉམས་ཀྱིས ||
གཟུང་བ་འཛིན་པ་རིག་པ་ཉམས ||
ཐམས་ཅད་དང་བཅས་བཞིན་རྟོགས་འགྱུར || (ཀ)

(Pramāṇa-viniścaya, chap. I, embodied in the Tibetan B̲s̲tan-h̲gyur, Mdo, Ce, folios 272, 274 and 273 respectively).

[1] I have consulted the Tibetan xylograph of this work embodied in the B̲s̲tan-h̲gyur of the India Office, London.

[2] I have consulted the Tibetan xylograph of the Nyāya-bindu embodied in the B̲s̲tan-h̲gyur of the India Office, London, as also the excellent edition of F. J. Sher-batski. The Sanskrit edition of the Nyāya-bindu and Ṭīkā (by F. J. Sherebatski) is also available now. Compare a "Bilingual Index of Nyāyabindu" by Dr. Satis Chandra Vidyābhūṣaṇa in the Bibliotheca Indica series.

krit: *Parārthānumāna*). Some of the subjects discussed in the work are noted below.

Perception.

Definition of Perception.

In chapter I, it is stated that all objects of man are accomplished by perfect or valid knowledge. Valid knowledge is of two kinds: (1) Perception (in Sanskrit: *Pratyakṣa*) and (2) Inference (in Sanskrit: *Anumāna*). Perception, which is knowledge derived through the senses, etc., is described as that which is free from preconception (*kalpanā*) and devoid of error (*abhrānta*). Preconception refers to the experiences of false images which appear real as if they were capable of being addressed and touched, *e.g.* the shadow of a tree may appear as the tree itself or a rope may appear as a snake. Error is caused by such causes as darkness, quick motion, journey by boat, shaking, etc.; for instance, to a man journeying by boat, trees on both banks appear to move. Perception is of four kinds: (1) perception by the five senses; (2) perception by the mind; (3) self-consciousness; and (4) knowledge of a contemplative saint. An object of perception is like itself (*sva-lakṣaṇa*) while an object of inference is like any one of its class (*sāmānya-lakṣaṇa*); for instance, a cow which I see is a peculiar one possessing an infinite number of qualities which distinguish it from all cows, whereas a cow which I infer is a general one possessing certain qualities in common with other cows: that is, perception is individual knowledge while inference is general knowledge. According to the proximity or remoteness of an object, perception of it varies. This is the peculiar characteristic of an object of perception, and this characteristic proves the object to be absolutely real (*paramārtha-sat*), as it shows that it possesses some practical efficiency, and this characteristic also shows that perception is a source of valid knowledge for it exactly corresponds to the object perceived.

Inference for one's self.

Definition of Inference for one's own self.

In chapter II, Inference for one's own self (*Svārthānumāna*) is defined as the knowledge of the inferable derived through the reason or middle term bearing its three forms or characteristics. In the instance 'this hill has fire, because it has smoke,' the knowledge of the hill as having fire is derived through smoke which is the reason or middle term.

Forms or characteristics of the middle term.

The three forms or characteristics of the reason or middle term are the following:—

(1) The middle term must abide in the minor term, *e.g.*

The hill has fire,
Because it has smoke,
Like a kitchen, but unlike a lake.

In this reasoning there must be 'smoke' on the 'hill.'

(2) The middle term must abide only in cases which are homologous with the major term, *e.g.* in the above reasoning 'smoke' abides in a kitchen which is homologous with things that contain fire

(3) The middle term must never abide in cases which are heterologous from the major term, *e.g.* in the above reasoning 'smoke' does not abide in a lake which is heterologous from things that contain fire.

Three kinds of the middle term.

The middle term is of three kinds according to the relation which it bears to the major term, thus:—

(1) Identity (in Tibetan: Raṅ-bshin, in Sanskrit: *Svabhāva*), *e.g.*

This is a tree,
Because it is śiṁśapā.

(2) Effect (in Tibetan: Ḫbras-bu, in Sankrit: *Kārya*), *e.g.*

Here there is fire, because there is smoke.

(3) Non-perception (in Tibetan: Mi-dmigs-pa, in Sanskrit: *Anupalabdhi*), which is of 11 kinds as follows:—

(i) Non-perception of identity (Svabhāvānupalabdhi), *e.g.*
Here is no smoke, because it is not perceived (though smoke is of such a nature that it is perceptible if existent).

(ii) Non-perception of effect (Kāryānupalabdhi), *e.g.*
Here there are no causes of smoke of unobstructed capacity, because there is no smoke here.

(iii) Non-perception of the pervader or container (Vyāpakānupalabdhi), *e.g.*
Here there is no Siṁśapā, because there is no tree at all.

(iv) Perception contrary to identity (Svabhāva-viruddhopalabdhi), *e.g.*
There is no cold sensation here, because there is fire.

(v) Perception of the opposite effect (Viruddha-kāryopalabdhi), *e.g.*
Here there is no cold sensation, because there is smoke.

(vi) Perception of contrary connection (Viruddha-vyāptopalabdhi), *e.g.*
Even the destruction of the past entity is not certain, because it is dependent on other causes.

(vii) Perception contrary to the effect (Kārya-viruddhopalabdhi), *e.g.*
Here there are no causes of cold of unobstructed capacity, because there is fire.

(viii) Perception contrary to the container (vyāpakaviruddhopalabdhi), *e.g.*
Here there is no icy sensation, because there is fire.

(ix) Non-perception of the cause (Kāraṇānupalabdhi), *e.g.*
There is no smoke, because there is no fire.

(x) Perception contrary to the cause (Kāraṇa-viruddhopalabdhi), *e.g.*
Hair on his body does not stand erect, because he sits near a fire.

(xi) Perception of effect contrary to its cause (Kāraṇa-viruddhakāryopalabdhi), *e.g.*
This place does not contain any person on whose body hair stands erect, because there is smoke here.

Inference for the sake of others.

Definition of Inference for the sake of others.

In chapter III, Inferençe for the sake of others (*Parārthānumāna*) is defined as the declaration of the three-formed middle term in words: that is, when the reason is set forth in words with a view to producing a conviction in others, it is said to be an inference for the sake of others.

Inference is a kind of knowledge; and words are here called inference by the attributing of effect to cause, for, though they are not themselves knowledge, they produce it. Inference for the sake of others is of two kinds: (1) positive or homogeneous (in Sanskrit: *Sādharmyavat*); and (2) negative or heterogeneous (in Sanskrit: *Vaidharmyavat*), as follows:—

(*a*) Sound is non-eternal,
Because it is a product,
All products are non-eternal as a pot (positive).

(*b*) Sound is non-eternal,
Because it is a product,
No non-non-eternal, *i.e.* eternal (thing) is a product as ether (negative).

Thesis.

The minor term (*Pakṣa*) is that to which the relation of the major term is to be proved, as—This hill has fire, because it has smoke. In this reasoning 'hill' is the minor term which is to be proved as having 'fire' which is the major term. A minor term and its corresponding major term combined together, constitute a proposition which, when offered for proof, is called a thesis.

Fallacies of the thesis or Pakṣābhāsa.

There are four fallacies of the thesis (*Pakṣābhāsa*).

A thesis is fallacious if it is incompatible with—

(1) Perception, *e.g.* Sound is inaudible;
(2) Inference, *e.g* Sound is eternal;
(3) Conception, *e.g.* The moon is not *luna* (Śaśi a-candra); or

(4) One's own statement, *e.g.* Inference is not a source of knowledge.

Fallacies of the middle term.

It has already been stated that the middle term must possess three characteristics. Fallacies of the middle term (*Hetvābhāsa*) occur even if one of the characteristics is unproved, uncertain or contradictory, thus—

A. Unproved (*asiddha*).

(1) Sound is eternal, because it is visible.

(Visibility of sound is admitted by neither party).

(2) Trees are conscious, because they die if their bark is taken off.

(This pecular kind of death of trees is not admitted by the opponent).

(3) The hill has fire, because it has vapour.

(Vapour as an effect of fire is questioned).

(4) The soul is all-pervading, because it is perceived everywhere.

(It is a matter of doubt whether the soul is perceived everywhere).

B. Uncertain (*anaikāntika*).

(1) Sound is non-eternal,
Because it is knowable.

(The knowable is too general, because it includes the eternal as well as the non-eternal).

(6) A certain man is omniscient,
Because he is a speaker.

(The reason is not general enough, for speakers are not necessarily either omniscient or non-omniscient).

C. Contradictory (*viruddha*).

(7) Sound is eternal,
Because it is a product.

(Here 'product' is not homogeneous with 'eternal,' that is, the middle term is opposed to the major term).

(8) Sound is eternal,
Because it is a product.

(Here 'product' is not heterogeneous from 'non-eternal').

Fallacies of the homogeneous example.

Example is of two kinds: (1) homogeneous and (2) heterogeneous. Fallacies of the homogeneous example occur as follows :—

(1) Sound is eternal,
Because it is incorporeal,
Like action.

(Action cannot serve as an example, because it is not eternal, that is, because it is excluded from the major term).

(2) Sound is eternal,
Because it is incorporeal,
Like atoms.

(Atoms cannot serve as an example, because they are not incorporeal, that is, because they are excluded from the middle term).

(3) Sound is eternal,
Because it is incorporeal,
Like a pot.

(Pot cannot serve as an example, because it is neither eternal nor incorporeal, that is, because it is excluded from both major and middle terms).

(4) This man is passionate.
Because he is a speaker,
Like the person in the street.

(The person in the street cannot serve as an example, as it is questionable whether he is passionate, that is, it involves doubt as to the validity of the major term).

(5) This man is mortal,
Because he is passionate,
Like the person in the street.

(This example involves doubt as to the validity of the middle term, that is, it is questionable whether the person in the street is passionate).

(6) This man is non-omniscient,
Because he is passionate,
Like the person in the street.

(This example involves doubt as to the validity of both the major and middle terms, that is, it is questionable whether the person in the street is passionate and non-omniscient).

(7) This man is passionate,
Because he is a speaker,
Like a certain person.

(This example is unconnected (*ananvaya*), for there is no inseparable connection between being 'passionate' and being a 'speaker').

(8) Sound is non-eternal,
Because it is a product,
Like a pot.

(This example involves the fallacy of 'connection unshown,' *apradarśitānvaya:* the connection should be shown as follows: All products are non-eternal like a pot).

(9) Sound is a product,
Because it is non-eternal,
All non-eternal things are products like a pot.

(The example involves the fallacy of inverted connection, *viparītānvaya*: the real connection should be shown as follows: All products are non-eternal like a pot).

Similarly there are nine fallacies of the heterogeneous example.

Refutation.

Refutation (*Dūṣaṇa*) consists in pointing out in the reasoning of an opponent any one of the fallacies mentioned above. The fallacies or semblances of refutation are the analogues or futilities called in Sanskrit *Jāti.*[1]

Concluding part.

In the concluding lines of the Nyāyabindu it is stated by the translators that "Dharmakīrti vanquished the entire Tīrthikas as Śākyamuni had subdued the large army of Māra; and as the sun dispels darkness, the Nyāyabindu has exterminated the Ātmaka theory (that is, the Tīrthika doctrine)—wonderful![2]

Dharmakīrti criticises Dignāga.

Implied contradiction.

The opposition of the middle term to the major term is a kind of fallacy called contradiction which is admitted by both Dignāga and Dharmakīrti. Opposition of the middle term to the implied major term (in the event of the major term being ambiguous) is noted by Dignāga in his Nyāya-praveśa[3] as another kind of fallacy called implied contradiction (in Sanskrit: *iṣṭa-vighāta-kṛt-viruddha*, and in Tibetan: chos-kyi-khyad-par-phyin-ci-log-tu-sgrub-par-byed-

---

[1] For Jāti *vide* Nyāya-sūtra, Book I, aphorism 58.

[2]
ཤཱ་ཀྱ་ཐུབ་པས་བདུད་ཀྱི་སྡེ་པོ་ཆེ ||
ཆོས་ཀྱི་གྲགས་པས་མུ་སྟེགས་མ་ལུས་པ ||
ཉི་མས་སྨག་རུམ་རིགས་པའི་ཐིགས་པ་ཡིས ||
བདག་གི་ལྟ་བ་རྫངས་རྒྱུང་ངོ་མཚར་ཉིད ||
(Nyāya-bindu).

[3] *Vide* Nyāya-praveśa, Fallacies of the Middle Term, concluding lines.

pa). Dharmakīrti in his Nyāya-bindu rejects this view saying that this second contradiction is included in the first kind.[1]

An illustration of the second or implied contradiction is given thus:—

> The eyes, etc., are for the use of another,
> Because they are composite things,
> Like a bed, seat, etc.

Here the major term "another" is ambiguous, inasmuch as it may signify either a composite thing (*e.g.* the body) or a non-composite thing (*e.g.* the soul). There would be a contradiction between the middle term and the major term if the word "another" were used by the speaker in the sense of a non-composite thing, but understood by the listener in the sense of a composite thing. The reasoning would then involve a contradiction of the middle term to the desired or implied major term.

Dharmakīrti[2] in his Nyāyā-bindu considers this case as an illustration of the first or natural contradiction A word, which is the major term of a proposition, can, as such, admit of only one meaning, and if there is ambiguity between the meaning expressed and the meaning implied the real meaning is to be ascertained from the context. If the meaning implied is the real one, there is a natural contradiction between the middle term and the major term.

Non-erroneous contradiction.

Dignāga[3] mentions yet another fallacy called the "non-erroneous contradiction" (*viruddhā vyabhīcāri*, called in Tibetan: h̲gal-wa-la-mi-h̲khrul-pa) which he includes among the

---

[1] तत्र च तृतीयोऽपि इष्टविघातकृद् विरुद्धः ।...स इह कस्मान्नोक्तः अनयोरेव अन्तर्भावात् ।

(Nyāya-bindu, Peterson's edition, Bibliotheca Indica series, chapter III, p. 413.

अयं च विरुद्ध आचार्य्य दिङ्नागेन उक्तः । स कस्मात् वार्त्तिककारेण सता मया नोक्तः ।

(Nyāya-bindu-ṭīkā, Peterson's edition, Bibliotheca Indica series, chapter III, p. 78).

Compare K. B. Pathaka's "On the authorship of the Nyāyā-bindu" in the Journal of the Bombay Branch of the Royal Asiatic Society, vol. XIX, p. 51.

[2] Nyāya-bindu, A.S.B., chapter III, pp. 113--114.

[3] *Vide* Nyāya-praveśa in the B̲stan-h̲gyur, M̲do, Ce, leaf 185. See *ante* Nyāya-praveśa, fallacy of the middle term.

विरुद्धाव्यभिचार्य्यपि संशयहेतुरुक्तः । स इह कस्मान्नोक्तः अनुमानविषये ऽसम्भवात् । ननु आचार्य्येण विरुद्धाव्यभिचार्य्यपि संशयहेतुरुक्तः । स तर्हि आचार्य्यं दिङ्नागेन कथं हेतुदोष उक्त इत्याह ।... तस्मादागमाश्रयमनुमानमाश्रित्य विरुद्धाव्यभिचार्य्युक्तः ।

(Nyāya-bindu-ṭikā, p. 84

Compare also Journal, Bombay Branch of the Royal Asiatic Society, vol. XIX, p. 40.

"fallacies of uncertainty." It takes place when two contradictory conclusions are supported by what appear to be valid reasons, *e g.*:

A Vaiśeṣika philosopher says :—

Sound is non-eternal,
Because it is a product.

A Mīmāṁsaka replies :—

Sound is eternal,
Because it is audible.

The reasons employed in the above cases are supposed both to be correct according, respectively, to the tenets of the Vaiśeṣika and Mīmāṁsā Schools, but as they lead to contradictory conclusions they are uncertain and, as such, fallacious.

Dharmakīrti[1] in the Nyāya-bindu rejects this fallacy of "non-erroneous contradiction," on the ground that it does not arise in connection with inference and is not based even on the scripture. A reason or middle term, which is valid, must stand to the major term in the relation of identity, casuality or non-perception, and must lead to a correct conclusion.

Two conclusions which are contradictory can not be supported by reasons which are valid. Two different sets of scripture too can not be of any help in the establishment of two contradictory conclusions inasmuch as a scripture can not override perception and inference, and is authoritative only in the ascertainment of supersensuous objects. The non-erroneous contradiction is therefore impossible.

The function of an example.

In opposition to Dignāga, Dharmakīrti[2] maintains that 'example' is not a part of a syllogism, as it is included in the middle term, *e.g.*

---

[1] Nyāya-bindu, chap. III, p. 115.

[2] त्रिरूपो हेतुरुक्तः । तावतैव अर्थप्रतीतिरिति न पृथग् दृष्टान्तो नाम साधनावयवः कश्चित् तेनास्य लक्षणं पृथग [न] उच्यते गतार्थत्वात् ।

(Nyāya-bindu, Peterson's edition, Bibliotheca Indica series, pp. 115—116).

The omission of न is perhaps an oversight. The न or negation appears in the Tibetan version which runs as follows :—

གཏན་ཚིགས་ཀྱི་མཚན་ཉིད་གསུམ་སྨོས་པ་དེ་ཙམ་གྱིས་དོན་རྟོགས་པས །
དཔེ་ཞེས་བྱ་བ་སྒྲུབ་པའི་ཡན་ལག་ནི་ལོགས་ཤིག་ཏུ་ཅི་ཡང་མེད་དེ ॥
དེས་ན་དེའི་མཚན་ཉིད་ལོགས་ཤིག་ཏུ་མ་བརྗོད་དེ་དོན་གོ་བའི་ཕྱིར ॥

(Nyāya-bindu, Sher-batski's edition; St. Petersburg, p. 193).

The hill is fiery,
Because it is smoky,
Like a kitchen.

In this reasoning the term 'smoky' includes a 'kitchen,' as well as other similar things, hence it is almost unnecessary to cite the example 'kitchen.' Nevertheless, says Dharmakīrti, the example has this much value[1] that it points out in a particular way what has been expressed in a general form by the middle term: thus, the general expression "all smoky things are fiery" is made more impressive by the particular example 'kitchen' which is smoky as well as fiery.

111. Hetu-bindu-vivaraṇa.

The **Hetu-bindu-vivaraṇa** is another excellent work on Logic by Dharmakīrti. The Sanskrit original of this work is lost, but there exists a Tibetan translation[2] in the Bstan-hgyur, Mdo, Ce, folios 355—375. The work in Tibetan is called Gtan-tshigs-kyi-thigs-pa signifying "A Drop of Reason." The work is divided into three chapters as follows:—

(1) Relation of identity between the middle term and the major term (in Tibetan: Raṅ-bshin-gyi-gtan-tshigs, in Sanskrit: *Svabhāva-hetu*); (2) Relation of effect and cause between the middle term and the major term (in Tibetan: Hbras-buhi-gtan-tshigs, in Sanskrit: *Kārya-hetu*); and (3) Relation of negation between the middle term and the heterogeneous major term (in Tibetan: Mi-dmigs-pahi-gtan-tshigs, in Sanskrit: *Anupalabdhi-hetu*).

112. Tarka-nyāya or Vāda-nyāya.

The **Tarka-nyāya** or **Vāda-nyāya** is another treatise on Logic by Dharmakīrti. The Sanskrit original of this work is lost, but there exists a Tibetan translation[3] in the Bstan-hgyur, Mdo, Ce, folios 384—416. The work in Tibetan is called Rtsod-pahi-rigs-pa, signifying the "Method of Discussion." The Tibetan translation was prepared by the great Indian sage Jñāna-śrī-bhadra and the Tibetan interpreter-monk Dge-wahi-blo-gros. The translation was retouched by the great Paṇḍita Dīpaṅkara (of Vikramaṇīpura in Bengal, born in 980 A.D. and started for Tibet in 1040 A.D.) and the interpreter-monk Dar-ma-grags.

---

[1] … उक्तम् अभेदेन … पुनर्विशेषेण दर्शनीयावुक्तौ ।
(Nyāya-bindu, p. 116).

[2] I have consulted the copy embodied in the Bstan-hgyur of the India Office, London.

[3] I have consulted the work embodied in the Bstan-hgyur of the India Office, London.

113. Santānāntara-siddhi.

The **Santānāntara-siddhi**, also called Tantrāntara-siddhi, is a philosophical treatise by Dharmakīrti. The Sanskrit original of the work is lost, but there exists a Tibetan version[1] in the Bstan-hgyur, Mdo, Ce, folios 416—420. The work in Tibetan is called Rgyud-gshan-grub-pa signifying "Proof of the Continuity of Succession." The Tibetan translation was prepared by the Indian sage Viśuddha Siṁha and the Tibetan official interpreter Dpal-rtsegs.

114. Sambandha-parīkṣā.

The **Sambandha-parīkṣā** is another philosophical treatise by Dharmakīrti. The Sanskrit original of the work is lost, but there exists a Tibetan translation[2] in the Bstan-hgyur, Mdo, Ce, folios 375—377. The work in Tibetan is called Hbrel-wa-brtag-pa signifying "Examination of Connection." The Tibetan translation was prepared by the Indian teacher Jñāna-garbha and the interpreter Vande-nam-mkhas.

115. Sambandha-parīkṣā-vṛtti.

The **Sambandha-parīkṣā vṛtti**[3] is a commentary on the Sambandha-parīkṣā by Dharmakīrti himself. The Sanskrit original of the work is lost, but there exists a Tibetan translation in the Bstan-hgyur, Mdo, Ce, folios 377—384. The work in Tibetan is called Hbrel-wa-brtag-pahi-hgrel-wa.

116. DEVENDRABODHI (ABOUT 650 A.D.).

Devendrabodhi, called in Tibetan Lha-dwaṅ-blo, was a contemporary of Dharmakīrti,[4] and so lived about 650 A.D. He wrote the following work on Logic:—

The **Pramāṇa-vārtika-pañjikā**, called in Tibetan Tshad-ma-rnam-hgrel-gyi-dkah-hgrel, signifying "An Explanation of Difficulties in the Pramāṇa-vārtika of Dharmakīrti." The Sanskrit original of this work is lost, but there exists a Tibetan translation[5] in the Bstan-hgyur, Mdo, Che, folios 1—380. The translation was

---

[1] I have consulted the Tibetan version embodied in the Bstan-hgyur of the India Office, London.

[2] I have consulted the copy embodied in the Bstan-hgyur of the India Office, London.

[3] I have consulted the copy of this work embodied in the Bstan-hgyur of the India Office, London.

[4] *Vide* Tārānātha's Geschichte des Buddhismus von Schiefner, pp. 186—187.

[5] I consulted the work in the monastery of Labrang in Sikkim in 1907.

prepared by the Indian sage Subhūti-śrī and the Tibetan interpreter-monk Dge-waḫi-ḇlo-groṣ.

This story [1] is told regarding the composition of the Pramāṇa-vārtika-pañjikā :—

Dharmakīrti chose Devendrabodhi to write a commentary on his Pramāṇa-vārtika. After Devendrabodhi had finished the commentary for the first time and had shown it to Dharmakīrti, the latter erased it with water. After he had compiled it a second time, Dharmakīrti burnt it in fire. He then compiled it a third time and gave it to Dharmakīrti with the observation; "Since the majority of men are incompetent and time is fleeting, I have written this commentary for the people of lighter understanding." This time Dharmakīrti allowed the work to exist.

117. Śākyabodhi (about 675 A.D.).

Śākyabodhi [2] is stated to have been a pupil of Devendrabodhi. He seems to have lived about 675 A.D He was the author of the following work :—

The Pramāṇa-vārtika(-pañjikā)-ṭīkā, called in Tibetan : Tshaḏ-ma-ṟnam-ḫgrel-gyi-ḫgrel-ḇśaḏ, which is an annotation on the Pramāṇa-vārtika-pañjikā of Devendrabodhi. The Sanskrit original of this work appears to be lost, but there exists a Tibetan translation [3] which covers volumes Je and Ñe of the Ḇstan-ḫgyur, Ṃdo. The translation was prepared by the interpreter Ḏge-waḫi-ḇlo-groṣ.

118. Vinīta Deva (about 700 A.D.).

Vinīta Deva,[4] called in Tibetan Dul-lha, lived in Nālandā during the time of king Lalita Candra, son of Govi Candra, and Dharmakīrti died during the time of Govi Candra. Vimala Candra, the father of Govi Candra, was married to the sister of Bhartṛhari, who sprang from the ancient royal family of Malwa. Supposing this Bhartṛhari to be identical with the famous grammarian of that name who died in 651—652 A.D.,[5] we may place his contemporary Govi Candra in the middle of the 7th century A.D. This is exactly the time when Dharmakīrti died. Hence we may conclude that Lalita Candra, son of Govi Candra,

---

1 *Vide* Tārānātha's Geschichte des Buddhismus von Schiefner, pp. 186—187.
2 *Vide* Tārānath's Geschichte des Buddhismus von Schiefner, p. 187.
3 I consulted this work in the monastery of Labrang in Sikkim in 1907.
4 *Vide* Tārānātha's Geschichte des Buddhismus von Schiefner, pp. 195—198, 272; Ḏpag-bsam-ljon-bzaṅ edited by Sarat Chandra Das, pp. xlviii, 108.
5 *Vide* Takakusu's I-tsing, p. lvii.

flourished towards the end of the 7th century A.D. Vinīta Deva, contemporary of Lalita Candra, must also have lived about this time, a view which harmonises with the date of Dharmakīrti on whose works Vinīta Deva wrote commentaries.

Vinīta Deva, who was the famous author of the Samayabhedoparacana-cakra, wrote the following works on Logic:—

Nyāya-bindu-ṭīkā, called in Tibetan: Rigs-paḫi-thigs-pa-rgya-cher-ḫgrel-wa, which is a detailed commentary on the Nyāyabindu of Dharmakīrti. The Sanskrit original of this work is lost, but a Tibetan translation[1] of it exists in the Bstan-ḫgyur, Mdo, She, folios 1—43. The translation was prepared by the Indian sage Jina Mitra and the interpreter of Shu-chen named Vande-ye-śes-sde.

Hetu-bindu-ṭīkā, called in Tibetan: Gtan-tshigs-kyi-thigs-pa-rgya-cher-ḫgrel-wa, which is a detailed commentary on the Hetubindu of Dharmakīrti. The Sanskrit original of this work appears to be lost, but there exists a Tibetan translation[2] in the Bstan-ḫgyur, Mdo, She, folios 116—205. The translation was prepared by the Indian teacher Prajñā Varma and the interpreter-monk of Shu-chen named Dpal-brtsegs-rakṣita.

Vādā-nyāya-vyākhyā, called in Tibetan: Rtsod-paḫi-rigs-paḫi-ḫgrel-wa, which is a commentary on the Vāda-nyāya (otherwise called Tarka-nyāya) of Dharmakīrti. The Sanskrit original of this work appears to be lost, but there exists a Tibetan translation[3] in the Bstan-ḫgyur, Mdo, Ze, folios 39—65. The work opens thus: "Who is self-perfected in sweet logical discussion, supreme in patience, affection, charity and self-restraint, and who is the most excellent of logicians—to him (Buddha) bowing down I compose a commentary on the text of Vāda-nyāya."

Sambandha parīkṣā-ṭīkā, called in Tibetan Ḫbrel-pa-brtag-paḫi-rgya-cher-bśad-pa, which is a copious commentary on the Sambandhaparīkṣā of Dharmakīrti. The Sanskrit original of this work is lost but there exists a Tibetan translation[4] in the Bstan-ḫgyur, Mdo, Ze, folios 1—24. The translation was prepared by the Indian sage Jñāna-garbha and the Tibetan interpreter Vande-nam-mkhas. The work opens thus:—

"Who is entirely unconnected with the world, and is yet designated as the supreme teacher of it—to him bowing down fully I explain the Sambandha-parīkṣā."

Ālambana-parīkṣā-ṭīkā, called in Tibetan Dmigs-pa-brtag-

---

[1] This work was brought down to Calcutta by the British Mission to Tibet during 1904. I examined it by permission of the Government of India. It is now deposited in the British Museum, London.

[2] I examined this work, by permission of the Government of India, when it was brought down to Calcutta by the British Mission to Tibet, 1904.

[3] I have consulted the India Office copy.

[4] I have consulted the India Office copy.

pahi-hgrel-bśad, is an annotation on the Ālambana-parīkṣā of Dignāga. The Sanskrit original of this work appears to be lost, but there exists a Tibetan translation[1] in the Bstan-hgyur, Mdo, Ze, folios 186—200. The translation was prepared by the Indian sage Śākya-siṁha and the interpreter Vande-dpal-brtsegs of Shu-chen. The work opens thus:—

"Meditating on the merciful Omniscient One, and saluting him by my head, I compose the Ālambana-parīkṣā-ṭīkā."

It ends thus:—

"Here is finished the Ālambana-parīkṣā-ṭīkā, which is a clean work of the teacher Vinīta Deva who weighed all sorts of ālambana (objects of thought), and is a lion of speakers confounding the brains of the Tīrthika elephants."

Santānāntara-siddhi-ṭīkā, called in Tibetan: Rgyud-gshan-grub-pahi-hgrel-bśad, being a commentary on the Santānāntara-siddhi of Dharmakīrti. The Sanskrit original of this work appears to be lost, but there exists a Tibetan translation[2] in the Bstan-hgyur, Mdo, Tshe, folios 1—21. The translation was prepared by the Indian sage Viśuddha-siṁha and the interpreter of Shu-chen named Dpal-rtsegs-rakṣita.

119. Ravi Gupta (about 725 A.D.).

Ravi Gupta,[3] called in Tibetan: Ñi-ma-sbas, was born in Kāśmīra. He was a great poet, dialectician and Tāntric teacher, who established 12 great religious schools in his native country and Magadha. He was a contemporary of king Bharṣa of Vārendra, and flourished before Jayanta, the author of Nyāya-mañjarī.[4] He must have lived in the first quarter of the eighth century A.D., for his disciple the famous Tāntric monk Sarvajña Mitra[5] lived in the middle of that century. Ravi Gupta is mentioned in the inscription of Vasanta Sena[6] as the *Sarva-daṇḍa-nāyaka* and *Mahāpratihāra* in the Gupta saṁvat 435 corresponding to 754 A.D. He was the author[7] of the following work on Logic:—

---

[1] I have consulted the India Office copy.

[2] I have consulted the India Office xylograph of the Tibetan version.

[3] *Vide* Tārānātha's Geschichte des Buddhismus von Schiefner, pp. 146, 147, 243; and Dpag-bsam-ljon-bzan, part i, pp. 90, 101, 118, xxxvii.

[4] एवेन रविगुप्तोऽपि परिच्छानमुखीकृतः ।
चपिकल्पचमादिम्नसुनप्रच्चपपण्डितः ॥

(Nyāya-mañjarī, chap. VII, p. 462, edited by M.M. Gaṅgādhara Śāstri).

[5] *Vide* Satis Chandra Vidyabhusana's Sragdharā Stotra, Introduction, p. xxx, printed in the Bibliotheca Indica series of Calcutta.

[6] Indian Antiquary, vol. IX, p. 167.

[7] For Ravi Gupta's Āryā-koṣa see Rockhill's Buddha, p. 228; and for his

Pramāṇa-vārtika-vṛtti called in Tibetan: Tshad-ma-rnam-hgrel-gyi-hgrel-pa, which is an annotation on the Pramāṇa-vārtika of Dharmakīrti. The Sanskrit original of this work appears to be lost, but there exists a Tibetan translation [1] in the Bstan-hgyur, Mdo, Tshe, folios 132—252.

120. JINENDRABODHI (ABOUT 725 A.D.).

In the Bstan-hgyur, Mdo, Re, there is the Tibetan version of a work called Viśālāmala-vatī-nāma-pramāṇa-samuccaya-ṭīkā. This version was prepared by the Tibetan interpreter Rdo-rje-rgyal-mtshan with the assistance of Dpal-ldan-blo-gros.

The author of the original work was Jinendrabodhi, called in Tibetan Rgyal-dwaṅ-blo-gros, who was comparable to the Bodhisattva (Bodhisattva-deśīya.). He is perhaps the same person who wrote the well-known Nyāsa on the grammar of Pāṇini in the eighth century A.D.

121. ŚĀNTA RAKṢITA (749 A.D.).

Śānta Rakṣita,[2] called in Tibetan: Shi-wa-htsho, was born in the royal family of Za-hor [in Bengal or near Lahor?]. The exact date of his birth is unknown, but it is stated that he was born at the time of Go Pāla who reigned up to 705 A.D. and died at the time of Dharma Pāla who became king in 765 A.D. He followed the Svatantra Mādhyamika school, and was a Professor at Nālandā. He visited Tibet at the invitation of King Khri sroṅ-deu-tsan who was born in 728 A.D. and died in 864 A.D. The king, with the assistance of Śānta Rakṣita, built in 749 A.D. the monastery of Sam-ye[3] in Tibet modelled after the Odantapura Vihāra of Magadha. Sam-ye was the first regular Buddhist monastery in Tibet and Śānta Rakṣita was its first abbot. He worked in Tibet for 13 years, that is, until 762 A.D. He was known there under the name of Ācārya Bodhisattva, and was the author of the following works on Logic:—

Vāda nyāya-vṛtti-vipañcitārtha, called in Tibetan: Rtsod-pahi-rigs-pahi-hbrel-pa-don-rnam-par-hbyed-pa, an elaborate commen-

---

works on Tantra, see Satis Chandra Vidyabhusana's Sragdharā Stotra, Introduction, pp. v—vii.

1 I have consulted the copy of the India Office, London.

2 *Vide* Dpag-bsam-ljon-bzaṅ edited by Sarat Chandra Das, C.I.E., Calcutta, p. 112.

3 For Sam-ye, བསམ་ཡས་ *vide* Csoma de Koros's Tibetan Grammar, p. 183; Sarat Chandra Das in the *Journal of the Asiatic Society of Bengal*, 1881, Part I, p. 226; and Waddell's Lamaism, p. 28.

tary on the Vāda-nyāya of Dharmakīrti. The Sanskrit original of this work appears to be lost, but there exists a Tibetan translation [1] in the B̲stan-h̲gyur, M̲do, Tshe, folios 21—131, and in the B̲stan-h̲gyur, M̲do, Ze, folios 65—186. The translation was prepared by the Indian sage Kumāra-śrī-bhadra and the Tibetan interpreter-monks venerable Śes̲-rab and H̲bro-seṅ-kar (who was a native of the province of H̲bro or Dö) in the holy monastery of B̲sam-yas̲ (Sam-ye). The work opens thus :—

"Who constantly dispersing darkness by the ray of the heap of various pure precious qualities, exerted himself in fulfilling the desire of various sentient beings and rejoiced to do good to the entire world—to that Mañju-śrī bowing down in reverence, I compose this concise and stainless Vāda-nyā-vṛtti-vipañcitārtha."

Tattva-saṁgraha-kārikā, called in Tibetan: De-kho-na-ñid-b̲sdus̲-pah̲i-tshig-leh̲ur-byas̲-pa, a work containing memorial verses on a summary of the Tattvas. The Sanskrit original of this work appears to be lost, but there exists a Tibetan translation [2] in the B̲stan-h̲gyur, M̲do, He, folios 1—146. The translation was prepared by the Indian Paṇḍita Guṇākara-śrī bhadra (belonging to the religious circle first instituted by the great king Lalitāditya in the incomparable city of Kāśmīra) and the great Tibetan interpreter the Śākya monk Lha-b̲la-ma-shi-wa-h̲od in the province of Guge (S.-W. Tibet). The work reviews various systems of philosophy such as the Sāṁkhya, Jaina, etc.[3]

---

[1] I have consulted the xylograph of this work contained in the India Office, London.

[2] I have consulted the work in the monastery of Labrang, Sikkim, which I visited in June 1907. For a detailed account of this work *vide* my "Sāṁkhya Philosophy in the Land of the Lamas" in the *Journal of the Asiatic Society of Bengal*, new series, Vol. iii, No. 8.

[3] Tattvasaṁgraha herein noticed is quite different from the Tattvasmmāsa, a Brāhmaṇic work on the Sāṁkhya philosophy, a manuscript of which is contained in the library of the Asiatic Society of Bengal.

Dr. George Bühler, during his explorations of the Bṛhat-jñāna-koṣa in the temple of Pārśva-nātha at Jesalmir, found in 1873 a *Pothi*, consisting of 189 ancient palm-leaves showing the characters of the 12th or 13th century, and bearing on the outside corner the title *kamala-śīla-tarka* (*vide* Dr. G. Bühler's correspondence with Rai Sarat Chandra Das, Bahadur, C.I.E., published in the *Journal of the Buddhist Text Society of Calcutta*, Vol. i, part ii, p. x). The real name of the work, according to Dr. Bühler, is *Tarka-saṁgraha*. Now, this Tarka-saṁgraha is nothing but Tattvasaṁgraha of Śānta Rakṣita with the commentary, by Kamala Śīla. The introductory part (*Maṅgala*) of the Tarka-saṁgraha, as noticed by Dr. Bühler, runs as follows :—

प्रकृतीशोभयात्मादि [क्रियया] रहितं चलम् ।
कर्म तत्फलसम्बन्ध व्यवस्थादिसमाश्रयम् ॥
गुणद्रव्यक्रियाजातिसमवायाद्युपाधिभिः ।
शून्यमारोपिताकारशब्दप्रत्ययगोचरम् ॥
स्पष्टलक्षणसंयुक्त प्रमाद्वितयनिश्चितम् ।
अणीयसापि नांशेन मिश्रीभूतापरात्मकम् ॥

The subject-matter of the work begins thus :—

" From *Pradhāna* (the primordial matter or nature) possessed of entire powers, all sorts of effects are produced. "

असंक्रान्तिमनाद्यन्तं प्रतिविम्बादिसंनिभम् ।
सर्व्वप्रपञ्च सन्दोहनिर्मुक्तमगतं परैः ॥
स्वतन्त्रश्रुतिनिःसङ्गो जगद्धितविधित्सया ।
अनल्पकल्पासंख्येय सात्मीभूत महोदयः ॥
यः प्रतीत्य समुत्पादं जगाद वदतां वरः ।
तं सर्व्वज्ञं प्रणम्यायं क्रियते तर्कसंग्रहः ॥

The introductory part in the Tattvasaṁgraha is identical with the above, as is evident from the Tibetan version extracted below :—

རང་བཞིན་དབང་ལྡན་གཉིས་ཀ་དང་ ||
བདག་སོགས་བྱེད་དང་བྲལ་གཡོ་བ ||
ལས་དང་དེ་འབྲས་འབྲེལ་བ་དག །
རྣམ་པར་བཞག་ལ་སོགས་པའི་རྟེན ||
ཡོན་ཏན་རྫས་དང་བྱ་བ་དང་ ||
རིགས་དང་འདུ་སོགས་ཁྱད་པར་གྱིས ||
སྤྱོད་དང་སྤྱོ་བཏགས་རྣམ་ཅན་ནི ||
སྒྲ་དང་ཤེས་པའི་སྤྱོད་ཡུལ་ཅན ||
མཚན་ཉིད་གསལ་དང་ལྡན་པ་ཡི ||
ཚད་ལ་གཉིས་ཀྱིས་གཏན་ལ་དབབ ||
ཆ་ཤས་ཤིན་ཏུ་ཕྲ་བས་ཀྱང་ ||
འདྲེས་པ་གཞན་གྱི་བདག་ཉིད་མིན ||
མི་འཕྲོ་ཐོག་མཐའ་མེད་པ་ཅན ||
གཟུགས་བརྙན་ལ་སོགས་དག་དང་འདྲ ||
སྤྲོས་པ་ཀུན་གྱི་ཚོགས་དང་བྲལ ||
གཞན་གྱི་རྟོགས་པ་མཛད་བཞེད་པ ||
བསྐལ་པ་གྲངས་མེད་མི་ཉུང་བས ||
ཐུགས་རྗེ་ཆེན་པོའི་བདག་གྱུར་པ ||
རྟེན་ཅིང་འབྲེལ་བར་འབྱུང་བ་ནི ||
གང་གིས་གསུངས་པ་སྨྲ་བའི་མཆོག ||
ཀུན་མཁྱེན་དེ་ལ་ཕྱག་འཚལ་ནས ||
དེ་ཉིད་རྣམས་ནི་བསྡུ་བར་བྱ ||

Dr. Bühler further observes that the first section of the Tarka-saṁgraha contains **ईश्वर-परीक्षा** (examination of God), **कपिलकल्पितात्म-परीक्षा** (examination of Kapila's doctrine of the soul), **औपनिषदकल्पितात्म-परीक्षा** (examination of the soul according to the Upaniṣads), **स्थिरभाव-परीक्षा** (examination of permanent

The work is divided into 31 chapters, *viz.* : (1) examination of nature (in Sanskrit : *Svabhāva parīkṣā*, in Tibetan : Raṅ-ḇshin-ḇṟtag-pa) ; (2) examination of the sense-organs (in Sanskrit : *Indriya-parīkṣā*, in Tibetan : Ḏwaṅ-phyug-ḇṟtag-pa) ; (3) examination of both (in Sanskrit : *Ubhaya-parīkṣā*, in Tibetan : G̱ñis-ka-ḇṟtag-pa) ; (4) examination of the theory that the world is self-existent (in Sanskrit : *Jagat-svabhāva vāda-parīkṣā*, in Tibetan : H̱gro-wa-raṅ-ḇshin-du-s̱mra-wa-ḇṟtag-pa) ; (5) examination of Brahma the presiding deity of sound (in Sanskrit : *Śabda-Brahma-parīkṣā*, in Tibetan : S̱graẖi-tshaṅs-pa-ḇṟtag-pa); (6) examination of the soul (in Sanskrit : *Puruṣa parīkṣā*, in Tibetan : S̱kyes̱-bu-ḇṟtag-pa) ; 7) examination of the Nyāya and Vaiśeṣika doctrines of the soul (in Sanskrit : *Nyāya-vaiśeṣika-parikalpita-puruṣa-parīkṣā*, in Tibetan : Rigs̱-pa-can-ḏaṅ-bye-brag-pas̱-kun-tu-ḇṟtags̱-paẖi-s̱kyes̱-bu-ḇṟtag-pa) ; (8) examination of the Mīmāṁsaka doctrine of the soul (in Sanskrit : *Mīmaṁsaka-kalpita-ātma-parīkṣā*, in Tibetan : S̱pyoḏ-pa-pas̱-ḇṟtags̱-paẖi-ḇdag-ḇṟtag-pa) ; (9) examination of Kapila's doctrine of the soul (in Sanskrit : *Kapila-parikalpita-ātma-parīkṣā*, in Tibetan : Ser-s̱kya-pas̱-kun-tu-ḇṟtags̱-paẖi-ḇdag-ḇṟtag-pa) ; (10) examination of the Digambara Jaina doctrine of the soul (in Sanskrit : *Digambara parikalpita-ātma-parīkṣā*, in Tibetan : Nam-m̱khaẖi-gos̱-can-gyis̱-kun-tu-ḇṟtags̱-paẖi-ḇdag-ḇṟtag-pa), (11) examination of the Upaniṣad-doctrine of the soul (in Sanskrit : *Upaniṣad-kalpita-ātma-parīkṣā*, in Tibetan : U-pa-ni-ṣa-di-kas̱-ḇṟtags-paẖi-ḇdag-ḇṟtag-pa) ; (12) examination of the Vātsīputra doctrine of the soul (in Sanskrit : *Vātsīputra-kalpita-ātma-parīkṣā*, in Tibtan : G̱nas̱-maẖi-bus̱-ḇdag-ḇṟtag-pa) ; (13) examination of the permanence of entities (in Sanskrit : *Sthira padártha-parīkṣā*, in Tibetan : Ḇṟtan-paẖi-ḏṅos̱-po-ḇṟtag-pa) ; (14) examination of the relation between *Karma* and its effect (in Sanskrit : *Karma-phala-sambandha-parīkṣā*, in Tibetan : Las̱-daṅ-ẖbras̱-buẖi-ẖbrel-pa-ḇṟtag-pa) ; (15) examination of the meaning of the word 'substance' (in Sanskrit : *Dravya-padārtha-parīkṣā* , in Tibetan : Ṟdsas̱-kyi-tshig-gi-don-ḇṟtag-pa) ; (16) examination of the meaning of the word 'quality' ; (in Sanskrit : *Guṇa-śabdārtha-parīkṣā*, in Tibetan : Yon-tan-gyi-tshig-gi-don-ḇṟtag-pa) ; (17) examination of the meaning of the word *Karma* (in Sanskrit : *Karma-śabdārtha-parīkṣā*, in Tibetan : Las̱-kyi-tshig gi-don-ḇṟtag-pa) ; (18) examination of the meaning of the word generality or genus (in Sanskrit : Sāmānya-śabdārtha-parīkṣā, in Tibetan : S̱pyihi-tshig-gi-don-ḇṟtag-po) ; (19) examination of the meaning of the words 'generality,' and 'particularity' (in Sanskrit :

entity), etc. The last colophon appears to him to be स्वत: प्रामाण्यवाद (examination of the doctrine of self-evidence). These are the very subjects treated in the Tattvasaṁgraha. So the two works are identical.

Sāmānya-viśeṣa-śabdārtha-parīkṣā, in Tibetan: Spyi-daṅ-bye-brag-gi-tshig-gi-don brtag-pa); (20) examination of the meaning of the word 'co-existent cause' (in Sanskrit: *Samavāya-śabdārtha-parīkṣā*, in Tibetan: Hdu-wahi-tshig-don-brtag-pa); (21) examination of the meaning of the word 'sound' (in Sanskrit: *Śabdārtha-parīkṣā*, in Tibetan: Sgra-yi-don-brtag-pa); (22) examination of the definition of perception (in Sanskrit: *Pratyakṣa-lakṣaṇa-parīkṣā*, in Tibetan: Mṅon-sum gyi-mtshan-ñid-brtag-pa); (23) examination of inference (in Sanskrit: *Anumānaparīkṣā*, in Tibetan: Rjes-su-dpag-pa-brtag-pa); (24) examination of other kinds of valid knowledge (in Sanskrit: *Pramāṇāntara-parīkṣā*, in Tibetan: Tshad-ma-shan-brtag-pa); (25) examination of the doctrine of evolution (in Sanskrit: *Vivartavāda-parīkṣā*, in Tibetan: Hgyur-war-smra-wa-brtag-pa): (26) examination of the three times (in Sanskrit: *Kālatraya-parīkṣā*, in Tibetan: Dus-gsum brtag-pa); (27) examination of continuity of the world (in Sanskrit: *Saṁsārā-santati-parīkṣā*, in Tibetan: Hjig-rten-rgyud-pahi-brtag-pa); (28) examination of external objects (in Sanskrit: *Vāhyārtha-parīkṣā*, in Tibetan: Phyi-rol-gyi-don-brtag-pa); (29) examination of Śruti or Scripture (in Sanskrit: *Śruti-parīkṣā*, in Tibetan: Thos-pa-brtag-pa); (30) examination of self-evidence (in Sanskrit: *Svataḥ-prāmāṇya-parīkṣā*, in Tibetan: Raṅ-las-tshad-ma-drtag pa); and (31) examination of the soul which sees things beyond the range of senses (in Sanskrit: *Anyendriyātītārtha-darśana-puruṣa-parīkṣā*, in Tibetan: Gshan-gyi-dwaṅ-po-las-hdas-pahi-don mthoṅ-wa-can-gyi-skyes-bu-brtag-pa).

122. Kamala Śila (about 750 A.D.).

Kamala Śila,[1] also called Kamala Śrīla, was a follower of Śānta Rakṣita. He was for some time a Professor of Tantras in Nālandā whence he was invited to Tibet by king Khri-sroṅ-deu-tsan (728—786 A.D.). While in Tibet he vindicated the religious views of Guru Padma-sambhava and Śānta Rakṣita by defeating and expelling a Chinese monk named Mahāyāna Hoshang. He was of wide fame and the author of the following works:—

Nyāya-bindu-pūrva-pakṣe saṁkṣipta, called in Tibetan Rigs-pahi-thigs-pahi-phyogs sṅa-ma-mdor-bsdus-pa, a summary of criticisms on the Nyāyabindu of Dharmakīrti. The Sanskrit original of this work appears to be lost, but there exists a Tibetan transla-

---

[1] *Vide* Dpag-bsam-ljon-bzaṅ, part i, p. 112, edited by Sarat Chandra Das, and also the *Journal of the Buddhist Text Society* of Calcutta, vol. i, part i., p. 10, and Waddell's Lamaism, p. 31.

tion[1] in the Bstan-hgyur, Mdo, She, Folios 106—115. The translation was prepared by the Indian sage Viśuddha Siṁha and the interpreter monk of Shu-chen named Dpal-rtsegs-rakṣita.

Tattva-saṁgraha pañjikā, called in Tibetan De-kho na-ñid-bsdus-pahi-dkah-hgrel, a commentary on the Tattva-saṁgraha of Śānta Rakṣita. The Sanskrit original of this work is lost, but there exists a Tibetan translation[2] of part I of this work in the Bstan-hgyur, Mdo, He, Folios 146—400, and part II of it in the Bstan-hgyur, Mdo, Ye, Folios 1—385. The translation was prepared by the Indian sage Devendra Bhadra and the interpreter monk Grags-hbyor-śes-rab.

123. Kalyāṇa Rakṣita (about 829 A.D.).

Kalyāṇa Rakṣita,[3] called in Tibetan Dge-bsruṅ, was a great dialectician and teacher of Dharmottarācārya. He flourished during the reign of Mahārāja Dharma Pāla who died in 829 A.D. He was the author of the undermentioned works[4]:—

Sarvajña-siddhi-kārikā, called in Tibetan Thams-cad-mkhyen-pa-grub-pahi-tshig-lehur-byas-pa, signifying "memorial verses on the attainment of omniscience." It is contained in the Bstan-hgyur, Mdo, Ze, folios 201—202, and begins with a salutation to Sarvajña.

Vāhyārtha-siddhi-kārikā, called in Tibetan phyi-rol-gyi-don-grub-pa-ces-bya-wahi-tshig-lehur, which signifies memorial verses on the reality of external things. The Sanskrit original of this work is lost, but there exists a Tibetan translation in the Bstan-hgyur, Mdo, Ze, Folios 202—210. The translation was prepared by the Vaibhāṣika teacher Jina Mitra of Kāśmīra and the Tibetan interpreter-monk Dpal-brtsegs-rakṣita.

Śruti parīkṣā, called in Tibetan Thos-pa-brtag-pahi-tshig-lehur-byas-pa, which signifies 'memorial verses on the examination of Śruti or verbal testimony.' The Sanskrit original of this work appears to be lost, but there exists a Tibetan translation in the Bstan-hgyur, Mdo, Ze, Folios 210—211.

---

[1] I have consulted the copy brought down by the British Mission to Tibet in 1904.

[2] I consulted this work in the monastery of Labrang, Sikkim, which I visited in June 1907.

[3] *Vide* Tārānātha's Geschichte des Buddhismus von Schiefner, pp. 216—219: and Dpag-bsam-ljon-bzaṅ, p. 114. The particle 'bsruṅ' signifies "protected" and is an equivalent for Sanskrit "Rakṣita." But Schiefner has taken it as an equivalent for "Gupta." This does not seem to be correct, for the Tibetan equivalent for Gupta is "sbas."

[4] I have consulted Kalyāṇa Rakṣita's works in volume Ze of the Bstan-hgyur lent to me by the India Office, London.

Anyāpoha vicāra kārikā, called in Tibetan Gshan-la brtag-pahi-tshig-lehur-byas-pa, which signifies 'memorial verses on the determination of a thing by the exclusion of its opposites.' The Sanskrit original of this work is lost, but there exists a Tibetan translation in the Bstan-hgyur, Mdo, Ze, Folios 211—213.

Īśvara-bhaṅga-kārikā, called in Tibetan Dwaṅ-phyug-hjig-pahi-tshig-lehur-byas-pa, which signifies 'memorial verses on the refutation of God.' The Sanskrit original of this work appears to be lost, but there exists a Tibetan translation in the Bstan-hgyur, Mdo, Ze, Folios 214—215

124. DHARMOTTARĀCĀRYA (ABOUT 847 A.D.).

Dharmottara [1] (Ācārya Dharmottara or Dharmottarācārya), called in Tibetan Chos-mchog, was a pupil of Kalyāna Raksita and of Dharmākara Datta of Kāśmīra. He appears to have flourished in Kāśmīra while Vana Pāla was reigning in Bengal about 847 A.D., and is mentioned by the Brāhmaṇa logician Śrīdhara [2] about 991 A.D. and by the Jaina philosophers Mallavādin the author of Dharmottara-ṭippanaka about 962 A.D.[3] and Ratnaprabha Sūri [4] the famous author of Syādvāda-ratnākarāvatārikā dated 1181 A D. Dharmottara was the author of the following works:—

Nyāya-bindu-ṭīkā, called in Tibetan Rigs-pahi-thigs-pahi-rgya-cher-hgrel-wa, a detailed commentary on the Nyāya-bindū of Dharmakīrti. The Sanskrit original [5] of this work was preserved in the Jaina temple of Śāntinātha, Cambay, and has been published by Professor Peterson in the Bibliotheca Indica series of Calcutta. There exists a Tibetan translation [6] in the Bstan-hgyur, Mdo, She, Folios 43—106. The translation was prepared by the Indian sage Jñāna-garbha and an interpreter-monk of Shu-chen

---

1 *Vide* Tārānātha's Geschichte des Buddhismus von Schiefner, p. 225; and Dpag bsam-ljon-bzaṅ, p. 114.

2 *Vide* Nyāya-kandalī, p. 76, Vizianagaram Sanskrit series.

3 The Jaina logician Mallavādin (q.v.) wrote a gloss called Dharmottara-ṭippanaka on Dharmottarācārya's Nyāyabinduṭikā. The year 884 in which Mallavādin flourished corresponds to 827 A.D. or 962 A.D. according as we take it to refer to Vikrama-saṁvat or Śakasaṁvat. On one supposition Mallavādin was a contemporary of Dharmottara and on the other he flourished a century later.

4 अथ धर्मोत्तरानुसारी प्राह । प्रयोजनमादिवाक्येन साक्षादाख्यायते इति न क्षमे ।
(Syādvāda-ratnākarāvatārikā, p. 10, Jaina Yaśovijaya series of Benares).

5 The palm-leaf manuscript of the Nyāya-bindu-ṭīkā preserved in Cambay bears the date of saṁvat 1229 or 1173 A.D. (Peterson's Third Report, p. 33).

6 I consulted the copy brought down by the British Mission to Tibet during 1904. The Tibetan version has also been edited by F. J. Sherbatski and printed in Russia.

named Dharmāloka, and afterwards recast by the Indian sage Sumati-kīrti and the Tibetan interpreter-monk Blo-ldan-śes-rab. Nyāyabindu-ṭīkā begins thus:—"Sugata, the conqueror of lust, etc., has overcome this world, the source of series of evils beginning with birth: may his words dispelling the darkness of our mind attain glory." [1]

Pramāṇa-parīkṣā, called in Tibetan Tshad-ma-brtag-pa, signifying 'an examination of Pramāṇa or the sources of valid knowledge.' The work begins with salutation to Sugata. The Sanskrit original of this work appears to be lost, but there exists a Tibetan translation[2] in the Bstan-hgyur, Mdo, Ze, Folios 215—253. The translation was prepared by monk Blo-ldan-śes-rab.

Apoha-nāma-prakaraṇa, called in Tibetan Gshan-sel-wa, signifying 'a treatise on the determination of a thing by the exclusion of its opposites.' The Sanskrit original of this work appears to be lost, but there exists a Tibetan translation[3] in the Bstan-hgyur, Mdo, Ze, Folios 254—266. The translation was prepared by the Kāśmīrian Paṇḍita Bhavyarāja and the interpreter-monk Blo-ldan-śes-rab, in the incomparable city of Kāśmīra.

Pāra-loka-siddhi, called in Tibetan Hjig-rten-pha-rol-grub-pa, signifying 'proof of the world beyond.' The Sanskrit original of this work appears to be lost, but there exists a Tibetan translation[4] in the Bstan-hgyur, Mdo, Ze, Folios 266—270. The translation was prepared by the great Paṇḍita Bhavyarāja and the interpreter-monk Tshab-ñi-ma-grags during the lifetime of Śrī Harṣa Deva (king of Kāśmīra, 1089—1101 A.D.) in the great incomparable city of Kāśmīra.

The work begins thus:—

"Some say that the world beyond is possessed of the characteristics of a complete separation from the link of consciousness which began from before birth and continued after death, etc."

Kṣaṇa-bhaṅga siddhi, called in Tibetan Skad-cig-ma-hjig-pa-grub-pa, signifying 'proof of the momentariness of things.' The Sanskrit original of this work appears to be lost, but there exists a Tibetan translation[5] in the Bstan-hgyur, Mdo, Ze, Folios 270—282. The translation was prepared by the Indian sage Bhavyarāja and the interpreter-monk Blo-ldan-śes-rab.

Pramāṇa-viniścaya-ṭīkā, called in Tibetan Tshad-ma-rnam-

---

1 जयन्ति जातिव्यसनप्रबन्ध प्रसूतिहेतोर्जगतो विजेतुः ।
रागाद्यरातेः सुगतस्य वाचो मनस्तमस्तानवमादधानाः ॥
(Nyāyabinduṭikā, chap. I).

2 I have consulted the India Office copy.

3 I have consulted the India Office copy.

4 I have consulted the India Office copy.

5 I have consulted the India Office copy.

ṅes-kyi-ṭīkā, which is a commentary on the Pramāṇa-viniścaya of Dharmakīrti. The Sanskrit original of this work appears to be lost, but there exists a Tibetan translation [1] in the Bstan hgyur Mdo, Dse, folios 346, and We, Folios 1--188. The translation was prepared by the Kāśmīrian Paṇḍita Parahita Bhadra and the Tibetan interpreter Blo-ldan-śes-rab in the model city of Kaśmīra. In the concluding lines of the work Dharmottara, the author of it is described as "the excellent subduer of bad disputants (quibblers)." [2]

125. Muktā-kumbha (after 900 A.D.).

Muktā-kumhha,[3] called in Tibetan Mu-tig-bum-pa, was the author of a work called Kṣaṇa-bhaṅga-siddhi-vyākhyā, which is a commentary on Dharmottarācārya's Kṣaṇa-bhaṅga-siddhi. Muktā-kumbha must have flourished after 847 A.D., when Dharmottara lived.

The Kṣaṇa-bhaṅga-siddhi-vyākhyā is called in Tibetan Skad-cig-ma-hjig-grub-pahi-rnam-hgrel. The Sanskrit original of the work appears to be lost, but a Tibetan translation[4] is embodied in the Bstan-hgyur, Mdo, Ze, Folios 282—301. This version was prepared by the Indian sage Vināyaka and the interpreter-monk Grags-hbyor-śes-rab.

126. Arcaṭa (about 900 A.D.).

Guṇa-ratna Sūri,[5] the famous Jaina author of the Ṣaḍdarśana-samuccaya-vṛtti, who lived in 1409 A.D., mentions the Tarkaṭīkā of Arcaṭa.[6] Arcaṭa is also mentioned by the Jaina philosopher Ratnaprabha Sūri,[7] the well-known author of Syādvādaratnākarāvatārikā, dated 1181 A.D. In the Jaina Nyāyāvatāra-vivṛti[8] it appears that Arcaṭa criticised Dharmottarācārya who lived about 847 A.D. Roughly speaking he flourished in the 9th century A.D.

---

1 I have consulted the India Office copy.

2 སྨྲ་ངན་ཚར་མཆོག་རྟོག་གེ་ངན་འཇོམས་མཆོག ། (Bstan-hgyur, Mdo, We, Folio 188)

3 The name Muktākumbha is restored from Tibetan.

4 I have consulted the work belonging to the India Office, London.

5 *Vide* Satis Chandra Vidyabhusana's Jaina Logic under "Guṇaratna Sūri."

6 *Vide* Dr. Suali's edition of the Ṣaḍdarśana-samuccaya-vṛtti, chapter on Bauddha darśana.

7 धर्मोत्तरार्चटप्रभृतयः प्रवराः । इह प्रेक्षावतां प्रवृत्तिः प्रयोजनवत्तया व्याप्ता... । (Syādvāda-ratnākarāvatārikā, chap. i, p. 17, published in Jaina Yaśovijaya granthamālā of Benares).

8 *Vide* Satis Chandra Vidyabhusana's edition of the Nyāyāvatāra with vivṛti which has been published by the Indian Research Society of Calcutta.

Arcaṭa was the author of the following work on Logic :—

Hetu-bindu-vivaraṇa, called in Tibetan G̱tan-tshigs̱-thigs̱-paẖi-ẖgrel-wa, being a commentary on the Hetu-bindu of Dharmakīrti. The Sanskrit original of this work appears to be lost, but there exists a Tibetan translation[1] in the ẞstan-ẖgyur, M̱do, She, Folios 205—375. It is divided into four chapters treating respectively of (1) Identity (in Tibetan : Raṅ-ḇshin, and in Sanskrit : *Svabhāva*) ; (2) Effect (in Tibetan : ẖḇras̱-bu, and in Sanskrit : *Kārya*) ; (3) Non-perception (in Tibetan : Mi-ḏmigs̱-pa, and in Sanskrit : *Anupalabdhi*) ; and (4) Explanation of Six Characteristics (in Tibetan : M̱tshan-ñid-drug-ḇśaḏ-pa, and in Sanskrit : *Ṣaḍ-lakṣaṇa-vyākhyā*). In the beginning of the work it is stated that Arcaṭa was a Brāhmaṇa, and from the concluding part it appears that he lived in Kāśmīra. The Tibetan version ends thus :—

"In the city of Kāśmīra, the pith of Jambudvīpa, the commentary (on the work) of Dharmakīrti, who was the best of sages, was translated. From this translation of Pramāṇa the pith of holy doctrines, let the unlearned derive wisdom."[2]

127. AŚOKA (ABOUT 900 A.D.).

Aśoka, otherwise known as Paṇḍita Aśokà or Ācārya Aśoka, is called in Tibetan Mya-ṅan-med. It is stated that through his spiritual instructions[3] Candra-Gomin (q.v.) was able to behold the face of Avalokiteśvara the Lord of supreme mercy and Tārā the saviouress.

Aśoka quotes Dharmottara[4] (q.v.) and must therefore have flourished after 847 A.D. We may approximately place him at about 900 A.D.

---

[1] The volume She, containing this work, was brought down by the British Mission to Tibet in 1904. I borrowed it from the Government of India.

[2] འཛམ་གླིང་སྙིང་པོ་ཁ་ཆེའི་གྲོང་ཁྱེར་དུ ||
མཁས་པའི་སྙིང་པོ་ཆོས་ཀྱི་གྲགས་པའི་འགྲེལ ||
དམ་ཆོས་སྙིང་པོ་ཚད་མ་བསྒྱུར་བ་ལས ||
སྙིང་པོ་མེད་པ་རྣམས་ཀྱི་སྙིང་པོར་ཤོག ||
(Bstan-hgyur, Mdo, She, folio 375).

[3] སློབ་དཔོན་ཙནྡྲ་གོ་མི་ནི། .... སློབ་དཔོན་མྱ་ངན་མེད་བླ་མ་ལ་ཆོས་ལུང་མནོས་ཏེ་བསྒྲུབས་པས་ཐུགས་རྗེ་ཆེན་པོ་དང་སྒྲོལ་མའི་ཞལ་གཟིགས།

Dpag-bsam-ljon-bzaṅ, p. 95, Sarat Chandra Das's edition, Calcutta).

[4] यदेतत् सकलमालोच्य भदन्तधर्म्मोत्तरेणोदसृतम् । न चावयवः क्रियावान् । अवयवेषु पि क्रियावत्सु विभागो जायते ।

(Avayavi-nirākaraṇa, in six Nyāya Tracts, edited by M.M. Hara Prasad Shastri, Calcutta p. 8.)

He wrote two logical treatises,[1] *viz.* *Avayavi-nirākaraṇa* (Refutation of the whole) and *Sāmānya-dūṣaṇa-dik-prasāritā* (Horizon of the refutation of generality extended). The first work, *viz.* Avayavi-nirākaraṇa, which begins with a salutation to Samantabhadra, upholds the theory that the whole (*avayavī*) is a mere collection of its parts (*avayava*) beyond which it has no separate existence.[2] There is no eternal relation[3] called inherence (*samavāya*) existing between a whole and its parts.

The second work, *viz.* Sāmānya-dūṣaṇa-dik-prasāritā, begins with a resolution to oppose those who maintain that there is a category named generality (*sāmānya*) which, being one and eternal, abides in many individual objects. It is argued that though we can see fingers as individual things, we cannot see fingerness as a generality pervading all fingers.

That Aśoka had to defend himself against the attacks of many Brāhmaṇa philosophers is evident from the last verse of his Avayavi-nirākaraṇa which runs as follows:—

"Having uprooted the numerous thorns of criticism fabricated by wicked intellects, I have cleansed the broad moral path of our Teacher. Let people removing their spites, move on by this path."[4]

128. Candra Gomin (Junior). (About 925 A.D.).

His life.

Candra Gomin,[5] called in Tibetan: Zla-wa-dge-bsñen, was born in a Kṣatriya family in the east as Vārendra (modern Rajshahye in Bengal). He was endowed with a very keen intellect and acquired distinction in literature, grammar, logic, astronomy, music, fine arts

---

1 The two treatises Avayavi-nirākaraṇa and Sāmānya-dūṣaṇa-dik-prasāritā are included in the "Six Nyāya Tracts," edited by M.M. Hara Prasad Shastri in the Bibliotheca Indica series, Calcutta.

2 ननु भवद्भिरसत्त्वेव अवयवी प्रतिज्ञायते स कथं प्रत्यक्षसिद्धः ।

(Avayavi-nirākaraṇa, p. 78).

3 व्यापकमित्यमेकञ्च सामान्यं यैः प्रकल्पितम् ।
मोक्षपन्थिविच्छिदे तेषां तदभावः प्रसाध्यते ॥

(Sāmānya-dūṣaṇa-dik-prasāritā, Calcutta, p. 64).

4 एवं मया बहुषु दुष्कृतिनिर्मितेषु
प्रत्युद्धृतेषु बहुदूषणकण्टकेषु ।
आचार्य्यनीतिपथ एष विशोधितोऽयम्
उत्सार्य्यमत्सरमनेन जनः प्रयातु ॥

(Avayavi-nirākaraṇa, p. 93).

5 *Vide* Tāranātha's Geschichte des Buddhismus von Schiefner, pp. 145—146, 148—158; and Dpag-bsam-ljon-bzaṅ edited in the original Tibetan by Sarat Chandra Das, Calcutta, pp. 95—96.

and the science of medicine. Under Ācārya Sthiramati he learnt the Sūtra and Abhidharma Piṭakas of the Buddhist scripture, and was converted to Buddhism by the Vidyādhara Ācārya Aśoka. He had an ardent faith in the Buddhist god Avalokiteśvara and the goddess Tārā.[1] He was offered in marriage a daughter of the king of Vārendra. Being told that she was named Tārā, which was the name of his tutelary deity, he, thinking it improper to accept her hand shrank from her with fear. Upon this the king became angry and put Candra Gomin into a chest which was thrown into the Ganges. The chest was carried down until it stopped at an island at the place where the Ganges flows into the ocean. Candra Gomin with deep reverence offered a prayer to goddess Tārā by whose blessing he got out of the chest He resided in the island, which was in course of time named Candra-dvīpa[2] or the island of Candra. He as a Buddhist devotee (*upāsaka*) established there stone-images of Avalokiteśvara and Tārā At first only fishermen (*kaivarta*) settled in the island, but afterwards other people came to live there. Gradually the island became a town.

There was another Candra Gomin called Candra Gomin the senior who went to Ceylon and on his way back found in Southern India, in the house of Vararuci, Nāga Śeṣa's (Patañjali's) Bhāṣya on Pāṇini's grammar. Finding that it contained "many words but few thoughts" he himself composed a commentary on Pāṇini, which was named Candra-vyākaraṇa.[3] Afterwards he came to Nālandā—the store-house of knowledge—and met there Candra-kīrti, the famous commentator on the Mādhyamika Philosophy of Ārya Nāgārjuna. Candra Gomin himself was a follower of the Yogācāra system expounded by Ārya Asaṅga. While Candra Kīrti and Candra Gomin entered upon philosophical discussions people used to observe[4]: "Alas! the text

---

[1] For Candra Gomin's "Ārya-Tārā-antarbali-vidhi" *vide* Satis Chandra Vidyabhusana's Sragdharā-stotra, Introduction, pp. xx. xxi.

[2] Candra-dvīpa is situated in the district of Barisal in South-eastern Bengal at a place where the Padmā, which is a main outlet of the Ganges, falls into the ocean. Vārendra, in which Candra Gomin was born, is identical with the Rajshahye division in North-eastern Bengal through which the Padmā flows.

[3] For Candra-vyākaraṇa *vide* Satis Chandra Vidyabhusana's Kaccāyana and "Sanskrit works on Literature, Grammar, Rhetoric and Lexicography, as preserved in Tibet" in the *Journal of the Asiatic Sciety of Bengal*, new series, Vol. iii, No. 2, 1907. The Candra-vyākaraṇa in the original Sanskrit has been printed in Germany.

[4] ཀྱེ་མ་འཕགས་པ་ཀླུ་སྒྲུབ་གཞེང་ ।།
ལ་ལའི་སྨན་ལ་ལ་ལའི་དུག །
མི་ཕམ་འཕགས་པ་ཐོགས་མེད་གཞུང་ །
སྐྱེ་བོ་ཀུན་ལ་བདུད་རྩི་ཉིད །

Dpag-bsam-ljon-bzaṅ, p. 96.

of Ārya Nāgārjuna is medicine to some but poison to others, whereas the text of invincible Ārya Asaṅga is very ambrosia to all men." It is further stated that Candra Gomin threw the original manuscript of his grammar into a well at Nālandā, thinking that it was not better than the one which Candra Kīrti had written. At that time Tārā and Avalokiteśvara appeared before him saying: "Though Candra Kīrti is overwhelmed with pride as a sage, your work is more useful than all others and will do immense good to the world." They raised the manuscript from this well, which was thence reputed as "Candra's well" (in Sanskrit: *Candra-kūpa* and in Tibetan: Tsandraḫi-khron-pa), the water of which was wont to be drunk by people in the belief that thereby their intellect would become sharp. Candra Kīrti was, however, a great admirer of Candra Gomin. When the latter arrived at Nālandā the monks refused to give him a reception, saying that it was not proper for priests to welcome a mere devotee (*upāsaka*). Hearing this, Candra Kīrti brought three chariots, two of which were occupied by himself and Candra Gomin respectively, while in the third was placed an image of Mañjuśrī, the Buddhist god of learning. The chariots passed through the town in a great procession, attended by the whole body of priests who came really to recite hymns to Mañjuśrī, but apparently to accord a fitting welcome to Candra Gomin.[1] It is not known as to whether the Candra Gomin lived at a time when Śīla, son of Śrī Harṣa, reigned in Kanoj and Siṁha of the Licchavi dynasty reigned in Vārendra. The famous poet Ravi Gupta was a contemporary of Bharṣa, son of Siṁha. Śrī Harṣa seems to be the same as king Harṣa Vardhana who was a contemporary of Hwen-thsang and reigned in 647 A.D. His son Śīla seems, on a rough calculation, to have reigned in 700 A.D., when his contemporary Candra Gomin must also have lived. Jaina Hema Candra Sūri, who lived during 1088—1172 A.D., refers to Candra Gomin while Jayāditya,[2] the famous author of the Kāśikā-vṛtti, who died in 661—662 A.D.,[3] does not mention him. This may be explained on the supposition that Candra Gomin lived after Jayāditya, but preceded Hema Candra.

The other Candra Gomin called Candra Gomin the junior seems to have lived about 925 A.D., as his preceptor Ārya Aśoka (q.v.) flourished about 900 A.D. It is not known with certainty as to whether Candra Gomin, the author of Candra Vyākaraṇa, was identical with the sage of that name who was a contem-

---

1 *Vide* Dpag-bsam-ljon-bzaṅ, pp. 95—96.

2 *Vide* Professor F. Kielhorn's "Indra Gomin and other grammarians" in the Indian Antiquary, Vol. xv, June 1886, pp. 181, 184.

3 *Vide* Takakusu's I-tsing, p. lvii.

porary of Candra Kīrti. But it may be asserted safely that Candra Gomin, the logician, was different from either.

Candra Gomin was the author of the following work on Logic: **Nyāyāloka-siddhi**, or Nyāya-siddhyāloka, called in Tibetan: Rigs-pa-grub-paḥi-sgron-ma, signifying "a lamp of logical reasoning." The Sanskrit original of this work appears to be lost, but there exists a Tibetan translation[1] in the Bstan-ḥgyur, Mdo Ze, folios 200—201. The translation was prepared by Paṇḍita Śr Sita-prabha and the interpreter-monk Vairocana.

129. PRAJÑĀKARA GUPTA (ABOUT 940 A.D.).

Prajñākara Gupta,[2] called in Tibetan Śes-rab-ḥbyuṅ-gnas-sbas, lived at the time of Maha Pāla, who died in 940 A.D. He was a lay devotee and is quite different from Prajñākara Mati, who was a monk and keeper of the southern gate of the university of Vikrama-śilā during the reign of Canaka in 983 A.D. Prajñākara Gupta was the author of the following works :—

Pramāṇa-vārtikālaṅkāra, called in Tibetan Tshad-ma-rnam-ḥgrel-gyi-rgyan, which is a commentary on the Pramāṇa-vārtika of Dharmakīrti. The Sanskit original of this work appears to be lost, but there exists a Tibetan translation[3] which is divided into two parts. The first part extends over Folios 1—352 of volume Te, and the second part Folios 1—328 of volume She of the Bstan-ḥgyur, section Mdo. The translation was prepared by the great Kāśmīrian Paṇḍita Bhavya-rāja and the Tibetan interpreter Blo-ldan-śes-rab. Subsequently, it was looked through by Sumati and the interpreter Blo-ldan-śes-rab. The translation has the advantage of having been assisted by numerous sages of the great monastery of Vikramaśilā in Middle India, under the supervision of the great wise Paṇḍita Śrī Śunaya-śrī Mitra and also of the wise Paṇḍita Kumāraśrī of the model city of Kāśmīra.

Sahāvalambha-niścaya, called in Tibetan Lhan-cig-dmigs-pa-ṅes-pa, signifying "the ascertainment of objects and their knowledge arising together." The Sanskrit original of this work appears to be lost, but there exists a Tibetan translation[4] in the Bstan-ḥgyur, Mdo, Ze, Folios 301—308. The translation was prepared by the Nepalese Paṇḍita Śānti Bhadra and the Tibetan

---

[1] I have used the India Office copy.

[2] *Vide* Tārānātha's Geschichte des Buddhismus von Schiefner, pp. 230, 235; and Dpag-bsam-ljon-bzaṅ, p. 116.

[3] I consulted this work in the monastery of Labraug in Sikkim, which I visited in June, 1907.

[4] I have consulted the India Office copy.

interpreter-monk Śākya-ḫoḏ of the village of Seṅ-ḏkar in the province of Ḫbro (Ḏo).

130. Ācārya Jetāri (940—980 A.D.).

Jetāri[1] or **Ācārya Jetāri**, called in Tibetan Ḏgra-las-rgyal-wa, was born of a Brāhmaṇa family. His father, Garbhapāda, lived in Vārendra at the court of Rājā Sanātana, who was a vassal to the Pala kings of Magadha. Being expelled by his kinsmen, Jetāri became a Buddhist devotee and worshipped Mañjuśrī, by whose grace he became a perfect master of sciences. He received from king Maha Pāla the royal diploma of Paṇḍita of the University of Vikramaśilā.

The famous Dīpaṅkara or Śrījñāna Atiśa is said, when very young, to have learnt five minor sciences from Jetāri. Maha Pāla reigned up to 940 A.D. and Dīpaṅkara was born in 980 A.D. Their contemporary, Jetāri, must have lived between those dates[2]

He was the author of the following works[3] on Logic:—

Hetu-tattva-upadeśa, called in Tibetan Ḡtan-tshigs-kyi-de-kho-na-ñid-ḇstan-pa, signifying "instruction on the real nature of the middle term in a syllogism." The Sanskrit original of this work appears to be lost, but there exists a Tibetan translation in the Ḇstan-ḫgyur, Ṃdo, Ze, Folios 344—354. The translation was prepared by the Indian sage Paṇḍita Kumāra-kalasa and the Tibetan interpreter-monk Śākya-ḫoḏ.

Dharma dharmi-viniścaya, called in Tibetan Chos-dan-chos-can-gtan la-ḏwab-pa, signifying "determination of the minor and major terms." The Sanskrit original of this work appears to be lost, but there exists a Tibetan translation in the Ḇstan-ḫgyur, Ṃdo, Ze, Folios 354—359.

Bālāvatāra-tarka, called in Tibetan Bis-wa-ḫjug-paḫi-rtog-ge, signifying "children's introduction to Logic." The Sanskrit original of this work appears to be lost, but there exists a Tibetan translation in the Ḇstan-ḫgyur Ṃdo, Ze, Folios 359—372. The translation was prepared by the Indian sage Nāga Rakṣita and the Tibetan interpreter of the province of Sum-pa (in Amdo) named Ḏpal-ṃchog-daṅ-poḫi-rdo-rje. The work begins thus:—

"Who by the lustre of his sermon has completely dispersed and cleared the veil of the gloom of ignorance, who is a single

---

[1] *Vide* Tāranātha's Geschichte des Buddhismus von Schiefner, pp. 230—233; and Ḏpag-bsam-ljon-bzaṅ, p. 116.

[2] *Vide* the "Journal" of the Buddhist Text Society of Calcutta, vol. i, part i, p. 8.

[3] The Volume Ze, of the Ḇstan-ḫgyur, Ṃdo, containing Jetāri's works, was lent to me by the India Office, London.

lamp to three worlds—may that Bhagavān long remain victorious."[1] It consists of three chapters named respectively: (1) Perception; (2) Inference for one's own self; and (3) Inference for the sake of others.

131. Jina (about 940 A.D.).

Jina, called in Tibetan Rgyal-wa-can, was the author of the following work:—

Pramāṇa-vārtikālaṅkāra-ṭīkā, called in Tibetan Tshad-ma-rnam-hgrel-gyi rgyan-gyi-hgrel-bśad, a voluminous work, the Tibetan version of which occupies volumes De and Ne of the Bstan-hgyur, section Mdo This version was prepared by Paṇḍita Dīpaṅkara Rakṣita of Vikramaśilā (who arrived in Tibet in 1045 A.D.) and the Tibetan interpreter, Byaṅ-chub-śes-rab of Shaṅ-shuṅ.

Jina, the author of the original work, is probably the same as Jina Bhadra of Koṅkana,[2] who was a contemporary of Vāgīśvarakīrti, about 940 A.D.

132. Ratnakīrti (about 940—1000 A.D.).

Ratnakīrti,[3] called in Tibetan Rin-chen-grags, was a Professor at the University of Vikrama-śilā. As he was a teacher of Ratnākara Śānti (q.v.) he must have flourished about 950 A.D. This Ratnakīrti, designated as *Mahāpaṇḍita*, deeply erudite, is different from the sage of that name who was patronised by King Vimala Candra of Bengal, Kāmarūpa and Tirhut about 650 A.D.

Ratnakīrti criticises the views of Dharmottara,[4] Nyāya-

---

[1] གང་གིས་གསུང་རབ་འོད་ཟེར་གཏི་མུག་གིས །།
མུན་པའི་རབ་རིབ་རྣམ་པར་གྲོལ་མཛད་གསལ །།
ས་གསུམ་གནས་ན་སྒྲོན་མ་གཅིག་པུ་ཡི །།
བཅོམ་ལྡན་འདས་དེ་ཡུན་རིང་རྒྱལ་གྱུར་ཅིག །།
(Bstan-hgyur, Mdo, Ze, folio 359).

[2] *Vide* Tārānātha's Geschichte des Buddhismus von Schiefner, p 235.

[3] *Vide* Tārānātha's Geschichte des Buddhismus von Schiefner, pp. 234—235, and 172, 174: also Dpag-bsam-ljon-bzaṅ, p. 105, edited by Sarat Chandra Das, Calcutta.

The colophons of *Apohasiddhi* and *Kṣaṇabhaṅga-siddhi* run as follows:—

कृतिरियं महापण्डितरत्नकीर्त्तिपादानाम् ॥

[4] नाकारस्य न वाह्यस्य तत्त्वतो विधिसाधनम् ।
बहिरेव हि संवृत्या संवृत्यापि तु नान्तरे ॥

bhūṣaṇa[1] and Vācaspati Misra[2] on the subjects of *apoha* (exclusion) and *kṣaṇa-bhaṅga* (momentariness).

He wrote two logical treatises,[3] *viz.* **Apohasiddhi** and **Kṣaṇabhaṅgasiddhi**, one of which begins with a salutation to Lokanātha and the other to Samanta Bhadra. The first work, which deals with the doctrine of *apoha*[4], propounds that a word while denoting a thing positive excludes it from all other things different from it, that is, a word bears a negative denotation along with a positive one. The second work[5] attempts, through affirmative and negative inferences, to prove that all things are momentary by showing that they do not require three moments for their production, continuance and destruction.

Ratnakīrti is said to have written two other treatises, *viz.* **Sthirasiddhidūṣaṇa**[6] and **Citrādvaitasiddhi**

133. Ratna Vajra (about 979—1040 A.D.).

Ratnavajra,[7] called in Tibetan Rin-chen-rdo-rje, was born in a Brāhmaṇa family in Kāśmīra. His ancestors were deeply versed in the śāstra of the Tīrthikas. His father, Hari Bhadra, was the first convert to Buddhism in his family. Ratnavajra, who was an *upāsaka* (lay devotee), studied by himself up to the 36th year of his life all the Buddhist sūtras, mantras and sciences. After this he came to Magadha and Vajrāsana (Buddha-Gayā)

एतेन यद् धर्म्मोत्तरः—आरोपितस्य वाह्यस्य विधिनिषेधौ। इत्यलौकिकम् अनागमम् अतार्किकीय कथयति तदपहस्तितम्॥

(Apohasiddhi, pp. 16—17).

1 यथाच न्यायभूषणेन स्वर्ग्यादिपदवत् तदुपकार्य्यांशेषवस्तुराशिपदवत्प्रसङ्गमनुक्तं तदभिप्रायानवगाहनफलम्

(Apohasiddhi, pp. 11, 14. Also Kṣaṇa-bhaṅgasiddhi, p. 58.)

यदप्यवोचद् वाचस्पतिः जातिमत्य व्यक्तयः...

(Apohasiddhi, p. 4, pp. 7, 8, 10). Also Kṣaṇa-bhaṅgasiddhi, p. 58, Calcutta edition.)

3 The Apohasiddhi and Kṣaṇa-bhaṅgasiddhi are included in the "Six Buddhist Nyāya Tracts," edited by M.M. Hara Prasad Shāstri in the Bibliotheca Indica series, Calcutta.

4 नास्माभिरपोहशब्देन विधिरेव केवलोऽभिप्रेतः। नापि अन्यव्यावृत्तिमात्रं किन्तु अन्यापोह विशिष्टो विधिः शब्दानामर्थः॥

(Apohasiddhi, p. 3, Calcutta edition).

5 प्रकृतेः सर्व्वधर्म्माणां यद्दोषाद्युपसिध्यते।
स एव तीर्थ्यनिर्म्माणो क्षणभङ्गः प्रसाधितः॥

(Kṣaṇa-bhaṅgasiddhi, p. 77, Calcutta edition).

6 Kṣaṇabhaṅgasiddhi, pp. 68, 71.

7 *Vide* Tāranātha's Geschichte des Buddhismus von Schiefner, p. 240.

where he beheld the face of Cakra-saṁvara, Vajravarāhī and many other deities, by whose grace he completely mastered the Buddhist śāstras. He received the royal diploma of the University of Vikramaśilā and was appointed a gate-keeper of the university. Afterwards he came back to Kāśmīra, whence he went through Udvāna (Kabul) to Tibet, where he was known by the name of Ācārya. He flourished during the reign of Canaka, and his approximate date may be placed between 970 A.D. and 1040 A.D. He was the author of the following work :—

Yukti-prayoga, called in Tibetan Rigs-pahi-sbyor-wa, signifying "application of reasoning" The Sanskrit original of this work appears to be lost, but there exists a Tibetan translation[1] in the Bstan-hgyur, Mdo, Ze, Folios 372—373. The translation was prepared by the Indian sage Śrī Śubhūti-śānta and the interpreter-monk of Shu-chen, named Tiṅ-ṅe-hdsin-bzaṅ-po.

134. Jina Mitra (about 1025 A.D.).

Jina Mitra[2] was a native of Kāśmīra who, together with Sarvajña Deva, Dāna-śīla and others, visited Tibet and helped the Tibetans in the work of translating Sanskrit books into Tibetan. Jina Mitra lived about 1025 A.D., when his contemporary king Mahī Pala reigned in Bengal. He wrote the undermentioned work on Logic :—

Nyāya-bindu-piṇḍārtha, called in Tibetan Rigs-pahi-thigs-pahi-don-bsdus-pa, which contains the purport of Dharmakīrti's Nyāyabindu. The Sanskrit original of this work is lost, but there exists a Tibetan translation[3] in the Bstan-hgyur, Mdo, She, Folios 115—116. The translation was prepared by the Indian teacher Surendrabodhi, and the interpreter of Shuchen, named Vande-ye-śes-sde.

135. Dānaśīla (about 1025 A.D.).

Dānaśīla,[4] also called Dānaśrīla, was born in Kāśmīra about 1025 A.D., when Mahī Pāla II was reigning in Bengal. He was a contemporary of Parahita Bhadra, Jina Mitra, Sarvajña Deva and Tilopā. He visited Tibet and co-operated in the propaganda

---

[1] I have consulted the Tibetan version in the possession of the India Office, London.

[2] *Vide* Tārānātha's Geschichte des Buddhismus von Schiefner, p. 226; and Dpag-bsam-ljon-bzaṅ, pp. xcvi, 115.

[3] I have consulted the India Office copy.

[4] *Vide* Tārānātha's Geschichte des Buddhismus von Schiefner, pp. 225—226; and Dpag-bsam-ljon-bzaṅ, p. xlvi.

of the translations of Sanskrit books into Tibetan. He was the author of the following work on Logic :—

Pustaka-pāṭhopāya, called in Tibetan Gleg-bam-bklag-paḥi-thabs, signifying the method of reading books. The Sanskrit original of this work appears to be lost, but there exists a Tibetan translation [1] in the Bstan-ḥgyur, Mdo, Ze, Folio 270. The translation was prepared by the author himself.

136. JÑĀNA-ŚRĪ MITRA (ABOUT 1040 A.D.).

Jñāna-śrī Mitra,[2] designated as a great pillar of the University of Vikramaśilā, was born in Gauḍa. He was at first admitted into the Śrāvaka school of Buddhism, but afterwards imbibed faith in the Mahāyāna. Dīpaṅkara or Śrī-jñāna Atiśa (born in 980 A D.) is said to have been much indebted to him. Jñāna-śrī Mitra was appointed a gate-keeper of the university of Vikramaśilā by Canaka who reigned in Magadha. Jñāna-śrī Mitra was attached to the University of Vakramaśilā even in 1040 A.D. when Dīpaṅkara Atiśa left for Tibet. Naropā while visiting Vikramaśilā got down from his conveyance leaning on the right arm of Atiśa and left arm of Jñāna-śrī Mitra. The Hindu philosopher Mādhavācārya in the 14th century quotes[3] Jñāna-śri, who is perhaps the same as Jñāna-śrī Mitra. He was the author of the following work on Logic :—

Kārya-kāraṇa bhāva-siddhi, called in Tibetan Rgyu-daṅ-ḥbras-buḥi-ṅo-wo-grub-pa, signifying 'establishment of the relation of cause and effect.' The Sanskrit original of this work appears to be lost, but there exists a Tibetan translation[4] in the Bstan-ḥgyur, Mdo, Ze, Folios 413—418. The translation was prepared by the great Indian sage Kumāra Kalasa and the interpreter monk Śākya-ḥod. Subsequently, it was retouched and published by the Nepalese Paṇḍita Ananta-śrī and the interpreter-monk afore-mentioned.

---

1 I have consulted the India Office copy.

2 *Vide* Tārānātha's Geschichte des Buddhismus von Schiefner, pp. 235—242 ; and Dpag-bsam ljon-bzaṅ. pp. 117—120.

3 *Vide* the Sarvadarśana-saṁgraha, chapter on Baudddha-darśana :—

तदुक्तं ज्ञानश्रिया

यत् सत् तत् क्षणिकं यथा जलधरः सन्तश्च भावा अमी ।
सत्ता शक्तिरिहार्थकर्मणि मितेः सिद्धेषु सिद्धा न सा ॥
नाप्येकैव विधान्यथा परकृतेनापि क्रियादिर्भवेत् ।
द्वेधापि क्षणभङ्गसङ्गतिरतः साध्ये च विश्राम्यति ॥

4 I have consulted the India Office copy.

137. Jñāna-śrī Bhadra (about 1050 A.D.).

Jñāna-śrī Bhadra,[1] called in Tibetan Ye-śes-dpal-bzaṅ-po, was a great logician. He was born in a Brāhmaṇa family of Kāśmīra[2] and became afterwards a convert to Buddhism. As junior to Naropā he lived about 1050 A.D. He visited Tibet where he was employed in translating Sanskrit books into Tibetan. In the land of the Lamas he was well known under the name of "Kha-che-jñāna-śrī"[3] or Kāśmīrian Jñāna-śrī. He was the author of the following work on Logic:—

Pramāṇa viniścaya-ṭikā[4] called in Tibetan Tshad-ma-rnam-par-ṅes-pahi-hgrel-bśad, which is a commentary on the Pramāṇa-viniścaya of Dharmakīrti and which begins with a salutation to Sarvajña. The Sanskrit original of this work appears to be lost, but there exists a Tibetan translation in the Bstan-hgyur, Mdo, We, Folios 188—322. The translation was prepared by the author himself with the co-operation of the interpreter-monk Chos-kyi-brtson-bgrus.

138. Ratnākara Śānti (about 1040 A.D.).

Ratnākara Śānti,[5] called Kalikāla-sarvajña, was known to the Tibetans as Ācārya Śānti or simply Śāntipa. He was ordained in the order of the Sarvāstivāda school of Odantapura, and learnt the Sūtra and Tantra at Vikramaśilā from Jetāri, Ratnakīrti[6] and others. Thereafter he was appointed by King Canaka (who died in 983 A.D.) to be a gate-keeper of the University of Vikramaśilā, where he defeated the Tīrthika disputants. At the invitation of the king of Ceylon he visited that island where he spread the Buddhist doctrine. He was the author of a work on

---

[1] Jñāna-śrī Bhadra was perhaps the same as Jñāna-siddha Bhadra mentioned in the Dpag-bsam-ljon-bzaṅ, p. 117.

[2] *Vide* the Colophon of Pramāṇa-viniścaya-ṭikā. *Vide* also Satis Chandra Vidyabhusana's "Indian Logic as preserved in Tibet, No. 3" in the Journal of the Asiatic Society of Bengal. New series, Vol. iii, No. 7, 1907.

[3] *Vide* Dpag-bsam-ljon-bzaṅ, p. 408.

[4] I consulted the Tibetan version of this work in the monastery of Labrang in Sikkim.

[5] *Vide* Tāranātha's Geschichte des Buddhismus von Schiefner, pp. 234, 235; and Dpag-bsam-ljon-bzaṅ, pp. 117, cx. The Tibetan equivalent for the name Ratnākara Śānti is རིན་ཆེན་འབྱུང་གནས་ཞི་བ །

[6] This Ratnakīrti is different from the sage of that name who was patronised by King Vimala Candra of Bengal, Kāmarūpa and Tirhut, about 650 A.D. (*vide* Tāranātha's Geschichte des Buddhismus von Schiefner, pp. 172, 174; Dpag-bsam ljon-bzaṅ, p. 105, Calcutta edition; and my discussion under the head Vinita Deva in the Buddhist Logic). This earlier Ratnakīrti, known through a commentary on the Madhyamakāvatāra, wrote Kalyāṇa-kāṇḍa and Dharmavi-niścaya embodied in the Bstan-hgyur, Mdo, Ku.

Chanda (prosody) called Chando ratnākara[1] and of the following works[2] on Logic:—

Viñapti-mātra siddhi, called in Tibetan Ṛnam-par-rig-pa-tsam-ñid-do-grub-pa, signifying 'establishment of a mere communication of knowledge.' The Sanskrit original of this work appears to be lost, but there exists a Tibetan translation in the Ḇstan-ḫgyur, Ṃdo, Ze, Folios 335—338. The translation was prepared by the Nepalese Paṇḍita Śânti Bhadra, and the Tibetan interpreter-monk Śâkya-ḫoḏ of the province of Ḫbro (Ḍo). Subsequently, it was published by the same Paṇḍita and Ḵlog-skya-śes-rab-ḇrtsegs̱.

Antar-vyāpti,[3] called in Tibetan Naṅ-gi-khyab-pa, signifying 'internal inseparable connection.' It is embodied in the Ḇstan-ḫgyur, Ṃdo, Ze, Folios 338—344. The translation was prepared by the Indian sage Kumāra Kalasa and the interpreter-monk Śākya-ḫoḏ. The work argues that the inseparable connection between the middle term and the major term can be conceived without the aid of an example in which the things signified by the two terms co-abide, nay, without the aid even of a minor term in which we are to prove the co-presence of the things, *e.g.* fiery because smoky.

139. Yamāri (about 1050 A.D.).

Yamâri was specially versed in Grammar and Logic. But he was very poor. Once, being unable to support his family and children, he came to Vajrāsana (Buddha-Gayā). There he related his poverty to a Yogin, who replied: "You Paṇḍits despise Yogins and do not solicit dharma from them, hence this has come to pass." Saying this, he uttered the Vasudhara benediction in virtue of which Yamāri rose to opulence. He afterwards received the royal diploma of the University of Vikramaśilā.[4] He lived during the time of Naya Pāla who reigned in 1050 A.D. He was the author of the following work:—

---

1 For an account of the Chandoratnākara see Satischandra Vidyabhusana's "Sanskrit works on Literature, Grammar, Rhetoric and Lexicography as preserved in Tibet," in J.A.S.B., New series, vol. III. no 2, 1907.

2 The volume Ze of the Ḇstan-ḫgyur, section Ṃdo, containing Ratnākara Śânti's works, was lent to me by the India Office, London.

3 The Sanskrit original of 'Antarvyāpti' or more fully 'Antarvyāpti-samarthana' has recently been edited by M.M Hara Prasad Shastri, M.A, C.I.E., of Calcutta, in the Bibliotheca Indica series. It begins thus:—इह सत्त्वमर्थक्रियाकारित्वं तदितरलक्षणायोगात्। तच्च क्रमयौगपद्याभ्यां व्याप्तं परस्परव्यवच्छेदलक्षणत्वादनयोः। प्रकारान्तरेण चरणासम्भवात्। It ends thus:—अन्तर्व्याप्तिसमर्थनं समाप्तमिति। कृतिरियं रत्नाकरशान्तिपादानाम्॥

4 *Vide* Tārānātha's Geschichte des Buddhismus von Schiefner, pp. 247, 253.

Pramāṇa-vārtikālaṅkāra-ṭīkā, called in Tibetan Tshad-ma-rnam-hgrel-rgyan-gyi-hgrel-bśad, which is an annotation on the Pramāṇa-vārtikālaṅkāra of Prajñākara Gupta. The Sanskrit original of this work appears to be lost, but there exists a very voluminous Tibetan translation which covers volumes Phe, pp. 104—342 and the whole of volumes Be, Me, and Tse of the Bstan-hgyur, Mdo. The translation was prepared by Paṇḍita Sumati and the interpreter Blo-ldan-śes-rab in the monastery of Sñe-thaṅ near Lhasa. The volume Be ends thus:—"From the immeasurable merit acquired by me by composing this regular annotation, may the world, subduing its adversary death, obtain the indestructible and perfected Nirvāṇa." [1]

140. ŚAṄKARĀNANDA (ABOUT 1050 A.D.).

Śaṅkarānanda,[2] called in Tibetan Bde-byed-dgah-wa, was born in a Brāhmaṇa family in Kāśmīra. He was learned in all sciences, and was above all an expert in Logic. He intended to write an original work on Logic refuting Dharmakīrti, but in a dream he was told by Mañjuśrī: "Since Dharmakīrti is an Ārya (an elect), one cannot refute him, and if thou seest mistake in him, it is the mistake of thine own understanding." Thereupon Śaṅkarānanda repented and composed a commentary on Dharmakīrti's Pramāṇa-vārtika in seven chapters. He flourished[3] during the time of Naya Pāla, who reigned in 1050 A.D. He was the author of the following works on Logic:—

Pramāṇa-vārtika-ṭīkā, called in Tibetan Tshad-ma-rnam-hgrel-gyi-hgrel-bśad, being an annotation on the Pramāṇa-vārtika of Dharmakīrti. The Sanskrit original of this work appears to be lost, but there exists a Tibetan translation[4] which covers volumes Pe, pages 103—354 and Phe, pages 1—104 of the Bstan-hgyur, Mdo.

---

1 ཚུལ་བཞིན་ཊཱི་ཀཱ་འདི་ནི་བྱས་པ་ལས ||
བསོད་ནམས་ཚད་མེད་བསགས་པ་གང་ཡིན་པ ||
དེས་ནི་འཇིག་རྟེན་གཤིན་རྗེའི་དགྲ་འཇོམས་ནི ||
མི་ཟད་རབ་བསྒྲུབ་གཉིས་མེད་ཐོབ་པར་ཤོག ||
(Bstan-hgyur, Mdo, Be, folio 303).

2 *Vide* Tārānātha's Geschichte des Buddhismus von Schiefner, pp. 247, 349; and Dpag-bsam-ljon bzaṅ, pp. 107, 120.

3 Some maintain that Saṅkarānanda was a personal pupil of Dharmakīrti. On this point Lama Tārānātha observes:—"The Brāhmaṇa Saṅkarānanda appeared at a much later time, and to call him a personal pupil of Dharmakīrti would be a great confusion."—Tārānātha's Geschichte des Buddhismus von Schiefner, p. 188.

4 I consulted this work in the monastery of Labrang, in Sikkim, in 1907.

Sambandha-parīkṣānusāra, called in Tibetan H̱brel-pa-ḇrtag-paẖi-rjeṣ-su-ẖbraṅ wa, which is a commentary on the Sambandha-parīkṣā of Dharmakīrti. The Sanskrit original of this work appears to be lost, but there exists a Tibetan translation [1] in the Ḇstan-ẖgyur, M̱do, Ze, Folios 24—39. The translation was prepared by the great Indian Paṇḍita Parahita, and the Tibetan interpreter-monk Ḏgaẖ-waẖi-ṟdo-rje.

The work begins thus :—

"By whom connection with the world has been renounced, in whom there are no "I" and "mine," who is called free from concerns—to that Omniscient One I bow down." [2]

Apohasiddhi, called in Tibetan Sel-wa-grub-pa, signifying "establishment of a thing by the exclusion of its opposites." The Sanskrit original of his work appears to be lost, but there exists a Tibetan translation [3] in the Ḇstan-ẖgyur, M̱do, Ze, Folios 308—334. The translation was prepared by the Kāśmīrian Paṇḍita Manoratha and the Tibetan interpreter Ḇlo-ḻdan-śeṣ-rab in the incomparable city of Kāśmīra.

The work opens thus :—

"The Omniscient One who is free from all mistakes and who looks to the interests of living beings in all times, saluting him and relying on his mercy, I elucidate the puzzle of 'self' and 'others' connected with the doctrine of *Apoha*." [4]

Pratibandha-siddhi, called in Tibetan H̱brel-pa-grub-pa, signifying "establishment of the causal connection." The Sanskrit original of this work appears to be lost, but there exists a Tibetan translation [5] in the Ḇstan-ẖgyur, M̱do, Ze, Folios 334—335. The translation was prepared by Paṇḍita Bhāgya-rāja and the interpreter Ḇlo-ḻdan-śeṣ-rab.

---

1 I have consulted the Tibetan version in the possession of India Office, London.

2
གང་གིས་འབྲེལ་བ་སྤངས་གྱུར་པ ||
འགྲོ་བ་བདག་དང་བདག་གི་མེ ||
གཟུང་འཛིན་མེད་པ་ཅན་གསུངས་པ ||
ཀུན་མཁྱེན་དེ་ལ་ཕྱག་འཚལ་ལོ ||

(Ḇstan-ẖgyur, M̱do, Ze, folio 24).

3 I have consulted the India Office copy.

4
ཀུན་མཁྱེན་འཁྲུལ་བྲལ་དུས་གསུམ་གནས་པ་ཡི ||
དོན་[illegible]མས་རྗེ་གཞན་གཟིགས་པ་ལ་བཏུད་དེ ||
བརྩེ་ལ་གནས་ནས་སེལ་བ་ལ་བརྟེན་པའི ||
བདག་གཞན་རབ་ཏུ་སྨྲ་བའི་འཁྲུལ་བསལ་བྱས ||

(Ḇstan-ẖgyur, M̱do, Ze, folio 308).

5 I have consulted the India Office copy.

141. Śubhakara Gupta (about 1080 A.D.).

Śubhakara Gupta was a disciple of Abhayākara Gupta, high-priest of the monastic University of Vikramaśilā. He flourished during the reign of Rāma Pāla[1] and resided for some time at the shrine of Eṭapurī erected by Rāma Pāla's wife. As the reign of Rāma Pāla commenced about 1080 A.D. Śubhakara Gupta must have lived at the end of the 11th century A.D.

He wrote a treatise on Logic in which he closely followed Dharmakīrti. His logicial views are quoted and criticised by the Jaina logician Haribhadra Sūri[2] who designates him as Śubha Gupta

142. Mokṣākara Gupta (about 1100 A.D.).

Mokṣākara Gupta, called in Tibetan Thar-paḥi-ḥbyuṅ-gnas-sbas, was the High-priest of the great monastery of Jagaddala[3] at the confluence of the Gaṅgā (Padmā) and the Karatoyā (perhaps near Bogra in North Bengal). He seems to have flourished early in the 12th century A.D., after the termination of the rule of the Pāla kings. He wrote the undermentioned work on Logic :—

Tarka bhāṣā, called in Tibetan Rtog-geḥi-skad, signifying 'technicalities of Logic.' The Sanskrit original of this work appears to be lost, but there exists a Tibetan translation[4] in the Bstan-ḥgyur, Mdo, Ze, Folios 373—413. The translation was prepared by the interpreter-monk Dpal-ldan-blo-gros-brtan-po without the co-operation of any Paṇḍita. The work is divided into three chapters named respectively : (1) Perception; (2) Inference for one's own self ; and (3) Inference for the sake of others. It begins thus :—

---

1 རཱ་མ་པཱ་ལའི་བཙུན་མོས་བཞེངས་པའི་ཨེ་ཊ་པུ་རིའི་ལྷ་ཁང་དུ་བསྒོམ་མཛད་ཅིང་སློབ་དཔོན་ཤུ་བྷ་ཀ་ར་གུཔ་ཏ
དང་བོད་ཀྱི་ཆ་ལོ་སོགས་དང་བཅས · · · ·

(Dpag-bsam-ljon-bzaṅ, p. 120, edited by S. C. Das).

2 Haribhadra Sūri observes :—

यथाह वार्त्तिकानुसारिणा शुभगुप्तेन । कल्पनाकारं स्वलक्षणादन्यत् विकल्पेन सामान्य-लक्षणात्मकम् उभयोरेकत्वाध्यासात् प्रतिभासते स्फुटतेव सत्यर्थे ययोरभ्रान्ति तत्र कल्पनाकारे संकेतः ।

(Anekāntajaya-patātākāṭikā, p. 117).

3 For the identification of Jagaddala see Rāma Pāla-carita.

4 I have consulted the India Office copy.

ཛ་ག་ཏྟ་ལའི་གཙུག་ཁང་ཆེན་པོའི་མཁས་པ་ཆེན་པོ་དགེ་བར་ཐར་པའི་འབྱུང་གནས་སྦས་པས་སྦྱར་བའི །

(Bstan-ḥgyur, Mdo, Ze, folio 413).

" Bowing down to the Teacher, the Lord of the world, I elucidate Tarkabhāṣā for the sake of introducing children of small intellect to the system of Dharmakīrti." [1]

---

1 བླ་མ་འཇིག་རྟེན་དབང་བཏུད་ནས
བྱིས་པ་ཡིད་གཞུངས་ཆུང་པ་རྣམས།
ཆོས་ཀྱི་གྲགས་པའི་ཞུགས་མཐུན་ཕྱིར
རྟོག་གེའི་སྐད་ནི་རབ་གསལ་བྱ། །

(Bstan-hgyur, Mdo, Ze, folio 373).

CHAPTER IV.

The Decline of Buddhist Logic.[1]

143. The contentious spirit of Buddhist Logic.

Antagonism between the Brahmaṇa and Buddhist logicians.

Unlike the Jainas, the Buddhists, in upholding their logical tenets, offered a bold challenge to the Brāhmaṇas. In the second century A.D., the Brāhmaṇic logician Akṣapāda brought out his comprehensive work on Logic called Nyāya-sūtra in which there was an explanation of sixteen categories, including four means of valid knowledge and five members of a syllogism. The Buddhist logician Nāgārjuna, who flourished in the 3rd century A.D., affirmed in opposition to Akṣapāda that a syllogism consisted of three members only. The Brāhmaṇic commentator Vātsyāyana (about 400 A.D.) attempted in vain to defend the position of Akṣapāda until he was overthrown by the Buddhist logician Dignāga who reduced the sixteen categories of Nyāya-sūtra to one, viz. *pramāṇa*, and the four means of valid knowledge to two, viz *pratyakṣa* and *anumāna*. "It was to dispel the error of Dignāga" that the *Brāhmaṇic* logician Uddyotakara wrote his Nyāya-vārtika about 635 A.D. He in his turn was assailed by the Buddhist logician Dharmakīrti who defended Dignāga.

After Uddyotakara there occurred a long gap in the succession of Brāhmaṇa writers on Logic until in the 9th century A.D. Vācaspati Miśra wrote his Nyāya-vārtika-tātparya-ṭīkā. By that time the Buddhist Logic had achieved a great triumph as is evident from the Buddhist writings of Devendra Bodhi, Śākya Bodhi, Vinīta Deva, Ravi Gupta, Jinendra Bodhi, Śānta Rakṣita, Kamala Śīla, Kalyāṇa Rakṣita and others. In the 9th and 10th centuries Dharmottara, Arcaṭa and other Buddhist logicians, having attacked the Brāhmaṇic authors, Udayanācārya, a Brāhmaṇa of Mithilā brought out, at the close of the 10th century A.D., his Ātma-tattva-viveka, etc., to refute the views of the Buddhists. Subsequently a large number of logicians such as

---

[1] *Vide* V. A. Smith's "Early History of India," my "Indian Missionaries to Foreign Lands in the Buddhistic Age"; my papers on "The influence of Buddhism on the development of Nyāya Philosophy" in the Journal of the Buddhist Text Society, part III for 1898, on "Anuruddha Thera—a learned Pāli author of Southern India in the 12th century A.D.," in J.A.S.B., Vol I, No. 4, 1905; and on "Ancient Indian Logic: an outline," published in Bhandarkar Commemorative Volume; Dr. Bunyiu Nanjio's Catalogue of the Chinese Tripiṭaka; Tāranātha's Geschichte des Buddhismus von Schiefner; and "Dpag-bsam-ljon-bzaṅ," edited by Sarat Chandra Das, Calcutta.

Jina Mitra, Prajñākara Gupta, Jetāri, Śaṅkarānanda and Mokṣākara Gupta appeared in the field to vindicate the Buddhist Logic from the attack of Brāhmaṇas. For nearly 800 years from 300 A.D. to 1100 A.D. the Buddhists fought valiantly against the Brāhmaṇas. But at last their principles of thought were almost entirely absorbed into the Brāhmaṇic Logic which left no room for an independent existence of the Buddhist Logic.

144. Loss of Royal Patronage.

Patronage in the past.

From time to time Buddhism received encouragement and favour from the rulers. As already stated the first, second, third and fourth Buddhist Councils were held in Rājagṛha, Vaiśālī, Pāṭalīputra and Jālandhara under the patronage of kings Ajāta śatru (about 490 B.C.), Kālāśoka (about 390 B.C.), Aśoka (255 B.C.) and Kaniṣka (about 78 A.D.) respectively. The Græco-Bactrian king Menander supported Buddhism, which he accepted as his religion about 150 B.C. King Śrī Harṣa of Kanauj (606—647 A D.) while revering Śiva and the Sun entertained a special faith in Buddha whose doctrines he defended with much care and enthusiasm.

The Buddhist logician Nāgārjuna (about 300 A.D.) received help from Sātavāhana, a king of the Andhra dynasty. Vasubandhu, another Buddhist logician, was patronised in the 5th century A.D. by certain kings of the Gupta dynasty, *viz.* Kumāra Gupta, Skanda Gupta, Pura Gupta and Bālāditya. Dignāga, the foremost of Buddhist logicians, was backed up about 500 A.D. by King Siṁha Varman of the Pallava dynasty.

Though Śaśāṅka Narendra Gupta, King of Central Bengal and a worshipper of Śiva, burnt the Bodhi tree at Buddha-Gayā, destroyed the foot-prints of Buddha at Pātalīputra and smashed numerous Buddhist temples and monasteries about 600 A.D., Buddhism could not be totally extirpated by him. The kings of the Pāla dynasty, who ruled in Bengal and Behar during 750—1119 A.D., were Buddhists who bestowed great patronage on the Buddhist teachers and monastic communities.

Persecution of Buddhism in Southern India.

Since the middle of the 6th century A.D. a great change took place in religion in the Deccan with the accession of the Cālukya kings on the throne at Vātāpi. Buddhism, which had a stronghold there, slowly declined and was gradually superseded by Jainism and Brāhmaṇism. During the two hundred years of Cālukya rule the Paurāṇic forms of Brahmaṇism grew in popularity.

Numerous temples dedicated to Śiva or Viṣṇu were built and many manuals of worship were compiled. The Rāṣṭrakūṭa King Amoghavarṣa, whose reign extended from 815 A.D. to at least 877 A.D., was a follower of Digambara Jainism. Under him and his successors Buddhism languished until it finally disappeared in the 12th century A.D.

Unlike the earlier kings the later rulers of the Pallava dynasty, from the 10th century onwards, became worshippers of Śiva, whose emblem the bull was adopted by them as their family crest.

Revival of Brāhmaṇism in Mithilā.

In 1019 A.D. Gāṅgeya Deva of the Cedi race set up a kingdom in Tirhut (Mithilā). He died in 1040 A.D. and was succeeded by his son Karṇa Deva who was a contemporary of Naya Pāla about 1038--1065 A.D.). Nānya Deva who was a Pramāra Kṣatriya of Karṇāta succeeded Karṇa Deva and reigned in Mithilā from 1089—1125 A.D. These kings, who overthrew Buddhism, brought about the revival of Brāhmaṇism in Mithilā.

Brāhmaṇic revival in Bengal.

Vijaya Sena, a member of the Karnāṭaka Kṣatriya race and a contemporary of Nānya Deva of Mithilā, wrested from the Pāla kings a large part of Bengal about 1119 A.D. Vijaya and his successors Vallāla Sena, Lakṣmaṇa Sena and others who ruled in Bengal up to 1197 A.D. re-established the Brāhmaṇic religion in Bengal in opposition to their predecessors the Pāla kings who had been Buddhists.

Buddhism having thus lost all patronage, the Buddhist Logic could not prosper.

145. Advent of the Mahomedans.

Mahomedans in Kāśmīra.

The Mahomedan invasion is said to have exerted a considerable influence on the disappearance of Buddhism from India. About 1021 A.D. the Hindu Shahiya dynasty of Kāśmīra was extirpated by the Mahomedans, and during the two centuries following there occurred great political disorders in the country. These circumstances led to the decline of Buddhism in Kāśmīra.

Mahomedans in Bengal and Behar.

Lama Tārānātha, while speaking of Kamala Rakṣitā, observes that Magadha, a stronghold of Buddhism, was attacked by the Turuṣkas (Mahomedans) at the end of the 10th century A.D. while the Buddhist University of Vikramaśilā was burnt by Bakhtiar Khiliji about 1197 A.D. A large proportion of the Buddhist population thought it expedient to embrace the Mahomedan faith. The Buddhists having in large numbers turned Mahomedans it became impossible for their Logic to attain a further development.

146. The Brāhmaṇic Preachers.

In Southern India

In the seventh century A.D. and onwards many Brāhmaṇic preachers began to flourish in Southern India to revive the Brāhmaṇic religion there. The attempts made by Kumārila Bhaṭṭa (about 630 A.D.) and Śaṅkarācārya (about 785 A.D.) to re-establish the Brāhmaṇic faith there are too well known to need a detailed notice. Early in the 12th century A.D. Rāmānuja, the celebrated Vaiṣṇava preacher, flourished in Srīperumātur, 18 miles east-north-east of Kāñcīpura (Conjeeveram), and converted the kings of the Cālukya and Cola dynasties to his religion.

In Northern India.

As regards Northern India, I have already referred to the efforts made by Udayanācārya of Mithilā in the 10th century to replace Buddhism by the Brāhmaṇic faith. It is a matter of common knowledge how in the 15th century A.D. Caitanya founded the Vaiṣṇava sect in Bengal and Śaṅkara Deva founded the Mahāpuruṣa sect in Assam. It is not necessary to give here a detailed account of the other sects that were founded in India to supplant Buddhism.

The Brāhmaṇic faith of new orders being thus established, there were left very few Buddhist writers who could continue to work in the field of Logic.

147. Shelter in Foreign Countries.

While Buddhism was undergoing persecution in India it was accorded a warm reception in foreign countries. Thousands of enterprising monks visited Nepal, Tibet, China, Mongolia, Corea, Japan, Ceylon, Burmah, Siam, Sumatra, Java, etc., where they were cordially welcomed and accepted as revered preceptors. The Buddhist monks being thus attracted in large numbers, to foreign countries, the field of Buddhist Logic in India was entirely deserted and suffered to grow wild and barren.

Spread of Buddhism in Asia, Europe and Africa.

Buddha instructed his followers, the monks, to take up the lives of missionaries, saying: "Go ye, Bhikkhus and wander forth for the gain of the many, the welfare of the many, in compassion for the world, for the good, for the gain, for the welfare of gods and men Proclaim, O Bhikkhus, the doctrine glorious. Preach ye a life of holiness, perfect and pure." Following this instruction many monks turned missionaries. From the *nirvāṇa* of Buddha to the middle of the third century B.C. the Buddhist missionaries were busily engaged in carrying on their propaganda in India. It was about 260 B.C. that Buddhism was carried abroad. The Maurya emperor Aśoka despatched missionaries not only to all his protected states such as those of the Gandhāras and Kāmbojas, but also to the

Hellenistic monarchies of the Yona country (Graeco-Bactria), Syria, Egypt, Cyrene, Macedonia and Epirus governed respectively by Diodotus, Antiochos Theos, Ptolemy Philadelphos, Magas, Antiogonos Gonatas and Alexander as is evident from his edicts.

Buddhism in Ceylon.

To preach Buddhism in Ceylon Aśoka sent his own son Mahinda and own daughter Saṅghamittā with a number of priests to that island. Among the numerous learned missionaries that subsequently visited Ceylon the names of Buddha Ghoṣa of Gayā (about 431 A.D.) and Anuruddha Thera of Kāñcīpura (12th century A D.) deserve a special notice.

Embassy at Rome.

Strabo the historican tells us that a Buddhist monk named Zarmana Chagos (Śramaṇācārya), a native of Barygaza (Broach) near Guzerat, went at the head of an embassy from the Indian king Poros to the court of Augustus Caesar at Rome about 29 B.C.

Buddhism in Khotan, etc.

During the reign of the Kuśāna king Kaniṣka and his successors, Buddhist missionaries went in large numbers to Khotan, Khasgar and other provinces of Central Asia.

Buddhist missionaries in China.

Buddhism was first known to China in the 2nd century B.C. But it was not till the time of Kaniṣka that arrangements could be made to send missionaries in large numbers to the celestial empire. It will be an impossible task to enumerate the missionaries that visited China during the thousand years of the Christian era. As late as in the 10th century A.D. Dharmadeva of Nālandā visited China where he translated many Sanskrit works into Chinese and received in 1001 A.D. a posthumous title of great honour. Dāna Pāla, a monk of Udyāna, who arrived in China in 980 A.D., was the recipient of a similar honour from the Chinese Emperor. Dharmarakṣa, a learned Buddhist monk of Magadha, who reached China in 1004 A.D. and received a special title of honour from the Chinese Emperor, translated numerous Sanskrit works into Chinese until he died in 1058 A.D. Instances may be enormously multiplied to show how Buddhist monks were received with honour in China.

Buddhist missionaries in Tibet.

In the 7th century A.D. Thon-mi-sam-bhota, a minister of king Sroṅ-tsan-gam-po of Tibet, visited Magadha, while in the 8th century A.D. the Indian sages Śānta Rakṣita and Kamala Śīla of the university of Nālandā and Guru Padma Sambhava of Udyāna was invited at the court of Khri-sroṅ-deu-tsan who ruled in Tibet from 728 A.D. to 864 A.D. About 1038 A.D. Lha-tsun-byaṅ-chub, a king of Tibet, sent an envoy named Rgya-tshon-seṅ-ge to invite Dīpaṅkara Śrījñāna or Atiśa of Vikramaśilā and to accompany him to Tibet. In the 9th, 10th, 11th and 12th centuries A.D. the number of Buddhist monks of Bengal and Behar that visited Tibet was enormously large. They were usefully employed with the co-operation of lamas to translate Sanskrit books into Tibetan. The Tibetan versions prepared by them were afterwards collected together to constitute the two encyclopaedias of Bkaḥ-ḥgyur and Bstan-ḥgyur that were edited by the great Tibetan sage Bu-ston of the monastery of Shālu near Tashi-lhun-po under orders of the Tibeto-Chinese-Mongol Emperor Kublai Khan in 1270 A.D.[1]

Buddhism in other countries.

Numerous Buddhist monks were also graciously received in Corea, Mongolia, Japan, Nepal, Burma, Siam, Java, Sumatra, etc.

148. Extinction of the Buddhists and their doctrines in India.

Disappearance of Buddhism as a separate organism.

I have shown that some of the Buddhists were received with hospitality in foreign countries while others became followers of Islam. The few that remained reverted to the Brāhmaṇic faith of the Tāntrika, Śaiva or Vaiṣṇava order. The Buddhist systems of thought were absorbed into the Brāhmaṇic systems, and the Modern School of Brāhmaṇic Logic was the result of a combination of the Brāhmaṇic *Nyāya* and the Buddhist science of *Pramāṇa*. The vitality of Buddhism as a separate organism was lost in the 13th century A.D. after which we hear no more of Buddhist logicians.

---

[1] ། མདོར་ན་བོད་དུ་བྱོན་པའི་པཎ་གྲུབ་ནི ། Indian Paṇḍitas, who were engaged in translating Sanskrit works into Tibetan, included the following:—

Śānta Rakṣita, Padma-sambhava, Dharmakīrti, Vimala Mitra, Buddha Guhya, Śānti Garbha, Viśuddhi Siṁha, Kamala Śīla, Kusara, Śaṅkara Brāhmaṇa, Śīla Mañju (of Nepal), Ananta Varman, Kalyāṇa Mitra, Jina Mitra, Surendra Bodhi Śīlendra Bodhi, Dāna Śīla, Bodhi Mitra, Muni Varma, Sarvajña Deva, Vidyākara Prabha, Śraddhākara Varma, Mukti Mitra, Buddha Śrī, Buddha Pāla, Dharma Pāla, Prajñā Pāla, Subhāṣita, Prajñā Varma, Dīpaṅkara Śrījñāna, Dāna Śrī, Smṛtijñāna-kīrti, Saṅgha Śrī, Jñāna Śrī of Kāśmīra, Candra Rāhula, Dhīra Pāla, Atulya Dāsa, Sumati Kīrti, Amara Candra, Bindu Kalasa, Kumāra Kalasa, Kanaka Varma, Sadbhārata, Jayānanta, Gayādhara, Amogha Vajra, Soma Nātha, Śūnyatā-samādhi Vajra, Jñāna Vajra, Prajñā Guhya, Mahāyāna Vajra, Bāla Candra, Mantra Kalukṣa, Sugata Śrī, Yamāri, Vairocana, Mañju Ghoṣa, Ravi Kīrti, Prajñā Śrījñāna, Gaṅgādhara, Dhana Gupta, Samanta Śrī, Niṣkalaṅka Deva, Jagat-mitra Nandi, Buddha Śrījñāna, Śākya Śrībhadra of Kāśmīra, Vibhūti Canda, Dāna Śīla, Saṅgha Śrī, Sambhoga Vajra, Ratna Śrī, Mahāsana of Nepal, Vajra Kīrti of Nepal, Gayā Śrī of Nepal, Kīrti of Nepal, Kumāra, Sanātana Śrī, Sādhu Kīrti, Vinaya Śrī, Śīla Śrī, Maṇḍala Śrī, Vimala Śrī, Darpaṇa Ācārya, Jaya Deva, Lakṣmīkara, Ratna Śrī, Ananta Śrī, Rāhula Śrī of Tāmra Dvīpa and Kīrti Paṇḍita.

(*Vide* Dpag-bsam-ljon-bzaṅ, p. 408).

PART III.

THE MODERN SCHOOL OF INDIAN LOGIC.

SECTION I.

Prakaraṇa—Manual of Logic.

CHAPTER I.

The Nyāya-Prākaraṇa reduces its Categories to one.

1. THE NEO-BRĀHMAṆIC AGE (CIRCA 900 A.D.—1920 A.D.).

In part II we have seen how Jainism and Buddhism exercised, for several centuries, a potent influence on the system of philosophy and culture of the Brāhmaṇas. In the Deccan, the decline of Buddhism commenced in the seventh century A.D., while in North India the Buddhists became almost extinct by 1200 A.D. The Brāhmaṇas, who survived them, organized their society on a secure basis. They took back into their folds some of their members who had embraced Buddhism or Jainism, but there arose the necessity of making strict rules for the maintenance of the integrity of their society and for the prevention of new admissions into it. It was at this period that different Brāhmaṇic legislators of different provinces composed treatises imposing laws, restrictions, and injunctions upon people of their province suited to their new local conditions. Thus there grew up a number of different schools of thought and culture, with local colourings of their own, which were quite different from the old schools so universal in their character and application. It may be observed that social exclusiveness became more marked in the Hindu Society at this period with the advent of the Muhammadans in India.

2. COMPOSITION OF THE *Prakaraṇas*, MANUALS OF LOGIC.

Placed in this new environment, the Brāhmaṇic writers, often under the patronage of local landholders, applied themselves to the study and teaching of Logic in quite a new spirit. The treatises on Logic, which were composed by them, borrowed their forms from the works of the mediaeval school, while for their subject-matter they went back to the works of the ancient school.

The works so composed in this period were technically called *Prakaraṇas*[1] or Manuals of Logic. In the Parāśara Upapurāṇa quoted in the commentaries on Nyāya-sāra and Saptapadārthī, the *prakaraṇa* is defined as a book which concerns itself with the topics of a portion of a śāstra which may deal even with matters not included in the śāstra, e.g. the Nyāya-sāra and Saptapadārthī—two very early manuals of Logic—treat in a very lucid way most topics of the Nyāya sūtra and Vaiśeṣika sūtra respectively, and at the same time some topics not included in those sūtras. Many matters which are elaborately treated in the works of the ancient school have been dismissed with scant ceremony in the logical manuals, while some subjects which were merely referred to in the former, have been clearly explained in the latter; for instance, the topics of *chala* (quibble), *jāti* (analogue) and *nigrahasthāna* (points of defeat), which occupied so much space in the works of the ancient school, drew very little attention from the authors of the manuals. On the other hand, the syllogism (*avayava*) which was briefly treated in the ancient works has been elaborately explained in the manuals. This treatment of certain subjects in preference to other subjects was most probably due to the influence of the Jaina and Buddhist systems of Logic which intervened. In respect of their styles also the ancient works differed considerably from the manuals: while the style of the former was mostly aphoristic, the style of the latter was expository. The *parakaraṇas* (manuals) are in fact remarkable for their accuracy and lucidity as well as for their direct handling of various topics in their serial orders. Definitions of terms are broad and accurate and not full of niceties.

3. FOUR CLASSES OF *prakaraṇas*.

The manuals of Logic called Prakaraṇas may be principally divided into four classes: (1) The Nyāya works treating only of the pramāṇa to which the remaining fifteen categories were subordinated; (2) the Nyāya works which embody in them the categories of the Vaiśeṣika philosophy; (3) the works which treat of six or seven Vaiśeṣika categories assimilating in them the Nyāya category of pramāṇa, and (4) the works which treat certain topics of the Nyāya and certain topics of the Vaiśeṣika. Most of the authors on manuals considered it necessary to combine such subjects of the Nyāya and Vaiśeṣika as would give us a complete

---

1 नन्वेवं शास्त्रप्रकरणयोः को भेद इति चेत् ।
शास्त्रैकदेशसम्बद्धं शास्त्रकार्यान्तरे स्थितम् ।
आहुः प्रकरणं नाम ग्रन्थभेदं विपश्चितः ॥
(Saptapadārthī, Vizianagram Sanskrit Series, p. 9).

theory of valid knowledge as well as of the objects which would give rise to that knowlege.

4. Nyāya-Prakaraṇa developing the category of *pramāṇa*.

The Jaina and Buddhist writers, who founded the Mediaeval School of Indian Logic, dealt with only one category, viz. *pramāṇa*, the means of valid knowledge. Following them some of the Brāhmaṇic writers chose only one category, viz. *Pramāṇa*, which they developed in such a way that it could assimilate in itself the remaining fifteen categories of the ancient school. Certain categories, such as *Prāmeya* (objects of knowledge), *jalpa* (wrangling), *vitaṇḍā* (cavil), *jāti* (analogue), and *nigrahasthāna* (the point of defeat) had to be excluded, while other categories were conveniently stuck on to *Pramāṇa* as its sub-divisions. These Brāhmaṇa writers, of whom accounts will shortly be given, were the true representatives of the Mediaeval School of Indian Logic. The earliest of these writers seem to have been Bhā-sarvajña,[1] who flourished about 950 A.D.

5. Bhā-sarvajña (about 950 A.D.).

The first Brāhmaṇic writer, who attempted to reduce the sixteen categories to one, was Bhā-sarvajña, the celebrated author of Nyāya-śāra.

His life.

Nothing is definitely known about the age in which he flourished or the country which he adorned by his birth He seems to me to have been a native of Kāśmīra. His name, which is very peculiar, bears a close resemblance to the names of Sarvajña Mitra[2] and Sarvajña Deva[3], who lived in Kāśmira about 775 A.D. and 1025 A.D. respectively.

His date.

As the reputed author of Nyāya-sāra, he is mentioned by the Jaina sages Guṇaratna[4] (1409 A.D.), and Maladhāri Rājaśekhara[5] (1348 A.D.).

---

[1] Bhāsarvajña's Nyāya-sāra with Jaya Siṁha's Nyāyatātparya-dīpikā has been edited by Dr. Satis Chandra Vidyabhusana and published in the Bibliotheca Indica Series of Calcutta.

[2] *Vide* Satis Chandra Vidyabhusana's edition of Sragdharā stotram, published in the Bibliotheca Indica series, Introduction, p. xxx.

[3] *Vide* Satis Chandra Vidyabhusana's "History of the Mediæval School of Indian Logic," pp. 134—135.

[4] भासर्वज्ञ प्रणीते न्यायसारेऽष्टादशटीकाः । तासु मुख्या टीका न्यायभूषणाख्या न्यायकलिका जयन्तरचिता न्यायकुसुमाञ्जलितर्कश्च ।

(Guṇaratna's Saddarśana-vṛtti, edited by Dr. L. Suali, p. 94).

[5] भासर्वज्ञो न्यायसारतर्कसूत्रविधायकः ।
न्यायसाराभिधे तर्के टीकाष्टादशस्फुटाः ॥

During their times there were already eighteen commentaries on the Nyāya-sāra. One of them is named Nyāya bhūṣaṇa, which I believe to be identical with the work of same name quoted by the Buddhist sage Ratnakīrti,[1] preceptor of Ratnākara Śānti,[2] who lived about 1000 A.D. This is therefore the latest date that we can assign to Bhā-sarvajña. The earliest limit may be fixed at 650 A.D. when there lived the Buddhist logician Dharmakīrti[3] whose controversy about the fallacy of "non-erroneous contradiction" (*viruddhāvyabhicāri*) is referred to in the Nyāya-sāra.[4] Bhā-sarvajña was evidently junior to Trilocana, whose fallacies of example have, according to Rāghava Bhaṭṭa, been quoted by him.[5] On these and other considerations I am inclined to believe that Bhā-sarvajña lived about 950 A.D.

Bhā-sarvajña who attempted to reconstruct Brāhmaṇic Logic on the plan of Buddhist Logic, must indeed have flourished in Kāśmīra in the 10th century A.D. when Brāhmaṇism and Buddhism flourished there side by side.

6. Bhā-sarvajña's Nyāya-sāra.

Nyāya-sāra follows no particular work.

The well-known logical treatise, which proceeded from the pen of Bhā-sarvajña, was designated as Nyāya-sāra, the Essence of Logic. It occupied a remarkable position in the history of Indian Logic. Following the method current in his time, Bhā-sarvajña undertook in his Nyāya-sāra, to treat only of *Pramāṇa* which he divided into three kinds: perception (*pratyakṣa*), inference (*anumāna*), and verbal testimony (*āgama*). This threefold division of Pramāṇa furnished a contrast to Akṣapāda who recognized a fourth

---

न्यायभूषणनाम्नी तु टीका तासु प्रसिद्धिभाक् ।

(Ṣaḍdarśana-samuccaya by Maladhāri Rājaśekhara' Sūri, published in the Yaśovijaya Granthamāla, Benares).

[1] Ratnakīrti observes:—

यदाह न्यायभूषणेन स्वर्थादिमयत्वे तदुपकार्य्याधेयत्वसुगामिपद्यप्रसङ्गमनुक्तं तदभिप्राया-नवगाहनफलं ...... ।

(Ratnakīrti's Apohasiddhi, edited by M.M. Hara Prasad Sastri, p. 11, A.S.B.)

[2] *Vide* Part II on Buddhist Logic.

[3] Dharmakīrti observes:—

विरुद्धाव्यभिचारी अपि संशयहेतुरुक्तः । ... ...

(Nyāyabindu, edited by Peterson, p. 115).

[4] Bhā-sarvajña writes:—

एकत्र तुल्यबलयोः विरुद्धहेतुद्वयोपनिपातो विरुद्धा व्यभिचारी इत्येके । ......

(Nyāya-sāra, edited by Satis Chandra Vidyabhusana, p. 12)

[5] *Vide* Rāghava Bhaṭṭa's commentary on the Nayā-sāra in reference to the passage:

अन्ये तु सन्देहद्वारेण अपरान् अष्टावुदाहरणाभासान् वर्णयन्ति ।

(Nyāya-sāra, p. 13, Vidyabhusana's edition).

kind named comparison (*upamāna*). It brought Bhā-sarvajña close to the Sāṁkhyas and Jainas who admitted three kinds of Pramāṇa, but distinguished him from the Buddhists who dealt with only two, viz. perception and inference. Like the Buddhist and Jaina writers, he divided inference into that for one's self (*svārthānumāna*) and that for the sake of others (*parārthānumāna*), and like them he gave an account of the fallacies of the minor term, the fallacies of example, etc. Quibble, analogue, etc., which had been prominent topics in the Nyāya-sūtra, were not altogether overlooked by Bhā-sarvajña who dealt with them in connection with an inference for the sake of others. Salvation (*mokṣa*) was described by him as the soul's attainment of eternal pleasure. In this respect he agreed with the Prābhākaras who affirmed that pleasure could be eternal, but differed from Akṣapāda who denied the eternality of pleasure.

The scheme laid down in the Nyāya-sāra, for the reduction of sixteen categories into one, may be exhibited in the tabular form thus :—

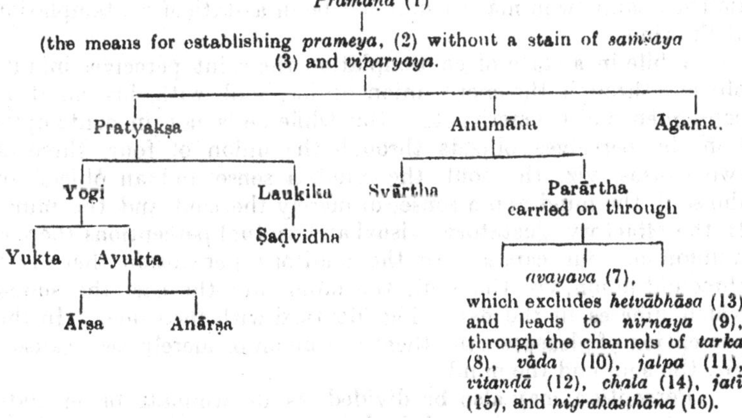

From the above it is evident that Bhā-sarvajña embodied in his *Pramāṇa* all the categories of the Nyāya-sūtra except *prayojana* (4) and *siddhānta* (6) which did not, according to him, constitute its integral parts and *dṛṣṭāntā* (5) which was included in *avayava* under the name of *udāharaṇa*.

7. Contents of the Nyāya-sāra.

Perception—*pratyakṣa*.

In the opening lines of the Nyāya-sāra, Bhāsarvajña says :—

Salutation.

"Bowing down to Śambhū (Śiva) the supreme Lord of the universe, who by nature knows all truths, I shall explain *Pramāṇa*, and its division and definition, in order that children may understand them well." [1]

Pramāṇa is defined in the work as the means of right knowledge freed from doubt and error. It is of three kinds, viz. perception (*pratyakṣa*), inference (*anumāna*), and verbal testimony (*āgama*).

Definition of Perception.

Perception, which is the means of direct cognition, may be either contemplative (*yogi-pratyakṣa*) or ordinary (*a-yogi pratyakṣa*). *The ordinary perception* is that which exhibits gross objects through their intercourse with our senses brought about by a favourable combination of light, space, time, nature, etc.

Intercourse.

The intercourse may be of six kinds, viz., (1) union, (2) united-inherence, (3) united-inherent inherence, (4) inherence, (5) inherent inherence, and (6) particularity—all of which have been explained before.

The *contemplative perception* exhibits objects which are too remote in time and space or too fine in nature. It is the perception of a saint, who may or may not be in a state of contemplation at the time.

While in a state of contemplation the saint perceives infinite objects through the mere union of his soul with his mind in consequence of his merit, etc. But while he is not in contemplation, he perceives objects through the union of four, three or two causes, viz. the soul, the mind, a sense and an object, or the soul, the mind and a sense, or merely the soul and the mind. In the olfactory, gustatory, visual and tactual perceptions there is a union of four causes. In the auditory perception there is a threefold union, viz. the soul, the mind and the ear (the sound which inheres in the ear being identical with the same). In the perception of pleasure, etc., there is a union of merely two causes, viz. the soul and the mind.

Kinds of Perception.

Perception may also be divided as determinate or mediate (*savikalpaka*) and indeterminate or immediate (*nirvikalpaka*). The determinate perception is knowledge of an object indicative of a relation of the object to its name, genus, quality, action, etc., e.g. this is Devadatta. The indeterminate perception is the knowledge which exhibits the mere essence of an object independent of its relation

---

[1] प्रणम्य शम्भुं जगतः पतिं परं
समस्ततत्त्वार्थविदं स्वभावतः।
शिशुप्रबोधाय मयाभिधास्यते
प्रमाणतद्भेदतदन्यलक्षणम्॥

(Opening lines, Nyāya sāra).

to a name, genus, etc., e.g. the knowledge produced by the first union of a sense with its object or the knowledge of a saint while he is in a state of contemplation.

Inference—*anumāna.*

Inference defined.

Inference (*anumāna*) is the means of knowing a thing beyond the range of the senses through its inseparable connection with another thing which lies within their range. "The hill is fiery, because it is smoky"—this is an inference in which we ascertain fire from smoke with which it is inseparably connected.

Invariable concomitance—*vyāpti.*

The inseparable connection (in Sanskrit *avinābhāva*) is also designated as pervasion or invariable concomitance (*vyāpti*). It is of two kinds: (1) affirmative (*anvaya*) and negative (*vyatireka*). The affirmative invariable concomitance (*anvaya-vyāpti*) is the accompaniment of the middle term by the major term in all cases. The negative invariable concomitance (*vyatireka-vyāpti*) is the accompaniment of the absence of the major term by the absence of the middle term in all cases. In the affirmative universal proposition "wherever there is smoke, there is fire"—smoke is the middle term which is in all cases accompanied by fire the major term; and in the negative universal proposition "wherever there is no fire, there is no smoke"—the absence of fire is in all cases accompanied by the absence of smoke.

Kinds of Inference.

Inference is of two kinds, viz. (1) inference for one's self (*svārthānumāna*) and (2) inference for the sake of others (*parārthānumāna*) The first does not stand in need of demonstration but the second does. The demonstration consists of a syllogism of five parts: (1) a proposition, (2) a reason, (3) an example, (4) an application, and (5) a conclusion. A proposition is the statement of the subject (minor term) of which something is desired to be established, e.g. sound is non-eternal. A reason is the statement of the mark which enables us to establish something. The reason may be exclusively affirmative (*kevalānvayi*), exclusively negative (*kevala vyatireki*) and affirmative negative (*anvaya-vyatireki*).

Terms of an Inference.

The subject or minor term (*pakṣa*) is that in which it is doubtful whether the quality of the major term abides. A homologue (*sapakṣa*) is that in which the quality of the major term is known, with certainty, to abide. A heterologue (*vipakṣa*) is that in which, it is known with certainty, that the quality of the major term does not abide. The essential nature of a syllogism (*pakṣa-dharmartā*) refers to the character of the pervasion of the middle term by the major term.

Take the following syllogism :—

The hill is fiery,
because it is smoky,
like a kitchen or like a lake.

Here "hill" is the subject or minor term on which the existence of fire is to be proved; "kitchen" is a homologue in which fire is known with certainty to abide; and "lake" is a heterologue in which, we are sure, fire does not abide.

Exclusively affirmative is the reason which abides in the minor term of which there are homologues but no heterologues, e.g., this is *nameable*, because it is knowable.

Kinds of the middle term.

Exclusively-negative is the reason which abides in the minor term of which there are no homologues and which is distinct from the heterologues, e.g. the earth is different from other elements, because it possesses *smell*.

Affirmative-negative is the reason which abides in the minor term and its homologues but does not abide in the heterologues of the minor term, which is not counterbalanced and the sphere of which is not opposed by evidences, e.g. the hill is fiery, because it is *smoky*.

Hetvābhāsa—fallacy of the reason.

Fallacy of reason.

Fallacy (*hetvābhāsa*) is that which possesses the appearance of a reason but not its essential characters. It is of various kinds as mentioned below :—

A. Unproved (*asiddha*).

Unproved (*asiddha*) is the reason whose existence in the minor term has not been known with certainty. It is of following kinds :—

(1) Unproved in respect of its nature (*svarūpāsiddha*), e.g. sound is non-eternal, because it is *visible*.

(2) Unproved on account of its abiding in a different locus (*vyadhikaraṇāsiddha*). e.g. sound is non-eternal, because a *pot* is a product.

(3) Unproved in respect of the substantive (*viśeṣyāsiddha*), e.g. sound is non-eternal, because it is a *visible thing* possessing generality [sound possesses generality (soundness), but it is not visible].

(4) Unproved in respect of the adjective (*viśeṣaṇāsiddha*), e.g. sound is non-eternal, because it possesses generality *which is visible* [soundness is not visible].

(5) Unproved in respect of a part (*bhāgāsiddha*), e.g. sound is non-eternal, because it is produced by effort. [The first

sound-wave is produced by effort, but the succeeding sound-waves do not, it is said, depend on it].

(6) Unproved in respect of the abode (*āśrayāsiddha*). e.g. there is primordial matter, because it evolves into the universe. [The Naiyāyikas do not admit that primordial matter (Prakṛti) is the prime source of the universe].

(7) Unproved in respect of a part of the abode (*āśrayaikadeśā-siddha*), e.g. the primordial matter, soul and God are eternal, because they are not products. [The Naiyāyikas admit the soul and God to be eternal but not the primordial matter *Prakṛti*].

(8) Unproved on account of the substantive being useless (*vyarthaviśeṣyāsiddha*), e.g. sound is non-eternal, because it possesses *generality* which is a product. [To say that "soundness is a product" is not only useless but also incorrect].

(9) Unproved on account of the adjective being useless (*vyartha-viśeṣaṇāsiddha*), e.g. sound is non-eternal, because it is a product *which is possessed of generality*. [It is superfluous here to say that "a product is possessed of generality].

(10) Unproved on account of the reason being doubtful (*sandig-dhāsiddha*), e.g. a person without ascertaining whether there is *smoke* or *mist* says: this place is fiery, because it *smoky*. [Here if the smoke turns out to be mist, the inference will be invalid].

(11) Unproved on account of the substantive being doubtful (*sandigdha viśeṣyāsiddha*), e.g Kapila is still overwhelmed with passions, because *true knowledge has not yet grown in him* who is a person. [It is doubtful as to whether true knowledge has not grown in him].

(12) Unproved on account of the adjective being doubtful (*sandig-dha-viśeṣaṇāsiddha*), e.g. Kapila is still overwhelmed with passions because he is a person *who is always devoid of true knowledge*. [It is doubtful as to whether he is always devoid of true knowledge].

The fallacies called *unproved* mentioned above are of two descriptions according as the lack of truth involved in them is recognized by both the parties or one of the parties engaged in a debate.

B. THE CONTRADICTORY (*viruddha*).

Contradictory (*viruddha*) is the reason which abides in the minor term as well as in the opposite of it.

If there are homologues to the minor term, the contradictory reason may be of four kinds as follows:—

(1) The reason which abides in the minor term as well as in its heterologue (but not in its homologue), e.g. sound is eternal, because it is a product [like ether (homologue)

and like a pot (heterologue). Productivity abides in sound as well as in its heterologue the pot].

(2) The reason which abides in the minor term as well as in a part of its heterologue (but not in its homologue), e.g. sound is eternal because it is a thing which possesses generality and is cognized by our external senses. [Here an instance of the heterologue is a pot (*a*) which is non-eternal, (*b*) which possesses generality *potness*, and (*c*) which is cognized by our external senses. "Pleasure" cannot be an instance of the heterologue, because though non-eternal it is not cognized by our external senses. So the reason abides only in a part of the heterologue. We cannot cite *potness* as a homologue, because though potness is eternal and cognized by our external sense, it does not possess generality *potness-ness*].

(3) The reason which abides in a part of the minor term as well as in a part of its heterologue but not in its homologue, e.g. sound is eternal, because it is a product of effort. [The first wave of sound is a product of effort, but the succeeding waves are not products of the same nature. So the productivity of effort abides only in a part of the minor term. Similarly it abides only in a part of the heterologue. "Pot" is a heterologue which is a product of effort, but "grass" is a heterologue which is not a product of effort.

(4) The reason which abides in a part of the minor term, but in the whole of its heterologue (and not in its homologue). e.g. the earth is eternal, because it is a product. [Productivity abides in the earth which is gross, but not in the earth which is subtle or atomic. At the same time it abides in all things which are non-eternal or heterologues to the minor term].

While there are no homologues, the contradictory reasons are four as follow:—

(1) The reason which abides in the minor term as well as in its heterologues, e.g. sound is a special quality of ether as it is knowable. [Knowableness abides in sound as well as in its heterologues such as smell. There are no homologues, because nothing but sound is a special quality of ether].

(2) The reason which abides in a part of the minor term and in a part of its heterologues, e.g. sound is a special quality of ether, because it is a product of effort. [Productivity of effort abides in the first sound-wave but does not abide in the succeeding sound waves, it abides in some heterologues as pot, etc., but not in other heterologues as the soul, etc.].

(3) The reason which abides in the minor term and in a part of its heterologues, e.g. sound is a special quality of ether,

because it is cognizable by the external senses. [All sounds are cognizable by the external senses. It is only some heterologues such as a pot, cloth, etc., that are cognizable by the external senses while other heterologues such as pleasure, pain, etc., are not so cognizable].

(4) The reason which abides in a part of the minor term, but in the whole of its heterologues, e.g. sound is a special quality of ether, because it does not arise from words. [Some sounds arise from words such as those which we read in books, while others do not, such as the sounds of a drum. No sound, which is not a special quality of ether, arises from words].

C. THE UNCERTAIN (*anaikāntika*).

Uncertain (*anaikāntika*) is the reason which abides in the minor term, its homologues and heterologues: its subdivisions are the following:—

(1) The reason which abides in the minor term, its homologues and heterologues, e.g. sound is non-eternal, because it is knowable.

(2) The reason which abides in the minor term, in a part of its homologues and in a part of its heterologues, e.g. sound is non-eternal, because it is perceptible. [(1) Perceptibility abides in "sound," (2) it abides in some of the non-eternal as a pot, but does not abide in some of the non-eternal as the binary compound of atoms, and (3) it abides in some of the eternal as generality, but does not abide in some of the eternal as ether]

(3) The reason which abides in the minor term and its homologues as well as in a part of its heterologues, e.g. this is a cow, because it has horns. [Horns abide in "this" as well as in its homologues cow, calf, etc. They abide with some of the heterologues such as a buffalo, but do not abide in other heterologues such as a horse].

(4) The reason which abides in the minor term and its heterologues and in a part of its homologues, e.g. this is not a cow, because it has horns.

(5) The reason which abides in a part of the minor term, a part of its homologues and a part of its heterologues, e.g. the earth is non-eternal, because it is perceptible. [Perceptibility abides in earth which is gross, but not in earth which is subtle (atomic). It abides in some homologues as a pot, but not in other homologues as a binary compound of atoms. Similarly it abides in some heterologues as generality but not in other heterologues as ether].

(6) The reason which abides in a part of the minor term, a part of its homologues and in the whole of its heterologues, e.g. space, time and mind are substances, because they are incorporeal. [Incorporeality abides in space and time but

not in mind which is an atom in dimension. It abides in some homologues as soul, ether, etc., but not in other homologues as earth, water, fire and air. It abides in all heterologues as quality, action, generality, particularity and inherence].

(7) The reason which abides in all homologues and heterologues, but only in a part of the minor term, e.g. ether, time, space, soul and mind are not substances, because they are devoid of special qualities of momentary character. [The devoidance of special qualities of momentary character abides in space, time and mind but not in ether and soul, sound and intelligence which are respectively the special qualities of ether and soul being momentary. It abides in all homologues as quality, action, generality, particularity and inherence, and also in heterologues as earth, water, fire and air]

D. NON-TRIED OR NON-CONCLUSIVE (*anadhyavasita*, or *anupasaṁhāri*).[1]

Non-tried (*anadhyavasita*) is the reason which abides in the minor term alone, without a definite connection with the major term. It is subdivided as follows :—

(1) The reason which abides in the minor term of which there are neither homologues nor heterologues, e.g. all are non-eternal, because they are existent. [" All " having included every thing there is no homologue or heterologue left behind. The reason " existence " does however abide in " all "].

(2) The reason which abides in a part of the minor term of which there are neither homologues nor heterologues, e.g. all are non-eternal, because they are products. [" All " which includes everything, has neither homologues nor heterologues. The reason " product " abides in non-eternal things but not in eternal things both of which are comprised by " all"].

(3) The reason which abides in the minor term of which there are both homologues and heterologues, e.g. sound is non-eternal, because it is a special quality of ether. [Sound which is a special quality of ether, has homologues which are however not qualities of ether].

(4) The reason which abides in a part of the minor term of which there are both homologues and heterologues, e.g. all substances are non-eternal, because they are possessed of

---

[1] Mr. V. P. Vaidya observes :—" This hetvābhāsa is mentioned by Bhā-sarvajña alone, except by Śaṅkara Miśra, who, about the 15th century, says that it is the same as anupasaṁhārī-anaikāntika, which latter did not take its name and form in the time of Bhā-sarvajña.

(Nyāya-sāra, p. 30, V. P. Vaidya's edition).

activity. [There is activity in earth but not in ether, although both are substances. There is no activity in quality and action which are homologues and in generality, particularity and inherence which are heterologues of the non-eternal].

(5) The reason which abides in the minor term and has homologues but no heterologues, e.g. all products are eternal, because they are originated. [There is no heterologue of "all products" which constitutes the minor term. Ether, which is a homologue, is not originated].

(6) The reason which abides in a part of the minor term and has homologues but no heterologues, e.g all products are eternal, because they are composed of parts. ["Pot" and intelligence are both products, one is composed of parts but the other is not. There is no heterologue of "all products" which constitutes the minor term. Ether is a homologue but it is not composed of parts]

E. Mistimed or incompatible reason (*kālātyayopadiṣṭa*[1] or *bādhita*).

Mistimed or incompatible is the reason which abides in the minor term as opposed by evidences. It is subdivided as follows:—

(1) Opposed by perception, e.g. this fire is non-warm, because it is a product.

(2) Opposed by inference, e.g. the atoms are non-eternal, because they are corporeal.

(3) Opposed by scripture, e.g wine should be drunk by Brāhmaṇas, because it is a liquid thing like milk.

(4) Partly opposed by perception, e.g. all heats are non-warm, because they have forms. [Heat of fire is warm but that of moon-stone is non-warm].

(5) Partly opposed by inference, e.g. fluidity, colour, taste, smell and touch abiding in eternal things are eternal, because they abide in atoms which do not occupy space, etc.

(6) Partly opposed by scripture, e.g. bodies of all celestial sages are earthy, because they are bodies like those of ours. [Bodies of some celestial sages are earthy, those of others watery, fiery, etc.]

F. Balancing the controversy (*prakaraṇa-sama*).

Balancing the controversy (*prakaraṇa-sama*) is the reason which possesses its three forms, but establishes one's own side as well as the opposite side, e.g.

---

[1] Mr. V. P. Vaidya observes:—"This fallacy is known in later works as *bādhita*. According to later writers "*kālātīta*" is the name of the fallacy.
(Nyāya-sāra, p. 31).

(1) Sound is eternal,
(2) because it is sound,
(3) like ether,
or,
(1) sound is non-eternal,
(2) because it is sound,
(3) like a pot.

G. Non-erroneous Contradiction—*viruddhāvyabhicārī.*

Some say that there is a fallacy called non-erroneous contradiction which occurs when there is an advancement of two contradictory reasons of equal characters, e.g. a disputant says:—

Ether is eternal, because it is an incorporeal substance, like the soul.

His opponent says:—

Ether is non-eternal, because it is the abode of a special quality cognized by one of our external senses, like a pot.

The non-erroneous contradiction is a fallacy with reference to one party, but is a good reasoning with reference to the other party.

Example—*udāharaṇa*.

An example (*udāharaṇa*) is the statement of a complete illustration It is of two kinds, viz. (1) homogeneous or affirmative (*sādharmya*), and (2) heterogenous or negative (*vaidharmya*). An affirmative example is the statement of an illustration in the positive or direct order, e.g.

(1) sound is non-eternal,
(2) because it possesses acuteness, etc.,
(3) whatever possesses acuteness, etc., is non-eternal, like pleasure, etc. (affirmative example).

Kinds of example.

A negative example is the statement of a complete illustration in negative or indirect order, e.g.

(1) Sound is non-eternal,
(2) because it possesses acuteness, etc.,
(3) whatever is not non-eternal does not possess acuteness, etc., like ether etc. (negative example).

A fallacious example (the fallacy or semblance of an example, *udāharaṇābhāsa*) is one which appears as an example but is really devoid of its essential character.

Fallacies of an affirmative example.

The fallacies of affirmative example are the following:—

(1) An example defective in the major term (*sādhya-vikala*), e.g. the mind is non-eternal, because it is corporeal like an *atom*.

(2) An example defective in the middle term (*sādhana-vikala*), e.g. the mind is non-eternal, because it is corporeal like an *action*.

(3) An example defective in both the major and middle terms (*ubhayavikala*), e.g. the mind is non-eternal, because it is corporeal, like *ether*.

(4) An example which is supportless (*āśraya-hīna*), e.g. the mind is non-eternal, because it is corporeal, like the *horn of a hare*.

(5) An example which is non-pervasive (*avyāpti*), e.g. the mind is non-eternal, because it is corporeal, like a *pot*. [There is no pervasion or universal connection between corporeality and non-eternality.]

(6) An example whose pervasion is inversely stated (*viparīta-vyāpti*), e.g.
   (i) the mind is non-eternal,
   (ii) because it is corporeal,
   (iii) whatever is non-eternal is corporeal like a *pot*. [This should have been stated thus: whatever is corporeal is non-eternal, like a pot].

Fallacies of negative example.

The fallacies of negative example are similarly of six kinds specified below :—

(1) An example of excluded major term, e.g. whatever is not non-eternal is not corporeal as an *atom*.

(2) An example of excluded middle term (*sādhanāvyāvṛtta*), e.g. whatever is not non-eternal is not corporeal, as an *action*.

(3) An example of excluded major and middle terms (*ubhayā-vyāvṛtta*), e.g. whatever is not non-eternal is not corporeal, as a *pot*.

(4) An example which is without support (*āśraya-hīna*), e.g. whatever is not non-eternal is not corporeal, as a sky-flower.

(5) A non-pervasive example (*avyāptyabhidhāna*), e.g. whatever is not non-eternal is not corporeal, as ether.

(6) An example with inverse pervasion (*viparīta-vyāptyabhi-dhāna*), e.g. whatever is not corporeal is not non-eternal, as ether.

Other fallacies of example.

Bhā-sarvajña[1] mentions another four kinds of fallacious examples of the affirmative form as follow :—

(1) An example of doubtful major term, e.g. this person will exercise sovereignty, because he is sprung from the lunar race, like a certain prince of that race.

(2) An example of doubtful middle term, e.g. this person is

1 Rāghava Bhaṭṭa in his commentary on the Nyāya-sāra says, that these eight kinds of fallacious examples (four of the affirmative form and four of the negative form) were laid down by Trilocana, who must therefore have flourished before Bhā-sarvajña. (Cf. V. P. Vaidya's edition of Nyāya-sāra, notes, p. 35).

not omniscient, because he is passionate like the man on the street.

(3) An example of doubtful major and middle terms, e.g. this person will go to heaven, because he has accumulated merits, like Devadatta.

(4) An example whose support is doubtful, e.g. this person is not omniscient, because he speaks evil, like Devadatta's son who will be born.

Similarly there are four kinds of fallacious examples of the negative form based on their doubtful character

Following Nyāya-sūtra.

Bhā-sarvajña [1] closely follows the Nyāya-sūtra in his explanation of *upanaya* (application), *nigamana* (conclusion), *nirṇaya* (ascertainment), *kathā* (disputation), *vāda* (discussion), *jalpa* (wrangling), *vitaṇḍā* (cavil), *jāti* (analogue), *nigrahasthāna* (point of defeat), etc.

Verbal testimony—*āgama*.

Kinds of verbal testimony.

Verbal testimony or reliable assertion (*āgama*) is the means of knowing things accurately through indicatory signs (or convention). It is of two kinds, according as the assertion refers to matter open to our senses or to matter beyond our senses. The authoritativeness of the first kind of assertion is evident from the action one takes on hearing the assertion, e.g. a boy runs to receive a mango when he is asked by his father to do so. The authoritativeness of the second kind of assertion is inferred from its having proceeded from a person who possesses supersensuous knowledge, and is, as such, reliable, e.g. one performs sacrifice on the strength of the Vedic injunction that a son is born when a sacrifice is performed for the same.

Other means of Knowledge.

The three means of right knowledge have been explained. All other so-called means are included in them, e.g. presumption (*arthāpatti*) and probability (*sambhava*) are included in inference, rumour (*aitihya*) and muscular movement (*ceṣṭā*), in verbal testimony, and negation or non-existence (*abhāva*) in any of the three according to circumstances. Muscular movement alleged to be a means of knowledge is only an action substituted for a word or assertion.

Emancipation—*mokṣa*.

Prameya.

The object of our knowledge (*prameya*) is of four kinds as follows :—

---

[1] Bhā-sarvajña uses the word *āgama* as a synonym for *śabda*. In reality one signifies "scripture" which enables us to know things beyond our senses, and the other signifies "the assertion of a reliable person."

(1) That which is fit only to be avoided, viz. misery or suffering (*duḥkha*), of which there are twenty-one varieties already explained.
(2) That which causes misery or suffering, viz. ignorance (*avidyā*), lust (*tṛṣṇā*), merit (*dharma*) or demerit (*adharma*).
(3) The cessation of misery or suffering.
(4) The means for the removal of misery or suffering, viz. the true knowledge of soul (*ātmā*).

Soul.

The soul is of two kinds, viz. the individual soul (*apara ātmā*) and the supreme soul (*para ātmā*). The individual soul, which has to undergo sufferings from the bondage of the world, attains final emancipation (*mokṣa*) through the knowledge of the supreme soul called Śiva. In the state of final emancipation the individual soul, being finally freed from misery, enjoys eternal pleasure.

8. Commentaries on the Nyāyasāra.

Of the eighteen commentaries on Nyāyasāra enumerated by Jaina writers some are noticed below :—[1]

(1) **Nyāya-bhūṣaṇa** the oldest commentary mentioned by Maladhāri Rāja Śekhara (1348 A.D.) and Guṇaratna (1409 A.D.) and quoted by the Buddhist sage Ratnakīrti in his Apohasiddhi (about 1000 A.D.), and by the Jaina sage Jayasiṁha Sūri, in his Nyāyatātparyadīpikā. No manuscript of it has yet been recovered.
(2) **Nyāyakalikā** by Jayanta, mentioned by Guṇaratna in the Ṣaḍdarśana samuccaya Vṛtti (1409 A.D.). No manuscript of it has yet been recovered.
(3) **Nyāyakusumāñjali tarka** mentioned by Guṇaratna in the Ṣaḍdarśana samuccaya Vṛtti (1409 A.D.). No manuscript of it has yet been recovered.
(4) **Nyāyasāraṭīkā** by Vijaya Siṁha Gaṇi. A manuscript of it has been recovered from Bikaner. (*Vide* S. K. Bhandarkar's Catalogue of MSS. in the Deccan College, 1888, p. 58).
(5) **Nyāyasāraṭīkā** by Jayatirtha (*vide* India Office Catalogue, No. 3132—1412).
(6) **Nyāyasārapadapañjikā** by Vāsudeva. A manuscript of it has been recovered from Kāśmīra. (*Vide* S. R. Bhandarkar's Catalogue of MSS. in the Deccan College, 1888, p. 95). Another manuscript of it written in Kāśmīrī character is to be found in the library of the Asiatic Society of Bengal bearing No. 1552. In the opening lines[2]

---

[1] *Vide* Rāja Śekhara's Ṣaḍdarśana samuccaya and Guṇaratna's Ṣaḍdarśana samuccaya vṛtti.

[2] The opening lines of the Nyāyasārapadapañjikā run as follows :—

देवदेवमभिवन्द्य भास्वरं
योगिवृन्दहृदयैकमन्दिरम् ।

Vāsudeva speaks of himself as the author of the work and in the colophon he is stated to be a native of Kāśmīra.

(7) **Nyāyasāravicāra** by Bhaṭṭa Rāghava. A manuscript of it dated [1] Saka 1174 A.D. 1252 is contained in the library of the Queen's College, Benares.

(8) **Nyāyatātparyadīpikā** [2] by Jayasiṃha Sūri, a Jaina of the Śvetāmbara Sect, who lived in the fourteenth century A.D. as his Kumārapālacaritra [3] is dated Saṁvat 1422 or A.D. 1365.

वासुदेवविदुषा विरच्यते
न्यायसारपदपञ्चिका मया ॥

[1] The Nyāyasāravicāra ends as follows :—

शके चतुःसप्तति संख्यके गतैः
शताधिकैरभ्यधिके च पञ्चभिः ।
द्विषाग्नितैस्तैश्च बभूव वत्सरैः
ध्रुवं विचारः परिशोधि राघवः ॥

इति सारंगसुतवादीन्द्रशिष्यन्यायनिपुणतर्कविचारचतुरभट्टराघवविरचिते न्यायसारविचारे तृतीयः परिच्छेदः समाप्तः ॥

The verse may be interpreted to give Śaka 1174 (A.D. 1252) or Śaka 1274, 1352 A.D.).

[2] Nyāyatātparyadīpikā with the text of Nyāyasāra has been edited by Satis Chandra Vidyabhusana and published in the Bibliotheca Indica series, Calcutta.

[3] श्रीविक्रमनृपाद् द्वि द्वि मन्वब्देऽयमजायत ।
ग्रन्थः सप्तविंशतीषट्शतश्लोकानुष्टुभाम् ॥

(Kumārapāla Caritra Praśasti, Chap. X).

CHAPTER II.

Nyāya-prakaraṇas embodying Vaiśeṣika categories.

9. The Nyāya incorporates the Vaiśeṣika.

Coalescence of the Nyāya and Vaiśeṣika.

The Vaiśeṣika philosophy rendered considerable help to the development of the Nyāya (Logic) and many of the sūtras of the Nyāya philosophy presuppose those of the Vaiśeṣika. In fact the Vaiśeṣika and Nyāya philosophies of the Ancient and Mediaeval periods supplemented each other in respect of their subjects and styles. Hence the two philosophies were called *samāna-tantra* or allied systems. At last the Vaiśeṣika and Nyāya philosophies actually coalesced. The six or seven categories of the Vaiśeṣika were entirely absorbed in the treatise on Nyāya philosophy and the Nyāya categories of pramāṇa in its developed form were actually absorbed in the treatises on Vaiśeṣika philosophy.

As instances of Nyāya absorbing the Vaiśeṣika categories, we may cite the cases of Tārkikarakṣā by Varadarāja and Tarkabhāṣā by Keśava Miśra. Varadarāja, who deals with all the sixteen categories of Nyāya, includes in the second category, viz. Prameya, not only the twelve objects of Nyāya, such as, "ātman," etc., but also the six categories of the Vaiśeṣika, such as dravya, etc. Keśava Miśra on the other hand brings the six categories of the Vaiśeṣika under "artha", which is one of the twelve objects included in the second Nyāya category "Prameya." A short account of the two works is given here

10. Varadarāja (about 1150 A.D.).

Varadarāja[1] wrote a work on Logic called Tārkikarakṣā, or "Protection of Logicians." He seems to have been a native of Andhra or Telingana, in the Madras Presidency. Varadarāja must have flourished after the 10th century A.D., possibly also after the 11th century A.D., as he mentions Trilocana, Vācaśpati Miśra,[2]

---

1. Varadarāja wrote a commentary on Udayana's Kusumāñjali called Nyāya Kusumāñjali ṭīkā. Compare

एतच्च ग्रन्थकृतैव स्वटीकितं न्यायकुसुमाञ्जलिटीकायामित्यास्तां तावत् ।

(Mallinātha's commentary on Tārkikarakṣā, edited by M.M. Vindhyeśvari Prasād, page 46).

2. आलोच्य दुस्तरगभीरतरान् प्रबन्धान्
वाचस्पतेर्वचनसश्च तथा परेषाम् ।

Udāyanācāryya, Śalikānātha, Viśvarūpa, Jayanta, Nyāyācāryya (Śivāditya), Bhā-sarvajña,[1] and Bhūṣaṇakāra. On the other hand, he is mentioned by Mādhvacāryya[2] in the Sarvadarśana saṁgraha, composed in the 14th century A.D. Very probably he flourished about 1150 A.D., shortly after which Jñāna Pūrṇa or Jñāna Deva, a disciple of Viṣṇu Svāmin, wrote a commentary on the Tārkikarakṣā called Laghudīpikā.[3] Viṣṇu Svāmin is said to have been the original founder of a Vaiṣṇava sect called in later times the Vallabhācāri. The immediate disciple of Viṣṇu Svāmin was Jñāna Deva who was succeeded consecutively by Nāma Deva and the junior Trilocana.[4] Perhaps there followed a few other preceptors before Vallabhācāryya, son of Lakṣmaṇa Bhaṭṭa of Andhra (Telingana), occupied the seat of guru at the end of the 15th century A.D. As Vallabhācāryya lived between 1450 and 1530 A.D., and as several preceptors intervened, the date of Varadarāja, if placed in 1150 A.D., will not be far wrong.[5]

11. Tārkikarakṣā.

Category.

The Tārkikarakṣā, which at once begins its subject, is divided into three chapters, the first of which deals with the first fourteen categories of Nyāya, viz. (1) *pramāṇa*, (2) *prameya*, (3) *saṁśaya*, (4) *prayojana*, (5) *dṛṣṭānta*, (6) *siddhānta*, (7) *avayava*, (8) *tarka*, (9) *nirṇaya*, (10) *vāda*, (11) *jalpa*, (12) *vitaṇḍā*, (13) *hetvābhāsa*, and (14) *chala*. The second chapter deals with the fifteenth category, viz. *jāti*, while the third chapter treats of the sixteenth category viz. *nigrahasthāna*.

शास्त्रे मयात्र समलङ्कृत वावदूके
नित्यं कथासु विजिगीषुभिरेव धार्य्यः ॥

(Tārkikarakṣā, p. 364, edited by M.M. Vindhyeśvarī Prasād, Benares).

[1] Varadarāja quotes Bhā-sarvajña thus :—

यथाह:,— तस्मै प्रमाणं शिव: । (Tārkikarakṣā, p. 58).

[2] *Vide* Sarvadarśanasaṁgraha, chapter on Pūrṇa-prajña-darśana in which we read :—

तार्किकरक्षायां च,——

सर्वज्ञ तद्गतद्रूप विकल्पानुपपत्तितः ।
सर्वज्ञसादिसिद्धश्च भङ्गो नित्यसमो भवेत् ॥

[3]
सर्वैश्वर्य्यं दिशाभासं सर्वविद्या निषेवितम् ।
श्रीपद्मेश्वरवरेः स्तनुं श्रीविष्णुस्वामिगुरुं गुरुः ॥

इति श्रीज्ञानपूर्णकृता वरदराजीयसारसंग्रहटीका लघुदीपिका समाप्ता ॥

[4] *Vide* Imperial Gazetteer.

[5] *Vide* Dr. Venis' prefatory notice to Tārkikarakṣā, edited by M.M. Vindhyeśvari Prasād, Benares.

Tārkikarakṣā incorporates the Vaiśeṣika categories.

Prameya, according to the Nyāya-sūtra, signifies *ātman*, *śarīra*, *indriya*, *artha*, *buddhi*, *manas*, *pravṛtti*, *doṣa*, *pretyabhāva*, *phala*, *duḥkha*, and *apavarga*, but, according to Varadarāja, it incorporates also the six predicaments of the Vaiśeṣika philosophy, viz. the substance (*dravya*), quality (*guṇa*), action (*karma*), generality (*sāmānya*), particularity (*viśeṣa*), and co-existence or inherence (*samavāya*).

The scheme of combination.

The categories of the Nyāya and Vaiśeṣika are thus combined together, but the combination is far from being satisfactory. It is evident that the categories of the Vaiśeṣika and objects coming under Prameya of the Nyāya overlap each other. Moreover there is hardly any truth in the statement[1] that the knowledge of the sixteen categories of Nyāya is the direct means of our attaining emancipation, whereas that of the seven categories of the Vaiśeṣika is only an indirect means, because *ātman* (the soul), *manas* (the mind), *buddhi* (intellect or knowledge), *duḥkha* (pain), etc., are included in both the Nyāya and Vaiśeṣika systems.

Varadarāja's scheme of combination of the Nyāya and Vaiśeṣika systems is shown below :—

Padārtha.

Pramāṇa, prameya, saṁśaya, prayojana, dṛṣṭānta, siddhānta, avayava, tarka, nirṇaya, vāda, jalpa, vitaṇḍā, hetvābhāsa, chala, jāti, nigrahasthāna.

1. Twelve objects of Nyāya. 2. Six categories of the Vaiśeṣika.

Valid knowledge—*pramāṇa*.

The Buddhistic definition of *pramāṇa* condemned.

The sixteen categories of Nyāya have already been explained. Varadarāja, in his Tārkikarakṣā, introduces here and there some peculiar discussions which are mentioned here. For instance, the Buddhists define valid knowledge (*pramāṇa*) as that which is not non-correspondent with our practical activity,[2] e.g. my knowledge of a cup of water is valid if the activity prompted by it is fruitful. Varadarāja condemns

---

1 मोक्षे साक्षादसाक्षाद्वयपादिदं कथितम् ।
तन्त्रान्तरानुसारेण षट्कं द्रव्यादि कथ्यते ॥
(Tārkikarakṣā, p. 130).

अविसंवादिविज्ञानं प्रमाणमिति सौगताः ।
Tārkikarakṣā, p. 13, edited by M.M. Vindhyeśvarī Prasād, Benares).

this definition by observing that it is too narrow. For instance, it cannot apply to our inferential knowledge of a thing that existed in the past or will exist in the future. We can test the validity of our knowledge only of a thing that exists in the present time. With regard to a past or future thing[1] we can draw an inference, but cannot prove the validity of the inference inasmuch as there is no practical activity prompted by it.

Inference—*anumāna*.

According to Varadarāja, inference (*anumāna*)[2] is the knowledge of a thing derived through its invariable concomitance with another thing. Invariable concomitance (*vyāpti*),[3] also called inseparableness (*avinābhāva*), is that relation which is devoid of condition (*upādhi*).[4]

Invariable concomitance, *avinābhāva* of the Buddhist, condemned.

The Naiyāyikas say that the invariable concomitance of one thing with another thing is based on their uniform agreement in presence and absence, e g. smoke is in invariable concomitance with fire, because where there is smoke there is fire and where there is no fire there is no smoke. In opposition to this definition the Buddhists[5] say that the invariable concomitance of one thing with another thing is really based on their mutual relation of cause

---

[1] अविसंवादकमिति तद्वत् ।
भूतभविष्यद्विषयेषु अनुमानेषु अव्याप्तेः ।

(Tārkikarakṣā, p. 14).

[2] व्याप्तिमच्छब्दसापेक्षं प्रमितेः साधनं विदुः ।
अनुमानमिति ।

(Tārkikarakṣā, p. 64).

[3] व्याप्तिः सम्बन्धो निरुपाधिकः ।

(Tārkikarakṣā, p. 65).

[4] *Upādhi*, condition, is thus defined :—

साधनाव्यापकाः साध्यसमव्याप्ता उपाधयः ॥

(Tārkikarakṣā, p. 66).

It is of two kinds: (1) sure (*niścita*) and (2) suspected (*śaṅkita*). I do not quote here the definition of these terms as they will recur in the Tattvacintāmaṇi.

[5] सौगतास्तु तादात्म्यतदुत्पत्तिभ्यामेवाविनाभावः । ... यथाहुः,—

कार्य्यकारणभावाद्वा स्वभावाद्वा नियामकात् ।
अविनाभावनियमो दर्शनान्न न दर्शनात् ॥

तदयुक्तम् । अकार्य्याकारणो रसादेरकारणाकार्यभूतरूपाद्यनुमानस्य लोके बहुलमुपलब्धेः ।

(Tārkikarakṣā, p. 82).

This verse is quoted from Dharmakīrti's Pramāṇa-vārtika-kārikā. The Tibetan version runs as follows :—

རྒྱུ་དང་འབྲས་བུའི་དངོས་པོའམ
རང་བཞིན་ངེས་པར་བྱེད་པ་ལས །

and effect or identity in essence, e.g. there is rain, because there was cloud (cloud being the cause of rain); and this is a tree, because it is a siṁśapā (śiṁśapā being a species of tree which is its genus).

Varadarāja condemns the Buddhists by saying that their definition is untenable. We infer the form of an orange from its taste, though between the taste and form there is neither the causal relation nor the relation of identity in essence.

Syllogism—*avayava*.

The Mīmāṁsā form of syllogism, *avayava*.

In explaining the seventh category, viz. *avayava*[1] parts of a syllogism, Varadarāja says that according to the Mīmāṁsaka, a syllogism, which consists of three parts may either begin with an example or end with the same, as follows:—

All that is smoky is fiery, as a kitchen,
The hill is smoky,
Therefore the hill is fiery.
or
The hill is fiery,
Because it is smoky.
All that is smoky is fiery, as a kitchen

The Saugatas (Buddhists) are said to maintain that a syllogism consists of only two parts, viz. an example and an application in the following form:—

All that is smoky is fiery, as a kitchen,
This hill is smoky.

The sign—*liṅga*.

Five characteristics of the middle term.

A sign, reason or middle term (*liṅga* or *hetu*) which is in invariable concomitance with the predicate or major term (*sādhya*), possesses five characteristics as follows:—

(1) *Pakṣadharmatā*, the existence of the sign in the subject or minor term, e.g. the hill has smoke.

མེད་ན་མི་འབྱུང་ངེས་པ་ཕྱིར༑
མ་མཐོང་ལས་མིན་མཐོང་ལས་མིན༑ ༎

(Pramāṇa-vārtika-kārikā, Bstan-ḥgyur, Mdo, Ce, leaf 196; also Prof. De La Vallee Poussin's French translation of Sarvadarśana-saṁgraha, p. 4, in La Bouddhisme).

1 त्रीनुदाहरणान्तान् वा यद्वोदाहरणादिकान् ।
मीमांसकाः सौगतास्तु सोपनीतिमुदाहृतिम् ॥
(Tārkikarakṣā, p. 175).

(2) *Sapakṣe sattvam*, existence of the sign in homologue, e.g. that which has smoke has fire, as a kitchen.
(3) *Vipakṣe asattvam*, non-existence of the sign in heterologues, e.g. that which has no fire has no smoke, as a lake.
(4) *Abādhita viṣayatvam*, the object of the sign not being incompatible, e.g. there is no incompatibility for smoke abiding in the hill.
(5) *Asatpratipakṣatvam*, there being no counterbalancing sign, e.g. there is nothing else which counterbalances smoke in respect of proving fire.

In the case of an exclusively affirmative or exclusively negative inference, the sign bears only four characteristics, as it does not then abide in the heterologue or homologue.

Upādhi.

In the logical work called Lakṣanamālā [1] a sign (*liṅga*) is defined as that which is in invariable concomitance with the major term freed from any condition (*upādhi*), e.g. smoke is the sign of fire, but fire is not necessarily a sign of smoke unless it is nourished by wet fuel (here wet fuel is the condition).

Debate—*kathā*.

Rules of debate.

In treating of the tenth category, viz. *vāda*, Varadarāja gives an elaborate exposition of debate (*kathā*) [2] which is defined as a number of sentences spoken by more persons than one as constituting the subjects for their judgment. The six requisites for a council of debate are the following :—

(1) A set of rules as to a certain thesis and its proof.
(2) The method to be followed in carrying on a particular debate.
(3) Specification of the disputant and his respondent.
(4) Election of the President and members of the Council.
(5) Determination of the points of defeat involved wholly or partly in a debate.
(6) Agreement as to the stage of termination of a debate.

Requisites of a debate.

Some logicians hold that the requisites for a council of detate are only four, viz. (1) the disputant, (2) the respondent, (3) the president, and (4) the members.

---

[1] निरुपाधिकसाध्यसम्बन्धशालि लिङ्गमिति लक्षणमालायाम् ।

(Tārkikarakṣā, page 179, edited by M.M. Vindhyeśvari Prasād Dvivedi, Benares). The Lakṣanmālā is said to be the works of Śivāditya Miśra.

[2] विचारविषयो नानावक्तृको वाक्यविस्तरः ।
कथा तस्याः षडङ्गानि प्राहुश्चत्वारि केचन ॥

(Tārkikarakṣā, p. 206).

If it is intended to record a debate, a writer (*lekhaka*) must be employed with the approval of the disputant and his respondent.

The disputant (*vādī*) must be equal to the respondent (*prativādī*) in respect of his learning. A debate, in which an expert stands against an ordinary person, is useless, inasmuch as the conclusion drawn from such a debate could have been obtained from the expert alone.

The members (*sabhya*), acceptable to both the parties and conversant with their tenets, must be freed from affection and aversion. They must be capable of receiving, retaining and demonstrating the purport of others' speech, while their number must be uneven and not less than three. Their duty is to control the debate, to point out the excellence or defect of the debates, to awaken one who is broken-hearted and to repeat a speech to one who is slow.

The president (*sabhāpati*) must be satisfactory to the disputant, the respondent and the members. Capable of showing favour or frown, he must not be influenced by affection or aversion. His duty is to announce to the council the conclusion of a debate when it comes to a close.

Persons coming by chance before a council of debate may, if the parties agree, point out irregularities, etc., in the debate. They cannot however be admitted into the council as its regular members to settle the main points at issue. This procedure applies to a council [1] of fair debate or discussion, but in the case of wrangling and cavil even chance-comers act as regular members.

Kind of debate.

A debate is of three kinds, viz. (1) discussion (*vāda*), (2) wrangling (*jalpa*), and (3) cavil (*vitaṇḍā*). A wrangling or cavil may be stopped by exposing the points of defeat (*nigrahasthāna*) which are necessarily involved in them.[2] A discussion end[3] only when one points out in it a fallacy of reason, *hetvābhāsa*, or a point of defeat called censuring the non-censurable. The seven points of defeat which may

---

[1] तथा च वदन्ति,——

रागद्वेषविनिर्मुक्ताः सप्तपञ्चत्रयोऽपि वा ।
यत्रोपविष्टा विप्राः स्युः सा यज्ञसदृशी सभा ॥
(Tārkikarakṣā, p. 208).

[2] एते सभ्यजिताः सर्वे समुद्भाव्याश्च निग्रहाः ।
विच्छेदकाः कथायां च द्वयोर्जल्पवितण्डयोः ॥
(Tārkikarakṣā, p. 362).

[3] वादे कथावसानस्य हेत्वाभासो हि कारणम् ।
तथा निरनुयोज्यानामनुयोग इति द्वयम् ॥
(Tārkikarakṣā, p. 363).

be pointed out in a discussion are :--(1) saying too little, (2) saying too much, (3) deviating from the tenet, (4) opposing the proposition, (5) silence, (6) repetition, and (7) the inopportune. The seven points of defeat which are not to be pointed out in a discussion are :—(1) evasion, (2) non ingenuity, (3) ignorance, (4) shifting the reason, (5) overlooking the censurable, (6) shifting the topic, and (7) the admission of an opinion.

The six points of defeat which are impossible in a discussion are :—(1) shifting the topic, (2) the unintelligible, (3) hurting the proposition, (4) renouncing the proposition, (5) the meaningless, and (6) the incoherent.

12. COMMENTARIES ON TĀRKIKARAKṢĀ.

Sārsaṁgraha.—A "summary of essences" (**sārasaṁgraha**), is the name of a commentary on the Tārkikarakṣā by Varadarāja himself. Varadarāja wrote also a commentary on *Nyāyakusumāñjali* called Sārsaṁgraha-tikā.

Laghudīpikā.—Jñānapūrṇa is the author of a commentary on the Tārkikarakṣā called Laghudīpikā, "a light lamp." He seems to have flourished in about 1200 A.D. as he was a disciple of Viṣṇu Svāmin,[1] who lived in about 1200 A.D. He mentions Jayanta[2] and Viśvarūpa.

Niṣkaṇtakā.—A commentary on Tārkikarakṣā called Niṣkaṇṭakā, the thornless, was composed by sage named Mallinātha, who lived in Kolācala. The sage in his commentary on Kirātārjunīya mentions Pijūṣavarṣa whose date is unknown. Mallinātha must have lived before śaka 1580 or A.D. 1658, when a manuscript of the aforesaid commentary on Kirātārjunīya was copied.[3] He seems to have preceded also Dinakara Miśra, whose commentary on Raghuvaṁśa was composed in 1385 A.D. Mallinātha is generally supposed to have lived in the 14th[4] century A.D. Mr. A. C. Burnell thinks that Mallinātha's son lived during the reign of Pratāpa Rudra,[5] of the Kākaṭiya dynasty in 1310 A.D.

---

[1] सर्वैश्वर्यं निजाबोधं सर्वविद्यानिधिश्रितम् ।
श्रीपद्मेश्वरसूरेः स्वगुरुं श्रीविष्णुस्वामिगुरुं नमः ॥

Colophon to Laghudīpikā on Tārkikarakṣā, page 364, edited by M.M. Vindhyeśvarī Prasād, Benares.

[2] तथिम् विश्वरूपजयन्तयोर्मते कथाभेदाधिक्षेपमाह ।

Laghudīpikā on Tārkikarakṣā, page 356, edited by M.M. Vindhyeśvari Prasād, Benares.

[3] The copy of the manuscript is preserved in Benares College.

[4] Macdonell's History of Sanskrit Literature, page 324.

[5] *Vide* preface to Vaṁśa Brāhmaṇa, edited by Mr. A. C. Burnell, and M.M. Vindhyeśvari Prasād's preface to Tārkikarakṣā, page 19.

13 KEŚAVA MIŚRA (ABOUT 1275 A.D.).

His life.

Keśáva Miśra was the author of a Nyāya treatise called Tarkabhāṣā. He was a native of Mithilā and a preceptor of Govardhana Miśra who wrote a commentary on Tarkabhāṣā, called Tarkabhāṣā Prakāśa. Padmanābha Miśra, author of Kiraṇāvalī Bhāskara and Kaṇāda-rahasya Muktāhāra, was an elder brother of Govardhana.[1] Hence it follows that Keśava Miśra, Padmanābha and Govardhana were contemporaries.[2] Sir Ramkrishna Gopal Bhandarkar in his Reports of Sanskrit Manuscripts, 1882-1883, observed Cinna Bhaṭṭa was the author of a commentary on Tarkābhāṣā called Tarkabhāṣā Praveśikā and that he lived in Vijayanagar at the Court of King Harihara at the latter half of the 14th century. Padmanābha, brother of Keśava, is said to have been younger to Vardhamāna whom he mentions in his Kiraṇāvalibhāskara. So Padmanābha lived between the beginning of the 13th century and end of the 14th century A.D. Probably he lived at the end of the 13th century A.D.

14. Tarkabhāṣā—TECHNICALITY OF LOGIC.

Categories—*padārtha.*

Keśava Miśra opens his work thus—"In order that even dull people may get admittance into the science of Logic, I bring out this Tarkabhāṣā (Technicality of Logic) replete with concise arguments."

Tarkabhāṣā incorporated the Vaiśeṣika categories.

The Tarkabhāṣā deals with the sixteen categories of the Nyāya sūtra, viz. (1) *pramāna*, (2) *prameya*, (3) *saṁśaya*, (4) *prayojana*, (5) *dṛṣṭānta*, (6) *siddhānta*, (7) *avayava*, (8) *tarka*, (9) *nirṇaya*, (10) *vāda*, (11) *jalpa*, (12) *vitaṇḍā*, (13) *hetvābhāsa*, (4) *chala*, (15) *jāti*, (16) *nigrahasthāna*. The second

---

[1] Govardhana Miśra, his Tarkabhāṣā Prakāśa, observes :—

विजयश्रीतनूजन्मा गोवर्द्धन इति श्रुतः ।
तर्कानुभाषां तनुते विविच्य गुरु निर्मितम् ॥
श्री विश्वनाथानुज पद्मनाभानुजो गरीयान् बलभद्रजन्मा ।
तनोति तर्कानधिगम्य सर्वान् श्रीपद्मनाभाद्विदुषोविनोदम् ॥
उपदिष्टा गुरुचरणैरस्पृष्टा वर्धमानेन ।
किरणावल्यामर्थास्तन्यन्ते पद्मनाभेन ॥

(Quoted in preface to Tarkabhāṣā, page 1, edited by Surendralal Goswami, Benares).

[2] Surendralal Goswamī's preface to Tarkabhāṣā, page 4.

The Tarkabhāṣā has also been edited with a learned introduction by Prof. D. R. Bhandarkar, in the Bombay Sanskrit Series. The book has been translated into English by M.M. Dr. Ganga Nath Jha, in the Indian Thought, Allahabad.

category, namely *prameya*, includes (*a*) *ātman*, (*b*) *śarīra*, (*c*) *indriya*, (*d*) *artha*, (*e*) *buddhi*, (*f*) *manas*, (*g*) *pravṛtti*, (*h*) *doṣa*, (*i*) *pretyabhāva*, (*j*) *phala*, (*k*) *duḥkha*, and (*b*) *apavarga*. The word *artha*, in the Nyāya sūtra signified five objects of sense, viz. (1) *gandha* (smell), (2) *rasa* (taste), (3) *rūpa* (colour), (4) *sparśa* (touch), and (5) *śabda* (sound). In order to incorporate the Vaiśeṣika categories into Nyāya, Keśava Miśra explained *artha* as signifying (1) *dravya*, (2) *guṇa*, (3) *karma*, (4) *sāmānya*, (5) *viśeṣa*, and (6) *samavāya*. Though the sixteen categories of the Nyāya are included in the six categories of the Vaiśeṣika, the two sets of categories are separately stated and the Vaiśeṣika categories are explained identically with *artha*. Keśava confesses that he adopts this overlapping division for a special purpose. The scheme of combination of the two sets of categories is shown below :—

(1) pramāṇa, (2) prameya, (3) saṁśaya, (4) prayojana, (5) dṛṣṭānta, (6) siddhānta,
(7) avayava, (8) tarka, (9) nirṇaya, (10) vāda,
(11) jalpa, (12) vitaṇḍā, etc.

(1) ātman, (2) śarīra, (3) indriya, (4) artha, (5) buddhi, (6) manas, (7) pravṛtti,
(8) doṣa, (9) pretyabhāva, (10) phala,
(11) duḥkha, (12) apavarga.

(1) dravya, (2) guṇa, (3) karma, (4) sāmānya,
(5) viśeṣa, (6) samavāya.

Instrument—*karaṇa*.

Under the first category, Keśava defines instrument (*karaṇa*) as a cause which is most effective in bringing about a result. A thing is said to be the cause (*kāraṇa*) of another thing, if it is a necessary antecedent of the latter, that is, if it necessarily exists before the latter and does not bring about anything else, e.g. threads constitute the cause of a cloth. Suppose an ass had existed at a place where a cloth was made ; the ass, whose existence there was not necessary, is not a cause of the cloth ; and the ass is an irrelevant antecedent. Similarly the colour of the threads is not a cause of the cloth, inasmuch as it brings about something else, viz. the colour of the cloth. In so far as the cloth itself is concerned, it is produced by the threads alone.

An effect (*kārya*) is defined as that necessary consequence which is not brought about by something else, e.g. a cloth is an effect of threads.

Cause—*kāraṇa*.

The cause is of three kinds as follows :—

(1) The material, constituent or inherent cause (*samavāyi kāraṇa*) is that in which an effect inheres, that which constitutes

the effect or that which forms the material out of which the effect is produced, e.g. threads are such a cause of the cloth. Inherence (*samavāya*) is the relation of two things which one, as long as it is not destroyed, continues to subsist in the other. The relation of inherence (*samavāya*) exists between its parts and a whole, the qualities and substance, action and an actor, the individual and a class, its specific qualities and the eternal substance.

(2) The non-material, non-constituent or non inherent cause (*asamavāyi kāraṇa*)—is that which inheres in the material cause and whose efficiency is well known, e.g. the conjunction of the threads is a non-material cause of the cloth, the colour of the threads is a non-material cause of the colour of the cloth. Colour inheres in threads and its efficiency in producing the colour of the cloth is well known.

(3) The efficient, instrumental or general cause is that which as a cause is distinct from both the preceding ones, e.g. the loom is the instrumental cause of the cloth. Of the several causes the most efficient is called an instrumental (*nimitta*) cause.

Perception—*pratyakṣa*.

Perception (*pratyakṣa*) is of two kinds :—

(1) *Nirvikalpaka*, non-determinate, non-effective or abstract, and (2) *savikalpaka*, determinate, reflective or concrete. The Buddhists admit only the first kind of perception and reject the second kind. They say that our perception is certainly indeterminate and individual, it has for its object an individual which alone can come in contact with our senses. A determinate perception (*savikalpaka pratyakṣa*) is according to them an impossibility, because it has for its object a generic entity which cannot come in contact with our senses. We can perceive an individual cow but cannot perceive the cowness generic to all individual cows. In fact the Buddhists altogether deny a genus or generic entity. If, for instance, the genus cowness at all exists, it is to be defined as that which is excluded by non-cowness, i.e. which is not horseness, tigerness, etc.

Now if we are unable to perceive cowness because it pertains to all cows, how can we perceive non-cowness which covers a still wider area ? Keśava's reply to the objection of the Buddhists is that even a genus is to be regarded as an entity, like an individual, which is, as such, capable of coming in contact with our senses.

Inference—*anumāna*.

Inference is consideration from sign. A sign (*liṅga*) is that which indicates the predicate (*sādhya*) by the force of their invariable concomitance, e.g. smoke is a sign of fire, inasmuch as there is an invariable concomitance of smoke with fire in the form "wherever there is smoke there is fire." Consideration (*parāmarśa*) is the knowledge that the sign pervaded by the predicate abides in the subject. Inferential knowledge (*anumiti*) is the knowledge which is derived through consideration, e.g. this hill has fire, because it has smoke, which is in invariable concomitance with fire. Invariable concomitance (*vyāpti*) is the constant association of the sign with the predicate, e.g. the co-presence of smoke with fire. The concomitance or co-presence must be natural and not conditional (*aupādhika*) [1]

Comparison—*upamāna*.

Comparison or analogy (*upamāna*) is the knowledge of a certain thing as similar to another thing, derived through the remembrance of an indicative declaration on the subject, e.g. a man who has heard from a forester that a bosgavaeus (*gavaya*) is like a cow, goes into a forest and sees an animal like a cow. Remembering the declaration of the forester, he ascertains that the animal he sees is a bosgavaeus. This knowledge is analogical or comparative knowledge derived through an analogy or comparison.

Word—*śabda*.

Word (*śabda*), if it is the assertion of a trustworthy person, is a means of right knowledge, e.g. the Veda is a means of right knowledge, inasmuch as it was spoken by God who is supremely trustworthy.

15. Commentaries on the Tarkabhāṣā.

There are numerous commentaries on the Tarkabhāṣā; such as, those by Nārāyaṇa Bhaṭṭa, Guṇḍu Bhaṭṭa, Bhinnī Bhaṭṭa, and Murāri Bhaṭṭa.

The following commentaries are also well known: **Ujjavalā** by Gopīnatha, **Tarkabhāṣā bhāva** by Roma Vilva Veṅkaṭa Buddha, **Nyāya saṁgraha** by Rāma Liṅga, **Sāramañjari** by Mādhava Deva, **Paribhāṣā darpaṇa** by Bhāskara Bhaṭṭa, **Tarkabhāṣā prakāśikā** by Bāla Candra, **Yuktimuktāvali** by Nāgeśa Bhaṭṭa about 1700 A.D. (Nāgeśa was a contemporary of Hari Dīkṣita, a grandson of Bhaṭṭoji Dīkṣita who lived between 1619 A.D and 1659 A.D.). **Tarkabhāṣāprakāśikā** by Cinna Bhaṭṭa about 1390 A.D. (Cinna Bhaṭṭa, son of Sahaja Sarvajña, and brother of Sarvajña, must have flourished about 1390[2] A.D. when his patron Harihara, King of

[1] A condition (*upādhi*) will be explained later.

[2] *Vide* Surendralal Goswami's preface to Tarkabhāṣā, page 3.

Vijayanagar, lived). **Tattva Prabodhini** by Gaṇeśa Dīkṣita, **Tarkabhāṣā-prakāśikā** by Kauṇḍinya Dīkṣita, **Tarkadīpikā** by Keśava Bhaṭṭa, **Tarkabhāṣā-prākāśikā** by Govardhana Miśra, **Tarkabhāṣā-prakāśikā** by Gaurīkānta Sārvabhauma, and **Nyāyapradīpa** by Viśvakarmā.[1]

1 *Vide* Surendralal Goswami's Preface to Tarkabhāṣā, pp. 9-13.

CHAPTER III.

The Vaiśeṣika Prakaraṇa embodying the Nyāya Category of Pramāṇa.

16. The Vaiśeṣika incorporates the Nyāya Category.

There appeared numerous treatises on the Vaiśeṣika philosophy which incorporated in them the Nyāya category of *pramāṇa*. In some of the treatises the Nyāya category of *pramāṇa* was included in the Vaiśeṣika category of *guṇa*, while others brought it under *ātman*, which was included in the category *dravya*. Some ingenious writers kept the categories of the Vaiśeṣika separate from the Nyāya category of *pramāṇa*, but they made them the subjects of distinct chapters of one and the same treatise. This incorporation of the Nyāya category of *pramāṇa* into the categories of the Vaiśeṣika philosophy must have commenced after the tenth century A.D. Lakṣaṇāvalī, written by Udayana in that century, deals with seven categories of the Vaiśeṣika, including *abhāva*, without any reference to the Nyāya category of *pramāṇa*. The Nyāya category of *pramāṇa* is included by Vallabhācarya in the Vaiśeṣika category of *guṇa*.

17. Vallabhācārya (about 12th century A.D.).

The exact date of Vallabhācārya is unknown. He seems to have lived in the twelfth century A.D. In the Nyāyalīlāvatī he mentions Kīrti (Dharmakīrti), Tutāti and Vyomācarya as well as Udayanācārya,[1] the famous author of Kiraṇāvalī, who flourished in 984 A.D. As Bhāsarvajña[2] and Bhūṣaṇa[3] are also mentioned, Vallabha could not have flourished before the 10th century A.D. The latest limit of his time is the 13th century A.D., when Vardhamāna Upādhyāya wrote a commentary on the Nyāyalīlāvatī called the Nyāyalīlāvatī-prakāśa. The Nyāyalīlāvatī is mentioned in a Kanarese poem written by a poet of the time of King Ciṅghaṇa of the Yādava dynasty who reigned in Devagiri

---

[1] यथा भेर्य्याकाशसंयोगस्योभयाश्रितत्वेऽपि नभसि शब्दजननियम इति किरणावलीकारः । *Nyāyalīlāvatī*, page 39, edited by Mangeśa Rāmakṛṣṇa Telang (Nirnaya Sagara Press, Bombay). Compare also pages 56 and 97 of the same.

[2] तदियमनाम्नातता भासर्वज्ञस्य यदयमाचार्य्यमप्यवमन्यते । *Nyāyalīlavatī*, page 33. Compare also page 40.

[3] तदिदं चिरन्तनवैशेषिकमतदूषणं भूषणकारस्यातिचापलम् । *Nyāyalīlāvatī*, page 33. Compare also pages 25, 46 and 102.

from 1210 to 1247 A.D.[1] This Vāllabhāchāryā is different from Vallabhāchārya who founded a Vaiṣṇava sect.

18. Nyāyalīlāvatī.

Subject of Nyāyalīlāvatī.

The Nyāyalīlāvatī, which is an expository treatise on Vaiśeṣika philosophy, opens with a salutation to Puruṣottama. It deals with six categories, viz. (1) substance (*dravya*), (2) quality (*guṇa*), (3) action (*karma*), (4) generality (*sāmānya*), (5) particularity (*viśeṣa*), and (6) inherence (*samavāya*). Under the category *guṇa* there comes *buddhi* (intellect or knowledge) which is divided as *vidyā*, right knowledge, and *avidyā*, wrong knowledge. The means for ascertaining right knowledge are called perception (*pratyakṣa*), inference (*anumāna*), comparison (*upamāna*), and verbal testimony (*śabda*). Presumption (*arthāpatti*), probability (*sambhava*), tradition (*aitihya*), are not separate means of right knowledge.

The scheme of amalgamation.

The Nyāya doctrine of *pramāṇa*[2] (means of knowledge) is thus included in the categories of the Vaiśeṣika philosophy. The scheme of incorporation is shown below :—

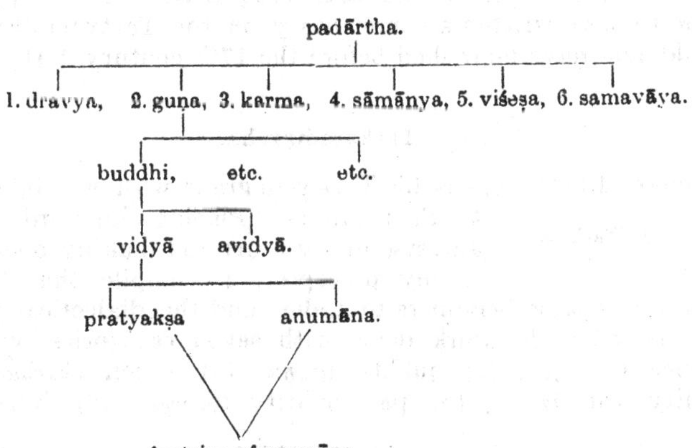

19. Commentaries[3] on the Nyāyalīlāvatī.

The following commentaries on the Nyāyalīlāvatī are available :—

---

[1] *Vide* Mr. M. R. Bodās's introduction to Tarkasaṁgraha, pp. 41-42.

[2] A valuable account of *pramāṇa* is available in the Sivajñāna Siddhiyār, and in the Maṇimekalai canto 29.

[3] *Vide* Maṅgeśa Rāmkṛṣṇa Telang, preface to Nyāyalīlāvatī, page 2.

(1) Nyāyalīlāvatī-prakāśa by Vardhamāna-Upādhyāya (about 1215 A.D.).
(2) Nyāyalīlāvatī-dīdhiti by Raghunātha Śiromaṇi (1500 A.D.).
(3) Nyāyalīlāvatī-kaṇṭhābharaṇa by Śaṅkara Miśra (about 1492 A.D.).
(4) Nyāyalīlāvatī-prakāśaviveka (gloss on Vardhamāna) by Mathurānātha Tarkavāgīśa (about 1570 A.D.).

20. Annam Bhaṭṭa (1623 A.D.).

Annam Bhaṭṭa is the author of an excellent Vaiśeṣika treatise called **Tarkasaṁgraha** and of a commentary thereon called **Dīpikā**, which two, taken together, are often designated as Annambhaṭṭīyaṁ. The Nyāya-pariśiṣṭa Prakāśa, a commentary on the Nyāya-pariśiṣṭa of Udayana, is also ascribed to him. The prevailing tradition in Southern India [1] is that Annam Bhaṭṭa was an Andhra (Telugu) of North Arcot (Chittur) district, who settled down in Benares at beginning of the 17th century A.D. He refers in his Dīpikā to King Tribhuvanatilaka, a Pallava chief of Kāñcī. A manuscript of Tarkasaṁgraha [2] was, as appears from Weber's Berlin Catalogue, copied in the year 1724 A.D.[3] He is supposed by some to have written a commentary on the Tattvacintāmaṇi. He could not have flourished before the 17th century A.D.

21. Tarkasaṁgraha.

Subject of Tarkasaṁgraha.

Annam Bhaṭṭa opens his Tarkasaṁgraha with a salutation [4] to Siva thus:—"Placing the Lord of the universe in my heart and making obeisance to my preceptor, I compile this Tarkasaṁgraha to enable beginners to understand the dialectical philosophy easily." The work deals with seven categories, viz. (1) substance (*dravya*), (2) quality (*guṇa*), (3) action (*karma*), (4) generality (*sāmānya*), (5) particularity (*viśeṣa*), (6) inherence

---

[1] The above information was supplied by Mr. Ramanan of Vedaraniyam (Tanjore) to Hon'ble Sir P. Aruṇāchalam, Kt., M A., C.S., Bar.-at-Law, of Colombo, who kindly communicated the same to me in August 1909.

[2] Tarkasaṁgraha was translated into English by J. R. Ballantyne in Benares.

[3] The colophon of the manuscript gives the date Saṁvat 1781 (A.D. 1724).

तपोमासस्य सिते पक्षे चन्द्रनामाभिधप्रके ।
वाराणस्यां मिते वर्षे स्वार्थमिन्दुर्षिमच वै ॥

Weber's Berlin Catalogue No. 683, p. 203.

[4] निधाय हृदि विश्वेशं विधाय गुरुवन्दनम् । बालानां सुखबोधाय क्रियते तर्कसंग्रहः ॥ Tarkasaṁgraha, opening lines, edited by Mr. M. R. Bodas, Bombay).

(*samavāya*), and (7) non-existence (*abhāva*). Quality is of twenty-four kinds, of which *buddhi* (intellect or knowledge) is one. *Buddhi* or knowledge is of two kinds, experience (*anubhava*) and *smṛti* (recollection). *Anubhava* or experience may be right or wrong. The right experience (*yathārthānubhava*) is of four kinds, *viz.* (1) perceptual knowledge (*pratyakṣa*), (2) inferential knowledge (*anumiti*), (3) comparative knowledge (*upamiti*), and verbal knowledge (*śabda*). The means by which these four kinds of knowledge are derived are called respectively (1) perception (*pratyakṣa*), (2) *anumāna* (inference), (3) comparison (*upamāna*), and verbal testimony (*śabda*).

Perception, inference, comparison and verbal testimony, together called *pramāṇa*, are thus included in *buddhi*, which is one of the twenty-four qualities. This sort of inclusion of the *pramāṇa* in the categories of the Vaiśeṣika is not altogether satisfactory, inasmuch as they do not completely fit into each other.

The scheme of incorporation is shown below :—

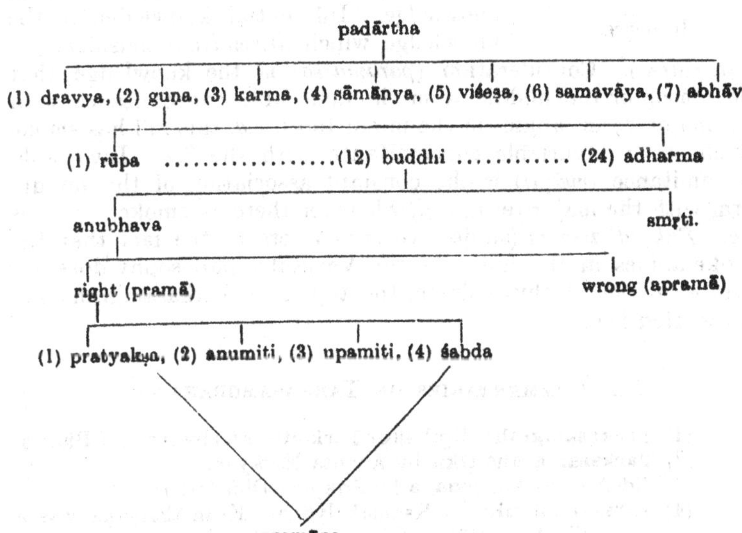

The seven categories and their numerous subdivisons are most lucidly treated.

Right knowledge.

A right experience (*yathārthānubhava*) is defined as the experience of a generic nature as abiding in its subject, *e.g.* in the case of a piece of silver, the experience that " this is silver," that is, this is the subject in which " silverness " abides, is a right experience.

Instrument and Cause.

An instrument (*karaṇa*) is defined as a special cause which is in operation, that is, which brings about an effect, *e.g.*, he cuts a tree with an axe. Here axe is the instrument. A cause (*kāraṇa*) is that which invariably precedes an effect, which cannot otherwise take place, *e.g.* "clay is the material cause of a pot."

An effect (*kārya*) is the counterpart of an antecedent which dissolves into non-existence, *e.g.*, "a pot is the effect of clay."

A cause is of three kinds: (1) a material or intimate cause (*samavāyikāraṇa*), (2) non-intimate or non-co-existent cause (*asamvāyikāraṇa*), and (3) the instrumental cause (*nimittakāraṇa*),[1] all of which will be explained later.

Perception.

Perception (*pratyakṣa*) is the knowledge which is produced from the intercourse of the sense organs with their objects. It is of two kinds: (1) indeterminate (*nirvikalpa*) and (2) determinate (*savikalpa*). The intercourse is of six kinds, which will be explained later.

Inference.

Inference (*anumāna*) is the means for deriving inferential knowledge. Inferential knowledge is the knowledge which arises from consideration (*parāmarśa*). Consideration (*parāmarśa*) is the knowledge that the reason or the middle term, in invariable concomitance with the major term, abides in the minor term, *e.g.* this hill has smoke which is in invariable concomitance with the fire. Invariable concomitance (*vyāpti*) is the constant association of the middle term with the major term, *e.g.*, wherever there is smoke, there is fire. *Pakṣadharmatā* (subjective law) refers to the fact that the smoke abides in the hill. As the Vaiśeṣika philosophy does not form a subject of this volume, the topics of Tarkasaṁgraha are not treated here.

22. Commentaries on Tarkasaṁgraha :—

(1) **Tarkasaṁgraha-dīpikā** (or Tarkadīpikā) by Annam Bhaṭṭa.
(2) **Tarkasaṁgraha-ṭīkā** by Ananta Nārāyaṇa.
(3) **Siddhānta-candrodaya** by Srīkṛṣṇa Dhūrjaṭī Dīkṣita.
(4) **Tarka-phakkikā** by Kṣamākalyāṇa. Kṣamākalyāṇa was a pupil of Jinalābha Sūri and wrote his commentary on both Tarkasaṁgraha and Tarkadīpikā in 1772 A.D.
(5) **Nyāya-bodhinī** by Govardhana Miśra.
(6) **Nyāyārtha-laghubodhinī** by Govardhana Raṅgācārya.
(7) **Tarkasaṁgraha-ṭīkā** by Gaurīkānta.

---

[1] Samavāyikāraṇa corresponds to Aristotle's *material* cause. Asamavāyikāraṇa corresponds to Aristotle's *formal* cause. Nimittakāraṇa corresponds to Aristotle's *efficient* cause. The final cause is the thing in its completeness, as a pot, when it has actually been made.

(8) **Padakṛtya** by Candraja Siṁha.

(9) **Tarkasaṁgraha-tattva-prakāśa** by Nīlakaṇṭha. [Perhaps he is the same person who wrote a commentary on the Mahābhārata in Mahārāṣṭra in the 16th century A.D.].

(10) **Nirukti** by Jagannātha Śāstrin

(11) **Nirukti** by Paṭṭābhiráma.

(12) **Tarkasaṁgraha-vākyārtha-nirukti** by Mādhava Padābhirāma.

(13) **Tarkasaṁgraha-candrikā** by Mukunda Bhaṭṭa Gāḍgil.

(14) **Tarkasaṁgrahopanyāsa** (**vākya-vṛtti**) by Meru Śāstri Goḍbolé.

(15) **Nyāya-bodhinī** by Śuklaratnanātha.

(16) **Tarkasaṁgraha-ṭīkā** by Ramānātha.

(17) **Tarkasaṁgraha-taraṅgiṇī** by Vindhyeśvarī Prasāda.

(18) **Tarkasaṁgraha-ṭīkā** by Viśvanātha.

(19) **Tarka-candrikā (prabhā)** by Vaidyanātha Gāḍgil.

(20) **Tarkasaṁgraha-ṭīkā (Hanumanti)** by Hanumat, son of Vyāsa. He was a Karnatic from Mysore who lived for some time in the Gwalior Court about 80 years ago.

(21) **Tarkasaṁgraha-vyākhyā** by Murāri.

(22) **Tarkasaṁgraha-ṭīkā**, author unknown.

(23) **Tarkasaṁgraha-śaṁku**, ditto.

(24) **Nyāya-candrikā**, ditto.

(25) **Tarkasaṁgrahopanyāsa**, ditto.

(26) **Tarkasaṁgraha-dīpikā-prakāśa** (gloss) by Nīlkaṇṭha Śāstrin, author of Tattva-cintāmaṇi-dīdhiti-ṭīkā.

(27) **Surata-kalpataru** (gloss) by Srinivāsa.

(28) **Ṭīkā** by Gaṅgādhara Bhaṭṭa.

(29) **Ṭīkā** by Jagadīśa Bhaṭṭa.

(30) **Ṭīkā** by Rāmarudra Bhaṭṭa.

(31) **Tattvārtha-dīpikā** by Vadhulavenkaṭa Guru.

(32) **Tarkasaṁgraha-dīpikā-prakāśa** by Nīlakaṇṭha. This Nīlkaṇṭha, who also wrote a commentary on **Tattva-cintāmaṇi**, is the last representative of the School of **Gaṅgeśa**; born at Pāṇya near Ahobala in the district of Kurnool, he died in Benares in 1840. His son (born 1816, died at Benares in 1887) wrote a commentary on the **Tarkasaṁgraha-dīpikā-prakāśa** of his father, entitled **Bhāskarodaya. Bhāskarodaya-ṭīkā** is a gloss on the Nīlkaṇṭhī-**ṭīkā** (see below No. 33) of **Tarkadīpikā** written by the son of Nīlakaṇṭha in Benares about 25 years ago.

(33) **Nīlakaṇṭhīṭīkā**, a gloss on Tarkadīpikā, by **Nīlkaṇṭha**, who was a Tailanga, and who wrote about 70 years ago, while residing at Benares.

(34) **Bhāṣyavṛtti** on Tarkasaṁgraha by Meru Śāstrī, who was a Maratha. He died in Benares about 60 years ago.

(35) **Tarkasaṁgraha-candrikā** by Mukunda Bhaṭṭa

23. VIŚVANĀTHA NYĀYAPAÑCĀNANA (1634 A.D.).

Viśvanātha Nyāyapañcānana, or simply Pañcānana, was the author of a Vaiśeṣika treatise called Bhāṣā-pariccheda [1] (determination of categories), and of a commentary on the same called Siddhānta-muktāvalī (rows of pearls of logical truths). Viśvanātha, as it appears from his Piṅgala-prakāśikā,[2] as also from other sources, was the son of Vidyānivāsa and a brother of Rudra Vācaspati. Vidyānivāsa lived in 1588 A.D.[3] when a book called Dānakāṇḍā was copied for him by a scribe called Kavicandra. Viśvanātha himself composed the Gautamasūtravṛtti at Vṛndāvana in the year 1634 A.D.[4] He was a native of Navadvīpa and an adherent of the Nyāya School of Raghunātha Śiromaṇi.[5]

24. BHĀṢĀPARICCHEDA.

Subjects.

Viśvanātha opens his Bhāṣāpariccheda with a salutation to Śrī Kṛṣṇa,[6] and while in his Siddhānta-muktāvalī he invokes the blessings of Śiva. The

---

[1] The Bhāṣāpariccheda has been edited and translated into English by Dr. G. Roer in the Bibliotheca Indica, Calcutta.

[2] In the Piṅgala-prakāśikā Viśvanātha says :—

विद्यानिवासतनोः कृतिरेषा विश्वनाथस्य ।
विदुषामनिन्द्यधिया चमत्कारा मुदे भविता ॥

[3] सर्वेषां गौडिरमाणां भट्टाचार्यमतानुगानां
एतद्विद्यानिवासानां दानकाण्डपुस्तकम् ।
व्योमेन्दुशरभौतांशमितशाके विशेषतः
शूद्रेण कविचन्द्रेण विलिख्य परिशोधितम् ॥

(*Vide* Eggeling's India Office Catalogue, Vol. III, page 409B ; and M.M. Hara Prasād Śāstrī's Nepal Catalogue, Preface, p. xvi).

[4] रसबाणतिथौ शकेन्द्रकाले
बहुले कामतिथौ शुचौ सिताहे ।
अकरोन्मुनिसूत्रवृत्तिमेतां
ननु वृन्दाविपिने स विश्वनाथः ॥

(*Vide* M.M. Hara Prasād Śāstri's article on Bhāṣāpariccheda in the J.A.S.B., Vol. VI, No. 7).

[5] एषा मुनिप्रवरगौतमसूत्रवृत्तिः
श्रीविश्वनाथकृतिना सुगमाल्पवर्णा ।
श्रीकृष्णचन्द्रचरणाम्बुज चञ्चरीक-
श्रीमच्छिरोमणि वचः प्रचयैरकारि ॥

(J.A.S.B., Vol. VI, No. 7, page 313).

[6] मथाद्या निखिलार्थिनाशिदम सन्दोहाः सदाभीष्टदाः ।
चन्द्रानप्रस्मराय यव मनसो हर्ति समर्थां दधुः ॥

Bhāṣāpariccheda deals with seven categories, viz. (1) *dravya* (substance), (2) *guṇa* (quality), (3) *karma* (action), (4) *sāmānya* (generality), (5) *viśeṣa* (particularity), (6) *samavāya* (inherence), and (7) *abhāva* (non-existence). *Dravya* or substance is subdivided *kṣiti* (earth), *ap* (water), *tejas* (light), *marut* (air), *vyoma* (ether), *kāla* (time), *dik* (space), *ātman* (soul), and *manas* (mind). The eighth substance called *ātman* or soul is the seat of intellect or knowledge (*buddhi*) and several other qualities. *Buddhi* is of two kinds: apprehension (*anubhuti*) and remembrance (*smṛti*). Apprehension includes perception (*pratyakṣa*), inference (*anumāna*), comparison (*upamāna*), and verbal testimony (*śabda*).

The scheme of amalgamation.

The Nyāya doctrine of *pramāṇa*, as represented by perception, inference, comparison and verbal testimony, is incorporated in the categories of the Vaiśeṣika philosophy. The scheme of incorporation is shown below.

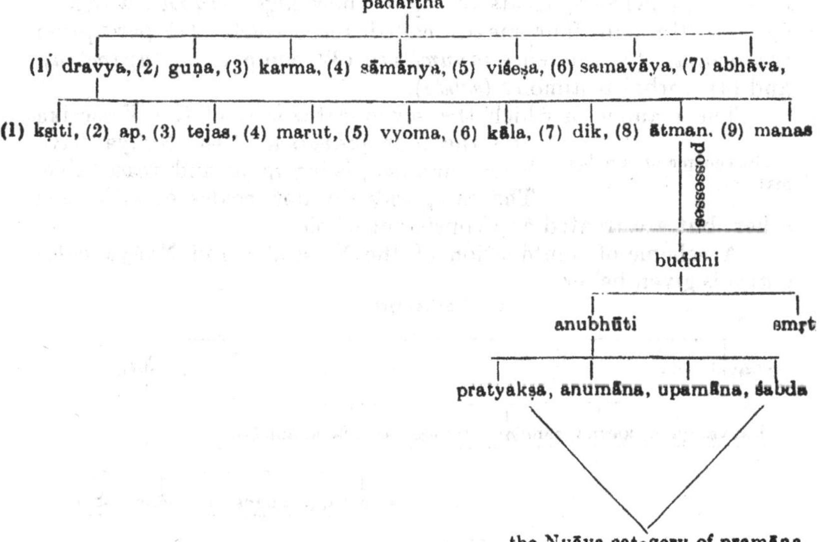

25. Tarkāmṛta (about 1635 A.D.).

The **Tarkāmṛta** [1] by Jagadīśa Tarkālaṅkāra is an important treatise on Vaiśeṣika philosophy, which begins with a salutation to

[1] Tarkāmṛita edited by Mahamahopadhyaya Maheś Chandra Nyāyaratna in Calcutta. It has been translated into Bengali by Babu Rājendra Nāth Ghose in Calcutta.

Viṣṇu.[1] A man who is desirous of attaining emancipation should, according to Jagadīśa, possess a true knowledge of the soul (*ātman*). In acquiring this knowledge, one should also be conversant with things which are connected with and opposed to the soul.

Subjects of Tarkāmṛta.

In the first part of the Tarkāmṛta called *Viṣaya-kāṇḍa* (section on subjects), Jagadīśa divides things into two kinds, viz. (1) positive (*bhāva*) and (2) negative (*abhāva*). The positive things or *bhāvas* are substance (*dravya*), quality (*guṇa*), action (*karma*), generality (*sāmānya*), particularity (*viśeṣa*), and inherence (*samavāya*). The negative things or *abhāvas* are of two kinds, viz. (1) relative non-existence (*saṁsargābhāva*), and (2) reciprocal non-existence (*anyonyābhāva*). The first kind is subdivided as: (1) antecedent non-existence (*prāgabhāva*), (2) subsequent non-existence (*pradhvaṁsābhāva*), and (3) absolute non-existence (*atyantābhāva*).

The second part of the Tarkāmṛta, called *Jñāna-kāṇḍa*, section on knowledge, treats of right knowledge (*pramā*), which is derived through four means called respectively, (1) perception (*pratyakṣa*), (2) inference (*anumāna*), (3) comparison (*upamāna*), and (4) verbal testimony (*śabda*).

The scheme of amalgamation.

The manner in which the seven categories of the Vaiśeṣika and the four *pramāṇas* of the Nyāya have been combined, is ingenious and reasonable. The categories do not coalesce with each other, but are treated as a consistent whole.

A scheme of combination of the Vaiśeṣika and Nyāya categories is given below :—

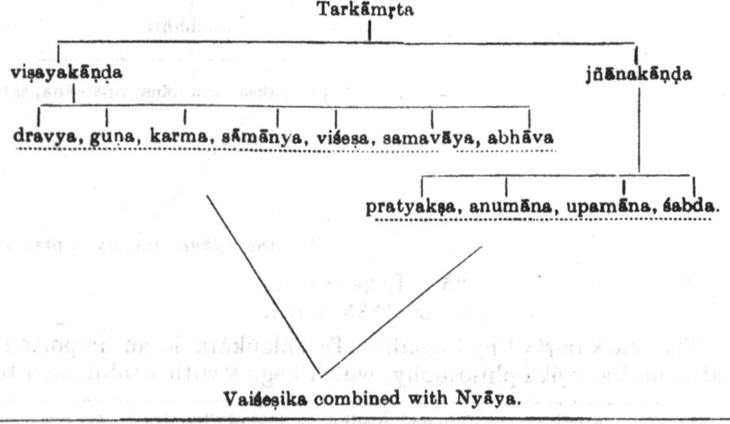

Vaiśeṣika combined with Nyāya.

---

1 श्रीविष्णोश्चरणाम्बुजं भवभयध्वंसैकबीजं परं ।
हृत्पद्मे विनिधाय तत्त्वरूपकतर्कामृतं तन्यते ॥

26. Laugākṣi Bhāskara.

Laugākṣi Bhāskara, well versed in Nyāya, Vaiśeṣika and Mīmāṁsā philosophies, was the son of Mudgala and nephew of the poet Rudra. His proper name was Bhāskara, his surname being Laugākṣi. From the fact that he mentions the temple of Viśveśvara and the pool of Maṇikarṇikā,—the two most sacred spots in Benares, —we may reasonably suppose that Laugākṣi Bhaskara lived in that sacred city.[1]

His age may be placed probably in the 17th century.

27. Tarkakaumudī.

His **Tarkakaumudī**, which opens with a salutation to Vāsudeva, pays due obeisance to Akṣapāda and Kaṇāda. He divides categories into seven kinds, *viz.* (1) substance (*dravya*), (2) quality (*guṇa*), (3) action (*karma*), (4) generality (*sāmānya*), (5) particularity (*viśeṣa*), (6) inherence (*samavāya*), and (7) non-existence (*abhāva*). *Buddhi* (intellect or knowledge), which is a quality of the soul, is of two kinds—apprehension (*anubhava*) and recollection (*smṛti*). Apprehension is of two kinds, (1) right apprehension (*pramā*) and (2) wrong apprehension (*apramā*). The means of acquiring right apprehension or *pramā* is *pramāṇa*, which is of two kinds, viz. (1) (*pratyakṣa*) and (2) inference (*anumāna*).

The doctrine of *pramāṇa*, which forms the main subject of the Nyāya philosophy, is thus amalgamated with the doctrine of seven categories, forming the subject-matter of the Vaiśeṣika philosophy.

---

[1] Laugākṣi Bhāskara mentions Maṇikarṇikā, the bathing place, and Viśveśvara, the presiding deity of Benares, in quite a familiar tone:—**यथा वा मणिकर्णिका, च विश्वेश्वर** etc. (Tarkakaumudī, page 6. edited by Vāsudeva Lakṣmaṇa Śāstrī Pansikar, Bombay).

CHAPTER IV.

Works treating of certain topics of the Nyāya and certain topics of the Vaiśeṣika.

28. The Nyāya and Vaiśeṣika promiscuously amalgamated.

Some manuals of Logic dealt neither with the entire categories of the Vaiśeṣika, nor with those of the Nyāya. Some important topics or sub-topics of the two systems were selected by them and elucidated in an abstruse and recondite style. These manuals assumed more or less the nature of critical notes on the important or controversial topics of the Nyāya and Vaiśeṣika philosophies. Śaśadhara's **Nyāya-siddhānta-dīpa** (about 1300 A.D.) is a most important work of this kind.

29. Śaśadhara
(about 1125 A.D.).

Śaśadhara, styled Mahopādhyāya Śaśadhara,[1] is reputed to have been a native of Mithilā. The time in which he flourished is not definitely known. Probably he flourished before Gaṅgeśa but after Udayana whose words he quotes under the designation of *kecit* (some). Śaśadhara and Maṇidhara were, according to a Bengali tradition, two logicians, whose definitions of *vyāpti* (invariable concomitance) were criticised by Gaṅgeśa Upādhyāya in the 12th century A.D., under the title of *siṁha-vyāghrokta-lakṣaṇa* or definitions as given by "the Lion" and "the Tiger." In reality it was the Jaina logicians, Ānanda Sūri and Amaracandra Sūri, who were called the Lion (*siṁha*) and the Tiger (*vyāghra*), *not* Śaśadhara and Maṇidhara. According, however, to the Bengali tradition, Śaśadhara lived in the 12th century A.D.

30. Nyāya-siddhānta-dīpa.

The only logical treatise of Śaśadhara that has come down to us, is **Nyāya-siddhānta-dīpa** (a lamp of logical truths) which opens[2] with a salutation to

Subjects of the work.

---

[1] *Vide* the colophon of the Nyāya-siddhānta-dīpa, in the possession of M.M. Vindhyeśvarī Prasād Dvivedi of Benares. It runs thus:—

इति महोपाध्याय शशधरकृतं न्यायप्रकरणं समाप्तम् ।

[2]
ध्वांधितमरविधाम्नां
गौतमनैकविद्याम्नायम् ।
नत्वा नित्यमधीशं
शशधर सर्वां प्रकाशयति ॥

From the manuscript of Nyāya-siddhānta-dīpa, in the possession of Asiatic Society of Bengal.

Adhīśa (Śiva). It deals with the topics of the Nyāya and Vaiśeṣika philosophy in a promiscuous way. This is evident from the titles of the various chapters of the work, *viz.* (1) invocation of blessings (*maṅgalācaraṇa*), (2) controversy on darkness (*andhakāra-vipratipatti*), (3) examination of causality (*kāraṇatā-vicāra*), (4) the power in generality as maintained by the Tautātikas (*jātī-śakti-vādi-tautāṭīkāmata*), (5) ascertainment of powers and conditions (*śakti-nirūpaṇa* and *upādhi*), (6) natural power (*sahaja-śakti*), (7) power of the content (*ādheya-śakti*), (8) nature of the mind (*manastattva-nirūpaṇa*), (9) word as a means of knowledge (*sahaja-pramāṇa*), (10) an aggregate of knowledge and action (*jñāna-karma-samuccaya*), (11) nature of emancipation (*apavarga-nirūpaṇa*), (12) the inseparable meaning (*siddhārtha*), (13) power of connected words (*anvita-śakti-vādimata*), (14) refutation of the perceptibility of air (*vāyu-pratyakṣa-tvādi-mata-khaṇḍana*), (15) controversy about indeterminate perception (*nirvikalpaka-vipratipatti*), (16) gold as a fiery thing (*suvarṇa-taijasa-prakaraṇa*), (17) the etymologo-conventional use of a word as "mud-born" (*paṅkaja iti padānām yogarūḍhitva-kathana*), (18) inference, consideration, etc. (*anumiti, liṅgaparāmarśādi-nirūpaṇa*), (19) determination of invariable concomitance (*vyāpti-nirūpaṇa*, etc.). The work ends with an examination of non-existence (*abhāva*) as a means of knowledge.

Commentary. There is a commentary on the Nyāya-siddhānta-dīpa called **Nyāya-siddhānta-dīpa-ṭīkā** by Śeṣānanta.

31. MĀDHAVĀCĀRYA (ABOUT 1331—1391 A.D.).

Mādhavācārya flourished in 1391[1] A.D. (1313 Śaka). He is the well-known author of Sarvadarśana-saṁgraha, Jaiminīya-nyāyamālā-vistara, Kathā-nirṇaya and Parāśarasmṛti-vyākhyā. He was elected[2] the head of the *smārta* order in the *maṭha* of Sringeri, in the Mysore territory, founded by Śaṅkara. He is said by some to have been brother of Sāyaṇa, while others hold that he was the same as Sāyana,[3] though essentially he was a writer on Mīmāṁsā

1 *Vide* Preface to Vivaraṇa-prameya-saṁgraha printed in the Vizianagaram Sanskrit Series.

2 Preface to Sarvadarśaṇa-saṁgraha, translated by E. B. Cowell and A. G. Gough, pp. vii–viii.

3 Perhaps Mādhava was born in the family of Sāyana. Compare—

श्रीमत्सायणदुग्धाब्धिकौस्तुभेन महौजसा ।
क्रियते माधवार्य्येण सर्व्वदर्शनसंग्रहः ॥
पूर्व्वेषामतिदुस्तराणि सुतरामालोड्य शास्त्राण्यसौ
श्रीमत्सायणमाधवः प्रभुरुपन्यास्थत् सतां प्रीतये ।

(Sarvadarśana-saṁgraha, opening lines).

philosophy. His preceptor was Sarvajña-viṣṇu, son of Śaṅgapāṇī.[1] He is mentioned here because he has supplied, among other things, some important information about the Nyāya philosophy. Besides giving a complete exposition of the Nyāya system under the head of Akṣapādadarśana, Mādhava throws a good deal of light on Logic of the Cārvākas and Buddhists.

32. Sarvadarśana-saṁgraha,—Akṣapāda Darśana.

Why Nyāya was so called ?

In the Sarvadarśana-saṁgraha under the title of Akṣapādadarśana, Mādhava has given a brief exposition of the sixteen categories treated in the Nyāya-sūtra. The Nyāya philosophy was so called, because it specially treated of *Nyāya*, otherwise called *avayava* (syllogism), which formed the predominant feature of the system and proved useful in the acquisition of all kinds of knowledge.[2]

Inference as a means of Right Knowledge.

The view of Cārvāka darśanta.

Cārvāka denies inference as a means of right knowledge. Those who maintain the authority of inference (*anumāna*), accept something as a sign or middle term, which is supposed to abide in the minor term, and to be in invariable concomitance with the major term. The invariable concomitance must be freed from all conditions, whether they are sure (*niścita*) or suspected (*sandigdha*). Now this concomitance by its mere existence cannot produce inference. The concomitance, if it is to produce inference, must be known. How do we then know this concomitance ? We cannot know the concomitance by means of perception, which does not cognize past and future events. We cannot employ inference, the validity of which has not yet been established. Verbal testimony, which is included in inference, cannot help us in this matter. Comparison is useless. Hence, the invariable concomitance of the middle term with the major term cannot be known by any of the so-called four means of knowledge.

---

[1] श्रीशार्ङ्गपाणितनयं निखिलागमज्ञं
सर्व्वज्ञविष्णुगुरुमन्वहमाश्रयेऽहम् ॥

(Sarvadarśana-saṁgraha, opening lines).

[2] ननु प्रमाणादिपदार्थषोडशके प्रतिपाद्यमाने कथमिदं न्यायशास्त्रमिति व्यपदिश्यते सत्यं तथाप्यसाधारणेन व्यपदेशा भवन्तीति न्यायेन न्यायस्य परार्थानुमानापरपर्य्यायस्य सकलविद्यानुग्राहकतया सर्व्वकर्म्मानुष्ठानसाधनतया प्रधानत्वेन तथाव्यपदेशो युज्यते। Sarvadarśana-saṁgraha, Akṣapādadarśanam, p. 130, edited by Tārānātha Tarkavācaspati, Calcutta.

Equipollent and non-equipollent concomitance.

Similarly, the invariable concomitance has also been described as freed from conditions (*upādhi*). A condition (*upādhi*) is that which constantly accompanies the major term, but does not constantly accompany the middle term, *e.g.* the hill has smoke because it has fire nourished by wet fuel (where wet fuel is a condition). A condition may be fully defined as that (1) which does not constantly accompany the middle term, (2) which constantly accompanies the major term, and (3) is constantly accompanied by the major term. That the condition must be equipollent in extension with the major term is evident from the statement of the Great Doctor (probably Udayanācārya) who says: "When an equipollent concomitance and a non-equipollent concomitance do both abide in an object, the non-equipollent concomitance, if it is not covered by the equipollent concomitance, is inadmissible, that is, not conducive to the true conclusion."[1]

A thing is said to be in equipollent concomitance (*samavyāpti*) with another thing, when the two are equal in their extensions, *e.g.*, "this is nameable because it is knowable," where "knowable" and "nameable" are equal in their extensions. Similarly, "this hill has smoke because it has fire nourished by wet fuel," where "smoke" and "fire nourished by wet fuel," are equal in their extensions; that is, wherever there is smoke, there is fire nourished by wet fuel; and wherever there is fire nourished by wet fuel, there is smoke.

A thing is said to be in non-equipollent concomitance (*viṣamavyāpti*) with another thing, when the two are unequal in their extensions, *e.g.*, "this hill has fire, because it has smoke," where the fire is greater in extension than smoke, that is, wherever there is smoke, there is fire, as in a kitchen, but wherever there is fire there is not necessarily smoke, as in a red-hot iron ball.

Now an equipollent concomitance and a non-equipollent concomitance do both abide in smoke in the following instances:—(1) the hill has smoke because it has fire, and (2) the hill has smoke because it has fire nourished by wet fuel.

In the first instance smoke is in non-equipollent concomitance with fire, whereas in the second instance smoke is in equi-

---

[1] Varadarāja in his commentary on Tārkikarakṣā called Sārasaṁgraha quotes this verse as an example of the fallacy *hetvābhāsā*, called *aprayojaka* (inadmissible), which is identified in the conditional (*upādhimāna*); quoted in the Sarvadarśanasaṁgraha chapter I, Cārvāka-darśana.

समासमाविनाभावावेकत्रस्तो यदा तदा ।
समेन यदि नो व्याप्तस्तयोर्हीनोऽप्रयोजकः ॥

The portion which is added to the middle term or subtracted from the major term is called an *upādhi* (condition), *anyathāsiddhi* (conditionality) or *aprayojaka* (inadmissible). Tārkikarakṣā, page 232, edited by Vindhyeśvarī Prasad, Benares.

pollent concomitance with "fire nourished by wet fuel." The first instance is inadmissible, because in it, the reason "fire" is not covered by the reason of the second instance, viz. "fire nourished by wet fuel."

Again (1) the hill has fire because it has smoke, (2) the hill has fire nourished by wet fuel, because it has smoke. The first is an instance of non-equipollent concomitance, while the second is that of an equipollent one. The first instance here, is not inadmissible, because the reason of it, viz. "smoke," is covered by the reason of the second instance, which is also smoke.

The middle term can on no account be greater in extent than the major term, but may be equal in extent to or less in extent than that term.

Upadhi.

Now this absence of conditions referred to above cannot be known through perception, specially in the cases of past and future instances. Cārvāka says that the step which the mind takes from the knowledge of smoke, etc., to the knowledge of fire, etc., can be accounted for by its being based on a former perception or by its being an error; and that in some cases this step is justified by the result is accidental, just like the coincidence of effects observed in the employment of gems, charms, drugs, etc. As it is impossible to know the concomitance which is invariable and unconditional, the inference as a means of knowledge cannot be established.

The Inference as a means of Right Knowledge cannot be denied.

The Buddhistic view.

The Buddhists maintain that the concomitance (*avinābhāva*), which is invariable and unconditional, is known through the relation of identity (*svabhāva*) or causality (*kārya-kāraṇa-bhāva*) No effect can, they say, be produced without a cause, for, if it could, it would destroy itself by putting a stop to activity of all kinds.

Causal relation and the relation of identity.

Through the relation of cause and effect, which is unalterable, we can ascertain that the middle term is in invariable concomitance with the major term. In like manner the invariable concomitance is known through the relation of identity, e.g., the *śiśu* is a tree, wherever we observe the attribute of a *śiśu* we observe also the attribute of "arboreity." A *śiśu* cannot lose its arboreity without losing its own self. Though there are differences between a *śiśu* and a tree, they are essentially the same. We are therefore quite competent to say that a *śiśu* is a tree and that the relation between the two is that of identity. We cannot however say, that a jar is a jar or that there is a relation of identity between the jars. We cannot predicate one thing of another thing, if there is no difference whatever between the two. It is therefore proved that we can infer one thing from another thing through the relation of cause and effect or when the two things are in essence the same.

The Buddhists further maintain that inference as a means of knowledge can on no account be denied. It would be a mere assertion, if a person were to say that inference is not a means of knowledge. To think of inference as a means of knowledge and yet to deny it involves him in an absurdity, as if, he were saying that his mother was barren.

SECTION II.

Tarka-Śāstra—the Science of Dialectics.

CHAPTER I.

Formation of the Tarka-Śāstra.

33. The Nyāya cannot be combined with the Vaiśeṣika.

In the previous section, while treating of the Prakaraṇas, we have found that it is impossible to combine the Nyāya with Vaiśeṣika, the categories of the two systems being altogether different. The sixteen categories of the Nyāya cannot assimilate the seven categories of the Vaiśeṣika nor can the latter assimilate the former. The Nyāya and Vaiśeṣika categories cannot be assimilated in any other way. It was, therefore, found necessary to keep them separate, though a futile attempt was made by the authors of the Prakaraṇas to combine in some way the categories of the Nyāya and Vaiśeṣika.

34. Adoption of *Pramāṇa* alone.

After their struggle with the Buddhists and Jains for over a thousand years the Brāhmaṇas found it expedient, in treating of the Nyāya, to take up only one topic, viz. *pramāṇa*, to the exclusion of the remaining fifteen topics. The division of *pramāṇa* into two sub-divisions, viz. Perception and Inference, was rejected. Akṣapāda's division of *pramāṇa* into four sub-divisions, viz. perception, inference, comparison, and verbal testimony, was retained. Great ingenuity was shown to establish the authorities of the four *pramāṇas*. Whole arguments from the Buddhistic and Jaina works were collected to establish inference while the works of the Mīmāṁsā philosophy were resorted to in establishing the authority of verbal testimony.

35. Adoption of the Vaiśeṣika Principles.

The theory of *pramāṇa* became very subtle when it adopted the principles of generality (*sāmānya*), particularity (*viśeṣa*), inherence (*samavāya*), negation (*abhāva*), etc. Thus in perceiving the colour of a jar we must admit a relation called inherence; an invariable concomitance may be of a general form or special forms; and whatever thing is perceptible by a sense, the non-existence of that thing is also perceptible by the same sense.

Thus the Nyāya theory of perception, etc., considered from the standpoint of the Vaiśeṣika philosophy, became very subtle and intricate.

36. Subtlety of meanings aimed at.

A hair-splitting subtlety in the discussion of meanings of terms is the distinguishing characteristic of the Tarka-śāstra (the science of dialectics). Thus Akṣapāda defines a proposition in quite a simple style as " the laying down of what is to be established." But in elucidating the meaning of a proposition Gaṅgeśa, Raghunātha, Gadādhara and others produce definitions which are terribly long and intricate. The subtle explanation is, however, an excellent training for the intellect.

37. Fine Definition of Terms.

The technicalities of Tarka-śāstra have repelled students of Sanskrit from its study. The immemorial practice has been for Naiyāyikas to explain verbally to their pupils the meaning of each term as it turns up in the course of their teaching.

The old works on Nyāya dealt with things, while the modern ones deal only with the verbal description or definition of things. Modern Logicians do not trouble themselves about the nature of things. They are satisfied if they can evolve a correct definition, and in their verbal definitions they evince a subtlety and skill, which to a certain extent compensate for the paucity of their materials.

38. The use of Technical Terms.[1]

In bringing out the subtlety of meanings and in giving fine definitions, the modern logicians have invented numerous technical terms of which some are given here.

ativyāpti—Being too wide.

anugata-dharma—Common property.

anugama—Generalisation.

anuyogitā—The quality of being an *anuyogi*. When a thing stands to another thing in a particular relation, that upon which it stands is called *anuyogi*, while it itself is called *pratiyogi* (counterpart) in regard to the relation. Thus a jar standing on the ground in the relation of union is called *pratiyogi* and the ground is the *anuyogi* of the relation.

anyathā-siddhi—Concomitant circumstances which are not causes.

---

1 *Vide* Rajendra Candra Śastrin's *Muktāvali* Vol. II, and Mahāmahopādhyāya Maheś Chandra Nyāyaratna's *Brief notes on the modern Nyāya system of Philosophy*, and also M.M. Gangānāth Jhā's *Indian Thought.*

avacchinna—That which is qualified or determined by some attribute.

avacchedaka—A quality or attribute which is determined by the special characters of a thing. Thus *daṇḍatva* is the special character of *daṇḍa* as a *hetu*.

avyāpti—Being too narrow.

kurvad-rūpatva—Causing activity, i.e. the property which abides in a cause actually producing its effect.

pratiyogi—The thing of which a negation is predicated, e.g. a jar is the *pratiyogi* of the negation of the jar.

vyāpti—Pervasion or invariable concomitance.

And there are numerous others.

Some of the characteristics of the Tarka-śāstra have been already given above.

Cintāmāṇi by Gaṅgeśa Upādhyāya is the earliest work on Tarka-śāstra, though Jānakīnā'ha Cuḍāmāṇi's **Nyāya-siddhānta-mañjari** is another excellent woık on the same subject.

CHAPTER II.

Tattva-cintāmaṇi the earliest Work on Tarka-śāstra.

39. IMPORTANCE OF TATTVA-CINTĀMAṆI.

The **Tattva-cintāmaṇi** ("a thought-jewel of truth"), otherwise known as **Pramāṇa-cintāmāṇi** ("a thought-jewel of valid knowledge"), of which a short summary in English is given in the following pages, was written by a Brāhmaṇa logician of Mithilā named Gaṅgeśa Upādhyāya. It introduces a new era in the development of Logic in India and is justly reckoned as the first work on the Modern School of Hindu Logic. In modern India Sanskrit scholarship is not considered of any worth unless it is accompanied by a knowledge of the Tattva-cintāmaṇi or at least a portion of it. The study of this work develops to an enormous extent the discursive faculty in the reader and enables him to argue with hair-splitting distinctions and subtleties.

The book, since its first composition in the 12th century A.D., has been a subject of close study by the Paṇḍits of Mithilā, and about the middle of the 15th century its study was introduced into Bengal by Vāsudeva Sārvabhauma, who had been educated in the academies of Mithilā. Since 1503 A.D., when the university of Navadvīpa was established, the Tattva-cintāmaṇi was much popularised in Bengal through the endeavours of the famous Raghunātha Śiromaṇi and others. Gradually the book was introduced into Madras, Mahārāṣṭra and Kāśmīra, and in a couple of centuries it became known all over India. The influence of this epoch-making book can be traced in the works on almost all the branches of Sanskrit learning that have appeared during the last five hundred years Unfortunately no attempt has yet been made to present the contents of the work in English, Bengali, Hindi or any other modern language, perhaps on account of the bewildering abstruseness of its style and thought.

40. GAṄGEŚA—THE AUTHOR OF THE TATTVA-CINTĀMAṆI. (1200 A.D.).

The Tattva-cintāmāṇi is the immortal work of Gaṅgeśa, also called Gaṅgeśvara, surnamed Upādhyāya, who was a Maithila Brāhmaṇa He was born in a village named Karion on the banks of the river Kamalā, twelve miles south-east of Darbhanga. It is said that Gaṅgeśa while young was altogether illiterate. He propitiated the goddess Kālī, on the cremation ground adjacent to his uncle's house, and acquired from her, as a boon, deep erudition in the science of Logic.

Gaṅgeśa mentions the name of Śivāditya Miśra,[1] the well-known author of Saptapadārthī, and makes frequent quotations from Ratna-kośa,[2] which is a work on the Vaiśeṣika philosophy. Nothing is definitely known about the Gauḍa Mīmāṁsaka[3] or Śrīkara[4] mentioned by him. Gaṅgeśa must have flourished after 1093-1150 A.D., the period when Ānanda Sūri and Amaracandra Sūri,[5] whose opinions he has quoted, flourished. As he criticises the Khaṇḍana-khaṇḍa-khādya, he must have been posterior also to Śrī Harṣa who lived in Kanauj in the Court of King Jayacandra in 1186 A.D.[6] The earliest date that has been assigned to Gaṅgeśa is before the first quarter of the 13th century A.D., when his son Vardhamāna Upādhyāya lived, in other words Gaṅgeśa is assigned to the last quarter of the 12th century A.D.[7]

---

[1] *Vide* Tattva-cintāmaṇi, pratyakṣa-khaṇḍa, p. 830.

[2] The Ratnakośa, a work on Vaiśeṣika philosophy, has been quoted not only by Gaṅgeśa in the Tattva-cintāmaṇi (śabda-khaṇḍa, ākhyāta-vāda, p. 830, and anumāna-khaṇḍa, p. 885), but also by Vardhamāna in the Nyāya-kusumāñjali and by Raghunātha Śiromaṇi in the Anumāna-dīdhiti. Glosses on Ratnakośa are said to have been written both by Harirāma and Gadādhara. This Ratnakośa is different from the Advaita-ratna-kośa—a work on the Vedānta philosophy by Akhaṇḍānanda—as well as from the Prameya-ratna-kośa, a work on Jaina philosophy by Candraprabha Sūri (1102 A.D.).

[3] *Vide* Tattva-cintāmaṇi, śabda-khaṇḍa, śabda-prāmāṇya-vāda, p. 88.

[4] *Vide* Tattva-cintāmaṇi, śabda-khaṇḍa, jāti-śakti-vāda, p. 569.

[5] *Vide* S. C. Vidyabhuṣaṇa's 'Indian Logic: Mediæval School', pp. 47-48. Ānanda and Amaracandra, nicknamed respectively Vyāghraśiśuka and Siṁhaśiśuka, have been referred to by Gaṅgeśa in the Tattva-cintāmaṇi under *siṁha-vyāghrokta-lakṣaṇa* of *vyāpti*. (*Vide* p. 396 above.)

[6] Khaṇḍana-khaṇḍa-khādya is quoted in the Tattva-cintāmaṇi, anumāna-khaṇḍa, p. 233, Bibliotheca Indica Series. For Śrī Harṣa and Jayacandra, see the Indian Antiquary, 1911-12: Prācīna-lekha-mālā, nos. 22-23; and B.B.R.A.S. of 1875, p. 279. Jayacandra was killed by Sahabuddin Ghori in 1194 A.D.

[7] According to the Dhanukhā inscription Maheśa Ṭhakkura, brother of Bhagīratha Ṭhakkura, the well-known author of a sub-commentary on the Tattva-cintāmaṇi, lived in 1556 A.D. Considering that in the succession of the generations of pupils Bhagīratha Ṭhakkura was seventh in descent from Gaṅgeśa Upādhyāya, and allowing an average life of thirty years for each generation, we may assume that Gaṅgeśa lived 180 years before Bhagīratha, that is, about the year 1376 A.D.

The succession of pupils from Gaṅgeśa is as follows:—

1. Gaṅgeśa; 2. Vardhamāna; 3. Yajñapati; 4. Hari Miśra; 5 Pakṣadhara; 6. (*a*) Vāsudeva, (*b*) Rucidatta, (*c*) Candrapati (?); 7. (*a*) Maheśa Thakkura, (*b*) Bhagīratha Ṭhakkura: 8. A pupil; 9. Bhavanātha; 10. Śaṅkara Miśra.

The inscription is found on a stone-slab attached to a well at the village Dhanukhā near Janakapura in Darbhanga. It runs thus:—

आसीत् पण्डितमण्डलाभरणितो भूमण्डलाखण्डलो,
ख्यातः खण्डवलाकुले निरवधिनाभक्तो महेशः कृती।
शाके रन्ध्रतुरङ्गमश्रुतिमदो संवचिते वाचवे,
वामदेवी कृपयाप्य येन मिथिलादेशः समस्तो जितः॥

[Those who maintain that Gaṅgeśa lived in the fourth quarter of the 12th century A.D.[1] base their contention on the mention of Vardhamāna, son of Gaṅgeśa, in the Sarvadarśana-saṁgraha in the 14th century A.D.[2] and upon an interpretation of the expression *śakābdā la saṁ 1509*, occurring in a manuscript of Pakṣadhara Miśra s commentary on Gaṅgeśa's Tattva-cintāmaṇi, as equivalent to 1278 A.D.[3] Now the verse on the authority of which Vardhamāna is supposed to have been mentioned in the Sarvadarśana-saṁgraha is obviously an interpolation, and the expression *śakābdā la saṁ 1509*, written in very modern characters, refers in my opinion *not* to Lakṣmaṇa saṁvat 159, corresponding to 1278 A.D., but to *śaka* year 1509 corresponding to 1587 A.D., the word *la saṁ* being either redundant or signifying simply a year. In fact, if Gaṅgeśa had been older than the author of the Sarvadarśana-saṁgraha, his work would have been reviewed, or at any rate referred to, in it.]

41. The Text of Tattva-cintāmaṇi.

Book I.—Perception—*Pratyakṣa-khaṇḍa.*

The Tattva-cintāmaṇi is divided into four books dealing respectively with (1) Perception (*pratyakṣa*), (2) Inference (*anumāna*), (3) Comparison (*upamāna*), and (4) Verbal testimony (*śabda*), which are the four means of deriving valid knowledge. The first book, which treats of perception, opens with stanzas saluting God Śiva.[4]

The śaka 1478 referred to here corresponds to 1556 A.D. That Maheśa Ṭhakkura was a brother of Bhagīratha Ṭhakkura appears from the opening lines of the Dravya-prakāśikā by the latter.

1 *Vide* M. M. Chakravarti's History of Navya-nyāya, J.A.S.B. for 1915, p. 265; Rājendra Nath Ghose's Vyāpti-pañcaka, Introduction, p. 33.

2 *Vide* Sarvadarśana-saṁgraha, Pāṇiniya-darśana.

3 प्रत्यक्षालोक (Pratyakṣāloka), which is a commentary on Gaṅgeśa's Tattva-cintāmaṇi by Pakṣadhara Miśra, was, according to its colophon, copied in the Śaka year 1509 (corresponding to 1587 A.D.) and *not* in the Lakṣmaṇa saṁvat 159 (corresponding to 1278 A.D.), as the date contained in the colophon runs thus :—

शुभमस्तु गौरस्य शकाब्दा ॥ ल सं १५०९ ते श्रावणस्य ९ ॥

4 गुणातीतोऽपीशस्त्रिगुणसचिवस्त्र्यक्षरमयः
चिदूर्मिर्यः सर्गस्थितिविलयकर्माणि तनुते ।
कृपापारावारः परमगतिरेकस्त्रिजगतां
नमस्तस्मै कस्मैचिदमितमहिमे पुरभिदे ॥ १ ॥
अन्वीक्षानयमाकलय्य गुरुभिर्ज्ञात्वा गुरूणां मतं
चिन्तादिव्यविलोचनेन च तयोः सारं विलोक्याखिलम् ।
तन्त्रे दोषगणेन दुर्गमतरे सिद्धान्तदीक्षागुरु-
र्गङ्गेशस्तनुते मितेन वचसा श्रीतत्त्वचिन्तामणिम् ॥ २ ॥

Invocation of Blessings—*Maṅgala-vāda.*

Salutation is offered to Śiva to invoke his blessings. The invocation is of three kinds, *viz* bodily, vocal, and mental. The bodily invocation consists in saluting a deity, the vocal in reciting the eulogy of the deity, and the mental in meditating on him. "All polite people," says Gaṅgeśa, "must observe the de orum of invoking blessings if they wish to bring their work to a successful completion" Though we do not find any explicit text in the Veda enjoining invocation of blessings, yet from the laudable practice of good people we can easily infer the implicit existence of such a text. It should be stated that the invocation of blessings is not the immediate cause of the completion of a work but is the means of removing obstacles which beset the work. In the case of an atheist finishing his work successfully without any invocation of blessings, we are to suppose that there were no obstacles in his way, or that he performed the invocation in his previous life. The case of a theist invoking blessings and yet failing to finish his work, is explained on the supposition that he encountered enormous obstacles which his feeble invocation could not remove. The Kādambarī, which opens with a profuse invocation of blessings, furnishes an illustration of a work remaining unfinished, owing to the excess of obstacles in its way.

The Validity of Knowledge—*Prāmāṇya-vāda.*

Pramā or valid knowledge.

In determining the true meaning of *pramāṇa* (the means of valid knowledge) one must understand the true meaning of the word *pramā* (valid knowledge) *Pramā* or valid knowledge is the knowledge of a thing as it is, it is the knowledge of the generic nature as abiding in its own subject, that is, abiding in every one of its individual embodiments. For instance, to know a piece of silver to be as such, is valid knowledge inasmuch as "silverness," which is a generic nature, really abides in the individual silver which is its subject.

How is valid knowledge derived and known?

Two questions arise here: (1) whence is the validity of knowledge derived, and (2) how are we conscious of the validity? To the first question the Mīmāṁsakas (*Prāabhākaras*) reply by saying that knowledge derives its validity from its own general grounds (or causes). As to the second question they say that knowledge is self-evident, that is, the very grounds out of which arises consciousness of knowledge, produce also the consciousness of its validity, and this consciousness of validity prompts us to activity.

Gaṇgeśa opposes the first reply by saying that if the validity of knowledge were derived from the general grounds of knowledge itself, then invalid knowledge would have been identical with valid knowledge. The second reply is also opposed on the ground that if we were conscious of the validity of knowledge along with our consciousness of knowledge itself, there could not have arisen in us doubt with regard to the validity of any kind of knowledge specially in the unhabitual condition But there often arises in us knowledge of a dubious character, and the Mīmāṁsakas cannot satisfactorily explain the production of this dubious knowledge or doubt. If there is consciousness of knowledge, there is, according to them, along with it a consciousness of its validity which leaves no room for doubt, and if on the other hand, there is no consciousness of knowledge, there cannot arise any consciousness of its dubiousness. Hence Gaṅgeśa concludes that the validity of knowledge is not derived from its general grounds (or causes). It is, according to him, derived through its special cause called instrument. The general grounds of knowledge are the union of the tactual surface with the mind and that of the latter with the soul, while the special causes are different. The special cause of perception is the intercourse of a sense-organ with its object without any hindrance, that of inference is consideration (or the knowledge of premisses), that of comparison is the knowledge of similarity, and that of verbal testimony is the knowledge of consistency. Our knowledge of colour, for instance, is valid if there is the contact of our eye with the colour without any hindrance. Gaṅgeśa further observes that our consciousness of the validity of a particular knowledge does not arise from our consciousness of the particular knowledge itself but from a different source, viz inference from the fruitful correspondence between our knowledge (idea) and the activity prompted by it. "This knowledge (idea)," says he, "is valid because it is conducive to activity which is fruitful; whatever is not conducive to activity which is fruitful, is not valid knowledge." Suppose, for instance, a person cognises from distance a white thing to be a piece of silver. His knowledge will be valid if it harmonises with his actual experience when he approaches the piece of silver. Our consciousness of the validity of a particular knowledge arises therefore from our consciousness of the fruitful correspondence or harmony between the particular knowledge (idea) and the activity which it leads to.

Invalid Knowledge—*Anyathākhyāti.*

apramā, anyathākhyāti, bhrama, or invalid knowledge.

Gaṅgeśa says that invalid knowledge or error, in Sanskrit *apramā, anyāthā-khyāti* or *bhrama*, is the knowledge (experience) of a thing as it is not,—it is the knowledge (experience) of a generic nature, which does not abide in its own subject, but which abides in the subject of another generic nature. For instance, to know a pearl to be a piece of silver is invalid knowledge, inasmuch as the generic nature "silverness" does not abide here in the piece of silver which is its own subject, but abides in a pearl which is the subject of another generic nature, *viz.* "pearlness."

How is activity, *pravṛtti*, caused?

The Mīmāṁsakas (*Prābhākaras*) do not admit invalid knowledge or error All knowledge, according to them, is valid and, as such, prompts us to activity. In the case of a person who takes a pearl to be a piece of silver by saying "this is silver," we should bear in mind that he acquires the knowledge of "this" (pearl) through perception and that of "silver" through recollection. But he, owing to some defect, is not conscious of the distinction between "this" (pearl) and "silver," that is, between "perception" and "recollection"; and this non-consciousness of distinction leads him to activity.

Gaṅgeśa opposes the Mīmāṁsakas by saying that the non-consciousness of distinction cannot account for the activity to which the person is prompted. There are here, according to the Mīmāṁsakas, grounds for activity, counter-activity and non-activity. The knowledge of "silver," for which the person is solicitous, must cause in him an activity, while the knowledge of "this" (pearl), for which he is not solicitous, must cause in him a counter-activity, and the non-consciousness of distinction (which is absence of knowledge) causes in him neither activity nor counter-activity, but leaves him in non-activity. The non-consciousness of distinction is not therefore the cause which leads him to activity.

According to Gaṅgeśa, when a person takes a pearl to be a piece of silver by saying "this is silver," he acquires the knowledge of both "this" (pearl) and "silver" by means of perception (the first through the ordinary intercourse between the sense-organ and its object, and the second through the transcendent intercourse whose character is knowledge). He, through some defect (of his eye, etc.), identifies "this" (pearl) with "silver," that is, becomes conscious of the generic nature "silverness" as abiding in "this" (pearl), which is not its own subject. Here his knowledge is invalid, or, in other words, he commits an error. When a person, on the other hand, takes a piece of silver to be silver by saying "this is silver," he identifies "this" with "silver," or, in other words, becomes conscious of the generic nature "silverness" as abiding in "silver" which is its own subject. His knowledge is valid.

Whether a particular knowledge is valid or invalid, it must be of a determinate character if it is to lead us to activity. Determinate knowledge is the knowledge of a generic nature as abiding in a subject. As already stated, when the generic nature abides in its own subject, the knowledge is valid: but when it abides in the subject of another generic nature, the knowledge is invalid. A valid determinate knowledge (*pramā*) leads us to activity which is fruitful, while an invalid determinate knowledge (*apramā*) leads us to activity which does not end in fruition. In explaining the cause of activity, whether fruitful or fruitless, we must assume determinate knowledge, and in accounting for fruitless activity we must assume error. Moreover, it is a matter of experience that in our consciousness, valid or invalid, of the form "this is silver," there is only one kind of knowledge, *viz.* determinate knowledge, and it will be cumbrous to assume two kinds, *viz.* perception and recollection.

Intercourse between Senses and their Objects—*Sannikarṣa.*

Ordinary Preception (*laukika-pratyakṣa*).

Perceptual knowledge, *(pratyakṣa).*

Perceptual knowledge, or, more simply, perception, has been defined (by Akṣapāda) as knowledge which arises from the intercourse of a sense with its object, and which is non-erratic, being either reflective (mediate) or non-reflective (immediate). This definition, according to Gaṅgeśa, is too wide in so far as it includes recollection and inference of the soul, and is also too narrow in so far as it excludes perception by God. To avoid such defects Gaṅgeśa proposes to define perception as a direct apprehension. When, for instance, a visual perception takes place, there arises in us a corresponding knowledge of the form "I apprehend direct." Perception is further defined by Gaṅgeśa as knowledge whose intrumental cause is not knowledge. The instrumental causes of inference, comparison and verbal testimony are respectively the knowledge of premisses, the knowledge of similarity and the knowledge of consistency; but the instrumental cause of the perception is a sense-organ which is not knowledge.

The word perception, which ordinarily signifies perceptual knowledge or rather the means by which we derive perceptual knowledge, does sometimes stand for the whole process in which a sense in intercourse with its object produces knowledge. The senses are six, *viz.* (1) the eye, (2) the ear, (3) the nose, (4) the tongue, (5) the tactual surface, and (6) the mind. Their objects are respectively the following:—(1) colour, (2) sound, (3) odour, (4) savour, (5) touch (of warmth, coldness, hardness, softness, etc.), and (6) feeling (of pleasure, pain, etc.). Correspondent with the senses there are six kinds of knowledge (perception), *viz.* the visual, auditory, olfactory, gustatory, tactual and mental (internal).

The intercourse, or rather the ordinary intercourse, which is the connection of a sense with its object, is of six kinds as mentioned below:—

(1) *Union* (*saṁyoga*), *e.g.* in the visual perception of a jar there is a union of our eye with the jar.
(2) *United-inherence* (*saṁyukta-samavāya*), that is, inherence in that which is in union, *e.g.* in the visual perception of the colour of a jar there is a union of our eye with the jar in which colour inheres.
(3) *United-inherent-inherence* (*saṁyukta-samaveta-samavāya*), that is, inherence in that which inheres in what is in union, *e.g.* in the visual perception of the "colourness" (the generic nature of colour) of a jar there is a union of our eye with the jar in which inheres colour wherein again abides "colourness" in the relation of inherence.
(4) *Inherence* (*samavāya*), *e.g.* in the auditory perception of sound there is the inherence of sound in the ether which pervades the cavity of our ear.
(5) *Inherent-inherence* (*samaveta-samavāya*), that is, inherence in that which inheres, *e.g.* in the auditory perception of "soundness" (the generic nature of sound), there is the inherence of "soundness" in sound which again inheres in the ether of our ear-cavity.
(6) *Particularity* (*viśeṣaṇatā*), *e.g.* in the perception of non-existence of a jar on a ground, there is a union of our eye with the ground which is possessed of non-existence of the jar.

Transcendent Perception (*alaukika-pratyakṣa*).

The supersensuous or transcendent perception does not take place through any of the six kinds of ordinary intercourse described above. But it is produced through an intercourse which is transcendent. The transcendent intercourse is of three kinds, *viz.* (1) the intercourse whose character is general (*sāmānya-lakṣaṇa*); (2) the intercourse whose character is knowledge (*jñāna lakṣaṇa*); and (3) the intercourse which is produced by meditation (*yogaja*).

Intercourse (*perception*) *whose character is general.*—In the perception of all individuals possessing a generic nature, the knowledge of the generic nature constitutes the intercourse. This is a transcendent intercourse whose character is general. When, for instance, there is an intercourse of our eye with a case of smoke, there arises in us a perception of smoke of all times and all places. The process by which this perception takes place is as follows:—

The intercourse between our eye and the case of smoke is an ordinary one called union (*saṁyoga*) and that between our eye and "smokeness" (the generic nature of smoke) is also an ordinary one which is called united-inherence (*saṁyukta-samavāya*). But the intercourse between our eye and all cases of smoke is not an ordinary one. It is a transcendent intercourse, as there is no ordinary union of our eye with all cases of smoke of all times and all places. The intercourse consists here of the knowledge of "smokeness", a generic nature which is possessed by all cases of smoke of all times and all places. This sort of intercourse which consists of the knowledge of a generic nature, is called a transcendent intercourse whose character is general The objection that if there were a transcendent intercourse (perception) whose character is general, we could become omniscient, inasmuch as in perceiving an object of knowledge we could perceive all objects of knowledge, is untenable because, though we can perceive all objects of knowledge comprehended under a generic nature, we cannot perceive their mutual differences, and as such cannot be omniscient.

Intercourse (perception) whose character is knowledge.—If in the perception of a thing the knowledge of the thing itself constitutes the intercourse, it is called an intercourse whose character is knowledge. On seeing a piece of sandal-wood we often say that it is fragrant. How does this visual perception of fragrance take place? The answer is that when the eye comes in union with the piece of sandal-wood, there arises within us a kind of knowledge (recollection) of fragrance which serves as the intercourse for our perception of the same. This is an instance of what is called in Western Psychology an "indirect perception".

Some say that the case cited above may be explained by the intercourse whose character is general, and there is no necessity for our assuming another intercourse whose character is knowledge. On seeing a piece of sandal-wood there arises in us the recollection of fragrance and "fragrancy" (the generic nature of fragrance), which abide in sandal-wood in the relations of inherence (*samavāya*) and inherent-inherence (*samaveta-samavāya*) respectively. From the recollection of "fragrancy", through the intercourse whose character is general, there arises in us the perception of all individual fragrances including the fragrance of this particular piece of sandal-wood.

In reply Gaṅgeśa says that, though, through the intercourse whose character is general, we can somehow explain the perception of fragrance, we cannot through this intercourse explain the perception of "fragrancy". Had there been a "fragranciness" (which is the generic nature of *fragrancy*), we could have, through the intercourse whose character is general, derived the perception of "fragrancy". But there is no generic nature of "fragrancy", which is itself the generic nature of fragrance. We cannot therefore perceive

" fragrancy " through the intercourse whose character is general. It is through the intercourse whose character is knowledge that we can perceive " fragrancy ", the recollection of which serves as the intercourse for such perception.

Intercourse (perception) produced by meditation.—It is of two kinds, *viz.* (1) the intercourse (perception) of an ascetic who has attained union with the Supreme Being, and (2) that of an ascetic who is endeavouring to attain such union. The first ascetic enjoys a constant perception of all things, while the second ascetic can secure perception only when he is attended with mediation.

Inherence—*Samavāya-vāda.*

In the visual perception of the colour of a jar, the intercourse that exists between our eye and the colour has been designated as united-inherence. It is not possible to understand the meaning of this term unless we understand the meaning of inherence. Inherence (*samavāya*) is an intimate relation between two things which cannot exist separately. Of the two things one exists only as lodged in the other. Such things are the whole and its parts, the substance and its qualities or action, the community and individuals, and the eternal substances and their final particulars. The relation that exists between these things is called inherence, *e.g.* threads inhere in the cloth, colour inheres in the jar, and so on. The knowledge of a whole as composed of parts, or of a substance as possessing qualities, etc. is determinate knowledge. In such knowledge we have to consider three things, *viz.* the subject, the predicate, and the relation that exists between them. For instance, in our determinate knowledge of the form "the man has a stick," the man is the subject and the stick is the predicate, while the relation that exists between them is union. Similarly in our determinate knowledge of the form " the flower has colour," the flower is the subject and the colour is the predicate, but the relation that exists between them is not union but inherence. When two things can be separated from each other, the relation between them is union, but when they cannot be mutually separated their relation is inherence. In fact colour is not united with flower but inheres in it.

The Invalidity of Non-perception—*Anupalabdhyaprāmāṇya-vāda.*

Some say that non-existence is not perceptible by any of our senses. and that the knowledge of non-existence of a thing arises through non-perception of the thing itself. For instance, the way in which the knowledge of non-existence of a pot arises is as follows : Had there been a pot here, it would have been perceived : since it is not perceived, there is no pot here. The non-perception of a pot is therefore the means of knowing the non-existence of the pot. Gaṅgeśa does not admit non-perception to be a means of knowledge. Non-existence, according to him, is perceived by our senses through the intercourse of particularity. For instance, in the perception of non-existence of a pot on the floor, there is the union of our eye with the floor in which abides non-existence of the pot as a particularity, that is, there is perception of the floor as possessed of the non-existence of the pot. The sense employed in the perception of a thing is the same as that which is employed in the perception of its non-existence. Whatever thing is perceptible by a sense, the non-existence of that thing is also perceptible by the same sense, *e.g.* a colour and its non-existence are both perceived by the eye, a sound and its non-existence by the ear, an odour and its non-existence by the nose, a savour and its non-existence by the tongue, warmth and its non-existence by the tactual surface, and pleasure and its non-existence by the mind.

Non-existence (or negation)—*Abhāva-vāda.*

Some say that there is no separate entity called non-existence (*abhāva*), that perception of what is ordinarily called the "non-existence of a thing" depends upon the locus (*adhikaraṇa*) of non-existence of the thing, and that the intercourse through which we perceive the thing, must be the same as that through which we perceive its non-existence, *viz.* union, etc. For instance, our perception of the non-existence of a pot (in the form "there is no pot on the floor") does not presuppose a separate entity called "non-existence", but rests entirely on "the floor" which is the locus of the non-existence of the pot, and is carried on through the intercourse of union.

Gaṅgeśa opposes the above view by saying that we must admit a separate entity called non-existence, that our perception of what is ordinarily called the non-existence of a thing, does not rest entirely on the locus of the non-existence of the thing, and that the intercourse through which we perceive the non-existence of the thing is not union etc., but particularity (*viśeṣaṇatā*). In the instance cited above our perception of the non-existence of the pot does not rest on "the floor", that is, the non-existence of the pot is not identical with the floor. Had the one rested on the other, or had the two been identical, there would have been perception of the non-existence of the pot even when the pot was on the floor, and further there would have been a disturbance of the relation of container and contained that exists between the two. Since this contingency is disastrous, we must admit that there is something on the ground which operates in our failure to perceive the pot. This something is "non-existence" which is a separate entity lying over and above the floor. Our failure to perceive a thing does not therefore rest on the mere locus of the thing, but on the locus as possessed of this something or "non-existence." The relation that exists between the locus and non-existence is that of particularity (*viśeṣaṇatā*). When we perceive the non-existence of a pot on the floor our eye comes in union with the floor on which abides the non-existence of the pot in the relation of particularity. The intercourse in this case is, therefore, of united particularity (*saṁyukta-viśeṣaṇatā*). Similarly the relation of particularity is to be associated with inherence, united-inherence, etc.

Every non-existence has a counterpart, *e.g.* with reference to the non existence of a pot and that of a piece of cloth, the pot and the piece of cloth are respectively the counterparts. The perception of a non-existence is subject to that of its counterpart. The process, by which we perceive non-existence through the relation of particularity, involves knowledge of its counterpart which is produced through memory or from any other source. In our perception of the non-existence of a pot on the floor, there arises in us first of all recollection of the pot, and as soon as our eye comes in union with the floor we perceive the non-existence of the pot on the same.

Non-existence is of two kinds: (1) universal, and (2) reciprocal. The universal non-existence is sub-divided into (*a*) the antecedent, (*b*) the subsequent, and (*c*) the absolute. The antecedent non-existence is that which has no beginning but has an end, *e.g.* a jar is in antecedent non-existence before it is made up. The subsequent non-existence has a beginning but no end, *e.g.* a jar is in subsequent non-existence after it is destroyed. The absolute non-existence is that whose counterpart is viewed in relation to all the three times—past, present, and future, *e.g.* there is no jar on the floor. The reciprocal non-existence is the non-existence of identity, *e.g.* a jar is not a pot.

Causes of Perception—*Pratyakṣa-kāraṇa-vāda*.

The causes of perception are the following:—

(1) A union of the mind with the tactual surface and the soul.

Causes of knowledge in general.

While a person is in deep sleep there is produced in him no knowledge, as there is then a union of his mind with the soul alone but not with the tactual surface. The mind abides at that time near the heart in a *nāḍī* called pericardium which is without a tactual surface. In recollecting a thing our mind is in union with both the tactual surface and the soul.

(2) A union of the mind with the senses and an intercourse of

the senses with their objects, *e.g.* in the perception of a colour there is a union of our mind with the eye which is in intercourse with the colour.

(3) Proportionate extension of the objects of sense, that is, the objects must not be of infinite extension as ether, or of no extension as atoms. The ether and atoms are not perceived but inferred, the former being the locus of sound, and the latter the final particulars of things.

Special causes of perception.

(4) An obviousness or manifest form of an object of sense, *e.g.* a colour, if it is to be perceptible, must possess obviousness. A meteor, which is obscured in the midday blaze, cannot be perceived. Similarly, a fire which exists in the latent condition in a heated frying-pan, is not perceptible.

(5) A special connection of light with the object of sense, *e.g.* a pot, if it is to be perceptible, must have sufficient light on its front rather than on its back.

Special causes of visual perception.

(6) Absence of obstacles, *e.g.* too much proxmity or too much distance, is often obstructive to our perception.

The Atomic Nature of the Mind—*Manoṇutva-vāda.*

The senses through the instrumentality of which we perceive colour, sound, odour, savour and touch, are the eye, ear, nose, tongue and tactual surface respectively. The sense which operates as an instrument in our perception of pleasure, pain, desire, aversion, intellect and volition, is the mind, which is called the internal sense in contrast to the other five senses which are external.

The mind is atomic in extension, inasmuch as we cannot perceive various objects at one and the same time. Although there may exist intercourse of our external senses with their corresponding objects, no perception will be produced until the mind comes in union with them. Had the mind been of infinite extension, or even of proportionate extension, it could have come into union with all the five external senses at once so as to give rise to the five kinds of perception simultaneously. But everybody is aware that it is impossible for more than one kind of perception to arise at one and the same time. This shows that the mind can come into union with only *one* external sense at a time, or in other words, the mind is atomic in extension.

Those who deny the atomic nature of the mind on the ground that sometimes, *e g.* in eating a large cake soaked in milk and sugar, we find the operations of the mind united with several senses simultaneously, should be told that the operations, which they suppose to be simultaneous, do really take place in succession, as the hundred leaves of a lotus are pierced one after another by a needle.

The Doctrine of Self-consciousness—*Anu-vyavasāya-vāda.*

Some philosophers maintain that any particular kind of knowledge performs by itself all its practical functions and does not depend upon another knowledge for the same. For instance, all practical functions connected with a pot can, according to them, be performed when there is knowledge of the pot, but we cannot perform those functions when there is no such knowledge It is therefore knowledge which performs all its practical functions. We must not however suppose that all practical functions are performed by all kinds of knowledge promiscuously. In fact each kind of knowledge is, by its very nature, related to a particular object which enables us to perform its corresponding functions.

Some others, who hold the doctrine of triangular perception (*tripuṭī-pratyakṣa-vādinaḥ*), say that each kind of knowledge is self-manifest and that it manifests itself in the form "I know this," which involves an assumption of a knower (the soul), a knowable (the object), and knowledge (the act), and as such performs all its practical functions.

Gaṅgeśa, in opposing the above views, says that a particular kind of knowledge cannot by itself perform its practical functions, but is dependent upon another sort called self-consciousness (*anu-vyavasāya*) which enables it to perform the same. Our knowledge, continues Gaṅgeśa, arises in the form "this" or "pot," but not in the form "I know this" or "I know the pot"; and until it assumes the latter form no practical functions can be performed. He therefore lays down that after the origination of knowledge of the form "this" or "pot," there arises another knowledge called self-consciousness of the form "I know this" or "I know the pot," which performs all practical functions. This latter variety, called self-consciousness, arises through the intercourse of the previous knowledge with our mind. The intercourse is united-inherence (*saṁyukta-samavāya*), inasmuch as there is a union of the mind with the soul in which resided the previous knowledge in the relation of inherence. In fact the latter knowledge or self-consciousness is the mental (or internal) perception of the previous knowledge.

Immediate Perception—*Nirvikalpaka-vāda.*

Perception is of two kinds, *viz.* (1) the immediate, non-reflective or abstract (*nirvikalpaka*) and (2) the mediate, reflective or concrete (*savikalpaka*). The immediate is perception of an indeterminate character. It is perception of a subject and its generic nature as separate from each other, *e.g.* the perception of a mere "pot" or mere "potness" without any mutual connection.

Even the mere "pot" or mere "potness" is of the form "something" of which it is absurd to talk as a "pot" or "potness." On the intercourse of a sense with its object the first perception that takes place is immediate or non-reflective. It is supersensuous, that is, not cognisable by any of our senses, not even by the mind. It has been defined as knowledge which is devoid of all connection with name, generic nature, etc., which indicates no relation and involves no specification.

Mediate Perception—*Savikalpaka-vāda.*

The mediate or reflective perception is of a determinate character. It indicates a subject and its generic nature through their relation to each other, *e.g.* "this is a pot" where "potness" (the generic nature) abides in "this" (the subject) in the relation of inherence. The perception of the form "this is a pot" is therefore mediate or reflective.

The doctrine of mediate or reflective perception may be set forth as follows :—

Immediate perception—the perception of "pot" and "potness" as separate from each other.

Mediate perception—the perception of "potness" as abiding in "this" in the form "this is a pot"

Self-consciousness—the mental perception of the knowledge of "potness" as abiding in "this," in the form "I know this is a pot."

Book II.—Inference—*Anumāna-khaṇḍa.*

The Determination of Inferential Knowledge—*Anumiti-nirūpaṇa.*

Inferential knowledge (*anumiti*) is that knowledge which is derived through another kind of knowledge, *viz.* that the middle term, in invariable concomitance with the major term, abides in the minor term, *e.g.*

The hill is full of fire,
because it is full of smoke.

Here "hill" is the minor term which is also called the subject, locus or side; "fire" is the major term, also called the predicate or probandum; and "smoke" is the middle term, also called the reason or mark. The knowledge of the form "the hill is full of smoke" is inferential knowledge inasmuch as it is derived through another kind of knowledge, *viz.* that of the smoke which, as being in invariable concomitance with fire, abides in the hill. This other knowledge, *viz.* that smoke, in invariable concomitance with fire, abides in the hill, is an instance of what is called *consideration, knowledge of premises* or *inference* (*parāmarśa* or *anumāna*). It is the intercourse or operation through which we arrive at the inferential knowledge. The whole process of arriving at that knowledge is also sometimes called inference.

Inference distinct from Perception.

Some say that perception is the only means of knowledge and that there is no separate means of knowledge called inference. Their reasons are as follows:—

(1) There cannot be any knowledge of the invariable concomitance between the middle term and the major term;
(2) The middle term may be erratic owing to its connection with a condition accepted or disputed; and
(3) We often associate the middle term with the major term through a mere probability which involves no certainty.

Gaṅgeśa sets aside the above view by saying that there are other means of knowledge over and above perception, and that inference is at any rate one means of knowledge. The doctrine of invariable concomitance, etc., will be treated later. In support of inference as a means of knowledge it will suffice at present to observe the following arguments:—

1. One cannot establish the invalidity of an inference unless one *infers* the invalidity from the similarity of the inference with things previously known as invalid. This process presupposes inference as a means of knowledge.

2. The statement that "inference is not a means of knowledge" is of no use to an expert who is aware of the invalidity of inference. It may be advanced usefully before a suspicious or an erring person. Now, how are we to know that the person is in suspicion or error? It is certainly not through perception but through inference.

3. "Inference is not a means of knowledge": is this statement valid or invalid? If it is valid, we must admit verbal testimony to be a means of knowledge. If on the other hand it is invalid, inference is to be admitted as a means of knowledge. Both the alternatives are incompatible with the opponent's view.

4. Moreover if inference is not valid, perception, too, cannot be valid. The validity being an object of inference, how can we, in the absence of inference, ascertain the validity of perception? If again perception were by itself valid, then there could not arise any doubt about its validity.

Perception is, therefore, not the only means of knowledge, but inference also is one of the means.

Inferential knowledge having been based upon an invariable concomitance of the middle term with the major term, it is necessary to define the phrase "invariable concomitance." In Sanskrit it is called *vyāpti* which is rendered by such expressions as pervasion, inseparable connection, perpetual attendance, constant co-presence, etc.

Five Provisional Definitions of Invariable Concomitance—*Vyāpti-pañcakam.*

1. Invariable concomitance is the non-presence of the middle term in the locus of the non-existence of the major term, *e.g.*

The hill is full of fire,
because it is full of smoke.

Diagram I.

Diagram II.

Here smoke (the middle term) is absent from all regions outside the region of fire (the major term) as shown in diagram I. Gaṅgeśa observes that the definition is defective inasmuch as it does not apply to an exclusively affirmative inference, such as "all are nameable, because they are knowable", illustrated in diagram II, in which outside the region of the nameable there is nothing from which the knowable may be absent.

2. Invariable concomitance is the non-presence of the middle term in that locus of the non-existence of the major term which is not the locus of the major term itself, *e.g.*

Diagram III.

This is occupied by the ape, because it is the tree.

Here "the tree" is the middle term, and "occupied by the ape" is the major term. In diagram III the tree is totally absent from the region not occupied by the ape. The part of the tree not occupied by the ape is excluded from the locus of the non-existence of the major term by the clause "which is not the locus of the major term itself." This definition too is defective, because it, like the previous one, does not apply to an exclusively affirmative inference.

3. Invariable concomitance is the non-co-presence of the middle term with that reciprocal non-existence whose counterpart abides in the locus of the major term, *e.g.*

> The hill is full of fire,
> because it is full of smoke.

In diagram I. we find that smoke is not co-present with anything which is non-existent in reciprocity to fire. Water, book, cloth, table, etc., are all non-existent in their reciprocal relation to fire, that is, they are not fire.

Gaṅgeśa observes that this definition too is defective, as it does not cover the case of an exclusively affirmative inference. In diagram II. we find that there is no reciprocal non-existence whose counterpart is the region of the nameable.

4. Invariable concomitance is the state in which the middle term forms the counterpart of that non-existence which abides in the locus of the non-existence of the entire major term, *e.g.*

> The hill is full of fire,
> because it is full of smoke.

Here smoke forms the counterpart of the non-existence of smoke which abides in the region of the non-existence of entire fire.

According to Gaṅgeśa this definition is defective, as it fails to explain the case of an exclusively affirmative inference. In diagram II. we find that there is no non-existence of the knowable which abides in the region of the non-existence of the nameable.

5. Invariable concomitance is the non-presence of the middle term in what is not the locus of the major term, *e.g.*

> The hill is full of fire.
> because it is full of smoke.

Here smoke is not present in anything which is not the abode of fire. This definition too, according to Gaṅgeśa, is defective, as it does not meet the case of an exclusively affirmative inference. In diagram II. we find that there is no non-presence of the knowable in what is not included in the region of the nameable.

Definition of Invariable Concomitance given by "Lion" and "Tiger"—*Siṁha-vyāghrokta-vyāptilakṣaṇa.*

1. Invariable concomitance is the state in which the middle term has not a locus in which there is the non-co-presence of the major term, *e.g.*

The hill is full of fire,
because it is full of smoke.

Here fire is always co-present with smoke in the locus of the latter. It never occurs that in the locus of smoke there is no fire.

2. Invariable concomitance is the state in which the middle term has not a locus which is different from the locus of the major term, *e.g.*

The hill is full of fire,
because it is full of smoke.

The locus of smoke is never different from that of fire, that is, the former never extends beyond the latter.

Gaṅgeśa observes that both these definitions are defective, inasmuch as their import is to show that the middle term has not a locus which is also not the locus of the major term. On the contrary we find that the middle term has often a locus which is not the locus of the major term. For instance, smoke on a hill has a locus which is not the locus of fire in a kitchen.

Non-existence whose Counterpart is Qualified by a Nature abiding in a Different Locus—*Vyadhikaraṇa-dharmāvacchinnābhāvaḥ.*

Most of the definitions of invariable concomitance given above were defective inasmuch as they did not cover the case of an exclusively affirmative inference. They involved such phrases as "non-existence of the major term" and "difference of locus of the major term" which could not apply to an exclusively affirmative inference in which the major term was all-pervading. To make the "non-existence of the major term" and "difference of locus of the major term" possible, even in an exclusively affirmative inference, some logicians assume a non-existence whose counterpart is qualified by a nature abiding in a locus different from the counterpart. The expression "there is no fire possessing the nature of a pot" signifies that "there is non-existence of a fire as qualified by the nature of a pot" which, according to them, is quite correct inasmuch as the nature of a pot abides in the relation of inherence in a pot and not in fire. Similarly "there is no nameableness possessing the nature of a pot" signifies that "there is non existence of nameableness as qualified by the nature of a pot." Though nameableness (major term) is all-pervading we have, they say, been able to talk of its non-existence by assuming the nature of a pot to abide in it (instead of it in the pot).

Gaṅgeśa opposes the above view in four ways:—(1) On the assumption of a non-existence of this form, invariable concomitance has to be defined as the state in which the middle term has not the co-presence with a non-existence whose counterpart is qualified by a nature which is the nature of the major term. This definition, in which the counterpart and the major term are identical, does not involve a non-existence of the form proposed. The definitions already condemned cannot also be defended by the assumption of this non-existence. (2) This sort of non-existence is not well known and cannot be established by any evidence. (3) The counterpart of the non-existence is said to be qualified by a quality which does not abide in it. This is impossible because our knowledge of non-existence depends on that of its counterpart as possessed of the nature. (4) And to assert a non-existence of this form is as absurd as to say that there is no hare-horn (*śaśa-śṛṅga*) in a cow.

Other Objectionable Definitions of Invariable Concomitance—*Pūrvapakṣaḥ*.

Gaṅgeśa examines and condemns twelve other definitions of invariable concomitance called objectionable definitions given by previous logicians.

The Conclusive Definition of Invariable Concomitance—*Siddhānta-lakṣaṇam*.

Invariable concomitance is the co-presence of the middle term with the major term which is not qualified by the nature of the counterpart of that absolute non-existence, which abides in the same locus with the middle term, but abides in a different locus in respect of that counterpart, *e.g.*

The hill is full of fire,
because it is full of smoke.

Diagram IV.

Diagram V.

Here there is co-presence of smoke (the middle term) with fire (the major term) which is not qualified by the nature of a pot, and the absolute non-existence, whose counterpart is the pot, abides in the same locus with smoke, but abides in a different locus in respect of the pot.

This definition covers the case of an exclusively affirmative inference inasmuch as it does not involve a non-existence of the major term, and the major term is not the counterpart of that non-existence which abides in the same locus with the middle term. Looking at diagram V, we find that there is co-presence of the knowable with the nameable which is not qualified by the nature of a pot (though the pot is qualified by the nature of the nameable), and the absolute non-existence, whose counterpart is the pot, abides in the same locus with the knowable, but in a different locus in respect of the pot.

Non-existence of the General Form—*Śāmānyābhāvaḥ*.

Some say that even the conclusive definition given above is defective inasmuch as in seeking to establish the invariable concomitance of smoke with fire we notice that fires are manifold owing to the difference of their loci, *e.g.* the fire of a kitchen, of a sacrificial ground, and so on. There is non-existence of these fires, except one, in the locus of a particular case of smoke. This, by making fire the counterpart of that non-existence which abides in the same locus with smoke, altogether upsets the conclusive definition.

Gaṅgeśa in reply says that though in the locus of smoke there is the non-existence of various fires, the natures which qualify the counterparts of those non-existences are not one and the same, *viz.* the nature of fire in general. They are different, that is, particular fires have particular natures, as for instance, the nature of the fire of a kitchen is different from that of the fire of a sacrificial ground, and so on. It is therefore necessary to admit a non-existence of fire of the general form—such as 'there is no fire' distinguished from non-existences of particular forms as 'there are not such and such fires.' A non-existence of the general form is the non-existence whose counterpart is not of a particular nature. Had the non-existence of the general form been a name merely for the sum total of particular non-existences then there would not have arisen in us a doubt of the form—'is not there a colour in air?' It is perfectly known to us that in air there are no particular colours as red, yellow, etc.; yet we entertain a doubt in our mind as to whether there is not in air a non-existence of colour of the general form.

Invariable Concomitance of Special Forms—*Viśeṣa-vyāptiḥ.*

It is to be admitted that there is non-existence of the fire of a hill in the locus of smoke of a sacrificial ground, and there is non-existence of the fire of a sacrifical ground, in the locus of smoke of a hill. There is no invariabie concomitance of smoke with fire if the two occupy different loci, that is, if the locus of smoke is different from that of the fire. But nobody can deny the invariable concomitance of smoke with fire if the two occupy the same locus, *e.g.* there is an invariable concomitance of smoke of a hill with the fire of the same. Though there is no invariable concomitance of all cases of smoke with all cases of fire, there is the concomitance of particular cases of smoke with their corresponding fires. The comprehensive connection of smoke with fire is not, by this particular concomitance, disturbed, for there is no smoke without fire.

This sort of invariable concomitance, called the invariable concomitance of special forms, may be defined as follows:—

1. Invariable concomitance is the co-presence of the middle term with the major term which is different from the counterpart of that absolute non-existence which does not abide in the locus of that counterpart, but abides with the middle term in the latter's own locus.

2. Invariable concomitance is the co-presence of the middle term with the major term, the locus of which is different from that of the counterpart of the reciprocal non-existence which abides in the locus of the middle term.

3. Invariable concomitance is the connection of the middle term with the major term which is different from the counterpart of that reciprocal non-existence which abides in the same locus with the middle term.

4. Invariable concomitance may also be defined as the co-presence of the middle term with the major term when there is no condition attached to the middle term.

5. Invariable concomitance is the co-presence of the middle term with the major term which co-abides with that absolute existence whose counterpart is that which is qualified by the nature of the counterpart of the absolute non-existence abiding in the same locus with the middle term.

6. Invariable concomitance is the possession of that nature which establishes the connection (that is, brings about the co-presence) of the middle term with the major term.

The Means of Apprehending Invariable Concomitance—*Vyāpti-grahopāyaḥ.*

Some logicians maintain that repeated observations of one thing as accompanying another thing are the means of apprehending invariable concomitance of the one with the other, *e.g.* we apprehend the invariable concomitance of smoke with fire after we have observed repeatedly that the one accompanies the other.

Gaṅgeśa opposes the above view on the following grounds:—

(1) Of the repeated observations each one separately cannot be the cause of apprehension of invariable concomitance owing to lack of unity among the observations. As the successive observations perish quickly there is nothing which unites them together to cause in us an apprehension of invariable concomitance. The impression left in our mind by the past observations are no doubt competent to produce recollection and recognition of equal things, but they cannot produce apprehension of invariable concomitance which involves unequal things such as occurrence of smoke in a kitchen, a sacrificial ground, a hill, etc.

(2) What again is the meaning of repeated observations? Does it mean observation in numerous places, or observation of numerous instances, or observation of the same instance numerous times? None of these alternatives are of any help to us in apprehending invariable concomitance. Can we establish invariable concomitance of colour with savour, even if we have observed them together in numerous places? Can numerous instances of colour observed along with savour in the same place (as a pot) entitle us to establish invariable concomitance between them? As regards the observation of an instance numerous times, it may be asked how many times? There is certainly no fixity as to the number of times There cannot in fact be an invariable concomitance of a pen with the floor even if they have been observed together a hundred times.

2. Some other logicians say that a reasoning (*tarka*) coupled with the observation of co-accompaniment (*sahacāra*) is the means of our apprehending invariable concomitance. For instance, smoke is in invariable concomitance with fire inasmuch as we observe the former co-accompanied by the latter; and by applying our reasoning we further find that had there been no inseparable connection between smoke and fire, we could have seen the former without the latter, but as such a contingency is an absurdity, there is certainly an invariable concomitance of smoke with fire.

According to Gaṅgeśa the above view is untenable inasmuch as a reasoning, being itself based on an apprehension of invariable concomitance, cannot be the cause of the same. Unless a person apprehends the invariable concomitance of one thing with another thing, his reasoning, which is to reveal the absurdity of all contrary apprehensions, cannot come into operation. We could argue *ad infinitum* without being able to ascertain whether reasoning preceded the apprehension of invariable concomitance, or the latter preceded the former.

Conclusion as to the Means of Apprehending Invariable Concomitance—*Vyāptigrahopāya-siddhānta*.

The observation of co-accompaniment attended with the absence of knowledge of exceptions is the means of apprehending invariable concomitance, *e.g.* there is invariable concomitance of smoke with fire as the former constantly accompanies the latter without any exceptions.

The knowledge of exceptions may assume the form of a certainty or doubt. In the former alternative we cannot at all apprehend invariable concomitance, and in the latter there is great difficulty in apprehending it. Doubt arises from two sources, *viz.* sometimes from the suspicion of a condition (*upādhi*) and sometimes from the recognition of common properties and non-recognition of special properties. As an instance of the latter source we may point out a tall object which in the twilight produces in us a doubt as to whether it is a man or a post, because we recognize in it tallness which is the common property of a man and a post without the recognition of locomotion, etc., which are the special properties of a man. As an instance of the former source, we may cite the case of a fire which, if wet fuel is attached to it as a condition, may be inseparably connected with smoke. In asserting the invariable concomitance of smoke with fire[1] we are therefore in doubt as to whether wet fuel is not a condition.

In certain instances the doubt does not arise at all on account of absence of such defects as myopia, long distance, etc. In certain other instances the doubt is removed by the employment of reasoning. For instance, our doubt as to whether there is invariable concomitance of fire with smoke, is removed by reasoning as follows: Had fire constantly accompanied smoke there would have been smoke in a red-hot iron-ball; but in it there is fire and no smoke; so there is no invariable concomitance of fire with smoke (but there is that of smoke with fire).

The reasoning which is to remove doubt, is to be carried on only as long as the doubt is not removed. The charge of *regressus ad infinitum* brought against the reasoning employed to establish invariable concomitance, does not apply to the present case, in which reasoning ceases with the disappearance of doubt and does not continue up to the commencement of the processes establishing invariable concomitance.

---

[1] There is invariable concomitance of smoke with fire but not of fire with smoke; that is, wherever there is smoke there is fire, but not *vice versa*.

Reasoning (or Confutation)—*Tarka.*

The processes of reasoning (or confutation) may be illustrated as follows :--

Interrogation.—Can smoke abide without fire ?

Reasoning.—If smoke could abide without fire, it would not have been a product of fire

Re-interrogation.—Is smoke a product of fire ?

Reasoning.—If smoke were produced neither from fire nor from non-fire, then it would have been a non-product. But it is not so.

Doubt.—Smoke then may have been produced either from fire or without a cause.

Incompatibility.—Why a person, who thus indulges in doubt, is nevertheless led on to activity ? If he doubts whether an effect may or may not be produced without a cause, why does he seek for a fire to obtain smoke, and for food to get satisfaction ? His own activity indicates that he is well aware of the connection between a cause and its effect. Why does he then entertain doubt ? It is incompatible with his own activity. There is no doubt that smoke as an effect cannot be produced without a cause. Smoke is in fact a product of fire without which it cannot abide.

Comprehensiveness of Invariable Concomitance—*Vyāptyanugamaḥ.*

Comprehensiveness (*anugama*) is the nature which exhibits in one form all the various kinds of invariable concomitance previously defined. The invariable concomitance involving reciprocal non-existence is a comprehensive one, and is on account of shortness to be accepted as the cause of inference. Of the five provisional definitions of invariable concomitance the third and the fifth, and of those of the invariable concomitance of a special form, the second and the third involve reciprocal non-existence. The conclusive definition of invariable concomitance may also be so modified as to involve reciprocal non-existence. Of these the third definition of the invariable concomitance of a special form is very short by far.

Intercourse whose Character is General—*Sāmānya-lakṣaṇa.*

We observed that there is invariable concomitance of smoke of a kitchen with fire of the same, and similarly there is invariable concomitance of smoke of a sacrifical ground with fire of the same. Though we thus observe that there is invariable concomitance of particular cases of smoke with particular cases of fire, we cannot infer fire on a hill by seeing smoke there, until we can establish the invariable concomitance of all cases of smoke with all cases of fire. We can establish the invariable concomitance of all cases of smoke with all cases of fire, if we assume the knowledge of "smokeness" (the generic nature of smoke) as the intercourse for our perception of all cases of smoke, and the knowledge of "fireness" (the generic nature of fire) as the intercourse for our perception of all cases of fire. This sort of intercourse which consists of the knowledge of a generic nature is called an intercourse whose character is general. It is described by some logicians as an ordinary intercourse of particularity, while others describe it as a transcendent intercourse. The logicians, who hold the first view, say that in perceiving a particular smoke by means of our eye there is the intercourse of union, while in perceiving "smokeness" there is the intercourse of united-inherence, and in perceiving all cases of smoke (at all times and in all places) through the knowledge of "smokeness" there is the intercourse of particularity. All these cases of intercourse are ordinary ones.

The logicians, who hold the second view, say that in the perception as a particular smoke and "smokeness" there are no doubt ordinary intercourses of union and united-inherence respectively, but in the perception of all cases of smoke through the knowledge of "smokeness" the intercourse is a transcendent one. It cannot be an ordinary intercourse because of all cases of smoke the present ones can be perceived by our eyes independent of the knowledge of "smokeness," while the past and future cases of smoke with which our eyes are not connected, cannot be perceived at all through any of the six ordinary intercourses. Therefore the intercourse, *viz.* the knowledge of "smokeness", through which we perceive all cases of smoke, is a transcendent one whose character is general. Hence the apprehension of invariable concomitance of a particular case of smoke with a particular case of fire refers through the intercourse whose character is general to all cases of smoke and all cases of fire.

Conclusion about the Intercourse whose Character is General.—*Sāmānya-lakṣaṇa-siddhāntaḥ.*

If the intercourse, whose character is general, were not accepted, there could not arise any doubt as to whether there were instances in which smoke (the middle term) did not accompany fire (the major term). As to the cases of smoke which were present, we could perceive their co-accompaniment with cases of fire, and they could leave no room for doubt regarding any case of exception. As for the past and future cases of smoke, or the cases of smoke of distant places, we could not know them as they were beyond the range of our eyes. In the absence of knowledge of those cases of smoke it would be impossible for us to entertain any doubt as to whether they constantly accompanied fire. Doubt being impossible, there could not be any reasoning employed to remove it. Hence we could not apprehend an invariable concomitance. But if the intercourse whose character is general, is admitted, we can explain the perception of all cases of smoke through the intercourse of "smokeness." It is possible for doubt to arise in respect of some of these cases of smoke through non-recognition of their special properties. We must therefore admit intercourse whose character is general.

The Conditional Middle Term—*Upādhi-vādaḥ*.

The middle term, if it is to be in invariable concomitance with the major, should be devoid of condition, that is, should be unconditional. A condition (*upādhi*) is that which constantly accompanies the major term, but does not always accompany the middle term, *e.g.*

The hill is full of smoke,
because it is full of fire (nourished by wet fuel).

Diagram VI.

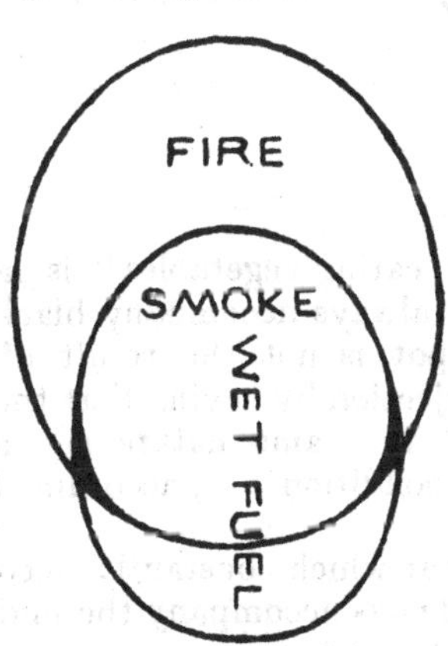

Here smoke is the major term, fire is the middle term and wet fuel is a condition. The wet fuel constantly accompanies smoke, but does not always accompany fire. For instance, the fire in an ignited iron-ball is not accompanied by wet fuel at all.

"Accompanying the major term" signifies the state of not being the counterpart of that absolute non-existence which abides in the locus of the major term, that is, the state of not being absent from the locus of the major term. "Not accompanying the middle term" is the state of being the counterpart of that absolute non-existence which abides in the locus of the middle term, that is, the state of being absent from the locus of the middle term. In diagram VI. "wet fuel" is not absent from the region of smoke, but it is present in some regions of fire and absent from the remaining regions of the same.

"Mitrā has many sons of whom one is black, and the rest fair-complexioned. The son conceived at a time when Mitrā ate vegetables, is black, but other sons that were conceived while she did not eat vegetables but drank milk, are fair-complexioned." In diagram VII. we find that "eating vegetable" is a condition which accompanies Mitrā's black son, but does not accompany her fair-complexioned sons.

Diagram VII.

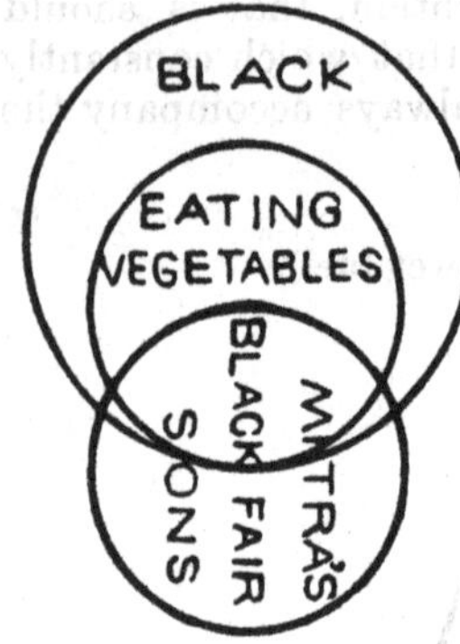

He is black,
because he is a son of Mitrā
(who eats vegetables).

Some say that "eating vegetables" is not a condition inasmuch as it does not always accompany blackness; for instance, the blackness of a pot is not the result of eating vegetables. Gaṅgeśa meets the objection by saying that the blackness marking Mitrā's son is not of the same nature as the blackness which abides in a pot. A "condition" is, according to him, to be clearly defined as follows:—

A condition is that which constantly accompanies the major term, but does not always accompany the middle term, in respect of an entity of a fixed nature.

Condition is of two kinds, *viz.* (1) sure, and (2) suspected. A condition is said to be "sure" when we know with certainty that it constantly accompanies the major term, but does not always accompany the middle term; and it is said to be "suspected" when there is doubt as to its accompanying the major term or as to its not accompanying the middle term. An instance of a suspected condition is given below:—

The earth has a maker,
because it is a product (caused by a body).

Here "caused by a body" is a condition which constantly accompanies a maker (if the maker is a person, but not if the maker is a collection of atoms), but does not always accompany a product (for instance, a product like a pot is caused by a body, but a product like a lightning is not so caused). The condition, *viz.* "causing by a body", is therefore a suspected one.

A condition is not in itself a defect, but its attachment to the middle term indicates that that term is erratic and the conclusion drawn therefrom wrong.

The State of Being the Locus or Minor Term—*Pakṣatā*.

The state of being the locus or the minor term (*pakṣatā*) has been defined by some logicians as the state in which it is doubtful whether the major term abides in it or not. Seeing that the connection of the major term with the locus or minor term, may not necessarily involve a doubt, Gaṅgeśa prefers to define the minor term as that whose connection with the major term is not known with certainty in consequence of the absence of a desire to know the connection. *E.g.* in the proposition "the hill is full of fire", the hill is the minor term whose connection with fire was hitherto neither investigated nor known. The minor term is so named not merely if there is an absence of knowledge of its connection with the major term, but also if the absence of knowledge is due to the absence of a desire to arrive at the knowledge. We cannot treat the minor term as such merely by establishing with it a connection of the major term if that connection has already been known, but we shall be justified in treating it as the minor term if there is in us a desire again to establish the connection.

A homologue, a similar locus, a homogeneous affirmative or positive example (*sapakṣa*), is that in which the major term is known with certainty to abide, *e.g.* the hill is full of fire, because it is full of smoke, as *a kitchen*.

A heterologue, a dissimilar locus, a heterogeneous or negative example (*vipakṣa*), is that in which the major term is known not to abide, *e.g.* the hill is full of fire, because it is full of smoke; where there is no fire, there is no smoke, as *a lake*.

Consideration or Knowledge of Premises—*Parāmarśaḥ*.

Consideration (*parámarṣaḥ*) is the knowledge that the middle term, in invariable concomitance with the major term, abides in the minor, *e.g.*

> The hill is full of fire,
> because it is full of smoke.

Here consideration consists of the knowledge that in the hill abides smoke which is in invariable concomitance with fire. This knowledge (consideration) is the cause of inference.

28

The ancients held that smoke actually perceived together with the knowledge that it is in invariable concomitance with fire was the cause of inference. But Gaṅgeśa opposes this view by saying that if smoke actually perceived were the cause, then inference could not take place from smoke that had been destroyed or that had not yet arisen. On hearing that there *will be* smoke here, a person can at once infer that there *will be* fire here, although he does not actually perceive the smoke which is not present. It is therefore not smoke itself but the knowledge of it that is the cause of the inference. In other words, the middle term actually perceived together with the knowledge that it is in invariable concomitance with fire, is not the cause of inference, but consideration or knowledge that in the minor term abides the middle term which is, in invariable concomitance with the major term, such a cause.

An Exclusively Affirmative Inference—*Kevalānvayyanumānam*.

Inference is of three kinds, *viz.* (1) an exclusively affirmative inference (*kevalānvayyanumānam*), (2) an exclusively negative inference (*kevalavyatirekyanumānam*), and (3) an affirmative negative inference (*anvaya-vyatirekyanumānam*).

The exclusively affirmative is an inference in which there is no negative example. It may also be defined as an inference in which the major term is not the counterpart of that absolute non-existence which has an abode; or, as an inference in which there is no non-presence of the major term, *e.g.*

This is nameable,
because it is knowable—(*vide* diagram II).

An Exclusively Negative Inference—*Kevalavyatirekyanumānam*.

An exclusively negative inference is the inference in which the major term has no affirmative example. It may also be defined as the inference in which the major term does not abide in anything else but in the minor term, *e.g.*

Diagram VIII.

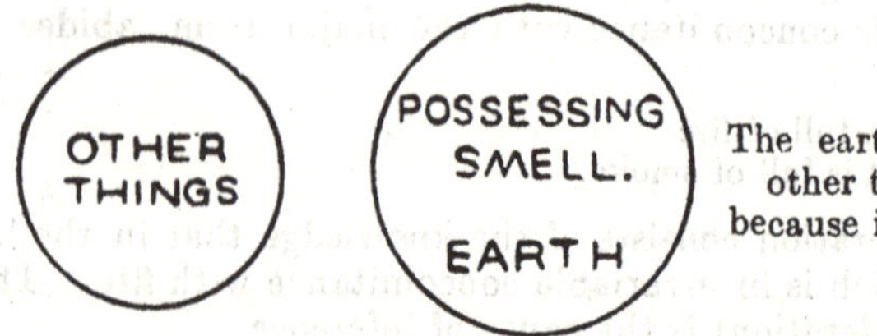

The earth is different from other things,
because it possesses smell.

An Affirmative-Negative Inference.

The affirmative-negative is an inference in which the major term has both affirmative and negative examples, *e.g.*

The hill is full of fire,
because it is full of smoke,
as a kitchen and not as a lake.

Presumption—*Arthāpatti.*

The Mīmāṁsakas say that presumption (*arthāpatti*) is a separate means of knowledge. On hearing that "Devadatta, who is fat, does not eat in the day", we at once conclude that he eats in the night. Since a person cannot become fat unless he eats either in the day or in the night, and, since he does not eat in the day, it follows by presumption that he eats in the night.

Gaṅgeśa does not admit presumption to be a separate means of knowledge, but includes it in the negative inference[1] which establishes the absence of the middle term through the absence of the major term. Here the absence of eating in the night would have been followed by the absence of that fatness which is attended with non-eating in the day.

Inference for One's Self—*Svārthānumāna.*

Inference is of two kinds: (1) inference for one's self (*svārthānumāna*) and (2) inference for the sake of others (*parārthānumāna*). A person having himself repeatedly observed in the kitchen and other places the invariable concomitance of smoke with fire, goes near a hill and sees smoke on it. He recollects that, wherever there is smoke, there is fire, and thereupon knowledge arises in him that "this hill has smoke which is in invariable concomitance with fire." This knowledge is called "consideration of the sign" (*liṅgaparāmarśa*) or simply "consideration" (*parāmarśa*), from which follows the knowledge that "this hill has fire", which is called inferential conclusion (*anumiti*). This is the process of inference for one's self.

Inference for the sake of Others—*Parārthānumāna.*

When a person, having inferred fire from smoke, demonstrates it to others by the employment of a syllogism, it is called "an inference for the sake of others." The process of this inference is as follows:—

---

[1] A person to be fat must take his food either in the day or in the night—(A proposition).
Devadatta, who is fat, does not take his food in the day—(E proposition).
Therefore Devadatta must take his food in the night. (This is a disjunctive categorical syllogism.)

(1) The hill is full of fire,
(2) Because it is full of smoke,
(3) All that is full of smoke is full of fire, as a kitchen,
(4) This hill is full of smoke,
(5) Therefore this hill is full of fire.

The demonstration given above produces in other people "consideration of the sign", which necessarily makes them admit that the hill has fire.

Syllogism—*Nyāyaḥ.*

Syllogism (*nyāya*) is the name for a collection of five sentences which give rise to knowledge that produces consideration. It is set forth as follows :—

(1) This hill is full of fire—*Proposition.*
(2) Because it is full of smoke—*Reason.*
(3) All that is full of smoke is full of fire, as a kitchen—*Example.*
(4) This hill is full of smoke—*Application.*
(5) Therefore this hill is full of fire—*Conclusion.*

After these five sentences have been employed there arises in the mind of the listener consideration of the form, 'this hill is full of smoke, which is in invariable concomitance with fire", from which follows the conclusion, "this hill is full of fire." Syllogism is therefore the name for the entire collection of these five sentences, each of which is called a part or member.

Parts of a Syllogism—*Avayavaḥ.*

A part or member (*avayavaḥ*) is a sentence that gives rise to knowledge which contributes to the production of an entire knowledge which produces consideration. On the employment of the five sentences there arises, at first, knowledge from each of them separately. Then arises collective knowledge from the five sentences combined together. This collective knowledge which produces consideration is based on each of the five sentences called a part or member. The parts are five, *viz.* (1) the proposition, (2) the reason, (3) the example, (4) the application, and (5) the conclusion.

The Proposition—*Pratijñā.*

The proposition (*pratijñā*) is a sentence which causes knowledge, whose object is the same as that of the conclusion and which contributes to the production of the entire knowledge which produces consideration, *e.g.*

This hill is full of fire.

It may also be defined as a sentence which gives rise to an inquiry necessitating the mention of the reason, *e.g.* this hill is full of fire. (Why so? because it is smoky.)

The Reason or Middle Term—*Hetuḥ*.

The reason or middle term (*hetuḥ*) is a word, with the instrumental or ablative suffix attached to it, which produces knowledge whose object is not the *probandum* (major term) but which contributes to the production of the entire knowledge that gives rise to consideration, *e.g.* because it is full of smoke (*i.e.* by or from smokiness).

The reason is of two kinds: (1) the affirmative (*anvayi*) and (2) the negative (*vyatirekī*). The affirmative reason is a member with the instrumental or ablative suffix attached to it, which produces knowledge that necessitates the mention of the member expressive of an affirmative invariable concomitance, *e.g.* because it has smoke (*i.e.* by or from "smokiness"), all that has smoke has fire, as a kitchen. The negative reason is a member with the instrumental or ablative suffix attached to it, which produces knowledge that necessitates the mention of the member expressive of a negative invariable concomitance, *e.g.* because it has smoke, (*i.e.* by or from "smokiness"), all that has no fire has no smoke, as a lake.

Example—*udāharaṇam*

The example (*udāharaṇam*) is a word which, while producing knowledge of connection of the form that the locus of the middle term is constantly occupied by the major term, causes another knowledge which proceeds from the sentence expressive of consideration,[1] *e.g.*

All that has smoke has fire, as a kitchen.
[So this hill has smoke].

Application—*upanayaḥ*.

The application (*upanayaḥ*) is a member which produces consideration, *e.g.* All that has smoke has fire, this hill too has smoke.

Conclusion—*Nigamanam*.

Conclusion (*nigamanam*) is a sentence which, while causing the knowledge which gives rise to consideration, produces knowledge of the major term as indicated by that of the middle term through its invariable concomitance with the major term and

[1] *i.e.* application (*upanayaḥ*), the sentence expressive of consideration.

its nature of abiding in the minor term, *e.g.* In this hill there is smoke, which is in invariable concomitance with fire. Therefore in this hill there is fire, or therefore this hill is full of fire.

Fallacies—*Hetvābhāsāḥ.*

A General Definition of Fallacy—*Hetvābhāsa-sāmānya-niruktiḥ.*

A person can ascertain truths and achieve victory by exposing fallacies in the argument of his opponent. It is therefore necessary to define a fallacy, which in Sanskrit is called ***hetvābhāsa***, a semblance of reason, a fallacy of reason or a fallacious reason.

A fallacy is an object of knowledge which obstructs an inference. It is in brief a defective reason. There are five kinds of fallacy or defective reason, viz. (1) the erratic or uncertain (***savyabhicāra*** or ***anaikānta***), (2) the contradictory (***viruddha***), (3) the counterbalanced (***satpratipakṣita***), (4) the unproved or inconclusive (***asiddha***), and (5) the incompatible (***bādhita***). The defects involved in the above reasons are respectively the following:—(1) the erraticalness or uncertainty (***vyabhicāra***), (2) contradiction (***virodha***), (3) counterbalance (***satpratipakṣa***), (4) absence of proof or inclusiveness (***asiddhi***), and (5) incompatibility, (***bādhā***).

The Erratic Reason—*Savyabhicāraḥ.*

The erratic (***savyabhicāra***) is a reason or middle term in which abides a character, the possession of which causes that presence of two alternatives which produces doubt in the ***probandum*** or major term. The nature refers to the constant accompaniment with, or absence from, both the major term and its non-existence. The erratic reason is subdivided into (1) that which is too general (***sādhāraṇa***), (2) that which is non-general or not general enough (***asādhāraṇa***), and (3) that which is non-exclusive (***anupasaṁhārī***).

A reason is said to be ***too general***, if it abides in the locus of the major term as well as in that of its absence, *e.g.*

> This hill is full of smoke,
> because it is full of fire.

Here the reason "fire" abides in the region of smoke (as in a kitchen) as well as in the region of the absence of smoke (as in an ignited iron-ball).

A reason is said to be ***non-general*** or ***not general enough***, if it abides neither in the locus of the major term nor in that of its absence, *e.g.*

> This hill is full of smoke,
> because it is full of ether.

Here the reason is ether, which has no locus. Ether abides neither in the locus of fire nor in that of the absence of fire.

A reason is said to be *non-exclusive*, if it is destitute of an example, whether affirmative or negative, *e.g.*

All things are impermanent,
because they are knowable.

Here we cannot cite any example, as "all things" is the subject.

The Contradictory Reason—*Viruddhaḥ*.

The contradictory (*viruddhaḥ*) is a reason which is the counterpart of that non-existence which constantly accompanies the major term, *e.g.*

This hill is full of fire,
because it is full of water.

Here the reason is contradictory, inasmuch as water is the counterpart of the *non-existence of water*, which constantly accompanies fire.

The contradictory may also be defined as a reason (middle term) which is constantly accompanied by the absence of the *probandum*, major term.

The Counterbalanced Reason—*Satpratipakṣitaḥ*.

If, at the time of the consideration of a reason which seeks to establish the *existence* of the *probandum* or major term, there occurs the consideration of another reason which seeks to establish the *non-existence* of that term, the first reason is a counterbalanced one,—in fact, *both* the reasons are counterbalanced, *e.g.*

One reason—Sound is eternal, because it is audible.
Opposite reason—Sound is non-eternal, because it is a product.

In the above instances, as consideration of both the sides prevails, there is no real inference. The inference from one reason being of as much force as that from the other reason, the two inferences neutralize each other.

The Unproved Reason—*Asiddhaḥ*.

The unproved (*asiddhaḥ*) reason is of three kinds: (1) unproved on the part of its locus or the subject (*āśrayāsiddhaḥ*), (2) unproved with regard to its own nature (*svarūpāsiddhaḥ*), and (3) unproved in respect of accompaniment (*vyāpyatvāsiddhaḥ*).

(1) A reason is said to be unproved on the part of its locus, if the characteristic distinguishing the locus does not belong to it, *e.g.*

This golden hill is full of fire,
because it is full of smoke.

Here the reason "smoke" is unproved, as its locus is unreal, on account of the "goldenness" not belonging to a hill.

(2) A reason is said to be unproved with regard to its own nature, if it does not abide in the locus or minor term, *e.g.*

The lake is full of fire,
because it is full of smoke.

Here the reason is unproved, as smoke from its very nature does not abide in a lake.

(3) A reason is said to be unproved in respect of constant accompaniment, if its generic nature is not useful in establishing its invariable concomitance with the major term. It is subdivided as follows:—

(*a*) Unproved on the part of the major term (*sādhyāsiddhi*) which occurs when there is a useless adjective appended to that term, *e.g.*

This hill is full of golden fire,
because it is full of smoke.

"Golden" is useless.

(*b*) Unproved on the part of the reason (*hetvasiddhi*) which occurs when there is a useless adjective appended to it. *e.g.*

This hill is full of fire,
because it is full of blue smoke.

"Blue" is useless.

(*c*) Unproved in respect of invariable concomitance (*vyāpyasiddhi*) which occurs when there is a condition attached to the reason, *e.g.*

This hill is full of smoke,
because it is full of fire nourished by wet fuel (which is a condition attached to the reason).

The Incompatible Reason—*Bādhitaḥ*.

An incompatible reason (*bādhitaḥ*) occurs when there is the knowledge that the major term, which is assigned to the minor term, does not really abide in it, *e.g.*

Fire is cold,
because it is a substance.

The incompatible reason, which is of ten kinds, occurs under the following circumstances:—

(1) The minor term being incompatible with perception (*pakṣaḥ pratyakṣa-bādhitaḥ*). *e.g.*

A pot is all-pervading,
because it is existent.

(2) The minor term being incompatible with inference (*pakṣaḥ anumāna-bādhitaḥ*), *e.g.*

A̓n atom has parts,
because it has a shape.

An atom has in fact no shape and no parts.

(3) The minor term being incompatible with verbal testimony (*pakṣaḥ śabda-bādhitaḥ*), *e.g.*

The golden mountain (Meru) is stony.
because it is a mountain.

(4) The minor term being incompatible with perception which establishes the counterpart of the major term (*pakṣaḥ sādhya-pratiyogi-pratyakṣa-bādhitaḥ*) *e.g.*

Fire is non-warm,
because it is a product.

(5) The minor term being incompatible with the inference which establishes the counterpart of the major term (*pakṣaḥ sādhya-pratiyogyanumāna-bādhitaḥ*), *e.g.*

Sound is inaudible,
because it is a quality (of ether).

(6) The minor term being incompatible with comparison which establishes the counterpart of the major term (*pakṣaḥ sādhya-pratiyogyupamāna-bādhitaḥ*), *e.g.*

Bos-gavaeus-ness is not the connotation of the term *bos-gavaeus*,
because it is a general notion.

(7) The minor term being incompatible with the evidence which is analogous to the evidence that establishes the major term *pakṣaḥ sādhya-grāhaka-pramāṇa-jātīya-pramāṇa-viruddhaḥ*), *e.g.*

The skull of a deceased person is pure,
because it is the limb of a being that had life, as a conch-shell.

[The scripture declares a conch-shell to be pure but not the skull of a deceased person.]

(8) The minor term being incompatible with perception which establishes the middle term (*pakṣaḥ hetu-grāhaka-pratyakṣa-bādhitaḥ*). *e.g.*

Water and air are warm,
because they are possessed of touch, unlike that of the earth.

(9) The minor term being incompatible with inference which establishes the middle term (*pakṣaḥ hetu-grāhakānumāna-bādhitaḥ*), *e.g.*

The mind is all-pervading,
because it is a seat of union which is a non-coexistent cause of knowledge.

(10) The minor term being incompatible with verbal testimony which establishes the middle term (*pakṣaḥ hetu-grāhaka-śabda-bādhitaḥ*), *e.g.*

The Rājasūya sacrifice should be celebrated by Brāhmaṇas,
because it is the means of conquering heaven.

[From verbal testimony the Rājasūya sacrifice is ascertained to be a duty of the Kṣatriyas and not of the Brāhmaṇas].

Fallacies are serviceable as they point out Inefficiency—*Hetvābhāsānām-asādhakatā-sādhakatva-nirūpaṇam.*

A fallacy when exposed is a good reply to an opponent, whose argument is thus pointed out to be inefficient. Quibbles and far-fetched analogies are not good replies as they are of no use in this respect. Far-fetched analogies are moreover self-destructive.

Inference of God—*Iśvarānumānam.*

By inference we can prove the existence of God, the Maker of the universe. The inference employed for this purpose is as follows :—

The universe has a maker,
because it is a product, as a pot.

The causes which operate in the case of a product may be stated thus :—

There must be (1) a direct knowledge (perception) by an agent himself of the materials which constitute a product, (2) a desire on the part of the agent to make it, and (3) an act of making it.

For instance, in making a product called a pot there are in the potter, (1) a perception of the pieces that constitute a pot, (2) a desire on his part to make it, and (3) his actual making of it.

Similarly in the case of a product called a binary atomic compound (*dvyaṇuka*) there must be (1) perception by an agent of the atoms which constitute the compound, (2) a desire in him to make it, (3) and his actual making of it. Now atoms are supersensuous, and, as such, cannot be perceived by man. Hence the maker of the binary atomic compound is an agent, who is not man but God.

Book III. Comparison—*Upamāna-khaṇḍa.*

How knowledge is derived through comparison.

A man, who does not know the signification of the word *bos-gavaeus*, hearing from an elder that the word *bos-gavaeus* signifies an animal which is like a cow, goes into a forest where he sees an animal like a cow. Recollecting the instructive assertion of the elder, he institutes a comparison by which he arrives at the conclusion that the animal which he sees is the thing signified by the word *bos-gavaeus*. The means by which this conclusion has been arrived at is called comparison (*upamāna*). This means is the knowledge of likeness between a cow and a bos-gavaeus The word comparison is ordinarily taken to signify the whole process.

The intercourse or operation (*vyāpāra*), in the case of comparison, consists in the recollection of the instructive assertion of the elder, *viz.* that the word *bos-gavaeus* signifies an animal which is like a cow. The result of comparison (*upamiti*) is the knowledge of the relation of a name to something so named.

Likeness explained.

The Mīmāṁsakas maintain that likeness (*sādṛśya*) is a distinct object which is not included in the seven categories of the Vaiśeṣikas. The signification of the word *bos-gavaeus* is, according to them, an animal which possesses likeness to a cow. Gaṅgeśa opposes this view by saying that it is cumbersome. A thing is said to bear likeness to another thing, if it, while possessing the special property of the latter thing, is different from the same in the generic nature. Such being the definition of likeness, we have to admit an infinite number of likenesses corresponding to the thing to which they refer. The real signification of the word *bos-gavaeus*, according to Gaṅgeśa, is not an animal which possesses likeness to a cow but an animal which possesses the generic nature of a bos-gavaeus (that is, which is a type of all *bos-gavaeus*). Hence the result of comparison consists of knowledge of the relation between the word *bos-gavaeus* and the animal which possesses the generic nature of a bos-gavaeus.

Comparison is not perception.

Some say that the knowledge of the signification of the word *bos-gavaeus* is derived through perception. This is absurd. Though the relation between the word *bos-gavaeus* and the animal called bos-gavaeus may be perceived in a particular case with which our eyes are in union, it is impossible for us to perceive such a relation in other cases which are beyond our eyes. Therefore the knowledge of signification of the word *bos-gavaeus* is not derived through perception, but through a separate means of knowledge, called comparison.

Comparison is not inference.

Neither can the knowledge of signification of the word *bos-gavaeus* be derived through inference, inasmuch as in the case of comparison knowledge is derived through the knowledge of likeness, independent of knowledge of invariable concomitance which is indispensable to an inference. Moreover in the case of knowledge derived through comparison there is in us a self-consciousness of the form "I *compare*", but not of the form "I infer."

Book IV. Verbal Testimony—*Śabda-khaṇḍa.*

Definition of Verbal Testimony—*Śabda-nirūpaṇam.*

Speech[1] (*śabda*) is a means of valid knowledge if it is uttered by a person as an outcome of the true knowledge of its meaning. *e.g.* the speech, the *horse runs*, is a means of valid knowledge if it has been uttered by a person who knows its meaning. The means by which or the process through which the valid knowledge is derived is called verbal testimony (*śabda-pramāṇam*). A speech uttered by a person who does not know its meaning may produce knowledge the validity of which is uncertain.

Verbal Knowledge—*Śabda-bodhaḥ.*

Any knowledge derived from a speech is called verbal knowledge (*śabda bodhaḥ*). It is the knowledge of the mutual connection of things signified by words which possess expectancy, consistency, contiguity and potentiality, and convey intention. The process through which verbal knowledge is produced is described as follows:—

In a speech—*ghaṭaḥ asti* (there is a pot)—are to be noted the following:

(i) At first there is the *hearing*[2] *of* (*śabdasya śravaṇam*) *words* in the speech, *viz. ghaṭa* + *ḥ* + *as* + *ti* (there + is + a + pot).

(ii) Then there is the *recollection of things* (*arthasya smaraṇam*) signified by the words, *viz.* the recollection of "pot" signified by the word *ghaṭa*, of "one" signified by *ḥ* (a modification of the first-case-ending *su*), of "existing" signified by *as* and of "the state of abiding" signified by *ti*, (a verbal termination of the third person, singular number, present tense).

(iii) Afterwards there is the knowledge of the *mutual connection of things* thus recollected (*saṁsarga-bodhaḥ*), that is, the knowledge that 'pot' as qualified by oneness is an abode

[1] "Speech" signifies "the knowledge of speech."

[2] The words need not always be actually *heard*, for sometimes we may recollect them from a written statement.

of existence. The knowledge in this third step is specially called a verbal knowledge.

(iv) Lastly there is *self-conciousness* (*anuvyavasāya*) of the knowledge in the following form: "I am the possessor of the knowledge of pot which as qualified by oneness is an abode of existence."

Speech as a means of Valid Knowledge—*Śabda-prāmāṇyavādaḥ*.

(*a*) *Can it be denied that speech is a means of valid knowledge?*

A means, otherwise called an instrument (*karaṇa*), is that cause which, when brought into operation, necessarily produces its effect. Speech is not, according to the Buddhists, such a means, inasmuch as it does not, even when uttered by a person who knows its meaning, produce knowledge, unless it is attended with expectancy, consistency, etc. Therefore "speech is not," say the Buddhists, "a means of valid knowledge."

Speech is indeed a means of valid knowledge, and Gaṅgeśa opposes the above view by asking whence, if the Buddhists do not admit speech to be a means of valid knowledge, they derive the validity of their own speech, *viz.* "speech is not a means of valid knowledge." The verbal testimony being denied, their speech cannot be proved as valid, and as such cannot be advanced against any party. On the contrary if their speech is admitted as valid, they will have to abandon their contention that "speech is not a means of valid knowledge." The contention of the Buddhists is therefore baseless, and speech is indeed a means of valid knowledge. But speech, if it is to be a means of valid knowledge, must not be a bare one: it should be attended with expectancy, consistency, etc.

Speech is mentioned as the means or instrument because it is the main cause in the production of valid knowledge, while expectancy, consistency, etc., are mere attendant causes or conditions. It should be stated here that only one cause without attendant conditions cannot produce any effect.

(*b*) *Is verbal testimony included in perception?*

The Buddhists, while not claiming their speech to be valid, say that it serves at any rate to produce in us a mental perception of the form "speech is not a means of valid knowledge" by causing the recollection of things signified by it. When we hear the speech, *viz.* "speech is not a means of valid knowledge," there arises in us a knowledge (recollection) of the things signified by it, and, through the intercourse whose character is knowledge. we actually perceive the thing in our mind. The function of verbal testimony being thus performed by mental perception, there is no necessity for assuming the former as a distinct means of valid knowledge.

(c) *Verbal testimony is not included in perception.*

Gaṅgeśa holds that speech which is attended with expectancy, etc., and produces recollection of things signified by it, must be accepted as a means of valid knowledge quite distinct from perception. Just as in the perception of a colour our eye is the means or instrument, its union with the colour is the intercourse, and the perceptual knowledge is the result, so in verbal testimony, speech is the means or instrument, the recollection of things signified by it is the intercourse and the verbal knowledge is the result. Speech therefore serves the same purpose in verbal testimony as the sense-organs do in perception, in other words, speech is the means of verbal knowledge, and considering the distinct nature of this means we must admit verbal testimony to be a distinct means of valid knowledge.

(d) *Is verbal testimony included in inference?*

The Vaiśeṣikas maintain that verbal testimony is not a distinct means of valid knowledge but is included in inference. In deriving knowledge from speech we first hear the words constituting the speech and then recollect the things signified by the words. The knowledge of the mutual connection of things thus recollected, which is designated as verbal knowledge, is, according to the Vaiśeṣikas, derived from inference. Suppose one utters a speech thus: "he beat the cow with a stick." On hearing this speech the listener may, say the Vaiśeṣikas, infer as follows :—

(1) The words constituting this speech must have been preceded by knowledge of the mutual connection of things as intended by the speaker and recollected by his words.—*proposition.*

(2) Because they are possessed of expectancy, etc., and convey the intention of the speaker.—*reason.*

(3) The words of all speeches possessing expectancy, etc. and conveying the intention of a speaker are preceded by the knowledge of the mutual connection of things as intended by the speaker and recollected by his words, just as the words of a speech, *viz*, " bring a pot " uttered by me (the listener),—*example.*

If we can thus derive knowledge of the speech by means of inference, there is, according to the Vaiśeṣikas, no necessity for admitting a separate means of knowledge called verbal testimony.

(e) *Verbal knowledge is not included in inference.*

Gaṅgeśa opposes the above view as follows :

The inference as shown above is not valid, inasmuch as it does not involve knowledge (recollection) of actual things as in the case of verbal testimony, but the knowledge of things recollected, *i.e.* the knowledge of knowledge (recollection) of the things. This is not only cumbersome but also fallacious. Our activity in respect of a thing arises from our knowledge of the thing itself, but not from our knowledge of knowledge of the thing, which, as in the case of knowledge of error, may not contain in itself the cause of activity. Moreover, verbal knowledge is not, like inferential knowledge, dependent on the knowledge of invariable concomitance between the words of a speech and knowledge of the mutual connection of things signified by them, but results immediately from the words as soon as expectancy, consistency, etc., existing among them have been known. Again, after verbal knowledge has been produced, there arises self-consciousness of the form "I know from *the speech*" but not of the form "I know through *inference*."

It has already been observed that a speech cannot produce verbal knowledge unless the words composing it possess expectancy, consistency, contiguity and potentiality and convey intention.

Expectancy—*Ākāṅkṣā-vādaḥ.*

A word is said to bear the relation of expectancy (*ākāṅkṣā*) to another word if it cannot without the latter produce knowledge of its interconnection in a speech. For instance. *Devadattaḥ grāmaṁ gacchati* (Devadatta goes to the village) is a speech in which the word *Devadattaḥ* (in the nominative case) is expectant for the word *gacchati* ('goes', the verb), and this latter in its turn is expectant for *grāmaṁ* ('village,' in the objective case). In the same way the crude word *Devadatta* is expectant for *ḥ* (the same as *su,* the first-case-ending), the crude word *grāma* for *am* (the second-case-ending) and *gaṁ* (the root) for *ti* (the verbal suffix). A crude word (*nāma*) and a case-ending (*vibhakti*), a root (*dhātu*) and a verbal suffix (*ākhyāta*), and a verb (*kriyā*) and a case (*kāraka*) are expectant for each other.

Consistency—*Yogyatā.*

Consistency (*yogyatā*) consists in a word not bearing a meaning which is incompatible with the meanings of other words in a speech. For instance, no verbal knowledge is derived from such a speech as *agninā siñca* (sprinkle with fire) because it is incompatible with fire being an instrument in the act of sprinkling. Consistency may be certain or doubtful, but in either case there will be verbal knowledge.

Contiguity—*Āsattiḥ.*

Contiguity (*āsattiḥ*) consists in the enunciation of words, which are connected with each other, without a long pause between them, *e.g.* the speech, *viz.* "bring water", will convey no meaning if one utters the word "bring" now, and the word "water" after an hour.

Intention—*Tātparyam*.

Intention (*tātparyam*), which indicates the wish of a speaker, consists in the utterance of a word to convey knowledge of a special thing. If at the time of eating a meal, one says "bring *saindhava*" we are to understand by the word *saindhava* a quantity of salt and not a horse.

The Non-eternity of Sound—*Śabdānityatā-vādaḥ*.

Sounds (*śabda*) such as *k*, etc., are multifarious, inasmuch as we find that a sound uttered by a man is different from the corresponding sound uttered by a parrot. On the ground that sounds are many, each of which is produced and destroyed, we must admit them to be non-eternal. In fact such an expression as 'the uproar that arose in the market has now ceased' proves beyond a doubt that sound is liable to destruction.

Sound destroyed and not concealed—*Ucchanna-pracchanna-vādaḥ*.

If sounds are destructible, their aggregates, the speeches, must also be so. The Veda, a collection of speeches, is consequently non-eternal. The Mīmāṁsakas say that, though the Veda as a collection of speeches is liable to destruction, as it has come down through succession of teachers, its continuity is uninterrupted. Gaṅgeśa opposes the above view by saying that from allusions occurring in the socio-religious institutes (*smṛti*) and from usages that have prevailed from olden times we can infer that once there existed certain branches of the Vedas which have since disappeared. Therefore the Veda is non-eternal.

The Veda is defined by Gaṅgeśa as a collection of valid speeches which are not the outcome of knowledge of things signified by words, and the things signified by which are not the objects of those kinds of knowledge which are derived from means other than verbal testimony.

Injunction—*Vidhi-vādaḥ*.

The Veda is the foundation of our good customs inasmuch as it is the source of all injunctions. An injunction (*vidhi*) is a speech which produces in a person such conviction as induces him to perform or desist from performing the act signified by the speech, *e.g.* "Let a person, who wishes to go to heaven, perform a horse-sacrifice" is an injunction. "Let not a man drink wine" is another injunction.

According to Kumārila the conviction, which in an ordinary speech represents the purpose of the speaker, and in the case of the Vedic speech (not emanating from any person) the potentiality of the speech itself, consists of an idea of the form: "this speech directs me to perform or to desist from performing the act signified by it."

Prabhākara says that the conviction consists of the belief that merit or demerit that accrues from the act signified by the speech, is capable of being earned by our efforts.

Gaṅgeśa, who is not satisfied with any of the above explanations, maintains that the conviction produced in the person consists of the consciousness (*a*) that the act signified by the speech is capable of being performed by him, (*b*) that the performance of it will fulfil the object of his desire, and (*c*) that no serious inconvenience will accompany the performance.

All logicians agree, however, in holding that the conviction is produced by the potentiality of the hortative particle *liṅ* (corresponding to the English word "let") in the speech itself.

Merit and Demerit—*Apūrva-vādaḥ.*

Prabhākara says that the conviction produced by a Vedic speech, consists first of the belief that the merit or demerit that accrues from the act signified by the speech, is capable of being acquired by our efforts. This belief is followed by the presumption that the act from which merit or demerit accrues, is such as can be performed by us. Gradually there arise two other beliefs, *viz.* (1) that the act, if performed, will fulfil the object of our desire, and (2) that there is no serious inconvenience involved in the act.

Gaṅgeśa opposes the above view by saying that it is cumbersome to assume that so many kinds of belief are produced from a speech to induce us to perform or desist from performing the act signified by it. Let us, for the sake of brevity, assume that the conviction produced by a speech consists merely of the belief that the act signified by the speech is such as can be performed by us. This belief in the theory of Gaṅgeśa includes in it two other beliefs, *viz.* that the act is capable of fulfilling our desire and that there is no serious inconvenience involved in it.

Potentiality—*Śakti-vādaḥ.*

The relation that exists between a word and the thing referred to by it is a special relation[1] called *indication* (*vṛtti*). It

[1] The relation is not an ordinary one, *e.g.* the word (sound) jar does not produce in us the recollection of either although the former abides in the latter in the relation of inherence (*samavāya*).

is on account of this special relation that we are, on hearing the word *pot*, able to recollect the thing known as a pot. This special relation possessed by a word is generally called its *potentiality* (*śakti*). Nice distinctions are however often made in this matter. The special relation is described as being of two kinds, viz. (1) signification (*saṁketa*) and (2) implication (*lakṣaṇā*). The signification is again subdivided into, (*a*) permanent and (*b*) occasional. The permanent signification which a word bears is called specially its *potentiality* (*śakti*). This potentiality, which is the capacity of a word to refer to (*i.e.* produce recollection of) a particular thing, depends upon the will of God manifesting itself in the form: "let such and such a thing be understood by such and such a word." For instance the potentiality of the word *pot* consists in its producing the recollection of an earthen vessel. The occasional signification is called *technicality* (*paribhāṣā*) which depends upon the will of man manifesting itself in the form: "such and such a thing is to be understood by such and such a word." A word is said to be *technical* if it produces recollection of a particular thing as desired by man. For instance *nadī* is a technical word for nouns ending in ī or ū. The distinction between the permanent and occasional significations is overlooked by those logicians who maintain that words derive their signification, or rather potentiality, not from the will of God but from the will of man. There is according to them as much potentiality in an ordinary word as in a technical one. The potentiality of a word is ascertained from the following sources:—

(1) *Grammar* (*vyākaraṇa*), *e.g.* in the sentence: *Caitraḥ pacati* (Caitra cooks). the potentiality of the crude word *Caitra*, the nominative case-ending *ḥ*, the root *pac* and the verbal suffix *ti* is ascertained from grammar.

(2) *Comparison* (*upamāna*), *e.g.* in the sentence: "a bos-gavaeus is like a cow," the potentiality of "bos-gavaeus" is ascertained through comparison.

(3) *Dictionary* (*koṣa*), *e.g.* the potentiality of the word *pika* to refer to the quality of blueness is ascertained from dictionary.

(4) *Reliable assertion* (*āpta-vākya*), *e.g* that the word *pika* signifies a black cuckoo is ascertained from the word of a competent scholar.

(5) *Usage* (*vyavahāra*), *e.g.* on hearing "bring a table," "take away a table," etc., and on seeing the table brought and taken away, one understands the potentiality of the word "table."

(6) *Context* (*vākya-śeṣa*), *e.g.* if in a sentence the meaning of the word *yava* (which may refer to a barley-corn or a panic seed) is not clear, we can ascertain its true meaning (as a barley-corn) by a reference to the remaining sentences in which it is spoken of as having ears.

(7) *Description* (*vivṛti*), *e.g.* when we describe a belligerent nation as a warlike one, we can understand the potentiality of the word "belligerent."

(8) *Association* with well-known words, *e.g.* the potentiality of the word *pika* to refer to a bird is easily understood when the word is associated with some well-known words such as : "in this mango-tree the *pika* sings sweetly."

We have seen that each word possesses the potentiality of producing the recollection of a thing dependent upon the will of God or man. Now the question arises as to whether the potentiality refers to the genus of the thing or to the thing as an individual. If we suppose that the potentiality refers to an individual, we shall have to assume, say the Mīmāṁsakas, an infinite number of potentialities corresponding to the individuals to which they refer. If, on the other hand, we assume that the potentiality refers to a genus, we shall have to assume only one potentiality corresponding to the genus which will also include individuals without which it cannot stand.

Gaṅgeśa opposes the above view by saying that we could not recollect individuals unless the potentiality resided in them. On the supposition of the potentiality referring to an individual, it is not, continues he, necessary to assume an infinite number of potentialities, as one and the same potentiality refers to all the individuals which are comprehended under one genus. Hence, he concludes that the potentiality really refers to the individuals coming under a genus and possessing a form.

Words possessed of potentiality may be specified as follows :—

(1) The *etymological* (*yaugika*) is a word which is understood by the potentiality of its component parts alone, *e.g.* the word *dātā* (giver) refers to the agent of giving.

(2) The *conventional* (*rūḍha*) is a word which is understood by the potentiality of its entirety independently of that of its parts, *e.g.* the word *go* signifies a cow (and not 'the agent of going' which is the meaning of its parts).

(3) The *etymologo-conventional* (*yoga-rūḍha*) is a word which is understood by the potentiality of the whole harmoniously with the potentiality of its parts, *e.g.* the word *paṅkaja* signifies a water-lily, which is born in the mud.

(4) The *etymological-conventional* (*yaugika-rūḍha*) is a word which is understood either by the power of its entirety or by that of its parts, *e.g.* the word *udbhid* signifies a germ, the sprouting of a seed or a sacrifice.

Implication—*Lakṣaṇā.*

By implication (*lakṣaṇā*) a word refers to a thing which is related to another thing which is the signification of the word, but which does not signify the intention of the speaker, *e.g.* the word 'Ganges' in the sentence, 'the cow-keeper dwells on the Ganges,' does not signify the current which is referred to by the potentiality of the word but signifies the bank which bears to the current the relation of proximity. Similarly the word 'crow' in the sentence, 'protect the curd from the crow' signifies by implication any thing that injures the curd.

Compound Words—*Samāsa-vādaḥ.*

In Sanskrit the compound word (*sāmasa*) is of six kinds, *viz.*: (1) an *attributive compound* (*bahuvrīhi*), (2) a *determinative compound* (*tatpuruṣa*) including the negative determinative compound (*nañ-tatpuruṣa*)), (3) a *descriptive compound* (*karmadhāraya*), (4) a *numeral compound* (*dvigu*) including the *unified numeral compound* (*samāhāra*), (5) an *aggregative compound* (*dvandva*) comprising the *mutually aggregative compound* (*itaretara*), the *unified aggregative compound* (*samāhāra*), and the *residual aggregative compound* (*ekaśeṣa*) and (6) an *indeclinable compound* (*avyayībhāva*).

In the attributive compound the first word possesses its fixed potentiality and the second word, which through its potentiality points out a thing, refers also by implication to another thing, *e.g citragum ānaya* (lit. bring the brindled-cow-man) signifies "bring the man having a brindled-cow." The first word *citra* (brindled) refers through its potentiality to the quality of "brindledness" while the second word *go* (cow) besides pointing out, through its potentiality, the thing called "cow" refers also by implication to its owner.

Grammarians maintain that, when two words are combined together to form an attributive compound, the combination possesses the potentiality of referring to a thing which is connected with but lies beyond the things signified by its component words, *e.g. citra-gu* (brindled-cow) refers to "ownership" over and above the quality of being "brindled" and the "cow." Gaṅgeśa holds that in an attributive compound all potentialities lie in the words which are combined together to form the compound, and there is no potentiality in the combination itself.

In the determinative compound the second word possesses its fixed potentiality while in the first word there are both potentiality and implication, *e.g. rāja-puruśaḥ* (a "king-officer", that is, an officer of the king) signifies an officer belonging to the king in which the word *rāja* refers to a "king" as well as to "connection with him."

In the descriptive compound in which the component words stand to each other in the relation of identity, there is no special rule for the possession of potentialities by them, *e.g. nīlotpalam* (blue-lotus). The same is the case with the numeral compound, *e.g. pañca-guvam* (five cows).

In the aggregative compound there is no special rule for the assumption of potentiality or implication by the component words, *e.g. yama-varuṇau* (Yama and Varuṇa).

In an indeclinable compound there are both potentiality and implication in the last word, *e.g. upakumbham* (near the jar).

Verbal Suffixes—*Ākhyāta-vādaḥ*.

A verbal suffix (*ākhyāta—ti, tas, anti*, etc.) used after a root, refers to the effort favourable to what is signified by the root, *e.g. Caitraḥ pacati* (Caitra cooks) signifies that Caitra is possessed of efforts favourable to cooking. If the agent is an inanimate thing the verbal suffix refers by implication to the operation favourable to what is signified by the root, *e.g, ratho gacchati* (a chariot moves) signifies that the chariot is possessed of the operation favourable to moving.

The Roots—*Dhātu vādaḥ*.

The root (*dhātu*) of a verb refers to the operation favourable to the effect of what is signified by the verb, *e.g.* the root *gam* (going) in the sentence, *viz. sa grāmaṁ gacchati* (he goes to the village) refers to moving, which is favourable to his connection with the village, which is the effect of his going. In the case of an intransitive verb the root refers merely to the operation, *e.g. sa tiṣṭhati* (he stays) in which *sthā* signifies merely 'staying.'

Prefixes—*Upasarga-vādaḥ*.

The prefix (*upasarga*) by itself does not bear any meaning but points out the speciality of meaning borne by the root that follows, *e.g. vi* in *vijayate* (completely conquers) signifies a completeness of conquest.

Validity of the Four Means of Knowledge—*Pramāṇa-catuṣṭaya-prāmāṇya-vādaḥ*.

Some say that a gesture (*ceṣṭā*) is a means of valid knowledge. But this is absurd, inasmuch as a gesture merely reminds us of words which produce knowledge. That a deaf person is sometimes prompted to activity by a gesture, must be due to the fact that he infers the desire of the man who makes the gesture. So a gesture is included in either verbal testimony or inference. Similarly tradition (*aitihya*) and rumour (*janaśruti*) are not distinct from verbal testimony while presumption (*arthāpatti*) and non-perception (*anupalabdhi*) are comprised in inference.

CHAPTER III.

COMMENTARIES ON THE TATTVA-CINTĀMAṆI.

42. THE POPULARITY OF TATTVA-CINTĀMAṆI.

The popularity of the Tattva-cintāmaṇi is attested in unmistakeable terms by the numerous commentaries, sub-commentaries and glosses that have grown around the book since its first appearance. The text of the work covers about 300 pages, but its expository treatises extend to ovèr 1,000,000 pages. In the following pages are enumerated some of the important expository treatises, and the accompanying table shows their mutual relationship.

43. THE MITHILĀ SCHOOL.

The Mithilā School of Nyāya flourished from the 12th to the 15th century A.D. The great masters were Gaṅgeśa, Vardhamāna, Pakṣadhara and others. Their style of writing was terse and they discussed the meaning of *vyāpti* more than did their predecessors. In the 16th century Nyāya studies waned in Mithila and made progress in Nadīa. The Principal Naiyāyikas [1] of Mithila School are mentioned below.

44. VARDHAMĀNA UPĀDHYĀYA (1250 A.D.).

Vardhamāna Upādhyāya was the son [2] of Gaṅgeśa Upādhyāya, and surnamed Mahopādhyāya [3] or Mahāmahopadhyāya [4]. He was the author of the following works:—

(1) Tattva-cintāmaṇi-prakāśa, commentary on Tattva-cintāmaṇi.

(2) Nyāya-nibandha-prakāśa, a commentary on Nyāya-vārttika-tātparya-pariśuddhi.

---

[1] *Vide* my *Logic in the University of Nadia* (1907), *Yaśovijaya Gani*, from the Journal and Proceedings of the Asiatic Society of Bengal, No. 9, 1910. Also *History of Navya-nyāya in Bengal and Mithila* by Rai Manmohan Chakravarti Bahadur and Catalogue of Sanskrit Manuscript in Madras Sanskrit College.

[2] Līlāvatī-prakāśa, Ind. Off. Cat., p. 668, No. 2080, verse 2:—

न्यायाम्भोज पतङ्गाय मीमांसापारदृश्वने ।
गङ्गेश्वराय गुरवे पित्रेऽत्रभवते नमः ॥ २ ॥

[3] *Vide* Sarvadarśana-saṁgraha, No. XIII, Pāṇini-darśana.

[4] Jaydeva speaks of Vardhamāna as Mahāmahopādhyāya-caraṇāḥ. *Vide* Tattva-cintāmaṇi, Bibliotheca Indica. 1—6—674.

(3) **Nyāya-pariśiṣṭa-prakāśa**, commentary on Udayanācārya's Nyāya-pariśiṣṭa.
(4) **Prameya-nibandha-prakāśa**, which may be the same as the Prameya-tattva-bodha.
(5) **Kiraṇāvalī-prakāśā.**
(6) **Nyāya-kusumañjalī-prakāśa.**
(7) **Nyāya-līlāvatī-prakāśa.**
(8) **Khaṇḍana-khaṇḍa-prakāśa.**

Vardhamāna Mahopādhyāya is named in the Sarva-darśana-saṁgraha of Mādhavācārya, under No. XIII, Pāṇini-darśana, so he must be older than the second half of the 14th century.[1] He must be older than Jayadeva, who commented on two of his Vaiśeṣika works. Jayadeva's time cannot be later than the third quarter of the 13th century. He speaks of Varddhamāna reverently as *Mahāmahopādhyāya-caraṇāḥ*: and so a fair interval must have elapsed between the two. Vardhamāna's time thus falls probably in the first quarter of the 13th century.

45. PAKṢADHARA MIŚRA (1275 A.D.).

Pakṣadhara Miśra whose early name was Jaydeva was born in Saisava, 16 miles east of Darbhanga, on the Kamalā. His father's name was Mahādeva Miśra and mother's name was Sumitrā. He was a pupil of his uncle Hari Miśra.[2] He was called Pakṣadhara on account of his gaining victory in a debate which he conducted for a fortnight or a pakṣa. With regard to Pakṣadhara it is observed: "Saṅkara and Vāchaspati are comparable to Śiva and Brihaspati, but there was none who could be compared to Pakṣadhara."[3] He was the author of the following works:—

(1) **Tattva-cintāmaṇyāloka.**
(2) **Dravya-padārtha** on the Dravya-kiraṇāvalī-prakāśa.
(3) **Līlāvatī-viveka** on the Līlāvatī-prakāśa.

In spite of his being a logician, he was the author of two charming Sanskrit plays, *viz. Prasanna Rāghava* and *Candrāloka*.[4]

---

[1] According to Rai Manmohan Chakravarti Bahadur he must be older than the second half of the 14th century A.D., *vide* his *History of Navya-nyāya in Bengal* (September 1915), p. 260.

[2] अधीत्य जयदेवेन हरिमिश्रात् पितृव्यतः ।
तत्त्वचिन्तामणेरित्थं व्यालोकोऽयं प्रकाश्यते ॥
(तत्त्वचिन्तामण्यालोक, opening lines).

[3] शङ्करवाचस्पत्योः शङ्करवाचस्पती सदृशौ । पक्षधरः प्रतिपक्षी लक्ष्यीभूतो न च क्वापि ।

[4] येषां कोमलकाव्यकौशलकला लीलावती भारती ।
तेषां कर्कशतर्कवक्रवचनोद्गारेऽपि किं हीयते ॥
(Prasanna Rāghava. Introduction).

Pakṣadhara had two disciples named Vāsudeva Miśra (his nephew), and Rucidatta Miśra. He must be older than *la sam* 1509 [1] the date of copying of his Pratyakṣāloka, which, according to some, corresponds with 1278 A.D. He might be placed in the third quarter of the thirteenth century.[2]

It is traditionally known that Pakṣadhara lived in the court of Raja Bhairava Sinha of Mithilā and was a class-fellow of Vidyāpati. But as Bhairava Sinha lived in 1435 to 1450 A.D., Pakṣadhara, if the tradition be true, must have lived in the middle of the 15th century A.D. He is said to have copied a manuscript of Viṣṇupurāṇa in 1452 A.D.[3]

46. VĀSUDEVA MIŚRA (ABOUT 1275 A.D.).

He was nephew and pupil of Jayadeva Miśra, and he wrote a commentary on the famous Tattva-cintāmaṇi of Gaṅgeśa Upādhyāya, called **Tattva cintāmaṇi-ṭīkā** in order to vindicate the work of his teacher, Jayadeva or Pakṣadhara Miśra.[4] He is called Nyāya-sidhāntā-sārābhijña (versed in the quintessence of logical truth) in the colophon of his work.[5] Being a nephew of Pakṣadhara he probably lived in the fourth quarter of the 13th century.

---

[1] R. Mittra. Notices V. p. 299, No 1976, (प्रत्यक्षालोक). The date is written curiously, and runs thus:—शुभमस्तु शकाब्दा ॥ ल सं १५०९ ॥ तं श्रावणस्य १ ॥ Some think that 1509=159=*la sam* 159+1119=1278 A.D. But I think it probable that 1509= 1509+78=1587 A.D., *la sam* means a year.

[2] It is traditionally known that Pakṣadhara was a contempotary of Vāsudeva Sārvabhauma and Raghunātha Śiromaṇi of Navadvipa: and it is asserted by the Darbhanga Rajas that Maheśa Ṭhakkura, from whom they trace their descent lived in 1556 A.D. during the time of Akbar; and that Śankara Miśra was a disciple of Maheśa Ṭhakkura. But the contrary evidence is equally strong. Rai Manmohan Chakraverti Bahadur fixes the date as given in the manuscripts of Pakṣadhara's Pratyakṣāloka to be Śāka *la sam* 159 or 1278 A.D. and Śaṅkara Miśra's Bhedaprakāśa as copied in Samvat 1519 or 1462 A.D. This date is accepted in this work.

[3] बाणैर्वेदयुतैः शशाङ्कनयनैः ख्याते शके श्रावणे ।
श्रीमद्गौडमहीभृतो गुरुदिने मार्गे च पक्षेऽसिते ॥

(A palm-leaf manuscript of Viṣṇupurāṇa from Mithilā, colophon).

[4] जयदेवगुरोर्वाचि ये केचिद्दोषदर्शिनः ।
प्रबोधाय मया तेषां टीकेयमभिधीयते ।

(Introductory verse).

[5] इति न्यायसिद्धान्तसाराभिज्ञमिश्रवर्य्यपक्षधरमिश्रभ्रातृपुत्रन्यायसिद्धान्तसाराभिज्ञवासुदेव-मिश्रविरचितायां चिन्तामणिटीकायाम्...

(Colophon of Anumānakhaṇḍa).

47. RUCIDATTA MIŚRA (ABOUT 1275 A.D.).

He was a pupil of Pakṣadhara or Jaydeva Miśra.[1] His parents were named Devadatta and Reṇukā and he had two brothers named Śaktidatta and Matidatta.[2] The name of his family is given as Sodarapurakula.[3]

Two of his works are now extant: (1) **Tattva cintāmaṇi-prakāśa**, a commentary on the famous work of Gaṅgeśa Upādhyāya, (2) **Nyāya-kusumāñjali-prakāśa-makaranda**, a commentary on the commentary of Vardhamāna on the Nyāya-kusumāñjalī of Udayanācārya.

A Ms. copy of a portion of his Tattva-cintāmaṇi-prakāsa is said to be as old as 1370 A.D.[4] He had the title Mahāmahopādhyāya added to his name. As a pupil of Pakṣadhara he may be placed in the fourth quarter of the 13th century A.D.

48. BHAGĪRATHA OR MEGHA ṬHAKKURA (ABOUT 1400 A.D.).

He was the second among the three elder brothers of Maheśa Ṭhakkura and he was the author of a commentary, called **Jalada**, on the Kusumāñjalī-prakāsa of Vardhamāna. It is also called **Kusumāñjalī-prakāśa prkāśikā**. Besides this, he prepared two other commentaries on Vardhamāna's work. They are (1) **Kiraṇāvalī-prakāśa-prakāśikā**; (2) **(Nyāya)-līlāvati-prakāśa-vyākhyā**. He seems to have lived about 1400 A.D.

49. MAHEŚA ṬHAKKURA (ABOUT 1400 A.D.).

He was born in Bhaur, 17 miles N.E. of Darbhanga on the Kamalā. He was son of Dhīrā and Candrapati,[5] and younger

---

1 अधीत्य रुचिदत्तेन जयदेवाख्यसद्गुरोः ।
चिन्तामणौ ग्रन्थमणौ प्रकाशोऽयं प्रकाश्यते ॥
(Tattva-cintāmaṇi-prakāśa, Introductory verse 2.)

2 श्रीदेवदत्ततनयो विनयोपगूढः
श्रीरेणुका विरलगर्भपुटोपजातः ।
श्रीशक्तिदत्तमतिदत्तसहोदरो यः
सोऽयं चकार रुचिदत्तकृती प्रकाशम् ॥
(Tattva-cintāmaṇi-prakāsa, Śabda-khaṇḍa, verse 2 at the end.)

3 इति श्रीसोदरपुरकुलसमुद्भूतमहामहोपाध्यायश्रीरुचिदत्तविरचिते तत्त्वचिन्तामणिप्रकाशे......(Colophon of Tattva-cintāmaṇi-prakāsa. Pratyakṣa-khaṇḍa.)

4 See Peterson's Sixth Report, p. 76, No. 190.

5 जनकविषयजन्मा राजसम्मान पात्रं

brother of Mahādeva, Bhagīratha and Dāmodara.[1] He belonged to the Khaṇḍwāl family. He wrote a commentary called **Darpaṇa** on the Āloka of Pakṣadhara Misra on Gangeśa's work, of which only the chapter on perception is extant. He was also the author of several Smṛti works, such as **Tīrtha-cintāmaṇi**.

His work on logic, the Darpaṇa, is held as an authority in Śaṅkara Miśra's Tri-sūtri-nibandha-vyākhyā.[2] He lived between Pakṣadhara and Śaṅkara or between 1270 and 1450 A.D.

One of his pupils, Raghunandanadāsa Rāya, was a great logician, who at the suggestion of Akbar went out to all quarters for discussion. Akbar, being pleased, installed him in the province of Mithilā, which he however made over to Maheśa Ṭhakkura, his teacher as preceptor's fee (गुरुदक्षिणा). So the latter became a landholder and founder of the Darbhanga Raj family.

50. Śaṅkara Miśra (1450 A.D.).

He was born in Sarisava in Darbhanga. He was the son of Bhavanātha Miśra, *alias* Ayācī Dube, who was eager to live on the bank of the Gangeś towards the close of his life, the Ganges being about 40 miles south of Darbhanga forming its southern boundary. He refers to his father's instructions in this introductory verses of several of his work[3]. He was nephew of Jīvanātha and pupil of Raghudeva Upādhyāya or Kaṇāda[4] as of well as Maheśa Ṭhakkura.

मवि...धीरचन्द्रपत्नीतनूजः ।
अवयवदनुमाना लोकमाश्रित्य नित्य-
प्रमथित बलदर्पो दर्पणं श्रीमहेशः ॥
(Anumānāloka-darpaṇa, verse 1 at the end)

ज्येष्ठा महादेवभगीरथदामोदरा यस्य वयोगुणाभ्याम् ।
(स) दर्पणं निर्मितवानमीषां सहोदरो विष्णुपरो महेशः ॥
(Anumānāloka-darpaṇa of Maheśa Ṭhakkura, verse 2 at the end.)

प्रकाशदर्पणोद्योतकल्पिकांश्चा हतोल्मषा ।
तथापि श्रीजगन्नाथमुद्दिश्यायं ममोद्यमः ॥
(Tri-sūtrī-nibandha-vyākhyā, Introductory verse 2.)
Quoted by H. Śāstri, Notices, Vol. III, pp. 68-9, No. 136.

अधीतमथापि ममार्जितं यशो
न शोचनीयं किमपीह भूतले ।
अतःपरं श्रीभवनाथ शर्मणो
मनोमनोवारिधि जाह्नवीतटे ॥
याभ्यां वैशेषिके तन्त्रे सम्यग् व्युत्पादितोऽस्म्यहम् ।
कणादभवनाथाभ्यां ताभ्यां मम नमः सदा ॥
(Vaiśeṣika-Sūtropaskāra, Intro. verse.)

He was a contemporary of Narendrasiṁha Rāya. He was the author of various works on various subjects.

(1) **Paṇḍita-vijaya**, in which he speaks of himself thus :

बालोऽहं जगदानन्दः न मे बाला सरस्वती ।
अपूर्णे पञ्चमे वर्षे वर्णयामि जगत्त्रयम् ॥

(2) **Ātma-tattva-viveka-kalpa-latā**, a commentary on Udayanācārya's polemical treatise.

(3) **Ānanda-vardhana**, a commentary on Śrī Harṣa's Khaṇḍana-khaṇḍa-khādya, which is referred to in Pragalbhācārya's commentary thereon.

(4) **Tattva-cintāmaṇi-mayūkha**, a commentary on Gaṅgeśa's famous work on Nyaya.

(5) **Tri-sūtri-nibhanda-vyākhyā**, a commentary on the commentary of Udayanācārya on the first three sūtras of Gotama.

(6) **Nyāya-līlāvatī-kaṇṭhābharaṇa**, a commentary on the Nyāya-līlāvātī of Vallabhācārya.

(7) **Bheda-prakāśa** or **Bheda-ratna-prakāśa**, a criticism of the non-dualistic Vedānta. It is criticised in its turn in the Saṁkṣepa-śārīraka of Sarvajñātma-muni.

(8) **Gaurī-digambara-prahasana**, a small comedy on the marriage of Śiva and Pārvatī, which was played at the instance of his father.[1]

(9) **Vaiśeṣika-sūtropaskāra**, a popular commentary on the Kaṇāda-sūtras.

(10) **Vedi-vinoda**, contains a discussion on the categories of Nyāya.

(11) **Bauddha-dhikkāra-tīkā**.

(12) **Abheda-dhikkāra**, a refutation of non-dualistic Vedānta.

Besides these, he wrote three important works on smṛti. He lived towards the close of the fifteenth century.

Śaṅkara must be older than 1462 A.D., in which year a MS. of the Bheda-prakāśa was copied. As Guru of the jurist Vardhamāna-Upādhyāya he cannot be much older than this time. He may be placed in the second and third quarters of the fifteenth century.

51. Vācaspati Miśra (The Younger or Junior) (about 1450 A.D.).

He is known as Abhinava Vācaspati Miśra. Though he is more famous as a smṛti-writer, yet he wrotes ten works in philosophy, as he himself has said in his Pitṛ-bhakti-taraṅgiṇī. He flourished in Mithilā about 400 years ago, and was the Pariṣad or court-officer of the kings Bhairavendra and Rāmabhadra (who reigned in the third and fourth quarters of the fifteenth century).

[1] H. Śāstri, Notices, vol III, p. 52, No. 83.

Of the ten works. four at least are traceable :—

(1) **Anumāṇa-khaṇḍa-ṭīka**, a commentary on Gaṅgeśa's famous work, giving the substance of both the Nyāya and the Mīmāṁsā views.
(2) **Khaṇḍana-khaṇḍoddhāra**. It is, as the name implies, a commentary on Śri Harṣa's famous criticism of the Nyāya-sūtras.
(3) **Nyāya-sūtroddhāra**, a gloss on the Nyāya-sūtras.
(4) **Śabda-nirṇaya**, a treatise on the nature of words.

No MS. has yet been found of this last work, but the name is known from his smṛiti work called Dvaita-nirṇaya.

52. Misaru Miśra (about 1475 A.D.).

He is the author of an original treatise on the Vaiśeṣika system, named **Padārtha-candra**. The work deals, as the name implies, with the seven categories. But the actual authorship of this work, like that of his work on smṛti (the **Vivāda-candra**), is attributed to Lachimā Devī, who was the chief queen of Candrasiṁha [1], the younger step-brother of Bhairavasiṁha Deva, So it seems that our author flourished in the third quarter of the 15th century.

It is to be noted here that Misaruka, the author of the Nyāya-dīpaka, is a different person.

53. Durgādatta Miśra (about 1550 A.D).

He wrote the **Nyāya-bodhinī** [2], an elementary work, on the first principles of the Nyāya and Vaiśeṣika systems combined. Though we have as yet no data to fix his exact time, it seems most probable that he flourished in the 16th century.

54. Devanātha Ṭhakkura (1562 A.D.).

He is the author of the **Tattva-cintāmanyāloka-pariśiṣṭa**, which, as the name implies, aimed at supplying the shortcomings of Jayadeva's Āloka on Gaṅgeśa's work. From the date of a copy

---

[1] श्रीचन्द्रसिंहनृपतेर्दयिता लखिमामहादेवी ।
रचयति पदार्थचन्द्रं मिसरुमिश्रोपदेशेन ॥
R. Mitra, Notices, IX, 12, No. 2901, introd. verse 2.

[2] R. Mitra, Notices, V, p. 84, No. 1764 and IX, p. 129, No. 3029: H. Śāstri Notices III, p. 75, No. 116.

of his work (*viz. la saṁvat* 443 or 1562 A.D.)[1] made by his order, it is ascertained that he must have lived in the third quarter of the 16th century.

55. MADHUSŪDANA ṬHAKKURA (1575 A.D.).

He is the author of the **Tattva-cintāmaṇyāloka-kaṇṭakoddhāra**,[2] a refutation of the hostile criticisms of Paksadhara in his Āloka on Gaṅgeśa's work.

His date must fall between that of the younger Vācaspati Miśra on whose Dvāita-nirṇaya he wrote another Kaṇṭakoddhāra and *la saṁvat* 491 or 1610 A.D., the date of a Ms. of his work. Thus roughly speaking, he flourished in the third quarter of the 16th century.

56. THE NADIA SCHOOL (1600—1800 A.D.).

The Nadia School of Nyāya flourished during the 16th, 17th and 18th centuries under the great masters Raghunātha Śiromaṇi, Mathurānāth Tarkavāgiśa, Jagadīśa Tarkālaṅkāra and Gadādhara Bhaṭṭācārya. They explained the Tattva-chintamaṇi of Gaṅgeśa in a critical way.

Before the Navadvīpa Naiyāyikas, the Mithilā Logicians stooped down. Raghunātha Śiromaṇi and others made the language of Nyāya quite stereotyped and made the use of *avacchedaka* and *avacchinna* very extensive. Their pride and abnormal growth of critical faculty put the logicians of all other provinces into the shade. The principal logicians of Nadīa School are mentioned below.

57. VĀSUDEVA SĀRVABHAUMA (ABOUT 1450—1525 A.D.).

Vāsudeva was born at Nadia in the middle of the 15th century A.D. His father, Maheśvara Viśārada, gave him a sound education in Sanskrit grammar, literature and jurisprudence. With a view to prosecuting his studies in Logic (Nyāya), Vāsudeva, while about 25 years old, went to Mithilā, where he was admitted into the academy of Pakṣadhara Miśra, the foremost logician of the place at that time. After finishing his studies in Mithilā he was subjected to a difficult test called Śalaka-parīkṣa, "probe-examination," in the course of which he had to explain any leaf of a manuscript that was pierced last by the probe as it was pushed into the manuscript. One by one he explained one hundred

---

[1] See R. Mitra, Notices, V, p. 84, No. 1704, IX, p. 129, No. 3029. See H. Śāstri, Notices, III, 75, No. 116.

[2] See Śāstri, Notices, III, p. 75, No. 116.

such leaves and his teacher was so much pleased that he conferred on him the title of Sārvabhauma.

Logical works brought to Nadia.

Finding that the Professors of Mithilā did not allow outsiders to copy their works on Logic, Vāsudeva committed to memory the entire Tattva-cintāmaṇi and the metrical portion of the Kusumāñjalī, and, being afraid that his life would be in danger on the way back from Mithilā, he, on the pretext of coming to Nadīa, went secretly to Benares where he studied for some years the Vedānta philosophy returning home at the close of the 15th century A.D.

The first academy of Logic in Nadia.

Having transcribed the above mentioned two works from memory Vāsudeva set up the first great academy of Logic in Nadia, where students flocked in large numbers. He had two distinguished pupils, *viz.* Raghunātha Śiromaṇi, the highest authority on modern Logic, and Chaitanya,[1] the founder of Vaisnavism in Bengal.

In his old age Vāsudeva is said to have accepted the Vaiṣṇava tenets preached by his pupil Caitanya. He passed the closing portion of his life in Orissa, where he was patronised by king Gajapati Pratāpa Rudra about 1520 A.D.[2] He was the author of a work on Logic called Sārvabhauma-nirukti, which is a commentary on Gangeśa.

Though an academy of Logic was thus for the first time opened outside Mithilā and schools of it gradually multiplied in the

---

[1] *Caitanya Caritāmṛta*, Madhya-līla, Chap. VI. Caitanya while beholding Jagannāth at Puri fell down senseless in consequence of his ecstacy. He was taken by Sārvabhauma to his house. He regained consciousness and Sārvabhauma asked him to be a student of Vedānta under him. Caitanya consented. After a course of studies for seven days Caitanya observed that the Vedānta Sūtras like the Upaniṣads were clear to him, but the commentaries of Śaṅkara as explained by Sārvabhauma, eclipsed the Sūtras. A discussion followed and Sārvabhauma became a convert to Vaiṣṇavism.

পূর্ব্বে মহাপ্রভু যবে
চলিলা দক্ষিণে।
প্রতাপরুদ্র রাজা
বোলাইল সার্ব্বভৌমে ॥ Madhya-lila, X.

नौमि तं गौरचन्द्रं
यः कुतर्ककर्कशाशयम् ।
सार्वभौमं सर्व्वभूमा
भक्तिभूमानमाचरत् ॥ *Ib.*, VI, 31.

[2] *Vide* Rajendra Lal Mitra's Notices of Sanskrit MSS., Vols. I–IX, L 2854; Śastri X-XI.

heart of Bengal, all was not gained. It yet remained for the academies of Nadia to acquire a university character and authority. To procure that power for Nadia, it was necessary that a representative from it should vanquish the teachers of Mithilā in philosophical controversy. That honour it was reserved for the genius and patriotic perseverance of Raghunātha Śiromaṇi to win for his country.

58. Raghunātha Śiromaṇi (1477--1547 A.D.).

Raghunātha was born in Nadia about the year 1477 A.D While he was about four years old he lost his father. His mother supported him with the greatest difficulty. When a boy of five years, Raghunātha once at the order of his mother had to fetch fire from the academy. He did not take with him any vessel for carrying the fire. Accordingly when a student in the academy offered him a spoonful of blazing charcoal, Raghunātha instantly picked up a handful of sand on which he asked the charcoal to be placed. Vāsudeva Sārvabhauma, being astonished at his marvellous presence of mind and thinking that some extraordinary work was reserved to be done by him, took up the entire charge of maintaining and educating the boy. While Raghunātha began to learn the consonants he used to ask why *k* should precede *kh*, and his teachers had to explain to him the rules of phonetics and grammar along with the alphabet. After finishing grammar, literature, lexicon and jurisprudence Ragunātha began assiduously to study Logic under Vāsudeva Sārvabhauma and discussed with him the knotty points of that branch of learning. He used sometimes to sit in deep mediation on problems of Logic under banyan trees in the neighbouring field, which he did not quit until his doubts were cleared. Soon he surpassed his teacher in many respects and demonstrated the worthlessness of the latter's commentary on Logic. To exact a charter for the academy of Nadiya to confer degrees, Raghunātha went with the permission of Vāsudeva Sārvabhauma to Mithilā in the disguise of a pupil, and entered the academy of the famous teacher, Pakṣadhara Miśra, who was still alive. Raghunātha who was blind of one eye was ridiculed by the students of the academy: "Indra is thousand-eyed, Siva is three-eyed, all others are two-eyed, verily why art thou one-eyed?"

However, getting admittance into the academy, Raghunātha very soon demonstrated his own worth and was promoted to the highest class. The teacher found him a hard pupil to deal with, and many were the controversies the brilliant pupil carried on with him. Matters soon came to a crisis. One day in the course of a hot and protracted disputation before all the numerous students and doctors, the renowned teacher, foiled and exasperated, insulted his brilliant pupil-polemic with the savagery of a schoolman. Raghunātha's nature rebelled against the treatment he had received—treatment undeserved by him and unworthy of the teacher. Brooding in silence over his wrongs, Raghunātha's proud nature proposed vengeance on his adversary, teacher now no longer. That very night, armed with a drawn sword, he went and hid himself in Pakṣadhara's house. At midnight, thinking the moment opportune, he went up the stairs and looking about descried Pakṣadhara lounging on the terrace with his wife at his side. Raghunātha hesitated in his fell purpose. It was a most glorious night in autumn when the full moon was shining in all her glory. The sky was serene and transparent and all nature was hushed, All were happy save the two unfortunate logicians—one brooding sadly on the imminent loss of his reputation and the other sorely anxious to achieve glory for himself. The young would-be murderer was perplexed for a while but instantly rushed in fury from his hiding place towards the couple. Suddenly he stopped. He was no hardened old sinner. He paused to listen. As the teacher and his wife were gazing at the full moon, the wife admired her beauty and asked her husband saying: "My lord, is there anything as bright as this grand queen of the night?" The teacher replied: "There is one thing, my dear, which is quite as bright, even more so: I was all the evening thinking of such a thing; there has come from Bengal a young logician who has for some time been a difficulty at Mithilā. He has this morning vanquished me by an obstinately conducted argument. His intellect in my opinion is more luminous than the full-moon herself." Raghunātha overheard this conversation. The sword fell from his involuntarily opened palm and he came and fell at the feet of his startled teacher. Pakṣadhara forgave him and embraced him warmly and on the next morning before the entire academy confessed himself beaten by the young Bengali logician. This confession in fact entitled Raghunātha to confer degrees. His triumph took place about the year 1514 A.D., from which the foundation of the university of Nadia is reckoned. On his return he established a college at Nadia.

The above story [1] is traditional only, but some particulars that he was blind of one eye are confirmed by contemporaneous writers.[2]

---

[1] This story about Raghunath Śiromaṇi and Pakṣadhara is widely known in this country. It appeared in "Mookerjee's Magazine," New series, Vol. 1, 1872, kindly lent to me by Babu Sanjib Chandra Sanyal. But depending on the date of manuscripts ascertained from the manuscripts themselves, we find that Raghunath and Pakṣadhara were not contemporaries.

[2] अभाग्यं गौड़देशस्य यत्र काणः शिरोमणिः ।

(Nyāya-khaṇḍana-khādya, leaf 43; ms. in possession of Vijayadharma or Dharmavijaya Sūri.)

Yasovijaya in another place speaks of Raghunātha as follows:—

"The ocean of Logic is hard to approach owing to the uproar of waves of the Dīdhiti-commentary (of Śiromaṇi); yet is not the water of that ocean capable of being drunk by our cloud-like genius?"[1]

Raghunātha must be earlier than 1602 A.D. in which year a manuscript of Kṛṣṇadāsa Sārvabhauma's sub-commentary on his Anumāna-dīdhiti was copied. He must have lived at the close of the 15th century and beginning of the 16th century when Caitanya lived. He died about 1547 A.D. at the age of 70 years.

(1) His foremost work is **Tattva-cintāmaṇi-dīdhiti.** It is a critical commentary on the Tattva-cintāmaṇi of Gaṅgeśa Upādhyāya. In this work Raghunātha calls himself "the crest-gem of logicians" (Tārkika-śiromaṇi). Elsewhere he is called crest-gem (Śiromaṇi). Mss. of this work are found all over India. It was commented upon by many writers, at least a dozen and half, of whom the majority came from provinces outside Bengal.

His other works are:—

(2) **Bauddha-dhikkāra-śiromaṇi** (which is a commentary on the Ātma-tattva-viveka of Udayanāchārya).
(3) **Padārtha-tattva-nirupaṇam** or **Padārtha-khaṇḍa.**
(4) **Kirāṇavalī-prakāśa-dīdhiti.**
(5) **Nyāya-līlāvatī-prakāśa-dīdhiti** (or °**vistārikā**).
(6) **Avacchedakatva-nirukti**, an original treatise.
(7) **Nañvāda**[2]
(8) **Ākhyāta-vāda.**[3]
(9) **Khaṇḍana-khaṇḍa-khādya-dīdhiti.**

59. HARIDĀSA NYĀYALAṄKĀRA BHAṬṬĀCĀRYA (1480—1540 A.D.).

Haridāsa Nyāyālaṅkāra was a pupil of Vāsudeva Sārvabhauma, and therefore lived about 1520 A.D.

Haridāsa Nyāyālaṅkāra must be older than Śaka 1521, or 1599 A.D., in which year a ms. of his Maṇyāloka-ṭippaṇī (*śabda*) was copied. He was the author of the following works:—

(1) **Kusumāñjalī-kārikā-vyākhyā**, a commentary on Udayana'ss Kusumāñjalī verses.

न्यायाम्बुधेर्दीधितिकारयुक्तिकल्लोलकोलाहलदुर्विगाहः ।
तस्यापि पातुं न पयः समर्थः किं नाम धीमत् प्रतिभाम्बुवाहः ॥

[1] (Aṣṭasāhasrī-vivaraṇa, leaf 82, ms. of Vijayadharma Sūri and Indravijaya Sūri.)

[2] Published in the Chowkhamba Series.

[3] Published in the Bibliotheca Indica Series.

(2) **Tattva-cintāmaṇi-prakāśa,** a commentary on Gaṅgeśa's famous work.

(3) **Maṇyāloka-ṭippaṇī** (or °**vyākhyā**), a sub-gloss on Jayadeva's commentary, the **Āloka.**

In the Śaṅkara Maṭha of Puri there is a copy of the second work prepared during 1599, 1600 and 1607 A.D.[1]

60. Jānakīnātha Śarmā (1550 A.D.).

He wrote the **Nyāya-siddhānta-mañjarī,** an elementary treatise on the four kinds of proof. Probably it was composed in 1550 A.D. This work mentions Śivāditya Miśra, Murāri Miśra and Cintāmaṇi. He has been commented upon a dozen times. He is called Bhaṭṭācārya Cūḍāmaṇi or Nyāya-cūḍāmaṇi.

61. Kaṇāda Tarkavāgīśa (about 1560 A.D.).

According to tradition Kaṇāda Tarkavāgīśa and Raghunātha Śiromaṇi were co-pupils of Vāsudeva Sārvabhauma. In the introductory verse of Bhāṣā-ratnam Kaṇāda salutes one Cūḍāmaṇi. Is this Jānakinath Cūḍāmaṇi? In that case Kaṇāda's date falls about 1560 A.D.

Kaṇāda wrote the following works:—

(1) **Maṇi-vyākhyā,**[2] a commentary on Gaṅgeśa's Tattva-cintāmaṇi.

(2) **Bhāṣā-ratnam,** on the seven Categories of the Vaiśeṣika system.

(3) **Āpa-śabda-khaṇḍanam,** another Vaiśeṣika work.[3]

62. Rāmakṛṣṇa Bhaṭṭācārya Cakravarti (about 1560 A.D.).

Hall says that he was the son of Raghunātha Śiromaṇi. He himself calls Śiromaṇi his Guru[4] or preceptor. He must be older

---

1 शाके त्रियुग्मविशिखक्षणदाधिनाथे
कन्दर्परायपदवीक इदं लिलेख ।
(Quoted in Navadvīpa-mahimā).

2 For the Maṇi-vyākhyā, see R. Mittra, Notices IV, p. 167, Sans. Coll. Cat. III, p. 327, No. 582 (Śaka 1705); and H. Śāstri, Notices V, p. 13, No. 14. For the Bhāṣā-ratna, see R. Mittra, Notices IV, p. 119, No. 1531, intro. verse 1:—

चूडामणिपदाम्भोजभ्रमरीभूतमौलिना ।
संचिन्त्य श्रीकणादेन भाषारत्नं वितन्यते ॥ १ ॥

For No. 3, See Peterson's Sixth Report, p. 74, No. 773.

3 For some traditionary account of Kaṇāda, see H. Shāstri's Introduction to his Notices, Vol. I, p. xviii.

4 Ind. Off. Cat. No. 2068, introd. verse 2;

than 1603 A.D., the date of a manuscript of his Guṇa-Śiromaṇi-prakāśa. He in all probability flourished in 1560 A.D. He was the author of **Guṇa-śiromaṇi-prakāśikā**[1] and possibly also of **Nyāya-dīpikā.**

63. MATHURĀNĀTHA TARKAVĀGĪŚA. (ABOUT 1570 A.D.).

Mathurānātha Tarkavāgīśa lived about 1570 A.D.[2] His father, Sri Rāma Tarkālaṅkāra[3], was a pupil of Raghunātha Śiromaṇi. Mathuranātha, who was a pupil of Sri Rāma Tarkālaṅkāra as well as of Raghunātha Śiromaṇi, wrote numerous valuable commentaries on Logic which are known under the general name of Māthurī. They are very lucid and easy, and for this reason are not much appreciated by the scholars of Nadia. He was the author of the following works :—

(1) **Tattva-cintāmaṇi rahasya.**[4] This work is familiarly known in Bengal as **Phakkikā** or **Māthurī**.
(2) **Tattvacintāmaṇy āloka-rahasya**, a sub-commentary on Jayadeva's Āloka.
(3) **Dīdhiti rahasya.**
(4) **Siddhānta-rahasya.**
(5) **Kiraṇāvali-prakāśa-rahasya**, a sub-commentary on Vardhamāna's work.
(6) **Nyāya-līlāvatī-prakāśa-rahasya**, a sub-commentary on Vardhamāna's **Prakāśa.**
(7) **Nyāya-līlāvatī-prakāśa-dīdhiti-rahasya.**
(8) **Bauddha-dhikkāra-rahasya.**
(9) **Ayur-daya-bāvanā.**
(10) (?) **ādi-kriya-viveka.**

Mathurānātha mentions Sundara Upādhyāya and Harinātha Upādhyāya, but nothing is known about these.

(?) यन्मूलमेव सुकृतानि तयोः कृतानि
व्यासादयः कवय नित्यमुदाचरन्ति ।
तज्ञाश्रयं गुणविवेचनमाकलय्य
ब्रूवे शिरोमणिगुरोरिव रामकृष्णः ॥ १ ॥

1 Ind. Off. Cat., No. 2069.

2 *Vide* Notices of Sanskrit Mss. in Bengal, 2nd series, Vol. I, p. xvi.

3 The beginning of the Tattva-cintāmaṇi-rahasya runs thus :—

न्यायाम्बुधिकृतावेतुं सेतुं श्रीराममणिसम्मतेः ।
तातं त्रिभुवनगीतं तर्कालङ्कारमादराद्वन्दे ॥ १ ॥
श्रीमता मथुरानाथ तर्कवागीश धीमता ।
विमृश्यैतत्व दर्श्यन्ते प्रत्यक्षमणिपङ्क्तिका ॥ २ ॥

4 This work has been published in the Bibliotheca Indica Series.

64. Kṛṣṇadāsa Sārvabhauma Bhaṭṭācārya (about 1575 A.D.).

Kṛṣṇadāsa Sārvabhauma was older than 1602 A.D., when the manuscript of his *Anumāna-dīdhiti-prasāriṇī*[1] was composed. As the note differs in reading the dīdhiti he must be considerably later than Raghunātha Śiromaṇi. Roughly speaking, he flourished in 1575 A.D. He was the author of the following works :—

(1) **Tattva-cintāmaṇi-dīdhiti-prasāriṇī**, a sub-commentary on Raghunātha's commentary.
(2) **Anumānāloka-prasāriṇī**, a sub-commentary on Jayadeva's Āloka (Anumāna-khaṇḍa).

65. Guṇānanda Vidyāvāgīśa (about 1570 A.D.).

He has been criticized by the Jaina logician, Yasovijaya Gani[2] (1608—1688 A.D.), in his Nyāya-khaṇḍana-khādya. Guṇānanda must be older than 1622 A.D., in which year a manuscript of his Gunavivṛti-viveka was copied. He was considerably later than Raghunātha Śiromaṇi whose works he commented on, and he may be placed roughly at about 1570 A.D. He was the author of the following works :—

(1) **Anumāna-dīdhiti-viveka.**
(2) **Ātma-tattva-viveka-dīdhiti ṭīkā.**
(3) **Guṇa-vivṛti-viveka.**
(4) **Nyāya-kusumāñjalī-viveka.**[3]
(5) **Nyāya-līlāvatī-prakāśa-dīdhiti-viveka.**
(6) **Śabdāloka-viveka.**

66. Rāmabhadra Sārvabhauma (about 1680 A.D.).

Rāmabhadra Sārvabhauma, son of Bhavanātha and Bhavānī praises his father's teachings as better than those contained in

---

[1] This work is being printed in the Bib. Ind. Series ; for No. 2 see p. 8 :—

विचारस्तु अनुमानालोकप्रसारिण्यामनुसन्धेयः ।

[2] Guṇānanda is mentioned by Yasovijya in his Nyāya-khaṇḍa-khādya, leaves 2, 11, 56, 70, 80. Satis Chandra Vidyabhuṣana's *Yasovijaya Gani* (1910,) p. 468.

[3] He was the author of Nyāya-kusumāñjalī-viveka, which begins :—

नमः कर्म्माधिष्ठात्रे वेदप्रामाण्यहेतवे
निरस्ताखिलबाधाय प्रमात्रे विश्वकर्म्मणे ॥
गुणानन्देन विदुषा विचार्य्य प्रतिपादितं
विविच्यन्ते प्रयत्नेन कुसुमाञ्जलिकारिकाः ॥

the Prakāśa and the Makaranda.[1] From his famous *tol* were produced such learned scholars as Jayarāma Nyāya-pañcānana and Jagadīśā Tarkālaṅkāra. He is older than 1613 A.D.[2], when, a manuscript of his Padārtha-tattva-vivecana-prakāśa was copied. He was later than Raghunātha. He probably flourished in 1680 A.D. He was the author of the following works:—

(1) **Dīdhiti-ṭīkā.**
(2) **Nyāya-rahasya.**
(3) **Guṇa-rahasya.**
(4) **Nyāya-kusumāñjali-kārikā-vyākhyā.**
(5) **Padārtha-viveka-prakāśa,** a commentary on Raghunātha Śiromaṇi's Padārtha-khaṇḍana.
(6) **Sat-cakra-krama-dīpikā.**

67. Jagadīśa Tarkālaṅkāra (about 1625 A.D.).

Jagadīśa Tarkalaṅkāra was the fourth in descent from Sanātana Miśra, the father-in-law of the famous Caitanya. As Caitanya was born in 1485 A.D., Sanātana must have lived about the same time. Allowing 30 years for each generation, we find that Jagadīśa was born about 1605 A.D. The date of his literary activity may be approximately fixed at about 1635 A.D. This date agrees well with the fact that a work of his named Kāvya-prakāśa-rahasya was copied by a pupil of his in Śaka 1599 or 1657 A.D.

Jagadīśa was a naughty boy in his early years. At the age of 18 years he began to learn the alphabet under an ascetic. Thereupon he entered the academy of Bhavānanda Siddhāntavāgīśa, where he finished his studies in Logic. Jāgadīśa Tarkālaṅkāra calls himself the pupil of a Sārvabhauma,[3] who should be identified with Rāmabhadra Sārvabhauma, as Jagadīśa quotes his Nyāya-rahasya with the remark that it was his Guru's.[4] Jagadīśa

---

1 The Kusumāñjali-vyākhyā, Sans. Coll. Ms. Cat. III. 318, intro. verses and 3:—

भवानीभवनाथाभ्यां पितृभ्यां प्रथमामहं ।
यत्प्रसादादिदं शास्त्रं करस्थौरोपमं क्षमम् ॥ २ ॥
मकरन्दप्रकाशे या व्याख्या मच्छिमतोऽथवा ।
ततोऽधिका पितुर्व्याख्यामाश्रित्य गुणसुन्दरम्: ॥ ३ ॥

2 Sans. Coll. Cat., III, p. 241, No. 399, final colophon.

इति श्रीरामभद्र सार्व्वभौमकृतपदार्थतत्त्वविवेचनप्रकाशः समाप्तः ॥
संवत् १६७० समये आश्विनमासकृष्णदशम्यां लिखितमिदं पुस्तकं परोपकारार्थम् ॥

3 The Maṇi-mayūkha, Sans. Coll. Cat., III, p. 324, No. 575, intro. verse 2:

सार्व्वभौमस्य गुरोः पदाब्जं विद्यार्थिनामाय कल्पतरोः प्रणम्य ।
विनिर्मितं श्रीजगदीशविप्रैर्विद्योत नामाद्य मणेर्मयूखः ॥ २ ॥

4 For his Guru's work, see the Śabda-śakti-prakāśikā, Cal. ed., p. 25 :—

इति गुरुन्यायरहस्ये चक्रवर्तिचरणाः ।

Tarkālaṅkāra was older than 1631 A.D., the date of a copy of his manuscript of Tarkāmṛta. As he was a pupil of Rāmabhadra Sārvabhauma, his date falls about 1625 A.D.

He was the author of the following works :—

(1) **Tattva-cintāmaṇi-dīdhiti-prakāśikā**, familiarly known as **Jāgidīśī**.[1]

(2) **Tattva-cintāmaṇi-mayūkha**, a commentary directly on Gaṅgeśa's works, of which only portions have survived.

(3) **Nyāyādarśa** or **Nyāya-sārāvalī**, dealing with the doctrine of causality.

(4) **Śabdaśakti-prakāśikā** on the force of words, etc., a grammatico-philosophical treatise.[2]

(5) **Tarkāmṛta.**

(6) **Dravya-bhāṣya-ṭīkā** or **Padārtha-tattva-nirṇaya.**

(7) **Nyāya-līlāvatī-dīdhiti-vyākhyā.**

68. Śabda-śakti-prakāśikā (Elucidation of the power of words).

In illustration of Jagadīśa's style of argument, I give below an English translation of the first five couplets of the Śabda-śakti-prakāśikā. This will give some idea of the *śabda*, verbal knowledge, as explained by Jagadīśa :—

Verbal Knowledge (*śabda-bodha*).

1. The Śabda-śakti-prakāśikā, delighting the learned, is composed by Jagadīśa, who was versed in debate as well as in the dogmas.

2. The goddess Sarasvatī who is gracious and approaches all persons and is able to fulfil their ends, makes herself manifest immediately, when she is worshipped.

or,

Words, which possess the three requisites of mutual interdependence, juxtaposition and compatibility in their signification, become at once a means of knowledge to any man who hears them.[3]

3. Knowledge of the mutual connection of things signified by correspondent words is neither perception nor inference, being limited in its scope.

4. Word or verbal testimony is the knowledge of the mutual connection of things signified (presented) by correspondent words. This knowledge is neither perception nor inference, for, in the case of

---

[1] Published in the Chowkhamba series.

[2] Printed in Calcutta (Saka 1769) and in Benares; later (1918) by the Calcutta University.

[3] This verse is capable of this double meaning.

perception, knowledge of things is derived through the contact of sense and in the case of inference through consideration (recognition of sign). Such is not the case here. Here arises the knowledge only of those things which are signified by corresponding words.

In the case of verbal testimony there is (1) the hearing of words, then (2) there is the recollection of things signified by the words, *e.g. ghato'sti*. Here from *ghaṭa* +*su*+*as*+*ti*, there is recollection of *ghaṭa* a pot, *su* one, *as* existing and *ti* abode; (3) there is knowledge of the mutual connection of the four things thus recollected, i.e. *ghaṭa* (pot) as the abode of oneness and existence. This is verbal knowledge, testimony or word.

Then there is mental perception (*anuvyavasāya*) of the knowledge thus: I am the possessor of the verbal knowledge of *ghaṭa*, as an abode of oneness and existence.

Some may say that verbal knowledge is simply the recollection of things signified by words. This is impossible, for there cannot be any recollection of the mutual connection of things if there was no perception of the mutual connection of those things. Hence it is necessary to admit an extra means of knowledge, namely, "verbal knowledge."

Verbal knowledge is not inference; compatibility pertains to things, whereas correspondence pertains to words. These two combined together do not abide in any one thing, and cannot therefore be the cause (sign) in an inference. Each one of these separately too cannot be the cause, for compatibility can abide in non-correspondent words where there is no verbal knowledge. Correspondence does not abide in things at all and cannot therefore be the cause in an inference.

There is a cow: hearing this expression we may, according to a modern Vaiśeṣika, make the following inference:—

The Vaiśeṣika position.

A cow is existent, because it is recollected by words conducive to the knowledge of the mutual connection between itself and existence, just like a pot.

Or we may say: A cow is existent because it is recollected by the word *go* connected with existence, just as an eye.

If we can thus draw knowledge of the expression by means of inference, what is the necessity for admitting a separate means of knowledge named verbal testimony?

Naiyāyika's reply.

In verbal testimony the recollection of things signified by words is the cause (sign), but not the knowledge of things recollected by words. In inference the knowledge of sign is the cause. Therefore, where we have such knowledge as "the word *cow* is not the thing of which I am reminded by the word *cow* connected with the word *existence*," we can draw (from the expression *there is a cow*) verbal knowledge but *not* inference, because there is no knowledge of the sign (middle term, reminding us of the connection of *cow* and *existence*) in the abode.

That is, where we have no previous knowledge of a cow as connected with existence, we can on hearing, "there is a cow", draw verbal knowledge, but not inference, because the knowledge of a cow as connected with existence is not recollected by me, not having seen *cow* and *existence* together previously. Therefore verbal testimony is a means of knowledge different from inference.

Inference cannot serve the purpose of verbal knowledge so far as mental perception of the knowledge (अनुव्यवसाय) is concerned. *There is a cow:* by this expression we first draw knowledge of the mutual connection of *cow* and *existence* (in the form: *a cow exists*), and then we have mental perception of the knowledge as: I hear that a cow exists. If you say that this form of mental perception is wrong and that verbal knowledge is really included in inference, I may say, as there is no fixed rule, that inference is included in verbal knowledge. Just as you incorporate verbal knowledge in inference by contriving a general proposition on the recollection of things through words, I shall include inference too in verbal knowledge by postulating correspondence between words recollected by things.

Objection.

In an inference where the thing signified by the major term is unfamiliar, knowledge of the general proposition (major premise) is derived by means of a heterogeneous example, *e.g.* "the lake has not smoke because it has not fire." This inference is carried on by a heterogeneous example, thus: "whatever has smoke has fire, as a hill." Here the knowledge of the major term, *viz.* the thing signified by "no smoke" (absence of smoke) did not exist before the inference was drawn, hence there was no knowledge of the word "no smoke" (absence of smoke) as also there was no knowledge of the thing of which it was a sign. Consequently the knowledge derived from the expression, "the lake has not smoke because it has not fire", is not drawn through verbal testimony but through inference. Therefore inference is to be admitted as a separate means of knowledge.

Reply 1.

It is true there was no knowledge of the thing signified by the major term, but the *word* of which the thing was a sign could be recollected by means of an association. Hence there is no necessity for admitting inference as a separate source of knowledge.

Reply 2.

All verbal testimony cannot be included in inference. The expression "being different from a *pot*" affords the verbal knowledge (testimony) of the form: "possessing distinction as counterpart of a pot.'

This knowledge cannot be drawn from inference, for inference cannot take place where there is no minor term, as here. Hence it is necessary to admit a separate means of knowledge named verbal testimony.

If you say that the knowledge can be drawn from inference thus: the distinction is counterpart of a pot as it is recollected by another word correspondent with the same distinction. This is absurd, for the inference merely affords knowledge of distinction which is counterpart of the pot, but not of the thing which possesses the distinction. But, if you admit a separate means of knowledge named verbal testimony, then the peculiar knowledge of the expression can be easily drawn from correspondence, etc.

Objection.

"Being different from a pot": here *different* may, by a secondary application (अनुव्यवसाय), refer to anything other than a pot, *i.e.*, non-pot. As a single word cannot afford any verbal knowledge, we may form connection with any other word, such as a "cloth." Consequently now we can make the inference of this form: "a cloth is non-pot."

Reply.

If you say so, statements arrive at absurdity, *e.g.* if the word "different" itself could afford the knowledge of "non-pot," the words "from a pot" would be useless. Similarly, if in the expression "there is (exists) a pot," a pot itself, by a secondary application, could afford the knowledge of "an existing pot," the word "is" (exists) would be useless.

Opinion of the Mīmāṁsakas.

Consciousness that it is the assertion of a competent person, is the cause of verbal knowledge. Knowledge of an expression is based on the belief that the expression is that of a competent person. On hearing the expression "there is a pot"—a listenor can derive verbal knowledge only if he is conscious that it is the expression of a competent person, otherwise not; or, in other words, the consciousness that a certain expression is that of a competent person precedes verbal knowledge. Now if the conclusion (*viz.*, that there is a pot) thus precedes verbal knowledge and there is no desire for drawing an inference, there cannot be any. Consequently it is to be admitted that verbal knowledge is a separate means of knowledge. Also that verbal knowledge is not right knowledge, for right knowledge concerns itself with things which are unknown, but not with things which are known to the competent person. Therefore verbal knowledge is not right knowledge.

Objection.

If right knowledge does not concern itself with things already known, then in the case of a series of perceptions right knowledge cannot abide in the series beginning with the second perception. For the thing already known by the first perception is the object of knowledge at the second perception.

Reply.

Right knowledge which concerns itself with things unknown is the correct knowledge which is different from that which is produced after knowledge of the same form in a series.

In the case of a series of perceptions, the series beginning with the second perception was produced no doubt after the first perception, but the first perception did not follow any. Therefore the first as well as the following perceptions are right knowledge. This rejects recollection as right knowledge, for all recollection takes place after a previous perception. Then verbal knowledge is also not right knowledge, for that succeeds a knowledge of the same form or kind, *viz.* the consciousness that it is the assertion of a competent person.

5. The belief that something has been asserted by a competent person cannot be the cause of verbal knowledge, because it depends on the meaning of a sentence. The meaning of a sentence remains really unknown before verbal knowledge occurs. And verbal knowledge occurs even when there is doubt as to whether a certain assertion is that of a competent person. If the cause of verbal knowledge was the belief that something was the assertion of a competent person who was aware of the meaning of a sentence as signifying connection of one thing with another thing, then verbal knowledge could not be inference as the knowledge of the conclusion preceded the same. In fact it is not necessary that the knowledge of the meaning of a sentence should precede verbal knowledge. Otherwise the Vedic text which is a competent assertion would be a mere reiteration, not being a source of right knowledge because it would indicate what was already known. Therefore the belief in the assertion of a competent person is not the cause of verbal knowledge.

Objection.

The belief, *viz.* it is the assertion of a competent person, is the cause of verbal knowledge which is derived from human speech, but not of that verbal knowledge which is derived from the Vedic text. Then the Veda will not be devoid of authority.

Answer.

It is cumbrous to suppose that consciousness of the assertion of a competent person is the cause in one place but not in the other. This difference of hypothesis is unnecessary. The belief that it is the assertion of a competent person is not the cause of verbal knowledge, because that knowledge takes place even where there is doubt of the connection of one thing with another or where there is doubt that a certain expression is the assertion of a competent person.

Objection.

In verbal knowledge, even if the assertion of a competent person is not the cause, context must be admitted to be the cause. Otherwise the word *ghaṭa* would have afforded the verbal knowledge, *viz.*, "an object connected with *ghaṭa*", even though we had not the belief that it was pronounced with the desire of expressing the same. Hence we must admit that, in ascertaining the meaning of expression *ghaṭa*, we must have knowledge of the context (intention) of the *form*: "it was pronounced, with the intention of expressing an object specified as *ghaṭa*.' Hence verbal knowledge is not inference, because the true meaning of the expression is contained in the context, and so conclusion precedes the so-called inference, which is absurd.

Answer.

Even if knowledge of the context was the cause of verbal knowledge, the true meaning of the expression (*viz.*, one thing as connected or qualified by another thing) is not contained in the former when there is the knowledge, *viz.*, the word *ghaṭa* is not pronounced with the desire of expressing an object specified as *ghaṭa*, even if there be verbal knowledge of *ghaṭa* (*viz.*, an object specified as *ghaṭa*); because there is knowledge of context of the form, it is pronounced with the desire of expressing an object specified as "knowable." But this does not take place; wherefore knowledge of context of the form: "it is pronounced with the desire of expressing an object specified as *ghaṭa*" must be admitted as the cause of the verbal knowledge of an object specified as *ghaṭa*. Now, the true meaning is not contained in the knowledge of the context. Therefore there is no harm in admitting an inference beyond verbal knowledge.

The word *saindhava* in the expression "bring *saindhava*" would indicate salt and not a horse if the expression is used at the hour of meal. Hence the cause of such verbal knowledge is admitted to be the knowledge of context of the form: "This word *saindhava* has been pronounced with the desire of indicating salt." That knowledge of context arises from knowledge of the particular occasion, such as that of meal, etc. Therefore in regard to verbal knowledge we may take knowledge of the occasion as the cause but not an extra cause named knowledge of context. If you say that knowledge of occasion is not comprehensive, hence knowledge of context should be adopted as being comprehensive, it would also be absurd, for knowledge of context too is non-comprehensive.

Suppose the belief: "it is pronounced with the desire of expressing an object called *ghaṭa*", exists elsewhere in the word *ghaṭam*, but not in the word which is heard now; or there exists in it the belief: "it is not pronounced with the desire of expressing an object called *ghaṭa*"; and suppose the belief, "it is," exists in the word *ghaṭam* which existed at another time, but not in the one which exists now, in such cases there is no verbal knowledge. Therefore each expression must be taken as indicating an object called *ghaṭa* which exists at the time of the expression. Hence owing to the expressions being different on different occasions, knowledge of context becomes different. Therefore we may rather admit knowledge of occasion as the cause, but not knowledge of context.

Refutation of Prabhākara.

Knowledge of context must be admitted as the cause of verbal knowledge, because where there is uncertainty or absence of knowledge of context there is no verbal knowledge. Moreover knowledge of context is the regulator of the knowledge of one meaning where a word admits of different meanings, and is the establisher of secondary meaning.

Therefore if knowledge of context is the cause of verbal knowledge, then the meaning of an expression having already been contained in the context, the conclusion is presupposed there. Therefore verbal knowledge is not inference. Though verbal knowledge is different from inference, it is not right knowledge because there is no "knowing what was unknown."

Naiyāyikas' reply.

Knowledge of context is not the cause of verbal knowledge. A poet uses a word in one sense, while a thoughtful person may take it in a different sense, though the poet had no knowledge of context in that sense. A parrot which has no knowledge of context utters words which produce verbal knowledge in us.

In the complete 'set' the author has said that verbal knowledge is produced by correspondent words. But it should be added that verbal knowledge arises from significant corresponding words. Now he gives the definition and division of significant words.

A certain word is significant in a certain sense, if that word with the association of another word produces verbal knowledge of the thing which is presented by its own power or by the power of its marks. Significant words are of three kinds: crude word, suffix and indeclinable. In the expression *paṭaḥ* (पटः), the word (पट) *paṭa* in association with the suffix *su* (सु) produces verbal knowledge of the form पटः (cloth) as possessing oneness, *i.e.* one piece of cloth.

69. Rudra Nyāyavācaspati.

Rudra Nyāyavācaspati was son of Vidyānivāsa Bhaṭṭācārya and grandson of Vidyāvācaspati [1] who had been honoured by the

[1] Vidyāvāchaspati is named as a smṛtic writer in Raghunandana's Durgotsava tattva.

king of Gauḍa. Viśvanāthā Siddhāntapañcanana was his younger brother, and Govinda Bhaṭṭācārya Cakravarti was his son. By order of his father, Vidyānivāsa, copies of the *Kalpa-taru*, the smṛtic digest of Lakṣmīdhara (Naiyatakālika and Dāna-khaṇḍas) were copied in Śaka 1510 or 1588 A.D. His time is further fixed by the poem composed in honour of Bhāvasiṁha, whose father, Mānasiṁha, was governor of Bengal, from the 38th to the 50th year of Akbar's reign or from 1593 to 1605 A.D. Rudra must therefore have lived at the beginning of the 17th century. Rudra Nyāyavācaspati should be distinguished from Rāmarudra Tarkavāgīśa, grandson of Bhavānanda Siddhāntavāgīśa whose philosophical treatise is often called *Raudrī*. Rudra Nyāyavāchaspati was the author of the following works :—

(1) **Tattva-cintāmaṇi-dīdhiti-parīkṣā.**
(2) **Kiraṇāvali-prakāśa-vivṛti-parīkṣā.**
(3) **Padārtha-khaṇḍana-vyākhyā.**
(4) **Bhāva-vilāsa,** a poem in praise of the prince Bhāvasiṁha, a son of Mānasiṁha, the Rājput Governor of Bihar and Bengal.
(5) **Bhramara-dūtam.**
(6) **Vṛndāvana-vinoda-kāvya.**

70. JAYARĀMA NYĀYAPAÑCĀNANA (ABOUT 1700 A.D.).

Jayarāma was a pupil of Rāmabhadra Sārvābhauma[1]. His title Nyāyapañcānana is sometimes shortened into Pañcānana.

Jayarāma, with Devanātha Tarkapañcānana, is mentioned as an authority in the rhetorical Eka-ṣaṣṭhyalaṅkāra-prakāśa, and in the Alaṅkāra-sāra-sthiti of Bhīmasena Dīkṣita[2], composed in Saṁvat 1712 during the rule of Ajitasiṁha in Jodhpur. He is older than 1659 A.D., the year in which the Padārthāmālā was composed. As pupil of Rāmabhadra Sārvabhauma, he lived about 1700 A.D.

He was patronised by Rājā Rāmkṛṣṇa of Krishnagar who obtained from the Pandits of Nadia the hereditary title of Nava-

---

1 The Anumāna-dīdihiti-gudhārtha-vidyotana (Ind. Off. Cat., p. 620, No. 7900, and Peterson's Sixth Report, p. 15) introd. verse :—

श्रीविश्वेशमशेषमङ्गलसुखं भूयोऽभिवन्द्यादरात्
बुद्ध्याधाय च रामभद्रचरणद्वन्द्वारविन्दद्वयम् ।
गूढाज्ञानघनावृतामविषयप्रौढोधिनौ दीधितिम्
तस्याः श्रीजयराम एष तनुते गूढार्थविद्योतनम् ॥ १ ॥

2 Madras Catalogue, No. 43037, introd. verse 2 :—

भक्तिनं भक्तिवात्सल्याद्या या [illegible] ।
मरणं जयरामगुरोश्चरणं स्मरणस्य सन्निधीकरणम् ।

dvīpādhipati (Lord of Nadia). Jayarāma's Nyāya-siddhānta-mālā was composed in Saṁvat 1750 or 1693 A.D.

He was the author of the following works:—

(1) **Tattva-cintāmaṇi-dīdhiti-gūḍhārtha-vidyotana,** a sub-commentary on Śiromaṇi's Dīdhiti.

(2) **Tattva-cintāmaṇyāloka-viveka,** a sub-commentary on Jayadeva's Āloka.

(3) **Nyāya-siddhānta-mālā,** a commentary on sūtras 4 to 7 of Gotama's Nyāya-sūtra.

(4) **Sabdārtha-mālā,** on śabda or words.

And in Vaiśeṣika—

(5) **Guṇa-dīdhiti-vivṛti,** a sub-sub-commentary on the Dīdhiti, the sub-commentary of Varddhamāna's commentary on Udayanācārya's Kiraṇāvalī.

(6) **Nyāya-kusumāñjalī-kārikā-vyākhyā,** a commentary on Udayanācārya's Kārikās or verses.

(7) **Padārtha-maṇi-mālā,** or **Padārtha-māla,** an original treatise examining the Vaiśeṣika categories. It was the best known of his works and was commented upon by Janārdana Vyāsa and Laugākṣi Bhāskara.

And in rhetoric:—

(8) **Kāvya-prakāśā-tilaka,** a philosophical commentary on the rhetorical work of Mammata.

71. Gaurīkānta Sārvabhauma (about 1725 A.D.).

Gaurīkānta Sārvabhauma was born in the northern part of Gaur[1] and got favours from the king for composing many nibandhas. He was older than 1714 A.D., the date of a manuscript of his Ānanda-laharī-tarī. He was later than Tāntrika Pūrṇānanda whose Shyama Rahasya is quoted in the said Tari and who wrote the Śākta-krama in 1571 A.D. Gaurīkānta must have flourished in the first quarter of the 17th century A.D. He was the author of the following works:—

(1) **Bhāvārtha-dīpikā,** a commentary on the Tarkabhāṣā of Keśava Miśra.

(2) **Sad-yukti-muktāvalī.**

---

[1] The Ānanda-laharī-tarī (R. Mitra, Notices VII, p. 245, No. 2490), endorse and colophon:—

यो नानाविधशास्त्रतर्कनिपुणश्चक्रे निबन्धान् बहून्
पूजां भूरिमहीभुजां सदसि यो लेभेऽतिधीमान् कविः ।
यो गौड़ोत्तरदेशदिग्गज इव श्री सार्व्वभौमो महान्
भट्टाचार्य्य इमां स एष विदधे टीकां मुदे वाग्विदां ॥ १ ॥

(3) **Ānanda-laharī-tarī.**
(4) **Vidagdha-mukha-maṇḍana-viṭikā.**

72. Bhavānanda Siddhāntavāgīśa (about 1625 A.D.).

Bhavānanda, as a preceptor of Rāghavendra, must be a generation older than the latter. Rāghavendra was a contemporary of Kṛpārāma favoured by the Delhi Emperors Jehāngīr and Shâhjehân. Bhavānanda must have lived in the first quarter of the 17th century. He was the author of the following works :—

(1) **Tattva-cintāmaṇi-dīdhiti-prakāśikā,** familiarly known as **Bhavānandī.**
(2) **Pratyak-āloka-sāra-mañjarī.**
(3) **Tattva-cintamaṇi-ṭīkā.**
(4) **Kāraka-vivecana.**

73. Harirāma Tarkavāgīśa (about 1625 A.D.).

Harirāma Tarkavāgīśa is sometimes called Tarkālaṅkāra, Tarkālaṅkāra-vāgīśa and Nyāyalaṅkāra-tarkavāgīśa. He was the teacher of Raghudeva Nyāyalaṅkāra and of Gadādhara Bhaṭṭācārya. He must be older than 1654 A.D., the date of a manuscript of his Vāda-buddhi-vicāra, a section of his Tattvā-cintāmaṇī-ṭīkā. As a teacher of Raghudeva, he might be placed in the first quarter of the seventeenth century. He was the author of the following works :—

(1) **Tattva-cintāmaṇi-ṭīkā-vicāra.**
(2) **Ācārya-mata-rahasya-vicāra.**
(3) **Ratna-koṣa-vicāra** or **vāda** as it is sometimes named.
(4) **Sva-prākāṣa-rahasya-vicāra** or **Bhaṭṭa-mata-siddhānta-vicāra.**

74. Viśvanātha Siddhāntapañcānana (about 1634 A.D.).

Viśvanātha was the son of Vidyānivāsa Bhaṭṭācārya and a younger brother of Rudra Nyāyavācaspati Bhattācārya. He composed his Bhāṣāpariccheda in 1634 A.D. He was the writer of the following works :—

(1) **Alaṅkārā-pariṣkāra.**
(2) **Nañ-vāda-ṭīkā.**
(3) **Nyāya-sūtra-vṛtti.**[1]

---

[1] Published under the authority of the General Committee of Public Instruction, Bengal.

(4) **Suvartha-tattvāloka** or **Kāraka-cakra.**
(5) **Nyāya-tantra-bodhinī** or **Nyāya-bodhinī.**
(6) **Padārtha-tattvāloka** a commentery on Raghunātha's Padārtha-khaṇḍana.
(7) **Bhāṣā-pariccheda.**[1]
(8) **Pingala prakāśa.**[2]

75. RĀMABHADRA SIDDHĀNTAVĀGĪŚA (ABOUT 1660 A.D.).

Rāmabhadra Siddhāntavāgīśa was a grandson of Jagadīśa Tarkālaṅkāra and was the author of a commentary called Subodhinī on the Sabda-śakti-prakāśikā of the latter. As Jagadīśa lived about 1635 A.D., his grandson Rāmabhadra flourished approximately about 1660 A.D. He calls himself Navadvīpīya [3] on a resident of Navadvīpa.

76. GOVINDA NYĀYAVĀGĪŚA (ABOUT 1650 A.D.).

Govinda Nyāyavāgīśa was a descendant of Vāsudeva Sārvabhauma and was the senior logician of his time. He was patronised by Rājā Rāghava of the town of Revi which was afterwards called Krishnagar. Rājā Rāghava dug a tank at Dignagara in 1669 A.D. Govinda calls himself son of Nyāyavācaspati [4] who is no other than Rudra Nyāyavācaspati. Roughly. he lived in 1650 A.D. He was the author of the following works:—

(1) **Nyāya-saṁkṣepa.**
(2) **Padārtha-khaṇḍana-vyākhyā.**
(3) Possibly **Samāsa-vāda.**

---

1 J.A.S.B., 1910, p. 313. M. M. Shastri's article on Bhāṣā-pariccheda Published in the Bibliotheca Indica Series of Calcutta.

2 In the Pingala-prakāśa Viśvanātha says :—

विद्यानिवाससूनोः कृतिरेषा विश्वनाथस्य ।

3 Sans. Coll. Cat., III, p. 226, No. 461, introd. verse 2 :—

गिरिमिव गुरुमिह नत्वा तत्कृतशब्दशक्तिप्रकाशिकायाः ।
श्रीरामभद्रकृती कुरुते टीकां मुदे सुधीयः ॥ २ ॥

and the final colophon :—इति नवद्वीपीय महामहोपाध्याय श्रीरामभद्रसिद्धान्त[-वागीश- in R. Mittra, No. 794] भट्टाचार्य विरचिता शब्दशक्तिप्रकाशिकासुबोधिनी समाप्ता ।

4 The Nyāya-saṁkṣepa (Ind. Off. Cat., p. 644, No. 1893), intro. verse 3 :—

न्यायवाचस्पतेः सूनोरियं गोविन्दशर्मणः ।
कृतिः कृतधियां भूयादमन्दानन्ददायिनी ॥

77. RAGHUDEVA NYĀYALAṄKĀRA (ABOUT 1650 A.D.).

Raghudeva was a disciple of Harirāma Tarkavāgīśa.[1] Raghudeva is older than 676 A.D., the date in which Anumiti-parāmarśa-vāda was copied. He is older than Yaśovijaya Gaṇi (1608-1688 A.D.) who quotes him in his Aṣṭa-sāhasrī-vīvaraṇa.[2] He probably flourished in 1650 A.D. He was the author of the following works :—

(1) **Tattva-cintāmaṇi-gudhārtha-dīpikā.**
(2) **Navīna-nirmāṇa.**
(3) **Dīdhiti-ṭīkā.**
(4) **Nyāya-kusumāñjali-kārikā-vyākhyā.**
(5) **Dravya-sāra-saṅgraha.**
(6) **Padārtha-khaṇḍana-vyākhyā.**

78. GADĀDHARA BHAṬṬĀCHĀRYA (ABOUT 1650 A.D.).

Gadādhara, whose father was Jīvācārya, was born in the middle of the 17th century A.D. in the district Lakshmipasa, Bogra, in Eastern Bengal. He came to Nadia and became a pupil of the famous logician Harirāma Tarkavāgīśa. On the death of the teacher, Gadādhara became the head of his academy. But the students in Nadia did not at first accept him as their teacher as he was a man of Eastern Bengal and did not belong to a family of hereditary Pandits. Gadādhara left the academy and established a new college on a public street, where he also set up a garden of flowers. As soon as any student came to collect flowers from the garden, Gadādhara used to deliver lectures on logic, addressing a tree there. Charmed with his exposition of the knotty points of logic, young men came and secretly enrolled themselves as his pupils. Soon after this he composed an excellent gloss on the Dīdhiti of Raghunātha Śiromaṇi which made his fame spread far and wide, and he was recognized as the chief logician of his time. Gadādhara has been called " the prince of Indian Schoolmen ", with whom modern Logic reached its climax. He was such a thoroughgoing logician that when asked on his death-bed to think of the prime cause of the Universe instead of thinking on God he is said to have repeated the words " atoms, atoms, atoms." He wrote numerous commentaries on Logic which are known under the general name of Gadādharī.

---

1 The Nañ-vāda-vyākhyā (Madras Catalogue, No. 4254) introd. verse, 1 :—

शिवं प्रणम्य तत् पश्चात् तर्कवागीश्वरं गुरुम् ।
क्रियते रघुदेवेन नञ्वादे सुविवेचनम् ॥ १ ॥

2 J.A.S.B., 1910, p. 468. Satis Chandra Vidyabhushana's article on Yasovijaya Gaṇi.

Gadādhara Bhaṭṭācarya must be older than 1625 A.D.,[1] the date of a manuscript of his Vyutpatti-vāda. His Śaktī-vāda was commented upon by a pupil of Jayarāma. He probably flourished in 1650 A.D. He is a resident of Navadvīpa and is often called Gauḍa-deśiya.

His collected works are called Gadādharī and are spread all over India, especially Southern India. He was the author of the following chief works :—

(1) **Tattva-cintāmaṇi-dīdhiti-prakāśikā.**
(2) **Tattva-cintāmaṇi-vyākhyā.**
(3) **Tattva-cintāmanyāloka-ṭīkā.**
(4) **Muktāvalī-ṭīkā.**
(5) **Ratna-koṣa-vāda-rahasya.**

Gadādhara Bhaṭṭacārya's other works are :—

(6) **Anumānā-cintāmaṇi-dīdhiti-ṭīkā.**
(7) **Ākhyāta-vāda.**
(8) **Kāraka-vāda.**
(9) **Nañ-vāda.**[2]
(10) **Prāmāṇya-vāda-dīdhī-ṭika.**.[3]
(11) **Buddhi-vāda.**
(12) **Muktī-vāda.**
(13) **Vidhi-vāda.**
(14) **Viś-ayatā-vāda.**
(15) **Vyutpatti-vāda.**
(16) **Śakti-vāda.**[4]
(17) **Smṛti-saṁskāra-vāda.**
(18) **Śabda-prāmānya-vāda-rahasya.**[5]

79. Nṛsiṁha Pañchānana (about 1675 A.D.).

Nṛsiṁha Pañchānana Bhaṭṭācārya was older than 1673 A.D. when his Bhūṣā was composed. He probably lived about 1675 A.D. He wrote **Nyāya-siddhānta-mañjarī-bhūṣā** a commentary on Jānakīnātha's work. He praises highly one Govinda[6] perhaps son of Rudra.

---

1 Gadādhara, lived in the time of Rāghava Rāy, grandson of Bhavānanda Rāy of Nadia Rāj, who built the Dighi of Dignaga, in Śaka 1591 (1669 A.D.) and also granted land in Śaka 1553.

2 Published in the Bibliotheca Indica series.

3 Published in the Śāstra Muktāvalī series of Kanci.

4 Published at Benares.

5 Published in the Śāstra Muktāvalī series of Kanci.

6 The Nyāya-siddhānta-mañjarī-bhūṣā, introd. verse 2 (Ind. Off. Cat., p. 641, No. 1976) :—

श्रीमच्छ्रीयुत गोवर्धनमखण्डबोधिप्रभावात् यत्कीर्त्तिता-

यत्कार्य्यं कृतिनः परं सुकृतिनो गोविन्दनामाभिधाः ।

80. Rāmdeva Cirañjīva (about 1700 A.D.).

Râmdeva who is generally known as Cirañjīva must be older than 1703 A.D., when his Kāvya-vilāsa was composed. He is generally believed to have lived about 1700 A.D. He was the author of the following works:—

(1) Vidvānāmoda-taraṅgiṇī.
(2) Kāvya-vilāsa.
(3) Mādhava-campu.
(4) Vṛtta-ratnāvalī.

81. Rāmarudra Tarkavāgīśa (about 1700 A.D.).

Ramrudra, or simply Rudra, was the grandson of Bhavānanda Siddhântavāgīṣa and son of Śrī Rāma or Rāmeśvara. He was probably a pupil of Madhusūdana. He probably lived about 1700 A.D. He was the author of the following works:—

(1) Tattva-cintāmaṇī-dīdhiti-ṭīkā,
(2) Vyutaptti-vāda-vyākhyā.
(3) Kārakādyartha-nirṇaya-ṭīkā.
(4) Dinakarya-prakāśa-taraṅgiṇī.
(5) Tattva-saṅgraha-dīpikā-ṭippaṇī.
(6) Siddhānta-muktāvalī-tīkā.

82. Śrī Kṛṣṇa Nyāyālaṅkāra (about 1650 A.D.).

Śrī Kṛṣṇa Nyāyālaṅkāra was a son of Govinda Nyāyavāgīśa and author of the Bhāva-dīpikā, a commentary on the Nyāya-siddhānta-mañjarī.

83. Jayarāma Tarkālañkāra (about 1700 A.D.).

Jayarāma Tarkālaṅkāra was born in the district of Pabna in Eastern Bengal. His father was a court pandit at Putia. He was a pupil of Gadādhara and wrote a commentary on the Śaktivāda in the year 1700 A.D.

तत्सनुर्मेधिर एष सुकृती भावं तु पञ्चाननो
बालानां चिरकांक्षया स्फुरयति श्रीमन्मायभिधान्विते ॥

And the final colophon: संवत् १०६० ज्येष्ठ वदि ४ ग्रन्थे समाप्तोऽयं पुस्तकः ॥

84. Rudrarāma (about 1750 A.D.).

Rudrarāma was a son of Bhavānanda Siddhāntavāgīśa and therefore lived about 1725 A.D. He was the author of :—

(1) **Vāda-pariccheda.**
(2) **Kāraka-vyūha.**
(3) **Citta-rūpa.**
(4) **Adhikaraṇa-candrikā.**
(5) **Vaiśeṣika-śāstrīya-padārtha-nirūpaṇa.**

85. "Buno"[1] Rāmanātha (about 1780 A.D.).

At the close of the 18th century there were two scholars in Nadia who both bore the name of Rāmanātha Tarkasiddhānta—one was versed in Logic and the other in Jurisprudence. The logician, who had his school in a wood on the outskirts of the town, was called *Buno* (wild) Rāmanātha in contradistinction to the jurist, who lived at the centre of the town.

Buno Rāmanātha was a pupil of Rāma Nārāyaṇa Tarkapañcānana. He was a man of extraordinary genius, but has left no work behind him. His circumstances were very poor, yet he did not seek help from any body. He had sometimes to live on boiled tamarind leaves only.

Once Mahārāja Śiva Chandra of Krishnagar, wishing to patronise him, came to Nadia and asked him ; " Are you in any difficulty ? " Buno Rāmanātha replied "No, thanks ; I have repeatedly gone through the Tattvacintāmaṇi but have met with no difficulty." Then the Mahārāja said ; " I did not enquire of any difficulty of yours in Logic, but I desire to know whether you have any pecuniary wants." The reply again was : " No, thanks."

86. Kṛṣṇa Kānta Vidyāvāgīśa (about 1780 A.D.).

He was a pupil of Rāma Nārāyana Tarkapañcānana and was equally versed in Logic and Jurisprudence. He wrote the following works :—

(1) **Nyāya-ratnāvalī.**
(2) **Dāyabhāga-ṭīka.**
(3) **Gopāla-līlāmṛta.**
(4) **Caitanya-candrāmṛta.**
(5) **Kāminī-kāma-kautuka.**

---

[1] *Buno* is the Bengali colloquial equivalent for Sanskrit *vanya* signifying "wild."

(6) Upamāna-cintāmaṇi-ṭikā.
(7) Śabda-sakti-prakāśikā-ṭīkā.

He flourished during the time of Maharajā Giriśa Chandra of Krishnagar. He was too conscious of his genius. On his death-bed when he found that his end was drawing nigh, he said :—

"Let many stars shine in the sky, let lamps too spread their lustre in every house, let the little fireflies glitter from quarters to quarters; alas! the sun having set, what things do not shine before people!" [1]

87. Rājacūḍāmaṇimakhin.

Writers of Navya Nyāya have spread all over the country. In Madras Rājacūḍāmaṇimakhin [2] who was a minister in the Court of Raghunātha Nāyaka of Tanjore, wrote a Tattva cintāmaṇi-darpaṇa in 1630 A.D.

88. Dharmarājādhvarin.

Dharmarājādhvarin, a native of Kaṇḍaramāṇīkkam, wrote a commentary on the Tattva-cintāmaṇī-prakāśa of Rucidatta.[3]

89. Gopīnātha Mauni.
(about 1650 A.D.).

He wrote Śabdāloka-rahasya, Tarkabhāṣā-ṭīkā, and Padārtha-viveka-ṭikā. He was a Maratha and lived in Benares during the time of Raja Jai Singh. He calls himself Lord of the Lily of Logic.[4]

---

1 अधिगगनमनेकास्तारका दीप्तिभाजः
प्रतिसदनमपि दीपा दर्शयन्तु प्रभुत्वम् ।
दिशि दिशि विलसन्तु क्षुद्रखद्योतपोताः
सवितरि परिभूते किन्न लोकैर्विलोकि ॥

2 अधीत्य निखिलं शास्त्रमप्पआदीक्षितेरहिनः ॥
राजचूडामणिमखी कुरुते मणिदर्पणम् ॥
तत्र कण्डरमाणिक्यग्रामरत्नमिवाश्रिता ।
मणिप्रकाशविवृतिर्धर्मराजेन तन्यते ॥
दृष्टानामपि टीकानां भङ्गं कुर्वन् क्वचित् क्वचित् ।
अनुमानप्रकाशस्य विवृतिं करवाण्यहम् ॥

4 Śabdālōka begins thus :—
समाप्तिमस्मिन् गहने प्रबन्धे परं परित्राणकरः प्रयासः ।
तथाप्यमन्ये मम चापलेऽस्मिन् सेवा ममाद्यम्बजनमम्बिकायाः ॥
उपदिष्टं पितृचरणैः स्वयमपि निर्दिष्टमितं यत्नैः ।
शब्दालोकरहस्यं गोपीनाथो विवेचयति ॥

90. KṚṢṆA BHAṬṬA ĀḌE.

Kṛṣṇa Bhaṭṭa Āḍe was a Maratha, who wrote a gloss on Gadādharī called Gadādharī-karṣikā[1] and one on Śiromaṇi's Tattvacintāmaṇi while residing at Benares, where he died about 150 years ago. The gloss has been printed in Telegu characters.

91. MAHĀDEVA PUNTAMKAR (ABOUT 1790 A.D.).

He was a Maratha resident in Poona and flourished about 125 years ago, during time of the end of the Peshawas (1795 A.D.) He wrote glosses on Bhavānandi-ṭīkā.[2]

---

and ends :—

पितुर्ज्ञानपदेर्वाञ्छामत्र व्याचख्यातवानहं

तत्र भ्रमापि मयाचावित्ति त्याज्या मनीषिभिः ॥

इति श्री महामहोपाध्याय न्यायकुमुदिनीपति श्रीगोपीनाथविरचितं शब्दालोकरहस्यं समाप्तं ॥

The MS., which is in Benares College, dated Saṁvat 1750, ends वन्दीदेव्यै नमः। विश्वेश्वराय नमः। अन्नपूर्णायै नमः।

Gopinātha was also the author of पदार्थविवेक टीका which begins :—

अभेद भावनोद्रेकादभेदं देहगोचरं

विभ्रतौ दम्पती कौचित् वाञ्छितार्थप्रदौ स्तुमः ॥

ends :—

राज्ञःश्रीजयसिंहस्य निदेशाद्वैरि संज्ञके।

सिद्धान्ततत्त्वसर्वस्वं गोपीनाथो विनिर्मिमे ॥

इति श्रीगोपीनाथ मौनिनः कृतौ पदार्थविवेकटीकायां द्रव्यपदार्थः।

[1] Kṛṣṇa Bhaṭṭa's Gadādharī-karṣikā begins thus :—

श्रीकृष्णं मुकुन्दरामस्य कृष्णो नारायणानुजः

गदाधरमतार्थानां टिप्पणीं तनुतेऽद्भुताम् ॥

राङ्गनाथो हृद्यशर्मा पण्डितेभ्यः कृताञ्जलिः

याचते भूय आत्मस्य दूष्यं बुद्ध्वा वचो मम ॥

[2] In one of the opening lines he states as follows :—

नत्वा पदाम्भोज युगं शिवस्य

स्मृत्वा गुरोर्वाचिकयुक्तिजातम् ।

कृत्वातिगूढार्थविभावनं च

व्याख्यायते वाग्भिरपक्षमत्र ॥

ends :—

श्रीमत् पुण्यस्तम्भोपनामकमुकुन्दपण्डितात्मजमहादेवपण्डितविरचिते भवानन्दीप्रकाशे उपाधिवादः समाप्तः ॥ गुर्जरोपनामककेशवपण्डितात्मजवासुदेवपण्डितस्य सत्यमिदं पुस्तकम् ॥

92. RAGHUNĀTHA ŚĀSTRI (PARVATA) (ABOUT 1815 A.D.).

He was a Maratha, who wrote a gloss on Gadādharī-pañcavāda [1] while residing at Poona about 70 years ago.

---

[1] व्याप्तिपञ्चकं, पक्षता, अवयव, सामान्य निरुक्ति।

CHAPTER IV.

Present state of the Science of dialectics.

(1700—1900 A.D.).

93. Patronage of the Maharaja of Nadia.

Nadia is still the best centre where students from all parts of India come to study Nyāya, for it represents the best traditions of Nyāya at the present time. Towards the end of the seventeenth century Mahārāja Rāmakṛṣṇa Rāya of Nadia, having granted valuable landed properties to the Pandits, specially the Nyāya Pandits of Nadia, enlisted their sympathy and was styled Navadvīpādhipatī, overlord of Navadvīpa.

Mahārāja Kṛṣnacandra Rāya of Nadia (1728—1782) was the last land-holder to encourage Pandits with monetary help. His council-room was adorned by Harirāma Tarkasiddhānta and Kṛṣṇānanda Vācaspati of Navadvīpa, Vaneśvara Vidyālaṅkāra of Guptipārā, Jagannātha Tarkapañcānana of Triveṇī and Rādhāmohana Goswami of Śāntīpura. There lived in the time of his son, Mahārāja Sivacandra Rāya (1782—1788) such famous Pandits as Śaṅkara Tarkavāgīśa and others. Māhāraja Iśvaracandra Rāya (1788—1802), Mahārāja Giriśacandra Rāya (1802-1842), and the Mahārājas of Burdwan and Nātore, gave a little encouragement, but it was not adequate.

94. The Portuguese take an interest in dialectics.

The Jesuit missionaries, who lived in India in the seventeenth and eighteenth centuries, took a great interest in Sanskrit and much valuable information is available from the accounts which they have left. The Portuguese Jesuits, while sending manuscripts from Pondicherry and Chandernagore to the King's Library at Paris, remark in 1732, that most of the manuscripts were collected from Navadvīpa. One missionary says: "The founder of the Nyāya School, which means disputation, is a famous Brāhmaṇa called Gautama." "Whatever research I made," says he, "I could not get his principles or aphorisms. I have obtained a commentary on them, which we have sent. The Nyāya School is the only one in vogue in the kingdom of Bengal, and it is for this reason that a large number of books by the authors of this sect are sent."

The missionary goes on to observe :—

"Gaṅgeśa is very famous: he is the author of the Cintāmaṇi, the name of which has clung to him. It is a book containing the whole of dialecties, according to Gotama's sentiments. Gaṅgeśa's dialectics have caused people to forget all the other parts of philosophy and to neglect the best authors, who are almost unknown since the decadence of letters under the Mogols." [1]

Father Pons remarks:—

"The School of Nyāya (reason or judgment) has surpassed all the others in Logic, especially from the time, some centuries back, that the Academy of Nadia, in Bengal, became the most celebrated of India, thanks to its famous Professors, whose works have spread in every direction.... Nowadays they teach in the Nyāya schools hardly anything else besides Logic, which the Brāhmaṇas have stuffed with an endless number of questions, a great deal more subtle than useful. It is a chaos of minutiæ, as Logic was in Europe about two centuries ago. The students spend several years in studying a thousand varieties of subtleties on the members of the syllogism, the causes, the negations, the genera, the species etc. They dispute stubbornly on suchlike trifles and go away without having acquired any other knowledge. The Nyāya has in consequence been given the name of *Tarkaśhāstram*." [2]

Anquetil Du Perron, who had known Father Mosac at Chandernagore since 1756, says that Father Mosac learnt Sanskrit at Nadia University and that his translation of the four Vedas, specially the Yajur Veda forms a part of his vast and learned collections.[3]

At the time the Portuguese searched for the books, the following works of Nyāya were prevalent in Bengal:—

(1) **Kusumañjāli,** of Udayana.
(2) **Commentary** on **Kusumāṇjali** by Vardhamāna.
(3) **Dravya-kiraṇāvalī** of Udayana.
(4) **Commentary on Dravya-kiraṇāvalī** by Vardhamāna.
(5) **Guṇa-kiraṇāvalī** of Udayana.
(6) **Commentary** on **Guṇa-kiraṇāvalī** by Vardhamāna.
(7) **Commentary** on **Gotama-sūtra** of Vacaspati.
(8) **Līlāvātī with Commentary.**
(9) **Vādārtha** in one volume comprising (i) **Devatā-vāda,** on the nature of the gods; (ii) **Mukti-vāda,** on salvation; (iii) **Prāgabhāva,** on future contingent things; (iv) **Visiṣṭha-**

---

[1] Written on the 16th January, 1732.

[2] Letter of Father Pons, missionary of the Society of Jesus, to Father Du Holde, of the same Society at Carical on the coast of Tanjour, in the East Indies, the 23rd of November, 1740 (translated by Father H. Hosten).

[3] Mosac died at Pondicherry, 4th December, 1779, aged 75, a humble, able and deeply learned missionary, he was little communicative though very conciliating. See Anquetil Du Perron. *Mem. de l' Ann. des Inscriptions et Belleslettres*, XLIX, p. 685. Anquetil Du Perron, *Zend Avesta*, I, pt. 1, p. xxxviii, Paris, 1771, translated by Father H. Hosten.

vaiśiṣṭha-vāda, on the qualities; (v) **Vidhi-vāda,** true meaning of laws, etc.

(10) **Bauddhādhikāra** of Raghunātha Śiromaṇi in the volume of Kusumāñjalī.

(11) **Vādārtha-khaṇḍana** showing that there is no other cause but God.

(12) **Ākhyāta-vāda** of Mathuranātha, on some points of grammar.

(13) **Apūrva-vāda,** on fate.

(14) **Śakti-vāda,** on power.

(15) **Siddhānta-muktāvalī.**

(16) **Cintāmaṇī** by **Gaṅgesa.**

(17) **Pratyakṣa and Aunumāna-khaṇḍa** by **Raghunātha.**

(18) **Commentary on Pratyakṣa and Anumāna-khaṇḍa** of Mathu-rānātha.

(19) **Mathurānātha on Vidhi-vāda.**

(20) **Bhavānanda on Anumāna.**

(21) **Bhavānanda on Śabda.**

(22) **Gadādhara the Master on the Pratyakṣa of Śiromaṇī.**

(23) **Gadādhara the Master on Anumāna of Śiromaṇi.**

(24) **Some special works of Gadādhara the Master.**

(25) **Jagadīśā on Anumāna of Śiromaṇī.**[1]

96. British Government encourages Nyāya.

India came into the possession of British in 1757 A.D. Since then the students of Navadvīpa have received grants from the British Raj. In the year 1829 this was stopped, but was again restored in 1830 by the Governor-General in Council at the request of H. H. Wilson, the great orientalist.[2]

---

[1] The manuscripts were bought by Jesuit missionaries of Pondicherry and Chandernagore for the library of the King of France. These were sent to Paris on the 16th and 24th January, 1732. They are also mentioned in Abbe Jourdain's Journal. The accounts about sending these have been translated by Father H. Hosten through whose kindness I got access to the account and lists of books.

[2] The correspondence quoted below shows how great was the work done at a nominal expense. At present Bengal Government spends 28,000 Rupees annually for Sanskrit Ṭols. In every Province including Benares, pecuniary aid is being given to Ṭols:—

THE SECRETARY OF THE BOARD OF REVENUE IN CALCUTTA.

The humble petition of Sib Chandra Siromoni and other students belonging to the Nuddea Sanskrit College.

RESPECTFULLY SHEWETH,

That your petitioners from the establishment of the College of Nuddea, they always received Sicca Rupees one hundred from the late zemindar Rajah Kissen Chunder Bahadoor, and during his zemindary being disposed off, your petitioners even obtained their said allowance from the Sirkar of the Honourable Company, but which being stopped from the month of June last, your petitioners had presented a petition before his Excellency the Governor-General in Council, and whereupon it was ordered that your petitioners must submit their representation through the Collector to the Board and then to the Government. Your poor petitioners in conformity of the said order, represented their case before the Collector at Nuddea and who has been pleased to report on the subject on the 27th

The Government is spending lots of money for the maintainance of the chairs of Nyāya in the Sanskrit College, Calcutta, at

day August 1829 has before the Commissioner W. Money of the Moorshidabad Division and who also being kindly pleased to report on the subject before your Board. Your petitioners do not know what they have stated within, but they your petitioners now confidently trust on the generousity of your Boardship.

As your petitioners hold the respective documents of obtaining their said allowance from the Sirkar of the Honourable Company and accordingly which they have even received without any molestation thereof.

Your petitioners therefore now most humbly pray, that your honour will be so kindly pleased as to take this your petitioners deplorable case into your worship's kind and merciful consideration and be pleased to do the needful order as to retain and continue their said pension as they have obtained all along and thereby they might be able to acquire a competent knowledge of their progress etc., and by such an act of benevolence your petitioners as in duty bound shall ever pray.

CALCUTTA,
February 1830.

To

A. STERLING, ESQ.

The humble petition of Sib Chandra Siromoni and other students belonging to the Nuddea Sanskrit College.

RESPECTFULLY SHEWETH,

That it is about a month ago your petitioners had presented a petition before His Excellency the Governor-General in Council respecting their allowance of Sicca Rupees one hundred which was restored by the late zemindar Rajah Kissen Chunder Bahadoor being since stopped; your (petitioner) being out of their pittance are under utmost trouble without any remedy thereof, the petition they your petitioners heard and believes has been referred to you for the adjustment of their prayer; if so the fact your petitioners humbly pray of your worship will be so kindly pleased as to do the needful order for the succession of their said allowance through the Collector of that district as that is has been all along carried and by your such an act of humanity your petitions shall ever pray for your welfare and increase of wealth.

CALCUTTA.

(No. 1031.)

To

W. W. BIRD AND W. FAME, ESQ.,

Sudder Board of Revenue.

GENTLEMEN,

With reference to your letter, dated the 12th February last, relative to a monthly allowance of 100 rupees paid from Treasury of the Colleetor of Nuddea for the support and instruction of students, resorting from distant parts of the country to that place, I am directed by the Governor in Council to transmit to you for information the accompanying copy of a letter and of its enclosures from the Deputy Persian Secretary to Government, dated the 16th ultimo, on that subject. You will be pleased to instruct the Collector to continue the pension in question to the Nuddea students and to discharge the arrears which may have accrued from the date on which the payment of it was stopped.

I have the honour to be,

Sir,

Your most obedient Servant,

(SD.) W. H. MACNAGHTEN,

Off. Deputy Secy. to Govt.

FORT WILLIAM,
The 3rd August, 1830.

Navadvīpa, Bhātpārā, Puri and other places. Public examinations have been instituted for the encouragement of Nyāya along with other branches of learning.

A subsidy has also been granted to the Asiatic Society of Bengal for publication of Sanskrit books, including dialectical works.

At present all the works and dialectics are being collected. English, French, German and other scholars are collecting Sanskrit books including books on dialectics.

There are heaps of manuscripts in the libraries of Europe, such as the British Museum, India Office, the Imperial Academy of Vienna, the Imperial Academy of St. Petersburg, Musée National of Paris, etc. Catalogues are being prepared, and great facilities are being given for the study of dialectical works.

97. Rise of Vernacular detrimental to Nyāya.

On account of the great attention given to vernaculars at the present day the study of Nyāya is declining. Great encouragement is being given to vernacular studies. The Dacca University Committee observes[1] that "the Bengali language has made great progress under British Rule, and its further development should be regarded as one of the duties of the state universities of the Bengal Presidency." The Calcutta University has already recognized—as the result of the zealous and devoted work of Sir Asutosh Mukerjee—the vernaculars up to the M.A. standard. Several well-organized societies such as the Bangīya Sāhitya Pariṣad and the Sāhitya Sabhā have been founded to cultivate the Bengali language. Nyāya written in Sanskrit is not much appreciated. Nyāya written in an easier language is acceptable, but even then the diction of such works cannot be easy.

97. The Universities on the Western Model.

As a result of long controversies dating from 1792 A.D. the Calcutta University was founded in 1854. The universities of Calcutta and other places have made suitable arrangements for the study of western learning. Nadia and other archaic universities are declining, being unable to make headway against the more scientific methods of study which are developing under the influence of Calcutta and of the other universities, established by the Imperial British Government, with the object of encouraging eastern and western learning side by side. In spite of the strenuous efforts made by the British Government to foster study and research in indigenous Logic, it is at its lowest ebb, as the degrees of

---

[1] Dacca University Committee Report, Chap. VII, p. 31.

a modern university are held in greater regard than those of the archaic universities of Mithilá and Nadia, because, it is often alleged, that in comparison with the Logic of Europe, Indian Logic though subtle, is cumbrous in its method, forbidding in its language, and less profitable in its material results.

APPENDIX A.

THE UNIVERSITY OF TAXILA.

A.

Taxila: Its political history.

(i) Persian conquest of Taxila.

Takṣaśilā or Taxila was the capital of a province of Gāndhāra and is situated near the river of Sadheri in the Rawalpindi district. The high antiquity of Taxila can be best gathered from the fact that it was famous in the time of Buddha as a University town in India and that Gāndhāra, of which it forms a part, is mentioned in both the Rig-veda and the Atharva-veda, and in the Upanishads and Buddhist literature. In historical times[1] we notice it came under the sway of Cyrus the Great (558—530 B.C.), who is said to have conquered it along with other provinces of Gāndhāra. It is said to have remained in the possession of his successor, Cambyses, who ruled the Persian empire from 530 to 522 B.C. It remained a Persian province for nearly two centuries; and after the downfall of the empire in 331 B.C., it, along with other provinces, came under the sway of Alexander the Great. Herodotus relates that Skylax was first sent by Darius (probably about 510 B.C.) to conduct a fleet of ships from a tributary of the Indus into the Gāndhāra country. Ctesias (415-319 B.C.) resided at the Persian Court for 17 years as physician during the reigns of Darius II and Artaxerxes Memnon, during which time Gāndhāra is said to have remained a Persian province. An interesting relic of Persian influence at Taxila is an inscription in Aramaic character of the fourth or fifth century B.C., which is the only Aramaic record that has yet been found in India.[2]

(ii) Greek régime: Alexander the Great.

Early in the spring of 326 B.C. Alexander with his army entered into the territories of the king of Taxila, who had already tendered his submission. Later on we find it to be a part of the Magadha Empire under the Mauryas, which is clearly evidenced by the fact that Aśoka was viceroy of Taxila. The territory of Gāndhāra, including Taxila, was again conquered by Euthydemus or Democritus and was subsequently wrested from the family of Greek princes by Eucratides. The inscriptions and coins further show that the family of Eucratides was supplanted

---

[1] E. J. Rapson's 'Ancient India.'

[2] 'A Guide to Taxila' by Sir John Marshall.

by the Śaka satraps in Taxila, but the princes continued to hold the Kabul valley until the last vestiges of their rule, which had survived the attacks of the Śakas, were swept away by the Kushans.

There is a copper-plate inscription of the satrap of Taxila, Pātilā by name, which records the deposit of the relics of Buddha and a donation made in the 78th year of some (Parthian ?) era (probably corresponding to 93 B.C.) during the reign of king Mogo or Manes. There has been discovered a column-inscription of one Heliodorus, a Greek native of Taxila and a Vaishnava convert which runs as follows :—

"This Garuda-column of Vāsudeva (Vishṇu) the god of gods, was erected here by Heliodorus, a worshipper of Vishṇu, the son of Dion, and an inhabitant of Taxila, who came as Greek Ambassador from the great king Antialcidas to king Kaśīputra Bhāgabhadra, the Saviour, then reigning, prosperously in the fourteenth year of his kingship."

B.

"Three immortal precepts (footsteps)....when practised lead to heaven—self restraint, charity, conscientiousness." [1]

Taxila the great seat of Hindu learning and culture.

Taxila was one of the great cities of the East, and was famous as the principal seat of Hindu learning in Northern India, to which scholars of all classes flocked for instruction, especially in medical science.[2] In the *Mahāvagga* VIII. 3 (Dr. Oldenberg's ed.), we find Jīvaka, who was a physician to Buddha, was educated in surgery and medicine at Taxila. Ample references have been met with in the Jātakas that people received education in lieu for school-fees or service rendered to their teachers. Jīvaka, the physician of Buddha is said to have received education by rendering service to the physicians at Taxila.[3] Generally the three Vedas and eighteen Vidyās or *sippas* were taught there.

Mutual exchange of Hindu and Greek culture at Taxila.

Philostratus in his life of Apollonius of Tyana gives an account of that philosopher s visit to India. The account tells us that the philosopher had a Babylonian guide, named Damis ; that Phrontes, king of Taxila, spoke in Greek and that up to 12 years of age he was educated in the Greek fashion and was sent afterwards to the Brahmins. Also that Taxila was about the size of Nineveh and walled like a Greek city

---

1 Sir John Marshal, K.C.I.E., in the journal of the Royal Asiatic Society, 1909, p. 1063.

2 *Vide* Archæological discoveries at Taxila by Sir John Marshall.

3 *Vide* my Buddha-deva, pp. 160—170 and 220—223, also Jātakas, Vol. I, p. 259, Vol. V, pp. 161, 210, 457.

and was the residence of a sovereign, who ruled over what of old was the kingdom of Porus. From Taxila to the hill of Saphoi the villagers also spoke Greek. That the people living in Saphoi knew the Pythagorean philosophy. We also learn from the narrative that the Greek and the Indian philosophers were mutually acquainted with each other's systems, and held each other in high honour. The Brahmins specially loved the Greeks and looked upon them as akin to themselves in mind and disposition. There was inter-communiaction between India, Babylon, and Egypt. Apollonius's journey shows that overland journeys from Babylon to India was constantly made by travellers. That the Babylonians were in the habit of making this journey regularly, is clearly indicated by the fact that Philostratus engaged the services of a Babylonian guide. That the Indian king showed much courtesy to the travellers and that such visits were frequently made, is clearly proved by the fact that travelling allowances paid to the guides formed a recognised and well-known item of expenditure of the frontier sovereign.

Arrian, Strabo, Ptolemy, Dionysius, Pliny, Fa-Hien and Hieun-Tsang all have spoken of this place. Hieun-Tsang, who visited Taxila in the 7th century A.D. says that the royal family was extinct; that formerly it was in subjection to Kapisa and latterly was a tributary to Kashmir, and that the nobles contended for power by force. After the 9th century we hear no more of Taxila.[1]

---

1 Beal's 'Buddhist records of the Western World'; 'Early History of India' by V. A Smith; Buddha-deva by Satis Chandra Vidyabhusan; Arrian, etc., Jātaka; Archæological Survey; B. C. Law's, 'Taxila,' volume 12, No. I, etc.

APPENDIX B

INFLUENCE OF ARISTOTLE ON THE DEVELOPMENT OF THE SYLLOGISM IN INDIAN LOGIC.[1]

1. Tarka-śāstra of Gotama (about 550 B.C.).

The Nyāya-sūtra, which is supposed to be the earliest work extant on Nyāya philosophy, treats of four distinct subjects, *viz.* (1) the art of debate (*tarka*), (2) the means of valid knowledge (*pramāṇa*), (3) the doctrine of syllogism (*avayava*), and (4) the examination of contemporaneous philosophical doctrines (*anya-mata-parīkṣā*). The first subject, ample references to which are met with in the old Brahmanic, Buddhistic, and Jaina works, seems to have been first handled by a sage named Gotama or Gautama, who is reputed to have flourished in Mithilā (North Behar) about 550 B.C. The second subject, which is also referred to in old books, was associated with the art of debate at a very early stage. These two subjects, combined together, constitute the Tarka-śāstra (the philosophy of reasoning), popularly known as Gautamī-vidyā (the Gotamide learning).[2]

2. The Nyāya-sūtra of Akṣapāda (about 150 A.D.).

The third subject, the doctrine of the Syllogism, does not appear to have been known in India a considerable time before the Christian era. The fourth subject refers to numerous philosophical doctrines that were propounded from time to time up to the second century A.D.[3] Gotama's Tarka-śāstra, after these two subjects had been introduced into it, became, about the second century A.D., designated as the Nyāya-sūtra—the aphorisms on logic. The term "Nyāya" in the sense of logic occurs in the Mahābhārata (Ādi-parva, adhyāya 1, verse 67; adhyāya 70, verses 42-4; and Sānti-parva, adhyāya 210, verse 22); Viṣnu-purāṇa (3rd pt., adhyāya 6); Matsya-purāṇa (3, 2); Padma-purāṇā (Uttara-

1 This is a reprint, in an altered form, of an article published in the Journal of the Asiatic Society of Great Britain and Ireland.

2 For Gotama or Gautama as the founder of Tarka-śāstra, see Naiṣadhacarita, Bk. xvii, verse 75; Padma-purāṇa, Uttara-khaṇḍa, ch. 263; and Skanda purāṇa, Kālikā-kaṇḍa, ch. xvii.

3 Some philosophical doctrines of the third and fourth centuries A.D. were incorporated into the Nyāya-sūtra of Akṣapāda by Vātsyāyana the first commentator (about 400 A.D.), through the introduction of certain sūtras of his own making fathered upon Akṣapāda.

khaṇḍa, ch. 263); Yājñavalkya-saṁhitā (I, 3), etc., in passages which are presumed to have been written after the second century A.D. We are not surprised to find that the Mahābhārata mentions even a syllogism,[1] called a speech of five parts, in which Nārada is said to have been an expert, when we consider that the Great Epic refers also to the voracious Romans called Romaka,[2] who, according to it, "came adorned with helmets and clad in endless garments to pay tributes" to Yudhiṣṭhira on the occasion of his coronation at Delhi. It is quite possible that the passage which refers to the syllogism was written after the intercourse of Rome with India had commenced and possibly after the second century A.D.

In the early commentaries[3] on the Nyāya-sūtra, the author of the sūtra is distincly named as Akṣapāda, while in the Padma-purāṇa[4] and other works Gotama or Gautama is credited with the authorship of the sūtra Ananta-yajvan,[5] in his commentary on the Pitṛmedha-sūtra, observes that Gautama and Akṣapāda were the same person, while the Nyāya-koṣa[6] mentions a legend to account for the name as applied, according to it, to Gautama. As no credible evidence has been adduced in either case, I consider the identification as fanciful, and maintain that Gotama or Gautama was quite different from Akṣapāda, but that both of them contributed to the production of the Nyāya-sūtra, one at its early stage and the other in its final form. Indeed, Akṣapāda, unlike Gotama or Gautama, is reported in the Brahmāṇḍā-purāṇa[7] to have been a son of Somaśarmā, who resided at Prabhāsa, near Broach, in Kathiawar, on the sea-coast.

3. When was the Syllogism first used in India?

Though Akṣapāda introduced into the Nyāya-sūtra the doctrine of the syllogism, he was by no means the first promulgator of the doctrine—nay, not even its first disseminator. The doctrine[8]

---

[1] Pañcāvayava-yuktasya vākyasya guṇa-doṣavit (Mahābhārata, Sabhāparva, adhyāya 51, verse 5).

[2] Auṣṇikānantavāsāṁśca Romakān puruṣādakān (Mahābhārata, Sabhāparva, adhyāya 51, verse 16).

[3] *Vide* the concluding verse of the Nyāya-bhāṣya (about 400 A.D.), the opening verse of the Nyāya-vārttika (about 630 A.D.), and the opening lines of the Nyāy-vārttika tātparya-ṭīkā (about 976 A.D.).

[4] Padma-purāṇa, Uttara-khaṇḍa, ch. 263.

[5] *Vide* Weber's *History of Indian Literature*, p. 85.

[6] Nyāya-koṣa, 2nd ed., Bombay.

[7] The Brahmāṇḍa-purāṇa, published under the name of Vāyu-purāṇa by A.S.B., adhyāya 23, verses 201-3.

[8] Seeing that the Greek word "Syllogismos" and the Sanskrit word "Saṁkhyā" or "Sāṁkhya" are identical in signification, one may say that Aristotle derived his doctrine of the Syllogism from the Sāṁkhya Philosophy of Kapila. But the Sāṁkhya Philosophy is not known to have dealt with the doctrine of the Syllogism at all.

was carried to great perfection in Greece by Aristotle in the fourth century B.C. (384–322 B.C.). That it was known even in India prior to Akṣapāda is apparent from a notice of the same in the Caraka-saṁhitā,[1] about 78 A.D. In fact, it is extremely difficult to ascertain the exact date at which the syllogistic reasoning was first used in India. It is also a problem of enormous difficulty to determine whether there is any genetical connexion between the syllogism as propounded in the Indian Logic and that propounded in the Greek Logic. Of the four subjects treated in the Nyāya-sūtra already referred to, the first, second, and fourth are undoubtedly of Indian origin. As to the third subject (syllogism), some scholars say that it, too, is of indigenous growth, as it forms a part of inference, a kind of *pramāṇa*, which originated in India. But on investigation into the history of the development of inference and the syllogism we find that in origin they were altogether distinct, though ultimately there was an amalgamation between them.

4. No connexion between an Inference and a Syllogism at their early stage.

The notice of inference (*anumāna*) in old books such as the Vaiśeṣika-sūtra (3, 1, 9 and 9, 2, 1) and the Caraka-saṁhitā (Sūtra-sthāna, ch. xi, and Vimāna-sthāna, ch. viii) is very meagre. The Nyāya-sūtra (1, 2, 5), which gives a more comprehensive account, defines inference as knowledge which is preceded by perception and as being of three kinds, *viz.*: (1) (knowledge which arises from the perception of what is) like the prior (*pūrvavat*), *e.g.* on seeing clouds one infers that there will be rain; (2) (knowledge which arises from the perception of what is) like the posterior *śeṣavat*, *e.g.* on seeing a river swollen one infers that there was rain; and (3) (knowledge which arises from the perception of what is) commonly seen (*sāmānyato dṛṣṭa*) *e.g.* on seeing an animal possessing horns one infers that it also possesses a tail. The inference, as illustrated here from the Nyāya-sūtra, was in essence a guess or conjecture which was neither a source of absolutely valid knowledge nor in any way connected with a syllogism. In order, therefore, to ascertain whether there is any genetical connextion between the syllogism of Indian Logic and that of the Greek Logic, I shall analyse here the two syllogisms side by side, with occasional references to the rules controlling them.

---

[1] Concerning the date of the Caraka-saṁhitā see *Journal Asiatique*, tom. viii, pp. 447-51, 1896, where M. Sylvain Lévi maintains on the authority of Chinese books that Caraka, the author of the Caraka-saṁhitā, lived at the Court of Kaniṣka (in Jālandhara, Punjab). I provisionally take the date of Kaniṣka to be 78 A.D.

5. *The Syllogism in Indian Logic conforms to the logical rules of Aristotle.*

A. CARAKA-SAMHITĀ (78 A.D.)

a. Demonstration and Counter-demonstration.

The Caraka-saṁhitā (Vimāna-sthāna, ch. viii), which contains the earliest information available on syllogism, analyses a demonstration (*sthāpanā*) and a counter-demonstration (*pratisṭhāpanā*) as follows :—

DEMONSTRATION (*sthāpanā*).

(1) Proposition (*pratijñā*). The soul is eternal.

(2) Reason (*hetu*). Because it is non-produced.

A. ARISTOTLE (384–322 B.C.)[1]

a. Demonstrative and Refutative Enthymemes.

Aristotle, in his Rhetoric (bk. ii, p. 194, Welldon's ed.), speaks of two species of enthymemes, *viz.* demonstrative and refutative, which correspond respectively to the demonstration and counter-demonstration of the Caraka-saṁhitā. The demonstrative enthymeme of Aristotle, like the demonstration of the Caraka-saṁhitā, consists in drawing conclusions from admitted propositions, while the

---

[1] Dr. B. M. Barua, a distinguished pupil of mine, differs from me on this point. He would however hold that syllogistic forms existed prior to the time of the Greek influence. As an authority he points out the following passages from the Mahāpadāna Suttantā (Dīgha. II, No. 1) where the *Dhammatā* doctrine put in the syllogistic forms involves the double process of deduction and induction :—

Deductive method :—

All Buddhas are equal in all respects,
One Buddha lost his mother on the seventh day of his birth,
All Buddhas lost their mothers on the seventh day of their birth,

Inductive method :—

All past Buddhas had lost their mothers on the seventh day of their birth,
The present Buddha lost his mother on the seventh day of his birth,
All future Buddhas will lose their mothers on the seventh day of their birth.

Thus by the law (*Dhammatā*) all Buddhas lose their mothers on the seventh day of their birth. This conclusion though formally correct is materially absurd.

My other pupil, Mr. Hire dra Lal Sen Gupta, M.A., a distinguished student of the Mahāyāna philosophy, in the Calcutta University, agrees with the above view and as illustrations he alludes to the numerous passages of controversy in the Dīgha Nikāya, Vol. I, Suttas 1 and 2, one of which having a crude form of syllogism thus:

My being wrong is a hindrance to me.
The sense of remorse is due to my being wrong.
The sense of remorse is a hindrance to me.

These illustrations according to Dr. Barua and Mr. Sen Gupta goes to prove that the ancient Hindus knew the syllogism before the Greeks came to India.

In reply I may say that one may use language involving Syllogism, yet one may not be aware of the art of Syllogism. Syllogism being a simple course of reasoning, men all over the world may use expressions illustrative of Syllogism. It was the Hindus and the Greeks that systematised the expressions and made a law out of them and I believe the Greeks preceded the Hindus in making that law.

(3) Example (*dṛṣṭānta*). That which is non-produced is eternal, as ether.

(4) Application (*upanaya*). The soul is non-produced.

(5) Conclusion (*nigamana*). Therefore the soul is eternal.

COUNTER-DEMONSTRATION (*pratiṣṭhāpanā*).

(1) The soul is non-eternal.

(2) Because it is cognized by the senses.

(3) That which is cognized by the senses is non-eternal, as a pot.

(4) The soul is cognized by the senses.

(5) Therefore the soul is non-eternal.

The Caraka-saṁhitā, which analyses demonstration and counter-demonstration into five members, does not give any clear definition of those members. "Dṛṣṭānta," which in the old Tarka-śāstra signified an instance familiar to the learned and the fool alike, was adopted designate the third member, although in its old sense it did not indicate the principle of connexion (between the middle term and the major term) involved in the member.

refutative enthymeme of Aristotle, like the counter-demonstration of the Caraka-saṁhitā, consists in drawing conclusions which are inconsistent with those of one's adversary.

The enthymeme is defined by Aristotle (in his Rhetoric, bk. i, p. 16, Welldon's ed.) as a syllogism with its constituent parts fewer than those of a normal syllogism, that is, a syllogism of which the major premise, minor premise, or the conclusion is suppressed as being well known to the audience, who can supply the same of their own accord.

The demonstration in the Caraka-ṣaṁhitā is obviously a combination of an enthymeme which comprises the first two parts of the demonstration and an example which comprises the last three parts of it. This is quite in conformity with the rule of Aristotle, who (in his Rhetoric, bk. ii, p. 184, Welldon's ed.) observes that an example may be used as a supplement to an enthymeme to serve the purpose of a testimony which is invariably persuasive. This rule may be illustrated as follows :—

Enthymeme.

(1) The soul is eternal,

(2) Because it is non-produced.

Example.

(3) That which is non-produced is eternal, as ether,

(4) The soul is non-produced,

(5) Therefore the soul is eternal.

B. AKṢAPĀDA (ABOUT 150 A.D.).[1]

b. Analysis into five members (Avayava).

Akṣapāda in his Nyāya-sūtra (1, 1, 32) mentions the five parts of a demonstration under the name of *avayava* (members) as follows :—

(1) Proposition (*pratijñā*). This hill is full of fire.

(2) Reason (*hetu*). Because it is full of smoke.

(3) Example (*udāharana*). That which is full of smoke is full of fire, as a kitchen.

(4) Application (*upanaya*). This hill is full of smoke.

(5) Conclusion (*nigamana*). Therefore, this hill is full of fire.

c. Example (udāharaṇa).

Akṣapāda calls the example an *udāharaṇa* which he divides into two kinds, *viz.* affirmative (*sādharmya*) and negative (*vaidharmya*). An affirmative example is defined in the Nyāya-sūtra (1, 1, 36) as a familiar instance, which, being similar to the minor term, possesses the property of that term as co-present (with the reason). A negative example is defined (in the Nyāya sūtra, 1, 1, 37) as a familiar instance, which is contrary to what has been stated in the case of the affirmative example, that is, in which there is an absence of the property implying an absence of the reason. The definition may be illustrated as follows :—

B. ARISTOTLE.

Analysis of syllogism and demonstration (analytics).

The term *avayava*, used by Akṣapada to signify parts or members of a syllogism or demonstration, corresponds to the term *analytics*, which refers to the section of the *Organon* in which Aristotle analyses the syllogism and demonstration into their principles (*vide* O.F. Owen's translations of the *Organon*, Prior Analytics, bk. i, ch. i, p. 80).

c. Example (paradeigma).

The affirmative example (*sādharmya udāharaṇa*), as defined by Akṣapāda, corresponds exactly to the example (*paradeigma*), as explained by Aristotle (in his Prior Analytics, bk. ii, ch. xxiv, p. 232). An example, according to Aristotle, occurs when the major term is shown to be present with the middle, through something similar to the minor; but it is necessary to know that the middle is with the minor, and the major with what is similar, *e.g.* :—

(1) That which is full of smoke is full of fire, as a kitchen.

(2) The hill is full of smoke.

(3) Therefore the hill is full of fire.

[1] Concerning the age of Akṣapāda, *vide* introduction to Daśapadārthī, translated by Mr. Ui and edited by Dr. F. W. Thomas (in the press).

Affirmative Example.

(1) The hill is full of fire.

(2) Because it is full of smoke.

(3) That which is full of smoke is full of fire, as a kitchen (affirmative conclusion).

(1) The hill is not smoky.

(2) Because it is non-fiery.

(3) That which is non-fiery is not smoky, as a lake (negative conclusion).

Negative Example.

(1) The hill is full of fire.

(2) Because it is full of smoke.

(3) That which is not full of fire is not full of smoke, as a lake.

The reason (*hetu*), as expounded by Akṣapāda (in the Nyāya-sūtra, 1, 1, 34, 35), is of two kinds, *viz.* affirmative and negative. An affirmative reason is the means which, through its homogeneity or connexion with the example, establishes what is to be established, while a negative reason is the means which, through its heterogeneity or separation from the example, establishes what is to be established. The definitions may be illustrated as follows :—

Affirmative Reason.

(1) The hill is full of fire.

(2) Because it is full of smoke.

(3) That which is full of smoke is full of fire as a kitchen.

Negative Reason.

(1) The hill is not full of smoke.

(2) Because it is not full of fire.

(3) That which is full of smoke is full of fire, as a kitchen.

The negative example and negative reason expounded by Akṣapāda (in the Nyāya-sūtra, 1, 1, 35, 37) possess apparently no counterparts in the *Organon* (Prior Analytics) of Aristotle. From the illustration of the example and reason (affirmative and negative) given by Akṣapāda it appears that he admitted the universal affirmative conclusion in what is called by Aristotle the "first figure" and the universal negative conclusion in the first and second figures. Now, if a conclusion in the first figure is to be negative, the major premise must be negative, and, if a conclusion in the second figure is to be negative, the minor premise must be negative (*vide* Prior Analytics, bk. i, chs. iv, v, pp. 85–94). Considering that the major and minor premises of Aristotle correspond respectively to the example and reason of Akṣapāda, it becomes absolutely necessary to admit a negative example and a negative reason as counter-parts of the negative major premises and the negative minor premise.

C. NĀGĀRJUNA (250-300 A.D.). MAITREYA (400 A.D.)[1]

d. Function of an Example.

The Buddhist philosopher Nāgārjuna, in his Upāya-kauśalya-hṛdaya-śāstra (Chinese version, ch. i, sect. 1), gives an elaborate explanation of example (*udāharaṇa*), which is either affirmative or negative, and which must, according to him be mentioned to make clear the reasons of the disputant and his respondent. The Buddhist philosopher Maitreya, in his Yoga-caryā-bhūmi-śāstra (Chinese version, vol. xv), treats of proofś (*sādhaka*) which include a proposition (*siddhānta*), a reason (*hetu*), and an example (*udāharaṇa*, affirmative or negative). Though in the commentaries (Nyāya-bhāṣya, 1, 1, 37, and Nyāya-vārttika, 1, 1, 37) on the Nyāya-sūtra the "application" and "conclusion" are considered as essential parts of a syllogism, inasmuch as these on the strength of the general principle involved in the example, reassert the reason and restate the proposition in a decisive way; Nāgārjuna and Maitreya, on the other hand, reject them as superfluous on the ground of their not being different from the reason and proposition.[2] The three members of a syllogism expounded by Nāgārjuna and Maitreya are as follows :—

C. ARISTOTLE.

d. Use of an Example.

The three members of a syllogism, as explained by Nāgārjuna, Maitreya, and others, constitute what is called an example. Aristotle, in his Rhetoric (bk. ii, p. 184, Welldon's ed.), observes that it is proper, in default of enthymemes, to make use of examples as logical proofs, these being the natural means of producing conviction. In the Prior Analytics (bk. ii, ch. xxiv, p. 233, O. F. Owen's ed.), it is further observed that the example differs from induction in that the latter proves the universal from a complete enumeration of individuals, while the former attempts to prove it from a single individual or from some selected individuals, and in that the induction steps at the universal, while the example draws syllogistically a conclusion in respect of the minor term, *e.g.* :

(1) That which is full of smoke is full of fire, as a kitchen.

(2) The hill is full of smoke

(3) Therefore the hill is full of fire.

The above may also be put in the reverse order as follows :

(1) The hill is full of fire.

(2) Because it is full of smoke.

(3) That which is full of smoke is full of fire, as a kitchen.

---

[1] *Vide* S. C. Vidyabhusana's *Medieval School of Indian Logic*, pp. 68, 73.

[2] It is perhaps the view of Nāgārjuna and Maitreya, and surely also of Dignāga, that is referred to under the name of "Bauddha" in the Nyaya-vārttika, 1, 1, 37.

(1) The hill is full of fire.
(2) Because it is full of smoke.
(3) That which is full of smoke is full of fire, as a kitchen.

We may also regard the syllogism expounded by Nāgārjuna and Maitreya as comprising an enthymeme and an example, for the example sometimes consists of only one proposition.[1]

D. Vasubandhu (about 450 A.D.).

e. Syllogism of two members.

Vasubandhu in his Tarka-śāstra (Chinese version, ch. 1) treats of syllogism as consisting of five members, but in his Ronki (Vādavidhi), as quoted by Kwei-ke[2] he is said to have maintained that a syllogism consists of two members only, *viz.* the proposition and the reason, and that the terms necessary for a syllogism are only three, *viz.* the minor, the major, and the middle. In the Nyāya-vārttika (1, 1, 37) and the Nyāya-vārttika-tātparya-ṭīkā (1, 1, 37)[3] Vasubandhu, designated as Subandhu, is stated to have held that a syllogism consists of only two members, and that the example is quite superfluous. The Jaina logician Siddhasena Divākara[4] (in his Nyāyāvatāra, v. 20) refers to Vasubandhu, when he says that according to experts in logic a

D. Aristotle.

e. A perfect Syllogism.

The form of syllogism laid down by Vasubandhu conforms in the main to the rules laid down by Aristotle with regard to a perfect syllogism, *viz.* that every syllogism consists of two premises and one conclusion, so that there are altogether three terms in a syllogism (*vide* Prior Analytics, bk. i, ch. xxv, pp. 140—2). A syllogism is defined by Aristotle (in Prior Analytics, bk. i, ch. i, p. 92) as a sentence (or speech) in which, certain things being laid down, something different from the premises necessarily results in consequence of their existence, *e.g.*

Premises.

(1) All that is full of smoke is full of fire.
(2) This hill is full of smoke.

---

[1] George Grote, in his *Aristotle*, vol. i, Analytica Priora, ii, ch. vi, p. 275, observes in a footnote as follows: "If we turn to ch. xxvii, p. 70, *a.* 30—4, we shall find *Aristotle* on a different occasion disallowing altogether the so-called syllogism from example."

[2] Sugiura's *Hindu Logic as preserved in China and Japan*, p. 32.

[3] *Vide* S. C. Vidyabhusana's "Vātsyāyana, author of the Nyāyabhāṣya" in the *Indian Antiquary* for April, 1915.

[4] Nyāyāvatāra (verse 20), edited by S. C. Vidyabhusana and published by the Indian Research Society, Calcutta. Siddhasena Divākara flourished about 500–33 A.D. *Vide* S. C. Vidyabhusana's *Medieval School of Indian Logic*, p. 15.

proposition can be proved without any example, if there is invariable concomitance of the middle term with the major term, and in the absence of such invariable concomitance the proof is impossible even with the example.

Such being the view of Vasubandhu, his syllogism is of the following form:—

(1) This hill is full of fire.

(2) Because it is full of smoke.

(3) All that is full of smoke being full of fire.

Conclusion.

(3) Therefore this hill is full of fire.

E. DIGNĀGA (ABOUT 590 A.D.).[1]

f. Inference for one's self and inference for the sake of others.

Asaṅga in his Prakaraṇāryavācā-śūtra (Chinese version, vol. xi) omits inference altogether and substitutes for it a syllogism of five members. Dignāga in his Pramāṇa-samuccaya retains inference under the name of an inference for one's self and affiliates syllogism to inference by calling it an inference for the sake of others.[2]

g. Definition of the minor term.

In the Pramāṇa-samuccaya,[3] ch. iii, Dignāga defines a minor term (*pakṣa*) as that of which the major term is chosen to be

E. ARISTOTLE.

f. The dialectic proposition and demonstrative proposition.

The distinction made by Dignāga between an inference for one's self and that for the sake of others corresponds exactly to the distinction made by Aristotle (in his Prior Analytics, bk. i, ch. i, p. 81) between a dialectic proposition and a demonstrative proposition.

g. Explanation of a proposition.

Just as in an inference for one's self the predicability of the major term in respect of the minor term is a matter of ques-

---

[1] *Vide* S. C. Vidyabhusana's *Medieval School of Indian Logic*, p. 80.

[2] Raṅ-don-ni tshul-*g*sum-*r*tag-las don-*m*thoṅ waho.
(Pramāṇa-samuccaya, ch. ii. Tangyur, *M*do, xcv, fol. 5).
Gshan-gyi-don-gyi-*r*jes- *d*pag-ni raṅ-gis *m*thoṅ-don-*g*sal-byed-yin
(Pramāṇa-samuccaya, ch. iii. Tangyur, *M*do, xcv, fol. 9).

[3] *Vide* Tangyur. *M*do. xcv, fol. 7.

predicated. The Jaina logician Siddhasena Divākara [1] (500–550 A.D.), in his Nyāyāvatāra, verse 14, says that in an inference for the sake of others the minor term is to be defined as that of which it is assumed that the major term is predicable. In an inference for one's self, on the other hand, the minor term is to be defined, according to old Indian logicians, as that of which it is questionable whether the major term is predicable.

tion or doubt, while in an inference for the sake of others it is a matter of assumption, so also in the *Organon* of Aristotle (Prior Analytics. bk. i, ch. i, p. 81) the dialectic is an interrogation of contradiction, while the demonstration is an assumption of one part of the contradiction. In the *Organon* (De Interpretatione, ch. xi, pp. 67–8, O. F. Owen's edition) a dialectic is stated indeed to be an interrogation, for a choice should be given from the interrogation to enunciate this or that part of the contradiction. This statement coincides with the definition of Dignāga, according to whom the debater chooses the major term as predicable of the minor.

h. Three characteristics of the middle term.

In an inference for one's self, as well as in that for the sake of others, the middle term, if it is to lead to a valid conclusion, must possess the following characteristics [2] :—

(1) The middle term must cover the minor term. *e.g.* the hill is smoky.

(2) The middle term must be present in places in which there is the major term, *e.g.* that which is smoky is fiery.

(3) The middle term must be absent from places where there is an absence of the major term, *e.g.* that which is not fiery (non-fiery) is not smoky.

h. The middle term in a syllogism.

The characteristics laid down by Dignāga correspond exactly to those laid down by Aristotle. In the *Organon* (Prior Analytics, bk. i, ch. iv, pp. 85-6. O. F. Owen's edition) it is stated that, when three terms so subsist with reference to one another that the minor is covered by the middle and the middle is or is not covered by the major, then there is necessarily a perfect syllogism of the major and the minor.

This statement may be illustrated as follows :—

---

[1] Sādhyābhyupagamaḥ pakṣaḥ (Nyāyāvatāra, verse 14, edited by S. C. Vidyabhusana). Sandigdha-sādhya-dharmatvam pakṣatvaṁ (quoted in the Tattva-cintāmaṇi, anumāna-khaṇḍa, p. 407, *Bibliotheca Indica*).

[2] (1) Phyogs-kyi-chos-ñid-daṅ, (2) *M*thun-pa*h*i-phyogs-ñid la yo*d*-par-ṅes-pa-daṅ, (3) Mi-*m*thun-pa*h*i-phyogs la-mo*d*-pa-ñid-du-ṅes-pa-yaṅ-ṅo, (Dignāga's Nyāya-pra.veśa, Tangyur, *M*do, xcv, fol. 183*b*).

The above characteristics, as applicable to an affirmative or negative conclusion, may be illustrated as follows: –

A

(1) This hill is fiery.
(2) Because it is smoky.
(3) That which is smoky is fiery.

B

(1) This hill is not smoky.
(2) Because it is non-fiery.
(3) That which is non-fiery is not smoky.

A

(1) That which is smoky is fiery.
(2) This hill is smoky.
(3) Therefore this hill is fiery.

B

(1) That which is non-fiery is not smoky.
(2) This hill is non-fiery.
(3) Therefore this hill is not smoky.

F. DHARMAKĪRTI [1] (600-50. A.D.).

Demonstration through three kinds of middle term.[2]

The Buddhist logician Dharmakīrtī, in his Nyāya-bindu, ch. ii, divides the middle term (*liṅga*, sign)[3] into three kinds in accordance with the relations which it bears to the major term. The relations are as follows:—

(1) Selfsameness, inherence, or "being the essence of that" (*svabhāva, samavāya, tādātmya*), which occurs when the predicate (or major term) is in essence wholly included in the subject, (or middle term), e.g. this is a tree, because it is *śiṁśapā*.

(2) Effect, also called "origination from that" (*kāryya, tadutpatti*), which occurs when the predicate (major term) and the sub-

F. ARISTOTLE.

Demonstration through the medium of essence and cause.

The two relations, *viz.* "selfsameness" (or "inherence") and "effect", as expounded by Dharmakīrti, correspond to the two relations, *viz.* "*per se*" (inherence) and "causal', as expounded by Aristotle in his Posterior Analytics (bk. i, ch. iv, pp. 253-5, and bk. i, ch. xxiv, p. 301).

(1) *Per se* (essence or inherence).—The predicate (major terms) is said to be related to the subject (middle term *per se* essentially), if the properties of the former are inherent in the definition of the latter.

(2) The causal.—The predicate (major term), which is essentially present with the subject (middle

---

[1] *Vide* S. C. Vidyabhusana's *Medieval School of Indian Logic*, pp. 103-5.
[2] Dignāga in his Pramāṇa samucaya, Chap. II.
[3] Triṇyeva ca liṅgāni, anupalabdhiḥ svabhāva-kāryye ceti (Nyāyabindu, ch, ii, p. 164, *Bibliotheca Indica*).

ject (middle term) stand to each other in the relation of cause and effect. *e.g.* all that is smoky is fiery.

(3) Non-perception[1] (*anupalabdhi*) *e.g.* whatever thing (being perceptible) is not perceived is non-existent.

term), is said to be the cause of the latter.

j. Nature of the universal preposition.

The relations which establish invariable concomitance of the middle term with the major term are the bases of universal propositions. "Invariable concomitance" is designated in Sanskrit as *vyāpti* (pervasion or co-presence), *nāntarīyaka* (non-separation), and *avinābhāva* (the relation owing to which one cannot exist without the other).

j. Nature of the universal proposition.

The proposition in which the predicate is related to the subject *per se* or *causally* is a universal one. Aristotle in his Posterior Analytics (bk. i, ch. iv, pp. 253-5, O. F. Owen's edition) calls that (the) universal (major term) which is predicated "of every" and "*per se*", that is, which being predicable of the middle term *per se* is predicated of it in every instance. In the Posterior Analytics (bk. i, ch. xxiv, p. 301) Aristotle further observes that the universal (major term) is the cause of the middle term, which is essentially co-present within it. In Prior Analytics, bk. i. ch. xxiv, pp. 138-9, Aristotle says that in all syllogisms we must have a universal proposition (premise) which is shown by the universal term.

---

[1] Dharmakīrti and his followers, who say that non-existence is *inferred* and not perceived, assume non-perception as a middle term (sign). But the majority of Indian logicians maintain that non-existence of a thing is *perceived* by the same sense by which the thing itself is perceived. Hence non-perception is not acknowledged by them as a middle term (sign).

G. Uddyotakara (600-50 A.D.)[1]

k. Syllogism from a sign (*liṅga-parāmarśa*).

Uddyotakara, who completely incorporated syllogism into inference in his Nyāya-vārttika,[2] defines inference as knowledge which is preceded by the perception of the middle term (sign) and recollection of its invariable concomitance with the major term in the following form: "I perceive that this hill has smoke, which I remember to be invariably concomitant with fire, and hence I infer that this hill has fire." The above may be properly put in the following form:—

(1) Whatever is smoky is fiery.
(2) This hill is smoky.
(3) Therefore this hill is fiery.

The first part (major premise) of the above inference is called *vyāpti* (a universal proposition); the second part (minor premise) is called *upanaya* (an application of the universal); and the third part is called *anumiti* (inferential knowledge or conclusion). The first two parts (premises) constitute what is

G. Aristotle.

k. Enthymeme from a sign.

Aristotle, in his Prior Analytics (bk. ii, ch. xxvii, pp. 238-40), speaks of two kinds of enthymemes, *viz.* the enthymeme from a sign and that from a likelihood. Now, the enthymeme from a sign[3] in the first figure (especially if the sign is infallible, *tekmerion*) leads to a conclusion which is necessarily true. It is this kind of enthymeme from a sign that corresponds to the syllogism from a sign[4] (*liṅga-parāmarśa*) as expounded by Uddyotakara.

Just as in the Nyāya-vārttika of Uddyotakara the syllogism (*parāmarśa*) comprises only the first two parts of an inference, so also in the Arabic Logic,[5] (*e.g.*in bk. iii of the Risalah Shamsiyyah, dated about 1250 A.D.) the syllogism (*qayas*) comprises only the two premises and not the conclusion. It may be added that the Arabic Logic of the schools of Baghdad (ninth century A.D.), Kufa (750 A.D.), and Bassora (700 A.D.) is re-

---

[1] *Vide* S. C. Vidyābhusana's "Uddyotakara, a contemporary of Dharmakīrti", in J.R.A.S., July 1914.

[2] Liṅga-liṅgī-sambandha-darśanāntaraṁ liṅga-darśana-sambandha-smṛtibhir liṅga-parāmarśo viśiṣyate . . . . Smṛtyanugṛhīto liṅga-parāmarśo 'numānam bhavati (Nyāya-varttika, 1, 1, 5, p. 47, *Bibliotheca Indica*).

[3] Dr. George Grote, in his *Aristotle*, vol. i, Analytica Priora, ch. vi, pp. 291-2, gives a lucid explanation of a sign.

[4] Dr. George Grote, in his *Aristotle*, vol. i, Analytica Priora, ch. vi. p. 292, states in a footnote as follows: "Aristotle throws in the remark (*a.* 24) that, when one premises only of the Ethymeme is enunciated, it is a sign: when the other is added, it becomes a syllogism. In the examples given to illustrate the description of the Enthymeme that which belongs to the first figure has its three terms and two propositions specified, like a complete and regular syllogism."

[5] The Risalah Shamsiyyah was published under tho name of "The Logic of the Arabians" in the *Bibliotheca Indica* series by Dr. A. Sprenger.

called by Uddyotakara *parāmarśa* [1](syllogism) or *liṅga-parāmarśa* (syllogism from a sign), and all the three parts combined together are designated as *parāmarūśa rūpanumāna* [2] (a syllogistic inference). Since the time of Uddyotakara no further development has been made in the form of the syllogistic inference, except that the three parts of it have been called respectively the instrument (*karaṇa*), operation (*vyāpāra*), and consequence (*phala*). The first two parts (premises) combined together have been uniformly designated as *parāmarśa* (syllogism or enthymeme).

puted to have been derived from the *Organon* of Aristotle, as taught in a developed form in the Syro-Persian School of Gundeshapur [3] in Susiana about 350 A.D.

According to certain Roman commentators [4] too, the premises alone constitute the syllogism.

6. *Migrations of the Logical Theories of Aristotle from Alexandria into India* (175 *B.C.*-600 *A.D.*)

Considering the antiquity of the syllogism as propounded by Aristotle and the close connexion that exists between it and the syllogism promulgated in the Hindu Logic, we may fairly conclude that the latter was greatly influenced by, if not based on, the former. Aristotle's works [5] were brought down to Alexandria (in Egypt) by Callimachus, the celebrated librarian of Ptolemy Philadelphus during 285–247 B.C., and it seems that copies of some of these works reached India through Syria, Susiana, Bactria, and Taxila in subsequent times. From the stages in the development of the syllogism in Hindu Logic, as indicated above, it will appear that Aristotle's works migrated into India during three distinct periods. The first period extends roughly from 175 B.C. to 30 B.C., when the Greeks occupied the north-western parts of

---

1 Tasmāt smṛtyanugṛhito *liṅga parāmarśo* 'bhiṣṭārtha pratipādako bhavatīti (Nyāya-vārttika, 1, 1, 5, p. 47, *Bibliotheca Indica*).

2 Tad idam antimam pratyakṣam pūrvābhyām. Pratyakṣābhyāṁ smṛtyanugṛhyamāṇam *parāmarśa-rupam anumānam* bhavati (Nyāya-vārttika, 1, 1, 5, p. 46, *Bibliotheca Indica*).

3 *Vide* C. Huart's *Arabic Literature*, pp. 137, 280.

4 George Grote, in his *Aristotle*, vol. i, Analytica Priora, i, ch. v, p. 206, says that Aristotle includes in a syllogism the two premises as well as the conclusion. But on the same page he quotes in a footnote the opinion of Julius Pacius (ad. Analyt. Prior i), who said that the syllogism consisted of the two premises alone and the conclusion was not a part thereof, but something distinct and superadded.

5 *Encyclopædia Britannica*, 9th ed., vol. i, p. 498.

India [1] and had their capital at Śākala, officially called Euthydemia (modern Sialkot) in the Punjab. The work of Aristotle of which we find a trace in this period is the Art of Rhetoric, which was evidently a favourite subject of study among the Indian Greeks, and from which the syllogism of five members as illustrated in the Caraka-saṁhitā, referred to above, seems to have been derived. It is worthy of note that the first trace in India of Aristotle's syllogism is met with in a work the author of which was the chief physician to King Kaniṣka, who reigned in the Punjab, if not exactly in the city of Śākala, at any rate near to it. The second period extends from about 39 B.C. to 450 A.D., when the Romans, masters of Alexandria, Syria, and Persia, carried on a brisk trade between Alexandria and India. The work of Aristotle which comes to our notice in this period is the Prior and Posterior Analytics (and possibly also the De Interpretatione), from which Akṣapāda, Nāgārjuna, Vasubandhu, and Dignāga seem to have, as shown above, borrowed the definition of some of the most important logical terms, the explanation of the various structures of the syllogism and the idea of a universal position, the basis of a true syllogism. The two chief among these logicians, Akṣapāda and Dignāga, were inhabitants of Kathiawar (Prabhāsa) and Conjeeveram (Kāñchī), which were the principal seaports on the eastern and western coasts of India, frequented by merchants and travellers from Alexandria. It is probable that the Prior Analytics was widely read in those days, either in the original or in vernacular translation. The introduction of different parts of the Greek Prior Analytics into Indian Logic must needs have been gradual, as these had to be assimilated into and harmonized with the parts previously ingrafted into Indian thought and language. The third period extends from about 450 A.D. to 600 A.D. when the Syro-Persian school of Gundeshapur, [2] established in Susiana (Persia) in 350 A.D. on the dispersion there of some of the best works of the school of Alexandria, was in the height of its glory and spread its light all around. But it is not quite certain whether any influence was exerted at this period.

I have endeavoured in the preceding pages to show that the works of Aristotle were very well known in India during the first six centuries of the Christian era. As regards the remarks of Cicero and Strabo, quoted by Sir A. Grant, that most of Aristotle's "writings had been lost," [3] I have to state that after the death of Aristotle his entire works were bought up by Callimachus [4] for the

---

[1] *Ibid.*, vol. xviii, p. 599. [2] *Vide* Huart's *Arabic Literature*, p. 137.

[3] Sir Alexander Grant's article on Aristotle in the *Encyclopædia Britannica*, 9th ed., vol. ii, p. 512,

[4] *Encyclopædia Britannica*. 9th ed., vol. i, p. 498.

library of Alexandria, where they were duly appreciated and whence they gradually spread to India and other countries. To the scholars at Athens and Rome these works were practically lost, until copies of some of them reached the island of Rhodes, where they were edited by Andronicus in 50 B.C. Even the edition of Andronicus was not available in the Middle Ages to the Greeks and Romans, who depended for their knowledge of Aristotle on the Latin translation of Boethius (480–525 A.D.). But the original works of Aristotle seem to have been carefully preserved in Alexandria, and on the downfall of the Greeks and Romans they found their way into Syria and Persia, whence they reached the Arabic school of Bagdad about the beginning of the ninth century A.D. The original Greek texts of Aristotle's works after these strange vicissitudes reached the country of their birth via Constantinople about 1204 A.D. The presumption, therefore, is that from the third century B.C. to 1200 A.D. Aristotle's works were more extensively read and better appreciated in the East than in the West.

APPENDIX C.[1]

THE UNIVERSITY OF NĀLANDĀ.

(About 300—850 A.D.).

Nālandā was a village which is identified with modern Baragaon,[2] 7 miles north of Rajgir, in Behar. Though occasionally mentioned in the Pāli literature, Nālandā was not of great importance before the rise of the Mahāyāna at the beginning of the Christian era. Nāgārjuna, about 300 A.D., and Ārya Deva, about 320 A.D., were the earliest scholars to take an interest in the educational institution at that village. A Brahmaṇa named Suviṣṇu, a contemporary of Nāgārjuna, is said to have established 108 temples there in order that the Abhidharma of the Mahāyāna might not decline.[3] About 400 A.D. the Chinese pilgrim, Fahian,[4] visited this place, which he calls "the village of Nalo." He saw there a tower which had been erected on the spot where Sāriputra, the right-hand disciple of Buddha, had entered Nirvāṇa. Early in the 7th century A.D. another Chinese pilgrim, the famous Hwen-thsang, visited Nālandā and halted[5] there 15 months to study the Sanskrit language under Sīlabhadra. According to him[6] the site of Nālandā was originally a mango garden which was bought by 500 merchants at a cost of ten crores of gold pieces and given to Buddha.[7] After the Nirvāṇa of Buddha, five kings, named Sakrāditya, Buddha Gupta, Tathāgata Gupta, Bālāditya, and Vajra, built five Saṅghārāma or monasteries at Nālandā. A king of Central India established another magnificent monastery, and began to build round these edifices a high wall with one gate. A long succession of kings continued the work of building, using all the skill of the sculptor, till at the time of Hwen-thsang in 637 A.D. the whole was "truly marvellous to behold." In the establishment were some thousands of monks, all men of great ability and learning. They were very strict in observing the rules of Vinaya, and were looked up to as models by all India. Learning and discussing, they found the day too short, day and night

---

1 From the author's "Indian Logic: Medieval School" (Appendix A).

2 *Vide* Cunningham's Ancient Geography of India, p. 468.

3 *Vide* Tārānātha's Geschichte des Buddhismus von Schiefner, pp. 70—86.

4 *Vide* Beal's Fa-hian, p. 111.

5 *Vide* Cunningham's Ancient Geography of India, p. x.

6 *Vide* Beal's Buddhist Records of the Western World, vol. ii, pp. 168—170.

7 It must have been given to a Buddhist saint of a later age and not to Buddha himself.

they admonished each other, juniors and seniors mutually helping to perfection. Learned men from different cities came to Nālandā to acquire renown, and some persons even usurped the name of Nālandā students in order that they might be received everywhere with honour. "Of those from abroad who wished to enter the schools discussion, the majority, beaten by the difficulties of the problems, withdrew; and those who were deeply versed in old and modern learning were admitted, only two or three out of ten succeeding.'[1] Hwen-thsang mentions some celebrated men of Nālandā, such as Dharmapāla and Candrapāla, Guṇamati and Sthiramati,[2] Prabhāmitra and Jinamitra, and Jñānacandra and Sīlabhadra.

Another Chinese pilgrim named I-tsing, who resided in Nālandā for ten years (probably 675—685 A.D.), says that there were eight halls and 300 apartments in the monastery of Nālandā with more than 3,000 resident monks. The lands in its possession contained more than 200 villages which had been bestowed upon the monastery by kings of different generations.[3]

Nālandā assumed the character of a university from about 450 A D.[4] Bālāditya, king of Magadha, who built a monastery at Nālandā, was a contemporary of the Hun king Mihirakula, who reigned first in Śākala and afterwards in Kāśmīra. Now Mihirakula[5] began his reign in 515 A.D., and his contemporary, Bālāditya, must also have lived about that time. There were three predecessors of Bālāditya who built monasteries at Nālandā. Of them, the earliest, named Śakrāditya, must have reigned about 450 A.D. if we suppose 25 years as the average duration of the reign of each of them. The year 450 A.D. is then the earliest limit which we can roughly assign to the royal recognition of Nālandā. The latest limit which we know with certainty is

---

1 *Vide* Watters' "On Yuan Chwang," vol. ii, pp. 164—165.

2 This Sthiramati seemed to be the one mentioned by I-tsing (*vide* Takakusu, p. 181), He flourished after Asaṅga and Vasubandhu.

3 *Vide* Takakusu's I-tsing, pp. xxxiii, 65 and 154.

4 *Vide* Watters' "On Yuan Chwang," vol. i, p. 289.

Takakusu, in his "Paramārtha's Life of Vasubandhu," published in the "Journal of the Royal Asiatic Society of Great Britain and Ireland," January 1905, maintains that Bālāditya came to the throne in 481 A.D., but this statement is by no means final. The date (452–480 A.D.) of Vikramāditya, Bālāditya's father, is also open to dispute.

5 Dr. D. B. Spooner observes :—

Nālandā, as is widely known, was one of the principal seats and centres of Buddhist culture and Buddhist learning in the Gupta period of Indian history, and for some centuries thereafter. The precise date of its foundation as "University" is now unknown, but from the circumstance that the Chinese pilgrim, Fa Hien, makes no particular mention of the place, whereas the pilgrim who followed him, Hieun Thsang, describes the place at length, leads modern scholars to infer that it must have risen in the interval between the visits of these two, namely, somewhere about the middle, perhaps, of the fifth century A.D. (p. 33 of the "Annual report of the Archæological Survey of India, Eastern Circle, for 1915–16.

750 A.D., when Kamalaśīla (*q.v.*) was the professor of Tantras at Nālanda. But as we read in the accounts of Vikramaśila that there was for some time an intercourse between that university and Nālandā, we may suppose that the latter continued to exist approximately until 850 A.D.

According to Tibetan accounts[1] the quarter in which the Nālandā University, with its grand library, was located, was called Dharmagañja (Piety Mart). It consisted of three grand buildings called Ratnasāgara, Ratnodadhi, and Ratnarañjaka, respectively. In Ratnodadhi, which was nine-storeyed, there were the sacred scripts called Prajñāpāramitā-sūtra, and Tāntrik works such as Samāja-guhya, etc. After the Turuṣka raiders had made incursions in Nālandā, the temples and *Caityas* there were repaired by a sage named Mudita Bhadra. Soon after this, Kukutasiddha, minister of the king of Magadha, erected a temple at Nālandā, and, while a religious sermon was being delivered there, two very indigent Tīrthika mendicants appeared. Some naughty young novice-monks in disdain threw washing-water on them. This made them very angry. After propitiating the sun for 12 years, they performed a *yajña*, fire-sacrifice, and threw living embers and ashes from the sacrificial pit into the Buddhist temples, etc. This produced a great conflagration which consumed Ratnodadhi. It is, however, said that many of the Buddhist scriptures were saved by water which leaked through the sacred volumes of Prajñapāramitā-sutra and Tantra.

1 *Vide* Pag-sam jon-zang, edited in the original Tibetan by Rai Sarat Chandra Das, Bahadur, C.I.E., at Calcutta, p. 92.

APPENDIX D.[1]

A LIST OF KINGS OF THE PĀLA DYNASTY OF BENGAL AND BEHAR.

(*From Tibetan sources.*)

In the Tibetan books,[2] such as Pag-sam-jon-zang, Lama Taranatha's Chos-byuṅ, etc., we find a short account of the kings of the Pāla dynasty of Bengal. Go Pāla, the founder of the dynasty, lived principally in Puṇḍra-vardhana. His successor, Deva Pāla, annexed Vārendra to his kingdom. Deva Pāla's grandson, Dharma Pāla, conquered Magadha and annexed it to Bengal. Dharma Pāla's power is said to have extended in the east to the ocean, in the west to Delhi, in the north to Jālandhara, and in the south to the Vindhya ranges. It is stated that during his reign Śānta Rakṣita died. Now Śānta Rakṣita visited Tibet during the reign of Thi-srong-deu-tsan in 749 A.D., and worked there for 13 years, that is, till 762 A.D. His death must therefore have taken place after 762 A.D. Dīpaṅkara Śrījñāna *alias* Atiśa, High-priest Vikramaśilā, who was a contemporary of king Naya Pāla of Magadha, visited Tibet in company with Nag-tsho-lotsava in 1040 A.D. during the reign of Lha-tsun-byaṅ-chub, son of Lha-lama-ye śes-ḥod, who held his court at Tholing in Ñāri. These facts throw a good deal of light on the dates of the Pāla kings.[3] It is further stated that the death of Mahī Pāla is exactly synchronous with that of the Tibetan king Khri-ral. Now Khri-ral (or Ral-pa-can) died in 899 A.D.[4] This fixes the date of the death of Mahī Pāla. As the period of reign of each of the kings that preceded and succeeded Mahī Pāla is definitely stated by Lama Tārānātha, and also by the author of the Pag-sam-jon-zang, there is no difficulty in ascertaining the dates of the Pāla kings. Proceeding in this way, we can fix the dates as follows :—

1.	Go Pāla	660—705 A.D.
2.	Deva Pāla	705—753 A.D.
3.	Rasa Pāla	753—765 A.D.

---

1 From the author's "Indian Logic, Medieval School" (Appendix B).

2 *Vide* Tārānātha's Geschichte des Buddhismus, von Schiefner, pp. 202—252; and Pag-sam-jon-zang, edited by Rai Sarat Chandra Das, Bahadur, C.I.E., pp. 112—121.

3 *Vide* the 16th volume of Kloṅ-rdol-gsuṅ-ḥbum, and Sarat Chandra Das's "Indian Pandits in the Land of Snow," pp. 50—76.

4 *Vide* the Chronological Table extracted from the Vaiduryakarpo in Csoma de Koros's Tibetan Grammar, p. 183.

4. Dharma Pāla .. .. 765— 829 A.D.
5. Masu Rakṣita .. .. 829— 837 A.D.
6. Vana Pāla .. .. 837— 847 A.D.
7. Mahī Pāla .. .. 847— 899 A.D.
8. Mahā Pāla .. .. 899— 940 A.D.
9. Śamu Pāla[1] .. .. 940— 952 A.D.
10. Śreṣṭha Pāla or Praiṣṭha Pāla 952— 955 A.D.
11. Canaka .. .. 955— 983 A.D.
12. Bhaya Pāla .. .. 983—1015 A.D.
13. Naya Pāla .. .. 1015—1050 A.D.
14. Āmra Pāla .. .. 1050—1063 A.D.
15. Hasti Pāla .. .. 1063—1078 A.D.
16. Ksānti Pāla .. .. 1078—1092 A.D.
17. Rāma Pāla .. .. 1092—1138 A.D.
18. Yakṣa Pāla .. .. 1138—1139 A.D.

The researches on the Pāla kings, by the late Dr. Rājendra Lal Mitra, arrived at a conclusion which is somewhat different from mine. Dr. Mitra's list of Pāla kings[2] is given below:—

1. Go Pāla.. .. .. 855— 875 A.D.
2. Dharma Pāla .. 875— 895 A.D.
3. Deva Pāla .. .. 895— 915 A.D.
4. Vigraha Pāla I .. .. 915— 935 A.D.
5. Nārāyaṇa Pāla .. .. 935— 955 A.D.
6. Rāja Pāla .. .. 955— 975 A.D.
7. ....Pāla .. .. 795— 995 A.D
8. Vigraha Pāla II .. .. 995—1015 A.D.
9. Mahī Pāla .. .. 1015—1040 A.D.
10. Naya Pāla .. .. 1040—1060 A.D.
11. Vigraha Pāla III .. .. 1060—1080 A.D.

---

[1] Probably the same as Nārāyaṇa Pāla who, in the Bhagalpur plate, is styled "the lord of Aṅga."

[2] *Vide* Dr. Rājendra Lāl Mitra's "Indo-Aryans," vol. ii, p. 232.

APPENDIX E.[1]

THE ROYAL UNIVERSITY OF VIKRAMAŚILĀ.

(About 800—1200 A.D.).

Vikramaśilā,[2] mentioned in Sanskrit Sragdharāstotra-ṭikā,[3] Vṛhat-svayambhū-purāṇa,[4] Tibetan Tangyur,[5] etc., was a great collegiate monastery, or rather University, founded by king Dharma Pāla at the close of the 8th century A.D. It was situated on a precipitous hill[6] in Behar at the right bank of the Ganges, possibly at Śila-saṁgama, now called Pātharghāṭā near Colgong in the Bhagalpur district. Dharmapāla endowed the university with rich grants sufficing for the maintenance of 108 resident monks besides numerous non-resident monks and pilgrims. At the head of the university was always a most learned and pious sage. Thus at the time of Dharma Pāla, Ācārya Buddha-jñāna-pāda directed the affairs of the university, and during 1034—1038 A.D. Dīpaṅkara or Śrījñāna Atiśa

---

1 From the author's "Indian Logic: Modioval School" (Appendix C).

2 *Vide* Tārānātha's Geschichte des Buddhismus, von Schiefner, pp. 234—242, 259—261; Pag-sam-jon-zang, pp. 113, 117, 118; and Sarat Chandra Das's article in the "Journal of the Buddhist Text Society of Calcutta", vol. i, part i, pp. 10—12; and his "Indian Pandits in the Land of Snow," pp. 50—76.

3 The colophon of the Sragdharā-stotra-tikā runs as follows:—

श्रीमद्विक्रमशीलदेवमहाविहारीय राजगुरुपण्डितभिक्षु श्रीजिनरक्षितकृता स्रग्धरास्तुति-टीका परिसमाप्ता (Sragdharā-stotra, edited in the Bibliotheca Indica series by Satis Chandra Vidyabhusana, p. 50).

4
नाराचस्थां नगर्यां च विहारे यत्र धार्मिके ।
तदा विक्रमशीलस्थि विहारे वसदुत्तमः ॥
धर्मश्रीमित्र नामाऽयं भिक्षुः पण्डितकञ्चुकः ।
धर्मं दिदेशयामास नामसङ्गीति च कथाम् ॥

(Vṛhat-svayambhū-purāṇa, edited by M. M. Hara Prasad Sastri, chap, vi, 320—321).

5 Numerous Sanskrit works such as तारैकविंशतिकास्तवे संक्षेप, तारा-विरजस्तोत्रम्, etc., were translated into Tibetan in the monastery of Vikramaśilā, as is evident from the Tangyur, Rgyud, La, Folios 11—26, 54, etc.

6 At the distance of a day's sail below Sultanganj there is a steep hill called Pātharghāṭā overhanging the Ganges, which here is *uttaravāhini* (or flows towards the north). This corresponds exactly with the account of Vikramaśilā given in Tibetan books. There are also ruins of Buddhistic images at Pātharghāṭā. For its old name Śilasaṁgama *vide* Francklin's "Site of Ancient Palibothra," pp. 54—55, Appendix, p. xiii. General Cunningham identifies Vikramaśilā with modern Silao, which is a small village three miles to the south of Bargaon (ancient Nālandā) and six miles to the north of Rajgir in the subdivision of Behar (*vide* Report of the Archæological Survey, vol. viii, p. 83). But this identification does not tally with the description found in Tibetan books, for the Ganges never passed by Silao, nor is there any hill near to it.

was at its head, and Sthavira Ratnākara was the superior of the monastery. The famous Tibetan scholar Nag-tshul-khrims-rgyal-wa, better known as Nag-tsho Lotsava, who came to take Dīpaṅkara Srījñāna *alias* Atiśa to Tibet, resided in the monastery of Vikramaśilā for three years, 1035—1038 A.D.[1] Kamalakuliśā, Narendra-śrī-jñāna, Dāna Rakṣita, Abhayakara Gupta Śubhakara Gupta, Sunāyakaśrī, Dharmākara Śānti and Śākyaśrī Paṇḍita also belonged to the university of Vikramaśilā. Provision was made specially for the study of grammar, metaphysics (including logic) and ritualistic books. On the walls of the university were painted images of paṇḍitas eminent for their learning and character. The distinguished scholars of the university received a diploma of "Paṇḍita" from the kings themselves. For instance, the distinguished logicians, Ācārya Jetāri of Vārendra and Ratnavajra of Kāśmīra, were granted such a diploma. The most erudite sages were appointed to guard the gates of the university. These were six in number, each of which had to be guarded by scholars designated "Gate-keepers" (called in Tibetan Go-sruṅ, corresponding, perhaps, to our Dvāra-paṇḍita). During the reign of Canaka (855—983 A.D.) the undermentioned eminent logicians acted as gate-keepers:—

(i) At the eastern gate	..	Ācārya Ratnākara Śānti.
(ii) At the western gate	..	Vāgīśvarakīrtī, of Benares.
(iii) At the northern gate	..	The famous Naropa.
(iv) At the southern gate	..	Prajñākaramati.
(v) At the first central gate	..	Ratnavajra of Kāśmīra.
(vi) At the second central gate	..	Jñāna-śrīmitra of Gauḍa.

The university of Vikramaśilā is said to have been destroyed by the Mahomedan invader Bakhtiar Khiliji[2] about 1203 A.D. when Sākya śrī-paṇḍita, of Kāśmīra, was at its head.

---

[1] *Vide* Kloṅ-rdol-gsuṅ-ḥbum, vol. xvi.

[2] *Vide* the Tibetan English Dictionary compiled by Rai Sarat Chandra Das, p. 869; Waddell's "Lamaism," p. 16.

The Turuṣkas or Mahomedans attacked Magadha several times. Thus Tārānātha, speaking of Ācārya Kamala Rakṣita who was at the head of the Vikramaśilā university at the end of the 10th century A.D., observes :—"A minister of the Turuṣka king, out of the Karṇa land in the west, together with 500 Turuṣkas, drew to Magadha to plunder. They plundered the sacrificial materials, but when they began to walk all in a body to the Ācārya (Kamala Rakṣita) the Ācārya got into a rage and walked up along, throwing a jug, filled with water, over which he had spoken the mantras. On the spot a great and indomitable storm collected, out of the wind came forth many black men armed with swords who fell upon the Turuṣkas; the minister himself perished spitting blood, and various contagious illnesses repulsed the others in such a way that none of them could reach their native country, and a great terror came over the Tīrthas and Turuṣkas—Tārānātha's Geschichte des Buddhismus, von Schiefner, pp. 266, 261.

APPENDIX F.

THE UNIVERSITY OF MITHILĀ.
(1175—1575 A.D.).

Modern history of Tirhut.

In the Rāmāyana, Mahābhārata and in Buddhistic literature, Mithilā or Tirhut figures as a renowned kingdom. Mithilā was protected on the north by the impenetrable jungles of the Himalayas. On the other three sides the three rivers Gandaki, Ganges and Kauśaki [1] surrounded it, while the land itself is intersected by small rivers. On account of the natural protection, Tirhut was not attacked by foreign invaders frequently though we hear that in the 13th century it was attacked by the ninth Malik Izzuddin-Tughril (1233-1244 A.D.) When Vijaya Sen was reigning in Bengal, Nānyadeva [2] of the Karṇatak dynasty was ruling in Mithilā in 1097 A.D. He was defeated by king Vijaya [3] from whom again Nānyadeva's son, Gangadeva, recovered Mithilā. Nānyadeva reigned for 36 years and died in 1125 A.D. He was succeeded by Gangadeva. He was succeeded by his son, Nrisiṁhadeva. The kings that succeeded Nṛsiṁhadeva were Rām Siṁha, Śakti Siṁha, Bhūpati Siṁha and Hara Siṁha. Their reign comprised 216 years. Roughly speaking the Karṇāta dynasty reigned from 1150-1395 A.D. Then the Kāmeśvara dynasty succeeded whose reign extended from 1350-1515 A.D. They are :—(1) Kameśvara, (2) Bhāgīśvara, (3) Gaṇesvara, (4) Vīsiṁhadeva (5) Kīrtisiṁha (6) Bhavasiṁhadeva, (7) Devasiṁha, (8) Śivasiṁha, (9) Padmasiṁha, (10) Harasiṁhadeva, (11) Nṛsiṁha or Narasiṁha, (12) Dhīrasiṁha, (13) Bhairava, (14) Rāmabhadradeva, (15) Lakṣmīnāthadeva. Then followed Maheśvara Ṭhakkura, who founded a line of Rajas in 1556, during the time of Emperor Akbar

---

1 History of Mithilā during the pre-Mughal period and History of Navya-Nyāya and Smṛit, November and December, 1915. Rai Monmohan Chakravarti Bahadur; *vide* also University of Nadia by Satis Chandra Vidyabhusana.

2
नन्देन्दुबिन्दुविधुसम्मितशाकवर्षे
सच्छ्रावणे सितदले मुनिसिद्ध तिथ्यां
स्वातौ शनैश्चरदिने करिवैरि लग्ने
श्रीनान्यदेव नृपतिर्व्यदधीत वास्तुम ॥

Vide the Rock Edicts on the ruined walls of the ancient fort of Simrāon.

3
त्वं नान्यवीर विजयीति गिरः कवीनां
श्रुत्वान्यथामनन निगूढ रोषः ।

Deopara Vijaya Sen Inscription.

which has continued up to the present time. Most of the later productions of Mithilā appeared in these periods.

The Modern School of Nyāya commenced with Gaṅgeśa on the eve of the 12th century. Similar is the case with Smṛti writers who began with Graheśvara in the 13th century.

Writers of the Mithilā in modern times.

The most important scholar of the Kāmeśvara period is Jagaddhara who besides writing commentaries on a variety of subjects, such as the Gītā, Devīmahātmya, Meghadūta, Gīta Govinda and Mālatī Mādhava and others, wrote original treatises on erotics (Rasika Sarvasva, Saṅgīta Sarvasva). The next is Vidyāpati whose name is associated with Maithili songs or Padāvalī generally. His works stirred up the later Vaiṣṇava writers of Bengal. The next scholar to be mentioned is Śaṅkara Miśra. His works on the Vaiśeṣika and the Nyāya are of high value. His other works on Smṛti are also of great value.

The next scholar of great importance is Vācaspati Miśra who flourished in the time of Bhairavendra and Rāmabhadra and wrote mainly on the Smṛti. But the great influence of the age did not spare him and he wrote also on Nyāya. His works on the latter subject are the Nyāya-sūtrādhāra, Khaṇḍana-khaṇḍādhāra and the Anumāna-khaṇḍa-ṭīka, his other works being the Nīti-cintāmaṇi, a work on the morals.

Many other scholars flourished at this time. But they are overshadowed by the glory and achievements of the scholars named above. It was an age of great scholastic activities. The glory of Mithilā was at its height, and its fame spread throughout all centres of oriental learning in India.

Thus Mithilā was the principal seat of Hindu learning in the 13th, 14th and 15th centuries A.D. and was the resort of a large number of students who flocked there from all parts of India to study specially Logic or Nyāya philosophy.[1]

---

[1] Students who finished their education in Mithilā had to undergo an examination called Needle Examination, Śalākā-parīkṣā. They were asked to explain the page pierced last by a needle. In this way they had to show their skill in any part of a book. After passing the examination they received the diploma of the Mithilā University.

APPENDIX G.

THE UNIVERSITY OF NADIA.

(1575—1920 A.D.).

Situation of Nadia.

Navadvīpa, which is popularly known as Nadia, is a small town in Bengal situated on the river Bhāgīrathī (Ganges) at the point of its junction with the Jalāṅgī. It occupies the north-western part of the Gangetic delta and literally signifies "a new isle." Once it was a very important centre through which trade was carried on by the Bhāgīrathī between Saptagrāma (a port on the river Sarasvatī, a little to the north-west of Huglī and nearly 15 krośas south of Nadia) and the United Provinces and by the Jalāṅgī between Saptagrāma and Eastern Bengal.

Traces of the Pala Kings in Nadia.

Nearly four miles to the east of the modern town of Nadia there is a small village called Suvarṇa-vihāra (golden hermitage) which is often pointed out as the place where the Buddhist Kings of the Pāla dynasty used to reside in the days of yore, when a branch of the Bhāgīrathī, flowing from the north of the modern village Māyāpur, rolled below the hermitage. Even now the ruins of the ancient buildings can be found here and there, silently testifying to the former grandeur of the place. The decaying stone column and fragments found here bear clearly the architectural designs of Buddhist India, which may be taken as proof that the place was once a temporary resort of the Pāla Kings. Relying upon these facts the existence of Nadia can be traced back to the 10th century A.D.

Nadia raised to the status of a town under the Sena Kings.

But, practically speaking, Nadia was unknown in history until it rose to importance for the first time in 1063 A.D. (or rather about 1106 A.D.) when, according to a local legend cited in the Imperial Gazetteer [1] of India and Statistical Account of Bengal [2] it was selected by Mahāraja Lakṣmaṇa Sena of Gauḍa [3] as the place of his residence in consideration of the sanctity of the Bhāgīrathī flowing by it. The ruins of the palace of Lakṣmaṇa Sena are still extant in Nadia at the south of the village Bilpukur and north of the village Samudragada

---

1 W. W. Hunter's Imperial Gazeteer of India, Vol. VII, p. 13.

2 W. W. Hunter's Statistical Account of Bengal, Vol. II, p. 142.

3 Lakṣmaṇa Sena is said to have reigned in Bengal between 1106 and 1138 A.D. For the date of the kings of the Sena dynasty, *vide* Rajendra Lal Mitra's Indo-Aryans, Vol. II, p. 256.

between the Bhāgīrathī and Jalāṅgī. About a mile to the north-east of Nadia there is a tank called Ballāla Dighi which is said to have been dug by Lakṣmaṇa Sena to commemorate the name of his father, the famous Ballāla Sena.

The Court of Lakṣmaṇa Sena.

Lakṣmaṇa Sena (1106–1138 A.D.), who raised Nadīa to the status of a town, is said to have been a great hero, whose prime minister was Halāyudha, the renowned author of Brāhmaṇa-sarvasva, Smṛti-sarvasva, Mīmāmsā-sarvasva, and Nyāya-sarvasva. The court of Lakṣmaṇa Sena was also adorned by Paśupati, the eldest brother of Halāyudha, who wrote a treatise on Hindu ceremonials called Paśupati-paddhati; Sūlapāṇī, the reputed author of Smṛti-viveka, Jayadeva, a native of Kendubilva, Birbhum and the well-known author of Gītagovinda; Dhoyi, the author of Pavanadūta; and Umāpati, the poet who made "language to sprout into luxuriant foliage"—all these flourished in the court of Lakṣmaṇa Sena.[1]

Nadia conquered by the Mahomedans.

Though Lakṣmaṇa Sena resided in Nadia, he greatly embellished the city of Gauḍa, which was the capital of Bengal at that time and was called Lakṣmaṇāvatī or Lakhnauti after his name. Lakṣmaṇa Sena was succeeded by Mādhava Sena (1138-39) Keśava Sena (1139) and Lakṣmaṇeya Sena *alias* Aśoka Sena (1139-1205 A.D.) The last king named Lakṣmaṇeya, designated by Mahomedan writers as Lakṣmaniya, was overthrown by Mahammad Bakhtiar Khiliji and was forced to run away to Vikramapura in Eastern Bengal about 1197 A.D. Bakhtiar Khiliji who marched with his troops from Behar to Nadia, plundered the latter town, and placing a Kazi there to look after its internal administration, himself proceeded to Gauḍa which he conquered. Subduing Gauḍa he chose it as the capital of whole Bengal which he ruled up to 1200 A.D. The Mahomedans ruled Bengal from 1198 to 1757 A.D., when the battle of Plassey took place and the country came into the possession of the British.

The nucleus of a University at Nadia.

During the Mahomedan rule from 1198 to 1757 A.D., Nadia became the greatest centre of Hindu learning in Bengal. In the 15th century A.D. the nucleus of a university was formed here. It is not known how much aid was directly given by the Mahomedan rulers towards the formation of this university, but it cannot be denied that their having expelled the Buddhists from every corner of Bengal and having stood as safeguards against all for-

---

[1] Baṭū Dāsa was the general of the army of Lakṣamaṇa Sena. His son, Śrīdhara Dāsa, who wrote a book named Sadukti-karṇāmṛta in 1209 A.D., has mentioned many of the learned men of his time.

eign invaders, enabled the Brâhmanas to lay the foundation of this new university on strictly orthodox Hindu principles.

Decay of the universities of Vikramaśilā and Mithilā.

Before the rise of the Nadia University in Bengal there were two famous Universities in Behar, *viz.* the Buddhist University of Vikramaśilā and the Brahmanic University of Mithilā. Vikramaśilā is said to have been burnt and destroyed by Bakhtiar Khiliji about 1198 A.D., when he marched from Behar towards Nadia, while the glory of the University of Mithilā was extinguished by the energy of the rising scholars of Nadia. Mithilā, which was a principal seat of Hindu learning in the 14th century A.D., was the resort of a large number of students who flocked there from all parts of India to study specially the Nyāya philosophy (Logic). Knowing her importance Mithilā guarded with extreme care and even jealousy her own teachings and did not permit any student to take away from any *tol*[1] any logical book or even notes of the lectures delivered there. Students were allowed to go away only with their diplomas. This rule was a great obstacle to the study and teaching of Logic outside Mithilā. This great inconvenience was at last removed by Raghunāta Śiromaṇi of Nadia, as already related in his life.

The chair of Logic in the Nadia University.

Raghunāthā Śiromaṇi of immortal memory founded in the University of Nadīa a special Chair of Logic which has since been occupied by the best and foremost logicians of Bengal. Ability to write works of original merit did not alone constitute the sole and sufficient qualification of an occupant of the chair but an exceptional dialectical skill was regarded to be the *sine qua non* for the candidate. Accordingly it was only those who in a large assembly of scholars could effectively silence their opponents in open debate, could with any chance of success lay a claim to the chair. The Nadīa University has produced numerous logicians of eminence since the time of Raghunātha Śiromaṇi, who was the

---

1 A *tol* consists generally of a thatched chamber in which the Pandit and the class meet, and a collection of mud hovels round a quadrangle, in which the students live in the simplest manner. Each student has his own hut, in which there is scarcely any furniture except his brass water-pot and mat. A student remains at the *tol* often for eight or ten years, according to whether he is studying law or logic. The Pandit does not always live at the *tol*, but comes every day on which study takes place, from an early hour till sunset. The huts are built and repaired at his expense. No fees are charged, and until recent years the Pandit even helped to provide his pupils with food and clothing. He himself obtained the necessary funds by grants and by the presents which his fame as a teacher ensured to him at religious ceremonies. The usual number of students in a *tol* is about twenty-five, though there may be more. These in most cases have no means of subsistence. The teacher provides them with shelter and free tuition, and food and clothes they obtain from him and also from shopkeepers and landholders and by begging at the chief festivals.

("Ancient Indian Education" by Rev. F. E. Keay, p. 52.)

founder and first occupant of the Chair of Logic. During recent times the following were the senior logicians of Bengal :—

(1) Harirāma Tarka-siddhānta (about 1730 A.D.).
(2) Ramanārāyaṇa Tarka-pañcānana (about 1760 A.D.).
(3) Buno Rāmanātha (probably 1770).
(4) Kṛṣṇakānta Vidyāvāgīśa (probably 1780 A.D.).
(5) Śaṅkara Tarkavāgīśa (about 1800 A.D.).
(6) Śivanātha Vidyāvācaspai (1810 A.D.).

This last mentioned gentleman was son of Śaṅkara Tarkavāgīśa and exhibited his dialectic skill in a debate with the famous Jagannātha Tarka-pañcānana of Bansberia. He was succeeded by

(7) Kāśīnātha Cūḍāmaṇi (about 1820 A.D.).
(8) Daṇḍī (about 1830 A.D.).
(9) Śrīrāma-Śiromāṇi—(author of Padārtha-tattva).

(10) Mādhava Tarka-siddhānta (about 1850 A.D.) was originally a court Pandit of Naldānga, but subsequently came to settle at Nadīa. He was the author of a commentary called Subodhā on the Padārtha-tattva. He was succeeded by

(11) Haramohan Cuḍāmaṇi, author of Sāmānya-lakṣaṇa, who was a contemporary of Mādhava Tarkasiddhānta and Prasanna Tarkaratna (1870 A.D.) Principal and founder of Paka-tol. About this time Golakanātha Nyāyaratna (about 1854 A.D.) was a great logician.

Pandit Harinātha Tarka-siddhāntā, who died in 1890 A.D. was a logician of high order, though not the senior logician. Subsequently Mahāmahopādhyāya Bhuvanamohana Vidyāratna, Mahāmahopādhyāya Rājakṛṣṇa Tarkapañcānana, Mahāmahopādhyāya Jadunātha Sārvabhauma and Mahāmahopādhyāya Kāmikhyānātha Tarkavāgisa became the senior logicians.

Competition for the Chair of Nyāya.

I happened to be present at the Council of debate, held at Rājbāti, Nadīa, in which Mahāmahopādhyāya Rājakṛṣṇa Tarkapañcānana was declared the senior logician in 1894 A.D. The rival candidate was Jadunātha Sārvabhauma. The Maharaja of Nadia opened the debate in the presence of Pandits and Professors, which was to decide the fate of the two candidates. The questions to be debated were (1) "Whether there is re-birth !" and (2) "Whether Nirvāṇa is possible !"

Kṣitīṣacandra Ray.

Mahāmahopādhyāya Jadunātha Sārvabhauma, whose erudition and energy were manifest to all and commanded the respect of every scholar, was first to take up the questions and lead the debate. He tackled the questions thoroughly and answered them from every possible point of view. But his exposition was of such an abstruse character that it was only the experts who could follow him. Then came the turn of Mahāmahopādhyāya Rājakṛṣṇa Tarkapañcānana, who took up the same questions and explained them fully, steadily and clearly. He elucidated each difficult word and that so thoroughly and clearly that every point in the argument was driven home to the audience. He then assailed the arguments put forward by his rival and thoroughly exposed his hasty exposition. Mahāmahopādhyāya Rajakṛṣṇa, in recognition of his lucid exposition and convincing logic, was declared senior logician by the Council.

Chair of Smriti.

In Smṛti there is a chair[1] of the Senior Smārta (Jurist), which was inaugurated by Raghunandana, the most famous jurist of his time. Raghunandana flourished in the sixteenth century A.D. His Jyotiś-tattva was compiled in 1489 Śaka or 1567 A.D. After him there flourished Srikṛṣṇa Sārvabhauma, Srikṛṣṇa Tarkālaṅkāra, Gopāla Nyāyālaṅkāra, Daitya Bīreśvara and Ramānanda Vācaspati, Bīreśvara Nyāyapañcānana, Kṛṣṇakānta Vidyāvāgīśa, Lakṣmīkānta Nyāyabhūṣaṇa, Brajanātha Vidyāratna, Mathurānātha Padaratna, Lālmohan Vidyāvāgīśa, Śivanātha Vacaspati, Mahāmahopādhyāya Kṛṣṇanātha Nyāyapañcānana and Jogendranātha Smṛtitīrtha.

Tāntrik studies flourished under Kṛṣṇānanda Agamvāgīśa and his followers.

Chair of Astronomy.

A chair of astronomy was established in Nadīa a long time ago. As late as 1718 A.D. there was born in Gārgya gotra an astronomer named Rāmarudra Vidyānidhi who was the author of Jyotiṣa-sāra-saṅgraha and Court-Pandit of Pañcakota. From the time of Mahārāj Kṛṣṇacandra Roy, Rāmarudra Vidyānidhi, who is related by blood with the compiler of this work, was also a Court-Pandit to the Raj-family of Krishnagar. He and his successors, Rāmakṛṣṇa Vidyāmaṇi, Prāṇanātha Vidyābharaṇa, Rāmajaya Śiromaṇi, Śridāma Vidyābhuṣaṇa, Tāriṇīcharaṇa Vidyāvāgīśa, Durgādāsa Vidyāratna and Pandit Biśvambhara Jyotiṣārṇava successively held the chair of senior astronomer in Nadia. Almanacs were prepared by them, which were supplied to the Nawab's Court in Murshidabad as well as to the East India Company, the Supreme Court, the High Court, the Bengal Government, etc. Pandit Viśveśvara Jyotiṣārnava, the brother of the compiler of this work, was the last senior astronomer, who supplied almanacs to the High Court, etc. The Navadvīpa Pañjikā under the imprimatur of Nava-dvīpādhipateranujñayā is accepted by all the landholders of Bengal.

---

[1] *Vide* Navadvipa Mahimā, by Kanti Chandra Rarhi and "Nadīa Kāhinī," by Kumudanath Mullick.

APPENDIX H.

THE TASHI LAMA'S VISIT TO INDIA.

Tashi Lama and his party.

During the year 1905, His Holiness the Tashi Lama, accepted the invitation of the Government of India to be present at the reception to be held by their Royal Highnesses, the Prince and Princess of Wales. With full staff His Holiness left Shigatse for India early in November (8th Nov.). The Government of India made ample provision for the reception and escort of the party. Accordingly Captain W. F. O'Connor, C.I.E., British Trade Agent, Gyantse (Tibet), Captain R. Steen, I.M.S., Medical Officer, Gyantse, Maharaj Kumar Sidkyong Tulku, C.I.E. of Sikkim, Professor Satis Chandra Vidyabhusana of the Presidency College, were deputed by the Government of India to receive the party.

In addition to this about sixty Lamas and laymen accompanied the party. From Shigatse to Darjeeling, the Tashi Lama travelled by easy stages halting at various stations. At Gangṭok His Holiness and his followers were the guests of the Maharaja of Sikkim who placed his palace at their disposal. The party then started for Darjeeling. Great was the excitement when the party arrived there about afternoon on Wednesday, the 29th November, 1905. Crowds went out to meet him. At Jalapahar and Ghoom, the Bhutias prostrated themselves as he passed, touching his garments and even his baggage to receive a blessing. Special arrangements were made at the Drumdruid Hotel, and His Holiness was received with a Tibetan salutation. The party started for Kurseong by a special train and a special trolly conveyed His Holiness to Siliguri where he was joined by Professor Satis Chandra Vidyabhusana. At Siliguri, all round the camp lay camps of devout Bhutias, who, clad in their motley dress, had ridden in for miles to pay their respects to the Lama. His Holiness and suite arrived at Rawalpindi on the 7th December at 2-30 P.M. and on the same day His Holiness had an audience with His Royal Highness the Prince and Princess of Wales. On the 10th December, 9-30 A.M, His Holiness left for Taxila, called in Tibetan Do-Jog, about 26 miles north of Rawalpindi, whence he started for Agra, which place he reached on 11th December. About five days after, 16th December, the party arrived at Benares where he was accommodated in the Hotel de Paris. On the same day the Lama visited the Buddhist ruins of Sarnath about 4 miles north of Benares. Here, on the 18th December, Captain O'Connor accompanied by Professor

Tashi Lama in India.

Satis Chandra Vidyabhusana and the tutor of the Lama went to the Government College to make a preliminary examination of the Brahminic Sanskrit manuscripts, copies of which had already been translated into Tibetan at various dates between 629 A.D. and 1400 A.D. At 4 P.M. the Tāshi Lama, together with his minister and the Māharāj Kumar of Sikkim, visited the College and examined the various Sanskrit manuscripts. The party started for Buddha Gaya where His Holiness was a guest of the Mahant. On the 20th December Captain O'Connor, accompanied by Professor Satis Chandra Vidyabhusana and others, made a preliminary inspection of the sacred sites in Buddha Gaya. The Tāshi Lama offered his worship to the Bodhi tree and the image of Buddha on the 21st December, one of the most auspicious days according to the Tibetan calendar. On entering the sacred shrine His Holiness bowed down before the great image and sat down himself. An hour after His Holiness came out of the temple and changed his dress for a yellow one and sat in meditation in the *vaijrāsana* under the Bodhi tree for about three hours from 9 A M. to 12 A.M., while his numerous devotees stood round him in deep silence. At noon the Lama opened his eyes and received ovations and gifts from his followers.

The Tāshi Lama left Buddha Gaya at 10 P.M. on the 25th December and reached Calcutta by a special train on the 26th at 7-30 A.M. He was greeted by a salute of 17 guns and was received by the Aide-de-Camp of the Viceroy. His Holiness was accommodated at Hastings House and was a guest of the Government of India. On the 2nd January His Royal Highness the Prince of Wales received a state visit from the Tashi Lama. His Highness appeared before the heir-apparent of the Imperial throne of Great Britain in all the dignity of his high place and made offerings to His Royal Highness. From the 5th to the 11th January, His Holiness attended the garden party at the Government House, witnessed illuminations and was greatly delighted with all he saw. His Holiness also received their Royal Highnesses when they paid their return visit. On the 11th January, His Holiness left Calcutta, and, on the eve of his departure, in appreciation of the great assistance rendered by Professor Satis Chandra Vidyabhusana, presented to him the Khatag or complimentary silken scarf. The departure was public and was honoured by 17 guns.

Tāshi Lama's departure.

Captain O'Connor accompanied His Holiness up to Siliguri and Lieutenant Bailey accompanied the Lama all the way up to Shigatse. On the way back His Holiness was hospitably received at Chumbi. The party reached Gyantse on the 3rd February.

APPENDIX I.

REMINISCENCES OF A VISIT TO LABRANG, PAMIYANGCHI AND PADANGI.

Journey to Labrang.

Having being associated with Rai Bahadur Sarat Chandra Das, C.I.E., in the compilation of the Tibetan Dictionary, I heard of the fame of Labrang and Pamiyangchi as two old monasteries.

About 1907 I learnt that there were two block prints of the *Bstan ḥ-gyur* and *Bka ḥ-gyur* at Labrang and Pamiyangchi and I undertook my journey there with the express purpose of examining the manuscripts and endeavouring to extend the knowledge of Sanskrit through the study of the Tibetan.

Teesta Bridge.

I started with credentials, from Mr. (afterwards Sir) A. Earle, Director of Public Instruction, Bengal, and Mr. C. H. Bompas, I.C.S., Deputy Commissioner of Darjeeling. On the 31st May, 1907, I left Darjeeling at 10 A.M. At the time of my departure from my residence at Darjeeling Rai Bahadur Sarat Chandra Das came to see me, offering me a dozen of oranges and a lantern. He said, "Accept these as a traveller's humble gifts." I received them with delight and found them very useful on the way.

Riding a distance of about 22 miles I arrived in the evening at the Teesta Bridge. This is a very important frontier station between Tibet, Sikkim, and India, and through it the British mission passed to Lhasa in 1903-04. There is a magnificent bridge over the river Teesta and there is a small bazar where edibles are procurable I was welcomed here by the Deputy Forest Ranger, who accommodated me in the upper flat of a new building erected by a Marwari trader in the centre of the bazar. Within a mile of the bazar there is a Triveni junction, where the Rangeet and another river flow into the Teesta. Nepalese and other hillmen attach great sanctity to these junctions, where they wash themselves every year at *Pous Sankranti* (about the middle of January) On this occasion they sacrifice goats and sheep and hold a fair which continues for three days. Teesta Bridge is a very charming place surrounded by hills and dales.

Rung-Po.

In the morning of 1st June, I left the Teesta Bridge Valley and following up the course of the river Teesta, by the Tibetan trade route, I arrived in the evening at the Rung-Po Valley. It is fifteen miles to the north of Teesta Bridge and is situated on the river Rung-Po, on which there is an artistic drawbridge. The source of the river, according to local information, lies on a snow-covered lake at Phari. The Rung-Po Valley commands a very conspicuous position in Sikkim on the way to the territory of the Grand Lama. The musical rippling of the river and the artless beauty of the hills surrounding the valley are imposing and impressive. The grandeur of the landscape, specially in the evening, can better be imagined than described.

There are very few human habitations here, still there is a bazar where rice, *dal*, *ghee* and even potatoes are available. Besides, there are a post office, a telegraph office, a medical hospital, a police station and an excise patrol and a magnificent Dak Bungalow—all testifying to the great importance of the place.

Gangtok.

In the morning of 2nd June I left Rung-Po Valley for Gangtok. The river Rung-Po falls into the Teesta at a place called Bhotang which is about a mile down the Rung-Po Valley. Again following up the course of the river Teesta, I arrived at a place called Singdom which is 7 miles up the Rung-Po Valley. Here there is a magnificent bridge over a small river which flowing from upper Sikkim, empties itself into the Teesta. Bidding farewell to my old friend —the Teesta—I pursued this new river which took me to a place called Khola Bridge, 12 miles north of Rung-Po Valley. This place derives its name from the beautiful bridge which is supported by a spring. Crossing this and several other bridges and passing through hills and dales, I arrived in the evening at Gangtok, 27 miles north of Rung-Po Valley. It is the present capital of Sikkim, situated on the peak of a hill girt by two rivers on its sides. There is a good road from Gangtok. The good-natured Maharaja of Sikkim and the intelligent Maharani are both very much interested in Buddhism and showed me the kindest consideration.

Mr. J. C. White, C.I.E., Political Resident of Sikkim, to whom I was already known in connection with the Tashi Lama's pilgrimage in India, received me very kindly and gave me letters of introduction to the Lamas at Labrang and Phodang, a copy of it is given below :—

ལམ་ཡིག།

༄༅། །འབྲས་ལྗོངས་ཀྱི་ཁྲབ་ཏྲོར་ས་ཧེབ་ནས། ལྷ་བྲང་འདུས་ཚོགས་
སྙན་གྲུས་ལགས་སུ། སྤབས་འབུལ་ ད་ལམ་འདི་ནས་འབའ་སྦུ་ཤོ་ དེ་སི་ཙན་སྡར་
དབི་ལྷི་ཡ་འབུ་སན་དེ་ བཞིན་དེ་ག་ ལྷ་བྲང་དུ་ བསྟན་འགྱུར་པོ་ཏི་ཇི་ཡོད་ཞིབ་ ཆ་ལྟ་
རྟོགས་བྱ་བར་ འགྲོ་རྩིས་ཡོད་ པ་དེ་ ལུགས་ སྐུ་ ཉིད་ རྣམས་ནས་པོ་ ཏི་ རྣམས་ ཀློག་

བཙུག་དགོས་དང་། ལྷག་པར་ཁོང་ལ་རོགས་རམ་གང་དགོས་ཅི་ཡོད་བྱ་དགོས་པ་
རེ་ཞུགས་ཐུགས་འཛགས་ཞུ། མེ་ལུག་ཟླ་བ་བཞི་པའི་ཚེས་ཉེར་ལྔ་ལ་སྒང་ཏོག་ཀོ་
ཋི་ནས། སྤྲུལ།

འབྲས་ལྗོངས་སྤྱི་ཁྱབ་ཧྲིར་ས་ཧེབ་ཀྱི་ས་ཡིག།

PASS-PORT.

From

WARA SAHIB,

Political Resident of Sikkim.

To

The Council of Monks,

Labrang.

Communication:

Now from here Satis Chandra Vidyabhusana is going to Labrang to see and examine Bstan-ḥ-gyur. how much of it is there. For that purpose the Lamas must let him read the Puthis. Moreover whatever assistance he wants must be given. In this direction keep your heart—I request.

Fire sheep year, fourth month, date 25th, from Gangtok Kuthi sent letter from

WARA SAHIB,
Political Resident, Sikkim,
1907

(SD.) G. J. WHITE,
Political Officer.
Gangtok, 4th June, 1907.

A similar letter was written to the Phodang Lama's monastery.

Hospitality of a lady.

I got this letter at about 2 P.M. and started in the company of my attendants towards Labrang. The weather that day was extremely foul and some inhabitants of Sikkim advised us not to set out that afternoon. But as the time at our disposal was rather short, and we could ill afford to lose even a single day, we felt constrained to start that very afternoon, even in the face of the stormy weather. We had not gone far when the sky began to pour forth in torrents. Taking the reins of the horse in one hand and the umbrella in the other we tried to brave the elemental frowns as best as we could. But we got terribly drenched and thoroughly exhausted after a short time, and to our consternation we saw the shades of the evening were falling fast. Swiftly we rode on but no trace of human habitation was to be found. At last the darkness of the night made it absolutely impossible for us to keep the horses on the roads, and every moment they began to stumble. Thoroughly exhausted and horribly frightened, we looked for human abodes but none could be found —it was dreary and desolate all around. We saw one or two lights on the way but we could never reach them, they seemed ever so far off and twinkled more like will-o'-the-wisp At last at about 11 we saw the unmistakable glow of a lamp, coming out from a humble cottage. The Lama, who was our guide and interpreter, knocked at the door, but the inmate would not open the door easily. "Are these ghosts or elves that come to me at so late an hour in the night?" That was the first murmur that reached our ears, and we came to know that it was a woman that spoke. We had no breath to argue with her. We begged and implored, and to our relief the door flew open and we saw she was preparing barley flour then. She received us very hospitably and gave us plenty of milk she had kept reserved for selling in the following morning. Our cook got this milk properly warmed on the fire and some of our attendants prepared tea with it. I drank a quantity of milk and felt somewhat refreshed. She supplied us with water which she kept in very big bamboos from which the soft portions had been carefully scooped out. These bamboos contained enough water for us to cleanse our hands and feet, etc. We learnt from her that her son was a Thapa Lama that is, one who is dedicated to the service of the church, which he serves for six days in the week, and is also allowed to keep his connection with his home to which he is allowed to return on the seventh day. Next morning we were going to take leave of her when she insisted on my divining some future truth with regard to her son. The inhabitants of the place have no other conception of a scholar than as an astrologer and a physician. Learning that I was a scholar, she had inferred that *ipso facto* I knew divination and pressed me with importunity to let her know whether her son was to be blessed with a child or not. I found myself in a queer position. I looked at the palm of her hands and said: "Your object will be fulfilled by the grace of Buddha whom you will adore with devotion for two years."

Then we took leave of her and arrived in the morning of the 4th at the Labrang Monastery. Subsequently I visited Phodang, which is only one mile from Labrang.

Labrang and Phodang.

Labrang, which is 77 miles north of Darjeeling, is situated on a beautiful hill overlooking the snowy range of Khangri. There is an old monastery belonging to the oldest religious sect of Tibet, named *Nying-ma-pa* or the unreformed sect. It contains images of Buddha, Bodhisatvas and saints, and a very large collection of the Tibetan Buddhist manuscripts and block prints including the encyclopædias of the Kangyur and the Tangyur.

Phodang is nearly a mile below Labrang. Here, too, there is an old monastery (which is being reconstructed) belonging to the Karma-pa sect of Tibet. This monastery is said to have been founded in 1725 A.D. by the then Maharaja of Sikhim who visited the headquarters of the Karma-pa sect in the north of Lhasa and was asked by the head of that sect to establish some Karma-pa monasteries in Sikkim. In the Phodang monastery too there are numerous images and books but the Tangyur is not to be found here. It is surprising to find that the veneration shown here by Lamas to Buddha is not so great as that shown to Karma-pa, the founder of the sect. Karma-pa's image adorns the very centre of the sanctuary, while on his left side is the image of the Indian saint Pe-ma-jungne (called in Sanskrit Padmasambhava) who founded Lamaism in Tibet about 747 A.D. To his left is the image of Sākya-Thub-pa or Buddha, who preached the doctrine of Nirvāṇa nearly 2,400 years ago. There are images of such saints as Srid-du-rim-po-che, Chong-kha-pa, Gye-chag-rim-po-che and others.

I examined a considerable portion of the manuscripts and block prints at Labrang where the Lamas gave me all possible help in the matter. I could not stay there for more than a week because the provisions I carried from Darjeeling and Gangtok were all exhausted. At Phodang and Labrang very few edibles are available, even rice, salt and oil are not obtainable there. The people pass their days round their blazing hearth and depend entirely upon *tsam-pa* or flour from the parched barley. A dish of bamboo offshoot being regarded as a great delicacy. Their only luxury is tea unmixed with milk or sugar. The Marwaris, whom one can see in almost every hill or wood where there are three or four householders or coolies, have totally failed in their enterprise here. I heard that a Marwari retail-dealer had once set up a small shop here, but finding demand of no kind had to break it up.

Both Phodang and Labrang are solitary places almost abandoned by men. On the way from Gangtok to Labrang—a distance of thirteen miles—I found no human habitation and came across only three cowherds who had come from distant villages to graze their cattle. Sikkim is very thinly populated. I asked an old man at Labrang why the road from Gangtok to that place was bad and there were no shops. The reply was: "because no Englishman treads the path. There are very few people here. Our only hope is that with the increase of population in the plains men might revert to the hills to make them comfortable."

I passed a week at Phodang and Labrang very happily. I have never seen people more simple or more charitable than the Lamas there.

Sikhim Monasteries.

Sikhim was inhabited by Lepchas who were a mild pastoral race without any settled government. Buddhism was unknown in the country and the only creed that seems to have prevailed was Bon which was a kind of devil worship. Sikkim emerges into the ken of history in 1641 A.D., when a man named Phun-tshog-nam-gyal, supposed to be of Tibetan origin, was, in fulfilment of a prophecy, made king by Lha-tsun-chen-po and two other learned priests who had come from Tibet to spread Lamaism. By efforts of the priests and their followers and patronage of the king and his successors Buddhism or rather Lamaism, was firmly established and became the state religion in Sikkim. People from Tibet, Bhutan, China, Mongolia and Nepal migrated to Sikkim and were mixed up with the Lepchas to give rise to a new race called Bhuteas. They profess Lamaism and have built numerous monasteries, temples, *chaityas*, etc. The Tibetan term for a monastery is *gompa,* meaning a solitary place or hermitage. There are 35 monasteries in Sikkim of which Sang-ngag-tsi-ling, Pamiangchi, Tashiding, Phodang and Labrang are the chief. These were visited by the writer of this both during his travels in Sikkim in June 1907 and October 1908. Sang-ngag tsi-ling, 47 miles west of Gantok and founded in 1697 A.D., is a most democratic institution which is open to all classes of Tibetans, Lepchas, Limbus, etc., both male and female. It consists of several two-storeyed stone-buildings with a spacious quadrangle and the largest collection of curios and arts. Pamiangchi, facing the Kanchanjangha peaks and founded in 1705 A.D., is an aristocratic institution whose gates are shut against women and which is supposed to be managed by celibate monks of pure Tibetan race. It has lately been reconstructed and consists of a grand three-storeyed stone building. Tashiding, situated on the confluence of the rivers Rathong and Rungeet, was founded in 1716 A.D. It is the holiest place resorted to by pilgrims from all quarters. Phodang, 13 miles north-east of Gangtok and facing the snow of Khangri, was founded in 1740 A.D. on the site once occupied by the fort of the Bhutanese invaders. All its Head Lamas were disturbed by evil spirits that appeared in the shapes of scorpions, rock-snakes, etc., until one named Dum-chot totally destroyed them by his magic powers. The monastery has recently been rebuilt, and its Head Lama at the time of my visit was the late Maharaj Kumar of Sikkim, Sid-kayong-tul-ku. Labrang, 2 miles above Phodang, is a very secluded monastery founded by a prince of Sikkim in 1844 A.D. All these monasteries, built on the traditions of old Buddhist monasteries, stand on the tops of hills, and belong to the Nying-ma-pa or Redhat sect, with the exception of Phodang which belongs to the Karmapa sect. They contain a large collection of Tibetan manuscripts and xylographs, but the famous encyclopædia called the Tangyur is contained only in Labrang and Pamiangchi. Almost every family in Sikhim is bound to spare at least one boy for devotion to the monastery, and he has to undergo various grades of training before attaining the exalted position of a Lama. It is to be regretted that the pure Lepchas are rapidly dying out, and the Bhuteas cannot stand the heat of Sikhim below the height of 6,000 feet. Since the termination of the wars with Nepal, the Nepalese have been rushing in large numbers and in a few years almost the whole of Sikhim will be occupied by them.

APPENDIX J.

REMINISCENCES OF A VISIT TO PAMIYANGCHI.

During the Puja vacation of the year 1908, I received a letter of invitation from the Maharaja and Maharani of Sikkim. His Highness the Maharaja Sir Thu-tob-nam-gyal, K.C.I.E., of Sikkim was very anxious to give me all comforts on the way to Pamiyangchi, and the Maharani, a daughter of the Prime Minister of Tibet, wrote to the authorities of the Pamiyangchi monastery on my behalf. I also received the following letter from Her Highness the Maharani of Sikkim enquiring the date on which I might start :—

Invitation from the Maharaja of Sikkim.

Bhutia Sa Tel
Year, 4th month.

Gangtok,
26th June, 1908.

My dear Professor,

Last year when you came up about this time to go through the Tengyur at Labrang, you told me that you were so much interested that you would come up again this year to Pamiangchi. Do you think that you will be able to do so, and if you do about what time will it be? You must let me know beforehand, as to when you intend coming up, so that I may make some arrangements about making your journey and sojourn in Sikkim as easy as we can. At present we are having copious rains here, but we are all in sound health. Trusting you also to be in perfect health.

I remain,
Yours truly.
ཡེ་ཤེས.
Maharani.

Mahamahopadhyaya Satis Chadra Vidyabhusana, M.A.,
Secy. to the Buddhist Shrine Restoration Society,
Calcutta.

The letter was very kind, and I at once made up my mind to undertake a journey to Pamiyangchi. I started from Darjeeling on the 10th of October with a passport from Mr. Crawford, Deputy Commissioner, Darjeeling, and on first setting foot on the territory of the Maharaja of Sikkim I was simply surprised to notice the extraordinary arrangements that had been made by the Maharaja to provide me with all possible necessaries and comforts on the way. The royal mandate had gone forth to furnish us with all possible help and at every stage of our halt, we found numbers of men waiting for us with various articles of provision and fuel—all much too great for us to carry. Rice, *dal*, oranges, fruits, vege-

Reception on the way.

tables, hay, butter, milk, etc., almost in cartloads, were placed freely and abundantly at our disposal. On the third day we arrived at Pamiyangchi. Here we saw three European Consuls, who had come here on a pleasure trip, mainly for sight-seeing. Pamiyangchi commands an excellent view of the lofty and snow-covered hills of Kinchinjanga, and the Europeans were enjoying themselves immensely seeing sights and taking photos. They were a large company, being attended by a good many servants and camp-followers. They were however badly in need of provisions, and as we had more than what was necessary for ourselves we gave them a quantity of our own.

Pamiyangchi Monastery.

When I reached the monastery I was wonder-struck at the majestic and imposing sight which was presented from the lofty heights of the peak of Pamiyangchi which commands an excellent prospect of the picturesque and snowy peaks of Kanchanjangha from which silver-white liquid streams seem to be perpetually running out. On entering the monastery I introduced myself to the monks and presented before them the following letter of introduction, which had been sent to me by the Maharaja of Sikkim before I started from Calcutta :—

(TRANSLATION.)

To

THE INCOMPARABLE SCHOOL OF PRECIOUS MONKS.

Communication:

From Calcutta, India, a Sanskrit Pandit named Satis Chandra Acharyya Vidyabhusana goes to have access to B̲s-tan-h̲-gyur. He being of a different kingdom, provide him with a good residence. Whatever necessary objects the Babu himself wants, be that done in a worthy way. Whatever may benefit and assist him that should be immediately rendered. This is very important. Bear this in mind. I beseech you.

From Gangtok Palace, Earth-Ape Year, month 8. date 8.

The monks received me well and gave me a ready access to the B̲s-tan-h̲-gyur Block Prints. They offered me a seat there for the night. But this I thankfully declined and put up in the Dak Bungalow. I stayed at Pamiyangchi for eight days during which time I had every opportunity and facility for making a searching examination of and for studying of the B̲s-tan-h̲-gyur.

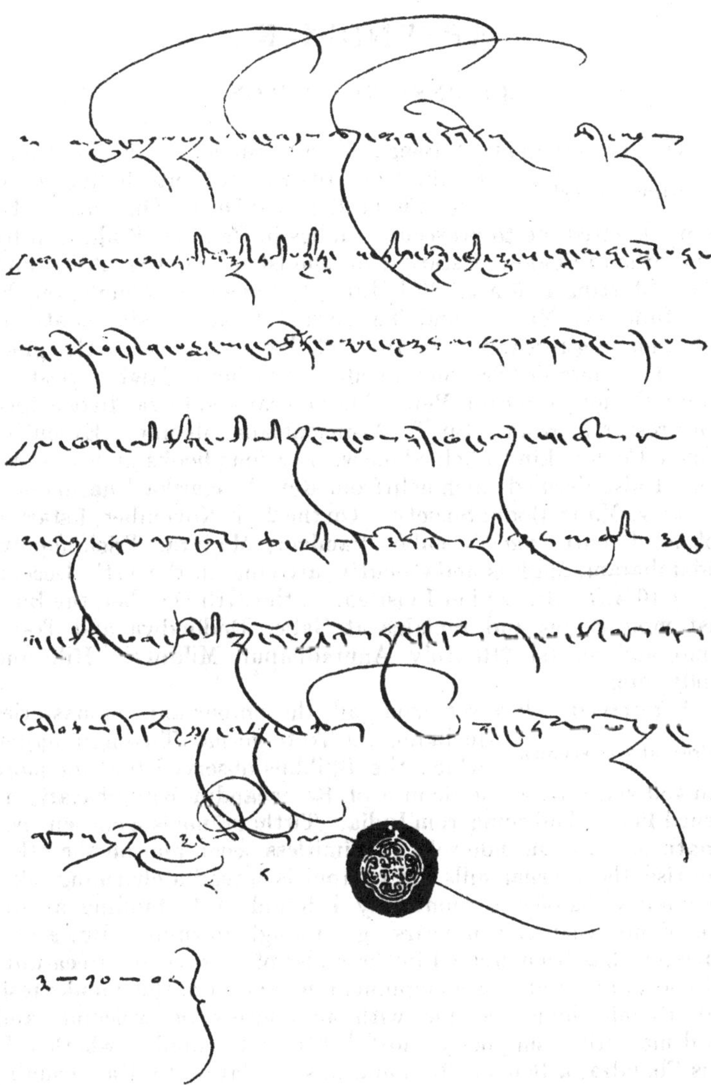

The original letter of introduction in Tibetan given by the Mahārājā of Sikkim.

APPENDIX K.

JOURNEY TO CEYLON

Experience in Ceylon.

The Government of Bengal in accordance with the advice of the Hon. Justice Sir Asutosh Mookerjee, Vice-Chancellor, and Dr. G. Thibaut, C.I.E., having deputed me to prosecute studies in Pali and Buddhism for six months in Ceylon, I started for the island on the 20th June, 1909. Starting at 6 P.M., 20th June, I arrived at Colombo on the 25th June via Madras and Tuticorin. I passed six months in Ceylon making researches in the Pali language under the guidance of Venerable Sri Sumungala Mahathero, High Priest of western Ceylon, and Prof. Venerable Nanisar and Deva Mitta helped in my research work. Sir P. Arunachalam, Member, Executive Council, Ceylon, kindly helped me with various books and information. I also derived much help from Rev. Anagarika Dharmapala, Secretary, Maha Bodhi Society. On the 25th November, I started back for Benares *via* Colombo, Pamban, Madura, Trichinopoly, Chidambaram, Madras and Calcutta, arriving on the 11th December, at 10 A.M. In Ceylon I visited, on the 27th October, the Buddhist monasteries and remains at Galle, Dodondwa and To-to-go-mo, and on 1st–7th July Anuradhapur, Mihintale Hill and Kandy, etc.

Address at To-to-go-mo.

I received addresses from all the important monasteries including the To-to-ge-mo (Tīrthagrâma), in which the Bhikkus observed that for more than 450 years after the demise of Rāmacandra Kavibhāratī, no learned Pandit had come from India. Tīrthagrāma is a chosen spot of nature. On one side rolls the limitless ocean and on the other side rise the eternal hills and in front is spread a charming lake. The stone-walls of the monastery I found still standing at the time of my visit eleven years ago, though in ruins. But a new monastery has been erected in the midst of a grove of areca-nut and cocoanuts and flowers innumerable, and here the monks resident therein honoured me with an address of welcome and asked me with a simplicity most befitting to monks, whether I, Satis Chandra, a Bengali Brahmin, was a relation to Rāmacandra—so green was the memory of the Kavibhāratī in their minds.

Departure.

The Venerable Sumungala Mahāthero convened on the day previous to my departure a grand meeting in which most of the learned gentlemen of Ceylon were present. I first addressed the meeting in English then read an address in Sanskrit in forty stanzas describing my reminiscences of Ceylon.

Estimate of Ceylon by common people.

One of the incidents on my way to Ceylon may here be narrated. At Tuticorin I stayed at a Dharamsala, which was a very big building consisting of long rows of rooms. The building covers a wide space and can accommodate over a thousand people. Any stranger would find food and lodging there for three days. Its doors remain open to all, night and day, and no question is asked of any one who enters its precincts. We were offered food and shelter when we went there. But, as we had enough provisions with ourselves, we would take no articles from them but merely sought shelter for the night. One elderly supervisor of the Dharamsala happening to find me a foreigner there was curiously speculating with a countryman of his as to where I lived, whither I was going and with what object. Wishing to satisfy his curiosity, I told him that I was an inhabitant of Calcutta and was going to Ceylon to learn Pali. He seemed to take my statement with a good big grain of salt and turned to his companion and spoke to him in Tamil, which I partly understood "Surely this is a good story-teller! No doubt he is a trader and is going to Ceylon for commercial purposes, but look you how he fables! Calcutta is the centre of learning and this man says he comes all the way from there to Ceylon of all places!" This conversation evidently shows how poor an opinion common people themselves have about Ceylon being a seat of learning, although scholars from Siam, Burma, Bombay, Calcutta and even Europe go there for the study of Pali and Buddhism.

How I lost my way and a strange Bengali song saved me.

Another of my reminiscences with regard to Ceylon is put down in detail, as the incident made a rather deep impression on my mind then. One evening I was taking my usual walk in the Victoria Park, which is surrounded on three of its sides by the sea. This is perhaps the most picturesque spot in all Ceylon, and is resorted to by all lovers of nature. Whilst taking my rounds amongst the beautiful pathways and groves of the park, the striking loveliness and singular attraction of this most wonderful work of nature, threw me in a fanciful reverie, and for a time I was lost to the world. When I came to myself, I realised that the park was almost deserted and I was the solitary figure present there. It was about 8-30 P.M. and I thought it expedient to return to my residence at once. But this I could hardly do. Having travelled through many pathways and groves I had completely lost sight of my direction and found myself in a labyrinth as it were. I then wanted to go near the sea, but the sea seemed to be on every side of me. I walked for a time towards one direction and then caught the noise of the roaring sea, and immediately receded, lest, in the darkness of the night, by one hasty step I might at once drop down into the waters below. Immediately turning back I travelled in the opposite direction and again the roar of the ocean frightened me away! To the right, and to the left, in my front, and behind my back, the sea seemed to be everywhere! Impatient and restless, I was getting excited and frightened when the short snatch of a popular Bengalee love-song reached my ears. I had been for one month in Ceylon and had not come across a single Bengalee. Hence I was beside myself with astonishment on catching the notes of the song there. The loneliness of the place, the helplessness of my position and the quaintness of the voice, heightened my sense of horror and astonishment and put me in mind of sirens about whom I had read many a tale describing how they beguile and seduce innocent victims. My hair stood on end as soon as I could see the singer, who seemed to be approaching towards me, I felt myself trembling, but I was not so thoroughly unnerved as not to make bold to ask him who he was. Somewhat to my surprise and relief, he answered me, much in the same way as a human being would do that he was a native of Malabar and a sailor by profession. Then my fear of sirens vanished and I learnt on further enquiry that he had been to France, England, Japan, Germany, Sweden, Belgium, Calcutta, and other places and had picked up a smattering and speaking knowledge of the language of every country he had visited. While he was in Calcutta, he used to stay at Mechuabazar and had learnt there the love-song of Rādhā and Kṛṣṇa, which he liked very much and used to sing whenever he was alone. The romantic grandeur of the picturesque park had let loose his sentiments and he was singing loudly this favourite song of his. At my request he showed me the way out of the park to the stand for carriages. Hardly any was available at this late hour of the night. Still I managed to secure one and reached home at about 10-30.

INDEX OF SUBJECTS.

Page

Abandonment of a proposition .. 35
Abhayadeva Sūri .. .. 196f.
—particulars about .. 196 (ftn. 2)
Abhayākara Gupta 347
Abhayatilakopādhyāya .. 151
Abhihitānvaya-vāda (connection of the expressed) 146
Abhinanda .. .. 147 (ftn. 2)
Absolute (Śūnyatā) 254
Absolute non-existence 184, 394, 416
—Deva Sūri on 203
Absolute truth 255
Abstract perception 383
Ācāra's monastery 272
Ācārya Buddhajñānapāda .. 519
Ācārya Bodhisattva 323
Action 37, 114
— bodily 58
— mental 58
— three kinds of 58
— vocal 58
Activity 58
—grounds for 410
Ādinātha or Ṛṣabhadeva .. 150
Admission 35
—of an opinion 89
Advaita-vedāntins 139
Affection 114
Affirmative-negative inference 131, 435
Affirmative reason 437
Agniveśa .. .. 25 (ftn. 1)
—in Tibetan .. 25 (ftn. 1)
Ahalyā .. .. .. 17f.
Ahalyā-sthāna (Ahiria) .. 18
Ahaṁkāra or Puruṣa of the Sāṁkhya philosophy .. 245 (ftn. 2)
Ajāta śatru .. 226, 349
Ajaya Deva 223
Ajita Siṁha 477
Akalaṅka Deva, age of .. 186
—works of 185

Page

Akhyāti (non-manifestation) .. 139
Akṣapāda (see Gautama, his doctrine embodied in Nyāya Sūtra of Akṣapāda) 16, 26, 47, 112, 348, 358, 359, 395
—age of .. .. 50, 502 (ftn. 1)
—Akṣapāda darśana .. 48, 398
—attacked by Jaina logicians 221 (ftn. 2)
—birth-place of 512
—compiler of the Nyāya Sūtra .. 50
—(his) definition of perception criticised by Dignāga 278
—designated as Naiyāyika .. 278
—different from Gautama .. 49
—(his) identification with Gautama 48
—not conversant with the Yogācāra .. .. 110 (ftn. 3)
—Nyāya philosophy as the philosophy of 48
—Nyāya Sūtra of 497f
—on the relation of thought and language.. 55
—real author of the Nyāya Sūtra 50
—redactor of the Ānvīkṣikī of Gautama.. 50
—son of Soma Śarmā 155
—(in) Tibetan 47
Akṣapāda and the Mīmāṁsakas, their definition of proposition criticised by Dignāga 283 (ftn. 2)
Alarka 10
Alaya-vijñāna, explanation of 249 (ftn.3)
Alexander 352
Amaracandra Sūri 207, 396, 406 (ftn. 5)
—details about .. 207 (ftn. 5)
Amradeva Sūri 210
Amṛtacandra Sūri 195
Analogue 65
—application of 816
—kinds of .. 67, 261, 288f.
—principles to be applied to .. 81f

Page

Analogue—
—test of .. .. .. 81f.
Ānanda .. 112 (ftn. 2), 406 (ftn. 5)
Ānanda Sūri .. 207, 396
—details about .. 207, (ftn. 5)
Ananta-vīrya .. 122 (ftn. 1), 98
Ananta-yajvan 408
Ancient School of Indian Logic, termination of 157
Andhra Dynasty .. 251 (ftn. 2, 3)
Andhras 272 273 (ftn. 1), 274, 274 ftn. 3)
Aṅga 160
Angīrasa, name of Buddha Gautama .. 19 (ftn. 2)
Āngīrasa tribe 19
Annambhaṭṭa 388
Anvivacanīya-khāyti (manifestation of the undefinable) .. 139
Annihilation of things impossible 105
Annihilationists followers of the Lokāyata philosophy .. 228f.
Antecedent non-existence 184, 416
—Deva Sūri on 203
Antigonos Gonetas 352
Antiochos 352
Anuruddha Thera 352
Ānvikṣikī (see Hetu-śāstra and Tarka-vidyā) 36
—accepting Vedas 39
—bifurcates into Philosophy and Logic 5
—Brāhmaṇa addicted to .. 37
—called Nyāya-Śāstra .. 8, 40
—called Nyāya-Śāstra when Nyāya constituted its special scope .. 40
—condemned by certain Brahmanas 36
—condemned by Manu .. 36
—condemned by Vālmīki .. 36
—condemned in certain circles .. 36
—dealt with two subjects .. 5
—Dharma should be ascertained by 38
—distinction between Ātma-vidyā and 5
—(as) expounded by Dattatreya .. 10f.

Page

Ānvikṣikī—
—followers of .. 107 (ftn. 1)
—formation of 5
—founding of 17
—generally designated as, in the first stage 40
—(in a) general sense 6
—held in high esteem in some quarters .. .. .. 37f.
—Kali satirising the founder of .. 37
—(in) Kauṭilīya 52, 7
—known as Nyāya-śāstra in the second stage .. 40
—(as the) lamp of all sciences .. 38
—(in its) logical aspects .. 7
—(in) Manu 4
—Mānavas' description of .. 5
—meant by Nyāya 20
—(as a) necessary study .. 38
—not a part of the original Āyurveda 26
—not in Brahma Sūtra .. 37
—opposed to the Vedas .. 36
—par excellence is Logic .. 6, 3
—penalties for studying .. 37
—philosophical aspect of .. 6
—principal topic of 27
—replacable by the word 'Darśana' 6
—(used in) special sense of Logic.. 7
—(as) Science of inquiry .. 4
—(as) Science of true reasoning .. 8
—(in) Sulabhā 12
—teachers of 9
—(in) Tibetan 7
—training prescribed in .. 37
—unfavourable criticism of .. 39
—useful for ascertaining truths .. 38
—utility of.. .. .. 37f.
—Vātsyāyana on 5
—Vyāsa arranges Upaniṣads with the help of 33
Ānvīkṣikī-vidyā of Gautama .. 50
—styled the Nyāya-sutras .. 50
Anvitābhidhāna-vāda (expression of the connected) 147

Page

Anya-mata-parīkṣā (examination of the doctrines of others) .. 51f.
Anyathā-khyāti (converse manifestation) 139
Apoha (knowledge of a thing by the exclusion of its opposites) criticised by Jayanta .. 149
Application (upanaya) 32, 61, 437 (ftn. 1)
—affirmative 61
—Deva Sūri on .. 202
—(as an) essential part of a syllogism 504
—kinds of 61, 395
—means of 395
—negative 61
—of the example 60
—of the reasoning of the disputant to his own case 236
Āraṇyakas (Forest treatises) .. 1
Arcaṭa 211, 331f., 348
Ardashīr 20
Argumentation (Tarka) .. 189
—Deva Sūri on 201
Aristotle .. .. 295 (ftn. 2)
—and Akṣapāda .. .. 502f.
—and Caraka Saṁhitā .. 500f.
—and Dharma-kīrti 503
—and Dignāga 506
—and Maitreya 504
—and Nāgārjuna 504
—and Uddyotakara .. .. 510f.
—and Vasubandhu 505
Art of Rhetoric 512
Ārya Asaṅga 249, 262, 265f., 334
—age of.. .. 265 (ftn. 5)
—logical views of .. .. 265f.
Ārya Deva .. .. 248, 261f.
—names of .. 261
Ārya Mahāsaṁghika and its subsects 247, 248
Ārya Sammitīya and its subjects .. .. 246, 247 (ftn. 2)
Ārya Sarvāstivāda and its subjects 246
Ārya Sthavira and its sub-sects 247, 248
Asat-khyāti (manifestation of the unreal) 139

Page

Ascertainment .. 33, 62
Aśoka 222, 226, f., 335, 349-51, 352-53
Assembly—
—(of) fools 29
—friendly 29
—hostile 29
—how to influence 29
—indifferent or impartial .. 29
—(of) wise men 29
Assumption, based on doubt .. 34
Aṣṭāvakra, his debate with Vandin 13ff.
—his ingenuity .. 16f, 114 (ftn. 1)
—shouts of victory for .. 15f.
—a violent debator .. .. 13ff.
Āsuri 10
Aśvaghoṣa 248
Atheistic doctrine 9
Ātmaka theory (i.e. Tīrthaka doctrine) 315
Ātma-khyāti (manifestation of the self) 138
Ātma-tattva-viveka, analysis of .. 145f.
Atom 105f
—what it is 105
Ātreya .. .. .. 11f.
—mentioned in Tibetan .. 11
—(the) original author the Caraka-saṁhitā 6
Attribution of censure .. 35
Augustus Caesar 352
Avadhi .. .. 169 (ftn. 1)
Avalokiteśvara .. 332, 334, 335
Avayava (members of a syllogism) 51
—corresponding to analytics .. 502
Avesta .. .. 20 (ftn. 4)
Avoidance of defeat 35
Ayodhyā .. 262, 265, 266
Āyurveda 11
—eight books of 11

Bakhtiar Khiliji 356
Bālāditya 349, 515
Bālāditya Narasiṁha Gupta .. 267[2]
Balancing the alternative .. 70
—(the) co-presence 71

Page

Balancing—
—(the) counter-example .. 73
—(a) deficit 69
—(the) demonstration .. 78
—(the) doubt 74
—(the) effect 81
—(the) eternal 80
—(an) excess 68
—(the) heterogeneity 68
—(the) homogeneity 67
—(the) infinite regression .. 73
—(the) mutual absence .. 72
—(the) non-difference .. 77
—(the) non-eternal 79
—(the) non-perception .. 79
—(the) non-produced 74
—(the) non-reason 75
—(the) perception 78
—(the) point at issue the controversial 75
—(the) the presumption .. 76
—(the) question 11
—(the) questionable 69
—(the) subject .. .. 34f.
—(the) unquestionable .. 70
Bāṇa, date of 124
Barygoza 352
Baṭū Dās .. .. 524 (ftn. 1)
Bauddhas' doctrine of the non-ātman .. .. 127 (ftn.)
Bde-byed-dyaḥ-wa 344
Begging the question 34
Being 253
Bengal, senior logicians of .. 526
Bhadanta, same as Dignāga .. 129
Bhadrabāhu 164ff. (ftn. 1, 2, 3)
—date of 164f., 164 (ftn. 1), 165 (ftn. 2)
—(his) explanation of Syādvāda .. 167f
—syllogism of .. .. 165f.
Bhadrabāhu the Junior, date of .. 165
Bhadra Pālita 272
Bhadreśvara Sūri 212
Bhagīratha Thākkurra 406 (ftn. 7)
Bhagīratha or Megha Thākkura .. 457
Bhāgya Rāja 345

Page

Bhairavendra .. 459, 522
Bharsu 335
Bhartṛhari 320
Bhāṣā-pariccheda (a manual of logic by Viśvanātha) .. 392
Bhāsarvajña 155, 357ff., 386
—date of 357
—life of 357
Bhaṭṭa Mīmāṁsakas 147
Bhavānanda Rāya .. 482 (ftn. 1)
Bhavānanda Siddhānta Vāgīśa .. 479
Bhavanātha .. 406 (ftn. 7)
Bhikṣu Nāga Sena 240
Bhoja Deva 251
Bhora Śilā .. 272 (ftn. 1)
Bhūṣana 386
Birth 58
—a source of pain 102
Blo-ldan-ses-rab .. 336, 344, 345
Bodhi Sattva of Za-hor .. 299
Body 57
—made of earth 99
Brahma, region of 3
Brahman (the Pervading Essence) 4
Brāhmaṇa and Buddhist logicians antagonism between .. 348f.
Brāhmaṇas 1
Brāhmaṇa Vasubhūti 160
Brāhmanic Sagės, conceits of .. 50
Brāhmaṇī Pṛthvī 160
Brāhmanism in Bengal, revival of 350
Brāhmanism in Mithila, revival of 350
Brāhmanism, in Northern India .. 351
—in Southern India 351
—preachers of 351
Brahmavidyā (the Divine Science) 4
Buddha Gautama 225
—date of .. .. 225 (ftn. 2)
Buddha Ghoṣa 352
Buddhism—
—at Rome 352
—disappearance of 353
—in Central Asia 352
—in Ceylon 352
—in China 352

Page

Buddhism—
—in other countries 353
—in Tibet .. .. .. 352f.
—persecution of 349
—reception in foreign countries of 351ff.
—royal patronage received by .. 349
—spread of, in Asia, Europe and Africa .. .. .. 351f.
—Śrāvaka School of 341

Buddhists—
—eighteen sects of .. .. 246f.
—heretical sects of 226

Buddhist and Jaina Scripture—
—condemned by Vācaspati Miśra 141

Buddhist Council .. .. 225f.
—account of .. 225 (ftn. 3)
—fourth 50

Buddhist denial of the soul—
—criticised by Uddyotakara .. 125

Buddhist doctrines of 'apoha,' 'kṣaṇabhaṅga' etc.— criticised by Udāyanacārya 143

Buddhist Logic 158
—contentious spirit of .. 348f.
—rise of 251
—triumph of 348

Buddhist Philosophy, four schools of 247

Buddhist Sabbath (uposatha) 232ff.
—preliminary acts of 233
—preparation for .. .. 232f.
—recitation of the code of monastic laws in (pātimokkhuddeśa) 233
—right season for 233
—three kinds of 233

Buddhist Sūtras, quoted by Brahmana authors .. 126 (ftn. 2)

Buno Rāmanātha 484

Burden and the burden-bearer 127 (ftn.)

Bu-ston 270, 353

Bzams-paḥi-ṇgon-pa 262

Caitanya .. 351, 462 (ftn. 1)

Cakra Saṁvara 340

Cālukya Dynasty 351

Page

Calukya kings 349

Canaka 336, 340, 341, 342, 520

Candra Dvīpa .. 334 (ftn. 2)

Candra Gomin 332

Candra Gomin the Junior .. 334f.
—date of .. .. .. 335f.
—life of .. .. .. 333f.

Candra Gomin the Senior, date of 335

Candra Gupta 261

Candra Gupta II 117

Candrakīrti 334

Candra Pati .. 406 (ftn. 7)

Candraprabha Sūri 206
—particulars about ..206 (ftn. 3)

Candra Sena Sūri 211

Candra Siṁha 460

Candra's well 335

Canonical Scriptures of the Jainas divisions of . .. 160f.

Canons of speech .. .. 12f.

Canons, logical subjects in ..161ff.

Canton 301

Caraka .. 25, 26, 499 (ftn. 1)
—according to Pāṇini .. 25
—borrowed terms from Vaiśeṣika philosophy and incorporated them into Vādamārga .. 27
—date of.. . .. 26 (ftn. 4)
—introduces terms unknown to Gautama into Vādamārga .. 27
—lived in the court of Kaniṣka 26 (ftn. 3)
—(a) name for śākhās of the Yajurveda 25
—(a) physician named .. 26
—(the) wandering sect named 26 (ftn. 1)

Caraka Saṁhitā—
—also called the Agniveśa-tantra .. .. 25 (ftn. 1)
—contains for the first time an exposition of the doctrine of syllogism 42
—(its) exact meaning unknown .. 26
—means the Āyurveda .. 26
—older in logical doctrines than Nyāya Sūtra 50

Page

Caraka Saṁhitā—
—terms explained in 27
Cārvāka .. .. 9, 398ff.
—followers of 9
—not the name of any individual 9
Cases for settlement (adhikaraṇa) 229f.
(A) Case presented by a disputant in a regular form (anuloma) .. 235
(A) Case presented through an analogy 238
(A) Case presented through a simple comparison .. .. 237f.
(A) Case presented through the fourfold method .. 239
Casuists 227
Category .. 374ff., 387, 393, 395
—defined in Nāgārjuna's Pramāṇa Vihetana 258
—definition of .. .. 54ff.
—examination of .. .. 90ff.
—reduced to one 357
—treatment of 53
Category of pramāṇa, (means of knowledge) in the prakaraṇas .. 357
Causality.. .. .. 400f.
Cause 390
—kinds of .. 382f., 390
Causes of Inference—
—ancient on 434
—Gaṅgeśa on 434
Cavil 62, 63
Caviller 63
Cedi race 350
Censuring the non-censurable .. 90
Ceylon—
—an incident of Dr. Vidyābhūṣaṇa in .. .. .. 541f.
—Dr. Vidyābhūṣaṇa's departure from 540
—Dr. Vidyābhūṣaṇa's experience in 540
—estimate of 541
Candra Kīrti .. 126 (ftn. 2)
Censurable 33
Chan Dynasty 268
Chinese Mission, sent to Magadha 301

Page

Choś-grags 303
Choś- mchog 329
Choś-mi-m Them-dpe-ltar-snaṅ-wa 296 (ftn. 1), 297 (ftn. 1)
Cinna Bhaṭṭa 384
Cirakārin (son of Gautama, see Gautama as mentioned in the Mahābhārata) 18
Clearing the meaning of terms .. 238
Cola Dynasty 351
Collective Nyāya (Saṁgraha) .. 171
Colour 57
Commentaries—
—nature of 115
—(as) store-houses of informations 115
Comparative estimate of the Ānvīkṣikī and the Nyāya .. 152
Comparison .. 33, 56, 384, 443
—Dignāga on 287
—(a) distinct means of right knowledge 94
—instrumental causes of .. 411
—(a) mere inference .. 94
—(a) mere perception .. 94
—not a means of right knowledge 93f.
—operation of 443
—process of 443
—really a means of right knowledge 94
—result of 443
—(a) Separate means of knowledge 99, 443
—special cause of 409
Complainant or Plaintiff (codaka) 231
Complaint (codanā) .. 23
Compound—
—attributive 452
—kinds of 452
—potentiality of aggregative .. 453
—potentiality of attributive .. 452
—potentiality of descriptive .. 452
—potentiality of determinative 452
—potentiality of indeclinable .. 453
Comprehensiveness .. 429
Conclusion (nigamana) 32, 61, 167, 237, 437

Page

Compound—
—as an essential part of a syllogism 504
—Deva Sūri on 202
—kinds of 259
Concrete cause 383
Condition (upādhi) 140, 376 (ftn. 4), 378, 399, 431, 432
—kinds of .. .. 432f.
—sure 432
—suspected 432
Conditionality 255
Conditional middle term .. 431
Conditional truth 254
Conflicting testimony 59
Confutation 61
Conjoined inherence (saṁyukta-samavāya) 130
Conjoined inherent-inherence (saṁyukta-samaveta samavāya) .. 130
Conjunction (saṁyoga) .. 130
Consideration (parāmarśa) 384, 390, 420, 433
Consistency 447
Context 113
Contiguity .. .. 447f.
Contradiction 34
Contradictory fallacy 63, 64
Contradictory reason .. 439
Controversial fallacy 63, 64
Council of Discussion—Deva Sūri on 204
Counter-activity
—grounds for . .. 410
Counter-balanced reason .. 439
Counter-demonstration .. 32
—analysis of 501
Counter-proposition 166
Counter-questioned fallacy ..63, 64
Cūḍāmaṇi 303
Cunningham .. 124 (ftn. 7)

Dad-pahi-śes-rab 275
Dāna Pāla 352
Dāna Śila .. .. 340f.
Dar-ma-grags 318

Page

Darśana—
—(a) branch of philosophy .. 6
—(an) explanation of the term .. 6
—literal sense 6
Dattātreya
—(his) parable of a tree .. 10f.
—(his) proper name 10
Death 58
Debate (vāda) 31
Debate—the art of (Tarka-vidyā), (see also Vāda-vidyā) 6
Debate—
—attending a place of .. 264
—categories for the knowledge of the course of 31
—(a) congenial 29
—(a) council of (pariṣad) .. 29
—(the) course of (see Vāda-mārga) 31
—defects of 163
—disputant of 379
—(the) expedients of (see Vādopāya) .. .. 30f.
—expedients in 163
—kinds of .. 29, 31, 379
—(a) hostile 29
—(the) limits of (see Vāda-maryādā) 31
—means of 264
—members of 379
—method of .. .. 28f.
—or dialogues in the Upaniṣads .. 23
—place of 263
—president of 379
—several terms of 162
—technical terms of .. .. 23ff.
—requisites of 378
—requisites of a council of .. 378
—respondent of 379
—rules of 378
—rules of, according to Deva Sūri 204f
—subjects of 263
—utility of (see saṁbhāṣā-praśaṁsā) .. .. 28f.
Debater—
—confidence of 264f

Page

Debater—
—qualifications of 264
Debts, three kinds of .. 102 (ftn. 1)
Defeat—
—points of (see points of defeat) .. 379
—eight kinds of 237
Defect of speech 34
—various types of 34
Definition 53
—of terms 238
—of the minor term and explanation of a proposition .. 506f.
Demonstration (sthāpanā) .. 32
—and counter-demonstration of Caraka-Saṁhitā compared with demonstration and refutative Enthymeme of Arts to the .. 500
—analysis of .. .. 500f.
—through three kinds of middle terms and through the media of essence and cause 508
Deprecating description .. 108
Description—
—kinds of 108
Desert (merit or demerit) .. 57
—grounds for the existence of 143 (ftn. 1)
Desire 57
—and aversion 113
Determinate 55
Determinate knowledge .. 414
Determinate perception (see Savikalpaka) 138
Deva Bhadra 211
Deva Nātha Ṭhākkura 460f.
Deva Pāla 517
Devardhi Gaṇi, known as Kṣamāśramaṇa 172
Devasena Bhaṭṭāraka .. 195
Deva Sundara 214
Deva Sūri—
—called Vādi-pravara .. 198
—on fallacies of Naya 203f.
—on non-existence .. 203
—on right knowledge 200ff.

Page

Deva Sūri—
—on superimposition .. 201
—on the method of debate .. 204
—on the soul 204
—(his) Pramāṇa-nayatatvālokālaṅkāra 200
Devendra Bodhi .. .. 319f.
Deviating from a tenet .. 90
Dgah-wahi-rdo-rje 345
Dge-brrun 328
Dgra-las-rgyal-wa 337
Dhammatā doctrine 500 (ftn. 1)
Dhammuttariya or Dhammottara 248 (ftn. 6)
Dhaneśvara Sūri .. 197 (ftn. 3)
Dhanukha Inscription 406 (ftn. 7)
Dharma Bhāṣaṇa 215f. 237 (ftn. 7)
—his references to other philosophers 215
—his references to works on logic 215
Dharma Deva 352
Dharmagañja 516
Dharma Ghoṣa 206
Dharmākara Gupta .. 329
Dharmakīrti 124, 133, 135, 136 (ftn.), 274 (ftn. 1), 303ff., 344, 346, 348, 358
—age of .. 124 (ftn. 3), 305f., 321
—birth-place of .. 303 (ftn. 4)
—criticises Dignāga 315f
—designated as a Bhikṣu, Sangata, Buddha or Śākya 130
—(his) division of the point of defeat (nigrahasthāna) criticised by Vācaspati Miśra .. 136
—triumph of 305
Dharmakīrti and Kumārila .. 304
Dharmapāla 117, 302f., 304, 323, 517, 519
—works of 303
Dharmarājādhvarin 485
Dharmarakṣa 352
Dharmaratna 300
Dharmavijaya .. 165 (ftn. 22)
Dharmottara .. 143, 338, 348

Page

Dharmottarācārya 329
Dialogue 62
—three kinds of 62
Digambaras .. .. 159[2]
Dignāga 116, 117, 125, 135, 307 (ftn. 2), 348, 349
—age of .. 116, 135, 272f[2]
—birth place of .. .. 512.
—called Bhadanta .. 125, 135 (ftn. 3)
—(his) definition of balancing the effect (kārya-sama) criticised by Vācaspati Miśra 135
—(as) founder of the Mediaeval Logic .. .. 158, 270ff.
—fuller accounts of .. 272 (ftn. 1)
—life of .. .. 272f.
—(a) portrait of 271
—(his) criticism of the definition of perception as given by Akṣapāda and Vātsyāyana 278
—(his) theory of examples 295ff.
—(his) theory of Nine Reasons criticised by Uddyotakara and Vācaspati Miśra .. 283 (ftn. 2)
—(his) views on inference 281ff.
Dignāga and Īśvara Kṛṣṇa 274f.
Dinakara Miśra 380
Dīnāra (the Roman coin denarius) imported into India 45 (ftn. 2)
Diodotus 352
Dīpaṅkara or Śrījñāna Atīśa 337, 341, 352, 517, 519f.
Direct knowledge (Pratyakṣa) 169, 174, 184
—Deva Sūri on 201
—kinds of 174
Discussion 62
—art of (Vāda-vidyā).. .. 6
(See also Tarka-vidyā)
Deva Suri on 204
—with whom to hold 104
Disjunctive categorical syllogism 435 (ftn. 1)
Disputation, methods of, as illustrated by the Kathāvattan ..235ff.
Dissentient 62

Page

Divine Science (Brahma-vīdya) 4
Doctrine of Impermanence .. 239
Doctrine of inter-relation leading to the doctrine of voidness 117 (ftn. 3)
Doctrine of momentariness 246, 262f.
—criticised by Vātysāyana .. 121
Doctrine of Mutual Dependence (Paticca samuppāda) 227 (ftn. 2)
Doctrine of Nyāya (method) 217 (ftn. 1)
Doctrine of Phonetic Explosion (sphoṭavāda) .. .. 131f.
Doctrine of Self-consciousness .. 418
Doctrine of Voidness .. .. 262f.
—time of .. 119 (ftn.)
Dogma 59
—hypothetical 60
—implied 60
—of all the schools 59
—peculiar to some schools .. 60
Doubt .. 33, 58f.
—Deva Sūri on 201
—grounds for 104
—impossibility of 103
—possibility of 104
—sources of 428
Dpal-ldan-blo-gros-brtan-po .. 349
Dravali (Drāvida) 305
Dress of monks 271
Dr. H Jacobi—
—on commentaries of the Nyāya Sūtra .. .. 116 (ftn. 1, 3)
—on the date of the Nyāya Sūtra 50 (ftn. 2)
—on Hari bhadra Sūri 209 (ftn.)
Dr. Sherbatski .. 120 (ftn. 3)
Dṛṣṭivāda .. 161, 161 (ftn. 3)
Dul-lha .. .. 320f.
Durgādatta Miśra 460
Dvividha Sambhāṣā (see Debate—kinds of) 29
Dwyiggñen 266
Ear 57
Eastern Cālukya dynasty 273 (ftn. 1)
(An) Ecclesiastical act .. 232

Page

Effect .. 280, 311, 382, 390
Efficient Cause .. 383, 390 (ftn. 1)
Ego 245, 246, 249
Ego or Ālaya—
—of the Vijñāna-vādins 245 (ftn. 2)
E. Harding—
—on the Sūtra of the Burden and the Burden-bearer .. 127 (ftn.)
Elements 57
Emancipation or release 57, 58, 246, 370
—attainment of 102
—definition of 103
—means of attainment of .. 103
Emperor Kublai Khan .. 353
Enthymemes .. .. 500f.
—definition of 501
Entreaty 113
Enunciation 53
Equipollent concomittance .. 399
Erratic fallacy 63
Erratic reason 438
—non-general 438
—too general 437
Etapurī 346
Eternalists (sassata-vādins)—
—followers of the Sāṁkhya philosophy of Kapila 228
Eternalists – non-eternalists (eka-ccasassatikā-ekacca-asassatikā)—
—followers of the Ānvīkṣikī of Medhātithi-Gautama .. 228
Evasion 89
Examination 53
—different means for .. 28
—four standards of .. 28
Example (dṛṣṭānta) 32, 59, 167, 258f., 366f., 437
—affirmative or homogeneous .. 502
—and major premise 503
—and paradigma .. .. 502f.
—converted into universal proposition .. .. 295f.
—function of 504
—heterogeneous or negative 61, 191, 159, 287, 290, 368, 502

Page

Example—
—heterogeneous, fallacies of .. 297f.
—homogeneous or affirmative 60, 191, 259, 286, 290, 368
—homogeneous, fallacies of 296f., 313ff.
—fallacies of 368f., 163, 176, 191, 289, 290, 311
—kinds of .. .. 286f.
—superfluous .. 193
—theory of .. ..295ff.
—uselessness of, according to Deva Sūri 202
Excellence of speech 34
Excess 113
Exclusively affirmative (anvayī) inference .. 130, 434
Exclusively negative (vyatirekī) inference .. 131, 434
Exercise 113
Existence, as a thing 97 (ftn. 1)
Expectancy 447
Explanation of the truths .. 261
Explanatory example .. 60
Extrinsic inseparable connection (bahir-vyāpti) 177
—Deva Sūri on 202
Eye .. .. 57, 111f.
—(a) material substance 111, 112
—(a) non-material substance .. 112

Fa-hian .. ..241 (ftn. 1), 252
—his description of Ārya Nāgārjuna .. .. 251 (ftn. 3)
Fallacy .. 63f., 362, 438ff.
—general definition of .. 438
—kinds of .. 192f., 260f.. 438
—of absence of connection .. 297
—of absence of disconnection .. 298
—of affirmative example 368f.
—of argumentation .. 193
—of balancing the controversy 367f.
—of balancing the predicate .. 260
—of balancing the point in dispute or begging the question .. 260
—of example 178, 193, 368, 369f.

Page

Fallacy—
—of false assumption .. 260
—of implied contradiction 315f.
—of included major term .. 297
—of included major and middle terms 298
—of included middle term .. 297
—of inverse connection .. 297
—of inverted negation .. 298
—of 'Naigama,' according to Deva Surī 203
—of negative example .. 369
—of non-erroneous contradiction 316, 368
—of perception 192
—of quibble in respect of a term 260
—of regressus ad infinitum .. 257
—of reason .. 63f., 90
—of reasoning (see fallacies of the thesis, middle term and example) 298
—of recognition 193
—of recollection 193
—of Sādhya-sama .. 256 (ftn. 1)
—of showing absurdity .. 260
—of the adoption of a fallacious reason 261
—of the collective, Deva Sūri on 203
—of the contradictory .. 260
—of the contradictory middle term 294f., 313
—of the contradictory reason .. 363
—of the contradictory reason, kinds of .. .. 363ff.
—of the excluded major term .. 296
—of the excluded major and middle terms 296
—of the excluded midde term .. 296
Fallacy of the heterogeneous example,—kinds of 180
Fallacy of the homogeneous example 178
—of contrary separation .. 180
—of separation unshown .. 180
—of six kinds 180
—unseparated 180

Page

Fallacy of the homogeneous example—
—of connection unshown .. 179
- of inverted connection .. 179
—three kinds of 179
—unconnected 179
Fallacy of the immediate, Deva Sūri on 203
Fallacy of the middle term or reason 178, 193, 293
Fallacy of the middle term or semblance of reason—
—contradictory 178
—kinds of 178
—uncertain 178
—unproved 177
Fallacy of the minor term 177, 193
—of the mistimed 260
—of the mistimed reason and its subdivision 367
—of the non-tried reason .. 366
—of the non-tried reason, subdivisions of .. .. 366f.
—of the practical, Deva Sūri on .. 203
—of the subtle, Deva Sūri on .. 204
—of the such-like, Deva Sūri on .. 204
—of the uncertain middle term 293f., 313
—of the uncertain reason .. 365
—of the uncertain reason, subdivisions of .. .. .. 365f.
—of the undistributed middle .. 260
—of the unproved middle term 293, 313
—of the unproved reason .. 362
—of the unproved reason, kinds of 362f.
—of verbal testimony .. 193
—of verbal testimony, Deva Sūri on 204
—services of 442
Faults 58
—subdivisions of 101
Fear 113
Firoz Shah Tughlak 223

Page

First academy of Logic in Nadia 462
Five Skandhas (aggregates of being) .. .. 126, 127 (ftn.)
Fixed signification of numbers .. 114
—Akṣapāda on .. .. 114.
Forefathers—
—(the) path of the 3
Form 111
Formal cause .. 390 (ftn. 1)
Fortuitous-originists (adhicca-samuppannika) .. 229
Four schools of Buddhists—
—(as) mentioned in the Chinese Tripiṭaka .. .. 243f.
Fruit 58
Future time 106

Gadādhara Bhaṭṭācārya .. 481
—date of 482
—(the) prince of Indian schoolmen 481
Gajapati Pratāparudra .. 462
Gāndhāra .. 265, 266, 351
Gaṇeśa Upādhyāya 155
Gaṅgā (Padmā) .. 346
Gaṅgā Deva 521
Gaṅgeśa .. 396, 405ff., 522
—date of .. 406 (ftn. 7), 407
—Portuguese account of .. 488f.
—succession of pupils from 406 (ftn. 7)
—Gāṅgeya Deva 350
Gangtok—
—Dr. Vidyābhūṣaṇa's journey to .. 531
—hospitality of a lady to Dr. Vidyābhūṣaṇa at .. .. 532f.
Garbhapāda 337
Gautama 21
Gauḍa .. 341, 524
Gaurī Kānta Sārvabhauma .. 478f.
Gautama (see Gautama Medhātithi)—
—(in) Avesta Gaotema .. 21
—believed to be the author of the Nyāya Sūtra 48

Page

Gautama—
—birthplace of 17
—Buddha 19
—(as) described in the Rāmāyaṇa 18
—(his) doctrine embodied in the Nyāya sutra of Akṣapāda (see Akṣapāda) 26
Gautama—
—Gotamaka, his followers .. 21
—(his) identification with Akṣapāda 48
—(and) Medhātithi the same person 18
—mentioned in old Persian scripture .. .. .. 20f.
—Naciketas 19
—Nodhā 19
—(his) theory of reasoning .. 20
—(his) theory of soul 20
—(his) wife Ahalyā .. .. .. 17f.
—(his) work on Ānvīkṣikī .. 20
Gautama-Medhātithi (see above)—
—age of 21
—(his) doctrines as reproduced in the Caraka Saṁhitā .. .. 25ff.
—family and tribe of 19
—(the) founder of Ānvīkṣikī .. 17ff.
—(and) Gautama or Gotama the same person (see Ahalyā) .. 20
—mentioned in the Mahābhārata 20
—(his) Nyāya .. 20
—terms unknown to 27
Gautamī-vidyā .. 20, 497
Generality (samavāya) 32, 333
Genus or type 111
Gestures 57
—as means of knowledge .. 453
God—
—(the) giver of fruits .. 101
—proof of the existence of .. 143f.
—path of 3
Gopāla 323, 517
Gopīnātha Maunī 485
Gotama (see Gautama) 37. 497 (ftn. 2)

Page

Gotama—
—descendants of 19
—Tarka Śāstra of 497
Gotamaka (see Gautama, his followers) 21
Govardhana Miśra 381
Govicandra 320
Govinda Nyāyavāgīśa .. 480
Grags-pa-rgyal-mtshan-dpal-le zan 289
Graheśvara 522
Graus-can-pa 278
Gser-gyi-go cha 275
Gtan-tshigs-ltar-snan .. 293 (ftn. 1)
Gtan-tsigs-ni-tshul-gsum 291 (ftn. 1)
Guge 324
Guṇānanda Vidyāvāgīśa .. 468
Guṇaratna 151, 206 (ftn. 4), 214, 357, 371
—his references to other philosophers .. .. 214f.
—his references to works on logic.. 215
Gupta Dynasty, kings of .. 349

Halāyudha 524
Haṁsa 210
Han Dynasty .. 243 (ftn. 1)
Hanumat 391
Haramohan Cūḍāmaṇi .. 526
Haribhadra 337
Haribhadra Sūri 152, 154, 208, 346
—age of 209
Haribhadra Sūri II 209 (ftn.)
Haridāsa Nyāyālaṅkāra Bhaṭṭācārya . .. 465
Hari Dīkṣita 384
Hari Miśra .. 406 (ftn. 7)
Harirāma Tarkavāgīśa .. 479
Harṣa Vardhana 335
Hbro or Do .. 324, 337, 343
Hellenestic monarchies .. 352
Hemacandra Sūri (surnamed Kalikāla Sarvajña) .. 205, 335
—details about 205
Hema (or Kanaka) Varmā .. 275
Heretical sects of the Buddhists 226, 220 (ftn. 2)

Page

Heretical—
—names and subdivisions of 226 (ftn. 2)
Heterogeneous or negative example 176
Heterologue .. 361, 433
Hetu (reason) 162
—(as) identical with valid knowledge 162
—(in the) sense of inference .. 162
—kinds of 162
Hetu-śāstra (see Ānvīkṣikī) .. 7, 25
Hetu-vidyā (see Ānvīkṣikī) 7, 240, 243, 274 (ftn. 3)
Hetu-vidyā-śāstra .. 274 (ftn. 3)
Hīnayāna .. 247, 272
—spread of 241
Hindu Logic—
—Aristotalian influence on .. 511f.
Hīravijaya 216
History of Jaina literature .. 172
Homogeneous example .. 176
Homologue .. 361, 433
Huen-Thsang 124, 241 (ftn. 1), 248, 261, 265, 266[3], 267, 274 (ftn. 3), 302, 302 (ftn. 4), 303, 306, 335
Hurting the proposition .. 84f.
Hymn 108

Idealism (vijñāna-vāda) .. 120f.
—in the Laṅkāvatāra .. 245
Identity 311
Ignorance 89
Illustrative description .. 108
Immediate perception .. 418f.
Immediate subsequency .. 113
Imperceptible reason in the affirmative form—
—three subdivisions of .. 191
Imperceptible reason in the negative form—
—seven subdivisions of .. 191
Implication (of a word) 450, 451f.
Imposition 218
Inadequacy 34
Incoherence 34
Incoherent 87

Page

Incompatible reason 440
—kinds of .. .. 440f.
Indeterminate perception (nirvikalpaka) 138
Indian Paṇḍits, as translator of Sanskrit works into Tibetan 353 (ftn. 1)
Indication 449
Indirect knowledge (parokṣa) 169, 189
—five kinds of, according to Deva Sūri 201
Indirect perception 413
Indirect valid knowledge—
—two kinds of 175
Individual 111
Indrabhūti Gautama—
—(a) disciple of Mahāvīra .. 159f.
—birthplace of .. ..
—date of .. ..
—parentage of 160
Indravijaya .. 165 (ftn. 2)
Inference 33, 56, 175, 189, 298, 361f., 376, 383, 390
—a posteriori 56
—a priori 56
—as a means of knowledge .. 420
—Cārvāka on .. ..398ff.
—cause of 433
—commonly seen 56
—demonstration of 361
—denied by Cārvāka .. ..398ff.
—Deva Sūri on 202
—Digṇāga on .. ..281ff.
—distinct from perception .. 420
—established .. .. 400f.
—for one's own self (svārthānumāna) .. 175, 192, 280, 310, 435
—for one's own self, Deva Sūri on 202
—for the sake of others (parārthānumāna) 176, 192, 282, 312, 435f.
—for the sake of others, Deva Sūri on 202
—for the sake of others, kinds of.. 312

Page

Inference—
—instrumental causes of .. 411
—kinds of 130f., 361, 260, 175, 192, 202, 280, 434, 435
—not a means of right knowledge 93
—really a means of right knowledge 93
—special cause of 409
—terms of .. .. 361f.
Inference for one's self and dialectic proposition 506
Inference for the sake of others and demonstrative proposition .. 506
Inference of God 442
Inferential knowledge. 384, 390, 419f.
Inherence (samavāya) 32, 130, 333, 383, 412, 414
—relation of 383
Inherence and union—
—distinguished 414
Inherent inherence .. 130, 412
Injunction .. 108, 448f.
—Gaṅgeśa on 449
—Kumārila on 449
—Prabhākara on 449
Inopportune 87
Inquiry 33
Inseparable connection or invariable concomittance (vyāpti) 177, 189, 361
—affirmative 361
—kinds of .. 177, 361
—negative 361
Instrument (karaṇa) .. 382, 390
Intellect 50
—impermanent .. 101, 112
—kinds of 395
—permanent 112
—(a) quality of a conscious agent, the soul 101
—(an) unconscious instrument .. 112
Intention 448
Intercourse (sannikarṣa)—
—kinds of .. 130, 360, 412
—produced by meditation .. 414

Page

Intercourse—
—whose character is general 412f.. 429, 430f.
—whose character is knowledge .. 413
Interrogation 33
Intervention 113
Intrinsic inseparable connection (antar-vyāpti) 177
—Deva Sūri on 202
Invalid knowledge .. ..409ff.
—Mīmāṁsakas on 410
Invariable concomittance (see Inseparable connection) 376, 384, 390
—Buddhist views on .. .. 400f.
—comprehensiveness of .. 429
—conclusive definition of .. 424
—defined by the 'Lion' and the 'Tiger' 423
—five provisional definitions of .. 421
—knowable .. .. 400f.
—means of apprehending ..426ff.
—nature of 140
—objectionable definitions of .. 424
—of special forms 426
—of the Buddhist condemned .. 376
—right means of apprehending .. 428
—unknowable .. ..398ff.
Inversion, Deva Sūri on .. 201
Invocation of Blessings .. 408
Invocation, kinds of 408
Irrelevancy 34
Iśvarabhaṅga (non-existence of God) criticised by Jayanta .. 150
Iśvara Sena .. 307 (ftn. 2)
I-tsing 306

Jagaddala .. .. 346 (ftn. 3)
Jagaddhara 522
Jagadīśa Tarkālaṅkāra .. 469f.
Jayāditya 335
Jaina Āgamas 172
Jaina Logic 158
—conciliatory character of .. 221f.
—not conflicting with the Brāhmaṇas .. .. 221f.
—permanency of 24

Page

Jainas 158, 273
—canonical scriptures.. .. 160f.
Jaina sects 159
Jainism—
—persecution suffered by .. 222f.
—rights and privileges of the laity of 223
—royal patronage enjoyed by .. 222
—support of the Jaina community received by 223
—unperturbed by the Mahomedans 223
Jalandhara.. 349
Jambudvīpa 332
Janaka 12, 13
Jānakīnātha Śarmā 466
Jātukarṇya, probably a compiler.. 50
Jātukarṇya Vyāsa 50
Jayadeva .. 455, 524
Jayanta .. 137 (ftn. 1),
—author of the Nyāya-mañjarī .. 146f.
—criticises the doctrines of Kalyāṇa Rakṣita and Dharmottara .. 149f.
—(his) criticism of Sphoṭa-vāda .. 149
—(his) criticism of the doctrines of apoha, kṣaṇa-bhaṅga, Iśvara-bhaṅga, etc. .. ..149f.
—date of 147
—(his) explanation of verbal knowledge .. .. ..147f.
—life of .. .. ..146f.
—(his) reproach of the Buddhists 150
—(his) review of some Buddhistic doctrines 150
Jayarāma Nyāyapañcānana .. 477f.
Jayarāma Tarkālaṅkāra .. 483
Jaya Siṁha Deva 199
Jaya Siṁha Sūri .. 206, 371, 372
Jehāṅgīr 479
Jehāri 337f., 342, 349
Jinadatta Sūri .. 152, 154
—date of .. .. 152 (ftn. 3)
Jinas .. 159, 274 (ftn. 3), 338
Jina Bhadra Gaṇikṣamā Śramaṇa 174, 181
Jina Bhaṭṭa 210
Jina Bhaṭṭa Sūri 390

	Page
Jina Mitra ..	340, 349
Jinendrabodhi ..	323
Jineśvara Sūri	197
Jīvita Gupta I	301
Jñānacandra	213
Jñānagarbha ..	250
Jñānapūrṇa or Jñāna Deva	374, 380
Jñāna Śrī Bhadra	342
—same as Jñānasiddha Bhadra	342 (ftn. 1)
Jñāna Śrī Mitra ..	211 (ftn. 3), 341
Jñātiputras	244
Judicial Council of monks (saṁgha)	231
—judge or umpire in	231 f.
—member of	231
Kākatiya Dynasty ..	380
Kālāśoka ..	226, 346
Kālidāsa	273
Kaliṅga	305
Kalyāṇa Candra	198
Kalyāṇa Rakṣita ..	143, 328
Kamala Rakṣitā ..	350
Kamala Śīla ..	327, 352, 516
Kāmbojas	351
Kāmeśvara Dynasty	521
Kaṇāda	395
—system of	304
Kaṇāda Gupta	304
Kaṇāda Tarkavāgīśa	466
—traditionary account of	466 (ftn. 3)
Kāñcī .	117, 272, 512
Kāñcīpura ..	117, 302, 351
Kaniṣka 26 (ftn. 3), 50, 241, 242,	349 352
—date of ..	241 (ftn. 1)
Kanoj	335
Kaṇva	45
Kaṇva Dynasty ..	251 (ftn. 3)
Kapila—	
—date of	10
—(his) doctrine of matter and soul	9f.
Kapilas	278
Karṇa Deva	350
Karṇāta Dynasty	521
Karṇātaka Kṣatriya race ..	350
Karatoyā	346
Kāryābhinirvṛtti—	
—(not in) Ānvīkṣikī	27[2]
—(a) part of the Vaiśeṣika Philosophy	27
Kāṣṭhāsaṁgha ..	169 (ftn.)
Kāśyapa	43
—hermitage of ..	39, 42
Kauśāmbī	117 (ftn. 2) 265, 266, 303
Kauśika	262
Kavicandra	396
Keśava Miśra	318
—life of	381
Kevala	169 (ftn.)1
Kha-che-jñāna Śrī	329
Khajjuttarā ..	112 (ftn. 2)
Kri-sroṅ-den-tsan	352
King Amoghavarṣa ..	223, 349
King Bhassa	322
King Candra Gupta	222
King Ciṅghana	386
King Dpal-lha-tsan-po ..	250
King Harihara	381
King Jayacandra ..	406, 406 (ftn. 6)
King Jaya Siṁha	205
King Jitāra	210
King Kaṇiṣka	512
King Khri-sroṅ-den-tsan	323, 327
King Kēma	222
King Lalitacandra	320
King Lalitāditya	324
King Muktāpīḍa	147
King Muñja	197
King Nemicandra	252
—date of ..	252 (ftn. 4)
—genealogy of ..	252 (ftn. 4)
King Poros..	352
King Rigs-ldan-rgyal-po ..	299
King Śrī Harṣa or Harṣavardhana	123
King Sroṅ-tsan-gan-po ..	305
King Tribhuvantilaka ..	388
King Vimalacandra of Bengal, Kāmarūpa and Tirhut	338, 342 (ftn. 6)
Kirti (see Dharmakīrti) ..	386

Page

Kīrti—
—time of 137
Kīrtivijaya 216
Klog-ṣkya-śeṣ-rab-brtrys .. 313
Knowledge (viññāna) 227
Knowledge 3
—basic 243
—distinguished from work ..)
—divisions of .. 227 (ftn.) 2
—from particular standpoint (Naya) 218
—(a) function of the intellect .. 112
—general grounds of 409
—kinds of 245, 389, 411
—objectified 245
—potential 245
—practical functions of .. 418
—presentative 245
—(a) quality of the soul .. 98
Koṅkana 338
Kṛpārāma 479
Kṛṣṇa Bhaṭṭa Āḍe 486
Kṛṣṇa Dāsa Sārvabhauma Bhaṭṭacārya 468
Kṛṣṇakānta Vidyāvagīśa .. 384f.
Kṣamākalyāṇa 390
Kṣaṇa-bhaṅga (the momentary existence)—
—criticised by Jayanta .. 149
Kṣirodadhi (khiroi) 17
Kṣitīścandra Roy 526
Kubja Viṣṇu Vardhana 273 (ftn. 1)
Kukutasiddha 516
Kumāra Gupta 267
Kumārajīva 252
Kumāra Kalasa 343
Kumāra-lābha .. 248 (ftn. 7)
Kumāra-pañha .. 114 (ftn. 1)
Kumāra Śrī 336
Kumārila Bhatta 138, 183, 273, 351
Kumārila and Dharmakīrti .. 304
Kumudacandrācārya 198
Kauṇḍa kuṇḍa .. 169 (ftn.)

Labrang .. .. 533f.
—Dr. Vidyābhūṣaṇa's journey to 530

Page

Labrang—
—monastery of 342 (ftn. 4), 344 (ftn. 4)
Lachimā Devī 460
Laghusamantabhadra .. 197f.
Lakṣaṇa Bhaṭṭa 374
Lakṣmaṇa Sena ..350, 523 (ftn. 3)
—court of 524
—successors of 424
Lalitacandra 321
Laugākṣī Bhāskara 395
Law of Extension 328
—application of 285
Lha-dvaṅ-blo .. .. 319f.
Liang Emperor Wu-fi 301
Licchavi Dynasty .. . 335
Likeness .. 113
—Gaṅgeśa on 443
—Mīmāṁsakas on 443
Limitation of the proposition (pratijñā-vibhakti) 166
Limitation of the reason .. 166
Logic (sophism) 229
—called Nīti or Nyāya .. 240
—called pre-eminently the Ānvīkṣikī 6
Logical theories of Aristotle migrated from Alexandria into India 511ff.

Logical works—
—brought to Nadia from Mithilā .. 462
Logic and Logicians—
—in the Laṅkāvatāra 244
Logic of Mithilā and Nadia .. 218
Lohācārya II .. 169 (ftn. 8)
Lokanātha 339
Lokāyata .. 5, 6. 9
Louis De La Vallée Poussin—
—on the Buddhistic doctrine of the soul .. .. 126 (ftn. 2)

Mādhavācārya 247 (ftn. 5), 248 (ftn. 3), 249 (ftn. 1, 6), 274 (ftn.), 306, 308 (ftn. 3), 341, 397f.
Mādhava Tarkasiddhānta .. 526

Page

Madhusūdana Ṭhakkura .. 461
Madhyadeśa .. 304 (ftn. 1)
Mādhyamika .. 135, 253, 249f.
—Chinese account of .. 253 (ftn. 2)
—criticised by Jayanta .. 150
—explanation of .. 249 (ftn. 6)
—expounders of 250
—founder of 250
—Indian account of .. 253 (ftn. 3)
—principal works of 250
—Tibetan and Chinese versions of 256
Mādhymika Buddhists .. 139
Mādhyamika doctrine of inter-relation—
—criticised by Vātsyāyana .. 117
Mādhyamika doctrine of Śūnyatā (voidness)—
—criticised by Vātsyāyana .. 118
Magadha 322, 339, 341, 350, 352^2
Mogas 352
Māgha .. .. 147 (ftn. 4)
Mahādeva Puntamkar .. 486
Mahāmahopādhyāya Jadunātha Sārvabhauma 526
Mahāmahopādhyāya Rājakṛṣṇa Tarkapañcānana 526
Mahāpāla 336, 337
Mahāpuruṣiya sect 351
Mahārāja Dharmapāla .. 328
Mahārāja Giriśacandra .. 485
Mahārāja Kumārapāla 205, 222
Mahārāja Kṛṣṇacandra Ray .. 488
Mahārājā of Sikkim—
—invites Dr. Vidyabhūṣaṇa .. 537
—original letter of introduction in Tibetan given by 539
Mahārāja Rāmakṛṣṇa Rāya .. 488
Mahārāja Śivacandra 484, 498
Mahāsāṃghikas 226
Mahāvīra or Vardhamāna .. 159
—date of .. 159 (ftn. 1)
—the founder of Jainism .. 158f.
Mahāyāna 126 (ftn. 2), 247^2, 272^2

Page

—canonical books of .. 242
—rise of 514
—spread of 241
Mahāyāna Hoshang .. 327
Mahendra Varman .. 222
Mahinda 352
Maheśa Ṭhakkura 406 (ftn. 7), 456 (ftn. 2), 457f.
Maheśvara Ṭhakkura .. 521
Mahipāla .. 340, 517
Mahipāla II .. 340
Mahomedans—
—in Bengal and Behar .. 350
—in Kāśmīra 350
Mahī Śāsaka sect 265
Maitreya 262
Maitreyanātha 120 (ftn. 3), 249
Major term .. 64^1, 128^2, 176
Maladhāri Srī Rāja Sekhara Sūri 153, 154, 155, 357, 371
Mallasena Sūri 212
Mallavādin 194f., 329 (ftn. 3)
Mallinātha .. 273, 380
Mālwa 320
Manaḥ-paryāya .. 169 (ftn. 1)
Māna Simha 477
Maṇidhara 396
Māṇikya Nandi—
—age of 188
—(his) parīkṣāmukha sūtra .. 188
—(his) references to contemporaneous systems of philosophy .. 193
Mañjunātha 300
Mañjuśrī 272, 274 (ftn. 3), 275, 335, 337, 344
Mañjuśrī Kumārabhūta .. 258
Manoratha .. 266, 345
Manu 4
Manuals of Logic—
—classes of 356
—composition of .. .. 355f.
Māra 315
Mark 113
Material cause 382f., 390 (ftn. 1)

Page

Mathurānātha Tarkavāgīśa .. 467
Mati .. .. 169 (ftn. 1)
Maticitra (Aśvaghoṣa) 241 (ftn. 1)
(The) Meaningless 82
Meaninglessness 34
Means 445
Means of right knowledge 54ff., 90ff., 370 387
—critical examination of 90 (ftn. 1)
—criticised by Nāgārjuna .. 257
—Dignāga on .. 276ff.
—impossibility of 91
—invalidity of .. .. 90f.
—kinds of .. 259, 360
—non-self established .. 257
—number of 95
—validity of .. 91f., 457
Medhātithi (see Gautama) .. 6, 20
—of Bhāsa 18
—(his) work on Ānvīksikī .. 20
Mediaeval School of Indian Logic 172, 270ff.
—(its) difference from the Ancient School 158
—early writers of .. 270ff.
—formation of .. .. 157f.
—founded by the Jainas and the Buddhists .. .. 157f.
—special features of . .. 157f.
Mediate perception .. 419
—doctrine of 419
Meeting of the question (āśaṅkā-pratiṣedha) 107
Memory .. .. .. 112f.
—belongs to the soul 112
—causes of .. 112 (ftn. 2)
—ground of .. .. 112f.
Menander 349
Merit and Demerit 114
—Gaṅgeśa on .. . 449
—Prabhākara on 449
Meru Śāstri 391
Method—
—fallacies of 203f

Page

Method of comprehending a thing from particular points of view—
—Deva Sūri on 203
Method of debate, Deva Sūri on .. 204
Method of description (Naya) seven kinds of 181
(The) Middle Path Doctrine (Madhyama-mārga) 253
—four aspects of .. .. 253f.
Middle term (hetu) .. 120, 128, 176
—affirmative negative .. 362
—characteristics of 310f. 377f., 202 (ftn. 1)
—conditional 431
—Deva Sūri on 202
—exclusively affirmative .. 362
—exclusively negative .. 362
—fallacies (see fallacy of the middle term) .. 293, 313, 315 (ftn. 3)
—kinds of .. 311, 362
—law governing 288
—law of extension of 283
—three characters of .. 280f., 291
Middle term and major term—
—relative extension of .. 292
—relation between 508
Migration of Aristotle's works into India—
—first period of 511
—second period of 512
—third period of 512
Milinda 240
Milinda and Nāga Sena—
—dialogue between .. .. 240f.
Mind 417
—(an) atom .. 98f., 101, 417
—mark of 57
—one in number 101
—whether a sense organ 280, 280 (ftn. 1)
Minor commentaries on the Nyāya sūtra .. .. .. 151f.
Minor term 60, 120, 176, 312, 361
Mirok 262
Misaruka 460

Page

Misaru Miśra 460
Mistimed 35
Mistimed fallacy .. 63, 64
Mithilā 497
—decay of 525
—modern history of .. .. 521f.
—modern writers of 522
—University of .. .. 521f.
Mithilā School of Logic 454ff.
—principal logicians of 454ff.
Modern School of Hindu Logic .. 405
Modern School of Nyāya .. 522
Moggaliputta Tissa 234
Mokṣākara Gupta .. 346f., 349
Monastery of Bsam-yas (Sam-ye) 324
Monastery of Labrang 289 (ftn. 1), 299 (ftn. 1), 319 (ftn. 5), 320 (ftn. 3), 324 (ftn. 2), 328 (ftn. 2), 336 (ftn. 3)
Monastery of Sam-ye (see Monastery of Bsam-yas) 323
Monastery of Śi-wahi-dge-inas .. 300
Monastery of Vikramaśila .. 336
Mudita Bhadra 516
Mudgala 395
Mukta kumbha 331
Munisundara Sūri 214
Muscular movement 370
Mu-tig-leum-pa 331
Mutual non-existence 184
—Deva Sūri on 203
Mya-ṅau-med 332

Nadiā—
—college at 464
—Mahomedan conquest of .. 524
—nucleus of a university at .. 524
—raised to the status of a town under the Sena kings .. 523f.
—situation of 523
—traces of the Pāla kings in .. 523
Nadiā School of Logic .. 461ff.
—principal logicians of 461ff.
—chair of Astronomy at .. 527
—chair of Logic at .. .. 525f.

Page

Nadiā University—
—chair of Smṛti at 527
—Tāntric studies at 527
Nāgadatta 272
Nāgārjuna 24 (ftn. 2), 106 (ftn. 1), 125, 248, 250, 251ff., 348, 349
—age of 117f., 252
—(his) criticism of the Nyāya doctrine of Pramāṇa 256
—legend about 258
—(his) letter to Sātavāhana 257 (ftn. 2)
—(his) logical theory of examples (udāharaṇa) criticised by Vātsyāyana 119
—(his) Mādhyamika-kārikā .. 253
—mentioned neither by Vātsyāyana nor by Uddyotakara by name .. .. 119 (ftn. 1)
—philosophical works of 253 (ftn.)
—(his) references to the logical doctrines of Akṣapāda .. 255f.
—Tibetan name of 252
—(his) Vigraha-vyāvartanī-kārikā 256
—(his) works on Tantra 252 (ftn. 6)
Nāgas 258
Nāgasena .. 112 (ftn. 2), 334
Nāgeśa 384
Nag-tshul-khrims-rgyal-wa .. 320
Naiyāyikas .. 139, 146, 244
—also called Yaugas .. 154 (ftn. 2)
—are Śaivas .. 154, 155
—characteristics of 155
Nālandā 261, 265, 272, 273, 303, 320, 323, 327, 334, 335, 352
—as a University 515
—celebrated men of 515
—Dr. Spooner's observation of 515 (ftn. 5)
—earliest scholars of 514
—Fa-hian's visit to 514
—Hwen-Thsang's visit to .. 514
—I-tsing's visit to 515
—kings building monasteries at .. 514
—monks at .. .. 514f.
—royal recognition of .. 515

Page

Nālandā—
—Saṅghārāmas or monasteries at 514
—situation of 514
—Tibetan account of 516
—University of (see University) 252, 302, 303, 352
Nāma Deva 374
Nanken 301
Nānyadeva 521
Nārada 408
—(an) expert in Nyāya Śāstra .. 43
—legends about .. 44, 44 (ftn. 2)
—(as a) logician doubtful ..
—(his) other works 45
—(the) real 45
—represents the philosophical culture of the first cent. A.D. .. 44
—shrouded in mystery .. 44
—(his) skill in syllogistic reasoning 43
—(his) visit to Śvetadvīpa .. 44f.
—(his) works in Smṛti .. 45
Nārada Smṛti—
—represents the theories of Smṛti and Nyāya of the early centuries of Christ .. .. 45 (ftn. 2)
Nārāyaṇa 153
Naropā 341, 342
Narrative description 108
Nature of the universal proposition—
—as understood by Dharmakīrti and Aristotle 509
Navadvīpa—
—university of 405
Naya (method) of description or mood of statements 161, 161 (ftn. 4), 170f.
—five kinds of .. .. 170f.
Nayapāla .. 343, 344, 350
Nedumāran Pāṇḍya 222
Negation—
—absolute .. 97 (ftn. 1)
—of correlation .. 97 (ftn 1)
—of identity .. 97 (ftn. 1)
—of the opposite .. 132, 287

Page

Negative reason 437
Negative things 394
Nemicandra Kavi 207
—details about .. 207 (ftn. 2)
Neo-Brahamanic age 355
Nilakaṇṭha 16 (ftn. 1), 391[2]
Ñi-ma-slas (a Tāntric teacher) .. 322
Nine reasons (see wheel of reasons) 283
—illustration of 284
—logic of 299
—(a) table of 284
Nine Sacred Works (Navadharmas) 242 (ftn. 3). 243
Nirgranthas 305
Nirgrantha putras 244
Nirukta kāras 138 (ftn. 1)
—criticised by Vācaspati Miśra .. 138
Nirvāṇa 255
Nirvikalpaka (indeterminate perception)—
—defined 137
Non-activity—
—grounds for 410
Non-analytical Naya (Nigama) .. 170
Non-being 253
Non-censurable 33
Non-equipollent concomittance .. 399
Non-erratic 55
Non-existence .. 56, 96., 370
—as a separate entity 415
—counterpart of 416
—Deva Sūri on 203
—included in inference .. 97
—kinds of 97, 184, 419f., 416
—(a) means of right knowledge .. 96
—not a means of right knowledge 96
—of the general form 425
—perception of 416
—subdivision of, according to Deva Sūri 203
—(as a) thing .. 97 (ftn. 1)
—whose counterpart is qualified by a Nature already in a different Locus 423
Non-ingenuity 89

Page

Non-material cause 383
Non-perception 281
—eleven kinds of 311
—invalidity of .. .. 414f.
—irregularity of 59
Non-reason (see fallacy) three kinds of .. .. 34, 39f.
Nose 57
Nṛga 134
Nṛsiṁha Deva and his successors 521
Nṛsiṁha pañcānana 482
Numbers doctrine of things fixed in 14f.
Nyāya (the science of true reasoning) 8
—adopts Pramāṇa alone .. 402
—called Gautamīvidyā and Akṣapāda-darśana 50
—causes of its present disregard 492f.
—(in) Chinese .. 40 (ftn. 2)
—competition for the chair of .. 526
—encouraged by the British Government .. .. 490ff.
—included among the fourteen principal sciences 382
—included in Ṣaḍdarśana by Jaina writers .. .. 153f.
—included in Ṣaḍdarśana by the Brāhmanic writers 153
—in the sense of logic not known to Pāṇini and Patañjali .. 41
—introduction of this word .. 40
—Mādhavācārya on .. 41
—Mahābhārata full of references to 39
—meaning of 40
—mentioned in the Veda and Cikitsā 39
—origin of the name of .. 40
—Pāṇini derives the word in the sense of justice .. 4, 41 (ftn. 4)
—patronised by the Mahārāja of Nadiā 488
—popularity of .. 39, 155f.
—Portuguese account of .. 489
—Portuguese interest in 488ff.
—recognised as a branch of Orthodox Learning .. 152ff.

Page

Nyāya—
—rise of vernacular detrimental to 402
—(in the) sense of Logic first in the Mahābhārata 42
—(in the) sense of logic in the Caraka Saṁhitā 42
—signifies just or justice in Artha Śāstra .. .. 41 (ftn. 6)
—spread of the study of .. 39
—supported by reasoning and scripture 39
—supports the Veda 39
—technical meaning of .. 40
—tenets of 39
—used in the sense of logic from about the first cent. A.D. .. 42
—three causes for its popularity 155f.
—(in) Tibetan 8
—Vātsyāyana on .. .. 40f.
—very popular about the 2nd cent. A.D. 42
—Viśvanātha on 41
Nyāya and Vaiśeṣika amalgamated 396
Nyāya and Vaiśeṣika categories impossible to assimilate .. 402
Nyāya-bhāṣya earliest commentary on 115
Nyāyabhūṣaṇa 338
Nyāya category of Pramāṇa incorporated in the Vaiśeṣika .. 386
Nyāya doctrine of tātparya (intention) 148
Nyāya lilāvatī commentaries on.. 387f.
Nyāya philosophy 279
—incorporates the Vaiśeṣika .. 373
—why termed Akṣapāda darśana.. 398
Nyāya-ratnāvalī (a prakaraṇa by Vallabhācārya) 387
Nyāya-sāra (a manual of logic by Bhā Sarvajña .. ..358ff.
—commentaries on .. .. 371f.
Nyāya Śāstra (see Ānvīkṣikī) .. 39
—antiquity of .. .. 41f.
—early teachers of .. .. 42f.
—first regular work on .. 46

Page

Nyāya Śāstra—
—science of right judgment or true reasoning .. .. 40[2]
—science of syllogism and of inference 41
—technical terms of, as used in the Caraka Saṁhitā 43
—(in) Tibetan .. 40 (ftn. 3)
Nyāya Siddhānta Dīpa (manual of logic by Śaśadhara).. .. 396f.
Nyāya Sūtra (see Nyāya Śāstra).. 46
—arrangement of categories in .. 52
—author of .. .. 47f.
—Bhāṣya (commentary) on .. 46
—contains the principles both of logic and philosophy .. 46
—criticised by Nāgārjuna .. 50
—Gautama and Akṣapāda both authors of 49
—(as) Gotama sūtra 48
—not the work of one person .. 46
—authorship of 498
—passage quoted from later Buddhist works in 46
—reviews doctrines of various periods 46
—subject-matter of .. 49, 50ff.
Nyāya theory of Pramāṇa criticised by Nāgārjuna 256
Nyāya-vidyā emanated from the mouth of Brahmā .. .. 38f.
Nyāya works found by Portuguese missionaries 489
Nying-ma-pa 533

Object of knowledge (see prameya) 375
—kinds of .. .. .. 370f.
Object of right knowledge .. 97
Objects of sense distribution of .. 100
Occasional signification .. 450
Odantapura Sarvāstivāda school of 342
Old man respect for 30
Opponent how to argue with .. 30f.
—how to vanquish 30

Page

Opposing the proposition .. 85
Opposition 113
Opposition to the counter-proposition .. .. .. 166f.
Ordinary Intercourse of Particularity 430
Originating cause 33
Overlooking the censurable .. 89f.

Padmanābha Miśra 381
Padma-saṁbhava .. 327, 352
Pain 58
Pakṣadhara Miśra 406 (ftn. 7), 455f.

Pāla Dynasty—
—kings of 349
—of Bengal and Behar .. 517f.
Pāla kings dates of .. .. 517f.

Pāli Buddhist Literature—
—logical topics in .. 227
—origin of .. .. 225f.
Pallava Dynasty kings of .. 350
Pallavas .. 273 (ftn. 1)
Pamiangchi 535
—Dr. Vidyābhuṣaṇa's reception on the way to . .. 537f.
—monastery of 538
Pañcaśikha 10
Panchen-shwa dmar 271
Paṇḍita Candra father of Jayanta 147
Paṇḍita Dīpāṅkara .. 318
Paṇḍita's red cap 271
Pāṇini 11
Parahita 345
Parahita Bhadra 340
Paramahaṁsa 210
Paramārtha .. 267, 301f.
Parīkṣā (see examination) .. 28

Pariṣad (council)—
—constituents of 22
—(a) council of debate .. 22
—various names of 22
Parivrājaka Karuṇānanda .. 303
Parokṣa and Pratyakṣa senses of, according to Umāsvāti and early Jaina writers 170

Page

Pārśvanātha 159
Parśvadeva Gaṇi 210
Pārtha Sārathi Miśra 273
Particularity (viśeṣa) .. 32, 412, 416
Parts 333
—alone are realities 105
Past time 106
Pāśupata Śaiva sect 155
Pāṭaliputra 349
Pātimokkha introductory part of 233f.
Perceptible reason in the affirmative form six subdivisions of .. 190
Perceptible reason in the negative form—
—six subdivisions of .. .. 190f.
Perception 33, 55², 298, 359ff.
—causes of .. 92, 416f.
—characteristic of an object of .. 310
—contemplative 360
—defined a knowledge .. 92
—(as) defined by Akṣapāda .. 130
—definition of .. 92, 310
—determinate 360
—different from inference .. 93
—Dignāga on .. .. 277ff.
—five special kinds of.. .. 92
—how it arises 57
—indeterminate 360
—instrumental causes of .. 411
—irregularity of .. ..
—kinds of 310, 360f., 383, 390
—ordinary 360
—parts taken by soul and mind in 92
—same as inference 93
—special cause of .. 92, 409
Perceptual knowledge.. .. 411
Permanent signification .. 450
Philosophy or darśana .. 5
Phodang .. 533f., 535
Phun-tshog-nam-gyal 535
Phyogs-glaṅ 272
Phyogs-ltar-snaṅ .. 290 (ftn. 1)
Pippalāda 22
Pījūṣa varṣa 380
Pleasure 58

Page

Pleasure—
—as the summum bonum .. 102
Pleasure and pain 113
Point of defeat or an occasion for rebuke .. 35, 66, 261, 264
—twenty-two kinds of .. 269
—varieties of .. .. 84ff.
Positive things 394
Possession 113
Posterior non-existence 97, 97 (ftn. 1)
Potentiality (of a word) 449ff.
—Gaṅgeśa on 451
—Mimāṁsakas on 451
—sources of .. .. 450f.
Prabhācandra .. 183 193f.
—his references to other philosophers 194
Prabhākara Mīmāṁsakas .. 148
Prabhākaras .. 139, 359
Prabhāsa .. .. 49 (ftn. 2)², 512
Practical direct valid knowledge.. 174
—Deva Sūri on 201
—subdivisions of, according to Deva Suri 201
Practical Naya 171
Pradyumna Sūri .. 196, 205
—particulars about .. 196 (ftn. 1)
Prahlāda 10
Prajñākara .. 187 (ftn. 1)
Prajñākara Gupta 187 (ftn. 2), 330f., 349
Prajñākara mati .. 126 (ftn. 2), 336
Prakṛti (primordial matter) .. 10
Pramāṇa (means of knowledge) 50f., 161
—four kinds of .. 170 (ftn.)
Prameya (object of knowledge) .. 51
Pratāparudra 380
Prayer 2
Predicate or major term 282, 285, 290
Prefixes 453
Present time—
—critical examination of 106 (ftn. 1)
—denied 106
—established 106

	Page
Present time—	
—indication	106
Presumption ..	33, 56, 370
—Mīmāṁsakas on	435
—not valid	96
—(a) special kind of inference ..	96
—validity of	96
Prior non-existence ..	97, 97 (ftn. 1)
Probability ..	56, 370
—(a) special kind of inference ..	96
Production of fruits—	
—time of	102
Prof. H. Ui—	
—on the date of the Nyāya sūtra	50 (ftn. 2)
Prof. L. Suali—	
—on the date of the Nyāya sūtra	50 (ftn. 2)
Proofs—	
—eight kinds of	264
—subdivisions of	366
Proposition 32, 60f, 166, 290, 312,	361, 436f.
Protector and Protégé ..	113
Ptolemy Philadelphos ..	352
Pudgalavada ..	127 (ftn.)
Pudgalavādins ..	127 (ftn.)
Puggalavādins	235
Punarvasu Ātreya—	
—(his) dissertation on the senses	11f.
—(the) original author of the Caraka Saṁhitā	11
Purpose	33, 592
Puragupta ..	227, 249
Puṣpapura ..	26 (ftn. 2)
Qualification or Particularity (Viśeṣaṇatā)	130
Quality (guṇa)	31
—kinds of	78
Questioning the validity of the example	167
Quibble	34, 65
—in respect of a genus ..	65
—in respect of a metaphor ..	65
Quibble—	
—in respect of a term ..	65
—three kinds of	65
Rabhasa Nandi	194
Rāghava Bhaṭṭa	358, 359 (ftn. 1)
Rāghava Rāya ..	482 (ftn. 1)
Raghudeva Nyāyālaṅkāra	220 (ftn. 5), 481
Raghunandana	527
Raghunandana Dāsa Miśra ..	458
Raghunātha Nāyaka ..	485
Raghunātha Sāstri	487
Raghunātha Śiromaṇi 405, 456	(ftn. 2), 463ff., 525
—date of	465
Raghuvratin	305
Rājacūḍāmaṇi Makhin ..	485
Rājā Ballāla Sena	153
Rājā Bhairava Siṁha.. ..	456
Rājagṛha	349
Rājā Rāghava	480
Rājā Rāmakṛṣṇa	477
Rājā Sanātana	337
Rājaśekhara ..	134, 213
Rāmabhadra ..	459, 522
Rāmabhadra Siddhānta Vāgīśa ..	480
Rāmacandra Kavibhārati ..	540
Rāmacandra Vidyāvāgīśa ..	468f.
Rāmakṛṣṇa Bhaṭṭācharya Cakravarty	466f.
Rāmānuja	351
Rāmapāla	346
Rāmarudra Tarkavāgīśa ..	477
Rāmadeva Cirañjiva	433
Rāmarudra Tarkavāgīśa ..	483
Rāmarudra Vidyānidhi ..	327
Rāṣṭrakūṭa king Kṛṣṇarāja I or Śubhatunga	222
Ratnākara Śānti ..	338, 342f., 358
Ratnakīrti	133, 134, 338f., 358, 371
—identification of ..	342 (ftn. 6)
Ratnaprabhā ..	147, 211
—particulars about ..	212 (ftn. 2)
—spiritual descent of ..	212

Page

Ratnavajra .. .. 339f.
Ravi Gupta 322
—date of 335
Reason (hetu.) (see middle term) 32, 32 (ftn. 2), 66², 166, 190, 258, 284f., 290, 361, 437
—and the minor premise .. 503
—affirmative .. 286, 503
—different phases of .. .. 190f.
—kinds of 286, 437
—negative 286, 503
—unproved in respect of constant accompaniment 440
—unproved in respect of invariable concomittance . .. 440
—unproved on the part of its locus 439
—unproved on the part of the major term 440
—unproved on the part of the reason 440
—unproved with regard to its own nature 440
Reasoning (casuistry) 229, 290, 429
—form of 290
—processes of 429
—theory of 5
Reasons—
—distinguished from Ānvīkṣikī and Ātmavidyā 5
—theory of 5, 22
Receipt 113
Reciprocal non-existence 394, 416
Recognition 101, 112, 189, 201
—(a) function of a conscious agent, the soul 112
—of common properties .. 59
—of properties not common .. 59
Recollection (smrti) .. 189, 201
Redundancy 34
Reflection 129
—Vācaspati and Jayanta on 129 (ftn. 3)
Refutation (Dūṣaṇa) .. 181, 298, 315
—semblance of .. 181, 298
Re-inculcation 108
Re-interrogation 33

Page

Rejoinder (uttara) 32
—causing entanglement or defeat on the disputant (niggaha) .. 236
—by the respondent (patikamma) 235f.
Relation of Identity 400
Relation—
—fundamental conceptions of .. 255
Relative non-existence .. 394
Renouncing the proposition .. 86
Repetition.. .. 34, 88f.
Resources for the accomplishment of an action 27
Respondent accused or defendant (cuditaka) 231
—three classes of 29
Rgyal-wa-can 338
Rgya-tshan-son-ge 352
Right knowledge 138, 174, 389, 394
—objects of .. .. 56ff.
—two kinds of .. 169, 174
Rigs-pa-can 278
Rigs-paḥi- yan-lag .. 289 (ftn. 3)
Rin-chen-grags 338
Rituals 2, 108
—three subdivisions of .. 108
Rnal-hbyor-pa 278
Root 453
Rucidatta .. 406 (ftn 7), 457
Rudra 395
Rudra Nyāyavācaspati .. 476f.
Rudrarāma 484
Rudra Vācaspati 392
Rumour 54, 370
—not a separate means of knowledge 95
—(a) special kind of verbal testimony 95
Rung po—
—Dr. Vidyābhūṣana's journey to.. 529f.

Sabda-śakti-prakāśikā (a logico-grammatical treatise of Jagadīśa Tarkālankāra) .. ..470ff.
Sadvāha or Śātavāhana .. 251
Sahabuddin Ghori .. 406 (ftn. 6)

Page

Sahaja Sarvajña 384
Saint Tirujñana Sambandar .. 222
Śakābda 241
Śākala 266
Śakrāditya 515
Śaktisvāmin 147
Śākyabodhi 320
Śākya hod 343
Śākya muni 315
Salvation (see emancipation) .. 359
Sāmantabhadra .. 182f., 333, 339
—age of 183
—(his) Āptamīmāṁsā .. 184f.
Saṁbhāṣā (see Vāda-vidhi and debate) .. .. .. 28f.
—method of .. .. 28f.
Saṁbhāṣā-praśaṁsā (see debate-utility of) .. .. 28f.
Saṁbhāṣā-vidhi (see Vāda-vidhi and Ānvīkṣikī)—the principal topic of 27
Saṁbhūtivijaya .. 164 (ftn. 4)
Sāṁkhya .. 5, 6, 10, 243, 278
—same as Upaniṣad and Vedānta .. .. 244 (ftn. 1)
Sāṁkhya Philosophy—
—the oldest work of .. 295 (ftn. 1)
Samprati 222
Sam-ye .. .. 323 (ftn. 3)
Śaṅkara Svāmin .. 302, 302 (ftn. 4)
Saṅgha 304
Saṅgha-bhadra .. 248 (ftn. 2), 266
—a contemporary of Vasubandhu 267 (ftn.)
Saṅghamittā 352
Saṅghārāma .. 248, 265
Sang-ngag-tsi-ling 535
Śaṅkarācārya 351
Śaṅkara Deva 351
Śaṅkara Miśra 366 (ftn. 1), 406 (ftn. 7), 456 (ftn. 2), 458 f., 522
Śaṅkarānanda .. 344f., 349
Sanskrit Buddhist Literature—
—logic mentioned in .. .. 242ff.
—origin of 242

Page

Śānta Rakṣita 271, 323, 327, 352, 517
Śāntideva .. 126 (ftn. 2)
Śānti Sūri 197
Sapta-bhaṅga Naya (sevenfold paralogism, see Syādvāda) .. 167f.
—particulars about .. 167 (ftn. 2)
Śaraha 251
Śāṛṅgapāṇi 393
Sarva-darśana-saṁgraha .. 398
Sarvajña 342
Sarvajña Deva .. 310², 357
Sarvajña Mitra .. 322, 357
Sarvajña Śrī Rakṣita 289
Sarvajña Viṣṇu 398
Sarvāstivāda 247
Sarvāstivāda sect 266
Śaśadhara 396
Śaśāṅka Narendra Gupta .. 349
Śā-skya monastery of Western Tibet 289, 300
Śātavāhana (see Sadvāha) 251 (ftn. 2), 349
Sautrāntika .. 135, 248
—criticised by Jayanta .. 150
—explanation of .. 248 (ftn. 3)
—founder of 248
Sautrāntikas—
—philosophical principles of .. 248
—sects belonging to 247
Savikalpaka (determinate perception)—
—definition of 137
Sāyaṇa 397
Saying too little 88
Saying too much 88
Scheme—
—for the reduction of sixteen categories into one 359
—of incorporation of the Nyāya and the Vaiśeṣika 375, 382 387, 389, 393, 394
Scholarly debate 240
School of Gangeśa .. 391
School of Raghunātha Śiromaṇi .. 392

Page

Scripture (Āgama) 189
—definition of 175
Seish 266
Self-consciousness 418
Seṅ-ḍkar 337
Senses 55, 57², 411, 417
—Ātreya's doctrine of .. 12
—five characteristic of knowledge corresponding to 100
—five in number .. 99, 100
—five objects of 100
—forms of 100
—grounds of their being five .. 100
—material 99
—materials of 100
—(as) modifications of touch 99, 99 (ftn. 1)
—objects of 57
—processes of 100
—sites of 100
Sentiments 57
Separation 113
Ser-ṣkya- wa 278
Śes-paḫi-ḍge-guas 275
Śes-rab-ḫbyuṅ-gnas-ṣbas .. 336f.
Settlement of cases—
—by a majority 230
—by an undertaking 230
—covering over with grass .. 230
—for the insane 230
—from recollection 230
—in presence 230
—seven rules for 230
—with the prospect of further inquiry 230
Seven categories of the Jaina philosophers 168
Sevenfold paralogism (syādvāda. 185
Shahiya Dynasty 350
Shāhjehān 479
Sha-lu 270
—monastery of 353
Shapur 20
Shifting the proposition .. 85
Shifting the reason .. 35, 36

Page

Shifting the topic .. 35, 86f.
Shi-wa-ḫtsho 323
Shu-chen 321, 322, 328, 329, 340²
Sh'-yen-töh-cia .. 251 (ftn. 2)
Siddharṣi .. 147 (ftn. 4)
Siddhasena Divākara .. 268 (ftn. 2)
alias Kṣapāṅkara 173 ff., 268 (ftn. 2)
—date of .. 173, 505 (ftn. 9)
—first Jaina writer on systematic logic 173
—founder of Mediaeval Logic .. 158
—(his) Nyāyā vatāra 174
—particulars about 173
—(a) pupil of Vṛddhavādi Sūri .. 173
Siddhasena Gaṇi 182
—a contemporary of Devardhi Gaṇi Kṣamā Śramaṇa .. 182
Sign (see middle term, reason) 113, 377, 383
Signification (of a word) .. 450
Signification (of letters) .. 131f.
Sikkim—
—Buddhism in 535
—monasteries in .. .. 534f.
Śīla 335
Śīlabhadra 302, 303
Śila Saṅgama .. 519 (ftn. 6)
Silence 89
Siṁha 335
Siṁha Giri or Siṁha Sūri 182, 182 (ftn. 3)
Siṁhavaktra 272
Siṁha Varman 349
Similar employment 113
Śiromaṇi—
—satirised by Yaśovijaya .. [illegible]8
Śivanātha Vidyāvācaspati .. 526
Six Systems 209
Six-winged disputation .. 82f.
Skanda Gupta .. 267², 349
Skin 57
Smell 57
Sñe-thaṅ monastery of .. 344
Soma Śarmā—
—father of Akṣapāda and Kaṇāda

Page

Sophists 227
Soul 181, 393
—(an) abstract conception of .. 4
—compared to a charioteer .. 3
—compromise between the two ideas of 4
—(a) concrete substance .. 4
—connection with a body .. 57
—destiny of 3
—Deva Sūri's views of .. 204
—different from body .. 3, 98
—different from mind 98
—different from the senses .. 93
—(the) enjoyer 7
—existence of 57
—evolution in the doctrine of .. 2
—good work of 3
—ideas of 4
—identical with the senses .. 97
—individual 371
—individuality of 99
—(in the) Kaṭhopaniṣad .. 3
—kinds of 371
—Lokāyata doctrine of .. 9
—marks or signs of 57
—pre-existence of 99
—(as consciousness) produced by the combination of elements .. 9
—qualities of 57
—(puruṣa) .. ..
—sāṁkhya doctrine of .. 10
—(in the) Śatapatha Brāhmaṇa .. 2
—(the) seat of knowledge (cognitions) 98
—science of (Ātmavidyā) .. 4
—seeing 6
—supreme 371
—theory of . .. 5
—two ideas regarding .. 4
—(in the) Upaniṣads 3
—(spirit) (in the) Vedas .. 2
—yoga doctrine of 11
Sound 57
—according to the Nyāya Sūtra .. 109
—artificial properties attributed to 110

Page

Sound—
—destroyed and not concealed .. 448
—cognised by the senses .. 109f.
—having a beginning .. – 109
—merely a manifestation of itself 109
—nature of 109
—non-eternal 109
—non-eternity of 448
—(a) product 109
—reasons for its being non-eternal 109f.
—substratum of 110
—traditionary teaching of .. 110

Speech—
—Buddhists on 445
—canons of a sound .. .. 12f.
—defect of 260
—excellence of 260
—(a) means of valid knowledge 444, 445
—opportune 260
Sphoṭa (the outburst of a conglomerate sound) 131

Sphoṭavāda (theory of phonetic explosion)—
—Jayanta's examination of .. 148f.
Śrī Candra .. 210, 211
Śrīdhara 213, 329
Śrī Harṣa 330, 335, 349, 406 (ftn. 6)
Śrī Kanṭha 151
Śrī Kṛṣṇa Nyāyālaṅkāra .. 483
Śrīlabdha 248
Śrīparvata or Śrīśaila 251 (ftn. 4)
Śripreramātur 351
Śrī Śūnya Śū Mitra 336
Sroṅ-tsan-gam-po 352
Śrughna .. .. 124 (ftn. 1)
Śruta .. .. 169 (ftn. 1)
Śruta Sāgara Gaṇi 215
Śrutya Prāmāṇya (denial of the authority of the Veda) criticised by Jayanta .. .. 149f.
Statement of the Conclusion .. 60
State of being the locus or the minor term 433
Sthavira Ratnākara 520

Page

Sthiramati .. 334, 515 (ftn. 2)
Sthitamati 266
Sthūlabhadra 161
Strabo 352
Straight or immediate Naya (Ṛjū-sūtra) 171
Subandhu same as Vasubandhu .. 128
Śubhakara Gupta 346
Śubhatuṅga .. 186 (ftn. 3)
Subject 290
Subjective law (Pakṣadharmatā) 390
Subsequent non-existence 184, 394, 416
—Deva Suri on 203
Substance (dravya) 31
Subtle śabda 171
Such-like śabda 171
Sudharma Svāmī .. 160 (ftn. 1)
Sufferings—
—channels of .. .. 132f.
—kinds of .. .. 132f.
Suitable śabda 171
Sulabhā 12
—(his) interview with king Janaka 12f.
—probably a fictitious person .. 24
Sumati 336, 314
Summary—
—of a dissertation on the senses 12
Summum bonum 54
Sumpa 337
Sundara 222
Sun Dynasty .. 243 (ftn. 1)
Śūnyatā or Nirvāṇa .. 127 (ftn.), 255
—of the Mādhyamikas 245 (ftn. 2)
Śūnyavāda .. 245 (ftn. 2)
Superimposition, three kinds of .. 201
Sūtra of the Burden-bearer 127 (ftn.) 2
Suvarṇa vihāra 523
Svatantra Mādhyamika school .. 323
Svāmin 117
Śveta dvīpa, identical with Syria 44 (ftn. 3)
Śvetāmbaras 159
Syādvāda (assertion of possibilities) 167f., 181, 184
- particulars about .. 167 (ftn. 2)

Page

Syllogism .. 258, 361, 377, 436, 497
—form of 290
—members of .. .. 60f.
—of five members .. 43, 269
—of ten parts 166
—criticised by Vātsyāyana .. 121f.
—essential nature of 361
—first introduction of .. 498f
—Greek influence in .. 500 (ftn. 1)
—Mīmāṁsā form of 377
—of two parts 260
—parts of 203, 289f., 436
—(a) Speech of five parts .. 43
—terms of .. 176, 189f.
Syllogism and Inference—
—connexion between 499
Syllogism from a sign—
—and Enthymeme from a sign .. 510
Syllogism in Indian Logic—
—conforms to the logical reebs of Aristotle .. 500ff.
Syllogism of two parts— ..
—and a perfect syllogism .. 505f.
Syllogism and Sāṁkhyā or Sāṁkhya .. 498 (ftn. 8)
Systematic Jaina Logic .. 172

Takṣaśilā 248
Tantrayukti (forms of scientific argument) 24
—added to the Carakasaṁhitā 24 (ftn. 1)
—in the Caraka Saṁhitā .. 25
—oldest work of Logic .. 25
—(in the) Suśruta-Saṁhitā 24f., 24 (ftn. 2)
—for the systematisation of debates 24
—technical terms constituting .. 25
Tāntrika Pūrṇānanda .. 478
Tārā 332, 334, 335
Tarka 37
Tarka-bhāṣā (a treatise by Keśava Miśra) 381
—commentaries on 384

Page

Tarka-bhāṣā—
—incorporates the Vaiśeṣika categories 381
Tarkakaumudī (a manual of logic by Laugākṣi Bhāskara) .. 395
Tarkāmṛta (a manual of logic by Jagadīśa Tarkālaṅkāra) .. 393f.
Tarka Saṁgraha (a manual of logic by Annam Bhaṭṭa) ..388ff.
—commentaries on .. .. 390f.
Tarka Śāstra—the science of diabetes .. ..402ff.
Tarkavidyā (see Vāda-vidyā and Ānvikṣiki) .. 7, 8 37
Tārkika—
—(as) indispensable member of a legal assembly 38
Tārkika-rakṣā (a treatise by Varadārāja) .. ..374ff.
Tārkikas 244
—Vyāsa against 37
Tashi-lhum-po 270
Tashiding 535
Tashi Lāmā—
—and his party 528
—departure of 529
—his reception of the Prince of Wales 529
—his visit to Buddha Gayā .. 529
—in Calcutta 529
—in India .. .. 528f.
—reception accorded to .. 528
Taste 57
Tathāgata .. .. 12.
Tattva-cintāmaṇi (the earliest work on Tarka Śāstra) ..405ff.
—popularity of 454
Taxila—
—antiquity of 494
—as the great seat of Hindu learning and culture 495
—Greek regime at .. .. 494f.
—mutual exchange of Hindu and Greek culture at 495
—Persian conquest of.. .. 494

Page

Taxila—
—Persian influence at.. .. 494
—political history of 494
Technicality 450
Technicalities of Logic in the Mādhyamika kārika 255
Teesta Bridge 530
Temple of Pārśvanātha 324 (ftn. 3)
Temple of Śāntinātha.. .. 329
Tenet or conclusion .. 33, 59
—four kinds of 33, 59
Terms—
—five definitions of 403
—meanings of 403
—of scientific argument .. 24
Terms technical .. 23, 403f.
—(used) in the) Brāhmaṇas and the Upaniṣads .. ..
—(used in the) Manusaṁhitā .. 23
—constituting the tantra-yukti .. 25
—(used in the) Rāmāyaṇa .. 23
Thāṅ Dynasty ..343 (ftn. 1), 266[2]
Thas-paḥi ḥbyuṅ-gnas ṣbas .. 346
Theory of Condition (upādhi)—
—Vācaspati Miśra on 140
Theory of cause and effect—
—Vacaspati Miśra on 140
Theory of Impermanence (kṣanika vāda) 121
Theory of perception as set forth by Dignāga—
—controverted by Uddyotakara .. 126
Theory of Proof 266
Theras .. 226, 246
Theravāda 226
Theravādin 235
Thesis (see proposition) 290, 312
—fallacies of .. 290f., 312
—two kinds of 264
Things—
—kinds of 394
Third Buddhist Council .. 234
Thogs-med 265
Thon-mi-sam-bhota 352

Page

Three characteristics of the middle term—
—and the middle term in a syllogism .. .. 507f.
Three Times 106
Tilakācārya 212
Tilopā 340
Tipiṭakas 226
Tirhut 350
Tīrtha 275[3], 303[2], 304, 305, 308, 315
Tīrtha dialecticians 272
Tīrtha-grāma 540
Tīrthakas .. 261, 339, 342
Tīrthaṅkaras 158
Tīrtha system—
—doctrines of 304
—followers of 304
Tol (a Sanskrit school) .. 525 (ftn. 1)
Tongue 57
To-to-go-mo—
—Dr. Vidyābhūṣaṇa receives an address at 540
Touch 57
Tradition 33
Transcendent Intercourse .. 430
—kinds of .. .. 412f.
Transcendent perception .. 412ff.
—consequence of 181
—process of .. .. 412f.
Transcendental direct valid knowledge .. 175, 201
—subdivisions of 201
Transcendental truth 254
Transmigration—
—belongs to the soul 101
—(the) path of .. 3, 57, 58
Triangular perception 418
Trilocana .. 358, 369 (ftn. 1)
—date of 134
—(a) writer on Vaiśeṣika philosophy 134
Trilocana the Junior 374
Trimalaya 303
Trividha paraḥ (see respondents)—three classes of 29

Page

Tsin Dynasty .. 243 (ftn. 1)
Turuṣkas 350
Tutārī 386
Udayakara 141
Udayana 155, 209 (ftn.) 348, 351, 386, 396, 399
—author of the Nyāya-vārtika-tātparya-ṭīkā-pariśuddhi .. 141
—better known as Ācārya .. 142
—combats the Buddhist .. 142
—(his) contention of the Buddhist doctrines 146
—(his) criticism of the doctrine of apoha, kṣaṇabhaṅga, etc. .. 143
—(his) Kusumāñjali 143
—opposes Kalyāna-rakṣita and Dharmottara 143
—(his) victory over the Buddhists causes his death 142
—(his) works 141
—(his) work Ātmatattva vidyā .. 145f.
Uddyotakara 119 (ftn.) 127 (ftn.), 155, 273, 306, 348
—attacked by Abhayadeva Sūri 221 (ftn. 2)
—author of the Nyāyavārtika .. 123
—(his) controversy with the Buddhists 125
—criticises Dignāga 129
—criticises Nāgarjuna .. 128
—(his) criticism of the Buddhist denial of the soul 125
—criticism of the theory of perception as held by Dignāga .. 129
—date of .. 123, 124
—(his) defence of the Nyāya-Sūtra and the Nyāyabhāṣya 287 (ftn. 2)
—(his) definition of Inference .. 130
—(his) explanation of perception .. 130
—(his) main object to write the subcommentary 125
—(his) Nyāya theory of signification of words 131
—on Dignāga's theory of perception .. 277 (ftn. 1)

Page

Uddyotakara—
—(as a) rescuer of the Nyāya .. 123
—residence of 124
—(his) theory of sufferings .. 132f.
—(his) theory of verbal knowledge 131
—various names of 124
Udyāna (Kabul) .. 340, 352[2]
Ujjayinī 301
Umāsvāti 161 (ftn. 4, 5), 164
—(his) doctrine of right knowledge 169f.
—(his) explanation of Naya (mood of statements) .. .. 170f.
—life of .. .. 168f.
—known as Vācaka Śramaṇa, Nāgara-vācaka and Umāsvāti Vācakācārya 168
—(his) particulars about 168 (ftn. 3)
Umā Svāmin (same as Umāsvāti) 168 (ftn. 3)
Uncertain 33
Uncertainty—
—Deva Sūri on 201
Unintelligible 87
Union .. 412, 414
United-inherent-inherence .. 412
United inherence .. 412, 414
Universal non-existence .. 416
Universal proposition—
—discovery of .. 295 (ftn. 2)
University of Nadia (see Nadia)—
—foundation of 464
University of Nālandā (see Nālandā) 271
University of Vikramaśilā (see Vikramaśilā) 271
Unnameable 55
Unproved reason 439
Upāṅga 160
Upaniṣads 134
Upendra 258
Uttara Tantra .. 24 (ftn. 2)

Vācaspati Miśra 120 (ftn. 3), 155, 183, 209 (ftn.), 247 (ftn. 2), 273, 282 (ftn.), 330, 348, 522

Page

Vâcaspati—
—author of the Nyāya-Vārtika-tātparya-ṭīkā 133
—(his) condemnation of the Buddhist and Jaina scriptures .. 141
—criticises Dharmakīrti .. 136
—(his) criticism of Dharmakīrti's division of the point of defeat (Nigrahasthāna) 136
—(his) criticism of Dignāga's definition of kārya-sama (balancing the effect) 135
—(his) criticism of the Niruktakāra's 138
—(his) explanation of determinate and indeterminate perceptions.. 137f.
—(on the) name Pakṣila Svāmī 115 (ftn. 2)
—opposes Dignāga 135
—place and time of 133
—(his) reference to the four Buddhist schools 135
—supports the Brahmanic interpretations of the Nyāya sūtra .. 133
—(his) theory of cause and effect 140f.
—(his) theory of condition .. 140
—(his) theory of right and wrong knowledge .. ..138ff.
—Trilocana, the preceptor of .. 134
—works of 134
Vācaspati Miśra, the junior 151, 459f.
Vaccagotta .. 117 (ftn. 3)
Vāda (discussion) 51
—subject of 51
Vāda-mārga (see debate-course of) 31
Vāda-maryādā (see debate-limits of) 31
Vāda-vidhi (see Ānvīkṣikī)—the principal topics of 27
(also see Sambhāsā and debate) 28
Vāda-vidyā (see Tarka-vidyā) .. 7
Vādopāya (see debate-expedients of) .. .. .. 30f.
Vāgīśvarkīrti 338
Vaibhāṣika 135

Page

Vaiśeṣikas .. 244, 247
—criticised by Jayanta .. 150
—explanation of .. 247 (ftn. 5)
—fundamental principal work of 247
Vaibhāṣika School of Philosophy—
—sects belonging to 246
Vaiśāli 349
Vaiśeṣika Philosophy .. 27, 278, 393
—incorporated into the Nyāya .. 373
—incorporates the Nyāya categories 386
Vaiśeṣika principles—
—adopted in Nyāya 402
Vaiyākaraṇa doctrine of apoha (exclusion) .. 132 (ftn. 1)
Vajrāsana (Buddhagayā) 339, 343
Vajra-varāhī 340
Valedictory description .. 108
Validity of knowledge .. 408f.
—consciousness of 409
—derived from its general grounds 408
—derived through the instrument 409
—Gaṅgeśa on 409
Valid knowledge (see right knowledge) .. 218, 375f., 408f.
—consequence of .. 181, 192
—Deva Sūri on .. ..200ff.
—defined by Māṇikya Nandi .. 189
—how derived and known .. 408f.
—kinds of .. 189, 310, 201
—objects of 192
—of the Buddhist condemned .. 375f.
Vallabhācārya .. 374f, 386f.
—founder of a Vaiṣṇava Sect .. 387
Vallāla Sena .. 350
Vāmana 267
Vana Pāla 329
Vandin (a famous sophist) .. 13
Varadārāja 373ff., 399 (ftn. 1)
Varāha Mihira 165, 165 (ftn. 2), 173
Vararuci 334
Vardhamāna 151, 386, 406 (ftn. 7), 405, 454f.
Vārendra 322, 333 334 (ftn. 2), 335, 337
Vasanta Sena 722

Page

Vasubandhu 116, 266ff., 272, 349
—age of 116
—biography of 267
—works of 267
Vāsudeva 372, 406 (ftn. 7), 456
Vāsudeva Sārvabhauma 405, 456 (ftn. 2), 461
Vasudhara Rakṣita 299
Vātāpi 349
Vātsīputrīya sect .. 135, 272
Vātsyāyana 46, 106 (ftn. 1), 155, 348
—age of .. ..116f.
—author of the Nyāya bhāṣya ..115ff.
—birthplace of 117
—criticises Nāgārjuna .. 117f.
—(his) criticism of the doctrine of momentariness 121
—(his) criticism of the Mādhyamika doctrine of inter-relation .. 117
—(his) criticism of the Mādhyamika doctrine of voidness (śūnyatā) .. 118
—(his) criticism of Nāgārjuna's logical theory of examples .. 119
—(his) criticism of the syllogism of ten parts .. ..121f.
—(his) criticism of the Yogācāra doctrine of Viññāna (knowledge) 120
—(his) definition of perception criticised by Dignāga 278
—designated as Drāmila .. 117
—followed Nāgārjuna and the Laṅkāvatāra 116
—(his) idea of emancipation .. 122
—(his) idea of God 122
—on mind as a sense-organ 280 (ftn. 1)
—(his) other name Pakṣila Svāmin 115
—precedes Dignāga and Vasubandhu 116
—(his) references to previous commentators .. 115 (ftn. 3)
—(in) Uddyotakara's Nyāya Vārtika .. .. 115 (ftn. 1)
Vaṭṭagāmaṇi 226
Vedānta 4
Vedāntins 273

	Page
Veda	1
—(its) authority established ..	107
—faultless	107
—faulty	107
—refers to unbelievers ..	9
—(its) reliability established ..	108
—subject-matter of	2
—two main divisions of ..	108
Vedic speech—	
—classification of	108
Veṅgi ..	273 (ftn. 1), 274
Verbal knowledge (śabda)	444, 470ff.
—cause of ..	..473ff.
—different from perception and inference ..	.. 470f.
—different from recollection ..	471
—Mīmāṁsakas on ..	.. 473f.
—Naiyāyikas on	471
—process of ..	444, 471
—Vaiśeṣikas on	471
Verbal Naya (śabda)	171
—three kinds of	171
Verbal suffix	453
Verbal testimony (Āgama śabda)	175, 192, 444
—Deva Sūri on	201
—Digṅāga on	287f.
—distinct from inference	95, 446
—distinct from perception ..	446
—included in inference according to the Vaiśeṣikas	446
—included in perception according to the Buddhists	445
—instrumental causes of ..	44
—kinds of	370
—(a) mere inference	94f.
—Mīmāṁsakas on	408
—special cause of	409
Vidyādhara Ācārya Aśoka ..	334
Vidyānanda ..	183 (ftn. 2)
—age of	187
—identical with Pātrakeśarī	187, 188 (ftn. 1)
—works of	187
Vidyānivāsa	392
Vidyāpati ..	456, 522
Vidyāvācaspati ..	476 (ftn. 1)
Vijaya Sena Sūri ..	212, 350, 521
Vijaya Siṁha	216
Vijñāna-vāda	135
—in Tibetan ..	245 (ftn. 1)
Vijñāna-vādins or yogācāras ..	146
Vikramāditya ..	173, 222, 267
Vikrama Saṁvat or Śaka era	329 (ftn. 3)
Vikrama Śilā ..	336, 342, 352
—decay of	525
—Mahomedan attacks on	520 (ftn. 2)
—situation of ..	519 (ftn. 6)
—university of	337, 338, 340, 341, 342, 343, 345, 350, 519f.
Vikramaśilā University—	
—destruction of	520
—gate-keepers of	520
—head of	519
—scholars of	520
Vimalacandra	320
Vinaya Vijaya	216
Vindhyavāsin	211
Vinīta Deva	320f.
Viṣṇu Svāmin	374
Viśvanātha	151
Viśvanātha Nyāyapañcānana ..	392
Viśvanātha Siddhānta-pañcānana	479f.
Viśveśvara Jyotiṣārṇava ..	527
Vyāsa—	
—signifies a compiler	50
Vyomācārya	386
Western Calukya Dynasty	273 (ftn. 1)
Wheel of reasons (see table of nine reasons) ..	285, 298
—analysis of	298
Whole ..	105, 333
—beyond its parts	105
Word ..	33, 56, 384
—compound (see compound) ..	452
—conventional	451
—connotes the genus	111
—denotes the individual ..	111
—does it denote 'apoha' (exclusion)	132

Page

Word—
—etymological 451
—etymological-conventional .. 451
—etymologo-conventional .. 451
—four kinds of 33
—how it signifies a thing .. 131
—presents the form 111
—signification of 111
—species of 451
—two kinds of .. 56. 110f.
Words and their meanings .. 106f.
—Jayanta on .. .. 147f.
—their connection conventional .. 107
—their connection natural .. 106
Wrangler 63
Wrangling .. 62. 63
Wrangling and Cavil—
—use of 104
Wrong knowledge or error .. 138f.
—nature of .. .. 138f.

Yādava Dynasty 386
Yajñapati .. 406 (ftn. 7)
Yama (the lord of death) .. 2
Yamāri .. .. 343f.
Yaśovijaya Gaṇi 217
—his references to other philosophers 219

Page

Yaśovijaya—
—his references to works on philosophy 219
—his reviews of other writers .. 218
—life of 217
—particulars about .. 218 (ftn. 3)
—spiritual descent of .. 217 (ftn. 2)
—works of .. .. 218f.
Yośodharma Deva 173
Ye-śes-dpal-bzañ-po 342
Yoga 5. 6. 11. 274 (ftn. 3)
Yogācārabhūmi Śāstra 274 (ftn. 3)
Yogācāra Buddhists 138
Yogācāras or Viññānavādins 146, 249. 278
—criticised by Jayanta .. 150
—explanation of .. 249 (ftn. 1)
—founds of 249
—in China. Tibet and Nepal 249 (ftn. 1)
Yogācāra-darśana 245
Yogācāra doctrine of Vijñāna (knowledge)—
—criticised by Vātsyāyana .. 124f.
Yogins 278

Za-hor 323
Zarmana Chagos 352
Zla-wa-dge-bsñen .. .. 333f.

INDEX OF BOOKS.

	Page
Abheda-dhikkāra	459
Abhidharma jñāna-prasthāna-śāstra	242
Abhidharma Mahāvibhāṣā	242 (ftn. 2), 247
Abhidhamma Piṭaka	226, 227 (ftn. 2), 242, 334
Abhidhammatthasaṅgaha	227 (ftn. 2)
Abhidhāna Cintāmaṇi ..	205
Abhidharmakośa ..	127 (ftn.)
Abhidharma-vibhāṣā	242[2]
Abhisamayālaṅkāra-kārikā	262[2], 262 (ftn. 5)
Ācārāṅga Sūtra	165
Ācārya-mata-rahasya-vicāra ..	479
Adhikaraṇa Candrikā	484
(?) Ādi-kriyā-viveka	467
Ādipurāṇa ..	176, 183
Advaitaratnakoṣa ..	406 (ftn. 2)
Ain-i Akbari ..	201 (ftn. 1)
Aitareya Brāhmaṇa ..	23, 23 (ftn. 6)
Akalaṅka stotra	185
Akbar	221 (ftn. 1)
Ākhyānamaṇikoṣa	210
Ākhyātavāda ..	465, 482
Ālambana-parīkṣā .	300, 301, 322
Ālambana-parīkṣā-ṭīkā ..	321[3]
Ālambana-parīkṣā-vṛtti ..	301
Ālambana-pratyayadhyāna-śāstra	300 (ftn 3)
Ālambana-Pratyayadhyāna Vyākhyā	303
Alaṅkāra-pariṣkāra	479
Alaṅkāra-sāra-sthiti	477
Āloka	458, 460, 465, 467, 468, 478
Amarakoṣa ..	7 (ftn. 1)
Ānanda-lahari-tarī ..	478, 479
Ānanda-vardhana	451
Ancient Geography of India	514 (ftn. 2, 4)
Ancient India by Rapson ..	494 (ftn. 1)
Ancient Indian Education	525 (ftn. 1)
Ancient Indian Logic..	348 (ftn. 1)
Anekānta-jaya-patākā	221 (ftn. 2)
Anekānta-jaya-patākā-ṭīkā	209 (ftn. 2)
Anekārtha saṃgraha	205
Aṅguttaranikāya III	21 (ftn. 2), 26 (ftn. 1) 227 (ftn. 2)
Antarvyāpti ..	343 (ftn. 3)
Anumāna-cintāmaṇi-dīdhiti-ṭikā..	482
Anumāna-dīdhiti ..	406 (ftn. 2)
Anumāna-dīdhiti-prasāriṇī ..	468
Anumāna-dīdhiti-viveka ..	468
Anumāna-khaṇḍa-ṭīkā	460, 522
Anumānāloka-prasāriṇī ..	468
Anumāna Sutta	220
Anumiti-parāmarśa-vāda ..	481
Anyāpoha-vicāra-kārikā	143, 150, 329
Apaśabda-khaṇḍana	466
Apoha-nāma-prakaraṇa	143, 150, 330
Apoha-siddhi	133 (ftn. 4), 134, 339 (ftn. 3), 345, 371
Āpta-mīmāṁsā	18[2], 184, 185, 186
Āpta-mīmāṁsālaṅkāra ..	186
Āpta-parīkṣā	187
Archæological Discoveries at Taxila	495 (ftn. 2)
Archæological Survey of Western India	49 (ftn. 2), 496 (ftn. 1), 515 (ftn. 5)
Arda-Viraf-Nāma ..	20 (ftn. 4)
Arabic Literature	511 (ftn. 3), 512 (ftn. 2)
Aristotle by Grote	505 (ftn. 1), 510 (ftn. 3, 4,) 511 (ftn. 4)
Arrian ..	496 (ftn. 1)
Artha Śāstra ..	24, 117
Ārya-koṣa ..	322 (ftn. 7)
Ārya Nāgārjuna Bodhisattva-Suhṛllekha ..	251 (ftn. 2)

Page

Ārya-Tārā-antarbali-vidhi 334 (ftn. 1)
Aśoka by V. A. Smith 234 (ftn. 1)
Aṣṭa-sāhasrī .. 186, 197
Aṣṭa-sāhasrikā prajñā-pāramitā 242 (ftn. 3)
Aṣṭa-sāhasrī - viṣamapada - tātparya-ṭikā .. .. 185 (ftn. 3)
Aṣṭa-sāhasrī-vivaraṇa .. 481
Aṣṭa-sāhasrī-vṛtti 218
Aṣṭaśatī .. 185 (ftn. 2)
Atharva-veda Saṁhitā 2 (ftn. 2)
Ātmakhyāti .. 195 (ftn. 6)
Ātma-tattva-viveka 143, 145, 348, 465
Ātma-tattva-viveka-dīdhīti-ṭīkā .. 468
Ātma-tattva-viveka-kalpa-latā .. 459
Avacchedakatva-nirukti .. 465
Āvaśyaka-laghu-vṛtti 212
Āvaśyaka-niryukti 181
Āvaśyaka-sūtra .. 165, 210
Avayavi-nirākaraṇa .. 338 (ftn. 1)
Āyur-daya-bāvanī 467
Ayurveda-saṁhitā 27

Bālāvatāra-tarka 337
Bauddha-dhikkāra 145
Bauddha dhikkāra-ṭikā .. 459
Bauddha-dhikkāra-rahasya .. 467
Bauddha-dhikkāra-śiromaṇi .. 465
B.B.R.A.S. (Journal) .. 406 (ftn. 6)
Bedā-vṛtti 303
Berlin Catalogue by Weber 388 (ftn. 3)
Bhagavad-gītā .. 4 (ftn. 2)
Bhāgavata-purāṇa .. 23 (ftn. 4, 6)
Bhagavatī-sūtra .. 161, 161 (ftn. 4)
Bhāmatī .. 127 (ftn.)
Bhāmati-ṭīkā .. 134
Bhatṛhari and Kumārila by K. B. Pāthak 186 (ftn. 3), 188 (ftn. 2, 3, 7)
Bhāṣāpariccheda 392f., 392 (ftn. 1), 480 (ftn. 1)
Bhāṣāratnam .. 466 (ftn. 21)
Bhāskarodaya 39
Bhāskarodaya-ṭīkā 391
Bhāṣya (Patañjali's) .. 41 (ftn. 5)
„ (Vātsyāyana's) .. 55

Bhāṣya-vṛtti 391
Bhāva-dīpikā 483
Bhāvārtha-dīpikā 478
Bhāva-vilāsa 477
Bheda-prakāśa ..456 (ftn. 2), 459[2]
Bheda-ratna-prakāśa 459
Bhikṣu Sūtra 240
Bhrama-pramathana-yukti-hetu-siddhi 261
Bhramara-dūtam 477
Bhūṣaṇa Sāra .. 220 (ftn. 6)

Bilingual Index of Nyāya-bindu, introduction 307 (ftn. 4), 309 (ftn 2)
Bis-wa hjug-pahi-ṛtog-ge .. 337
Bkah-hgyur .. 11 (ftn. 3), 352 530
Bodha-siddhi .. .. 141[2]
Bodhi-caryāvatāra-ṭīkā 126 (ftn. 2)[2]
Bodhisattva-caryā-nirdeśa 249, 262
Brahmajāla-sutta 20, 21 (ftn. 4), 227 (ftn. 4)
Brāhmaṇa Sarvasva 524
Brahmāṇḍa Purāṇa 155 (ftn. 1), 498 (ftn. 7)
Bṛhadāraṇyakopaniṣad 3 (ftn. 3)
Bṛhad-jñāna-koṣa .. 324 (ftn. 3)

Brief notes on the modern Nyāya system of Philosophy by MM. Maheścandra Nyāyaratna 403 (ftn. 1)
Bsaṇ-hgyur, Bstod-pa 253 (ftn.)
Bśes-pahi-ṣpriṅ-yig .. 215 (ftn. 1)
Bstan-hgyur 7 (ftn. 7), 8 (ftn. 7), 54 (ftn. 2), 55 (ftn. 1), 241 (ftn. 1), 249 (ftn. 4), 251 (ftn. 2), 256, 256 (ftn. 2), 257, 262 (ftn. 5), 270, 276 (ftn. 1), 289 (ftn. 1), 299[2], 300[2], 300 (ftn. 1), 301[3], 306 (ftn. 7), 307 (ftn. 3, 4), 308 (ftn. 1), 309 (ftn. 1, 2), 316 (ftn. 3), 318 (ftn. 2, 3), 319 (ftn. 1, 2, 3), 320, 321[4], 322[2], 323[2], 324[3], 328[6], 328 (ftn. 4), 329[5], 330[4], 331[2], 332, 336[3], 337[5], 337 (ftn. 3), 338, 340[2],

Page

341[2], 342, 341 (ftn. 6), 343[2], 343 (ftn. 2), 344[2],345[5], 346, 352, 530, 538[2]

Buddha by Rockhill 246 (ftn. 2), 322 (ftn. 7)

Buddha Deva 495 (ftn. 3), 496 (ftn. 1)

Buddhism by Schlagintweit 249 (ftn. 1, 5)

,, by Wassilief 248 (ftn. 6)

Buddhist India by Rhys Davids .. 242 (ftn. 4), 248 (ftn. 3)

Buddhist Records by Beal 124 (ftn. 7), 173 (ftn. 5), 241 (ftn. 1), 243 (ftn. 3), 247 (ftn. 1), 248, (ftn. 2, 7, 8), 249 (ftn. 4), 251 (ftn. 1), (261 (ftn. 2), 265 (ftn. 2, 7), 266 (ftn. 1), 274 (ftn. 3), 302 (ftn. 5), 303 (ftn. 1), 496 (ftn. 1), 514 (ftn. 6)

Buddhi-vāda 482

Caitanya Candrāmṛta.. .. 484

Caitanya Caritāmṛta .. 462 (ftn. 1)

Candrāloka 455

Cāndra Vyākaraṇa .. 334 (ftn. 3), 335

Caṅ-shwo (or here) tso-li-ein 302 (ftn. 1)[2]

Caraka Saṁhitā 9 (ftn. 4), 20, 26 (ftn. 5), 31 (ftn. 3)[2], 42 (ftn. 2), 51[4], 221, 499 (ftn. 1), 500[4], 501[2], 512

Catalogue by Eggeling 392 (ftn. 3)

Catalogue of the Chinese Tripiṭaka 240 (ftn 2), 242 (ftn. 2), 243 (ftn. 1, 4, 5), 244 (ftn. 2), 247 (ftn. 3, 4), 248 (ftn. 1, 2), 249 (ftn. 4), 252 (ftn. 5), 253 (ftn. 2), 256 (ftn. 2), 259 (ftn. 1), 261 (ftn. 1, 5), 262 (ftn. 2), 265 (ftn. 6, 8, 9), 266 (ftn. 2) 267 (ftn. 2, 4), 268 (ftn. 1), 272 (ftn. 3), 289 (ftn. 1), 300 (ftn. 2, 3), 301 (ftn. 3)[2], 302 (ftn. 3, 4, 5), 348 (ftn. 1)

Caturviṁśati-jina-stuti .. 183

Caturviṁśati-prabandha 165, 208 (ftn. 4), 213

Chāndogyopaniṣad 3 (ftn. 2), 45 (ftn. 4)

Page

Chandonuśāsana-vṛtti .. 205

Chandoratnākara .. 343 (ftn. 1)

Chinese Tripiṭaka .. 26, 243

Choṣ-byuṅ .. 305 (ftn. 1), 517

Choṣ-daṅ-choṣ-can-gtan-la-ḍwal-pa 337

Cintāmaṇi 404

Citrādavaita siddhi 394

Cittarūpa 438

Commentary on the Ṛgveda by Sāyana 45 (ftn. 3)

Comparative studies in Vaiṣṇavism and Christianity by B.N. Seal 44 (ftn. 3)

Cūrṇika of Nandī-sūtra 161 (ftn. 2)

Daṁśana-sāra 195

Dānakāṇḍa 392

Dānakhaṇḍa 477

Darpaṇa 458

Darśana-siddhi (or Samyaktva-prakaraṇa) 206

Daśabhūmīśvara .. 242 (ftn. 3)

Daśapadārtha 503

Daśa-śruta-skandha-sūtra .. 165

Daśa-vaikālika-niryukti 164, 165[4]

Daśa-vaikālika-niryukti-ṭīkā 208 (ftn. 4)

Daśa-vaikāilika-sūtra 164

Dāyabhāga-ṭīkā 484

De Interpretatione 512

De-kho-na-ñid- bsdus - pahi - dkaḥ - ḥgrel 328

De-kho-no- ñid- bsdus- pahi- Tshig-lehwi-byaṣ-pa 324

Devabhadra and his Nyāyāvatāra ṭippana .. 211 (ftn. 1)

Devapratiṣṭhā-tattva 153

Devīmāhātmya 522

Devīpurāṇa .. 145 (ftn. 4)

Dhamma saṅgaṇī .. 227 (ftn. 2)

Dharmādharma-viniścaya .. 337

Dharma-dhātu-stava .. 253 (ftn.)

Dharma Saṁgraha .. 249 (ftn. 2)

Dharma-viniścaya .. 342 (ftn. 6)

Dharmottara-ṭippanaka 105[3], 222, 329 (ftn. 3)

Page

Dialogue of the Buddha by Rhys Davids .. 9 (ftn. 5)
Dictionary of Religion 254 (ftn. 2)
Dīdhiti .. 478[2], 481
Dīdhīti-rahasya 467
Dīdhīti-ṭīkā .. 469, 481
Die Handschriften-Verzeichnisse by Weber .. 197 (ftn. 3, 4)
Digambara Paṭṭāvalī .. 168 (ftn. 3)
Dīgha Nikāya 227 (ftn. 2), 500 (ftn. 1)
Dinakarya-prakāśa-tippaṇī .. 483
Dīpikā 388
Diṭṭhivās .. 161 (ftn. 3)
Dmigs-pa-btrag-pa 301
Dmigs-pa-brtag-pahi-hgrel-bśad .. 321
Dpag-bsam-ljon-bzan 274 (ftn. 1), 320 (ftn. 4), 322 (ftn. 3), 323 (ftn. 2), 327 (ftn. 1), 328 (ftn. 3), 329 (ftn. 1), 333 (ftn. 5), 335 (ftn. 1), 336 (ftn. 2), 338 (ftn. 3), 340 (ftn. 2, 4), 341 (ftn. 2), 342 (ftn. 1, 3, 5, 6), 344 (ftn. 2), 348 (ftn. 1), 353 (ftn. 1)
Dravya-bhāṣya-ṭīkā (or Padārtha-tattvanirṇaya) 470
Dravya-kiraṇāvalī-prakāśa .. 455
Dravya-padārtha 455
Dravya-parīkṣā .. 407 (ftn.)
Dravya-sāra-saṃgraha .. 481
Dṛṣtivāda .. 161, 161 (ftn. 3)
Durgotsava-tattva .. 476 (ftn. 1)
Dus-brum brtag-pa 301
Dvaita-nirṇaya .. 460, 461
Dvāśraya mahākāvya.. .. 205
Dvātriṁśat-dvātriṁśikā .. 174
Dvātriṁśikā 212
Dvyardha-śatikā .. 118 (ftn. 3)
Dwaṅ-phyug-hjig-pahi-tshig - bhur - byas-pa 329

Early History of India by Smith 221 (ftn. 1), 267 (ftn. 3), 301 (ftn. 3), 348 (ftn. 1), 496 (ftn. 1)
Early History of the Dekkan by R. G. Bhandarkar 186 (ftn. 4), 251 (ftn.. 2)

Page

Edicts of Aśoka .. 49 (ftn. 2)
Eka-ṣaṣṭhyalaṅkāra-prakāśa .. 47)
Encyclopædia Britannica 511 (ftn. 5), 512 (ftn. 1, 3, 4)
Encyclopædia of Religion and Ethics 227 (ftn. 1)
Epigraphia Indica .. 221 (ftn. 1)
Explanation of the Can-lun 302 (ftn. 1)

Fa-hian .. 514 (ftn. 4)
Fa-hian and Sungyun by Beal 248 (ftn. 3)
Fāṅ-pien-sin-lun 259
Filosofia Indiana 26 (ftn. 4), 119 (ftn.)

Gacchotpatti prakaraṇa 208 (ftn. 4)
Gadādhari-pañcavāda.. .. 487
Gaṇapāṭha .. 41 (ftn. 5)
Gaṇḍa-vyūha .. 242 (ftn. 3)
Gandhahasti-mahābhāṣya .. 182
Gāthāsāhasrī .. 208 (ftn. 1, 4)
Gaurī digambara-prahasana .. 450
Gautama-dharma-sūtra 7 (ftn. 3), 8 (ftn. 4), 48 (ftn. 4)
Gautama-sūtra-vṛtti 392
Geschichte des Buddhismus by Schiefner 246 (ftn. 2), 248 (ftn. 5, 7, 8), 249 (ftn. 4), 251 (ftn. 4, 5), 252 (ftn. 2, 4), 261 (ftn. 3), 265 (ftn. 4), 274 (ftn. 1), 274 (ftn. 2), 303 (ftn. 3), 307 (ftn. 1), 319 (ftn. 4), 320 (ftn. 1, 2, 4), 322 (ftn. 3), 328 (ftn. 3), 329 (ftn. 1), 333 (ftn. 5), 336 (ftn. 2), 337 (ftn. 1), 338 (ftn. 2, 3), 339 (ftn. 7), 340 (ftn. 2, 9), 341 (ftn. 2), 342 (ftn. 5, 6), 343 (ftn. 4), 344 (ftn. 2, 3), 348 (ftn. 1), 514 (ftn. 3), 517 (ftn. 2), 519 (ftn. 2), 520 (ftn. 2)

Gītā 522
Gīta Govinda .. 522, 524
Gbs-bam-bklag-pahi-thabs .. 241
Gopāla-līlāmṛta 484
Grimm's Phonetic Law of the Indo-European Languages 1 (ftn. 1)

Page

Gslase-la-bstag-pahi-'tshig-bhur-byas-pa 329
Gshan-sel-wa 330
Gtan-Tshigs-kyi-de-kho-na-ñid-bstan-pa 337
Gtan-tshigs-kyi-hkhor-lo-gtan-la-dwab-pa 299
Gtan-tshigs-kyi-thigs-pa .. 318
Gtan tshigs-kyi-thigs-pa-ugya cber-hgrel wa 321
Gtan-tshigs-thigs-pahi-hgrel-wa .. 332
Guide to Taxila by Marshall 494 (ftn. 2)
Guṇa-dīdhiti-vivṛti 478
Guṇa rahasya 469
Guṇa Śiromaṇi prakāśa 467
Guṇa-vivṛti-viveka 468
Gurugītā 153
Gurvāvalī Sūtra .. 164 (ftn. 4)
Gyen-min-gshihi-ein lihi-lun .. 300

Harṣā-carita .. 123 (ftn. 4)
Hastābala 250
Hayaśīrṣa-Pañcarātra .. 153 (ftn. 3)
Hbrel-pa-brtag-pahi-rgya-cher-leś-ad-pa 321
Hbrel-pa-brtag-pahi-rges-su-beran-wa 345
Hbrel-pa-grub-pa 345
Hbrel-wa-brtag-pa 319
Hbrel-wa-brtag-pahi-hgrel-wa .. 319
Hetu-cakra .. 300 (ftn. 1)
Hetu-cakra-hamaru .. 299 (ftn. 1)
Hetu-dvāra-śāstra .. 299 (ftn. 1)
Hetu-vidyā nyāya-praveśa-śastra .. 302
Hetu vindu .. 321, 332
Hetu vindu-ṭikā 321
Hetu vindu-vivaraṇa .. 318, 332
Hetu-tattva-upadeśa 337
Hhien-yān-Stan-ciāo-ben .. 266
Hindu Logic as preserved in China and Japan 262 (ftn. 3), 265 (ftn. 1), 267 (ftn. 5), 289 (ftn. 1), 302 (ftn. 1), 505 (ftn. 2)
Historical Record of the Jainas 199 (ftn. 1), 200 (ftn. 2)

Page

History of Ancient Sanskrit Literature by Max Müller 22 (ftn. 2), 25 (ftn. 2)
History of Indian Literature by Weber 10 (ftn. 5), 48 (ftn. 4), 498 (ftn. 5)
History of Logic by Dr. Robert Adamson .. .. 52 (ftn. 1)
History of Mithilā during the pre-Moghal period .. 521 (ftn. 1)
History of Navya-Nyāya in Bengal and Mithilā by M. Chakravarty 454 (ftn. 1), 455 (ftn. 1)
History of Navya Nyāya and Smṛti .. .. 521 (ftn. 1)
History of Sanskrit Literature by Macdonell 1 (ftn. 1), 10 (ftn. 2), 380 (ftn. 4)
History of the Medieval School of Indian Logic 26 (ftn. 3), 357 (ftn. 3)
Hjig-rten-pha-rot-grub-pa .. 330
Hwenthsang's Life by Beal 251 (ftn. 4)

Illustration of the Literature and religion of the Buddhists 242 (ftn. 3)
Imperial Gazeteer of India 523 (ftn. 1)
Indian Antiquary 116 (ftn. 4), 198 (ftn. 3), 199 (ftn. 1), 200 (ftn. 1, 2), 206 (ftn. 1), 209 (ftn. 3) 214 (ftn. 3), 267 (ftn. 3)[2], 322 (ftn. 6), 335 (ftn. 2), 406 (ftn. 6), 505 (ftn. 3)
Indian Logic—Medieval school by Dr. Vidyābhūṣaṇa .. 406 (ftn. 5)
Indian Paṇḍits in the Land of Snow 517 (ftn. 3), 519 (ftn. 2)
Indian Thought .. 403 (ftn. 1)
Indo-Aryans 518 (ftn. 2), 523 (ftn. 3)
Inscription of Rudradamana 49 (ftn. 2)
Introduction à l'Étude des Traites Medicaun Sanskritas 252 (ftn. 6)
Introduction to the Kūṭadabha-Sutta by Rhys Davids 9 (ftn. 5)
Introduction to the Pañca-siddhāntikā .. .. 174 (ftn. 1)

Page

Introduction to Ṣaḍdarśana Samuccaya .. .. 210 (ftn 1)
Introduction to the Sragdharā-stotra .. .. 252 (ftn. 6)
Iśvarabhaṅga kārikā.. 143, 150, 329
I-tsing 241 (ftn. 2), 247 (ftn. 1, 2), 275 (ftn. 2), 289 (ftn. 1), 299 (ftn. 1), 300 (ftn. 3), 301 (ftn. 2), 302 (ftn. 5), 303 (ftn. 2) 306 (ftn. 2, 5), 320 (ftn. 5), 335 (ftn. 3), 515 (ftn. 3)
Jaiminīya Nyāya-mālā vistara .. 397
Jaina Inscription .. 221 (ftn. 1)
Jaina Logic by Dr. Vidyābhūṣaṇa 331 (ftn. 5)
Jaina Sthānāṅga Sūtra.. .. 51
Jainistic Notices 210 (ftn. 4), 211 (ftn. 1)
Jalada.. 457
Jambudvīpa-Samāsa .. 169 (ftn.)
Jātakas 495 (ftn. 3), 496 (ftn. 1)
Journal Asiatique 26 (ftn. 3), 499 (ftn. 1)
Journal of the American Oriental Society 50 (ftn. 2), 116 (ftn. 3), 120 (ftn. 3), 261 (ftn. 4)
Journal of the Asiatic Society of Bengal 232 (ftn. 1), 241 (ftn. 1), 249 (ftn. 6), 253 (ftn.), 262 (ftn. 1), 272 (ftn. 1), 323 (ftn. 3), 324 (ftn. 2), 334 (ftn. 3), 342 (ftn. 2), 343 (ftn. 1), 348 (ftn. 1), 407 (ftn. 1), 454 (ftn. 1), 480 (ftn. 1), 481 (ftn. 2)
J.B.B.R.A.S. 183 (ftn. 3), 187 (ftn. 5), 88 (ftn. 1², 2, 3, 7), 199 (ftn. ?), 241 (ftn. 1), 273 (ftn. 7), 306 (ftn. 3), 316 (ftn. 1, 3)
Journal of the Buddhist Text Society of Calcutta 227 (ftn. 2), 348 (ftn. 1), 242 (ftn. 1), 246 (ftn. 2), 247 (ftn. 5), 248 (ftn. 3, 5), 249 (ftn. 1, 6), 253 (ftn. 1, 2?), 324 (ftn. 3), 327 (ftn. 1), 337 (ftn. 2), 519 (ftn. 2)
Journal of the Pali Text Society 226 (ftn. 4) 251 (ftn. 2)

Page

Journal of the Royal Asiatic Society 7 (ftn. 9), 26 (ftn. 1), 267 (ftn. 3), 3?4 (ftn. 1), 495 (ftn. 1), 510 (ftn. 1), 126 (ftn. 2), 225 (ftn. 2), 220 (ftn. 2), 241 (ftn. 1, 2), 242 (ftn. 2 (243 (ftn. 3), 246 (ftn. 2), 267 (ftn.), 267 (ftn. 2), 515 (ftn. 4)
J A.S.G.B. I .. 497 (ftn. 1)
J.R.S.B. 18 (ftn. 3), 19 (ftn. 4)
Jyotiṣa-sāra-saṃgraha 527
Jyotiṣ-tattva 527

Kādambarī-kathā-sāra 147 (ftn. 2)
Kalpa Sūtra 159 (ftn. 1), 164 (ftn. 1), 165, 172(ftn. 1)
Kalpataru 477
Kalyāṇakāṇḍa .. 342 ftn. 6)
Kamala-śīla-tarka .. 324 (ftn. 3)
Kāmandakīya Nītisāra 23 (ftn. 6)
Kāma Śāstra 117
Kāminī-kāma-kautuka .. 484
Kaṇādarahasya-muktā-hāra .. 381
Kaṇāda Sūtra 459
Kaṅgyur 533
Kaṅkhā-vitaraṇī .. 232 (ftn. 1)
Kaṇṭakoddhāra 461
Kārakādyartha-nirṇayaṭīkā .. 483
Kāraka-vāda 482
Kāraka-vivecana 478
Kāraka-vyūha 484
Kārikās 478
Kārya-kāraṇa-bhāva-siddhi .. 341
Kāśika-vṛtti 335
Kathākoṣa .. 188 (ftn. 4)
Kathānirṇaya 397
Kathāvatthu 235 (ftn. 1), 239 (ftn. 1)
Kathāvatthuppakaraṇa 234 (ftn. 2)
Kauśika Sūtra of the Atharva veda .. 10 (ftn. 5)
Kaṭhopaniṣad 3 (ftn. 4), 23, 23 (ftn. 4)
Kauṭilya .. 23 (ftn. 12)
Kāvyānuśāsana vṛtti 205
Kāvya-prakāśa-rahasya .. 469
Kāvya-prakāśa-saṅketa 207 (ftn 1)
Kāvya-prakāśa-tilaka 478

Page

Kāvyavilāsa 483
Khaṇḍanakhaṇḍādhāra .. 522
Khaṇḍanakhaṇḍakhādya 406 (ftn. 6), 459
Khaṇḍanakhaṇḍakhādya-dīdhiti .. 465
Khaṇḍana khaṇḍa-prakāśa .. 455
Khaṇḍana khaṇḍoddhara .. 460
Kharatara-gaccha-paṭṭāvalī 164 (ftn. 1), 208 (ftn. 4)
Khorda Avestā 20
Khuddaka Nikāya 229
Kiraṇāvalī .. 141, 478
Kiraṇāvalī-bhāskara 381
Kiraṇāvalī-prakāśa 455
Kiraṇāvalī-prakāśa-didhiti .. 465
Kiraṇāvalī-prakāśa-parīkṣā .. 457
Kiraṇāvalī-prakāśa-rahasya .. 467
Kirātārjunīya 380
Kloṅ-rdol-gsuṅ-hbum 517 (ftn. 3), 520 (ftn. 1)
Koṣakāraka Śāstra 248
Kriyāratna-samuccaya .. 214
Kṣaṇabhaṅga-siddhi 133 (ftn. 4), 134, 143, 150, 330, 331, 339 (ftn. 3, 6)
Kṣaṇabhaṅga-siddhi-vyākhyā .. 331
Kusumāñjalī 17, 141 143, 155 (ftn. 3), 373 (ftn. 1), 462
Kusumāñjalī-kārikā-vyākhyā .. 465
Kusumāñjalī-prakāśa 457
Kusumāñjalī-prakāśa-parīkṣā .. 457

Laghīyastraya .. 185, 194
Laghu-dīpikā .. 374, 380
Laghuvṛtti .. 214 (ftn. 1)
(The) Logic of the Arabians 510 (ftn 5)
Lakṣāṇāratī 386
Lakṣaṇamālā .. 378 (ftn. 1)
Lakṣmīdhara 477
Lalitavistara 242 (ftn. 3), 243 (ftn. 1)
Lamaism by Waddell 271 (ftn. 1), 323 (ftn. 3), 327 (ftn. 1), 520
Laṅkāvatāra Sūtra 116[2], 118 (ftn. 3), 121, 121 (ftn. 2), 242 (ftn. 3), 243 (ftn. 3), 249, 249 (ftn. 3)[2]
Le Buddhisme d'aprés les Sources Bramaniques 306 (ftn. 7), 30 (ftn. 3)

Page

Lecture on the Story of Hemacandra by Peterson (in the Bombay Gazette, Aug. 29, 1895) 205 (ftn. 1)
Līlāvatī-prakāśa 455
Līlāvatī-viveka 455
Lhan-cig-dmigs-pa-ṅes-pa . 336
Life of Buddha by Rockhill 11 (ftn. 3)
List of Antiquities in Madras by Sewell .. 251 (ftn. 3), 273 (ftn. 1)
Logic of nine reasons and fourteen fallacies .. 300 (ftn. 1)
Loka-prakāśa .. 216 (ftn. 1)

Mādhava-campu 483
Madhyama-hṛdayakārikā .. 250
Mādhyamika kārikā 250
Mādhyamika philosophy .. 334
Madhyama-pratītya-samutpāda .. 250
Mādhyamika Sūtra 116[2], 118 (ftn. 3)
Mādhyamikāvatāra tīkā .. 250
Mādhyamika vṛtti 126 (ftn. 2), 250
Madhyāntavibhāga Śāstra 262 (ftn. 4)
Mahābhārata 7 (ftn. 5, 9), 8 (ftn.), 12 (ftn. 1), 13 (ftn. 1), 16 (ftn. 2), 18 (ftn. 1), 20, 23 (ftn. 4, 7, 8, 10, 11, 12, 13), 42 (ftn. 2), 51, 114 (ftn. 1), 244 (ftn. 1), 407, 521
Mahābhāṣya of Patañjali 129 (ftn. 3)
Mahāpadāna Suttanta 500 (ftn. 1)
Mahāsamaya Sūtra 249
Mahāvagga 495
Mahāvaṁsa 225 (ftn. 2), 226 (ftn. 3, 4), 246 (ftn. 2), 248 (ftn. 6)
Mahāvastu .. 26 (ftn. 1)
Mahāvyutpatti 7 (ftn. 7), 11 (ftn. 1), 25 (ftn. 1), 40 (ftn. 3), 43 (ftn. 2), 47 (ftn. 1), 54 (ftn. 2), 55 (ftn. 1)
Mahāyānābhidharma - saṁyukta-saṅgīti śāstra 265
Mahāyāna-samparigraha-śāstra .. 265
Majjhima Nikāya 229 (ftn. 1), 239 (ftn. 1)
Makaranda 469
Mālatīmādhava .. 251 (ftn. 4), 522

Page

Mallinātha's commentary on the Meghadūta .. 273 (ftn. 5)
Maṇimekalai .. 387 (ftn. 2)
Maṇi-vyākhyā .. 466 (ftn. 2)
Manual of Buddhism by Hardy 225 (ftn. 1)
Manusaṁhitā 7 (ftn. 2, 8), 8 (ftn. 1), 23 (ftn. 4, 5, 9, 11, 12), 56
Maṇyāloka-ṭippaṇī .. 465, 464
Matsyapurāṇa .. 20, 42 (ftn. 1)
Medieval School of Indian Logic 221 (ftn. 1), 504 (ftn. 1), 505 (ftn. 4), 506 (ftn. 1), 508 (ftn. 1), 514 (ftn. 1), 517 (ftn. 1), 519 (ftn. 1)
Meghadūta .. 273 (ftn. 2), 522
Mem. de l'Ann. des Inscriptions et belles letters .. 489 (ftn. 3)
Milinda pañha 240
Mīmāṁsā sarvasva 524
Mīmāṁsāvārtika .. 132 (ftn. 1)
Mookerjee's Magazine .. 464 (ftn. 1)
Muir's Sanskrit Texts .. 2 (ftn. 2, 3)
Muktāvalī .. 403 (ftn. 1)
Muktāvalī-ṭikā 482
Muktivāda 482
Mūlamadhyama-vṛtti 250
Mūlamadhyamaka vṛtti-akutobhaya 250
Muṇḍakopaniṣad .. 4 (ftn. 2)

Nadiā Kāhinī .. 527 (ftn. 1)
Nāgasena Bhikṣu Sūtra .. 240
Naiṣadha-carita .. 153, 497 (ftn. 2)
Naiyatakālika 477
Nāmamālā 205
Nandi Sūtra .. 161 (ftn. 1)
Nañ-gi-khyab-pa 343
Nañvāda .. 465, 482
Nañ-vāda-ṭikā 479
Navadvīpa-mahimā .. 527 (ftn. 1)
Navadvīpa-pañjikā 527
Navīna-nirmāṇa 481
Nighaṇṭu śeṣa 205
Nīlakaṇṭha ṭīkā 391
Nirukti 391²

Page

Nirupama Stava .. 253 (ftn.)
Niṣkaṇṭakā 380
Nīti-cintāmaṇi 522
Notices of Sanskrit MSS. by H. Sāstrī 459 (ftn. 1), 460 (ftn. 1), 461 (ftn. 1, 2), 466 (ftn. 2)
Notices of Sanskrit MSS. by R. Mitra 460 (ftn. 1), 461 (ftn. 1), 462 (ftn. 2), 478 (ftn.), 466 (ftn. 2)²
Notices of Sanskrit MSS. in Bengal (467 (ftn. 2)
Nyāsa 323
Nyāya .. .. 302 (ftn. 1)
Nyāya-bhāṣya 52 (ftn. 1), 57, 97 (ftn. 1), 115, 115 (ftn. 3), 116 (ftn 2), 117 (ftn. 4), 119 (ftn. 1), 121², 155, 155 (ftn. 2), 302, 498 (ftn. 3), 504
Nyāya-bhūṣaṇa .. 358, 371
Nyāya-bindu-piṇḍārtha .. 340
Nyāya-bindu-pūrvapakṣa-saṁkṣipta 327
Nyāya-bindu-ṭīkā 194, 195, 222, 321, 329 (ftn. 3, 5), 330
Nyāya-bodhinī .. 390, 391, 460
Nyāya-cakra 195
Nyāya-candrikā 391
Nyāyādarśa or Nyāya-sārāvalī .. 470
Nyāya-dīpikā .. 215, 460, 467
Nyāya-dvāra-tarka-śāstra 289 (ftn. 1)
Nyāyālokasiddhi or Nyāyasiddhyāloka 336
Nyāya-kalikā 371
Nyāya-kandali .. 329 (ftn 1)
Nyāya kaṇikā .. 134, 140
Nyāya karṇikā .. 216, 217 (ftn. 1)
Nyāya khaṇḍa-khādya 218, 219 (ftn. 4), 468 (ftn. 2)
Nyāya-koṣa 48 (ftn. 5), 498 (ftn. 6)
Nyāya-kumuda-candrodaya or Candrodaya 194
Nyāyakusumāñjali 380, 406 (ftn. 2), 457*b*
Nyāyakusumāñjali - kārikā - vyākhyā 469, 478, 481

Page

Nyāyakusumāñjali-prakāśa .. 455
Nyāya kusumāñjalī-prakāśa-makaranda 457
Nyāya-kusumāñjali-tarka .. 371
Nyāya-kusumāñjali-ṭikā 373 (ftn. 1)
Nyāya-kusumāñjali-viveka .. 468
Nyāyalaṅkāra 151
Nyāya-līlāvatī .. 386, 387f., 459
Nyāya-līlāvati-dīdhiti 388
Nyāya-līlāvati-dīdhiti-vyākhyā .. 470
Nyāya-līlāvati kaṇṭhābharaṇa 388, 459
Nyāya-līlāvati-prakāśa 386, 388 455
Nyāya-līlāvati-prakāśa-didhiti-rahasya 467
Nyāya-līlāvati-prakāśa-dīdhiti-viveka 468
Nyāya-līlāvati-prakāśa-rahasya .. 467
Nyāya-līlāvati-prakāśa-viveka .. 388
Nyāya līlāvatī prakāśa-vyākhyā .. 457
Nyāyamañjarī 132 (ftn. 1), 147 (ftn. 3, 4, 7), 148 (ftn. 1), 149, 150, 153 (ftn. 4)
Nyāyāmirta-taraṅginī 218
Nyāya-nibandha-prakāśa 151, 454
Nyāyānusāra Śāstra 24
Nyāyapariśiṣṭa .. 141, 388, 455
Nyāyapariśiṣṭa prakāśa 388, 455
Nyāyapradīpa .. 218, 385
Nyāyapraveśa 210, 221, 289 (ftn. 1[2])[2], 295 (ftn. 1), 300 (ftn. 1[2], 2), 302, 315 (ftn. 3), 316 (ftn. 3)[2]
Nyāyapraveśaka Sūtra .. 208
Nyāyapraveśa-tarka-śāstra 289 (ftn. 1), 302, 302 (ftn. 4)
Nyāyapraveśa-tippana .. 210
Nyāyapraveśa-vṛtti 210
Nyāyarahasya .. 218, 469[2]
Nyāyarahasya-dīpikā .. 151 (ftn. 2, 3)
Nyāya-ratnāvalī 484
Nyāyārtha-laghubodhinī .. 390
Nyāya-saṁkṣepa 480
Nyāya-saṁgraha 384
Nyāyasāra 221 (ftn. 1), 356, 357[3], 358, 366 (ftn. 1), 367 (ftn. 1), 369 (ftn. 1), 371ff., 372 (ftn. 2)

Page

Nyāyasārapada-pañjikā .. 371
Nyāyasāra-ṭikā 371
Nyāyasāra vicāra 372
Nyāya-sarvasva 524
Nyāya Śāstra .. 107 (ftn. 1)
Nyāya-siddhānta dīpa .. 396f.
Nyāya-siddhānta dīpa ṭikā .. 397
Nyāya-siddānta mālā 478
Nyāya-siddhānta-mañjarī 404, 466, 483
Nyāya-siddhānta-mañjarī-bhūṣā .. 482
Nyāya Sūtra 16 (ftn. 1), 20, 84 (ftn. 1), 97, 101 (ftn. 1), 105, 106 (ftn. 1), 109, 109 (ftn. 1), 112 (ftn. 1), 114 (ftn. 1), 115[3], 116, 117 (ftn. 5), 136 (ftn. 1), 154 (ftn. 1), 155, 221, 280 (ftn. 1)[5], 283 (ftn. 1, 2), 288 (ftn. 3), 301, 302, 302 (ftn. 1), 315 (ftn. 1), 348, 356, 359[2], 370, 460[2], 478, 497[2], 499, 502[2], 503[2], 504
Nyāya-sūtradhāra 522
Nyāya Sūtra in the Indian thought 40 (ftn. 4)
Nyāya-sūtra-vṛtti 17, 41 (ftn. 2), 52 (ftn. 1), 479
Nyāya-sūtroddhāra 480
Nyāyatantra-bodhinī or Nyāya-bodhinī 480
Nyāya-tātparya-dīpikā 221 (ftn. 1) 357 (ftn. 1), 371, 372 (ftn. 2)
Nyāyavārtika 57, 97 (ftn. 1), 119 (ftn. 1), 124, 125, 130, 131[2], 132, 132 (ftn. 1), 133, 138, 155, 273 (ftn. 3), 277 (ftn. 1), 287 (ftn. 2), 288 (ftn. 1), 348, 498 (ftn. 3), 504 (ftn. 2), 505
Nyāyavārtika-tātparya-ṭikā 97 (ftn. 1), 129 (ftn. 3), 131, 134 (ftn. 6), 135, 135 (ftn. 2, 3), 138, 140[2], 155, 273 (ftn. 4), 282 (ftn.), 283 (ftn. 1), 284 (ftn.), 348, 498 (ftn. 3), 505
Nyāya-vārtika-tātparya-pariśuddhi 454
Nyāyāvatāra 122 (ftn. 1), 166, 173, 173 (ftn. 1)[2], 174, 200, 206 (ftn. 4),

Page

208 (ftn. 4), 221, 331 (ftn. 8), 565 (ftn. 4), 507

Nyāyâvatāra-tippana 211

Nyāyāvatāra-vivṛti 179, 180, 211, 206 (ftn. 4)², 208 (ftn. 4²), 331

Nyāya-vindu 309 (ftn. 2)², 316 (ftn. 2), 317 (ftn. 1), 327, 329, 340, 508

Nyāya-viniścaya .. 185, 198, 200

Nyāya-viniścaya-vṛtti 198

Nyāya-vṛtti 151²

On Yuan Chwang 242 (ftn. 1), 248 (ftn 4), 249 (ftn. 1, 9), 251 (ftn. 1), 261 (ftn. 1), 262 (ftn. 4), 265 (ftn. 3), 266 (ftn. 1), 272 (ftn. 2), 515 (ftn. 1, 4)

Organon 502², 503², 506²

Padakṛtya 391

Padārtha-candra 460

Padārtha-khaṇḍana 480

Padārtha-khaṇḍana-vyakhyā 477, 480, 481

Padhārtha-maṇi mālā .. 478

Padārtha-tattva 526

Padārtha-tattvāloka 480

Padārtha-tattva-nirūpaṇa or Padārtha-khaṇḍa 465

Padārtha-tattva-vivecana-prakāśa 469

Padārtha-viveka-prakāśa .. 469

Padārtha-viveka-ṭīkā 485

Padma Caritra 195

Padmapurāṇa 10, 20, 42 (ftn. 5), 497, 497 (ftn. 2), 498 (ftn. 4)

Pag-sam-jon-zang 516 (ftn. 1), 517², 517 (ftn. 2), 519 (ftn. 2)

Pāli-kathāvatthuppakaraṇa .. 51

Pāli Mahāvagga .. 11 (ftn. 3)

Pañcatantra .. 179 (ftn. 2)

Paṇḍitavijaya 459

Pāṇini 23 (ftn. 8), 303, 323

Pāṇini by Goldstucker 41 (ftn. 4)

Paraloka siddhi 330

Parāśara-smṛti-vyākhyā .. 397

Page

Parāśara Upapurāṇa 356

Paribhāṣā-darpaṇa 384

Parīkṣā-mukha-pañjikā .. 198

Parīkṣā-mukha-śāstra 188 (ftn. 5, 7)

Parīkṣa-mukha-sūtra 185, 188, 193, 194, 198, 200

Pariśiṣṭa Parvan .. 159 (ftn. 1)

Parivāra .. 229 (ftn. 3)

Pārtha Sārathi's Gloss on Kumārila Bhaṭṭa's Vārtika on the Sūtra of Jaimini .. 273 (ftn. 6)

Pārtha-vijaya 134

Paśupati-paddhati 524

Paṭicca-samuppāda 227

Pātimokkha of the Vinaya-Piṭakam 229 (ftn. 3), 232 (ftn. 1), 271

Paṭṭāvalī of the Kharataragaccha 160 (ftn. 5), 172 (ftn. 1), 209 (ftn. 3), 214 (ftn. 3)

Paṭṭāvalī of the Sarasvatī gaccha 169 (ftn.)

Pavanadūta 524

Persia by Dr. K. Geldner 20 (ftn. 4)

Phyi-rol don-grub-pa ces-bya-wahi-tshig-bhur 328

Piṅgala-prakāśa 480

Piṭakas 272, 304

Pitṛbhakti-taraṅgiṇī 459

Pitṛmedha Sūtra .. 48 (ftn. 4), 498

Points of controversy by Shwe Zan-Aung 235 (ftn. 1), 239 (ftn. 1)

Posterior Analytics .. 508, 509², 517

Prabandhacintamaṇi 152 (ftn. 3), 173 (ftn. 4), 195 (ftn. 1)

Prabhākara-caritra 195

Prabhāvaka-caritra 173 (ftn. 3), 208 (ftn. 4)

Prācīna-lekha-mālā .. 406 (ftn. 6)

Pradeśa-vyākhyā-ṭippanaka .. 210

Prajñāpanā Sūtra .. 161 161 (ftn. 4)

Prajñāpāramitā .. 250, 516

Prakaraṇārya-vācā Śāstra 265, 506

Prakāśa .. 153, 469

Pramāṇa-cintāmaṇi 405

Pramāṇa-mīmāṃsā .. 205 (ftn. 2)

Page

Pramāṇa-naya-tattva-lokālaṅkāra 170 (ftn.), 198, 200, 211, 213

Pramāṇa-nyāya-praveśa (or Nyāya-praveśa-nāma, Pramāṇa-prakaraṇa) 300 (ftn. 1), 302

Pramāṇa-parīkṣā .. 187, 330

Pramāṇa-samuccaya 116 (ftn. 2), 274 (ftn. 2), 275[3], 284 (ftn. 1), 299, 307 (ftn. 2), 508 (ftn. 2)

Pramāṇa-samuccaya vṛtti 299, 300

Pramāṇa-śāstra-nyāya-praveśa (or Pramāṇa-śāstra-nyāya-praveśa-nāma) .. 300 (ftn. 1)

Pramāṇa-vārtika 198, 222, 319, 323, 344[2]

Pramāṇa-vārtikā-kārikā 307, 308

Pramāṇa-vārtikālaṅkāra 336, 344

Pramāṇa-vārtikālaṅkāra-ṭīkā 338, 344

Pramāṇa-vārtika-pañjikā .. 319

Pramāṇa-vārtika-pañjikā-ṭīkā .. 320

Pramāṇa-vārtika-ṭīkā 198, 222, 344

Pramāṇa-vārtika-vṛtti .. 323

Pramāṇa-vidhvaṁsana .. 128

Pramāṇa-viheṭana 128 (ftn. 4), 257, 258

Pramāṇa-viheṭana-ṭipanaka-vṛtti (or Pramāṇa-vidhvaṁsana-saṁbhāṣita-vṛtti) 257, 257 (ftn. 1)

Pramāṇa-viniścaya .. 308 (ftn. 3), 331

Pramāṇa-viniscaya-ṭīkā 330, 342 (ftn. 2)

Prāmāṇya-vāda-dīdhiti-tīkā .. 482

Prameya-kamala-mārtaṇḍa 188, 193

Prameya-nibandha-prakāśa .. 455

Prameya-ratna-koṣa .. 206, 406 (ftn. 2)

Prameya-ratna-mālā 198

Prameya-tattva-bodha .. 455

Praśamarati .. 169 (ftn.)

Prasanna Rāghava 455

Praśnopaniṣad .. 22 (ftn. 3)

Pratibandha-siddhi 345

Pratyakṣāloka .. 456 (ftn. 2)

Pratyakṣāloka-sāramañjarī .. 479

Pratyeka buddha caritra .. 212

Prāyaścitta 185

Prior Analytics 504, 505[2], 506, 509, 510, 512

Pūjā-prakaraṇa .. 160 (ftn.)

Pustaka-pāṭhopāya 341

Page

Questions of King Milinda 113 (ftn.), 240 (ftn. 1, 3, 4)

Raghuvaṁśa 380

Rāmāyaṇa 7 (ftn 4), 8 (ftn. 5), 23 (ftn. 5, 6, 9, 12, 13), 51, 521

Rāmapāla-carita .. 246 (ftn. 3)

Rasika-sarvasva 522

Ratnakaraṇḍaka 183

Ratnākarāvatārikā 213

Ratnākarā-vatārīkā-pañjikā 213 (ftn. 1)

Ratnakoṣa .. 406 (ftn. 2)

Ratna-koṣa vāda rahasya .. 482

Ratnakoṣa-vicāra or vāda .. 479

Ratnāvalī .. 251 (ftn. 4)

Ratnāloka-dhāraṇī .. 29 (ftn. 1)

Report on Sanskrit MSS. by Peterson 168 (ftn. 3), 181 (ftn. 1), 182 (ftn. 3), 186 (ftn. 3), 194 (ftn. 4), 195. (ftn. 1, 2, 5, 7), 196 (ftn. 1, 2), 197 (ftn. 1, 2, 5), 198 (ftn. 2), 199 (ftn. 1, 2), 200 (ftn. 1), 205 (ftn. 1, 2, 3), 206 (ftn. 3, 4[3]), 207 (ftn. 1[2], 2, 4, 5), 208 (ftn. 1, 2, 3), 209 (ftn. 3[2]), 210 (ftn. 1, 2, 3, 5), 211 (ftn. 1, 4), 212 (ftn. 1, 2, 3[2]), 213 (ftn. 3), 214 (ftn. 2), 215 (ftn. 1), 218 (ftn. 3), 329 (ftn. 5), 457 (ftn. 5), 466 (ftn. 3), 47

Report of Sanskrit MSS. by R. G. Bhandarkar 160 (ftn. 2), 164 (ftn. 3), 165 (ftn. 2), 173 (ftn. 4), 183 (ftn. 3), 185 (ftn. 1), 197 (ftn. 4), 198 (ftn. 3), 201 (ftn. 1), 206 (ftn. 2), 207 (ftn. 3), 214 (ftn. 3), 381

Report II by Weber 212 (ftn. 2), 213 (ftn. 4), 214 (ftn. 3)

Report of the Archaeological Survey .. .. 519 (ftn. 6)

Rgyal-dwaṅ-blo-gros 323

Rgyu-daṅ-ḥbras-buḥi-ṅo-wo-grub-pa 341

Rgyud-gshan-grub-pa 319

Rgyud-gshan-grab-paḥi-ḥgrel-bśad 322

Rhetoric .. 500, 501[2], 509

Page

Rigs-pa grub pahi-sgron-ma .. 336
Rigs-pahi-sbyor-wa 340
Rigs-pahi-thigs-pa 300
Rigs-pahi-thigs-pahi-don-bsdus-pa 340
Rigs-pahi-thigs-pahi-phyogs-sna-ma-mdor-bs dus-pa 327
Rigs-pahi-thigs-pahi rgya-cher-hgrel wa 329
Rigs-pahi-thigs-pa rgya cher-hgrel-wa 321
Rigveda Saṁhitā 2 (ftn. 1), 9 (ftn. 1), 19 (ftn. 3)
Rnam-par-rig-pa-tsam-ñid-do-grub-pa 343
Ronki .. 267, 268, 269, 505
Ronshin 267
Ronshiki 267
Ṛṣibhāṣita-sūtra 165
Ṛṣimaṇḍala prakaraṇa vṛtti .. 165
Rtog-gehi-skad 346
Rtsod pa-bzlog-pahi-tshig-bhur-byas-pa 256
Rtsod-pahi-rigs-pa 318
Rtsod pahi rigs-pahi-hbrel-pa-don-ruam-par-hbyed-pa .. 323
Rtsod-pahi-rigs-pahi-hgrel-wa .. 321

Śabda-kaustubha .. 148 (ftn. 1)
Śabdāloka-viveka 468
Śabdanirṇaya 460
Śabda-prāmāṇya-vāda-rahasya .. 482
Śabda-śakti-prakāśikā 470, 480
Śabda-śakti-prakāśikā ṭīkā .. 485
Sacred Literature of the Jainas 161 (ftn. 3)
Ṣaḍdarśana-samuccaya 154 (ftn. 3), 208 (ftn. 4)[2], 209 (ftn.)[2], 214 (ftn. 1), 222, 371 (ftn. 1)
Ṣaḍdarśana-samuccaya-vṛtti 151 (ftn. 2, 3), 214, 331 (ftn. 6), 371[2], 371 (ftn. 1)
Saddharmapuṇḍarīka .. 242 (ftn. 3)
Sadukti-karṇāmṛta .. 524 (ftn. 1)
Sad-yukti-muktāvalī 478
Sahāvalambha-niścaya .. 336

Page

Śākta-krama 478
Śakti-vāda .. 482, 483
Śālistambha-sūtra .. 126 (ftn. 2)
Samādhi-rāja .. 242 (ftn. 3)
Samāja-guhya 516
Samantapāsādikā 232 (ftn. 1), 267 (ftn.)
Sāmānya-dūṣaṇa-dik-prasāritā 333 (ftn. 1)
Sāmānya-lakṣaṇa 526
Samaya-prābhṛta .. 195 (ftn. 6)
Samaraiccakahā .. 209 (ftn.)
Samāsa-vāda 480
Samayabhedoparacana-cakra .. 321
Saṁbandha-parīkṣā 194, 221, 319, 321, 345
Sambandha-parīkṣānu-sāra .. 345
Sambandha-parīkṣā-ṭīkā .. 321
Sambandha-parīkṣā-vṛtti .. 319
Sambandhoddyota .. 194, 221
Saṁkṣepa Śārīraka 459
Sāṁkhya Kārikā 10 (ftn. 1), 274 (ftn. 4), 295 (ftn. 1)
Sāṁkhya-tattva-kaumudī .. 134
Sammati-tarka .. 221 (ftn. 2)
Sammati-tarka-sūtra .. 173, 197
Saṁyutta Nikāya .. 127 (ftn.)
Saṅgīta-sarvasva 522
Śaṅkara-bhāṣya on the Vedānta-sūtra .. .. 6 (ftn. 7)
Saptapadārthī 356
Santānāntara-siddhi or Tantrāntara-siddhi .. 319, 322
Santāntara-siddhi-ṭikā .. 322
Sapta bhaṅgī taraṅgiṇī 167 (ftn. 2)
Saptadaśa-bhūmi-śāstra-yogācārya 240, 262, 262 (ftn. 4), 263
Sapta-padārtha 406
Sāramañjarī 384
Sāra-Saṁgraha ..380, 399 (ftn. 1)
Sarasvatī-gaccha-paṭṭāvalī 165 (ftn. 1)
Sārasaṁgraha-ṭīkā 380
Sārvabhauma-nirukti .. 462
Sarvābhisamaya-sūtra 126

Page

Sarvadarśana Saṁgraha 41 (ftn. 3), 48, 126 (ftn. 2), 127 (ftn.), 186 (ftn 5), 167 (ftn. 1), 168 (ftn. 2), 198, 247 (ftn. 5), 248 (ftn. 3), 249 (ftn. 1, 6), 306 (ftn. 7), 308 (ftn. 3), 377 (ftn.), 397, 398 ff., 407 (ftn. 2), 454 (ftn. 3). 455
Sarvajña-siddhi-kārikā .. 328
Sarvānukramaṇikā 45
Sarvārtha-siddhi .. 168 (ftn. 1)
Śāstra on the Meditation of the three worlds .. 301 (ftn. 2)
Śāstra-vārtā samuccaya 221 (ftn. 2)
Śataka-śāstra 261
Śatapatha Brāhmaṇa 3 (ftn. 3), 4 (ftn. 1), 19 (ftn. 4)
Śata-śāstra-vaipulya-vyākhyā .. 303
Ṣaṭ-cakra-krama-dīpikā .. 469
Ṣel-wa-grub-pa 345
Siddhānta-candrodaya .. 390
Siddhāntamuktāvalī 392
Siddhāntamuktāvalī-ṭīkā .. 483
Siddhānta-rahasya 467
Śikṣā-samuccaya .. 126 (ftn. 2)
Site of Ancient Palibothra 589 (ftn. 6)
Śivajñānasiddhiyār .. 387 (ftn. 2)
Six Buddhist Nyāya Texts 339 (ftn. 3)
Six Nyāya Tracts by H. P. Śāstri 322 (ftn. 4), 333 (ftn 1)
Six Systems of Indian Philosophy 148 (ftn. 1)
Ṣkad-cig-ma-ḥjig-grub-paḥi-ruam-ḥgrel 331
Ṣkal-cig-ma-ḥjig-pa-grub-pa .. 330
Skandapurāṇa 8 (ftn. 3), 497 (ftn. 2)
Śloka-vārtika 187
Smṛti-saṁskāra-vāda 482
Smṛti-sarvasva 524
Smṛti-viveka 524
So-sor-thar-pa .. .. 232 (ftn. 1)
Sragdharā Stotra. Introduction to .. 322 (ftn. 5, 6), 334 (ftn. 1)
Sragdharā-stotram .. 357 (ftn. 2)
Sragdharā-stotra-ṭīkā 519
Śrīpaṭṭāvalī-vācanā .. 160 (ftn. 5)

Page

Śrutiparīkṣā .. 143, 150, 328
Statistical Account of Bengal 523 (ftn. 2)
Sthānāṅga Sūtra 161 (ftn. 5)[2], 167 (ftn. 1), 170 (ftn.), 221
Sthira-siddhi-dūṣaṇa 339
Surbodhā 526
Subodhini 480
Sukṛta Saṁkirtana .. 152 (ftn. 3)
Sukṛa Saṁkirtana .. 208 (ftn. 2)
Sum-paḥi-chos-byuṅ 241 (ftn. 1), 242 (ftn. 1)
Surata kalpataru 391
Sūrya-prajāpati-sūtra 165
Sūtra-kṛtāṅga-sūtra .. 165, 221
Sūtrālaṅkāra ṭikā .. 262 (ftn. 4)
Sūtra piṭakas 334
Sūtra Upadeśa 242
Sutta Piṭaka 226, 227, 229[2], 242
Suvarṇa prabhāsa .. 242 (ftn. 3)
Suvartha tattvāloka or Kāraka-cakra 480
Sva-prakāśa-rahasya-vicāra or Bhaṭṭa-mata-siddhānta-vicāra .. 479
Svarūpa-sambodhana 185
Svayambhū Stotra 183
Syādvādakalika 213
Syādvāda-ratnākara 198
Syādvāda-ratnākarāvatārikā 329, 331

Takakusu .. .. 515 (ftn. 2)
Tangyur 506 (ftn. 3), 519 (ftn. 5), 533, 534, 535
Tantra 516
Tantrayukti 51
Tapāgaccha-paṭṭāvalī 159 (ftn. 1), 161, 208 (ftn. 4)
Tāraikaviṁśatikāṅga-sūtra Saṅkṣepa .. .. 518 (ftn. 5)
Tārā-triratna Stotram 519 (ftn. 5)
Tarka bhāṣā 215, 218, 346, 373, 381 ff., 478
Tarka bhāṣā bhāva 384
Tarka bhāṣā prakāśa 381
Tarka bhāṣā prakāśikā 384[2], 385

	Page
Tarkabhāṣā-praveśikā ..	381
Tarkabhāṣā-ṭīkā	485
Tarka-candrikā (Prabhā) ..	391
Tarkadīpikā ..	385, 391[2]
Tarkakaumudī	395
Tarkāmṛta ..	393 (ftn. 1), 393f.. 470
Tarkanyāya or Vāda-nyāya ..	318
Tarka-phakkikā	390
Tarka-rahasya-dīpikā	214
Tarka-saṁgraha 324 (ftn. 3), 387 (ftn. 1),	388 ff.
Tarka-saṁgraha-candrikā ..	391[2]
Tarka-saṁgraha-dīpikā ..	390
Tarka-saṁgraha-dīpikā-prakāśa ..	391[3]
Tarka-saṁgraha, saṅku ..	391
Tarka-saṁgraha-taraṅgiṇī ..	391
Tarka-saṁgraha-tattva-prakāśa ..	391
Tarka-saṁgraha ṭīkā ..	390[2], 391[4]
Tarka-saṁgraha-vākyārtha-nirukti	391
Tarka-saṁgraha-vyākhyā ..	391
Tarka-saṁgrahopanyāsa ..	391[2]
Tarka Śāstra ..	268[2], 301, 505
Tarkaṭīkā	331
Tārkika-rahasya ..	373[2], 374ff.
Tārkika-rakṣā ..	399 (ftn. 1)
Tā-shaṅ-ö-phi-tā matsā-tsi-hen ..	266
Tathāgata-guhyaka ..	292 (ftn. 3)
Tattvacintāmaṇi 155, 208, 376 (ftn. 4), 388, 405, 406 (ftn. 1, 2, 3. 4, 5, 6), 454 (ftn. 4), 456, 461,	462, 465, 466, 484
Tattvacintāmaṇi-darpaṇa ..	485
Tattvacintāmaṇi-dīdhiti ..	465
Tattvacintāmaṇi-dīdhiti-gūḍhārtha-vidyotana	478
Tattvacintāmaṇi-dīdhiti-parīkṣā ..	477
Tattvacintāmaṇi-dīdhiti-prakāśikā	470, 479, 482
Tattvacintāmaṇi-dīdhiti-prasāriṇī	468
Tattvacintāmaṇi-dīdhiti-ṭīkā ..	483
Tattvacintāmaṇi-gūḍhārtha-dīpikā	481
Tattvacintāmaṇi-mayūkha	459, 470
Tattvacintāmaṇi-prakāśa	454, 457, 466, 485
Tattvacintāmaṇi-rahasya (Phakkikā or Māthurī)	467
Tattvacintāmaṇi-ṭīkā	479[2], 456
Tattvacintāmaṇi-ṭīkā-vicāra ..	479
Tattvacintāmaṇi-vyākhyā ..	482
Tattvacintāmaṇyāloka ..	455
Tattvacintāmaṇyāloka-kaṇṭakoddhāra	461
Tattvacintāmaṇyāloka-prakāśa ..	460
Tattvacintāmaṇyāloka-ṭīkā ..	482
Tattva-cintāmaṇyāloka-rahasya ..	467
Tattvacintāmaṇyāloka-viveka ..	478
Tattva-prabodhinī	385
Tattvārtha	187
Tattvārtha-bodhavidhāyinī ..	197
Tattvārtha-dīpikā	391
Tattvārtha-śloka-vārtika	187 (ftn. 4)
Tattvārtha-ṭīkā ..	182, 182 (ftn. 1)
Tattvārthādhigama-sūtra 168 (ftn. 1), 169 (ftn.),	182[2]
Tattvārtha-dīpikā	182[2]
Tattvārtha-sāra	195
Tattvārtha-vārtikālaṅkāra 168 (ftn. 1),	169 (ftn.)
Tattvārtha-vārtika-vyākhyānālaṅkāra	185
Tattvasamāsa ..	324 (ftn. 3)
Tattvasaṁgraha 222, 324 (ftn. 3)[2],	326 (ftn.), 328
Tattvasaṁgraha-dīpikā-ṭippanī ..	483
Tattvasaṁgraha-kārikā ..	324
Tattvasaṁgraha-pañjikā ..	328
Taxila by Law ..	496 (ftn. 1)
Thems-cad-ḿkhyan-pa-grub-pahi-tshig-bhur	328
Thos-pa brtag-pahi-tshig bhur-byas-pa	328
Tibetan Catalogue by Cordier	262 (ftn. 2)
Tibetan Dictionary	530
Tibetan Grammar 306 (ftn. 1),	323 (ftn. 3)
Ṭīkā (on Tarkasaṁgraha) ..	391[5]
Tipiṭaka	226, 227, 242
Ṭippanaka..	195
Tīrthacintāmaṇi	458

Page

Tirthakalpa .. 159 (ftn. 1), 169

Tirthika works 289

Translation of the Mahāvaṁsa 226 (ftn.), 226 (ftn. 1, 2), 234 (ftn. 1)

Translation of the Nyāya-praveśa

—by Hwen-thsang .. 300 (ftn. 2)

—by I-tsing .. 300 (ftn. 2)

Translation of the Vinaya Texts by Rhys Davids .. 232 (ftn. 1)

Travels of Fa-hian and Suṁg-yun by Beal .. .. 252 (ftn. 3)

Tripiṭaka 272

Triṣaṣṭi-śalāka-puruṣa-caritra .. 205

Trisūtri-nibandha-vyākhyā 458, 459

Tshad-ma-brtag-pa 330

Tshad-maḥi-bstan-bcos-rig-pa-la-ḥjug-pa 300

Tshad-maḥi-Mdo-kun-las-bhus-pa 276

Tshad-ma-kun-las-btus pa .. 276

Tshad-ma-kun-las-btus-peḥi-bgrel-wa 299

Tshad-ma-rigs-par-ḥjug-paḥi-sgo.. 280

Tshad-ma-rnam-ḥgrel-gyi dkah-ḥgrel 319

Tshad-ma-rnam ḥgrel-gyi-ḥgrel-bśad 320, 344

Tshad-ma-rnam-ḥgrel-gyi-ḥgrel-wa 308

Tshad-ma-rnam-ḥgrel-gyi-lshing .. 307

Tshad-ma-rnam-ḥgrel-gyi-ḥgrel-pa 323

Tshad-ma-rnam-ḥgrel-gyi rgyan .. 336

Tshad-ma-rnam-ḥgrel-gyi-rgyan-gyi-ḥgrel-bśad 338

Tshad-ma-rnam-ḥgrel-rgyan-gyi ḥgrel bśad 344

Tshad-ma-rnam-nes-kyi-ṭikā .. 331

Tshad-ma-rnam-par-ḥjoms-pa-mdor-bśad-paḥi-ḥgrel .. 257

Tshad-ma-rnam-parnes-pa .. 309

Tshad ma-rnam-parnis-paḥi-ḥgrel-bśad 342

Ueber das Lebens des Jaina Mönches Hemacandra .. 205 (ftn. 1)

Ujjvala 384

University of Nadia (see Nadia) 521 (ftn. 1)

Page

Upāli-vāda Sutta 229

Upamiti-bhava-prapañca-kathā 147 (ftn. 4)

Upaniṣads by F. Max Müller 45 (ftn. 4)

Upamānacintāmaṇi-ṭīkā .. 485

Upāsakādhyayana 183

Upāyakauśalya-hṛdaya-śāstra, 259, 504

Upāyakausalya Sūtra.. .. 119

Utpāda-siddhi-prakaraṇa .. 211

Uttarādhyayana Sūtra .. 165

Uvāsagadasāo .. 182 (ftn. 3)

Vādabuddhivicāra 479

Vāda-mahārṇava .. 196, 197[1], 124

Vādanyāya .. 321[2], 324

Vādanyāya-vṛtti-vipañcitārtha 323, 324

Vādayāya-vyākhyā 321

Vāda-pariccheda 484

Vāda-vidhi.. .. 124 (ftn. 1)

Vāhyārtha-siddhi kārikā .. 328

Vaiduryakarpo .. 517 (ftn. 4)

Vaiśeṣika philosophy by Prof. H. Ui 40 (ftn. 2), 256 (ftn. 2), 300 (ftn. 1), 302 (ftn. 1)

Vaiśeṣika-śāstrīya-padārtha-nirūpaṇa 484

Vaiśeṣika Sūtra .. 356, 499

Vaiśeṣika-sūtropadeśa .. 459

Vaiyākaraṇa-bhuṣaṇa-sāra 132 (ftn. 1), 148 (ftn. 1)

Vākyapadīya .. 148 (ftn. 1)

Vaṁsa Brāhmaṇa .. 380 (ftn. 5)

Varāhapurāṇa .. 45 (ftn. 1)

Vārtika on the Nyāya Sūtra 259 (ftn.)

Vātsyāyana, author of the Nyāya-bhāṣya .. .. 116 (ftn. 4)

Vāyupurāṇa .. 498 (ftn. 7)

Vedi-vinoda 459

Vibhāṣā-śāstra 248

Vibhāṣa-vinaya .. 266 (ftn. 2)

Vicārāmṛta-saṁgraha 208 (ftn. 4)

Vicāra-ratna-saṁgraha 169 (ftn. 2)

Vicāra-sāra-prakaraṇa 159 (ftn. 1), 208 (ftn. 4)

Vicāra-śreṇi .. 159 (ftn. 1)

Page
Vidagdha-mukha-maṇḍana-vitikā 479
Vidhi-vāda .. 482
Vidvānamoda-taraṅgiṇī .. 483
Vidyāmātra-siddhi - śāstra - vyākhyā .. 303
Vienna Oriental Journal 195 (ftn. 3)
Vigraha-vyāvartanī-kārikā .. 257[2]
Vijñapti-mātra siddhi .. 343
Vinaya-piṭaka 225 (ftn. 3), 226, 229 (ftn. 3)[2], 242
Vinaya-vibhāṣā .. 241
Viśālāmalavatīmānca - pramāṇa - samuccaya-ṭīkā .. 323
Viṣayatā-vāda .. 482
Viśeṣāvaśyaka-bhāṣya .. 181
Viṣṇupurāṇa 42 (ftn. 3), 456, 497
Viśvasāra-tantra .. 153
Vītarāga-stuti .. 212
Vivādacandra .. 466
Vivādaśamana-śāstra .. 257
Vivaraṇa-prameya-saṁgraha 397 (ftn. 1)
Viveka-vilāsa 153, 154
Vṛhadgaccha .. 212
Vṛhatsvayambhūpurāṇa .. 519

Page
Vṛndāvana-vinoda-kāvya .. 477
Vṛtta-ratnā vali 483
Vṛtti on Gaṇadharasārdhaśatakam .. .. 160 (ftn.
Vyāptipañcaka .. 407 (ftn. 1)
Vyavahāra sūtra 165
Vyutpatti-vāda 482
Vyutpatti-vāda-vyākhya .. 483

Wassilief .. .. 306 (ftn. 1)

Yājñavalka Saṁhitā 8 (ftn. 6), 23 (ftn. 5, 11), 42 (ftn. 6), 152 (ftn. 1), 498
Yast .. .. 20 (ftn. 3)
Yogācārabhūmi Śāstra .. 504
Yogācāra philosophy 303
Yoga Śāstra .. 205
Yukti-muktāvali .. 384
Yukti-prayoga 340
Yuktyanuśāsana 183
Yuka Pon.. .. 263 (ftn. 3)

Zend Avesta .. 489 (ftn. 3)
Zu-shih-ben 268

INDEX OF AUTHORS.

Page

Abhayadeva Sūri 199
Abhayatilakopādhyāya .. 151
Abhinanda . 147 (ftn. 2)
Ācārya Dignāga .. ..270ff.
Akalaṅka Deva .. 168 (ftn. 1)
Akhaṇḍānanda .. 406 (ftn. 2)
Amaracandra Sūri 207
Amṛtacandra Sūri 195
Ānanda Sūri 207
Ananta Nārāyaṇa 390
Ananta Śrī 341
Anantavīrya .. 188 (ftn. 6). 198
Annam Bhaṭṭa .. 388, 390
Arcaṭa .. .. .. 331f.
Ārya Āsaṅga .. .. 265f.
Ārya Deva .. .. 250, 261f.
Aśoka .. .. .. 332f.

Bāla Candra 384
Bāṇa .. .. .. 123[2]
Bhadrabāhu .. 122 (ftn. 1)
Bhāsa 20
Bhāsarvajña 155
Bhāskara Bhaṭṭa 384
Bhaṭṭa Rāghava 372
Bhavya 250
Bhavyarāja .. 330[2], 336
Bhīma Sena Dīkṣita 477
Bhimi Bhaṭṭa 384
Blo-ldan-śes-rab 262 (ftn. 5), 309, 330[2], 331 336[2]
Brahmanemi Datta .. 188 (ftn. 4)
Buddhaghoṣa 232 (ftn. 1), 267 (ftn.)
Buddha Pālita 250
Byaṅ-chub śes-rab 338

Candra Gomin .. ..333ff.
Candraja Siṃha 391
Candra Kīrti .. 126 (ftn. 2), 250
Candraprabha Sūri 166 (ftn. 1), 206, 406 (ftn. 2)

Page

Candra Sena .. 205 (ftn. 3), 211
Caraka 50
Chos-kyi-brtson-bgrus 342
Chos kyi rin-chen 300
Ci-cia-ye 259
Cinna Bhaṭṭa .. 381, 384

Dad-pa-Śes-rab 300
Dāna Śīla 340
Devabhadra 211
Devardhi Gaṇi 172
Devasena Bhaṭṭāraka 195
Deva Sūri .. .. ..198ff.
Devendrabhadra 328
Devendrabuddhi .. 319f., 348
Dge-śes-sisi-gyaṅ 300
Dge-wahi-blo-gros .. 307, 318, 320[2]
Dharma-bhūṣaṇa .. 215, 273 (ftn. 7)
Dharmakīrti 124, 133. 136 (ftn.), 303ff., 340, 345
Dharmapāla 302
Dharmottara .. 150, 329ff.
Dhoyī 524
Dignaya 42, 135
Dīpaṅkara Rakṣita 338
Dpal-brtsegs rakṣita .. 321, 322, 328
Dpal mchog-daṅ-pohi-rdo-rje .. 337
Dpal-ldan-blo-gros 323
Dpal-rtseges-rakṣita 328
Dpal-trsegs 319
Dr. J. Jolly .. 45 (ftn. 2)

Gadādhara .. .. 406 (ftn. 2)
Gaṅgādhara Bhaṭṭa 391
Gaṅgeśa Dīkṣita 385
Gaṅgeśa Upādhyāya 155, 404, 405ff.
Gaurī Kānta .. 390, 385
Gautama .. .. 48 (ftn. 4)
Govardhana Miśra .. 385, 390
Grogs-hbyor śes-rab .. 328, 331
Gser-gyi-go-cha 300

	Page
Guṇākara Śrībhadra ..	.. 323
Guṇaratna	.. 151, 214, 331
Guṇḍu Bhaṭṭa	 384
Hanumat ..	 391
Haribhadra Sūri 152, 154, 160 (ftn. 6), 206 (ftn. 4), 208f.	
Harirāma..	.. 406 (ftn. 2)
Ḥbro-seṅ-kar	 324
Hemacandra Sūri	 205
Hema (or kanaka) Varma	.. 300
Hwon-thsang	.. 300 (ftn. 2), 302
Iśvara Kṛṣṇa	274 (ftn. 4), 295 (ftn. 1)
I-tsing ..	.. 300 (ftn. 2)
Jābāla ..	 9
Jagadīśa Bhaṭṭa	 391
Jagadīśa Tarkālaṅkāra	.. 393
Jagannātha Śāstrin	 391
Jānakinātha Cuḍāmaṇi	.. 404
Janārdana Vyāsa	 478
Jayadeva ..	 524
Jayānanta ..	.. 250, 256
Jayanta ..	 371
Jayasiṁha Sūri	 372
Jayasoma Sūri	.. 164 (ftn. 2)
Jaya Tīrtha	 371
Jetāri ..	 337
Jina ..	 338
Jinabhadra Gaṇi	 181
Jinadatta Sūri	.. 152, 154
Jina Mitra ..	.. 321, 328, 340
Jinaprabha Sūri	159, (ftn. 1), 169
Jinendrabodhi	.. 323, 348
Jñāna Candra	 213
Jñāna Garbha	256, 319, 321, 329
Jñāna Pūrṇa	.. 374, 380
Jñāna-śrī Bhadra	.. 318, 342
Jñānaśrī Mitra	 341
Kalyāṇa Candra	 198
Kalyāṇa Rakṣita	.. 150, 328f., 348
Kamala Śīla	324 (ftn. 3), 327f., 348
Kapila ..	.. .. 9f.

	Page
Kātyāyana	.. 41 (ftn. 4)
Kātyāyanī-putra	.. 242, 247
Kaunda Bhaṭṭa	 132
Kauṇḍinya Dīkṣita	 385
Kauṭilya ..	 24
Ka-wa-dpal-brtsegs	 256
Keśava Bhaṭṭa	 385
Keśava Miśra	.. 373, 381ff., 478
Khu-mdo-sde-dpal	 256
Kṛṣṇa ..	 250
Kṣamākalyāṇa	 390
Kumārajīva	.. 261, 267
Kumāra-kalasa	.. 337, 341
Kumāra Śrībhadra	 324
Kumārila Bhaṭṭa	138 (ftn. 1), 273
Kundakundācārya	.. 195 (ftn. 6)
Laugākṣi Bhāskara	.. 395, 478
Laghu Sāmantabhadra	185 (ftn. 3), 197
Lha-bla-ma-shi-wa-ḥod	.. 323
Mādhavācārya	 198
Mādhava Deva	 384
Mādhavapadābhirāma	.. 391
Māhopādhyāya Dharma-sāgara Gaṇi	.. 164 (ftn. 4)
Maitreya ..	 262
Maladhāri Śrī Rājaśekhara Sūri 153, 154, 155	
Mallaṣena Sūri	 212
Mallavādin ..	 194
Mallinātha	273, 373 (ftn. 1), 380
Mammaṭa ..	 478
Maṇibhadra	.. 214 (ftn. 1)
Māṇikyanandi	.. 185, 188
Mathurānātha Tarkavāgīśa	.. 388
Meru Śāstri..	 391
Meru Śāstri Godbole ..	.. 391
Merutuṅga ..	.. 159 (ftn. 1)
Mokṣakara Gupta	 346
Muktākumbha	 331
Mukunda Bhaṭṭa	 391
Mukunda Bhaṭṭa Gāḍgil	.. 391
Munisundara Sūri	.. 165 (ftn.)
Murāri ..	 391
Murāri Bhaṭṭa	 384

	Page
Nāga Rakṣita	337
Nāgārjuna ..	..50, 250, 256, 334
Nāgeśa Bhaṭṭa	384
Nārāyaṇa	153
Nārāyaṇa Bhaṭṭa	384
Nemicandra Kavi ..	207, 210
Nilakaṇṭha	391
Padmanābha Miśra	381
Pakṣadhara Miśra ..	407 (ftn. 3)
Paṇḍita Amara Gomin	262 (ftn. 5)
Parahita Bhadra	309
Paramārtha ..	267, 268, 301f.
Pārśvadeva Gaṇi	210
Pārthasārathi Miśra	273
Paśupati	524
Patañjali	41 (ftn. 4, 5)
Pattābhirāma	391
Prabhā Candra 193, 208 (ftn. 4), 273 (ftn. 7)	
Pradyumna Sūri ..	173, 196
Prajñākara Gupta ..	331f., 344
Prajñākaramati ..	126 (ftn. 2)
Prajñā Varma	321
Pūjyapāda Svāmin ..	168 (ftn. 1)
Rabhasa Nandi	194
Raghunandana ..	153 (ftn. 3)
Raghunātha Śiromaṇi..	388, 406 (ftn. 2)
Rāja Śekhara	134, 147 (ftn. 6) 213
Rāma Liṅga	384
Ramānātha	391
Rāmarudra Bhaṭṭa	391
Ratnākara Śānti	342
Ratnakīrti ..	133, 338
Ratnaprabha Sūri	166 (ftn. 1), 211, 331
Ratna Vajra	339
Ravi Gupta ..	322f., 348
Rdo-rje-rgyal-mtshan	323
Romavilva-Veṅkata Buddha ..	384
Śākya bodhi ..	320, 348
Śākya-hod	337[2], 341, 343
Śākya Siṁha	322
Samanta Bhadra ..	182ff., 185
Saṅghabhadra	248
Śaṅkara Miśra	388
Śaṅkarānanda	344
Śaṅkara Svāmin ..	289 (ftn. 1), 320
Śānta Rakṣita ..	323f., 348
Śānti Bhadra ..	336, 343
Śāntyācārya ..	147 (ftn. 4)
Sarvajñātma Muni	459
Śaśadhara	396
Śes-rab	323
Sha-ma-dge-bsñen-siṅ-rgyal ..	299
Siddharṣi	147 (ftn. 4)
Siddhasena Divākara ..	..173ff.
Siddhasena Divākara-vyākhyānaka	206 (ftn. 4)
Siddhasena Gaṇi ..	168 (ftn. 3), 182
Śīlabhadra	303
Śivāditya Miśra ..	378 (ftn. 1), 406
Śrī Candra	210
Śrīdhara Dāsa ..	524 (ftn. 1)
Śrīkaṇṭha	151
Śrīkṛṣṇā Dhūrjaṭi Dikṣita ..	390
Śrīnivāsa	391
Śrī Śitaprabha	336
Śrī Śubhūti Śānta	340
Śrutasāgara Gaṇi	215
Stou-gshon	300
Subandu	123
Śubhakara Gupta	346
Subhūti-śri-Śānti ..	307, 320
Śuklaratna Nātha	391
Śūlapāṇi	524
Surendrabodhi ..	340
Sureśvarācārya	306
Thān-yāo	259
Thasam-tsan	300
Tilakācārya	206 (ftn. 5), 212
Tiṅ-ṅe-ḥdsin-bzaṅ-po	340
Tsab-ñi-ma-grags	330
Udayana	386
Umāpati	524
Vācaspati Miśra ..	131, 133ff
Vācaspati Miśra—the Junior	151, 303

	Page
Vadhulaveṅkaṭa Guru	.. 391
Vaidyanātha Gaḍgil ..	.. 391
Vairocana ..	 336
Vande-dpal-brtsegs ..	.. 322
Vande-nam-ṃkhaṣ ..	319, 321
Vande-ye-śeṣ-sde ..	321, 340
Varadā rāja ..	..373ff.
Vardhamāna	151, 388, 406 (ftn. 2)
Vasubandu	124 (ftn. 1), 266ff., 300, 371
Vātsyāyana	40 (ftn. 1), 52 (ftn. 1)
Vidyānanda	186, 273 (ftn. 7), 306
Vijayasiṁha Gaṇi ..	.. 371
Vijñāna Bhikṣu ..	244 (ftn. 1)
Vimala Dāsa ..	167 (ftn. 2)

	Page
Vimokṣa Prajña ..	.. 257
Vināyaka	.. 331
Vinaya Vijaya ..	.. 216
Vindhyeśvari Prasād ..	.. 391
Vinīta Deva ..	.. 348
Viśuddha Siṁha ..	319, 322, 328
Viśva Karmā ..	.. 385
Viśvanātha	52 (ftn. 1), 151, 391
Viśvanātha Nyāya pañcānana ..	392
Yamāri	.. 343
Yaśovijaya Gaṇi ..	.. 217
Yayanta	146 (ftn.)
Yuan Chwang ..	40 (ftn. 2)

INDEX OF QUOTATIONS.

Abhidhāna-cintāmaṇi— *Page*

—वात्स्यायनो मल्लनाग .. 117 (ftn. 2)

Abhisamayālaṅkāra-kārikā—

—धर्मज्ञानान्वयज्ञान .. 263 (ftn. 2)

—पूर्वेण बाधिधौतक्ता .. 262 (ftn. 6)

—स्वप्नोपमेषु धर्मेषु .. 263 (ftn. 1)

Acāra-dinakara—

—सुगुण दिङ्निवायं कालिय 161 (ftn. 1)

Address of Udayana—

—ऐश्वर्यमदमत्तः सन् .. 142 (ftn. 3)

Ādipurāṇa—

—चन्द्रांशु शुभ्रयशसं .. 194 (ftn. 3)

—भट्टाकलङ्कं श्रीपाल .. 188 (ftn. 1)

Alaṅkāra-sāra-sthiti—

—शक्तिर्न शक्तिवाद व्याख्या 477 (ftn. 2)

Amarasvāmi-carita—

—स्तौमि श्रीहरिभद्रं तं .. 209 (ftn. 3)

Ananadalahari-tarī—

—यो नानाविधशास्त्रतर्कनिपुण 478 (ftn. 1)

Anekānta-jaya-patākā—

—उक्तञ्च वादिमुख्येन .. 209 (ftn. 2)

—यथोक्तं वार्त्तिकानुसारिणा 209 (ftn. 2)

Anekāntajaya-patākā-ṭikā—

—यथोक्तं वार्त्तिकानुसारिणा शुभगुप्तेन 346 (ftn. 2)

Antarvyāpti—

—अन्तर्व्याप्तिसमर्थनं समाप्तम् 343 (ftn. 3)

—इह सत्यमर्थक्रियाकारित्वं 343 (ftn. 3)

Anumāna-dīdhiti-gūḍhārtha-vidyotana—

—श्रीविश्वेश्वरमशेषमङ्गलभुवं 477 (ftn. 1)

Anumāna-dīdhiti-prasāriṇī—

—विचारस्तु अनुमानालोक 468 (ftn. 1)

Anumāna khaṇḍa—

—इति न्यायसिद्धान्तसाराभिज्ञ 456 (ftn. 5)

Anumānāloka-darpaṇa— *Page*

—जनकविषयजन्मा राजसम्मानपात्रं 457 (ftn. 5)

—ज्येष्ठा महादेवभगीरथ .. 458 (ftn. 1)

Apohasiddhi—

—कृतिरियं महापण्डित .. 338 (ftn. 3)

—नाकारस्य न बाह्यस्य .. 338 (ftn. 4)

—नास्माभिरपोहशब्देन विधिरेव 339 (ftn. 4)

—यथाच न्यायभूषणेन 339 (ftn. 1), 358 (ftn. 1)

—यत्तु त्रिलोचनः । अश्वत्वगोत्वादिना 134 (ftn. 3)

—यदप्यवोचद् वाचस्पति .. 339 (ftn. 2)

Āptamimāṁsā—

—अद्वैतैकान्तपक्षेऽपि .. 182 (ftn. 5)

—भावैकान्ते पदार्थानाम् उपयोगात्र सर्वथा .. .. 184 (ftn. 1)

—स्याद्वादसर्वथैकान्त 183 (ftn. 1)

Āptamīmāṁsālaṅkṛti-ṭikā—

—येनाशेष कुनीति वृत्तिसरित 183 (ftn. 2)

Arthaśāstra of Kauṭilya—

—त्रयी वार्त्ता दण्डनीति .. 5 (ftn. 1)

—धर्माधर्मौ त्रय्याम् शस्त्रदान्वीक्षिकी मता .. .. 7 (ftn. 6)

—प्रदीपः सर्वविद्यानाम् .. 38 (ftn. 4)

—शास्त्रं विप्रतिपद्यत .. 41 (ftn. 6)

—संघमुख्यश्च संघेषु .. 42 (ftn. 1)

—सांख्यं योगो लोकायतं .. 5 (ftn. 4)

—आन्वीक्षिकी त्रयी वार्त्ता 5 (ftn. 2)

Aṣṭasāhasri—

—यथोपयोगेऽपि पुनः .. 187 (ftn. 1)

—प्रज्ञाकरस्येदं वचः क्रमप्रतीतिरेव स्यात् 187 (ftn. 2)

—यदुक्तं धर्मकीर्तिनाऽतद्रूप परावृत्त 187 (ftn. 1)

Page

—यदुक्तं बृहदारण्यकवार्तिके आत्मापि सदिदं ब्रह्म .. 187 (ftn. 4)

—श्रीमदकलङ्कविवृतां .. 187 (ftn.)

—श्रीमदकलङ्कशशधरकुल 186 (ftn. 6)

—श्रीवर्द्धमानमभिवन्द्य समन्तभद्र 186 (ftn. 6)

Aṣṭasāhasrī-vivaraṇa—

—ऐन्द्रमहः प्रणिधाय न्याय 220 (ftn. 4)

—न्यायाम्बुधिदीधितिकारयुक्ति 218 (ftn. 2), 465 (ftn. 1)

Aṣṭasāhasrī-viṣama-pada-tātparya-ṭīkā—

—देवं स्वामिनममलं विद्यानन्दं 197 (ftn. 6)

Ātma-tattva-viveka—

—बहुतरपटतन्त्रप्रान्तरध्वान्तभीत 141 (ftn. 2)

Avadāna Kalpalatā—

—भगवद्भाषितं तत्तु .. 174 (ftn. 2)

Āvaśyaka niryukti—

—छव्वास सयाइं नवुत्तराइं 159 (ftn. 2)

Avayavinirākaraṇa—

—एवं मया बहुषु दुर्मतिनिर्मितषु 333 (ftn. 4)

—तदेतत् सकलमालोक्य .. 332 (ftn. 4)

—ननु भवद्भि रसन्नेवापयवी 333 (ftn. 2)

Bhadrabāhu-carita—

—मृते विक्रमभूपाले .. 159 (ftn. 2)

Bhāgavata—

—न वक्तव्यमिदास्माभिः .. 49 (ftn. 2)

—स्त्रियो बालाश्च वृद्धाश्च .. 49 (ftn. 2)

Bhāgavatapurāṇa—

—षष्ठमत्रेरपत्यत्वं वृतः .. 10 (ftn. 4)

—स्तूयमानो जनैरेभिः .. 6 (ftn. 5)

Bhagavatī Sūtra—

—अथवा हेऊ चउव्विहे णत्थि भं हेऊ 162 (ftn. 1)

Bhāmatī—

—नरेश्वरा यच्चरितानुकारम् 134 (ftn. 1)

—यथाह धर्मकीर्तिः तस्माद्यार्थेन च ज्ञाने 306 (ftn. 6)

—स्याद्वादसर्वथैकान्त .. 183 (ftn. 1)

Page

Bhāṣāpariccheda—

—अस्माद्या निखिलार्चितस्त्रिदश 392 (ftn. 6)

—रसबाणतिथौ शकेन्द्रकाले 392 (ftn. 4)

Bhāṣāratna—

—चूडामणिपदाम्भोज .. 466 (ftn. 2)

Brahmāṇḍa purāṇa—

—वने त्वाङ्गिरसः श्रेष्ठो .. 19 (ftn. 2)

—सप्तविंशतिमे प्राप्ते उलूको वत्स एव च 49 (ftn. 1)

Bṛhadāraṇyaka—

—अरे:यमात्माऽनन्तरोऽबाह्यः 9 (ftn. 2)

—आत्मा वारे द्रष्टव्यः .. 6 (ftn. 1)

—तदेतत् क्षत्रस्य क्षत्रम् .. 3 (ftn. 1)

—श्वेतकेतुर्ह आरुणेयः .. 22 (ftn. 2)

Bṛhadāraṇyaka-vārtika—

—चिच्चैव त्वविनाभावाद् .. 306 (ftn. 4)

Caitanya Caritamṛta—

—नौमि तं गौरचन्द्रं .. 462 (ftn. 1)

—পূর্ব্বে মহাপ্রভু যবে .. 462 (ftn. 1)

Caraka Saṁhitā—

—अथात् इन्द्रियापक्रमणीयमध्यायं 11 (ftn. 2)

—एवं प्रमाणैः श्रुतिभिः .. 28 (ftn. 3)

—चतुस्त्रिंशद् विचित्राभि भवन्त्येतानि कृत्स्नशः .. .. 24 (ftn. 1)

—द्विविधमेव खलु .. 28 (ftn. 1)

—हेतुर्नामोपलब्धि कारणम् 28 (ftn 2)

Caturviṁśati-prabandha—

—शरगगनमनुमितादौ श्रेष्ठा 213 (ftn. 4)

Commentary on Tārkikarakṣā

—एतच्च ग्रन्थकृतैव स्पष्टीकृत 373 (ftn. 1)

Commentary on Utpāda-siddhiprakaraṇa—

—श्रीमांश्चन्द्रकुलेऽभवद् .. 205 (ftn. 3)

Dāna-kāṇḍa—

—सर्वेषां मौलिवराणां .. 392 (ftn. 3)

Daśa-vaikālika-niryukti—

—तेउ पदस्स विभत्ती .. 166 (ftn. 1)

Daśa-vaikālika ṭīkā—

—तीर्थे वीरविभोः सुधर्मगणभृत् 206 (ftn. 5)

Page

Daśa-vaikālika-vṛtti—

—बालश्रीहवसूर्याचा: .. 160 (ftn. 6)

Deopara Vijaya Sena Inscription—

—त्वं नान्यवीरविजयीतिगिरः कवीना 521 (ftn. 3)

Devīpurāṇa—

—शम्भोः कृपामनुप्राप्य .. 154 (ftn. 4)

Dhanukhā Inscription—

—आसीत् पण्डितमण्डलाग्रगणितो 406 (ftn. 7)

Dharmābhyudaya Mahā-kāvya—

—आनन्दसूरिरिति तस्य बभूव शिष्यश्री व्याघ्रसिंहशिशुकाविति सिद्धिराजः 207 (ftn. 4)

—सिद्धान्तोपनिषन्निषण्णहृदयो 208 (ftn. 3)

Gacchotpatti-prakīrṇaka—

—पंचसए पचतीए .. 208 (ftn. 1)

Gadādharī-karṣikā—

—श्रीकृष्णं मुकुन्दरामस्य .. 486 (ftn. 1)

Gandharva-tantra—

—गौतमप्रोक्तशास्त्रार्थनिरताः 17 (ftn. 3), 36 (ftn. 3)

Gautama Dharma Sūtra—

—राजा सर्वस्येष्टे ब्राह्मणवर्जं प्रत्यवहृत्य भिक्षां गमयेत् .. 37 (ftn. 3)

Gautama-sūtra-vṛtti—

—एषा मुनिप्रवरगौतमसूत्रवृत्तिः 392 (ftn. 5)

Gloss on Bhavānandi-ṭīkā—

—नत्वा पदाम्भोजयुगं शिवस्य 486 (ftn. 2)

—श्रीमत्पुण्यस्तम्भोपनायक 486 (ftn. 2)

Gotama-stotra—

—श्रीमन्तं मगधेषु गोर्वर इति प्राप्तोऽभिरामः श्रिया .. 160 (ftn. 4)

Guru-śiromaṇi-prakasa—

—यन्मूलमेव सुकृतानि तयोः कृतानि 467 (ftn.)

Gurvāvalī Sūtra—

—अवधिमः पूर्वश्रुतां द्वितीयः श्रीस्थूलभद्रश्च ददातु शर्म .. 164 (ftn. 5)

—उभावपि षष्ठपट्टधरौ 164 (ftn. 4)

Page

—येनार्दितश्चतुरशीति सुवादिलीला शिष्या बहवोऽभवन् विदिताः 199 (ftn. 2)

—रसरसमनुमितवर्षे २४६६ 214 (ftn. 4)

Harṣa-carita—

—कवीनामगलद्दर्पो .. 123 (ftn. 3)

Hayaśīrṣapañcarātra—

—गौतमस्य कणादस्य .. 153 (ftn. 3)

Introductory verses to Saṅkara Miśra's works—

—अधीतमध्यापितमर्जितयशो 458 (ftn. 3)

Jaina Harivaṁśa Purāṇa—

—अथ सप्तर्षिसम्पन्नं .. 159 (ftn. 3)

Jambudvīpa-samāsa—

—कृतिः सिताम्बराचार्यस्य 169 (ftn.)

Jyotirvidābharaṇa—

—धन्वन्तरिः क्षपणकोऽमरसिंह 174 (ftn. 2)

Kādambari—

—रजोजुषे जन्मनि सत्त्ववृत्तये 194 (ftn. 1)

Kalpasūtra-subodhikāvṛtti—

—प्रतिष्ठानपुरे वराहमिहिरभद्रबाहु 165 (ftn. 3)

Kātantra—

—अम्बवधिरः .. 19 (ftn. 5)

Kathāvatthuppakaraṇa—

—गो च भयम् तथा तत्थ .. 234 (ftn. 2)

Kathāvatthuppakaraṇa - aṭṭaha - kathā—

—एवं तेन, धुलेन निम्मत्ते 234 (ftn. 2)

Kathopaniṣad—

—शान्तसंकल्पसुमनाः आत्मा भवति गौतमः .. .. 19 (ftn. 1)

Kāvyālaṅkāra sūtra vṛtti—

—साभिप्रायत्वं यथा सोऽयं संप्रति चन्द्रगुप्ततनय .. .. 267 (ftn. 1)

Khuddakapātha of the Pāli Sutta-piṭaka—

—एकं नाम किं ? पच्चुपादानक्खन्धा 114 (ftn. 1)

Kriyāratna-samuccaya—

—काले षड् रसपूर्वे २४६६ 214 (ftn. 5)

Page

Kṣaṇabhaṅga-siddhi—
—क्षतिरियं महापण्डितस्य 338 (ftn. 3)
—त्रिलोचनस्याप्ययं संक्षिप्तार्थः 134 (ftn. 4)
—प्रकृतेः सर्वधर्माणां .. 339 (ftn. 5)
—यच्चात्र न्यायभूषणेन .. 339 (ftn. 1)
—यदप्यवोचद् वाचस्पतिः 339 (ftn. 2)
Kumārapāla-carita-praśasti—
—श्री विक्रमनृपाद् द्वि द्वि 372 (ftn. 3)
Kusumāñjali—
—अस्माकन्तु निसर्गसुन्दर चिराच्चेतो निमग्नं त्वयि .. 145 (ftn. 2)
—इत्येव श्रुतिनीति संप्लवजलैर्भूयोभिराक्षालिते .. 145 (ftn. 1)
—व्याघातावधिराशङ्का .. 31 (ftn. 2)
—सापेक्षत्वादनादित्वाद् .. 144 (ftn.
Kusumāñjali-vyākhyā—
—भवानीभवनाथाभ्यां .. 469 (ftn. 1)

Laghu-dīpikā—
—तस्मिन् विश्वरूपजयन्तयोर्मते 380 (ftn. 2)
—सर्वैश्वर्यनिवासम् .. 380 (ftn. 1)
Lakṣaṇāvalī—
—तर्काम्बराङ्क प्रमितेष्व .. 142 (ftn. 1)
Lalitavistara—
—निर्घण्टौ निगमे पुराणे .. 243 (ftn. 2)
Laṅkāvatāra Sūtra—
—अनुत्पन्नास्तु धर्माणाः .. 46 (ftn. 1)
—आलयविज्ञाने पुनर्निरूप्यमाने 245 (ftn. 2)
—कथं हि ग्राह्यते तर्कः .. 244 (ftn. 4)
—दृष्टान्तहेतुभिर्युक्तः .. 244 (ftn. 5)
—निर्व्यापारं क्षणिकं .. 246 (ftn. 1)
—नैयायिकाः कथं ब्रूहि .. 244 (ftn. 3)
—बुद्ध्या विविच्यमानानां 46 (ftn. 1), 120 (ftn. 2)
—सांख्या वैशेषिका नग्ना .. 244 (ftn. 2)
Last words of Kṛṣṇakānta Vidyāvāgīśa—
—अधिगगनमनेका .. 485 (ftn. 1)
Līlāvatī-prakāśa
—न्यायाम्भोजपतङ्गाय .. 454 (ftn. 2)

Mādhyamika kārikā—
—प्रदीपं स्वपरात्मानौ .. 256 (ftn. 2)
—विग्रहे यः परीहारं .. 256 (ftn. 1)
Mādhyamika Sūtra—
—अनिरोधमनुत्पादम् .. 254 (ftn. 4)
—गतं न गम्यते तावत् .. 47 (ftn.)
—न सन् नासन् न सदसन् 46 (ftn. 2)
—न सम्भवः स्वभावस्य .. 118 (ftn.)
—न हि स्वभावो भावानां 46 (ftn, 2)
—यथा माया यथा स्वप्नो 47 (ftn.), 118 (ftn. 2)
—रूपादि व्यतिरेकेण .. 117 (ftn.6)
Mādhyamikā-vṛtti—
—अतो भावाभावान्तद्वयरहितत्वात् 249 (ftn. 6), 253 (ftn. 2)
—अनक्षरस्य धर्मस्य .. 255 (ftn. 2)
—आर्यं समाधिराजे चोक्तं भगवता 254 (ftn. 1)
—एवं प्रत्ययमुपादानमुपादाता 119 (ftn.)
—इदं सत्ये समुपाश्रित्य .. 254 (ftn. 3)
—यथैव गन्धर्वपुरं मरीचिका 118 (ftn. 2)
—अतः प्रतीत्य समुत्पादः सर्वधर्मनिःस्वभाव योगेन इति .. 118 (ftn. 3)
Mahābhārata—
—अवाप्युदारक्षौमाम् .. 19 (ftn. 2)
—अहमासं पण्डितको सृगालत्वं मम द्विज .. .. 36 (ftn. 3)
—औष्णिकानन्तवासांस .. 498 (ftn. 2)
—क्षीरोदधेरुत्तरतो .. 44 (ftn. 3)
—चतुर्थश्चौपनिषदो धर्मः .. 20 (ftn. 2)
—तत्रोपनिषदं तात .. 38 (ftn. 6)
—तस्मिन् यज्ञे प्रवृत्ते तु .. 39 (ftn. 4)
—तुल्यं शौचं तपोयुक्तं .. 6 (ftn. 4)
—न्यायतत्त्वात्मविज्ञान .. 39 (ftn. 2)
—न्यायतन्त्राण्यनेकानि 39 (ftn. 3), 42 (ftn. 10)
—न्यायशिक्षा चिकित्सा .. 39 (ftn. 1)
—वेदोपनिषदां वेत्ता यथावत् कृतनिश्चयः 43 (ftn. 3)

Page

—मालिनीमभितो राजन् 43 (ftn. 1)

—मेधातिथिर्महाप्राज्ञो .. 18 (ftn. 4)

—यातकानामिदं शास्त्रं .. 37 (ftn. 1)

Mahāvagga—

—चङ्करक्खस्स कायं .. 19 (ftn. 2)

Mahāvīracarita—

—इन्द्रभूतिप्रभृतीनां .. 160 (ftn. 1)

Mandhara-Stuti—

—रक्षिया काशीमठं .. 217 (ftn. 3)

Manimayūkha—

—सार्वभौमस्य गुरोः पदाब्जं 469 (ftn. 3)

Manu Saṁhitā—

—आर्षं धर्मोपदेशंच .. 38 (ftn. 1)

—त्रैविद्येभ्यस्त्रयीं विद्याद् 4 (ftn. 3), 38 (ftn. 2)

—त्रैविद्यो हैतुकस्तर्की 22 (ftn. 4), 38 (ftn. 3)

—प्रत्यक्षमनुमानंच .. 23 (ftn. 3)

—योऽवमन्येत ते मूलं .. 36 (ftn. 1)

—हिमवद्विन्ध्ययोर्मध्यं .. 304 (ftn. 1)

Mārkaṇḍeyapurāṇa—

—पृथु ताम यथा योगी .. 10 (ftn. 5)

Matsyapurāṇa—

—चमत्कारं च वक्त्रेभ्यो .. 38 (ftn. 8)

Muṇḍakopaniṣad—

—भिद्यते हृदयग्रन्थिः .. 6 (ftn. 3)

Naiṣadha-carita—

—मुक्तये यः शिलात्वाय 17 (ftn. 4), 37 (ftn. 4)

—मानुं प्रयच्छति न पक्षचतुष्टयं तां 153 (ftn. 2)

Naiṣadha-carita—Nārāyaṇa's commentary on—

—मतानां सांख्यादिषड्दर्शनानां 153 (ftn. 2)

Nañ-vāda-vyākhyā—

—शिवं प्रणम्य तत्पदान् .. 481 (ftn. 1)

Nārada-smṛti-pariśiṣṭa—

—सद्द्वादशसुवर्णास्तु .. 45 (ftn. 2)

Navadvīpa-mahimā—

—शाके त्रियुग्मविशिखक्षणदाधिनाथे 466 (ftn. 1)

Nitisāra of Kamandaka—

—आन्वीक्षिक्यात्म विज्ञानम् 4 (ftn. 3)

Nyāyabhāṣya—

—अवयवविपर्यासवचनं .. 115 (ftn. 3)

—इमास्तु चतस्रो विद्या .. 5 (ftn. 3)

—उपनयनञ्चान्तरेण न वैधर्म्यमात्रस्य वेति .. .. 119 (ftn. 1)

—तदेतन्मन्तव्यम् .. 278 (ftn. 4)

—तच नानुपलब्धेन .. 40 (ftn. 4)

—त्रिविधा चास्य शास्त्रस्य 53 (ftn. 1)

—दशदाड़िमानि षड़पूपाः 117 (ftn. 1)

—परमतमप्रतिसिद्धम् .. 24 (ftn. 3)

—प्रमाणैरर्थपरीक्षणं न्यायं 41 (ftn. 1)

—यत् पुरुषधर्मो ज्ञानम् .. 6 (ftn. 6)

—योऽक्षपादमृषिं न्यायः .. 47 (ftn. 2)

—बुद्ध्या विवेचनात्तु भावानां 120 (ftn. 1)

—सर्वेषामेकार्थ समवाये .. 42 (ftn. 8)

—सेयमान्वीक्षिकी 40 (ftn. 1), 116 (ftn. 5)

Nyāya-dīpikā—

—न याति न च तत्रास्ते .. 273 (ftn. 7)

Nyāya-kandali—

—श्रीमज्जिनप्रभविभोरधिगत्य 213 (ftn. 3)

Nyāya-karṇikā—

—इत्थं नयार्थकवचकुसुमैर्जिनेन्दु 216 (ftn. 2)

—सर्वे नया अपि विरोधभृतो मिथस्ते 216 (ftn. 3)

Nyāya-khaṇḍanakhādya—

—अभाग्यं गौड़देशस्य 218 (ftn. 1), 464 (ftn. 2)

—ऐङ्कारजापरमाप्य कवित्ववित्व 219 (ftn. 5)

—जानेहि हन्तिनियमोगदित 220 (ftn. 2)

—यत्त्वेवं सति तत्रये भावभूतस्तूल 220 (ftn. 3)

—सत्यंनैव क्षणभङ्गो वक्तव्य 220 (ftn. 1)

Nyāyakusumāñjali-viveka—

—नमः कर्मण्यधिष्ठात्रे .. 468 (ftn. 3)

Nyāya-līlāvatī—

—यदिदं चिरन्तन वैशेषिक 380 (ftn. 3)

Page

—तदियमनाम्नातता भासर्वज्ञस्य 386 (ftn. 2)
—यथाभेर्य्याकाश संयोगस्य 386 (ftn. 1)

Nyālāloka—
—कृत्वा न्यायालोकं प्रवचनरागाद् 219 (ftn. 2)
—प्रणम्य परमात्मानं .. 219 (ftn. 1)
—यदुक्तं बौद्धप्रधानेन, चित्रमेव हि संसारं .. .. 219 (ftn. 3)

Nyāyamañjarī—
—अक्षपादप्रणीतो हि .. 47 (ftn. 5)
—अत्र कीर्तिराह द्वाविंशति धा 137 (ftn. 1)
—अथोच्यते अनादिरेवैषा 26 (ftn. 2)
—एतेन रविगुप्तोऽपि .. 322 (ftn. 4)
—एतेषां धर्म कीर्तेऽपि .. 137 (ftn. 3)
—नास्त्यात्मा फलभोगमात्रमथ च स्वर्गाय चैत्यर्चनं .. .. 151 (ftn. 1)
—पञ्च चैताः कल्पना भवन्ति 129 (ftn. 3)
—यथाह नारदः सारस्तु व्यवहाराणां 44 (ftn. 1)
—यदपि उच्यते-नानिष्पन्नस्य 147 (ftn. 3)
—वादेष्वप्रजेयो जयन्त इति यः ख्यातः सतामग्रणीः .. 147 (ftn. 1)
—षट् पक्ष्यामुभयोरसिद्धिः 84 (ftn. 1)

Nyāya-praveśa-pañjikā—
—दुर्वारमारधारि कुमतदप्रभेद 210 (ftn. 2)

Nyāya-saṁkṣepa—
—न्यायवाचस्पतेः सूनो .. 480 (ftn. 4)

Nyāyasāra—
—अन्ये तु सन्देह द्वारेण .. 358 (ftn. 5)
—एकत्र तुल्यलक्षणविरुद्ध 358 (ftn. 4)
—प्रणम्य शम्भुं जगतः पतिम्पर 155 (ftn. 4), 360 (ftn. 1)

Nyāyasāra-pada-pañjikā—
—देवदेवमभिवन्द्य भास्वरं 371 (ftn. 2)

Nyāyasāra-vicāra—
—शके चतुःसप्तति संख्यके शतेः 372 (ftn. 1)

Nyāya-siddhānta-dīpa—
—इति महोपाध्याय .. 396 (ftn. 1)
—ध्वसितनरसिद्धान्तध्वान्तं 393 (ftn. 2)

Page

Nyāya-siddhānta-mañjarī-bhāṣā—
— श्रीमच्छ्रीयुतगौड़मण्डलमहीविख्यात 482 (ftn. 6)

Nyāya-sūcī-nibandha—
—न्यायसूचो निबन्धोऽसां .. 133 (ftn. 3)

Nyāya Sūtra—
—इन्द्रियार्थ सन्निकर्षोत्पन्नं 278 (ftn. 4)
—न प्रदीपप्रकाशवत्सिद्ध 25 (ftn. 7)
—न सन् नासन् न सदसद् 46 (ftn. 2)
—न स्वभावसिद्धिः 46 (ftn. 2), 118 (ftn.)
—नियमहेत्वभावाद् .. 121 (ftn. 1)
—नोत्पत्तिविनाश .. 121 (ftn. 1)
—मन्त्रायुर्वेदप्रामाण्यवच्च .. 50 (ftn. 1)
—मायागन्धर्वनगर .. 46 (ftn. 2)
—वर्तमानाभावः पततः .. 47 (ftn.)
—बुद्ध्या विवेचनात्तु .. 46 (ftn. 1)
—स्फटिकेऽपि अपरोत्पत्ते 46 (ftn. 1), 121 (ftn. 1)
—स्वप्न विषयाभिमानवत् 118 (ftn. 1)

Nyāya-sūtra-vṛtti—
—एषा मुनिवरगौतम सूत्रवृत्तिः 48 (ftn. 3)

Nyāya-vārtika—
—अनुमेयेऽथ तत्तुल्ये .. 288 (ftn. 2)
—अपरे तु मन्यन्ते प्रत्यक्षं कोऽन्यो भदन्ताद्दन्तुमर्हति .. 129 (ftn. 1)
—अतो प्रमाणाभिज्ञता भदन्तस्य 125 (ftn. 2)
—इति श्रीपरमर्षिभारद्वाज 124 (ftn. 4, 5)
—उपनयनिगमने .. 119 (ftn. 1)
—एतेन तयोः सम्बन्धिः .. 128 (ftn. 4)
—एष पन्थाः शून्यं गच्छति 124 (ftn 6)
—तथा भारं वो भिक्षवो पुग्गलो तिस्स वचनीयं .. .. 126 (ftn. 1)
—तथा सिद्धो दृष्टान्त इत्यन्ये 128 (ftn. 3)
—तदिदमन्तिमं प्रत्यक्षम् .. 511 (ftn. 2)
—तदेतस्मिन्नवयवत्रये एवं 128 (ftn. 1)
—तस्मात् स्मृत्यनुगृहीतो लिङ्ग 511 (ftn. 1)
—न चात्मानमनभ्युपगच्छता 125 (ftn. 3)
—यदक्षपाद प्रतिमाः 115 (ftn. 1), 123 (ftn. 1)

Page

—यदक्षपादःप्रवरो मुनीनां 47 (ftn. 3), 125 (ftn. 1), 273 (ftn. 3)

—यदपि वादविधौ .. 124 (ftn. 1)

—लिङ्गलिङ्गीसम्बन्ध .. 510 (ftn. 2)

—स्मृत्यनुमानदित्वौ लिङ्ग परामर्शोऽनुमानम् 130 (ftn. 1)

Nyāya-vārtika-tātparya-ṭikā—

—यच्च सुबन्धुना प्रतिज्ञादयः 128 (ftn. 2)

—यत्र भगवता अक्षपादेन 47 (ftn. 4), 115 (ftn. 2)

—अस्माभिः

—आप्तवाक्याविसंवादः .. 288 (ftn. 1)

—आहुः असाधनाङ्गवचनम् 136 (ftn. 2)

—तस्माद् यदुक्तं कीर्तिना 137 (ftn. 2)

—त्रिलोचन गुरून्नीतमार्गानु 134 (ftn. 2), 137 (ftn. 5)

—न सुखादिप्रमेयं वा .. 280 (ftn. 1)

—नित्यानित्यप्रयत्नोत्तममध्यम 285 (ftn. 1)

—प्रमेयकृतकानित्यकृत .. 285 (ftn.)

—यथाहुः निष्प्रकारा: । निर्विकल्पकबोधेन .. .. 138 (ftn. 1)

—यद्यपि भाष्यकृताकृतव्युत्पादनम् 133 (ftn. 1)

—व्यवसायात्मकं पदं साक्षात् 137 (ftn. 4)

—संप्रति दिग्नागस्य लक्षणम् 129 (ftn. 2)

—साध्येनानुमानात् कार्य .. 136 (ftn.)

Nyāya-vārtika-tātparya-ṭikā-pariśuddhi—

—मातः सरस्वति पुनः पुनरेष नत्वा 141 (ftn. 1)

Nyāyāvatāra—

—अत्र व्याप्तिव साध्यस्य .. 268 (ftn. 2)

—आप्तोपज्ञमनुल्लङ्घ्य .. 175 (ftn. 1)

—साध्याभ्युपगमः पक्षः .. 507 (ftn.)

—सनिश्चयवदन्येषां .. 286 (ftn. 2)

Nyāyāvatāra-ṭippana—

—ननु चार्थक्रिया सामान्यमेव 211 (ftn. 3)

Nyāyāvatāra-vivṛti—

—अवयवापेक्षया अवयवमध्यमोत्कृष्टा 166 (ftn. 1)

—प्रमाणेत्यादि अनेन च .. 206 (ftn. 6)

Nyāya-vindu—

—उत्क्रमभेदेन पुनर्विशेषेण 318 (ftn. 1)

—तत्र च तृतीयोऽपि .. 316 (ftn. 1)

—त्रिरूपे हेतुरुक्तः । तावतैव 317 (ftn. 2)

—त्रीण्येव च लिङ्गानि .. 508 (ftn. 3)

—त्रैरूप्यं पुनर्लिङ्गस्य .. 202 (ftn. 1)

—विरुद्धाव्यभिचारी अपि .. 358 (ftn. 3)

—स्वयमिति वादिना .. 124 (ftn. 2)

Nyāya-vindu-ṭikā—

—अयं च विरुद्ध आचार्य 316 (ftn. 1)

—अयमपि जाति असमग्रधाम 330 (ftn. 1)

—विरुद्धाव्यभिचार्यपि .. 316 (ftn. 3)

Padārtha-candra—

—श्रीचन्द्रसिंह नृपतेर्दयिता 460 (ftn. 1)

Padārtha-tattva-vivecana-prakāśa—

—इति श्रीरामभद्र सार्वभौम 469 (ftn. 2)

Padārtha-viveka ṭikā—

—अभेदभावनोद्रेकाद् .. 486 (ftn.)

—राज्ञः श्रीजयसिंहस्य .. 486 (ftn.)

Padmapurāṇa—

—अङ्गानि चतुरो वेदान् .. 38 (ftn. 7)

—कणादेन तु संप्रोक्तं 17 (ftn. 1), 48 (ftn. 1)

Pañcasiddhāntikā—

—सप्ताश्विवेदसंख्यं शककालम 174 (ftn. 1)

Pāṇḍavapurāṇa—

—अकलङ्कोऽकलङ्कः स .. 186 (ftn. 1)

—समन्तभद्रो भद्रार्थो .. 182 (ftn. 4)

Pāṇini's Aṣṭādhyāyī—

—अध्यायन्यायोद्याव संहाराश्च 41 (ftn. 4)

—कठचरकाल्लुक् .. 25 (ftn. 2)

—छन्दसि पुनर्वसोरेकवचनम् 11 (ftn. 4)

—क्रतुकथकादि सूत्रान्तात् ठक् 41 (ftn 4)

Pañjikā on Syādvāda-ratnākarāvatārikā—

—स्याद्वादरत्नाकर इत्यस्मि 198 (ftn. 4)

Parāśara Saṁhitā—

—कणादितायधो येऽन्ये .. 22 (ftn. 5)

Parikṣāmukham saṭikam—

—वैजेय प्रियपुत्रस्य .. 198 (ftn. 2)

Page

Parīkṣāmukha Sūtra—
—परीक्षामुखमादर्श .. 193 (ftn. 2)
—सह क्रमभाव नियमो .. 189 (ftn. 2)
—साधनात् साध्य विज्ञानम 189 (ftn. 1)
—साध्याविनाभाविलेन .. 193 (ftn. 1)

Parivāra—
—चक्षीरसो साक्यमुनि .. 19 (ftn. 2)

Pārśvanātha-carita—
—तर्कग्रन्थविचारदुर्गमवनो विजय श्रीसंपदं संव्यधात् .. 197 (ftn. 3)
—पुंसां विग्रहजं विकारमखिलं शौर्य-दास्यमशिश्रियत् .. 196 (ftn. 2)
—षड्नितिकीलनलना विलास 207 (ftn. 1)

Peterson's Report V—
—इति धर्मोत्तर टिप्पनके .. 195 (ftn. 2)
—संवत् १२३१ वर्षे भाद्रपद शुदि 195 (ftn. 2)

Piṅgala prakāśikā—
—विद्यामिवासस्थलो: 392 (ftn. 2), 480 (ftn. 2)

Prabhāvakacar—
—चन्द्राष्टशिववर्षेऽत्र .. 199 (ftn. 1)
—शववेदेश्वरे वर्षे .. 206 (ftn. 1)
—शिखिवेदशिवे जन्म दीक्षा श्रीदेव-सूरय: .. .. 200 (ftn. 2)

Pramāṇa-mīmāṁsā—
—वाचकमुख्य विरचितानि 186 (ftn. 2), 205 (ftn. 2)

Pramāna - naya - tattvālokālankāra—
—अन्यथानुपपत्त्येकलक्षणं हेतोः .. 202 (ftn. 3)
—विविधं साधनमभिधायैव 202 (ftn. 2)
—मन्दमतींस्तु व्युत्पादयितुं 203 (ftn. 1)

Pramāṇasamuccaya—
—आत्मेन्द्रियमनोऽर्थ सन्निकर्षाद् 279 (ftn. 1)
—कार्यतान्यतलेशेन यत् .. 135 (ftn. 4)
—केचिद् धर्मान्तरं मेयं धर्मिणा गमयिष्यति .. 281 (ftn. 1)
—तत्र यः सन् सजातीये .. 283 (ftn. 3)
—प्रत्यक्षमनुमानञ्च .. 277 (ftn.)

—प्रत्यक्षं कल्पनापोढ़ .. 277 (ftn. 1)
—श्वपचे सम्भवन् द्वेधा .. 283 (ftn. 1)
—सामान्य विशेषापेक्षञ्च .. 279 (ftn. 1)
—स्वरूपेणैव निर्देश्य .. 282 (ftn. 2)

Pramāṇa-vārtika-kārikā—
—भेदश्च भ्रान्तिविज्ञानै: .. 306 (ftn. 7)

Pramāṇa-viniścaya—
—नान्योऽनुभाव्यो बुद्ध्यास्ति भेदवानिव लक्ष्यते .. .. 308 (ftn. 3)

Prameya-kamala-martanda—
—तथा अर्थापत्तिरपि प्रमाणान्तरं 194 (ftn. 2)
—रजोजुषे जन्मनि सत्त्ववृत्तये 194 (ftn. 2)

Prameya-ratnakosa—
—प्रमेयरत्नकोशोऽयं .. 206 (ftn. 4)

Prameya-ratnamālā—
—अकलङ्कवचोऽम्भोधे: .. 188 (ftn. 6)

Prasanna Rāghava—
—येषां कोमलकान्तकौशलकला 455 (ftn. 4)

Praśastapāda-Bhāṣya—
—अक्षाणि इन्द्रियाणि .. 279 (ftn. 1)
—पञ्चावयवेन वाक्येन .. 282 (ftn. 1)
—सामान्यविशेष द्रव्यगुण .. 279 (ftn. 1)

Praśasti of Pāṇḍava-caritra—
—शैशवेऽभ्यस्तनां तर्क: .. 211 (ftn. 2)

Pratimā Nāṭaka—
—भोः काश्यपगोत्रोऽस्मि .. 18 (ftn. 2)

Pratyakṣāloka—
—शुभमस्तु श्रीरस्तु शकाब्दा 407 (ftn. 3), 455 (ftn. 1)

Rāmāyaṇa—
—ऐतिह्यमनुमानञ्च .. 23 (ftn. 2)
—धर्मशास्त्रेषु मुख्येषु .. 36 (ftn. 2)
—मिथिलोपवने तत्र राजपुत्र महायशा: 17 (ftn. 6)
—न नास्ति परमित्येतत् .. 9 (ftn. 3)

Ratnākarāvatārikā-tippana
—तेनान्यापोहविषयाः प्रोक्ताः 198 (ftn. 1), 213 (ftn. 5)
—रत्नाकरावतारिकावरटिप्पन तत् 213 (ftn. 6)

Page

Ratnāvalī—
—न चाभावोऽपि निर्वाणं 255 (ftn. 1)

Ratnāvatārikā—
—तथा च अयमः स्वरूपादुद्भवत् 147 (ftn. 5)

Rock Edicts on the ruined walls of the ancient part of Simraon—
—मन्देन्दुबिन्दुविधुमम्मितशाकवर्षे 521 (ftn. 2)

Śabdāloka—
—पितुर्ज्ञानपतेरत्र व्याख्यान 486 (ftn.)
—सतामस्मिन् गदने प्रबन्धे 485 (ftn. 4)

Śabdaśaktiprakāśikā—
—इति पुनर्न्यायरत्नस्ये .. 469 (ftn. 4)

Ṣaḍdarśana-samuccaya—
—यथादौ नैयायिकानां नित्यबुद्धि समाश्रयः .. .. 154 (ftn. 2)
—अयमाचार्यरचितो .. 147 (ftn. 6)
—जैनं सांख्यं जैमिनियं .. 153 (ftn. 1)
—प्रत्यक्षं कल्पनापोढम् .. 209 (ftn. 1)
—भासर्वज्ञो न्यायसारतर्के 357 (ftn. 5)
—बौद्धं नैयायिकं सांख्यं .. 152 (ftn. 2)

Ṣaḍdarśana-samuccaya-vṛtti—
—एषां तर्कग्रन्थन्यायसूत्र 151 (ftn. 2, 3)

Ṣaḍdarśana-vṛtti—
—भासर्वज्ञप्रणीते न्यायसारे 357 (ftn. 4)

Syādvāda-ratnākara—
—यदत्र शक्तिसंसिद्धौ .. 147 (ftn. 6)

Sāmānya-dūṣaṇa-dikprasārikā—
—व्यापकनित्यमेकत्र .. 333 (ftn. 3)

Sāṁkhya-bhāṣya—
—एकमेवाद्वितीयं तत्व .. 244 (ftn. 1)

Sāṁgatva-prakāśa—
—तथा श्लोकवार्तिके विद्यानन्दापरः 188 (ftn. 1)

Saptapadārthī—
—नन्वेवं शास्त्रप्रकरणयोः .. 356 (ftn. 1)

Sarvadarśanasaṁgraha—
—तदुक्तं ज्ञानश्रिया यत् सत् तत् क्षणिकं यथा .. .. 341 (ftn. 3)
—तार्किकरक्षायां च धर्मस्य तदतद्रूप 371 (ftn. 2)

Page

—ननु प्रमाणादि पदार्थ षोडशके ... (ftn. 2)
—न याति न च तत्रासीद् 274 (ftn.)
—श्रीमन्न्यायपदुग्धाब्धि .. 397 (ftn. 3)
—श्रीशार्ङ्गपाणितनयं .. 398 (ftn. 1)
—समासमाविनाभावः .. 399 (ftn. 1)

Saṭīka Utpāda-siddhi-prakaraṇa—
—द्वादशवर्षशतेषु श्रीविक्रमतो 211 (ftn. 4)

(A) Saying—
—शङ्करवाचस्पत्योः .. 455 (ftn. 3)

Siddha-Hema-Śabdānuśāsana-bṛhat-ṭikā—
—अनुमस्रवादिनं तार्किकाः 195 (ftn. 4)

Siddha-jayantī-carita-ṭikā—
—यत्प्रज्ञाप्रसरेऽतिशायिनि तथा प्रालेय शैलोज्ज्वले .. 160 (ftn. 3)

Skandapurāṇa—
—गौतमः स्वेन तर्केण 17 (ftn. 2), 48 (ftn. 2), 37 (ftn. 3)

Ślokavārtika—
—तमानुमानमेवेदं .. 287 (ftn. 3)
—शब्दानुमानयोरैक्यं नैकान्त्यविषयाश्रयात् .. .. 288 (ftn.)

Ślokavārtika-ṭikā—
—परार्थानुमानम् .. 282 (ftn. 1)

Śrāddha-prati-kramaṇa-sūtra-vṛtti—
—विख्याततपेत्याख्या जगति इत्तिमिमामकृत कृतिदुष्ट .. 214 (ftn. 2)

Sragdharā-stotra-ṭikā—
—श्रीमद्विक्रमशीलदेवमहाविहारीय 519 (ftn. 3)

Sthānāṅga Sūtra—
—चउव्विहे णाए पन्नत्ते .. 163 (ftn. 1)
—छव्विहे विवादे पन्नत्ते .. 163 (ftn. 2)
—दसविहे दोसे पन्नत्ते .. 163 (ftn. 3)
—पमाणे चउव्विहे पन्नत्ते .. 161 (ftn. 5)

Subodhinī—
—इति नवद्वीपीय महामहोपाध्याय 480 (ftn. 3)
—गिरिमिव मुकमिव .. 480 (ftn. 3)

Page

Sukhabodhikā-ṭīkā to Kalpa sūtra—
—वलदिपुरम्मि नयरे . 172 (ftn. 1)

Sūkti-muktāvalī—
—कर्त्तुं त्रिलोचनादन्यः .. 134 (ftn. 5)

Suśruta Saṁhitā—
—असद्वादिप्रयुक्तानां .. 24 (ftn. 4)
—द्वात्रिंशद् युक्तयो .. 24 (ftn. 2)

Sūtrakṛtāṅga—
—सस्सिस्सभावं न गिरा गरीए सउणी-पञ्जरं जहा .. 162 (ftn. 2)

Sūtrakṛtāṅga-niryukti—
—अस्यिसय किरियाणं .. 167 (ftn. 1)

Śvetāśvataropaniṣad—
—अजामेकां लोहितशुक्लकृष्णां 10 (ftn. 3)
—ऋषिं प्रसूतं कपिलं .. 9 (ftn. 6)

Syādvādamañjarī—
—श्रीमल्लिषेण सूरिभिरकारि 212 (ftn. 4)

Syādvāda-ratnākarā·vatārikā—
—अत्र धर्मान्तरानुसारी प्राह 329 (ftn. 4)
—अथैव अथचतुरः पुनराह 331 (ftn. 7)
—पक्षादिप्रयुक्तयस्य पञ्चप्राह्या: 166 (ftn. 1)
—प्रमाणे च प्रमेये च .. 211 (ftn. 5)

Taittirīya Āraṇyaka—
—स्मृतिः प्रत्यक्षमैतिह्यम् .. 23 (ftn. 1

Tarkabhāṣā—
—ऐन्द्रहन्दनतं नत्वा .. 218 (ftn. 4)
—पूर्वं न्यायविशारदत्व विरुद्धं 217 (ftn. 4)

Tarkabhāṣā-prakāśa—
—विजय श्रीतनुजन्मा तन्यते पद्मनाभेन 381 (ftn. 1)

Tarkakaumudī—
—यथा सा मणिकर्णिका .. 395 (ftn. 1)

Tarkāmṛta—
—श्रीविश्वेश्वरपादाम्बुजं .. 394 (ftn. 1)

Tarkasaṁgraha—
—तपोमात्सचिते क्षणे .. 388 (ftn. 3)
—निधाय हृदि विश्वेशं .. 388 (ftn. 4)
—प्रकृती शोभयात्मादि क्रियते तर्कसंग्रहः 234 (ftn. 3)

Tārkikarakṣā—
—अविसंवादि विज्ञानमिति 376 (ftn. 1), 375 (ftn. 1)
—आलोच्य दुस्तरगभीरतरान् प्रबन्धान् 373 (ftn. 2)
—एते सम्बन्धिनः सर्वे .. 379 (ftn. 2)
—तथा च स्मरन्ति, रागद्वेषविनिर्मुक्ताः 379 (ftn. 1)
—चौमुदाहरणान्तान् वा .. 377 (ftn. 1)
—निरुपाधिकसाध्यसम्बन्ध 378 (ftn. 1)
—मोक्षे साक्षादनङ्गत्वाद् .. 375 (ftn. 1)
—यथाहुः तन्मे प्रमाणं शिवः 374 (ftn. 1)
—वादे कथावसानस्य .. 379 (ftn. 3)
—विचारविषयो नाना .. 378 (ftn. 2)
—व्याप्तिग्रहणसापेक्षं .. 376 (ftn. 2)
—व्याप्ति सम्बन्धो निरुपाधिकः 376 (ftn. 3)
—साधनाव्यापकाः साध्य .. 376 (ftn. 4)
—सौगताश्च तादात्म्यतदुत्पत्तिभ्यां 376 (ftn. 5)

Tattvacintāmaṇi—
—गुणातीतोऽपीशस्त्रिगुणसचिव श्रीतत्त्वचिन्तामणिम् .. 407 (ftn. 4)
—सन्निकर्षसाध्यधर्मत्वम् .. 507 (ftn. 1)

Tattvacintāmaṇi-darpaṇam—
—अधीत्य निखिलं शास्त्रम् 485 (ftn. 2)
—अधीत्य यच्चिदत्तेन .. 457 (ftn. 1)
—इति श्रीसोदरपुरकुलसमुद्भूत 457 (ftn. 3)
—तत्र कण्ठरमाणिक्य ग्राम 485 (ftn. 3)
—श्रीदेवदत्ततनयो .. 457 (ftn. 2)

Tattvacintāmaṇi-rahasya—
—न्यायाम्बुधिकृतासेतुं .. 467 (ftn. 3)

Tattvacintāmaṇi-ṭīkā—
—जयदेव गुरोर्वाचि .. 456 (ftn. 4)

Tattvacintāmaṇyāloka—
—अधीत्य जयदेवेन .. 455 (ftn. 2)

Tattvārthādhigama Sūtra—
—अनुमानोपमानागमार्थापत्ति 169 (ftn. 2)
—चतुर्विधमित्येके .. 170 (ftn.)

Page

—नैगमसंग्रह व्यवहारर्जु सूत्रशब्दा 170 (ftn. 2)

—न्यग्रोधिका प्रसृतेन विस्तरता स्वहस्त-माखातिना ग्राह्यम् .. 168 (ftn. 3)

—यथार्थाभिधानं शब्द .. 171 (ftn. 1)

—यथा वा प्रत्यक्षानुमानोपमाना..प्रवचनैः 170 (ftn.)

Tattvārtha ṭikā—

—तत् पादरजोऽवयवः .. 182 (ftn. 2)

Triloka Sāra—

—पञ्चवस्य वस पञ्चमास .. 159 (ftn. 1)

Tri-sūtrī (nibandha-vyākhyā)

—प्रकाशदर्पणोद्योत .. 458 (ftn. 2)

Udānaṁ—

—याव सम्मासम्बुद्धा लोके 229 (ftn. 2)

Upadeśa mālā ṭikā—

—शिष्यः श्रीमुनिचन्द्र सूरिगुरुभि इत्ति-विशेषार्थिनाम् .. 199 (ftn. 2)

Upadeśa mālā viśeṣa Vṛtti—

—बाल्यादपूर्वाग्रमपि छिद्रनाशः 206 (ftn. 4)

Upadeśa mālā vṛtti—

—श्रीरत्नप्रभ सूरिभिः प्राभृते 212 (ftn. 1)

Upāsakādhyayana—

—येनाज्ञानतमो विनाश्य निखिलं भव्यात्मचेतोगतं .. 183 (ftn. 2)

Page

Uttarādhyayana bṛhadvṛtti—

—यस्याभूद्गुरुरागमे गुणनिधिः 197 (ftn. 4)

Vaiśeṣika Sūtra—

—आत्मेन्द्रियमनोऽर्थ सन्निकर्षात् 279 (ftn. 1)

Vaiśeṣika Sūtropaskāra—

—याभ्यां वैशेषिके तन्त्रे .. 458 (ftn. 4)

Vākyapadīya—

—न सोऽस्ति प्रत्ययो लोके 187 (ftn. 3)

Vāsava datta—

—न्यायस्थितिमिवोद्योतकर 123 (ftn. 2)

Vedānta Sūtra—

—अपरिग्रहाच्चात्यन्तमनपेक्षा 37 (ftn. 2)

Vicāra sāra prakaraṇa—

—पंचेव य च वरिससए .. 173 (ftn. 2)

Viṣṇu purāṇa—

—तस्माल्लोकेषु ते मूढ .. 44 (ftn. 2)

—वार्षैर्वेदयुतैः सरम्भुनयनैः 456 (ftn. 3)

Vṛhatsvayambhū purāṇa—

—वाराणस्यां नगर्यां च .. 519 (ftn. 4)

Yajñavalka Saṁhitā—

—अयन्तु परमो धर्मो .. 0 (ftn. 2)

—चत्वारो वेद धर्मज्ञाः .. 22 (ftn 6)

—पुराणन्यायमीमांसा .. 38 (ftn. 5)

INDEX OF SANSKRIT TERMS.

Page

Akevala jñāna (defective knowledge) .. .. 161 (ftn. 5[2])
Akṛtabhyāgama (gain of unmerited action) .. 99, 101
Akṣapāda darśana (the philosophy of Akṣapāda) .. 48
Akhyāti (non-manifestation) .. 134
Agni (fire god) 19
Aṅkābhidhāna (distinctionary of numbers) .. 16 (ftn. 1)
Ajīva (soul-less) 168
Aja-bhāga (the unborn part) .. 2
Ajñāna (ignorance) .. 84, 269
Anuloma sambhāṣā (congenial debate) 29
Anulomaitta (propitiating the authority) 163
Anuvāda (re-inculcation) .. 108[2]
Atikrāntāvekṣaṇa (retrospection) 25
Aticchandas (a kind of metre) .. 15
Ativyāpti (being too wide) .. 403
Atīta kāla (mistimed) 35
Atīta vākya (irrelevant talk) .. 264
Atideśa (extended application) .. 25
Attā (soul) .. 127 (ftn.)
Atyantābhāva (absolute negation) 97 (ftn. 1), 189, 203, 394
Adṛṣta (desert) 143[2], 143 (ftn. 1)[2], 144
Adoṣodbhāvana (allegation of an unmerited action) 136
Adrikalpa (like a rock) .. 273
Adharma (demerit) .. 371, 389
Adhika (saying too much) 84, 261, 269
Adhikaraṇa (subject) 25
Adhikaraṇa (hypothetical dogma) 59
Adhikaraṇa (cases for settlement) 229[2]
Adhikaraṇa (locus) 415
Adhikaraṇa - samatha - dhamma (rules for the settlement of cases) 230[2]

Page

Adhikaraṇa siddhānta (conclusion accepted hypothetically) .. 259
Adhicca-samuppannika (fortuitous originists) 229
Adhyātma vidyā (spiritual science) 4
Adhvaryu (priest) 14
Anadhyavasāya (uncertainty) .. 201
Anadhyavasita or Anupasaṁhāra (non-tried) 366
Ananubhāṣaṇa (silence) 84, 261, 269
Ananvaya (unconnected) 179, 297, 314
Ananuyojya (non-censurable) .. 33
Anāgatāvekṣaṇa (anticipation) .. 25
Anāpanna (not guilty) .. 231
Anārṣa (non-saintly) 359
Anitya (non-eternal) .. 284 285[4]
Antya-sama (balancing the non-eternal) 67
Anindriya-nibandhana (not through sense-organs) .. 201
Anirvacanīya-khyāti (manifestation of the undefinable) .. 189
Aniścita (uncertain) 293
Anugata dharma (common property) 4032
Anugama (generalisation) 403 429
Anutpatti-sama (balancing the non-produced) .. 67, 268 289.
Anupalambha (voidness of the world) 146
Anupalabdhi (imperceptible) 190, 203, 258, 281, 311, 332, 453, 509
Anupalabdhi-sama (balancing the non-perception) 67
Anupalabdhi-hetu (relation of negation) 318
Anupalabhya pramānya-vāda (invalidity of non-perception) .. 414
Anupasaṁhāri (non-exclusiveness) 438
Anubhava (experience) 389[3], 395

Page

Anubhūti (apprehension) .. 393[2]

Anumata (assent) 25

Anumāna (inference) 23[3], 27[2], 28, 32, 33, 50, 54, 130, 162[3], 169, 175[2], 189, 192, 201, 209 (ftn. 1), 215, 219, 221, 229, 310, 259, 264, 265, 266, 259, 277, 280, 298, 348, 358, 359, 360, 361[2], 376[2], 383, 387[2], 389, 390, 393[3], 394[2], 395, 398, 407 440

Anumāna khaṇḍa (chapter on inference) 419

Anumāna parikṣā (examination of inference) 327

Anumānā bhāsa (semblance of inference) 298

Anumiti (inferential knowledge) 384, 389[2], 397, 419, 435, 510

Anumiti nirūpaṇa (determination of inferential knowledge) .. 419

Anumeya (inferred) 282

Anuyoga (interrogation) 33, 234

Anuyogī (a thing in a particular relation to another) .. .. 403[3]

Anuyogitā (quality of being in a particular relation) 403

Anuyojya (censurable) 33

Anuloma (regular form) 235

Anubandha (adjunct) 27

Anuvādādhikaraṇa (a case in which one party accuses another party of the violation of a rule of good conduct) 229

Anuvijjaka (judge or umpire) .. 231[2]

Anuvyavasāya (self-consciousness) 418, 445, 471, 472, 473

Anuvyavasāya vāda (doctrine of self-consciousness) 418

Anuṣṭubh (a kind of metre) .. 275

Anekānta (uncertain) 25

Anaikānta (erratic) 438

Anaikāntika (uncertain) 178, 313, 365

Antarvyāpti (intrinsic inseparable connection 177, 178, 202, 268 (ftn. 2)

Andhakāra-vipratipatti (controversy on darkness) 397

Page

Anyathākhyāti (caverse manifestation) 139, 140

Anyathākhyāti (invalid knowledge) .. .. .. 409[3]

Anyathāsiddhi (conditionality) 399 (ftn. 1), 403

Anyamata parīkṣā (examination of contemporaneous philosophical doctrines) .. 49, 51, 497

Anyāpoha (mutual non-existence) 184

Anyendriyātītārtha - darśana - puruṣa-parīkṣā (examination of the soul which sees things beyond the range of senses) 327

Anyonyābhāva or Anyāpoha (mutual non-existence) 184, 394

Anvaya (affirmation) 361

Anvaya-vyatirekī (affirmative-negative) 130, 361

Anvaya-vyatirekī anumāṇa (affirmative-negative inference) .. 434

Anvaya-vyāpti (affirmative inseparable connection) 361

Anvayī udāharaṇa (homogeneous example) 259

Anvayī (exclusively affirmative) 130, 191, 86[2], 437

Anvita-śakti-vādimata (opinion of those who hold the power of connected words) 397

Anvitābhidhāna-vāda (expression of the connected) 147

Ap (water) .. .. 393[2]

Apakarṣa-sama (balancing the deficit) 67, 261

Apadeśa (specification) .. 25

Apara ātmā (individual soul) .. 371

Apavarga (exception) 25, 375, 382

Apavarga nirūpaṇa (nature of emancipation) 397

Apasiddhānta (deviating from the tenet) 84, 269

Apārthaka (incoherent) 84, 117, 150, 269, 261

Apūrva vādaḥ (doctrine of merit and demerit) 449

Page

Apekṣā (inter-relation) 117, 118 (ftn. 3)
Apoha (negation of the opposite) 132[2], 143[2], 146, 149, 276, 287, 339[2], 345
Apratipatti (not understanding an argument) 136
Apratibhā (non-ingenuity) 84, 261. 269
Apratibhāna (non-ingenuity) .. 137
Apradarśita vyatireka (fallacy of separation unshown) .. 180
Apradarśitānvaya (fallacy of connection unshown) .. 179, 315
Apramā (error) 138, 389, 395[2], 409[2], 410
Aprayojaka (inadmissible) 399 (ftn. 1)[2]
Aprāpta kāla (inopportune) 65, 84, 261, 269
Aprāpti sama (balancing the mutual absence) 67, 261, 268, 288
Abādhita viṣayatvam (object of the sign not being incompatible) 378
Abhāva (non-existence) 56, 95, 97, 97 (ftn. 1), 170, 184[2], 203, 219, 370, 386, 389[2], 393[2], 394[3], 395, 397, 402, 415
Abhāva vāda (doctrine of non-existence) 415
Abhinibodha or Mati (knowledge of existing things acquired through the senses and the mind) 161 (ftn. 5)
Abhihitānvaya vāda (connection of the expressed) 147
Abhyanujñā (admission) .. 35
Abhyupagama (implied dogma) .. 39
Abhyupagama siddhānta (conclusion assumed) 259
Abhrānta (devoid of error) .. 310
Amūḍha-vinaya (settlement for the insane) 230
Ayukta (erroneous) 359
Ayogi-pratyakṣa (ordinary perception) 360
Artha (object) .. 373, 375, 382
Artha vāda (description) .. 108[2]
Arthasya smaraṇam (recollection of a thing) 444

Page

Arthāntara (shifting the topic) 35, 84, 269
Arthāpatti (presumption) 25, 33, 56, 95, 370, 387, 435[2], 453
Arthāpatti sama (balancing the presumption) .. 67, 269, 289
Arhat (one freed from all faults or obstructions) 201
Alaukika pratyakṣa (transcendental perception) 412
Avagraha (distinguishing) 201, 201 (ftn. 1)
Avacchinna (determined) .. 404
Avacchedaka (that which determines) 404
Avadhi (knowledge of things beyond the range of perception) 161 (ftn. 5), 169 (ftn. 1)
Avadhi jñāna (limited knowledge) 201
Avayava (member of the syllogism) 49, 51, 52, 60, 105, 203, 356, 359[2], 377[3], 258[2], 333, 497, 502[3], 374, 375, 381, 436[2], 487 (ftn. 1)
Avayavin (whole) .. 105, 338
Avarṇya sama (balancing the unquestionable) 67, 261, 268, 289
Avasarpaṇī kāla (period of involution) 158
Avāya (arriving at) 201
Avijñātārtha (the unintelligible) 84, 261, 269
Avidyā (ignorance) .. 371, 387[2]
Avinābhāva (pervasion) 189, 361, 376[2], 400, 509
Aviśeṣa sama (balancing the non-difference) .. 67, 268
Avyatireki (unseparated) .. 180
Avyaya (indeclinable) 110 (ftn. 1)
Avyayī-bhāva (indeclinable compound) 452
Avyāpti (non-pervasive) .. 369
Avyāpti (being too narrow) .. 404
Avyāptyabhidhāna (non-pervasive example) 369

Page

Asakkaittā (taking some time in making oneself ready) .. 163
Asiddha (unproved) 362
Asti (it is existence) 184
Aśvinīkumāras (the twin gods) .. 14
Asat (absent) .. .. 284[6]
Asat khyāti (manifestation of the unreal) 139
Asataḥ sajjāyate (effect springs up from nothing) 140
Asat pratipakṣatvam (there being no counterbalancing sign) .. 378
Asamavāyi kāraṇa (non-material cause) 383, 390
Asādhanāṅga vacana (improper reason) 136
Asādhāraṇa (not general) 294, 438
Asiddha (unproved) 178, 293, 313, 438, 439[2]
Asiddhi (absence of proof) .. 438
Asu (breath, life) 2
Ahaṁ (ego) 245
Ahaṁkāra (ego) .. 245 (ftn. 2)[2]
Ahetu (fallacy) .. 34, 51[2]
Ahetu sama (balancing the non-reason) 67, 261, 268

Ākāṅkṣā (expectancy) .. 447
Ākāṅkṣā vādaḥ (expectancy) .. 447
Ākāśa (ether) 105, 219, 265
Ākṣepa (refutation) 43
Ākhyāta (verbal suffix) 447, 453
Ākhyātavāda (doctrine of verbal suffix) 453
Āgama (verbal testimony) 162, 170, 189, 192[2], 201, 203, 215, 219, 221, 259, 266, 264, 265, 358, 359, 360, 370[2], 370 (ftn. 1)
Āgamākhya pramāṇa nirṇaya (determination of the nature of valid knowledge derived from verbal testimony) 200
Āgamābhāsa (fallacy of verbal testimony) 193
Ācāra (practice) 249
Ācārya (head of the church) .. 223

Page

Ātman (soul) .. 2, 3, 278
Ātma-khyāti (manifestation of the soul) 138
Ātma-vidyā (the science of soul) 4[8]
Ātma sambandha (concerning one's self) 264
Ātmā (soul) 4, 5, 146, 204, 126[2], 127 (ftn.)[2], 219[2], 371[2], 375[2], 382, 386, 393[3], 394
Ādityas (a group of gods) .. 15
Ādeśa (substitution) 111
Ādheya śakti (power of the content) 397
Ānvīkṣikī (the science of logic) 1, 4[2], 38, 39, 40[2], 152
Ānvīkṣikī vidyā (the science of logic) .. .. 49, 50[2]
Āpattādhikaraṇa (case in which a monk has actually transgressed an established rule of good conduct) 229
Āpanno (guilty) 231
Āpta vākya (reliable assertion) ... 450
Āptopadeśa (reliable assertion) 27, 28, 51
Ābhāsa (fallacy) .. 188, 192, 203
Ārya (reliable person) 56
Āryas (the civilised) .. 107
Ārṣa (saintly) 359
Ālambana (objects of thought) .. 322
Ālaya (ego) 245 (ftn. 2)[4]
Ālaya vijñāna (the abiding cognition, or ego) 146, 245, 245 (ftn. 1)
Āśaṅkā (questioning the validity of the instance) 167
Āśaṅkā pratiṣedha (meeting the question) 167
Āśraya-hīna (supportless) .. 369[2]
Āśrayāsiddha (unproved in respect of the abode) .. 363, 439
Āśrayaika deśāsiddha (unproved in respect of a part of the abode) 363
Āsattiḥ (contiguity) .. .. 447[2]
Āsrava (action) 168
Āsana (seat) 233

Page

Āharaṇa (complete example) 163, 221, 234
Āharaṇa-taddeśa (limited example) 163[2]
Āhnika (diurnal portion) .. 46
Itaretara (mutually aggregative compound) 452
Itaretarābhāva (mutual non-existence) 203
Indra (lord of gods) 142
Indriya (senses) .. 1, 375, 382
Indriya nibandhana (through sense-organs) 201
Indriya parīkṣā (examination of the sense-organs) 326
Iṣṭa-vighāta-kṛtviruddha (implied contradiction) 315
Isvara (God) .. 122, 143, 155
Iśvara parīkṣā (examination of God) .. .. 325 (ftn.)
Iśvara bhaṅga (non-existence of God) 150
Iśvarānumānam (inference of God) 442
Īhā (inquiring) 201
Ukthādi-gaṇa (a group of words beginning with Uktha) 41, 41 (ftn. 5)
Ucchanna-pracchannavāda (doctrine of the sound as destroyed or concealed) 448
Uccheda-vāda (annihilationism) .. 228
Utukkhāna (naming the season) .. 233
Utkarṣa sama (balancing the excess) 67, 261
Uttara (rejoinder) .. 27, 32, 51
Uttara (posterior) .. 190, 191[2]
Uttara-pakṣa (reply) 25
Uttara-vahinī (flowing towards the north) .. .. 519 (ftn. 6)
Utpatti (origination) 219
Utsarpaṇī kāla (period of evolution) 158
Udaka (water) 233
Udāharaṇa (example) 60, 119, 121, 191, 221, 259, 264[2], 266, 268, 359, 368, 437[2], 502[3], 504[2]

Page

Udāharaṇābhāsa (fallacious example) 368
Uddeśa (enunciation) .. 25, 53
Uddhāra (citation) 25
Upadeśa (instruction) .. 25
Upanaya (application) 27, 32, 60, 119[2], 119 (ftn. 1), 120, 122, 176, 191, 202, 203, 234, 236, 266, 370, 437[2], 437 (ftn. 1), 501, 502, 510
Upanyāsopanaya (anecdote used as an example) 163
Upapatti sama (balancing the demonstration) .. 67, 268
Upamāna (comparison) 25, 50, 51, 54, 125, 162, 170, 221, 259, 265, 266, 268, 287, 359, 384[2], 387[2], 389, 393[2], 394[2], 407, 443, 450
Upamāna-khaṇḍa (section of comparison) 443
Upamiti (comparative knowledge) 389[2], 443
Upaniṣad kalpita ātma parīkṣā (examination of the Upaniṣad-doctrine of the soul) .. 326
Upalabdhi (perception) .. 190
Upalabdhi sama (balancing the perception) .. 67, 289
Upasarga (prefix) 453
Upasarga vāda (doctrine of prefixes) 453
Upādhi (condition) 140[3], 376, 376 (ftn. 4), 378, 384, 399[2], 399 (ftn. 1), 400, 428, 431
Upādhi māna (conditional) 399 (ftn. 1)
Upādhi vāda (doctrine of the conditional middle term) .. 431
Upāya (favourable condition) .. 27
Upālambha (attribution of censure) 35
Upāsaka (devotee) 304, 334, 335, 339
Upāsanā (prayer) .. .. 2[2]
Uposatha (Buddhist sabbath) 232[2], 233[3]
Ubhaya parīkṣā (examination of both) 326
Ubhaya vikala (defective in both) 369

Page

Ussakkaitha (gaining enthusiasm) 163

Ūrddhvatā (heterogenous) .. 192

Ūha (argumentation) 189

Ūhya (ellipsis) 25

Ṛju-sūtra (straight method of description) 161 (ftn. 1), 170, 171, 181, 216

Ṛju-sūtrābhāsa (fallacy of the straight) 203

Ṛṣi-ṛṇa (debt to sages) 102 (ftn. 1)

Ṛṣi (sage) .. 56, 107

Ekacca-sassatika-ekacca-asassatikā (eternalist-non-eternalists) 228

Ekānta (certain) 25

Evaṁbhūta (such-like) 161 (ftn. 4), 171², 181, 216

Evaṁbhūtābhāsa (fallacy of the such-like) 204

Aitihya (tradition) 23², 32, 33, 51, 56, 95, 370, 387, 453

Opamma-samsandana (a case presented through analogy) .. 238

Oṁ namaḥ Śivāya (hail, obeisance to Śiva) 155

Ovāda (arrangement) 233

Aupameya (comparison) 27, 32, 33, 51

Aupaniṣadakalpitātma-parīkṣā (examination of the soul according to the upaniṣads) .. 325 (ftn.)

Aupādhika (ceditional) .. 384

Auṣadha (medicine) 34

Kathā (discourse) 51, 62, 235, 370, 378²

Kapila-kalpitātma-parīkṣā (examination of Kapila's doctrine of the soul) ..325 (ftn.), 326

Karaṇa (instrument) 27², 382², 390, 445

Karma (work) 3

Karma (rituals) 2²

Karma (action) 27, 32, 279, 287, 326², 375, 382, 387², 388, 389, 393², 394², 395

Karma (merits and demerits) 127, 204, 245

Karmadhāraya (descriptive compound) 452

Karma-phala saṁbandha-parīkṣā (examination of the relation between karma and its effect) .. 326

Karma-śabdārtha parīkṣā (examination of the meaning of the word karma) 326

Kalpanā (reflection) 125, 129, (ftn. 3)², 32)

Kavi (poet) 185

Kāraka (case) 447

Kāya-viññāṇa (tactual perception) 227

Kāraṇa (cause) 189, 190², 191², 382², 390, 511

Kāraṇata-vicāra (examination of causality) 397

Kāraṇa-doṣa (defect of arguing) .. 163

Kāraṇa-viruddha-kāryopalabdhi (perception of effect contrary to its cause) 312

Kāraṇa-viruddhopalabdhi (perception contrary to the cause) .. 312

Kāraṇānupalabdhi (non-perception of the cause) 312

Kārya (action) 27

Kārya (causality) 134

Kārya (effect) 189, 190², 191², 140, 258, 280, 311, 332, 382, 390, 508

Kārya-kāraṇa (causal relation) .. 140²

Kārya-kāraṇa-bhāva (causality) .. 400

Kārya-phala (effect) 27

Kārya-yoni (material cause) .. 27

Kārya-viruddhopalabdhi (perception contrary to the effect) .. 311

Kārya sama (balancing the effect) 67, 135², 135 (ftn. 4), 268, 289

Kārya-hetu (relation of effect) .. 318

Kāryānupalabdhi (non-perception of effect) 311

Kāryābhinirvṛtti (the aggregate of resources for the accomplishment of an action) .. 26², 27²

Kāla (time) 27, 106, 219, 393²

Page

Kālatraya-parīkṣā(examination of the three times) 327

Kālātīta (mistimed) 63, 115 (ftn. 3), 367 (ftn. 1)

Kālātyayopadiṣṭa or -bādhita (mistimed or incompatible) .. 367

Kiccādhikaraṇa (case relating to the formal procedure of an ecclesiastical act) .. 230, 232

Kutārkika (quibbler) 273

Kumāra-pañha (*Pali*) (novice's question) .. 16 (ftn. 1)

Kurvad-rūpatva (causing activity) 404

Kṛta (produced) 285

Kṛtaka (product) 284

Kṛta-hāni (loss of merited action) 99, 101

Kṛttikā (constellation) .. 14

Kecit (some) 396

Kevala (absolute) .. 169 (ftn. 1), 175

Kevala-jñāna (absolute knowledge) 160, 161, (ftn. 5)

Kevala-vyatireki (exclusively negative) 361

Kevala-vyatirekyanumāna (exclusively negative inference) .. 434[2]

Kevalānvayi (exclusively affirmative) 361

Kevalānvayanumāna (exclusively affirmative inference) .. 434[2]

Kevalin (one who has attained absolute knowledge) 160

Keśī (a presiding deity) .. 15

Koṣa (dictionary) 450

Kaivarta (fisherman) 334

Kriyā (action) .. 129 (ftn. 3)[2]

Kriyā (verb) 447

Kṣaṇa-bhaṅga (momentariness) 143[2], 145, 149, 339

Kṣaṇikatva (momentariness) 121, 219

Kṣaṇika-vāda (doctrine of momentariness) .. 52, 121, 262

Kṣaṇika-vādin (upholder of the doctrine of momentariness) .. 121

Kṣatrasya kṣatram (strength of the kṣatriya) 3

Page

Kṣiti (earth) .. .. 393[2]

Khaṇika-kathā (doctrine of impermanence) 239

Khyāti-vijñāna (potential knowledge) 245

Gaṇa-dhara (leader of the assembly) 160

Gavaya (bos gavaeus) .. 384

Guṇa (quality) 27, 31, 129 (ftn. 3[2]), 279, 287, 375, 382, 386[2], 387[3], 388, 389, 393[2], 394[2], 395

Guṇa-guṇi-bheda-bhaṅga (a substance is not distinct from its qualities) 145

Guṇa-śabdārtha-parīkṣā (examination of the meaning of the word Guṇa) 326

Guru (preceptor) 216

Guru-dakṣiṇā (preceptor's fee) .. 458

Gautami-vidyā (Gotamide science) . 20

Ghāna-viññāṇa (olfactory perception) 227

Cakkhu-viññāṇa (ocular perception) .. .. 227, 227 (ftn. 3)

Cakṣuḥ (eye) 111

Cań-li (*Chinese*) (right or justice) 40

Catukka-naya-saṁsandana (case presented through the four-fold method) 239

Candra-kūpa (Candra's well) .. 335

Cikitsā (the science of medicine).. 39

Ceṣṭā (muscular movement) .. 370

Ceṣṭā (gesture) 453

Cuditaka (defendant) 231

Codaka (complainant) .. 231

Codanā (complaint) 231

Caitya (tower) 150

Chanda (vote by proxy) .. 233

Chandas (prosody) 343

Chandaṁ danami (I give authority) 233

Chandaṁ me ārocehi (do ye con-

Page

vey my authority to the council) 233
Chandaṁ me hara (do ye receive my authority) 233
Chala (quibble) 23, 34, 52, 65, 162, 212, 221, 234 (ftn. 2), 258, 356, 359, 374, 375, 381

Jagat-svabhāva-parīkṣā (examination of the nature of the world) 326
Jagatī (a kind of metre) .. 15
Jana-śruti (rumour) 453
Jalpa (wrangling) 23, 31, 51, 52, 62, 63, 258, 357, 359, 370, 374, 375, 379, 381
Jalpa-vitaṇḍā (wrangling and cavil) 104
Jāti (analogue) 51[8], 52, 65, 135
Jāti (genus) 129 (ftn. 3)[2], 219, 212, 258, 259, 288[2], 276, 315, (ftn. 1), 315 356, 357, 370, 374, 375, 381
Jāti-śakti - vādi - tantātīkā-mata (power in generality as maintained by Tantāṭikas) .. 397
Jātyuttara (analogous rejoinder) 119
Jijñāsā (inquiry) .. 33, 122
Jina (conqueror of passions) 158, 159
Jivhā-viññāṇa (gustatory perception) 227
Jīva (soul) 168, 181
Jñāta (example) 163
Jñāna (knowledge) 2[2], 3, 161, 161 (ftn. 5)
Jñāna-karma-samuccaya (aggregate of knowledge and action) .. 397
Jñāna-kāṇḍa (section on knowledge) .. .. .. 394[2]
Jñāna-lakṣaṇa (imagination) .. 140
Jñāna-lakṣaṇa (intercourse whose character is knowledge) .. 412

Ñāa (=Sans. *jñāta*) (example) .. 163

Tol (school) .. 525 (ftn. 1)
Takka (*Prak.*) (debate) 162, 227
Takki (argumentationist) 21, 227[2]
Takkika (logician) .. 227, 229[2]

Page

Tajjāta-doṣa (defeat arising from a disputant being agitated in mind) 163
Tatpuruṣa (determinative compound) 452
Tattva-jñāna (right knowledge) .. 138
Tattva-vyākhyāna (explanation of truth) 259
Tathātā (suchness) 255
Tadutpatti (effect) 508
Tantra-yukti (terms of scientific argument) .. .. 24[3]
Tarka (debate) 23, 37, 38, 52, 61, 61 (ftn. 1), 162, 189, 201, 215, 244, 258, 359, 374, 375, 381, 427, 429, 497
Tarka-puṅgava (bull in discussion) 272
Tarka-vidyā (logic) .. 7, 40
Tarkābhāsa (fallacy of argumentation) 193
Tarkin (logician) 38
Tassa pāpiyya sikā (settlement with the prospect of further inquiry) 230
Tātparya (intention) .. 148, 448
Tādātmya (inherence) 508
Tādātmyābhava (negation of identity) .. .. 97 (ftn. 1)
Tārkika (logician) .. 37, 244[2]
Tiṇa-vatthāraka (settlement by covering over with grass) .. 230
Tipiṭaka or Piṭakattaya (the three baskets of Buddhist teachings) 226
Tiryak (homogeneous) .. 192
Tīrthaṅkara (builder of a landing place in the sea of existence) .. 158
Tuṣānala (penetentiary rite of putting an end to one's life in a slow fire) .. .. 142[2]
Tūṣṇīṁ bhāva (speechlessness) .. 137
Tṛṣṇā (lust) 371
Tejas (light) .. .. 393[2]
Trayī (the three Vedas) .. 5

Page

Trasareṇu (triad or tertiary compound) .. .. .. 106[2]

Tripiṭaka or Piṭakatraya (three baskets of Buddhist teachings) 226

Tripuṭī - pratyakṣa - vādin (supporter of triangular perception) . 418

Trividha-paraḥ (three classes of respondents) 29

Daṁsana (*Prak.*) (philosophy) 5 (ftn. 5)

Darśana (Philosophy) 5, 5 (ftn. 5), 6, 152

Daśāvayava-vākya (syllogism of ten parts) 166

Dassana (*Pali*) (philosophy) 5 (ftn. 5)

Dik (space) .. .. 393[2]

Digambara-parikalpita-ātma - parīkṣā (examination of the Digambare Jaina doctrine of the soul) 326

Dīnāra (the Roman coin *denarius*) 45 (ftn. 2)

Duṣṭa-vākyānusaraṇa (adoption of a fallacious reason) 259

Duḥkha (pain) 132, 371, 375[2], 382

Duḥkha-satya (misery as a pain) 127 (ftn.)

Dūṣaṇa (refutation) .. 181, 298, 315

Dūṣaṇābhāsa (semblance of a refutation) 181, 298

Dṛṣṭānta (familiar instance) 27, 32, 52, 59, 128, 128 (ftn. 4), 167, 176[2], 177, 191[2], 203, 258[2], 265, 268 (ftn. 2), 286, 290, 359, 374, 375, 381, 501[2]

Dṛṣṭāntābhāsa (fallacy of example) 178, 193

Deva-ṛṇa (debt to gods) 102 (ftn. 1)

Deśa (place) .. 27, 219

Doṣa (defect) .. 163, 375, 382

Dravya (substance) 27, 31, 129 (ftn. 3), 219, 279, 287, 373, 375, 382, 386, 387[2], 388, 389, 393[3], 394[2], 395

Dravya (cause) 171

Dravya-padārtha-parīkṣā (examination of the meaning of the word substance) 326

Dravyāstikāya (a group of substance) 216

Page

Dvandva (aggregative compound) 452

Dvātriṁśadākāra - śrauta - yutaya (the thirty-two forms of set argument) 42

Dvigu (numeral compound) .. 452

Dvividha-sambhāṣā (two kinds of debate) 29

Dvyaṇuka (dyad or binary compound) 106, 442

Dhammatā (law) .. 500 (ftn. 1)

Dharma (duty) 38

Dharma (predicate) .. 190, 290

Dharma (doctrine) .. .. 305[2]

Dharma (merit) 371

Dharma-putra (foster son) .. 208

Dharmin (subject) 290

Dhātu (root) .. 447, 453

Dhātu-vādaḥ (doctrine of roots)

Dhāraṇā (recollecting) .. 201

Dhāraṇi (numonics) 304

Dhvaṁsa (destruction) .. 219

Naya (method of comprehending things from particular standpoints) 168, 174, 181[2], 182, 203[2], 215, 216[2], 218

Nayātma-svarūpa-nirṇaya (determination of the nature of one-sided knowledge) 200

Nayābhāsa (fallacy of Naya) .. 203

Nava-dharma (nine sacred works) 242 (ftn. 3)

Nāntarīyaka (non-co-presence) .. 504

Nāma (name) 129 (ftn. 3)[2], 171

Nāma (crude word) 447

Nāma (valid knowledge) .. 161

Nārada (a celestial sage) .. 14

Nāsti (it is not, non-existence) .. 184

Niḥśreyasa (summum bonum) .. 54

Nigamana (conclusion) 27, 32, 42, 60, 119[2], 167, 176, 191, 202, 203, 237, 266, 268, 370, 437[2], 501, 502

Niggaha (=Sans. *nigraha*) (defeat) 234, 234 (ftn. 2), 236

Page

Nigraha (defeat) 51

Nigraha-doṣa (defect of understanding) 163

Nigraha-sthāna (point of defeat) 35, 44, 51[3], 52, 65, 66, 136, 136 (ftn. 1), 150, 212, 258, 259, 264, 268, 269, 356, 357, 359, 370, 374, 375, 379, 381

Nitya (eternal) .. .. 285[4]

Nitya-sama (balancing the eternal) 67, 269

Nidāna (the introductory part of the Pātimokkha) 233

Nidarśana (example) 25

Nindā (deprecation) 108

Nimitta (efficient cause) 383

Nimitta-kāraṇa (instrumental cause) 390

Niyoga (injunction) 25

Niranuyojyānuyoga (overlooking the censurable) 84

Niranuyojyānuyoga (censuring the non-censurable) 264

Nirarthaka (meaningless) 84, 261, 269

Nirartha-khaṇḍana (rejoinder on the ground of meaninglessness) 268

Nirukti (explanation) .. 487 (ftn. 1)

Nirjara (destruction of the consequences of action) .. 168

Nirṇaya (ascertainment) 23[2], 52, 62, 258, 359, 370, 374, 375, 381

Niryukti (commentarie) .. 165

Nirvacana (etymological explanation) 25

Nirvāṇa (Buddhist emancipation) 159[2], 159 (ftn. 1[2], 2), 160[2], 160 (ftn. 1)

Nirvikalpa (indeterminate) .. 55

Nirvikalpaka (indeterminate) 134, 137[2], 138[2], 138 (ftn. 1), 179, 360, 383, 390, 418

Nirvikalpaka-vāda (doctrine of indeterminate perception) .. 418

Nirvikalpaka-vipratipatti (controversy about indeterminate perception) 397

Page

Niścita (sure) .. 376 (ftn. 4), 398

Niḥkṣepa (imposition) .. 218

Nīti or Nyāya (logic) 240[2], 240 (ftn. 3)

Naigama (non-analytical method of description) 161 (ftn. 4), 170[2], 181, 216

Naigamābhāsa (fallacy of the Naigama) 203

Nairātmya-vāda (doctrine of non-soul) .. .. 127 (ftn.)

Naiyāyika (logician) .. 41 (ftn. 5), 244

Nyāya (logic) 20, 38, 39[2], 40[2], 152, 240[2], 240 (ftn. 3[3]), 497

Nyāya (syllogism) .. 41 (ftn. 2), 436[4]

Nyāya-tattva (categories of logic) 39

Nyāya-pūrvāṅga (first part of logic) .. .. 41 (ftn. 2)

Nyāya-vidyā (science of logic) .. 38

Nyāya-vaiśeṣika-parikalpita-puruṣa-parīkṣā (examination of the Nyāya and Vaiśeṣika doctrine of soul) 326

Nyāya-śāstra (science of logic) 39, 40, 116

Nyāya-sūtra (science of true logic) 8

Nyāya-svarūpa (essential form of a syllogism) .. 41 (ftn. 2)

Nyāyāvayava (members of a syllogism) .. 42, 289, 289 (ftn. 3)

Nyāyāśraya .. 41 (ftn. 2)

Nyāyottaraṅga the last part of logic) .. 41 (ftn. 2)

Nyāyya (reasonable) .. 41 (ftn. 5)

Nyūna (saying too little) 84, 261, 269

Pakkha (*Prak*.) (party) .. 162

Pakṣa (party) 162

Pakṣa (minor term) 176[3], 177, 193, 292, 268, 268 (ftn. 2), 283, 291, 312, 361, 506

Pakṣatā (nature of the minor term) 433[2], 487 (ftn. 1)

Pakṣa-dharma (law of extension of the minor term) 283

Pakṣa-dharma-cakra (wheel of reasons put in order) .. 299 (ftn. 2)

Page

Pakṣa-dharmatā (essential nature of a syllogism) .. 361, 377, 390

Pakṣa-prayoga (use of the minor term) 203

Pakṣābhāsa (fallacy of the minor term) 176, 177, 193, 290 (ftn. 1), 312

Pakṣaḥ anumāna-bādhitaḥ (minor term being incompatible with inference) 441

Pakṣaḥ pratyakṣa-bādhitaḥ (minor term being incompatible with perception) 440

Pakṣaḥ śabda-bādhitaḥ (minor term being incompatible with verbal testimony) 441

Pakṣaḥ sādhya-grāhaka-pramāṇa-jātīya-pramāṇa-viruddhaḥ (minor term being incompatible with the evidence which is analogous to the evidence that establishes the major-term) 441

Pakṣaḥ hetu-grāhaka-pratyakṣa-bādhitaḥ (minor term being incompatible with perception which establishes the middle term) 441

Pakṣaḥ hetu-grāhakānumāna-bādhitaḥ (minor term being incompatible with inference which establishes the middle term) .. 442

Paṅkaja iti padānām yogarūḍhitva-kathana (etymologo-conventional use of a word as mud-born) 397

Paṅkti (a kind of metre) .. 14

Paccanika-niggaho (adverse controversy) 237

Pañcāvayava (five parts of a syllogism) 286

Pañcāvayava-vākya (speech of five parts) 43

Pañjikā (commentary) .. 213

Paṇḍita (scholar) .. 240

Patikamma (rejoinder) .. 235

Page

Paticca-samuppāda (=Sans. *Pratītya samutpāda*, doctrine of mutual dependence) .. 227 (ftn. 2)

Patiññā (=Sans. *Pratijñā*) (proposition) .. 234, 234 (ftn. 2)

Patiññaya kāretabbaṁ (settlement by an undertaking) .. 230

Patta (sacred chair) 199

Pattakallaṁ (in season) .. 233

Pathamo niggaho (first defeat) .. 237

Pada (word) .. 110[2], 149

Pada-sphoṭa (word-explosion) 148, 149

Padārtha (category) 25, 381, 387. 389, 393

Padīpa (lighting a lamp) .. 238

Pamāṇa (valid knowledge) .. 161

Para-ātmā (supreme soul) .. 371

Paratantra (conditional) 245, 245 (ftn. 1)

Parama-nyāya (conclusion) .. 42

Paramātmā (supreme soul) .. 143

Paramāṇu (atom) 105

Paramārtha (transcendental) 254, 255

Paramārtha-sat (absolutely real).. 310

Para-saṁbandha (concerning others) 264

Parāmarśa (consideration) 384, 390[2], 420. 433[2], 435, 510. 511[2]

Parāmarśānurūpānumāna (syllogistic inference) 511

Parārthānumāna (inference for the sake of others) 175, 192, 202, 276, 282. 307, 309, 310, 312. 359[2], 361, 435[2]

Parikalpita (false) 245, 245 (ftn. 1)

Pariccheda (chapter) 184, 200

Pariniṣpanna (perfect) 245, 245 (ftn. 1, 2)

Paribhāṣā (technicality) .. 450

Pariṣad (council of debate) 7, 22[2]. 24. 29[2]. 263

Pariharaṇa-doṣa (avoidance of charges) 163

Parihāra (avoidance of defeat) .. 35

Parikṣā (examination) 20, 27, 28[2]. 51. 53, 90

Page

Parokṣa (indirect knowledge) 161 (ftn. 5)[2], 169[2], 170[2], 170 (ftn. 1), 174, 175, 188, 189, 201[2], 215
Parokṣa-jñāna (indirect knowledge) 219
Paryanuyojyopekṣaṇa (admission of an opinion) 84
Paryanuyojyopekṣaṇa (overlooking the censurable) 269
Paryāstikāya (group of attributes) 216
Parvata (a celestial sage) .. 14
Pātimokkhuddesa (recitation of the code of monastic laws) .. 233
Pāramārthika (transcendental) 175, 201[2], 203
Pāramārthika-doṣā (transcendental condition) 4
Pāramārthika-pratyakṣa (transcendental perception) .. 170 (ftn. 1)
Pāramārthika-pratyakṣa-pramāṇa (transcendental perception) .. 181
Pāriśuddhi (purity) 233
Pārṣad (council) 22
Pāśupata (follower of Paśupati).. 154
Pitṛ-ṛṇa (debt to our progenitors) 102 (ftn. 1)
Pitṛ-yāna (path of the forefathers) 3
Puggala (soul) .. .. 235[3]
Putreṣti (sacrifice for the sake of a son) 107
Pudgala (burden-bearer) 126, 127 (ftn.)
Pudgala-vāda (doctrine of the burden-bearer) .. 127 (ftn.)
Punarukta (repetition) 84. 255, 269
Purākalpa (narration).. .. 108
Puruṣa (soul) .. 10, 245 (ftn. 2)[2]
Puruṣa-parīkṣā (examination of the soul) 326
Pubba-karaṇa (preparation) 232, 232 (ftn. 1). 233
Pubba-kicca (preliminary acts) 232 (ftn. 1), 233[2]
Pūrva (prior) .. 190[2], 191
Pūrva-pakṣa (question) 25. 424

Page

Pūrvavat (à priori) 56, 116 (ftn. 1), 260, 499
Pothi (book) .. 324 (ftn. 3)
Pauṣa saṁkrānti (the last day of the month of Pauṣa) .. 530
Prakaraṇa (expository treatise) .. 205
Prakaraṇa-sama (begging the question) 34, 63, 67, 260, 268, 367
Prakāśa (chapter) 215
Prakṛti (primordial matter) 10, 363[2]
Prakṛti (illustration) . .. 108
Pratijñā (proposition) 27, 32, 60, 121, 166, 203, 265, 266, 436[2], 500, 502
Pratijñāntara (shifting the proposition) 84, 264
Pratijñā-vibhakti (limitation of the proposition) 166
Pratijñā-virodha (opposing the proposition) .. 84, 269
Pratijñā-sannyāsa (renouncing the proposition) .. 84, 137, 269
Pratijñā-hāni (hurting the proposition) 34, 44, 84, 261, 268, 269
Prati tantra (dogma peculiar to some school) 59
Pratitantra-siddhānta (conclusion accepted by a particular school) 259
Prati-dṛṣtānta-sama (balancing the counter-example) .. 67, 261, 268
Pratiyogi (counter-part) 403[2], 404
Pratilomaittā (making the authorities hostile) 163
Prativādī (opponent) .. 204, 379
Pratiṣedha (negation) .. 190
Pratisthāpanā (counter-demonstration) 27, 32, 500, 501
Pratyakṣa (perception) 27[2], 28, 32, 33, 50, 54, 125, 129. 130, 134, 150, 161 (ftn. 5), 162, 169[2], 170, 174[2], 188, 189, 201, 209. (ftn. 1), 215, 221, 259, 264, 265, 266, 276, 277, 279, 298, 306, 307, 309, 310, 348, 358. 359[2], 360. 383[2], 387[2], 389[3], 390. 393[2], 394[2], 395, 407, 411

Page

Pratyakṣa-kāraṇa-vāda (causes of perception) 416

Pratyakṣa-jñāna(direct knowledge) 219

Pratyakṣa-lakṣaṇa-parīkṣā (examination of the definition of perception) 327

Pratyakṣa-vyavasthā (system of perception) 309

Pratyakṣa-svarūpa-nirṇaya (determination of the nature of perception) 200

Pratyakṣābhāsa (fallacy of perception) 192, 298

Pratyanuyoga (re-interrogation) .. 33

Pratyabhijñāna (recognition) 189, 201, 215

Pratyabhijñānābhāsa (fallacy of recógnition) 193

Pratyaya (inter-relation) 117, 118 (ftn. 3)

Pratyuccāraṇa (repetition) .. 25

Pradeśa (determination) from a statement to be made) .. 25

Pradhāna (Primordial matter) .. 325

Pradhvaṁsābhāva (posterior non-existence) 97, 97 (ftn. 1), 184, 203, 394

Pramā (right knowledge) 138[2], 389, 394, 395[2], 408[3], 411

Pramāṇa (means of right knowledge) 23, 28, 43, 49, 50, 51[3], 52, 84, 84 (ftn. 1), 113, 155, 158[4], 161, 162[2], 168, 169, 174[3], 181[3], 182, 189[3], 200, 201[3], 201 (ftn. 1), 203, 212[2], 218[3], 256[3], 257[11], 258, 259, 276[2], 277[2], 307[2], 309, 330, 348, 357[4], 358, 359[4], 381, 386[6], 387[2], 389[3], 393[2], 394, 395[2], 402[6], 408, 497, 499

Pramāṇa-catuṣṭaya-prāmāṇya-vādaḥ (doctrine of the validity of the four means of knowledge) .. 453

Pramāṇa-śāstra (science of right knowledge) 158

Page

Pramāṇa-sāmānya-lakṣaṇa (general characteristics of valid knowledge) 215

Pramāṇa-siddhi (establishment of proof) 307

Pramāṇa-svarūpa (characteristics of valid knowledge) .. 188

Pramāṇa-svarūpa-nirṇaya (determination of the nature of valid knowledge) 200

Pramāṇāntara-parīkṣā (examination of other kinds of valid knowledge) 327

Prameya (object of knowledge) 23, 49, 51[2], 52, 56, 97, 113, 158[2], 257[2], 258, 284, 357[2], 359, 370, 373[2], 374, 375, 381

Prayojana (purpose) 23, 28, 33, 52, 59, 122, 258, 359, 374, 375, 381

Pralaya (dissolution of the world) 105

Pralāpita (irrelevant talk) .. 137

Pravṛtti (exertion) 27, 375, 382, 410

Pravṛtti-vijñāna (continuous flow of momentary cognitions) 146, 245[4], 245 (ftn. 1)

Prasaṅga (connected argument) .. 25

Prasaṅga-samā (balancing the infinite regression) .. 67, 268, 289

Praśāstṛ-doṣa (defeat arising from the authorities) 163

Prāgabhāva (prior non-existence) 97, 97 (ftn. 1), 189, 203, 394

Prāna (breath) 2

Prāpti-sama (balancing the co-presence) .. 67, 261, 288

Prābhākarāḥ (the Mīmāṁsakas) .. 408

Prāmāṇya-vāda (the doctrine of the validity of knowledge) .. 408

Pretyabhāva (condition after death) 375, 382

Phala (result) 188, 375, 382, 511

Phala-pramāṇa-svarūpādyābhāsa-nirṇaya (determination of the consequences and fallacies of knowledge) .. 200

Page

Bandha (bondage) 168
Bahir-vyāpti (extrinsic inseparable connection) .. 177, 178, 202
Bahuvrīhi (attributive compound) 452
Bādhā (incompatibility) .. 438
Bādhita (incompatible) 367 (ftn. 1), 438, 440[2]
Buddhi (intellect) 52, 112, 375[2], 382, 387[2], 389[4], 393[3], 395
Brahman (the pervading essence) 4
Brahma-pariṇāma-vāda (doctrine of the transformation of Brahman) 32
Brahma-vidyā (divine science) .. 4
Brāhmaṇa (ritual) 108

Bhāgāsiddha (unproved in respect of a part) 362
Bhāra (burden) .. 127 (ftn.)
Bhāva (entity itself) .. 171, 184, 394[2]
Bhāṣya (commentary) 116, 121
Bhikkhu-gaṇanā (counting the number of monks) 233
Bhūmi (stage) 249
Bhayaitta (creating divisions) .. 163
Bhaitta (serving the authorities) 163
Bhaiṣajya (medicine) 34
Bhrama (error) .. 138, 409
Bhrānta (erring) 273
Bhrānti (blunder) 273

Maṅgala (benedictory portion) 324 (ftn. 3)
Maṅgala-vāda (invocation of blessings) 408
Maṅgalācaraṇa (invocation of blessing) 397
Matānujñā (admission of an opinion) 84, 261, 269
Mati (knowledge of existing things acquired through the senses and the mind) .. 169 (ftn. 1)
Mati-kamma (deliberation) .. 231
Mati-bhaṅga-doṣa (defeat arising from the failure of the disputants memory) 163

Page

Madhyama (middle) 249
Manas (mind) 116, 201, 278, 280 (ftn. 1), 375[2], 382, 393[2]
Manaḥ (intelligence) 2
Manaḥ-paryāya (knowledge derived from reading the thoughts of others) 161 (ftn. 5), 169 (ftn. 1), 201
Manas tattva-nirūpaṇa (determination of the nature of the mind) 397
Manoṇutva-vāda (atomic nature of mind) 417
Mano-viññāna (mental perception) 227
Mantras 15
Marut (air) .. .. .. 393[2]
Mahāpratihāra (the great gatekeeper) 322
Mahābhadra-kalpa (the very blessed cycle) 225
Mahāyāna (the Great vehicle) .. 241[2]
Mithyā-jñāna (error) 138
Mīmāṁsaka-kalpita-ātma - parīkṣā (examination of the Mīmāṁsaka doctrine of the soul) .. 326
Mukti (emancipation) .. 219[2]
Mokṣa (emancipation) 57, 122, 123, 168, 181, 359, 370, 371
Mleccha (non-Aryan) .. 56, 107

Yajña (sacrifice) 516
Yatnaja (product of effort) .. 285[3]
Yathārthānubhava (right experience) .. .. 389[2]
Yama (the god of death) .. 14
Yava (grain) 107
Yukta (right) 359
Yukti (continuous argument) 23, 27, 28
Yuga-pradhāna (foremost man of the age) 164
Yūpa (stake) 15
Yebhuyyasikā (settlement by a majority) 230
Yoga (union of words) .. 25
Yoga (concentration) .. 245, 249
Yoga-rūḍha (etymologo-conventional) 451

Page

Yogācāra (practice of meditation) 249

Yogācāra or Vijñāna-vadin (a sect of Buddhist philosophers who maintain that cognitions alone are real) 146

Yogin (contemplative).. .. 359

Yogi-pratyakṣa (contemplative perception) 360

Yogyatā (consistency) . 447[4]

Yaugika (etymological) .. 451

Yaugika-rūḍha (etymological conventional) 451

Rudra (a sect of gods) .. 15

Rūḍha (conventional) 451

Rūpa (form) .. 126[2], 389

Rūpa (matter) 238

Lakkhaṇāyutti-kathā (definition of terms) 238

Lakṣaṇa (definition) 53

Lakṣaṇa-doṣa (defect of definition) 163

Lakṣaṇā (implication) 450, 451[2]

Laghu-ṭikā (light commentary) .. 211

Liṅga (sign) 175, 190, 290, 377[2], 383, 508

Liṅga-parāmarśa (remembrance of a sign; a syllogism from a sign). 130 (ftn. 1), 435, 510, 511

Liṅga-parāmarśādi-nirūpaṇa (determination of the consideration of the sign, etc.) 397

Liṅgasya trai-rūpyam (three characteristics of the middle term) 291 (ftn. 1)

Lekhaka (writer) 379

Lokāyata (casuist) .. 240 (ftn. 3)

Laukika (personal) .. 175, 359

Laukika-pratyakṣa (ordinary-pratyakṣa)

Vacana-śodhana (clearing the meaning of terms) 238

Vajra (thunderbolt) 272

Vanya (wild) .. 484 (ftn. 1)

Page

Varṇa-sphoṭa (letter-explosion) .. 148

Varṇya-sama (balancing the subject) 34, 67, 289

Vartamāna (present time) 106 (ftn. 1)

Vasu (a sect of gods) 15

Vastu-doṣa (defect of the subject) 163

Vastu-prativikalpa-vijñāna (objectified knowledge) 245

Vāk-chala (quibble in respect of a term) 260

Vākovākya (grammar, rhetoric or debate) .. .. 45, 45 (ftn. 5)

Vākya (sentence) 149

Vākya-doṣa (defect of speech) 34, 259

Vākya-praśaṁsā (excellence of speech) 34, 259

Vākya-sphoṭa (sentence-explosion) 148, 149

Vākya-śeṣa (context) .. 25, 459

Vājapeya (a sacrifice) 14

Vāda (discussion) 23, 31, 49, 51[5], 52, 62[2], 104, 204, 229, 258, 359, 370, 374, 375, 378, 379, 381

Vāda-maryādā (limits of debate).. 31

Vāda-mārga (course of debate) 27[4], 31, 51

Vāda-vidyā (art of discussion) 7, 26, 27, 28

Vāda-viśadī-karaṇa (elucidation of debate) 259

Vādī (disputant) .. 195, 204, 379

Vādi-prativādi-nyāya-nirṇaya (determination of the right procedure of a disputant and his opponent) 200

Vādopāya (expedients of debate) 30,

Vāyu-pratyakṣatvādimata-khaṇḍana (refutation of the perceptibility of air) 397

Vārttā (commerce) 5

Vātsīputra-kalpita-ātma-parīkṣā (examination of the Vātsīputra doctrine of the soul) .. 326

Vāhyārtha-parīkṣā (examination of external objects) 327

Page

Vāhyārtha-bhaṅga (things possess no external reality) .. 145
Vāhyārtha-vāda (doctrine of the external world) 220
Vāhyārtha-siddhi (validity of external things) 219
Vikala (defective) 201
Vikalpa (alternative) 25
Vikalpa-sama (balancing the alternative) 67, 289
Vikāra (modification) 111
Vikṣepa (evasion) .. 84, 269
Vigraha (in a spirit of opposition) 29
Vigraha-sambhāṣā (hostile debate) 29
Vijñāna (knowledge) .. 120, 126², 245
Vijñāna-vāda (idealism) 120, 120 (ftn. 3)³, 220, 245²
Vijñāna-vādin (see *Yogācāra*) .. 146
Viññāna (knowledge) 227, 227 (ftn. 3)
Vitaṇḍā (cavil) 23, 31, 51, 52, 62, 63, 240 (ftn. 3), 258, 357, 359, 370, 374, 375, 379, 381
Vitarka (speculation) 162
Vidyā (knowledge) 387²
Vidhāna (arrangement) .. 25
Vidhi (injunction) .. 108², 190, 448
Vidhi-vāda (doctrine of injunction) 448
Vipakṣa (counter-proposition) 166, 283, 284, 361, 433
Vipakṣa-pratiṣedha (opposition to the counter-proposition) .. 166
Vipakṣe asattvam (non-existence of the sign in heterologues) .. 378
Viparīta-khaṇḍana (contrary rejoinder) 268
Viparīta-vyatireka (of contrary separation) 180
Viparīta-vyāpti (inverse pervasion) 369
Viparīta-vyāptyabhidhāna (example with inverse pervasion) .. 369
Viparītānvaya (of inverted connection) 179, 297, 315
Viparyaya (reversion) .. 25, 201, 359

Page

Viparyaya-khaṇḍana (rejoinder on the basis of reversion) .. 268
Vipratipatti (misunderstanding an argument) 136
Vibhakti (case-ending) .. 447
Vibhāṣā (commentary) .. 247²
Viyakka (speculation) 162
Viraha (separation) .. 209 (ftn.), 210²
Viruddha (contradictory) 63, 178, 260, 294, 313, 363, 438, 439²
Viruddha-kāryopalabdhi (perception of the opposite effect) .. 311
Viruddhāvyabhicāri (non-erroneous contradiction) 316, 358, 368
Virodha (contradiction) .. 438
Vivarta-vāda-parīkṣā (examination of the doctrine of evolution) .. 327
Vivādādhikaraṇa (case pertaining to differences of opinions) .. 229
Vivṛti (description) 451
Viśeṣa (particularity) 27, 32, 138, 192, 279, 287, 375, 382, 387², 388, 389, 393², 394², 395, 402
Viśeṣaṇatā (qualification or particularity) 130, 412, 415, 416
Viśeṣaṇāsiddha (improved in respect of the adjective) .. 362
Viśeṣa-vyāpti (invariable concomittance of special forms) .. 426
Viśeṣyāsiddha (unproved in respect of the substantive) .. 362
Viṣama-vyāpti (non-equipolent concomittance) 399
Viṣaya (object of knowledge) 188, 192
Viṣaya-kāṇḍa (section on subject) 394²
Viṣaya-svarūpa-nirṇaya (determination of the nature of objects of knowledge) 200
Vīmaṁsā (casuistry) 227
Vīmaṁsī (casuist) .. 21, 227
Vṛtti (commentary) 214
Vṛtti (indication) 449
Vṛhatī (a kind of metre) .. 15
Vedas 14

Page

Vedanā (feeling) .. 126[2], 238
Vaidharmya (heterogeneous) 176, 191, 264, 287, 290, 368, 502
Vaidharmya dṛṣṭāntābhāsa (fallacy of the heterogeneous example) 179, 180, 297
Vaidharmyavat (negative inference) 312
Vaidharmya-sama (balancing the heterogeneity) .. 67, 266, 289
Vyakti (individual) 219
Vyatireka (relating to things) .. 192
Vyatireka (negative) 361
Vyatireka-vyāpti (invariable separation) 180, 361
Vyatirekī (exclusively negative) 130, 191, 286, 287, 437
Vyatirekī-udāharaṇa (heterogeneous example) 259
Vyadhikaraṇa - dharmāvacchinnābhāva (non-existence whose counter part is qualified by a nature abiding in different locus) 423
Vyadhikaraṇāsiddha (unproved on account of abiding in a different locus) 362
Vyabhicāra (erraticalness) .. 438
Vyartha-viśeṣaṇāsiddha (unproved on account of the adjective being useless) 363
Vyartha-viśeṣyāsiddha (unproved on account of the substantive being useless) 363
Vyavasāya (ascertainment) .. 33
Vyavahāra (practical method of description) 161 (ftn. 4), 181, 216, 450
Vyavahārābhāsa (fallacy of the practical) 203
Vyākaraṇa (grammar) .. 450
Vyākhyāna (description) .. 25
Vyāghāta pradarśana (showing absurdity) 260
Vyāghra (tiger) 396
Vyāghra-śiśuka (tiger cub) .. 207
Vyāpaka (pervader) .. 189, 220

Page

Vyāpaka-viruddhopalabdhi (perception contrary to the container) 312
Vyāpakānupalabdhi (non-perception of the pervader) .. 311
Vyāpāra (operation) .. 443, 511
Vyāpti (invariable concomittance) 140, 177[2], 179, 189[2], 292, 361, 376, 384, 390, 396, 404, 406 (ftn. 5), 421, 454, 509, 510
Vyāpti-graha (indication or the process of ascertaining the middle term and the major term) .. 218
Vyāpti-grahopāya (means of apprehending invariable concomittance) 426
Vyāpti-grahopāya-siddhānta (conclusion as to the means of apprehending invariable concommittance) 428
Vyāpti-nirūpaṇa (determination of invariable concomittance) .. 397
Vyāpti-pañcakam (five provisional definitions of invariable concomittance) .. 421, 487 (ftn. 1)
Vyāptyanugama (comprehensiveness of invariable concomittance) 429
Vyāptyasiddhi (unproved in respect of invariable concomittance) 440
Vyāpya (pervaded) 189, 190[2], 191, 220
Vyāpyatvāsiddha (unproved in respect of accompaniment) .. 439
Vyāvahārika (practical) 170, 171, 174
Vyāvahārika-daśā (practical condition) 4
Vyoma (ether) .. .. 393[2]
Vrata (religious vow) 164, 205

Śakti (strength) 171
Śakti (potentiality) .. .. 450[2]
Śakti-nirūpaṇa and upādhi (ascertainment of power and condition) 397
Śakti-vāda (doctrine of potentiality of word) 449

Page

Śakya-prāpti (capacity of the example to warrant the conclusion) 122
Śakra (strong) 171
Śaṅkita (suspected) .. 140, 376 (ftn. 4)
Śarīra (body) .. 375, 382
Śabda (sound) .. 109, 448
Śabda (verbal testimony) 50², 125, 175², 287, 370 (ftn. 1), 387, 389³, 393², 394, 407, 444, 465, 470
Śabda (verbal method of description) 161 (ftn. 4)², 170, 171, 181, 216
Śabda (word) .. 33, 51, 54, 384²
Śabda-khaṇḍa (book of verbal testimony) 444
Śabda-nirūpaṇam (definition of verbal testimony) 444
Śabda-pramāṇa (verbal testimony as a means of valid knowledge) 397, 444
Śabda-prāmāṇya-vāda (speech as means of valid knowledge) .. 445
Śabda-bodha (verbal knowledge) 444², 470
Śabda-Brahma-parīkṣā (examination of Brahma the presiding deity of sound) 326
Śabdasya śravaṇam (hearing of a word) 444
Śabdānityatā-vāda (doctrine of the non-eternity of sound) .. 448
Śabdābhāsa (fallacy of verbal testimony) 204
Śabdārtha (words and their meanings) 106
Śabdārtha-parīkṣā (examination of the meaning of the word 'sound') 327
Śalākā-parīkṣā (probe-examination) 461, 522, (ftn. 1)
Śaśa-śṛṅga (hare horn) .. 424
Śākhās (spiritual genealogy) 25, 168
Śāstra (scripture) 23²
Śāstraja-śabda (spiritual testimony) 175

Page

Śūnyatā (voidness) 52, 118 (ftn. 3), 245, (ftn. 2,²), 254, 255
Śūnya-vāda (doctrine of voidness) 119 (ftn.), 262
Śeṣavat (a posteriori) 56, 116 (ftn. 1), 260, 499
Śaivas (followers of Śiva) .. 154
Śrāvaka (layman) 223
Śrāvaṇa (audible) 285
Śrāvikā (laywoman) 223
Śruta (knowledge of things acquired through reasoning and study) .. 161 (ftn. 5), 169 (ftn. 1)
Śruta-kevalin (one versed in the 14 pūrvas of the Dṛṣṭivāda) .. 164
Śruti-parikṣā (examination of scripture) 327
Śrutyaprāmāṇya (denial of the authority of the Veda) 143, 149

Ṣaṭ-pakṣī-kathā (six-winged disputation) 82
Ṣaḍ-darśana (six systems of philosophy) 152⁴, 153
Ṣaḍ-darśana-vicāra (criticism of the six systems of philosophy) .. 153
Ṣaḍ-lakṣaṇa-vyākhyā (explanation of six characteristics) .. 332

Sakala (perfect) 201
Sakala-tārkika-cakra-cūḍāmaṇi (the crest-gem of the circle of all logicians) 185
Saṅgha (council) .. 230², 231², 232
Sat (present) 284³
Sataḥ sajjāyate (effect pre-exists in its cause) 141
Sat-pratipakṣa (counter-balance) 438², 439
Sativinaya (settlement from recollection) 230²
Sadasat (partly present and partly absent) 284⁶
Sadyaska (a kind of sacrifice) .. 14
Saṅdigdha (doubtful) 398

Page

Sandigdha - viśeṣaṇā - siddha (unproved on account of the adjective being doubtful) .. 363
Sandigdha - viśeṣyā siddha (unproved on account of the substantive being doubtful) .. 363
Sandigdhā-siddha (unproved on account of the reason being doubtful) 363
Sandhāya (peacefully) .. 29
Sannikarṣa (intercourse) 130, 411
Sapakṣa (homologue of the reason) 283, 284, 361, 433
Sapakṣe sattvam (existence of the sign in the homologue) .. 378
Saptabhaṅgī-naya (sevenfold paralogism) 203, 212, 221
Sabhā (council) .. 22, 27
Sabhā-pati (president) .. 204, 379
Sabhya (member) .. 204, 379
Samabhirūḍha (subtle verbal method of description) 161 (ftn. 4), 171[2], 181, 216
Samabhirūḍhābhāsa (fallacy of the subtle) 204
Samayocita - vākya (opportune speech) 259
Samavāya (inherence) 27, 32, 130, 134, 219, 287, 333, 375, 382, 383[2], 387[2], 389[2], 393[2], 394[2], 395, 402, 412, 413, 414 449 (ftn. 1), 508
Samavāya-vāda (doctrine of inherence) 414
Samavāya-śabdārtha-parīkṣā (examination of the meaning of the word 'co-existent cause') .. 327
Samavāyābhāva (absolute non-existence) 184
Samavāyi-kāraṇa (material cause) 382, 390
Samaveta-samavāya (inherent inherence) 130, 412, 413
Sama-vyāpti (equipotent concomitance) 399
Samāna-tantra (allied system) .. 373

Page

Samāropa (superimposition) .. 201
Samāropita (charged).. .. 140
Samāsa (compound) 452
Samāsa-vādaḥ (doctrine of compound words) 452
Samāhāra (unified aggregative compound) .. .. 452[2]
Samiti (council) 22
Samuccaya (aggregate) .. 25
Saṁkramaṇa-doṣa (diversion to other subjects) 163
Saṁketa (signification) .. 450
Saṁkhyaikānta (final signification of numbers) 114
Saṁkhyaikānta-vāda (doctrine of the fixity of things signified by numbers) .. 16 (ftn. 1)
Saṁgāmāvacara-bhikku (member of a council) .. .. 231[2]
Saṁgraha (collective method of description) 161 (ftn. 4), 170, 171, 181, 216
Saṁgrahābhāsa (fallacy of the collective) 203
Saṁjñā (sensation) .. .. 126[2]
Saṁbhava (probability) 25, 56. 95, 170, 370, 387
Saṁbhava (the originating cause) 33
Saṁbhāṣā (method of debate) .. 28
Saṁbhāṣā-praśaṁsā (utility of debate) 29
Saṁbhāṣā-vidhi (method of debate) 26, 27[3]
Sammajjanī (cleansing the ground) 232
Sammukhābhinaya (settlement in presence).. 230
Saṁyukta-viśeṣaṇatā (united particularity) 416
Saṁyukta-samavāya (conjoined inherence) .. 130, 412, 413, 413
Saṁyukta - samaveta - samavāya (conjoined inherent inherence) 130, 412
Saṁyoga (conjunction) 130, 412[2]
Saṁvara (restraint) 168
Saṁvṛti (veil) 146

Page

Saṁvṛti (illusory) 203
Saṁvṛti (conditional) 254
Saṁśaya (doubt) 25, 33, 51, 52, 58, 103, 122, 201, 258, 359, 374, 375, 381
Saṁśaya-vidhi (method of debate) 51
Saṁśaya-vyudāsa (dispelling all questions) 122
Saṁśaya-sama (balancing the doubt) 34, 67, 260, 261, 268, 289
Saṁsad (council) 22
Saṁsarga-bodhaḥ (knowledge of the mutual connection of things) 444
Saṁsargābhāva (negation of correlation) .. .. 97 (ftn. 1), 394
Saṁsāra (path of transmigration) 3
Saṁsāra-santati-parīkṣā (examination of continuity of the world) 327
Saṁskāra (impression) .. 126[2]
Saṁhitā (hymn) 108
Sarva-tantra (dogma of all schools) 59
Sarva-tantra siddhānta (conclusion accepted by all schools) .. 259
Sarva-daṇḍa-nāyaka (the leader of all daṇḍas) 322
Savikalpa (determinate) .. 55
Savikalpaka (determinate) 134, 137[2], 138, 138 (ftn. 1), 179, 360, 383, 390
Savikalpaka-pratyakṣa (determinate perception) 383
Savikalpaka-vāda (doctrine of the determinate) 419
Savyabhicāra (erratic) 33, 63, 438[3]
Savyabhicāra (undistributed middle) 260
Śāśvata- vāda (eternalists) .. 228
Sahakāri-kāraṇa (causality) .. 134
Sahacāra (simultaneous) 190, 191[2], 427
Sahaja śakti (natural power) .. 397
Sādṛśya (likeness) 443
Sādhaka (theory of proof). 266, 504
Sādhana (medicine) 34
Sādhana (middle term) 180[3], 190, 290

Page

Sādhana-vikala (defective in the middle term) 369
Sādhanāvyāvṛtta (example of excluded middle term) .. 369
Sādharmya (homogeneous) 176, 191, 264[2], 287, 290, 368, 502
Sādharmyodāharaṇa (affirmative example) 502
Sadharmya-dṛṣṭāntābhāsa (fallacy of the homogeneous example) 178, 296 (ftn. 1)
Sādharmya-vat (positive inference) 312
Sādharmya-sama (balancing the homogeneity) .. 67, 268, 289
Sādhāraṇa (general) .. 293, 438
Sādhu (monk) 223
Sādhya (major term) 175, 176[2], 177[2], 178[4], 179, 180[3], 189, 264, 268, 268 (ftn 2), 282, 285, 290, 377, 383
Sādhya-vikala (example defective in the major term) 368
Sādhya-sama (counter-questioned) 63, 67, 256, 260, 268, 289
Sādhyāsiddha (unproved on the part of the major term) .. 440
Sādhvī (nun) 223
Sāmānya (generality) 27, 32, 138, 192, 279, 287[2], 295, 333, 375, 382, 387[2], 388, 389, 393[2], 394[2], 395, 402, 487 (ftn. 1)
Sāmānyato dṛṣṭa (commonly seen) 56, 116 (ftn. 1), 260, 499
Sāmānyato-' dṛṣṭa (not commonly seen) 56
Sāmānya-lakṣaṇa (like any one of its kind) 310
Sāmānya-lakṣaṇa (intercourse whose character is general) 412, 429
Sāmānya-lakṣaṇa-siddhānta (conclusion about the intercourse whose character is general) .. 430
Sāmānya-viśeṣa (general particular) 177
Sāmānya-viśeṣa-śabdārtha parīkṣā (examination of the meaning, of

Page

the words 'generality' and 'particularity') 327

Sāmānya-śabdārtha-parīkṣā (examination of the meaning of the word 'generality') 326

Sāmānyābhāvaḥ (non-existence of the general form) 425

Sāmprata (suitable) .. .. 171[2]

Sāmvyavahārika (practical) .. 201

Sāmvyavahārika-pratyakṣa (practical perception) .. 170 (ftn. 1)

Sāvaka (layman) 229

Siddha-sādhana (demonstration of what has already been established) 256

Siddhānta (conclusion) 27, 32, 33, 52, 59, 258, 259, 264, 359, 374, 375, 381, 504

Siddhānta-lakṣaṇa (conclusive definition) 424

Siddhārtha (inseparable meaning) 397

Simha (lion) 396

Simha-vyaghrokta-lakṣaṇa (definition as given by the Lion and the Tiger) .. .. 396, 406 (ftn. 5)

Simha-vyaghrokta-vyāpti-lakṣaṇa (definition of invariable concomittance given by the Lion and the Tiger) 423

Simha-śiśuka (lion cub) .. 207

Sukha (pleasure) 280

Suddhika-samsandana (simple comparison) 237

Suvarṇa-taijasa-prakaraṇa (section on gold as a fiery thing) .. 397

Sūtrānta or suttānta (original text) 248[2]

Sota-viññāna (auditory perception) 227

Skandhas (aggregates of beings) 126[2], 127 (ftn.)[2]

Stuti (validiction) 108

Sthāpanā (demonstration) 28, 42, 43, 51, 171, 500[2]

Sthira-padārtha-parīkṣā (examination of the permanence of entities) 326

Pag

Sthira-bhāva-parīkṣā (examination of permanent entities) 325 (ftn.)

Sthūla-hasta (rugged hand) .. 273

Sparśa (tangible) 285

Sphoṭa (outburst of a conglomerate sound) 131, 132[2], 148[2], 149[4]

Sphoṭa-vāda (doctrine of phonetic explosion) .. .. 131[2]

Smaraṇa (recollection) .. 201

Smaraṇa-pratyabhijñāna-tarkānumāna-svarūpa-nirṇaya (determination of the nature of recollection, recognition, argumentation, and inference) 200

Smaraṇābhāsa (fallacy of recollection) 193

Smṛti (scripture) 23

Smṛti (memory) 112[2], 189, 215, 393[2], 395

Syād-asti (may be, it is) .. 184

Syād-nāsti (may be, it is not) .. 184

Syād-vāda (see Sapta-bhangi naya) 184, 219

Syād-vāda-śruta (perfect knowledge of things taken from all possible standpoints) .. 181

Svataḥ-prāmaṇya-vāda (doctrine of self-evidence) 326 (ftn), 327

Svabhāva (relation of identity) 140, 191[2], 258, 280, 311, 332, 400, 508

Svabhāva-parīkṣā (examination of nature) 326

Svabhāva-viruddhopalabdhi (perception contrary to identity) .. 311

Svabhāva-hetu (relation of identity) 318

Svabhāvānupalabdhi (non-perception of identity) 311

Svarūpa (specific individual) .. 129

Svarūpāsiddha (unproved in respect of nature) .. 362, 439

Sva-lakṣaṇa (like itself) .. 310

Sva-samjñā (special term) .. 25

Svārthānumāna (inference for one's own self) 175, 192, 202, 276, 280, 307, 309[2], 310, 359[2], 361, 435[2]

Page

Hāra (bearer) .. 127 (ftn.)

Hīnayāna (the little vehicle) .. 241

Hetu (middle term or reason) 5, 22, 27², 28, 32, 32 (ftn. 1), 60, 121, 162², 166, 175, 176², 177², 178³, 180, 190³, 193, 202⁴, 258, 264², 265, 266, 268², 268 (ftn. 2), 284, 286, 290, 291, 377, 437², 500, 502, 503, 504

Hetu (means of knowledge) 51, 161, 162, 189

Hetu (cause) 240 (ftn. 3)², 404

Hetu-cakra (wheel of reasons) 299 (ftn. 2)

Hetu-dṛṣṭānta (reason and example) 276

Hetu-doṣa (committing fallacies) .. 163

Hetu-prayoga (use of the middle term) 203

Hetu-vāda (theory of reasons) .. 23

Page

Hetu-vādin (logician) 39

Hetu-vidyā (logic) .. 240 (ftn. 3)

Hetu-vibhakti (limitation of the reason) 166

Hetu-śāstra (logic) .. 7, 37, 40

Hetvantara (shifting the reason) 35, 84, 269

Hetvartha (implication) .. 25

Hetvasiddhi (unproved on the part of the reason) .. 440

Hetvābhāsa (semblance of a reason) 51², 52, 63, 84, 137, 178, 193, 258, 259, 269, 293 (ftn. 1), 313, 359, 362, 374, 375, 379, 381, 399, (ftn. 1), 438²

Hetvābhāsa-sāmānya-nirukti (general definition of fallacy) .. 438

Hetvābhāsānām asādhukatā-sādhakatva-nirūpaṇam (determination of the serviceableness of fallacies) 442

TIBETAN INDEX.

This index is intended to facilitate the finding of all references and all general matter contained in the volume connected, in any way, with Tibet, its language and literature. It is meant for those who wish to consult the work not for its main subject, logic, but for the data it contains in connection with Tibetan studies. For this reason, in this index, only such names, whether Tibetan or Indian, have been given as are referred to in some specific Tibetan connection. Only those works are quoted of which the Tibetan versions are mentioned. Indian paṇḍits collaborating in Tibetan translation, but whose Tibetan names are not given, are excluded. On the contrary the names of Tibetan interpreters have all been given. A list of Indian translator-paṇḍits may be found on p. 353. Also excluded are the details contained in appendices H, I and J except a very few items. A list of errata, as far as observed, but only in Tibetan words, or connected with them, is added. The plan of the index is as follows:—

I. Logical terms—Tibetan, Sanskrit, English.

II. Initial words of Tibetan quotations.

III. Books.
1. Titles of Logical Books—Tibetan, Sanskrit, English.
2. id. —Sanskrit only.
3. References to (a) the Tanjur.
(b) the Kanjur.
4. References to other Tibetan works.
5. References to other Indian works.
6. References to 'Tibetan books' in general.
7. Modern books quoted.

IV Proper names.
1. Tibetan.
2. Indian.
3. Modern authors.

V. Place names.
1. Tibetan spelling.
2. English spelling.

VI. Residuals.
1. Tibetan.
2. English.

VII. Errata.

J. v. M.

I. LOGICAL TERMS.

Page

ཀུན་བརྟགས་ parikalpita, fanciful, erroneous, false .. 245 *n* 1

ཀུན་རྫོབ་བདེན་པ་ samvṛti satya, conditional truth .. 254 *n* 2

ཀུན་གཞི་རྣམ་པར་ཤེས་པ་ ālaya-vijñāna, knowledge which constitutes the basis or foundation of all, the basic knowledge .. 245 *n* 1

སྐྱེས་བུ་བརྟག་པ་ puruṣa-parīkṣā, examination of the soul .. 326

ཁྱད་ *or* བྱེ་བྲག་ viśeṣa, particularity 287

ཁྱབ་ vyāpti universal, invariable, inseparable connection between the middle term and the major term 292

གྲངས་ཅན་པ་ (see སེར་སྐྱ་བ་) sāṁkhya *or* kāpila.. 278

གྲུབ་པའི་མཐའ་ avayava, siddhānta, established tenet, member 54 *n* 2, 258

དགོས་པ་ prayojana, motive, purpose 54 *n* 2, 258

འགལ་བ་ viruddha, the contradictory 294

འགལ་བ་མི་འཁྲུལ་པ་ viruddha-vyabhicāri, non-erroneous contradiction 316

འགྱུར་བར་སྨྲ་བ་བརྟག་པ་ vivartavāda-parīkṣā, examination of the doctrine of evolution 327

འགྲོ་བ་རང་བཞིན་དུ་སྨྲ་བ་བརྟག་པ་ jagat svabhāva-vāda-parīkṣā, examination of the theory that the world is self-existent 326

རྒྱུ་ལྟར་སྣང་བ་ hetvābhāsa, fallacious middle term, fallacy 54 *n* 2

སྒྲ་ཡི་དོན་བརྟག་པ་ śabdārtha-parīkṣā, examination of the meaning of the word 'sound' 327

སྒྲ་ལས་བྱུང་བ see ཡིད་ཆེས་ཚིག

སྒྲའི་ཚངས་པ་བརྟག་པ་ śabda Brahma-parīkṣā, examination of Brahma, the presiding Deity of Sound .. 326

བསྒྲུབ་པར་བྱ་ *or* ཆོས་ sādhya or dharma, major term or predicate .. 290

བསྒྲུབ་པར་བྱེད་ *or* གཏན་ཚིགས་ sādhana, hetu, linga, middle term, reason, mark 290

བསྒྲུབ་བྱ་ *or* དཔག་བྱ་ sādhya, anumeya, major term, syllogism .. 282

བསྒྲུབ་བྱ་མཚུངས་ sādhya-samā .. 289

ངག་དོན་ *see* ཡིད་ཆེས་ཚིག

མངོན་སུམ་ pratyakṣa, perception 55 *n* 1, 276, 277 *n* 1, 298, 307, 309

མངོན་སུམ་གྱི་མཚན་ཉིད་བརྟག་པ་ pratyakṣa-lakṣaṇa-parīkṣā, examination of the definition of perception 327

མངོན་སུམ་གཏན་ལ་དབབ་པ་ pratyakṣa-vyavastha, system of perception 309

མངོན་སུམ་ལྟར་སྣང་ pratyakṣābhāsa, fallacy of perception .. 298

ཆ་ཤས་ siddhānta, avayava, member of syllogism, tenet, syllogism 54 *n* 2, 258

ཚད་པའི་གནས་ nigraha sthāna, a reason why one may be declared unfit to continue the controversy, point of defeat 54 *n* 2

ཆོས་ *or* བསྒྲུབ་པར་བྱ་ dharma *or* sādhya, predicate *or* major term 290

ཆོས་ཀྱི་ཁྱད་པར་ཕྱིན་ཅི་ལོག་ཏུ་སྒྲུབ་པར་བྱེད་པ་ iṣṭa vighāta-kṛt-viruddha, implied contradiction .. 315, 316

ཆོས་ཅན་ *or* ཕྱོགས་ dharmin *or* pakṣa, subject *or* minor term .. 290

ཆོས་མཐུན་པ་ sādharmya, homogeneous 290

ཆོས་མཐུན་དཔེ་ལྟར་སྣང་བ་ sādharmya-dṛṣṭāntābhāsa, fallacies of the homogeneous example .. 296

ཆོས་མཐུན་མཚུངས་ sādharmya-samā 289

ཆོས་མི་མཐུན་པ་ vaidharmya, heterogeneous 290

ཆོས་མི་མཐུན་དཔེ་ལྟར་སྣང་བ་ vaidharmya-dṛṣṭāntābhāsa, fallacy of the heterogeneous example 297 *n* 1

Page

ཆོས་མི་མཐུན་མཚུངས་ vaidharmya-samā 289

འཇིག་རྟེན་རྒྱུད་པའི་བརྟག་པ་ saṁsārā-santati-parīkṣā, examination of the continuity of the world .. 327

རྗེས་དཔག་ *see* རྗེས་སུ་དཔག་ anumāna, inference 280, 298

རྗེས་དཔག་ལྟར་སྣང་ anumānābhāsa, fallacy of inference 298

རྗེས་སུ་འགྲོ་བ་ཕྱིན་ཅི་ལོག་པ་ viparītānvaya, fallacy of inverse connection 297

རྗེས་སུ་འགྲོ་བ་མེད་ ananvaya, absence of connection 297

རྗེས་སུ་དཔག་ *see* རྗེས་དཔག་

རྗེས་སུ་དཔག་པ་བརྟག་པ་ anumānaparīkṣā, examination of inference 327

བརྗོད་པ་ jalpa, wrangling 54 *n* 2

བརྗོད་མཚུངས་ varṇyasamā 288, 289

ཉེར་འཇལ་ upamāna, comparison .. 287

གཉིས་ཀ་བརྟག་པ་ ubhaya-parīkṣā, examination of both [nature and sense-organs] 326

གཏན་ཚིགས་ hetu, reason, middle term 258, 286

གཏན་ཚིགས་ *or* བསྒྲུབ་པར་བྱེད་ hetu, liṅga, sādhana, middle term, reason, mark 290

གཏན་ཚིགས་ལྟར་ སྣང་ [བ་] hetvābhāsa, fallacy of the middle term 293 *n* 1, 258

གཏན་ཚིགས་དང་དཔེ་ hetu-dṛṣṭānta, reason and example .. 276

གཏན་ཚིགས་ [ཀྱི་] ཚུལ་གསུམ་ liṅgasya trairūpyam, three characteristics of the middle term .. 291 *n* 1

གཏན་ཚིགས་རིག་པ་ hetu-śāstra, hetu-vidyā, science of reasoning .. 7 *n* 7

གཏན་ལ་ཕབ་པ་ nirṇaya 258

གཏན་ལ་དབབ་པ་ nirṇaya, demonstration, ascertainment .. 54 *n* 2

རྟགས་ mark 298

རྟོག་གེ་ tarka, corroborating a proposition by showing that its denial is impossible, *reductio ad absurdum*, confutation, 54 *n* 2, 258

རྟོག་གེ་རིག་ tarka-vidyā, art of debate .. .. 7 *n* 10

ལྟ་བ་ darśana, philosophy .. 5 *n* 5

ལྟག་གཅོད་ jāti, analogue, far-fetched analogue, .. 258, 276, 288

ལྟག་ཆོད་ jāti, evasive answer, analogue .. .. 54 *n* 2

སྟོང་པ་ཉིད་ śūnyatā [śūnya-vāda], the absolute, the void .. 254 *n* 2

བརྟན་པའི་དངོས་པོ་བརྟག་པ་ sthira-padārtha-parīkṣā, examination of the permanence of entities .. 326

ཐལ་བ་མཚུངས་ prasaṅga-samā .. 289

ཐུན་མོང་ sādhāraṇa, the too general 293

ཐུན་མོང་མ་ཡིན་ asādhāraṇa, the not general enough 294

ཐེ་ཚོམ་ saṁśaya, doubt.. 54 *n* 2, 258

ཐེ་ཚོམ་མཚུངས་ saṁśaya-samā .. 289

ཐོས་པ་བརྟག་བ་ śruti-parīkṣā, examination of śruti or scripture .. 327

དུས་གསུམ་བརྟག་པ་ kālatraya-parīkṣā, examination of the three times 327

དོན་རྟོགས་མཚུངས་ arthāpatti-samā 289

དོན་དམ་པའི་བདེན་པ་ paramārtha satyā, transcendental truth 254 *n* 2

འདུ་ཁྱད་ samavāya, inherence .. 287

འདུ་བའི་ཚིག་དོན་བརྟག་པ་ samavāya-śabdārtha-parīkṣā, examination of the word 'co-existent cause' 327

ནམ་མཁའི་གོས་ཅན་གྱིས་ཀུན་ཏུ་བརྟགས་པའི་བདག་བརྟག་པ་ digambara-parikalpita-ātma-parīkṣā, examination of the Digambara Jaina doctrine of the soul .. ..

གནས་མའི་བུས་བདག་བརྟག་པ་ Vātsīputra-kalpita-ātma-parīkṣa, examination of the Vātsīputra doctrine of the soul 326

རྣམ་རྟོག་མཚུངས་ vikalpa-samā .. 289

Page

རྣམ་པར་རྩོད་པ་འ་མཐའ་ vitaṇḍā .. 258

རྣམ་པར་ཤེས་པའི་སྨྲ་བ་ *see* རྣལ་འབྱོར་པའི་སྨྲ་བ་ vijñāna vāda (yogācāra-darśaṇa), the doctrine of idealism 245 *n* 1

རྣམ་བཞིན་ svabhāva, identity .. 258

རྣལ་འབྱོར་པ་ yogin, yogācāra .. 278

རྣལ་འབྱོར་པའི་སྨྲ་བ་ *see* རྣམ་པར་ཤེས་པའི་སྨྲ་བ་ yogācāra darśaṇa, yogācāra [in Tibet yogācārya], practice of meditation 245 *n* 1, 249, 249 *n* 1

དཔག་བྱ་ *or* བསྒྲུབ་བྱ་ anumeya *or* sādhya, predicate *or* major term 282

དཔེ་ dṛṣṭānta, example 54 *n* 2, 128 *n* 4, 258, 286

དཔེ་བརྗོད་ dṛṣṭānta, example .. 290

སྤྱི་ sāmānya, generality .. 287

སྤྱི་དང་བྱེ་བྲག་གི་ཚིག་གི་དོན་བརྟག་པ་ sāmānya-viśeṣa-śabdārtha-parīkṣā, examination o the words 'generality' and 'parti.ula:ity' 326, 327

སྤྱིའི་ཚིག་གི་དོན་བརྟག་པ་ sāmānya śabdārtha parikṣā, examination of the meaning of the word 'generality' or 'genus' 326

སྤྱོད་པ་པས་བརྟགས་པའི་བདག་བརྟག་པ་ mīmāṃsaka-kalpita-ātma-parīkṣā, examination of the mimāṃsaka doctrine of the soul.. .. 326

ཕྱི་རོལ་གྱི་དོན་བརྟག་པ་ vāhyārtha-parikṣā, examination of external objects 327

ཕྱོགས་ *or* ཆོས་ཅན་ pakṣa *or* dharmin, minor term *or* subject .. 290

ཕྱོགས་ཆོས་ pakṣa-dharma, law of extension of the middle term .. 283

ཕྱོགས་ལྟར་སྣང་ pakṣābhāsa, fallacy of thesis .. .. 290 *n* 1

ཕྲད་མཚུངས་ prāpti-samā .. 288

བྱེ་བྲག་ *or* ཁྱད་ viśeṣā, particularity 287

དབང་ཕྱུག་བརྟག་པ་ indriya parīkṣā, examination of the sense-organs .. 326

དབུ་མ་ mādhyamika .. 249

འབྲས་བུ་ kārya, effect 258, 280, 311, 332

འབྲས་བུའི་གཏན་ཚིགས་ kārya-hetu, relation of effect and cause .. 318

འབྲས་མཚུངས་ kārya-samā .. 289

མ་སྐྱེས་མཚུངས་ anutpatti-samā .. 289

མ་གྲུབ་ asiddha, the unproved .. 293

མ་ངེས་པ་ aniścita, the uncertain .. 293

མ་བརྗོད་མཚུངས་ avarṇya-samā .. 289

མ་ཕྲད་མཚུངས་ aprāpti-samā .. 288

མི་དམིགས་ anupalabdhi, non-perception .. 258, 281, 311, 332

མི་དམིགས་པའི་གཏན་ཚིགས་ anupalabdhi-hetu, relation of negation .. 318

དམིགས་པ་མཚུངས་ upalabdhi-sāma [*sic.*] 289

སྨྲ་བའི་མཐའ་ vāda 258

རྩོད་པ་ anvīkṣikī, vāda, logic, discussion .. .. 7 *n* 1, 54 *n* 2

རྩོད་པའི་མཐའ་ jalpa 258

ཚད་མ་ pramāṇa, source of right cognition, means of right knowledge 54 *n* 2, 258

ཚད་མ་གྲུབ་པ་ pramāṇa-siddhi, establishment of pramāṇa .. 307

ཚད་མ་ [ག] ཞན་བརྟག་པ་ pramāṇāntara-parīkṣā, examination of other kinds of valid knowledge 327

ཚན་སེལ་བ་ apoha, negation of the opposite .. .. 276, [287]

ཚར་གཅད་པ་ nigraha sthāna .. 258

ཚིག་གི་དོན་བཅུ་དྲུག་ ṣoḍaśa padārthāḥ, the sixteen categories [in Akṣapāda's Nyāya-sutra] 54 *n* 2

ཚིག་དོར་ chala, quibble 54 *n* 2, 258

མཚན་ཉིད་དྲུག་བཤད་པ་ ṣaḍ-lakṣaṇa-vyākhyā, explanation of six characteristics 332

རྫས་ dravya, substance .. 287

རྫས་ཀྱི་ཚིག་གི་དོན་བརྟག་པ་ dravya-padārtha-parīkṣā, examination of the meaning of the word 'substance' 326

Page

གཞན་གྱི་དོན་གྱི་རྗེ[ས་]དཔག་ parārthānumāna, inference for the sake of others 276, 282

གཞན་གྱི་དོན་གྱི་རྗེས་སུ་དཔག་པ་ parārthānumāna, inference for the sake of others 309

གཞན་གྱི་དོན་གྱི་ཚིག་ parārtha-vākya, words for the sake of others .. 307

གཞན་དབང་ paratantra, dependent on others, conditional ..245 *n* 1

གཞན་གྱི་དབང་པོ་ལས་འདས་པའི་དོན་མཐོང་བ་ཅན་གྱི་སྐྱེས་བུ་བརྟག་པ་ anyendriyātītārtha-darśana-puruṣa-parīkṣā, examination of the soul which sees things beyond the range of senses 327

གཞན་སེལ་བ་ apoha, negation of the opposite .. .. 287, [276]

གཞལ་བྱ་ prameya, object of right cognition, object of right knowledge .. .. 54 *n* 2, 258

ཡིད་ཆེས་ཚིག་ *or* སྒྲ་ལས་བྱུང་བ་ *or* ངག་དོན་ śabda, credible word *or* verbal testimony 287

ཡོངས་གྲུབ་ pariniṣpanna, complete in itself, perfect .. 245 *n* 1

ཡོན་ཏན་ guṇa, quality 287

ཡོན་ཏན་གྱི་ཚིག་གི་དོན་བརྟག་པ་ guṇa-śabdārtha-parīkṣā, examination of the meaning of the word 'quality' 326

རང་[གི་]དོན་[གྱི་]རྗེས་[སུ་]དཔག་[པ་] svārthānumāna, inference for one's self .. 276, 280, 307, 309

རང་བཞིན་ svabhāva, identity 280, 311, 332

རང་བཞིན་གྱི་གཏན་ཚིགས་ svabhāva-hetu, relation of identity .. 318

རང་བཞིན་བརྟག་པ svabhāva-parīkṣā, examination of nature .. 326

རང་ལས་ཚད་མ་བརྟག་པ་ svataḥ-prāmāṇya-parīkṣā, examination of self-evidence 327

Page

རིགས་བསྟན་བཅོས་ nyāya-śāstra, science of right judgment, of true reasoning .. 40, 40 *n* 3

རིགས་པ་ nyāya, true reasoning .. 8 *n* 7

རིགས་པ་ཅན་ naiyāyika .. 287, 287 *n* 3

རིགས་པ་ཅན་དང་བྱེ་བྲག་པས་ཀུན་ཏུ་བརྟགས་པའི་སྐྱེས་བུ་བརྟག་པ་ nyāya-vaiśeṣika-parikalpita-puruṣa parīkṣā, examination of the Nyāya and Vaiśeṣika doctrines of the soul .. 326

རིགས་པའི་བསྟན་བཅོས་ *see* རིགས་བསྟན་བཅོས་

རིགས་པའི་ཡན་ལག་ nyāyāvayava, the (five) parts or members of a syllogism; syllogism .. 42 *n* 9, 289 *n* 3

ལས་ karma, action 287

ལས་ཀྱི་ཚིག་གི་དོན་བརྟག་པ་ karma-śabdārtha parīkṣa, examination of the meaning of the word 'karma' 326

ལས་དང་འབྲས་བུའི་འབྲེལ་པ་བརྟགས་ karma-phala-sambandha-parīkṣā, examination of the relation between karma and its effect .. 326

ལེན་པའི་རྣམ་པར་ཤེས་ pravṛtti-vijñāna, knowledge as received, presentative knowledge which produces the external world drawing us toward it.. .. 245 *n* 1

སུན་འབྱིན་ dūṣaṇa, refutation .. 298

སུན་འབྱིན་ལྟར་སྣང་བ་ dūṣaṇābhāsa, fallacy of refutation 298

སུན་འབྱིན་དུ་རྒོལ་བ་ vitaṇḍā, cavil or reducing a proposition *ad absurdum* without caring to establish one's own view .. 54 *n* 2

སེར་སྐྱ་པས་ཀུན་ཏུ་བརྟགས་པའི་བདག་བརྟག་པ་ kapila-parikalpita-ātma-parīkṣā, examination of Kapila's doctrine of the soul 326

སེར་སྐྱ་བ་ *see* གྲངས་ཅན་པ་ Kāpila *or* Sāṁkhya 278

ཨུ་པ་ནི་ཥ་ད་ཀྱིས་བརྟགས་པའི་བདག་བརྟག་པ་ Upaniṣad-kalpita-ātma-parīkṣā, examination of the Upaniṣad doctrine of the soul.. .. 326

II. TIBETAN QUOTATIONS.

	Page
ཀུན་མཁྱེན་འཁྲུལ་བྲལ་ ..	345 *n* 4
ཀྱེ་མ་འཕགས་པ་ ..	334 *n* 4
གང་གིས་འབྲལ་བ་ ..	345 *n* 2
གང་གིས་གསུང་རབ་ ..	338 *n* 1
གང་ཚེ་དོན་དང་ ..	278 *n* 1
གལ་ཏེ་ཆོས་ཀྱི་ ..	305 *n* 2
མངོན་སུམ་རྟོག་པ་ ..	277 *n* 1
མངོན་སུམ་དང་ནི་ ..	276 *n* 4
རྒྱུ་དང་འབྲས་བུའི་ ..	376 *n* 5
སྒྲ་ལས་བྱུང་བ་ ..	287 *n* 3
སྒྲུབ་པ་དེང་ནི་ ..	289 *n* 2
མཁས་པ་དགའ་བ་ ..	258 *n* 1
འཁྲུལ་པའི་ང་བ་ ..	299 *n* 3
ཆོས་ཅན་གྱི་ཆུ་ས་པ་ ..	258 *n* 2
ཇི་ལྟར་རྟོག་གེ་ ..	244 *n* 4
རྗེས་དཔག་རྣམ་གཉིས་ ..	280 *n* 2
རྗེས་དཔག་བྱ་དང་ ..	288 *n* 2
ཉེར་འཇལ་བཞིན་དུ་ ..	287 *n* 2
གཏན་ཚིགས་ཀྱི་མཚན་ ..	317 *n* 2.
གཏན་ཚིགས་བསྒྲུབ་པའི་ ..	286 *n* 1
རྟགས་ནི་འཁྲུལ་པ་ ..	281 *n* 1
སྐྱེ་བ་རྣམས་ཀྱང་ ..	244 *n* 3
དམ་བཅས་པ་ཡང་ ..	124 *n* 1
དེ་ཕྱིར་དཔེ་ནི་	286 *n* 3
དེ་བཞིན་གཤེགས་པ་ ..	252 *n* 1
དེའི་ཚེ་གཞན་དུ་ ..	305 *n* 1
དེར་གང་མཐུན་ཕྱོགས་ ..	283 *n* 3
བདག་དང་དབང་པོ་དང་ཡིད་དང་	279 *n* 1
བེད་སོགས་གཞལ་བྱ་ ..	280 *n* 1
མདོར་ན་བོད་དུ་ ..	353 *n* 1
རྣམ་ཤེས་འཁྲུལ་པས་ ..	306 *n* 7
དཔེ་ཞེས་པ་ནི་	128 *n* 4, 258 *n* 4
སྒྲ་དང་ཁྱད་པར་ ..	279 *n* 1
ཕྱོགས་ཀྱི་ཆོས་ཉིད་ ..	507 *n* 2
ཕྱོགས་ཆོས་མཐུན་ཕྱོགས་ ..	283 *n* 1
ཕྱོགས་རྣམས་ཀུན་གྱི་ ..	276 *n* 3
བུ་མ་བྱེད་མ་བྱེད་ ..	275 *n* 1
བྱས་ན་རྣམ་པར་ ..	244 *n* 6
བྱས་སོགས་བཞིན་དུ་ ..	287 *n* 1
བྱེ་བྲག་པ་རྣམས་ཀྱི་མདོ་ལས་	279 *n* 1
བླ་མ་འཇིག་རྟེན་ ..	347 *n* 1
བློ་ཡིས་ཉམས་སྨྱོང་བ[? = བློས་]	308 *n* 3
བློ་ཡིས་རྣམ་པར་ ..	120 *n* 2
དབང་པོ་དང་དོན་ (སྐྱེས་པའི)	278 *n* 3
དབང་པོ་དང་དོན་ (བྱུང་བའི་)	55 *n* 1
འབྲས་ཉིད་གཞན་གྱི་ ..	135 *n* 5
ཚད་མ་རྣམ་འགྲེལ་ [? རྣམས་འགྲེལ་]	307 *n* 4
ཚད་མར་གྱུར་པ་ ..	276 *n* 2
ཚུལ་བཞིན་ཏེ་ཀྲ་ ..	344 *n* 1
[འ]ཇ་ག་ཏུ་ལའི་ ..	346 *n* 3
འཛམ་གླིང་སྙིང་པོ་ ..	332 *n* 2
གཞན་གྱི་དོན་གྱི་ ..	282 *n* 1, 506 *n* 2
གཞལ་བྱ་བྱས་མི་ ..	285 *n* 1*
ཡིད་ཆེས་ཚིག་ནི་ ..	288 *n* 1
རང་གི་ངོ་བོ་ ..	282 *n* 2
རང. དོན་ནི་ཚུལ་ ..	506 *n* 2
རང་བཞིན་དབང་ལྡན་ ..	325 *n* 3*
རང་གི་རྟོག་པ་ ..	278 *n* 1
རང་ལ་ངེས་བཞིན་ ...	286 *n* 2
ཏུ་མ་པུ་ལའི་	346 *n* 1
རིགས་པ་ཅན་རྣམས་ ..	278 *n* 3
རིགས་པ་ཆེན་པོ་ ..	308 *n* 2
རིགས་པའི་ཡན་ལག་ ..	42 *n* 9
སློབ་དཔོན་ཆོས་མཆོག་ ..	331 *n* 2
སློབ་དཔོན་ཛྙ་གོ་མི་ ..	332 *n* 3
ཤཱ་ཀྱ་ཐུབ་པ་མི་ ..	315 *n* 2

III. BOOKS.

1. *Logical Works, Tibetan.*

	Page
སྐད་ཅིག་མ་འཇིག་གྲུབ་པའི་རྣམ་འགྲེལ་ kṣaṇa-bhaṅga-siddhi vyākhyā, commentary on the kṣaṇa-bhaṅga-siddhi	331
སྐད་ཅིག་མ་འཇིག་པ་གྲུབ་པ་ kṣaṇa-bhaṅga-siddhi, proof of the momentariness of things	330

Page

གླེགས་བམ་བཀླག་པའི་ཐབས་ pustaka-pāṭhopāya, the method of reading books 341

རྒྱུ་དང་འབྲས་བུའི་ངོ་བོ་གྲུབ་པ་ kārya-kāraṇa-bhāva-siddhi, establishment of the relation of cause and effect 341

རྒྱུད་གཞན་གྲུབ་པ་ santānāntara-siddhi, proof of the continuity of succession 319

རྒྱུད་གཞན་གྲུབ་པའི་འགྲེལ་བཤད་ santānāntara-siddhi ṭikā, commentary on the above 322

ཆོས་དང་ཆོས་ཅན་གཏན་ལ་དབབ་པ་ dharma-dharmi-viniścaya, determination of the minor and major terms 337

འཇིག་རྟེན་ཕ་རོལ་གྲུབ་པ་ pāra-loka-siddhi, proof of the world beyond 330

གཏན་ཚིགས་ཀྱི་འཁོར་ལོ་གཏན་ལ་དབབ་པ་ *or* ཕྱོགས་ཆོས་དགུའི་འཁོར་ལོ་ hetu-cakrahamaru *or* pakṣa dharma-cakra, the wheel of reasons put in order 299, 299 *n* 1, 2, 3

གཏན་ཚིགས་ཀྱི་ཐིགས་པ་ hetu-bindu vivaraṇa, a drop of reason .. 318

གཏན་ཚིགས་ཀྱི་ཐིགས་པ་རྒྱ་ཆེར་འགྲེལ་པ་ hetu-bindu-ṭikā, detailed commentary on the above .. 321

གཏན་ཚིགས་ཀྱི་དེ་ཁོ་ན་ཉིད་བསྟན་པ་ hetu-tattva-upadeśa, instruction on the real nature of the middle term in a syllogism.. .. 337

གཏན་ཚིགས་ཐིགས་པའི་འགྲེལ་པ་ hetu-bindu-vivaraṇa, commentary on the hetu-bindu 332

རྟོག་གེའི་སྐད་ tarka-bhāṣā, technicalities of logic 346

ཐམས་ཅད་མཁྱེན་པ་གྲུབ་པའི་ཚིག་ལེའུར་བྱས་པ་ sarvajña-siddhi-kārikā, memorial verses on the attainment of omniscience 328

ཐོས་པ་བརྟག་པའི་ཚིག་ལེའུར་བྱས་པ་ śruti-parīkṣā, memorial verses on the examination of śruti or verbal testimony 328

དུས་གསུམ་བརྟག་པ་ trikāla-parīkṣā, examination of [the] three times .. 301

དེ་ཁོ་ན་ཉིད་བསྡུས་པའི་དཀའ་འགྲེལ་ tattva-saṁgraha-pañjikā, commentary on the tattva-saṁgraha .. 328

དེ་ཁོ་ན་ཉིད་བསྡུས་པའི་ཚིག་ལེའུར་བྱས་པ་ tattva-saṁgraha-kārikā, memorial verses on a summary of the tattvas 324

ནང་གི་ཁྱབ་པ་ antar-vyāpti, internal inseparable connection .. 343

རྣམ་པར་རིག་པ་ཙམ་ཉིད་དུ་གྲུབ་པ་ vijñapti-mātra-siddhi, establishment of a mere communication of knowledge 343

ཕྱི་རོལ་གྱི་དོན་གྲུབ་པ་ཞེས་བྱ་བའི་ཚིག་ལེའུར་ vāhyārtha-siddhi-kārikā, memorial verses on the reality of external things .. ., 328

ཕྱོགས་ཆོས་དགུའི་འཁོར་ལོ་ *see* གཏན་ཚིགས་ཀྱི་འཁོར་ལོ་གཏན་ལ་དབབ་པ་ pakṣa-dharma-cakra

བྱིས་པ་འཇུག་པའི་རྟོག་གེ་ bālāvatāra-tarka, children's introduction to logic 337

དབང་ཕྱུག་འཇིག་པའི་ཚིག་ལེའུར་བྱས་པ་ Iśvara-bhaṅga-kārikā, memorial verses on the refutation of God .. 329

འབྲེལ་པ་གྲུབ་པ་ pratibandha-siddhi, establishment of the causal connection 345

འབྲེལ་པ་བརྟག་པ་ sambandha-parīkṣā, examination of connection .. 319

འབྲེལ་པ་བརྟག་པའི་འགྲེལ་པ་ sambandha-parīkṣā-vṛtti, commentary on the above 319

འབྲེལ་པ་བརྟག་པའི་རྒྱ་ཆེར་བཤད་པ་ sambandha-parīkṣā-ṭikā, copious commentary on the above .. 321

འབྲེལ་པ་བརྟག་པའི་རྗེས་སུ་འབྲང་བ་ sambandha-parīkṣānusāra, commentary on the above 345

དམིགས་པ་བརྟག་པ་ ālambana-parīkṣā,

Page

examination of the objects of thought 301

དམིགས་པ་བརྟག་པའི་འགྲེལ་[པ་] ālambaṇa-parīkṣā-vṛtti, commentary on the above 301

དམིགས་པ་བརྟག་པའི་འགྲེལ་བ་བཤད་ ālambaṇa-parīkṣā-ṭīkā, annotation on the above .. 321, 322

རྩོད་པ་བཟློག་པའི་ཚིག་ལེའུར་བྱས་པ་, vigraha-vyāvartanī-kārikā, memorial verses on quelling disputes 256, 257

རྩོད་པའི་རིགས་པ་ tarka-nyāya *or* vāda-nyāya, method of discussion 318

རྩོད་པའི་རིགས་པའི་འགྲེལ་པ་ vāda-nyāya-vyākhyā, commentary on the above 321

རྩོད་པའི་རིགས་པའི་འགྲེལ་པ་དོན་རྣམ་པར་འབྱེད་པ་ vāda-nyāya-vṛtti-vipañcitārtha, elaborate commentary on the above 323

ཚད་མ་ཀུན་ལས་བཏུས་པ་ *see* ཚད་མའི་མདོ་ *etc.*, pramāṇa-samuccaya, compilation on pramāṇa, valid knowledge .. 42 *n* 9, 135 *n* 5, 276

ཚད་མ་ཀུན་ལས་བཏུས་པའི་འགྲེལ་པ་ pramāṇa-samuccaya-vṛtti, commentary on the above 299, 300

ཚད་མ་བརྟག་པ་ pramāṇa parīkṣā, examination of pramāṇa or the sources of valid knowledge .. 330

ཚད་མ་རྣམ་འགྲེལ་གྱི་དཀའ་འགྲེལ་ pramāṇa-vārtika-pañjikā, explanation of difficulties in the pramāṇa-vārtika 319

ཚད་མ་རྣམ་འགྲེལ་གྱི་འགྲེལ་བ་ pramāṇa-vārtika-vṛtti, annotation on the pramāṇa-vārtika 308, 308 *n* 2, 323

ཚད་མ་རྣམ་འགྲེལ་གྱི་འགྲེལ་བཤད་ pramāṇa-vārtika (-pañjikā)-ṭīkā, annotation on the pramāṇa-vārtika-pañjikā .. . 320, 344

ཚད་མ་རྣམ་འགྲེལ་གྱི་རྒྱན་ pramāṇa-vārtikālaṅkāra, commentary on the pramāṇa-vārtika 336

Page

ཚད་མ་རྣམ་འགྲེལ་[གྱི་] རྒྱན་གྱི་འགྲེལ་བཤད་ pramāṇā - vārtikālaṅkāra - ṭīkā, annotation on the above 338, 344

ཚད་མ་རྣམ་འགྲེལ་གྱི་ཚིག་ pramāṇa-vārtika [kārikā], memorial verses explanatory of pramāṇa or sources of knowledge .. 307, 307 *n* 4

ཚད་མ་རྣམ་ངེས་ཀྱི་ཊཱི་ཀཱ་ pramāṇa-viniścaya-ṭīkā, *see below*, commentary on the pramāṇa-viniścaya 330, 331

ཚད་མ་རྣམ་པར་ངེས་པ་ pramāṇa-viniścaya, determination of pramāṇa or sources of knowledge 308, 309, 308/9 *n* 3

ཚད་མ་རྣམ་པར་ངེས་པའི་འགྲེལ་བཤད་ pramāṇa-viniścaya-ṭīkā, *see above*, commentary on the pramāṇa-viniścaya 342

ཚད་མ་རྣམ་པར་འཇོམས་པ་མདོར་བཤད་པའི་འགྲེལ་ pramāṇa-vidhvaṁsana-tippitaka-vṛtti, *or* Pr°-viheṭana-teppitaka-vṛtti, *or* Pr°-vidhvaṁsana-sambhāṣita-vṛtti, a magic-stick commentary on Pr°-viheṭana *or* Pr°-vidhvaṁsana .. 257

ཚད་མ་རིགས་པར་འཇུག་པའི་སྒོ་ nyāya-praveśa, door of entrance to logic 289

ཚད་མའི་བསྟན་བཅོས་རིགས་པ་ལ་འཇུག་པ་ pramāṇa-śāstra nyāya-praveśa, an entrance to the science of logic 300, 300 *n* 1

ཚད་མའི་མདོ་ཀུན་ལས་བཏུས་པ་ *see* ཚད་མ་ཀུན་ *etc.*, pramāṇa-sūtra samuccaya, compilation of aphorisms on pramāṇa, valid knowledge 276, 276 *n* 4

གཞན་ལ་བརྟག་པའི་ཚིག་ལེའུར་བྱས་པ་ anyāpoha-vicāra-kārikā, memorial verses on the determination of a thing by the exclusion of its opposites 329

གཞན་སེལ་བ་[ཞེས་བྱ་བའི་རབ་ཏུ་བྱེད་པ་] apoha-namā-prakaraṇa, treatise on the determination of a thing by the exclusion of its opposites .. 330

Page

[ཡངས་པ་དང་དྲི་མ་མེད་པ་དང་ལྡན་པ་ཞེས་བྱ་བ་ཚད་མ་ཀུན་ལས་བཏུས་པའི་འགྲེལ་བཤད་] viśālāmala-vatī-nāma-pramāṇa samuccaya-ṭīkā 323

རིགས་པ་གྲུབ་པའི་སྒྲོན་མ་ nyāyāloka-siddhi *or* nyāya-siddhyāloka, a lamp of logical reasoning 336

རིགས་པའི་ཐིགས་པ་ nyāya-bindu, a drop of logic 309

རིགས་པའི་ཐིགས་པ་རྒྱ་ཆེར་འགྲེལ་བ་ nyāya-bindu-ṭīkā (two different works), detailed commentary on the above 321, 329

རིགས་པའི་ཐིགས་པའི་དོན་བསྡུས་པ་ nyāya-bindu-piṇḍārtha, purport of the above 340

རིགས་པའི་ཐིགས་པའི་ཕྱོགས་སྔ་མ་མདོར་བསྡུས་པ་ nyāya-bindu-pūrva-pakṣe saṁkṣipta, summary of criticisms on the above 327

རིགས་པའི་སྦྱོར་བ་ yukti-prayoga, application of reasoning .. 340

སེལ་བ་གྲུབ་པ་ apoha-siddhi, establishment of a thing by the exclusion of its opposites 345

ལྷན་ཅིག་དམིགས་པ་ངེས་པ་ sahāvalambha-niścaya, the ascertainment of objects and their knowledge arising together 336

2. *Logical Works, Sanskrit.*

(Translated into Tibetan.)

Page

[Abhidharma-]jñāna-prasthāna-śāstra .. .. 247 *n* 3

[Abhidharma-mahā-]vibhāṣā [-śāstra] .. .. 247 *n* 4

Abhisamayālaṅkāra-kārikā 262, 262 *n* 5

Ālambana-parīkṣā .. 300, 300 *n* 3 (*perhaps identical with* Ālambana-pratyaya-dhyāna-śāstra).

Ālambana-parīkṣā-ṭīkā 321/322

Ālambana-parīkṣā-vṛtti 301, 301 *n* 1

Antar-vyāpti 343

Anyāpoha-vicāra-kārikā .. 329

Apoha-nāma-prakaraṇa .. 330

Apoha-siddhi 345

Bālāvatāra-tarka 337

Dharma-dharmi-viniścaya .. 337

Hetu-bindu-ṭīkā 321

Hetu-bindu-vivaraṇa .. 318, 332

Hetu-cakra-hamaru .. 299, 299 *n* 1, 3

Hetu-tattva-upadeśa 337

Īśvara-bhaṅga-kārikā 329

Kārya-kāraṇa-bhava-siddhi .. 341

Kṣana-bhaṅga-siddhi 330

Kṣaṇa-bhaṅga-siddhi-vyākhyā .. 331

Mūla-madhyamaka-vṛtti-akuto-bhaya 250

Page

Nyāya-bindu 309, 309 *n* 2, 315, 315 *n* 2, 317 *n* 2

Nyāya-bindu-piṇḍārtha .. 340

Nyāya-bindu-pūrva-pakṣe-saṁkṣipta 327

Nyāya-bindu-ṭīkā 321, 329, 329 *n* 6

Nyāyāloka-siddhi *or* Nyāya siddhyāloka.. 336

Nyāyānusāra-śāstra *or* Koṣa-kāraka-śāstra .. .. 248 *n* 1

Nyāya-praveśa *or* Nyāya-praveśo-nāma-pramāṇa-prakaraṇa, *perhaps* Nyāya-dvāra-tarka-śāstra: 289, 289 *n* 1, 2; 300, 300 *n* 1, 302, 302 *n* 4, 507 *n* 2

Pāra-loka-siddhi 330

Pramāṇa-nyāya-praveśa *see* Nyāya-praveśa

Pramāṇa-parikṣā 330

Pramāṇa-samuccaya 275, 277 *n* 1, 278 *n* 1, 2, 3; 279 *n* 1, 280 *n* 1, 2; 281 *n* 1, 282 *n* 1. 2; 283 *n* 1, 3; 285 *n* 1, 286 *n* 1*, 2, 3; 287 *n* 1, 2, 3; 288 *n* 1, 2; 506 *n* 2

Pramāṇa-samuccaya-vṛtti .. 299

Page

Pramāṇa-śāstra-nyāya-praveśa *see* Nyāya praveśa.
Pramāṇa-vārtika [-kārikā] 306 *n* 7, 307, 376 *n* 5
Pramāṇa-vārtikālaṅkāra .. 336
Pramāṇa-vārtikālaṅkāra-ṭīkā 338, 344
Pramāṇa-vārtika-pañjikā .. 319
Pramāṇa-vārtika (-pañjikā)-ṭīkā .. 320
Pramāṇa-vārtika-ṭīkā 344
Pramāṇa-vārtika-vṛtti 308, 323
Pramāṇa-viniścaya 308/309, 308 *n* 3
Pramāṇa-viniścaya-ṭīkā 330/331, 342
Pratibandha-siddhi 345
Pustaka-pāṭhopāya 341
Sahāvalambha-niścaya .. 336
Sambhandha-parīkṣā 319
Sambhanda-parīkṣānusāra .. 345
Sambhanda-parīkṣā-ṭīkā .. 321
Sambhanda-parīkṣā-vṛtti .. 319

Page

Santānāntarā-siddhi 319
Santānāntara-siddhi-ṭīkā .. 322
Sarvajña-siddhi-kārikā .. 328
Śruti-parīkṣā 328
Tarka-bhāṣā 346
Tarka-nyāya *or* Vāda-nyāya 124 *n* 1, 318
Tattva-saṁgraha *or* Tarka-saṁgraha .. .. ..325 *n*
Tattva-saṁgraha-kārikā .. 324
Tattva-saṁgraha-pañjikā .. 328
Trikāla-parīkṣā .. 301, 301 *n* 2
Vāda-nyāya *see* Tarka-nyāya.
Vāda-nyāya-vṛtti vipañcitārtha 323/324
Vāda-nyāya-vyākhyā 321
Vāhyārtha-siddhi-kārikā .. 328
Vijñapti-mātra-siddhi 343
Viśālāmala- vatī - nāma - pramāṇa - samuccaya-ṭīkā 323
Yukti-prayoga 340

3A. *References to the Tanjur.*

Page

Tibetan Tanjur—
general .. 519, 530 *et seq.*, 537 *et seq.*
collection of 352
mdo, on the yogācāra school 249 *n* 4
British Mission Copy—
in British Museum 321 *n* 1, 2 ; 328 *n* 1, 329 *n* 6, 332
India Office Copy 300 *n* 3, 301 *n* 1, 2 ; 302, 302 *n* 4, 307 *n* 3, 308 *n* 1, 309 *n* 1, 2 ; 318 *n* 2, 3 ; 319 *n* 1, 2, 3 ; 321 *n* 3, 4 ; 322 *n* 1, 2 ; 323 *n* 1, 324 *n* 1, 328 *n* 4, 330 *n* 2, 3, 4, 5 ; 331 *n* 1, 4 ; 336 *n* 1, 4 ; 337 *n* 3, 340 *n* 1, 3 ; 341 *n* 1 ; 343 *n* 2 ; 345 *n* 1, 3, 5 ; 346 *n* 4
Sikkim, Labrang, Copy 299 *n* 1, 319 *n* 5, 320 *n* 4, 324 *n* 2, 336 *n* 3, 342 *n* 4, 344 *n* 4, 530–538
Single Volumes—
ཙནྡ་པ་, ka ཀ་ = 1 .. 253 *n* 6*
མདོ་, ka ཀ་ = 1 .. 262 *n* 5
,, tsa ཙ་ = 17 256 *n* 2
,, ha ཧ་ = 29 128 *n* 4, 257, 258 *n* 1, 2, 4

Page

མདོ་ gi གི་ = 33 241 *n* 1, 251 *n* 2
,, ku ཀུ་ = 61 342 *n* 6
,, ce ཅེ་ = 95 42 *n* 9. 124 *n* 1, 135 *n* 5, 270, 275, 276, 276 *n* 1, 2, 3; 289, 289 *n* 1, 299, 299, *n* 1, 2 ; 300, 301, 306 *n* 7, 307, 307 *n* 4, 308, 308 *n* 3, 309, 316 *n* 3, 318, 319, 376 *n* 5, 506 *n* 2, 3 ; 507 *n* 2
,, che ཆེ་ = 96 .. 319
,, je ཇེ་ = 97 .. 320
,, ñe ཉེ་ = 98 .. 320
,, te ཏེ་ = 99 .. 336
,, the ཐེ་ (misprint *she*) = 100 336
,, de དེ་ = 101 .. 338
,, ne ནེ་ = 102 .. 338
,, pe པེ་ = 103 .. 344
,, phe ཕེ་ = 104 .. 344
,, be བེ་ = 105 344, 344 *n* 1
,, me མེ་ = 106 .. 344
,, tse ཙེ་ = 107 .. 344
,, tshe ཚེ་ = 108 322, 323, 334

Page

མདོ་ dse ཛེ་ = 109 .. 331
,, we ཝེ་ = 110 331 *n* 2, 342
,, she ཞེ་ = 111 321, 322, 328, 329, 332, 332 *n* 2, 340
,, ze ཟེ་ = 112 324, 328, 328 *n* 4, 329, 330, 331, 336, 336 *n* 1, 4; 337, 337 *n* 3, 338 *n* 1, 340. 341, 343, 345, 345 *n* 2, 4; 346, 346 *n* 3, 347 *n* 1
མདོ་ ḥe འེ་ = 113 .. 328
,, ye ཡེ་ = 114 .. 328
,, re རེ་ = 115 .. 323
,, he ཧེ་ = 119 .. 324
,, go གོ་ = 123 7 *n* 7, 8 *n* 7, 54 *n* 2, 55 *n* 1

3B. *References to the Kanjur.*

Page

འདུལ་བ་, ga ག་ = 3 .. 11 *n* 3
མདོ་, ca ཅ་ = 5 120 *n* 2, 244 *n* 3, 4, 6
collection of 352
general 530–538

4. *Other Tibetan Works.*

Page

ཀློང་རྡོལ་གསུང་འབུམ་ .. 517, 520 *n* 1
ཆོས་བྱུང་ *see* also under Tibetan names *s. v.* Tāranātha 305 *n* 1, 517
འཇམ་དཔལ་རྩ་རྒྱུད་ mañju-śrī-mūla-tantra .. .. 252 *n* 1
དཔག་བསམ་ལྗོན་བཟང་ *see* also under Modern Authors, *s. v.* Das, Sarat Chandra, 305 *n* 1, 2; 320 *n* 4, 322 *n* 3, 323 *n* 2, 327 *n* 1, 328 *n* 3, 329 *n* 1, 332 *n* 3, 333 *n* 5, 334 *n* 4, 335 *n* 1, 336 *n* 2, 337 *n* 1, 338 *n* 3, 340 *n* 2, 4; 341 *n* 2, 342 *n* 1, 5, 6; 344 *n* 2, 346 *n* 1, 348 *n* 1, 353 *n* 1, 516 *n* 1, 517, 517 *n* 2, 519 *n* 2
བཻ་ཌཱུར་དཀར་པོ་ 517
ཤེས་རབ་སྡོང་བུ་ prajñā-daṇḍa 252 *n* 1
བཤེས་པའི་སྤྲིང་ཡིག་ suhṛllekha 251 *n* 2
སུམ་པའི་ཆོས་བྱུང་ 241 *n* 1; 242 *n* 1
སོ་སོར་ཐར་པ་ pātimokkha 232 *n* 1

5. *Other Indian Works.*

Page

Amarakoṣa.. .. 7 *n* 1, 10
Mahārāja-kanika-lekha 241 *n* 1
Mahāvyutpatti 7*n*7, 8*n*7, 11*n*1, 25*n*1, 40*n*3, 43*n*2, 47*n*1, 54*n* 2, 55*n* 1
Laṅkāvatāra sūtra 120 *n* 2, 243 *n* 3, 244 *n* 3, 4, 6
Pātimokkha .. 232 *n* 1
Suhṛllekha .. .. 251 *n* 2

6. *Tibetan Books in general.*

Page

T. authorities on the sūtra of " the burden and the burden-bearer " 127
T. accounts of Nālandā .. 516
T. books .. .. 11, 241 *n* 1
T. books on the Pāla dynasty of Bengal 517
Some books of T. on date of Buddha .. .. 252 *n* 1
T. books on yogācāra 249
Sanskrit books translated into Tibetan .. .. 352, 519 *n* 5, 6
T. literature about Madhya-deśa 304 *n* 1
T. translations of Vasubandhu's works 267
T. versions of Asaṅga's works .. 265

7. *Modern Books.*

(See Modern Authors.)

	Page
Bilingual Index of the Nyāyabindu, Vidyābhūṣana	370 n 4, 309, n 2
Buddhism, Schlagintweit	249 n 1, 5
Catalogue du Fonds Tibétain, Cordier ..	257 n 1, 262 n 2
Geschichte des Buddhismus, Tārānātha, Schiefner, see under Tibetan names s. v. Tārānātha.	
Indian Logic as preserved in Tibet, No. 3, Vidyābhūṣana	262 n 1, 342 n 2
Indian Pandits in the Land of Snow, Sarat Chandra Das	517, 519 n 2
Lamaism, Waddell	271 n 1, 323 n 3, 327 n 1, 520 n 2
Life of Buddha, Rockhill	11 n 3, 246 n 2, 322 n 7
Sāṁkhya Philosophy in the Land of the Lamas, Vidyābhūṣana	324 n 2
Sanskrit works on Literature, Grammar, Rhetoric and Lexicography as preserved in Tibet, Vidyābhūṣana	334 n 3, 343 n 1
Sragdharā Stotra, Vidyābhūṣana	322 n 5, 7
Tibetan-English Dictionary, Sarat Chandra Das ..	520 n 2, 530
Tibetan Grammar, Csoma de Körös	306 n 1, 323 n 3, 517

IV. PROPER NAMES.

1. *Tibetan.*

[Abbreviations : Chinese : C ; Editor : e ; Interpreter : i ; King : k ; Monk : m ; Official : o ; Scholar : s ; Tibetan : T ; Translator : t ; Venerable : v ; Very Venerable : vv.]

	Page
ཀ་བ་དཔལ་བརྩེགས་ T i	256
ཀླུ་སྒྲུབ་ Nāgārjuna, date of ..	252
ཀླུའི་རྒྱལ་མཚན་ T o i	250
ཀློག་སྐྱ་ཤེས་རབ་བརྩེགས་	343
རྐང་མིག་ཅན་ Akṣapada ..	47 n 1
ཁ་ཆེ་ཧྲུ་ན་ཤྲཱི་ = ཡེ་ཤེས་དཔལ་བཟང་པོ་	
ཁུ་མདོ་སྡེ་དཔལ་ i	256
ཁྲི་རལ་ *or* རལ་པ་ཅན་ k	517
ཁྲི་སྲོང་དེ་ཙུ་ཙན་[ཟླ་བཙན་] k	323, 327, 352, 517
གྲགས་པ་རྒྱལ་མཚན་དཔལ་བཟང་ Sāskya m	289
གྲགས་འབྱོར་ཤེས་རབ་ i m ..	331, 328
དགའ་བའི་རྡོ་རྗེ་ T i m	345
དགེ་བའི་བློ་གྲོས་ T i m ..	307, 318, 320
དགེ་བཤེས་སེང་གུང་ C s	300
དགེ་བསྲུང་ Kalyāṇa Rakṣita ..	328
དགྲ་ལས་རྒྱལ་བ་ [Ācārya] Jetāri ..	337
རྒྱ་བཙན་སེང་གེ་ envoy	352
རྒྱས་ཀ་ཅན་ Jina	338
རྒྱལ་དབང་བློ་གྲོས་ Jinendrabodhi ..	323
རྒྱུན་ཤེས་ཀྱི་བུ་ Ātreya ..	11 n 1
ཆོས་ཀྱི་བརྩོན་འགྲུས་ i m	342
ཆོས་ཀྱི་རིན་ཆེན་ Dharmaratna vv C m e T t	300
ཆོས་གྲགས་ Dharmakīrti ..	303
ཆོས་མཆོག་ Dharmottara	329, 331 n 2
ཉི་མ་སྦས་ Ravi Gupta	322
ཏཱ་ར་ནཱ་ཐ་ Lama	246 n 2, 248 n 5, 7, 8; 249 n 4, 251, 251 n 1, 4, 5; 252, 252 n 2, 4; 261 n 3, 265 n 4, 272 n 1, 274 n 2, 303 n 3, 305 n 1, 307 n 1, 319 n 4, 320 n 1, 2, 4; 323 n 3, 328 n 3, 329 n 1, 333 n 5, 336 n 2, 337 n 1, 338 n 2, 3; 339 n 7, 305 n 1, 340 n 2, 4; 341 n 2, 342 n 5, 6; 348 n 4, 344 n 2, 3; 348 n 1, 350 514 n 3, 517, 517 n 2, 519 n 2 520 n 2
ཏི་ལོ་པ་	340

Page

ཉིང་རེ་འབྱོན་བཟང་པོ་ i m of Shu-chen 340
སྟོན་གཞོན་ t m 300
ཐར་པའི་འབྱུང་གནས་སྦས་ Mokṣākara Gupta 346
ཐོགས་མེད་ Asaṅga 265
ཐོན་མི་སམ་བྷོ་ཊ་ minister .. 352
དད་པ་ཤེས་རབ་ t i 300
དད་པའི་ཤེས་རབ་ t i 275
དར་མ་གྲགས་ [སྙམ་ ?] i m .. 318
དུལ་ལྷ་ Vinīta Deva 320
བདེ་བྱེད་དགའ་བ་ Śaṅkarānanda .. 344
རྡོ་རྗེ་རྒྱལ་མཚན་ T i 323
ན་རོ་པ་ 341, 520
ནག་ཚོ་ལོ་ཙཱ་བ་ 517
དཔལ་མཆོག་དང་པོའི་རྡོ་རྗེ་ T i .. 337
དཔལ་ལྡན་བློ་གྲོས་ 323
དཔལ་ལྡན་བློ་གྲོས་བརྟན་པོ་ i m .. 346
དཔལ་རྩེགས་ T o i 319
དཔལ་བརྩེགས་རཀྵི་ཏ་ T i m of Shu-chen 321, 322, 328
དཔལ་ལྷ་ཙན་པོ་ k 250
ཕྱོགས་གླང་ Dignāga .. 272–301
 portrait of 271
 nick-name of 272
བན་དེ་ནམ་མཁས་ i .. 319, 321
བན་དེ་དཔལ་བརྩེགས་ *see* དཔལ་བརྩེགས་ i of Shu-chen 322
བན་དེ་ཡེ་ཤེས་སྡེ་ i of Shu-chen 321, 340
བུ་སྟོན་ great T. sage .. 270, 353
བེ་རོ་ཙ་ན་ i m 336
བྱང་ཆུབ་ཤེས་རབ་ T i 338
བྱམས་པའི་མགོན་པོ་ Maitreya-nātha *or* Maitreya .. 262, 262 *n* 5
བློ་ལྡན་ཤེས་རབ་ T i m 262 *n* 5, 309, 330, 331, 336, 344, 345
དབྱིག་གཉེན Vasubandhu .. 266
འབྲོ་སེང་དཀར་ v i m 324
མིས་སྦྱིན་གྱི་བུ་ Nārada .. 43 *n* 2

Page

མུ་ཏིག་བུམ་པ་ Muktā-kumbha .. 331
མེ་བཞིན་འཇུག་ Agniveśa .. 25 *n* 1
མྱ་ངན་མེད་ Paṇḍita *or* Ācārya Aśoka 332
རྩོད་པའི་ཁྱུ་མཆོག་ Tarka-puṅgava, Fighting Bull, nickname of Dignāga 272
ཚབ་ཉི་མ་གྲགས་ i m 330
ཚུལ་ཁྲིམས་རྒྱལ་མཚན་ i m t .. 301
ཞ་མ་དགེ་བསྙེན་སེང་རྒྱལ་ T i .. 299
ཞི་བ་འཚོ་ Śānta Rakṣita .. 323
ཟླ་བ་དགེ་བསྙེན་ Candra Gomin 332, 332 *n* 2, 333
ཡེ་ཤེས་དཔལ་བཟང་པོ་ Jñāna-śrī Bhadra 342
རལ་པ་ཅན་ *or* ཁྲི་རལ་ k 517
རིགས་ལྡན་རྒྱལ་པོ་ k 299
རིན་ཆེན་གྲགས་ Ratnakīrti .. 338
རིན་ཆེན་རྡོ་རྗེ་ Ratnavajra .. 339
རིན་ཆེན་འབྱུང་གནས་ཞི་བ་ *see* ཨ་ཀ་ར་ཤཱན་ཏི་ Ratnākara Śānti .. 342 *n* 5
ཤཱཀྱ་འོད་ T i m of Hbro 336, 337, 341, 343
ཤེས་རབ་ v i m 324
ཤེས་རབ་འབྱུང་གནས་སྦས་ Prajñākara Gupta 336
སློང་ཙན་གསལ་པོ་ k. contemp. of Dharmakīrti 305, 306, 352
སློབ་དཔོན་ Ācārya, Tib. name of Ratnavajra 340
གསེར་གྱི་གོ་ཆ་ Hema (*or* Kanaka) Varma, Indian sage .. 275, 300
ལྷ་བླ་མ་ཞི་བ་འོད་ great T i Śākya m .. 324
ལྷ་བླ་མ་ཡེ་ཤེས་འོད་ 517
ལྷ་དབང་བློ་ Devendrabodhi .. 319
ལྷ་བཙུན་བྱང་ཆུབ་ k .. 352, 517
ཨ་ཙ་ར་ཤཱན་ཏི་ *or* ཤཱན་ཏི་པ་ *see* རིན་ཆེན་འབྱུང་གནས་ཞི་བ་ Ratnākara Śānti 342

2. *Indian.*

Page

Acārya, T name for Ratnavajra .. 340
Atiśa (Śrī Jñāna Atiśa), visits Tibet 341

Page

Ārya Deva, Tāranātha on .. 261
Ātreya .. .. 11, 11 *n* 3
Dānaśīla *or* Dānaśrīla, visits Tibet 340

Page

Dharmakīrti, quoted .. 124 *n* 1
Dignāga epithet of 272
Dīpaṅkara, starts for Tibet .. 318
Haṁsa, killed in Tibet .. 210
Jina Mitra, visits Tibet .. 340
Jñāna-siddha Bhadra, perhaps identical with Jñāna-śrī Bhadra 342 *n* 1
Kamala Śīla (Śrīla), called to Tibet 327
Kaniṣka, date of .. 241 *n* 1
Nāgārjuna, quoted 128 *n* 4, 250
Nāgārjuna, Tārānātha's date of 252, 252 *n* 4

Page

Muktākumbha, name restored from the Tibetan .. 331 *n* 3
Paramahaṁsa, killed in Tibet .. 210
Ratna Vajra, see Ācārya.
Saṅghabhadra, existence of his work in Tibetan .. 248 *n* 1
Śaṅkara Svāmin, Tibetan knowledge of .. .. 302, 302 *n* 4
(Tārānātha, see under Tibetan names).
Tarka-puṅgava, see Dignāga.

3. *Modern Authors.*

Page

Cordier, P., Tibetan catalogue 257 *n* 1, 262 *n* 2
Csoma de Körös, A., Tibetan Grammar 55 *n* 1, 306 *n* 1, 323 *n* 3, 517
Das, Sarat Chandra, various, 43 *n* 2, 47 *n* 1, 242 *n* 1, 274 *n* 2, 275 *n* 1, 305 *n* 1, 320 *n* 4, 323 *n* 2, 3; 324 *n* 3, 327 *n* 1, 332 *n* 3, 338 *n* 3, 348 *n* 1, 516 *n* 1, 517 *n* 2, 517 *n* 3, 519 *n* 2, 520 *n* 2, 530
Rockhill, W. W., Life of Buddha 11 *n* 3, 246 *n* 2, 322 *n* 7
Ross, E. D., Mahāvyutpatti, 7 *n* 7, 8 *n* 7, 40 *n* 3, 43 *n* 2, 47 *n* 1
Schiefner, A., Tārānātha, Geschichte des Buddhismus, see under Tibetan names *s.v* Tārānātha.

Page

Schlagintweit, E., Buddhism, 249 *n* 1, 5
Sherbatski, F. J., Nyāya-bindu 309 *n* 2, 329 *n* 6
Vidyābhuśana, Satis Chandra, various, 7 *n* 1, 7, 10; 40 *n* 3, 241 *n* 1, 262 *n* 1, 307 *n* 4, 309 *n* 2, 322 *n* 5, 7; 324 *n* 2, 334 *n* 3, 343 *n* 1, 342 *n* 2
Waddell, L. A., Lamaism 271 *n* 1, 323 *n* 3; 327 *n* 1; 520 *n* 2
Wassiljew, W. .. 251 *n* 1, 306 *n* 1

V. PLACE NAMES.

1. *Tibetan Spelling.*

Page

བཀྲ་ཤིས་ལྷུན་པོ་ .. 270, 353
གུ་གེ་, in W. Tibet 324
ཇ་རི་, [?] Tholing in 517
སྐྱི་ནང་, monastery near Lhasa .. 344
ཐོ་ཞིང་ [?], in Ñari 517
འབྲོ་, province, translators of 324, 337, 343
ཙནྡྲ་ཝི་ཁྲོན་པ་, Candra-kūpa .. 335

Page

ཞ་ལུ་, near Tashi Lhunpo 270, 338
ཞང་ཞུང་, interpreter of .. 338
རྒྱ་ཆེན་, interpreters of 321, 322, 328, (See errata) 329, 340
ཟ་ཧོར་, Bodhisattva t of 299, 323
ཞི་བའི་དགེ་གནས་, monastery .. 300
ཞམ་པའི་དགེ་གནས་ monastery .. 275

	Page
ས་སྐྱ་, monastery ..	289, 300
སུམ་པ་ province in Amdo ..	337
སེང་དཀར་, village ..	337
བསམ་ཡས་, holy monastery	323, 323 n 2, 324
སྙེ་མ་, Nyethang near ..	344

2. *English Spelling.*

	Page
Amdo, province of Sum-pa in ..	337
Do-jog, Taxila ..	528
Labrang, in Sikkim	289 n 1, 299 n 1, 319 n 5, 320 n 4, 324 n 2, 328 n 2, 336 n 3, 342 n 4, 344 n 4, 530–536
Padangi ..	530, *et seq.*
Pamiyangchi	530, *et seq.*, 537–539
Sikkim, see Labrang ..	537–539
Tibet, spread of Mahāyāna in ..	241
Buddhist Missionaries in ..	352
Enterprising monks visiting ..	351
Śānta Rakṣita visits ..	517
Western Tibet, Saskya monastery in ..	289, 300

VI. RESIDUALS.

1. *Tibetan.*

	Page
སྒོ་སྲུང་ dvāra-paṇḍita ?, gate keeper	520
རྡོ་རྗེ་ vajra, thunderbolt ..	272
པཎ་ཆེན་ཞྭ་དམར་ paṇḍita's red cap ..	271
སྦས་ gupta ..	328 n 3
ལམ་ཡིག་ ..	531
བསྲུང་ rakṣita, protected	328 n 3

2. *English.*

	Page
Illustration, likeness of Dignāga	271
Mahārājā of Sikkim, letter from	538, 539
Mahārānī of Sikkim, letter from	537
Tashi Lama, visit to India	528, 529

VII. ERRATA.

PAGE:	FOR:	READ:
124, n 1:	Dhamakirti,	Dharmakīrti.
245, n 1:	ཡོང་མ་ཀྱབ་	ཡོང་མ་ཁྱབ་
252, n 1:	སྔ་འདམ་	ང་འདམ་
252 3 n 6:	B̲san-h̲gyur,	B̲stan-h̲gyur.
257, § 82:	ṭeppitaka,	ṭippiṭaka
276, l. 15/16:	r̲je d̲pag,	r̲jes-d̲pag.
288, n 1:	དཔག་པའི་ཉེད་	དཔག་པ་ཉིད་
298, bottom:	Mṅon-sum ltar-naṅ,	Mṅon-sum-ltar-snaṅ.
299, l 5:	ṇ do,	ṇ do, Vol. ce.
299, bottom:	h̲grel-wa,	h̲grel-pa.
300, § 98:	D̲ge-śes	D̲ge-bśes.
301, § 100:	br̲tag-pallis h̲grel,	br̲tag-pah̲i-h̲grel-pa.
301, § 101:	Dus-bsum,	Dus-gsum.

PAGE:	FOR:	READ:
303, *n* 3:	vou,	von.
307, *n* 4:	ཚད་མ་རྣམས་འགྲུལ་	ཚད་མ་རྣམ་འགྲེལ་
308, *n* 3, l. 2, fr. b.:	ལྷུན་	ལྷན་
309, l. 5:	rnan-par	rnam-par.
309, *n* 2:	Sher-batski, Shére-bataki,	Sherbatski.
317, *n* 2:	*id.*	*id.*
319, § 114, § 115:	Hbrel-wa	Hbrel-pa.
321, passim:	*id.*	*id.*
323, last line:	hbrel,	hgrel.
323, *n* 3:	Koros,	Körös.
325, Tib. l. 4, fr. b.:	འབྲུལ་	འགྲེལ་
326, l. 26:	Tibtan,	Tibetan.
326, l. 2 fr. b:	po,	pa.
327, l. 12:	shan,	gshan.
327, l 23:	drtag,	brtag.
330, § 129, l. 13:	She,	The.
337, l. 9 fr. b.:	Bis-wa,	Byis-pa.
342, § 137, last l.:	bgrus,	hgrus.
343, l 4:	do,	du.
335, *n* 4, l. 1:	མཁྱུན་	མཁྱེན་
353, *n* 1, l. 1:	ཀྱན་པ་དེ་པ་ཊ་	ཀྱོན་པའི་པཊ་
517, l. 11:	Thi-srong,	Khri-sroṅ.
517, l 17:	lama,	bla-ma.

Passim, See Index V. I. ཞུ་ཆེན་ is not the name of a country, but a title: great revisor. Certain other irregularities have not been indicated, as this index enables the reader to draw his own inferences.

Tattvacintāmaṇi (Gaṅgeśa)

1. Maṇi-vyākhyā (Kaṇāda Tarkavāgīśa Bhattàcharyya).
2. Tattvacintāmaṇi-dīdhiti (Raghunātha Tārkika-śiromaṇi)
   1. Tattvacintāmaṇi-dīdhiti-ṭikā (Rāmarudra Tarkavāgīśa).
   2. Tattvacintāmaṇi-dīdhiti-prakāśikā (Gadādhara Tarkavāgīśa).
   3. Dīdhiti-ṭikā (Raghudeva Nyāyālaṅkāra).
   4. Tattvacintāmaṇi-dīdhiti-prakāśikā (Rudra Nyāyavācaspati).
   5. Tattvacintāmaṇi-dīdhiti-gūḍhārtha-vidyotana (Jayarāma Nyāyapañcānana).
   6. Tattvacintāmaṇi-dīdhiti-prakāśikā (Jagadīśa Tarkālaṅkāra).
   7. Dīdhiti-ṭikā (Rāmabhadra Sārvabhauma).
   8. Dīdhiti-rahasya (Mathurānātha Tarkavāgīśa)
      1. Anumāna-dīdhiti-viveka (Guṇānanda Vidyāvāgīśa).
   9. Tattvacintāmaṇi-dīdhiti-prasāriṇī (Kṛṣṇadāsa Sārvabhauma).
   10. Tattvacintāmaṇi-dīdhiti-prakāśikā (Bhavānanda Siddhāntavāgīśa).
3. Tattvacintāmaṇi-prakāśa (Haridāsa Nyāyālaṅkāra Bhaṭṭācārya).
4. Anumāna-khaṇḍa (Vācaspati Miśra).
5. Tattvacintāmaṇi-mayūkha (Śaṅkara Miśra).
6. Tattvacintāmaṇi-prakāśa (Vardhamāna Upādhyāya).
7. Tattvacintāmaṇi-āloka (Pakṣadhara Miśra)
   1. Tattvacintāmaṇi-āloka-rahasya (Mathurānātha Tarkavāgīśa).
   2. Maṇi-āloka-ṭippaṇī (Haridāsa Nyāyālaṅkāra Bhaṭṭācārya).
   3. Tattvacintāmaṇi-āloka-kaṇṭakoddhāra(MadhusūdanaṬhakkura).
   4. Āloka-darpaṇa (Maheśa Ṭhakkura).
   5. Tattvacintāmaṇi-āloka-pariśiṣṭa (Devanātha Ṭhakkura).
   6. Anumāna-āloka-prasāriṇī (Kṛṣṇadāsa Sārvabhauma).
   7. Śabda-āloka-viveka (Guṇānanda Vidyāvāgīśa).
   8. Pratyakṣa-āloka-sāra-mañjarī (Bhavānanda Siddhāntavāgīśa).
   9. Tattvacintāmaṇi-āloka-ṭikā (Gadādhara Bhaṭṭācarya)
8. Tattvacintāmaṇi-prakāśa (Rucidatta).
9. Tattvacintāmaṇi-mayūkha (Jagadīśa Tarkālaṅkāra).
10. Tattvacintāmaṇi-āloka-viveka (Jayarāma Nyāyālaṅkāra).
11. Tattvacintāmaṇi-ṭikā (Bhavānanda Siddhāntavāgīśa).
12. Tattvacintāmaṇi-ṭikā (Harirāma Tarkavāgīśa).
13. Tattvacintāmaṇi-gūḍhārtha-dīpikā (Raghudeva Nyāyālaṅkāra).
14. Tattvacintāmaṇi-vyākhyā (Gadādhara Bhaṭṭācārya).

96A. Hetu-Cakra—The Wheel of Reasons.

(Nine possible relations between the Middle Term and the Major Term in a syllogism.)

1

Sound is eternal,
Because it is knowable,
Like ether and like a pot.
Here the 'knowable' (which is the reason or middle term) abides in all things homogeneous with, and all things heterogeneous from, the 'eternal' (which is the major term).
The reason or middle term is too general.
Truth is uncertain.

2

Sound is non-eternal,
Because it is produced,
Like a pot, but unlike ether.
Here the 'produced' (which is the reason or middle term) abides in all things homogeneous with, but does not abide in any thing heterogeneous from, the 'non-eternal' (which is the major term).
The reasoning is valid. Well!

3

Sound is a product of effort,
Because it is non-eternal,
Like a pot, unlike lightning and unlike ether.
Here the 'non-eternal' (which is the reason or middle term) abides in all things homogeneous with, and some things heterogeneous from, the product of effort (which is the major term).
Truth is uncertain.

4

Sound is eternal,
Because it is produced,
Unlike ether and like a pot.
Here the 'produced' (which is the reason or middle term) abides in nothing homogeneous with, but in all things heterogeneous from, the 'eternal' (which is the major term).
The reason or middle term is contradictory to the major term.

5

Sound is non-eternal,
Because it is audible,
Like a pot and like ether.
Here the 'audible' (which is the reason or middle term) abides in nothing homogeneous with, and in nothing heterogeneous from, the 'non-eternal' (which is the major term).
The reason or middle term is not general enough.
Truth is uncertain.

6

Sound is eternal,
Because it is a product of effort,
Unlike ether, like a pot, and unlike lightning.
Here the 'product of effort' (which is the reason or middle term) abides in nothing homogeneous with, but in some things heterogeneous from, the 'eternal' (which is the major term).
The reason or middle term is contradictory to the major term.

7

Sound is a non-product of effort,
Because it is non-eternal,
Unlike lightning, unlike ether, and like a pot.
Here the 'non-eternal' (which is the reason or middle term) abides in some things homogeneous with, and in all things heterogeneous from, the 'non-product of effort' (which is the major term).
Truth is uncertain.

8

Sound is non-eternal,
Because it is a product of effort,
Like a pot, unlike lightning, and unlike ether.
Here the 'product of effort' (which is the reason or middle term) abides in some things homogeneous with, but in nothing heterogeneous from, the 'non-eternal' (which is the major term).
The reasoning is valid. Well.

9

Sound is eternal,
Because it is corporeal,
Unlike ether, like atoms of dust, unlike action and like a pot.
Here the 'corporeal' (which is the reason or middle term) abides in some things homogeneous with, and in some things heterogeneous from, the 'eternal' (which is the major term).
Truth is uncertain.

Analysis of the Wheel.

1

Sound is eternal (S is P),
Because it is knowable (S is R).
(*a*) The knowables are all eternals, as ether (R is all P), that is, all eternals are knowables as ether.
(*b*) The knowables are all non-eternals, as a pot (R is all non-P), that is, all non-eternals are knowables as a pot. Symbolically :
S is P
Because S is R—right }
R is all-P— right } reasoning is unsound.
R is all non-P—wrong }

2

Sound is non-eternal (S is P),
Because it is produced (S is R).
(*a*) The produced are all non-eternals as a pot (R is all-P), that is, all non-eternals are produced, as a pot.
(*b*) No non-eternals are non-produced, as ether, that is, non-produced are no non-eternals as ether (R is no non-P). Symbolically :
S is P
Because S is R – right }
R is all-P— right } reasoning is sound.
R is no non-P— right }

3

Sound is a product of effort (S is P),
Because it is non-eternal (S is R).
(*a*) The non-eternals are all products-of-effort, that is, all products-of-effort are non-eternals, as a pot (R is all-P).
(*b*) Some non-products-of-effort are non-eternal, as lightning, that is, the non-eternal is some non-product-of-effort as lightning (R is some non-P).
(*c*) Some non-product-of-effort is not non-eternal, as ether, that is, the non-eternal is not some non-product-of-effort as ether (R is not some non-P). Symbolically :
S is P
Because S is R—right }
R is all-P— right }
R is some non-P } wrong } reasoning is unsound.
R is not some non-P } }

4

Sound is eternal (S is P),
Because it is produced (S is R).
(*a*) The produced are not eternal, as ether (R is no P), that is, the eternal are not produced, as ether.
(*b*) The non-eternals are all produced (R is all non-P), that is, the produced are non-eternals, as a pot. Symbolically :
S is P
Because S is R—right }
R is no P— wrong } reasoning is unsound.
R is all non-P—wrong }

5

Sound is non-eternal (S is P),
Because it is audible (S is R).
(*a*) The audibles are no non-eternals as a pot (R is no P), that is, the non-eternals are no audibles, as a pot.
(*b*) No non-non-eternal (that is, no eternal), is audible, as ether, that is, no audible is non-non-eternal, as ether (R is no non-P). Symbolically:
S is P
Because S is R—right }
R is no P— wrong } reasoning is unsound.
R is no non-P—right }

6

Sound is eternal (S is P),
Because it is a product of effort (S is R).
(*a*) The products of effort are no eternals (R is no P), that is, the eternals are no products of effort, as ether.
(*b*) The products of effort are some non eternals, as a pot (R is some non-P), that is, some non-eternals are products of effort, as a pot.
(*c*) The products of effort are not some non-eternals, as lightning (R is not some non-P), that is, some non-eternals are not products of effort, as lightning. Symbolically :
S is P
Because S is R— right }
R is no P— wrong }
R is some non-P } —wrong } reasoning is unsound.
R is not some non-P } }

7

Sound is a non-product of effort (S is P),
Because it is non-eternal (S is R).
(*a*) The non-eternals are some non-products of effort, as lightning (R is some P), that is, some non-products of effort are non-eternals as lightning.
(*b*) The non-eternals are not some non-products of effort, as ether (R is not some P), that is, some non-products of effort are not non-eternals, as ether.
(*c*) The non-eternals are all non-non-products of effort as a pot (R is all non-P). Symbolically:
S is P
Because S is R—right }
R is some P } }
R is not some P } **—right** } **reasoning is unsound.**
R is all non-P—wrong }

8

Sound is non-eternal (S is P),
Because it is a product of effort (S is R).
(*a*) The products of effort, are some non-eternals, that is, some non-eternals are products of effort as a pot (R is some P).
(*b*) The products of effort are not some non-eternals, as lightning (R is not some P), that is, some non-eternals are not products of effort as lightning.
(*c*) The non-eternals are not products of effort, as ether, that is, the products of effort are no non-eternals, as ether (R is no non-non-eternals, as ether (R is no non-P). Symbolically :
S is P
Because S is R—right }
R is some P } }
R is not some P } right } reasoning is sound.
R is no non-P } right }

9

Sound is eternal (S is P),
Because it is corporeal (S is R).
(*a*) The corporeals are some eternals, as atoms (R is some P), that is, some eternals are corporeals, as atoms.
(*b*) The corporeals are not some eternals, as ether (R is not some P), that is, some eternals are not corporeals, as ether.
(*c*) The corporeals are some non-eternals, as a pot (R is some non-P).
(*d*) The corporeals are not some non-eternals, as an action (R is not some non-P). Symbolically :
S is P
Because S is R—wrong }
R is some P } }
R is not some P } —right }
R is some non-P } } reasoning is unsound.
R is not some non-P } —wrong }